PENGUIN CANADA

COMPANY OF ADVENTURERS

PETER C. NEWMAN is one of Canada's most successful and honoured writers. The former editor in-chief of the *Toronto Star* and *Maclean's* magazine has also been the recipient of a dozen of North America's most coveted literary and journalism awards, and his twenty-two books have sold more than two million copies. He currently lives in London, England.

Also by Peter C. Newman

COMPANY
OF
ADVENTURERS

How the Hudson's Bay Empire
Determined the Destiny of a Continent

Peter C. Newman

PENGUIN
CANADA

PENGUIN CANADA

Published by the Penguin Group

Penguin Group (Canada), 10 Alcorn Avenue, Toronto, Ontario, Canada M4V 3B2
(a division of Pearson Penguin Canada Inc.)

Penguin Group (USA) Inc., 375 Hudson Street, New York, New York 10014, U.S.A.
Penguin Books Ltd, 80 Strand, London WC2R 0RL, England
Penguin Ireland, 25 St Stephen's Green, Dublin 2, Ireland (a division of Penguin Books Ltd)
Penguin Group (Australia), 250 Camberwell Road, Camberwell, Victoria 3124, Australia
    (a division of Pearson Australia Group Pty Ltd)
Penguin Books India Pvt Ltd, 11 Community Centre, Panchsheel Park, New Delhi – 110 017, India
Penguin Group (NZ), Cnr Airborne and Rosedale Roads, Albany, Auckland, New Zealand
    (a division of Pearson New Zealand Ltd)
Penguin Books (South Africa) (Pty) Ltd, 24 Sturdee Avenue, Rosebank, Johannesburg 2196, South Africa

Penguin Books Ltd, Registered Offices: 80 Strand, London WC2R 0RL, England

Company of Adventurers (vol. I) first published in Viking Canada hardcover, 1985;
    published in Penguin Canada paperback, 1986, 1987.

Caesars of the Wilderness (vol. II) first published in Viking Canada hardcover, 1987;
    published in Penguin Canada paperback, 1988.

Empire of the Bay (compilation of vols. I and II) first published in Penguin Canada paperback, 1998.

Merchant Princes (vol. III) first published in Viking Canada hardcover, 1991;
    published in Penguin Canada paperback, 1992.

Published in this edition, 2005

(WEB) 10 9 8 7 6 5 4 3 2 1

LIBRARY AND ARCHIVES CANADA CATALOGUING IN PUBLICATION

Newman, Peter C., 1929–
    Company of adventurers : how the Hudson's Bay empire determined the destiny
of a continent / Peter C. Newman.

Includes index.
ISBN 0-14-305147-4

1. Hudson's Bay Company—History. 2. Northwest, Canadian—History.
3. Fur trade—Canada—History. 4. Canada—Discovery and exploration. I. Title.

FC3207.N492 2005   971.2'01   C2004-905812-6

Visit the Penguin Group (Canada) website at **www.penguin.ca**

*This book is dedicated
to the adventurers, traders and roustabouts
who hugged the memory of their time on Hudson Bay
as they would an extra blanket on a bitterly cold night:
glad that they had been there,
and gladder still to have returned.*

Forts of the Hudson's Bay Company

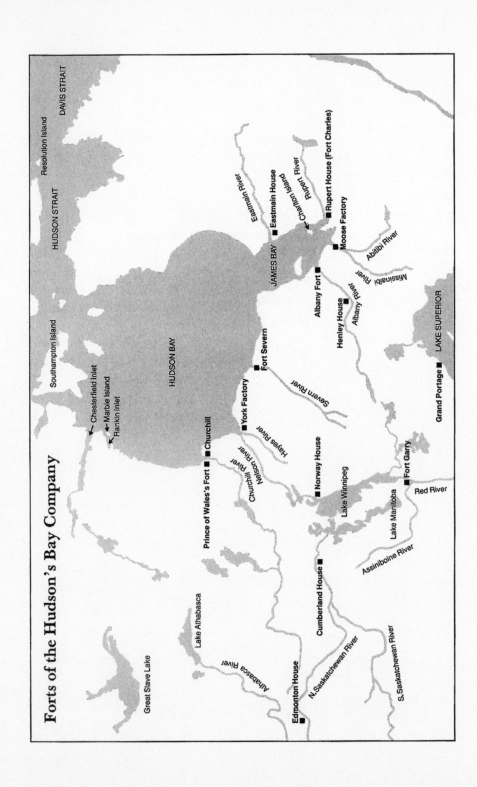

DAVIS STRAIT

Resolution Island

HUDSON STRAIT

Southampton Island

Chesterfield Inlet

Marble Island

Rankin Inlet

HUDSON BAY

Prince of Wales's Fort ■

Churchill ■

York Factory ■

Hayes River

Churchill River

Nelson River

Great Slave Lake

Lake Athabasca

Athabasca River

Edmonton House ■

N. Saskatchewan River

S. Saskatchewan River

Cumberland House ■

Assiniboine River

Lake Manitoba

Lake Winnipeg

Norway House ■

Fort Garry ■

Red River

Grand Portage ■

LAKE SUPERIOR

Severn River

Fort Severn ■

Henley House ■

Albany Fort ■

Albany River

Missinaibi River

Abitibi River

Moose Factory ■

JAMES BAY

Charlton Island

Rupert River

Rupert House (Fort Charles) ■

Eastmain House ■

Eastmain River

CONTENTS

INTRODUCTION

THE SAD LOOKING GENT on the jacket of this book is Henry Hudson, who gave his name (and life) to the inland sea that juts so distinctively into the northeastern arm of the Canadian subcontinent. His previous exploits included a voyage of discovery from what is now New York up the Manna-hata River. And, yes, that was how both the Hudson River and Manhattan Island got their names. The ambitious explorer was next hired by a prestigious group of British financiers to map the North West Passage, that illusory maritime link to the riches of India and Cathay that intrigued European navigators for most of three centuries, prompting them to risk their cockleshell hulls against the fearsome ice barrier of an impassable waterway.

Hudson set off on his ill-fated voyage from London in 1610, aboard the *Discovery*, entered the bay that now bears his name and headed south, convinced he had just rounded the top of the American continent. Instead, he found himself trapped in a cul-de-sac (James Bay) where he spent the winter in frigid, indescribable misery. That sojourn was relieved only once when a visiting Indian arrived with a sledful of deer meat and two beaver hides, which Hudson traded for a knife, a mirror and a few buttons. That was the Bay's first fur trade. In spring the *Discovery* floated free of ice, but instead of returning to England, Hudson tacked endlessly from shore to shore, searching for an outlet to the Orient. His crew finally mutinied and forced him into a lifeboat. He was never seen again.

The painting on the jacket, by British court artist the Honourable John Collier, which depicts Hudson, his son John and eight loyal crew members cast adrift by the mutineers, bears mute testimony to his courage and foolhardiness. Out of his geographical legacy eventually grew the Hudson's Bay Company, the magnificent Company of Adventurers that is the subject of the pages that follow.

I spent more than half a decade researching and writing the three volumes that constitute this book: *Company of Adventurers, Caesars of the Wilderness* and *Merchant Princes*. Chronicling the lively history of the Hudson's Bay

Company (later turned into a television documentary by John McGreevey) proved to be the grandest and most complicated literary undertaking of my life. During that lengthy stretch of intense preoccupation with the details of the Company's sometimes glorious and more frequently precarious existence, I often wondered if it was worth my time and energy to resurrect the lives of anonymous fur traders who had huddled under the polar moon in centuries past. Their challenges were daunting and their stories were compelling, but their greatest achievement was survival—just being there and living to tell the tale.

Yet the more I dug into the project, I came to realize that this feat was paralleled by the history of Canada, that those of us who were born in this magnificent land or came here as involuntary exiles have been quick to adopt the survival syndrome. It became my fierce conviction that in a precarious country like Canada, which has so much more geography than history, it was essential to illuminate the past, not backlit by hindsight but as it really happened. My books set out to measure the impact of the HBC on Canada's evolution, not only its first commercial stirrings but its influence on the national psyche.

More than any of my other books, this project enveloped me, kidnapping my emotions and channelling my thoughts backwards through time to the birth of the Company of Adventurers in 1670. My first discovery was that its founder, Prince Rupert of the Rhine, had grown up in Czechoslovakia (like me), having been born in Prague's Hradčany Castle to royal parents whose lineage reached back to Charlemagne. The Bohemian prince was a Renaissance man, having been an admiral, freebooting pirate, erotic painter, metallurgist, inventor of the torpedo as well as surgical instruments, and the field marshal who restored Charles II to the British throne. His reward was the royal charter that established "The Governor and Company of Adventurers of England Trading into Hudson's Bay" with himself as its founding governor. Named Rupert's Land, the real estate grant he received from the king (the largest in history) was described in the royal charter as all of the land covered by the rivers flowing into Hudson Bay. That gargantuan freehold was the equivalent of nearly 40 percent of modern Canada: everything west of Kenora; all of northern Ontario, Quebec, Manitoba, Saskatchewan and Alberta; a huge chunk of the eastern portion of the Northwest Territories; plus much of Minnesota and North Dakota and later Oregon. That slab of geography amounted to one-twelfth of the earth's land surface or ten times the size of the Holy Roman Empire at its height.

The HBC's second governor, the Duke of York, reluctantly gave up his position to become king of England as James II. He was succeeded as governor by John Churchill, the Duke of Marlborough, whose epic military victories triggered two centuries of British imperialism. The duke's direct descendant, nine generations removed, was Sir Winston Churchill, Britain's great wartime prime minister. (When he retired from politics in 1955, Churchill accepted only one post in any commercial enterprise, though many were offered. He became grand seigneur of the Hudson's Bay Company and remained so until his death.) Another early HBC director was the famed architect Sir Christopher Wren, builder of St. Paul's Cathedral, who chaired the Company's meetings when Prince Rupert was otherwise engaged. No commercial enterprise has enjoyed a more illustrious birth, and I have tried to make the most of it.

In the course of my research, my then wife Camilla and I eventually interviewed five hundred men and women who had either worked for the Company or were touched by its activities. We ranged the country like a bureau of missing persons, coaxing memories out of aloof Highlanders who had given the best of their lives to the Bay and unexpectedly found eager listeners for the tall tales they had almost forgotten. Their voices dominate the manuscript, and the descriptions of their first-hand experiences, especially in the Canadian North, constitute a Canadian epic of astonishing proportions. In the research for this book, I owe a primary debt to the fur traders themselves, jabbing their quill pens impatiently into half-frozen inkwells by candlelight, meticulously recounting details of their daily exertions, their scribbles being carefully gathered and lovingly preserved in the HBC Archives.

Out of those archives and our interviews, I wrote the three thick volumes of text and an illustrated version of my Hudson's Bay histories (*Empire of the Bay*), which eventually totalled 1,588 pages, or more than 700,000 words, just short of Leo Tolstoy's *War and Peace*.

I never ceased to wonder about the hold that the HBC exercised over its "servants," as it was pleased to call its employees. Some of its bachelor officers willed it their life savings; one woman executive told me that she loved the Company more than either of her husbands. Others, who put in long, slow lives in dreary wilderness postings, confided to me that they were "damn well going to retire early"—after only thirty-eight years in the service. Serving under the crimson ensign of the HBC (the only commercial banner permitted to include the Union Jack) became a fever in the blood.

The one emotion the HBC never engendered was neutrality. The Inuit and Indians, touched by its inevitable presence but feeling exploited by the harsh terms at its local trading depots, insisted that the initials really spelled out the Hungry Belly Company, while Indian women, speaking from experience, denounced it as the Horny Boys' Club. Equally appropriate, because the HBC seemed to have been there forever, was the claim that the initials stood for Here Before Christ or, more appropriately, Here Before Canada. (Edmonton, which became one of the Company's most important inland depots, proclaimed that HBC really meant Here Before Calgary, which was born much later as a railway town.) No one touched by the Hudson's Bay Company's Darwinian will to survive remained unaffected. No wonder that being a Bay man was tantamount to joining a quasi-religious order, even if in modern times the Company was reduced to selling socks and underwear.

Another motivating impulse for this project was my conviction that Canada lacks heroes. We import too many of our role models from the United States. Whenever I am asked what Canada needs most, I usually reply, "Our own Walt Disney." What I mean is someone whose artistry will ensure that our own myths and legends are embedded in the Canadian imagination. For examples of Canadian heroes I refer readers to my chapters on Pierre-Esprit Radisson, Samuel Hearne, George Simpson, Donald Smith and John Rae.

My approach to the writing of history stresses the interplay of feisty characters with remarkable circumstances. Academic historians quarrel with such a simplistic reading of events, and I do not deny for a moment that their dedication to documented detail is an essential element in any attempt to reconstruct what really happened. My argument with their approach is that truth is not necessarily the sum of all the ascertainable facts and there is room for both styles of historical writing, mine and theirs. The problem is that most academic historians are also teachers of the old school who insists that their students feed back to them exactly what they have been taught. While I hesitate to encroach on any sacred academic turf, I do not believe that professors hold a monopoly on either the primary sources or the history that's written, and certainly not on the imagination used in reconstructing it. Having little patience with cant or the musty scholarly ruminations that the poet Dylan Thomas once described as being the preserve of scholars "smelling of water biscuits," I imbued the tales that follow with the bounce and bravado they deserve.

In their various Penguin and Viking editions, my HBC chronicles sold half a million copies. Each volume was a prime selection of the Book of the Month

Club; publication in the United Kingdom and the United States followed, with astonishingly favourable reviews. That generous reception was not based on any spectacular scandals or sexual innuendos I unearthed in the history of the fur trade. It was simply that readers responded to my version of storytelling, which was dedicated to one over-arching objective: to destroy forever the stereotypic notion that Canadian history is dull and not worth telling and retelling.

My real problem was how to sort out all those masses of names, dates and faces into a coherent narrative. I remember feeling a little better about the many filing cabinets of documents I had accumulated after reading in *The Spectator* an interview with the British historian A.J.P. Taylor, who declared on his seventy-fifth birthday that "history is not a catalogue, but a convincing version of events." That rang true. All the historians I admire—Taylor himself, Francis Parkman, G.M. Trevelyan, Pierre Berton, Alan Moorehead and, above all, Barbara Tuchman—managed to capture on the printed page the enthusiasm of storytellers, to spin the web accurately without being swamped by detail. If I have a literary credo, it is an echo of Tuchman's evocative declaration in her collection of essays *Practising History*: "In my mind is a picture of Kipling's itinerant storyteller of India, with his rice bowl, who tells tales of ancient romance and legend to a circle of villagers by firelight. If he sees figures drifting away from the edge of the circle in the darkness, and his audience thinning out, he knows his rice bowl will be meagerly filled.... I feel just as urgent a connection with the reader."

Events happen in sequence or simultaneously, but never in categories. Thus it was impossible to fit the HBC story into any neat set of orderly revelations. Instead, at each pivotal stage of the Company's evolution, I chose a compelling individual as my focus. This allowed me, through one character sketch at a time, to freeze-frame the landscape of the Company's activity at that particular moment. I then attempted to recreate the world in which these animators lived and acted to discover how they were altered by their peculiar fates: the weight of their collective heritage pitted against their individual impulse; the tug of the Company's past competing with the pull of the new continent's future.

This is a journalist's book, a search for the stories, the themes, the personalities who dominated the more than three centuries of the Company's stormy stewardship. I believe that is a valid approach to a complicated subject because it is rooted in my own desire to make sense of the tantalizing moments that gave the HBC's history meaning and the beguiling individuals who gave it excitement. The hard-bitten Bay men profiled in this volume are as true to life as I could make them. I carefully limited myself to the available evidence.

Like all my works, I have no more claimed the credentials of a professional historian than I assumed the mantle of a political scientist when I wrote my political books or pretended to be an economist when I was chronicling my various studies of the Canadian establishment. I regard the much-maligned profession of journalism as an honourable craft that requires no apologies.

I am delighted that Penguin has decided to reissue my books in this omnibus edition and am grateful to the firm's editorial director Diane Turbide for steering it through to publication. Now, a new generation of readers can follow the remarkable exploits of the Company of Adventurers that became a country: Canada.

A puff of onshore wind ruffles the low-lying vegetation; nothing else moves. There is no enduring memory of the great events that took place here because there is no one left to remember them. Every so often native trappers wander by, the juice of wild blueberries purpling their faces. The abandoned pastures hum with the liquid accent of the Swampy Cree as they circle KICHEWASKAHIKUN, the now-empty "Big House" still standing on the shores of the Hayes River. They sing as they walk by because they believe the huge depot to be the home of evil spirits.

This is York Factory, once the Company's great tidewater headquarters on Hudson Bay. The most essential HBC destination, then and now, York Factory is where history and present-day reality come together. This was where the Company first perfected the fur trade as a world-scale enterprise; it was from here that most of its pathfinders set off to probe its inland empire; and it is here that its vulnerability to change is most dramatically on view.

Formerly the busiest of the HBC's trading posts, the depot building's hundred vacant windows yawn in the silver afternoon, reminding outsiders that here was the centre of North American commerce, the overseas headquarters of the Company of Adventurers.

The first white man to winter near this spot, halfway up Hudson Bay's west coast, was Sir Thomas Button, who searched in 1612 for the doomed explorer Henry Hudson and for a navigable North West Passage. Seven more decades elapsed before an expedition headed by Pierre Radisson, travelling under the French flag, returned to the site; two years later, the HBC built its first permanent trading station and named it York Factory after the Company's Governor, the Duke of York. (It was called a "factory" not because anything was manufactured there but because this was where the factor lived.)

In the next dozen years, York Factory would become a pawn in the tangled wars between the English and the French for control of Hudson Bay, changing hands six times. During the early 1690s it was the only bay post not held by the French. Then Pierre Le Moyne d'Iberville, the most astute military genius Canada has produced, captured the fort for New France in an epic sea battle as the thunder of cannon fire rolled along Hudson Bay's growling cliffs and ships-of-the-line foundered in frigid waters almost as deadly as the combat itself. Returned to English possession by the Treaty of Utrecht in 1713, York Factory was sacked nearly seventy years later by a valiant raiding party of French marines who had dashed north from the West Indies *during the American Revolution. Joseph Colen, the* HBC *Chief Factor in charge of rebuilding it (and York Factory's first resident intellectual; he moved in with a library of fourteen hundred books), decided to shift operations to the present site. He gave the refurbished post the only name that seemed to fit: "New York."*

For 249 years the Hudson's Bay Company sent supply ships to Five Fathom Hole from its docks in London. Then in 1931, the traffic stopped. From being district headquarters York Factory had been downgraded to just another hbc trading post, but the decline really dated back to 1871, when railway construction reached the Red River, providing a new and cheaper method of supplying the Company's western network. The trade's headquarters was shifted to the site of present-day Winnipeg. The last brigade of York boats set off from Norway House three years later, and York Factory was reduced to handling local traffic.

The great seaboard fort fell into disuse. Most of its buildings were pulled down, razed or ravaged by vandals. Nearly seven hundred Cree still followed their ancestors' tradition and came to trade at York Factory in 1936, but twenty years later their total was down to seventy and, in 1957, the HBC abandoned its once-proud headquarters.

Only the great white depot building remains, its door barricaded in a useless gesture against natural and human intruders. For decades the building has withstood the assault of wind, frost and the occasional marauders (mostly American goose-hunters) who rolled old cannon balls along its polished floors at beer-bottle tenpins, smashed mickeys of whisky against its satiny spruce walls, tore off its siding to burn as fuel and used its elegant pantries as pissoirs. The depot is still standing only because its builders placed the structure on top of a complex system of drainage ditches and compensated for permafrost heave by mounting it on replaceable wooden sills instead of masonry that would inevitably have crumbled.

The Cree who once flocked here have retreated inland to Shamattawa and the reserve at Split Lake. Now and again a polar bear pads around the sacred confines of the depot's courtyard, searching for meat and companionship.

At the hub of a vanished empire, York Factory is an apt example of the Company's penchant for sloughing off past hindrances and expediently renewing itself in other places, other guises. For more than three centuries, the Company has shuttled between splendour and dust, unstoppable momentum and impending collapse.

I DREAMS OF EMPIRE

The Bay Men

The Hudson's Bay Company turned much of the upper half of North America into a company town writ large, in which customers displayed individuality and imagination at their own risk.

FOR A TIME THEY were trustees of the largest sweep of pale red on Mercator's map, lording it over a new subcontinent, building their toy forts and seducing the Indian maidens they playfully called their "bits of brown." They were displaced Scots and Englishmen—mostly gentle Orkney carpenters, ambitious Aberdeen clerks and black-sheep progeny of Anglican clergymen—toiling for fur in the service of the Governor and Company of Adventurers of England Trading into Hudson's Bay.

Through the polished-brass telescope of imperial history, the Hudson's Bay Company appears a majestic, fiercely patrician enterprise, grandly fielding its own armies and navies, minting its own coins, issuing its own medals, even operating according to a calendar dating from its own Creation. But for the generations of lumpen fur traders who scratched for a living in the North American wilderness, the reality was often harsh and disillusioning. They neither struck metaphorical gold nor found a land to build a dream on. Yet there was a certain valour in their stand against the vastness of the untamed land. Those who were touched by it hugged the memory of their time on Hudson Bay as they would an extra blanket on a bitter night—glad that they had been there, gladder still to have returned. The men in the little bush forts huddling beneath the pewter sky developed the camaraderie of a lengthy sea voyage, marked forever by their time "on the bay."

ROOTED IN THE NEW WORLD'S NORTHERN SWAMPS, the early HBC was more of an independent beaver republic than a business firm. As John Buchan, First Baron Tweedsmuir and the author-statesman who served as Governor General of Canada in the late 1930s, astutely observed: "The Hudson's Bay is *not* an ordinary commercial company, but a kind of kingdom by itself, and it needs statesmen to administer it." It did not always find them, but during the first two centuries of its dominance, nothing stopped the HBC's march as it commandeered a domain that eventually stretched over a twelfth of the earth's surface. The Company's trading posts reached from the white shores of the Arctic Ocean to the sweaty docks of San Francisco and westward to balmy Hawaii, and its influence spread far beyond that.

HBC's amazing realm eventually encompassed nearly three million square miles—ten times the size of the Holy Roman Empire at its height. When Sir George Simpson, its overseas Governor, attended a civic dinner at Christiania in Norway during his 1838 world tour, he was toasted as "head of the most extended dominion in the known world—the Emperor of Russia, the Queen of England and the President of the United States excepted."

Much of modern Canada emerged from the HBC; it was the presence of the Hudson's Bay Company's traders that kept the Canadian West out of the grasp of American colonizers pushing northward. It was the 1870 sale of Company territory to the new nation of Canada that let the former colonies fill in their western and northern boundaries, and three of the early HBC trading posts—Fort Garry (Winnipeg), Fort Edmonton and Fort Victoria—grew into provincial capitals. Its officers charted the Arctic coast and mapped the British Columbia interior. The Company's servants introduced to Canada sheep farming and dandelions, originally imported to provide food and wine.

Bearing in mind the fact that the HBC was heir to the Montreal-based North West Company which it absorbed in 1821, the Company's impact on the formation of present-day Canada has been incalculable. The Hudson's Bay Company determined the country's political and physical shape, endowing the new nationality with a mentality that endures to this day. University of Alberta historian John Foster had the HBC in mind when he wrote: "For nearly all regions of Canada, recorded history begins with the fur trade. Its history is a kaleidoscope of experiences, ranging from the demi-heroic achievements of individuals to the machinations of empires headquartered in distant homelands."

All that power prompted resentment. The initials HBC were (and are) just as often defined for the inquiring tenderfoot as "the Hungry Belly Company" as by the more benign "Here Before Christ."*

A pugnacious relic of the high afternoon of Empire and the oldest continuous capitalist corporation still in existence, the HBC is the ultimate example of corporate Darwinism. It has always managed to adapt itself to successive sets of altered circumstances. The Company has weathered 315 years of war, rebellion, ambush, siege, bumbling bureaucracy and coupon-clipping neglect. Unlike the splendiferous and much more ambitious Cecil Rhodes, Stamford Raffles, Rajah Brooke and the East India nabobs, the HBC has not only endured but, until lately, also prospered. Despite recent years of humiliating financial losses, the Company remains a major economic force as the world's largest private fur auctioneer, Canada's most widespread department store chain and a significant international player in real estate and oil—still stuffing $5 billion in sales into its coffers every year. It has survived by turning nearly every necessity into an opportunity and by never moving too fast. The HBC motto should really have been "Wait and Seize."

"What the HBC gave with one hand, it seemed to take back with the other," French-Canadian novelist Gabrielle Roy has argued, voicing the sentiment of many of its subjects. A more specific *cri de coeur* comes from Blair Stonechild, a full-blood Cree who heads the Department of Indian Studies at the Saskatchewan Indian Federated College in Regina: "The Company takes the view that it treated Indians fairly, using the rationale that it did not attempt to exterminate them, as was done in the U.S. It is the difference between being in the fire and being in the frying pan."

THE HISTORY OF the Hudson's Bay Company has been played out in the vast mysterious hinterland that Canadian poet Al Purdy once described as being "north of summer." Canadians' romance with their North has not been defused by time, even if they themselves seldom venture into latitudes higher than their summer cottages. "Because of our origin in the northern frontier," wrote historian W.L. Morton, "Canadian life to this day is marked by a northern quality. The line which marks the frontier from the farmstead, the wilderness from the baseland, the hinterland from the metropolis, runs

* A young Inuit girl in the mid-1970s wrote to the editor of *Inuit Today* claiming the initials should really stand for Horny Boys' Club.

through every Canadian psyche." The same resonance of spirit has been caught so evocatively in Canada's unofficial national anthem, Quebec folksinger Gilles Vigneault's *Mon pays, c'est l'hiver.*

It was partly this sense of quintessential northernness that made the Hudson's Bay Company such a subliminally essential element pervading the Canadian consciousness. Imprisoned in paved cities and blinkered by urban impulses, the modern Canadian is barely aware that the geographical centre of the country is at Baker Lake, originally an HBC trading post nuzzling Chesterfield Inlet, west off Hudson Bay.

The Canadian North is usually defined by its size (1.5 million square miles north of 60°), its low temperatures (the cold can be so intense it burns the flesh) and its isolation. Yet what makes life there unique is the quality of the silence—very different from the inert void of space or the foreboding hush of a battlefield. The North is suffused with a tumultuous stillness, almost deafening in its intensity, that conveys a warning to the visitor: this land has entered into only a temporary truce with man's presence. It is not a place to seek or to find tranquillity and will shake pomposity out of anyone's boots. The North is attractive mainly for what Hugh Stewart, an old Arctic hand, has called "the moral alternative it offers."

In winter, the North shines with a dozen recognizably different shades of white; in autumn, the neon-red brilliance of bearberries lights up the countryside for miles around, accented by cloud or hill shadows. Along the treeline, the pastel hues of the land are heightened here and there by a cluster of spruce. In February, the calm radiance of an afternoon can instantaneously vanish in a blizzard so thick that snow-walkers cannot see as far as their feet. At high noon on a sparkling patch of snow, the light can literally blind.

To describe this frozen country as forbidding seems beside the point, yet it is an unfailingly fascinating landscape. An omnivorous Arctic fox, his wise countenance as world-weary as a long-tenured professor's, materializes out of rocky scrub that looks as if it could not sustain a field mouse. Fox fur was used by the natives to wipe babies' bottoms until first Edwardian duchesses and then the fancy high-steppers of Harlem and streetwalkers of Paris adopted white boas as their trademark—and created a market.

The northern furies seldom disturbed the Company's well-moneyed English proprietors. The Governors (roughly equivalent to chairmen of the board), Deputy Governors (presidents) and the Committeemen (the seven directors) who ran the burgeoning enterprise from the City, London's financial district for three centuries, never heard the castanet tail-slap of an alarmed beaver in a wilderness pond or felt the chill of autumn's early frost closing in on Hudson Bay. Nor did they want to.

They were the ultimate absentee landlords. No Governor visited Hudson Bay until 264 years after the Company's incorporation, when Sir Patrick Ashley Cooper, the twenty-ninth man to hold the office, made a brief ceremonial procession through its posts.

The London-based proprietors exercised authority from afar according to the Bertrand Russell definition of power as "the production of intended effects." Fortunately for them, the hardy men at the outposts were resistant enough to interpret London's orders none too literally. Instead, they invested considerable energy trying to educate various governors about the essential contradictions that made life so difficult on the bay. Somehow the long-distance marriage worked, with each side maintaining a mixture of a mutual respect for and proper distrust of one another.

For their part, the London Committeemen were always careful to confine their dispatches to detail rather than policy.* There was little flavour of mani-fest destiny in their often mundane instructions, for they were creating a merchant empire dedicated strictly to profit. They betrayed scant urge to seek title to its spiritual dimension. At the same time, no money-saving wrinkle was too much trouble to claim the management's attention. A May 29, 1680, directive to John Nixon, then in charge of the bay posts, instructs him on how to economize on food imports by raising his own pigs. "Upon Hay Island where our grand Factory is," it runs, "you may propergate swine without much diffi-culty, wch is an excellent flesh, and the creature is hardy and will live where some other creatures cannot."

Such irrelevant nonsense (the climate could not possibly sustain forage for pigs to survive, like European wild boars, unsheltered for a winter) tended to fix in the minds of the bay-side traders a stereotype of the London governors as superannuated financiers with abalone-shaped jowls and little common sense. Most of them had indeed simmered up in the lugubrious universe of upper-crust England, where a discreetly arched eyebrow could ruin a man's or a country's credit. But except for the trio of lordly personages who established

---

* The occasional directive was totally misguided, such as the 1784 decision to send 150 copies of *The Country Clergyman's Advice* to Parishioners for distribution among Indians who could not read any printed work, let alone English parochial flummery.

the Company's original claims (Prince Rupert, the Duke of York and the Duke of Marlborough) the HBC governors were tough-minded City financiers who supported Lord Palmerston's stern edict: "We have no permanent friends nor perpetual enemies: our interests are permanent."

Unlike some of their contemporaries, they did not subscribe to the unblushing credo that Providence was the ultimate source of British authority. But if they would not bow to "heaven's command" in spreading British munificence around the world, they most assuredly recognized the connection between harvesting profits overseas and furthering England's diplomatic interests abroad. John S. Galbraith, the California historian who wrote a book (*The Hudson's Bay Company as an Imperial Factor*) to document the thesis that "the expansion of the British Empire has been largely motivated by the energies of the mercantile class," argued that largely unknown merchants were more influential in shaping Imperial policy than the statesmen who got the kudos. It seemed a point beyond contention to the men who directed the affairs of the HBC that their corporate objectives and England's priorities of state were one and the same.

A clue to why the HBC's operational code evolved as it did—the notion that moderation in the conduct of the whole enterprise was not just a safe course between extremes but a secular mandate on how to conduct one's life—was that, as it matured, the Bay came more and more under Scottish influence. Sparse of speech but swift in action, the tight-lipped individualists who came to North America from the distinctive parishes of Scotland had temperaments ideally suited for the fur trade: a meld of persistence and self-sufficiency. Intellectually armed by the Shorter Catechism, they made up in loyalty and moral fibre what they lacked in creativity and exuberance.

Nearly all the great names in the HBC's annals grew up in Scotland; not just Sir George Simpson, Donald Smith and Sir James Douglas, the trio who dominated the Company's nineteenth-century history, but others: Chief Factor Robert Campbell, who spent eleven years fur trading and map making among hostile Indians of the unknown Yukon; Chief Factor Alexander Hunter Murray, who plunked down Fort Yukon in Russian territory and told Imperial Russia to like it; John McLean from the Isle of Mull, who unlocked the savage country of Ungava; Thomas Simpson, descendant of Duncan Forbes of Culloden, who mapped some of the most forbidding parts of the Arctic coast; James Leith of Aberdeenshire, who left half his estate for the propagation of the Protestant faith among the Indians; John Stuart of

Strathspey, who first penetrated the region that became northern British Columbia; and many, many more.

They became citizens of the New Land, in the early years mating with the Indian tribes with whom they traded. When the Scottish Marquis of Lorne, then Governor General of Canada, made his first national tour in 1881 and found himself at Rat Portage in northwestern Ontario, he asked the local HBC Factor to introduce him to a "typical" Indian. The Bay man motioned for the fiercest-looking brave to come forward: "Would ye come here for a minute, Macdonald?"

The introduction of the Scottish strain via the HBC into the complicated weave that makes up the tartan of the Canadian character must be ranked as one of the Company's enduring legacies. "Canadians like to see themselves as the Scots of North America," concluded Ronald Bryden, director of the Graduate Centre for the Study of Drama at the University of Toronto, "canny, sober, frugal folk of superior education who by quietly terrible Calvinist virtue will inherit the 21st century." The residual Calvinism of the early Scots was the real religion of the first Hudson Bay posts: inbred obedience to authority and eagerness to bear the burden of Calvinism's earthly path to salvation—hard work.

On other continents, West European civilization had been spearheaded by devoted missionaries, followed by glory-driven soldiers and flinty-eyed traders. In the Canadian North and West, the order was precisely the reverse—traders, soldiers, then missionaries. The Company's backhanded attitude towards itin-erant men of God was summed up in an 1863 directive from Alexander Grant Dallas, then Chief Factor of Victoria, who allowed that as a general rule the Company ought to be civil to and assist the missionaries, but not allow them to trespass too far upon its resources.*

To take the place of organized religion and to impose its authority, the Company at irregular intervals issued its own commandments prescribing how its men should behave. A typical set of paper tablets, proclaimed on

---

* Just to cover all the eventualities, God was enlisted in the Company's business affairs to the extent that His helping hand was extolled no fewer than three times in the official Bill of Lading forms then in use: "Shipped, by the Grace of God, in good order and well-conditioned by .... in the Hudson's Bay Company service for and on account of the Honourable Governor and Company of Adventurers of England trading into Hudson Bay, in and upon the good ship .... now riding at anchor at .... in North America and, by God's Grace, bound for .... All which goods and merchandise I promise to deliver according to the order of the Governor and Committee of the Honourable Hudson's Bay Company (the dangers of the seas only excepted). And so God send the good ship to her desired port in safety. Amen."

September 26, 1714, directed its men "to live lovingly with one another, not to swear or quarrel, but to live peaceably, without drunkenness or profaneness." The traders were forbidden "to embezzle gunpowder" and neither were they "to meddle, trade or affront any Indians, nor to concern themselves with women—which Frenchmen did, thereby cutting themselves off through jealousy ... Men going contrary to be punished before Indians."

Such Company edicts comprised the true gospel. As late as 1921, N.M.W.J. McKenzie wrote in *The Men of the Hudson's Bay Company*, "you might break all the ten Commandments in one clatter, but to break any of the rules of the Company, *that* was quite another thing."

EXCEPT FOR SERVANTS from the Orkney Islands, the early Bay men came from no specific social stratum of England or Scotland. Not satisfied to waste their careers serving time in the stultifying occupations then available in a crowded and fluctuating domestic labour market yet not rash enough to volunteer for the military, they signed on with the intention of saving enough money to return, marry well and settle into small-scale but independent pursuits.

But once they found themselves on Hudson Bay—living out their first five-year hitches and having to exist near the limits of human endurance—they were never the same again. Some hurried home on the first supply ship due out after the expiration of their contracts. Most stayed, or came back after a visit home, caught despite themselves in the dream and drama of the Company of Adventurers. They were, one after the other, transmogrified into Company men, faithful to a corporate ethic they perceived as being somehow more alluring than merely a return on investment, even though this was how their efforts were invariably judged. They continued in the trade, braving conditions of life and work beyond the call of duty, firm in their conviction that even when their dreams proved flawed, particular circumstances were at fault rather than the great enterprise itself.

Stoicism was a prized virtue, even at the top. When Colonel John Crofton came to Rupert's Land in 1846 with his 6th Regiment of Foot, the Royal Warwickshires, to help defend the Red River settlement, he travelled up the thirty-four portages from York Factory to Fort Garry with Sir George Simpson, who was by then sixty years old. The daily canoe journey was strenuous enough, but camping on wet ground every night without a tent was far worse. "One night," the Colonel confided to his journal, "when wet and cold, old

Sir George turned to me and said: 'I wish to heaven you'd say, "This is dreadful, horrid work"—for I want to grumble, but not to be the first to do so.'" Neither man voiced a whimper of public complaint.

Despite the drawbacks of climate and the primitive facilities, postings at the forts tended to be viewed as the real world, while sojourns back to England, Scotland or, later, to urban Canada made the HBC traders feel ill at ease and out of place. They would arrive, after a lengthy assignment in the service, to pay their respects to the London Committeemen, shifting restlessly in uphol-stered armchairs and standing about in Sabbath waistcoats that might have been in vogue a decade or two earlier, giving off a distinctly musty odour. Accustomed to silence and not knowing what to say to whom, they were reduced from knights of the bay to shuffling misfits. No wonder they signed up again, abandoned their patrimonies and rushed back to the new continent where they could stand tall in silent valleys that marched towards the Rocky Mountains or dip their canteens in northern waters that no one else knew.

Yet for all its freedoms, it was a life that imprisoned the soul. With some exceptions, the Bay men became internal exiles in both their homelands, original and adopted. Never part of any society outside the fur trade, they gradually pruned their ancestral roots, becoming bitterly aware of the true nature of any voluntary emigration: that one is exiled *from*, never *to*, and that disinheritance and marginality are all too often the price of freedom. More than one loyal HBC trader faced the end of his days with few close friends or blood relatives he wished to acknowledge and so bequeathed whatever worldly goods he had gathered to the only family he had: the Company. "They were comfortably settled but apparently at a loss what to do with themselves," Sir George Simpson commented about his own retired factors. "They sigh for the Indian Country, the squaws, and skins and savages."

INDENTURED TO THEIR CORPORATE LUST for beaver pelts—the commodity that allowed the HBC traders to produce handsome profits of at least £20 million by 1857—the Hudson's Bay Company provided ultimate proof of Adam Smith's contention that England was a nation of shopkeepers on an imperial scale.

The HBC was far more interested in making profit than in making history. Once the Treaty of Utrecht had been signed and the Hudson Bay territories were officially tucked beneath England's wing, the vanities of Empire touched the HBC and its proprietors only tangentially. The notion that the Company of

Adventurers might be destined for such lofty purposes as colonizing the New World, converting "the savages" or discovering the North West Passage tested the upper limits of its governors' condescension. Such postulations of glory were reserved for early-morning conceits, discarded while toying at breakfast with the silver salvers keeping their devilled kidneys warm. At serious times of the day the proprietors went on doing what they knew best: turning furs into money.

Unlike their competitors in France, they never did seem to feel themselves charged with the concurrent missions of extending their monarch's territorial reach. As private capitalists, they were unhampered by the parasitic aristocrats who haunted their French rivals beholden to the court at Versailles. Operating under the strict discipline of strained balance sheets, the Bay men bent their efforts towards maximum gain quietly enough to avoid stirring up homegrown competitors who might challenge their questionable monopoly. "Throughout the Company's history, we have to remind ourselves that it existed not for the advancement of geographical knowledge nor to win the admiration of later generations, but to make money," K.G. Davies, the British historian, shrewdly noted, "and that an important part of making money is not losing it. This objective, if limited, was legitimate, and was undoubtedly achieved ..."

The single-minded drive for greater revenues coloured everything the Company did. For the first two hundred years of its existence, the HBC was dedicated to maintaining its vaunted fur trade monopoly; as soon as that carefully nurtured domain was overrun by floods of immigrants determined to turn the southern portion of the fur preserve into farmland, the Company switched to building up new monopolies devoted to supplying settlers with their goods and to gaining exclusive jurisdiction over water transportation on the Red, Saskatchewan, Athabasca and Mackenzie river systems.

This ability to evolve and thrive without competition was fortified from the beginning by a series of determined attempts to diversify the HBC's economic base. Some commodities that came their way as by-products of occupying the North, such as goose quills, walrus tusks, bear grease, whale oil and sealskins, were traded from the start, but the English governors were endlessly puzzled that the New Land seemed to contain no precious metals. They dispatched Samuel Hearne, James Knight and others on monumental journeys to find and claim nonexistent mountains of copper. Except for two coal mines the Company later developed on Vancouver Island near Nanaimo and Fort Rupert, the hunt for minerals proved fruitless.

Exports to England at one time or another included such diverse items as buffalo wool and buffalo tongues, eiderdown from ducks, narwhal tusks, smoked, dried and salted salmon, turpentine distilled from coniferous trees and Labrador tea—the leaves of a local plant that produced a passable beverage but proved much more useful in keeping rats out of granaries, moths out of clothes closets and fleas out of beds. The trade in all these items produced nothing but headaches. A similar result was achieved in 1921, when the HBC decided to breed reindeer on Baffin Island: 550 of the animals were transported from Norway and the Hudson's Bay Reindeer Company was incorporated under the direction of the well-known Arctic explorer Vilhjalmur Stefansson. But the project failed when there proved to be no suitable moss for the animals to chaw, and when the Lapps who had been hired as herders turned out to be fishermen.

The most bizarre HBC sideline was selling ice to Californians during the 1850s. At the time, San Francisco's population had swollen because of the 1848 Gold Rush, and all the available ice had to be shipped around Cape Horn from north of Boston. In 1854, James Douglas, the HBC's West Coast Governor, leased out for $14,000 a year the ice fields under the Company's jurisdiction to a former U.S. naval captain named W.A. Howard, who represented a group of San Francisco entrepreneurs. Their ice ship, the *Fanny Major*, put into Frederick Sound (in what is now Alaska), where Captain Howard hired five hundred Stikine Indians to cut and load chunks of the blue glacier. The first shipment of three hundred tons sold so quickly that Howard and his backers rushed to buy six more ice ships and decided to share their profitable mode of natural air conditioning and food preservation with Hong Kong and Honolulu. That was a mistake. The ice melted on the way across the Pacific, and the ships arrived with wet, empty holds. The business collapsed in 1856 when the senior San Francisco shareholder embezzled the funds and absconded to China.*

A far more serious and very much more profitable venture was a scheme organized during the stormy stewardship of the British financier Sir Robert Molesworth Kindersley, the HBC's twenty-seventh Governor, to supply France, Russia and Romania with food and munitions during the First World War. (The venture was actually the brainchild of Jean Monnet, who later became

---

* In the western Arctic, hosts still advise their guests they will never have a hangover if they use glacial ice in their drinks—implying that the rattle in their glasses has recently been hacked from local glaciers.

the first head of the European Common Market.) Through an elaborate maze of subsidiaries and overseas agencies, the Hudson's Bay Company arranged credits for the French administration and operated a fleet of nearly three hundred merchant ships. The HBC became a massive mover of edibles, fuel, lumber, ammunition and troops. More than thirteen million tons of supplies were delivered to France alone. By the spring of 1918, the private armada was discharging eleven thousand tons of freight daily at French ports. The HBC fleet's captains evaded German submarines whenever possible, but 110 vessels flying the Company's flag were sunk. The HBC applied its northern shipping experience to delivering similar cargoes to Tsarist Russia and, at Winston Churchill's request, took charge of supplying the White Russian armies following the Bolshevik Revolution. It was on the Archangel run that the HBC supply ship *Nascopie*'s deck gun sank a German submarine.

Apart from these and many other attempts to diversify,* the HBC has always devoted inordinate, almost obscene energy to trimming costs. One early result of this obsessive penny-pinching was that long after the Age of Steam, the posts around Hudson Bay were still operating on Iron Age technology. "Even a casual observer of fur trade society recognized that as the Nineteenth Century wore on, life in posts like York Factory got more and more out of touch with life in Britain," noted Michael Payne in his social history of York Factory. "In 1844 a Scottish friend of James Hargrave [the resident Chief Factor] wrote him a letter calling York Factory a 'heavy, lumbering, lazy' sort of place quite distinct from the 'velocified' world of Britain ... The world of work at a fur trade post remained essentially 'pre-industrial.'"

Salaries were (and are) kept at a minimum. David Thompson, whose pioneering maps of Western Canada were standard reference works for three-quarters of a century, was fired by the HBC after twenty-three years' service because the London Committeemen thought he was spending too much time shooting the sun instead of trading pelts. Such impersonal cost cutting left no detail untouched. In an official memorandum headed *sauces*, Sir George Simpson reprimanded Hargrave at York Factory on March 3, 1843, for spending too much on condiments. "I consider it quite unnecessary," scolded the parsimonious Governor, "to indent [requisition] for Sauces & Pickles on public account ... I never use fish sauce in the country, and never saw anyone

---

* Another was the establishment in 1964 of the U-Paddle Canoe rental service, which allows latter-day *voyageurs* to pick up their boats at one northern HBC store and deposit them at another.

use it or pickles either. From the quantity of Mustard indented for, one would suppose it is now issued as an article of trade with the Indians!"

Simpson also had a nasty habit of inducing his traders to re-engage for as little as three-quarters of the prevailing rates by renewing contracts for officers and men during the winter when they were isolated and could not take advantage of a competitive market.

Few Bay men beat the system. One who tried was John McKay, who invited his rivals from the North West Company to celebrate Christmas in 1799 at Osnaburgh House. "I had the honour of my neighbours company to dinner," he smugly reported. "Your Honours has the honour of bearing the expence." More typical was the pathetic 1789 journal entry of Thomas Stagner, the Factor at Manchester House on the North Saskatchewan River: "This being Christmas Morning, our small stock of flour, afforded us, a cake to eat, with a little tea & chocolate ... No one can know what it is to want bread, but those who experience it—which we here, daily do, in this Wild Country; particular Holidays only excepted."

A twentieth-century version of the Company's single-minded devotion to business that continued into the 1960s was the habit of not heating its northern stores, keeping them so cool, in fact, that inside walls and nailheads would be coated with ice. "The reason was that they didn't want anybody hanging around ... they wanted everybody out trapping," recalls Stuart Hodgson, who served twelve years as Commissioner of the Northwest Territories. "I remember going over to Repulse Bay in 1965 to see old Henry Voisey, and he complained they were going to heat his store the next year. When I told him it was about time, he said: 'What the hell do you mean it's about time? It's going to be terrible. I won't be able to get people out of here to do some work.'" E.J. (Scotty) Gall, who spent forty-four years with the HBC in the western Arctic, was proud of the unheated stores he ran for a quarter of a century and considered his hunters good workers only if they were on the trapline or out hunting. "I never encouraged them to hang around."

THE HBC'S REMARKABLE LONGEVITY has been due in no small measure to several lucky geographical accidents.

By choosing to settle the deserted shores of Hudson Bay rather than more attractive landfalls to the south, the early traders appropriated the overwhelming advantage of being able to deliver their goods into the very heart of the new continent, at the mouths of wide rivers that flowed through a fur-rich hinterland stretching back to the foothills of the Rocky Mountains. (An astounding 43 percent of Canada's territory drains into Hudson Bay, compared with only 10 percent into the much more populated St Lawrence.)

The trip from the loading docks on the Thames to the anchorage at Five Fathom Hole off York Factory was equal to the sailing time required to reach Montreal. By the end of the journey up the St Lawrence, however, the goods were still very far from the Lake Winnipeg streams that flowed to the beaver ponds of the northern forests. Hudson Bay's southwestern shore is 1,500 miles closer than the storehouses of Montreal to the Saskatchewan River system, then the richest beaver country. Until the advent of the railways, the Montreal-based fur merchants had to store and finance trade goods for two full years before reaping any harvest. It simply was not possible to make the round trip of thousands of miles inland by canoe during the time needed for the supply ships to arrive, unload and leave the St Lawrence before freeze-up. It was the capital burden of this lengthy overhead period, as much as any other reason, that defeated the North West Company. Being all too aware of the HBC's geographical advantage, the bold Nor'Westers tried unsuccessfully to negotiate their own access into Hudson Bay, even attempting to buy out the HBC.

The other great geographical advantage that allowed the fur trade to flourish was that most of Canada's huge drainage system is interconnected with relatively short portages—the main exceptions being the nine-mile Grand Portage west from Lake Superior and the twelve-mile Methy Portage into the Mackenzie Basin, first crossed by Peter Pond in 1778. Apart from these twenty-one-mile land barriers, it is possible to cross the upper half of the continent east of the Rockies by canoe.* "Canada's almost total navigability by canoe," noted Eric W. Morse, a modern explorer who has paddled most of the water routes, "is related to the fact that half of its surface lies on the world's oldest land mass, the Precambrian Shield, whose peaks and precipices have in

---

* Writing in the March 3, 1975, issue of *The New Yorker*, John McPhee documented how easily the continent can be crossed by its water routes: "A friend of mine who grew up in Timmins, a remote community in Ontario, once told me about an Indian friend of his boyhood who developed an irresistible urge to see New York City. He put his canoe in the water and started out. From stream to lake to pond to portage, he made his way a hundred miles to Lake Timiskaming, and its outlet, the Ottawa River. He went down the Ottawa to the St. Lawrence, down the St. Lawrence to the Richelieu, up the Richelieu to Lake Champlain, and from Lake Champlain to the Hudson. At the 79th Street Boat Basin he left the canoe in custody of attendants, and walked into town."

billions of years been ground to gentler gradients. The great contribution of
the Shield in making throughways is the chain of vast, connected lakes which
it caused to be formed around its edge. Great Bear, Great Slave, Athabasca,
Winnipeg, Lake of the Woods, Superior and Huron all have one side, or end,
in granite. As the rains and ice-melt for thousands of years poured down from
the steep edges of the Shield, water courses in softer soil were formed, draining to the sea. In this way were born great arterial rivers such as the
Mackenzie, the Churchill, the Winnipeg and the Ottawa."

Three large lakes—Superior, Winnipeg and Athabasca—were all eventually
controlled by the HBC as staging areas for the fur trade. During the summer, the
Canadian Shield is laced by impatient rivers, some as wide as the Danube yet
so remote they have yet to be named, all racing to tidewater at Hudson Bay.
Nature could hardly have planned to meet the Company's corporate objectives
more effectively: here was a huge subcontinent for the taking with a ready-
made, free transportation system; frigid enough that its animals grew thick
pelts; fertile enough to sprout an immense boreal forest that provided those
animals with shelter; rugged enough to keep out permanent settlers.

It was the fur trade moving up the beaver-choked rivers that determined
Canada's political boundaries. As Harold A. Innis noted in his monumental
The Fur Trade in Canada, "Canada emerged as a political entity with boundaries largely determined by the fur trade ... not in spite of geography but
because of it." Such nation building was no altruistic act of statesmanship by
the HBC. Except for its inland community at Red River, a bizarre experiment
by the utopian-minded Lord Selkirk, the Company was dead set against
settlers. They upset the animals. The Company pushed westward not to plant
colonies but to control competing trappers. By thus exhibiting a highly visible
presence west of the Lakehead, it prevented American farmers and mountain
men from pushing north and, after amalgamation with the Nor'Westers in
1821, stretched its own version of the Canadian nation from Hudson Bay and
the Gulf of St Lawrence to the Pacific.

That sometimes great notion was ultimately nailed down by the building
from Montreal to Vancouver of the transcontinental Canadian Pacific
Railway. As Pierre Berton wrote in *The Last Spike,* the second volume of his
perceptive study of the CPR: "For the next half century [1880–1930], this single
corporation would be the dominant force west of Ottawa. Already its initials,
CPR, had entered the national lexicon; soon they would be as familiar to most
Canadians as their own. In the decades to follow they would come to symbol-

ize many things to many people—repression, monopoly, daring, exploitation, imagination, government subsidy, high finance, patriotism, paternalism, and even life itself. There were few Canadians who were not in some manner affected by the presence of the Canadian Pacific; indeed, no other private company, with the single exception of the Hudson's Bay, has had such an influence on the destinies of the nation."

Irene Spry, the talented godmother of Canadian fur trade students, has pushed this argument one step further: "There is little doubt that the forces of American manifest destiny would have taken the West into a continental orbit, and if Canada had *not* been coast to coast, the pitiful little settlements in the St. Lawrence Valley would have been absorbed by the Americans long ago."

At the same time, both the CPR and the HBC—those ubiquitous sets of initials that richly earned the scepticism due any externally owned monopoly—ignited the resentment inherent in the master-servant relationship between the Central Canadian and the Western Canadian settlements that has accounted for many of the country's regional conflicts ever since. Too many Central Canadians still view the West as a kind of afterthought, a cranky child of the East. In fact, the fur-trading West was from the beginning politically and economically quite distinct—a different nation altogether from the farms and villages of the St Lawrence Valley, the Atlantic provinces or the nascent manufacturing industries around Lake Ontario. A proud society that existed on its own terms, this pre-agricultural West saw the birth of many genuine grievances against the metropolitan East.

"MY COUNTRY HAS NO HISTORY, only a past," complained New Brunswick poet Alden Nowlan. That may be true, if history is thought of as pompous successions of grandiloquent men, rosters of events or attempts to turn back economic tidal waves. But history always adds up to more than the ascertainable facts. The sudden promptings of blind accident or coalitions of individual yearnings that defeat armies—such quixotic forces also drive history's unpredictable chariots.

In the case of the Hudson's Bay Company, history was made by an enterprise of marginal economic and geographical significance that gradually evolved into one of the central formative influences in the founding of a nation—and, equally important, in the profound impact it had on the mentality of its inhabitants.

A loose federation of regions on the cold periphery of world civilization, Canada has always had trouble organizing itself to deal with crises threatening its national integrity, and as a result Canadians feel they are a marginal people with few core values to call their own. But they do share a distinctive mentality that, if often the despair of its more restless animators, has allowed this brave huddle of like-minded survivors to prosper in North America's attic.

It is the original implanting of that special mentality within the Canadian psyche, a combination of creative deference and cautiously progressive pragmatism, that is the Hudson's Bay Company's most pervasive legacy.

This prevailing ethic (ideology is too strong a term, philosophy too pretentious) was very different from the aggressive egalitarianism of the American frontier. Canada had few vigilantes, no Davy Crocketts or Daniel Boones. In sharp contrast to that of the United States, the Canadian experience flowed from the principles of allegiance rather than social contract and was founded on the organic growth of tradition rather than the assertion of revolutionary will. This was why, as historian William Kilbourn has noted, the original British North America Act set down common objectives of peace, order and good government in contrast to the individualistic emphasis in the American Declaration of Independence on life, liberty and the pursuit of happiness.

The fur trade in general and the Hudson's Bay Company in particular exercised a profound influence in the sculpting of the Canadian soul. "The shape of the indigenous Canadian imagination," concluded Abraham Rotstein, the University of Toronto economist who is an expert on both the fur trade and Canada's identity, "took root in the experiences of the fur trade, both for the French period and after the Conquest. Voyageurs, rapids, the outlying frontier, courageous exploration of rivers, long portages, relations with distant Indian tribes, these and other features of the fur trade are echoed today in the Canadian self-image. The vivid response in Canadian public opinion to such issues as pipelines and northern development bears the stamp of this legacy of 'nordicity' ... The fur trade, in short, more than virtually any other single experience, is the primary matrix out of which modern Canada emerged."

THE HUDSON'S BAY COMPANY turned much of the upper half of North America into a company town writ large, in which customers displayed individuality and imagination at their own risk.

The first HBC forts were the ultimate expression of what Northrop Frye, the eminent Canadian literary critic, dubbed "the garrison mentality." Frye described these small, isolated communities as "surrounded with a physical or psychological 'frontier,' separated from one another and from their American and British cultural sources: communities that provide all that their members have in the way of distinctively human values, and that are compelled to feel a great respect for the law and order that holds them together, yet confronted with a huge, unthinking, menacing, and formidable physical setting ... A garrison is a closely-knit and beleaguered society, and its moral and social values are unquestionable. In a perilous enterprise, one does not discuss causes or motives: one is either a fighter or a deserter."

During the HBC's first half-century, its outposts were garrisons in more than a metaphoric sense, and later, as they began to soften into trading towns, very little changed. The prevailing ethic remained deference to authority inside the ramparts and deference to nature beyond them. This orderly attitude, rooted in collective survival rather than individual excellence, still colours what most Canadians do and, especially, don't do.

Another element injected into the Canadian mentality by the HBC is the notion that monopoly or a mixture of private and public enterprise works better than individual ventures. This concept was derived from the enormous size of the continent, its climatic challenges and the fact that the only alternative to the Indian/Inuit mode of living off the land was to field such a huge economic infrastructure that over the long term only a state enterprise or a monopoly could afford it.

Coming from a mixed English/Scottish tradition, the early HBC traders set out a primitive form of capitalism in the cold-frame latitudes around Hudson Bay. They stressed life's sombre virtues—the notion that there is no feeling more satisfying than a hard day's work well done and that the good man always earns more than his keep. In dramatic contrast to the shotgun individualism of the American West, the idea was to be *careful*, plainly dressed and quiet spoken, close with one's money and emotions. Flashes of pleasure and moments of splendour had to look accidental, never planned.

Such a gloomy credo could have been carved in stone for the Thomson family—Roy, the Scottish-Canadian press potentate who was appointed to the British House of Lords, and his son, Kenneth, who purchased control of the HBC in 1979 for $640 million cash. "They say business is the law of the jungle," Roy Thomson once mused. "I think it is the law of life. If you want to live and you want to prosper, you have to be ambitious. You've got to be ready to sacrifice leisure and pleasure. I was forty years old before I had any money at all.

But these things don't happen overnight. How many people are there who will wait that long to be successful, and work all the time? Not very many. Maybe they're right. Maybe I'm a bloody fool. But I don't think I am."

Amen.

VIEWED THROUGH THE SEPIA GLOW of retrospect, the HBC was a mercantile colossus, straddling oceans, spanning continents and only recently reduced to more modest circumstances. Yet in terms of manpower and gross revenues, the very opposite was true. The Company has always been large in terms of the square miles it controlled, but until the mid-twentieth century it was never very big. At the height of its geographical presence, when its domain covered a quarter of North America, the HBC had fewer than three thousand employees, and as late as 1811 when it was competing head to head with the rambunctious platoons of Nor'Westers fanning out from Montreal, a staff of only 320 manned its seventy-six posts.*

The Company's exponential fiscal growth occurred not during its historic heyday but in the early 1980s when its personnel roster nudged 50,000—an army of clerks and generals as large as the late and glorious East India Company at the height of its powers. Gross revenues first exceeded $1 billion in 1977 and the Company's highest profit ($80.3 million) was recorded in 1979. By the end of 1984, the payroll was down to 42,500 people and profits had been replaced by a three-year losing streak of nearly $350 million that saw the control shares Lord Thomson of Fleet had purchased for $37 plummet to as low as $15.†

Donald McGiverin, the modern-day Governor who headed the Company in its best and worst years (having force-marched total sales from less than $500 million to nearly $5 billion), remained philosophical in the face of adversity, blaming the economic recession that hit every merchandiser and the fact that too much debt (a peak of $2 billion in 1982) was acquired for expanding the business: "I regret that the recession took place and I wish Canada

* The natural tendency to exaggerate the Company's power and size found its most absurd expression in a novel published by Jules Verne in 1873. In *The Fur Country*, the best-selling author of *Twenty Thousand Leagues Under the Sea* assured his readers that the Hudson's Bay Company at that time employed "about a million men in its territories."
† In 1970, when the HBC's headquarters was moved from London to Winnipeg, 7 percent of its stock was held in Canada; by Dec. 31, 1984, only 3.8 percent of the shares were still owned in the United Kingdom.

were not overstored. But in the tradition of this Company you have to build forts in order to *be* there, even if they are hard to maintain for a while. This is still a great Company. We must be doing something right when we have $5-billion worth of business with the public ... This is not what I had in mind, but the chief executive officer never has a bulletproof vest."

By the winter of 1984–85, McGiverin, a gregarious merchandiser with a kindly disposition, was having private as well as public troubles: his weekend hideaway at Palgrave, deep in the Ontario bush, was being overrun by beavers. "The little buggers keep eating away at my only apple tree," he complained after having tied steel plates around its gnawed trunk. He defended his domain against the industrious rodents with every available weapon, including dynamite to bust their dams. But the beavers, perhaps driven by tribal memory of the millions of their ancestors who gave their all to the Company of Adventurers, would not leave the Governor in peace. Sometimes, late at night while reading in bed, trying to find solace from the brutal competition of the marketplace, McGiverin thought he heard trees falling. Those damn beavers will get him yet.

Beyond the Westering Sea

"Whosoever commands the seas, commands the trade; whosoever commands the trade of the world, commands the riches of the world—and consequently, the world itself."
—Sir Walter Raleigh

THEY CAME in ungainly three-masted ships with brave bowsprits and shuddering shrouds to claim a New World.

The chimera of a North West Passage had haunted Europeans for most of three hundred years, its discovery eventually becoming as much the pursuit of personal fulfilment as a feat of navigation. In the foreword to *Northwest Passage*, American novelist Kenneth Roberts caught the true nature of this operatic quest: "On every side of us are men who hunt perpetually for their personal Northwest Passage, too often sacrificing health, strength, and life itself to the search; and who shall say they are not happier in their vain and hopeful quest than wiser, duller folks who sit at home, venturing nothing and, with sour laughs, deriding the seekers for that fabled thoroughfare?"

The search took on almost religious overtones, with many icebound mariners comforting themselves with the thought that the Creator had placed daunting natural obstacles in the way because the richest reward would go to those who dared and suffered most. In cockleshells of ships more suitable for cruising the relatively benign coastal waters of Europe, they set out to test their souls against the elements. Many never returned. Most of those who wintered on the new continent soon regretted their vows, offering their Deity secret bargains to swap their pretensions to glory for mere survival.

By the dawn of the sixteenth century, nearly every European monarch whose kingdom was washed by the sea had commissioned adventurous captains to seek lucrative landfalls beyond the setting sun.

Their rhumb line was set by the scatterbrained Italian mariner Christopher Columbus, who had crossed the great Western Ocean four times to confirm his conviction that he had found "the islands at the end of the Orient." He mistook Haiti for Japan, was more fascinated by the ornaments "worn in the noses of the natives" than in discovering new territory and, when he found no gold, recommended to Queen Isabella that she encourage the barter of local "cannibal-slaves" for Spanish cattle.

Until the Spanish found silver and gold, Europe's outward-bound mariners were searching not for a new continent but for a fast route to the treasures of India and Cathay. The idea of reaching the Far East by sailing west was still unproved, and for the next three centuries expeditions of varying skill but equal determination would try to butt their way past or through the land barrier blocking access to Asia. A cargo of Oriental silks or cloves from the spice islands of the East Indies could yield tenfold profits for the importer. European tastebuds craved exotic condiments to mask the taste of tainted meat in summer or, even worse, the salted cuts in winter. The land route to China was long, tedious and infested by Islamic tax collectors, but Magellan's sea alternative past the furies of Cape Horn was estimated to be two thousand leagues (six thousand miles) longer than a direct passage—if there were one.

Determined skippers bent their ships' topgallants, heading due west, hopeful they could find the secret seaway through the cursed land barrier. Every deep cove was thought to be a passage to India. Inevitably, ships heading confidently up some bay, inlet or river would heave-to, as their captains entered in log-books the oft repeated lament: "Once more, we are embayed ..."

"They had not expected to find North America in the first place, impudently lying across their path to the Orient," Daniel Francis has pointed out in *Battle for the West*, "and when they discovered it was not just an oversized island but an entire continent stretching almost from pole to pole, they were infuriated." Ownership of the New World had originally been claimed by Spain and Portugal, their authority stemming from a series of arrogant papal bulls and the Treaty of Tordesillas (1494), which divided between the Iberian powers the unknown territory along a meridian lying 370 leagues west of the Cape Verde Islands, with a line drawn roughly from Brazil to Newfoundland.

This sweeping claim held fast through most of the 1500s, even though it was violated as frequently as it was respected.

THE NOTION OF A NEW WORLD on the far shore of the Atlantic had intrigued European navigators ever since the restless Vikings had probed the western edges of that misty sea. They left little to posterity but a few stone ruins and an anonymous chronicle, *The King's Mirror,* which would forever frame the romantic essence of their journeys. "If you wish to know what men seek in that land, why men journey thither in so great peril of their lives, it is the threefold nature of man that draws him ... One part thereof is the spirit of rivalry and the desire for fame; for it is man's nature to go where there is likelihood of great danger, and to make himself famous thereby. Another part is the desire for knowledge; for it is man's nature to wish to know and see those parts of which he had heard ... The third part is the desire of gain; for men seek after riches in every place where they learn that profit is to be had, even though there is great danger in it."

For three interminable centuries, brave and otherwise rational men cast common sense aside to embark on improbable voyages into the void. They were lured by the fact that the once nebulous concept of a short route to the Far East had grown increasingly specific, even if little of the rumoured geographical detail was accurate. Brooding savants of the day who themselves seldom ventured to sea postulated that since the amount of the earth's water was bound to be equally divided between the northern and southern hemispheres, the capacity of land masses also had to coincide. Portuguese navigators who had circled Africa to reach the Orient perceived that the Asian coastline veered eastward at its upper extensions, while Spanish galleon captains in the Pacific, tacking north of Panama, reported the American coastline bending steadily westward. From this scanty data flowed the conclusion that the two land masses were joined at the top, and that the new continent was really a giant peninsula jutting out of Asia, with rivers crossing it affording easy access to Cathay.

The magnetism of the North was not limited to the swing of compass needles. Fishermen from St Malo and Bristol had glimpsed the New World while harvesting the profusion of sea life on the shallow Grand Banks. This revived the long-dormant saga of how the Vikings reached Greenland, there to establish Christian settlements prosperous enough to pay tithes to the Pope as well as taxes to the King of Norway and even to dispatch a small contingent to the Crusades.

The first organized voyage to the northern gate of this new land mass was that of John Cabot. A silk-clad Venetian dandy who had immigrated to England in 1495, Cabot was sponsored by Henry VII. Seven years earlier the English king had turned down a plea from Bartholomew Columbus to underwrite his brother Christopher's impending journey, and he was determined not to be outdone by his Spanish rivals again. Henry granted Cabot and his sons the right to govern whatever lands they might find, plus a trade monopoly subject to a 20 percent tax payable to the Crown. An experienced explorer who had already visited Mecca and contemplated caravans winding their solemn way from "Xanadu," Cabot had constructed a magnificent globe of the earth with land masses converging at each pole and the Asian continent bulging obligingly into the Atlantic. He used this fanciful construct, plus the privilege of the royal charter, to extract the necessary financing from Bristol merchants and, after one false start, set off in May 1497 aboard the fifty-ton *Matthew* to seek his fortune. Thirty-five days later he made a landfall, probably on the east coast of either Newfoundland or Cape Breton Island. He claimed the territory for his royal sponsor and a scant two weeks later was back in England.

Hailed as the conqueror of a New World, Cabot was awarded £10 by Henry and became the idol of his day, with crowds of admirers surrounding him on the Bristol docks, aping his every gesture. He enthralled his entourage by describing how, when anchored off the new-found-land, his crew had dipped buckets into the sea and hauled them up brimming with silvery cod, swearing that the fish were so plentiful "that at times they even stayed the ship's passage." Cabot had indeed found treasure; for centuries afterward, Bristol merchants would exploit the fishing grounds fully.

The following summer a convoy of Bristol settlers led by Cabot and reportedly accompanied by a Venetian bishop planned to establish a permanent community in the new territory before sailing the rest of the way to Chipangu (Japan). The five-ship flotilla set off with great fanfare amid all the appropriate blessings but ingloriously sank, except for one vessel that limped back to Ireland. Cabot, safe home, died quietly in England the next year.

Cabot's son Sebastian chose a different path to the Asian mainland by organizing expeditions to search for a North *East* Passage and succeeded in establishing lucrative trade links with Russia through Archangel, on the White Sea. To exploit that commerce, a group of London merchants gathered under the banner of the Muscovy Company and received in 1555 the first

English charter granted to an overseas trading company. In return for weapons and other items of relatively advanced technology, the czars agreed to export squirrel, tallow, wax, deerhide, beaver, marten, flax and cordage. (It was Russian rope trimming the sails of Elizabeth I's rampaging navy that helped defeat the Spanish Armada in 1588.) This Russian trade proved so profitable that further exploration was shelved, but the Muscovy Company's prized monopoly was soon threatened, particularly by the belligerent sea-beggars of the Netherlands.

The transatlantic voyages that followed, mainly from France, England and the Netherlands, consisted of a succession of curiosity-driven navigators claiming hesitant outposts on the inhospitable eastern seaboard of the new land. The first northern settlements had been founded by Basque fishermen during the third quarter of the sixteenth century as temporary wintering stations for the fleets of whaling galleons sailing out of Biscay. At about the same time, the Oxford-educated privateer Sir Humphrey Gilbert planted a short-lived colony in Newfoundland (the first English settlement in North America), but two of his vessels later foundered, and he was last seen aboard his sinking flagship shouting grandly into the wind: "We are as near heaven by sea as by land!"

The saddest early attempt at colonization was the doomed undertaking of the splendidly named Troilus de La Roche de Mesgouez, the first viceroy of New France, who chose to colonize, of all places, the treacherous sands of Sable Island, off Nova Scotia. There he settled his ragged crew of three hundred "vagabonds and beggars," who promptly proceeded to massacre their leaders and one another.

Gradually becoming aware that they were dealing with a separate continent and not a protrusion of Asia, European mariners determined to find an easier passage round the land barrier than the fog-bound and violent Strait of Magellan between the mainland's southernmost tip and the inhospitable Tierra del Fuego islands. Jacques Cartier tacked up the beckoning St Lawrence River, convinced he had found a passage to Cathay.*

One theory current at the time held that the new continent was bisected by three great bays—the Gulf of Mexico on the southeast, the Gulf of

---

* Time did not shake this belief. More than a century later, René-Robert Cavelier, Sieur de La Salle, who later explored the Mississippi to its delta, was granted a site by the Sulpician Fathers at the rapids where the St Lawrence narrows and named the tiny settlement *La Chine* (now Lachine), certain he was on his way to China and the Orient.

California on the southwest and the still unnamed Hudson Bay on the northeast, with the latter two connected in some undetermined fashion. Because both coasts of South America had been avidly explored without discovery of this mythical waterway's outlets, attention turned to the northern continent, and the hunt for the North West Passage started in earnest.

The two qualifications for northern exploration seemed to be courage bordering on the foolhardy and a literary obsession for recording everyday minutiae. Journals proliferated on the shelves of printers in London and on the continent, weighty sagas documenting the adventure and hardship of the search for the elusive Passage. None of these accounts of tragic escapades, which recounted every pang of conscience and twitch of frozen toe, deterred successive waves of nautical speculators from seeking the prize. Sir Walter Raleigh best expressed the sentiment of outward-bound Europeans: "Whosoever commands the seas, commands the trade; whosoever commands the trade of the world, commands the riches of the world—and consequently, the world itself."

Sir Martin Frobisher, a dour fortune hunter who headed three absurd expeditions into the Arctic, voiced another reason for all the fuss when he declared that discovering the North West Passage was "the only thing of the world that was left yet undone." A typical Elizabethan sea-dog and captain of his own ship at twenty, Frobisher never cloaked his appetites in piety, believing that privateering was a fit profession for a gentleman—even if the English geographer Richard Hakluyt described him as "the most infamous for outrageous common and daily piracies." After trying unsuccessfully for fifteen years to obtain the necessary financing, Frobisher presented his scheme for a voyage of discovery to the directors of the Muscovy Company. They at first turned him down, but he caught the interest of a City broker named Michael Lok who had himself captained a merchantman in the Levant Company's trade. Both men had enough friends at court to apply royal pressure on the Muscovy directors and enlist their participation. Elizabeth I herself subscribed £100 to the Frobisher expedition in the full expectation that he would return with a hoard of silver from Lima and trunks laden with Manila gold. The funds proved adequate to afford Frobisher some unusual comforts, including "duck upholstery for his bedding" and "a bottell of aquavite."

His three ships dropped down the Thames tide on June 7, 1576, firing a smoky cannonade as they passed the royal Palace at Greenwich: "Her Majestie beholding the same, commended it and bade us farewell, with shaking her

hand at us out the window." Off Greenland (which Frobisher alarmingly
mistook for the mythical "Friesland"), one of his vessels was swamped by a
storm, and its captain, unnerved by the ice, turned back. Twenty-eight days
later, aboard the ten-ton *Gabriel*, Frobisher sighted land. Convinced that they
had discovered the northern equivalent of Magellan's passage round the lower
tip of South America, Frobisher's pilot George Best proudly reported: "So this
place he named Frobisher's Straits—like as Magellan at the southwest end of
the world, we having discovered the passage to the South Sea."

When he returned to London two months later without pursuing his find,
Frobisher was carrying a heavy black rock he had picked up during a brief landfall at Hall Island. The wife of Michael Lok, his financial backer, happened to
throw a chip of it into the dining-room fire. It burned with a strange flame,
and when it was coated in vinegar "glisttered with a bright Marquesset of
gold." Lok promptly took samples to London assayers, who just as promptly
declared them worthless. But an Italian metallurgical charlatan named John
Baptiste Agnello pronounced that the rock fragments contained traces of gold.
(When Lok demanded how Agnello had found what his colleagues missed, the
alchemist soothingly assured the financier it was "necessary to know how to
flatter nature.")

Lok eventually unearthed another imaginative metallurgist who also
perceived the "gold," and the Queen granted the prospectors a charter and
£1,000 to establish the Cathay Company, naming Lok its first governor.
Frobisher was promoted to high admiral and set out the following April with
three new ships and twelve dozen Cornish miners. The expedition returned
with two hundred tons of ore, making the run home in only twenty days, and
reported with mounting excitement that the stones of the islands they passed
"glitter in the sun like gold." Assays this time claimed that the rock contained
up to £53 of gold per ton. Aboard the fifteen ships of the 1578 expedition that
followed were four hundred men (including an Anglican divine, the Reverend
Mr Wolfall), heavy tunnelling equipment and a prefabricated bunker designed
to winter a hundred miners. After dropping off his supplies on an island in
Countess of Warwick Strait, Frobisher sailed 180 miles into what would later
be named Hudson Strait, convinced that he was on his way to the South
Seas—until the floating ice stopped him cold.

The miners dug up nearly two thousand tons of the ore. Wintering plans
were happily abandoned and the flotilla returned in triumph to discharge its
cargo at a special smelter built on the Thames. But the ore turned out to

contain no gold (the crushed rock was eventually put to use paving the streets of London), and the unfortunate Lok found himself languishing in debtors' prison.* Frobisher nimbly escaped his critics and he was awarded a gold chain by Elizabeth I—the only gold he ever found. He presented his sovereign with a narwhal tusk and an Eskimo, complete with kayak. The Queen was so delighted with her new charge that she allowed the Arctic hunter to spear swans along the Avon River, customarily a royal prerogative. Frobisher went on to greater joy, serving as vice-admiral under his friend Sir Francis Drake in privateering ventures off the West Indies, winning rich laurels for his inspiring command of a squadron during the defeat of the Spanish Armada. He died from wounds in 1594 during an assault on the Spanish-held fortress of Crozon, in Brittany. The most enduring legacy of his northern adventures was the maxim credited to George Best, who rose from pilot to command of the *Anne Francis* on Frobisher's third expedition. This wise navigator had good reason to coin a new version of the enduring aphorism: "All is not gold that shineth."

Seven years after Frobisher's anticlimactic return, Elizabeth granted a similar exploration charter to John Davis, a mathematically inclined navigator eager to prove his theories about the precise location of the North West Passage. He staged three modest expeditions, uneventful except that, for once, they turned a tidy profit from the codfish and sealskins brought back. He observed that at the outlet of what is now Davis Strait there was "a furious overfall ... like the rage of the waters under London Bridge"—the riptide ebbing out of Hudson Strait.

There followed two brief probes of northern channels by Captain George Weymouth (1602) and John Knight (1606), each sponsored by the newly founded East India Company, anxious to locate a quicker route to the gold of the Philippines and the silks of China.

These desultory forays gave way to methodical exploration in the epic voyages of Henry Hudson, who gave his name (and life) to the inland sea that would eventually yield access to a fortune in furs.

A seasoned mariner who had been hired by the Muscovy Company to reach Cathay via the North Pole, Hudson turned this apparently impossible

---

* The diggings (including a still existing jetty) were revisited by Charles Francis Hall in 1861, the Rawson-MacMillan Sub-Arctic Expedition of 1927 and by Dr Walter Kenyon of the Royal Ontario Museum in 1974. Chemical analyses of the ore showed it to be a combination of amphibolite and pyroxenite, which modern miners call "fool's gold." What glistened turned out to be flecks of biotite mica.

assignment into a profitable venture by discovering a bay teeming with whales on Spitzbergen, a wind-whipped archipelago off Norway. Hired away by the rival Dutch East India Company, Hudson sailed northward along the American east coast, putting in at what is now New York and sailing 150 miles up the Manna-hata River as far as the site of Albany. That journey led in 1626 to the famous purchase of Manhattan Island from local Canarsee Indians for trinkets and cloth worth twenty-four dollars.

Hudson's successful exploits brought him to the attention of James I, who refused to sanction his return to Amsterdam. A syndicate of English courtiers—the Earl of Northampton, Lord Keeper of the Privy Seal; the Earl of Nottingham, Admiral of England; the Earls of Suffolk, Southampton and Salisbury; Sir Thomas Smith; John Wolstenholme of the new East India Company; and the scholarly Sir Dudley Digges—joined to sponsor Hudson's next trip to map the North West Passage.

The enduring mystery of Hudson, who commanded the most lavishly financed single-ship expedition of his day, was why he deliberately gathered such a devil's brew of ill-assorted malcontents instead of recruiting some of the qualified seamen then readily available for hire on the London docks. Among them were his mate, Robert Juet, a thug who held Hudson in low esteem; John King, the quartermaster, a moody troublemaker; the haberdasher Abacuck Prickett; and a florid young rogue named Henry Greene, who did not board the fifty-ton *Discovery* at St Katharine's Pool along with the others but was mysteriously plucked off a dock at Gravesend, twenty miles down the Thames.

Given this motley assemblage, Hudson might have been able to mould them into an effective crew with determination and discipline. Instead, he went against the prevailing ethic of his age by trying to run the expedition as a floating democracy, seeking mutual consent for major decisions. This only infuriated the crewmen, barely able to conceal their contempt for the vacillating captain. Stuck among the floes of Ungava Bay, Hudson offered to turn back, if that was the will of the majority, but he was interrupted by the need to save the ship from being crushed by a rogue iceberg. After that, Hudson arbitrarily set his course to the northwest, but his authority had been fatally undermined. Once past the islands he named for his backers, Nottingham and Digges, Hudson realized he was in open water again, and his dark spirits lifted. He felt that he had won the Passage. Before him lay an open ocean; scuds of water birds mewed their wild calls, as if to lure him deeper into the beckoning bay.

The *Discovery* ran southward, heeling happily, along four hundred miles of forbidding coastline. Hudson noticed the shore veering to the southwest, then almost due west. He judged himself to be sailing across the top of the continent. The approach to Cathay could be only a few watches away. Past Cape Jones he saw the shore sharply dropping away, first to the south, then to the southwest and finally, worst of all, due north. This was no North West Passage, he realized with dawning horror, but the bottom pocket of a huge bay. Instead of sailing out of this obvious cul-de-sac, Hudson panicked. He criss-crossed what is now James Bay, aware that his food supplies would scarcely last the coming winter, yet unable to break out of his predicament. It was September by then and the early winter gales nearly broached the *Discovery*, her lee scuppers foaming in the rushing waves. Juet rebelled, and Hudson threw the mate in irons, then put him on trial. Some of the crew were preparing to break open the arms locker and assume command. With the prevailing north winds threatening to founder the ship on the wilderness beaches of James Bay, Hudson turned back to find shelter inside what is now Rupert Bay and hauled the ship into shallow water. Philip Staffe, the ship's carpenter, erected a small lean-to of tamarack on the frozen shore, and there they huddled against the winter, emerging only to hunt birds and fill buckets with snow for water.

Because they had been bound for the South Seas, few members of the crew had heavy clothes, and as the furious winter gales buffeted the inadequate shelter, frostbite, scurvy and death became frequent visitors. The first to go was John Williams, the ship's gunner. Instead of following the custom of the sea and auctioning the dead man's clothing, Hudson gave Williams's coat to Henry Greene, the dissolute malingerer who had joined the expedition separately. When Greene failed to show any gratitude, Hudson snatched the garment away from him and awarded it to Robert Bylot, the deckhand he had promoted as his mate. The only interruption to such petty infighting was the appearance of an Indian dragging a sled with two deer and a pair of beaver hides on it. Hudson gave the visitor a knife, a looking-glass and some buttons for the pelts, initiating the bay's fur trade.

By June 18, 1611, the *Discovery* had floated free of ice and the survivors re-embarked, desperate to head home. Instead of rationing the remaining food, Hudson handed out all the maggoty hardtack and mouldy cheese, failing to allay the suspicion that he had retained a hoard of supplies for himself and his favourites. Hudson resumed his wanderings, erratically tacking across James Bay with no apparent destination in mind. He undercut his authority one more time by demoting Bylot and making the carpenter Philip Staffe, who could neither read nor write, his new mate. At the same time, he confiscated all the navigation equipment aboard so that his crew could only guess the course he was steering. Certain that their captain intended to play out what was left of their lives aimlessly cruising the cursed bay, the crew turned mutinous. Six days out of Rupert, Greene and Juet organized the takeover, bundling a dazed Hudson into the ship's shallop, followed by his young son John and half a dozen scurvy-ridden tars. Only Staffe, the loyal carpenter, volunteered to join the doomed party.

The *Discovery* towed the lifeboat into clear water. Then, as the ship's mainsail ballooned under a following sou'wester, the dinghy was cut loose. Hudson raised his own sail and caught up with his disloyal crew who were busy looting the ship and gorging on his hidden cache of beer and biscuits. Guilty at the reappearance of their commanding officer, the mutineers trimmed the *Discovery*'s sails and raced away as if fleeing from the devil himself.

Henry Hudson and his eight companions perished without hope.* The history-book image of Hudson is the Collier portrait of him surrounded by icebergs, his bearded countenance downcast, his hand on the tiller of his tiny shallop, his haunted eyes gazing into the blank distance, overwhelmed by the self-pity of knowing he is facing certain death on the unknown coast of a merciless sea.

The conspirators aboard the *Discovery* hacked their way home, stopping off at Digges Islands to hunt for provisions before they were chased away by local Eskimos. Rations were so short that the starving sailors were reduced to chewing candles and sucking picked-over gulls' bones dipped in vinegar. They had ceased to care "which end of the ship went forward." It was only the stamina and navigational instincts of Robert Bylot, Hudson's erstwhile mate, that brought them back to England. Tried for murder instead of mutiny, the crewmen were acquitted.

---

* The only clue to Henry Hudson's final resting place is an obscure entry in the log of Captain Thomas James, the Bristol sailor who wintered on Charlton Island in James Bay in 1631–32. On nearby Danby Island, he found "some stakes driven into the ground." They were "about the bigness of my arms and had been cut sharpe at the ends with a hatchet." This could only have been the work of Europeans, and history records no unaccounted-for presence except that of Henry Hudson and his sad remnant of loyalists. Historian Richard Glover remembers several HBC men telling him about the first white man the Eskimos saw on Hudson Strait. He was dead, but in the boat with him was a live white boy. They did not know what to do with him, so they tied him up in dog harness, outside their tent. And that was that. No more was recalled.

The *Discovery* was back in Hudson Bay the following summer, under the command of Sir Thomas Button, a Welsh sea captain who enlisted the most distinguished patrons for any northern voyage. The charter signed by James I for the "Company of Merchants, Discoverers of the North West Passage" enjoyed the supreme protection of Henry, Prince of Wales, and included among its investors the Archbishop of Canterbury, Sir Francis Bacon (then Solicitor General), the mathematician Henry Briggs and the geographer Richard Hakluyt, as well as six dozen assorted lords and knights plus one lady. Button's commission was to find the source of the strange tides ebbing from the west that the Hudson expedition's survivors reported as certain evidence of the Passage's existence. Enlisting Bylot as his navigator, Button sailed straight across Hudson Bay only to sight its western shore just above the estuary of what was later called the Churchill River. He then veered south and anchored off a great stream he named the Nelson, after one of his officers who died there. Button and his crew thus became the first white men to winter anywhere near the future site of York Factory. After spring breakup, Button nosed north on the bay, tracing the shoreline of Southampton Island before heading for England. His faith was undiminished. "I do confidently believe there to be a Passage," he declared, "as there is one between Calais and Dover." During the next two decades, nine plucky explorers followed Button, all but one of them English.

The exception was the Danish pathfinder Jens Munk, who had already tried to locate a North East Passage, fought pirates in the North Sea, commanded an Arctic whaler and served in the Royal Danish Navy in several senior capacities. Ordered by King Christian IV to plot the exact Mercator projections of the Passage westward out of Hudson Bay, he rounded up an able-bodied crew of sixty-three aboard two naval ships, the *Unicorn* and *Lamprey*, and set off on May 30, 1619, for what turned out to be one of the most harrowing epics of survival in the history of northern exploration. The party landed without incident at the mouth of the Churchill River and dug in for the winter. At first, the profusion of wild berries, ptarmigan, the beluga whales, visiting polar bears and plentiful firewood made it seem a perfect landfall. Then the Hudson Bay winter set in, with ice "forty fathoms deep" and the wind biting exposed skin. "I gave the men wine and strong beer," Munk noted in his log, "which they had to boil afresh, for it was frozen to the bottom." The Danes were soon writhing with scurvy, that dreaded disease of early maritime expeditions caused by the lack of ascorbic acid (Vitamin C). It loosened men's teeth, stiffened their joints and if unchecked caused internal bleeding and death. Munk described the "peculiar illness" as causing "great pains in the loins, as if a thousand knives had been thrust there. At the same time the body was discoloured as when someone has a black eye, and all the limbs were powerless; all the teeth were loose, so that it was impossible to eat."* By summer only Munk and two crewmen were still alive. Sixty-one sailors had died, and no one had the strength to bury them. Below decks, the Danish captain recorded his awful plight: "As I could no longer stand the bad smell of the dead bodies that had remained on the ship so long, I managed to crawl out of my berth. For surely it would not matter where I died … I spent the night on deck, wrapped in the clothing of those who were already dead." In spring Munk crawled over the rotting bodies to munch a few blades of grass. By mid-July, with the two other survivors, he refloated the *Lamprey,* and in an astounding feat of seamanship and navigation the three emaciated Danes managed to sail safely to Copenhagen, 3,500 miles away. Munk's log book, published in 1624, remains a classic epic of endurance. In one chilling entry the stalwart captain, who had been cajoling his men to hang on to life longer than their bodies would allow, finally saluted his own mortality: "Herewith, good-night to all the world—and my soul into the hand of God …"

BEING A PRACTICAL PEOPLE, the Danes opted to surrender to others the honour of charting the North West Passage, but English sailors could not bear to leave the prize unclaimed. They were driven by that combination of curiosity and stubbornness that Napoleon would later brand the rarest form of audacity—the courage of the early morning.

Next in line for the northern prize was the duo of Luke Foxe and Thomas James, whose nearly parallel tracks through Hudson Bay lent their voyages a strange echo effect. They copied each other in equipment—the *Charles* and the *Henrietta Maria,* both eighty-ton pinnaces with twenty-man crews, provisioned for eighteen months—and both captains carried letters of introduction from Charles I to the Emperor of Japan. They left their home ports of London and Bristol within days of each other during the spring of 1631 and headed for

---

* That so many men perished from scurvy, when fresh meat was available, has been the Munk expedition's unsolved mystery. It has been suggested that while some scurvy did indeed occur, most of the men died of trichinosis, from improperly cooked polar bear meat. The key to the puzzle may be Munk's off-hand comment that his own meat was more thoroughly cooked than that of the others because he liked it well done.

identical destinations. But the two captains themselves were very different. Foxe was all dash and daring, a rough self-educated mariner who picked up most of his knowledge of the new continent by visiting local globemakers' shops. James, on the other hand, was a cultivated Welshman, a barrister-at-law educated at London's Inner Temple, who had his personal quadrant fashioned of pearwood and spent as much effort polishing the entries in his log book as searching for the Passage. Well schooled in what was then the art (rather than the science) of navigation, James was described by a contemporary as "a heroicke soule," yet he was surprisingly accident-prone for an explorer. He once, for instance, almost managed the difficult act of self-immolation while up a tree on Charlton Island.

With a lilt of language that presaged the cadence of the Welsh songster Dylan Thomas, James began his chronicle: "Many a Storme, and Rocke and Mist, and Wind, and Tyde, and Sea, and Mount of Ice, have I in this Discovery encountred withall; Many a despaire and death had, almost, overwhelmed mee...."* In his writings, the icy wind became "Satan's malice," and when James observed a storm overtaking his ship, he rushed below to rhapsodize: "... there came a great rowling sea out of the NNE and by eight a clock it blew very hard at SE.... the sea was all in a breach; and to make up a perfect tempest, it did so lighten, snow, rain and blow, all the night long, that I was never in the like ... nor I, nor any that were then with me, ever saw the sea in such a breach. Our ship was so tormented, and did so labour; with taking it in on both sides, and at both ends; that we were in a most miserable distress, in this so unknown a place.... the sea, indeed, so continually over-rackt us, that we were like Jonas in the Whales-Belly."

Not to be outdone, Foxe in his terser log entries painted his version of the evocative landscape. "This delicate morning," a typical notation begins, "the sun rose clear, and so continued all this cold virgin day ... This evening the sun set clear; the air breathed gentle from the east. We lay quietly all night amongst the ice ..." Foxe, gulping down polar bear steaks or gaping awestruck at the gaudy gossamer of the Northern Lights, exulted in the natural wonders of his environment. "So long as I am sailing," he wrote, expressing the prayer of all good sailors, "I bless God and care not." One warm day, while coasting down the bay's wooded western shore on a broad

---

* Samuel Taylor Coleridge, more than a century later, used the James chronicle as inspiration for some of the more lurid imagery in *The Rime of the Ancient Mariner*.

reach with the life-giving sun glinting on the water around him, Foxe recorded a prayerful gasp of satisfaction: "God, hold it."

When they were not preoccupied with their literary pursuits, the two navigators followed each other from Churchill down as far as Cape Henrietta Maria, so named by James, who continued sailing southward. Foxe veered due north and after poking his bow past the Arctic Circle into what is now Foxe Basin, sailed for home, icicles hanging from his rigging. Despite the publication of his memoirs in which he billed himself as "North-West Foxe," the London navigator soon lapsed into obscurity.

His Bristol compatriot decided to winter on Charlton Island in the part of the great bay that would be named after him. James realized that the only way to save his vessel from being pounded to bits by the winter surf and ice was to sink it. Taking his auger down to the ship's bilges, he drilled holes to allow the vessel to settle on the sandy bottom from which it might be deballasted and refloated after breakup. The winter on Charlton was the usual dismal nightmare, with four men dying of scurvy and James noting: "I caused the surgeon to cut the hairs of my head short, and to shave away all the hair of my face; for that it was become intolerable, that it would freeze great with icicles."

By spring the crew was able to refloat the *Henrietta Maria*, but James almost missed sailing home. On June 25 he scrambled up the island's tallest pine and told one of his seamen to set a neighbouring evergreen afire as a signal to attract any well-disposed Indians who might be nearby. Not surprisingly, the branches under James's feet also caught fire, as did most of the island, very nearly roasting the captain. Four months later, the *Henrietta Maria* was welcomed back to Bristol. James received more acclaim than Foxe because he and his crew had stayed to suffer through the long sub-Arctic winter. The exuberant memoir that followed (*The Strange and Dangerous Voyage of Captain Thomas James*) outsold Foxe's inferior effort. It was notable for identifying the potential of Hudson Bay's shores and the islands as "the home of many of the choicest fur-bearing animals in the world." James went on to battle privateers off the English coast in command of the saucily christened *Ninth Whelp of the Lion*. The two navigators died within weeks of each other in 1635.

They had recorded no dramatic discoveries, but their paths had made known the bay's uncharted western shore, providing conclusive evidence that it hid no seaway to the Orient. "Even if that merely imaginary passage did exist," James flatly predicted, "it would be narrow, beset by ice, and longer than the route to the east by the Cape." Another century would go by before the search for the North West Passage was resumed, but now the dimensions of Hudson Bay had been mapped and its fur potential recognized. The commercial exploitation of that great inland sea was about to begin.

A Bounty of Beaver

"The beaver, by its defencelessness, no less than by its value, was responsible for unrolling the map of Canada."   —Eric W. Morse

SELDOM HAS AN ANIMAL exercised such a profound influence on the history of a continent. Men defied oceans and hacked their way across North America; armies and navies clashed under the polar moon; an Indian civilization was debauched—all in quest of the pug-nosed rodent with the lustrous fur. In the conduct of this feverish enterprise, which stretched from the early 1650s to the late 1850s, the cartography of world trade routes was filled in and the roots of many a dynastic fortune were planted.

There was nothing genteel about the hunt. Beaver became the breathing equivalent of gold. Men risked their lives and reputations for a scramble at the bonanza, caught up in a trade that transformed one of nature's gentlest creatures into a *casus belli*.

Paradoxically, the beavers themselves, peering myopically from the portcullises of their mud-and-twig castles, led the interlopers ever deeper into North America's hinterland. As the streams draining into the St Lawrence Valley were trapped out, the traders and their Indian middlemen were obliged to keep pressing westward and northward: the best pelts were always round the next bend of the river. The beaver is a non-migratory animal which needs relatively large spaces to keep it happy, so that once a creek was "beavered out," the hunters had to move on, deeper and farther into the New Land. Just as the stalking of elephants for their ivories lured white hunters into the heart of Africa, so the pelts of the beaver drew the traders from both Hudson Bay and the St Lawrence towards the snow-capped Rocky Mountains and eventually to the shores of the bottle-green Pacific.

It was the confluence of three separate trends that transformed a marginal barter for furs by sixteenth-century seamen into an important export. First, there was the undiminishing supply of beaver provided by an immense drainage system containing nearly half the world's fresh water; second, the flourishing and astonishingly durable demand for the products of the beaver's coat in the European market; and third, the availability of an inexpensive and willing labour force—Indians with an insatiable passion for the cornucopia of European trade goods.

Without anyone being particularly aware of it, the hunt for beaver turned into the quest for a nation. As the modern explorer Eric W. Morse noted in his classic study of fur trade canoe routes: "The beaver, by its defencelessness, no less than by its value, was responsible for unrolling the map of Canada."

Basque and Iberian fishermen had already swapped furs informally, but the first documented beaver-pelt transaction took place in the summer of 1534, when Jacques Cartier, the St Malo navigator, tacked into the Baie de Chaleur, a narrowing inlet between the present-day provinces of Quebec and New Brunswick. There the French explorer encountered a beached fleet of fifty Micmac canoes, their owners enjoying a picnic on the strand. "They made frequent signs to us to come on shore, holding up some furs on sticks," Cartier noted in his ship's log. The ensuing bargaining grew so spirited that the Indians traded even the robes off their backs for European beads and knives.

Fur-trade historian W.A. MacKay relates that as the ships pulled away accompanied by the fleet of gesticulating Indians, Cartier observed that his satisfied if naked customers were leaping and dancing in their canoes—and parenthetically noted that they were a small tribe. This prompted MacKay to comment wryly: "Any tribe that practises dancing in canoes is bound to be small."

EVER SINCE ADAM AND EVE, ejected from Eden, first donned the skins of wild beasts, fur has been a spectacular talisman. In the delicate interplay between sensibility and fashion, practicality and luxury, the wearing of furs has retained a savage symbolic undercurrent of potency, success and brute strength— bestowing on its wearer an aura of wild beauty, magic powers and social cachet. In Sung times, Chinese emperors decapitated courtiers churlish enough to wear sea otter robes without imperial permission. In the original French fairy tale, Cinderella's slipper was made of squirrel fur *(vair)* and not glass *(verre)*, contrasting the sensuality of the medieval image with its brittle modern version.

Fur was, of course, worn for warmth, but its varieties were inextricably bound up with social distinctions, in the belief that each pelt perpetuated the essence of its original animal nature. A coat fashioned of rabbit or polecat skins might be just as warm but lacked the metaphysical zap of lion, leopard or fox. At Troy, Agamemnon wore a lion skin while Paris preferred leopard, but that great prince of Israel, the wise King Solomon, stuck to beaver.* Medieval edicts governed precisely who could wear what skin. The Westminster Church Council proclaimed in 1127 that abbesses and nuns could not wear winter garments any more precious than lamb or black cat. By 1337, edicts were passed stating that only nobles (and clerks earning more than £100 annually) could adorn themselves with certain furs. But a thriving black market in second-hand furs obliterated these official barriers and many a grandee was heard to complain that it was becoming impossible to distinguish an innkeeper's wife from a gentlewoman. By the middle of the fifteenth century, the once-plentiful beaver was extinct in England; mayors and sheriffs were permitted to sport marten and squirrel. Edward III decreed that rare furs, such as ermine and sable, should be restricted to royalty, the nobility and persons who gave at least £100 a year to the Church. Ladies wearing furs had to be of blameless or at least noble birth.

Yesterday's velvety beavers were nothing like today's Disneyfied replicas of Davy Crockett's coonskin cap, with the ringed tail bobbing down the back. The true beaver hat was made not from the glossy long-haired pelt but from the fine thick underhair, shaved and sheared from the skin. Unlike that of most animals, the beaver's undercoat is covered with tiny barbs that allow the downy fibres to be matted and beaten, then shellacked and shaped into a lustrous, wonderfully soft and durable felt.

The production of felt from fur is an ancient human technology, its discovery credited to central Asian nomads such as the Scythians, whose descendants roof their tents and wagons with heavy waterproof felt made by combing out sheep's wool, wetting it, rolling and beating it with sticks and, finally,

---

* Fur trade historians lament that there is no mention of beavers on the Ark but console themselves with the fact that when scouring the Black Sea, Jason and the Argonauts took time out to exchange Greek pottery for beaver pelts.

pressing it flat between reed mats. Felt was used by the Greeks and Romans for waterproof cloaks and as padding under metal armour. Its manufacture eventually became a specialty of the back-alley artisans of Constantinople. The Crusaders picked up the technique and took it back to Europe, mainly to France, where felt making flourished. The Turkish artisans were themselves driven into Russia, but after the sacking of Kiev by Tartars in 1240, escaped to Western Europe and joined their fellow felt makers in France. There, the finest felt hats were turned out at Rouen, Caudebec and other towns in Normandy, largely by Huguenots. But increasing prejudice against them and the heresy of their pragmatic faith culminated in the St Bartholomew's Day massacre in Paris and other towns, so that scores of the Protestants fled to Holland and England. The Edict of Nantes, which allowed Huguenots freedom of conscience, ended these conflicts in 1598. To protect themselves, Protestant towns were permitted to have their own armed forces and assemblies, and walled Atlantic towns, such as La Rochelle, became home ports for roaming privateers. But the Edict of Nantes was revoked in 1685 and up to half a million Huguenots emigrated, including an estimated ten thousand hatters, so that by 1701 France was forced to import its fashionable hats from England. Samuel Smiles, who chronicled the sorry exodus, concluded that "Hat-making was one of the most important manufactures brought to England by the Huguenots, who alone possessed the secret of the liquid composition which served to prepare rabbit, hare and beaver skins ... After the Revocation, most of the hatmakers went to London, and took with them the secret of their art, which was lost to France for about forty years.* During this period, the French nobility, and all persons making pretensions to dress, wore none but English hats. Even the Roman cardinals got their hats from the celebrated manufactory at Wandsworth, established by the refugees."

Before the invention of the umbrella, beaver headgear provided an elegant way to keep dry, but there was much more to the fashion than mere practicality. It was more mania than swank. Men and women could be instantly placed within the social structure according to their hats; meticulous etiquette prevailed about how the headpieces were worn and the sweeping gesture with which they were removed and parked so that they would mark their owners' station in life. The precise technique used in doffing a beaver expressed

---

* The lead fumes inhaled during the felt-making process drove practitioners of the art into early senility; thus the saying, "mad as a hatter."

minute shadings of deference. "To own a fine beaver was to prove one's standing as a man—or woman—of the beau monde," U.S. historical writer Walter
O'Meara has pointed out. "To appear without one was to be quite hopelessly
out of style—and there was only one kind of fur out of which a beaver hat
could be made, and that, quite naturally, was the beaver's."

Beaver hats became the rage in Stuart England, the fashion having been
copied from the superb beaver bonnets worn by the victorious Swedish
cavalrymen in the Thirty Years' War. Beavers assumed a variety of shapes
and meanings, from plumed ceremonial models to tricorner pointed toppers.*
So valuable did the beaver headpieces become that they were willed by fathers
to eldest sons. Samuel Pepys boasted in one of his 1662 diary entries that he
had paid eighty-five shillings for his beaver hat. It was such a precious object
that he kept a spare rabbit version for bad weather.

Styles varied not only according to the wearer's social schedule and station
but with changing political regimes. During the reign of the first two Stuarts,
the elaborate, blocky, wide-brimmed "Spanish Beaver" was in vogue, but
with the beheading of Charles I and the austere stewardship of Oliver
Cromwell, the severely unadorned conical beaver came into its own. This
Puritan headgear was followed, during the Restoration, by the adoption of the
feathered fedora-like slouch adapted from the French court. "Every major
political upheaval," noted Murray G. Lawson, who traced fashion's erratic
patterns, "brought in its train a corresponding change in hat styles."

Beaver pelts became so valuable that sand from the floor in the warehouses where they were stored was sifted to salvage every last hair. In France
the hat gained such status that generous trade-ins were given for worn
models on new purchases. They were sold in Spain, then trimmed of the
most worn parts for resale in Portugal. Finally, a little the worse for wear,
they were swapped for ivory in Africa.

NORTH AMERICA'S RIVERS, flowing under succulent clumps of aspen, willow
and white birch, were progressively denuded of animals, as Indians rushed to
swap pelts for trade goods. "The beaver does everything perfectly well,"
marvelled a Montagnais chief. "He makes us kettles, axes, swords, knives, and
gives us drink and food without the trouble of cultivating the ground ..."

---

* The fur "muff," an outgrowth of the beaver-edged angel sleeve, became a popular fashion
item for both men and women. This led to the breeding of tiny "muff dogs," personal pets small
enough to be carried along as one's (presumably "muff-broken") canine companion.

Beaver became such a valued commodity that it was literally turned into money. For a century and a half, the standard of currency was not cash but beaver skins. "Made-beaver" (M-B), a prime quality skin from an adult beaver or its equivalent in other furs or goods, was the fixed unit of barter.* At the fur-gathering end of the commerce, all goods were quoted in terms of their beaver equivalents, so that two otter skins, eight pair of moose hooves or ten pounds of goose feathers each equalled one made-beaver. A moose hide or the fur of a black bear would fetch goods worth the equivalent of two made-beavers. Indians could get an impressive array of outdoor goods for their catch.

ANOTHER PART OF THE BEAVER that sparked dreams of fortune in men's eyes was its pear-shaped perineal scent glands located in the anal region of both sexes. They contain a bitter orange-brown alkaloid substance called *castoreum*, which proved to be a surprisingly effective medicine. It cured headaches, helped reduce fever and possessed many other magical healing qualities.†

Solomon was reported to have used Spanish castoreum for his migraines, Hippocrates mentioned it favourably in 500 B.C. and Pliny recommended it for allaying hysteria. It was used as a nostrum for mental illness, an anti-spasmodic by anxious midwives and a palliative for epilepsy and tuberculosis. Joanne Franco, an early enthusiast of the medical sciences, confided in 1685 that "Castoreum does much good to mad people, and those who are attacked with pleurisy give proof of its effect every day, however little may be given to them. Castoreum destroys fleas; is an excellent stomachic; stops hiccough; induces sleep; strengthens the sight, and taken up the nose it causes sneezing and clears the brain…. A Jew of my acquaintance who visited me occasionally, … communicated to me a secret which he had learnt from his ancestors, who themselves got it from Solomon who had proved it. He assured me that in order to acquire a prodigious memory and never to forget what one had once read, it was only necessary to wear a hat of the beaver's skin, to rub the head

---

* When coins were eventually introduced to facilitate the fur trade, they were made-beaver tokens. Minted of brass or stamped out of the copper bindings of kegs shipped to the bay from London, they were imprinted with whatever fraction of a made-beaver they represented and could be spent like cash inside HBC stores. A prime-quality beaver usually represented a dozen tokens; a bear skin, twenty. The last tokens were aluminum pieces for use in the white fox trade, issued in the eastern Arctic by the HBC in 1946. The standard fluctuated from time to time and from factory to factory, depending on the trading circumstances.
† There is a strong basis for this in fact. Modern chemical analysis has shown castoreum to contain acetylsalicylic acid, the main component of Aspirin and other headache remedies.

and spine every month with that animal's oil, and to take, twice a year, the weight of a gold crownpiece of castoreum."

From the very beginnings of the fur trade, the pear-shaped "beaver stones" were treasured almost as much as the furs. Between 1808 and 1828, the HBC exported nearly ten tons of castoreum out of the Athabasca district alone. Because of the gooey substance's proven curative powers, the prosaic beaver became an object of folk fantasy. The *Latin Bestiary of the Twelfth Century* claimed that when the beaver notices it is being pursued by a hunter, "he removes his own testicles with a bite, and casts them before the sportsman, and thus escapes by flight. What is more, if he should again happen to be chased by a second hunter, he lifts himself up and shows his members to him. And the latter, when he perceives the testicles to be missing, leaves the Beaver alone ... The creature is called a Beaver (Castor)* because of the castration."

There are no accurate calculations of how many beavers sacrificed their glands or became hats, but in 1854, when the fashion in beaver hats had already passed its height,† 509,000 pelts were auctioned off in London alone, and HBC accountants calculated from 1853 to 1877 they had sold three million skins. The beaver had once colonized nearly every river bed from the Rio Grande to the Arctic Ocean, with estimates of the rodent's original North American population ranging between sixty million and four hundred million. Robert J. Naiman, a biologist with the Woods Hole Oceanographic Institution in Massachusetts, believes that in 1670 there were at least ten million beavers within the boundaries of present-day Canada.

What changed the odds against the beaver was the invention of the steel trap by Sewell Newhouse at Oneida, New York, in 1823. Instead of lashing ice chisels to sticks and trying to spear the animals as they repaired the holes in their lodges, hunters could now set dozens of traps, bait them with castoreum and collect the carcasses. The record catch was made by Alexander Ross, a canny Yankee trapper who in 1824 led a twenty-man expedition into the

---

* The word comes from the old Sanskrit word Kasturi meaning "musk"; "beaver" is likely derived from the Sanskrit word for "brown."
† Beaver felt declined in value after the mid-nineteenth century when silk velour was found to be a less expensive and socially acceptable substitute. When Prince Albert, Queen Victoria's consort, appeared in public in a silk topper, the industry seemed doomed. But in 1843, Archibald Barclay, the Hudson's Bay Company's London-based secretary, had a brilliant suggestion. "We have been trying some experiments on the beaver," he informed the Committeemen confidentially, "with a view of testing the article to be used as ... *fur!*"

Bitterroot Mountains along what is now the Montana–Idaho border. The group caught as many as 155 beavers in a single day and came back with five thousand pelts.

While it was an uneven contest, most Indians respected the beaver's intelligence and believed the animal had sacred origins. According to Ojibway legend, the Great Spirit sent the beaver to dive beneath the waters then covering the surface of the earth to dredge up mud to form land surfaces. The Algonquin believed that it was the clapping of the beavers' tails that made thunder and the Crow venerated the animals, convinced they would be reincarnated as beavers. There were tales of marriages between beavers and Indian women, and lively legends of beaveroid offspring.

Among the Ojibway, a young man might ask for a daughter's hand in marriage by saying to her father: "I love your daughter. Will you give her to me, that the roots of her heart may entangle with mine, so that the strongest wind that blows shall never separate them?" If the father approved, he would throw a beaver robe over the couple. That act marked them as man and wife.

Indian legends relate that beavers had originally been endowed with the power of speech, but exhibited so many other noble qualities that the Great Spirit took away this gift to prevent them from becoming superior in understanding to mankind. None of this veneration stopped the slaughter, but after skinning and eating a beaver, Indian families took care not to feed its bones to the dogs, depositing them instead in the pond that had been the beaver's home.

Invading fur traders dismissed such spiritual ritual as flummery—and added the beaver to their menus. The early trappers pounded the beaver meat with wild fruit, then dipped the mixture into tallow and packed it into hot deer bladders for a delicious repast. It was the scaly stern appendage that popularized the beaver among Catholic missionaries and their converts. In 1704, Michel Sarrazin, Louis xiv's chief physician in New France, sent a petition to the Académie Royale des Sciences in Paris, which conveniently decreed that the beaver's hairless tail really made it a fish. This ruling, later approved by the Faculty of Divinity at the University of Paris, guaranteed the beaver's inclusion as a proper dish on Friday dinner or Lenten menus.

Early naturalists fantasized that the paddle-tailed animals lived in multistorey condominiums in which "their republics are well governed," and there were engravings of beavers officiously marching around, lugging smoothly planed wooden boards on their shoulders to build their dams. In his *Universal*

Dictionary of Trade and Commerce (1751), Malachy Postlethwayt postulated that beavers eat only fish—except those he accused of being "lazy beavers" which lived on land and went near water only to drink. The aquatic variety, according to Postlethwayt, gathered every spring, "and, walking two by two, they go in a body to hunt for animals of their own species; and all those they can catch they lead into their dams, where they make them work like slaves."

Samuel Hearne, the young Royal Navy seaman who became one of the HBC's most daring explorers, contemptuously dismissed the notion of such a hierarchy within the beaver world, pointing out that some animals found with hairless backs got that way because of the mange, not by carrying heavy boards on their shoulders. "I cannot refrain from smiling," he wrote in his *Journey to the Northern Ocean*, "when I read the accounts of different authors who have written on the economy of those animals, [as] ... Little remains to be added beside a vocabulary of their language, a code of their laws, and a sketch of their religion ... Their plaistering the inside of their houses with a composition of mud and straw, and swimming with mud and stones on their tails, are still more incredible.... It would be as impossible for a beaver to use its tail as a trowel, except on the surface of the ground on which it walks, as it would have been for Sir James Thornhill to have painted the dome of St. Paul's cathedral without the assistance of scaffolding."

One of the few fur traders who took the trouble to domesticate beaver kits thoroughly enough so that they answered to their names, Hearne was fascinated by the playful creatures. He studied even what he called their dunging habits. "In respect to the beaver dunging in their houses, as some persons assert, it is quite wrong, as they always plunge into the water to do it ... I had a house built for them, and a small piece of water before the door, into which they always plunged when they wanted to ease nature; and their dung being of a light substance, immediately rises and floats on the surface then separates and subsides to the bottom. When the Winter sets in so as to freeze the water solid, they still continue their custom of coming out of their house, and dunging and making water on the ice; and when the weather was so cold that I was obliged to take them into my house, they always went into a large tub of water which I set for that purpose; so that they made not the least dirt."

Except for Grey Owl, an eccentric Englishman named Archie Belaney, who masqueraded as an Indian and shared his living quarters with a family of beavers, few people have successfully tamed the little beasts. Dr John Knox, Danish ambassador to Canada in the 1950s, spent most of his spare time in the

Gatineau Hills north of Ottawa patiently observing beavers, with mixed results: "Anxious to learn more about their ways when confined to the lodge and the waters under the ice, I called on my forest friends one Saturday in December, when the pond was icebound and the cold was biting my fingers," he related. "It was obvious that in two places the beavers had, until recently, managed to keep openings in the ice. I broke the ice at one of these places and waited patiently for a beaver to come out. Though I could hear one moving around under the ice, he appeared only after I had moved to the other hole on the far shore of the pond. Aided by a sixth sense, he came out of hole number one when I was watching hole number two. Sitting up on his haunches, scratching his belly, he sniffed against the wind and directed a sly look in my direction across the pond. That entire afternoon he would invariably choose the better hole of the two—where I would not be at that moment."

Beavers are difficult to domesticate partly because they must spend most of their waking hours chewing wood. Maud Watt, wife of the HBC factor at Rupert House on James Bay, kept a beaver kit in her house in the 1920s. After it chewed through most of the family's furniture, the Watts decided to deport the offending creature to Akimiski Island. During the short trip, the little passenger chewed right through its wooden cage and gnawed a hole in the bottom of the boat. The craft just made it to shore before sinking.

The saddest and all too frequent use for the beaver's magnificent teeth is to chew off its own leg to escape old-fashioned steel traps.

A touching instance of how the animals look after one another was the observation by Dan McCowan, a Canadian naturalist, of two beavers swimming in a small lake near Banff, Alberta. The hindmost swam touching the leader's tail with its nose; once, when the rear beaver swam abreast, it bumped into a rock and quickly realigned itself in the nose-to-tail position. Having reached shore, the duo started munching contentedly, but when McCowan walked up to have a look, the leading beaver swished back into the lake. The other stayed stock-still, unable to flee. It was blind.

The beaver's brainpower has not been tested, but its instincts and behaviour certainly seem more advanced than those of most rodents, and it is one of the few animals that manipulates the environment so explicitly to suit its needs. "It does act intelligently," concluded E.R. Warren in *The Beaver and Its Works*, "not with the human intelligence some writers would ascribe to it, but it does things in which it is guided by something more than instinct alone."

A nocturnal animal that passes more than half its waking life tucked away in its underwater lodge, the beaver is deceptively unimpressive looking, with a dumpy figure, webbed feet, no neck to speak of and squinty little eyes.* Its weight varies between 40 and 60 pounds, though Vernon Bailey of the U.S. Biological Service once caught a 110-pounder on the Iron Ore River in Wisconsin.[†]

The beaver's broad, scaly tail, about a foot long, six inches wide and three-quarters of an inch thick, is useful for submerged steering, for propping the animal up while it is cutting trees and for slapping the water as a warning of approaching danger. It also acts as a radiator, allowing beavers to disperse excess body heat. But it is not, as some early naturalists maintained, used as a trowel during dam construction or as a punt for ferrying kits ashore. The rudder-like appendage can be manoeuvred with considerable dexterity, so that when the beaver is towing a leafy branch, for example, it angles its tail to overcome the torque of its forward motion.

The animal is an eating machine, even if it is not always hungry. It *must* chaw continually with its chisel-like teeth or it will perish. Its four self-sharpening incisors, coated with bright orange enamel, can grow up to a length of seven inches and if not worn down by constant gnawing will eventually pierce the beaver's skull. The incisors can chop their way through a six-inch tree in five minutes. Trees up to forty-two inches in diameter have been felled by these determined lumber-rats, their heads tilted as they chew against the grain, spitting out the chips.

The naturalist Ernest Thompson Seton has observed that a beaver can cut down a tree as fast as a man with a dull hatchet. The beaver squats on its tail at the foot of the tree and, clasping the trunk with its forepaws, cuts two horizontal grooves three inches apart with its incisors, then pries out the wood between cuts. The animal then positions itself at the opposite side of the tree

---

* Although they lack obvious star quality, they have been celebrated in various art forms, such as *The Revolt of the Beavers*, a play presented by Washington's Federal Theater Project in 1937, and Stan Kenton's dam-busting *Eager Beaver*, a rhythmical riff first recorded on November 19, 1943.

† That was a midget compared with pre-history's giant beavers (*Castoroides ohioensis*), which walked tall during the Pleistocene epoch. These Brobdingnagian rodents were up to nine feet long and weighed as much as a full-grown grizzly. Samples of the giant beaver's lower incisors measure 9.69 inches. Dr Richard Harrington, chief of the paleobiology division of the National Museum of Natural Sciences in Ottawa, recently discovered remains of these behemoths in the Old Grow Basin of the Yukon. Their incisors were highly prized as cutting tools by the first North American Indians.

and connects up to the previous trench at a slightly higher level. Seton estimates that the average beaver fells 216 trees a year.*

When beavers are not eating, they are grooming. As soon as it wades to shore, the beaver will raise itself erect on its tail, scratch its belly and shake its ears dry by hopping from side to side. Then it waterproofs its fur, tuft by tuft, by smearing it with the greasy discharge of special oil glands stored in pockets near the anus. It dips its forepaws into the glandular excretion and spreads the musky substance over its fur. Then, using the second and third toes of its hind feet, which are split to form a primitive comb, it fastidiously preens its coat until it is smooth and glossy. This grooming not only produces an oiled pelage so essential to aquatic animals, but it helps get rid of annoying beetles snuggling in the underhair.

When on land the beaver walks with an awkward gait but it undergoes a metamorphosis under water, becoming as sleek as a seal and fast as a torpedo. It can remain submerged under water without a breath for as long as fifteen minutes, a feat made possible by relatively large lungs and an oversize liver that allow the beaver to extend oxygen storage. The animal's respiratory system tolerates high doses of carbon dioxide, and when under ice, the beaver will sometimes wait while an exhaled breath-bubble is oxygenated by the water, then re-inhale it to extend time under water. With its thick fur and layers of fat that insulate better than a diver's wet suit, the beaver comes very close to being nature's scuba diver. Its webbed hind paws act like flippers; valvular ears and nose close off automatically beneath the surface and transparent goggle-like eyelids permit underwater vision. Tight folds of skin behind the incisors shut water out of the mouth, allowing the beaver to chew tree bark while under the surface. It has its own sonar: the animal's auditory nerves are so finely tuned it can detect threatening vibrations through the water. The beaver's sense of smell is acute but, just to make sure, it will always feed on the lee side of potential enemies.

Beavers mate for life, and the ladies seem to rule the roost. According to Lars Willson, a zoologist who has studied their behaviour, the female beaver

---

* The myth persists that beavers are intelligent enough to determine the direction in which their chosen trees will fall. The reason most shore trees tumble into the stream where they can be towed to the dams is that their upper branches, reaching for sunlight, tend to grow faster on the water side. Top-heavy, they usually topple in the direction most convenient for the beaver, but occasionally the tree falls the wrong way, once in a while right on top of the dumpy little lumberjack.

initiates the relationship by beating off stray males who waddle into her territory, testing their vigour to make sure she chooses the strongest. Once set to
raise a family, the couple never quarrels again. After pairing takes place, the
male defends his pond, his lodge and his mate against randy strangers. If he is
killed, the female scurries off to a neighbouring lodge, ferrying her kits in her
teeth to the new location. Beavers communicate through auditory signals such
as whines, bellows and tail whacks, as well as complicated paw-mark messages
on the soft mud pies they leave on the sides of canals.

Alexander Henry, the elder (a fur trader captured by Ojibway in 1763),
reported that "the beaver is much given to jealousy. If a strange male
approaches, a battle immediately ensues. The female remains an unconcerned
spectator, careless to which party the law of conquest may assign her ... The
male is as constant as he is jealous, never attaching himself to more than one
female, while the female, on her side, is always fond of strangers."

In the mated pair, amatory foreplay is quickly resolved because beaver sex
leaves little time for diversionary antics. Beavers make love face to face, *vis-à-
vis* and *ventre-à-ventre*, swimming on their sides while spiralling through the
water in an aquatic ballet that requires total concentration and commendable
technique.*

Kits weigh a pound at birth, arriving in litters of up to nine, and can
manage a basic dog-paddle the day after they are born. The mother makes a
nursery for her brood by splitting aspen and birch sticks into long fibres that
allow the moving water beneath to cleanse the cradles. The newcomers enjoy
their youth, cavorting in the water, chasing each other and learning to slap
their tails for protection. Daily gnawing lessons are a compulsory part of the
cycle.

But at the age of two, everything changes. The young beavers are driven
out of the lodge, forced to strike out on their own to build lodges downstream

---

* Beavers have seldom been observed in the sex act. One exception was the commentary of
Frank Kahan, an Arlington, Washington, researcher who reported in the *American Journal of
Mammology* (vol. 21, 1940): "While the female was swimming the male clasped her above the
hips with his fore limbs and turned on his side, hanging on while the female swam slowly for
a moment. Then they churned the water and dived with a splash. Upon coming to the surface
they swam to shore, climbed out and sat side by side combing themselves. A few minutes later
the female entered the water, the male followed and the same performance was repeated." In
both males and females, sexual organs are enclosed within a cloacal chamber, so that it is
impossible to tell one from another, even with the beaver in hand. The beavers themselves
have no such problem.

from their parents. Reluctant to face the wet, cruel world, the befuddled adolescents sometimes try sneaking back into the nest but are rebuffed, and if they persist, they are killed. With more kits on the way and food supplies limited, the whole colony would be endangered by their continued presence.

The beaver has been called the only animal besides man that can manufacture its own environment. The snug lodges where the beavers live are marvels of animal architecture, the protective dams as much as a mile long and forty feet thick. Their foundations are twigs stuck into the river bottom, anchored down with stones and mud; the self-supporting structure may rise to twelve feet or more. The outer walls of the lodges are intricately interlaced branches and trimmed tree trunks, insulated with tufts of grass patiently patted into place by beaver snouts. The miracle of the beaver lodge is how its builders know precisely where to locate exits and breathing chimneys; how they sense exactly how thick the ice will be each winter so that they can place their living platforms above it. The members of a beaver colony put up caches of poplar and willow to feed on during freeze-up. The sides of the colony's lodge are plastered with mud, which washes into the cracks between branches and twigs. When it freezes, the mixture congeals into a wall solid enough to keep out predators, except for man. Their secret is the network of peripheral dams the beavers erect up- and downstream from their lodges to control water levels to the nearest inch. The dams can be as much as six feet high, eighteen feet wide and consist of 250 tons of material. They hold water at five-foot level differentials, and the total effect is of miniature castles complete with moat, underwater entrances and dry, well-ventilated sleeping chambers along passageways sometimes twenty feet long. Beavers sleep on mats made from patted-down twigs and wide blades of grass; bedding is regularly changed when it gets fouled by mud.

The original explorers brought back tales of beaver lodges three storeys high, complete with windows, balconies and distinctively separate sleeping lairs and rooms for dining or nesting. Contemporary research proves them at least partly correct. Frank Conibear, inventor of a more humane trap, spent thirty years in the Canadian North and examined the interior of many beaver lodges. In his book, *The Wise One*, he wrote: "In my youth the Indians who were my companions along the trap-line told much of the ways of beaver. In speaking of the beaver lodges, they described the larger ones as containing usually three rooms, a room for sleeping, a room for eating in, and a smaller [underwater] room where the beaver passed their excrement, which was cleaned out at regular intervals. In addition to these rooms, the mother of the family in the spring hollowed out for herself an additional small room in the thick part of the partition, in which to have her young. In my own observations of beaver I have never found anything which caused me to doubt the genuineness of either of these items of information. On the contrary, I have seen what I believe to be proof that the Indians, with centuries of beaver lore behind them, were, as always, right."

The beaver's most sophisticated engineering feat is the canal system that supports the colony. Intricately designed ditches divert water, collect seepage from swamps and help the beaver float food supplies homeward. Canals six feet wide and more than six hundred feet long have been found, some elaborately controlled by spillways and crude locks. "These canals," the naturalist A. Radclyffe Dugmore has noted, "are a demonstration of the highest skill to be found of any animal below man ... It is doubtful whether man in his lowest form does such extraordinary work and with such remarkable success."

"THE HISTORY OF CANADA," noted H.A. Innis in his classic *The Fur Trade in Canada*, "has been profoundly influenced by the habits of an animal which very fittingly occupies a prominent place on her coat of arms. The beaver was of dominant importance in the beginnings of the Canadian fur trade. It is impossible to understand the characteristic developments of the trade or of Canadian history without some knowledge of its life and habits."

A glorified water rat with a flat tail, *Castor canadensis* has richly earned its pride of place as Canada's national emblem.

Messrs Radishes
& Gooseberries

"Glib, plausible, ambitious, supported by unquestionable physical courage, they were the completely equipped fortune hunters." —Douglas MacKay

MOUNTING GEOGRAPHICAL EVIDENCE to the contrary, the settlers in the St Lawrence Valley who made up the colony of New France still believed it would eventually be possible to reach China overland from Montreal. An explorer named Jean Nicollet, who discovered Lake Michigan in the 1630s, spent a decade trekking through the wilderness of America's Northwest with a robe of Chinese damask carefully packed in his knapsack so that he would be properly attired to greet the mandarins of Cathay.*

Successive French officials resident in Quebec confirmed the existence of Hudson Bay, firmly believing it was connected to an unspecified Oriental sea. The century-old dream of Jacques Cartier was still alive, and it did not really end until 1742, when Louis-Joseph and François La Vérendrye brought back Cree reports of a great mountain range blocking the continent's western gate.

Of the many fur traders, missionaries, confidence men and royal emissaries sent inland from New France to take the measure of *le pays d'en haut*, two men stood out among the rest: Pierre-Esprit Radisson and Médard Chouart, Sieur Des Groseilliers. Every Canadian schoolchild knows them as "Radishes and

---

* At Green Bay in what is now Wisconsin, Nicollet finally put on his damask robe. He struck such terror in the gathered Winnebagos that they thought he was a god and promptly concluded a peace treaty.

Gooseberries"* though few grasped the full impact of their exploits. This astute pair of *coureurs de bois* were the first Europeans to penetrate deep into the forest belt of the North, first to negotiate treaties with the Cree, first to explore the upper reaches of the Mississippi and Missouri and first to establish the durable trading pattern responsible for creation of the Hudson's Bay Company. The American historian Agnes Laut refers to Radisson and Groseilliers slipping nimbly "between the Sun King and His Britannic Majesty, between Jesuit camp and Recollect clique, between New England and Old England, between New France and Old France, between Catholicism and Protestantism, giving merry chase to the wits of monarchs, fur-trading barons, governors, and churchmen."

The two are invariably mentioned in tandem, but they were very different in age (Radisson was twenty-two years the junior), temperament (Groseilliers was the steadfast organizer, Radisson the mercurial merchandiser) and outlook (Radisson wanted to make history, his confrère to forget it).

If Radisson is inevitably ranked as the more prominent of the two, it is mainly because he left behind jovial jottings of his journeys, colouring valid geographical detail with tales of birds so fat they could scarcely fly and Indians who could shoot three ducks with one arrow.† It was he who issued the famous boast: "We were Caesars, being nobody to contradict us." While it is unwise to accept Radisson at his word, the lives and times of the two men provided the essential link between the trapping of animals as a subsistence activity and the exploitation on a grand scale of the furry riches of North America's streams and lakes. "A more daring pair of intentional promoters cannot be found in the history of commerce," wrote Douglas MacKay in *The Honourable Company*. "Glib, plausible, ambitious, supported by unquestionable physical courage, they were the completely equipped fortune hunters."

---

* The members of Charles II's court could not or would not pronounce the two men's names correctly and the HBC minutes contain eight different spellings of "Groseilliers," with the record keepers eventually settling on "Gooseberries." In Radisson's case, the problem was with his first name—which was cited so often as Peter that in his will, written in his own hand, dated July 17, 1710, he refers to himself as Peter Radisson. The only posthumous mention of his widow (his third wife), in the HBC minutes on January 2, 1732, refers to her as Elizabeth Radiston.

† The original copy in French of Radisson's *Voyages* was lost, but one contemporary translation survived in the papers of Samuel Pepys. It was discovered by chance, just before being sold to a fish-and-chip shop as wrapping paper, and now reposes in the Bodleian Library at Oxford.

MÉDARD CHOUART ARRIVED in Quebec during his late teens from the Marne country in north-central France, where his parents managed a farm known in the surrounding villages as *Les Groseilliers* (Gooseberry Bushes). By 1646, the youngster had become a disciple of the Jesuit fathers and was serving as a lay assistant at their Huron mission near Georgian Bay. Back in Quebec, he married Hélène, the daughter of a river pilot named Abraham Martin (whose land would achieve historical fame a century later as the Plains of Abraham) and settled down in a seigneury near Trois-Rivières. Better educated than most of the other *coureurs de bois* who populated the young colony, he was a natural leader, resentful of imagined injustice and proud enough of his sliver of land to call himself Sieur Des Groseilliers, attaching the name of his parents' farm to his new estate. After his first wife's death, he married Marguerite Hayet, half-sister of a local roustabout named Pierre Radisson.

Radisson served a more savage apprenticeship. At the age of fifteen while out on a duck shoot, he was ambushed by a band of roving Mohawks who took him to their village on Lake Champlain. Adopted by the family of a warrior who had nineteen white scalps to his credit, Radisson quickly learned the Mohawk language and ways of hunting. He began to understand the psychology of being Indian that would later help him act as an effective interlocutor for the fur traders. Going along on Mohawk war parties pillaging the villages of hostile tribes, he became, in effect, a white Indian. But the memories of life in New France were too sweet to forget. While hunting with three Mohawks and a captive Algonquin, he and the prisoner escaped after crushing the skulls of their sleeping companions. They were tracked down and quickly recaptured. The Algonquin was executed on the spot while Radisson was placed on the village scaffold. His soles were seared with heated irons and a red-hot sword was driven through one of his feet. His fingernails were pulled out, each one more slowly than the next; then the raw fingertips were dipped into canisters of live coals. Children were beginning to chew his tortured hands when he was rescued by his adopted family. But the nightmare of that ordeal never left him. After two more years of life as a Mohawk slave, he escaped to Fort Orange, the Dutch trading post on the site of modern Albany, New York, where he acted as an interpreter until he returned to Trois-Rivières. Though still less than twenty-one years old, Radisson was toughened beyond his years and fully primed for his travels inland.

Groseilliers had meanwhile paddled into the land of the Huron to persuade them to bring more pelts down to the St Lawrence. In the Green

Bay area, he picked up stories about a legendary Eldorado of untouched beaver preserves north of Lake Superior. It was into this country that the two "brothers," as they started to call each other, ventured in the early spring of 1659. During the winter that followed, in the long evenings around campfires with the Huron, and later with the Sioux and the Cree, the two traders heard tales of the wealth of beaver ponds between Lake Superior and Hudson Bay's southwestern shore.* Visiting Cree from that mysterious region had collected the glossiest pelts Radisson and Groseilliers had ever seen, claiming they came from massive rivers rising beyond the nearby divide of ice-scoured granite that flowed north into an inland sea.

Although the rich bales of fur the two brought back to Quebec probably saved the colony's struggling economy, the governor, the Marquis d'Argenson, arbitrarily confiscated most of the pelts and briefly jailed Groseilliers for trading without a licence. Concerned that exploration of the Hudson Bay route might shift the focus of the fur trade away from the St Lawrence, the French governor refused to grant the *coureurs de bois* permission to reconnoitre the distant territory, which left them little choice but to try their luck in New England. That switch in loyalties was to have momentous consequences, the first of a chain of events that reached its climax a century later with the British conquest of New France.

During the next three years the pair persuaded several Boston punters to sponsor voyages into Hudson Bay—though only one (in 1663, under the command of Capt. Zachariah Gillam) actually made it into Hudson Strait, before being forced back by ice. This abortive attempt caught the attention of Colonel George Cartwright, a commissioner sent by Charles II to enlist support from the truculent New Englanders and extract taxes from the new colony. The colonel persuaded the two renegades to sail with him to England, planning to introduce them to his influential friend Sir George Carteret in the hope of enlisting royal support for exploration of what he visualized as a beaver-packed passage to the South Seas. Like nearly every other enterprise involving young Radisson, their transatlantic voyage turned out to be high adventure: the *Charles*, which was supposed to carry the party smartly back to

---

* Radisson claimed in his reminiscences written a decade later that they had actually travelled to the shores of Hudson Bay, but the time sequence involved makes this highly unlikely, since they did not leave Superior until breakup in late April and were back in Quebec by August 19.

England, was captured by Dutch privateers, and her passengers were unexpectedly put ashore in Spain, so that it took almost twice the usual time to reach London.

THE LONDON that Radisson and Groseilliers encountered in the autumn of 1665 was a grotesque caricature of Dante's Inferno, devastated by the bubonic plague that had already carried off one-sixth of its half-million citizens.* Normal life had been disrupted by the horror of carts collecting the daily dead.

As Cartwright accompanied the visitors on the boat voyage up the Thames to Oxford, where the court had temporarily fled, they passed through a chilling landscape of lifeless streets and looted houses. There were smoke-wreathed barges anchored in mid-stream, crowded with families trying to avoid the pestilence. As their shallop passed under the arches of London Bridge, they were given perfumed handkerchiefs to cut the stench of putrefaction coming from the "plague pits" where victims were dumped. They could see the wild-eyed prophets of doom parading on the empty streets, with scrawled signs proclaiming even more horror in the offing.† One lunatic, wearing only a loincloth and carrying a brazier of hot coals on his head, ran about Westminster shouting: "Oh, the great and dreadful God!"

The two woodrunners were about to meet a king of England who deftly balanced his roles as a debauched playboy and as an enlightened statesman. Charles II has deservedly been credited with resurrecting the Royal Navy and reviving English theatre and science. He not only restored the Crown but with his talented advisers moved England towards a constitutional monarchy without a revolution, yet he headed the most blasé court of voluptuaries in Europe and was himself absorbed in endless horizontal rendezvous with his

---

* The plague was carried by lice and fleas which fed on rats, slowly killing them. As the rodents died, the insects fled the cooling bodies and transferred their attentions to humans, feeding on their blood and causing fatal infections. There was no immunity to the plague except escape, but according to street gossip, its effects could be ameliorated by catching a pox of almost equal ferocity, such as syphilis. The rumour was false, but that did not discourage a run on London's bawdy houses.

† They were right. Within a year, on September 2, 1666, a fire that started in the king's bakery shop in Pudding Lane engulfed London. It raged for five days, razing an estimated thirteen thousand wooden houses and eighty-eight churches. That catastrophe was followed in 1667 by the humiliation of a Dutch fleet sneaking up the Thames, sailing to Chatham harbour and sinking half a dozen Royal Navy ships at their moorings, then towing the flagship, *Royal Charles*, back to Holland.

round of thirty-nine frisky mistresses.* The Earl of Rochester, a notorious court wag of the period, summed up the king with the appropriate comment that he was a monarch "who never said a foolish thing, nor did a wise one"— to which Charles riposted: "My sayings are my own, but my actions are my ministers." Although he regularly attended Privy Council sessions and demonstrated a lively instinct for politics as the art of making the necessary possible, he had a remarkably small tolerance for ennui. He spent more time egging on the mischief of his courtiers than delving into serious affairs of state, depending on his natural charm and highly developed survival instinct to preserve the Stuart dynasty.

Charles's other ruling passion was money; he could never get enough. Although Parliament voted him an annual stipend of £1,200,000 and he received a dowry worth £800,000 when he married the pious Portuguese Infanta, Catherine of Braganza, his costs ran very high. He even returned Dunkirk to the French in exchange for £400,000 and finally accepted a secret £2,000,000 bribe from Louis xiv. Not only did he have to provide for his mistresses (who could not always be fobbed off with titles) but the royal purse also had to absorb most of the cost of the Royal Navy and the upkeep of Whitehall, then Europe's most commodious palace.†

---

* When asked about this precise total of his amours, Charles replied that it reminded him of the 39 Articles of the Church of England. How he had time or energy to spare for governing after dealing with these devouring Restoration beauties is a mystery. Their portraits picture them as remarkably interchangeable, nearly all sharing the round faces, pouting mouths and flaxen curls so fashionable in those circles at the time. But at least two women stood out in the crowd. Barbara Villiers, Lady Castlemaine, a hot-tempered nymphomaniac who enjoyed royal favour longer than any of her rivals, had no hesitation in taking other lovers, among them Jacob the Rope Dancer, whose gymnastics inspired in her the urge to know "how he might be under his tumbling clothes." The other was Nell Gwyn, an actress with bouncy breasts and wit to match, who was not quite, according to Charles II's biographer Antonia Fraser, "the golden-hearted prostitute of popular imagination. Or rather, she may have had a heart of gold, but she also liked the stuff for its own sake." Charles II publicly acknowledged fourteen children from these and other liaisons, prompting the saying that he was truly the father of his people.

† The compound was an agglomeration of galleries, courtyards, gardens, public service buildings and regal dwellings sprawling over twenty-three acres. (The Vatican at the time covered less than fourteen, Versailles only seven.) One visiting diplomat complained that of Whitehall's more than two thousand rooms, not one was really cozy or comfortable. Its architecture, a jumble of Dutch brick, Tudor stone and Elizabethan half-timber, was dominated by Inigo Jones's great Banqueting Hall with its magnificent Rubens ceiling. Stretching half a mile along the Thames and reaching to the present site of No. 10 Downing Street, the original Whitehall, or most of it, burned in 1698.

Charles II was the first English monarch to maintain close personal connections with London's City financiers and waged war against Holland mainly for commercial reasons. Mercantile concerns became national interests, and very much a part of that trend was the expansion of English trade into the colonies of Africa, India and North America. This was one reason Radisson and Groseilliers—who brought with them a novel scheme for exploiting the assets of the new continent across the Atlantic that did not call for heavy financial outlays to establish large permanent colonies—were guaranteed a receptive audience even before the details of their plan were known. The other reason their timing fitted in so well with the mood of the English court was that, despite the plague and other distractions, the Restoration of Charles II had aroused in England's ruling circles a spirit of commercial innovation perfectly attuned to the impending exploitation of Hudson Bay.

The Restoration was the green end to England's hardest winter—a freeing of the spirit after a decade of Cromwellian suppression, when even amusements as innocent as maypoles were pulled down, theatres were closed and stained glass and stone church carvings sledge-hammered. It was judged illegal to go walking on Sundays except to a religious service in one's own parish. Without a king, a proper Parliament or a functioning Church of England to channel or deflect popular emotions, the prevailing Puritanism became a source of bitterness rather than of enlightenment. The euphoria of the Restoration led to outbursts of creativity everywhere, among its main agents of change being Sir Christopher Wren (architecture), Grinling Gibbons (ornamental wood carving), Henry Purcell (music), Sir Isaac Newton (gravity), Edmund Halley (comets), William Congreve (theatre), Robert Boyle (chemistry) and Samuel Pepys (honest gossip). The most profound economic change that accompanied this renascence in science and the arts was the renewed emphasis on royal charters for overseas trading monopolies.

It was the confluence of these new attitudes, plus new technologies in shipbuilding, navigation and felting, that set the stage for the arrival of the two *coureurs de bois* at the English court.

At the time, the expanding fortunes and recently liberated energies of the land-owning class were being reflected in their search for private investment that would marry trade and profit. The East India Company, which was sending its thirty ships around the Cape on lucrative voyages of ten thousand miles, provided a sterling example of what might be achieved. The new Hudson Bay project, it was rumoured, would not only yield fabulous wealth in fur and copper but offer easy entry to the long-sought North West Passage that would dramatically shorten the costly journeys to Cathay and the Spice Islands.

It is not clear whether it was Robert Boyle (then secretary of the Royal Society) or Sir George Carteret (the king's most trusted financial adviser) who actually introduced Radisson and Groseilliers to Charles II, and there is no record of their conversation among the dreaming spires of Oxford. But talk they did, on October 25, 1666, and from that exchange flowed the royal prerogatives that made the Company of Adventurers possible. Intrigued by glowing rhetoric about "the Bay of the North" and by Radisson's testimony that he had travelled a river that discharged "North West into the South Seas," into which they went and returned "North East into Hudson Bay," Charles II detected in the visitors' flowery description how a new pattern in fur trading might be developed for England's benefit. Peaceful Indians might be enticed to paddle their pelts down the many rivers to Hudson Bay, where they would be met by ships coming from the northern waters with goods to trade.

The immediate effect of the encounter was that Radisson and Groseilliers were granted royal protection and a weekly pension of forty shillings, and were placed in the care of a young banker named Sir Peter Colleton. The king began to discuss the idea of outfitting a royal ship for a voyage into Hudson Bay, and in the process piqued the interest of the Duke of Cumberland, Earl of Holderness and Count Palatine of the Rhine—better known to history as Prince Rupert.

II ASSUMPTION OF EMPIRE

A Princely Undertaking

"A soldier's life is a life of honour, but a dog would not lead it."
—Rupert of the Rhine

THE LAST OF THE CLASSIC KNIGHTS ERRANT, Prince Rupert of the Rhine buoyed the frail fortunes of the Hudson's Bay Company during the first dozen years of its existence, providing the royal patronage and the romantic impulse without which the tiny enterprise would have foundered.

A latter-day Renaissance man, the dark and handsome prince earned distinction as a cavalry leader, king's admiral, freebooting pirate, chemist, metallurgist, inventor, artist and entrepreneur. Rupert was accurately described by Lord Tweedsmuir, a former Governor General of Canada, as having had "one of the most varied careers that ever fell to the lot of man." Never popular in the raffish Restoration court because he was neither by birth nor inclination an Englishman and because his unquiet but disciplined spirit made his hedonist peers uncomfortable, the prince remains a puzzling historical figure, not as prominent or as widely understood as he deserves to be. Oliver Cromwell, who broke Rupert's cavalry at Marston Moor, dismissed him as a man who had his hands very deep in the blood of many innocent people and the Lord Protector's fellow Roundheads sanctimoniously condemned him as the most diabolical of the Cavaliers. Typical of the times was the lambasting by the anonymous 1644 pamphleteer who, after accusing the "Robber Prince" of every evil there was, demanded: "How many towns hast thou fired? How many virgins hast thou ruined? How many Godly ministers hast thou killed?"

Such denunciations bothered Rupert not one whit. Sensitive to his inner drives and passions but outwardly impervious to his legions of detractors, the Bohemian prince was a military genius who marched to his own drum corps. Preferring to be feared rather than loved, he was scornful of court intrigues and thus very often their victim. "A man of intense loyalties but few friends, proud, reserved and morose, uncompromising, unpolitical, undiplomatic, single-minded in his chosen craft of war, which he saw as a personal adventure, such was Prince Rupert of the Rhine," asserted British historian Hugh Trevor-Roper. "Though he lived long in England, he seems never to have understood it, or loved it, or its people: only his uncle, Charles I, and—to a lesser extent—his cousin Charles II who, on his Restoration, would reward his services with offices and revenues. For the rest, he lived to himself, in a private world, with his blackamoors and his poodles, his books, his laboratory and his instruments of art."

An incongruous pastiche of Galahad and Cyrano, the Bohemian prince enlisted his panache in the unpredictable causes of his cousins, the English Stuart kings, drawing his sword to defend the divine right of Charles I yet devoting himself equally to the preservation of Parliament under Charles II Driven out of his father's adopted land when he was less than a year old and forced to flee his British uncle's kingdom a quarter-century later, Rupert spent more than half his life in exile, searching for familiar touchstones that might grant his restless soul the solace of hearth and home. Deprived of a natural sanctuary, he opted for a nomadic existence fighting for (or against) various armies and navies manned by the English, the French, the Dutch and the Italians. He was never a ruler, always the prince.

A streak of stubbornness was developed early in Rupert's character. One of his tutors recalled that the teenage prince, while out hunting with his dog, had chased a fox into its burrow and then become stuck. After considerable effort, the teacher succeeded in pulling out Rupert, dog and fox—all three still firmly attached to each other.

One of those rare warriors at home in the world of ideas, Rupert found no sequestered oasis away from the battle zones but took on the status-quo thinkers of his time with all the dramatic dash of his cavalry charges. "Because he was abreast of contemporary thought," noted biographer George Edinger, "he was ahead of contemporary opinion. He is perhaps the only leader of men, certainly the only royal prince, whose views advanced with his years. He began life, the champion of causes lately lost; and ended it, the protagonist of others yet to be won."

During the last decade and a half of his life, while actively pursuing the business of the Hudson's Bay Company, Rupert set up a laboratory and metal forge in his lodgings at Windsor Castle. His inventions and innovations add up to an impressive tally. He is credited with fashioning the first primitive torpedo, the forerunners of the modern revolver and machine gun, a new method of manufacturing hail-shot, a useful new alloy of copper and zinc still called "Prince's Metal," tear-shaped glass globules known as "Rupert's Drops," that led to the making of bulletproof glass, a new means of boring cannon to ensure truer aim, a naval quadrant that made it possible to take observations at sea in rough weather, and a "diving engine" successfully used to retrieve pieces-of-eight from the sunken Spanish treasure ship *Nuestra Señora de la Concepcion* off Hispaniola. In the autumn of 1667, faced by a brain operation to ease his agonizing migraines, the prince put his ingenuity to work designing and forging the surgical instruments used to relieve the pain under his periwig.

In his alternate incarnation of artist, Rupert worked out a new means of drawing buildings in perspective and a technique for painting on marble; his best-known marble "canvas" is an erotic depiction on the theme of *The Woman Taken in Adultery*. His main artistic coup involved importing into England the art of mezzotint, a method of engraving on copper achieved by scraping away parts of the roughened surface, first taught him by the German artist Ludwig von Siegen. Rupert's prints and etchings reveal a fine hand, and according to P.H. Hulton, Assistant Keeper of Prints at the British Museum, his mezzotints are among the finest ever produced.

Considered the scientific equal of Sir Isaac Newton or Sir Christopher Wren and a founding Fellow of the Royal Society, Rupert took his experiments so seriously that he became the butt of royal jests. Charles II and the Duke of Buckingham would often pay surprise visits to his laboratories to torment the prince, his soot-covered face knotted in concentration as he bent over his fire with vials and beakers. To rid himself of these and less majestic intruders, Rupert kept handy a supply of sulphur powder to throw into his forge-fire; the resultant cloud of noxious fumes drove out the curious interlopers, and the king vowed never again to enter that "alchemist's hell."

GENEALOGISTS HAVE TRACED Rupert's lineage back to Attila, Charlemagne and William the Silent, one of the "Sea Beggars" who founded the Netherlands. His father was Frederick V, Elector Palatine, one of the seven German rulers entitled to choose the Holy Roman Emperor; his mother was

Elizabeth, the daughter of James I of England and VI of Scotland. Responding to the call of the Protestant nobles of Bohemia (later part of Czechoslovakia), the young couple became the little kingdom's monarchs in 1619, and only six weeks after their coronation, Elizabeth gave birth to a son. The first royal prince to be born in Bohemia for more than a century, he was swaddled in Cambrai lace and rocked in a cradle of ivory filigreed with gold. The young prince was named Ruprecht von Wittelsbach, and the christening was a grand state occasion. The Russian ambassador presented the Bohemian crown with fifty carriages, each bearing gifts of red leather chests brimming with valuable furs, while the homage of other plenipotentiaries was borne in coaches drawn by trained polar bears and tame black stags. The arrival of each well-wisher was heralded by flourishes of trumpets and kettledrums, harmonizing with the peal of bells from the Lower Town. The court attracted Moravian hawkboys, young nobles who carried birds of prey in upraised salutes as a symbol of the kingdom's new vitality, their aristocratic gaze translated onto canvas by the great Czech painter Wenceslas Brožik.

Despite the seamless joy of the celebrations, local Jesuits, loyal to Rome and aware of the political momentum gathering outside Bohemia's borders, coined a disquieting title for Rupert's father, referring to him as "The Winter King" who would vanish as surely as the snow. The Jesuits were secretly in league with the Habsburg emperor in Vienna who was plotting to bind his Bohemian subjects closer to his crown.

The Bohemians and Austrians clashed that autumn along the White Mountains stretching behind Hradčany Castle, and the Habsburg mercenaries overwhelmed the brave defenders in an hour. While loyal Moravian Calvinists and the Palatine royal guard fought a courageous rearguard action on the castle grounds, a quick-witted chamberlain remembered the baby Rupert and hid him in the last of the royal carriages clanking and lurching across the Charles Bridge. And so the dream of Bohemian independence had been crushed—not for the last time—only three days before a blizzard that might have bogged down the Austrian invaders. The savage Thirty Years' War that followed reduced a generation of Central Europeans to terror as hired gangs of pikemen, indiscriminately waving crosses and swords, committed the most brutish slaughters, all in the name of a distant god.

Rupert and his fleeing parents found temporary refuge with the queen's brother-in-law, the mean-spirited Elector George of Brandenburg, who reluctantly permitted the exiles to occupy an empty castle at Kustrin. Three years later, the family found refuge in Amsterdam, where Rupert was first officially recognized by England when he was granted a royal "pension" of £300 by his uncle, Charles I. The youngster studied at the University of Leyden, specializing in mathematics, military architecture and draughting. He spent much of his spare time in rough canvas clothes haunting the Dutch docks and taverns where sailors congregated at big oak tables, smoking their clay churchwardens and spinning yarns about palmy faraway landfalls.

The *émigré* family threw itself on the fiscal mercies of its royal relatives, and in 1636 Rupert and his brother Carl Louis were invited to visit London. Even at sixteen, Rupert impressed the English court with his sense of adventure and strength of character. Much fuss was made over the handsome young hotspur, and he was even offered the chance to lead an expedition to Madagascar, off Africa's east coast, with the promise that he could be king of the island should he succeed in conquering it. That quixotic notion was vetoed by his mother, and he reluctantly returned to Holland, where he joined the Life Guards of that enlightened military strategist, the Prince of Orange. Dispatched under Swedish patronage to besiege the Austrians at Vlotho in Westphalia, Rupert was captured and spent the next three years imprisoned in the brooding Danube fortress of Linz.

Here the Rupert saga slips into steamy soap opera. The prison's governor, Count von Kuefstein, had a dark-eyed daughter named Susanne who was asked to minister to the prisoner, and she promptly fell in love with him. Their mutual crush quickly spun into an intense but short-lived romance, consummated in Rupert's non-monastic cell above the rolling Danube. Alas! The young prince was ransomed by his uncle and recalled to England to help fend off the king's enemies, but he never forgot his sweet sojourn in Linz.

It was in prison that Rupert also acquired the first of his many pets, a dog he referred to as "my rare bitch Puddle" and a tame hare that could open the prince's interior cell door with its snout at his bidding.

WHEN CHARLES I RAISED HIS STANDARD at Nottingham in 1642, he vowed that he would return to London on his own terms and named the twenty-two-year-old Bohemian prince his General of Horse, with a command independent of the other royal military and political advisers. The young warrior became a master of the lightning cavalry charge, coaching his men to hold their fire until the most propitious instant. He drove back the Parliamentary forces at every encounter, briskly capturing Bristol, England's second-largest city, raising arms and money, enforcing his military priorities and extending his influence in every direction. A grateful Charles soon appointed him his commander-in-chief. An extraordinary marksman (on one occasion he hit the weathercock on the church steeple at Stratford with one musket shot), Rupert pioneered many of the tactics of modern-day guerrilla fighting, living off the land and striking at the most unexpected moments. He was particularly known for his unorthodox manner of obtaining firsthand intelligence about his enemy's strength and intentions. Just before the battle of Warwick he disguised himself as a cabbage vendor and drove a cart into the town to examine the fortifications and troop deployments.

Mounting court intrigue and Rupert's own insensitivity to the political dimensions of the situation in which he found himself gradually undermined his prestige and authority. As the war's most audacious and most successful commander, he attracted the blame for its savagery, and like most other military potentates blinded by the hubris of too many easy victories, he eventually overstepped himself. Rupert had rashly promised Charles he could hold Bristol against any odds, but once typhus started and an outlying fortress was captured, he pronounced the city indefensible and surrendered in four days. "I have no stomach for sieges," the chastened cavalry commander confessed in a rare display of introspection into both his tactics and personality, when he was reprimanded by the king.

Prince Rupert was to serve the Stuart family's cause with undiminished loyalty for another thirty-six years, first as commander of the royal fleet during the Second Civil War, and later as a blue water pilot gathering spoils for the court of the exiled Charles II in daring raids across the Mediterranean and Caribbean seas. Recalled to England at the time of the Restoration by a grateful king, Rupert was granted an annual pension of £1,500, appointed to the Privy Council, named Admiral of the Fleet and for six years held the important portfolio of First Lord of the Admiralty. He fought the Dutch in three minor wars and helped restore discipline to the Royal Navy—in one instance by throwing two mutineers over the side of his flagship with his own hands. He was tolerant of drinking at sea as long as it inflamed rather than dulled the fighting spirit, and when there were complaints about excessive liquor consumption, he scoffed at the charges, replying with the memorable riposte: "God damme, if they will turn out every man that will be drunk, they must turn out all the commanders in the fleet."

STILL IN HIS EARLY FORTIES, Rupert appeared an outmoded figure to the City and within the Restoration court, an all too visible reminder of wars best forgotten, an embarrassment to a society trying to compromise its recent past. The martial magic was gone, and the garlands of war that trailed his name had been won against too many of his current compatriots. There was a tragic tinge to his demeanour. Here was a man who had validated both his physical courage and his social prestige, yet he had always been a prince without a principality, a grandee of empire without a hectare to call his own.

Although something of a recluse, Rupert did join the royal court in the giddy frolics at the summer resort of Tunbridge Wells. There he met and wooed Margaret Hughes, a spirited and beautiful actress who had commenced her career with the opening of the Drury Lane Theatre in 1663. He eventually purchased for her a magnificent country seat near Hammersmith and had a daughter (appropriately named Ruperta) by her, but they never married. He later formed a passionate liaison with Francesca Bard, daughter of an Irish peer, and had a son by her named Dudley, but again no wedding followed.

After these infatuations had exhausted themselves, Rupert settled permanently into moody bachelorhood as Governor of Windsor Castle. He concentrated on his art and scientific experiments, but an inadequate personal income and his dreams of empire found him devoting more time and energy to the prospect of overseas trade. Fur-pelt was becoming a strategic staple because its water-resistant qualities were valuable to soldiers trying to keep their powder dry.

The rise of the Dutch commercial empire, based on maritime security and the attendant decline of the Hanseatic League in the Baltic, had driven up fur prices, forcing England to look elsewhere not only for cheaper pelts but also for a more secure and controllable supply of vital timber, copper and cordage for the Royal Navy.

Rupert's meetings at his Windsor apartments with Radisson and Groseilliers ignited his determination to wrest the lucrative North American fur trade from the French. Closely questioning the renegade traders from New France about Indian reports of gold and copper, Rupert (then also Governor of the Mines Royal) was excited by the prospect that the back country beyond Hudson Bay might yield not only fur but as much mineral wealth to the Stuart dynasty as the mines of Mexico and Peru had produced for the kings of Spain. He took the visitors at their word, listening with rapt attention as Radisson described the fur harvest and the copper outcrops he had seen north of

Lake Superior, and set about organizing a private syndicate to finance an exploratory journey to Hudson Bay.

The original ledgers have been lost, but the earliest subscribers are known to have included at least half a dozen of the Adventurers who later congealed as the Hudson's Bay Company. Using cash advanced by Charles's banker, Sir Robert Vyner, Customs Commissioner Francis Millington and Admiralty Paymaster John Fenn, Rupert's group envisioned a voyage to North America in the spring of 1667, but the first vessel lent to the expedition proved inadequate, and the journey was postponed for a season. "The full complement of original investors," according to Fulmer Mood, a University of California historian, "grew in almost organic fashion from a rudimentary nucleus into a financial entity that was, in social, political and religious composition, and functions, fairly complex ... The process is not unlike that which happens when a crystal, in suitably prepared mother liquid, grows from a small to a great size by progressive accretions."

The syndicate had been recruited by Rupert, but it was his personal secretary, Sir James Hayes, who fleshed out the details. The prince had persuaded Charles to lease the associates a two-masted ketch, the *Eaglet*, for a nominal £6 2s. 6d. The even smaller forty-five-ton *Nonsuch** was purchased for £290 from Sir William Warren, a wealthy London timber merchant who had repossessed the vessel from the Royal Navy the previous autumn.

By May 1668 the ships had been outfitted; grocers, chandlers, sailmakers, ropemakers, vintners, butchers, haberdashers, timber merchants and ironmongers furnished the *Eaglet* and *Nonsuch* as floating department stores. Into the little ships were stowed hundreds of items, including hatchets, spears, scrapers, muskets, blunderbusses, pistols, gunpowder, eighteen barrels of shot, paper, quills, ink, thirty-seven pounds of tobacco, compasses, flags, lanterns, ropes, pitch, tar, axes, saws, hammers, anchors; "shirts, socks and mittens and

---

* Royal Navy records list the *Nonsuch* as having had a beam of fifteen feet, a draft of six feet six inches and an overall deck length of fifty-three feet. This would be about half the size of the *Mayflower* (1620) and slightly shorter than the sixteen-oared knoors used by the Vikings. In modern terms, the *Nonsuch* was not as long as the twelve-metre sloops in the America's Cup races. A *Nonsuch* replica, built by the HBC to celebrate the Company's three hundredth anniversary in 1970, was authentic enough except for a 90-h.p. diesel engine and some electronic equipment. After sailing around the United Kingdom, the vessel was loaded on a merchant ship at Bristol for the Atlantic crossing. She toured twenty-eight ports along the St Lawrence and the Great Lakes as well as the waters of Puget Sound and the coast of British Columbia. A truck then took her to a permanent concrete berth at the Manitoba Museum of Man and Nature in Winnipeg, moored to a re-creation of London's Deptford docks.

other slopsellers' wares"; four dozen pairs of shoes; malt for ship's beer, eight gallons of lemon juice to ward off scurvy, five thousand needles; food such as biscuits, raisins, prunes, peas, oatmeal, salt beef and pork; wines and brandy; fifty-six pounds of cork; and a trumpet. Both vessels also carried necklaces of wampum, the standard currency of the Indian trade, consisting of small shell beads that had been brought to England by Groseilliers. Radisson was instructed by the associates to sail on the *Eaglet* with Captain William Stannard and to winter on Hudson Bay; Groseilliers, aboard the *Nonsuch* with their old shipmate Captain Zachariah Gillam, was to bring home the pelts from the first summer's trade and return again with provisions. The captains were enjoined to treat the Frenchmen "with all manner of civility and courtesy, they being the persons upon whose credit we have undertaken this expedition." The sailing instructions, drafted by Rupert's secretary, Sir James Hayes, covered every contingency: "We do also declare that if by accident you meete with any Sea Horse or Mors teeth [narwhal horn] ... it is to be made good to our account." As the expedition's British commanders, the captains were ordered to build fortifications, trade cautiously, hunt whales, prospect for minerals and, as an afterthought, to remember "the discovery of the passage into the South Sea, and attempt it as occasion shall offer." The *Nonsuch* also carried a French surgeon named Pierre Romieux* and a crew of eight.

After a farewell banquet in his Spring Gardens home, Rupert and the syndicate members were rowed down the Thames to see the ships off at Gravesend. On the misty morning ebb-tide of June 3, 1668, the *Eaglet* and *Nonsuch* were piloted out of the river by Isaac Manychurch for a fee of £5. By evening they had reached the open sea and turned north in a fresh breeze; ten days later they rounded the Orkneys and headed due west towards the New World. Four hundred leagues off Ireland, they were struck by a storm that nearly broached the low-waisted *Eaglet*, forcing her to turn back.

Six weeks later, Gillam sighted the coast of Labrador and turned north, navigating the *Nonsuch* skilfully under clouds of seabirds over the "furious overfall" into Hudson Strait. The tiny ketch sailed past the Belchers and found refuge in the same river mouth where Henry Hudson had wintered more than half a century before. It was promptly named Rupert River, after the expedition's Royal sponsor. The crew chopped down scores of spruce trees and

---

* He is referred to in the ship's roster as Peter Romulus, while Chouart Sieur Des Groseilliers is reduced to Mr Groselyer.

cleared a site; the *Nonsuch*, its keel grating on the gravel of the river bed, was hauled up and careened on the river bank; a stockade and house were built of vertical logs chinked with moss and a roof fashioned from local thatch. A twelve-foot-deep cellar was dug below the frost line to store the beer, pike were gill-netted in the river and hundreds of geese and ptarmigan were killed and hung for the winter.

The long season that followed was cold and monotonous, but Groseilliers had experienced far worse, and his bush-honed talents, as well as the ship-master skills of Gillam, made their survival more pleasant and possible. The men developed only a touch of scurvy of the gums, helped along by Groseilliers's bitter-tasting concoctions of spruce beer and by the lemon juice brought along on the voyage. That spring nearly three hundred James Bay Indians came to trade. Advised by Groseilliers, Gillam made a "League of Friendship" with the chief and "formally purchased" the land. Although there was some pilfering from the stockade and the ship, the British muskets, hatchets, scrapers, needles and trinkets were easily and profitably traded for valuable prime-coat beaver—that is, fur the Indians had worn so that the guard hairs were loosened and the inner down could be combed out more easily for felt-making. "This visit," historians Toby Morantz and Daniel Francis noted in *Partners in Furs*, "was different from earlier ones. Now the white man came, not in search of a passage to China, but rather intent on establishing trading settlements, claiming ownership of the land and bartering for furs. The James Bay Indians accepted the newcomers, not because they were naive or helpless, but because the Europeans brought rare and useful items to trade for the most common of New World commodities, furs."

On June 14, 1669, pursued by millions of ravenous mosquitoes, the crew of the *Nonsuch* fled Rupert River. Gillam sailed quickly north, but ice at the top of the bay slowed his passage and it was not until mid-August that he reached open water. Two uneventful months later, the *Nonsuch* cast anchor back in the Thames, and Groseilliers, glad to find Radisson still alive, welcomed his partner warmly.

The return of the fur-loaded little ketch caused minimal stir; its cargo, bartered for goods originally purchased for £650, brought £1,379 on the London fur market, and the ship was resold for £152. Wages of £535 plus the required startup investments, customs duties, the damage to the *Eaglet* and other expenses had failed to make the voyage profitable. But the backers were pleased. The thesis that Radisson and Groseilliers had been expounding for more than a decade had been proved correct: it was entirely practicable to sail into Hudson Bay, winter on its shores and return with a profitable cargo of fur.

Rupert led the delighted backers in obtaining from Charles II the loan of another, larger ship, the pink* *Wivenhoe,* and commissioned construction of a seventy-five-ton frigate especially for the new trade, christened the *Prince Rupert.* To promote further shareholding in the Company, the early Adventurers paid out £34 for hats made from some of the hundred pounds of best Hudson Bay beaver fur kept back from sale, both as trophies for themselves and as gifts for prominent patrons and suppliers who might be interested in financing the Company.

At the age of fifty-one the Bohemian soldier-scientist was becoming such a hero to London commerce that a few months after the return of the *Nonsuch* Rupert was invited to lay the cornerstone of London's new Royal Exchange. The stage was now set to exploit the commercial opening pioneered by the *Nonsuch* voyages. What the Adventurers trading into Hudson Bay really wanted was a royally approved monopoly over the kingdom of fur they had so daringly discovered.

ON FRIDAY, MAY 2, 1670, in Whitehall Palace, they got their wish. Charles II awarded Rupert and his fellow Adventurers a charter as "true lords and proprietors" of all the sea and lands of Hudson Bay and its entire drainage system.

By any standard, the royal declaration in favour of his cousin that established history's oldest continuing capitalist company was an extraordinary document.† The HBC charter was one of the most generous gifts ever presented

---

* A pink is a flat-bottomed, narrow-sterned three-master with a triangular sail as mizzen.
† The claim that the Hudson's Bay Company is the world's oldest continuing commercial enterprise requires some qualification. Several business partnerships, such as the Löwenbrau brewery in Munich (1383), the Banco di Napoli (1539) and Joseph Travers & Sons Ltd. in Singapore (1666) are older, but they have not maintained an unbroken operation under the same name or form of organization. The only real rival for the claim is the Swedish concern Stora Kopparberg, established in 1288—but it altered its business from copper mining to iron manufacturing, the development of water power and making chemicals. Probably the first recorded example of joint stock company (in that it existed as an independent business unit apart from its owners), Stora Kopparberg issued negotiable share certificates in 1888; its 1,200 medieval lots in the Great Copper Mountain were exchanged for stock certificates worth 1,000 Swedish crowns each. The first printed share certificates were issued by the Dutch East India Company in 1606. The HBC was a joint-stock company, which meant that transfer by investors had to be made in the Company's London office where a ledger was kept of the proprietors and their claims. Printed share certificates were not issued until 1863.

by a monarch to his subjects, but its benefits are more visible in retrospect than they were at the time.

It was a fairly routine (and inexpensive) grant for the king to bestow. Its purposes fitted in precisely with the objectives of the English mercantilism of the day: to direct trade policies in a way that would allow private investors to minimize their risks and maximize their profits. They, and not the state, would bear the costs of developing markets for British goods in barely accessible colonies with inhospitable climates and independently minded natives. Similar gifts had been granted to slave traders and gold hunters of West Africa, and only two years earlier Charles II had transferred the Indian island of Bombay (part of the dowry received when he married Catherine of Braganza) to the East India Company for an annual rental of £10.

What made Charles II hesitate for most of a year before actually signing the document requested by Rupert and his impatient associates was the possible effect this particular grant might have on his friendship with Louis XIV of France, who was not only an ally but was also the provider of the pension that allowed the English sovereign to act independently of Parliament. Charles had recently bound himself to the French court by the Treaty of Breda, which returned most of the Cromwellian conquests in America to France. Apart from the northward claims of New France, Louis XIV had himself, on April 27, 1670, granted a charter over roughly the same territory as Rupert's to an obscure Dutch mariner, Jan Van Heemskerk. That claim was based on the exploits of the captain's great-uncle, a confused navigator claiming to have made "a voyage for Holland to the East Indies, entering by way of Formosa in the South Sea and departing to the north of California, reaching Holland by way of Hudson Bay."*

Royal assent was finally granted on the second day of May, partly because Rupert could justifiably claim that this was the only reward he had requested from Stuart monarchs despite his life-long dedication to their cause. Another reason, not sufficiently documented, may be that the king was promised a monetary reward for signing the Hudson's Bay Company charter.†

---

* Van Heemskerk sailed from Brest with three vessels on August 14, 1670, determined to copy his great-uncle's remarkable geographical manoeuvre in reverse. His quandary was resolved when the little fleet sank during a storm in the Bay of Biscay.

† In her authoritative *Conquest of the Great North-west*, Agnes C. Laut quotes a Company minute to the effect that in 1684, Sir James Hayes, then Deputy Governor of the HBC, was ordered to present Charles II "his dividend in gold in a faire embroidered purse."

The contents of the HBC charter itself, at least as far as its provisions for a monopoly were concerned, differed hardly at all from those of many similar royal grants.* Because capital gains from overseas voyages were at best uncertain and investments had to be secured over the often lengthy period between the launching of an enterprise and its payoff, it was not unusual for merchants of the day to demand monopolistic protection for their ventures so that potential rivals and interlopers could be kept away. "The granting of such wide territory and such rich resources was no mere favouritism," Arthur S. Morton noted in his *History of the Canadian West.* "It carried with it the obligation first of all to put out the private capital to make the natural resources available, and then to use these to establish settlements and to govern the colony."

Apart from its leathery durability, what set the HBC charter apart from similar documents was the formidable dimension of the estate it unknowingly granted. By setting the geographical limits of the territory at the sources of the streams that drain into Hudson Bay, the grant enclosed a virtual subcontinent of 1.5 million square miles, its eastern boundary extending back to the height of land in the unexplored reaches of Labrador, its southern extremities stretching along a huge territory just above the headwaters of the St Lawrence's many tributaries. Then it swept into the Red River Valley, south past the 49th parallel, vaulting west to the very peaks of the Rocky Mountain divide. Only the wild lands around the great streams gushing northward (the Coppermine and the Mackenzie) and the rivers flowing westward into the Pacific (the Columbia, the Fraser, the Skeena and the Yukon) were excluded.

Named Rupert's Land, this huge freehold was the equivalent of nearly 40 percent of modern Canada: all of northern Ontario and Quebec; all of Manitoba; southern Saskatchewan and Alberta; a huge chunk of the eastern portion of the Northwest Territories; plus much of the American states of Minnesota and North Dakota. Even these gargantuan boundaries did not entirely accommodate the limits set out in the document. Because it was open-ended in defining the outer limits of the Company's trade, the charter in effect granted a monopoly over trade originating anywhere west of Hudson Bay, so that if the North West Passage had actually existed where navigators

---

* Other, earlier enterprises that received similar sanctions included the East India Company, chartered by Elizabeth I on Dec. 31, 1600; the Dutch East India Company (1602); the Danish East India Company (1634); and the French East India Company (1664). None survived past 1858. Scores of smaller enterprises were chartered to exploit the Antilles, Bermuda, Senegal, the West Indies, Cape Verde and Virginia.

of that day thought it did, the HBC would have possessed control of trade rights, based on discovery, all the way to the shores of Cathay.*

The commercially minded Adventurers had no intention of disturbing their monopoly by sponsoring the discovery of a North West Passage. But the charter's preamble did praise "Our Deare and entirely Beloved cousin Prince Rupert" and his associates, who had "at theire owne great cost and charge undertaken an expedicion for Hudsons Bay in the North west part of America for the discovery of a new Passage into the South Sea and for the finding of some Trade for Furrs Mineralls and other considerable Commodityes and by such theire undertakeing have already made such discoveryes as doe encourage them to proceed further in pursuance of theire said designe by meanes whereof there may probably arise very great advantage to us and our Kingdome."

Nor was the document particularly clear on how strenuous an effort at colonization was required of its recipients. The HBC staunchly resisted admitting anyone other than its own traders into Rupert's Land for another 142 years— the first real settlers being the ragged band of Red River immigrants brought by Lord Selkirk in 1812—but in any case there were no sanctions applied or available to spur the Company to create a more hospitable haven.†

Unlike some of the joint-stock charters of the time, the HBC grant makes no mention of any religious obligations, although a set of accompanying instructions drawn up by Charles II's Colonial Office did contain this injunction: "You are to consider how the Indians and slaves may be best instructed in and united to the Christian religion; it being both for the honour of the Crown and of the Protestant religion itself, that all persons within any of our territories, though never so remote, should be taught the knowledge of God, and be made acquainted with the mysteries of salvation."

But again, there was no enforcing clause accompanying this mandate, and except for one chaplain sent out for a three-year stint in 1683 and another one-season experiment in 1693, the notion of spreading Christianity to the natives or anyone else remained a dead letter. From the very outset, the whole

---

* No explorer from the east found his way across the continent until Alexander Mackenzie did it in 1793. Because he was in the employ of the North West Company at the time, he carefully noted that he had come "from *Canada* [not Hudson Bay] by land."

† This was partly a matter of climate. Alternative destinations for would-be colonists were available in the Carolinas, Bermuda, Antigua and Barbados. Even Newfoundland, which had a settled population, was refused the status of a colony because of the rigours of its weather and the infertility of its soil. The Commissioners for Trade and Plantations ruled in 1675 that "all inhabiting in that country must be discouraged."

business of the Company was business, not the dissemination of the British way of life or the proclamation of the gospel of Christ.

Quite apart from Charles II's cavalier dismissal of French claims in granting the Charter, the English monarch omitted any reference to the well-established occupancy of the Indian inhabitants. The only proviso was that the Company not make war against another Christian monarch without his permission. Although the document clearly recognized that the fur trade depended on the continuing presence of the indigenous peoples, no attempt was made to draw them into any "league of friendship" as informal treaties were then known. The HBC was, in effect, being handed a vast hunting preserve, to dispose of and exploit at will.

Certainly, the price exacted by the Charter for these considerable privileges amounted to a bit of Restoration hokum. In return for his splendid gift, Charles II required the Company merely to yield and pay two elks and two black beavers "whensoever and as often as wee our heires and successors shall happen to enter into the said 'Countryes Territoryes and Regions hereby granted.'"* This bizarre bit of bounty was actually paid only four times. The royal rent ceremony was first performed in 1927 when the Prince of Wales (the future Edward VIII) visited his ranch in Alberta; the second time in 1939 for George VI; the third time in 1959 for Queen Elizabeth II; and the last time in 1970 for the Queen and Prince Philip. The 1970 ceremony was unique in that live black beavers were presented for the first (and last) time.†

---

* The ceremonial fee amounted to a puckish codicil by Charles II. But ever conscious of its precious charter, the HBC took its "rent" payment deadly seriously. "We kept stuffed elk's heads and beaver pelts in most of our western stores, just in case the Queen should put down somewhere, because the continuation of our Charter depended on making the presentation," Sir Eric Faulkner, former Deputy Governor of the HBC, recalled in 1981. "In case she put down in Saskatoon or Winnipeg, somebody was always ready to rush out and present the items to her, otherwise our Charter was forfeit and enemies of the Company would damn well see that it *was* forfeited. So my recollection is that there were some rather moth-eaten pelts in some of the stores. But this only applied to Rupert's Land. She could slip into Toronto or Vancouver and that was all right. It was only if she set foot in what was formerly Rupert's Land that we were in trouble."

† The ceremony, held on the rainy afternoon of July 14, 1970, on a dais outside Lower Fort Garry near Winnipeg, was unique in another respect. The animals were feeling particularly perky in their presentation tank that day, and just as the Queen bent over to accept the symbolic rent, the beavers, not versed in court etiquette, released their tensions by first having a tussle and then by making love. "Whatever are they doing?" Her Majesty demanded of Lord Amory, the HBC governor, who was presiding over the ceremony. "Ma'am, it's no good asking me," intoned the Governor, peering down at his coupling charges with undisguised disgust. "I am a bachelor." The Queen assumed her customary mid-distance gaze and murmured, "I *quite* understand."

Despite the inclusion of subsequently discovered weak spots, the charter had been drafted with a great deal of thought and attention to legal tradition, and even though the circumstances surrounding its land grant changed drastically, the validity of the document was never successfully challenged.* This was a remarkable achievement in view of the fact that the authority bestowed on the Company was almost feudal in its prerogatives. No British subject (much less anyone else) was allowed to trade within the Company's territory, and if that regulation was violated, all the goods of the trespasser would be confiscated, with half going to the king and half to the Company. The HBC had the absolute right to administer law and to judge all cases, civil or criminal, on the spot. It was empowered to employ its own armies and navies, erect forts and generally defend its fiefdom in any way it chose.

The original Adventurers who came to possess this remarkable document certainly had no doubt about its worth. The five sheepskin parchment sheets bearing its seven thousand words of text were locked away in an iron-bound chest kept in Rupert's apartments at Windsor Castle.† In the context of its time, the HBC charter's provisions conformed to the purposes of both its sponsors and its recipients. But even at its granting it was an important document, easily ranking, as Canadian historian Barry M. Gough has observed, with "the passing of the Navigation Act of 1660, the establishment of Carolina, the capture of New York, the acquisition of Bombay and Tangier, the attempt to create a Dominion in New England, the reorganization of the East India Company, and the founding of the Guinea Company. With the establishment of this Company to engage in the fur trade of Hudson Bay, the interests of the two parties were united—that of the adventurers for profit and that of the government for the development of trade, which in mercantilist terms was seen as an expedient of strategic expansion to check the French in North America. And along with this, England had opportunities for Arctic discovery and scientific inquiry."

PRINCE RUPERT HAS BEEN ACCORDED most of the credit for founding the Hudson's Bay Company. In fact, he directly subscribed to less than 3 percent

---

* Between 1690, when the privileges were confirmed by Act of Parliament, and 1870, when the Company gave up its monopoly, the Charter was formally recognized in five major international treaties and at least nine Commons bills at Westminster.

† The original charter, under glass and kept at a constant temperature, is now stored in the HBC's Toronto boardroom.

(£270) of its founding capital, and although he certainly ranked as the Company's chief sponsor, his co-adventurers were a distinguished and potent coalition of dukes, earls, baronets and knights of the realm, joined by some of the most influential of the whiggish merchant princes then beginning to dominate the City of London's blossoming financial district.

The original shareholders were promoters and imperialists in the grand style. "Profit and power ought jointly to be considered," mused Sir Josiah Child, the exalted Governor of the East India Company, to his bustling City cohorts. The post-Restoration investment climate could not have been more welcoming. The HBC took shape just as more and more members of the landed gentry turned their attention to investments abroad and much of Whitehall's hierarchy of courtiers devoted their energies to lobbying for royal charters that could be exploited by floating joint-stock companies. These new corporate innovations were designed to spread the risk through absorption of the suddenly available venture capital. The first exchange, dedicated to dealing solely in the marketing of joint-stock investments, had opened in Amsterdam during the 1602 rush to raise the six million guilders required by the Dutch East India Company, whose grandiose new charter encompassed half the earth's surface: the trade and navigation east of the Cape of Good Hope and west of the Strait of Magellan.*

The Bank of Sweden was about to be established but England did not officially follow suit for another twenty years.† It was during the Restoration that state debtors and private financial creditors began to recognize some common concerns, so that not only Prince Rupert but also Charles II and his brother James, Duke of York, became focal points for City investment decisions in both the public and purely commercial spheres.

---

* The exchange got off to a roaring start with traders gathering on the New Bridge, in front of the future site of the Central Station. The market received a boost when shares were issued for the Dutch *West* India Company, which may have been the only stock market issue ever floated to admit openly that its business was piracy. Within a surprisingly short time of its opening, the Amsterdam Exchange adopted most of the fast-money techniques that continue to characterize its modern counterparts: put-and-call options, short and long purchases, fractional share deals and so on. Joseph de la Vega, who wrote history's first market tip sheet, complained that the stock market was "a touchstone for the intelligent and a tombstone for the audacious."

† The Bank of England's formation in 1694 followed the loan of £1.2 million to King William III by a group of City merchants in return for a bank note monopoly and the right to accept deposits. They began to finance governments through bond issues, thus creating a permanent national debt that grew to £800 million by 1815.

In its royal genesis, the HBC was an instrument of foreign trade policy—one side of the imperial coin, the East India Company being the other. The hope was to outmanoeuvre the French, busy exploiting the empire of the St Lawrence, by squeezing them between British-backed fur-trading ventures moving north from the Duke of York's fiefdom on the Hudson River and south from Hudson Bay. The intent was also to command the market in fur, a luxury prized in the Baltic in Russia, then such a strategic source of naval supplies. The confidence with which the original Adventurers risked their means was based on the assurances of royal support they received through their fellow shareholders Lords Arlington and Ashley, then members of the influential Cabal that maintained Charles II in power. No fewer than six of the original HBC investors sat on the King's Privy Council. They, and Prince Rupert's own personal access to royal attention, made it very clear that the HBC could depend on the monarch's support. Quite apart from his territorial ambitions overseas, Charles was more than a little anxious to create additional revenues for himself beyond the reach of Parliament. He had already contrived to extract a duty of 4.5 percent from the reluctant plantation owners of the West Indies and no doubt regarded the favourable prospects of the Hudson's Bay Company as one eventual source to finance his extravagances.

Risks were minimized by keeping the initial capitalization low, £10,500 compared with £100,000 for the lavish Royal African Company. The dozen-and-a-half original investors all knew one another through common interests. Most of them had shared investments before, mainly in spearheading the Carolina colony or Barbados plantations, or in providing capital for the Royal African, the Levant and Royal Fisheries companies. Nearly all of them had been staunch Royalists during the Civil War, and eight were founding members of the recently chartered Royal Society of London for Improving Natural Knowledge.

Stuart expansionists all, with a healthy entrepreneurial greed, they shared the vision that pelts taken from the new continent's beavers—animals they had never actually seen and could hardly describe—would make them rich while at the same time advancing the cause of English economic influence.

THE ORIGINAL ADVENTURERS appointed seven Committeemen, who gathered once a week to consider the Company's slowly expanding affairs either at Rupert's lodgings in Spring Gardens or in the Chamber of the King's Wardrobe, a sort of bursar's office by the Whitehall Palace gates. The domestic operation of the royal household was being managed by Sir George Carteret, who took an increasingly active role in the HBC's policy formation and became Deputy Governor in 1674.

"Absolutism, pomp, formality and a sense of personal responsibility for retainers—all characteristics of feudalism—marked the rule of the Hudson's Bay Company from the beginning," Agnes C. Laut wrote in *The Adventurers of England*. "They were not merely merchants and traders; they were courtiers and princes as well."

One early item not expanded upon in the Committee's agenda concerned the "sundry charges" paid to Rupert as a reward for having obtained the Company's charter. At an agreed signal during one 1671 Committee meeting, Rupert feigned a spell of indisposition, excused himself and left the room. His friend the Earl of Shaftesbury raised the issue of the Prince's compensation and a substantial sum was voted to him, but the exact amount was not recorded.

Rupert was no titular governor; his contributions went far beyond the exchange of court gossip, which was the second most popular indoor sport of his day. He interceded again and again with Charles II on the Company's behalf, procuring, for example, an exemption from having to pay duty on trade goods sent out to Hudson Bay.

Early board minutes record gifts of "beaver stockings for the King," "silver tankards, hogsheads of claret" and "cat skin counterpanes for his bed" to friends of the Company. All the Adventurers had to take oaths of corporate fidelity,* and careful provisions were made for possible injuries to the officers and servants being sent into Hudson Bay. The loss of a toe by frostbite was assessed at £4, while more serious (or less frequent) injuries were to be settled on the more enduring basis of a yearly £30. This set the tone of parsimonious paternalism that was to pervade the HBC's regulations from the beginning. Any officer who died in the Company's service was granted a "funeral by torch-light to St. Paul's—Company and crew marching in procession. Cost not to exceed £20."

FOUR WEEKS AFTER the HBC was awarded its formal charter, the frigate *Prince Rupert* and the pink *Wivenhoe* cast away from Ratcliffe Wharf below the

---

* The first oath of fidelity and secrecy reads as follows: "I do swear to be true and faithful to the Company of Adventurers; the secrets of the said Company I will not disclose, nor trade to the limits of the Company's charter, so help me God."

Tower, bound for Hudson Bay, under orders to establish a permanent trading post on the Nelson River.

Prince Rupert and the newly incorporated Committeemen tendered a boisterous farewell banquet to the voyage's leaders: Zachariah Gillam, formerly of the *Nonsuch* and now skipper of the *Prince Rupert*, which also carried Groseilliers; Robert Newland, commander of the *Wivenhoe*, with Radisson aboard; and their newly chosen overseas Governor, a cashiered Quaker named Charles Bayley.*

The Royal treasure hunt was now on in earnest, but the choice of Bayley—the only Governor of an overseas English protectorate ever to be installed in his position straight out of jail—was peculiar. Not much is known of Charles Bayley's early life except that he first saw the light in the London parish of St Paul's Covent Garden during the 1630s and that he had some vague connection with the Stuarts, probably as a childhood playmate of the future Charles II. His French mother was lady-in-waiting to the future king's own French mother, Henrietta Maria, daughter of Henry IV of France, and presumably there was some backstairs royal blood in the infant. Enticed or kidnapped aboard a ship bound for America while still in his teens, Bayley was forced to endure fourteen years' hardship as a bond servant in Virginia, where he came under the sway of the Quaker missionary Elizabeth Harris.†

Bayley returned to England at the time of the Restoration and immediately went to Rome as part of a hare-brained mission led by an over-zealous Quaker named John Perrot to convert the Pope to their faith. The duo was apprehended and confined to a madhouse, where Bayley fasted in protest for twenty days and began to grow his beard. Eventually, they were thrown out of Italy, but

---

* The title "Governor" properly applied only to the head of the entire Company, but it was used indiscriminately during most of the 1700s and 1800s to describe officers in charge of major posts and the early supervisors of the whole Hudson Bay area—thus "Governor of Rupert's Land." The title ended with William Tomison, who held the newly created position of "Chief Inland" from 1778 until his retirement in 1803. The York Factory command was made subordinate to the "Chief Inland" in 1786.

† Founded by the London preacher George Fox, the Quakers (also known as the Society of Friends) began as a militant sect protesting against established church conventions, preferring the guidance of "inner light" and individual God-given inspiration over scriptural authority. Fox was arrested eight times. Instead of quietly teaching his creed, he and his disciples would attend regular churches to heckle resident reverends during their sermons. Because they believed that each human being could contact God directly and that no one man was therefore any more important than any other, the early Quakers had little respect for earthly authority and suffered much persecution.

Bayley continued to proselytize his wild faith as he walked barefoot across France. He was frequently arrested and finally jailed when he returned to England for refusing to take the oath of allegiance. His eccentric actions forced the more temperate Quakers to excommunicate him. From various dungeons he wrote letters to his boyhood friend Charles II, warning the king of dangers to his throne and cautioning the monarch that unless he avoided "rioting and excess, chambering and wantonness" he would be "threatened with a share in the whirlwind of the Lord" that was coming to the nation. The royal response was unsubtle and swift—Bayley was transferred from ordinary jails to the Tower of London, where he languished from 1663 to 1669. He was never accused of any specific crime or even examined. The legal problem, presumably, was that it was difficult to charge him with sedition or treason because he was advocating a course of action intended to *keep* the king on his throne. Bayley maintained his correspondence for years, penning direct missives from "the King of Heaven" to "the King of England," and was described by contemporaries in the Tower as "an old Quaker with a long beard" on the edge of madness.

Then a highly unexpected turn of events transformed the discredited zealot into a respected overseas administrator. No evidence exists to document this transmogrification. (According to one whimsical theory, he was a good choice for Hudson Bay because, having spent most of his adult life in prison, he was unlikely to be homesick.) The king released Bayley from the Tower on condition that he "betook himself to the navigation of Hudson Bay and the places lately discovered and to be discovered in those parts," and that he was assured of "conditions and allowances ... agreeable to reason and with the nature of his employment." Almost certainly, the go-between was his jailer Sir John Robinson, then both Lieutenant (Chief Administrator and keeper of the crown jewels) of the Tower and Deputy Governor of the HBC. Whatever the process, a very changed Bayley sailed to Hudson Bay in 1670, commander of the first expedition under Company colours. The party landed at the estuary of the Nelson River and nailed the King's Arms to a tree, claiming the territory. Bayley had time for little more than formalities before an autumn gale drove the *Wivenhoe* back into deep water. Her captain decided to winter 720 miles away across the bay at Charles Fort (soon to be renamed Rupert House) where the *Prince Rupert* with Radisson and Gillam aboard was already safely tucked in for the winter.

The new Governor confirmed the treaties Gillam and Groseilliers had negotiated with local Indians the previous season, and the little colony settled into peaceful hibernation. Scurvy was kept to a minimum with generous daily quaffs of spruce brew, though the captain of the *Wivenhoe* and his mate died of influenza. The Indians who came to barter for steel knives and iron axes brought not only furs but fresh deer meat, wild fowl, sturgeon, whitefish and trout. Life took on decidedly civilized overtones as the sailors baked venison pie and pickled the fall geese in brine. The pigs and chickens brought out from England were slaughtered over the winter. In spring two small boats were launched to range down the coast, with Bayley and Radisson trading beaver skins at the mouth of the Moose River.

Over the next nine years, with only one brief interruption, Bayley conducted the business of the fledgling Company with imagination and sound judgment, establishing its presence at the estuaries of the major rivers flowing into James Bay and Hudson Bay (the Albany, Moose, Severn, Eastmain and Nelson) and founding a depot on Charlton Island to supply the James Bay outposts. He staked out the matrix of the Company's "factory" system, which meant that trade would be carried on from coastal forts instead of from aboard ship, allowing the Company to maintain constant contact with its customers. Bayley won the confidence of the Indians by fair trading and even favourably impressed the Jesuit missionary Charles Albanel and the explorer Louis Jolliet, sent north by the authorities in New France to stake a claim over Hudson Bay for the French crown. Despite his background as a religious fanatic, Bayley seemed to have acted as a decidedly calming influence—except on Radisson and Groseilliers, who never trusted him. The feeling was mutual.

The two *coureurs de bois* who pioneered the Hudson Bay route now felt isolated and unappreciated in the service of the HBC. Their every suggestion that its trade be expanded to the interior met with suspicious whispers that they were really determined to desert and entrust their newly won knowledge to the French.

That was precisely what happened. Influenced by the stern invocations of the visiting Jesuit, Father Albanel, offers of four hundred *louis-d'or* and the restoration of their former estates, plus the promise that their skills and knowledge would be more profitably employed in the service of France, they switched sides in 1674. Radisson, in his autobiographical *Voyages*, claimed that he had been faithful to the Company and had quit only for reasons that "tended to the ruin of the beaver trade and that on all occasions we were look'd upon as useless persons that deserved neither reward nor encouragement."

Five years later, Bayley's term came to an abrupt end when he was recalled to London and accused of unspecified irregularities, mainly on the basis of charges from disgruntled subordinates. Before he could clear his name, he suddenly died on January 6, 1680. Two nights later, Charles Bayley was buried at Company expense (exceeding the official limit, at £31 0s. 9d.) in St Paul's Covent Garden, his body borne through the gloom of London's streets by torchbearers from the crew of the ship that had brought him home. At the cold graveside, Prince Rupert and the Committeemen genuinely grieved the passing of the mad Quaker who had found salvation as the first Governor of Rupert's Land.

FURTHER VOYAGES yielded growing returns, and the Dutch merchants who controlled much of the European fur trade quickly accepted the HBC as their major source of supply. Huguenot hatmakers came to value the rich Hudson Bay beavers over the fur from New France or Albany on the upper Hudson River. London began to challenge Amsterdam, Paris and Vienna as the preeminent European fur market. The nascent HBC was rapidly developing into a tidy little operation, its management (mainly Prince Rupert and Sir James Hayes) determined to see it survive and gradually weaned away from royal prerogatives to unsentimental business methods. Separate ledgerkeeping for profit and capital accounts was instituted, and the joint stock holdings of the original Adventurers were sweetened by calls for temporary loans (an early form of preferred stock) to finance individual voyages, paid back out of the proceeds. Any cash surpluses were reinvested in expanding the arc of posts around Hudson Bay. Most of the annual "courts" were held at Rupert's lodgings in Spring Gardens. Many important decisions were taken at these early policy sessions: instead of using coloured beads, silk ribbons and tinkling trinkets, the trade with the native peoples would be based on utilitarian goods such as knives, axes, muskets, flannel and wool, copper kettles and so on; ships would be leased rather than owned; the charter would be deposited for safekeeping in Rupert's apartments at Windsor Castle and "an iron chest with a great lock" ordered to prevent it from falling into competitors' hands; the sale of furs would be split into two auctions "by candle" at Garraway's Coffee House.

Built at the time of the Restoration by Thomas Garraway, the coffee house (at No. 3 Exchange Alley, off Cornhill near the Royal Exchange) was celebrated for its fine cherry brandy, pale ale, punch and tobacco. According to the raffish merchant and novelist Daniel Defoe, who frequented it, Garraway's was the place where all the most influential citizens gathered, including Sir Josiah Child, the swashbuckling godparent of the East India Company. Here, in the spring of 1651, took place a momentous event in British history: the first tasting of a new beverage brewed from shredded, dried leaves imported by the East India Company—a soothing drink known as "tea." It was an immediate success, and Garraway's resultant popularity made the tavern a good choice for the fur sales. Bidding was "by candle," in which one of two procedures was used to determine the buyer. A one-inch candle was lit, an upset price of seven shillings was called, and bids were made on separate lots of furs; the highest bidder at the point when the candle guttered out got the goods. Alternatively, a pin was stuck into the tallow and the last bidder before it fell out was declared the purchaser.

The first HBC sale on January 24, 1672, turned out to be a noisy assembly of merchants and gallants led by Prince Rupert and his cousin the Lord High Admiral, the Duke of York. The Restoration poet John Dryden was a sceptical onlooker, later sourly musing:

Friend, once 'twas Fame that led thee forth,
To brave the tropic heat: the frozen North.
Later 'twas gold. Then beauty was the spur,
But now our gallants venture but for fur.

Not satisfied with their existing charter, Rupert and his fellow Adventurers applied to Charles II on December 11, 1673, for a patent to extend their monopoly over "Buss Island." It was granted two years later, and the quirky document eventually came into the possession of the Earl of Arlington, who willed it to the Duke of Grafton, who in turn presented it to the Northamptonshire Record Society. That sheet of parchment is all that remains of the dubious venture, since Buss Island did not, in fact, exist. Marked on charts of the Atlantic Ocean for three centuries (slightly east and south of Iceland), it had been "discovered" by the crew of the *Emmanuel*, one of the vessels attached to Sir Martin Frobisher's third expedition. (The *Emmanuel* was a buss—a stout, three-masted Dutch fishing boat of sixty tons burden; hence the name.) Henry Hudson searched for the elusive Outcrop on his way to discover the Hudson River in 1609, and Captain Zachariah Gillam claimed to have sighted it during his passage to Hudson Bay aboard the

Nonsuch fifty-nine years later. Thomas Shepard, the mate of the *Nonsuch,* was actually hired to lead an expedition to Buss but was dismissed for "ill behaviour" before he could depart. Ownership of the mysterious island was carried as an asset on the Company's books well into the 1800s, and critics continued to believe that succeeding governors kept its exact location secret to perpetuate their monopoly. In 1791, Captain Charles Duncan, a progressive navigator on loan to the HBC from the Admiralty, had the nerve and good sense to report after a long voyage trying to trace the mysterious place: "I strove as much as the winds would permit me to keep in the *supposed* latitude of the supposed Buss Island, but it is my firm opinion that no such Island is now above water if ever it was."

PRINCE RUPERT'S SUCCESS in attaining the supplementary charter for Buss Island was the last royal favour granted him. After 1675 he retired more and more into seclusion in his Windsor Castle apartments. He was still Vice-Admiral of England and used his good offices to authorize the flying of the King's Jack on the HBC supply ships but was being frequently overruled on substantial issues by, of all people, Samuel Pepys, then Secretary of the Navy. Because too many high-born Royal Navy officers knew very little of their craft, Pepys had recommended that every candidate for lieutenant be eligible only after he had served three years at sea, at least one of them as a midshipman. Rupert objected that such service as a midshipman was "beneath the quality of a gentleman," but his uncharacteristically reactionary view did not prevail. Besides, as the historian Thomas Macaulay dryly noted, "There were gentlemen and there were seamen in the navy of Charles the Second. But the seamen were not gentlemen; and the gentlemen were not seamen."

By the autumn of 1682, Rupert's health began to give way, his old war wounds reasserting themselves. The Cavalier cause for which the Bohemian warrior had fought had been triumphant for more than two decades, but its animating purposes were all but forgotten, its leaders all but dishonoured. No more church bells rang to warn of Rupert's approach, as the wrinkled, rheumy-eyed prince hobbled around the Berkshire countryside accompanied only by a black dog loping at his heels and a majestic hawk on his wrist.

In mid-November Rupert returned to his town house in Spring Gardens and collapsed while out for an evening of theatre. His condition was diagnosed as pleurisy with a high fever. On Saturday, November 25, the HBC Committee met to re-elect Rupert as Governor but he did not have the strength to attend.

On November 29, 1682, Rupert died—eighteen days short of his sixty-third birthday—refusing to be bled and expiring fully in command of himself.*

The funeral was staged at Westminster Abbey a week later, with the court ordered to observe full mourning—three weeks in purple and three weeks in black. Two companies of Foot Guards, followed by the prince's watermen, footmen, huntsmen, grooms, gentlemen servants, pages, physicians, lawyers and chaplains, led the procession. Then came his secretaries, pursuivants, heralds and so on up the social ladder—to the barons, bishops, earls, dukes and the Marquess of Halifax, Lord Privy Seal. The coffin was borne by stalwart Yeomen of the Guard from Windsor Castle, and behind them, after another bevy of grieving nobles, with head bowed slow-marched the Chief Mourner, William, Earl of Craven, the loyal retainer from the days of exile—paying his final homage to the last of the Winter Queen's sons.

The body was laid to rest in Henry VII's chapel, but no monument survives to mark Rupert's tomb. Only a bittersweet epitaph identifies the final resting place of the Hudson's Bay Company's founder and first Governor: "A soldier's life is a life of honour," it reads, "but a dog would not lead it."

A DOZEN YEARS AFTER the granting of its charter, the Company was generating a yearly profit of 200 percent on invested capital and was only two years away from declaring its first hefty dividend. The main problem was finding a worthy successor to Prince Rupert.

It was a sign of how closely the enterprise stayed tied to the politics of the Stuart court that, instead of reaching into the City where a rapidly emerging mercantile class could have provided a dynamic alternative, the Committeemen decided to approach James, Duke of York, brother of the king and his most likely successor. The decision was not automatic and took six meetings to confirm but finally, in January 1683, Deputy Governor Sir James Hayes and Sir Christopher Wren, the architect who served as a member of the

---

* An autopsy revealed the presence of "bones" in Rupert's brain and heart, presumably the calcification of a blood clot and of a mitral valve ring. Rupert's will left most of his possessions (valued at £10,415) divided equally between his first mistress, Peg Hughes, and the nine-year-old Ruperta. His daughter married Brig.-Gen. Emanuel Scrope Howe, later ambassador to the court of Hanover, thus joining the Bromley family, which is still extant. Dudley, Rupert's son by Francesca Bard, inherited one of his residences but was killed at the age of twenty by a Turkish scimitar at the siege of Buda in 1686. Rupert's most prized possession, his mother's pearl necklace, was sold by his executor, Lord Craven, to Nell Gwyn for £4,520.

Committee between 1679 and 1683, were instructed to attend on His Royal Highness and petition that the second man in the kingdom take the Company under his patronage and protection. The duke accepted the position, but when Hayes returned to Whitehall with a batch of instructions and commissions to be initialled, James imperiously waved him away, declaring that although he had also been appointed Governor of the Royal African Company and of the Royal Fisheries Company, he never, but *never,* signed any documents.

While the Company found itself temporarily on the winning side in the struggle for the English Crown, the Duke of York proved to be as ineffective and short-lived a Governor as he was later king of England. His lack of enthusiasm for the HBC stemmed in part from his desire to stay on good terms with Louis XIV of France and the conflict of interest he felt from the competing beaver preserves he owned in the upper parts of the Hudson River Valley. He had sent ships of war to capture the territory from the Dutch and renamed New Amsterdam, the capital of the little colony, New York after himself.

The Duke of York's contemptuous neglect of the Company of Adventurers undoubtedly was rooted in his personality. The second son of Charles I, James was a stiff and stubborn bigot with popping eyes and a tongue too large for his mouth, so that he could hardly drink a glass of wine or water without slobbering all over himself, gulping the liquid down as if he were eating it. Incapable of a graceful gesture, he had little sense of humour and was so obsessed with the sanctity of the monarchy and the doctrine of Divine Right that even when he was alone with his brother Charles, he would spring respectfully to attention whenever affairs of state were being discussed. His fierce loyalty to the Church of Rome was equalled only by his personal paranoia. His fear of enemies, even before he succeeded in making them, was so intense that a French envoy reported James had been busy fortifying the great naval base at Portsmouth on the *landward* side.

James's sex life was as untidy and overpopulated as that of his brother, but not nearly so pleasant. He had two wives, at least twenty children and a series of mistresses who must have been chosen by his priests, as Charles once sniffed, "by way of penance." Catherine Sedley, one of the deadliest blossoms in his bouquet of thistles, was a lean, ugly sadist who was herself puzzled by the violence of the future king's passion. "It cannot be my beauty," she mused, "for I have none; and it cannot be my wit, for he has not enough to know that I have any."

The only good thing about the Duke of York's tenure as Governor of the Hudson's Bay Company was its brevity—only two years, from January 1683 to February 1685. After that date he held on to his stock but resigned to become king of England. The only other mention of James II in Company minutes occurs on October 31, 1688, when Sir Edward Dering, then Deputy Governor, paid the king his HBC dividend of 150 guineas in gold. Five days later, his royal mandate shattered by his inability to seek consensus (much less find it), James fled England, dropping the Great Seal into the Thames on his way to exile.

THE SOUR TASTE left behind by the Duke of York's flaccid stewardship and the strain in relations between France and England made the Committeemen seek the very best-connected candidate for the HBC governorship. There was only one choice. At a dinner on April 1, 1685, Sir James Hayes approached the Right Honourable John, Lord Churchill (later Duke of Marlborough), to assume the post, and the very next day he was sworn into office. Then thirty-five years old, Churchill was about to be appointed a major-general in the army that would defeat the insurgents led by the bastard son of Charles II, the tragic Duke of Monmouth. Churchill was busy consolidating his position in the front ranks of Restoration military commanders and backstage political manipulators. The second son of an impoverished Stuart administrator named Sir Winston Churchill, he originally found a place at court as a page to the Duke of York and was eventually commissioned an ensign in the King's Own Company of Footguards. An imposing youngster with blue eyes and a clear, ruddy complexion, he quickly became embroiled in the court's sexual intrigues, fighting at least two duels over various transferable ladies, and even shared a mistress—the delicious Barbara Villiers, Lady Castlemaine—with Charles II. (Once, when the two young lovers were at play and the king unexpectedly entered the anteroom to the bedchamber, Churchill demonstrated his grasp of appropriate tactics by diving through the open window to the courtyard below. The lady in question was so grateful for his instant, if slightly retroactive, discretion that she gave him £4,500; this sum, lent out at high rates, became the foundation of Churchill's fortune.)

Shortly afterwards he met Sarah Jennings, a maid of honour in Charles II's court and one of its few members who deserved the title. A handsome woman with an indomitable will, she fell in love with Churchill when she was a pert fifteen and married him three years later. The two were inseparable, mutually reinforcing each other's ambitions, and remained wildly in love even though they had very different temperaments. John was determinedly cool and always collected; Sarah was the opposite, full of spirit with temper to match. In a flash of anger at her husband, she once cut off her straw-blonde hair, knowing it was an object of the Duke's admiration. When Marlborough saw her in the shorn state, he betrayed no emotion, pretending not to have noticed the rape of the locks. Ashamed of herself, Sarah never alluded to her rash act. After the Duke's death, when she was searching through a strongbox containing his most prized personal possessions, she found her fall of hair where it had been treasured in silent homage for more than thirty years.

John Churchill rose ever higher in the royal service, eventually attaining a bewildering array of titles and honours, including Duke of Marlborough, Marquess of Blandford, Earl of Marlborough, Baron Churchill (of Sandridge), Lord Churchill (of Eyemouth in Scotland), Prince of the Holy Roman Empire and Prince of Mindelheim. His stunning success in ten major military campaigns raised England to the forefront of the world's nation-states. It broke the domination of Louis xiv's France over Europe and opened the gate to two centuries of successful British imperialism. Yet his epic military victories at Blenheim (1704), Ramillies (1706), Oudenarde (1708) and Malplaquet (1709) were only the most visible manifestations of his career, overshadowing his behind-the-scenes diplomatic authority, which for a long while (certainly during the early tentative reign of William iii and Mary) made him virtually the uncrowned king of England. A brilliant political strategist and supreme military tactician, Marlborough viewed the world in stark primary colours, refusing to recognize pastel tones of any kind and, like most other self-made men, came to worship his creator. Because he was not only a duke but also a prince of the tiny principality of Mindelheim (in Swabia, west of Munich), he insisted that he be addressed as "Your Highness" and treated as an equal on his travels among the kings, princes and margraves of Europe.

Armed with the booty of war, he built himself appropriately magnificent dwellings—Marlborough House, designed by Sir Christopher Wren, in London and Blenheim Palace, designed by Sir John Vanbrugh, in the country, a baroque structure of outrageous proportions that enclosed seven acres of floor space and prompted even house-proud Sarah to complain that it was a "wild and unmerciful" dwelling.

According to his splendid descendant nine generations removed, Sir Winston Churchill,* the Duke was "a greater do-er than he was a man," but

---

* After he retired from politics in 1955, Sir Winston accepted an honorary post from only one commercial enterprise, although many offers were tendered. He became Grand Seigneur of the Hudson's Bay Company and remained so until his death.

there is little doubt that during his seven years as the HBC's Governor, Marlborough rescued the Company from the neglect of his predecessor and placed it on a solid political footing. If Rupert was the HBC's princely founder, the Duke of Marlborough was its noble preserver, assuring the fledgling enterprise of his protection at a time when he was rapidly broadening his civilian and military power base. He applied his influence to have a hundred marines detailed to protect the HBC supply ships on their transatlantic voyages and arranged for several Royal Navy ships to help defend the Company's northern domain. A grateful Company presented him with a gold plate worth a hundred guineas and named a mighty northern river in his honour.

Probably the most significant achievement during Marlborough's important stewardship was the backhand confirmation of the Company's charter by Parliament. The Skinners Company, the Company of Feltmakers in London and competing American fur merchants all had good reasons to complain about the Company's tendency to monopolistic practices, but the sum of their demands was abolition of the HBC monopoly itself because it was based on an antique royal charter that had never received Parliament's approbation. To head off these and other dissenters, the Committeemen petitioned Westminster for an act confirming their charter. It was passed in 1690 with token opposition, but it was to be valid for only seven years. When the arguments were rekindled in 1697, the London fur merchants renewed their complaints. Uncertain it would carry the day, the Company did not even try to revive the act and lay low though everyone concerned tacitly assumed that the charter would remain in force.

One of the unanswered charges that emerged out of the 1690 hearings was that the Company's Committeemen had been guilty of "stock-jobbing" by paying out inordinately large dividends and then unloading their shares. It was true. The Company paid no dividends in the fourteen years after the granting of its charter, but in 1688—even though French disruptions of the trade on Hudson Bay had caused a cumulative loss of £118,014 over the preceding six years—a fat 50 percent payout was distributed to its tight circle of eight dominant shareholders, including the Duke of Marlborough.

This was followed by another 25 percent declaration and, in 1690, by the largest bonus in the Company's history: a 74 percent dividend, together with a stock bonus of 200 percent in the form of a convertible dividend scrip. Vague explanations were floated that this would bring the HBC's capitalization more into line with the Committeemen's estimates of what the stock was really worth, yet such a forecast of the Company's potential earnings was so far removed from the facts (in the next five years, further losses of £97,500 would be recorded) that a less benign explanation for the extraordinary bonanza seems more likely. British historian K.G. Davies noted that within the next two years, six of the eight Committeemen who voted themselves the bloated dividends had resigned from the Company and sold their stock. "On this evidence," he concluded, "sharp practice cannot be ruled out; nor can opportunism." Watering of the stock (which raised the Company's capitalization from £10,500 to £31,500) increased the value of Marlborough's shares by 400 percent. During the next two years, the HBC quotations at Jonathan's informal stock exchange doubled in value, presumably because investors thought they might be due for another 150 percent dividend. Instead, there followed twenty-eight years of no dividend payments at all.

This was mainly the result of the havoc the French wrought on the fur trade in Hudson Bay, partly due to the economic recession and the currency crisis that cut into an already oversupplied fur market. One reason the HBC endured the drought was that no one was certain precisely how a royally chartered joint-stock company could be wound up. Yet such a drastic course must have been tempting because only through liquidation could the HBC's debts—up to a crippling £30,000 by 1698—have been eliminated.

The exception was the dividend presented to the royal successor of the unhappy, exiled James II. On September 16, 1690, six of the Company's Committeemen, led by Deputy Governor Sir Edward Dering, called on the new king, William III, at Kensington Palace and presented him with three hundred gold guineas.*

Marlborough resigned as Governor in 1692, having fallen into temporary disfavour (he was actually imprisoned in the Tower for six weeks) and become embroiled in political problems that required his full attention. Political power was passing from the regal palaces to the grand country mansions of the Whig aristocracy, and the source of the pivotal commercial decisions was moving from royal favouritism to the London financial houses. As always, the HBC adapted itself to current trends and appointed as its next Governor a banker and fiscal manipulator named Sir Stephen Evans, who would be Governor for two terms stretching over sixteen years. He was the first and the most peculiar of the succession of City men who were to guide the Hudson's Bay Company during the next two centuries.

---

* The HBC shares originally granted to James II were deemed to be the property of the British royal house. Dividend payments were made to the monarchy until 1764 and the sovereign was officially listed as an HBC proprietor until 1824.

Battling for the Bay

Forced marches through waist-deep snow,
the hollow boom of cannon fire and the terror
of guerrilla attacks on the inadequately armed
forts became commonplace on the once dormant bay.

DURING THE HARD-SCRABBLE DECADE before Sir Stephen Evans assumed the helm of the London-based Committee and for the five years that followed, the trading posts on Hudson Bay unexpectedly joined the mainstream of world history. They became royal pawns in the escalating hostilities between France and England that led to an official declaration of war on May 17, 1689. Even though the writ of European monarchs carried little sanction on the gravelly shores of the bay, the traders who manned the wilderness forts found themselves caught up in operatic clashes not of their own making.

After 1682 the European tug-of-war shifted overseas, as French flotillas and overland raiding parties from Montreal attacked and pillaged the HBC's fur factories. Because the HBC traders were far more interested in staying alive to collect their pay than in sacrificing their lives to defend storehouses full of pungent pelts, they accepted defeat with more relief than shame. Except for the sea battles of 1696 and 1697, they seldom bothered to call for help from the Royal Navy. Individual sieges by land were fierce enough to inflict serious casualties on both sides. Some of the posts changed hands half a dozen times.

Yet neither France nor England could determine precisely how much money and manpower the sub-Arctic war was worth. Even the most ambitious fur lords of New France were torn between trying to advance their cause in Hudson Bay and expanding their commercial interests in the warm and infinitely more welcoming climate of the Illinois country south of Lake Superior and beyond. Apart from these considerations—and the serious problems posed by trying to mount marine engagements in a body of water littered with navigational hazards—there was one other reason that prevented either side from pushing to ultimate victory. While most of the battles for Hudson Bay were being fought, the price of beaver pelts on European markets wilted to new lows, mainly because of over-production from New York and other colonies.

The superior warriors from Quebec won most of the bay battles, but failed to follow their brilliant tactical successes with enduring strategic consolidation; the English company limited its concern to survival, but not at any cost. The HBC fought back only hard enough to keep at least one post in its possession at all times (either Albany or York) and concentrated on lobbying royal courtiers and influencing peddlers in the back rooms of St James's and Versailles. Such bland quiescence tallied precisely with the glut in the fur market; in those circumstances, more profit was to be made in controlling distribution of the furs than in harvesting them. What, after all, was the point of victory if it yielded only an increase in the backlog of unsaleable pelts? Better to guard capital and wait out the storm.

Still, forced marches through waist-deep snow, the hollow boom of cannon fire and the terror of guerrilla attacks on the inadequately armed forts became commonplace on the once dormant bay. "All in all, the men in London who guided the Company's affairs before 1763," noted Grace Lee Nute, the Minnesota historian, "never knew what news their captains would bring next from the bay, nor what their servants, staggering into London after months or years in the hands of French conquerors, would report concerning ownership of Bay forts."

In charge of these forts between 1683 and 1686 was Henry Sergeant, an irascible and high-handed Englishman whose small claim to immortality was that he brought the first white women to Hudson Bay: his wife, her companion (a gentlewoman named Mrs Maurice) and their maid.* The overseas Governor, crossly referred to in HBC minutes as "Sergeant and the whole parcel

---

* It was a long while before any other women followed the Sergeant precedent. In April 1684, when Elinor Verner, the wife of an experienced HBC trader placed in charge of Fort Rupert, applied for permission to join her husband, it was denied. Never known for acting hastily, the HBC did not appoint its first woman manager of a northern post for another three centuries: in October 1983, a Cree named Donna Carrière was placed in charge of the Company's store at Weagamow Lake in northwestern Ontario.

of women appertaining to him," also employed three menservants. His private quarters at Albany Fort had a four-poster bed complete with heavy curtains and a valance. Sergeant's lackadaisical surrender of his home fort to the French after not quite one day's perfunctory fighting prompted the Company to sue him for cowardice and £20,000. The case was never heard, but the charges rang true.

WITH RADISSON PLEDGED TO THE SERVICE of New France, the London Committeemen were aware that the immunity to competition of their northern monopoly was bound to be short-lived. The first agent of their discomfiture was an unusually talented financier from Amiens named Charles Aubert de La Chesnaye, who arrived from France in 1655 as the agent of a group of Rouen hatters and furriers.

A stern and pious merchant, La Chesnaye lived so modestly that the curtains in his home were patched together from old tablecloths and he spent most of his working life wearing the same pair of red flannel trousers. Married three times, he sired eighteen children and remained the outstanding leader of the early New France business community until his death in 1702. Like so many members of France's third estate, he was dissatisfied with his bourgeois status and gave himself a title after acquiring several seigneuries to gain the prestige due a landowner. Montreal's first important venture capitalist, the leathery old trader controlled a significant economic empire as well as holding mortgages on many of the growing community's houses.*

La Chesnaye first met Radisson during a visit to Paris in 1679. That get-together triggered the eventual formation of La Compagnie du Nord as New France's thorny challenge to the HBC. Radisson agreed to lead an expedition to Hudson Bay in return for a quarter of the profits. By 1682, La Chesnaye had organized a flotilla of two small fishing ships and twenty-seven men, carrying Radisson and Groseilliers with orders to establish the Compagnie du Nord's first permanent station at the mouth of the Hayes River.

Radisson had camped at the nearby Nelson River with Charles Bayley a decade earlier and was aware that the upper reaches of the Hayes were

---

* In his last will he asked forgiveness for any wrongs, great and small, he might have committed in his business dealings and requested that he be buried in the paupers' cemetery at Hôtel-Dieu—presumably so that he could appear before his Maker as a simple man of God. To be on the safe side, he followed the custom of arranging for the posthumous celebration of daily mass, in perpetuity, to guarantee the calm repose of his capitalistic but cautious soul.

connected to the wider Nelson, but that because the smaller stream was easier to navigate, most natives preferred to switch to it on the final leg of their journey down to the bay. The adjacent estuaries of these two important rivers, whose sources lie hundreds of miles upstream in prime fur country, would be the site of the bay's major battles, and York Factory, the post that sprouted there, quickly became the area's main settlement. York's initial colonization resembled the speeded-up antics of the silent films' Keystone Kops; its location was moved ten times as its procession of occupants behaved with something considerably less than the cool bravado normally associated with conquerors of a new land.

Edward H. Borins in his thesis *La Compagnie du Nord, 1682–1700* makes a telling point about the whole era. "*The Compagnie du Nord's* fatal error proved to be its decision to compete with the English by sea. Had the company concentrated its efforts on its posts in James Bay and contented itself with small but regular profits, it might well have survived," he concludes. "But the *Compagnie du Nord's* directors, who seemed inclined to take gambles, chose to invest all their capital in the expeditions of the early 1690s, which failed. Therefore, the Canadians, who were so well adapted to the rigours of the fur trade, lost to the English, who were far superior in naval skills, which proved to be the decisive factor in the exploitation of the Hudson Bay trade."

The sequence of events began with Radisson's arrival on August 21, 1682, in the two fishing smacks whose crews included his nephew, Groseilliers's son Jean-Baptiste Chouart. Three days earlier another expedition, inbound from Boston aboard the sturdy *Bachelor's Delight*, had put in upstream on the Nelson. Its crew of fourteen, skippered by Benjamin Gillam, son of the original commander of the *Nonsuch*, had settled in for the winter unaware of the French visitors camped on the nearby Hayes. Although they were described as "all bachelors and very resolute fellows" and carried a "charter" from the governor of Massachusetts, the Bostonians were clearly inspired by the revenue-hungry Zachariah Gillam, back in the Company's employ as captain of the supply ship *Prince Rupert*—even then heading for the Nelson from London, carrying John Bridgar, appointed York's first Governor.

Radisson went up country to contact families of Cree with furs to trade while Groseilliers stayed behind to erect a small fort on the south shore of the Hayes. Eight days upriver, Radisson found an Indian encampment and concluded an informal treaty that he later claimed gave New France exclusive trading rights in the area. The day he arrived back at the bay, he heard cannon fire, which upon investigation turned out to be a burying party of the Bostonians paying final tribute to one of their companions who had died on September 12. Radisson paddled over to the Nelson with a few men to investigate. His outrage at finding a band of competing traders was larded with a generous helping of bluff. He told the youthful Gillam that he not only held a commission from the king of France to build a great post and forbid any aliens from trading, but that fifty French marines were encamped on the next river to enforce his royal mission. An uneasy pact was negotiated, beguiling Gillam into Radisson's power.

As the woodrunner and his companions were leaving the little camp, congratulating themselves on the successful ruse, they spotted a large ship under full sail entering the Nelson River. She was the *Prince Rupert* out of London, carrying the official HBC party. To stop them from proceeding farther upriver—where they would be seen by the Bostonians, who would quickly realize that the English had a lot more firepower than the French—Radisson lit a large bonfire and piled it high with smoke-producing grass, hoping to persuade the lookouts aboard the *Prince Rupert* that the tiny clearing was really an Indian encampment. The trick worked. The *Prince Rupert* dropped anchor.

The following morning the dinghies were lowered and a landing party left the *Prince Rupert* to investigate. Radisson posted his men in the bush and positioned himself boldly on shore, a true Caesar of the wilderness deigning to greet the puzzled intruders. Informing the luckless Bridgar that the land had already been claimed for the king of France, he professed to have been in residence for a year, in command of three hundred troops dedicated to enforcing occupation of the area by his most Christian Majesty, Louis XIV.

There followed an impasse that could not be readily resolved since the season was too far advanced for the HBC servants to exercise any option but to winter ashore. All but nine crew members disembarked and began to build winter shelter. Then an act of God intervened: a violent swirl of ice caused the *Prince Rupert* to drag anchor, drift out to sea and sink with all aboard, among them old Zachariah Gillam. The HBC men were now at Radisson's mercy for their future and food supplies.

The uneasy winter truce was broken in February when Radisson and his confrères easily captured the Bostonians' ramshackle stockade; shortly afterward, Bridgar and his men were similarly overrun. Their winter abode was burned (but its trade goods fastidiously saved) as the victorious Frenchmen made ready to build a permanent post and to export their furs. Most of the prisoners were eventually dispatched to Company posts at the Bottom of the Bay aboard a leaky vessel hammered together from the remains of Radisson's two fishing smacks.

Leaving their young relative Jean-Baptiste Chouart in charge, Radisson and Groseilliers boarded *Bachelor's Delight,* the only seaworthy ship that remained of the assembled craft. They loaded the two thousand pelts traded during the winter and sailed off in triumph for Quebec. Once again, the authorities of New France acted against their own interests, confiscating the ship and charging the two preening woodsmen the standard 25 percent duty exacted on local fur catches. That was too much for Médard Chouart, Sieur Des Groseilliers. At sixty-five, he was worn out and frustrated by the succession of shortsighted Quebec intendants. He retired in disgust to his modest seigneury at Trois-Rivières, where he died peacefully in 1696.

It was also too much for Radisson. As soon as he learned that the tax collectors rather than he and his brother-in-law were to receive the quarter-share of profits from the hard-won furs, he began to plot reconciliation with his one-time English employers. After a quick reconnoitre in France, Radisson realized the authorities there were much more anxious to appease the king of England than reward their baywise emissary's exploits. Lord Preston, the adroit diplomat then British ambassador to the Court of Versailles, was instructed by Sir James Hayes of the HBC to seek out the renegade trader "who, it is believed, could be brought over again to our service if he were so entreated by your Lordship." Preston was told that Radisson was holding court on the third floor of a house in the Faubourg St-Antoine and sent his aide, a Captain Godey, to negotiate. Godey described Radisson as being "apparelled more like a savage than a Christian. His black hair, just touched with grey, hung in a wild profusion about his bare neck and shoulders. He showed a swart complexion, seamed and pitted by frost and exposure in a rigorous climate. A huge scar, wrought by the tomahawk of a drunken Indian, disfigured his left cheek. His whole costume was surmounted by a wide collar of marten's skin; his feet were adorned by buckskin moccasins. In his leather belt was sheathed a long knife."

Since he could not get any pledges of favourable French action, Radisson was easily seduced by the English overtures, confiding to his journal: "I yielded to these solicitations and am determined to go to England forever, and so strongly bind myself to his Majesty's service ... that no other cause could ever detach me from it." He was welcomed back to London by most of the HBC Committeemen, who swallowed their scepticism after he revealed that his nephew was still in Port Nelson guarding a magnificent hoard of skins awaiting shipment. Rewarded with a silver tankard, £200 in Company stock and the grand if slightly hollow title of Superintendent and Chief Director of Trade at Port Nelson, Radisson sailed again for the bay, this time aboard the aptly named *Happy Return*. His arrival under English colours understandably confused his patient nephew, who by then had garnered a valuable booty of twenty thousand pelts and was now being asked to turn them over to the hated HBC—from under whose corporate snout most of them had been snatched in the first place. No record of the two men's conversation exists, but at the end of it, both the furs and young Jean-Baptiste were taken over by the Hudson's Bay Company.

That season alone, more than seven hundred Cree in three hundred canoes arrived to barter for 300 guns, 10,000 knives and hatchets, 247 hogsheads of tobacco and 15 gross of pipes, 390 blankets and a cornucopia of household items that were becoming regular features of the interchange. Radisson repeated his lucrative visits to the bay for three more years, but since the French government had put a price on his head, he maintained an uncharacteristically unheralded presence there and eventually retired to London. By the close of the seventeenth century, he was sixty-four years old and being only vaguely credited for his exploits on the Company's behalf. Penny-pinching Committeemen with short memories cut his pension, and it took Radisson five years of tedious legal procedures to win it back. The one-time Caesar of the wilderness was reduced to begging the Company for a job as its London warehouse-keeper. Being refused, he had to make do with a pension of £12 10s. per quarter. Pierre-Esprit Radisson died in 1710, his zest for life long since extinguished, his grave unmarked. The only subsequent entry in the minute books of the Company he established was the payment of a paltry £6 for his funeral expenses.

THE HBC POSTS ON THE BAY were becoming far too prosperous for the French to ignore. They were returning an annual £20,000 and diverting a growing proportion of the trade that had originally gone to Montreal. La Compagnie du Nord had little trouble persuading Brisay de Denonville, the governor of New France, to mount a military expedition overland to capture the forts of the English intruders. By March 1686, the little army had been assembled in Montreal: seventy Canadian irregulars, a few native guides, thirty French soldiers and their leader, the Chevalier de Troyes, a Parisian company commander who had arrived in Quebec only eight months before. The troop started out on sleds, dragging thirty-five canoes that they used as soon as spring breakup allowed them to paddle—up the Ottawa River to Lake Temiskaming and down the Abitibi and Moose rivers to James Bay. The eight-hundred-mile journey remains an epic of bush travel and was one of North America's earliest and most successful commando assaults. Because no large expedition had ever travelled this route north overland, no portages had yet been cut. With the canoes and loads of supplies the men had to struggle between various lakes and rivers, stumbling over fallen trees, slippery rocks and tangled underbrush. Eighty-two days out of Montreal, they neared the first of the HBC's installations, Moose Factory, tucked behind its square palisade, eighteen feet high and protected by bastions at each corner. The little fort's defences were impressive, but they were designed to repel attacks from the sea. Since no visitors, friendly or otherwise, could get through Hudson Strait until late summer, few lookouts had been posted and the seven-pound bastion-cannons had been left unloaded. The local Governor, John Bridgar, had sailed for Rupert House the previous day with most of his officers, leaving behind a garrison of sixteen leaderless men. Their main protection was the three-storey redoubt inside the fort, armed with three cannon.

The French attack was launched by two of the Le Moyne brothers, Pierre d'Iberville and Jacques de Sainte-Hélène. Squad leaders under de Troyes, they tippytoed inside Moose Fort while the HBC men were asleep and roped the cannon together so that even if the Bay men managed to stir themselves enough to fire the weapons, the recoil would only bring down the palisades. The dawn attack that followed lasted a scant two hours. The most dramatic moment in the brief scrap was the solo stand of the twenty-four-year-old Pierre Le Moyne d'Iberville, who had been leading the way inside the redoubt when the gate was shut behind him; he had to hold off the entire garrison, sword in one hand and musket in the other, while his companions forced the gateway open again. Shouting the war whoop of the Iroquois, the one hundred Frenchmen quickly overwhelmed the stunned HBC traders, who surrendered in the name of arithmetic and expediency.

De Troyes decided to follow up his easy triumph with an assault on Rupert House, seventy-five miles up the east coast of James Bay. Leaving forty men to guard the captured fort, he set off with the others in his war canoes and soon sighted not only the fort but also the supply ship *Craven*, which had brought Bridgar and his officers from Moose. The main body of Montreal troops attacked the fort and took it handily—a forgotten ladder was still conveniently propped against the side of the redoubt. Up they swarmed to drop lighted grenades down the chimney on the sleeping Englishmen.

D'Iberville was assigned capture of the *Craven*. He silently boarded the ship, shot the one sailor dozing at anchor watch, then stamped his feet on the deck, giving the customary signal to wake crews at times of emergency. As the first three sleepy heads appeared through the companionway, each was greeted with the blunt end of a musket; the rest of the crew meekly surrendered. The captured Bay men were escorted back to Moose while d'Iberville took charge of the *Craven* for an assault on the more heavily armed HBC fortress at the mouth of the Albany River. The main problem was finding it, because the site, a short distance up the river, was not visible from its sea side. The fort's occupants resolved that quandary for their would-be invaders by blithely firing their routine sunset gun just as the attackers were about to sail off in frustration.

Albany was the best protected of the bay forts, but de Troyes and d'Iberville had brought along the heavy siege guns from Rupert House. They mounted them on a patch of frozen gravel outside the palisade and patiently lobbed 140 shots into the fort. As the attacking troops shouted *Vive le Roi!*, an echo of their war cry could be faintly heard—so faintly, in fact, that d'Iberville realized it was emanating from the fort's cellar where the cowardly defenders were huddled in refuge instead of firing back. None of the HBC regulars had dared mount the barricades to lower the Company flag. The cannonade stopped only when the bravest Englishman present made an unexpected appearance. Through the gate the resident chaplain hove into sight, holding aloft a maid's white apron tied to his walking stick.

Henry Sergeant agreed to rendezvous with de Troyes, choosing the middle of the Albany River as a neutral venue. Two small boats set out, one from each river bank. Having lost his fort, Sergeant seemed concerned mainly with the etiquette of the occasion. A bottle of vintage claret tucked under his arm, Sergeant proposed that the two leaders drink a toast to their respective sovereigns. De Troyes's more mundane concern was to prevent the English Governor from noticing how famished and exhausted his men were after their three successive sieges, and how easily they might have been overrun. The only concessions the Englishman won were that they could keep their personal possessions and that they would be shipped to Charlton Island to await the next Company supply ship.

Leaving forty men under d'Iberville to consolidate his gains, de Troyes and most of the other victors marched back to Quebec, where they were welcomed by Brisay de Denonville—though in his report to Versailles, the Governor hedged his bets by stating that the HBC posts had been attacked without his direct orders. The French king was only too delighted with the results of the expedition, but to placate James II of England, then still an uneasy ally, he agreed to sign a treaty of neutrality that guaranteed the status quo on Hudson Bay. On the bay itself D'Iberville fretted away the winter, longing for action. Finally he too returned to Quebec and later went to France where he obtained a fast new frigate, the *Soleil d'Afrique,* and a commission to bring out the captured furs.

Not yet thirty, he was appointed commander-in-chief of Hudson Bay. D'Iberville was soon anchored off Charlton Island, loading up the *Soleil d'Afrique* with the accumulated pelts. He set off in a small sloop to gather the furs from Albany and had collected that load too, but just as he was about to leave, he unexpectedly found himself in the shadow of two incoming English warships, the imposing eighteen-gun *Churchill* and the smaller frigate *Yonge.*

The vessels, crewed by eighty-five men, had been sent out by the Company to recapture Albany, and they carried aboard a new Governor, Captain John Marsh, plus the first and only Admiral in the HBC's service. He was William Bond, a veteran bay mariner who had been given the grandiose title to underscore his authority. France and England were not yet officially at war so the two majestic ships peacefully continued sailing up the river.

D'Iberville quickly anchored below the fort. He had only sixteen men under his command but an ingenious mind with which to lead them. He ordered a war party out in canoes to cut loose the river's channel markers. The HBC ships promptly ran aground. By the time they were sufficiently lightened to be floated off, the French had consolidated their land defences. The newcomers parked on an island a short distance from the main fort. Since they hadn't had an opportunity to see inside, the HBC men had no idea they outnumbered the defenders more than four to one. D'Iberville maintained the illusion of superiority by assigning snipers to prey on the British camp. He flatly refused to allow the hungry arrivals the right to hunt for fresh game, thus encouraging the spread of scurvy. Governor Marsh was one of the first victims. Admiral Bond and his mate slipped away on a partridge hunt but were taken captive, as was a search party sent after them, plus a delegation of seventeen men later dispatched to plead for Bond's release. D'Iberville finally administered the *coup de grâce* by dragging a couple of cannon up a bluff overlooking the Englishmen's island. Using extra powder to produce loud reports, he pumped enough rounds into the camp to force its surrender, then sailed home in triumph, his fleet loaded down with prisoners and a well-deserved bounty of fur.

By this time William of Orange was ruler of England and the simmering hostilities with France boiled over into open war. At the urging of the Duke of Marlborough, the English king listed French actions in James and Hudson bays as a major *casus belli*. With d'Iberville vowing to put a permanent end to the English presence, the site of the northern war moved, as if by unspoken agreement, towards the most valuable prize of all: the English traders' bayside headquarters at York Factory. In 1690, d'Iberville arrived off Five Fathom Hole with three small ships and dreams of repeating his triumphs of James Bay, but he found the Factory guarded by a thirty-six-gun man-of-war borrowed from the Royal Navy. Too heavily outgunned to risk a head-on clash, he instead skipped down the bay and quickly captured Fort Severn and its rich store of pelts.

Two years later, the English finally retaliated. Because most of the French fleet had been defeated at La Hogue, London strategists convinced themselves that their rivals could spare no ships to defend Hudson Bay and defiantly dispatched three Company frigates and a fire ship—eighty-two guns in all, with 213 marines and supplies for two years. The war party was led by James Knight, a promoted shipwright wise in the ways of the bay and determined to protect the Company's interests. His first assignment was to recapture Fort Albany, where he had served as Chief Factor a decade earlier.

After wintering on the east coast of James Bay, Knight arrived at Albany late in the spring of 1693; he landed his men and marched towards what he assumed to be an abandoned fort. His troops were met by salvoes of heavy, if irregular, gunfire. On June 23, the guns fell silent. Knight advanced into the fort, discovering to his chagrin that it was occupied by a lone demented French blacksmith chained inside the blockhouse cell. Prolonged interrogation of the unhinged smith revealed that the fort had, in fact, been defended by a cadre of five starving survivors who had magnified their defensive efforts by loading and firing their dead comrades' guns to frighten the English into leaving instead of laying a long siege. Exhausted and discouraged by the odds they were facing, the remaining Frenchmen decided to escape and, on the night of June 22, had wormed their way through their attackers' ranks to start the long trek to Quebec. Knight's triumph was thus muted, though he did have as a consolation prize thirty thousand beaver skins from the Albany warehouse.

By 1694, d'Iberville was back at York Factory aboard one of his two modest warships, facing the thirty-two cannon and fourteen brass swivel-guns of the HBC's most important post. York Factory was at the time being defended by a ghost army called the Independent Company of Foot, commanded by Philip Parsons, its Deputy Governor. Not a single professional soldier had been recruited, and the grandly named I.C.F. consisted of little more than fur traders desultorily trained in small arms drill. The slapdash army's first encounter with the wily d'Iberville proved a predictable disaster. Removing the guns from his ships to the shore, d'Iberville mounted them in such a way that their trajectories reached behind the Factory's artillery, which was permanently pointed out to sea. Then he lobbed in a few experimental shots. By the early evening of October 14, he was ready to order a full-scale bombardment, but decided to send an emissary into the Factory first to discuss surrender terms. Much to his surprise, they were accepted with only one proviso: that all hands be allowed a good night's sleep, uninterrupted by the bark of the siege guns. The cannon stayed silent overnight and, following a leisurely breakfast, the fifty-three defenders ignominiously surrendered. D'Iberville renamed the site Fort Bourbon and left for France at the end of the summer with a valuable load of pelts. Ten months later, during his absence, an English sortie by three Royal Navy frigates under Captain William Allen easily recaptured the fort. After a full decade of fighting and winning, the French once again lacked any toehold on the bay.

THE SEASON AFTER THAT, the Hudson Bay war grew serious. In the greatest Arctic sea battle in North American history, the two sides clashed in a drama that determined ownership of York Factory for the next sixteen years. The engagement should by rights have consolidated d'Iberville's reputation for courage and innovation, but since the battle-prize was only a fur trading post on the margin of civilization, his remarkable exploits were almost ignored.

In the summer of 1697, the king of France dispatched the most formidable fleet ever sent to Hudson Bay. Under the command of d'Iberville aboard the forty-four-gun *Pélican*, the ships were stuck for three weeks among the floes blocking Hudson Strait. When the flagship broke loose, she laid a southwesterly course for the Nelson River, and by September 3, d'Iberville dropped anchor at Five Fathom Hole. The following morning at 9:30, just after he had sent a shallop ashore with twenty-five men to reconnoitre the British-held fortress, he spied the silhouettes of three peaked sails on the horizon. Certain that this was the balance of his fleet, d'Iberville raised anchor and sailed out to meet his mates, yardarms aflutter with signal flags. No response. The trio of newcomers was almost alongside his gunwales when he realized that this was an enemy fleet: two armed freighters—the *Dering* and the *Hudson's Bay*— flying the flag of the Company of Adventurers and a proud man-o'-war, the Royal Navy frigate *Hampshire*. Among them, the English ships boasted 118 guns and full complements of sailors and marines, while the *Pélican* was sadly short-handed: some of her best men were ashore, forty prostrate sailors lay in the sick bay with scurvy, and twenty-seven of her most able sea-hands had been transferred to another of the French ships during a stopover in Newfoundland.

Caught between the English-held fort on land and English cannon facing him at sea, d'Iberville had two choices, surrender or fight—and for him that was no choice at all. He ordered the stoppers torn off his guns, sent his battery-men below, had ropes stretched across the slippery decks to provide handholds and aimed his prow at the enemy. As he swept by the *Hampshire*, Captain John Fletcher, its commanding officer, let go a broadside that left most of the *Pélican*'s rigging in tatters. At the same time, the two HBC ships poured a stream of grapeshot and musket fire into the Frenchman's unprotected stern.

The battle raged for four hours. The blood of the wounded French sailors bubbled down the clinkerboards through the scuppers into the sea. The ships's superstructure was reduced to a bizarre accumulation of shattered wood; a lucky shot from the *Dering* had blown off the *Pélican*'s prow so that she appeared dead in the water.

In a brief respite, when the two tacking flagships were close enough for the commanding officers to see one another, Fletcher called across from the *Hampshire* demanding d'Iberville's surrender. The Frenchman made an appropriate gesture of refusal, and the English captain paid tribute to his opponent's courage by ordering a steward to bring him a bottle of vintage wine. He proposed a toast across the gap between the two vessels, raising his glass in an exaggerated salute. D'Iberville reciprocated. The ships were so close and the two hulls had so many holes in them that the opposing gun crews could see into each other's smoky quarters. Minutes later, d'Iberville came up on Fletcher's windward quarter and let go with one great broadside, the storm of fire pouring into the English hull, puncturing her right at the waterline. Within three ship's lengths, the *Hampshire* foundered, having struck a shoal, and eventually sank with all hands.

It was barely noon and the desperate splashings of drowning seamen still echoed in the freshening autumn wind as d'Iberville manoeuvred his crippled ship to direct the force of his guns against the *Hudson's Bay*. The Company ship let go one volley and surrendered. During a squall, the *Dering* fled for shelter in the Nelson River. As the *Pélican*'s crew began boarding the vanquished *Hudson's Bay*, a sudden storm came in off the open water, the shrieking wind melding with the screams of the wounded as the rough heaving of the ships battered their bleeding limbs against bulkheads and splintered decks. The *Hudson's Bay* was lucky enough to be driven almost ashore before she sank, so that those aboard could wade to land, but the *Pélican* dragged useless anchors along the bay-bottom silt in the teeth of the hurricane-strength onshore winds. Finally, her rudder broken, she nosed her prow into a sandbar six miles from the nearest bluff. Her lifeboats had been shot away; rescue canoes from shore were swamped as soon as they were launched. The survivors were forced to swim ashore, towing the wounded on a makeshift raft of broken spars. Eighteen more men drowned, and the others stumbled on shore to find the inhospitable land swathed in snow, with nothing but a bonfire and sips of seaweed tea to comfort them.

The belated French ships arrived within a few days but could not land their troops because of York Factory's cannon. D'Iberville and his tiny band of survivors crept up close to the palisade. They made as much noise as they could, drawing the fire of the English long enough to allow the French ships to land troops and guns. Finding himself in the chronic condition of HBC factors of the day—surrounded by d'Iberville's gunners—Henry Bayley, then in charge of York Factory, took the simplest way out: he decided to surrender. Granted only their personal belongings, the HBC men marched out of their fortified sanctuary the following afternoon, drums beating a fast step and a Company flag flapping in the breeze. They retreated with dignity if not a little apprehension into the wilderness of the surrounding forest to face the hazards of the Hudson Bay winter.

The French victory was complete. With frost already in the air, d'Iberville made for home. Sailing out of Hudson Bay for the last time, he was bound for further triumphs in Louisiana and the West Indies before expiring of malarial fever at forty-seven in Havana. His posthumous reputation, which should have ranked him as a minor Nelson or Wellington, was diluted by the fact that the scene of his victories was so far removed from Versailles. A soldier of fortune on his own account as well as his king's, he won France's highest decoration, the Cross of Saint Louis, but was never granted the opportunity to practise his genius on the battlefields of Europe.

York Factory remained under French rule until the Treaty of Utrecht unctuously returned it to the HBC in 1713. Except for the occasional skirmish and commando raid,* the royal charter was never again challenged by a foreign power. It was somehow typical of both the Company's unwarlike character and its enduring diplomatic shrewdness that even though the English lost every important battle, when all the fighting and all the negotiating were done, the Hudson's Bay Company reigned supreme over the territory of its choice, and returned to the happy drudgery of the fur trade.

---

* In the summer of 1709, a force of a hundred Montreal traders and Mohawk Indians attacked Albany Fort. Warned by a visiting hunter, HBC Governor John Fullartine repulsed the assault, killing sixteen attackers and saving the Company's only remaining foothold.

The Century of the Lakes

Sir Bibye Lake believed that if circumspection in the conduct of the Hudson's Bay Company's affairs was desirable, silence was even better.

THE INDIVIDUAL MOST DIRECTLY RESPONSIBLE for translating the beaver catch into an impressive cash flow was Sir Bibye Lake, a nimble City financier whose family achieved effective control in 1697 and ran the Hudson's Bay Company as a private fiefdom for most of a century. Except for two brief gaps totalling eight years, Lake family oligarchs were either Governor or Deputy Governor of the Company continuously for eighty-seven years. In a remarkable feat of corporate endurance, Sir Bibye himself guided the HBC's fortunes for an unmatched span of thirty-one years.

The Lake family's record in salvaging the HBC's fortunes was all the more remarkable because of the Company's depleted circumstances when they first acquired its stock. Their timely intercession fitted in well with the Hudson's Bay Company's uncanny good luck in attracting precisely the style of management appropriate for its crisis of the moment.

It was under the stewardship of Sir Bibye Lake that profit, not mock heroics, became the HBC's motivating force. Financial discretion, backed by solid London capital, repeatedly triumphed over valour. Thus was perfected the creative somnambulism that would be the Company's hallmark.

THAT THE DISPOSITION OF THE WILDERNESS around Hudson Bay could become the specific subject of two articles in the Treaty of Utrecht, which in 1713 ended the thirteen-year War of the Spanish Succession, was more the result of the persistence of the Company's petitioners than of its importance as real estate in the conduct of Britain's *realpolitik*. Even in this context, the day-to-day bustle of the City fur markets and London dockside seemed only tenuously connected with the glamour of the sealed royal parchments of 1670 and the glory of the courtier-statesmen who had originally formed the Company of Adventurers.

In the short term, the war had been bad for business. At this low point in its history, the Company could not afford to pay its tradesmen, found it had to dip into the vaults of its bankers to settle wartime excise bills and was reduced to the desperate expedient of borrowing to pay interest on existing debt. Anthony Beale, the Governor of its only surviving fort, Albany, was owed £600 in back pay. Although £100 was borrowed to buy off Pierre Radisson, the Company's irrepressible co-founder, his pension was almost constantly in arrears and the HBC could not raise the extra £40 he was demanding to damp down his public innuendos about the Company's looming insolvency.

According to historian E.E. Rich, the HBC's survival at the turn of that century depended on "the connivance of a bankrupt Governor." He was Sir Stephen Evans, a goldsmith and Member of Parliament whose judgment seemed equally dubious in life as in his pitiful, unnecessary death. As a long-time HBC banker, he did manage to cover some of its cash shortfalls (at reasonable profit to himself) and originally underwrote its business of importing Russian hemp from Peter the Great for the Royal Navy, although he was soon squeezed out by a ring of naval contractors.

A strangely erratic speculator, Evans was the younger brother of one of Marlborough's generals. He lacked dash and verve and could not keep his mind on any one business for very long. In 1694 he had been dropped from the Customs Board of the House of Commons for poor attendance. As HBC Governor, he paid so little attention to its affairs that he attended only three of the monthly Committee meetings during 1702 and 1703; Thomas Lake, the Deputy Governor, was the real day-to-day manager of the Company. Frequently the aging Sir Christopher Wren—his newly completed dome of St Paul's the shining glory of the City—would fill in when both Evans and Lake were absent.

Sir Stephen, who presided over the Company's affairs for all but four years between 1692 and 1712, was not above using the HBC's good offices for his own purposes. He floated a questionable insurance fund for setting up apprentices in trade and helping to finance their marriages. This eccentric scheme was somewhat less than honest and cost the Company £900, which Lake tried to recover from Evans in City court. Meanwhile Sir Stephen had gone bankrupt from one of his other and even more questionable ventures, which involved a scheme floated at Lloyd's Coffee House to insure merchants against the outbreak of foreign wars. By January 1712, Lake and the other Committeemen won the claim against their quixotic Governor before the Guildhall Commissioners, but they could recover only £11 before the star-crossed Sir Stephen tricked his creditors by committing suicide.

Even this irrevocable act did nothing to improve Evans's reputation for inept decision making. Posthumous examination of his jumble of holdings revealed that the whole thing might have been prompted by a ghastly mistake: he still had £3,574 in HBC Governor's stock stashed away in a forgotten hoard. One theory was that the meticulous Lakes, father Thomas and son Bibye, had become so exasperated with their doddering chief that, to kick him out of the Governor's chair, they conspired to allow him to believe himself bankrupt, not realizing the desperate act of which he was capable.

What kept the Company alive at this point was the Lakes' stubborn lobbying for return of the HBC lands from the French. It clearly required subsidizing the ministry of Robert Harley, Earl of Oxford, whose Secretary of State, Lord Bolingbroke, leader of the British negotiations at Utrecht, archly complained: "There is nothing more persistent in the world than these claims of the Hudson's Bay Company. We are desirous greatly to see all these smug ancient gentlemen satisfied."

When the Treaty of Utrecht was finally signed, the French resigned themselves not only to the "cession" of Newfoundland, but also to the full restoration of the Hudson Bay territories.* This was particularly significant to the HBC Committeemen, because their failure in 1690 to obtain parliamentary confirmation of their charter for longer than seven years had left their monopoly claims hanging by the unravelling thread of a royal prerogative granted nearly half a century before. All now depended upon building up squatters' rights on the shores of Hudson Bay. The treaty not only inaugurated an unprecedented thirty-one years of peace between France and England, but it also marked incontrovertible international recognition of the HBC's "title"— the claim to exclusive use of its huge overseas territories.

---

* The tenth clause of the Treaty of Utrecht provided that: "The said most Christian King shall restore to the Kingdom and Queen of Great Britain to be possessed in full right for ever, the bay and streights rivers and places situate in the said bay and streights, and which belong there-unto no tracts of land or of sea being excepted, which are at present possessed by the subjects of France ..."

This might logically have triggered the HBC to undertake some exploration activity, but instead, Bibye Lake and his fellow financiers limited their objectives to remaining solvent and easing back out of public view. Relaxed in their tranquil possession of power, the HBC Committeemen were well content to float along on a policy characterized by E.E. Rich as "unobtrusive sanity."

Throughout the crisis years of the War of the Spanish Succession, the price of HBC shares had responded to the bitter circumstances, with quotes on the new London Stock Exchange dropping to 50 percent of par value. After 1700, in their customary cavalier style, the HBC Committeemen simply stopped having the official price quotations published. By then the stock was rarely traded. Thomas and Bibye Lake held the controlling fistful, while many of the rest of the shares were retained, magpie-style, through fiscal splendour and adversity alike, and passed on as dusty family heirlooms to parishes, deacons, widows and eldest sons. In each of two typical years (1709 and 1711), only one transaction was recorded in the HBC stock transfer book. The Company's General Courts, as the annual conclaves of stockholders continued to be called, were desultory formalities. At the 1707 meeting, only seven shareholders presented themselves, all of them members of the retiring Committee. They promptly re-elected one another plus their two absent colleagues and adjourned the meeting.

Many of the shareholders were not only apathetic, they were dead. The ledgers show that, of forty-nine holders of stock in 1713, seventeen were deceased. The holdings purchased in 1674 by chemist-philosopher Robert Boyle still stood in his name, for example, though he had died in 1691. The trustees, in most cases the Governor or Secretary acting for the estate, sleepily controlled nearly half the Company's nominal capital—an enviable state of affairs in any company.

The long drought in dividend payments was symptomatic of the change in the Company's character. It had, quite simply, gone into City limbo. Instead of continuing as a fairly popular and fairly risky venture-stock on the London Exchange, the HBC had evolved through the cunning of the Lake family into the closed proprietorship it was to remain until Lord Selkirk's takeover in 1809. Adam Smith, the leading economic prophet of the day, accurately described it as "very nearly to the nature of a private copartnery."

WHEN THE BRITISH FUR TRADE is set in its early eighteenth-century perspective, it shows why the HBC, having lost its original court-connected sponsorship, exercised so little domestic political influence. In part it was the result of the reluctance of HBC governors to budget any significant sums for parliamentary bribes. Kings and lords continued to be subsidized, but not the Commons. Generally, it was far better to lie low and not attract interest, only collect it. The governors had the example before them of the East India Company, an overly visible organization which learned to its cost that if politicians could not be bought, they most certainly had to be rented.

At the heart of the matter was a continuing battle between the Court and the City. To retain its parliamentary charter, the East India Company had become so involved in "subsidizing" Parliament and the Crown that a clamour arose from those not exposed to its largess that they too should share the bounty. When the East India Company drew the line, the House of Commons set up an inquiry into East India Company bribery. Presenting their findings in 1695, the parliamentarians reported that the East India Company had been doling out £90,000 a year, £10,000 of which had been going annually into the Royal Household.

The East India Company was allowed to save some face when it generously agreed to lend the bulk of its capital to the Bank of England. But this was not enough, and shrewder heads reasoned that the East India Company could do with a little competition. In 1698 the New East India Company was chartered alongside the old, but "not without heavy bribery of ministers." The new company's terms were almost the same as those of the old, except more evangelical—ships were required to carry a chaplain, and provision had to be made for the maintenance of local ministers and schoolmasters. Directors were required to hold £1,000 of stock, and members of the New East India Company traded co-operatively as individuals, not as a company. The overburdened companies were merged in 1708 in exchange for the transfer of their capital to the National Debt through the Bank of England, which was given the monopoly of joint-stock banking.

Inspired by the East India experience and by the insolvency of the Royal African Company, the HBC soldiered gingerly onward from year to year, earnestly avoiding public gaze. Still another reason for its retreat into the calm backwaters of superannuated investments was that, essential as the fur business was to the New World, it accounted for an insignificant portion of Britain's overall trade. Although there were no firm statistics (since with the advent of bonded warehouses in London, where silks and furs were held for re-export, no figures on total trade could be made available), the true import of skins, hides and furs from all sources accounted for less than .5 percent of the total value of Britain's incoming trade between 1700 and 1750. Although much has been made of the Company's monopoly, only half of the skins sold at London auction houses originated in Company lands. Because of its superior capitalization the HBC could ride any market at will.

The most significant competition came out of Boston, New York and the colonies of Maryland and Virginia, famous for the quality of their deerskin. Not all fur went into hats and luxury garments; lower-grade skins were shaved and made into footwear. At first, the superior quality of the Hudson Bay furs had placed them in a class apart (and many still went directly to Moscow or Leipzig), but that distinction soon lost its edge as the immigrant Huguenot hatters learned ways to make beaver-wool from almost any grade and variety of skin. Glue could be added even to rabbit to make a passable imitation; however, such plebeian headgear had an unfortunate propensity to droop and disintegrate in the rain.

Despite its negligible size, the fur trade slotted neatly into England's mercantilist policies, which were designed to perpetuate a self-contained empire, aggressively maintained on four vital pillars: England's own growing manufacturing might; the sugar and molasses trade of the West Indies; the degrading but lucrative slave and gold traffic with African chiefs; and the products of the New World's forests, farms and oceans.

It was to preserve this precariously balanced parallelogram that there was a movement in the 1760s by City sugar traders to bargain away Canada so that control of Guadeloupe could be retained instead. Because the French-held islands in the West Indies had progressed much faster than their English-held counterparts, the trading equations had been thrown out of balance and pamphleteers on both sides of the Atlantic began to debate which of the two colonies—a lucrative 688-square-mile island or an apparently empty northern wilderness—would make the more lasting contribution to British interests.

The case for Guadeloupe was based partly on the notion that if the farmers, trappers and fishermen of the New World were deprived of their West Indian markets, they might turn to manufacturing and cut into the monopoly of the mother country. One pamphlet compared Canada, "which produces nothing but a few hats," with Guadeloupe, rich in "that article of luxury, sugar, the consumption of which is daily increasing both in America and Europe." Another unattributed argument cited in favour of retaining Canada was that "a northern colony is preferable to a southern, being healthier and more suited to the development of a white race."

ONE REASON Canada was not unceremoniously dumped in the 1760s was that, half a century before, Sir Bibye Lake had begun the process that was to build the Hudson's Bay Company's toehold into the depot of a continental trading system. Lake could hold his own against the sugar barons, but English politicians came to see the Company as the only countervailing force to claims on the continent's western territories by the troublemakers and land dealers in the Thirteen Colonies. The Committeemen suffered from few illusions that this state of affairs would bear long-term diplomatic consequences, but there is little question that, without their Governor's financial cunning, the HBC would not have survived.

Sir Bibye had been inaugurated into the Hudson's Bay orbit by his father, Thomas Lake, a well-connected London barrister-financier who began buying the Company's stock on May 13, 1697, and rapidly became its largest shareholder. Named Deputy Governor in 1710, Thomas Lake brought his only son Bibye into the Company with a grant of £1,000 in stock. He had sponsored his election to the HBC Committee in 1708 and sent him to Holland to represent the Company in the early stages of the Utrecht peace negotiations, for which the twenty-six-year-old barrister was given a gratuity of £50. Two years later, the young man replaced his father as Deputy Governor and on November 21, 1712, succeeded the ill-starred Sir Stephen Evans as Governor. It was no plum: no dividends had been paid since 1691; the parliamentary confirmation of the Company's charter was still hanging; unsold furs were piled high in its London warehouses; and its activities in the New World were confined to the holding operation at Albany.

In 1711, on the death of his father, young Lake succeeded as heir to the baronetcy that Charles II had granted his loyalist great-uncle. Lake's royal connections were striking. His uncle Warwick Lake, mp for Middlesex, had been a supporter of the Glorious Revolution, and a family cousin, Dr John Lake, later Bishop of Chichester and reputedly a good Anglican, had served as tutor to the Duke of York's young daughters, the future queens Mary and Anne. Like his father, Bibye Lake had been trained for the Bar in London's Middle Temple, but his interest was quickly caught by the allure of overseas trade. He eventually became a major shareholder in both the East India Company and the up-again, down-again Royal African Company of which he was subsequently named Sub-Governor. He inherited tracts of virgin land in Acadia and Maine granted to his grandfather, Thomas Lake of Boston. Not only did his successful intervention during the Utrecht negotiations help restore the HBC's

North American possessions, but prices on the London fur market also picked up, and in 1718 Sir Bibye summoned the Company's thirty-five surviving shareholders to declare a 10 percent dividend—the first return on their capital for twenty-eight years. (From an original capitalization of £10,500, not all of which had been taken up, the Company was by then recording delectable annual profits of more than £6,000 on yearly turnovers of £30,000.)

Sir Bibye Lake believed that if circumspection in the conduct of the Hudson's Bay Company's affairs was desirable, silence was even better. His insistence that every decision aggrandize the Company's profits while absolute secrecy was imposed would characterize the rule of every governor who succeeded him. This obsession with concealment was such that even the most mundane comments, such as the record of tides through Hudson Strait, the weather observations by the Company's factors, the location of HBC outposts and details of prevailing trade methods with the Indians were kept locked within corporate archives. Letters written home by the servants on Hudson Bay were censored, and the captains of Company ships were ordered to subject all passengers to the indignity of having their personal luggage searched before returning up the Thames. The maritime commanders' own logs and charts were whisked off to the vaults in Fenchurch Street before anyone but the Committeemen could read them, even when they detailed important geographic discoveries. "What little exploration was carried out by Company servants rarely became public knowledge," wrote Glyndwr Williams, the noted HBC historian. "Printed maps of the Bay remained as crudely inaccurate as they had been a century before."

Lake knew the legal value of the HBC's royal charter, which had escaped parliamentary scrutiny in 1697. Members of the HBC's august Committee were warned that under no circumstances were they to discuss the contents of that hallowed document with outsiders. Company employees engaged in the fur trade itself were searched for contraband pelts on leaving or entering their posts. Each employee had to swear formally to maintain secrecy about "all matters pertaining to the Company"—an oath that was enforced by withholding a portion of their wages until retirement.

The HBC's financial dealings were similarly obscured. Stock transfers were handled privately between existing investors. In the most comprehensive guide to the City's main financiers, published in 1740, Sir Bibye Lake is listed only as a director of the Royal African Company, though he was spending nearly all his time on HBC affairs.

Sir Bibye's extravagant stipulations and precautions flowed from the natural reticence imposed on the proprietors of any lucrative monopoly; foreign rivals and domestic interlopers were perceived as potential poachers, even when their interest remained cursory. By the softest, surest pussyfooting, the HBC was able to circumvent the avalanche of criticism that eventually helped drive the Royal African and South Sea companies out of business. Unlike its overseas rivals, the Company neither requested nor received any government subventions, so that even if it failed to live up to the extravagant mandate of its charter, at least its operations were not a burden on the national treasury.

Sir Bibye was brilliant in his choreography of the HBC's relations with London furriers and skinners, who bought largely for re-export. His manipulations may have provided welcome fodder to the HBC's critics, but it was during Lake's tenure that the Company was transformed from a dubious enterprise dependent for survival on each season's fur sales to a gilt-edged investment company with a proper portfolio and substantial backing in the City. Silence was indeed golden.

No one gained more from this metamorphosis than Sir Bibye himself. Minute books of the time record a series of almost annual "gratuities" voted to him in recognition of the HBC's new and happier fiscal state. He was not averse to using the Company's cash reserves to finance his outside ventures, borrowing from the HBC treasury against anticipated dividends. These loans amounted to as much as £20,000 each, and in 1738 some of the more independent Committeemen secured a Chancery Injunction to prevent him from selling £12,222 in stock he was holding at the time. (He transferred it to his chosen nominees anyway.)

Sir Bibye identified himself so strongly with the Company that he had considerable trouble differentiating between his corporate and his personal interests. When in doubt, he opted for the latter. In April 1718 he borrowed £17,000 from the Company at 3 percent per annum, which it in turn was forced to raise at 5 percent. He was constantly manipulating his HBC stock, selling in May and repurchasing in July, so that he would receive maximum dividends without tying up his capital. Sir Bibye had also borrowed from the Company the £11,000 he paid for his country retreat in Derbyshire, a debt that had not yet been repaid at the time of his death.

Although he was canny enough to steer the Company through the bullish speculation that climaxed with the bursting of the South Sea Bubble in 1720, he came very close to endangering its capital structure with a flamboyant scheme that would have grossly multiplied his own fortune by diluting the value of HBC stock. The basic idea (approved by the Company's Committee on August 30, 1720) was sound enough. The capitalization of £10,500 had been raised only once—to £31,500, in 1684—so that the Company's book value had not caught up to the expanded assets. To remedy this imbalance, Sir Bibye proposed a daring manoeuvre that would have benefited the Company's existing shareholders (himself chief among them) far more than its treasury. He proposed trebling the existing capital base of 315 shares at £100 each to 945 shares (£94,500), with each existing shareholder given, free of charge, 3 new shares for each £100 held, for a total share value of £378,000—a 1,200 percent dilution on top of the split. Three more shares were to be optioned to each of the fortunate proprietors on the basis of a 10 percent down payment. It was little wonder that the ecstatic stockholders voted their imaginative Governor a lavish gratuity of five hundred gold guineas. But the unrealistic anticipation of South Sea profits deflated the British financial markets; when the bubble popped, share values in the absurdly capitalized South Sea Company dropped from £1,000 to £100. Lake's scheme brought £3,150 in cash into the HBC, largely from existing share-holders, so Sir Bibye eventually withdrew the second part of the bargain. Each proprietor was thus credited with £30 for each £10 paid in, the excep-tion being the stock held by George I. The King was thenceforward paid dividends on a holding of £2,970, so that the royal dividends at that point amounted to as much as the monarchy's original investment half a century before. By the end of the complicated shuffle, the HBC's capitalization totalled £103,950, which raised it closer to the value of its assets, although only £3,150 in new cash had actually been injected into its treasury.

Sir Bibye was to spend twenty-three years after the South Sea episode as the HBC's Governor. His smooth helmsmanship left a permanent imprint on the manner of the Company's approach to its several constituencies. Whether they were bartering with the Cree on Hudson Bay or blandishing the Bank of England for the season's working capital, Company officers handled each situation with a mixture of sobriety and shrewdness that exasperated their detractors and pleased their shareholders. The generous dividend flow, which had begun to gush so freely in Sir Bibye's time, was not disrupted again until forty years after his death, when French warships again captured the bay.

Lake's influence on the HBC was so overwhelming that it outlasted his governorship by nearly half a century.* Seven years after he died in 1743, his son Atwell was named Governor and served for the next decade, commuting to London from his estate of Edmonton in Middlesex. Atwell's younger brother, Bibye, served a grand total of thirty-nine years (1743–1782) as a Company Committeeman, the last dozen of those years as Governor. Sir Atwell's eldest son, James Winter Lake (who continued to live at the Edmonton estate), was a member of the Committee for forty-five years, serving as Deputy Governor and, from 1799 until his death in 1807, as Governor. (During James Lake's time as Deputy Governor, the Company established a trading post on the North Saskatchewan River to compete with the North West Company's Fort Augustus and named it Fort Edmonton in honour of the Lake family estate. The tiny settlement grew to be the capital of Alberta.)

The extended domination of the Lake family—and particularly the tenure of Sir Bibye himself—was marked by consolidation, efficiency and prosperity, but also by a narrowness of outlook that prevented exploration inland from Hudson Bay or northward in search for a passage to the Orient. The real paradox of Sir Bibye's remarkable career was how, without venturing farther from London than his country estate, he was able to instil in the HBC Factors, an ocean away, his stubbornly maintained ethic. In this he was aided by the constancy of the seasonal and commercial cycles into which life on Hudson Bay was divided and the unchanging nature of the quest for fur.

---

* His longevity was rivalled but not surpassed by Lord Strathcona, the veteran fur trader who rose to the governorship in 1889 at the advanced age of sixty-nine. He held onto that office until he died twenty-five years later in 1914. John Henry Pelly, a former East India Company trading captain, was forty-five when he took over in 1822, to become an essential partner with Sir George Simpson in exploiting the amalgamation with the North West Company. He rose to become Governor of the Bank of England and led the HBC through most of its thirty years of greatest influence.

III | ANCHORING OF EMPIRE

Asleep by the Frozen Sea

"The Company have for eighty years slept at the edge of a frozen sea; they have shewn no curiosity to penetrate farther themselves, and have exerted all their art and power to crush that spirit in others." —Joseph Robson

IT OWNED THE WORLD'S most valuable land monopoly—a third of the still-to-be-explored northern part of the American continent. Yet during most of the eighteenth century, the Company was hived into a handful of economically marginal and physically unprepossessing outposts around Hudson Bay, squeezed between the boreal forest and an inhospitable sea.

Sir Bibye Lake and his fellow proprietors, preoccupied with smoothing the fluctuations in London's money and fur markets, hinted at invincibility in the field and omnipotence at home, but the Company's true position could more accurately be gauged by its sparse representation on the bay itself—at one point fewer than thirty shivering souls. Between 1693 and 1714, the French almost succeeded in elbowing the Company away from the bay altogether, with only Albany Fort's garrison of twenty-seven defenders doggedly flying its banner. The diminutive scale of the forces that tussled over control of the huge territory was dramatically illustrated in 1714, when James Knight, the veteran HBC administrator, was sent from London to reclaim York Factory from its French occupiers. Bearing a royal mandate which rested on the grandiose terms of the Treaty of Utrecht, he found a quaint cluster of rickety shacks manned by a wretched crew of just nine French defenders, including a chaplain, a surgeon and an apprentice. In a vivid dispatch to his principals in London, Knight complained that York's facilities were "nothing but a confused heap of old rotten houses without form or strength very not sufficient to secure your goods from the weather, not fit for men to live in without being exposed to the frigid winter. My own place I have to live in this winter is not half so good as our cowhouse was in the Bottom of the Bay, and I have never been able to see my hand in it since I have been there without a candle. It is so black and dark, cold and wet withal, nothing to make it better but heaping up earth about it to make it warm."

Except for the very occasional foray, the Company's disposition was to sit quietly on the periphery of the bay, routinely manning its trading posts.

The dynamics of the fur trade had grown static, if not altogether comatose. Hardly anything interrupted its monotonous rhythm, unless it was some outrage of the interlopers from Montreal or a diplomatic spat in Leipzig. The financial reporting and management methods put in place by Sir Bibye Lake functioned as if the perpetual Governor had perfected a perpetual money machine. As long as the Company's profits were reflected in respectable dividends and the Indians continued to fetch the furs, there was judged to be no particular need to expand the Company's activities, no purpose in initiating grand new policies on a search for the North West Passage, inland exploration or very much else.

HUDSON BAY IS AN INLAND SEA nearly as large as the Mediterranean; its shoreline meanders for 7,600 miles, a distance only 300 miles shorter than the earth's diameter at the equator, but during the eighteenth century, the HBC governors dispatched no more than two hundred men at a time to exploit their immense holdings. John Oldmixon, in his 1708 study *The British Empire in America*, admitted that he should have led off his book with a description of the Hudson's Bay Company's territories, but explained, "There being no Towns nor Plantations in this Country, but two or three poor Forts to defend the Factories, we thought we were at Liberty to place it where we pleas'd, and were loath to let our History open with the Description of so miserable a Wilderness." Except for Albany Fort and the recaptured York Factory (1714), occupation of Hudson Bay by the Company for more than fifty years was limited to trading-depots at Moose Factory, Rupert House and Churchill (Prince of Wales's Fort), with outstations at Eastmain and, later, Henley House and Severn.

It was by a quirk of geography and navigational limitations that this initial British occupation of Canada came through its north-central back door, a territory that nearly three centuries later would still be struggling unsuccessfully for economic viability. "The search for the North West Passage," noted

University of Winnipeg geographer Dr Tim Ball, "coupled with the practice of latitude sailing and efforts to avoid the North Atlantic Drift, resulted in early explorers to Canada arriving via the Davis and Hudson straits into Hudson Bay, so that the earliest trading-posts were established on its shores."

Except for its relative proximity to Britain and the fact that the estuaries of several large river systems emptied into it, inviting the movement of goods to and from the continent's interior, Hudson Bay was hardly a comfortable choice.

The November 1754 issue of *The Gentleman's Magazine* carried the sensible suggestion that "the countries bordering on Hudson Bay might serve as an English Siberia, where we might hold our convicts, instead of hanging them by thousands at home, or transporting them to corrupt the natives of our colonies." Then it righteously added: "Convicts should always be sent to a country barren, and in a manner uninhabited, because there they cannot corrupt by their bad example; are secure from their former temptations; and must be industrious—and consequently have the best chance of reforming, and growing good." The Public Records office of Northern Ireland in Belfast contains documents that outline a similar proposal, suggesting that the Irish government take over Hudson Bay and turn it into a huge penal settlement, administered by one simple rule-of-thumb: the worse the criminal, the farther north he should be sent "with the most enormous and confirmed offenders handed over to the Eskimos as slaves."

The HBC posts were not prisons. They were more reminiscent of lunar colonies. During their tours of duty (three, or more usually five years), the Bay men had to be utterly self-reliant. Except for the brief annual visit of a solitary Company supply ship (weather, ice and French raiders permitting), the tiny posts were on their own. Pride in being thrust into such self-reliance seemed to have its therapeutic aspects because many loyal Company men signed up for term upon term. One servant named John Paterson stayed at Churchill for seventeen years without requesting a visit home—a measure of his family life in Britain, perhaps, or of the defiant euphoria of sheer survival.

The daily and seasonal cycle of events at the HBC's outposts was meticulously recorded by the resident Factor in each post's journal, laboriously lettered with goose-quill pen and thawed ink, either in his own hand or, at the larger posts, dictated to his "writer." Entries in these journals, dispatched to London once a year on the returning supply ships, consisted of weather information and trade figures, along with deferential descriptions of the duties performed by each "officer" and "servant." The reports were similar in style to ships' logs—brief and impersonal, justifying rather than explaining, documenting their authors' adherence to standing instructions, scrupulously avoiding innovation.* These laboriously maintained volumes were coffined in "packets"—wooden boxes 1½ feet by 2 feet by 4 feet—into which mail was collected from each post. Year after year, generation after generation, these packets were shipped across the North Atlantic with the season's fur catch. Each was perused by the Committeemen before they issued the next season's instructions. Then regardless of the content and quality of the dispatches, the books were solemnly interred in the Company's confidential vaults, where they would remain, inaccessible, for the next two centuries.†

Each Wednesday noon, the Governor, Deputy Governor and half a dozen Committeemen would gather at Hudson's Bay House in the heart of London's financial district and spend the afternoon issuing their various decrees.

Because the Company's strictly observed policy was neither to allow public access to its factors' journals nor to welcome any visitors to the bay's shores, the only firsthand description published and circulated about the HBC's activities in the first half of the eighteenth century was that of an early corporate renegade: Joseph Robson's *An Account of Six Years Residence in Hudson's Bay*. Robson had first entered the Company's service as a stonemason in 1733 for a three-year term and had returned overseas in 1744 as the Surveyor and Supervisor of Buildings. After completing the first authentic charts of the lower fifty miles of the Nelson River and mapping York Factory, he was transferred northward to Churchill and ordered to carry out similar surveys. There he came up against Robert Pilgrim, the resident Factor. A rheumatic former ship's steward who seemed to be bitterly at odds

---

* Although local factors exercised great power over everyday events, they had almost no policy functions, even to decide who should run their posts. Each Factor was left to make his own day-to-day decisions like the captain of a ship at sea. In 1742, when the factors at Moose and Albany protested that the appointment of captains of supply ships to positions on the posts' governing councils was an infringement of their independence, they were rebuked and told to devote their limited talents to fostering the fur trade and leave the London Committee to settle policy matters.

† Again and again, exasperated factors urged the Committeemen to take the trouble to read their journals, feeling that the nature of the questions that kept flowing from London clearly indicated that their dispatches had not been adequately studied. The Committeemen sometimes acted more like schoolmasters than governors, not so much concerned with the contents of the bayside journals as with their form. "Your general letter is not wrote in paragraphs which you must not fail to observe for the future, answering distinctly each paragraph of our letter," they admonished James Isham, when he was in charge of York Factory.

with everyone he met, Pilgrim traded unfairly with the Indians, neglected the maintenance of his post's buildings and was particularly incensed at Robson's direct and often angry criticism of his methods. Just before Robson returned to England, his dealings had deteriorated to near-mutiny, and Pilgrim whined to the London Committee that Robson and two of his companions had "declared themselves Your Honours' Enemies." In his book published five years later, Robson severely criticized the HBC's slipshod trading practices and its haphazard construction methods at Prince of Wales's Fort. He alleged that penetration up the rivers into the continent was easy, that corn and other vegetables could be cultivated as far north as York Factory and that local mining and fishing enterprises as well as permanent colonies could be established on Hudson Bay. It was the mean-spirited blockade of innovation at any level, he claimed, that had hindered such possibilities. "The Company have for eighty years slept at the edge of a frozen sea," he wrote in what became a rallying cry for the growing legion of the HBC's self-appointed critics. "They have shewn no curiosity to penetrate farther themselves, and have exerted all their art and power to crush that spirit in others."

HIS ACCUSATIONS WERE TRUE enough, but Robson was so anxious to discredit the Company that he minimized the difficulties of expanding the operations on the bay. Chief among the problems was the region's dismal climate.

Few places on earth experience such extreme weather fluctuations. Because it is out of reach of moderating ocean currents, Hudson Bay is more frigid than the iceberg-packed Arctic Ocean or the North Pole itself. Temperatures of −82°F have been recorded—colder than most polar lows. For nine months of the year, the sun hugs the horizon; the fierce winds snarl across the beaches and eskers, and on overcast days drifting snow creates a disorienting white void that obliterates all points of reference. "Rich as the trade to these parts have been or may be," wrote John Oldmixon, "the way of living is such that we can not reckon any man happy whose lot is cast upon this Bay ... for that country is so prodigiously cold that nature is never impregnated by the sun; or, rather, her barren womb produces nothing for the subsistence of man."

Oldmixon's distressing description was not based on his own observations but on the verdict of those familiar with the bay's climatic tantrums.* Their

* The first hundred years of the Company's occupation of the bay is known to meteorologists as the Little Ice Age. Samuel Champlain found "bearing" ice on the shores of Lake Superior in June 1608, while a lake in Scotland was reported frozen over in August 1675.

reports were hardly encouraging. Captain Christopher Middleton, one of the company's most experienced sea captains and a dogged bay explorer, wintered at Churchill in 1741–42 and kept a detailed weather log. On October 11, Middleton proposed a birthday salute to George II. He noted in his journal later the same evening that "the wine with which the officers drank the aforesaid healths, and which was good port wine, froze in the glass as soon as poured out of the bottle."* By the end of the month, the snow was twelve feet deep and the men had to use axes to hack ice off the *inside* walls of the Factor's house. William Wales, the London astronomer who visited the same post twenty-seven winters later, left behind a graphic description: "The head of my bed-place, for want of knowing better, went against one of the outside walls of the house; and notwithstanding they were of stone, near three feet thick, and lined with inch boards, supported at least three inches from the walls, my bedding was frozen to the boards every morning; and before the end of February, these boards were covered with ice almost half as thick as themselves. Towards the latter end of January, when the cold was so very intense, I carried a half-pint of brandy, perfectly fluid, into the open air, and in less than two minutes it was as thick as treacle; in about five it had a very strong ice on the top; and I verily believe that in an hour's time it would have been nearly solid."

Factors' journal entries for the period reflect not merely bleak temperature levels but the awesome furies of a Hudson Bay winter: "Insufferable cold. Almost froze my arm in bed"; "Very troublesome to write, ink freezing on my pen"; "Frozen feet and no wonder, as the thermometer for the last three nights was −36, −42 and −38"; "Men cannot see a hundred yards to windward— neither can one get out of our gates for snow"; "Some quicksilver that had been put out some time ago for trying the cold was observed to be frozen while the thermometer was only 36 below zero, which proves the weather to have been six degrees colder than per thermometer"; "Rain froze as it fell—if we have one hour fine weather, we have ten bad for it"; "Hail the size of a Musket Ball"; "Twenty-one years in this country and never see or hear so dismal a night ..."

Samuel Hearne, the good-natured northern explorer who regularly wintered at Prince of Wales's, described in detail the fort's spring snowfall in a

---

* The apparent anomaly of wine which pours from the bottle but freezes immediately in the glass can be explained by the fact that wine which is corked is held under pressure and can be kept below its freezing-point without solidification (i.e., supercooled). When the cork is removed and the pressure released, the liquid forms an icy slush as it is poured into the glass.

letter to Humphrey Marten, then in charge of York Factory: "The winter in general has been the mildest I ever knew at Churchill and till the first of March the least snow that has been remembered, at which time a violent snow came on the NNW and lasted four days without intermission. The snows were higher than the house—consequently, all the windows of the upper as well as the lower storey were entirely blocked up ... The depth of drift in the yard is about twenty-two feet."

The brief summers brought little respite. Temperatures could rise as high as 80°F, but the numbing agony of the winter's cold was replaced by intolerable plagues of "mosketos" and "sand flyes."* Writing in *Hudson's Bay, or Every-Day Life in the Wilds of North America*, Robert Ballantyne complained how "day and night, the painful, tender little pimples on our necks and behind our ears were constantly being retouched by these villainous flies. It was useless killing thousands of them; millions supplied their place. The only thing, in fact, that can protect one during the night (*nothing* can during the day) is a net of gauze hung over the bed, and as this is looked upon by the young men as somewhat effeminate, it was seldom resorted to."

While he was at Churchill, James Knight gave way to near-hysteria in his August 11, 1717, journal entry describing the hellish insects: "Here is now such swarms of a small sand flyes that wee can hardly see the sun through them and where they light is just as if a spark of fire fell and raises a little bump which smarts and burns so that we cannot forbear rubbing of them as causes such scabbs that our hands and faces is nothing but scabbs. They fly into our ears nose eyes mouth and down our throats as we be most sorely plagued with them ... Certainly these be the flyes that was sent as plagues to the Egyptians as caused a darkness over the land and brought such blotches and boils as broke out over them into sores."

Knight, who dominated the HBC's overseas history during the first two decades of the eighteenth century, also penned the classic definition of another of the region's peculiarities, permafrost, when he noted that "the summer never thaws above the depth of what the following winter freezes." Permafrost in the Hudson Bay area inhibits efficient drainage so that little

---

* The black flies of Hudson Bay can be vicious, leaving their victims with a toxin that produces an influenza-like sickness. The number of mosquitoes defies description. A mathematician who accompanied the Curran-Caulkins expedition of 1912 estimated there were fifteen million mosquitoes per cubic yard of free air on the east coast of James Bay.

plant life can flourish. Rain and snow are permanently trapped in shallow lakes and ponds; the east wind snaps the earth's outcrops into a brown cement, turning the landscape into a bleak tableau of muskeg and rock.

The dramatic natural event of the year, then and now, is breakup, when spring runoffs and warming currents combine to soften and fragment coastal ice, forcing the polar bears ashore, where the huge carnivores den and whelp their pups before returning to the floes in the fall. The spring sun once again warms the soul and the rivers draining the Canadian Shield's winter accumulations become torrents as they rampage towards the bay. On May 7, 1715, when the Hayes River thawed inland before its mouth was clear of ice, Knight, then York Factory's Governor, was sitting down to dinner when a flash flood forced him and his entire garrison "to leave the factory and betake our selves to the woods and gett on trees ... the water rising above nine foot upon the land and continued up for six days, wee looking every minute when the factory would be tore to pieces. The ice lay heap'd and crowded at least twenty foot higher than the factory ..."

Knight shifted York Factory's buildings to higher but still temporary ground. When a similar catastrophe overtook the post on May 7, 1788, causing "almost universal destruction," Joseph Colen, then resident at York, took advantage of the flood to choose for the Factory a more enduring site. Observing that "water is as true a level as can be found," he splashed about in his canoe until he located the highest dry promontory where new, more protected permanent buildings could eventually be constructed.

Nature's malevolence in the bay lowlands was the private, if universal, nightmare of those who had invested their lives in the Company's service. But it was the sailors in the HBC's employ who spread the region's reputation as an "evil vortex" at the edge of the known world. In addition to the usual hazards and privations faced by mariners of the day, they encountered conditions that often turned their six-month voyages into endurance tests. One hazard unique to the bay was that shore ice, broken up by winter gales into huge floes, would pile up, sheet upon sheet, and coagulate into solid rafts up to thirty feet thick. These could hole a sailing ship on contact. Icebergs, drifting down from Davis Strait, shut off the Atlantic entrance and exit of the bay for all but three months of the year. The bergs, no respecters of calendar dates, could be deadly even during the navigation season.

These dangers were at least visible, but the sailors, dependent on rudimentary navigational aids in unmarked waters, also found themselves travelling so close to the north magnetic pole that their compass needles tended to dip downward and lose directional stability. Even when veterans of many passages learned to compensate for this disorienting phenomenon, magnetic storms and the large iron-ore bodies on the floor of Hudson Bay sapped compasses of navigational value. Existing charts of the bay looked like children's drawings, so that ships' captains had to rely on a combination of intuition and prayer. They posted crowsnest look-outs trained to spot changes in water colour that might warn of submerged dangers.* To these uncomfortable problems were added an unusually high incidence of cloudiness that prevented celestial sightings and (except for the long, curving and hilly bight in the south-eastern part of the bay) flat coastlines that provided no easily identifiable reference points. The warmer winds rising from the water meeting the cold land in fall and early winter produced impenetrable fog banks, as did the warm, moist offshore winds in spring and early summer. These pleasant offshore breezes could be deadly, carrying many a canoeist out into Hudson Bay beyond rescue. Early harbours were marked only by barely distinguishable cairns and the pine flagpoles of each HBC post. Another questionable aid to navigation was the firing of cannon, both from shore and ship's decks, to help locate the forts. The original beacons guiding ships seeking Moose Factory were tall trees stripped of their branches, with the local Cree occasionally assigned to raise a flag when they sighted an incoming ship.†

Despite these hazards, the number of accidents was surprisingly small. During more than three hundred years of dispatching its fleet into the bay, the Company lost only thirteen ships. The fact that nearly half of these sank in the twentieth century is a reflection of the modern arrogance of confronting nature. In the past the practice during storms had been to grapple the ships

---

* The government of Canada did not install navigation lights, beacons and buoys in Hudson Bay until 1914. Then, because of wartime security, all aids were extinguished the following year—and not relit until 1932. As recently as 1965, only the principal harbours had been surveyed; two years earlier, aerial reconnaissance between the Belcher Islands and Hudson Bay's eastern shore had revealed numerous islets and above-water rocks, unreported in more than three centuries of navigation. These included a rock pinnacle sweeping 120 feet up from the sea-bed to the surface, just north of Grey Goose Island, which sank the M/V *North Star* in 1961.
† The last prominent beacon, the seventy-five-foot foremast of the sunken schooner *Fort Severn*, was put in place by the Company in 1953. A similar navigational aid (a ninety-six-foot mast) had been erected on North Bluff near the mouth of the Moose River, but it blew down during a 1922 gale. The beacon at Marsh Point, which splits the mouths of the Nelson and Hayes rivers, is still in place.

onto ice, on the theory that, as when fighting an opponent much stronger, the advantage of greater strength can be negated by hanging on.

Like the rest of the HBC trade, shipping settled into its own predictable annual cycle. Two or three square-riggers would ghost out of Gravesend in May, tack northward along Britain's eastern shore and, after loading up with fresh water and recruits in the Orkneys, bear away across the Atlantic. The voyage took about twelve weeks. Its landfalls were uncertain. Churchill had fair holding ground and Moose offered reasonable refuge below the Factory, but at all other ports of call the silted mudflats deposited by river outflows kept seaborne visitors at a distance. At York Factory, vessels anchored seven miles out at Five Fathom Hole and at Albany, an awkward fifteen miles from the post. Smaller, shore-based sloops unloaded the trade goods and ferried out the season's fur catch.

Because of distances and climate, the posts were almost as separate from one another as from England. It took the Bay men most of a century to organize an informal system of exchanging winter packets of mail between settlements. With no emergency assistance available from either side of the Atlantic, each post had to calculate the limits of its survival, and little was left to chance. Every incoming item was carefully logged and stored, to be produced at the appropriate occasion. Turnaround time was at a premium, as fussy clerks pored over lengthy rosters listing nails, muskets, sealing wax, beads, axe heads and all the sundry items required for trade and survival during another twelve months' isolation. The ships' captains, proud men who tended to patronize their shore-bound colleagues, did little to disguise their impatience to be away from that bleak wilderness. Every hour counted; the days grew shorter as the nippy dawns of September signalled the urgency of their departure.

Their return to England was a forced dash through an ice-ridden Hudson Strait, past Resolution Island into the angry Atlantic. It would be late October before they could butt their way around the Kentish coast and tie up at their assigned slips on the welcoming Thames.

This drawn-out schedule meant that the reports addressed to the HBC's Committeemen were as much as fifteen months out of date. "It was on the basis of intelligence thus hopelessly stale that they made their decisions," noted historian Richard Glover. "If in doubt about some point of policy, they put a question to the Governor of one of their forts, twelve months must pass before they could send instructions based on his reply, and their decision could not begin to be carried into effect till the situation it was intended to meet had had ample time in which to alter."

LIFE ON THE BAY, once the season's supply ships had weighed anchor and set off, flying for home, settled into dreary routine. Endurance was the prime virtue. Like the inhabitants of a closed Darwinian archipelago, the Bay traders assumed local coloration, appearing, according to York Factor James Isham, "more like beasts than men, with the hairy cloathing we wear."

Winter dress consisted of a combination of pelts that must have made the Hudsonians resemble a surrealistic mutation of every fur-bearing animal within trapping range. The outer garment was of mooseskin, with cuffs and a cape of beaver, marten or fox. The breeches were cut from deerskin and lined with flannel over three layers of cut-up blankets. Shoes consisted of a shaped piece of tough leather wrapped around the instep and fastened securely. This whole ensemble, which made movement ponderous, was in fact the standard winter *indoor* uniform. It was merely underwear for the outdoors.

Winter wood- and food-gathering excursions required the addition of yet more protection, though limbs and faces often froze. According to astronomer William Wales, venturing outdoors entailed adding "a beaver skin which comes down so as to cover their neck and shoulders, and also a neck cloth or cravat made of a white fox's skin, or, which is much more complete, the tails of two of these animals sewed together at the stump ends. Beside these they have shoes of soft tanned mooseskin and a pair of snow shoes about four feet or four and a half feet long."

Cleanliness was a forgotten divertissement. Isham describes in his York journal that fur traders commonly had "a beard as long as Captain Teach's,* and a face as black as any chimney sweeper's." Soap was a rare luxury, seldom indulged, and so if the Bay men rarely saw the colour of their own skin, it was probably merciful.

---

* The beard in question was that of a firebrand pirate named Edward Teach, also known as Blackbeard. "Teach allowed his beard to grow untrimmed," notes Hugh F. Rankin in *The Golden Age of Piracy*. "It was long and rose on his face almost to the level of his eye ... Before an impending engagement, he exaggerated an already frightful appearance by tucking slow-burning matches under his hat, wreathing his face in wispy curls of smoke, as if he were the Devil himself, fresh from Hell's outer reaches." The much-married Captain Teach (one contemporary claimed that of the pirate's fourteen wives, "a dozen might still be living") was shot dead in North Carolina in November 1718.

Their dwelling places, defiantly called "forts," were makeshift huts of fir or pine logs laid one upon the other, crudely caulked and enclosed by palisades. Because urgency for shelter did not permit the wood to season before construction, the timbers shrank and cracked open the caulked seams. "In summer," Joseph Robson wrote, "the water beats between the logs, keeping the timber continually damp; and in the winter the white frost gets through, which being thawed by the heat of the stoves, has the same effect, so that with the water above and the damp below, the timber both of the foundation and superstructure rots so fast that in twenty-five or thirty years the whole fort must be rebuilt with fresh timber."

Added to the discomfort of draughts knifing through the widening chinks between the logs was the smoke belching from the none-too-sophisticated brick stoves.* As soon as the night fires were banked, chimneys would be closed with iron gates to retain whatever heat had been coaxed from the hard-won fuel. The daylight hours were no more cheerful; windows were boarded up for the winter with three-inch shutters. Iron shot was heated red-hot in the stoves and hung around the room, but nothing really helped.

Occupants were frequently laid up, unable to work because their joints were too seized up to flex. Aching with arthritis and chilblains, they found their only cheer was that of the bottle, but even this was often frustrated by the temperature. Because of their low alcohol content, wine and beer quickly froze solid and turned insipid when thawed over a stove. One inspired solution put into effect at Prince of Wales's Fort in 1741 was to bury the kegs in an eight-foot-deep pit, cover them with fresh horse dung and hope they would stay unfrozen. They did.

The only accommodation with a touch of refinement was the Factor's or Governor's House, particularly at Prince of Wales's Fort, where the quarters were spacious enough for entertaining the post's officers on Wednesday and Saturday evenings. There was also opportunity to do a little fancy trapping. Moses Norton, the Factor, boasts in his November 1, 1759, journal entry of how he entertained himself by catching three foxes in the fort's yard by dangling bait on fish-hooks out of his bedroom window. Norton, a notorious

---

* An essential winter-related mission was felling trees for the wood-burning stoves, with the lumber crews forced to move ever further inland to find enough fuel. A "stout" winter's supply at Prince of Wales's Fort was calculated to be "two large piles each forty-three yards round" and Joseph Isbister estimated that providing firewood for the fort took at least nine months of the year. Coal was eventually brought in, as ship's ballast.

womanizer, had a more comforting time of it than any of his compatriots. He maintained a harem of at least five Indian wives.

The fort itself was an anomaly in the fur trade. Built on the site first occupied by James Knight in 1717, with four angular bastions, each mounting forty cannon, Prince of Wales's Fort had been commissioned by Sir Bibye Lake in 1732 and took forty years to complete.* It was intended to become the most secure fortress in North America, a formidable star-shaped pile of dressed masonry more than three hundred feet square, with walls up to forty feet thick. No written justification for its construction survives, but Lake, who did not expend Company funds freely, had at least three purposes in mind: that the fort could serve as a major provisioning point for exploitation of northern mineral resources; that it would become a profitable fur-trading centre, due to its location bordering the lands of the Cree, Chipewyan and Eskimos; and, most importantly, that it would act as the strategic centre for the HBC's defence of its trade and territories. Not one of these objectives was realized. Arthur S. Morton, an astute historian of the Canadian West, has speculated that "the plan must have had to do with the ships taking refuge in the commodious harbour under the shelter of the fortifications. In that case their crews would go to manning the fort ... In case of meeting the enemy in overpowering numbers, they could find safety in the Churchill River, the crews man the fort, and present an impregnable front to the foe."

Even this strategy seems questionable. Because it was on the wrong river— the Nelson drained a much larger hinterland—fur returns at Prince of Wales's never exceeded half the take at York Factory. Gathering in only about ten thousand made-beaver per season, the garrison was reduced to fewer than forty men—a ridiculous one-to-one ratio with the number of the fort's artillery pieces. The fort was supposed to be an answer to France's Louisbourg, but even if it were reinforced with an extra hundred men off the Company's ships, it could still not have held off an attack of any size or intensity.

---

* Building went on intermittently until 1771. J.B. Tyrrell, the Canadian explorer, toured the ruin in 1892, recording this description: "It is 310 feet long on the north and south sides, and 317 feet long on the east and west sides, measured from corner to corner on the bastions. The walls are from 37 to 42 feet thick, and 16 feet 9 inches high to the top of the parapet, which is 5 feet high and 6 feet 3 inches wide. On the outside the wall was faced with dressed stone, except towards the river, while on the inside undressed stone was used. The interior wall is a rubble of boulders held together by a poor mortar. In the parapet are forty embrasures and forty guns; from six to twenty-four pounders are lying on the wall near them, now partly hidden by low willows, currant and gooseberry bushes."

TRYING TO DIVINE the daily lives of the men who endured on the bay during the eighteenth century, the dispassionate observer finds it difficult to escape the conclusion that their main preoccupation was eating and drinking. Factors, anxious to fill the pages of their journals, often described menus at their posts, detailing the remarkable quantity, if not variety, of the food consumed. James Knight at York Factory records that during three days of feasting at Christmas in 1715, he allocated to each mess hall of four men a helping of four geese, a large slice of beef, four hares, seven pounds of fresh pork, two pounds of drippings, a pound of butter, three and a half pounds of fruit preserves, four pounds of flour and a hogshead of strong beer. Records at Moose Factory show that on Christmas Day, 1705, each four-man mess had been doled out enough victuals to make the York Factory rations look like a snack. The bill of fare read: five geese, twelve partridge, sixty fish, eight pounds of mutton, three pounds of suet, two pints of rice, twenty pounds of flour, two pounds of bacon, eight pints of oatmeal, four pounds of biscuit bread, two pounds of cheese, two pounds of raisins, a pound and a half of butter and one piece of salt beef. This was special fare, but the daily rations were only slightly more modest. Andrew Graham, who spent most of his life on Hudson Bay, complained that "the major part of the people can not use all their allowance but are forced to give it to the natives."

Since food was one of the few human appetites that could safely and prodigiously be satisfied within the confines of their circumstances, the catering at such feasts seems only slightly incongruous with the otherwise desolate lives of the HBC outlanders. Provisioning was partly from the holds of the annual supply ships, with beef, pork, cheese, flour, oatmeal, peas, malt, vinegar, raisins, butter and spices being the main staples, though cases of sherry, port and other civilizing potables were provided for the Factor's tables. The goods did not always arrive intact. This was particularly true of the salted beef and pork, which were often maggoty or just plain putrid. "In opening the cask of hogs' cheeks," complained Anthony Beale at Prince of Wales's Fort, "we find the whole cask to be infected. I had some of them dressed at my table but it was so bad it could not be eat. Therefore ... must be obliged to give it to starved Indians."

The imports were supplemented by "country provisions." Most of the Committeemen never did comprehend that even if northern England and the bay were astride similar latitudes, it was impossible for their expatriates to reproduce English vegetable and flower gardens—even if, as one London-based financial knight noted in his fanciful description of the primordial soil around York Factory: "Such rich mould has laine fallow, it may be from the Creation."

The growing season (sixty days at best) was desperately short and the only crop regularly supported by the thin layer of soil that surrounded the HBC posts was wild dandelion.* The weed was used for a bitter but vitamin-rich salad, was occasionally fermented into wine and proved to be a useful anti-scorbutic. The season was too frosty for grain crops, but local gardeners could cultivate potatoes up to the size of hens' eggs as well as limited pickings of radishes, turnips and lettuce. The greatest problem was maintaining cattle for milk and horses as draught animals. There was little hay to provide winter fodder, and the beasts could not forage for themselves. Moses Norton, the oddly playful Factor at Prince of Wales's Fort, tried taming caribou to pull sleds, but they refused to be domesticated.†

The most important indigenous source of food was the seasonal bird hunts. Wild geese and partridge, ducks and curlew were taken in the spring and autumn, while the willow ptarmigan (an Arctic grouse) was caught in huge nets baited with the gravel the birds' gizzards need to aid digestion. (The net was stretched over a heap of gravel and held in place by a stake that could be jerked away at the appropriate moment.) Isham refers to catching seventy or eighty birds at one haul. The explorer Thomas Button and his crew shot 21,600 during his one season on the bay, and the eighteenth-century account of Nicolas Jérémie claims that during the winter of 1709–10, the eighty men then stationed at York Factory (temporarily renamed Fort Bourbon) consumed 90,000 ptarmigan and 25,000 hares.

Local fish, mainly Arctic char (referred to as "salmon"), were cured in a very peculiar way, as an official Company guidebook documents:

Take whole salmons split them up ye back (not through ye belly) and take ye bone clear out, wash and clean them thoroughly, then double

---

* There is circumstantial evidence that the Bay men grew so fond of their dandelion brew that when they began to journey southward, they took the sticky yellow pompon with them—as a crop that eventually blighted suburban lawns.

† In 1767, Norton sent a pair of live moose to London as a gift to the HBC Committeemen. One died in transit, but the other became a burden on the Company's coffers. A board minute nervously notes that she cost £9 10s. 11d. in feed from October 1767 to February 1768, when the problem was solved by presenting the beast to George III. The King promptly passed the buck, shipping the hairy expatriate upriver to the Royal enclosures at Richmond Park.

them together, and lay them to drein in ye shade, a whole day, then at night begin to salt them. Put a little bay [leaf], and a common salt at ye bottom of ye tub, after which open ye salmon and lay them in with ye skin downward, then sprinkle it with ye same salt, and lay them one upon ye other, ye skin still downward, and continue sprinkling with salts between each fish, till ye tub is full. Let them lye so for ten days, to be kept in a cool place, then provide casks, and put ye fish therein, in ye same manner laying them open with ye skin downwards, without anymore salt, and head them up being well pressed down then take ye pickle out of ye tubs, and put it into ye cask's at ye bung hole, keeping them every day fill'd up for ten days. Then stop them up close.

For variety, caribou and moose meat could be traded from the Indians. Many of the caribou were slaughtered while crossing rivers. Indian women and children would gather on both shores, shrieking, hollering and throwing stones so that the confused animals would be forced to remain in deep water, unable to flee or defend themselves. The commotion set up by the women and children was no benign baying at the moon; this was a fierce and primitive pageant that chilled the marrow of any HBC man who heard it. Into this madness would paddle the Indian hunters with spears and sticks sharpened in bonfires. They were soon consumed by the lust of the moment, killing the hapless caribou as much for pleasure as for sustenance, oblivious of anything but the ecstasy of their slaughter. Here was an assertion of their superiority, a feeling they could not achieve from the passive acts of trapping or fishing. The Cree tried to strike the beasts in their unprotected kidneys, driving their spears straight in, then twisting upward, massacring their prey in an orgy of murderous pleasure.

Deer tongues were a particular delicacy. Food was such a priority that its trade sometimes took precedence over fur. During the largest single month's business recorded at Prince of Wales's Fort (November 1774), the Indians brought in only six hundred made-beaver, but they also traded 9,651 pounds of deer flesh, eight hundred deer tongues, twenty-four hares and one great shaggy muskox.

The Bay men, particularly recruits from the Orkneys' rocky shores, were offered daily fare much superior to any nourishment they might have expected to get at home. No wheat was grown on the islands off northern Scotland; few farmers could afford to slaughter domestic animals, and the sheep fed mostly on seaweed, which made the mutton practically unpalatable. In this and other ways life on Hudson Bay, although hellish at times, was fairly bearable by comparison with life in eighteenth-century Britain. Orkney roofs of thatch produced draughty homes not much better than their bay counterparts. Much of London's housing stock had been renewed in brick following the Great Fire of 1666, but those Bay men from the British capital left behind a city that offered few comforts. The Industrial Revolution was still in its nascency, with most of English society divided into patrician, property-owning families and a labouring class that drifted aimlessly from job to job, with all but the particularly skilled alternating between casual farm work, odd jobs and petty pilfering. A posting on the bay could be a godsend for some. The middle class, which would eventually contribute most HBC recruits, was as yet only a small group.

Despite the relative abundance of nourishment at the bay, almost constant dissatisfaction was expressed by the Company's servants. Apart from the monotony and the natural tendency of isolated men to take out their frustrations on the only corporate scapegoat available, part of this trouble stemmed from the salting method used to preserve food between hunting and fishing seasons. In the fall of 1757 when the Prince of Wales's messes had been served greasy, salted-down Arctic char every Monday and Friday for months, Ferdinand Jacobs, the fort's Governor, found the men, one dinner hour, "flinging it in one another's faces, and turning up their noses at it." Five years earlier, under Joseph Isbister, one of Jacobs's predecessors, partridge had been the object of a similar disturbance. "In my absence," he wrote in his journal, "some of the corrupted ones stird up most of our men to throw away all their partridges ... when Mr. Walker and I came into the Factory, we was surprised to see the partridges strowed about in the dirt and gravel. I toke one of them up in my hand, smelt it and found it as sweet as when it was killed." Isbister, like a boarding school headmaster faced by naughty boys, accused his men of "behaving in a mutinous manner" and threatened "to whip and cane them all." One dissatisfied diner, James Flat, was in fact flogged for his partridge protest, and the gastronomic uprising was quickly quashed.

Another reason for the men's crankiness may have been the difference they could observe between their own rations and the delicacies reserved for the Factor's table. Andrew Graham, who served in various capacities on the bay from 1767 to 1791, observed that the Chief Factor's table "is always handsomely supplied with provisions, very seldom having less than three dishes; and on particular occasions, fourteen or sixteen.... The officers have wines and French brandy plentifully allowed them; and the men London porter, and

British spirit (raw gin) served out at the discretion of the Chief."

One advantage of the bay diet was that it contained enough fresh meat and vegetables to discourage scurvy, the scourge of explorers, mariners and other adventurers in the pre-refrigeration age. (The Royal Navy did not start issuing lemon juice on a daily basis until 1793.) A common local panacea, called wishakapucka (Labrador tea), was claimed to cure everything from "giddiness in the head" to "fainting fitts," not to mention "gangrenes, contusions and excorations." More serious medical complaints included "country distemper" (a form of fever combined with catarrh) and syphilis. The factors argued that venereal disease was endemic among the Indians, and their journals frequently complain about repentant sinners coming down with "the Clap" or being "in a salivation for the venereal disorder." Apart from that particular curse, the occasional accident and frequent cases of frostbite, the Bay men enjoyed remarkably good health. In his characteristically exuberant style, Samuel Hearne caught this mood in a letter to York's Factor, Humphrey Marten: "Myself and people are as usual all in good health, but that is no wonder since the pureness of the air and the wholesomeness of the diet makes it the health-iest part in the known world and what is very extraordinary at this place some of us think we never grow any older."

The daily cycle of assigned work was devoted mainly to self-preservation, but garrisons had every Sunday and half of each Saturday free, and holidays were celebrated at the slightest excuse. Besides Christmas, New Year's Day and Easter, there were St George's Day (April 23), Guy Fawkes Day (November 5), royal birthdays, accession dates and May 2—"Bay Day"—the anniversary of the Company's Charter. Card and dice games were popular and, in the summers, football games of a sort were played using inflated whale bladders.

Religion was an afterthought.* The London Committee, buttonholed by the Society for the Promotion of Christian Knowledge, piously required that

---

* There were few resident chaplains on the bay during the British occupation. One early exception was the Reverend Thomas Anderson, who helped draw up the surrender terms—in Latin—of York Factory to the French in 1693. Sundays at most bay posts were made even more leisurely by the erratic pattern of local religious services held at the discretion of the Factor in charge. Samuel Hearne, a deist and follower of Voltaire, contented himself with reading only a sermon and did not demand that his Prince of Wales's garrison pray in unison.

Much later, when Bishop J.N. Provencher, as Apostolic Vicar of Hudson Bay, wanted to take up residence at York Factory, the Company refused his request with the curt comment that the conflict among opposing beliefs would be harmful to the spiritual and material welfare of the Indians.

all its servants worship on Sunday mornings at divine service conducted by resident factors—unless, of course, the heathen should choose the Sabbath to arrive with a particularly appealing canoe-load of pelts.

Such evangelical diversions did little to relieve the men's frustrations. They were trapped in an inhospitable climate, at the edge of an unknown universe. The monotony of the seasons—there were two, a long winter and a short spring—and their own aimless activity produced lethal doses of cabin fever for which there was only one cure: alcohol. The Company quickly realized that liquor was a greater enemy than the climate to its trade on the bay, but no matter how many prohibitions it proclaimed and no matter how often it paid off informers to halt the smuggling of brandy casks on outgoing ships, the booze flowed steadily across the Atlantic. Exceptional was the Company servant who failed to organize surreptitious caches of several gallons or so of brandy for his private stock.

As early as 1682, the HBC had shipped 440 gallons of brandy to its posts, mainly for use as part of the trading ceremony with the Indians. Each subsequent liquid cargo was accompanied by long written instructions such as this 1692 notice sent to George Geyer, then Governor at York Factory: "Whereas we have sent you a very large quantity of new french brandy, which we procured with great difficulty, our desire is that what you shall not have emediate use for it in the Factory to trade either with the Natives or our Servants." Anthony Beale, an HBC apprentice who rose to be Governor of Albany, received an even sterner admonition on June 10, 1713: "... Trade as little brandy as possible to the Indians, we being informed it has destroyed several of them."

But by the middle of the eighteenth century, the French traders operating out of Montreal had introduced enough brandy and rum into the native economy that little fur could be traded with the abstinence requested by the HBC's absentee landlords. As suited their style of pragmatic entrepreneurship, the London Committeemen accepted the fact that liquor was a necessary part of their operations and became canny about its use and manufacture. Since brandy from France was expensive and scarce because of the frequent conflicts between Versailles and the British throne, the HBC governors abandoned the French product and introduced a mixture they christened English Brandy. This was cheap (almost raw) London gin to which were added drops of any of several tinctures (usually iodine) to duplicate the rich auburn colour of the real brandy. "We have sent in the medicine chest a bottle of tincture to colour the English Brandy," explained an official communication dated May 2, 1735, from Hudson's Bay House in London to Thomas Maclish, then Governor at Albany. "When there shall be occasion, four or five drops thereof are sufficient to colour a pint and so in proportion for a larger quantity." This raw recipe worked, but the iodine was soon replaced with molasses that not only coloured the rotgut but gave the potent brew a touch of sweetness.

With kegs of "brandy" freely available for the Indian trade, the Company instituted regular rations (one quart each Wednesday and Saturday) for its own personnel. According to account books at Prince of Wales's Fort, by 1721 the *official* average per capita staff consumption amounted to seven and a half gallons per year, but because there were several teetotallers, it was probably closer to ten gallons—not counting the active illicit trade.

There was no great consistency in the Company's policy. Despite the London Committee's sanctimonious protestations against the evils of alcohol, servants who performed beyond the call of duty were rewarded by local trading post commanders with extra rations. Thomas Smith, a stonemason at Prince of Wales's Fort, for example, was granted an extra ten gallons of brandy a year in return for risking his life blowing up rocks for the Fort's walls—an activity that the local Factor's journal laconically noted resulted in regular wounds to "the head, legs and hands that were not mortall."

The factors complained in their journals to London about "the sots" they had been assigned and urged the Committeemen to recruit fresh-faced country lads "not debauched by the voluptuousness of London." The effects of so much drink—by 1766, York Factory alone was storing 2,474 gallons of "brandy"— were occasionally bizarre, such as this incident detailed in the York Fort journal about the would-be suicide of a "servant" named James Robertson: "... This evening James Robertson, whose hand was cut off ye 3d. of this instant, made an open confession. He went out of ye Factory with a full resolution to lay violent hands on himself. He had saved half pint of brandy for six days before to drink in the cold air, so as to make himself elevated ... he likewise carried a piece of rope, but after he had drank the brandy, he throw'd the rope away ... so went to ye steel trap with a design to make away with himself ... But after he had been fast in the trap for almost two hours by his own confession without attempting to get out of the said trap and by that time the fumes of the brandy having evaporated and come a little to his sences he got himself out of ye trap."

The demand for liquor grew so fast that by the end of the eighteenth century the Company shipped to its post at Churchill a dismantled still, capable of turning molasses into a hundred gallons of "cordials." But for undetermined reasons, the machinery was never installed and was returned to England the following year. A highly successful brewing operation was by then flourishing at every HBC outpost, with the Company supplying most of the required malt. The recipe for spruce beer, a valuable anti-scorbutic, was literally explosive because gunpowder was used to accelerate the aging process:

> To brew this beer, the kettle being near full of water, cram the kettle with small pine; from one experiment you will judge the quantity of pine that will bear a proportion to your water. Let the tops of the pine be boiled in the water until the pine turns yellow, and the bark peels, or the sprigs strip off readily on being pulled; then take off your kettle, and the pine out of the water, and to about two gallons of liquor put a quarter of a pint of molasses. Hang your kettle on, giving the liquor off, put it into a cask in which you have before put cold water, the quantity of about two gallons. Then take a gun with a small quantity of powder, and no wad; fire into the bunghole. It will set the liquor a working; in about twenty-four hours stop the cask down, and the liquor will be ready to drink.

One dramatic instance of the corruption of discipline by alcohol occurred on Christmas Day 1735, when the newly rebuilt post at Moose was ravaged by fire. The blaze had been set in the cookhouse and quickly spread through the wooden palisades. According to resident Factor Richard Staunton, "drunkenness and debochery" caused the misfortune: "Vice and ignorance predominated to a monsterous degree of wickedness both amongst the English and Indians." He reported that the Indians had brought their women into the post and thereby gained influence over the English and themselves learned "much villainy."

Moose Factory was one of the Company's earliest settlements, dating back to its choice in 1673 as the principal factory at the Bottom of the Bay. It quickly evolved into the equivalent of a provincial capital, becoming the transportation hub for the chain of southern outposts and the magnet for Indians from the mesh of rivers that empty into James Bay. After being destroyed by the French under the Chevalier de Troyes, it was rebuilt in 1730, but Moose was never a happy post. It became the most "corrupted" (which in the parlance of the day meant that it had "gone Indian") of all the HBC factories. The guzzling of brandy remained the biggest problem. "Many of the accidents at Moose were alcohol-related," concluded Frits Pannekoek in his study, "Corruption at Moose," published in *The Beaver* magazine. "One man consumed so much 'bumbo'—that fur-trade mixture of rum, water, sugar and nutmeg—that he fell off the sloop and promptly drowned. With some regret and much haste, his mates lost no time in auctioning off the contents of his chest. The chief factors were always afraid that the men on watch, who were too often drunk, would, spitefully or accidentally, set fire to the buildings. The courage to commit suicide could also be found in the bottle. 'Brandy-death' was common, and known in Rupert's Land as a Northwester's Death."

In order to reform the social disorder at Moose, the London Committeemen dispatched a tough disciplinarian named James Duffield, whose disruption of the local pattern of co-existence with the Indians drove the community to anarchy. He personally patrolled the post's grounds from sunrise past sunset, armed with a brace of pistols and a stout cane for self-defence, strenuously enforcing his myriad regulations—which the militant Company servants interpreted as a loss of their previous liberties.

In that dreadful winter of 1741, Duffield devised an intriguing method for preventing any of the malcontents from setting fire to his post. Each evening before his uneasy slumber, he would lash the most likely troublemaker to the stove so that he would be among the first victims of any conflagration. To prevent late-night drunken brawls with local Indian women, he had the doors to the men's cabins removed. When a particularly outspoken mutineer with the unlikely name of Porto Bello swore to hang himself unless Duffield relaxed his disciplinary measures, the Factor calmly provided him with a rope, and when that produced a meek complaint that it really wasn't long enough, the Factor handed him a longer one.

Curiously, Duffield blamed most of the troubles at Moose on the dominance of the Masons, the secretive organization that had influenced the HBC's founding father, Prince Rupert, and many of the crowned heads of Europe. Duffield's journal contains the bitter complaint that he felt he had been "dropp'd down amongst a nest of free and accepted Masons, without being initiated by ye bretheren, but as an intruder on their laws, by virtue of ye Compys authority: and therefore at all events I was to be hoodwink'd and kept from discovering their secret measures … such a scandalous society."

The unhappy Duffield was recalled to London in 1744, but the disciplinary problems at Moose and many of the other bay forts continued. "For the most part," notes historian Glyndwr Williams, the Factors "ruled by a series of compromises. Conventions and practices developed in the Bay outside the range of knowledge and approval of the distant London Committee. This is not to say that life at the posts was a squalid orgy, with drunken servants forcing Indian women into prostitution, and robbing the Company at every turn. The Company could not have survived if this were so, but it is no more of a caricature than the assumption that the garrisons lived by the letter of the Company's annual instructions. What had evolved was a local and distinctive lifestyle, based on a combination of trading considerations, sexual needs and the requirements of a harsh physical environment."

This trade-off—the acceptance of Company edicts in principle and their evasion in practice—resulted in a devil's brew of distrust and tension between its servants and officers. On one occasion, the Chief Factor at York went to Churchill to have a key made because he could not trust his own armourer. Punishments, which took the form of fines and canings, occasionally acquired some odd twists, as when Henry Pollexfen, Factor at Moose in 1757, resented being asked for a new work assignment by one of his crew. "I desired him not to be saucy nor to give me any ill language, and I gave him a little blow on the head," Pollexfen noted in his journal. In return, the Factor was himself knocked to the ground. He promptly placed the unruly servant in irons until he could be sent back to England.

The main reason why this potentially explosive set of human relationships functioned surprisingly well was the kind of men the HBC hired. Because England spent most of the eighteenth century at war, military service was difficult to avoid and career choices were limited. Unlike some of the other far-flung trading companies, which tended to pick as their officers cultured English gentlemen whose education as generalists hardly fitted them for life in the wilderness, the HBC depended for most of its recruits on the unexcitable Orkneymen. Dour they might be, but the Orkneymen's own sea-borne history had implanted character traits well fitted for survival under stress. Canny moderation, self-control, resourcefulness and rivalry without animosity characterized their approach to life.

It was not an easy route to great fortune, but service with the HBC was sometimes the only hope for the fourth son of a farmer or fisherman. Chief Factors in the eighteenth century were paid £100 to £300, though they could usually make as much again by private trapping; sloop captains received £40, and each rank was paid on a descending scale, with apprenticed clerks earning about

£15 a year. Skilled tradesmen could make up to £36 per annum, but an ordinary labourer started at £6 a year, with annual increments of 40 shillings a year to a maximum of £14.

In London unskilled workers earned 10 shillings a week but, unlike the HBC employees, received no free board and lodging. Henry Kelsey, who first penetrated the Canadian prairies and remained in the Company's employ for thirty-eight years, including a term as Governor of Albany, earned a lifetime total of less than £2,500 and two suits of clothes. The main fiscal advantage of service on the bay was that the men hoarded most of their earnings—none more assiduously than Anthony Henday, who saved £113 of the £120 he was paid during twelve years of service.*

The Company could be heartless. Few of its Factors contributed more to its economic well-being than Andrew Graham, whose several volumes of observations of nature were classic works. He served on the bay from 1749 to 1775, holding in turn all the major posts including the governorships of York Factory and Churchill. During all that time he asked the London Committeemen for only one personal favour: that he be allowed, at his own expense, to send his daughter (by his Indian mistress) to England for her education. "I will with pleasure give my security for her maintenance," he pleaded. "I have settled one thousand pounds upon her, and if you choose it shall be lodged in your hands. You are many, if not all of you, fathers; let then what would be the feelings of your own paternal hearts on such an occasion plead in my behalf, and let not humanity and Christianity be forgot. Let me then have cause to bless your goodness."

The reply was short and not sweet: "In regard to your request respecting sending from Hudsons Bay the infant child you mention, it being of such tender age we must decline such permission until a farther opportunity, as we think its safety much to be apprehended by the voyage for want of the care that may be necessary to a female child."

There is no record of the father's reaction, but it is more than a little ironic that it was Graham, probably more than any other Factor, whose loyalty had been unbending. It was he who had attempted to stem the private trading in

---

* Inexplicably, the Company did not pay its employees if, in the line of duty, they were held prisoner by French or other raiders. This was one reason why Edward Umfreville, one of the most articulate of the HBC's servants, decided to switch loyalties to the North West Company. Captured by the French at York Factory on August 24, 1782, his wages promptly ceased. He left the Company on February 27, 1783, after he was returned to England from France.

furs that was undermining the Company's bayside profits. His detailed descriptions of how the illicit trade was carried out (3,136 skins from one post alone) helped reduce the traffic, though it never ceased to be a problem. This black market came very close to being institutionalized into an elaborate system of bribes for the supply ships' crews. Servants caught attempting to enrich themselves privately were liable to be lashed, though many Factors engaged in the same shadowy commerce with impunity. James Knight, for example, while he was in charge of York Factory, sold his own furs at the Company's auctions, and the record books for 1718 show Mrs Knight at a London address being credited with £52 2s. 9d.

Like other aspects of life on the bay, private trading illustrated the distance between theory and reality. This was most apparent in the difference between the London Committeemen's optimistic perception of how their overseas possessions could be defended and the flimsy military capabilities of those on the ground. The Company's precise tactics were clouded in ambivalence, both among the armchair strategists in London and the men in the trenches abroad, but there definitely was a military dimension to its occupation of Hudson Bay. The adventurers had landed as conquerors, brandishing their Royal Charter, and the carrying of the flag of trade into any new territory was seldom far removed from the profession of arms.

The Company's wilderness settlements were eventually modelled on contemporary defensive architecture, much like those erected at the other side of the world by the East India Company. They were situated inside a quadrangle of wooden bastions mounting various gauges of cannon, joined by palisades of upright logs, sometimes with iron points. The main buildings were meant to be unassailable redoubts with parapets pierced by embrasures for fixed eight-pounders, but were more often flimsily protected shacks. The area required for a clear field of fire inside the stockades inevitably grew crowded with outbuildings, workshops and piles of winter firewood that any attacking force could easily set aflame, destroying the entire "fort." The outer bastions were used as storehouses for pelts rather than as serious defence points. Prince of Wales's, the only fort worthy of the name, was considerably weakened against possible siege because the twenty-four-foot-wide moat was just a shallow ditch and had initially been built with a *fixed* bridge. This would-be moat was a source of constant annoyance because its banks kept crumbling, structurally weakening the fort's palisades.

Depending on the prevailing circumstances and the militancy of the local

Factor, the Company's servants were expected to take part in regular musket drills, to practise firing the heavy guns and to repel whatever invaders might happen by. The journals of the period deal less with the military aspects of such operations than with minute enquiries into the extent of the Company's liability should any servants or officers be killed or injured in its defence. "It should be remembered," notes Michael Payne, social historian of Prince of Wales's Fort, "that the men garrisoning the fort had signed on with the company as tailors, masons, blacksmiths and labourers and not as soldiers. Their desire to court death or dismemberment in the defence of their employer's property was probably slight. The Company, recognizing this fact, offered cash benefits for those wounded in defence of its forts, and money for the estates of those killed. A sum of £30 was to be paid to any man who lost an arm or a leg in the defence of a company fort, and for those who died an equal sum of money would be paid to their beneficiaries. Other injuries would be compensated for as the Committee saw fit. All cases of injuries were at the 'Charge of the Company.'"

THE BEST OF THE BAY MEN displayed an esprit de corps comparable to that of the Royal Navy. The wilderness was their ocean, their outposts the ships. Such an analogy was deliberately fostered. Like the Hudson's Bay Company, the Royal Navy reaches back to the dawn of British world span, each providing an essential impetus to the affairs of empire. Like the Royal Navy, the HBC evolved from royalist mercenary beginnings to play out its role of innocent pomp while undertaking grave circumstance.* "The service assumed an anthropomorphic character," commented the Welsh bard James Morris in a description of naval traditions published in the magazine *Encounter,* "hard-drinking but always alert, eccentric but superbly professional, breezy, naughty, posh, kindly, Nelsonically ready to disobey an order in a good cause, or blow any number of deserving foreigners out of the water. To Britons and to foreigners alike, in the meridian years of Empire the Royal Navy *was* Britain, and the truest national anthem was not *God Save the Queen,* but *Rule Britannia.*"

---

* It was an obscure Sultan of Morocco during the 1880s who took the true measure of Britain's senior service when, after a tour of the Royal Navy's latest battleship, he was asked what had impressed him the most—the powerful turret guns, the massive engines, the torpedo boats carried aboard or perhaps the electric light throughout. "The captain's face," was his reply.

Seniority, sobriety and the ability to keep neat journals brought command in the service of the Company. Instead of elaborate sets of King's Regulations and the threat of court martial, it was often the Factor's fists that ruled. Social stratification was strengthened by the strict rule that all "commissioned gentlemen" had to be addressed as "Mr" by both subordinates and superiors. The arrival and departure of a post's commanding officer demanded cannon salutes. Even if the setting was bush-primitive and the facilities were threadbare, every attempt was made to duplicate in the North American bush the grand protocol and mannered grandeur of the Royal Navy.

This depended on a rank structure with the subtlest of shadings. The choice of thwarts in a canoe, entitlement to a segregated campfire, even the location of pews at the occasional Sunday worship all signalled one's position in the hierarchy.* "Gentlemen had to be just that, socially as well as administratively superior to the servants whose labour they commanded," concluded Philip Goldring in a study of the HBC's labour practices. "Everybody found reason to be grateful for superiority over someone else." HBC Governor Sir George Simpson articulated this attitude most directly in a scathing comment on staff members who were promoted beyond their capabilities—men who "came into the Country as labouring men, but either through favour or cunning got advanced to the rank of Clerks and thereby became useless."

Designations of rank varied with the evolving sophistication of the fur trade, but the basic structure consisted of nine gradations:

Labourers. Sometimes called "middlemen," they performed the basic physical drudgery—shovelling snow, portaging boats, cutting firewood, loading and unloading ships.

Apprentices. Frequently the country sons of HBC traders, they were paid lower wages than labourers but enjoyed better prospects of promotion. They acted as understudies and assistants to other ranks.

---

* A list of 105 Rules and Regulations, issued in 1887, defines privileges and duties so precisely that even the amount of pepper allocated to each rank is listed. Commissioned officers were allowed twice as much as clerks, who in turn could use twice as much as postmasters. The most noticeable dietary difference was in tea rations, with officers getting ten times as much as interpreters.

Craftsmen or Tradesmen. They were the cattlekeepers, carpenters, black-smiths, coopers, boatbuilders, fishermen, store porters, net-menders, tinsmiths and cooks.

Guides and Interpreters. Tenured time-servers who knew native languages and dialects, they performed minor but invaluable inter-locutory functions in the fur trade. One indication of how minute were the gradations between the HBC ranks was the 103rd Resolution of the HBC Council, adopted in 1824: "In order to draw a line of distinction between Guides, Interpreters and the Gentlemen in the service, no Guide or Interpreter, whether at the Factory Depot, or inland, be permitted to Mess with commissioned Gentlemen or Clerks in charge of Posts."

Postmasters. Usually promoted labourers, they had little to do with the mail but occupied the only ambiguous stratum between servants and officers, as they were frequently placed in charge of small outposts.

Apprentice Clerks. Dewy-cheeked lads in their mid-teens who came to Hudson Bay fresh from English schools, they were equally eager to probe the secrets of the fur trade and the mysteries of young Indian women. Their apprenticeships lasted five years, their virginity much less.

Clerks. The lowest of the officer (non-servant) class, they were placed in charge of smaller units and were the cadre out of which future leaders were recruited. Their pay was three times that of apprentice clerks.

Chief Traders. Thirteen to twenty years as a clerk with what the Company judged to be the appropriate skills and attitudes could bring promotion to the level of Chief Trader and responsibility for the actual fur bartering.

Chief Factors. Only Chief Traders were eligible to become Chief Factors. The title seemed to be freely interchangeable with "Factor" or "Governor" during most of the eighteenth century, although there was only one *real* Governor, who ran the Company and resided in London.

Men's dress reflected their rank and occasionally became absurd. In 1783, when the Company's posts were being raided by the French, a directive was drafted to outfit all servants in regimental uniforms.* The order (which was never carried out) cited three reasons for the battle dress:

"1. To excite emulation and ambition as well as proper confidence in our men.
"2. It would give the Indians an idea of our determined resolution of defending ourselves to the utmost, and thereby securing them strongly in our interest.
"3. By a spirited unexpected uniform appearance, it might give the enemy an opinion of our having received succors and tend to dishearten them or strike them with a sudden panick, as we read of numerous instances from similar causes."

Much of the HBC's routine and ritual was modelled on Royal Navy custom. The Company's own flags flew on ships and stores.† The paramilitary atmosphere was emphasized by naming even the least prepossessing moose pasture outposts "forts." The martial air of the daily routine was unrelenting. The so-called forts (few of which were ever successfully defended against attack) were built on the typical imperial plan found in Cape Colony, India, Hong Kong and Australia: officers' quarters in the centre of the courtyard with a bachelors' hall and the men's huts banked against the outer palisades. A powder magazine was tucked safely away on the periphery, and armed bastions faced

---

* Such parish bluff survived into the 1940s, when the Company was still differentiating the ranks of its employees in Northern services by forcing them to wear peaked caps decorated with enamelled badges and various configurations of gold braid. The once-rigid rank structure is still to be found in the graveyards, now tucked behind respectful but incongruous white picket fences at the posts. Crude time-worn crosses, mottled with lichen and twisted to crazy angles by the heaving permafrost, mark the servants' graves. The officers repose in calm dignity and posthumous glory beneath granite or even marble headstones on which have been carefully carved not just their names and dates but the highest rank they achieved in the service of the Company.
† By a special warrant dated July 21, 1682, Prince Rupert, Vice-Admiral of England (who also happened to be Governor of the HBC at the time), granted the Company the right to use the Red Ensign ("King's Jack"), with the letters HBC on the fly, at its forts and on its ships entering Hudson Strait. No other private concern enjoyed the same privilege. The Governor's standard, consisting of the Company coat of arms on a field of white, has been in use at least since 1779.

each other diagonally across the enclosure. Like the Navy, the Company recognized spontaneous valour or oncoming senility with its own medals* and counted elapsed time on its own calendar.† Its motto, *Pro Pelle Cutem*, was a less straightforward choice. A whimsical derivation of the vengeful biblical "an eye for an eye" sentiment, it meant, roughly, "a skin for its equivalent." The original saying was probably intended to convey the risks incurred by the early adventurers, as in "we risk our skins to get your pelts" and meant "a skin for a pelt." A more earthy application to the fur trade was "we skin you as you try to skin us," or, during the days when liquor became the effective medium of exchange, "a skin for a skinful."

The naval atmosphere of the northern posts was reinforced by the fact that changes in shift, meals and bedtimes were signalled by the sounding of ships' bells. In both services, the bell was a symbol of a disciplined and punctual workforce. "The day was arranged rather like watches on a ship," according to historian Glyndwr Williams. "Many of the officers went into the Company as the equivalent of midshipmen, spent thirty years or more on the bay, with rigid discipline and long periods of isolation, rose up through the ranks to the equivalent of post captains or rear-admirals, then went on the half-pay list. The key characteristic was continuity."

As in the Royal Navy, discipline depended on maintenance of as much distance between officers and men as physical circumstances would allow. This was achieved through the provision of distinct quarters and different messing arrangements; officers were served by stewards at separate tables while servants drew their rations from large communal pots. Anyone late for a meal had to absent himself politely and go hungry; as in a naval wardroom, no strident discussion was allowed in the messes.

Cultivating the pride of privilege and the cap-doffing subservience required to maintain such rigid social equations in a rough land was not always easy, especially because most of the Company's Chief Factors and Traders (unlike most Royal Navy officers, who seemed to be bred for their billets) could not claim particularly impressive class credentials. Even though fur trade society

---

* Nine special medals were struck, including a silver George III medal that the HBC awarded to Indians who brought the most trade to Company posts. Long-service medals were issued until 1965.

† To place things in their proper perspective, the HBC calendar dates back to the birth of the Company in 1670 instead of to the nativity of Jesus of Nazareth; 1985, for instance, is still referred to in correspondence with northern stores as "Outfit 315."

was highly structured, status differentiations reflected rank rather than family tree, school tie or even military title. Much later, when Jonas Oxley, who had served as a lieutenant in the British army, objected to serving under a Company officer named Joseph Greill who had been only a sergeant—and in a regiment of German mercenaries at that—Sir George Simpson, the then Governor, wrote him a curt reply: "Sir, your impertinent and ridiculous note of this evening shall be treated with the sovereign contempt it merits. Your honor and rank in his majesty's service are quite immaterial to me & all I require of you is to do your duty faithfully as a Clerk in the service of the Honourable Company."

NOT A SINGLE EMPLOYEE during the eighteenth century asked to remain on Hudson Bay following his retirement from the service. The early HBC men thought of themselves as sailors ashore on a sea coast rather than as settlers, however temporary, on the edge of an exciting new land.

Light years removed from the sherry-tippling gentility of their overlords, they were nevertheless subject to strict control by the London-based Committeemen. In the hierarchical society of eighteenth-century England, such an impotent existence was accepted as part of the given social order, rousing little if any resentment. The traders were too preoccupied with staying alive.

The struggle was not so much against distant authority as against rugged geography and a merciless climate—a contest with the elements that yielded few victories, only the postponement of defeats.

The Salty Orcadians

"They pulled the wilderness round them like a cloak, and wore its beauty like a crest." —Bernard De Voto

BECAUSE HISTORY DEMANDS DOCUMENTATION, most Hudson's Bay Company chroniclers have concentrated on two mines of information: the official corporate minutes that hint at the austere manipulations among London-based Committeemen and the self-justifying daily journals kept by Chief Factors and explorers in the field.

But most of the Company's servants—the men who actually staffed the posts—fit into neither of these categories. They kept no records, got on with their jobs and left behind only a scattered legacy of their own memories as having been part of a grand enterprise. Yet they did most of the real work, and it was their loyalty to the Company they served and their canny attitude towards the Indians with whom they traded that allowed the HBC to rule its distant domain and barter in good faith with the native harvesters of fur.

During the 1700s, more than three-quarters of these unknown soldiers were recruited from the Orkneys, a cluster of sixty-five bleak islands off Scotland's north coast. If the combination of determination and oatmeal* produced the ideal Scot, the Orkneyman was a product of sandstone and spindrift. The Orcadians' penchant for uncomplaining servitude plus the fact that they were used to labouring at home under conditions as rigorous as those on Hudson Bay made them ideal for manning the distant swampy ramparts of the HBC's early empire. They were cheaper to hire than Englishmen and more tractable

---

* Dr Samuel Johnson defined oats as "food for men in Scotland, and horses in England."

than the Irish; and they had yet to share the aspiration for self-determination that infected the tight-lipped Highlanders.

Many original HBC servants had been recruited from the bands of scavenging urchins who roamed the Thames docks. But John Nixon, the HBC's second overseas Governor (1679–83), complained about "our London born childring" pestering him, and asked for country lads instead. The Company did recruit a few "Oliver Twists" from charity schools to serve seven-year terms of indenture, but the naval press gangs stalking the London docklands deprived the HBC of its pick of the best available manpower.

In their annual ritual, the HBC supply ships would slip anchor, edge out of Gravesend at the mouth of the Thames, then heeling over in a freshening breeze, race northward along England's east coast, past Newcastle and Aberdeen, across to Stromness. The Orkney Islands' tiny harbour town was the last stopping point for fresh water* and provisions before crossing the North Atlantic by the great circle route.[†] Since the ships were there anyway and because the Company was always short of capable and willing servants, local Orkney lads were enlisted after 1702. Their prowess was so impressive that Stromness quickly became the HBC's main recruiting ground. Of the 530 employees on the Company's overseas payroll in 1799, 416 were Orcadians. Stromness had a population of 1,400 at the time, with many a rich shopkeeper but only half as many young men as women; most of the able-bodied males had departed for Hudson Bay.

Orkneymen enlisted in the Company's service at £6 a year, with small increases at the end of each five-year hitch. After 1779, they were offered a £2 bonus for inland service and a scheme of modest premiums based on their posts' fur returns. Because they were granted "all-found" (free food and board) and had no place or need to spend money at the bay, they could look forward to returning to their native hearths and local lasses with enough savings to

---

* The water was drawn from Login's Well, near the granite quays of the settlement. The well was sealed in 1931, but its life-giving water had sustained HBC ships for most of two hundred years. Its water had also slaked the thirst of the crews of Captain Cook's *Resolution* and *Discovery* during their homeward voyage of 1780 and of the outward-bound voyagers aboard *Erebus* and *Terror* before they were led into the doomed search for the North West Passage by Sir John Franklin in 1845.

† This was true to their concept of latitude sailing and the desire to avoid direct confrontation with the Gulf Stream/North Atlantic Drift. The general route to North America from the Orkney Islands was to the Isle of Sheep and the southern tip of Greenland, bringing ships into Davis Strait and then on through Hudson Strait.

purchase fishing boats or small holdings. Many brought home new blood as well. By the end of the 1770s, so many of these hardy expatriates had fallen in love with Indian women that a small college was founded at St Margaret's Hope in South Ronaldsay to school their offspring.

Recruits from the northern isles were not all Orkneymen. In 1806, a recently arrived HBC servant named John Fubbister stumbled into the post of Alexander Henry, a North West Company fur trader at Pembina, and begged for help. Henry recalled the encounter in vivid detail: "I was surprised at the fellow's demand. I told him to sit down and warm himself. I returned to my own room, where I had not been long before he sent one of my people, requesting the favor of speaking with me. Accordingly I stepped down to him, and was much surprised to find him extended on the hearth, uttering dreadful lamentations; he stretched out his hands toward me, and in piteous tones begged to me be kind to a poor, helpless, abandoned wretch, who was not of the sex I had supposed, but an unfortunate Orkney girl, pregnant, and actually in childbirth. In saying this she opened her jacket, and displayed a pair of beautiful, round, white breasts; she further informed me of the circumstances that had brought her into this state. The man who had debauched her in the Orkneys ... was wintering at Grandes Fourches [an outpost on the Red River]. In about an hour she was safely delivered of a fine boy, and that same day she was conveyed home in my cariole, where she soon recovered."

The only postscript to this odd incident was the terse entry in the journal of a Company trader named John Kipling, who noted that one of his fellow HBC men "turned out to be a woman, and was delivered of a fine boy in Mr. Henry's house. The child was born before they could get her breeches off." (John Fubbister was really Isabel Gunn. The father of her baby, Jany, was identified as an Orcadian named John Scarth, an experienced HBC veteran who returned home in 1812. Isabel stayed at Albany until 1809, working as a nurse and washerwoman.)

Some of the more sanctimonious London Committeemen were not amused. Shortly afterward, David Geddes, the resident recruiting agent at Stromness, received a stinging complaint about the quality of recent Orkney recruits: "Of late, many men have been sent out, who on their arrival were found totally unfit for the Service. The Board will not consider themselves bound by any agreement you make, unless the men engaged by you are *stout, able, and active.*"

Most of the human traffic between the Orkneys and the bay was more mundane, with local HBC representatives screening applicants and giving them rudimentary medicals. Notices of incoming ships and Company hiring requirements were posted on church doors in the islands' various parishes, so that local boys attending divine service knew when, where and how to apply. The annual arrivals and departures of the ships quickly developed into the highlight of the sombre Stromness social calendar.

Visiting captains gathered local supporters, playing up parental feelings as they invited the families of departing youngsters to dine aboard in their private cabins. Wardrooms were used as public reception areas, and nightly dances transformed docksides into a carnival. When it was time to leave, the Company flag, with its red cross and four rampant beavers, was run up the harbour tower. The low hills protecting Stromness reverberated as the island's thirty-two-pounder fired farewell salutes to the departing ships, borne by the racing ebb tide past Hoy Sound into the grey Atlantic. The enduring final glimpse of his home ground for many a young Orkneyman was the crowd of burghers gathered on the point of Ness, waving handkerchiefs and cheering in a thin and fading chorus as the ships raised sail and set course for the New World.

Signing on to serve five years at a time in the flourishing ring of outposts on Hudson Bay—Rupert, Moose, Severn, Albany, Prince of Wales's Fort and York Factory—the youngsters were quick to adapt to the climate and cramped circumstances. "The Orcadian was the perpetual migrant," Richard Glover has written of the islanders of that era. "Women went into domestic service in Edinburgh, Newcastle, and London. Men found outlets in the Iceland or Greenland fisheries and also turned to the Hudson's Bay Company, for even the wilderness of North America offered them a higher standard of living and a better chance of saving money than a labouring life at home."

Most of those who stayed became slaves to subsistence farms, tilled with near-prehistoric implements, fertilized by seaweed and yielding crops that hardly fed their cultivators. While a few fertile farms raised cattle and sheep, the main cash crop was kelp, burned for its iodine. One minor source of income was the breeding of a particularly ugly and brutish kind of coarse-haired pig; its bristles, twisted into ropes, were used by the islanders to pluck birds' eggs from cliffside nests in spring. Farmhouses were meticulously constructed from flagstone chinked with peat since there was little money to buy the lime for mortar that might have made insulation more adequate and rooms drier. The beasts of the field were allowed inside during winter to add their body warmth to the household.

Apart from such domestic discomforts, the Orcadians had to suffer through winters bound to reaffirm an only slightly facetious island saying—that its sons moved to Hudson Bay to get warm. Less than eight degrees south of the Arctic Circle, the Orkneys straddle the 59th parallel, sharing the latitude of some of Hudson Bay's more northern posts. At the stormy apex where the Atlantic crashes into the Norwegian Sea, then sweeps down to meld with the North Sea, the Orkneys are swept by prevailing winds that blow so fiercely few trees ever take root. The islands' rocky eastern shores are whipped by avalanching water as the tides of the North Atlantic slam into the ebb and flow of the North Sea, reaching the Orkneys with equal strength from opposite directions.* Temporarily calm anchorages can suddenly be filled or emptied by cascades of water that flow in and out at sixteen knots or more. The seas are so turbulent that salt crystals are permanently suspended in the atmosphere, their refraction splitting the sun's rays into an intensified glow. That particular quality of light and a topography both gentle and jagged give the islands an aura of unyielding beauty.

The characteristics that made the island lads so sought after as HBC labourers were their natural frugality, adaptability and inbred obedience to authority which made them docile without being servile. If not particularly imaginative or enterprising, they were possessed of a strong sense of self-sufficiency. Authenticity mattered to them more than originality, and they felt instinctively mistrustful of self-aggrandizement or virtuosity. Shy to express emotion, they would conceal minor crimes such as theft—even as its victims—feeling it was sinful to be the instrument of another's suffering.

Because of its remoteness, the great movements of history bypassed Orkney, but the islands presented such a peril to navigation that a steady supply of shipwrecked sailors marrying local girls kept the culture from becoming too inbred. The islanders' linguistic ability and a parish school system that encouraged Orcadians to master the rudiments of reading, writing and arithmetic produced recruits with skills particularly suited to the dogged ledgerkeeping of the fur trade.

The austere and highly structured life at the little log outposts on Hudson Bay required their inhabitants to practise a system of working relationships

---

* According to H. Lamb's *Climate, History and the Modern World*, "A bizarre occurrence—serious for the individuals concerned—presumably resulting from the great southward spread of the polar water and ice was the arrival about the Orkney Islands a number of times between 1690 and 1728, and once in the river Don near Aberdeen, of an Eskimo in his kayak."

based on the mutually acceptable interplay of discipline and deference between Company officers and servants. Unlike the independent-minded Highlanders or the orphaned exiles from London (where tension between social classes was beginning to foster egalitarian demands), the Orcadians did not feel uncomfortable "knowing their place"—providing, of course, that the bounds of obligation and service were well respected and annual salaries were credited on time. One example of how structured the fur trade society had become was the nightly encampments of the first HBC brigades travelling inland; they were divided into three campfires, one for the Indians, another for Company servants and the third and grandest for the accompanying HBC officer or Chief Factor.

Another quality highly appreciated by early bayside governors was the Orcadian affinity for the sea. Patient fisherfolk, splendid boatmen and wise sailors, they knew how to read the wind, estimate a tide or ride out a storm. Latter-day Vikings, they manned the sloops that connected the HBC's early posts and headed north to hunt for whales and Eskimo customers. Paradoxically, it was the islanders' spreading reputation as able seamen that eventually deprived the HBC of their services. British admirals, hard pressed by Napoleon's navies, needed more and more Orkneymen to man the lower decks. Seafarers they might be, but warriors they were not. To escape the rounding up of involuntary candidates for the press gangs, able-bodied Orkneymen hid themselves in glens on the moorland, inside hollowed-out peat stacks, in secret compartments under the floorboards of their houses or in age-old cliff-caves invisible from the sea, where their anti-English slogans still adorn the walls.

Within the Hudson's Bay Company, opinion of the Orcadians' effectiveness was at times sharply divided. Samuel Hearne, the explorer who led a group of them inland to establish Cumberland House, noted in his journal that "the Orkneymen are the quietest servants and the best adapted for this country that can be procured. Yet they are the slyest set of men under the sun and their universal propensity to smuggling, and clandestine dealings of every kind, added to their clannish attachment to each other, puts it out of the power of any one Englishman to detect them." Sir George Simpson, the greatest of the overseas governors, disparaged the Orcadians for their "slow, inanimate habits," and one officer, William Walker, priggishly requested that he be recalled "if any person from the Orkney Isles should be placed over me." The London Committeemen accused the Orkney servants of cowardice during the

HBC's battles with the French, and Colin Robertson, who was to command the Company's Athabasca district, condemned them as being fit only to serve at bayside posts.

Some of this criticism was justified. The penny-pinching Orkney expatriates took much greater pride in returning home with a nest egg than in exploring the new continent or trying to extract the last pelt from visiting Cree. Yet Philip Turnor, the first of the Company's bona fide surveyors, noted in his 1779 journal that the very Orcadians condemned by Hearne were "a set of the best men I ever saw together, as they are obliging, hardy, good canoe men." Ten years later, Edward Umfreville, the HBC officer who had switched to the North West Company and had competed against the Orcadian labourers along the Saskatchewan rivers, wrote that "they are a close, prudent, quiet people, strictly faithful to their employers, and sordidly avaricious. When these people are scattered about the country in small parties among the Indians, the general tenor of their behaviour is conducted with so much propriety, as not only to make themselves esteemed by the natives, and to procure their protection, but they also employ their time in endeavouring to enrich themselves."

More specific praise came from Sir John Franklin, who commanded a crew of Orcadians during his first northern trek: "It is not easy for any but an eyewitness to form an adequate idea of the exertions of the Orkney boatmen. The necessity they are under of frequently jumping into the water to lift the boats over the rocks compel them the whole day to remain in wet clothes, at a season when the temperature is far below the freezing point. The immense loads they carry over the portages is not more a matter of surprise than the alacrity with which they perform these various duties."

Whether they lauded or damned them, few HBC officers bothered to identify their Orcadian servants by name, relegating them to the role of a collective presence, like domestic staff in a noble house. The main exceptions were the very few islanders who stayed with the Company long enough to crack the officers' ranks. The first of this select group was Joseph Isbister, son of a Stromness merchant, who became Chief Factor at Albany and Governor at Prince of Wales's Fort. Even more successful was William Tomison from South Ronaldsay, who joined the HBC in 1760 as a labourer and stayed on for the next fifty-one years, rising to be the Company's first "Chief Inland." *The New Orkney Book*, a collection of essays by some of the islands' most notable sons, states with pride that "From the western Arctic to Red River, and from Red River to Ungava, Orcadians of the eighteenth and nineteenth centuries made paths, hewed clearings, built portages, erected buildings, and planted gardens in the wilderness that was Rupert's Land."* In the enduring phrase of the American historical essayist, Bernard De Voto, they constituted a legion of brave and hardy men who "pulled the wilderness round them like a cloak, and wore its beauty like a crest."

The flood of Orkneymen into the HBC continued well into the twentieth century, but soon after the Battle of Waterloo their proportion diminished. The North American offspring of Orcadians and native women took some of their places; Canadian voyageurs recruited from Montreal occupied others. To bypass the press gangs, the Company sought staff in other countries during times of prolonged British conflict—in Ireland during the Napoleonic Wars and in Norway at the time of the Crimean War. But when the Earl of Selkirk required sturdy pioneers to establish his colony at Red River, his vanguard of seventy was recruited at Stromness.

As Sir George Simpson, himself a West Highlander, took over more and more of the Company's affairs, the recruiting emphasis changed, and the supply ships that called at Stromness in 1860 picked up as many new servants from the Highlands, the Hebrides and the Shetlands as from the Orkneys. In 1891, the HBC captains stopped calling altogether.

For most of two long centuries, the storm-battered islands that guard Scotland's rugged north coast had sent their best sons into Hudson Bay, but the Orkneymen's diaspora left little permanent imprint on either the Company they served or the land they helped exploit.

---

* Only a few Orcadian place names survive in modern Canada—Orkney and Kirkwall in Ontario, Binscarth and Westray in Manitoba, Birsay and Orkney in Saskatchewan and Scapa in Alberta. There is a Stromness Bay on Victoria Island in the western Arctic.

A Savage Commerce

"European records made a big thing of how impressed the Indians were with their trade goods; Indian oral tradition tells the reverse—how impressed the Europeans were with the furs that the Indians didn't value particularly highly."   —Professor Jennifer Brown

THE INDIANS, who along with the Orcadians were the proletariat of the fur trade, seldom troubled the consciences or inhabited the journals of the HBC. With some exceptions, Company factors and factotums treated their presence as an amorphous, slightly out-of-focus collective reality not far removed from the backdrop of local vegetation and animal life: an offstage Greek chorus supplying an endless abundance of furs.

They are the ghosts of Canadian history.

Canada's Indian nations were not conquered like the American Sioux or massacred like the Andean Incas, yet their lives were torn apart by the arrival of the white man; they became (like the Welsh, in the telling phrase of the late Gwyn Thomas) "a people deeply wounded in their minds."

The Indians' loss of a continent and its rich resources has yet to be adequately documented. "The picture of the Indian as a human being presented by writers of Canadian history is confusing, contradictory and incomplete," concluded Nova Scotia historian James W. St. G. Walker, after studying the literature. Unlike their voluble white counterparts, who seemed to spend more time scribbling entries in their ledgers and journals than swapping furs, the Indians made much history but wrote very little. They lived within a hallowed oral tradition, masterfully employing the spoken word. Their chiefs were capable of magnificent oratory; individual bands would stage four-day-long miracle plays from memory; and family heads could recite ritual prayers by the hour without the omission of a single syllable. But because they had no written record—only tribal memories and sustaining myths—they were dismissed as having no past. Even the few conscientious white chroniclers who tried to understand their vanishing culture were almost invariably fooled, because most Indians, considering it more important to give a pleasing answer than an informative one, told the white man precisely what they thought he wanted to hear.

Since he was so different, the "red man" was regarded by his white contemporaries as inferior, treacherous, barbaric and fickle. A "pagan," he did not subscribe to Christian ideals, refused to observe the European sabbath, allowed his women to go naked and tortured his prisoners—all traits considered decidedly un-English and therefore "savage" and beyond the pale. (Ironically, many so-called civilized Englishmen referred to Scottish Highlanders as "savages" well into the eighteenth century.) There was not even a hint of hesitation about the manifest destiny of European civilization spreading across the continent. The only good Indian, in their thinking, was the stout chap willing to go along with that inevitable tidal wave of empire. Commercial pacification on such a massive scale required its clearly defined heroes and antagonists. The French claimed the former by preserving the memory of mutilated Jesuit martyrs, while the English created the latter by subscribing to the veracity of lurid descriptions of Indian survival habits such as this report about hard times at York Factory in the early 1700s: "When at the point of starvation, the father and mother kill their children and eat them, and then the stronger of the two eats the other. I have seen a man who had eaten his wife and their six children, and he said his heart had not failed him until he came to eat the last child, as he loved him more than the others, and when he was opening the head to eat the brains, he was touched by the natural affection of a father for his children, and had not strength to break the bones to suck the marrow."

The basic pattern of the Hudson Bay trade was one of mutual exploitation, yet there were few places on earth where commerce came to terms with an indigenous population under less violent circumstances. The exchange of peltry for trade goods resulted in a balanced reciprocity of purpose: two radically different cultures and totally dissimilar economies finding common ground in order to attain their diverse objectives. The ledgers of the Company may provide the figures and totals, but they reveal very little about the transactions' social implications.

One whimsical example of how profoundly the two cultures differed enlivens a memoir by American painter George Catlin, who observed the behaviour of a group of Indians he guided through Paris in the early 1840s. The natives were not particularly overawed by large buildings nor wildly impressed by the carriages and litters; they managed to suppress any sign of enthusiasm for white women and retained their dignity even when pawed over by various impertinent royal personages assembled to inspect them—but they were utterly flabbergasted by the way Parisian women treated their dogs. The visitors were unable to understand the affection showered on the pooches when they had seen orphanages filled with unwanted children. They could not comprehend the horror on a saleswoman's face when they tried to buy the main course for a traditional dog feast. One of the Indian visitors carefully produced a table of Parisian dog-walking habits that ironically presaged later anthropological reports on North American Indians:

Women leading one little dog	432
Women leading two little dogs	71
Women leading three little dogs	5
Women with big dogs following (no string)	80
Women carrying little dogs	20
Women with little dogs in carriages	31

The French visit was followed by a tour of England by a dozen Chipewyan from the HBC territories in 1848. All but three died of pneumonia and English cooking.

TOO OFTEN the folk memory of the Indian–HBC trading relationship is reduced to the nature of a simple swap: furs for trinkets. That may have been temporarily true during initial European contact, but as the interchange between societies grew in frequency and intensity, it evolved its own complicated cultural repertoire.

The tribes saw themselves not as fur suppliers to the HBC or as trappers for gain but as part of an interlocked, animate universe in which every animal was treated as a relative of man. Hunting was very much a spiritual experience. They communicated in dreams with the sacred "keepers of the game" who told them where to hunt and sought permission to kill from the animals themselves. They knew that they would be granted the bounty of pelts only if they proved worthy of it. When the invading Europeans demanded that the Indians slaughter the creatures of the woods merely for profit, they could not know how very much they were asking.

The main reason the fur trade operated as smoothly as it did was that, without really being aware of it, the HBC factors tapped into an existing Indian economic network dating back as much as five thousand years. It extended from Hudson Bay across the prairies, inland from the Pacific, from the St Lawrence to the Great Lakes, and eventually right across the continent. The greatest of these networks, formed by tribal alliances and the natural water routes connecting them, was the Mandan trading empire. This shrewd tribe of Plains Indians once spread its influence from the Missouri River to the Spanish settlements of early Mexico, as far east as Lake of the Woods and north into present-day Saskatchewan and Alberta. The Mandan tribes lived in semi-permanent, domed earth-lodge villages and evolved such sophisticated business patterns that they organized annual fairs featuring chanting dancers offering special bargains. One incentive to traders completing the trek across the plains to the Mandan villages was the attitude towards the women of the tribe. HBC servant Richard White noted in his journal that the Mandan were "a sensible people, and agreed their women should be made use of ..."

The Mandan had a well-deserved reputation as canny traders with their nomadic neighbours, often exacting markups of 100 percent or more. The Crow sold horses to the Mandan at double the price they had paid the Shoshoni for them, and the Mandan in turn at least doubled the price to the Cree. These trading links were jealously guarded against efforts of white intruders to short-circuit them.* The network that terminated at Hudson Bay had the scantiest population yet the richest fur supplies, stretching all the way back to the Athapaskan region in the west as well as along the waterways south and east of the bay. From the first tentative trades in the 1600s until 1763, the Cree along with the Assiniboine and Chipewyan exercised a virtual monopoly on trade with York Factory and most of the other Hudson and James Bay posts. It wasn't until the HBC permeated the interior that nearly every other tribe in the American Northwest became their trading partners, such as the Ojibway, the various Athapaskan tribes, members of the Blackfoot confed-

---

* The fur merchants of New France were the beneficiaries of a similar sequence of alliances, at first with the Huron and later with the Iroquois, threatening those tribes trading at the bay with punitive raids by their resentful neighbours.

eracy, the Chinook, Haida and Nootka of the Pacific coast, and the Carrier and Chilcotin of inland British Columbia. Early HBC journals are filled with admonitions from "savages" advising against any ventures to the interior because of great danger from hostile tribes. In reality, this was the Cree way of maintaining a comfortable monopoly; they were especially anxious that no enemies of the Mandan be supplied with guns.*

Until the Company circumvented the Cree by setting up its own inland operations, these and other native middlemen exacted high tribute for their services. Guns received in trade at York Factory for fourteen beaver pelts were peddled to the Blackfoot for fifty. The northern Chipewyan paid nine furs for the hatchets that had cost the Cree three made-beaver. Michael Asch, a University of Alberta anthropologist, contends that these middlemen had genuine economic power and that their image as the fur trade's unwilling victims is false: "I have never seen a finer sense of profit than in a trading Indian. He knew exactly the effort that went into getting a gun from York Factory, had a highly developed idea of what the traffic would bear and was aware not only of the utility of what he bought but also of the social status that would accrue, and he built that into his price."

The Swampy Cree who dominated the trade out of Hudson Bay were a powerful coalition of nomadic bands, encompassing in their Algonkian language grouping the caribou-hunting Woodland Cree of northern Saskatchewan and the buffalo-hunting Plains Cree of the Qu'Appelle River region. All had successfully adopted ways of life that blended with their varied environments. The bands who chose to live permanently around the HBC posts became known as the "Home Guard" Indians, as contrasted with the "Upland" Indians who would gather for the annual trading sessions. Jennifer Brown, the University of Winnipeg historian who has examined the records, makes a strong argument for the mutuality of these transactions: "The Indians saw themselves as partners, not as the exploited victims of the fur trade. The European records made a big thing of how impressed the Indians were with their trade goods; Indian oral tradition tells the reverse—how impressed the Europeans were with the furs that the Indians didn't value particularly highly. So there was a sort of mutual exploitation going on, based on a lack of knowledge about how each side perceived the value of the goods it was trading."

---

* The Mandan were almost wiped out by a smallpox epidemic that came up the Missouri by steamboat, and by U.S. cavalry raids. By 1837 there were only a hundred survivors of what had once been North America's richest economic culture.

Some Indian academics take a more severe view of the relationship. "The Indian people inadvertently became dependent on European goods for their own survival," states Blair Stonechild, a Cree who heads the department of Indian Studies at the Saskatchewan Indian Federated College in Regina. "Some goods such as knives and kettles made life easier, but soon items such as traps and rifles became necessary to ensure the economic and political welfare of Indian groups and so-called 'traditional enemies' among Indians developed. One example of this phenomenon was the Cree-Déné animosity, some of which arose out of trade-based conflicts in the mid-1700s. Indians identified bows and arrows with hunting, not human carnage, but the arrival of the rifle brought a marked increase in human violence."

Stonechild and others point out that even if the actual trading pattern was not unjust, the economic base of the Indian survival mode was undermined through the massive slaughter of fur-bearing animals and, later, through depletion of the buffalo for pemmican supplies. Dr Oliver Brass, a fellow faculty member of Stonechild's who has four degrees, is from Peepeekisis, one of the File Hills reserves in Saskatchewan. He rarely shops at The Bay, insisting that the Company was a corrupting and co-opting influence. Brass claims that Indians in the United States have been able to remain far more distinctive and independent because they had to wage an armed struggle to survive.

The difference in the way Indians were treated in the evolving countries that would later become the United States of America and Canada is a recurring theme in native history. Stan Cuthand, a Saskatoon-based professor of Indian studies whose father, Jose, starred in Buffalo Bill's Wild West Show, contends that the fate of Canadian natives has been the more humiliating. "In Canada, the Indians were not directly shot at, but they were degraded and had no choice about the way they were treated. It was a case of *cultural* genocide, and the Hudson's Bay Company was certainly part of that process."

However one views such strong interpretations, there was a very real contrast in the ways indigenous people were treated. This was especially true of the territory under HBC control, where strict Company rules and regulations prevented the spawning of a vigilante mentality, whereas settlement of the American West amounted to military conquest of Indian lands. "On the other hand," Stonechild points out, "one should note that Indian treaties and sovereignty received earlier recognition in the United States because of the conflict nature of Indian/white relations and early resort to the judicial system for clarification of Indian rights. In Canada, because of the omnipotence of the Indian Act, questions of aboriginal rights and status of treaties were never fully addressed."

The invasion of white trappers in the United States—the notorious "mountain men"—and colonists anxious to grab Indian acreage guaranteed violent confrontation.* "Military action was personal and vital, not imposed in drilled ranks and chalked white pantaloons for some remote dynastic or territorial ambition of a monarch," wrote Barbara Tuchman in her wise *Practising History.* "Conquest of the plains took fifty years of incessant warfare. Eventually, when the Civil War released armed men to the frontier, the struggle was won by the fort, the repeating rifle, starvation, treachery, the railroad, the reservation policy and, ultimately, the extermination of the buffalo which had provided the Plains Indian with food, shelter, and clothing. The last battle was fought in 1890—less than one hundred years ago."

ONE REASON the swampy cree and most other North American Indians were so eager to swap beaver was that the white man's goods transported them instantly from the Stone Age into the Iron Age. That quantum leap had immeasurable social consequences, but at the level of conducting their daily lives, it meant that meals could be cooked in copper pans over fires instead of in birch bark cauldrons containing red-hot rocks, and that fish could be caught on strong metal hooks instead of threaded carved beaver teeth or bird bones. Describing the impact of one such item, the axe, on his people, Chief Dan George, the Canadian activist and actor, once explained: "Imagine its impact on a people whose main implement was still a sharpened stone. Five strokes of an axe and a sapling is down; one day, and a stockade is built—the Iron Age attached to a wooden handle! ... The Industrial Revolution came across the ocean under canvas, and the Indian wanted a part of it for good

---

* The worst examples of cruelty probably occurred in the New England states, where "sniping redskins to watch them spin" became a popular frontier pastime. Canadians have no reason to feel smug on this account. The once-populous Beothuk Indians, a gentle and peaceful people who originally inhabited Newfoundland, were similarly slaughtered, being hunted by local trappers and fishermen for sport. Between 1613 and 1829 they were wiped out, and not a single white "hunter" was ever punished or charged with any crime. A trapper named Noel Boss boasted of having killed ninety-nine Beothuks, but only wounded his hundredth victim—a young girl called Shanawdithit who survived briefly to become "the last of the Beothuks" in 1829.

reason. So he became a fur trader, a year-long job that began in winter with the laying of the traps … You came down to the forts in the early summer and you wanted the whole bazaar—guns, blankets, axes—even the trinkets and love beads for the long winter nights."

The transfer of technology was not all one-sided. Indian families provided the white man with the means of moving inland by introducing him to snow-shoes, birch bark canoes, moccasins and toboggans. They taught the early trader how to harvest wild rice, make clothes from deer or caribou hides and how to put up pemmican, a mixture of dried meat, fat and berries that, pounded and packed into ninety-pound bags, became the staple food of the inland fur trade.

Although they were dealing with a foreign culture, the Cree were surprisingly canny shoppers. Not only did they successfully play off the French against the English and vice versa but they refused to trade items they considered unnecessary, such as dolls, raisins and metal shields; faulty guns were returned, as was tobacco that had been damaged in flooded warehouses.

The act of bartering goods for furs evolved a culture of its own, distinct from the two societies involved and yet very much an expression of their particular and respective priorities and values. The Company was generally fair in its dealings, but that attitude had little to do with decency or altru-ism and everything to do with preserving the natives as a cheap and convenient labour force. The relationship was somewhat akin to that of a modern-day agricultural implements dealer living in an isolated rural community, his livelihood very much dependent on the health of the crops of his customers who in turn can achieve price efficiency only by unrestricted use of the dealer's technology—even if the dealer has to lend them machinery in bad times.

Carol Judd, an Ottawa historian who has examined the HBC's personnel policies, takes a realistic view of the Company's motives in dealing with the Cree of Hudson Bay. "The Company exchanged as many furs for as few or as inexpensive trade goods as it possibly could," she wrote. "At the same time, it perceived itself as humane, fair, even generous: feeding starving natives, healing their sick, providing employment, educating their children. It also introduced schemes for conserving fur-bearing animals and, whenever monop-oly conditions prevailed, it stopped selling liquor to the Indians. Beneath the humanistic veneer, the Company did all of these things because they were essential to its own long term economic and political interest … To the Company the only good Indian was tending his trapline—starving and sick Indians could not trap furs."

Each side approached the transaction from a different premise. The English and Scottish traders operated in the European tradition that endowed the accumulation of material objects with social approbation and viewed the gaining of profits as the ultimate goal, but most Indian people admired the sharing, not the ownership, of goods. Despite their roles as middlemen among their own peoples, they had no framework within which to calculate fur prices that fluctuated as a result of the balance between European supply and demand. They therefore tacitly elected to regard the fur trade's equivalent of price—the standards of trade per made-beaver—as an immutable measure. In Professor Abraham Rotstein's telling analogy, it "was equivalent to the way we think of three feet adding up to one yard. If they believed, for example, that three beaver skins were worth one axe head, then that was that."

Rotstein, who mapped the price levels of HBC goods, discovered that the official rates of exchange for thirty-one of the fifty-five major trading goods were not altered for more than a century (and the others were changed only slightly) no matter how much the price of the trade goods purchased from English manufacturers went up or down or how quotations on the London fur market fluctuated. In 1785, for example, beaver skins sold on the London market for twenty shillings a pound; in 1790, for thirteen shillings; in 1793 for ten shillings.

The ritual of the trading process itself was rooted in the ancient formalities of tribal councils—the ceremonial format for renewing the peace alliances that governed Indian life. (Modern stereotyped terms such as "burying the hatchet," "smoking the peace-pipe" and "an Indian giver" came into the language from these ceremonies.) The ritual began every June or July, even before the Indians arrived at any fort, their canoes assembling upstream just out of sight to plan a grand entrance; only then would the flotilla sweep noisily around the bend of the river. The boats of the trading captains led the way, flying a Union Jack or a small flag of St George. The outriders chanted and fired their fowling pieces in an exuberant salute to the process about to begin. Having waited a long winter and spring for this day, the trading post men would spring into action, raise the Company flag and respond with a volley or two from their own saluting guns.

After the Indian party had landed, cleared a site, pitched its tepees and lit campfires, the Trading Captains* and their lieutenants would come calling on the Governor or Chief Factor. Because most tribes recognized no hereditary command structures, these Captains were chosen for each voyage on the basis of their familiarity with canoe routes and knowledge of the white man. Since they taxed their followers a beaver skin per canoe, the Captains attempted to recruit large flotillas, which would also elevate their prestige in the eyes of the HBC.

The initial encounter in the fur exchange was an elaborate greeting procedure that was part of Indian religious ritual: the smoking of the peace-pipe. The Captain and the Chief Factor would puff, pause and pass the pipe, then puff again—saying nothing. The buzz of deerflies and mosquitoes and the spank of the Company flag in the summer wind were the only sounds heard for most of an hour. The peace-pipe used in these preliminaries was carved of a special stone mined in northern Minnesota. Its four-foot stem was decorated with bear claws and eagle talons, its bowl filled with tamped-down Brazil tobacco leavened with dried local herbs. HBC trader Edward Umfreville, who was a frequent witness, described the ceremony which began with the Factor, "who takes the pipe in both hands, and with much gravity rises from his chair, and points the end of the stem to the East, or sunrise, then to the Zenith, afterwards to the West, and then perpendicularly down to the Nadir. After this he takes three or four hearty whiffs, and having done so, presents it to the Indian leader, from whom it is carried round to the whole party ... When it is entirely smoked out, the Factor takes it again, and having twirled it three or four times over his head, lays it deliberately on the table; which being done, all the Indians return him thanks by a kind of sighing out of the word 'Ho!'"

Then the talk would slowly begin. In a *sotto voce* chant, his eyes fixed on the ground, the Trading Captain would describe how many canoes and how much fur he had brought with him and what had happened upcountry since his last visit. Then he would tentatively enquire, as a throwaway line, how the white man was feeling and what kind of goods he might like to trade. That was

* William Asikinack (Blackbird) of the Saskatchewan Indian Federated College points out that this term was not an internal designation by Indian tribes. As far as they were concerned, each individual could do his or her own bargaining. When people wanted to trade collectively, the person who had the ability to negotiate and to get the best possible "price" for fur was chosen by the group. In the original language of the Ojibway, the only name this person would have was "leader" and this would be only for the specific notion of trade at any given time.

the signal for the Chief Factor to bid his visitors a generous welcome, explaining in great detail why he loved the Indians and how he would always be kind to them. It was all part of a liturgical foreplay leading to a dénouement both sides knew would eventually be based on mutual, if unexpressed, self-interest.

At some point in the proceedings, the Trading Captain would be outfitted (at the HBC's expense) in a uniform befitting his station: a red or blue cloth coat lined with baize, decorated with stripes of broad and narrow orris lace, with regimental cuffs and collar. He would wear a matching waistcoat and breeches; a white open shirt with sleeves narrowed at the wrists with lace; yarn stockings, one blue, the other red, tied below the knees with worsted garters; a hat, bedecked with three colourfully dyed ostrich feathers, a sash around its crown with the ends hanging down each side to his shoulders and a small silk handkerchief tucked into the hatband's knot. For his part, the Chief Factor would bedeck himself in equally elaborate plumage. His suit of black or dark blue might be set off by a white silk shirt, velvet frock coat and a long cloak made of Royal Stewart or some other appropriate tartan, lined with scarlet or blue coating. Such cloaks had soft Genoa velvet collars fastened across by mosaic-ornamented gold clasps and chains.

Once this elaborate costuming was accomplished, everyone could relax and nibble on bread and prunes. Then the visitors were presented with gifts, usually including a two-gallon barrel of liquor and a fathom or two of tobacco, which came in long, twine-like rolls.* Having accepted these and other offerings, they marched back to their camp in predetermined formation. The parade was led by an HBC servant carrying the Ensign, while another beat time on a snare drum; Company men followed bearing the gifts, and behind them came the Chief Factor and the Trading Captain, conversing as they walked— men of the world exchanging prospects and pleasantries under the noonday sun. Then followed the Indian lieutenants and sundry camp followers. Once back inside their compound of tepees, the Indians turned the long night into a gaudy extravaganza of singing, dancing and arm-wrestling—the jubilant

---

* Although tobacco had been cultivated by North American Indians since prehistoric times, they much preferred the white man's milder mixture and soon stopped growing their own. Only the Blackfoot people continued to raise small plots of ceremonial tobacco until 1940. The Company at first imported Bermuda tobacco but in 1684 switched to a substance known as Brazil tobacco, which actually came from Trinidad and from the valleys of the Amazon. The use of tobacco had highly symbolic overtones. If passed from band to band without being smoked, it could be the sign for war.

release of pressures from the winter in the bush. The bonfires were reflected in increasingly glassy stares as the liquor took hold and the fights started in earnest, old scores being settled and new ones started, with many a bitten-off nose or ear to show for it.

Under the sober morning sun, the ceremonies resumed with yet another round of peace-pipe, bread and prunes. Then the Trading Captain would proudly launch his oration:

> You told me last year to bring many Indians to trade, which I promised to do; you see I have not lied; here are a great many young men come with me; use them kindly, I say; let them trade good goods, I say! We lived hard last winter and hungry, the powder being short measure and bad—being short measure and bad, I say! Tell your servants to fill the measure, and not to put their thumbs within the brim; take pity on us, take pity on us, I say! We paddle a long way to see you; we love the English. Let us trade good black tobacco, moist and hard twisted; let us see it before it is opened. Take pity on us; take pity on us, I say! The guns are bad, let us trade light guns, small in the hand, and well shaped, with locks that will not freeze in the winter, and red gun cases. Let the young men have more than measure of tobacco; cheap kettles, thick and high. Give us good measure of cloth; let us see the old measure; do you mind me? The young men love you, by coming so far to see you; take pity, take pity, I say; and give them good goods; they like to dress and be fine. Do you understand me?

The Chief Factor would respond by proclaiming the deep affection of the great men of England for the Indians, detailing the trouble and danger with which they had sent the big ship yearly full of goods to supply their wants. He exhorted the Indians not to be lazy but to trap more beaver, haranguing them about the smallness of the measures offered by the traders from Montreal, emphasizing the largess of the Company's larder. As he talked, the assembly approached the post's trading window, a hole in the wall of the storehouse that served the very important psychological purpose of separating the two parties in the transaction. Only the Trading Captain was allowed inside, so that he could inspect the procedure and assess the measure as each member of his canoe flotilla presented his furs and was given the requested goods in return.

Hatchets and ice chisels (for trapping beaver), knives, files, flints, kettles, cloth, beads and tobacco were the standard items, with each Indian trading the equivalent of about a hundred made-beaver a season. They were little inclined to hoard or "put away for a rainy day," so that as the resident HBC factors accurately observed, giving the visitors more goods in exchange for their furs would only have resulted in fewer furs being brought in. This was no impulse buying: the choosing of barter items could take up to five days. It was an awkward, slow and suspicion-laden process, especially when compared with the haphazard free-for-all bush exchanges of the *voyageurs* from Quebec, who often used liquor at the time of the actual barters (instead of before) to mellow their customers.

In the last two decades of the eighteenth century, a new trade item rapidly gained popularity. This was the famous Hudson's Bay "point" blanket, so named because its size and trading value was marked right in the weave with small black stripes—three points, or stripes, equalling three made-beaver, and so on. Manufactured by Thomas Empson of Witney, in Oxfordshire, of quality wool pounded with wooden mallets to prevent shrinking, the blankets made valuable winter clothing. They were often cut into leggings and hooded coats, their snowy colour enabling hunters to stalk their winter prey without being seen. (The colourful stripes were added later.)

The most sought-after item in the white man's inventory was the gun, but the easy assumption that it quickly replaced the bow and arrow ignores the many disadvantages of the flintlock muskets traded by the HBC for most of the first two centuries. The awkward muzzle-loader required more than a dozen motions to prime and fire. Its barrel would occasionally blow up, killing or maiming the owner; wet powder or a misplaced gunflint would render the weapon useless; unlike individually marked arrows, musket-balls did not identify the owners of felled game; and, worst of all, the noise of one shot might scare away nearby animals.* For these and other reasons, the gun did not become a prime hunting weapon among the Indians until the introduction of the repeating rifle in the 1860s. Instead, its earliest importance was as a symbol of authority and as an instrument of war. Braves on the warpath improved their aim by holding their fire until they quite literally saw the whites of their

---

* The early guns were so ponderous to use that a German writer in 1640 boasted that his prince's musketeers, in a battle lasting six hours, had fired their pieces five times. The accuracy of the weapon was so poor that according to one contemporary estimate a soldier was obliged to fire away his own weight in lead for every enemy killed.

enemies' eyes and learned to reload faster by carrying extra balls in their mouths and spitting them down the gun barrels. The weapons were lovingly protected with coatings of wolf grease and became objects of such reverence that they were thought to have extrasensory qualities. Guns were shot into the air to drive off thunder and lightning; a meeting attended by warriors with empty guns was a sure sign of trust and friendship. The gun became "the great persuader," used by the Cree to raid south and west over the Prairies, down the Mackenzie to its delta and up the Peace River into the Rocky Mountains. The Chipewyan used the weapons to oppress the Athapaskan tribes, the Dogrib, the Slavey and the Yellowknives.

The most persistent legend about the gun trade—which every Indian swears is true and every HBC man swears is not—claims that the early flintlocks were bartered for a pile of pelts equal to the length of the barrel. According to the elaboration of this tale, the Company kept introducing longer and longer gun barrels to take in more furs. The length of the barrel was indeed increased from the original thirty-seven inches to forty-four inches and later to sixty-six inches, but the reason stated was that the length gave the slow-burning powder more time to ignite, raising muzzle velocity. (Indian hunters sometimes sawed off the gun barrels because the long weapons were hard to handle in the bush.) The very idea of trading guns for piles of furs, thus bypassing carefully preset measures of trade, is dismissed by students of the HBC as "unhistorical rubbish" and the physical dimensions of such an exchange would seem to support their scepticism. To make up the five-and-a-half-foot pile of furs reaching to the top of the longest gun barrel would have required at least four hundred beaver skins. No Trading Captain was uninformed enough to agree to such an exchange when the going rate was the equivalent of about a dozen made-beaver per gun.*

Another contentious fur trade issue was the way the Company covered its overhead, the fluctuating cost of maintaining its ships and forts plus the

---

* The only modern HBC man to experiment with duplicating the exchange, to quash the myth once and for all, was Hugh Ross, post manager at Temagami in Northern Ontario. It took 170 skins to reach the muzzle of a sixty-dollar rifle, "and at that point the damn things kept slipping all over the place, so I couldn't make a pile more than halfway up the gun," he reported. Yet, as late as 1976, at the hearings of the Mackenzie Valley Pipeline Inquiry, Henry Simba, a resident of Kakisa Lake, testified: "You bought a gun with skins, piled to the height of the gun, even before you received it . . . I saw two people buy guns like that, trapping all winter long. They just piled all their cache for the whole winter and got the gun."

expenses of the gifts and other facilities granted visiting Indians. Because both sides in the exchange had agreed not to vary the accepted standards, the HBC traders introduced a concept called "overplus" to take up the fiscal slack. "The official standard did remain unchanged for long periods," according to Professor Glyndwr Williams, "but there was another, local, more flexible standard of trade, and it was the difference between the two standards which was the overplus."

Arthur Ray, who has made the most complete study of the Company's trading records, has estimated that between 1725 and 1735 traders at York Factory advanced their standards 50 percent above the official rates. Between 1735 and 1755, when the French expanded into the York Factory hinterland, the markup level at the post declined to 33 percent. Following the French withdrawal, an advance of 50 percent was again exacted until the Nor'Westers ended the company's monopoly in the 1780s. At the same time, the HBC traders were often guilty of placing a heavy thumb on the scales when weighing gunpowder or shot, cutting shorter lengths of tobacco and deliberately mismeasuring bolts of broadcloth and duffle material—and later, diluting brandy with water. Why the Indians complained only mildly about these departures from the accepted trading standards remains a mystery.

On the other side of the ledger from the questionable practice of charging overplus, the Company gave its preferred customers considerable credit and looked after their subsistence needs during periods of hardship and starvation. In 1748, for example, a hundred Cree were fed through a long harsh winter at Fort Albany and nearly as many again at Moose Factory. Hunters who had suffered a poor season were often advanced equipment and supplies until they could resume their trapping. This private form of social welfare was certainly helpful, but it also placed the Indians under severe restraint and obligation. Yet that obligation was mutual. The debt load did give them a certain measure of power over the traders: the hunter who starved to death was the worst credit risk—so the HBC became committed to his welfare.

The gist of the credit relationship was plainly articulated more than two and a half centuries later, after the pattern had been well established. One HBC district manager, James Ray, defended his doling out of several tens of thousands of dollars in credit, advances and outright gifts by noting: "The natives are our asset ... we must keep them alive for future profits, even though we carry them at a loss till such time shall come."

Mutual exploitation was paralleled by mutual dependence. As the trade developed, the Indians lost their self-sufficiency, involuntarily revolutionizing their way of life so that trade goods became necessities instead of novelties. At the same time, the traders began to realize just how indebted they had become to their customers. Merchant adventurers they might be, but they were heavily outnumbered and totally dependent for their survival on maintaining the good will of their Indian hosts.

Surveying the end-effects of the fur trade, University of Toronto political economist Mel Watkins observed: "If you look at the range of contacts between white and native peoples, the least of the evils was the fur trade. Compared to any other contacts, it was relatively benign. Of course, who came out of it better is unambiguous—the HBC moved on to other things, while the Indian was reduced to a lumpen condition."

Only one voice among the loyal Company men of the early fur trade was raised to suggest that Indian contact with the HBC had been a mixed blessing. Samuel Hearne, the HBC explorer and blithe spirit who survived the Barrens in the late eighteenth century, wrote in his diary of that time on the bay: "I must confess that such conduct [encouragement of the fur trade] is by no means for the real benefit of the poor Indians—it being well known that those who have the least intercourse with the Factories are by far the happiest."

THE MOST CONTROVERSIAL aspect of the Indian–white relationship had little to do with business, yet it touched the most sensitive nerve of the isolated society that grew up around the fur trade. Because liaisons between Indian women and HBC traders were officially considered a menace to the security of the Company forts, London perfunctorily decreed they never should and never would take place. The men of the HBC may have been loyal but they were not monastic, and no head office directive was more widely or happily ignored.

Quite apart from the sensual pleasures involved, HBC men who dallied with daughters of prominent Indian families gained a concentrated course in wilderness survival. Growing up in the relatively urban environment of the British Isles provided no training in snaring rabbits with willow twigs, readying raw furs for market or chewing tough moosehide into pliable moccasins. More important, these liaisons allowed the traders entry into Indian society; the women acted as interpreters and mentors, true partners in a relationship which, when it worked, went far beyond sexual congress.

On the most elementary level, it provided the HBC men with cheap scalp insurance. Through a simple ceremony *à la façon du pays*—an impromptu marriage without benefit of clergy—they took "country wives," acquiring personal security and the inestimably beneficial support system of the country wife's family. For their part, the women won access to the relative comforts of living year-round at or near the HBC forts; they gained social prominence and, usually, some form of special consideration for their relatives at the Company stores.

The Indian leaders perceived most of these live-in arrangements as advantageous, because their society operated along strong kinship lines and such semi-permanent partnerships extended family allegiances into the white man's valuable networks. This was, of course, not universally true, but it did happen often enough. Trading Captains calling at Company posts sometimes paid local factors the honour of offering their daughters in country marriages to forge blood-brotherhoods. At another level, living within the intimacy of these wilderness pairings was an ideal way to pass the long postings. The most effective traders were often the veterans of such tacit marriages. "About the only way you could learn the grunts and twists that go with most Indian talk is from a sleeping dictionary," inelegantly concluded a free trader named Andrew Garcia, who spent his life on the bush frontier.*

Although the HBC did not officially sanction marriage between its employees and Indian women until well into the nineteenth century, Sir George Simpson, its outspoken Governor, set down the Company's blunt policy when he wrote to the London Committee from Fort Wedderburn in the Mackenzie River District on May 15, 1821: "Connubial alliances are the best security we can have of the good will of the natives. I have therefore recommended the Gentlemen to form connections with the principal Families immediately on their arrival, which is no difficult matter, as the offer of their Wives and Daughters is the first token of their friendship and hospitality."

---

* According to Walter O'Meara's *Daughters of the Country*, two of Garcia's buddies settled in very direct fashion a feud over an Indian girl they both loved. The partners, known only as Fink and Carpenter, had been in the habit of demonstrating their trust in each other by filling a cup full of whisky and taking turns shooting it off each other's heads. To settle the love match, therefore, they decided to prove their good will by repeating their familiar performance. Fink won the coin toss for the first shot. "Hold your noodle steady, Carpenter," the gunman commanded, "and don't spill the whisky." A trigger squeeze later, Carpenter was stone dead with a bullet hole in his forehead. "Aw, shucks, Carpenter," Fink reproached his late partner, "you spilled the whisky ..."

Individual tribes, bands and families had their own sexual rules and customs, but most girls were fairly uninhibited before their weddings, suffering from few of the premarital constraints that characterized the upright young ladies of eighteenth-century England and Scotland. After marriage, the Indian girls became the "property" of their husbands, who could lend them out, or sell them or beat them if they were found to have played false. The restraints of marriage could be severe, but divorce was often as unceremonious as pushing the rejected wife outdoors and telling her not to come back. Some of the more curious native rites were not shared with the white men, though Alexander Henry the Younger once witnessed a Mandan orgy he described with vicarious gusto: "About midnight we were awakened by some extraordinary noise in the village. On going to the outer porch door I saw about 25 persons of both sexes, entirely naked, going about the village singing and dancing. At times they withdrew in couples, but soon rejoined their companions in the dance and song. During this short separation from the rest they appeared to be very closely engaged, and not withstanding the night was dark I could perceive them occupied in enjoying each other with as little ceremony as if it had been only the common calls of nature."

While Indian women were at the mercy of an *ad hoc* social structure devised primarily to meet the needs and desires of European males, Sylvia Van Kirk, in her important study of women in fur-trade society, *Many Tender Ties*, maintains that they played an active part in the promotion of its material and cultural changes. "Generally, the women agreed to being offered to the white men and should they be refused, they could become very indignant at this insult." In the longer term, suggests Van Kirk, "... the norm for sexual relationships in fur trade society was not casual, promiscuous encounters but the development of marital unions which gave rise to distinct family units ... The marriage of a fur trader and an Indian woman was not just a 'private' affair; the bond thus created helped to advance trade relations with a new tribe, placing the Indian wife in the role of cultural liaison between the traders and her kin. In Indian societies, the division of labour was such that the women had an essential economic role to play. This role, although somewhat modified, was carried over into the fur trade where the work of native women constituted an important contribution to the functioning of the trade."

The relationship, once again, was a case of mutual exploitation but the odds were uneven. Their terms of service ended, most HBC men would vanish on the September supply ships, leaving their country wives no choice but to rejoin their tribes in a state of widowhood and await another husband. This traders' habit of what was called "turning off"—discarding their mates to suit their transient needs—was the worst aspect of the interchange. One Hudson Bay country wife named Mademoiselle Censols was reputed to have gone through eight "husbands." There were many long and happy unions, but George Nelson, a contemporary observer, quoted the bitter lament of an Indian who hoped to pass off his second wife to a white man because he considered her to have been debauched by past associations with them: "They take women, not for wives—but use them as Sluts—to satisfy the animal lust, and when they are satiated, they cast them off, and another one takes her for the same purpose—and by and by casts her off again, and so she will go on until she becomes an old woman, soiled by everyone who chuses to use her. She is foolish—she has no understanding, no sense, no shame."

Country marriages were the preferred life-style, but prostitution also flourished around the bay, as did various forms of venereal disease. The Chipewyan were known to take their women hundreds of miles to indenture their bodies to the traders' demands. Ferdinand Jacobs, when he took over from James Isham at York Factory in 1761, complained that "the worst Brothel House in London is not so common a stew as the mens house in this Factory." Alexander Henry the Younger, who found more than one Indian chief's daughter in his bed, documented one of the many swaps of women for horses: "On the 12th, one of my men gave a mare that cost him ... currency equal to £16 13s. 4d. for one single touch at a Slave [Slavey tribe] girl."

A limited slave trade in Indian women did take place, mostly in the form of white men buying female war captives from friendly tribes. Henry's journal records instances of Indians "who have disposed of their women to HBCO.'s people in barter for bear meat," and he cites the case of a spirited young mare being traded for "a young wife about eight years of age." (The highest bids seem to have been for sterile women who did not burden their mates with unwanted children.) Describing the pattern during the early operations of the Hudson's Bay Company, when the traffic in women was lucrative enough to attract tribes from the distant western plains, American historian Walter O'Meara wrote that "female captives taken in slave raids by the Blackfoot were sold to the Cree or Assiniboine, who in turn disposed of them on the Bay. During the long journey from the Saskatchewan River to York Fort, the women were passed around the camp at night. On arrival at York they were traded, along with beaver pelts and buffalo robes, to the factors of 'the

Honourable Company.' Those for whom there was no sale were said to have been destroyed."

The Hudson's Bay Company journals and archives are silent on these sexual transactions. Officially, there was no intercourse between Company men and Indian women.

Liberated from Presbyterian mothers who would not allow them even to play cards on Sundays and stern fathers who equated sensuality with sinfulness, the young HBC clerks suddenly found themselves surrounded by attractive tawny-skinned women willing and proud to express their uninhibited sexuality. Love-making on the frontier did not carry much emotional baggage, being routinely offered and casually accepted. The lure of these "bits of brown" or "smoked bacon"—as the women were then crudely called—demurely asking some lonely fur trader to dry his breeches in front of their tepee fire must have been difficult to resist. The women were there, every day and every night, within sight and sound of the forts, an overpowering presence, causing yearnings that erupted into mad dark evenings of ecstasy and pain. By guttering candlelight in a trader's wood-gathering camp and by firelight among the country family members, the rough or sweet enchantments of intimate moments became a phenomenon that pervaded HBC life through the centuries.

MORE CREDIT for the relatively benign treatment meted out to the Indian peoples by the Company must go to the HBC men on the spot than to their English overlords. Again and again, local factors urged London to adopt more enlightened policies. The most eloquent appeal came from William Auld, an Edinburgh surgeon who had become Chief Factor at Churchill. He wrote to the London Committee: "Your servants of every rank, your Chief Factors and Traders alike with myself are utterly disqualified for wringing from the bloody sweat of these poor creatures any more advantages worth a moment's consideration and we recoil with horror at the thought of these *advantages* being rejected at the judgement seat of Heaven where your Honours as well as ourselves must deliver in the accounts of our government. There, distinctions of colour cease and it will avail but little if we transgress the rights of our coppered Indians to satiate rapacious Tradesmen of a fairer hue...."

IV MARCH
OF EMPIRE

ELEVEN

Pathfinders

The HBC traders felt uneasy away from the tang of salt water, suspecting they might starve once removed from the protection of their forts—fears that were compounded by tall tales of upcountry famine and cannibalism earnestly recounted by visiting Cree.

AND SO THE COMPANY MEN perched on the desolate perimeter of Hudson Bay, sitting out the first half of the eighteenth century. The slowly revolving cycle of the fur trade—the spring and autumn goose hunts, winter ptarmigan and rabbit shoots, freeze-up and breakup, the summer curse of the mosquitoes, the annual arrival and departure of the supply ships—these and other minor interruptions only rarely disturbed what was otherwise a dreary survival mode, fostering from one generation to the next not only a fixed sense of place but a rigid state of mind.

It was a mood of inertia so pervasive that the HBC residents found themselves in a society under a siege of their own making. The Bay men kept their thoughts focused homeward, as if the unexplored regions behind and beyond the bay were occupied by the land-equivalents of the allegorical creatures in the "Here Be Dragons" admonitions of early sea charts. A 1782 map of North America, published in London by Thomas Conder, depicted all the land west of Hudson Bay as a blank, with the notation: "These parts intirely unknown."

To remain rooted in their primitive sanctuaries, where they could preserve the tenuous umbilical link to their mother civilization, was an obsession. Almost without exception, the few hardy souls who made flash trips inland instinctively rushed back home with the determination of spawned-out Atlantic salmon spurting down to the sea.

Then, as the vigorous entrepreneur-traders from Montreal began to divert fur and intercept Indians bound for the HBC posts, the Company men realized they had to venture inland for sheer commercial survival. They began to range into the mysterious hinterland, coming to terms with its gargantuan dimensions and settling posts at its river junctures. They started to penetrate the straggling black spruce curtain of the Canadian Shield, becoming adept woodsmen and swift canoe travellers, gradually mastering their new environment.

This was no sudden metamorphosis. During the seven decades between the signings of the Treaty of Utrecht in 1713 and the Peace of Paris in 1783, the fur trade and the Hudson's Bay Company itself were transformed. For the first time since its founding, the HBC began to take full measure of the empire granted by Charles II's casual charter. Such a dramatically expanded landscape called not just for new skills and fresh assumptions but for a different breed of men.

When the HBC first ventured overseas, the North American continent was still presumed to be bisected by the mythical Strait of Anian, connecting the Pacific with a western outlet of Hudson Bay somewhere near Roes Welcome. The main reason for this speculation was that Luke Foxe, the British navigator, had reported upon returning from Hudson Bay in 1632 that the wide range of local tides pointed to the existence of an ocean passage nearby. Cartographers from Juan de la Cosa, in 1500, to Jonathan Carver, in 1778, depicted Anian on their maps. Navigators vainly sought to find and control the secret passage to break the Spanish hold on Pacific-Orient trade.

Apart from a dash to the mouth of the Churchill River from York Factory by two HBC captains, John Abraham and Michael Grimington, in 1686,* only the journey of the boy explorer Henry Kelsey four years later into buffalo country disrupted the bay-bound isolation. The HBC traders felt uneasy away from the tang of salt water, suspecting they might starve once removed from the protection of their forts—fears that were compounded by tall tales of upcountry famine and cannibalism earnestly recounted by visiting Cree. (The Indians were understandably loath to have their delicate trading relationships with farther-flung tribes thrown out of balance by foreign penetration.) As late as 1749, James Isham, the Governor of York Factory and a seventeen-year Company veteran, testified before a British parliamentary committee that

---

* The following year, Abraham left the employ of the HBC and, along with another ex-captain named John Outlaw, attempted to claim the river for private trade. They were caught in the ice of Hudson Strait, rescued by a Company supply ship, taken to York Factory and summarily returned to England.

inland posts were not practicable because the rivers were too full of shoals for trans-shipping supplies, no corn could be grown to maintain permanent settlements—and even if these difficulties were overcome, nothing would be accomplished beyond diverting the fur trade away from existing HBC posts.

The Company's Committeemen were all too ready to be convinced. They were caught up in the belief that the fur trade could remain profitable only so long as the wilderness south and west of Hudson Bay was kept inviolate. Any disruptions—particularly the influx of large-scale trade through a North West Passage—would menace their monopoly. The London governors treated reports and rumours of goods-laden French free-traders moving westward from Montreal as a harmless and temporary aberration, certain that the fiscal instability of these freelance operations would inevitably cause their collapse. They took great pains to perpetuate the isolation of their posts; in 1725, for example, when a trader named John Butler wanted to send his son "up into the Country with the Northern Indians in order to learn the Language," they disapproved the idea: "We do hereby order you not to suffer him or any other Person to be absent from his Duty on such pretence …"

The fact that the Committeemen were proved wrong on every one of their assumptions was due not so much to their lack of foresight as to what Professor Richard Glover described as "the fog of war—the way in which a commander must grope for knowledge of his opponent, fight for the very information without which he cannot fight, and at times put all to the touch without the knowledge that makes the difference between success and failure. Few commanders in the field have been as handicapped by this fog of war as the Hudson's Bay Company in the long struggle for the fur trade with their competitors from Montreal …" One solution might have been to appoint a resident overseas Governor with full executive authority to make decisions according to local conditions. No individual was entrusted with such powers, however, from the tenure of Charles Bayley in the 1670s, and his two immediate successors, to the creation in 1810 of the HBC's Northern Department under its own authority, headed by William Auld.

The Company continued to operate precisely as a landed Scots estate, whereby his lordship entrusted all the details of trade and management to his hard-headed "factor" but kept the profit strictly to himself. It was no internal change of attitude but external pressure that finally lifted this siege mentality. Determined to break the French hold on North America, the English government, encouraged by commercial rivals jealous of the HBC monopoly, pushed the Company into taking up those conditions of its original charter dealing with sea and land exploration. When the HBC's neglect of its obligations was brought up during the 1749 parliamentary hearings, the Company was forced, in self-defence, to remind the MPs of the wanderings of its apprentice Henry Kelsey, more than half a century earlier.

KELSEY IS EITHER BILLED as "The Discoverer of the Canadian Prairies" or dismissed by historians such as Lawrence Burpee, who concluded that his narrative was "too unsubstantial to afford any safe ground for historical conclusions."

Kelsey would later in his career become one of the HBC's senior overseas governors, spending nearly forty years in faithful, prosaic anticlimax to his 1690 mission. He was sent, not on a voyage of exploration, but "to call, encourage and invite the remoter Indians" to bring their furs eastward to the bay. North America's first travelling salesman, he carried a packet of trade samples such as twenty pounds of Brazil tobacco, glass beads, hatchets and kettles. Heading southwest from York Factory, he reached a sheltered bend in the Saskatchewan River below what is now The Pas, Manitoba, and after a successful wintering continued westward into the Assiniboine country, reaching the buffalo-rich Touchwood Hills southeast of present-day Saskatoon. Kelsey was gone for two years, but apart from his attempts to make trade treaties and to mediate between warring tribes, not much evidence of his exploits survives beyond a journal, much of it in amateurish doggerel, written to while away the hours spent hunched in a canoe.

Kelsey did accompany Indians on a bison hunt, was the first Bay man to view the Prairies and arrived back at York Factory at the head of a "good fleet of Indians."

Yet, judging by the lack of follow-up, his journey might never have happened. "What, if anything, the Company made of Kelsey's journey is totally obscure," commented Glyndwr Williams. "It failed to use, publish or even preserve the notes of his findings. No evidence of his wanderings appears on contemporary maps; the episode was an isolated and soon-forgotten feat in an era when Company servants were reluctant to move away from the bayside posts."

A SIGNIFICANT BUT MYSTERIOUS FIGURE in the long roster of errants who risked themselves on the land's illusory mercies, James Knight spent four eventful decades in the Company's service. Originally apprenticed as a ship-wright at Deptford, he joined the HBC in 1676 and was sent to the bay as a staff carpenter. The energetic Knight proved himself so capable that only six years later he was named Chief Factor at Albany. But after his return to England he was accused of private trading in furs and summarily dismissed. His exile proved temporary. During the last quarter of the seventeenth century, when the French held most of Hudson Bay and the Company was organizing an attack flotilla to recapture Albany, Knight (described at that point in the HBC minute book as "… of London, Merchant") was rehired to lead the expedition. He had waited a month before accepting—a deliberate delay that would bring him a £500 bonus if he succeeded*—and sailed off in June 1692 with a four-ship convoy and 213 men, the most formidable expedition the Company ever sent into the bay. Knight's troop quickly recaptured the almost-abandoned Albany; he stayed on as its Governor until 1697, when he returned to England, wealthy enough to acquire £400 in HBC stock.

That purchase, plus Knight's practical experience, was recognized in 1711 when he became one of the very few overseas Bay men to be honoured with a seat on the London Committee.[†] Duly promoted in Company minutes to "… of London, Gentleman," he acted as Sir Bibye Lake's adviser during the Utrecht negotiations and, once the Treaty had been signed, in 1713, was charged with returning to the bay to accept the surrender of York Factory from the French commander Nicolas Jérémie.

Knight was by then well past seventy years old, but his imperious nature had not mellowed. He not only forbade the members of his garrison to drink, use profanity or have contact with the Indian women but actually tried to *enforce* such restrictions. His elaborate plans for reinvigorating the fur trade were set back when Captain Joseph Davis returned to England without unloading his 1715 supply ship, the *Hudson's Bay III*. He had scudded back and forth along the coast for three weeks, trying to find an entrance to the Hayes

---

* The crusty Knight drove a hard bargain. By stalling negotiations, he won the promise not only of the monetary bonus but also of a share in the profits of any new trade in furs, "sea horse teeth" (walrus ivory or narwhal tusks), minerals, oil and bones that his efforts might stimulate, plus a free beaver coverlet for his bed and the right to keep any presents that the vanquished French might choose to give him.

† Only two others shared this distinction during the eighteenth century: John Fullartine (on the Committee 1711–14), who had served twice as Governor of Albany, and George Spurrells (1756–65), who had commanded thirty-five successful supply voyages into Hudson Bay.

River, and at one point his ship had actually been spotted from shore as she was anchored in the mouth of the river. The ship would probably have reached York Factory on the flood tide if her misguided captain had simply allowed her to drift gently towards shore instead of setting sail for his return voyage. Knight was beside himself, furiously scratching in his journal that "none but a Sott or a Madman would have done it!"

With no replenishment of its badly depleted stores, York Factory faced a bleak winter. Fourteen bushels of turnips were forked out of the gardens, and none of the resident sheep or goats survived through to spring breakup. As word spread that the English were back in charge, the up-country Indians returned to trade. Many arrived without their bows and arrows, in the certain expectation they could barter their furs for powder and new guns. When told there were no goods available, they refused to leave. Although worried that their families might starve if they did not return home, they feared the three-month journey even more—they could not face a winter unarmed, either travelling or at the post's gates. By mid-August, there were more than a thousand angry, starving Indians camped along a hundred miles of riverbank up from York. The HBC men dared not venture outdoors to hunt or even to collect firewood, and Knight ordered that no meals be cooked in case the smell of food incited violence. Several Indians prostrated themselves in a death vigil in front of the fort's entrance, and a band that had already massacred several of the garrison's Frenchmen in 1712 was rumoured to be preparing another attack. Knight blustered and bluffed his way through the predicament, promising that new supplies from England were due at any moment—but he was simultaneously rushing to complete a high wooden inner palisade so he would have some semblance of defence if no ship arrived. The structure was finished on August 31, 1716, and three days later a most welcome cannon salute was heard out at sea.

Next morning, the lifting fog revealed an HBC supply ship at anchor near Five Fathom Hole, complete with a new, sharper-eyed captain. The HBC men pretended nonchalance, but the Indians whooped it up, yelling and dancing on the shore long into the night, their animated silhouettes reflected against the bonfires and torches beside the cold black water.

HAVING RESOLVED HIS MOST PRESSING PROBLEM, Knight turned to the more complicated challenge posed by the Montreal free traders. He had been at Utrecht while Sir Bibye Lake lobbied against allowing the French to hunt, or even travel, within the Company's land limits, but now that he was on the spot, Knight realized that the diplomatic punctiliousness that had seemed paramount in Utrecht was hardly applicable here. With a trading post built only seven days' paddling up the Albany River, the French and their Huron and Algonquin allies were hemming in the HBC posts with increasingly effective competition, siphoning off the flow of prime furs to Hudson Bay.

Since Knight had not enough men or arms to force a confrontation with the French, he decided to try outflanking "the woodrunners" by seeking new fur-trading grounds to the north, out of reach of their Montreal-based routes.

West beyond the Churchill River was the land of the Chipewyan. This tribe tended to shy away from contact with the HBC posts because they as yet lacked the firearms with which they were periodically ambushed by the gun-toting Cree. To negotiate peace between the two tribes and to measure the potential fur yield of the Chipewyan territories, Knight dispatched a small peace mission into the wild country northwest of York Factory. The expedition was led by William Stuart, a Company servant only semi-literate in English but fluently articulate in Cree. He left no journals of his year-long absence, but his voyage pushed into brief prominence one of the most remarkable personalities of the early Canadian fur trade: Thanadelthur, the Slave Woman.

There is no description of her appearance, though Chipewyan legend stresses her youth and attractiveness. More to the point, she was self-possessed, shrewd and plucky, one of the very few Indian women to stamp her individuality on native history. Originally a member of a clan of Chipewyan known as the Slaves,* as a teenager she had been captured by the Cree in the spring of 1713, had escaped and eventually stumbled into a goose-hunter's tent at Ten Shilling Creek near York Factory. Knight was impressed with her intelligence, and when she declared herself anxious to help him make peace with her people to provide them access to the Company's valuable trade goods, Knight entrusted her to Stuart as his interpreter. He gave Thanadelthur samples of HBC trade goods and instructed her to tell her people of his promise to build a fort closer to them, at the mouth of the Churchill River, the following summer.

---

* The Slaves occupied the western half of Great Slave Lake's shores and, except for their feud with the Nahanni, had a reputation of being peaceable and inoffensive, protected by their prowess in witchcraft. They caught woodland caribou by running them down on snowshoes or snaring them with the help of dogs in the spring, and fished with lines made of twisted willow bark and hooks fashioned from ptarmigan claws.

The Stuart expedition, which initially included 150 Cree, headed north and probably reached Great Slave Lake. But they were too large a group to be sustained by the land and within a few months they drifted apart, breaking into smaller squads, hunting along the way. The mission's failure seemed certain when the main party came across the bodies of nine Chipewyan massacred by their former companions. Fearing revenge, the remaining Cree wanted to flee, but Thanadelthur assumed command and persuaded them to wait ten days until she went to her people to negotiate a peace. She tracked the Chipewyan to their camp and, as Stuart reported, "made herself hoarse with her perpetual talking." She persuaded her brothers to forget past grievances and make peace with the Cree in order to gain access to the white men's goods. With theatrical precision, she duly reappeared on the tenth day, silhouetted on the horizon backlit by the dawn, with two Chipewyan emissaries by her side. When Stuart welcomed them into his tent, she gave a hand signal and a hundred northern young men materialized out of the morning mist at the edge of the clearing. Thanadelthur mounted a high rock platform and encouraged her brothers to approach more closely. As Chipewyan legend has it, "when she beheld her people coming, she sang with joy."

According to the less lyrical Stuart, she "made them all stand in fear of her as she scolded at some and pushing of others … and forced them to ye peace. Indeed, she was a divellish spirit and I believe if there were but fifty of her Country Men of the same carriage and resolution, they would drive all the [Southern] Indians out of their country …"

Stuart and his new allies marched back into York Factory on May 7, 1716. Thanadelthur spent the summer and fall instructing her fellow Chipewyan how to cure furs for trade purposes, and when one elder suggested that less-than-prime pelts be surreptitiously bartered to the HBC, she "ketcht him by the nose, pushed him backwards and called him a fool." On one occasion her temper flared at her benefactor, James Knight, when he caught her giving away a kettle he had presented to her. She flew into a rage, claiming the kettle had been stolen, and warned the greybeard Governor that if he ever set foot north of the Churchill River, she would order her people to kill him. "She did rise in such a passion as I never did see the like before," Knight marvelled in his journal, adding: "So I cuffed her ears for her." The next morning, Thanadelthur came to him begging forgiveness, slyly assuring Knight that he was like a father to her and diplomatically reiterating that all Indians everywhere would always love him.

Shortly after these diversions and her marriage to a Chipewyan Lothario, Thanadelthur taught herself fluent English and began to spin into Knight's attentive ear alluring tales of rich mineral deposits. Like all Bay men since Prince Rupert, he had long dreamed of such an El Dorado and had even brought with him "Cruseables, melting Potts, borax &c., for the Trial of Minerals" from England to York Factory. Thanadelthur's promise to lead Knight to the mineral showings went unfulfilled because she took ill and died on February 5, 1717.

Disappointed but only temporarily deterred from his great purpose, the doughty old Governor established a permanent post at the mouth of the Churchill River, fulfilling his pledge to the Chipewyan and hoping to tempt them into trade. Churchill was meant to provide a harbour for the Company's whaling fleet and, most important of all, to be the northern jumping-off point for Knight's intended quest for the legendary mines of the Copper Indians. Certainly its blasted environs offered few attractions, prompting Knight to confide to his journal: "York Fort is badd but this is tenn times worse!"

Thanadelthur had described to Knight a broad strait in her country through which great tides ebbed and flowed, suggesting the existence of the ever-elusive North West Passage. But the HBC veteran was much more enthralled by her tales of "Yellow mettle" and "black pitch"—possible references to Klondike gold and the Athabasca tar sands. Her disjointed narrative had been peppered with vague tales of a lost tribe of bearded white giants gathering bags of pure gold and mining mountains of copper somewhere beyond the northern horizon. Joseph Robson reported that the gossip among HBC posts at the time was that "Governor Knight knew the way to the place as well as to his bedside." One group of visiting Chipewyan drew him a rough map of the Copper Indians' country,* sketching a specific route to the Coppermine, four-teen river-crossings to the north and west of Churchill. They assured him that just beyond these copper hills lay the Great Western Sea and that inhabitants there had spotted strange vessels, which Knight took to be Japanese or Tartar ships at the western end of the North West Passage.

Hardly able to contain his excitement, the credulous veteran hurried back to England in the fall of 1718 to obtain the Committee's backing for a major voyage of discovery. While Knight had earned the respect of the HBC's governors and was a particular favourite of Sir Bibye Lake, he was returning to England at an

* The Copper Indians were really the Yellowknives, a tribe with characteristics similar to the Chipewyan; they lived farther north in the vicinity of Great Bear Lake and the Coppermine River.

awkward time. The war-weary nation had enjoyed less than five years' peace since 1688, and trade prospects were only slowly recovering. Yet, reluctantly persuaded by their elder colleague's faith in the existence of distant lucre, the London Committeemen granted Knight their blessing and the funds to outfit two vessels, the hundred-ton frigate *Albany* and the forty-ton sloop *Discovery*, with a twenty-seven-man crew between them, plus two captains and ten "landsmen passengers." Knight was directed to explore the west coast of Hudson Bay north of the sixty-fourth parallel and plant the Company flag on the mineral treasures assumed to exist en route, the search for the Strait of Anian being very much a secondary goal. Knight was granted a one-eighth interest in his own discoveries, given enough brick to build a portable shelter and supplied with great iron-bound chests in which to stow the expected hoards of gold and copper.

The HBC Committeemen's instructions contained a highly unusual codicil: Knight's captains were expressly forbidden to land at any Company post on Hudson Bay or even to trade south of latitude 64° north where commercial contact had already been made. This was presumably put in to avoid exacerbating the quarrel between Knight and his York Factory Deputy and successor, Henry Kelsey, the one-time boy explorer. After arriving in London, Knight lost no time in filing a complaint with the Committee, accusing Kelsey of conniving with the Indians in the theft of Company goods. His charges were not taken very seriously, and Kelsey was confirmed as Governor of York, but there was strong mutual distrust between the two. The younger and intensely ambitious Kelsey thought he had made history with his wilderness trek into the interior but complained he had not been sufficiently recognized by the HBC hierarchy; the old Governor, who had held every honour within the Company's grant, felt on the other hand that he had yet to make any history or earn much of a fortune.

Neither man would attain his goal. Knight was to die in frigid isolation on one of Hudson Bay's bleakest outcroppings; Kelsey would be recalled to England under a cloud of unsubstantiated suspicion and vanish from the Company's books with no official mention of his thirty-eight-year loyal service, of his magnificent journey inland or his important role in reinvigorating the HBC trade after 1714.*

---

* Kelsey's subsequent application for return to Hudson Bay was refused. The only other reference to Henry Kelsey in the HBC archives is a petition of his widow, Elizabeth, pleading for funds "to buy her son, John Kelsey, clothes, she being wholly incapable to do it herself." The Company awarded her six guineas.

More puzzling still was the uncharacteristically desultory way in which the Committeemen dealt with their former colleague's tragic disappearance. Although the outcome of the Knight expedition ranked second only to the Franklin tragedy in the number of men lost, no one seemed particularly concerned about their fate. Without ever resolving the reason for their disappearance, on September 29, 1722, the Company wrote off their two ships and crews in its books as "being castaway to the northward in Hudson Bay ..." Joseph Stephens and Samuel Hearne stumbled on the physical remains of the expedition forty-eight years later, on Marble Island, but that discovery did little to clear up the mystery of Knight's voyage.

ON JUNE 4, 1719, Sir Bibye Lake and his Committeemen rattled down the bumpy road to Gravesend in a convoy of carriages to bid farewell to James Knight and the two HBC ships, manned by their forty treasure-seekers. They tipped the men for drinks, bought fresh vegetables for the officers and wished the proud octogenarian "Godspeed."

On June 19, Henry Kelsey left York Factory to sail north in the hoy *Prosperous*. Accompanied by the Churchill-based *Success*, he set sail to explore the coastline north of Marble Island, which would be Knight's landfall later that summer. The two groups knew nothing of each other's itinerary, though Kelsey was probably prospecting for the same copper mines. His voyage also had a darker purpose: trading two Indian slaves for two Eskimos he hoped to train as interpreters. The Company later claimed before the 1749 British parliamentary committee that Kelsey had been under orders to search for the North West Passage, but according to Professor Glyndwr Williams this was his "least concern." Knight's movements are not known because no record survived his death, some time between the summer of 1719 and the summer of 1721.

The fact that it took the HBC nearly half a century to locate the expedition's remains and document its tragic demise defies explanation. Between 1719 and 1721, Kelsey and his emissaries sailed north three times, but except for the casual complaint of one HBC captain ("Mr. Handcock tells me the Goldfinders winter'd where we had been last Summer and had traded with those Indians and spoiled our trade"), there is no record of any effort to find the missing explorers. In the summer of 1721, Eskimos offered Kelsey objects clearly belonging to the Knight expedition, but instead of waiting out the winds to land at Marble Island, he returned by mid-August. Later evidence indicated that some of Knight's men were still alive at the time.

Radisson (standing) and Groseilliers

Trading Ceremony at York Factory, 1780s

Brigade of Boats: York boats on the Lower Saskatchewan River

Governor George Simpson on a Tour of Inspection

Nineteenth-century portrayal of Henry Hudson cast adrift by his mutinous crew with his son John and a few loyal sailors

Prince Rupert (1619–1682)

*The signing of the Hudson's Bay
Company Charter by Charles II, on
May 2, 1670, in Whitehall Palace*

The battle between the Hampshire and the Pélican, 1697

D'Iberville's bombardment of York Factory in 1697 after the sinking of the Hampshire

PLANS of YORK and PRINCE of WALES's FORTS

A . Magazine .
B . Store House .
C . Dwelling House .
D . Offices .
E . What is built of Stone Tarras .
F . Governors Cook: Room .
G . 1 Raveline to defend the Gate .

Fig.II.

PRINCE of WALES's FORT.

South Bastion

G

K

V V V

L

A

H

C

I

B

The Original Plans Rampart was 42 Feet, but the Gor.' was sure that 25 Feet would do very well. I was order'd therefore to lay the Foundation 23 Feet thick as H.I.K. When the Cannon was try'd they ran of the Wall or L was pulld down & Built up according to the first Plan H.I. and K not done yet.

Scale 114 Feet in one Inch

Fig.I.
YORK FORT.

Hayes's River

The North Channel

Water Mark

Water Mark

High Water Mark

Low Water

South

Battery of 4 Guns

Wood Pile

Battery of 10 Guns

A Run of Water

Scale 118 Feet in one Inch.

A southwest view of Prince of Wales's Fort

Mr. Samuel Hearne, late Chief at Prince of Wales's Fort, Hudson's Bay, 1796

Portaging trade goods on the way to the fur country

Coat of arms of the North West Company

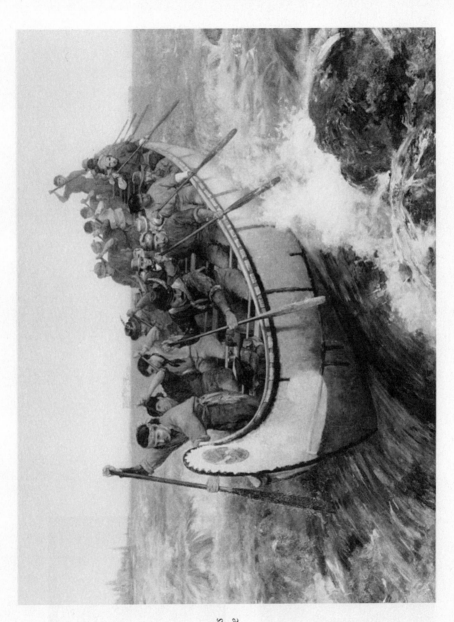

*Shooting the rapids
in a freight canoe*

Simon McTavish

Beaver Club medals

The following summer, Kelsey ordered John Scroggs to cover the same territory for trade leads—but issued no instructions to watch for survivors. Scroggs
was an indifferent navigator and, after fumbling about at the entrance to
Chesterfield Inlet, sailed south and set a boat ashore on Marble Island at a spot
where the spar from a ship's foremast had been found floating on his outward
voyage. His shore party retrieved from local Eskimos parts of a cabin lining, a
medicine chest and ice-poles, all belongings of Knight's crews. Without trying
further to find the ships or any survivors, Scroggs hurried back to Churchill
and reported that all of Knight's men had been massacred by the "Eskemoes,
which I am heartily sorry for their hard fortune."

In the packet of instructions from London to York Factory that arrived in
the summer of 1721, Kelsey was told by the Committeemen not to winter
north of Churchill ("at the hazard of your life") but there was no mention of
Knight, despite the fact that by then he and his men had spent two whole
years in the same locale. The following summer the sloop *Whalebone* sailed
north to trade with the Eskimos, still lacking instructions to seek Knight.
According to the authoritative compilation in Alan Cooke's and Clive
Holland's *Exploration of Northern Canada*, between 1720 and 1764 twenty-
three HBC vessels as well as six discovery ships from England operated in northwestern Hudson Bay—and at least eight of their crews went ashore at Marble
Island. While collecting driftwood, seamen sent ashore from the *California*, on
August 13, 1747, even found "a piece of oak about two feet in length with such
trunnel holes as are made in ship's sides," and the vessel's log noted that the
object in all probability had come from one of Knight's ships.

The HBC trading sloop *Churchill* logged landings on Marble Island twice in
the 1750s *after* the *California*'s discovery, but no attempt was made to confirm
the Knight find. As W. Gillies Ross and William Barr, two Canadian geographers who studied Knight's disappearance, have pointed out: "The total length
of coastline on Marble Island is approximately thirty-two miles. Two groups of
men walking in opposite directions around the shore could have circled the
island easily in a day … Assuming that the men were honest, sober, of normal
vision, and unhindered by fog, it seems inconceivable that they could have
missed the Knight relics, which were numerous, large and prominent." It was
not until July 20, 1767—forty-eight years after Knight vanished—that some
HBC sailors off the *Success* spotted the expedition's remains, including "eight
chaldrons (288 bushels) of good burning coal" and three large anchors. Two
weeks later, Samuel Hearne, then mate of the *Churchill*, arrived on Marble

Island and found the ruins of a stone house, an anvil and some muskets. These items were sent to London without a hint that they might have belonged to Knight. Two years later Hearne returned to Marble Island, located the wreckage of the *Albany* and *Discovery* five fathoms deep in a cove on Marble's stony southeast shore and, by interrogating local Eskimos, finally reconstructed the expedition's last days.

The natives confirmed to Hearne that Knight had been driven ashore by a storm and had built a house. By the second winter illness had reduced the survivors to only five men. The last two had expired in abject misery: "Many days after the rest, [they] frequently went to the tip of an adjacent rock, and earnestly looked to the South and East, as if in expectation of some vessels coming to their relief. After continuing there a considerable time together, and nothing appearing, they sat down close together and wept bitterly. At length, one of the two died, and the other's strength was so far exhausted that he fell down and died also, in attempting to dig a grave for his companion."*

This may indeed have been the tragic finale of the Knight expedition, but the sequence of events leading up to such a miserable ending makes little sense. Marble Island is within easy sight of the mainland. Rankin Inlet is less than ten miles away.† Knight's men were reported by their Eskimo observers to be at work lengthening one of their longboats in their first season on Marble Island. Why would they sit out two summers in ever-declining numbers within sight of shore? They were about four days' sail from Churchill, the post that Knight himself had founded. Scroggs's report that they were murdered by the Eskimos hardly seems credible—the bodies were eventually found scrupulously buried; logically, a sudden massacre would have left the survivors too demoralized for large-scale interment duties. Besides, it is unlikely that the Eskimos were devious enough to invent a sympathetic chronicle of the expedition's decline if they had been the murderers. It seems equally baffling that Knight, whose compulsion to record the minutiae of all his activities fills many a journal now in the HBC archives, would not have left a record of his experiences or tried to send a written message out with the Eskimos who occasionally supplied the dying men with whale blubber and

* Glover makes a strong case that the sad duo saw the sails of Henry Kelsey's hoy *Prosperous* and were forced to watch her bear away and disappear over the horizon.
† The gap is so easily traversed that during the 1760s whalers would call at Marble Island and set fires to attract Eskimos in kayaks from the mainland to trade venison for European artifacts.

seal flesh. One explanation might be Knight's inherent fear of the Ice People, which he described in his journal at the time he was building the post at Churchill: "Them natives to the Norward are more savage and brutelike than these and will drink blood and eat raw flesh and fish and loves it as well as some does Strong Drink." That fright was physically expressed in the way Knight planned his Marble Island survival house—a brick bunker designed for defence and positioned so that it would be difficult to approach it undetected across a nearly featureless terrain.

Reconstructing the fate of the Knight expedition, it is impossible not to conclude that the HBC really did not want the old explorer to succeed. A note in a pamphlet published in 1743 by Captain Christopher Middleton, the veteran Hudson Bay skipper, maintained that "the Company were against him [Knight] going, but he was *opiniatre*, they durst not disoblige him, lest he should apply elsewhere." In his book about the HBC, Joseph Robson noted that when word of Knight's disappearance reached England, "some of the Company Committeemen said upon this occasion that they did not value the loss of the ship and the sloop as long as they were rid of those troublesome men."

Knight's disappearance endures as one of the Arctic's mysteries and an unexplained exception in the HBC's usually precise dealings with its senior Factors.

Marble Island remains a haunted place. It was used as a Company whaling post until 1772, but nine voyages in more than eight years yielded only five whales. Fourteen more seamen perished when two American whalers (the *Orray Taft* and the *Ansel Gibbs*) were wrecked off its desolate south shore in 1873. The aura of dread abides. Marble Island is seldom visited, but those few modern-day Inuit who go there crawl up its ghostly beaches on knees and elbows, obeying the legend that some terrible event will strike the person who walks ashore. No one knows whether they are assuaging the unquiet spirits of their ancestors or paying tribute to the futile endurance of Knight and his doomed crew.

THE NEXT IMPETUS to Arctic exploration came from an unexpected quarter. Peter the Great, the six-and-a-half-foot tyrant who ruled Russia for thirty-six years, enjoyed the plebeian pastime of quaffing mugs of beer in the taverns of St Petersburg. There, from visiting shipwrights and sailors, he learned about others' efforts to plot a water route across the roof of the world. At the time, he was rebuilding the Russian navy, having launched fifty-two ships-of-the-line as well as hundreds of galleys and other craft so rapidly that he had had to recruit foreign officers to command them. One was a Dane named Vitus Jonassen Bering, a native of the Jutland port of Horsens, who had first gone to sea in the early 1700s aboard the supply ships of the Dutch East India Company. Invited to become a sub-lieutenant in Russia's fledgling fleet, he changed his name to Ivan Ivanovich, fought with distinction in the Baltic, Black and White seas and rose rapidly in rank to Captain (Second Class). Temporarily denied advancement, he resigned to study exploration on an estate at Vyborg, on the Gulf of Finland.

Invited back by Peter the Great in 1724, he became a Captain (First Class) and was ordered to head a secret expedition into terra incognita eastward beyond the Asian continent. His main assignment was to probe what is now the Alaskan coast to see if he could pinpoint the western outlet of the so-called Strait of Anian. Bering's four-year trudge from St Petersburg six thousand miles eastward to the harsh Kamchatka Peninsula was a logistical nightmare, eventually involving one hundred men, two dozen boats and a thousand horses. The expedition set sail in July 1728. Bering reached latitude 67° north and discovered St Lawrence Island, now a part of Alaska, and the Diomede Islands, but missed the mainland of America by a few miles. On his return to St Petersburg in 1730 he wrote a report of which a copy fell into the hands of a French geographer, Jean-Baptiste Du Halde. Bering believed that he had found a new ocean route from the Baltic to Japan and, blaming himself for having been overly cautious in turning back so soon, recommended to the Russian Admiralty that he be sent out again to explore the new-found coast to establish the separation of the continents. It took three years to draw up orders, and when Bering got them they included detailed instructions to Christianize the natives of Siberia, build a chain of lighthouses on Russia's Pacific coast and establish a postal system as he went along in order to mail reports of his expedition back to St Petersburg. It was the most ambitious, most expensive and most foolhardy Arctic foray ever mounted. As time went on and as more and more bureaucrats and specialists added their pennyworth to the planning, the logistics became a nightmare. An odd assortment of expectations and abilities, this Bering party eventually numbered nearly three thousand men. It included two landscape painters, three bakers, seven priests, a dozen doctors, fourteen bodyguards, four thousand horses, an awkward convoy of fifteen-foot telescopes mounted on wheels, plus a library of several hundred volumes.

The motley caravan took half a wretched decade to cross the northern steppes and tundra, their horses gradually becoming supper instead of motive power. Thousands of Siberian exiles were conscripted to drag barge-loads of useless supplies against the angry currents of ice-cold tributary rivers. Bering eventually reached salt water and set sail from Petropavlosk in June 1741. By now Bering was a harried and exhausted man of sixty. He was captain of the *St Peter*, with Aleksei Chirikov commanding the companion vessel, the *St Paul*. The ships soon became separated, never to meet again. Chirikov reached the American shore by July. Anchoring near Sitka, he sent out two boats to find safe harbour. The boats were seized and their crews massacred by the natives. He then cruised aimlessly along the shores for about a month and turned for home. On July 16 Bering had sighted the North American coast near Kayak Island on the Gulf of Alaska. Only a few weeks later, with his crew weakened by scurvy and exhaustion, Bering's voyage of discovery ended ignominiously when the *St Peter* went aground on an isolated rocky promontory of Bering Island. It provided so little building material that shallow pits had to be dug into the sand as temporary shelters. By the end of November, the survivors found their will to endure at such a low ebb that Arctic foxes began swarming into their dugouts, gnawing on the dead and attacking the dying. The sand pits had to be reinforced with frozen corpses and carcasses of clubbed foxes. Bering himself died on the morning of December 19, the sand from his shelter trickling into his nostrils, expiring as much from the sorrow of failure as from frost and hunger.

The only positive commercial legacy of this inglorious expedition was that its few bedraggled survivors (who had fashioned a boat from the wreckage, loaded it with furs and eventually reached Petropavlovsk in the summer of 1742) received such good prices for their haul that many of them returned to initiate a lively commerce in blue fox and sea otter. This trade culminated in the establishment of the Russian-American Company, which would eventually give the HBC stiff competition on Canada's West Coast. English captains, sailing to Russia's European ports in the hemp trade, brought word to London about that country's accelerating tempo of northern exploration, and the information prompted the Committeemen to reconsider their own expansion plans on Hudson Bay.

THE CHIEF ELEMENT in the mix of slowly fermenting forces that would eventually drive the Bay men inland was the remarkable advance westward of the

nimble traders from Montreal. While the French and English had been grap-
pling for control of Hudson Bay, the colonists who had settled the shores of
the St Lawrence almost succeeded in encircling Hudson Bay by land. Daniel
Greysolon, Sieur Dulhut, a dashing leader of the early *coureurs de bois*, had
been licensed as early as the 1670s to push past Lake Superior in the search for
lucrative furs and the Great Western Sea. He built a rough-hewn stockade on
the northeast side of Lake Nipigon (to intercept the Assiniboine and Cree
trappers on their way to Albany) and by 1688 had penetrated with his partners as far west as Rainy Lake, only two hundred miles east of where Winnipeg
now stands. The Treaty of Utrecht formally prohibited France from contending ownership of the land around the bay, but the Quebec traders redoubled
their overland efforts. By 1728, the Compagnie du Nord appointed Pierre
Gaultier de Varennes, Sieur de La Vérendrye, commander of *les postes du nord*.
Born in Trois-Rivières, son of the district's governor, he was schooled in
France and had fought in Europe with the armies of France at Malplaquet
against Marlborough (and was left for dead on that blood-soaked ground with
eight sabre cuts in his body). Drawn by the magnet of discovering the alluring
"sea of the west," he sailed back across the Atlantic. During the 1730s and
early 1740s he and his four sons established seven trading forts, planting the
first semi-permanent white settlements in Western Canada. Harassed by his
angry financial backers (who wanted him to make money, not discoveries),
distracted by colonial governors uncertain of their own authority and by his
own irresolution in the face of daunting odds, La Vérendrye was never able to
realize his potential as an explorer but did lay down the matrix of Montreal's
future inland trade across the routes to Hudson Bay. "He was," wrote Lawrence
Burpee in the *Canadian Geographical Journal*, "in a real sense the discoverer of
Western Canada; first to descend the Winnipeg River, first to see Lake
Winnipeg, first to cross the great plains to the Missouri."

The more important immediate effect of La Vérendrye's enterprise was to
slash the HBC's fur harvest drastically. York Factory, for example, which then
accounted for half the Company's take, slipped from shipping 52,000 made-
beaver in 1731 to only 37,000 the following year, as La Vérendrye and his sons
probed as far west as the Black Hills of South Dakota.

The HBC met its burgeoning competition from the Montreal pedlars by
reducing prices on some of its most popular trade goods. This list shows the
difference in prices by made-beaver equivalents:

	Pedlar price	HBC price
Guns	20	14
Ice chisel	4	1
Knife	2	4
Ball	10	1 lb.
Powder	¼ lb.	1 lb.
Cloth1	½ yds. per 10 M-B	1 yd. per 3 M-B
Blanket	10	7
Tobacco	¼ lb.	¾ lb.

The Indians took happy advantage of the escalating rivalry, playing off one set of European traders against the other and becoming participants in the contest themselves, with the Cree and Assiniboine benefiting most as middlemen. The French were willing to trade on the Indians' home ground, eliminating their need to pack, paddle and portage for weeks to Hudson Bay and back. Added to this was the Montreal traders' generosity with French brandy, which was becoming the fur trade's most desirable staple. The English equivalent was much inferior, though in tobacco the advantage was the other way. Company-dispensed Brazil brand was much preferred to the French product, which was said to taste like sawdust.

The French frequently became victims of the tribal feuds they helped generate, while the English concentrated on promoting commerce. On an individual level, the French traders played dangerous games by carrying off young Indian women against their will, forcing them to share their beds, while the English and Scots were usually careful to secure bedmates according to the formalities of Indian society—by purchase or the consent of fathers, husbands and, often, the women themselves. Even if the ravished Indian girls might be pardoned for missing the subtle difference, it was often sufficient to allow HBC traders to pass through Indian territory unmolested, while the *coureurs de bois* were getting into brawls and stumbling into ambushes. For example, in 1758 Fort Bourbon, near the northwest side of Lake Winnipeg, was plundered by the Indians, while Joseph Smith of the HBC, bound for the country of the Assiniboine, sauntered safely by.

In 1743 the Company decided to experiment with the opening of Henley House, its first post away from Hudson Bay, at the junction of the Albany and Kenogami rivers. The tiny settlement was put in place by Orkneyman Joseph Isbister, then Chief Factor at Albany, when he heard that the French had established their own trading post 120 miles upstream from his home fort. London approved his move but insisted that the little outpost's main function should be defensive rather than commercial. The fiercely independent Isbister ran Albany (and Henley, where William Lamb was nominally in charge) like military garrisons, using a cat-o'-nine-tails to impose his edicts against strong drink. He rigidly policed Company regulations against the harbouring of Indian women at HBC posts, but since he allowed one exception (himself), his moral authority was hardly convincing. When William Lamb followed Isbister's sexual example at Henley, Woudbee, the Captain of the Albany Home Guard Indians, was so enraged that in December 1754, accompanied by his sons Snuff-the-Blanket and Sheanapp, he plundered the post and massacred its occupants. The three were apprehended and jailed in separate cells at Albany. Before interrogating the prisoners, Isbister first went outdoors and fired two shots into the sky. Then he told each of the captives that the other two had confessed and been executed and that there was no further point denying the crime. The ensuing confessions were authentic—but so was the provocation. Lamb had appropriated against their will two Indian women for the winter, one of them Woudbee's daughter, the other one of his son's wives. When the Woudbee men arrived at the post, Lamb had haughtily dismissed their protests and refused to welcome them, insisting they camp outside the stockade. The massacre ensued. The three Indians were hanged on June 21, 1755.*

Henley House was not resettled until 1759, when within a few weeks a raiding party once again massacred its master, George Clark, and his assistant. This time the apparent motive was carrying off the trade goods, though HBC men then believed the attack was actually staged by French traders led by Louis Ménard from Nipigon. Henley House was reopened in 1763, following the end of the Seven Years' War. It never became an important post, but the violence of its brief history helped delay the HBC's move inland.

---

* Isbister was reprimanded by London not so much for the executions as for his unwillingness to re-establish the Henley post. He was recalled the following year for his own safety and in 1760 emigrated to Quebec City, where he lived on the rue des Remparts. He died eleven years later of "decay and wore-out lungs."

The Dobbs Intervention

"When the Sky falls,
a great number of Larks may be catched ..."

—Captain John Merry

WHAT FINALLY HELPED turn the tide upriver was a drawn-out campaign against the Hudson's Bay Company staged by a persistent Irishman named Arthur Dobbs. The avowed purpose of Dobbs's intervention was to force the Company into an active search for the North West Passage, but this worthy undertaking was mixed with selfish commercial impulses. Even though the eventual effect of the Dobbs initiative was to force the Company into the outward exploration that helped save its charter, loyal HBCers two centuries later still dismiss him with the vitriol due a brigand.

From two only tenuously connected facts—that the North West Passage had not been found and that the HBC owned most of the land around its eastern egress—Dobbs concluded that either the Company had kept the existence of the waterway secret for its own commercial reasons or that it had not been discovered because the Adventurers were not adventurous enough. He seized on British expansionist sentiments and built his anti-HBC stand into a national crusade of no mean impact. As noted by his biographer, Desmond Clarke, Dobbs "viewed the Hudson's Bay Company, like many others, as a fat, wealthy monopoly sated with profits, and sleeping in inglorious ease while the French increased their power and influence in Northern Canada ... Dobbs was in every sense a carrier and exponent of the imperial energies that intended to make the Pacific a British instead of a Spanish lake."

Most historians stress the romantic aspect of Dobbs—a visionary trying to resurrect the tradition of the Elizabethan buccaneers who blended religion, patriotism and profit into a pageant of exploration—or they picture him as a busybody, a schemer dedicated to transferring the HBC monopoly to his own control. Whatever his motive, Dobbs's campaign was based on what at the time appeared to be scientific observations. The basis for his conviction that the North West Passage did indeed exist was his study of the height and direction of the flood-tides on Hudson Bay's western shores. Geographers of the time thought that those tides, if they were indeed flowing directly from the Pacific, would understandably be at much higher levels than if they were merely the distant eddy from an Atlantic surge, their source a thousand miles to the east. When the British navigator Luke Foxe had been bumbling around Hudson Bay in the summer of 1631, he reported a flood-tide of eighteen feet at latitude 64°10′ north. The leap in logic seemed simple enough: by following that tide to its source, any explorer would inevitably be drawn into the North West Passage. One other observation supported the belief that Hudson Bay was a strait instead of an inlet: black whales were often seen off its western shores but had never been sighted passing into the bay from the North Atlantic.

Enticing as Dobbs's various arguments may have sounded, they were derived from a selective reading of sometimes questionable sources. The high tide in Roes Welcome, for example, is caused by water rushing past White Island, tunnelled through Frozen and Fisher straits, neither of which had been discovered when Dobbs was formalizing his plans. The whales came not from the Pacific but from Baffin Bay through Hudson Strait during spring breakup. Dobbs drafted an elaborate seventy-page abstract outlining his theories, but he made his real impact through the access he gained to British politicians.

The son of the high sheriff of County Antrim in the north of Ireland, Dobbs multiplied his family wealth by marrying the heiress Anne Osburn and sat in the Irish House of Commons from 1721 to 1730. Tutored in part by a very young Jonathan Swift, then serving as a village parson, Dobbs won appointment to the post of Surveyor-General of Ireland, expanding his interest in science and meteorology. Doggedly ambitious, he became friendly with Lord Conway, a cousin of Sir Robert Walpole, the British prime minister. Seeking to widen his influence, Dobbs crossed in 1730 to London where he was introduced to many of the City's leading functionaries. Bursting with brilliant if sometimes oddball schemes, he wrote essays on free trade and on the

Aurora borealis and penned a plan to attack Quebec that was successfully carried out twenty-five years later. He also began to advocate a resumption of the search for a North West Passage. Colonel Martin Bladen, a Lord Commissioner of the Board of Trade and Plantations, passed him on to Sir Charles Wager, First Lord of the Admiralty, who in turn persuaded Samuel Jones, the HBC's Deputy Governor, to grant him an audience. Jones expressed no interest and refused to let Dobbs examine the Company's charter. (Colonel Bladen later got a copy for him.) Dobbs then tried to persuade the South Sea Company to send whalers from Davis Strait into the bay with instructions to find the Passage, but there were no takers. Dobbs finally confronted Sir Bibye Lake and pointed out that the Charter specifically charged the Company with furthering the search. Lake, whose contempt for meddlers in the HBC's corporate realm was matched only by his passion for silent diplomacy, treated the voluble Irishman as a noisy pest.

Dobbs had meanwhile made contact with Captain Christopher Middleton, one of the HBC's most experienced supply ship veterans, who agreed to share his knowledge of Hudson Bay. The Irishman also enlisted the active support of a few City financiers, who recognized that his efforts might help them make a dent in Lake's cosy fur monopoly. To this mercantilist appeal Dobbs added a dollop of anti-Spanish sentiment as a sop to Britain's more nationalistic politicians and seasoned the brew with pious references to evangelizing "the savages"—not forgetting a nod towards finding new outlets for English woollens.

It is easy to sympathize with Dobbs's frustration. His efforts, if fully exploited, would have benefited no group more than the HBC's shareholders, yet the Company's governors refused to take him seriously. Lake did order Richard Norton at Churchill to have a whaling sloop seek an opening up the bay's west coast near Roes Welcome, but the voyage lasted only six weeks, did not reach within two hundred miles of the Welcome and came back with only three barrels of blubber and twenty pounds of walrus ivory. That this was really a commercial voyage and not a journey of discovery was betrayed by the fact that the sloop-master and crew were signed on for 10 percent of its trade profits. Lake promptly reported the fruitless trip to Dobbs and excused the Company from further exploration ventures.

Realizing that the Company had been trifling with him, Dobbs brought Captain Middleton into the fight and during the next dozen years maintained the most concentrated attack ever mounted on the HBC. It was his linking of the search for a North West Passage with his attack against the HBC monopoly that garnered the support of City barons and Westminster backbenchers. When Dobbs petitioned the Royal Navy to mount a full-scale expedition in search of the Passage, the Admiralty's Sir Charles Wager demurred for financial reasons, though he agreed with Dobbs that "the Hudson's Bay Company do not desire to have any body interfere with them in the fur trade in those parts; they seem to be content with what they have, and make, I believe, considerable profit by it."

Middleton, who became a tragic victim of the Dobbs intervention, had served aboard privateers before joining the HBC as second mate of the *Hannah*, later becoming her captain. His observations of magnetic variations in the bay were published in the *Philosophical Transactions of the Royal Society*, which elected him a member. A thoroughly competent navigator of impeccable integrity, Middleton was caught up voluntarily in Dobbs's manoeuvrings because he believed in the existence of the Passage and felt ideally equipped to find it. His appeals to be appointed the commanding officer of a voyage of discovery into the bay reached the ear of George II, who casually approved the idea. Middleton was allocated a converted bomb-vessel, the *Furnace*, and an ex-collier, the *Discovery*, but had to rely on press gangs to recruit most of his crew. Their participation in the gallant venture was ensured only by posting armed guards at the gangways before the ships' departure. Middleton complained later that "no ship was ever pester'd with such a set of rogues, most of them having deserved hanging before they entered with me." Although this was the first Royal Navy expedition to leave England in search of the North West Passage, it aroused so little interest that the only newspaper report about its departure, in the *Daily Post* of June 3, 1741, managed to scramble the facts by reporting: FURNACE AND DISCOVERY BOUND TO RUSSIA TO FIND OUT A NORTH WEST PASSAGE TO INDIA.

Middleton realized that any worthwhile exploration would require wintering on Hudson Bay, and that meant obtaining the Company's support when his ships put in at Prince of Wales's Fort, the stone fortress near the mouth of the Churchill River on which HBC masons had been labouring for a decade. Pressured by the Royal Navy, the HBC sent a niggardly note to its local Factor advising that Middleton should be sheltered, but only if "by inevitable necessity [he was] brought into real distress and danger of his life or loss of his ship." But when Wager, at the Admiralty, heard about the HBC's attitude, he attacked it for conduct "very unbecoming for a Company which subsists by his Majesty's favour, having only an old charter which no doubt they made several breaches in." Lake relented by amending the instructions to grant Middleton "the best assistance" in the Company's power.

The two ships arrived within hailing distance of Prince of Wales's Fort on August 8, 1741, and Robert Pilgrim, the resident Factor, promptly fired a volley across the ships' bows. The baffled vessel commanders could only respond by raising white surrender flags. This incident—Company cannon firing at Royal Navy ships with impunity—appropriately summed up the intensity of the HBC's proprietary impulse. That impulse would not be diluted during the more than three centuries of the Company's occupation of Hudson Bay.

MIDDLETON NEGOTIATED PERMISSION to house his crew in the remains of the old factory founded by James Knight at Churchill, six miles upstream from Prince of Wales's Fort. Two weeks later, Pilgrim was replaced by James Isham, a talented naturalist who shared Middleton's appetite for scientific investigation. The two reached a sensible compromise: the Royal Navy crew would not trade in furs, and the HBC residents would help provision them through the winter. It was an arrangement that would eventually create problems for both men.

Middleton moved into the relative comfort of the fort to join Isham in taking astral observations. The two groups shared the chilly misery of a Hudson Bay winter in a semblance of camaraderie, fuelled magnificently by the Royal Navy's generous liquor rations. Bountiful quantities of grog were issued to mark every "holiday," many of them self-proclaimed. The Christmas revelries staged by Middleton lasted a full fourteen days, with the men being given "strong beer and brandy every day all the time." The little post had temporarily become a pub. Isham's tailor froze to death in a drunken stupor, and three of his troop had to be arrested for their own protection when in the afterglow of a night's brandy-swilling they grandly declared they were going "to sleep by the river." The ships' surgeons were kept busy amputating frozen toes and fingers, and vainly trying to hold back the scurvy that eventually claimed the lives of eleven sailors.

The two commanders genuinely liked each other, but Isham's patient hospitality was stretched to the limit when Middleton recruited five of his best men into the Navy. They parted gladly on the last day of June 1742, and despite a crew so incapacitated by illness that only five men were fit enough to climb aloft and reef sails, Middleton struck out for the Arctic. He probed and named Wager Inlet and sailed to the sandy terminus of Roes Welcome, being so disappointed it wasn't the Passage that he named it Repulse Bay.

On the way back, the two ships carried out a perfunctory probe of the bay's menacing and shallow western shore; they stayed three leagues out to sea, thus missing the entrance to Chesterfield Inlet. With this one exception, Middleton's charts were later proved to be remarkably accurate. He had sailed farther north in the bay than any white man before him and had brought his ships home safely, even though on the return voyage only two men were well enough to handle the wheel. Yet Middleton was immediately challenged by Dobbs for not pursuing his exploration and accused of having been bribed by the HBC.

Dobbs had changed tack. Instead of concentrating on opening up the Passage, he was now determined to break the HBC's trade Charter so that inland settlements could be put in place before the next phase of exploration began. At the same time, members of Middleton's crew, including his former mate John Rankin, began sabotaging their captain, claiming that he had indeed been paid by the HBC to falsify his report. Middleton's 150-page reply to these and other accusations, filed with the Admiralty, clearly vindicated him, but he was never again given an important command. Only seven years after his historic voyage, Middleton (now forgotten by Dobbs) was retired on a paltry pension of four shillings a day. He died in 1770, according to a report in the 1784 edition of the *Monthly Review*, "in the utmost penury and distress, having long before been drove to the necessity of parting with Sir Godfrey Copley's Gold Medal, which had been presented to him by the Royal Society in 1742, for his account of Hudson Bay. His children, four daughters, brought up in ease and elegance by the product of his labours in the early part of his life, all died before him, some of them, at least, in a more wretched situation than himself ..."

Dobbs's obsession suffered a setback with Walpole's fall from power in 1742, but he was no longer isolated, having consolidated his contacts in the City by becoming an active partner in a scheme to purchase a large tract of North Carolina wilderness. He set about publishing what became his best-known book, which tried to make up for its dubious literary distinction by the length of its title: *An Account of the countries adjoining to Hudson's Bay, containing a description of their lakes and rivers, the nature of the soil and climates, their methods of commerce &c shewing the benefit to be made by settling colonies and opening a trade in these parts; whereby the French will be deprived in a great measure of their traffic in furs, and the communication between Canada and the Mississippi be cut off: with an abstract of Captain Middleton's Journal and observations upon his behaviour during his voyage and since his return, the whole intended to shew the great probability of a North-west Passage, so long desired; and which (if discovered) would be of the highest advantage to these kingdoms.*

The volume was a somewhat disjointed attack on "the darling monopoly" and "avarice" of the HBC, "who, to deter others from trading or making settlements, conceal all the advantage to be made in that country ..." Even if Dobbs used exaggeration as his main literary device, the core of his sermon was perfectly accurate—that if the Company did not drastically alter its tactics, the French would occupy the new continent's central plains. The message struck a sympathetic chord in liberal-minded Englishmen who loathed both monopolies and the French. The first book published about the HBC, it revealed the extravagant terms of the original Charter but grossly overestimated the Company's annual profit at 2,000 percent. Its most valuable historical contribution was the description of the extraordinary exploits of a "French Canadese Indian" named Joseph La France.

The son of a French trader and an Ojibway mother, La France had been a rambunctious renegade existing on the fur trade's illicit fringes. When the authorities in Montreal put a price on his head, La France decided to walk to Hudson Bay and join the English. The journey to York Factory via the Nelson River took him three years, but he emerged from the scrub forests with a crude map and some intriguing observations on the continent's potential wealth. Even if it placed Lake Winnipeg perilously close to California, his was the first map of a water route from Lake Superior to Hudson Bay. La France advised the HBC to move inland and lower its standard of trade, but no one except Dobbs took him seriously.

In the spring of 1745, a £20,000 prize for discovery of the North West Passage was offered by Parliament. News of the reward revived Dobbs's spirits. He organized the North West Committee, which handily raised £7,200 to equip a new expedition into Hudson Bay from City merchants anxious to form their own North American trading company. Its ships, the *Dobbs* and the *California*, were commanded by William Moor and Francis Smith, who shared a common background as mates on HBC supply ships but little else. The two men quarrelled continually, agreeing only to winter at York Factory before launching their explorations. James Isham, who had extended a hand of friendship under similar circumstances to Captain Middleton, had been moved south to York and, having been reprimanded for being too co-operative the first time, resolved not to sweeten his welcome. This created awkwardness because the ships' captains held commissions from the Admiralty empowering them to act as privateers and, as such, they had the right to call for aid from British subjects overseas. Isham was not impressed. He greeted the arrivals at York Factory not only with cannon shot but by removing the buoys leading to the anchorage at Five Fathom Hole so that one of the ships ran aground in the mud.

The crews settled in for the winter at Ten Shilling Creek in log-tents provided by Isham, but the captains continued feuding. They could not even decide how to divide the Indians' partridge hunt between them and asked Isham to adjudicate. Smith and Moor paced their ramshackle abodes dreaming up new quarrels and during one two-month period exchanged not a single word. Deranged by cabin fever, Smith finally abandoned the shelter, abandoned Moor, abandoned his wife, Kitty, and sought asylum at the Factory. When the vessels left the following spring, Isham did not, as was customary at the time, consign the seafarers to the protection of the Almighty.

After a half-hearted exploration of Chesterfield Inlet, the ships' longboats ventured up Wager Inlet, which led them to a dead-end stream at Brown Lake. The *California*'s subsequent return across the Atlantic was so stormy that only Smith was well enough to take the helm and he had to commandeer a Royal Navy crew in the Orkneys to pilot his ship back to the crowded Thames.

Once again, Dobbs applied his self-serving logic to the expedition's inconclusive outcome: the existence of the Passage had not been *disproved*—therefore it must exist. He petitioned the King in Council to grant his North West Committee trading arrangements similar to those of the HBC, in effect demanding precisely the kind of monopoly he had been condemning. At the time, British merchants, especially in the burgeoning ports of Liverpool and Bristol, were engaged in a coordinated attack on the perpetuation of London-based trading monopolies, including the overextended Royal African Company, which collapsed in 1750. Eventually, seventeen petitions questioning the HBC's charter reached Parliament from Britain's leading industrial ports, and a special committee was struck to hear the complaints. Headed by Lord Strange, the group listened to a long litany of criticism inspired by Dobbs and his entourage, including that of Joseph Robson, the unhappy Prince of Wales's Fort stonemason, and John Hayter, a former house carpenter at Albany, who insisted that wheat could be cultivated inland if only the Company had the nerve to move there.

The HBC's Governor, Thomas Knapp, did not deign to appear but sent the special committee a stack of documents, including a suddenly resurrected description of Henry Kelsey's epic journey and the log of every ship that had ever stuck its bow north of Churchill. James Isham, the dependable old trouper, crossed the Atlantic to testify on the Company's behalf, providing a calm rationale for its status-quo policies. Finally, the HBC's solicitor went so far as to pledge a careful move towards cautious expansion.

After hearing twenty-two witnesses, Lord Strange ruled that there was no case for annulling the HBC Charter or interfering with the Company's trade position—in other words, no case for doing anything. The parliamentarians realized that even if Dobbs's mythical passage did exist, it would not be commercially navigable, and that in view of the climate and geography of Hudson Bay, the Company's understandable accent on survival could not be condemned. The verdict seems to have hinged on the dispassionate conviction that since the northern fur trade had to be supported by a chain of permanent forts, only a monopoly or the government itself could finance this far-away commerce. The Royal African Company, whose slavery monopoly was successfully challenged at about the same time, had no permanent posts but did have militantly dissatisfied shareholders. By contrast, the HBC's shareholders throughout the Dobbs intervention met only to praise their Committeemen, boasting that "Mr. Dobbs cannot produce any single Adventurer that makes any complaint." In an aphoristic condemnation of Dobbs's fantasies, Deputy Governor John Merry sarcastically scribbled in the margins of the Irishman's pamphlet advocating the harvesting of huge, imaginary quantities of timber on Hudson Bay: "When the Sky falls, a great number of Larks may be catched ..."

The main effect of the parliamentary inquiry was to expose the Company to unprecedented publicity. Its shareholder lists, business methods, standards of trade, profit margins (30 percent on an annual outlay of £27,000) and anti-exploration policies had become a matter of public debate. This was aggravated by the publication of Robson's critique in 1752, which put forth his famous accusation that the Company was asleep at the edge of a frozen sea. As for the disgruntled Dobbs, he retired to his "rural amusements" in Carrickfergus to study the swarming habits of bees and leave the search for the Passage to "some more happy Adventurer." The pugnacious Irishman was named Governor of North Carolina in 1754 and died there eleven years later, still sighing over the elusive Passage to the South Sea.

Exploration continued in desultory fashion until a century later, when the search for survivors of Franklin's expedition triggered the activity that finally sketched in the awesome dimensions of the continent's northern margin. One explorer, Charles Duncan, felt the disappointment of not finding the Passage so keenly that on the way home to England he was stricken by "brain fever" and made so many attempts to jump overboard that he had to be lashed to his bunk. John Bean, a Company sloop captain accompanied by Moses Norton, spent a harsh season searching for the Passage and bitterly concluded: "This fly-away River resembles old Brazil—not to be seen but by some chimerical persons." Norton, who as Governor at Churchill was to send Samuel Hearne on his overland journey, also sailed 130 miles up Chesterfield Inlet into the dead-end flats of Baker Lake, eliminating that possibility as a western outlet of the Hudson Bay. He realized early on that the only way to fix the position of North America's Arctic coast would be by a land route.

Exhausted by Dobbs's assaults, the Company assured its factors: "We have nothing more at heart than the preservation of our factories, the security of our people and encrease of our trade." At the same time, the parliamentary hearings had convinced the Committeemen that if their territory were not explored, the Company's vaunted charter would prove to be no more than a scrap of old parchment. It could no longer protect them: royally chartered companies had clearly become historical anomalies, and Parliament was already demanding that the Company define precisely the extent of its land claims.

It would be another two decades before the HBC seriously began moving inland with the establishment of a permanent post at Cumberland House, but one immediate effect of the public outcry was that the London Committee authorized a journey into the interior by a volunteer from York Factory to "draw down many of the natives to trade." The long trek, undertaken by a former smuggler and HBC net-mender named Anthony Henday, was to be the first officially sanctioned inland journey since the peace mission of William Stuart and Thanadelthur into the land of the Chipewyan and Henry Kelsey's meandering westward probe and back half a century before.

Although the immediate trigger for Henday's historic run may have been the Dobbs affair, it was also a response—twenty-three years after the fact—to the founding by Pierre Gaultier de Varennes, Sieur de La Vérendrye and his sons of trading posts a thousand miles to the southwest at Fort La Reine on the Assiniboine and at Fort Pasquia near The Pas. Because these "woodrunners" occupied many of the traditional canoe routes along which furs were brought out to Hudson Bay, the Company was anxious to make contacts beyond the range of French penetration, where, as the younger Chevalier de La Vérendrye put it, "the Cree of the Mountains, Prairies and Rivers rendezvous every spring to deliberate as to what they shall do—go and trade with the French or with the English."

Like Kelsey before him (and Hearne after him), Henday travelled as super-cargo with a group of Indians heading to their home country. After four months hunched in a canoe and toiling across the rolling parkland, they reached a patch of bald prairie near the present site of Edmonton. Instead of empty wilderness, he encountered French traders busy loading their canoes. "I don't very well like it," he recorded apprehensively in his journal. "Having nothing to satisfy them on what account I am going up the country and very possably they may expect me to be a spy ..." His competitors left him alone, mainly because he was accompanied by a large troop led by a Cree named Attickasish who, Henday noted, "has the charge of me." His constant companion was a Cree woman who acted as his food gatherer and cook and was officially listed as his interpreter, though Henday referred to her in the version of his journal not sent to London as "my bed-fellow."

On October 1, 1754, seven stern hunters dressed in bison skins and armed with bone-tipped spears rode into Henday's camp, located southeast of the present-day site of Red Deer, Alberta. They were Bloods from the powerful Blackfoot Confederacy that reigned supreme in the Western Prairie and controlled the approaches to the mysterious foothill country. After much preliminary prying, they escorted Henday to their main camp, a wilderness city of more than two hundred painted tepees pitched in two long rows. The encampment was abuzz with excitement as the white man was led to the great meeting hall, a buffalo-hide lodge that could seat fifty elders. Sweetgrass smoke was wafted about and calumets were lit and served in a hush as the rulers of the plains quizzically examined the stranger who had come from the shore of the inland sea. Boiled buffalo meat was served in baskets of woven grass, and the gift of a dozen buffalo tongues, the tastiest of local delicacies, was formally presented to Henday. But when the visitor began to bargain with the Blackfoot chief to send some of his men back with him to York Factory, Henday was rebuffed first by silence and later with the sensible explanation that the Blackfoot would not leave their horses or abandon the buffalo hunt, that they did not know how to use canoes and that they had heard of many

Indians starving on their journeys to Hudson Bay. A chastened Henday, who
was a better bush traveller than negotiator, confided to his journal, "Such
remarks I thought exceeding true." Though the conversations continued over
the next six months, the Blackfoot chief's only concession was to present
Henday with two comely young women.

The Henday expedition, which at times was reduced to only eleven Cree,
including five women and four children, continued moving west, reaching
the site of the present town of Innisfail, Alberta, less than forty miles from the
future location of the famous trading post, Rocky Mountain House. The
geographical co-ordinates of Henday's westernmost location—51°50´N,
114°W—placed him within clear view of the Rocky Mountains, but his
journal is curiously silent on his reaction to such a dramatic sighting. Like
every other explorer of his day, Henday hoped to discover a western ocean, not
a massive rock barrier, and when facing the immensity of the Rocky
Mountains that stretched like a continent unto themselves, he may have
chosen to deny their existence. "The water very salt, smells like Brine," he
scribbled in his journal while tramping through the rolling western parkland.

On the return journey, his accompanying flotilla sometimes swelling to
sixty canoes, Henday realized that the Cree were too established in their role
as fur-trade middlemen to permit interior Indians to undertake the long
Hudson Bay journey themselves. The documentation of that elementary
proposition, which would eventually prompt the HBC to appreciate some of the
complexities of the inter-tribe fur trade, was the most valuable contribution of
Henday's long mission. That and his report about the sophistication of the
French traders at Fort Pasquia: "The French talk several languages to perfection; they have the advantage of us in every shape, and if they had Brazile
tobacco would entirely cut our trade off." Significantly, Henday's own Cree
companions twice traded their furs to the French for brandy.

When the salute guns boomed York Factory's welcome on June 23, 1755,
Henday had been away for a year and had completed an astonishing journey.
James Isham questioned the traveller closely and accepted the burden of
Henday's report,* suggesting to London that the HBC dispatch several men
inland with roving commissions to bring the Indians out to trade and "root the

* Henday's original journal was never found, but four copies survive in the HBC Archives in
Winnipeg, though they contain serious inaccuracies and contradictions. Historian Glyndwr
Williams has argued convincingly that Henday tried to paint his achievements in "a dishon-
estly optimistic light."

French out." The Committeemen balked at such heresy, rewarded Henday with a £20 bonus—and promptly went back to sleep.

Henday made several more inland probes but seven years later he left the Company, heartbroken at not being promoted above the rank of net-mender and angry at being abused by supply ship crews for not wanting to buy their bayside luxuries. In the autumn of 1755, even as Henday was sailing out of Hudson Bay for the last time, history was on the march, all but obliterating the memory of his great exploit. The Royal Navy was already at sea with the Duke of Newcastle's orders to intercept supplies from France for its American colonies, so that without any formal declaration, the Seven Years' War had begun, threatening the existence of the French fur trade.

The surrender of Quebec in 1759 convinced the London Committeemen that their golden age of monopoly had finally dawned, that the "woodrunners" would somehow vanish and leave all the furs to them. Yet by 1764, the western trading routes were once again crowded with Montreal canoes. The new inter-lopers were of a much more impressive cut than their French predecessors, who had been limited in their thrust westward by a meddlesome Versailles bureaucracy and the stingy budgets of hard-pressed colonial administrators. Not only had these restraints been lifted, but Montreal was bursting with freshly landed entrepreneurs with access to capital and a thirst for new conquests—feisty Scots quartermasters and adventurous Irish hawkers, as well as shrewd Yankee veterans of the Mississippi fur trade. London had petulantly dropped any attempt to enforce a monopoly in the fur trade, so that suddenly the western territories were open to all comers. The geography of the fur trade was about to undergo a sea change.

Samuel Hearne's Odyssey

This was no North West Passage;
It was a rocky suburb of Hell.

SOUTH OF RUPERT'S LAND, the Union Jack now snapped and fluttered from hundreds of whitewashed flagstaffs in what was called "Canada." The three remaining barriers to freedom of trade in the Americas were the half-serious claims by Spain (based on the Papal Bull of 1493), by Russia (based on Bering's discoveries along the West Coast) and the HBC monopoly in the north. By 1774, Spanish navigators had charted the Pacific rim up to the Queen Charlotte Islands, while Russian fur traders were pushing southward from Alaska. It was becoming evident that the North West Passage, even if it did exist, was located north of the continent and was very much longer and less accessible than had been hitherto suspected. The elusive Passage now took on a new imperialist dimension: its discoverers and claimants would be able to command the Canadian subcontinent and gain considerable advantage in the contest for sovereignty on North America's Pacific Coast.

Exploration accelerated as the Montreal traders followed the setting sun. Alexander Mackenzie, hardiest of the North West Company's travellers, would soon stand near Bella Bella on the Pacific Ocean and, using a pomade of vermilion face-paint and bear grease, leave his proud mark: "... from Canada, by land, the 22nd of July, 1793."

In London, the HBC perspective was shifting under the influence of Samuel Wegg, who became Deputy Governor in 1774 and Governor six years later, temporarily breaking the Lake family domination. Unlike his predecessors, Wegg welcomed geographers, naturalists and explorers into the Company archives. He served as Treasurer of the Royal Society for thirty-four years and became an indefatigable member of the select Thursday Club, which met at the Mitre Tavern on Fleet Street to discuss the disposition of the Empire over claret and a haunch of venison.* "The achievement of Samuel Wegg was that he helped the Company of his day to distinguish between information which because of its commercial importance was properly confidential and that which was not," wrote Glyndwr Williams. "The charter was no longer attacked—it was simply ignored by the traders who inherited the old French routes west from Montreal and pushed on towards the Pacific."

Two unconnected events prompted the Hudson's Bay Company to take a more active stance in exploring its own hinterland. Alexander Cluny, who described himself as "an old experienced trader" (though he had spent only one short season on the bay), published a detailed pamphlet about North America. Nothing if not ingenious, Cluny advocated turning Hudson Bay into a metropolis with no fewer than a dozen towns and the setting up of a whale fishery that would employ eight hundred ships and sixteen thousand men. Cluny riveted the attention of the HBC Committeemen when he described large lumps of virgin copper he had allegedly picked up north of the bay. Cluny's mythical find turned suspiciously real when at about the same time Moses Norton, the Governor at Prince of Wales's Fort, then visiting London, plunked down a chunk of rich copper ore on the polished mahogany Committee-room table. Norton reported that the metal had recently been brought out of the north country by two Chipewyan—Matonabbee and Idotliaze—dispatched by him to search the northern rivers five years earlier. The natives reported that the rivers between the copper mines were thick with beaver.

Hardly able to contain their impatience, the London governors ordered Norton to mount an expedition "far to the north, to promote an extension of our trade, as well as for the discovery of a North West Passage [and] Copper Mines ... taking observation for determining the longitude and latitude, and also distances, and the course of rivers and their depths."

In the discussion that followed, the man picked to lead the HBC venture was Samuel Hearne, an enthusiastic young sailor then serving under Norton as mate of the trading brigantine, *Charlotte*.

---

* Various guest lists included Captain William Bligh (of *Bounty* fame), Benjamin Franklin and Captain James Cook.

HEARNE HAD GROWN UP in England's capital, where his father was secretary of the London Bridge Water Works Company. When his mother, Diana, was widowed, the family moved to Beaminster in Dorset. Young Samuel's schooling was sporadic, and he proved equally incapable of mastering the fundamentals of spelling, grammar or mathematics. According to normal practice for ambitious boys of his class, Hearne volunteered for the Royal Navy at the age of twelve. He was taken on as a boy servant to Captain Samuel Hood, then in command of HMS *Bideford,* a frigate on convoy duty in the Bay of Biscay and the Mediterranean. Hearne spent half a dozen years at sea, growing inured to the foul diet, harsh discipline and tensions of the lower deck. He took part in several fire fights with French transports off Cape Finisterre, the capture of two privateers and the bombardment of Le Havre. When the Seven Years' War ended in 1763, Hearne, having no hope of preferment, left the Navy and three years later joined the HBC as mate on the little sloop *Churchill,* then engaged in the northern whaling trade.

In the late summer of 1768, Prince of Wales's Fort received its first distinguished visitor, William Wales, the British astronomer-mathematician sent to Hudson Bay by the Royal Society to observe the transit of Venus across the face of the sun.* His stay presented Hearne with the opportunity to improve his knowledge of surveying and chartmaking, which he had already gleaned while serving with the Royal Navy. The following spring, Hearne, twenty-four and in full vigour, was distressed at being transferred to the Company's hundred-ton whaling brig *Charlotte,* not as her captain but still as mate. He found himself serving under Joseph Stephens, whom he described as "a man of the least merit I ever knew," and promptly appealed to London for a more senior assignment "where there is greater probability of my making some returns, and giving satisfaction to my Employers."

The real reason Hearne's superior, Moses Norton, picked him to lead the trek inland was only partly based on the youthful seaman's proven abilities. The two men despised one another, and the best solution was geographical separation. In his posthumously published journal, Hearne described the

---

* Wales sailed around the world as chief astronomer on Captain James Cook's second expedition and later became mathematical master at Christ's Hospital, where he numbered among his students Charles Lamb, Leigh Hunt and Samuel Taylor Coleridge. Because of the schedules of supply ships, Wales had to spend a full year (September 1768 to September 1769) at Churchill to record a celestial event that lasted only seven hours—most of it invisible because of cloud cover.

Prince of Wales's Governor as "one of the most debauched wretches under the sun, who wished to engross every woman in the country to himself. He kept for his own use five or six of the finest Indian girls, took every means in his power to prevent any European from having intercourse with the women of the country, even owned a box of poison to be administered to anyone who refused him his wife or daughter. He showed more respect to one of his favourite dogs than he ever did to his first officer." Hearne accused Norton of, among other villainies, poisoning two of his women "because he thought them partial to other men more suitable to their ages." His portrait of Norton as living "in open defiance of every law, human and divine" is a little too one-dimensional to be entirely believable, but it is the only source available.

The son of a former overseas governor of the HBC, young Norton had been educated in England. Back on the bay in the Governor's chair, he provided himself with elegant private apartments, furnished with leather-bound books, paintings, an organ and a parrot. The Company left him in charge of Prince of Wales's Fort for more than a decade, and in only one instance was his behaviour questioned: his London principals warned Norton to conduct his trade "in the best manner, so as not to give the Indians any disgust."

Whatever the truth about Norton's disposition, Hearne was delighted to leave the relative comfort of the fort for the unpredictable wilds.

SAMUEL HEARNE'S THREE JOURNEYS inland took him into the brutally beautiful Barren Ground, which sprawls across the top of North America like some discarded purgatory. At its southern edges, in sheltered hollows, gale-blasted evergreens peter out into scatterings of dwarf spruce that take three centuries to grow to the height of a man, like natural bonsai shaped by some horticultural deity. Northward, the underbrush gives way to a topographical void under featureless skies. A relic of the Pleistocene Epoch, the mainland section of the Barrens rolls on for half a million square miles in a rough upside-down triangle formed by Hudson Bay, the saw-toothed perimeter of the Arctic Ocean and the Mackenzie River system. "Viewed by a summer traveller on the ground," wrote Farley Mowat, "the tundra gives the feeling of limitless space, intensified until one wonders if there can be an end to this terrestrial ocean whose waves are the rolling ridges. Perhaps nowhere else in the world, except far out at sea, does a man feel so exposed. On the northern prairie it is as if the ceiling of the world no longer exists and no walls remain to close one in."

Two hundred years after Hearne's audacious probes, this land mass had yet
to be crossed on foot by more than half a dozen white men. It is an Arctic
desert, its annual precipitation averaging eleven inches—less than falls on the
outer edges of the Sahara. Because only the top few inches of the ground in
the Barrens ever thaws, even this light sprinkling does not drain away but lies
in huge muskeg patches and an endless chain of shallow lakes, which when
frozen over resemble hammered pewter.

In late spring and early fall, the lake surfaces flicker with the wings of
migrating ducks and geese. Even in winter there are sporadic touches of life,
with small herds of muskox exploiting their uncanny ability to forage
beneath the snow. For brief weeks, summer suffuses the mossy ground
mattress with a carpet of miniature bloom and brings the return of the
Barrens' most important seasonal inhabitants, the caribou herds. No estimate of the caribou which roamed the north in Hearne's time is possible, but
contemporary accounts indicate they were beyond counting. They migrated
with the wildfowl, thronging to the Arctic prairie in spring to give birth,
marching back to the forest for winter, their numbers darkening the horizon.
Once in perfect balance with their two main predators (wolves and human
hunters), the caribou in modern times have been indiscriminately slaughtered.* "The natives gave fresh caribou meat to whalers and fur traders,
exchanging flesh for firearms," Dr Albert Hochbaum, the well-known
Manitoba naturalist-painter, has observed. "The deer supplied energy to run
the dog teams, which steadily required more bloody red fuel as their size and
numbers were increased to meet the HBC demand for fur. Ammunition
became a major trade item as millions of rounds were available to fire the
ever-more-efficient breech-loading rifles. Then came the gasoline engine,
which consumed time and space—the two most precious commodities to the
caribou. No part of the north country remains safe or secret from anyone
from anywhere. Now, suddenly, there is an overwhelming incursion of
bureaucracies—federal, provincial, territorial, corporate, Canadian and

---

* A bizarre example of this careless butchery occurred in northern Manitoba during the
Second World War, when the U.S. Army Air Force was occupying Fort Churchill. There were
so many caribou migrating through the area in the 1940s that some years it took several days
for them to file by. Many were used by machine-gunners for target practice and their frozen
bodies propped up in parallel lines to mark the boundaries of the landing strips in the snow.
Pilots took off and landed between this gruesome guard of honour instead of the usual spruce
tree markers.

foreign—each in its own way coveting some part of the land that belonged to the caribou."

Historically, the only inhabitants of the southern Barrens were the Chipewyan, named for the Cree term meaning "pointed skins"—a reference to the poncho-style caribou-hide shirts worn by Chipewyan of both sexes, cut with a point or tall at the back and front.

Because they compete for caribou, the Chipewyan have been almost constantly at war with the Eskimos. They blamed their enemies' conjuring for any illness or death among the elders and tried to drive the ice people ever northward, ambushing any hunting parties that followed caribou into the southern Barrens. In 1756 at Knapp Bay north of the Churchill River, the Chipewyan massacred more than forty Eskimos for no other reason than the fact that two of their elders had died of mysterious illnesses the previous season.

The antagonism worked both ways. The last authenticated massacre of Indians by Eskimos took place on the Peel River at Fort McPherson in 1850. A group of Indians were fishing when the northern caribou hunters came in to trade. That night, with no warning and no apparent reason save proximity, the Eskimos attacked and killed all the Indians except one little girl who had hidden in the undergrowth.

This traditional enmity has survived into the twentieth century even though no one seems certain exactly how it started. One explanation is that of Dr Robert McGhee, an archaeologist with the National Museum of Man, who has postulated that "Their mutual hostility can be best understood within the context of Indian hostility against other Indian groups, Inuit against other Inuit—the hostility between most neighbouring groups living in tribal societies. The main cause of trouble seems to have been covetousness of one's neighbour's wife, or of his other possessions. In addition, they shared a shamanistic theory of disease caused by sorcery. Neighbouring groups were generally thought of as adept sorcerers, and often blamed for disease or other misfortunes, which exacerbated hostilities. In specific cases, there was probably also economic competition for hunting grounds, good fishing spots and resources such as native copper."

The important point is that Hearne found these pristine people warring. The edge of the Barrens was no Eden, but very much the same thing was going on between bands and tribes in the rich south-land. These struggles were mostly stand-offs; a coup of some kind was much more important than seizing land or bringing home a particularly desirable woman. In their study of human aggression, *The Imperial Man*, Lionel Tiger and Robin Fox have documented that at the primitive level there never was much "war," but many raids and skirmishes: "The actual violence took much less time than the elaborate male rituals of violence, of preparation and celebration. In many cases there was nothing obvious to fight about ... Sometimes 'real' causes could be assumed—disputes over territory, hunting rights, water holes, women, real or imagined insults to tribal honor. But for the most part, enemies were what were traditionally defined as such. No Shoshone needed any 'real' cause for fighting the Sioux: they existed to be fought. A great deal of this fighting was highly ritualized so that the men could get the maximum satisfaction from their sense of danger and exercise of courage, while neither side lost too many lives ... The showing of courage and skill and the braving of dangers were more important than the wholesale slaughter of the enemy."

Chipewyan life revolved around hunting. Men became heads of families and chiefs because of their skill in tracking and killing game. They followed the migrating caribou, spearing them in summer and snaring them in enclosures during winter. In rutting time the caribou were lured to their death by decoys, hunters who tied antler stems to their waists and rattled them to reproduce the sound of bulls fighting for a female's favour. When a curious bull appeared, he was shot by an arrow. (The Chipewyan used bone rather than stone arrowheads because bone tips break off and work themselves toward the animal's heart.) A lone hunter, disguised under a caribou skin and a set of antlers, would infiltrate a herd and kill its fattest member. Traditionally every part of every animal was used, with the caribou foetus considered a particular delicacy. Even the skeleton of the caribou was reduced to bonemeal and added to stews for nutritious flavouring.

The Chipewyan dwelt in a universe of animalistic spiritualism, their lives permeated by ritual and superstition. It was wrong, for example, to stretch two nets across a stream because one would be jealous of the other and neither would catch fish. Women would never eat the gristly muzzle of the caribou for fear of growing beards, and young men were afraid that eating bear feet might insult the bear's spirit and slow their own running. It was believed that the dead travelled in stone boats to a beautiful island abounding with game, but that only the good would reach the island; sinners would be capsized and struggle in the water forever.

According to Chipewyan legend, the birth of the world occurred in the cave of a lone Indian woman who rescued a dog-like animal. When she made love with it, the animal was magically transformed into a handsome young man whose sexual ecstasy equalled her own. At daybreak he resumed the dog's form, and "the mother of the world" scarcely remembered or understood the dreams of her night's passion until she gave birth to a superior being who grew so tall his head reached the clouds. With a huge walking stick he marked out the earth's lakes and rivers. Then he killed his dog-father and tore him to bits, and the entrails became fish, the flesh caribou and the skin birds. The tall man told his mother that her future offspring would have the ability to kill as many animals as they required, assuring the abundance of game and orderliness in the world.

Whenever two parties of Chipewyan met in the Barrens they would advance to within a stone's throw and sit on the ground in silence. Elders from each group would then rise and recite the litany of deaths and misfortunes visited on their band since the last encounter. After much wailing and prolonged, cathartic crying, pipes would be passed and gifts exchanged—and only then would real conversation begin. Unlike some of the Cree, the Chipewyan, too proud to become hired hunters and provisioners, never surrendered their independence to the HBC. Instead of loitering around Churchill or Prince of Wales's Fort, they preferred to roam the Barrens, trading with the tribes of the Far West and exacting costly commissions for Company goods.

Because the Chipewyan were so unpredictable—appearing unheralded once a year out of the forbidding Barren Grounds with tales of vast mineral treasures and distant seas—the early HBC traders treated them with attention and curiosity. The Company men were also beguiled by the Chipewyan's sex lives. The HBC journal writers described at such length and in such detail the Indians' sexual proclivities that one is tempted to conclude that much of their knowledge must have come from firsthand research.

They knew most about the Cree around them on the bay. James Isham, for instance, noted in high dudgeon that at York Factory "maidens are very rare to be found at thirteen or fourteen years of age, and … none at fifteen." Hearne described how it was common for a Cree to make free with his brother's wife or daughter, and how "many of them cohabit occasionally with their own mothers, and frequently espouse sisters and daughters."

No such sexual transgressions were observed among the Chipewyan. Here was male frontier fantasy at its best, or worst: a tribe that openly treated its women as slaves and concubines. Wives could be jettisoned by the simple expedient of administering a good drubbing and turning them out. In return for supplying game and protection, some of the Chipewyan men maintained harems of up to eight wives. New sex mates were won by barter or physical contest. The first man thrown to the ground in these flash wrestling bouts was the loser. An opponent could most readily be downed by grabbing his hair (and so they kept it cut short) or by twisting his ears, which were often greased. No one seemed to care how the women felt, and there was no recourse or appeal once a woman had been won or lost. "On these occasions," Hearne reported, "their grief and reluctance to follow their new lords has been so great, that the business has often ended in the greatest brutality; for in the struggle I have seen the poor girls stripped quite naked, and carried by main force to their new lodgings." The only relief women enjoyed was during their menstrual cycles when they went to live away from the main tents. It was an essential escape, and Hearne slyly noted: "I have known some sulky dames to leave their husbands for five days at a time, and repeat the farce twice or thrice a month, while the poor men never suspected the deceit."

Chipewyan women had clear brown skin but, according to Hearne, did not meet the white man's standard of beauty: "Ask a northern Indian what is beauty, and he will answer—a broad flat face, small eyes, high cheek bones, three or four lines across each cheek,* a tawny hide and breasts hanging down to the belt."

"Chipewyan women ranked lower than in any other tribe," observed Diamond Jenness in his definitive study of Canadian Indians. "Separated from all boy companions at the age of eight or nine, married at adolescence often to middle-aged men, and always subject to many restrictions, they were the first to perish in seasons of scarcity. In winter they were mere traction animals; unaided, they dragged the heavy toboggans. In summer, they were pack animals, carrying all the household goods, food and hides on their backs." It was nothing out of the ordinary for a Chipewyan woman to be lugging a 140-pound pack in summer and dragging twice as much on a sled in winter.

In the harsh climate of the Barrens, life was so brutish and short that alluring girls turned into cackling crones by the age of thirty. They were obliged to draw sleds, dress skins, cook meat, pitch tents, mend breeches and keep their

---

* A tattoo acquired by pushing an awl through the skin, withdrawing it and rubbing charcoal into the raw wound.

men satisfied. The sexist attitude of the day was summed up by Matonabbee, the Chipewyan chief, who explained to Hearne: "Women were made for labour; one of them can carry or haul as much as two men can do. They also pitch our tents, make and mend our clothing, keep us warm at night ... Though they do everything, [they] are maintained at a trifling expense; for as they always cook, the very licking of their fingers in scarce times is sufficient for their subsistence."

TO VENTURE ACROSS THE BARREN GROUNDS in Samuel Hearne's time meant stepping off the edge of the known world. It also meant having to cross the gravelly, spongy sphagnum the latter-day explorer R.A.J. Phillips described as being very like trying to wade through "porridge sown with razor blades."

Hearne himself explained the effect of trudging through this cursed terrain when, halfway through his appalling forty-mile-a-day return journey from the Coppermine, he looked down at the tatters of his lower extremities, shook his head in despair and noted in his journal that he had acquired an advanced case of "foundered feet."

Still, the mood was festive as Hearne set off on his first expedition during a pre-dawn snowflurry on November 6, 1769. Accompanied by two Company servants and a pair of Cree hunters from Prince of Wales's Fort, he left at the same time as a group of Chipewyan led by an Indian known as Captain Chawchinahaw. Only three weeks later, two hundred miles north of the fort, Chawchinahaw and his band abruptly plundered Hearne's food stocks, then decided to turn southwest, mockingly suggesting that Hearne and his companions find their own way home. As the Indians decamped, "making the woods ring with their laughter," Hearne's survival instinct asserted itself. Deprived of provisions and flintlocks, the five survivors set off south, escaping starvation by snaring a few rabbits and gnawing the boiled hide of their jackets. It was a mortifying experience, but Hearne's skills had been sharpened; by the time he stumbled back into his home fort, he had been transformed from an ineffectual camp-follower to a resourceful man-of-the-land.

By February 1770 Hearne was itching to set off again, and Norton once more chose his companions, this time placing him under the dubious protection of a hired Indian named Conne-e-quese who claimed to have seen the Arctic copper mines. With their usual shrewdness, the northern Indians had come to realize that the white man would reward them for telling him exactly what he wanted to hear; they saw nothing wrong in spinning a few tall tales about rich copper mines in return for free guns and other supplies. The small party, equipped with one moosehide tent, a Hadley quadrant and a few guns and trinkets, struck north towards Baker Lake. The "Keewatin" or north wind blew, and prodigious cold chilled the travellers to their marrow. Pulling air into their lungs became a major undertaking. It was so bitterly cold that Hearne was able to trap several marten by falling on top of them and holding them down for a few minutes until he could feel them stiffen, frozen to death.

By June the spruce had thinned out. They were on the edge of the Barrens, Hearne stumbling along, weighed down by a sixty-pound shoulder sack and his awkward quadrant, his face smeared with goose grease to ward off the swarms of mosquitoes and flies so thick they shadowed the sun. Finding no game to shoot, the party was soon reduced to munching cranberries and chewing scraps of hide and burned bones from long-abandoned fires. Hearne was now at Yathkyed Lake, deeper into the Barrens than any white man before him. Here his group was joined by parties of roaming Chipewyan, who eventually swelled the aggregation to nearly six hundred. The incompetent Conne-e-quese, no longer certain where he was or whether the copper outcrops really existed, decided they would winter with the nomads. Hearne had no choice but to go along. Shortly afterward, his quadrant was destroyed by a gust of wind as he was setting up a sighting. Hearne was at Dubawnt Lake, far from his home fort; his few trade goods were long gone, and his companions were grumbling about how useless he was. His future course was decided for him when several of the Indians stole his personal possessions. Instead of getting angry, Hearne played on Chipewyan psychology by exclaiming that the lighter load would make his journey pleasanter and politely asked for the return of his razors, his awl, a needle and some soap. Taken aback by the unexpected civility, they agreed, and Hearne smugly noted in his diary that even if they returned only one of his razors, "they chose to keep the worst."

The heralding chill of winter was in the air; Hearne was lost and alone. Having deprived him of his possessions, the Indians dropped away. Fearing that he would soon freeze or starve, Hearne permitted himself a rare note of self-pity, complaining to his journal: "I never saw a set of people that possessed so little humanity, or that could view the distress of their fellow creatures with so little feeling and unconcern …"

He had no snowshoes, no tent or warm clothes. He trudged south for three days, falling asleep later and later each night, trying to hold off the moment when his will power would be exhausted and he would collapse into delirium, surrendering himself to the long Arctic slumber from which there is no waking.

Then occurred one of those theatrical entrances that characterize the Hudson's Bay chronicles. On September 20, 1770, just a day before Hearne might have frozen to death, there materialized out of that uninhabited void a tall, dark apparition. It was Matonabbee, the greatest of the Chipewyan chiefs. Samuel Hearne had found his mentor and soulmate. The two men would forge a unique partnership evolving into mutual admiration and even love. Hearne praised Matonabbee for a "scrupulous adherence to truth and honesty that would have done honour to the most enlightened and devout Christian," describing his personality as an admirable mixture of "the vivacity of a Frenchman and the sincerity of an Englishman with the gravity and nobleness of a Turk."

A handsome six-footer with a hawk nose and brooding eyes, Matonabbee was born at Prince of Wales's Fort, the son of a Cree slave-girl and a local Chipewyan hunter. Adopted by Richard Norton (Moses's father), the young Matonabbee learned to speak Cree and some English, as well as teaching himself the workings of the fur trade. He was probably the only Chipewyan of his time who felt at home both on the Barrens and inside the HBC forts. He had been to the Coppermine country, distributing Company trade goods to the distant Copper and Yellowknife Indians, and was practised at maintaining the uneasy peace between the errant tribes of the Barrens and the sullen western Cree of Athabasca. He was proclaimed "Captain" of the Chipewyan by HBC traders, though that tribe did not recognize any overall leadership function outside the hunt and its dealings with the Company.

And so Matonabbee plucked Hearne from the shores of eternity, provided him with otter robes, directed him to woods where they made snowshoes and sleds, then guided him back to Prince of Wales's Fort. The two men agreed en route to strike out for the Coppermine River together. Only twelve days after his return from this second gruelling journey, Hearne slipped silently out of the Company post. This time he went alone, attaching himself to Matonabbee and his accompanying retinue of up to eight wives and nine children, thus becoming a member of the Indian's extended family. "Probably no Canadian explorer depended so much upon one Indian for the success of his venture," notes historian Maurice Hodgson, who continues, "It is impossible to conceive of the success of Hearne's last expedition without [appreciating] the degree to which Hearne allowed himself to be physically and psychologically captured by the Indians, and more specifically by his attachment to, and affection for, Matonabbee."

At the time, this was a most unusual arrangement. Englishmen simply did not subordinate themselves to natives they were still pleased to call "red savages." Hearne gave himself up to the natural rhythms and diet of the Barrens; he turned over to Matonabbee the success of his mission and his personal safety. His final and successful Coppermine journey, which lasted nineteen months, saw Hearne reduce his travelling party to the minimum— himself—and melding into the nomadic bands of accompanying Indians so effectively that he nearly became one of them.*

One reason Hearne was able to surrender his individuality so completely was that he felt himself more of an observer than a participant, living out most of his emotions in the entries of his journal. That painfully honest chronicle of his epic journey—published twenty-three years later as *A Journey from Hudson's Bay to the Northern Ocean*—turned out to be as important a legacy as the journey itself. The perceptiveness that allowed Hearne to view each new experience without the inhibitions of his time made his diary a classic in the literature of northern discovery. The candid quality of his observations came through in such jottings as this graphic description of native ingenuity: "When I was on my passage from Cumberland House to York Fort, two boys killed a fine buck moose in the water, by forcing a stick up its fundament; for they had neither gun, bow, nor arrows with them."

He was amazed but not shocked when the Indian wife of a Company servant named Isaac Batt, who had recently lost an infant, was forced "to suckle a young Bear," and seemed absolutely mesmerized by the Indian medicine men's cure for constipation: "For some inward complaints, such as, griping in the intestines, difficulty of making water, etc., it is very common to see those jugglers blowing into the anus, or into the parts adjacent, till their eyes are almost starting out of their heads: and this operation is performed indifferently on all, without regard either to age or sex. The accumulation of so large a quantity of wind is at times apt to occasion some extraordinary emotions, which are not easily suppressed by a sick person; and as there is no vent for it but by the channel through which it was conveyed thither, it sometimes occasions an odd scene between the doctor and his patient ..."

---

* All that Hearne carried with him into the wilderness, apart from his quadrant, was some tobacco, a few knives, one spare coat, a pair of drawers, a blanket, his gun and ammunition, and "some useful ironwork."

He happily gorged with his companion on delicacies such as deer entrails, buffalo foetuses, the genitals of unborn caribou and baby beaver torn from their mothers' wombs. He grew especially fond of a Chipewyan version of haggis: caribou meat was first cut into bite-sized pieces and given to small boys to chew. The softened bits were then stirred in with the half-digested contents of the animal's stomach with enough water added so that the whole mess would boil up into a mush, then stuffed into the stomach lining and cured over a smoky fire.*

Such a menu, together with the unrelenting hardship of crossing the Barrens, might have brutalized another man, but it served only to open Hearne's eyes to the logic of that nude landscape. His salvation was that he rarely grew cynical, taking pleasure out of even the most disconcerting experiences. When he first encountered the Copper Indians deep in the northern Barrens, they encircled him and poked his bodily parts. After the most intimate examination they pronounced him to be a perfect human being—except for his skin, which they thought looked like boiled meat, and his blond hair, which they agreed among themselves was the colour and texture of a piss-stained buffalo tail. "As I was the first [white man] whom they had ever seen, and in all probability might be the last," he benignly noted in his journal, "it was curious to see how they flocked around me, and expressed as much desire to examine me from top to toe, as an European Naturalist would a non-descript animal."

It took Matonabbee and Hearne four months to reach the Thelewey-aza-yeth River, where tent poles were cut, meat was dried and birch bark collected for making portage-fording canoes before the plunge northward into wild Slave country. At times they were accompanying an unruly mob of as many as sixty Chipewyan, and even though he displayed the same stoicism as his companions, Hearne retained his British sense of civility and never lost sight of his own objectives. They were a ragged little army following their stomachs, their timing and direction dependent on the migrating caribou. Hearne tagged along, scratching in his journal, lugging a thirty-year-old Elton quadrant, trying to puzzle out exactly where he was. At Clowey Lake, Hearne's

---

* Hearne drew the line only at eating lice and warble flies, which the Indians happily nibbled after picking them off their garments and out of their hair. Hearne diplomatically explained to Matonabbee that he did not want to become addicted to the taste of the insects because he could not obtain a handy supply once he was back in London. He got so used to eating such delicacies as raw deer brains that, years afterward at fine London restaurants, he would order his trout and salmon "not warm to the bone."

party was joined by a foraging band of mysterious Indians who refused to explain why they were heading north.

Hearne loped northward, trying to keep from slipping into one of the many potholes that dot the terrain. At one point progress was slowed when the thighs and buttocks of one of Matonabbee's wives froze, producing blisters the size of sheep's bladders. The travellers nudged one another, jeering at her for having belted her clothes so high. "I must acknowledge that I was not in the number of those who pitied her," Hearne primly noted in his journal, "as I thought she took too much pains to shew a clean heel and a good leg; her garters being always in sight, which, though by no means considered here as bordering on indecency, is by far too airy to withstand the rigorous cold of a severe winter in a high Northern latitude."

Of more concern to Hearne was another Chipewyan woman who gave birth on the trail: "The instant, however, the poor woman was delivered, which was not until she had suffered all the pains usually felt on those occasions for nearly fifty-two hours, the signal was made for moving when the poor creature took her infant on her back and set out with the rest of the company; and though another person had the humanity to haul the sledge for her (for one day only), she was obliged to carry a considerable load beside her little charge, and was frequently obliged to wade knee-deep in water and wet snow."

Hearne missed little, describing even the ethos of muskox dung: "It is perhaps not generally known, even to the curious, therefore may not be unworthy of observation, that the dung of the muskox, though so large an animal, is not larger, and at the same time so near the shape and colour of that of the Alpine hare, that the difference is not easily distinguished but by the natives, though in general the quantity may lead to a discovery of the animal to which it belongs."

One of Hearne's more alluring observations was of the "Alarm Bird," a boreal owl used by the Copper Indians to detect approaching strangers.* "When it perceives any people, or beast, it directs its way towards them immediately, and after hovering over them some time, flies round them in circles, or goes ahead in the same direction in which they walk. They repeat their visits frequently; and if they see any other moving objects, fly alternately from one party to the other, hover over them for some time, and make a loud

---

* Hearne's "Alarm Bird" was probably the short-eared owl, *Asio flammeus*, a common summer inhabitant of the Barren Ground.

screaming noise, like the crying of a child. In this manner they are said sometimes to follow passengers a whole day."

The expedition had to devote inordinate time to Matonabbee's wives. His roster varied between two and eight, with various unblushing brides dropping out or joining the caravan at unpredictable intervals. Hearne had difficulty distinguishing their separate identities because of the Chief's habit of calling them all "Marten"—presumably to minimize domestic jealousies. At one point, when the youngest and comeliest Marten eloped with a muscular traveller, Matonabbee was disconsolate; he stood howling in the middle of the half-million square miles of Barrens and wanted to call off the expedition and go home. Hearne persuaded him to stay by appealing to the strength of his vow when he undertook the journey. By calming Matonabbee's distress, Hearne successfully drew him into the European value system. Their relationship worked both ways. Still, when it came to the occasional showdown, there was no question that Hearne was considered the outsider. At one point the Chipewyan ambushed a party of Indians, plundered their possessions and gang-raped their women, treating them, according to Hearne, "in so barbarous a manner as to endanger the lives of one or two of them." When the HBC explorer objected, the Chipewyan not only did not stop, "they made no scruple of telling me in the plainest terms that, if any female relation of mine had been present, she would have been served in the same manner."

The caravan slanted north and west, dropping most of the wives and children at a camp near Kathawachaga Lake ("Congecathawachaga" in Hearne's diary) while preparations went on for the final dash towards the Arctic Ocean. The strangers who had integrated themselves with the main convoy now made for themselves inch-thick wooden shields, carved and painted with primitive spirit-symbols Hearne recognized as having nothing to do with hunting. He gradually realized that the newcomers—Copper Indians from the east—were taking over the direction of the expedition and that their purpose was to massacre Eskimos known to be frequenting the Coppermine River. Matonabbee himself was not particularly anxious to participate in a killing spree, and Hearne, after making several exasperated objections, scribbled defensively in his diary: "I did not *care* if they rendered the name and race of Esquimaux extinct."

The war party sped north, covering eighty miles in four days, and crossed the Coppermine River at Sandstone Rapids, about forty miles south of Coronation Gulf. Instead of a wide and accommodating passage that could be used by Company ships, Hearne found himself on the bank of a broad, rock-strewn stream with turbulent rapids and no sign of an ebbing tide that might have led to the Arctic Sea. This was the shank of the 1771 summer season, yet on July 3, a raging snowstorm obliterated their tracks. Huddling in the lee of boulders, the warriors shivered in the teeth of the blizzard and dreamed of their prey. Scouts sent ahead found the quarry and reported that an Eskimo hunting camp of five tents had been set up at a cataract of the river which Hearne would later appropriately christen Bloody Fall. At this news the Chipewyan tensed, then set about painting their faces, tying up their hair, removing their leggings and finally stripping down to their breechcloths. Gliding silently from stone to stone, they crept along the riverbank. Hearne had been told to stay behind, but nervous that he might be killed by one of the escaping Eskimos, he went along, armed with a spear.

Just after midnight on July 17 the massacre began. The Indians slithered right up to the tents and hurled themselves at the sleeping Eskimos. The scene was more reminiscent of an abattoir than of a battle, with the panic-stricken victims rearing out of their cozy tents and being impaled on out-thrust spears. More than twenty men, women and children, their faces still sweet from interrupted slumber, were slain within minutes, their death rattles despoiling the Arctic silence. A young Eskimo woman ran desperately towards Hearne, the one man not engaged in the killing. A Chipewyan wheeled and plunged a spear into her side. "She fell down at my feet," Hearne wrote later, "and twisted around my legs, so that it was with diffi-culty I could disengage myself from her dying grasps. Two Indian men were pursuing this unfortunate victim, and I solicited very hard for her life. The murderers made no reply until they had stuck both their spears through her body and transfixed her to the ground. They then looked at me sternly in the face and began to ridicule me by asking if I desired an Eskimo wife; mean-while paying not the slightest heed to the shrieks and agony of the poor wretch who was still twining around their spears like an eel. Indeed, after receiving much abuse from them, I was at length obliged to desire only that they would be more expeditious in despatching their victim out of her misery; otherwise I should be obliged, out of pity, to assist in the friendly office of putting an end to a fellow creature who had been so cruelly wounded. On this request being made, one of the Indians hastily drew his spear from the place where it was first lodged, and pierced it through her breast near the heart. The love of life, however, even in this most miserable state, was so predominant that though this might justly be called the most merciful act that could be done for the poor creature, it still seemed to be unwelcome. Though much exhausted by pain and loss of blood, she made several efforts to ward off this friendly blow."

The aftermath was even worse. Hearne mercifully leaves out the details from his journal, remarking only that "the brutish manner in which these savages used the bodies that had been so cruelly bereaved of life was so shocking that it would be indecent to describe it ..."

Except for the spearing of an old man "until his whole body was like a cullender" and the murder of one elderly half-blind Eskimo woman who had been fishing nearby by stabbing her in the non-vital parts so she would die slowly, the ghastly encounter was now over. Hearne composed himself, noting somewhat ambivalently: "I am confident that my features must have expressed how sincerely I was affected by this barbarous scene."

The killing had stopped, but the plunder continued. Their blood-lust played out, the Chipewyan destroyed all evidence of the Eskimos' very existence, hurling their tent poles into the river, even though they might well have been useful. Then the satiated victors sat down for a feast of fresh char.

Within the hour the marauders reverted to being explorers, hiking the eight miles from Bloody Fall to the Arctic Ocean. Although some later explorers, including John Richardson and Eric Morse, have questioned whether Hearne actually descended the river or merely viewed its mouth from atop a nearby hill, Denis St-Onge, a veteran of the Geological Survey of Canada who spent a decade combing the same patch of wilderness, has no doubt about what happened. "Hearne was there," he has maintained. "His descriptions of Coronation Gulf are much too accurate for him not to have seen its shore. He was right there, on this silly mudflat at the end of the Coppermine, and if he tasted the water it would have been fresh, because the river flows into a huge delta where the tide is less than one metre."

Hearne had reached the Arctic Sea at the western end of Coronation Gulf. Here was the destination of all his efforts: journey's end, the ocean he had spent so many agonizing months trying to reach. He stood there, transfixed by disappointment in what he saw: a waddle of seals on a nearby floe and a flight of curlew wheeling over the sterile marshland. Nothing else. This was no North West Passage; it was a rocky suburb of Hell. The fabled Coppermine, its mouth blocked by a ridge and impassable shoals, would never accommodate Company ships or anything else.

It was one o'clock on the bright morning of July 18, 1771, and the dream of finding a channel across North America had just ended.

Men would cast themselves into the quest for another one hundred and thirty-five years, but no one would ever equal Hearne's walk.

Hearne snapped out of his reverie and, being a good Company man, did the only sensible thing: "erected a mark, and took possession of the coast on behalf of the HBC."

On the way back, three days' march up the Coppermine then east across Burnt Creek past the September Mountains, Hearne was guided by Matonabbee to the copper hills that garnished so many Indian legends.* After a four-hour search they found only one sizeable chunk of loose metal—a four-pound lump the shape of "an Alpine hare couchant." There was much evidence that ore had been taken out of the ground, but with winter coming and the Chipewyan impatient to be back with their women, Hearne had little time for mineralogy.†

The Indians tramped flat out back to their family camp, and for the first time Hearne began to lag behind, his feet punctured by gravel that ate into his flesh, his toenails peeling away. Each step he took left a footprint of blood. Hearne's return journey took nearly another year, partly across a frozen Great Slave, the world's eleventh-largest lake, three hundred miles long and two thousand feet deep. On June 29, 1772, eighteen months and twenty-two days after he had left Prince of Wales's Fort, Hearne found himself only ten miles from the fort. In the hunter's way, he settled in to savour one last camp on the land, planning to make the most of his entrance the following morning. As he sat by the feeble embers of the campfire, he scratched a final triumphant entry into his travel journal: "Though my discoveries are not likely to prove of any material advantage to the Nation at large," he wrote, "or indeed to the Hudson's Bay Company, yet I have the pleasure to think that I have fully complied with the orders of my Masters, and that it has put a final end to all disputes concerning a North West Passage through Hudson's Bay."

Hearne's odyssey has rarely if ever been matched. His round trip of about

* According to mythology, the copper mines were discovered by a woman who for several seasons guided the Indians to the richest ore. But when they took sexual liberties with her, she vowed in revenge to stay at the mines and sit on the copper deposits until both she and the deposits sank into the ground. When the Indians came back the following season, she was buried to her waist, and there was much less metal; when they returned a year later, both the woman and the copper were gone.
† John Franklin explored the same site in 1821, and many mineral claims in the area were filed between 1913 and 1968, though at only one spot (Hope Lake) was a shaft ever sunk.

3,500 miles, the equivalent of the distance as the crow flies from Gibraltar to Moscow, or Quebec City to Juneau, Alaska, was an epic adventure on a grand scale. This intrepid naif had been the first white man to reach the Arctic Ocean by land, discovering en route Great Slave Lake and the Mackenzie River system. He pioneered a new technique of exploration—the propensity to go native.

THE COMPANY RESPONDED to Hearne's magnificent achievement in its customary cavalier style. He was paid a £200 bonus and promptly posted back to his former job as mate of the *Charlotte*, but the fact that he had traversed a region half the size of "European Russia" was not lost on the London governors. He had come to their notice, not merely as a promising neophyte but as a dependable explorer ready to take on other assignments.

His circumstances were improved a year and a half later by the sudden death of the tyrannical Prince of Wales's Governor, Moses Norton. Suffering from an untreated intestinal infection, Norton called his officers and concubines to his private quarters on December 29, 1773, rudely proclaiming the details of his last will, which left all his goods to a wife in England he hardly ever saw, except for the miserly sum of £10 a year to clothe his several Indian women on the bay. As he lay there, alternately cursing his illness and writhing in the painful spasms of its effects, Norton spied a subordinate and one of his younger Indian wives whispering together. "Goddamn you for a bitch!" he bellowed in what turned out to be his valedictory. "If I live, I'll knock your brains out!"

"A few minutes after this elegant apostrophe," Hearne cheerfully reported, "he expired in the greatest agonies that can possibly be conceived."

The Blood
Feud Begins

*It was an uneven battle fought with all the passion of a Sicilian vendetta.
But in the process of trying to outdo one another, the competing fur traders
roughed out the contours of upper North America.*

SIX MONTHS BEFORE MOSES Norton's death, an HBC bookkeeper named
Matthew Cocking lurched into York Factory after a lengthy journey up
country to report with grave concern that the Montrealers were monopolizing
the fur trade of the Saskatchewan River area and were poised to cut off the
HBC from its main supply of furs. This hardy scribe, who had little idea of how
to steer a canoe, had managed to penetrate as far as the Eagle Hills (just south
of present-day Battleford), had hunted with the Blackfoot, observed the flow
of the fur trade but, unlike his emotional and romantic predecessors, came
back to record in his precise copper-plate script the operational details of the
inland panorama. "The natives are very dilatory in proceeding," he noted.
"Their whole delight is to sit smoking and feasting. Yesterday I received an
invitation to no less than ten feasts." He was disturbed by his camping
companions. "I get no rest at nights," he priggishly complained, "for
Drumming, Dancing, &c."

Cocking's accountant's-eye view of the wood buffalo country, his tidy
reconstruction of the extent to which the pedlars were controlling the fur
trade and his exact descriptions of how this rich fur country could be exploited
confirmed the London Committeemen's inclination to act—that, plus the
actuarial evidence supporting his contention that the pedlars were drying up
the fur traffic to the bay. York Factory's return in 1773 was only eight thousand
made-beaver, down from an annual average of thirty thousand made-beaver in

the decade before 1766. There had been a running argument within Company circles about inland posts since Anthony Henday's journey. The specific decision to move, taken in May 1773, was based on recommendations from Andrew Graham, the Chief Factor at York Factory, and firsthand testimony from Isaac Batt, one of the HBC's most experienced inland travellers.

And so, London woke from its slumbers and ordered Cocking and Hearne to establish Cumberland House, the HBC's first permanent western inland settlement.*

At this time "Canada" extended only from the Detroit River east to the Gaspé and as far north of the St Lawrence River as Lac St-Jean. The land to the north and west of the St Lawrence Valley belonged either to the HBC or to nomadic tribes. The HBC had been able to butt heads with the Montreal-based competition in this huge domain by sending its emissaries inland to lure the Indians out to Hudson Bay, where they could still obtain the best bargains and the heavyweight goods that the pedlars did not carry.† But after 1770 the free-lance traders began to form partnerships, temporary coalitions of interests that allowed them to carry on their business much more aggressively. In the nick of time, just before these annually financed "outfits" were consolidated into the North West Company, the Hudson's Bay Company finally snapped out of its reverie of more than a century and set out to claim Prince Rupert's empire.

During the next half-century, HBC traders would march across the continent, eventually commandeering the vast territory from the Great Lakes to the Pacific. "The Company's success sprang in no small degree from the

---

* Upon his return, Cocking settled at York Factory for most of the next decade. He died in York, England, in 1799, providing in his will £6 annually for each of his three half-breed daughters—specifically requesting that part of his legacy might be "laid out in gingerbread, nuts, etc., as they have no other means of obtaining these little luxuries, with which the paternal fondness of a Father formerly provided them ..."

† The pedlars often catered to individual Indian needs more astutely than did the HBC. Garments called "surcoats" were made in Montreal, for example, and shipped west without sleeves attached; the sleeves were sold separately in three lengths, so that the clothing conformed more closely to customers' sizes. But some of the HBC trade goods had advantages of their own. Because the best pelts for feltmaking were the furs off the Indians' backs, the Company provided woollen blankets made to native specifications—the ubiquitous Bay blankets dyed with bands of black, yellow, scarlet and green still sold today. The French trades provided no equivalent. The HBC also stocked lightweight copper pans and kettles while the competing traders continued to supply massive iron cookware completely unsuitable for long portages. English rum was a cheap product of the West Indian slave colonies, while French brandy (though much superior) had to be tediously aged in casks.

timely foundation of Cumberland House in 1774," Richard Glover has pointed out. "Had this step not been taken when it was, the Company's chance of surviving and triumphing in its struggle with its rivals would have been much reduced. The margin by which it survived and won was small enough as things were."

SAMUEL HEARNE HAD WINTERED at York Factory, preparing for his excursion inland and recruiting a reluctant clutch of Orkneymen to accompany him. They set off in the spring of 1774 as passengers in deep-laden canoes with Indians returning to their hunting grounds, each canoe carrying 180 pounds of Brazil tobacco, pouches of gunpowder, shot and six-gallon kegs of brandy as well as some building supplies. Every advantageous trading site Hearne saw along the way was already occupied by pedlars hawking rum, knives, flint, awls and needles.

About sixty miles west of the modern-day location of The Pas, in the evergreen slough of northwestern Manitoba at Pine Island Lake (now Cumberland Lake in Saskatchewan), Hearne finally found his spot. He decided to clear ground for a permanent post to be called Cumberland House. It was a good choice. Cumberland was strategically situated at convenient river connections to Lake Winnipeg, the Rockies and the Nor'Westers' route towards the Athabasca country, yet it was only 450 miles, about forty days' paddling time, from its supply base at York Factory. (The pedlars were five months' travel away from Montreal. A low-slung log bunker, thirty-eight by twenty-six feet, with a leaky plank roof and moss as caulking was eventually completed.

Wood-smoke curling from its makeshift chimney, the first full-fledged inland post of the Hudson's Bay Company opened for business. New supplies (including thirty-five gallons of brandy) arrived from York, but no extra food was brought in and they almost starved the first winter. When one of Hearne's nine fellow residents, Robert Longmoor, went out to hunt game and came back "with both his Big Toes much froze," Hearne had to "open them up" and pack the inner rind of larch-tree roots close to the bone, because this was "generally used among the Natives to prevent mortification."

Faced for the first time with having to winter in the wilderness not with indigenous Indians but among white men who had never before strayed from the shore of the bay, Hearne emerged as a resolute leader. He rotated the members of his little band in twelve-hour shifts, insisting that they never let down their guard. Despite his stern regime, none of the Orkneymen deserted to the pedlars. Some 150 rival traders had set up their bivouacs nearby. The "distant civility" with which the Company directed its servants to treat the Montrealers had been maintained. With spring breakup, Hearne proudly led a fur-burdened flotilla of thirty-two canoes down to York Factory. His mission to Cumberland House had succeeded,* and although he was ambitious to push the HBC farther inland, the 1775 supply ship from London brought him a promotion. At the age of thirty he was given command of his former home base at Prince of Wales's Fort.

DURING HEARNE'S FIRST AUTUMN as Governor, his old friend Matonabbee, by then the acknowledged chief of all the northern Indians, arrived leading three hundred Chipewyan with a goodly pile of prime pelts. He knew he had brought out the largest Chipewyan fur haul in a hundred years and was not about to go unrewarded. The ensuing orgy of gift-giving (quite apart from the trade goods owed for the furs) was without precedent in HBC annals, and at least part of Hearne's generosity must have been prompted by his gratitude for his comrade's guidance to the Coppermine and back. After dressing him up as a Captain and completely outfitting his six wives, Hearne also gave Matonabbee "seven lieutenants coats, fifteen common coats, eighteen hats, eighteen shirts, eight guns, 140 pounds weight of gunpowder with shot, ball, and flints in proportion; many hatchets, ice chisels, files, bayonets, knives; and a great quantity of tobacco, cloth, blankets, combs, looking-glasses, stockings, handkerchiefs; besides numberless small articles such as awls, needles, paint and steels."

Not satisfied, Matonabbee started to bargain, brazenly demanding gifts of "twelve pounds of powder, twenty-eight pounds of shot and ball, four pounds of tobacco, more articles of clothing, and several pieces of ironwork, to give to two men who had hauled his tent and other lumber the preceding Winter." Hearne later complained to his journal: "This demand was so very

---

* The oldest permanent settlement in Saskatchewan, Cumberland House was moved a mile upstream in 1789 and remained an important distribution depot until it was overshadowed by Norway House in northern Manitoba; it finally became a pemmican storehouse for passing brigades. By the mid-1850s Cumberland House had been reduced to just another outpost on the margin of civilization instead of the entry-point to a continental empire. As late as 1905 three steamboats worked out of the settlement, but its importance as a regional distribution centre gradually declined. It remains an HBC post, and local Indians still trap the muskrat marshes that supported Hearne's original little community.

unreasonable, that I made some scruple, or at least hesitated to comply with it, hinting that he was the person who ought to satisfy those men for their services; but I was soon answered, That he did not expect to have been denied such a trifle as that was; and for the future he would carry his goods where he could get his own price for them. On my asking where that was? he replied, in a very insolent tone, To the Canadian Traders."

All told, Matonabbee received goods the equivalent of 1,100 made-beaver—the largest single barter up to that time. That even a friend of the HBC, born at one of its posts and long engaged in its service, would threaten to switch loyalties was a dangerous indication of how vulnerable the Hudson Bay trade had become to the incursion of the pedlars. Freshly returned from Cumberland House, Hearne knew precisely how powerful the competition was.

The next half-decade was the happiest of Hearne's life. His governor's quarters were turned into a miniature zoo. Hearne's menagerie included tame lemmings, imported canaries, horned larks, foxes, eagles, snow buntings,* squirrels and several beavers.[†] The beavers were so domesticated that "they answered to their names and followed as a dog would do. They were as pleased at being fondled as any animal I ever saw. During the winter they lived on the same food as the women and were remarkably fond of rice and plum pudding."

Hearne's other relaxations included watching Indians fashion flutes from the wing-bones of whooping cranes and reading the astringent essays of Voltaire. For the first time in his adventurous life, Hearne felt secure enough to fall in love. The object of his affections was Mary Norton, the polygamous Governor's young daughter. Sixteen and as innocent as a freshly opened flower, she would, he confided to his journal, "have shone with superior lustre in any other country: for if an engaging person, gentle manners, an easy freedom, an amiable modesty, and an unrivalled delicacy of sentiment, are graces and virtues which render a woman lovely, none ever had greater pretensions to general esteem and regard...." The intrepid explorer settled into a life of peaceful domesticity with this benevolent and humane woman, the offspring of the irascible Moses Norton.

---

* Hearne noted that the snow buntings were excellent mimics—"When in company with canary birds, quickly learning to imitate their song."
† Hearne wrote: "The beaver were so fond of their company that when the women were absent for any considerable time, the animals displayed great signs of uneasiness and on their return shewed equal marks of pleasure by crawling on their laps, sitting erect like a squirrel and behaving to them like children who see their parents but seldom."

Unfortunately, their idyll was brutally interrupted by the last, and most improbable, attack on Hudson Bay.

The revolution in the Thirteen Colonies, which began while Hearne was still at Cumberland House, had grown into the War of American Independence. For a month in 1779 a combined French and Spanish fleet commanded the English Channel, and an invasion seemed imminent. The major English naval success was in the West Indies; Hearne's former captain, now Rear-Admiral Lord Hood, accepted the surrender of the French flagship, the 110-gun *Ville de Paris*, following a fierce engagement on April 12, 1782, that broke the French line of battle and scattered its twenty-six surviving warships. Three of the vessels—the seventy-five-gun *Sceptre* and two frigates of thirty-six guns each, the *Astrée* and *Engageante*—were ordered to mount an attack on the posts of Hudson Bay.

The ships were well equipped, carrying three hundred marines, two eight-inch mortars, three hundred bombs and four cannon, but why these fast-sailing, copper-bottomed men of war should be detached for half a year at a time when the French might have regained at least some of their influence in the Caribbean Sea remains obscure. "Weighed in any sane strategical balance, the French attack ... was pure nonsense," according to historian Richard Glover. "As such it offers a specially glaring example of that tendency which Mahan so eloquently deplored in French naval policy, a weakness for frittering resources away on commerce destruction, instead of seeking to dispute, to win and to hold, the command of the sea."

The French fleet sailed due north. Its commander, Jean François de Galaup, Conte de La Pérouse, later noted in *La Gazette de France*, that his main concern was not with waging war but with navigation: "I burned with impatience to arrive speedily at Prince of Wales. This was the first place which I proposed to attack; I had not an instant to lose, the rigour of the season obliging all ships to abandon these seas by the first days of September; but my impatience was put to a new proof. On the 3rd of August, sailing with security enough in the Bay of Hudson, I was enveloped in a fog, and immediately surrounded with large islands of ice, which extended beyond our view ... But on the 5th of August the bank of ice, in which I was engaged, opened a little, and I determined to force through it by a press of sail, whatever risque my ships might run. I was happy enough to accomplish it; and on the 8th of August in the evening, I saw the colours of Fort Prince of Wales."

With less than a month of navigable weather left open to him, the French admiral must have looked up at the massive battlements and wondered how he could successfully lay siege to this impressive wilderness apparition. The fort was known to have limestone embrasures up to forty feet thick and forty guns, and by those standards should have been the continent's most impregnable stronghold. La Pérouse's ships approached within a league and a half (about five miles), carefully staying out of artillery range; the French admiral raised English pennants to divert its gunners and lowered his boats to sound the harbour entrance.

Nothing stirred. Instead of displaying evidence of a hectic round of preparations for its defence, the fort appeared to be steeped in stony indolence.

At two o'clock in the morning of August 9, 1782, La Pérouse sent off 150 armed men in six longboats to land just below the fort's battlements and ordered the *Sceptre* to slip within firing range. Still no response from shore. The landing party reported that the fort betrayed no intention of trying to marshal any defences. Instead of the expected onslaught, the silence was deafening. Hardly believing his good fortune or suspecting a ruse, La Pérouse sent an emissary accompanied by a drummer to seek a parley.

The fort's gates were immediately thrown open and a white tablecloth run up its flagpole. The incredulous French conquerors marched in and raised the fleur-de-lys. The "invincible" fortress had fallen without a shot, its only casualties being the post's two horses, which the French promptly shot and made into soup.

La Pérouse and Hearne amicably negotiated the terms of surrender, which was unconditional except that it allowed the English to keep their personal possessions. Hearne's lightning capitulation has puzzled historians, particularly since the map-maker David Thompson, later a junior at the fort, alleged that the men "begged of Mr. Hearne to allow them to mow down the French troops with the heavy guns loaded with grapeshot, which he absolutely refused ..."

In fact, Hearne, who could see at once that the visiting ships had hostile intent, had served long enough in the Royal Navy to realize the havoc the vessels' naval cannon could inflict—particularly since he was in command of a garrison of only thirty-eight men. Each gun required a crew of about ten men, and Hearne was grievously over-gunned and understaffed; further, many of the pieces defending the fort were of museum quality, dating back to the reign of William and Mary. The fort itself had been poorly designed to withstand a siege; its embrasures were ill-built, it had no defensible moat and no internal water supply. La Pérouse accurately pointed out that the *Sceptre's* seventy-four guns could quickly have firebombed the HBC men into submission. Hearne might well have put up token resistance but waging uneven military encounters was not his forte, and he had no wish to risk the lives of his men in a battle he could not win.

If all Englishmen had lived by Hearne's rules, pragmatism would have become Britain's state religion. As an archetypical Company man, Hearne was more concerned with keeping a proper tally of the pillage than with trying to stop it. His report of the incident includes a meticulous account of the furs and other stock carried off by the French—leaving the observer to wonder who had time to count the 17,350 goose quills he reported missing.

La Pérouse and his men spiked the cannon, blew up the arches of the magazines in the bastions, and torched anything that would burn. The great fort, which had taken thirty-eight years to build, took half a day to destroy. It would never be occupied again, its battlements a bleak monument to man's presumptions about the invulnerability of citadels. The French admiral was reasonably gracious in victory, distributing powder and shot to a group of Indians who happened to witness the fort's destruction so that they would not starve on the way back to their hunting grounds. The HBC men were herded onto the French ships, and the victorious flotilla weighed anchor to sail to its next objective: the fur-rich storehouses at York Factory. From plans he found at Prince of Wales's Fort, La Pérouse knew that the HBC post was manned by sixty Englishmen armed with twenty-five cannon and a dozen swivel guns. It was supplied with thirty head of cattle and had adequate water sources within its stockades.

With less than three weeks of open navigation remaining on the bay and scurvy sweeping the men on his lower decks, La Pérouse rushed his advantage and landed an attack group of 250 men, plus mortars, cannon and eight days' provisions, at the Nelson River estuary behind York Factory. An HBC turncoat named John Irvine was bribed to guide them across the isthmus between the Nelson and the Hayes rivers, but the path was so swampy that the Frenchmen wasted three days hacking and sloshing their way to their goal. Having watched the French ships arrive, resident Governor Humphrey Marten hurriedly loaded most of the post's furs aboard the HBC supply vessel *Prince Rupert,* which on a moonless night slipped away past the French ships and headed straight for England.

At eleven o'clock on the morning of August 25, 1782, the French troops rallied for their assault outside the factory gates. Marten, having acted as the good Company man and saved the bulk of the furs from being captured by the French, now felt there was no reason to risk having his men killed defending an empty warehouse. "Their numbers appeared so formidable," he later noted, "that it was thought prudent to demand a parley." A less charitable reconstruction was offered by Edward Umfreville, then York Factory's second-in-command: "During their approach, a most inviting opportunity offered itself to be revenged on our invaders, by discharging the guns on the ramparts. But a kind of tepid stupefaction seemed to take possession of the Governor at this time of trial, and he peremptorily declared that he would shoot the first man who offered to fire a gun. Accordingly ... he ... held out a white flag with his own hand, which was answered by the French officer showing his pocket handkerchief.... the place was most ingloriously given up in about ten minutes, to a half-starved, wretched group of Frenchmen, worn out with fatigue and hard labour, in a country they were entire strangers to."

And so York Factory changed hands for the eighth time. With the nip of winter already in the air, La Pérouse's men hurriedly pillaged its stores, burned the timber palisades and scuttled back to their ships. Although the French commander's main fear during the brief York Factory campaign was that the Company men might tempt the Cree with brandy and gunpowder to take arms in their defence, he again carefully saved from the wholesale destruction a cache of powder, shot and firelocks so that Indians who had taken refuge in the nearby woods would not be caught without supplies for the winter. Most of the HBC prisoners, including Hearne, were shifted to the Company's sloop *Severn*, which had been anchored off York Factory at the time, and La Pérouse even towed the vessel as far as Cape Resolution. When the French cut the little sloop loose for her voyage across the Atlantic, Umfreville noted that La Pérouse's "politeness, humanity and goodness secured him the affection of all the Company's officers; and on parting at the mouth of Hudson's Strait, they felt the same sensation which the dearest friends feel in an interview preceding a long separation." Hearne and the French admiral had become friendly during their brief time together; La Pérouse had read parts of the explorer's journal and was so taken with it that he chivalrously insisted its early publication be the essential precondition of returning it to Hearne.

The London Committeemen seemed only mildly chagrined by the plunder of their main outposts, even though the surrender of their possessions caused the Company a loss estimated at £14,580 and halted the payout of dividends for four years. Hearne and Humphrey Marten were appointed to reoccupy their former posts and, although the HBC governors decided not to rebuild Prince of Wales's Fort, tried to carry on business as usual. But the stench of ignominious defeat was not that easy to dispel. The Chipewyan trade with Prince of Wales's had been disrupted and would never again reach its former levels. The inland HBC traders who once had come out for supplies now found only burned, empty posts. Besides losing prestige and two seasons' fur returns, the remaining Company men were so strapped for goods that they were forced to purchase ammunition from the hated pedlars to survive the winter. Their most faithful Indian allies on the Saskatchewan, who had boasted that the Englishmen were their countrymen, now moved within the trading sphere of the Montreal-based partnerships.

At Prince of Wales's Fort the Home Guard Indians, no longer in contact with their HBC confrères, scattered into the wilderness. Mary Norton, who had led a sheltered life—first pampered by her father and then indulged by her lover Hearne—was frightened by the French conquerors and bolted into the Barren Ground. Distraught and unaccustomed to the harsh demands of nomadic life, she soon starved to death among her Indian relations.

Another victim was the proud Matonabbee. His authority had become so dependent on the English presence, his sense of honour so closely bonded with the HBC and particularly to Hearne himself, that with the fort destroyed and, as he believed, its occupants taken out on the foreign ships to be drowned, there seemed no reason to continue living in shame. His spirit broken, Matonabbee decided that his sad circumstances demanded self-destruction. After he hanged himself, six of Matonabbee's beloved Martens and four of their children, bereft of their protector, starved to death during the winter of 1783.

At about this time, the Chipewyan were ravaged by a smallpox epidemic spreading north from the Mississippi region; it claimed a staggering toll among the tribes of the Canadian northwest, including nearly half the Chipewyan. The journal of William Walker, then an HBC officer, paints a pathetic landscape of "Indians lying dead about the Barren Ground like rotten sheep, their tents left standing and the wild beasts devouring them." An even more dramatic description is contained in the journal of David Thompson, who reported that from the Chipewyan, the plague "extended over all the Indians of the forest to its northward extremity, and by the Sieux over the Indians of the Plains and crossed the Rocky Mountains. More men died in proportion than Women and Children, for unable to bear the heat of the fever they rushed into the Rivers and Lakes to cool themselves, and the greater part thus perished. The countries were in a manner depopulated, the Natives allowed that far more than one half had died, and from the number of tents which remained, it appeared that about three-fifths had perished; despair and despondency had to give way to active hunting both for provisions, clothing and all the necessaries of life; for in their sickness, as usual, they had offered almost everything they had to the Good Spirit and to the Bad to preserve their lives, and were in a manner destitute of everything."

By the fall of 1783 Hearne was back on Hudson Bay, greeted by the chilling news of the tragic deaths of the two people he most loved—his gallant comrade, Matonabbee, and the beguiling Mary Norton. Too bereft to express his own feelings for her, he instead entered in his journal a quote from the Restoration poet Edmund Waller, that ends with the line: "Here rests the pleasing friend and faithful wife."

"Reason shrinks from accounting for the decrees of Providence on such occasions as this," he wrote bitterly in his journal, adding a quizzical philosophical note about Matonabbee's having acted so much like a defeated Roman general falling on his own sword: "Poor man! He was a stranger to the lenity of European warriors, but naturally thought the French had taken us all out to sea in deep water and murdered us ... He is the only Northern Indian who, that I ever heard, put an end to his own existence."

The balance of Hearne's service was merely an assignment to be performed, no longer a vocation to be cherished. He erected a wooden hut that had been prefabricated in London ("a brown-paper building," he called it), five miles upstream from the destroyed fort, on the site James Knight had occupied sixty-five years before, and tried somewhat listlessly to reawaken Churchill's prospects. But with the move of the trade inland, the post had become dormant, to be run eventually by a single post-master; its decline into oblivion was halted only during the twentieth century by its revival as a grain port, air hub and terminus of the Hudson Bay Railway.

Devastated by the smallpox epidemic and disillusioned by the HBC's inability to defend Prince of Wales's Fort, the Chipewyan now seldom emerged from the Barrens, preferring to trade at Fort Chipewyan on the Athabasca, a rudimentary post founded by the independent trader Peter Pond near what is now Old Fort Bay.* Downstream was Lake Athabasca, the hub of the mighty Slave,

---

* One of the Canadian frontier's more eccentric characters, Peter Pond spent his early life as a shoemaker, soldier and sailor, drifting into the Mississippi fur trade during the 1770s, having already killed a competitor in a duel. He moved north into previously untapped areas and in 1779 came out of the Chipewyan country with an astounding eighty thousand prime beaver skins. He was later accused of murdering a fellow-trader—the Swiss entrepreneur Jean-Etienne Waddens—and of being involved in yet another white killing and was eventually banished from the woods. He was the first to map the Mackenzie River system and to identify the tar sands of northern Alberta, later found to contain one of the largest reservoirs of oil in the earth's crust.

Peace and Mackenzie river systems that drain the virgin beaver country of northern Alberta. Battling their way up the treacherous Peace into the Buffalo Head Hills and eventually to within sight of the awesome Rocky Mountains, the Montreal pedlars opened for trade a huge watery delta that proved to be the continent's richest storehouse of quality furs.

The Treaty of Paris (1783) ended the fighting, but peace did not filter through to the Canadian fur trade. The American Revolution had driven more and more of the eastern traders deep into the Canadian northwest where nothing disturbed their entrepreneurial inclinations. Aided by their mastery of the water routes, the feisty pedlars were now rampaging across the continent in solid control of the inland fur trade. By 1779, their seasonal, short-term partnerships had been formally amalgamated into the North West Company, dedicated to capturing control of Canada's fur trade from the venerable but vulnerable HBC.

Not so much a financial vehicle as a loose confederation of common interests, the North West Company enjoyed the advantage of being able to make decisions on the spot. Its inland partners and Montreal-based agents met each summer at Grand Portage on the northwest shore of Lake Superior to plan the next season's fur harvesting strategies and ways of outflanking the still-powerful but pompously inflexible Hudson's Bay Company.*

The Company's London-based Committeemen, who had successfully held the reins of their field operations as long as they were confined to the shores of Hudson Bay, found themselves attempting to rule a commercial empire they could no longer control. To keep up with leap-frogging Nor'Westers, the HBC in 1786 appointed William Tomison its first inland Governor, thereby relegating the bay posts to a subordinate trans-shipment function. But as Tomison moved upstream on the North Saskatchewan River (from Manchester House to Buckingham House to Edmonton House), the London-based governors lost track of what was happening and where, certain only that their commercial survival depended on outrunning their new rivals. Initially, whenever the two companies occupied adjacent posts, their traders had been friendly, often exchanging books and joining in football games. But as the supply lines grew longer† and each company's

---

* The Nor'Westers moved their base forty miles north to Fort William, now Thunder Bay, in 1805.
† The distance from the North West Company forts on the Athabasca River to Montreal was three thousand miles, one way.

resources became increasingly strained, they began to wage a war of attrition that would eventually exhaust them both.

The continent-wide confrontation, which quickly became one of the deadliest feuds in commercial history, was seen simply as a duel between the dull but dependable functionaries of the HBC and the dashing but extravagant fortune-seekers of the North West Company. Such oversimplifications did little to explain the significant differences between the two sets of traders, who shared very little except the quest for fur. The location of their home-bases—Montreal/Fort William and London/York Factory—also determined the character and function of their operations.

The HBC continued its century-old trading pattern in and out of Hudson Bay, but with one great difference—most of the furs had to be collected at posts inland rather than being transported to the bay by unpaid Indian paddlers. That meant having to set up, for the first time, a transportation network between the bay and the inland posts. In this, the Nor'Westers had a distinct advantage because they already had easy access to both the technology and the raw material required to make canoes.*

There were no birch trees on the shores of Hudson Bay. The canoes built by the local Cree, makeshift at best, were not more than eighteen feet long with a carrying capacity of less than 350 pounds. These craft might have been suitable for the HBC trade if the Indians had been willing to become dependable hirelings, and to perform the necessary ferrying function. But such notions of servility were foreign to their nature; the receipt of free goods or payment of wages imposed no clearly recognized obligations. The usual result of assigning either a load of trade goods or a consignment of furs to the Indians' care was that neither was ever seen again. In 1775, Hearne had thought that one way to resolve this dilemma would be to have light timber skiffs built in England for assembly at York Factory, but when the ungainly craft arrived the HBC men refused to board them. By importing the necessary materials from

---

* One of the two main types they used was the *canot du maître*, up to forty feet in length, with a capacity of four tons and manned by ten paddlers. At the western end of Lake Superior, the goods were re-embarked into *canots du nord*, smaller vessels with half the carrying capacity but light enough for two men to lift across portages. Birch bark was the only indigenous material strong enough to carry economical loads, yet sufficiently light to be spun away from rock outcrops with a flick of the steersman's wrist. Cedar frames were bent (using heat) into halfcircles, and the bark was sewn on with wattape made from spruce roots and then caulked with spruce gum. Two large canes shaped the gunwales and shorter rods of beechwood were formed into paddlers' thwarts.

their land-bound posts and teaching themselves the art of canoe-making, the HBC's traders were gradually able to overcome this early crisis, though for bulk freight they eventually settled on York boats, the double-ended, forty-foot-long craft originally designed at Albany in 1746. Descended from sturdy inter-island skiffs, they had a gaff-rigged sail and, being flat-bottomed, could be rolled on logs across portages while fully loaded.

At the time the HBC was facing its first major assault from the North West Company, it suffered not only from a shortage of usable canoes but also from a lack of crews to man them. For one thing, the NWC had a much larger manpower pool from which to draw recruits. Quebec after the conquest was estimated to have a population of about sixty thousand, and it increased rapidly thereafter with the highest birthrate ever recorded. As late as 1799, the HBC still had only 498 men posted in North America.* Space for bringing new employees across the Atlantic was severely limited by the fact that most of the supply ships' holds were crammed with trade goods, not recruits. England was at war for twenty-eight of the forty-seven years between the founding of Cumberland House and the amalgamation of the two companies in 1821. Orkney seamen were liable to press gangs. The wars of 1778–1783 and 1793–1815 had stripped the Orkneys of seamen at such a rate that at one point the HBC was permitted to recruit only locals shorter than five-feet-four—the height restriction of the Royal Navy. The Company's agent in the Orkneys could meet his recruitment quota only by taking on boys twelve to fourteen years old. Another disruption was that gunsmiths in England had been seconded to the war effort, leaving for the fur hunt mostly badly made muskets that tended to explode and take part of a hand with them.

The obvious alternative—to hire voyageurs from Montreal—was not practical because of the complications caused by the short navigation seasons of Hudson Bay and the St Lawrence, and also because the HBC traders did not trust their NWC counterparts, whose short tempers ignited more violence and distrust among the various tribes than the HBC was willing to tolerate.

Most of the Nor'Westers were bellicose risk takers unhampered by the discipline of a strict corporate structure. Steeped in the frontier ethic of sacrificing long-term stability for short-term gain, they based much of their commerce on an explosive mixture of rum and violence, indiscriminately exploiting Indian

---

* Of the total, 180 were still employed on the bay. At this time there were 1,276 Nor'Westers engaged in the fur trade, 903 of them west of Grand Portage.

trappers and seducing their women. Edward Umfreville, an HBC officer who defected to the NWC, complained that "The Hudson's Bay traders have ingratiated themselves more into the esteem and confidence of the natives than the Canadians.... The great impudence and bad way of living of the Canadian traders have been an invincible bar to the emolument of their employers."

In practical terms, the carefree behaviour of some of the Montreal traders meant that, fearing possible reprisals, few dared to winter in the same locality twice. This precluded them from establishing stable business patterns. Although the Nor'Westers enjoyed a longer trading season (from April to October) than their bay-bound competitors and travelled through land that abounded with fish and game (in contrast to the "starving country" west of Hudson Bay), these advantages were overshadowed by the length of their supply line. Manufactured goods had to arrive in Montreal from overseas by November of one year so they could be sorted, bagged and baled for the voyage inland the following April. Taken by cart, and later canal, around the Lachine rapids, they were tallied and packed into the big freight canoes. Forty days and thirty-five portages later, they arrived at the tip of Lake Superior for transshipment to the smaller "northern" canoes. Only then could the Nor'Westers make for the fur country, still a thousand miles to the west, where they wintered. They then had to double back along the same route, so that a single transaction often took up to twenty-four months to complete. William McGillivray, one of the North West Company's guiding spirits, complained about the difficulties of having to compete against a company that imported its goods at less than half the expense incurred by the Nor'Westers.

It was an uneven battle fought with all the passion of a Sicilian vendetta. But in the process of trying to outdo one another, the competing fur traders roughed out the contours of upper North America.

AN EARLY CASUALTY of the fur trade wars was Samuel Hearne. Now Governor of a narrowing fiefdom, he hunched in his Churchill hut, feeling far removed from the action and, though not yet forty, a full generation behind the youngsters taking over the fur trade. There was almost no Home Guard left around Churchill to stimulate local commerce; only a few Chipewyan still made the seven-month round trip to the bay; the whale fishery to the north bore lean results; and the bored Orkneymen in Hearne's service indulged in illegal private trading. Once the Company's showpiece, the post had become a dingy liability. Not surprisingly, the fretful London Committeemen blamed

Hearne for the slack. Stung by their criticism and still grieving for his soul-mates, Matonabbee and Mary Norton, who had defined his life, Hearne requested home leave. On August 16, 1787, he sailed out of Hudson Bay for the last time.

The valour of his Coppermine journey had scarcely prepared Hearne for the vanities of London society. The only surviving portrait of Hearne painted after his return to England depicts him as a pasty-faced and slightly wall-eyed dandy, done up in a lace blouse and blond wig. Yet in the field, fellow fur traders remembered him as a handsome and robust wilderness man with a ruddy complexion, who stayed in condition by racing against moose.

He chose to reside in modest quarters in Red Lion Square, spending most of the time preparing his journal for publication. He drew £600 from his savings with the Company, was reported to have joined the Bucks Club* and expended considerable energy defending himself from the harsh harassment of Alexander Dalrymple, who had published a pamphlet entitled *Memoir of a Map of the Lands about the North Pole* in which he questioned Hearne's accuracy as a surveyor.

The former chief cartographer of the East India Company and the future hydrographer of the British Admiralty, Dalrymple may have been history's busiest armchair geographer. Having drafted charts of a vast, mythical Pacific continent named the Great South Land, he was furious with Captain Cook when that doughty navigator not only could not locate it but proved it did not exist. The disinherited seventh son of a Scottish baronet, Dalrymple was an energetic manipulator who advocated exploitation of a land-bound "North West Passage" *through* America instead of around it. This scheme called for a grand amalgamation between the Hudson's Bay Company and the East India Company, then holding a monopoly on trade to both China and India. It proposed combining their assets and spheres of influence to eliminate the Russian middlemen who were beginning to reap extraordinary profits from the American–Asian fur trade. Dalrymple visualized the furs being collected at a Pacific port located an "expedient distance from Hudson Bay," for trans-shipment to China. Conjuring up his improbable dreams behind the Ionic

---

* The Order of the Bucks, a spurious offshoot of the Freemasons, was primarily a drinking club that met at various London pubs, its adherents exchanging bawdy tales and smashing glasses in the fireplaces. The only membership rule seems to have been that no Buck could wear the same waistcoat to more than one Bacchanal.

façade of East India House on London's Leadenhall Street, the cartographer pored over Hearne's charts and journals, borrowed from Samuel Wegg, the HBC Governor, and decided to make a few alterations.

Dalrymple still hoped to discover an easy passage from Hudson Bay to the West Coast and hated to admit that Hearne's observations shattered that possibility. If he could nudge Hearne's route map a few degrees southward, he reasoned, there was always a chance that a channel still existed to the north. The first part of his wish came true when he correctly calculated that Hearne had committed errors in his observations at the mouth of the Coppermine River. By recording his position as 71°55′N and 120°30′W (instead of 67°48′N and 115°47′W), Hearne had placed himself to be more than two hundred miles farther north than he actually was.

The error was excusable. Hearne had been reduced to making many observations by dead reckoning. His only instrument, an Elton quadrant that had been lying around York Factory for thirty years, was smashed on his way back to Hudson Bay. The Hearne observations were corrected half a century later by an 1821 expedition led by John Franklin across part of the same territory. Equipped with every advantage then known to science, Franklin returned to a hero's welcome and a knighthood.* In vivid contrast, Hearne lived out his days working on his journal, noting that it was not meant "for those who are critics of geography" but for readers who might be "gratified by having the face of a country brought to their view." His health and his money gave out before the book was published.

Having spent so much of his life outside the money economy, Hearne tended to lend what modest funds he had with more generosity than discretion. The eighteenth century's equivalent of Lawrence of Arabia, Hearne had dared the impossible and succeeded, but in the process he assimilated the survival techniques of a civilization so foreign to his own that he found it impossible to thrive within the urban sophistication of England. It was only with the help of his old friend, the astronomer William Wales, that he was able to negotiate a good contract with the publishers of *Cook's Third Voyage*.

---

* Joseph Burr Tyrrell, the pioneering Canadian surveyor who traversed similar ground in 1893, wrote: "It has been my good fortune to travel over parts of the same country through which Hearne had journeyed 123 years before me, and into which no white man had ventured in the intervening time. The conditions which I found were just as he describes ..." In the mid-1950s, the Geological Survey of Canada still carried notations on maps of the terrain crossed by Hearne warning: "relief data incomplete" and "highest elevation unknown."

His £200 advance for *Journey to the Northern Ocean* was relatively generous—certainly so when compared with the £10 Jane Austen was paid for some of her early novels. But only a month after he signed the publishing contract and a full three years before his book was actually printed, Hearne died of dropsy, a condition usually associated with cirrhosis of the liver.

Neither the man nor his book enjoyed more than a brief posthumous following. Hearne's austere style of northern travel was sniffed at by the traditionalists who still subscribed to more formal schools of discovery, even if their bravura approach was about to lead a whole generation of valiant men seeking the North West Passage to their deaths. Hearne's picaresque approach to life and his disregard for timetables and drawing room niceties made him something of an outcast even among his peers. It was the final irony of Hearne's magnificent but muted career that the chief disciple of his gentle, naturalistic approach to exploration would be Dr John Rae, a nineteenth-century HBC Chief Factor whose main claim to fame would be his discovery of the doomed Arctic expedition of Sir John Franklin, who was the most flamboyant exponent of the old-school-tie approach to exploration.

"Hearne was a contradictory mixture of indecision and persistency, and his weakness seemed always on the verge of overwhelming his strengths—but ... he had a habit of coming out on top," concluded Gordon Speck, his biographer. Had Samuel Hearne's exploits been sponsored by a less circumspect agency than the Hudson's Bay Company, his magnificent Coppermine journey would have made him an international folk hero.

Instead, his only monument is the elegantly hand-chiselled graffito—SL. HEARNE JULY ye 2 1767—he himself carved into the smoothly curving granite on tidewater at Sloops Cove, within sight of the long-abandoned palisades guarding Prince of Wales's Fort. The fortress's restored splendour haunts Hudson Bay to this day—silent and foreboding, its blocks of stone square and solid as if cut by the very hand of rectitude.

March of Empire

"We know only two powers—God and the Company."   —John Rowand
Chief Factor, Edmonton House
Hudson's Bay Company

BY THE END of the eighteenth century, the Company of Adventurers could look back on the conquest of Hudson Bay and salute the successful launch of a reassuringly profitable commercial enterprise. The tentative probes by Groseilliers, Radisson, Bayley, Knight, Kelsey, Henday and Hearne had been amply rewarded. What was now emerging on their parchment maps was the outline of a great inland trapping preserve, all theirs, but increasingly menaced by the freebooters from Montreal.

The pioneering traders who sat out their lives in the forts around the bay may have been unremarkable men, castaways in a tight-fisted land, yet they achieved something truly magnificent.

They endured.

Although colonies are founded as fragments of the mother societies from which they spring, a scarcely perceptible sea-change took place on the shores of Hudson Bay that transformed the early squatters and their spartan ethic. Despite the Company's rigid control, their individual attachments to their motherland eroded. To survive, they began to borrow from native lore, becoming more attuned to the cadence of their self-imposed exile, growing in confidence and sense of purpose as their mission expanded to the taming of a sub-continent.

The sleep by the frozen sea and its haunting, ice-bound serenity was over. From among the ranks of the Bay men in the next century would spring a dynasty of merchant princes who gave voice and deed to transforming these first awkward stirrings into the world's largest commercial empire—and, eventually, into a new nationality.

From the founding of the rival North West Company in 1783 to the surrender of the HBC's monopoly in 1869—the Hudson's Bay Company aroused every emotion except indifference. The profit-haunted puritans who were the Company's field hands subordinated their personal impulses to remarkably single-minded corporate principles designed to maximize dividends, minimize personal profiles and perpetuate the powers of the royally chartered monopoly. Those who were outside the faith—the HBC's competitors, its parliamentary opponents and the would-be colonizers of its territories—found "the Company of Adventurers of England Tradeing into Hudsons Bay" anything but benign. In an open letter to Lord Palmerston, the British prime minister, Andrew Freeport, an observer of the HBC's methods, noted that "the management of their affairs ... is like a commercial tomb, closed with the key of death to all except a favoured few ... its councils unfathomable and its secrets unknown."

Suspended in doldrums of time, place and spirit—asleep "at the edge of a frozen sea," as their critics rightly charged—the Bay men watched the coalescing of their Montreal-based rivals into the North West Company. The energetic young competitors threatened to cut off their fur supplies by establishing inland trading posts along the rivers feeding Hudson Bay. And still they watched. At first, the HBC reacted not at all, trusting the kindly Providence that had, it seemed, always blessed its uncomplicated commerce. Doing nothing about something as important as a dynamic rival determined to undermine the Company's business created a soporific inertia of considerable power. This was typical of the HBC's operational code—to allow their trading rivals enough latitude to hang themselves. Only when it looked as if the royal adventurers themselves were about to be terminated did the Company spring into action. It took more than a decade for the feud between the two outfits to be fully joined. But once it was, the forests exploded.

As they launched their own long march inland, the HBC traders encountered a breed of buccaneers very different from themselves. Instead of being servants indentured to distant governors, the Nor'Westers were the rampaging free enterprisers of the North American frontier—brave men who had transcended their Presbyterian ethic to mix a little Methodism in their madness. Having adopted a crude form of commercial chutzpah far removed from the grand strategies of British mercantilism and even farther removed from the elegant principle that one should grow rich strictly from other people's labours, these brawny wintering partners were not afraid to plunge into the mosquito-plagued portages of the inland waterways or to spend months in frost-caked lean-tos if it would boost their personal share of profits. This unquenchable impulse—that it was essential to work for oneself and not, like their HBC competitors, for absentee landlords who knew little about the going rate for stamina and defiance—was the incentive that allowed the Nor'Westers to dominate the fur trade and to stay on top for most of four decades.

The Nor'Westers' remarkable exploits were inextricably woven into those of the HBC, and vice versa. They followed their gutsy instincts, convinced that their unorthodox methods were the only right way of doing things and that no matter how much the Hudson's Bay Governors might wish it, dominance over *le pays sauvage* could no longer be held by waistcoated financiers lounging around mahogany Adam tables in London's marble halls. Although the Nor'Westers could never obtain a charter to prove it, their hunting grounds eventually extended by right of possession farther than the immense Rupert's Land domain of the Hudson's Bay Company. It was they who developed the first transcontinental trading system. Their profits reflected their fortitude; more than three-quarters of the subcontinent's fur trade moved to their accounts within fifteen years of the NWC's formation. In what turned out to be premature gloating, one of the Montreal Nor'Wester agents proclaimed in feigned protest that *of course* he and his partners did not want to see the HBC go out of business—slyly adding that the Company of Adventurers provided a most useful "cloak to protect the trade from more active opponents."

THE COMMERCIAL WARFARE between the Hudson's Bay and North West companies meant that Canada, which has prided itself on having undergone no revolutions or wars of independence and prissily set itself apart as always having been a "peaceable kingdom," experienced its own equivalent of the American Wild West. The competing fur brigades fought bloody but contained skirmishes in the forests and along the rivers west of the Great Lakes. It was somehow typically Canadian that this struggle was not, as in the American West, concerned with noble assertions of individual liberty against land-hungry cattle barons and black-hatted railway promoters—or even a brave push for collective independence—but was rather an internecine feud between two houses of commerce locked in mortal combat for greater profits.

There was no other commercial feud to equal it.

Ostensibly, the struggle between the HBC and the North West Company was a corporate contest for markets and furs, but it quickly turned into a quest for power and territory. The competition for beaver pelts grew so intense that the northern reaches of America's forests became a battleground.

Both sides settled their accounts in blood. Snipers rode the riverbanks. Loaded cannon were used to reclaim stolen cargoes. Murder and ambush, arson and theft, kidnapping and destruction of property became so common that the act of maiming a competitor was regarded as a condition of doing business. Anarchy escalated to such a degree that in 1803 Britain's Parliament passed the Canada Jurisdiction Act, intended specifically to prevent the abuses that characterized the lawless conflict between the fur-trading companies. But without a resident police to enforce it, the legislation had little effect. In the first eighteen years after these provisions were passed, there is no record of anyone actually being convicted under the law—even though this was the period of the most vicious fighting in the Canadian Northwest.

In one assault, European mercenaries captured the Nor'Westers' main wilderness stronghold. Both sides abused their prisoners, and on the rustic outskirts of the HBC's Red River Colony, twenty settlers and the resident Governor were shot and their bodies mutilated by retainers of the North West Company. Worst of all, by concentrating on massive quantities of liquor as an irresistible lure in the frantic contest for the Indian trappers' bounty, the traders of both companies debauched a civilization, leaving in their wake a dispirited people and nearly destroying a once-proud culture. "It was a bitter war in which each party wielded weapons of trade and violence mercilessly in turn," summarized the Harvard historian Frederick Merk. "From the arsenal of war were drawn raids, the levelling of each other's trading posts, incitation of the Indians and half-breeds to open fighting and secret stabbing and shooting in the shadows of the forest."

Only after the spiral of violence had exhausted itself by the early 1820s in the amalgamation of the two companies' 173 posts under the name and dominance of the HBC did it become clear how close the hostilities between the two firms had come to escalating into all-out war. When the NWC eventually turned in its weapons, the inventory of the Columbia Department alone revealed that its Pacific Coast traders had been armed not only with the usual array of rifles and other small arms but with thirty-two cannon ranging from eighteen-pounders to half-pound swivel guns.

Having won the corporate battle, the Hudson's Bay Company now enjoyed the spoils, lording it over an empire more than twice the size of the princely domain it had originally been granted by Charles II, which had encompassed the then unmapped territory covered by the many rivers draining from nearly every point of the compass into Hudson Bay. The Company's new monopoly stretched from Labrador through to the Pacific Coast and across the continent's northern reaches. The HBC held joint occupancy in what are now the American states of Oregon, Washington, Idaho, Wyoming, and Montana with outposts as far away as Alaska, Hawaii and San Francisco. This was the moment of the HBC's greatest glory, the time when it held sway over nearly one-twelfth of the earth's land surface. No other commercial enterprise ever achieved comparable sway over so much territory. (The HBC cagily protected its empire against the encroachment of ambitious outsiders by manipulating fur prices, so that challengers soon lost the fiscal will to perpetuate the contest.) During most of the half-century it ruled over this enormous domain, the Company's authority was supreme: it exercised nearly every mandate of a sovereign government, with Sir George Simpson acting as uncrowned king.

It was under Simpson's rigorous stewardship that the HBC exerted its maximum impact on the formation of the Canadian character. As already pointed out, much of the northern half of North America became a company town, whose inhabitants displayed individuality and imagination at their own risk. Because the little trading posts (or forts, as many were grandly called) were owned and operated by the Company, the prevailing ethic was deference to authority inside their toy ramparts and deference to nature beyond them. These attitudes—the importance of allegiance, of stressing collective survival over individual excellence, of faith in protocol, of respect for the proper order of things—still colour what Canadians do and, especially, don't do.

The most significant historical contribution of both the Hudson's Bay and North West companies was simply that they existed when they did along the still only vaguely defined boundary separating British North America from the United States. "Between 1821 and 1869, it was the skill and perseverance with which the Hudson's Bay Company protected its monopoly trading area between the Great Lakes and the Rocky Mountains that prevented an influx of American settlers that could easily have made the Canadian prairies a second Oregon," noted Dr W. Kaye Lamb, who has written extensively on the fur trade. "And if this had not been so, it is unlikely that Canada as we know it today would now exist."

The two companies acted as willing surrogates of the British Empire, occupying for their own purposes the lands beyond its North American colonies. They thus safeguarded these territories until Canada's own awakened imperialistic aspirations took over; this was in time recognized as an essential stage in nation-building.

Similarly, the very fact that these corporate hierarchies existed on the northern side of the border, while the early American fur industry was dominated by individualistic mountain men who competed with Indians for each pelt and liked nothing better than "sniping redskins to watch them spin," fathered permanent characteristics in both societies. The Americans conquered their frontier, sharpshooters against tomahawks, across the ill-famed "Bloody Ground," with the U.S. Cavalry verging on committing genocide in its sixty-nine major attacks on the red man. In sharp contrast, both the Nor'Westers and the Bay men recognized the Indians as long-term trading partners. They formed a relationship based on mutual exploitation. This meant that the Indians were able to trade near-worthless pelts (they had previously killed animals mainly for food) for such desirable goods as axes, guns, blankets and sewing needles; the corporate representatives, on the other hand, got the furs at a fraction of their value on European markets. All parties in the transaction thus had a permanent stake in each other's welfare and in conducting the barter with a modicum of fair play.

The two fur companies fought one another as if they were pursuing a Sicilian vendetta. But they never shot their customers. Frederick Merk, the American history professor who has studied the fur trade of both countries, concluded that the "striking contrast between British and American Indian relations was no mere temporary phenomenon disappearing with the passing of the fur trade. It persisted as long as the red man and the white faced each other in the coveted land of the Far West. Trapper and trader gave way on both sides of the international boundary to miner and cattleman and they in turn to the pioneer farmer. These harbingers of a new day on the American side entered a region of already established strife and perpetuated there traditions two centuries old of Indian massacre and border retaliation. On the Canadian side civilization entered a region reduced by the Hudson's Bay Company to a tradition of law and order...."

THE DEBT TO WATER in the nation's history is another dominant trait within the Canadian character nurtured by the fur trade. Novelist Clark Blaise has spoken of "the parenting effect of water on the Canadian imagination" and no politician jealous of his mandate has ever advocated the export of a drop of the stuff. "Water is very special to Canadians," Dr Derrick Sewell, a geography professor at the University of Victoria and specialist on water usage, has commented. "There is no Indian word for wilderness, because while we may regard it as something separate from us, for them the wilderness is every-thing—their dwelling place and source of food, part of their being. To some degree, Canadians view water with that kind of internal attachment."

The birchbark canoes of the fur trade were propelled by the brawn and sixth sense of the voyageurs, who were so sensitized to thousands of miles of river subtleties that they would use clumps of weeds streaming in fast currents as telltales of their progress. It was this flowing intimacy with the millions of square miles of wilderness that first created the notion that Canada might possess a geographical unity all its own.

The land (for its animals) was the quest of these hardy sojourners, but they depended on water for transportation and supply lines. The setting for nearly all this book is the network of lakes and rivers that interlaces Canada's western and northern heartland. Unlike most countries, Canada was first penetrated by water instead of on horseback. The animals could not cover enough of the rough terrain or find enough nourishment to survive in the Precambrian Shield—a rolling quagmire of rock, matted undergrowth, lakes and streams that covers nearly half the Canadian subcontinent.

Four key lakes—Huron, Superior, Winnipeg and Athabasca—were the interconnected hubs whose spokes radiated into the bountiful fur forests. Onward along three waterways—Hudson Bay, the St Lawrence and the Columbia—ran the transport routes to market. The water-highways developed by the early fur traders included many a portage around rapids, waterfalls and beaver dams, but in the entire length of the continent, the system was inter-rupted by few major land gaps, the longest of them being the twelve-mile Methy Portage in the Churchill river system at the crest of the Hudson Bay and Mackenzie Basin watersheds. "The waterways were almost miraculous in their range and intricacy, and the birchbark canoe a miracle of efficiency," noted the historian Chester Martin. "A trader could embark at Cumberland House [an HBC trading post on the Saskatchewan River not far west of Lake Winnipeg] and, with no portage longer than a single day, could reach the Arctic Ocean, the Pacific, the Atlantic, or the Gulf of Mexico."

THE FUR TRADERS who people this book possessed an inordinate capacity for living in desolation. Their stoicism may have bordered on masochism and yet it was much grander than that; any new challenge, however awkward or dangerous, could not go unaccepted. They were the true caesars of the wilderness—dispossessed Scots and Englishmen seized by the excitement of exploring a New World, determined to live out their boldest fantasies and win fortune in the process.

Their lives were hard and their isolation was hermetic: at Fort Good Hope on the Mackenzie River it took two years for a reply to be received from a letter to England. To the few outsiders who visited their domain, the traders seemed a species apart, men who had voluntarily stepped outside the bounds of civilized society. "I hate the sight of these forts," complained Frederick Ulric Graham, a British baronet who accompanied Simpson on one of his inland journeys. "All the white men living in them look as if they had been buried for a century or two, and dug up again, and had scarcely yet got their eyes open, for they look frightened when they see a stranger."

Their lives may indeed have been harsh, but the best of them savoured the sights, sounds and fragrances of a bewitching land where a man could lose his soul or grasp rare understanding of life's wonders and nature's cycles. The wild flowers forced their green energies through the snow. Deer, moose and ginger fox would watch them from the aromatic forest. The silence of the wild land could cloak emotions or become the catalyst for exhilarating self-discovery. Pretensions fell away like chips from a sculptor's block; character and capabilities were laid bare as stone.

Flashes of humiliation and self-hatred, the cursed immensity of the country, the feats of accomplishment performed without peers to validate one's bravery or compassion—those were the worst emotional ordeals.

Their collective endeavours mapped a continent and claimed an empire, yet with the exception of such grand personages as Sir George Simpson and Lord Selkirk (the utopian Scot who planted Western Canada's first settlement) the men and women portrayed in this book were not aristocrats, innovators or daredevils. They were survivors. They patterned their behaviour around each day's mundane events, leading expedient lives, with the maintenance of shelter and the hunting of food as prevailing priorities. Inclement weather might obliterate overnight a promising pattern of animal tracks, and *that* was often a far weightier matter than the balance-sheet considerations of their distant overlords. Time was as much of a problem as distance, with crucial canoe routes seldom open before mid-May and often frozen shut again by late September. Climate was always the final arbiter of the available options.

The streak of yearning for the freedom of wilderness existence so boldly personified by the men and women who people the pages that follow has endured within the nation's psyche. Most modern Canadians have forgotten or never known about these valiant caesars of the wilderness, yet their lives are marked by the same seasonal rhythms, equally touched by the shared loneliness—the ineffable "northernness" that forms the Canadian character.

V EMPIRE AT RISK

The Nor'Westers

Never able to establish themselves on Hudson Bay, the Nor'Westers stepped over the edge of the horizon and explored virgin lands beyond the known world.

LIKE CRUSADERS of the Middle Ages they ultimately failed in their quest and soiled the banner under which they set out to conquer a continent. But between 1783 and 1820, the Nor'Westers braved the wilderness and won. Operating out of their counting houses in Montreal and a hundred or so outposts connected by an inland navy of two thousand canoeists, they challenged the power and majesty—the very existence—of the Hudson's Bay Company and fought the Royal Adventurers to a standstill.

THE NORTH WEST COMPANY was the first North American business to operate on a continental scale. Its vast holdings were administered with greater efficiency and larger civil budgets than the provinces of Lower and Upper Canada. The NWC's wilderness headquarters, first at Grand Portage and later at Fort Kaministikwia (renamed Fort William in honour of William McGillivray, the company's second chief executive officer), could accommodate nearly two thousand people at the height of the trading season, its fifteen-foot palisade of pointed timbers enclosing Canada's first inland metropolis.

The logistics of fur and goods purchasing and the need to co-ordinate a precariously overextended transportation network led to the development of a remarkably sophisticated trading system. The brigades of canoes, loaded to the gunwales with kegs of liquor and packs of trade goods, pushed up from the St Lawrence along the Ottawa and Mattawa rivers, over the height of land and across Lake Nipissing, down the French River to Georgian Bay,

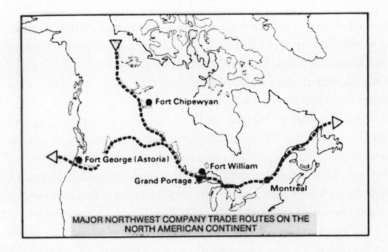

MAJOR NORTHWEST COMPANY TRADE ROUTES ON THE
NORTH AMERICAN CONTINENT

through the company's primitive wooden lock at Sault Ste Marie and into Lake Superior. At their northwestern terminus on Superior, the trade goods were trans-shipped into the smaller *canots du nord*, then paddled and portaged up through Rainy Lake, Lake of the Woods and the Winnipeg River into Lake Winnipeg for dispersal along the South and North Saskatchewan rivers and up the Red. The canoes also headed northwest up the Churchill River towards the dreaded Methy Portage that linked the river systems with outlets in the Arctic and Pacific watersheds.

Bringing the furs back to Montreal—the gathering point for their ultimate destination at London's auction markets—meant backtracking over the same route. By the time the Nor'Westers were fully exploiting the prime fur-bearing grounds of the Athabasca Country, the supply line was more than three thousand miles long. These horrendous distances, plus a climate that reduced the period of navigation on northern rivers to less than half the year, created the company's greatest dilemma. Up to thirty months might elapse between the purchase of trade goods and the sale of the furs for which they had been bartered. Every possible shortcut was explored, including an investment of £12,000 "toward making Yonge Street a better road" so that goods in winter could be shipped more efficiently from the town of York (now Toronto) to Georgian Bay.

The Nor'Westers' outposts stretched from Nasquiscow Lake in central Labrador to Fort St James west of the Rockies, north to Fort Good Hope, south to Astoria at the mouth of the Columbia River on the Pacific, across the Prairies and Great Lakes. As well as maintaining posts at nearly every important river junction in what is now northern and western Canada, the NWC established strings of trading forts in present-day Oregon, Washington, Idaho, Montana, North Dakota, Minnesota and Wisconsin. The supply lines converged on a cluster of forty warehouses at Lachine, a cart ride from the partners' headquarters in Montreal.

The most remarkable feature of this wilderness empire was its roots in original exploration. The pathfinders and mapmakers of the North American continent's upper latitudes were the fur traders of the North West Company. With a few dramatic exceptions such as Samuel Hearne, Peter Fidler and Dr John Rae, the HBC's officers for most of a century were content to remain ensconced around Hudson Bay, prepared to allow others to determine the lay of the land. The Nor'Westers were a more venturesome breed. Peter Pond was the first white man into the Athabasca Country in 1778, and half a decade later the various partnerships exploring the continent's outlying regions had become united in a transcontinental trading company determined to take on the HBC and its hoary charter. The Nor'Westers numbered among their officers some of history's most courageous explorers. Sir Alexander Mackenzie was the first European to cross North America north of Mexico; he and Simon Fraser hacked their way to the mouths of the torrential rivers that now bear their names. By 1805, the Nor'Westers had started trading past the Great Divide, and Western Canada's founding geographer, David Thompson, was well into his most productive decade of drafting the first workable maps of North America, which included his discovery of the Mississippi's headwaters.

The NWC traders who preceded and followed these and other daring explorers left behind a legacy of alcoholism, syphilis, Mixed Blood babies—and the precise path for the Hudson's Bay Company's subsequent march inland. There was little doubt, as fur-trade historian H.A. Innis put it, that "the North West Company was the forerunner" of Canadian Confederation, but its more direct accomplishment was to place the huge dominion of land beyond the HBC's territory under the protection of the British Crown.

That these enterprising expansionists deemed each new North West Company outpost to be an extension of the British monarch's reach was the company's most curious gift to posterity, since the Nor'Westers were nearly all either Scots or French—both victims of English imperialism. But they needed London. The manufactured goods essential to the fur trade, such as blankets, axes and particularly the much-sought-after guns, had to be purchased in

England. London was, of course, also the chief market for dressed pelts, though the Nor'Westers later managed to sidestep that monopoly by trading some of their more valuable sea otter skins directly to Canton in southeast China, navigating half the globe to do so.

The impact of the transcontinental trading routes was pervasive enough to work the magic that helped save Western Canada from being absorbed into the United States. The land had already been claimed through right of exploration by the Nor'Westers and later by occupation of the Hudson's Bay Company. It was a puny scattering of tiny outposts that held the line, but it was enough.

The Nor'Westers' impulse to explore uncharted territories was less the product of an altruistic desire to advance the frontiers of knowledge than a result of the company's infrastructure and the stretch of its traplines. The NWC's profitability depended on constantly moving onward and outward to tap newer and richer animal preserves. That, in turn, meant maintaining an ever-lengthening transportation system with large and multiplying overhead expenditures. Unlike the more sedentary Bay men, the Nor'Westers were constantly in motion. As the beaver lodges in relatively accessible corners were trapped out, the canoes moved ever farther afield—and the longer the network, the less viable it became. No wonder the North West Company's official motto eschewed Latin subtleties, encapsulating its hopes in a one-word, no-nonsense exclamation: "PERSEVERANCE"!

Throughout its glory days, the North West Company sought in vain what the Hudson's Bay Company took for granted: direct sea access into the continent's midriff and a monopoly sanctioned by royal decree over the trading area within its jurisdiction. "The rivalry was not between two commercial enterprises at all," Daniel Francis, a popular historian of the fur trade, has commented. "Rather, it was a rivalry between two great geographic possibilities. Would the resources of the western hinterland flow southeastward across the Great Lakes and down the Ottawa River to Canada? Or would they take the shorter route north and east, through the stunted forest of the Shield to the swampy shores of Hudson Bay? For almost half a century the answer hung in the balance." Because the Bay route reduced the cost of transportation by more than fifteen hundred canoe-miles, the geographical advantages clearly lay with the London-based Company. Never able to establish themselves on Hudson Bay, the Nor'Westers stepped over the edge of the horizon and explored virgin lands beyond the known world.

Within two decades of their original amalgamation, the Nor'Westers controlled 78 percent of Canadian fur sales and could caustically claim that the Hudson's Bay Company was doing business "as if it were drawn by a dead horse." They ruled the West. Despite perilously overextended supply lines, during the decade and a half after the turn of the century the Nor'West part-ners earned net profits estimated at £1,185,000. This meant that original investments of £800 returned £16,000. The NWC also achieved a well-balanced diversification in its fur offerings. In a typical year (1798) their catch included: 106,000 beaver skins, 2,100 bear, 5,500 fox, 4,600 otter, 17,000 musquash (muskrat), 32,000 marten, 1,800 mink, 6,000 lynx, 600 wolverine, 1,600 fisher, 3,800 wolf, 700 elk hides and 1,900 deer hides. Five hundred buffalo robes were a bonus.

They not only grew rich, they also became powerful, forming the fledgling colony's first indigenous commercial Establishment. Unlike the Bay men who went back across the Atlantic at the expiration of their contracts, most Nor'Westers settled down and stayed on. Many of the NWC partners built elegant houses at the foot of Montreal's Mount Royal, capricious castles meant both to display their newly won riches and to proclaim their intention of establishing family dynasties. Their profits helped build the Bank of Montreal into what was briefly North America's largest financial institution, and their favourite hearth, that saturnalian dining phenomenon known as the Beaver Club, became for its time the most exclusive fraternity on the continent.

These knights of the forest regarded themselves as inheritors of that mantle of esteem once worn by gladiators and noblemen, or, more appropriately, Highland clan chieftains—living proof to a hesitant colonial society that ability and application could be spectacularly rewarded. "Sometimes one or two partners, recently from the interior posts, would make their appearance in New York," observed the American historian Washington Irving. "On these occasions there was a degree of magnificence of the purse about them, and a peculiar propensity to expenditure at the goldsmith's and jeweller's for rings, chains, brooches, necklaces, jewelled watches, and other rich trinkets, partly for their own wear, partly for presents to their female acquaintances; a gorgeous prodigality, such as was often to be noticed in former times in Southern planters and West India creoles, when flush with the profits of their plantations."

Irving made fun of "the swelling and braggart style" of "these hyperborean nabobs," noting that the Nor'Westers were not merely traders but in fact proprietors. In sharp contrast to even the most senior employees of the HBC, who laboured for overseas patrons and paltry wages, the ranking Nor'Westers controlled their own destinies. An uneasy alliance of up to three dozen partners, among them Montreal-based Scottish promoters and merchants, the NWC may not have been blessed with a royal charter but its shareholders reaped regal profits. The cost of one share averaged £4,000, and yet yearly dividends of £400 were routinely disbursed at a time when clerks at the NWC's trading posts were being paid £100 per annum.

No wonder the North West Company partners behaved as though they were chiefs of a transcontinental clan, claiming all the traditions and especially the loyalties due in such a feudal structure. Their escutcheons and rituals were designed to strengthen the notion that only within the confines of the corporation could its partners discover and exploit their true natures. Any deviation from set standards was considered treachery. No clan operated with more ruthless efficiency than the North West Company of Montreal.

The organization's hierarchy was not as refined as that of the HBC, which maintained ranks so minutely structured that by accepted protocol Chief Factors, when ordered to perform a duty, had to be "requested," Chief Traders "directed" and non-commissioned officers "instructed"—even when they were talking to one another in the bush. Highlanders entered the NWC as clerks, rising in rank to masters of minor trading posts and eventually, if they produced results, to wintering partners. This latter category, which had no early equivalent within the HBC, gave officers in the field the double incentive of sharing in profits and having a direct voice in formulating policies that would multiply revenues. They were owners as well as operators. At the top of the pyramid were the Montreal agents or directors, who received commissions for their commercial services besides owning a controlling interest of the shares.

This visible, tightly knit command structure helped ignite the NWC's vibrant *esprit de corps*, but what made most of the senior partners so devoted to the common cause was that they belonged not just to the same company or even to the same clan, but often to the same family. At one time or another, there were on the NWC rolls seven Simon Frasers, four Finlays, five Camerons, six McTavishes, seven McLeods, eight McGillivrays, fourteen each of Grants and McKenzies and so many McDonalds that they had to differentiate themselves by including home towns in their surnames, as in

John McDonald of Garth.* It seemed at times that every partner in the North West Company was a blood relative to every other, most of them linking their family trees with that of Simon McTavish, the company's chief founder and guiding spirit. McTavish married a daughter of the trader Charles Chaboillez, whose other daughter became the wife of Roderick McKenzie, a first Cousin of Sir Alexander Mackenzie. Simon McTavish's nephew William McGillivray, later the leading partner in the concern (joining his brothers Duncan and Simon), married a sister of John McDonald of Garth, nephew-in-law of McTavish and a cousin of Patrick Small, whose daughter married David Thompson. McTavish had three nephews, two grandnephews, three nephews-in-law, two brothers-in-law, three cousins and one "distant cousin" in the company.

These family connections at least partly compensated for the North West Company's inherent instability as a constantly shifting set of partnerships among the internationally minded Montreal money men and the more earthy and less sophisticated wintering partners. At least eight different agreements were negotiated, and each time the inlanders believed their interests were being subordinated to those of the metropolitan agents who were determined not only to dominate the St Lawrence fur trade but to create business empires of their own. Most of the Montrealers, especially the Frobishers (Benjamin, Joseph and Thomas) and the various McGillivrays (who were all former traders), tried to keep themselves sensitive to the winterers' problems. But officers in the field seldom appreciated the grave difficulties involved in obtaining extended credit sources for the fur trade, the tricky and sometimes questionable tactics required to keep governments in line and the fiscal acrobatics necessary to maintain the prosperity of as volatile an enterprise as the North West Company.

---

* John McDonald of Garth, whose grandfather was wounded at Culloden, was one of the Canadian fur trade's more contentious characters. He often boasted that, as lords of the isles at the time of the Great Flood, the McDonalds had had their own ark on Loch Lomond, and the subsequent survival of their strongest men and fairest women rendered them superior to all Scotland's other clans. Although he was of small physical stature even for that time and was handicapped by a withered right arm, he enjoyed combat and fought several duels, one of them with a Hudson's Bay Company trader named William Tomison over the possession of a well. After his retirement from the NWC at the end of twenty-three years in the fur trade, he built himself a laird's home in Ontario's Stormont County, had sixty tenants cultivating his land and was named a justice of the peace.

SIMON MCTAVISH, who masterminded the firm's evolution for most of thirty years, remains a shadowy figure in Canadian history. Yet if Paul de Chomedey de Maisonneuve can be credited with the physical founding of Montreal, then it was McTavish with his genius for business organization who transformed the community into a major commercial centre. He repeatedly crowded out smaller Montreal partnerships and struck treaties with American fur companies, hiving their activities into the upper regions of the Mississippi and keeping them there with the persuasively domineering bluster that became his trademark and his chief negotiating weapon. His tenacity, territorial ambition and imperial lifestyle earned him the aristocratic sobriquet "Le Marquis," and he abundantly lived up to both the grandeur and the snobbishness his nickname implied. Lord Selkirk, the Scottish visionary whose colony would ultimately threaten the North West Company, observed during an 1804 visit to Montreal, "McTavish is entirely unequalled here in acuteness and reach of thought—he is admitted to have planned the constitution of the old North West Company by means of which that vast undertaking is kept together."

Born in 1750 on Lord Lovat's estate in Stratherrick, Simon McTavish was the son of a lieutenant in the old 78th, or Fraser's Highlanders, and emigrated to the American colonies at thirteen to apprentice in the Albany fur trade. Described even at that age as a charming young man who loved "good wine, good oysters and pretty girls," he moved to Montreal in about 1775 and began to haggle with the independent traders ranging into the continent's far corners, pushing the idea that the economies of scale inherent in a joint venture would benefit them all, particularly in the face of the HBC's implacable monopoly. By 1790, his firm McTavish, Frobisher & Company dominated the newly formed North West partnership, and he held the controlling interest. The coalition performed economic miracles, but it never achieved the calm possession of authority that the HBC could grandly assume; there were always upstarts ready to finance expeditions inland, knowing the NWC's tenure had no legitimacy beyond tenacious occupancy. The firm's facilities and communications lines were so stretched that it never ceased to be vulnerable.

Instead of relying on royal charters or bureaucratic niceties to enforce their rule over the territories in which they traded, the Nor'Westers under McTavish's direction used the much more direct technique of physically evicting intruders. In 1801, for example, a Montreal free-trader named Dominique

Rousseau sent a canoe inland under the command of a Monsieur Hervieu, who eventually set up a tiny emporium just beyond gunshot range of the NWC stronghold at Grand Portage. Duncan McGillivray, Simon McTavish's nephew and a senior NWC partner, immediately ordered him off the site. But Hervieu refused to move until he was shown title to the land, accurately pointing out that he had as much right to be there as anyone else. This legalistic demand for a document the Nor'Westers had never been able to obtain so infuriated McGillivray that he stuck his dagger into Hervieu's tent and slashed it beyond repair, bellowing that the free-trader's throat would be cut next if he ventured farther inland. Hervieu's boss, Rousseau, later took McGillivray to court and won £500 in damages. That legal victory emboldened him to try again, and in 1806 Rousseau dispatched two canoes under a Monsieur Delorme to trade north of Superior. On the trail from the lakehead, the little expedition was intercepted by Alexander McKay, a Nor'Wester with a mordant sense of humour. Instead of threatening the visitors, McKay ordered his crew to fell trees across the narrow creeks along Delorme's route, and the intruders were soon hopelessly entangled in branches. Frustrated beyond endurance and sensing that their persistent enemy was ready to block their watery path all the way to the Pacific, Delorme and his companions stepped out of their canoes, abandoned their trade goods and walked back to Montreal. Rousseau threatened another court case, but it was never heard; instead, the Nor'Westers paid Delorme back for the jettisoned goods—at the lower Montreal prices, of course.

By the 1790s, more than a hundred canoes were being sent inland annually from Lachine. For the next decade and a half McTavish's influence multiplied exponentially. He was recognized as Montreal's most important and richest merchant. In 1793, at a mature forty-three, he married the beautiful seventeen-year-old Marguerite Chaboillez and purchased, for £25,000, the seigneury of Terrebonne. When he was told that Castle Dunardary, the ancestral home of the chief of the Clan McTavish in Argyll, was due to go under the auctioneer's hammer, he bought that too and received permission to use the clan's armorial bearings. In Montreal, the newlyweds at first occupied a substantial house on Rue St Jean Baptiste, but in 1804 McTavish decided to build his love a northern palace. Angled into a plateau below Mount Royal (between today's Peel and McTavish streets) to allow an unobstructed vista of the St Lawrence River and the rounded mountains beyond, the mansion boasted a flamboyant four-storey façade marked by twin conical towers roofed in tin and a vaulted living-room that promised to become the focal point of Montreal society.

The fur barons tried hard to emulate their role models, the Scottish clan chiefs, by building themselves huge overdone pavilions and carefully keeping score of one another's ostentations. Joseph Frobisher, a Yorkshireman who passed as a Lowland Scot and became McTavish's senior partner, erected an impressive rockpile called Beaver Hall, whose sweeping driveway lined with Lombardy poplars welcomed every dignitary visiting Montreal. William McGillivray moved into Château St Antoine, and many of the lesser partners purchased seigneuries along the St Lawrence.* There was a golden autumn quality about their sybaritic lives, with even their most delightful diversions pervaded by a subtle end-of-season mood.

The fur trade was a demanding but highly seasonal enterprise. While the rivers were frozen the Montreal-based *nouveaux riches* devoted their energies to outdoing one another at lavishly catered sleigh rides, card tournaments, private musical recitals and masked balls. One former winterer shod his favourite horse with silver and galloped through the city's poorer districts, scattering showers of coins. He also loved riding into particularly fancy restaurants and ordering the animal a full-course meal. It was a comfortable if self-indulgent existence, but like veterans who can never transcend their time in the trenches, the citified Nor'Westers yearned to recapture the wild freedom and excitement of the frontier. Something, anything, to make the adrenalin pump again.

Those urges found their outlet in February 1785 with the founding of the Beaver Club, which became the quintessential NWC institution. Nothing like it could have been created by the prosaic ramrods then in charge of the Hudson's Bay Company. Despite its astronomical liquor consumption, the Beaver Club was much more than an urban watering hole. Here the Nor'Westers could abandon artificial dignities and re-create those heady times that had given meaning to their lives. Because it was only among their own that such nostalgia was lifted above its more mundane level of providing an excuse to get drunk and break furniture, membership in the Beaver Club was

* The only remaining public monument of the fur-trade fortunes is Montreal's McGill University. James McGill had been in the fur trade but gained most of his wealth from banking, timber and land speculation. He bequeathed his summer home, Burnside, plus £10,000, for the establishment of a university—assets that by 1981 were worth $150 million, making McGill the best-endowed university in the country.

limited to fifty-five fur traders who had spent at least one full season in *le pays d'en haut.** Club rules were simple but rigidly followed. On admission, each new member had a gold medal struck, engraved with his name, initial wintering date and the club motto: "Fortitude in Distress." These baubles were worn at fortnightly evening meetings, and there was a nominal cash penalty for leaving one's medal at home. The repasts were convened at prestigious local dining-rooms such as Richard Dillon's Montreal Hotel at Place d'Armes or the Mansion House at 156 St Paul Street, where meals were served on the club's own crested crystal and china with matching silver cutlery. The menu consisted of such country delicacies as wedges of pemmican, venison steaks, roasted beaver tails and pickled buffalo tongues. But it was the attendant ritual that really counted. Five toasts were proposed: the Mother of All Saints; the King; the Fur Trade in All Its Branches; Voyageurs, Wives and Children; and Absent Members. Any reveller who deviated in the order of these salutes was fined six bottles of Madeira. Each round was climaxed by the dashing of glasses into the fireplace. After that, a peace pipe was passed around and the serious reminiscing and drinking began.

Usually no one was sober enough to keep minutes of the proceedings, but George T. Landmann, a visiting British officer, left this description of a typical meeting in his *Adventures and Recollections:* "In those days we dined at 4 o'clock, and after taking a satisfactory quantity of wine, the married men ... retired, leaving about a dozen to drink to their health. We now began in right earnest and true Highland style, and by 4 o'clock in the morning, the whole of us had arrived at such a state of perfection, that we could all give the war-whoops as well as Mackenzie and McGillivray, we could all sing admirably, we could all drink like fishes and we all thought we could dance on the table without disturbing a single decanter, glass or plate ... but on making the experiment we discovered that it was a complete delusion,

---

* Paradoxically, this eliminated Simon McTavish, who had taken many inland journeys but had never wintered in Indian Country. Eight years after the club's inception, McTavish was allowed to join, perhaps partly because of his proclivity for settling social accounts by winning duels. He had fought a successful duel at Detroit in 1772 against the American land speculator William Constable, and when a Montreal physician named George Selby challenged him because the socially ambitious doctor had not been invited to one of McTavish's balls, the Marquis (who was a crack shot) deliberately missed, leaving the social climber's honour and body intact.

David David was the only Jewish member of the Beaver Club. His medal sold in 1986 at an auction in London for $19,000.

and ultimately, we broke all the plates, glasses, bottles, etc., and the table also, and worse than that all the heads and hands of the party received many severe contusions, cuts and scratches…. I was afterwards informed that one hundred and twenty bottles of wine had been consumed at our convivial meeting."

Landmann's diary noted the presence of a dozen guests at the gathering, which translated into an incredible ten bottles of wine each—but that tally did not include the large quantities of ale, porter, gin and brandy also downed on these occasions. A bill dated September 17, 1808, recorded that thirty-two invitees consumed twenty-nine bottles of Madeira, nineteen bottles of port, fourteen bottles of porter and twelve quarts of ale, as well as unspecified quantities of gin, brandy and negus—a concoction of wine, hot water, sugar and nutmeg. Among the notables who attended Beaver Club dinners were Lord Selkirk, the Arctic explorer Sir John Franklin, the Irish poet Thomas Moore, the American fur magnate John Jacob Astor, Colonel Isaac Brock, then commanding the Montreal garrison, and the Duke of Kent, later the father of Queen Victoria. When the resident Governor-in-Chief, Lord Dalhousie, came to dine on May 14, 1824, he presented each of his companions with a specially designed silver snuff box.

A highlight of the Beaver Club gatherings was the restaging of *le grand voyage*. Using that narrow window of opportunity between being uproariously drunk and actually passing out, the Nor'Westers would stumble around until they were seated on the floor, arranged two abreast, pretending they were steering a fast-moving *canot du nord*. Grasping fire-tongs, pokers, walking sticks, swords and other likely looking implements as imaginary paddles, they bawled voyageur songs as they stroked ever faster, their eyes glazed, their faces beet-red with exertion. But even make-believe northern canoes must eventually encounter rapids—and that required a change of tactic. With the false shrewdness of the very drunk, the Nor'Westers would consider the possibilities, then clamber up on the dinner-tables and ride the rapids by "shooting" to the floor astride empty wine casks, bellowing a variation on Indian war whoops that verged on Highland battle cries. By this time it might have been four or five in the morning, and the rented dining-room resembled the field hospital of a vanquished army. The few members still upright would adjourn the meeting and stagger home.

The Beaver Club's final gathering was held on March 5, 1827, three years after the death of the elder Alexander Henry, the last of its original members. By then the meeting had mellowed into a sedate gentlemen's soirée, a decline attested to by the fact that the thirty-two men who were there emptied only sixty-eight bottles.*

THE CLUB'S WILDERNESS OUTSTATION, the place the Nor'West partners treated as the inland nerve centre of the fur trade, was Grand Portage near the head of Lake Superior. But when the boundary settlements between the United States and British North America made it clear that the NWC post would fall south of the new border, the company moved its quarters forty-five miles northeast to the mouth of the Kaministikwia River. There a thousand men built a new trans-shipment centre eventually known as Fort William, and every summer the voyageur-manned canoes would converge on the fort from Lachine and the far-flung hunting grounds. There too assembled the Montreal and wintering partners, laden with gear and self-importance, to negotiate new contracts for the season's catch. "They ascended the rivers in great state," wrote Washington Irving about the partners' processions to Fort William. "They were wrapped in rich furs, their huge canoes freighted with every convenience and luxury, and manned by Canadian voyageurs, as obedient as Highland clansmen. They carried up with them cooks and bakers, together with delicacies of every kind, and an abundance of choice wines for the banquets which attended this great convocation. Happy were they, too, if they could meet with some distinguished stranger, above all, some titled member of the British nobility, to accompany them on this stately occasion, and grace their high solemnities."

Fort William's 125 acres accommodated forty-two buildings massed in a rectangle paralleling the landing docks. Because transportation costs were so high, the Nor'Westers maintained their own workshops, including a cooperage for making kegs and a boatyard for building and repairing canoes. All the warehouses, dormitories and offices were linked to the Great Hall, where the senior partners lived, ate, sat in council and celebrated their large and smaller triumphs. Spacious enough to seat two hundred at a formal dinner, this building was enhanced in its elegant Georgian symmetry by a balconied façade sixty feet long. Off the main dining-room were four lavishly furnished lodgings for

---

* A modern version of the Beaver Club was inaugurated by Her Majesty Queen Elizabeth II at Montreal's Queen Elizabeth Hotel in 1959 and eventually enlisted nearly a thousand members in forty countries. A major meeting of the Beaver Club was held at the Queen Elizabeth during the Fifth Annual Fur Trade Conference at Montreal in 1985, but it was closed in 1997.

the Montreal agents. The Great Hall's décor included a stern-looking bust of Simon McTavish, a life-size portrait of Lord Nelson and a painting of the Battle of Trafalgar (both attributed to William Berczy), as well as arrays of glittering silver candlesticks and crystal decanters. The NWC's executives dined in comfort every evening, the seating plan tailored to their station within the company's hierarchy. Wild duck, lake trout and buffalo humps were featured, with mutton, beef, fowl, vegetables and butter brought in fresh from the rudimentary farm outside the fort's gates. The daily ration at these sumptuous meals was the equivalent of several pounds of buffalo meat or two whole geese a man, washed down with West Indies rum and French brandy by the barrel.

Each season's rendezvous was climaxed by a gala summer ball. An impromptu orchestra that combined the not always compatible tones of bagpipes, violins, flutes and fifes bleated the lively strains of "The Reel of Tulloch," "The Flowers of Edinburgh" and "The Dashing White Sergeant." Senior partners had first pick among "the ladies of the country" invited to these extravaganzas, and the revelry lasted long into the night. These galas displayed a vigorous mélange of traditions: Scottish reels, Quebec jigs and the more sedate Ojibway steps. While their partners whirled around, the Indian women stood in one place, bobbing up and down in time to the music, lifting both feet off the ground at the same time—all executed with rhythmic pacing and dignity. As the hour grew late and the liquor took hold, mock canoe races would be staged, with traders taking their escorts for a "paddle" around the room, ending up in laughing mêlées of buckled legs and groping hands. "At night *bourgeois* and clerks danced in the Great Hall," wrote Marjorie Wilkins Campbell, the unofficial historian of the North West Company, "singing tender Scottish ballads and naughty French songs to the sensuous slipslap of moccasined feet ... now and again a Chippewa girl's throaty murmur blended with a man's exulting laughter in one of the cabins or from under the canoes beached along the riverside."

When the partners had slept off the after-effects of these revelries, wintering preparations got under way. Brigades of canoes heavy with furs were dispatched at two-day intervals on the return journey to Lachine; the inland partners led their flotillas laden with trade goods into the great Northwest, ready to face another winter trading season. By the end of August, fewer than two dozen maintenance personnel remained at the fort.

The winterers scattered across the Indian Country led isolated but endurable lives. Almost entirely cut off from the outside world, they created a universe of their own that often included country brides and families. Unlike the HBC, the North West Company placed no restrictions on their traders' taking Indian wives until 1806. These relationships, which were formed at every level of the enterprise, were based on more than sexual gratification, and became vital to the fur trade. The women acted as interpreters, mentors and, through their kinship links, vital conduits into Indian society. Women dressed the hides, made the moccasins, pounded the pemmican, netted the snowshoes and acted as porters when no animal power was available. "What did the Indian women get in return for their labour?" inquired Margaret Atwood in a remarkable essay on the period. "Sometimes they got syphilis or smallpox. They got copper pots instead of birchbark ones, and they got cheap cotton and blanket cloth. They got needles and thread and the pleasure of sewing the coloured trade beads—'mock coral, barley corn, mock garnet, enamelled, blue agate,' and the many more listed in the company's inventories—into beautiful patterns for their men's clothes. They also got acknowledgement of a kind: the company knew their importance, as it knew the importance of the beaver and buffalo."

There is evidence that an active trade in female slaves was sponsored by some of the NWC winterers. When Archibald McLeod, who later became a senior member of the Beaver Club, was stationed at Fort Alexandria on the upper Assiniboine, he noted in his diary: "I gave the Chef de Canard's widow to the amount of 28 plus, & took the Slave Woman, whom next fall I shall sell for a good price to one of the men." James McKenzie, who participated in the Northwest fur trade for twenty-seven years, described in his journal entry of April 9, 1800, how complicated some of these human transactions could become: "This Indian brought his daughter, who deserted in the course of the winter from Morin, at Slave Lake, in order to be returned to her husband.... Mr Porter wrote me, by Morin's orders, to sell her to the highest bidder and debit [sic: credit] Morin for the amount. Two advantages may be reaped from this affair; the first is that it will assist to discharge the debts of a man unable to do it by any other means, for he is neither good middleman, foreman, steersman, interpreter or carpenter; the second is that it may be the means to tricking some lecherous miser to part with some of his hoard. I therefore kept the woman to be disposed of in the season when the Peace River bucks look out for women, in the month of May."

There were examples of women and girls as young as nine or ten being traded for horses or kegs of rum, but such transactions were a perversion of

Indian custom. More common was the taking of "country wives" in temporary marriages that customarily lasted the length of a Nor'Wester's posting—although many such liaisons endured the stretch of their partners' lives. If the traders' diaries are to be believed, some of these matings were entered into by the men with considerable initial reluctance. Alexander Henry the Younger, who travelled the Northwest accompanied by a tame dancing bear, left behind a sixteen-hundred-page journal describing his encounters with the Plains Indians. Occasionally he would come across some exceptional scenes, such as this one that he recorded in his diary: "[The Gros Ventres] appear to be destitute or ignorant of all shame or modesty. In their visits to our establishments women are articles of temporary barter with our men. For a few inches of twist tobacco a Gros Ventre will barter the person of his wife or daughter with as much sang-froid as he would bargain for a horse. He has no equal in such an affair, though the Blackfoot, Blood, or Peigan is now nearly as bad—in fact, all those tribes are a nuisance when they come to the forts with their women. They intrude upon every room and cabin in the place, and even though a trader may have a family of his own, they insist upon doing them the charity of accepting of the company of at least one woman for the night. It is sometimes with the greatest difficulty that we can get the fort clear of them in the evening and shut the gates...."

On New Year's Day, 1801, Henry awoke with a chief's dark-eyed daughter in his bed. "Liard's daughter took possession of my room," he complained, "and the devil himself could not have got her out." After a month of sparring, he accepted the young woman as his companion. Four years later, while he was away from his post at Fort Pembina, Henry's in-laws were massacred by a raiding party of Sioux. When he later rode out to survey the remains of his family's camp beyond the fort's gates, Henry found only his father-in-law's torso, the skull having been carried off by the raiders as a water dish. "I gathered up the remaining bones of my *belle-mère* in a handkerchief," he lamented, "then I gave a party of three hundred Assiniboines Saulteaux and Cree a nine-gallon keg of gunpowder and a hundred musket balls. 'Go,' I encouraged them. 'Revenge the death of my *beau-père* and his family.'"

A more gentle view of the wild country can be glimpsed in the journals of Daniel Williams Harmon, the God-fearing Vermont-born trader who spent two decades in the Northwest bemoaning, among other things, the loose morals of frontier society. His Sunday-school ethics were particularly affronted by the wanton matings of some NWC traders and their disregard for the sanctity of the Sabbath. After four years of successfully combating temptation, Harmon found himself reluctantly capitulating to the charms of a fourteen-year-old Mixed Blood named Elizabeth Duval. The couple spent the next decade and a half moving from one NWC post to another. In 1819 Harmon was due to leave the fur trade, and there is a moving entry in his diary as he tries to decide how he can follow the usual custom and abandon his country wife. "The union which has been formed between us in the providence of God," he confided to his diary, "has not only been cemented by a long and mutual performance of kind offices, but, also, by a more sacred consideration. We have wept together over the early departure of several children, and especially, over the death of a beloved son. We have children still living, who are equally dear to us both. How could I spend my days in the civilized world, and leave my beloved children in the wilderness? How could I tear them from a mother's love, and leave her to mourn over their absence, to the day of her death?" Harmon opted to take his beloved Elizabeth and their fourteen children out with him; they were officially married at a Vermont Congregational church. The couple founded the New England town of Harmonsville and later moved to Sault au Récollet near Montreal, where Harmon died impoverished but not alone.

Harmon was not the only Nor'Wester to take his wife east. NWC traders George Nelson, James Hughes and J.D. Cameron all took their Indian wives out of the wilderness country, and many more took Métis or Mixed Blood wives with them when their service was complete.

The sons of many North Country liaisons were absorbed into the fur trade, while some of the daughters were sent to the East for convent educations. Because local NWC forts were being charged with maintaining too many wives and children, during its 1806 conclave at Fort William, the Montreal company adopted a new regulation that prohibited its employees from "marrying" pure-blood Indian women (at a fine of £100) to lessen the burden of having to feed and clothe families at company forts. One reason behind this reform was the growing number of retired NWC voyageurs who had chosen to live with women of the country. They had fathered large families and were willing to settle permanently in the Fur Country.

These canoemen provided the essential link with the heartland. It was one of the great ironies of the rampaging empire founded by the Montreal fur traders that it was held together by a remarkable ragbag of magnificent river rats, using the most primitive mode of locomotion there is: raw muscle.

The Magnificent River Rats

Their exuberant and highly un-Canadian sense of daring propelled them to risk everything for a cause as ephemeral as their own brotherhood.

NO SMEAR OF THEIR SWEAT or echo of their ribaldry reaches out to us, yet in their time they were cockleshell heroes on seas of sweet water.

Unsung, unlettered and uncouth, the early fur-trade voyageurs gave substance to the unformed notion of Canada as a transcontinental state. The traditional postcard pastiche of slap happy buffoons with sly moustaches and scarlet sashes, bellowing dirty *chansons* about pliant maidens—that was not who they were. Their eighteen-hour paddling days were more wretched than many men then or now could survive. They were in effect galley slaves, and their only reward was defiant pride in their own courage and endurance.

Because they could boast of their exploits to no one but themselves, the voyageurs, like a wild and worn-out professional hockey team perpetually on the road, had to concoct their own sustaining myths. No voyageur ever reported meeting a small bear, a tame moose or a wolf that wasn't snarling with blood-lust.

Running through mosquito clouds along boggy portages with 180 pounds or more on their shoulders, strong-arming four tons of cargo through icy rapids while, as one trader told it, "not only hanging on by their hands and feet but by their 'eyebrows,'" the canoemen cherished these daily victories, which became grist for the self-justifying legends that kept them going. The tally of hardship was most clearly visible at the steepest of the killing portages—the plain wooden crosses, sometimes thirty in a group, marking the spot where drowning, stroke, heart attack or strangulated hernia had finally claimed their victims. Out in that witches' brew of a wilderness, they outran their souls and maimed their bodies, and nobody was there to salute them or mark their passage.

Listed in the company ledgers as "engagés," the voyageurs were peons and free spirits at one and the same time. Hired to man the canoes through season after season in the Fur Country, they eagerly signed up for unimaginable toil that cracked their backs and ruptured their intestines but never broke their spirit.*

"They had the pride of champions," noted Hugh MacLennan in *The Rivers of Canada*. "They sprang from European peasants who had never been allowed to leave their villages or their lords' estates ... but in the West of Canada they were their own masters and lived with the freedom of kings. In the Canadian service far more licence was granted to an independently minded Voyageur than was ever given within the service of the Bay. That is why the Nor'Westers became such great explorers." Indeed, it had been voyageurs (plus some even less acknowledged Indians) who manned the canoes that carried Mackenzie, Fraser, Thompson and the other trail-blazers to fame.

Resident officers of the Hudson's Bay Company, which had to hire Orkneymen and the less tractable Indians instead of voyageurs to man their boats, complained about not having an equivalent to "those natural water Dogs" in their service. The most astute endorsement was delivered by Ramsay Crooks, an executive of the American Fur Company, who requested that voyageurs be exempted from a ban proposed by the United States Congress on Nor'West traders in the upper Mississippi Valley. "It will still be good policy to admit freely & without the least restraint the Canadian boatmen," he wrote. "These people are indispensable to the successful prosecution of the trade, their places cannot be supplied by Americans, who are for the most part ... too independent to submit quietly to a proper control ... 'tis only in the Canadian we find that temper of mind, to render him patient, docile and persevering. In short they are a people harmless in themselves whose habits of submission fit them peculiarly for our business and if guided as it is my wish they should be,

---

* The voyageurs are sometimes confused with *coureurs de bois*, a description reserved for the itinerant, illicit fur gatherers who flooded into the Superior Country during the late 1600s and early 1700s to outrun the Indian middlemen then dominating the trade. The voyageurs' powers of endurance are difficult to exaggerate. Northern historian Alan Cooke, who has portaged a canoe upstream, once observed that the work "may be unfavourably compared with the labour of Sisyphus, whose boulder was, at least, neither fragile nor perishable. The course of his work did not lie along the bed of a mountain stream nor, in the legend, is there any mention of mosquitoes and black flies.... All other discomforts of wilderness travel pale beside the continuous torment offered by the hordes of biting insects—this scourge being beyond easy description."

will never give just cause of alarm to the Government of the Union." The Canadian identity has seldom since been more perceptively defined.

The voyageurs were not universally revered. Many of the more fastidious NWC partners dismissed them as filthy and profane, much too volatile and sensual to suit the proprietors' Presbyterian predilections. David Thompson disdainfully reported that he had managed to sign up a whole crew of voyageurs for a tough winter journey to the Missouri River because the men wanted to experience for themselves the fabled sexuality of the Mandan women. The most damning indictment was that left by Daniel Harmon: "They are not brave; but when they apprehend a little danger, they will often, as they say, play the man. They are very deceitful, and exceedingly smooth and polite, and are even gross flatterers to the face of a person, whom they will basely slander, behind his back.... A secret they cannot keep. They rarely feel gratitude, though they are often generous. They are obedient, but not faithful servants. By flattering their vanity, of which they have not a little, they may be persuaded to undertake the most difficult enterprises ... all their chat is about horses, dogs, canoes, women and strong men, who can fight a good battle."

The *esprit de corps* that drove the voyageurs to their prodigious physical feats had no clear origins. They could be tender, shyly gathering wild roses to brighten the breakfast table of a trader's wife, or thoughtlessly brutal. They followed the code of the frontier.

There was a strong streak of vanity in the voyageurs' make-up, so much so that before putting into any inhabited port, they stopped to shave, slip on their cleanest shirts and stick plumes in their headgear. Only then would they sweep towards the dock, their boats deliberately angled on collision course. By adroitly backpaddling at the last possible moment, the canoeists would settle their craft, becalmed, at their exact landing spot and each would step ashore with the exaggerated swagger of a lion tamer.

The voyageur subculture was based on custom, dress and circumstance. But it was language that was their unifying ethos; for neither the Indians nor the Nor'Westers enjoyed their advantage of having French as a mother tongue. Unlike the servants of the HBC, the voyageurs were not formless juniors trying to create themselves in the image of their employers. They shared drinks but few assumptions with the *bourgeois* (the NWC's commanding officers, wintering partners and Montreal agents) and were virtually never promoted out of their canoes into more responsible shore billets. If the forts of the Hudson's Bay

Company suffered from the harsh discipline that turned them into shore-bound Royal Navy frigates, the rowdy voyageurs' favourite hangout, *la cantine salope*, the harlots' tavern at the NWC's summer headquarters, probably had few equivalents this side of a modern motorcycle gang's safe house.

Respect for authority was not the voyageurs' strong suit. They could be reduced to belly-pumping laughter by collapsing a dozy *bourgeois's* tent over his head or by "accidentally" dunking him in an icy stream if he "forgot" to share his private liquor reserve. The dripping, shivering trader would then find himself taunted by derisive catcalls claiming he had just been "baptized." Occasionally, the canoeists would salute a naïve *bourgeois* by "naming" a lobstick after him. A voyageur would climb the tallest nearby pine, lop off all but the top branches and carve the *bourgeois's* name into the trunk. That ceremony was followed by the firing of guns, loud cheers—and a demand for free drinks from the newly honoured potentate. Most of the *bourgeois* travelled with a personal manservant, but they were not, as an envious HBC surveyor named Philip Turnor reported, carried ashore in feather beds to share the night with female travelling companions.

The universe that counted among voyageurs was self-contained within their canoes. Seniority, muscle and a sixth sense about river navigation determined rank and pay. At the bottom of the scale were the *milieux* who squatted, two abreast, on the middle thwarts and paddled all day according to orders from the *avant* (bowsman) and the *gouvernail* (steersman). These veterans could read the sky and understand the river's moods; they knew how to spot *le fil d'eau*—the safest entry point for shooting rapids. Each brigade of four to a dozen canoes was under the direction of a *guide*, an experienced riverman responsible for daily travel schedules and the safety of the cargo. Paid at least three times as much as the lowly *milieux*, the *guides* were permitted to eat with the *bourgeois* at Fort William and sleep in tents, while their crews had to shelter beneath overturned canoes.

There was one other, pivotal distinction. The voyageurs were divided into two mutually exclusive societies. Those crews taking the freight canoes as far as the head of Superior (or Rainy Lake) were called *les allants et venants* (the goers and comers) or, more frequently, derisively dismissed as *les mangeurs de lard*—a reference to the pork they mixed with their corn gruel. They were usually hired on a per-trip basis and drifted in and out of the trade as the spirit moved them. The aristocrats of the waterways were *les hommes du nord*, the Northmen who wintered in the Fur Country and delivered the payloads. They were the tough professionals who could make their paddles hum, living as close to nature as Indians. There was one other tiny elite—the crack crews of the express canoes, the light craft reserved for delivering messages and conveying visiting dignitaries.

The exploits of these early voyageurs were so remarkable that in retrospect they appear as giants; in fact, because every pound of excess weight aboard a canoe counted, the ideal voyageur was a compact five foot five. Many a farm boy cursed as he faced the mirror and saw himself grow past the physical limit of the voyageur ideal. Because it was usually the eldest son who inherited the farm while his brothers had little training and few alternatives to fall back on, there was strong family pressure on younger siblings to sign up for the fur trade. Grandfathers who claimed they had followed La Vérendrye westward, cousins and uncles who had worn the voyageur sash filled the tedium of winter nights with many a tall tale of life in *le pays d'en haut,* the wild country north and west of Superior. Sometimes there was little choice. Fathers occasionally signed their sons into the service for three-year stints at whatever wage the *bourgeois* might find appropriate.

At the peak of its activities, the North West Company employed more than eleven hundred voyageurs (and thirty-five *guides*), half of them confined to the shuttle run between Lachine and the head of the Great Lakes. Most of the recruits arrived (with letters of recommendation signed by their local *curés*) from the villages near Montreal—Sorel, Vaudreuil, Longueuil, Rigaud, Île-Perrot, Châteauguay, Chambly and Pointe-Claire—but Trois-Rivières and Quebec also contributed their share. Nearly all were French, but contracts have been found for Englishmen, Germans, Scots and one West Indian named Bonga.

These contracts (usually signed with a bold X) spelled out not only their pay and length of servitude (three years in the North Country) but even such exact terms as the goods they were granted upon joining. A typical winterer might be given two blankets, two shirts, two pairs of trousers, two handkerchiefs and fourteen pounds of tobacco, though the generosity of distribution depended on each man's rank and experience. Jean-Baptiste Rolland, for example, who signed up on April 24, 1817, as a *milieu* for three years at Lake Huron in the service of a *bourgeois* named Guillaume, was paid £30 a year and given two rods of trade cloth, a three-point blanket, bits of cotton, a pair of shoes, one towline, two pounds of soap and three pounds of tobacco.

The voyageurs also pledged themselves "to serve, obey, and faithfully carry out all that the said Bourgeois or any of their representatives to whom they might transfer the present engagement [require], to lawfully respect and honestly do by him, their profit, avoid their damages, to warn them if it comes to his knowledge, and in general all that a good hired man should and is obliged to do; without being allowed to do any personal trading, to be absent from or to leave the aforesaid service, under the penalties set forth by the Laws of this Province, and to lose his wages." This was a vicious enough form of indenture, but what made it worse was that, once inland, the voyageurs were encouraged to go into debt at company stores (which indulged in exorbitant markups) as a way of keeping a grip on their future. Once in hock, they had to work out their debts by further service. The sanctity of their contracts was seldom challenged.

Such peonage must have roused natural resentment, but there were very few documented instances of mutiny. At Rainy Lake on August 3, 1794, the NWC's Duncan McGillivray found a strike in progress, with several brigades of voyageurs refusing to budge unless their wages were increased. It didn't last long. The canny McGillivray noticed some of the ringleaders hesitating and later noted in his journal: "Their minds were agitated with these scruples at the very time that they insisted on a compliance with their demands, and tho' they endeavoured carefully to conceal it, yet a timidity was observed in their behaviour which proved very fortunate for their Masters, who took such good advantage of it, that before night they prevailed on a few of the most timid to return to their duty, and the rest, being only ashamed to abandon their companions, soon followed the example."

Except for such occasional glimpses, there are few firsthand records of the voyageurs' temperament or physical appearance. Dr John J. Bigsby, secretary of the commission that defined the boundary between Canada and the United States following the Treaty of Ghent in 1814, left behind in one of his diaries a rare description of their tortured features. "One man's face," he wrote, "with a large Jewish nose, seemed to have been squeezed in a vice, or to have passed through a flattening machine. It was like a cheese-cutter—all edge. Another had one nostril bitten off. He proved the buffoon of the party. He had the extraordinary faculty of untying the strings of his face, as it were, at pleasure, when his features fell into confusion—into a crazed chaos almost frightful; his eye, too, lost its usual significance; but no man's countenance ... was fuller of fun and fancies than his, when he liked. A third man had his features wrenched to the right—exceedingly little, it is true; but the effect was remark-able. He had been slapped on the face by a grizzly bear. Another was a short, paunchy old man, with vast features, but no forehead—the last man I should have selected; but he was a hard-working creature, usually called 'Passe-partout,' because he had been everywhere, and was famous for the weight of fish he could devour at a meal.... Except the younger men, their faces were short, thin, quick in their expression, and mapped out in furrows."

They kept their hair long so that a shake of the head would help drive away the marauding summer insects. Short and bulky like Belgian workhorses, they took the pride of dandies in their simple but distinctive dress code. They wore deer- or moose-skin moccasins with no socks, corduroy trousers and sky blue *capots* (hooded frock coats with brass buttons) over red-and-black flannel shirts. The pants were tied at the knees with beadwork garters and held around the waist with crimson handwoven sashes—the famous *ceintures fléchées*. One variation was an embroidered buckskin coat, its seams decorated with bear hair; when caught by the wind after a rainstorm, the garment would make a strange and desolate sound like the ground drumming of a grouse. Choice of hats expressed at least a touch of individuality. Some wore high, scarlet-tasselled night bonnets, others coarse blue cloth caps with peaks, or toques or colourful handkerchiefs wound into turbans. The Northmen proclaimed their vanity by sticking what they called "ostrich plumes" into their headgear, though these were usually dyed chicken feathers—and, sometimes, fox tails.

Almost as much a part of them as their clothes were the voyageurs' canoes. Perfected by the Algonquin tribes of the eastern woodlands, these frail but versatile craft provided the day's transportation, the night's shelter and the centrepiece of pride and conversation. Fashioned from the bark of yellow birches, they were amazing vessels, weighing less than three hundred pounds (six hundred when wet) yet capable of carrying four tons of crew and freight. Birch bark rots slowly, if at all, and is tolerant of frost and heat; it consists of individually layered skins, so that it can be trimmed to any desired shape and thickness without losing tensile strength. Only an axe, a crooked knife and a square or an Indian awl, plus some spruce roots and pitch (spruce gum) were required to build canoes that lasted several seasons. The birch skin was folded around a cedar frame into which were fitted spruce or ash ribs, gunwales, thwarts, stem and stern pieces. Tree roots were used for sewing the birch bark, and resinous gum for caulking its seams.

The large freight canoes (*canots de maître*) that set off from Lachine were thirty-six (occasionally forty) feet long and five feet wide, driven by a dozen men and capable of carrying seventy ninety-pound cargo packages. The smaller *canot du nord*, twenty-four feet long with a beam of just over four feet, required half the crew yet could still hold a ton and a half of freight. Despite their impressive capacities, the vessels were so frail that crewmen did not dare change their paddling positions, and during landings the canoe was never dragged ashore. At the appropriate moment, the crewmen would leap out and gently guide their craft towards the river bank. (These boats were perilously easy to tip. Hugh Mackay Ross, a twentieth-century HBC trader who tried paddling one, wrote in his memoirs: "You really had to keep your tongue in the middle of your mouth; otherwise the canoe would capsize.")

The prow and stern of each vessel were routinely painted with the company flag (its initials in gold letters on the fly of a Red Ensign), a rearing horse or the head of an Indian in war dress, but the best art was reserved for the paddles. The red-cedar paddles came in lengths up to nine feet, depending on their user's position, their surfaces stained a bright blue or green, ornamented by red or black designs. The standard stroking cadence of forty-five dips to the minute could drive a canoe at nearly six knots, though the crews of the express boats were expected to push themselves to a superhuman sixty strokes a minute. The only other way to increase speed was to hoist sail in a following wind. The sail, made of the oilcloth used to cover the freight packages and attached to a temporary mast and boom fashioned from trimmed branches lashed to the thwarts and gunwales, was a jury-rig at best and not often used. But in the right wind and with the proper course and set, the winged canoes could surf along at an expeditious eight knots.

EVERY SPRING the voyageurs would gather at Montreal's Old Market to spend a few days drinking, sparring and relaxing before they took the nine-mile dirt road that bypassed the Lachine Rapids, leading to the North West Company's main staging area and starting point for the brigades west.

The surrounding woods and meadows were still more in bud than leaf as the hectic preparations began for the grand departure. "No camel train across Asia Minor moved with the surety and efficiency of the canoe brigades in the great days of the Canadian fur trade," Leslie F. Hannon noted in an essay on the period. "No European coach or wagon could survive a single mile of the route: there were no roads, only rocks, rapids and white water all the way. Yet cargo losses per voyage were as low as one-half of one percent."

The *bourgeois* appeared appropriately pompous as they paraded their "wilderness look"—ruffles and lace, a brass-handled pistol stuck theatrically into the belt. They gave elaborate farewell picnics for their hangers-on, the coterie of junior partners, clerks, fusty subalterns with small lives and the

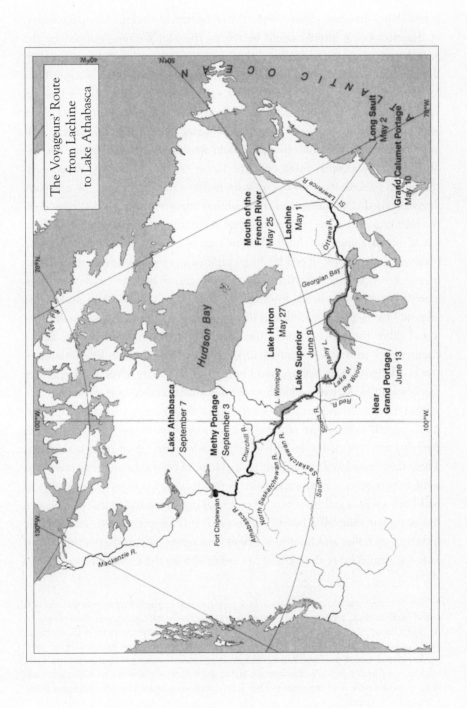

The Voyageurs' Route
from Lachine
to Lake Athabasca

ATLANTIC OCEAN

40°W.
50°N
70°W.

Long Sault
May 2

Grand Calumet Portage
May 10

St. Lawrence R.

Ottawa R.

Lachine
May 1

Mouth of the
French River
May 25

Georgian Bay

Hudson Bay

Lake Huron
May 27

Lake Superior
June 9

Rainy L.

Lake of
the Woods

Near
Grand Portage
June 13

L. Winnipeg

Red R.

Souris R.

South Saskatchewan R.

Saskatchewan R.

North Saskatchewan R.

Churchill R.

Methy Portage
September 3

Lake Athabasca
September 7

Athabasca R.

Fort Chipewyan

Mackenzie R.

20°N
100°W
130°W
100°W.

ladies-always-in-waiting who formed their Montreal circles. An undercurrent of destinies being altered could be felt as the Nor'Westers, gripped by the pageantry of the moment, offered their jaunty Gaelic toast, "On to the High Kanadushka!"—vowing to open up a continent with God knew what riches.

Between rounds of nibbling nippy cheese and gorging themselves on smoked sturgeon, venison and bear steaks washed down with the finest claret and Madeira, the *bourgeois* supervised loading of the freight canoes, self-importantly making certain that bow packs were properly stored before the rest of the cargo was gently fitted onto the flimsy cedar floor boards. When each canoe was packed, its gunwales only six inches above the water, the company flag was raised at the prow and the boatmen impatiently circled offshore until the brigade was in all respects ready.* Just before the final departure signal there would be a momentary hush. The *milieux* hunched over in their starting postures; the *bourgeois* tipped his beaver hat in a farewell salute to shorebound friends; lovers exchanged a final glance. Then the chief *guide,* holding a steersman's pole over his head, lowered his arms in a sudden chop and yelled *"Avant!"* Every paddle sliced into the water, the first of countless strokes that would drive the canoes almost the distance of an Atlantic crossing before coming back to this welcoming hailport. As the brigades—in line formation, two boatlengths apart—disappeared beyond a bend in the river, the voyageurs' mood was jolly. A cloud of laughter seemed almost visible in their wake.

Past Dorval Island and the steep-roofed seigneury mansions they went, following the north shore of Lake St Louis upstream to the first rapids at Ste Anne's (now Ste-Anne-de-Bellevue) at the western tip of Montreal Island. There they halted at a small stone chapel to pray, offer alms and take communion for their time in *le pays d'en haut.* Before leaving Lachine, each canoeman had been given a gallon of rum, the official ration for the journey. Typically, the voyageurs sampled a hearty portion of it on the spot, as if to exorcise the influence of home and family, of priests and saints. When they set off again, only the thin echo of the bells of Ste Anne's broke the crystal silence.

---

* Each voyageur was allowed forty pounds of personal luggage, including his blanket. As well as the packs of trade goods, provisions for the crew had to be carried because there would be no time to hunt along the way. Boat repair materials (*watape* or fine spruce roots for sewing in bark patches, and pine-gum for waterproofing the seams), towlines, the *bourgeois*'s tent, axes, kettles, kegs of liquor and large bailing sponges completed the standard equipment list. Early brigades consisted of as few as four canoes, but at the height of the NWC's trading cycle, each brigade numbered at least ten canoes. They left Lachine at two-day intervals to stagger traffic through the portages.

Though they were about to launch themselves along the subcontinent's main transportation artery, they passed few settlements. Ever so rarely was there visible on the far horizon a curling wisp of delicate smoke from a woodsman's hearth, reminding the voyageurs they were not completely beyond the tendrils of white civilization. The Ottawa route, pioneered by Samuel de Champlain in the early 1600s, remained the primary access into the Great Lakes region until the advent of the railways and major canal building. From Lachine to height-of-land on the Ottawa meant a climb of 659 feet, and the subsequent drop to Georgian Bay was 99 feet. That required passage of thirty-six portages, but it was still three hundred miles shorter than going up the St Lawrence and through Lakes Ontario and Erie.

After entering the mouth of the Ottawa (then called the Grand River or *Grande Rivière des Algonquins*), the voyageurs soon encountered the Long Sault Rapids, and doffed their headgear in respect to Adam Dollard des Ormeaux and his seventeen compatriots, besieged there by a war party of Iroquois in 1660.* Just above the rapids, the voyageurs first sighted the furrowed brow of the Precambrian Shield, that rugged mantle of rock, muskeg and water that gives Canada much of its topography, resources and character.

The journey from Lachine to the head of Lake Superior took seven to eight weeks, which meant covering an average of about twenty-five miles a day. That was a considerable feat, since portages of various lengths and encumbrances had to be negotiated along the way. Portaging meant that the canoe and its load were lifted separately around waterfalls and impassable rapids for distances of a few yards to twelve miles—along bush trails, up creviced cliffs and through bogs, with the men often knee-deep in mud, slithering over slimy boulders. Each crew member would tuck one of the ninety-pound bales[†] into the small of his back, part of its weight borne by a leather tumpline stretched across his forehead so that some of the strain could be absorbed by neck muscles. Then his partner would settle another bale between the carrier's shoulder blades, and the loaded man would dogtrot along the portage trail,

---

* They were all dead after a week's battle, except for nine bitter-enders who were captured, then ritually tortured and eaten. Traces of the bloody struggle were discovered by Pierre Radisson, one of the founding spirits of the Hudson's Bay Company, and the site became a shrine. Quebec historians have postulated that Dollard deliberately sacrificed himself to fend off an attack on Montreal.

† Their size depended on their contents, but each bale weighed exactly ninety pounds whether it contained trade goods or pelts. This was a subtle anti-pilfering technique because it was immediately obvious if a bale suddenly seemed lighter than the rest.

knees and back bent, legs pumping, arms swinging free, looking for all the world like a hunchback ape scurrying for cover.

Humping 180 pounds across impassable terrain sounds difficult enough, but ambitious voyageurs could earn a Spanish silver dollar by carrying an extra bale to accelerate the portage crossing. Many did. Pierre Bonga, the only black West Indian known to have been a voyageur, once lugged 450 pounds across an NWC portage, and a Mistassini Indian named Chief Solomon Voyageur is said to have carried the equivalent of eight packs over a half-mile stretch. The most unusual test of strength was the improbable feat of a river man named Montferant, who was reported to have carried loads weighing over 500 pounds across the portage at Grand Calumet from four o'clock one morning to half past ten that night without a rest stop.

The brigades tried hard to avoid portages, preferring to brave all but the worst rapids—a daring option, since the boats they were paddle-handling between the unforgiving rocks were so frail they were susceptible to damage even by a moccasined foot. A frigid dunking of a sweat-soaked body was the lightest penalty for such daring.

Between portages they relentlessly pushed westward, boosting their spirits by mimicking the waterfowl, perfecting the "yole" cry of the loon and the high piercing song of the gulls. To offset the tedium of paddle strokes—as silent and regular as heartbeats—they sang. Like the heave-away sea shanties of the clipper-ship deckhands, the melodies were work songs, a way to ease the tedium of repetitive labour while endowing it with a comforting cadence. In his essay on voyageur songs, the old-world explorer J.G. Kohl noted: "Their song is like the murmur of the river itself. It seems endless. The singers are satisfied when they have found some pleasantly-sounding words which they can adapt to a favourite melody or a refrain giving a good turn to the paddling. The refrain and its constant repetition occupy so much time and place that the story itself in the song at length appears to be a mere makeweight.... After each short line comes the refrain, and the story twines itself along like a slender creeping-plant."

Though some songs were filled with *double entendres* more profane than sacred, most of the ditties were romantic re-creations of heroic events. A typical ballad concerned Jean Cayeux, who was fatally wounded by a band of Iroquois while trying to defend his family. As he lay bleeding, he dug his own grave and before sliding into it composed a lament, laboriously writing the words in blood on birch bark. The voyageur's unofficial anthem was an evocative melody called "À la Claire Fontaine," which tells how love expired because of the late delivery of a rose bouquet. Music was in the canoemen's souls. At night they loved listening to the rasp of a homemade violin or the twang of a mouth harp. One voyageur dragged part of a wooden door to Fort Edmonton so that he would have a platform to tap-dance on.

When sundown made further progress impossible, the canoes put in to shore. Before it was time to rest, boat hulls had to be patched, an exacting job by torch-light. The evening meal consisted of cooked dried peas or cornmeal mixed with water and bits of lard or suet, a gruel not dissimilar to what the Americans called hominy. Occasionally this tasteless diet was supplemented with a voyageur variety of bread known as *galette*. The recipe was simple: a hole was punched in one of the flour bags, a little water poured in and salt added. The main flavour-ing came from the cook's unwashed hands, when he kneaded the dough and shaped it into flat cakes to be baked in frying-pan grease. The voyageurs loved flipping these primitive flapjacks by the light of their torches, telling a few more thigh-slappers, smoking one last pipeful, then relaxing their knotted muscles and lamed backs in sleep. With the *bourgeois*'s tent in place, the men tucked in under their upside-down canoes and pulled tarpaulins over their exhausted limbs.

By four in the morning or even earlier, the camp would be stirring with shouts of *"Star Levé!"* (a contraction of *"C'est l'heure à se lever"*). As the rays of the approaching dawn threw trees into relief with just enough light to navi-gate by, the brigade would depart, paddling quietly through the mist. No one sang until after the eight o'clock breakfast stop. Lunch was either eaten under way or when the crews landed just long enough to boil some tea water and reheat the leftover gruel. Rest periods of five minutes every hour allowed the paddlers to light their pipes, so that distances came to be measured by the number of pipes instead of miles.

FOUR WEEKS OUT OF LACHINE, the canoes swept through the awesome beauty of Georgian Bay's North Channel, squeezed past St Joseph Island to Sault Ste Marie and entered the world's largest lake, Superior.*

---

* At 31,700 square miles, Lake Superior ranks ahead of every other inland body of water except the Caspian, which is classified as a sea rather than a lake. After 1799, the Nor'Westers eliminated the portage at Sault Ste Marie by building a primitive wooden canal. Because Superior was the hub of the NWC's empire, the company eventually built its own fleet of schooners to ferry heavy goods around the upper lakes. They included the ninety-ton *Recovery*, which survived the War of 1812 by being demasted, covered with pine boughs and hidden inside one of the deep bays of Isle Royale.

Hugging the lofty cliffs of Superior's north shore and bucking angry head-winds, which the voyageurs tried to assuage by sprinkling flecks of tea or tobacco on the boiling sea, the canoes made the final 450-mile dash to Grand Portage, the open sesame to the West first used by Radisson and Groseilliers. Their faces furred with untidy beards, their clothes stiff with two months' sweat, the travellers would land at Pointe aux Chapeaux (today's Hat Point) to wash and change into their finery before racing into the oval harbour of the depot at Grand Portage. The steersman would raise the company flag (stowed since leaving Lachine), the accompanying *bourgeois* would adjust his beaver hat and the vermilion-tipped paddles would glint in the sun as in one final burst of speed the canoes completed their epic voyage.

The cedar-picket stockade of this busy NWC emporium surrounded the complex of sixteen buildings that comprised the main transfer point between the freight canoes arriving with the Montreal trade goods and the North Country canoes bringing in the furs. The crude warehouses and dining-hall where the partners and their clerks discussed policy and celebrated the season's winnings were made of hand-sawn planks, with sloping shingle roofs and window casements painted a deep red, then known as Spanish Brown and later used to paint railway boxcars. Swarms of wild dogs roamed the fort, yelping and begging for scraps. Outside the stockades lived the cows, horses—and the voyageurs.

Even though they had lugged their precious loads from opposite sides of the continent, the canoeists rarely enjoyed the relative comfort of the trading post. Few Indians or voyageurs were permitted to enter the fort at Grand Portage or the enclosure of the later headquarters, Fort William. There, the exceptions were delinquents destined for the *pot au beurre*—the "butter tub," where they were confined overnight to cool off after particularly vicious brawls. The "butter tub" may have been used as a jail, but it was more of a privy. A blacksmith named Alexander Fraser, who had been caught trading a few moose skins to barefoot passersby so they could fashion new moccasins, was sentenced to twenty days in the *pot au beurre*. In pleading for mercy, he left behind an eloquent third-person deposition, picturing life in that hellhole: "It was a small square building made of hewn logs, without any light, wherein was a quantity of human excrement. That, after being a short time in this confinement, the stench of the place, and the bruises he had received, made this deponent conceive that if he were kept there much longer his health would be destroyed." Gasping for breath, Fraser promised to work a year for no wages if he were released. That offer failed to soften the heart of his overseer, who allowed him out only after the unfortunate Fraser had promised to renew his voluntary contract for *three* full years.

Forced to camp outside the fort's wooden walls, the voyageurs were encouraged to spend their earnings at Boucher's House, a canteen operated by a semi-independent trader named Jean-Marie Boucher, and to run up debts at a nearby "company store." The result was that many voyageurs remained indentured most of their working lives.

Having little else to do, the pork-eaters and *hommes du nord* drank and picked fights. Few rendezvous went by without bullies on both sides dealing out knife wounds, gouged eyes, torn ears and bitten-off noses. What little relief they found was at the harlots' tavern, where they could purchase rum at the equivalent of eight dollars a quart, extra food rations and the temporary favours of Ojibway or Chippewa women. "They have a softness and delicacy in their countenance," confessed a trader named Peter Grant about these resident *poules*, "which rival the charms of some of our more civilized belles."

Before the Lachine brigades could start back with their canoe-loads of fur, they had to lug the trade goods north to Pigeon Lake, a storage depot nine miles inland. That steep trek, usually scheduled before they had recovered from their hangovers, seemed the harshest of their ordeals. It was easier, they sighed, to reach heaven than Pigeon Lake.

By the first week of August, the winterers were growing restive, aware that they had to reach the Athabasca forests within the next two and a half months or face frozen rivers and starvation. The small, manoeuvrable canoes could carry cargoes of three thousand pounds with crews of five, yet their shallow eighteen-inch draft made most streams accessible. (Because there were few birch trees available along the Red and Assiniboine rivers, some local canoes were fashioned out of willow frames over which were stretched raw buffalo hides, fur side in. These floating robes were not good for voyages of any length and had to be unloaded at least once a day to be dried in the sun or over a fire, or they would sink.)

Eventually, an advance storage depot was built on Rainy Lake so that the Athabasca brigades could save fifteen days in each direction by exchanging their loads there instead of going on to Grand Portage. Fort Chipewyan on Lake Athabasca was sixteen hundred miles, or 75 days, from Superior, and the NWC's farthest outpost, Fort Good Hope near the Mackenzie Delta, was a full thousand miles north of Lake Athabasca, which enjoyed only 150 ice-free days. At the topographical dividing point that marked the height of land where the rivers began their long descent to Hudson Bay and the Arctic Ocean, the northern voyageurs paused for a unique ceremony. The senior *guide* would sharpen his knife, cut a bough from a scrub cedar, dip it in ditch water and command each novice in the canoe train to kneel. Thoroughly "blessed" by the wet branch, the newcomers swore allegiance to the Northmen's code of honour: that they would never allow another novice to pass this way without administering a similar oath, and never kiss a voyageur's wife without her permission. The simple cere-mony meant more than just another excuse for a celebratory round of drinks. It was no light privilege to stand up and tell the world: *"Je suis un homme du nord!"*—and this was the moment of transmogrification. These tough hombres were willing to risk everything except their pride. "It is questionable," wrote Thomas L. McKenney, an early traveller who witnessed one of the ceremonies, "whether [Napoleon] Bonaparte ever felt this superiority in all departments of mind which so distinguished him, or his achievements, to an extent of greater excitement, than does this poor man … in the animating and single belief in his supremacy as a north western voyageur."

Paddling towards Lake Winnipeg was at least a downstream run, but on one stretch of the Winnipeg River ten portages had to be crossed in a single day. When the waterways widened into lakes, the little boats were swung abreast, lashed together, sails hoisted, and the voyageurs would drift north, smoking their pipes, regaling one another with escapades of their recent stay at Grand Portage. The danger in crossing the immense but shallow Lake Winnipeg was its bathtub effect—wind gusts could tip a loaded canoe without warning. That didn't stop the brigades from challenging each other to races. The usual paddling pace of forty-five per minute quickly accelerated to fifty, sixty, even sixty-five. One marathon went on for two days and nights and was called off after forty hours of continuous paddling only because Duncan McGillivray, the accompanying *bourgeois*, ordered a halt. "On the second night of the contest," he later recalled, "one of our steersman being overpowered with sleep fell out of the Stern of his Canoe which being under sail advanced a considerable distance before the people could recover from the confusion that this accident occasioned; in the meantime the poor fellow almost sinking with the weight of his clothes cried out to two Canoes that happened to pass within a few yards of him to save his life *pour l'amour de dieu*; but neither the love of God or of the blessed Virgin, whom he powerfully called to his assistance, had the least influence on his hard hearted Countrymen who paddled along with the greatest unconcern, and he must have certainly perished if his own Canoe had not returned in time enough to prevent it."

Near the mouth of the Winnipeg River at Bas-de-la-Rivière (later called Fort Alexander) the brigades took on supplies of pemmican. This was the fuel of the Northwest fur trade, the propellant that fed the beasts of burden who manned the canoes. Because every day, almost every hour before freeze-up counted, because the canoes did not have the space to carry adequate food supplies and because there was no time in the eternal rush of the voyageur's sunrise-to-sunset schedule to hunt, pemmican became as essential a part of the fur business as the trade goods. In terms of its bulk, weight and energy-giving properties, it was a remarkably cost-efficient food, with canoemen apparently content to down only a pound and a half of the mundane but highly nutritious substance a day.

Supplied from the plains of the Red and Assiniboine rivers, pemmican, which looked a bit like dehydrated dog food, was made from pulverized buffalo meat mixed with melted tallow and the Saskatoon berries then common on the Prairies. (This fruit was a valuable source of vitamin C that helped prevent scurvy.) The ingredients for a ninety-pound bag of pemmican were simple: one buffalo to sixteen pounds of berries. The animal's flesh was cut into flakes or thin slices and hung out to dry in the sun or preferably over fires, a procedure that also served to keep at least some flies out of the mixture. After the meat chunks were thoroughly desiccated, Indian women spread them out and pounded them with stones or wooden flails until they were reduced to a pulp. The animal's hide had meanwhile been sewn into a rawhide sack, which then was half filled with the pulverized shreds. The buffalo's fat, which had been boiling in huge kettles, was now poured hot into the rawhide bags; the berries were stirred in and the sack was sewn shut, its seams sealed with tallow.

Pemmican was eaten either raw, sliced, coated with flour and fried, or cut up into a thick soup called *rababoo*. It required no preservatives and seemed to last forever.* There was considerable dispute about exactly how palatable the stuff really was. Those who ate it staunchly declared there wasn't anything else quite like it, claiming it tasted like nothing but pemmican. The liveliest description of that unmatched flavour is in H.M. Robinson's *The Great Fur*

---

* The *Winnipeg Free Press* of August 10, 1934, reported the discovery by William Campbell of twenty bags of pemmican that had been cached on his northern Manitoba farm eighty years before. After munching a sample, Campbell observed: "It still tasted like meat and retained some of its flavour."

Land: "Take the scrapings from the driest outside corner of a very stale piece of cold roast beef, add to it lumps of rancid fat, then garnish all with long human hairs and short hairs of dogs and oxen and you have a fair imitation of common Pemmican."

Tons of this precious food were required annually for distribution along the northern canoe routes, and the native peoples quickly realized that they controlled a major staple of the fur trade, just as valuable a barter item for liquor, tobacco and knives as animal pelts. To preserve their monopoly, Indians, and later Métis, would occasionally burn the scrub off the land surrounding the trading posts to keep the buffalo herds in their own territories. When pemmican supplies ran out, the voyageurs survived by roasting beaver tails, fishing, shooting the occasional duck or bear, or chewing on herbs and roots. Once in a rare while they would enjoy such local Northwest delicacies as buffalo tongues, dried moose noses or the boiled fetal calf of a buffalo. But most of the time, it was pemmican all the way.

FROM LAKE WINNIPEG, the NWC brigades went south via the Red River towards the upper reaches of the Mississippi; southwest on the Souris River into Missouri Country; or northwest along one of the tributaries of the Saskatchewan River system. With a combined length greater than that of either the St Lawrence or the Danube, the North and South Saskatchewan rivers connect the Lake Winnipeg region with the Rocky Mountains through Blackfoot Country. Starting as glacier melt in those distant plateaus, the sister rivers traverse the Prairies in a huge horizontal Y before joining just east of Prince Albert. Their final cascade into Lake Winnipeg is through the dramatic Grand Rapids, which before damming was an extraordinary sight. The river, a powersurge five hundred feet wide, tumbled through high rock chambers in a drop of more than seventy-five feet in less than three miles.

The Grand Rapids portage brought the voyageurs to Cumberland House, an NWC pemmican depot beside the Hudson's Bay Company post originally built by Samuel Hearne in 1774. It would be September by then, and there was a frigid tang of autumn in the air as the wind scudded across the spruce forests under the flaxen rays of the cooling sun. The brigades toiled ever westward, those on the Saskatchewan's upper flank running near the edge of the prairie grasslands and the northern wood country. Canoe brigades ascending the North Saskatchewan were occasionally met by NWC wintering partners from nearby posts bringing saddle horses to allow the accompanying *bourgeois* a spot of buffalo hunting.

The main route out of Cumberland House led to the great Churchill River, which roared down to Hudson Bay from the divide at Lac La Loche, site of the infamous Methy Portage, the longest and toughest on the trade routes. Conquering its twelve-mile trail and climbing its six-hundred-foot elevation under 180-pound packs of freight and furs earned voyageurs the ultimate badge of courage. Crossing this formidable rampart put the canoes in the Athabasca Country, whose gloomy forests eventually yielded more than half the North West Company's profits.

Winter was a frustrating interlude of hunting, gathering firewood, and transporting routine cargoes by dogsled instead of canoe. The voyageurs decked out their animals in gaudy belled harnesses and embroidered felt coats, fitting them with tiny deerskin booties to protect soft paw pads from cracked ice. Travelling mostly at night to avoid snow glare, the men provided the essential courier service between the snowbound foils, fighting cold so intense a veteran trader cried out that "one ought to have his Blood composed of Brandy, his Body of Brass and his Eyes of Glass."

After three or more years in the wilderness the Northmen would return to Montreal, but it was no easy adjustment. River life may have been brutal, but it obeyed natural laws at odds with those of the city. Like sailors at the end of a long passage, the voyageurs, especially the Northmen who had crossed the Hudson Bay divide, found they had become a race apart, outcasts from a world they never made. "Their arrival at Lachine," wrote William George Beers, the observant Montreal dentist who later popularized lacrosse, "is a time of great excitement. The wild picturesque appearance of the men, and the distance they have come, awakens a sympathy for them, and hundreds will go out from town to see them. Their appearance in the city is very odd. They go along the streets, gaping and staring at everything, in such haste and excitement that they run against people and stumble over little obstructions. They ... roar aloud with laughter at the extensiveness of the ladies' hoops, and the peculiarity of their hats; look in the windows at the jumble of new things, to them, and have hearty laughs at what they consider the absurdities and curiosities of city people."

GIVEN THEIR ABHORRENCE of discipline, the voyageurs must have suffered a shock to their independent spirits when for five action-filled months they found themselves in an incongruous role: they became soldiers for Britain, defending Canada against the Americans in the War of 1812. The Corps of Canadian Voyageurs, formed as an auxiliary unit on October 1, 1812, and disbanded March 14, 1813, was commanded by twenty-seven volunteer *bour-geois* itching in their tailored tunics. Joseph McGillivray, one of the ensigns, reported on the comic tableau of his troops parading with British regulars. "They talked incessantly, called each other pork-eaters, and quarrelled about their rations," he wrote in his diary. "They were guilty of much insubordina-tion, and it was quite impossible to make them amenable to military law. They generally came on parade with a pipe in their mouths and their rations of pork and bread stuck on their bayonets. On seeing an officer, whether general, colonel, or subaltern, they took off their hats and made a low bow, with the common salutation of *Bon jour, Monsieur le Général,* or *le Colonel,* as the case might be, and, if they happened to know that the officer was married, never failed to inquire after the health of *Madame et les enfants* ... when called to order by their officers and told to hold their tongues, one or more would reply, 'Ah dear captain, let us off as quick as you can; some of us have not yet break-fasted, and it's upwards of an hour since I had a smoke.'"

The voyageurs fought as members of larger units in the battle at Crysler's Farm and the capture of Prairie du Chien. Their best-known exploit was a lightning raid on the pivotal American trading post at Michilimackinac (Mackinac) then commanding the straits between Lakes Huron and Michigan. Under strict orders from Major-General Isaac Brock to capture this strategic fortification, 180 voyageurs and 300 Indians joined 45 British regulars stationed at St Joseph's Island on a three-day expedition to lay siege to the American position. The decisive factor in the garrison's surrender was the presence of two iron six-pounders, artillery pieces lugged along by the voyageurs. Their natural sense of theatrics plus only the vaguest of instincts for self-preservation in the face of danger would have made any enemy flinch.*

---

* That untypical interlude was followed much later by a bizarre incident involving so-called voyageurs in an expedition up the Nile. In 1884, Moslem rebels led by the charismatic Mohammed Ahmed, known as the Mahdi, determined to dislodge British and Egyptian forces from the Sudan, had cornered General Charles George "Chinese" Gordon and his troops in Khartoum, a provincial capital on the sixth cataract of the Upper Nile. Sir Garnet Wolseley, the British general charged with organizing an expeditionary force to rescue Gordon, realized he would have to transport his troops up 860 miles of shallow, treacherous rapids above Aswan and remembered the voyageurs from his previous service in Canada, while suppressing the Riel Rebellion on the Red River. Four hundred "voyageurs" (really rivermen then employed in the lumber trade along the Gatineau and Saguenay) were recruited and placed in charge of the troops who paddled eight hundred whalers (enlarged lifeboats) up the turbulent river. The rescuers reached their objective—but it was too late. On January 26, 1885, two days before the expedition arrived, the rebels broke into the city and put Gordon to the sword.

THE VOYAGEURS VANISHED from Montreal's hinterland after the demise of the North West Company in 1821. Their songs were heard no more along the rivers and portages. Their lives may not have been blessed with a surfeit of grace, but their legacy endures: their exuberant and highly un-Canadian sense of daring propelled them to risk everything for a cause as ephemeral as their own brotherhood. They have since retreated from the map of their country's consciousness as if they had never existed, leaving history to hand down no precise tally of their achievements.

One problem in attempting retrospectively to plumb the voyageurs' psyches is that there exist no firsthand records of their exploits, no diaries, no letters, nothing but a few songs and the folk memory of men in scarlet sashes having done impossible things. Their own voice is permanently silent.

Only once was a voyageur actually questioned about his brave calling. In 1822, an anonymous septuagenarian who had been a voyageur hitched a ride from Norway House to Red River with the former NWC trader Alexander Ross. "I have now been," the old man told Ross, "forty-two years in this country. For twenty-four, I was a light canoeman; I required but little sleep, but sometimes got less than I required. No portage was too long for me; all portages were alike. My end of the canoe never touched the ground till I saw the end of it. Fifty songs a day were nothing to me. I could carry, paddle, walk, and sing with any man I ever saw. During that period, I saved the lives of ten *Bourgeois*, and was always the favourite, because when others stopped to carry at a bad step, and lost time, I pushed on—over rapids, over cascades, over chutes; all were the same to me. No water, no weather, ever stopped the paddle or the song. I had twelve wives in the country; and was once possessed of fifty horses, and six running dogs, trimmed in the first style. I was then like a *Bourgeois*, rich and happy: no *Bourgeois* had better-dressed wives than I; no Indian chief finer horses; no white man better-harnessed or swifter dogs. I beat all Indians at the race, and no white man ever passed me in the chase. I wanted for nothing; and I spent all my earnings in the enjoyment of pleasure. Five hundred pounds, twice told, have passed through my hands; although now I have not a spare shirt to my back, nor a penny to buy one.

"Yet, were I young again, I should glory in commencing the same career again, I would willingly spend another half-century in the same fields of enjoyment. There is no life so happy as a voyageur's life; none so independent; no place where a man enjoys so much variety and freedom as in the Indian country. *Huzza! Huzza! pour le pays sauvage!*"

Big Mack

Thorny as the thistles of his native Scotland, Alexander Mackenzie was as immovable as the mountains he crossed. If there ever was such a quality as mulish intelligence he personified it ...

ONE WORD DOMINATED the concerns and conversations of Nor'Westers huddled around summer campfires and crude winter hearths: Athabasca. That vaguely defined territory edging up to the shadows of the Rocky Mountains became the touchstone for the company's aspirations to greatness.

The full measure of the Athabasca Country—what would later be called the Mackenzie River Basin—was difficult to grasp, and is still. In the Western Hemisphere, only two drainage basins—the Amazon's and the Mississippi's—exceed the size of the Mackenzie's, which covers an area the equivalent of Western Europe. Three time zones are required to encompass Athabasca's dimensions, and the Mackenzie, from its headwaters on the Finlay River to the Arctic Ocean, flows for 2,635 miles—farther than Africa's Niger or Russia's Volga.

What attracted the Nor'Westers into the Athabasca Country was a simple law of nature. Covered by matted forests that provided a prime habitat, chilled by sub-Arctic temperatures that induced its profusion of animals to grow thick, rich pelts, Athabasca was one of the world's most lucrative fur farms. The other overwhelming advantage for the Montrealers was that Athabasca was legally a no-man's land. The HBC's charter covered only the territory with rivers emptying into Hudson Bay. Beyond the Methy Portage, the domain of Athabasca clearly drained in other directions. The HBC was aware of Athabasca's riches (having sent an illiterate explorer named William Stuart to that far kingdom as early as 1714), but the Company of Adventurers seemed at that point psychologically unable to field the logistics required to venture that far inland. This was difficult to comprehend because from their starting point in the middle of the continent, the HBC traders were already halfway there. By contrast, the Nor'Westers had to travel forty-three hundred miles from Lachine to the Mackenzie, crossing sixty lakes and 330 portages along the way.

The Nor'Westers had been nibbling at the Far West long before their official amalgamation into one company. An early Nor'Wester named Peter Pangman had marked a spruce tree within sight of the Rockies in 1790, but it was a charismatic murderer named Peter Pond who first plunged into Athabasca.

This combative Connecticut Yankee left home to join the army and escape his father's shoe repair shop at sixteen, noting the event in his diary using his own strange and barely decipherable phonetic spelling. "Beaing then sixteen years of age I gave my Parans to understand that I had a strong desire to be a Solge.... But thay forbid me, and no wonder as my father had a larg and young famerly I just begun to be of sum youse to him in his afairs. Still the same Inklanation & Sperit that my Ancestors Profest run thero my Vanes. It is well known that from fifth Gineration downward we ware all Waryers Ither by Sea or Land and in Dead so strong was the Propensatey for the arme that I could not with stand its Temtations."

After serving in the Seven Years' War, during which he won field commission as an acting captain, Pond went into the Mississippi fur trade but left for the Canadian Northwest in 1775 following the fatal wounding of another trader in a sunrise duel. ("We met the next morning eairley and discharged pistels in which the pore fellowe was unfortenat.") The Saskatchewan River tributaries were by that time swarming with independent traders. At the mouth of the Sturgeon River near modern-day Prince Albert, Saskatchewan, for example, seven different partnerships were represented. In the spring of 1778, the frontiersmen working out of this post pooled the season's remaining trade goods and chose Pond to lead an exploratory five-canoe probe into the heart of the Athabasca territories. This foray was nothing more than a pragmatic response to the circumstances in which the winterers found themselves, but the tactic was to prove an essential breakthrough for the Nor'Westers. If the assault on Athabasca were started at mid-continent instead of from the head of Lake Superior, the anticipated fur trade could become a practical proposition. Pond pushed up the Churchill River, his voyageurs paddling through virgin spruce forests until they reached Methy Portage. The first white men to struggle up the cliff towering six hundred feet over the Clearwater as it flows towards the Athabasca River, they marvelled at the verdant panorama. One lyrical description of the view from the top of Methy was that of Lieutenant John Henry Lefroy, a Royal Artillery surveyor who visited the site in 1844: "It is celebrated for the view from the north end. It is a wide and regular valley, of great depth, stretching for a distance of thirty miles to the west. The sun was just setting as I arrived there, the light glancing from the nearer foliage, and filling the distance with golden haze; there is not that variety in the autumnal tints of a forest here which makes those of Canada so wonderful, but quite enough to compose a very beautiful picture. A portion of wood in the distance was burning, and there was an uncommon felicity in the manner in which the columns of smoke rose up against a dark mass of Pines which crossed the valley behind them. The Clearwater river winds through the midst, sometimes expanding into a placid little lake, then diminishing to a thread of light barely caught among the trees. Upon the whole I have seen few views more beautiful."

After setting up a crude log cabin forty miles south of Lake Athabasca, Pond and his voyageurs settled in for the winter's trading with the Chipewyan. On July 2, 1779, they were back at Cumberland House, starving but hauling 140 packs of superb dark pelts, having been forced to leave an equal quantity behind in a secret cache because the little brigade would have sunk under the full load.

Pond spent the following season in Athabasca with similarly impressive results and became a full partner in one of the first NWC amalgamations.* Caught by an early freeze-up, he spent the winter of 1781–82 at Lac La Ronge, where he met Jean-Etienne Waddens, the Protestant son of a Swiss professor, who had come to Canada with Wolfe's army.† The opportunities of the fur trade quickly led Waddens into a share of the new North West Company, but he was part of a faction that opposed the granting of the entire Athabasca district to Pond. One March night the two men quarrelled and Waddens was

---

* During his journeys, Pond observed outcroppings of tar sand, the black gold that would eventually become the impetus for grand-scale oil extraction. At the time, he was impressed with the dark substance oozing from the banks of the Athabasca River only because it was useful for caulking canoes.
† In 1761 Waddens had married Marie-Josephte Deguire, and their daughter Veronique became the wife of the Reverend John Bethune, Montreal's first Presbyterian minister. The Bethunes' son Angus was an active NWC partner and great-grandfather of Norman Bethune, the Canadian surgeon who became a hero of the Chinese Revolution.

fatally wounded, though the exact circumstances of the fight were never established and the murder might have been committed by a Pond subordinate with the grand name of Toussaint le Sieur. Pond escaped retribution and fled the Northwest. Five years later the intemperate Yankee was back in the Athabasca Country trading opposite John Ross, who had left the NWC to join an ambitious competing fur partnership called Gregory, McLeod & Company. During a quarrel with Pond about supplies, Ross was killed, though it was one of Pond's men, a Canadian named Péché, who was charged (but not convicted).

By this time, Pond was forty-six, an old man in the brotherhood of the trade, and his reputation for violence had lost him the respect of his peers. He did spend one more season in the Athabasca Country, working on a chart he swore would revolutionize the geography of the day and teaching all he knew to an eager neophyte named Alexander Mackenzie.

Pond kept busy that long winter drafting a map depicting a mythical North West Passage, convinced by his conversations with local Copper Indians that the Pacific Ocean lay within easy access of the rivers linked to Lake Athabasca. He planned to present his theory to Catherine II, Great Empress of all the Russias, who was known to be interested in northern exploration. Working by the flicker of candlelight and using ink that often had to be thawed, Pond drew and labelled the two "Great Rivers" he postulated ran to the Pacific. The geography of his scratchings proved to be mostly imagination, but he inspired the eventual discovery by the twenty-four-year-old Mackenzie of the river that now bears his name, and his subsequent push to the Pacific. In the spring of 1788, Pond left the Fur Country forever, to die in impoverished anonymity nineteen years later in the wilds of New England. His protégé, Mackenzie, journeyed to the NWC's Superior headquarters, determined to obtain official blessing for his dream of seeking the Pacific using one of Pond's suggested routes.

ALEXANDER MACKENZIE is a legitimate Canadian hero, having been the first to pass the test of crossing the country that two centuries later would confer similar status on his handicapped successors: Terry Fox, Steve Fonyo and Rick Hansen. Mackenzie's physical feat of having been the first white man to take an expedition across the upper continent—thirteen years before Meriwether Lewis and William Clark led a much larger and better-equipped force to the more southerly American shore of the Pacific—overshadowed his considerable contributions to the politics of the fur trade, to international diplomacy and to Arctic literature. The first Nor'Wester more interested in creating a global British commercial empire than in the gathering of pelts, he envisaged the linking of the North American fur trade to the exotic commerce of the Orient, with Britain's growing manufacturing strength forming the third side of the triangle. It was a dream of high statesmanship. "At one moment," wrote Dr W. Kaye Lamb, the former dominion archivist, in a perceptive essay introducing the explorer's journal, "Mackenzie is hard put to it to overcome a few yards of rapid current, at another he is thinking of trans-Pacific commerce with Canton. He may be standing waist deep in a rushing river, holding on to a wrecked canoe, but this battered craft is still the needle drawing behind it a thread which, knotted with those drawn across the world's greatest oceans by Cook and Vancouver, will form the basis of a network on which Canada still depends for economic survival. Mackenzie may have been, from a military point of view, almost unarmed, yet the permanent effects of his penetration of territory were at least comparable to Marlborough's leading an army to Blenheim."

The official portrait of Mackenzie by Sir Thomas Lawrence that now hangs in the National Gallery of Canada reveals a sensitive, almost pious face, its set jaw contradicting the dreamy eyes—a self-contained man fully aware of his worth. There is no texture of wilderness in Mackenzie's features, little residue of his superhuman struggles down wild rivers, yet the man's virility and physical prowess shine through. He once snowshoed seven hundred miles to attend a Christmas dinner, and paddled a freight canoe seventy-two miles in one stretch of daylight, against headwinds and in temperatures so frigid his voyageurs resorted to wearing mittens. Like most of his confrères, he enjoyed several open-air romances but did not marry until he was forty-eight, settling down at last with a perky fourteen-year-old Scottish lass. Thorny as the thistles of his native Scotland, Alexander Mackenzie was as immovable as the mountains he crossed. If there ever was such a quality as mulish intelligence he personified it, convinced that his inherent arrogance sprang from superior intellect.

In his daily dealings with Indians and voyageurs he was often suspicious and curt, treating them as inferior creatures to be manipulated for his own purposes. Unlike Samuel Hearne, who surrendered himself to his soulmate and guide, Matonabbee, Mackenzie never developed a bond of friendship with English Chief, the leader of the Indians who accompanied him to the Arctic Ocean. "The English Chief was very much displeased at my reproaches," Mackenzie noted in his journal, "and expressed himself to me in person to that effect. This was the very opportunity which I wanted, to make him acquainted with my dissatisfaction for some time past … he accused me of speaking ill words to him … [and] concluded by informing me that he would not accompany me any further … [later] I sent for the English Chief to sup with me, and a dram or two dispelled all his heart-burning and discontent … I took care that he should carry some liquid consolation to his lodge, to prevent the return of his chagrin."

Although he was always careful to husband his energies and planned his life with a sure instinct for beneficial self-preservation, his natural reserve would occasionally break. In the spring of 1797, while the NWC canoe brigades were preparing to leave Lachine, Mackenzie and William McGillivray, then sharing Montreal lodgings, lunched with George Landmann, the visiting officer from the Royal Engineers. "We sat down," Landmann later reported, "and without loss of time, expedited the lunch intended to supersede a dinner, during which time the bottle had freely circulated, raising the old Highland drinking propensity, so that there was no stopping it; Highland speeches and sayings, Highland reminiscences; and Highland farewells, with the doch and dorich, over and over again, was kept up with extraordinary energy, so that by six or seven o'clock, I had, in common with many of the others, fallen from my seat. To save my legs from being trampled on, I contrived to draw myself into the fire-place, and sat up in one of the corners, there being no stove or grate … I there remained very passive, contemplating the proceedings of those who still remained at table, when at length Mackenzie … and McGillivray … were the last retaining their seats. Mackenzie now proposed to drink to our memory, and then give the war-whoop over us, fallen foes or friends, all nevertheless on the floor, and in attempting to push the bottle to McGillivray at the opposite end of the table, he slid off his chair, and could not recover his seat whilst McGillivray, in extending himself over the table in the hope of seizing the bottle which Mackenzie had attempted to push to him, also in like manner began to slide to one side, and fell helpless on the floor."

Just why this singular but fallible man fought with such unremitting fierceness to achieve his vision of the fur trade can never be fully ascertained. His unusual apprenticeship seems to have been devised for straightforward commercial ambitions—the natural quest of an expansion-minded business executive determined to extend his territory. Certainly, he was obsessed with serving the best economic interests of Britain by squaring the circle of the island nation's trade routes—in effect discovering the North West Passage that

English seamen had been trying to find for nearly two centuries, even if that channel now ran by land and water through the middle of the continent.

Born to a prominent Stornoway family in 1764, Mackenzie was left mother-less very young. His father emigrated to New York, where he eventually became an officer in the Loyalist forces fighting the American insurgents. Young Alexander was reared mainly by two aunts, who sent him to Montreal for his schooling. At fifteen, he joined a counting house headed by John Gregory, a pioneer of the inland fur barter, whose canoe brigades had been among the first to reach the Saskatchewan Valley. Mackenzie spent five formative years learning the business side of the trade, and when Gregory decided to join the Nor'Westers, Mackenzie went along as a partner.

His posting to the Athabasca Country, first as Peter Pond's assistant and later as his successor, was one of those satisfying coincidences of history that fix an individual precisely at the time and place in which circumstances allow him to realize his aspirations. Pond's theory that two broad rivers connected Great Slave Lake north of Lake Athabasca with the Pacific Ocean by only six paddling days to the west was a bit of geographical fancy because it assumed that the northern extensions of the Rocky Mountains ended at 62° north and that Great Slave Lake was at least a thousand miles farther west than it actu-ally was. But in happy ignorance Mackenzie resolved to follow one of Pond's mysterious streams to its mouth and stake a claim to the Pacific shore.

So excited was he by the secret instructions he received to this effect at the 1788 summer meeting in Grand Portage that he returned to Athabasca in a record fifty-two days, cutting two weeks off the usual travel time. His first cousin Roderick McKenzie,* assigned to be his assistant, built Fort

---

* The resident intellectual of the Northwest fur trade, Roderick McKenzie started a library at the new Fort Chipewyan, arranging to have an eclectic collection of books shipped, paddled and portaged from England. The library grew so large it eventually had to be catalogued and housed in its own building. Under McKenzie, the desolate fort (the only NWC post that was painted inside) was known as "Little Athens" and became an important social influence. After a decade a new post was built across the lake, on the site of the present Fort Chipewyan.

The last of the original buildings at the second fort, the residence of the former Chief Factor, was torn down in 1964. Except for some fading footpaths, all that remains of this once-great facility is the base of the sundial that marked the time of day until the 1940s. Indians at the isolated settlement, 380 miles north of Edmonton, in the spring of 1987 settled one of Canada's largest outstanding land claims. After twenty years of negotiation, local Cree were given $26.6 million cash plus hunting rights to three million acres of nearby Wood Buffalo National Park. Fort Chipewyan has only five miles of streets and one general store— plus a beer parlour named for the old explorer: The Peter Pond Hotel.

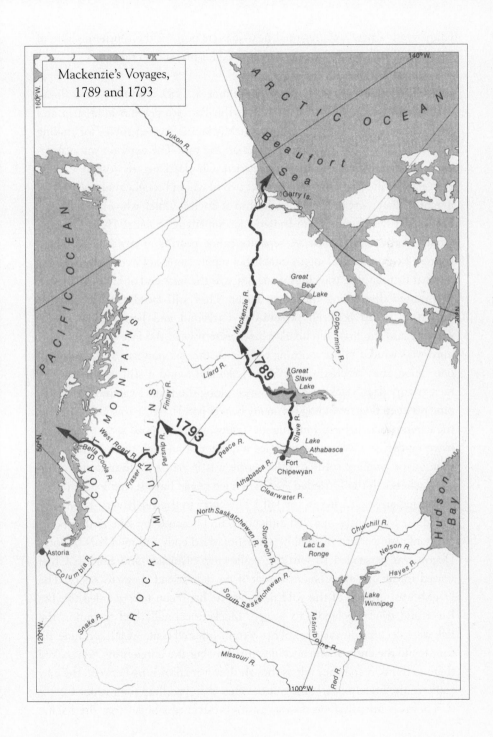

Mackenzie's Voyages,
1789 and 1793

Chipewyan, a new NWC regional headquarters post on the southern shore of
Lake Athabasca, while Mackenzie prepared for his dash to tidewater.

AT NINE O'CLOCK ON THE MORNING of June 3, 1789, a flotilla of four flimsy
canoes unceremoniously departed from the Fort Chipewyan mud strip and
pushed off into the lake. In his pocket Mackenzie carried rubles for trading
with the Russians he expected to meet on the way. The explorer was accompanied by the voyageurs François Barrieu, Charles Ducette, Joseph Landry,
Pierre de Lorme and John Steinbruck, two of whom brought their wives, and
a small Indian party under the leadership of English Chief, who eighteen years
before had been among the Indians accompanying Samuel Hearne to the
mouth of the Coppermine. A separate canoe bearing an NWC clerk named
Laurent Leroux went along to establish a supply camp at Great Slave Lake.

   That first day, the travellers made it across the west end of Lake Athabasca
and started descending the Slave River. They still faced the sixteen-mile
stretch of rapids between present-day Fitzgerald and Fort Smith. It was
snowing and the little birchbark canoes were toys in the face of a vindictive
northwest wind. On the morning of June 9, after six portages and the loss of
one canoe, they reached Great Slave Lake and found it still frozen. For the
next twenty days Mackenzie led his men along the lake's swampy shore, slipping between floes, avoiding the many beaver ponds, trying to snatch sleep in
the extended daylight of June nights. Temperatures dropped so fast that each
morning the lake was edged with ice a quarter of an inch thick—this at the
time of the summer solstice. (Mackenzie was in fact travelling during what
geographers call the Little Ice Age, when ice would have stayed longer in the
spring and arrived earlier in the fall.) The entry to the Big River—later to be
called the Mackenzie—proved difficult to find because the lake at that point
is a confusing pattern of shallows, marshes, dead ends and mud bars. A local
Dogrib was persuaded to join the wallowing cavalcade and English Chief
vowed to cut the newcomer's throat if he didn't lead them to safety. The
Dogrib was terrified of the wild monsters he had been told guarded the Big
River and tried repeatedly to escape; Mackenzie finally had to pinion the
fellow by sleeping on the edge of his vermin-infested coat. At last, on June 29,
they found the entry and headed downstream, but the unrelenting rain soaked
them to the skin and they felt as though they were drowning between the clay
banks of the broad river, bailing more often than paddling their canoes.

   The river initially flowed west, raising Mackenzie's hopes that the Pacific

Ocean might appear around one more bend. But then the stream turned due north, and by July 10 (at a latitude of 67°47′N) Mackenzie realized that this was no shortcut to a still distant ocean. "It was evident," he noted in his journal, "that these waters emptied themselves into the Hyperborean Sea; and though it was probable that we could not return to Athabasca in the course of the season, I determined to penetrate to the discharge of them."

By this time not only the cowed Dogrib but all the Indians and the voyageurs had seen enough. They begged Mackenzie to turn back, and to their surprise he promised he would, if they didn't touch an ocean shore within a week. "I also urged the honour of conquering disasters and the disgrace that would attend them on their return home without having obtained the object of the expedition," he noted later in his journal. "Nor did I fail to mention the courage and resolution which was the peculiar boast of the Northmen...."

The puny expedition had by now lost most of its sense of purpose and direction; the battered canoes meandered unresisting down the broad torrent hissing under their narrow beams. Only the occasional abandoned native settlement broke the monotony of steep banks dotted with dwarf trees. The few fox or hare they shot had a strange whitish grey hue and unusual socks of downy fur covering their feet. As the season advanced, the sun merely teased the horizon, and their meagre provisions were nearly exhausted. Out of desperation, Mackenzie kept landing to climb nearby hills to see where the river was leading them, but the view was never clear enough to show the way.

The air of doom hanging over the cursed river grew more tangible as the Indians spotted a deserted encampment, its tent poles fashioned from whalebone. They knew then that they had entered the land of their ancestral enemies, the Eskimos. Time was measured in hours instead of days now, and Mackenzie's observations placed the forlorn brigade at about 69° north, just downstream from present-day Inuvik. They pressed on, heading west through freezing shallow water. Dispirited beyond the point of fear, they landed at what is now called Garry Island, but it was too foggy for them to estimate their position.

That night (July 14, 1789), it finally happened. At four in the morning Mackenzie awakened and sat bolt upright; his belongings were wet. Since there was no wind, the only explanation had to be an incoming tide—the conclusive signature of an ocean. After a few hours of paddling out from the dank coast into the Beaufort Sea, Mackenzie and his men hurried away from the godforsaken shore, knowing they had beaten the odds, but to little purpose.

By September 12 they were safely back at Fort Chipewyan. They had been gone 102 days. They had covered more than three thousand miles, survived unspeakable hardships—and discovered only that what they were seeking must be elsewhere.

WHEN MACKENZIE REPORTED his meagre findings to the following summer's NWC conclave at Lake Superior, he was politely ignored. That not-unexpected reaction hardly upset him, because by then the disappointed explorer had another expedition in mind. On his return journey, Mackenzie had learned that nomadic bands of Eskimos traded with white men in ships to the west-ward, though local Indians warned him the natives of that far country were giants with wings who could kill with their eyes. Shortly afterward, during one of his journeys out of the Athabasca, Mackenzie had met Philip Turnor, a surveyor for the Hudson's Bay Company, who persuaded him that he needed to study surveying and astronomy in England if he intended to become a serious explorer. Turnor had located the true position of Fort Chipewyan at longitude 111° west, which, if true, meant that it was considerably farther from the Pacific than Pond had originally postulated. Mackenzie's mercenary instincts were also aroused; he was pleased to learn that the British Parliament had posted an award of £20,000 to the discoverer of the North West Passage.

After a winter in England spent honing his surveying skills, Mackenzie returned to the Athabasca determined to follow Pond's second "Great River" of the Northwest to its mouth. He moved out to winter at a fork of the Peace River.

ON MAY 9, 1793, Mackenzie departed on his greatest adventure. With him was an NWC clerk named Alexander McKay, six voyageurs (Jacques Beauchamp, François Beaulieux, Baptiste Bisson, François Courtois, Charles Ducette and Joseph Landry), two Indians and a large friendly dog. They were crowded into a specially built twenty-five-foot canoe light enough for two men to portage, yet capable of carrying three thousand pounds of pemmican, beans, flour, rum, guns and trade goods. As they paddled west under a cool spring sun, the customarily stoical Mackenzie was moved to write in his journal: "This magnificent theatre of nature has all the decorations which the trees and animals of the country can afford it. Groves of poplar in every shape vary the scene; and their intervals are enlivened with vast herds of elks and buffaloes. The whole country displayed an exuberant verdure; the trees that bear a blossom were advancing fast to that delightful appearance, and the velvet rind of their branches reflecting the oblique rays of a rising or setting sun, added a splendid gaiety to the scene."

By mid-May they were under the brow of the still snowbound Rockies. Game seemed plentiful, but Mackenzie was nervous that gunfire might frighten local Indians. Finally it was the dog that chased down a buffalo calf for the evening's repast. The gorges narrowed the next day, squeezing the river into rapids between perpendicular cliffs. The crew had to disembark, towing the canoe with a 180-foot line while Mackenzie led his troops up impossible rock-faces, cutting miniature ledges as he ascended the slippery slope. The men stepped from his shoulders to the shaft of his axe, embedded in whatever root he could reach, creeping up the near-vertical surface, trying not to glance at the waters raging below. The canyons of the Peace echoed with the rumble of distant rockslides as the stream disintegrated into a sequence of waterfalls. They struck out overland, chopping their way through the brush and forest on the bone-chilling margin of the Rockies. Sulphur pools bubbled unheeded as they hacked their way through moss-hung branches, advancing less than three miles a day. They collapsed exhausted by four o'clock in the afternoon, sleeping where they fell, their backs wedged against large tree trunks as protection from rock- and mud-slides. Their moccasins were in useless tatters; every step was agony. In case they perished among the slides of these malignant hills Mackenzie scribbled a note, stuffed it into an empty rum keg and kicked the thing into the river.

They were near the height of land now, marching silently through the halo of clouds that blotted out the earth except for mountain peaks that appeared to float in these elevated misty seas. At the juncture of the Parsnip and Finlay rivers they halted, not sure which way to go. Then, heeding the advice of an old Beaver Indian they had met along the way, they turned south into the Parsnip. The turbulent tributary was in flood, inundating the beaver meadows that lined its banks, and their progress was halted by so many rapids that the crew threatened mutiny. The travellers were too dispirited to talk or even pray.

Then, some unexpected luck. Camped in that high hard land was a small band of Sekanis, people of the rocks. Understandably nervous about this unexpected incursion of palefaced scarecrows, they took up their weapons, but Mackenzie reassured them with the simple gesture of walking up to the closest warrior and placing an arm around his shoulders. In the translated conversation that followed, one of the Indians recalled obtaining bits of iron from other tribes that had gone down to a big stinking lake (the Pacific Ocean) to trade with white men who arrived in ships "as big as islands," but he would not or could not tell how to get there. Mackenzie tried to bribe him with hunks of pemmican, beads, a knife—but no, he claimed he knew nothing about the "Great River" flowing into that stinking lake.

The phrase "Great River" was used so often in the interchange between the Sekanis and the expedition's interpreter that Mackenzie memorized it. Next morning he was feeding bits of sugar to a young Sekani boy when he overheard one of the adults mentioning the "Great River." He confronted the man and had him sketch its location on bark with a chip of charcoal. The drawing showed a route farther along the Parsnip, across a chain of small lakes and portages, down to the "Great River," which the Indian warned was the home of warlike tribes who lived in houses built on islands. The stinking lake, he estimated, was a moon's journey away.

Setting out with renewed vigour, the expedition reached the little lakes, where a well-travelled path of 817 paces led across a ridge to a sister body of water. Each was a source of rivers that flowed in opposite directions. Mackenzie was jubilant: he had reached the Arctic-Pacific divide. All he had to do now was to follow the new river to the sea—downstream all the way.

Next day Mackenzie and his men celebrated their luck, shooting down the river, their reflexes dulled by their easy passage. Suddenly the canoe was deep in white water exploding into rapids. The boat slammed into a rock, almost went over on its port side, was thrown onto a gravel bar and then back into the maelstrom, where its stern was pounded against a boulder—the force of the impact heaving it against the opposite shore and caving in the bow. Trying to steady what was left of their craft, one of the voyageurs grabbed the over-hanging branch of a tree, but instead of holding the boat inshore, it catapulted him into the bush. The canoe, still somehow floating, was tossed into a shallow cataract that damaged its bottom, then spewed it out into a calm eddy. Some supplies and many musket balls were lost; the canoe had been reduced almost to kindling.

That night the shaken voyageurs gathered for comfort around an early campfire. It was almost their last. One of the voyageurs carelessly puffed a pipe while strolling over the gunpowder spread out to dry—very nearly, as Mackenzie noted in his diary, putting "a period to all my anxiety and ambition." Next morning they rebuilt the canoe, which now looked more like a patchwork quilt than a boat, and resumed their voyage. On this western slope of the Rockies there was little indigenous food supply; Mackenzie buried a ninety-pound sack of pemmican one night, and his men built a campfire over the hole to hide any trace of the cache for their return journey. Farther along, now on the Fraser, the travellers entered the land of the Carriers, a fierce tribe of Indian middlemen who did not welcome white traders. After being greeted by a volley of arrows, Mackenzie landed on the opposite shore and beckoned to the chief, spreading beads on the ground in a gesture of giving—but first stationing one of his sharpshooting voyageurs in the brush to cover him in case of trouble. After some hesitation, the Carriers crossed the river in a dugout canoe and the palaver began. Drawing pictures in the mud to make themselves understood, the Indians told Mackenzie the "Great River" was blocked by cascades that could not be crossed. The stinking lake could be reached only by land.

Mackenzie was puzzled. For six years he had been dreaming that Pond's "Great River" would carry him to the Pacific. Should he now abandon that quest for an alternative route scratched on a forlorn beach by an Indian with uncertain motives? He decided to do just that, partly because the Fraser was veering south instead of west and partly because he knew he could not keep his men on the river much longer. "I determined to proceed with resolution, and set future events at defiance," he boasted in his journal.

After reaching a point on the Fraser about midway between the present-day towns of Quesnel and Williams Lake, he headed back up the river to somewhere near its junction with a western tributary, which Mackenzie called the West Road River (also known as the Blackwater). He and his men cached their canoe and much of their food and powder and set off westward on foot along a trail to the north of the West Road. The land route was so hard to follow when they found it on July 4 that Mackenzie enlisted a guide who promptly threatened to desert. To ensure his presence overnight, Mackenzie took him to bed, confiding to his journal: "My companion's hair being greased with fish oil, and his body smeared with red earth, my sense of smelling threatened to interrupt my rest; but these inconveniences yielded to my fatigue, and I passed a night of sound repose." The Nor'Westers were passed along to a relay of guides and, once over the coastal range, entered the rain forest of the Pacific, warmed and wetted by milder breezes that made the cedar, hemlock and fir grow too large to hug. Welcomed by local Bella Coola Indians who lived in a highly developed, salmon-dependent culture, the explorers were feasted; their hosts even lent them a replacement canoe for the final dash to

the ocean along North Bentinck Arm and down Dean Channel. The tang of
salt spray was in the air now; the pearly sky was flat. It was a moment for drums
and flags—but understatement was the order of the day. Mackenzie's journal
barely mentioned his first hint of the Pacific. It was casually tossed in at the
end of a lengthy diversion about local architecture: "In the house there were
several chests or boxes containing different articles that belonged to the
people whom we had lately passed. If I were to judge by the heaps of filth
beneath these buildings, they must have been erected at a more distant period
than any which we had passed. From these houses I could perceive the termination of the river, and its discharge into a narrow arm of the sea."

Next day Mackenzie set out to touch the ocean, guided by his Bella Coola
friends. They reached King Island at the top of Fitz Hugh Sound and were
confronted by three canoes of Bella Bellas, hostile natives whose chief menacingly recounted a mysterious tale of an earlier unpleasant confrontation with
white men, and threatened Mackenzie's crew. The Nor'Westers escaped by
paddling to a nearby cove, where they spent an uneasy night. Two more war
canoes appeared next morning and his crew begged Mackenzie to flee before
they were all slaughtered. As he was leaving, he made his best-remembered
statement. On the southeast face of the large rock that had served as his
nocturnal rampart, the proud Highlander used a mixture of vermilion and bear
grease to daub, in large letters, the laconic summary of his incredible journey:

ALEX MACKENZIE
FROM CANADA
BY LAND
22d JULY 1793*

---

* Patterning himself on Mackenzie, William Clark, who with Meriwether Lewis was the first
American explorer to reach tidewater on the Pacific, carved into a tree the words: "WM. CLARK,
DECEMBER 3D 1805 BY LAND FROM U.STATES IN 1804&5." Meriwether Lewis was more wordy.
As the party was about to leave on the return journey to St Louis, he posted a sign that read:
"The object of this last is that through the medium of some civilised person who may see the
same, it may be made known to the world that the party consisting of the persons whose names
are hereunto annexed and who were sent out by the Government of the United States to
explore the interior of the continent of North America, did penetrate the same by way of the
Missouri and Columbia Rivers, to the discharge of the latter into the Pacific Ocean, at which
they arrived on the 14th day of November, 1805, and departed on their return to the United
States by the same route by which they had come."

Next morning the party started home, and thirty-three days later the ten men and the large friendly dog were back in Fort Chipewyan. Having covered 2,811 miles, Mackenzie jotted a final entry in his journal: "Here my voyages of discovery terminate. Their toils and their dangers, their solicitudes and sufferings, have not been exaggerated in my description. On the contrary, in many instances, language has failed me in the attempt to describe them. I received, however, the reward of my labours, for they were crowned with success."

He had been the first across the North West Passage, that mysterious and, as it turned out, barely existent route to the Orient that had been the chief geographical goal of European explorers ever since Christopher Columbus first set out to seek it three centuries before. "Mackenzie," Hugh MacLennan has noted, "introduced a new reality, just as Columbus's lost quest drew an entire hemisphere into the story of civilization. How strange that a Canadian birch-bark canoe without a name, last in a long succession of canoes from Champlain's first one, should have earned a place in the company of ships like the *Santa Maria* and *Golden Hind!*" Still, Mackenzie had not pioneered a feasible new trading route, nor could he claim to have discovered the Bella Bella country. The white men encountered there by the Indians had sailed into the same channel forty-nine days earlier in a cutter charting the inlet for Captain George Vancouver, then on a voyage of exploration on behalf of George III.

The anticlimax of having to spend the winter in the mundane preoccupations of the fur trade taxed Mackenzie's nerves. Physically exhausted and emotionally crippled by having led two expeditions dedicated to the glory of extending British commerce and failing both times, he imploded into what seems to have been a nervous breakdown. He spent that long, lonely season pacing the floor of his snowbound hut, trying aimlessly to complete his appointed task of producing a fair copy of his wilderness journals, and finding it impossible to concentrate. Writing to his cousin Roderick, Mackenzie

---

The American expedition, consisting of forty-five men and a Newfoundland dog, spent two years in the field and all one winter on the Pacific shore. Although Lewis and Clark quickly established themselves as twin icons in the American exploration hall of fame, at least one contemporary observer, David McKeeham, wrote to remind them of Mackenzie's greater, if less heralded, achievement: "Mr. M'Kenzie with a party consisting of about one fourth part of the number under your command, with means which will not bear a comparison with those furnished you, and without the *authority*, the *flags*, or *medals* of his government, crossed the Rocky mountains several degrees north of your route, and for the *first time* penetrated to the Pacific Ocean. You had the advantage of the information contained in his journal, and could in some degree estimate and guard against the dangers and difficulties you were to meet...."

confided his innermost thoughts, disjointedly apologizing that the draft of his revised journal was not enclosed for his cousin's perusal: "Last fall I was to begin copying it—but the greatest part of my time was taken up in vain speculations—I got into such a habit of thinking that I was often lost in thought nor could I ever write to the purpose—what I was thinking of—would often occur to me instead of that which I ought to do—I never passed so much of my time so insignificantly—nor so uneasy—Although I am not superstitious—dreams amongst other things—caused me much annoyance—I could not close my eyes without finding myself in company with the Dead—I had visions of late which almost convince me that I lost a near relation or a friend—It was the latter end of January when I began my work—thinking then I had time enough—though the reverse is the fact—and I will be satisfied and so must you, if I can finish the copy to give you reading of it in the Spring—I find it a work that will require more time than I was aware of—for it is not a quarter finished."

In an even more telling sequel, he explained to McKenzie why he was determined to attend the following summer's NWC conclave at Grand Portage: "I am fully bent on going down. I am more anxious now than ever. For I think it unpardonable in any man to remain in this country who can afford to leave it. What a pretty Situation I am in this winter. Starving and alone, without the power of doing myself or body else any Service. The Boy at Lac La Loche, or even my own Servant, is equal to the performance of my Winter employment."

STILL ONLY THIRTY YEARS OLD, Mackenzie left Athabasca the next summer, vowing to quit that accursed country forever and to turn his attention to a continental strategy for the fur trade. At the Grand Portage meetings the NWC partners were reasonably impressed with the tally of his performance, voting him an extra share of stock as a reward, particularly since he had achieved what the Hudson's Bay Company, originally chartered to discover the North West Passage, had failed to accomplish. Some of his more practical colleagues, however, carped at the exorbitant mark-up on his glory, noting that the Mackenzie expedition had cost £1,500 without adding a single pelt to their storehouses. The winterers at that 1794 gathering, unhappy about their share of profits and feeling frustrated that the Montreal agents were supplying goods inferior to those of the HBC, cornered Mackenzie with their complaints. They found him, if not rebellious, at least open to suggestions for drastic reform of the Canadian fur trade. It was Mackenzie's contention that the company should negotiate a merger with the Hudson's Bay Company, and that the joint organization should plunge into the Pacific trade before it came to be dominated by the aggressive Americans. On his way east from Superior, Mackenzie stopped off at Newark (Niagara-on-the-Lake) and called on John Graves Simcoe, Lieutenant-Governor of Upper Canada, to advocate his radical proposal. That November, back in Montreal, he prepared a lengthy treatise of his views for Lord Dorchester, then Governor-in-Chief of British North America. The expanded, royally chartered fur monopoly he visualized would have opened a transportation route through the Rockies and established a large harbour on the Pacific to take control of the West Coast trade across the ocean to China, the whole network being controlled, round Cape Horn, from London, with an amalgamated NWC and HBC at the heart of the empire.*

Simon McTavish had very mixed feelings about the Mackenzie proposals. It was clearly in the Marquis's self-interest to keep Montreal—and thereby his personal influence—dominant in the fur trade. The highly profitable infrastructure he had set in place would topple if Hudson Bay and the Pacific Coast became the transportation hubs of the amalgamated companies. Yet there was no doubt the shorter routes offered decisive cost savings, and so McTavish did the only sensible thing—he became determined to claim a Pacific port and, more immediately, to negotiate for direct access to Hudson Bay. Earlier he had spent several winters in London, appealing to William Pitt for repeal of the HBC charter. When the British Prime Minister pointed out that this would require an Act of Parliament he was not prepared to sponsor, McTavish lost patience and in 1803 dispatched an armed detachment and a supply ship to establish four outlaw trading posts on Hudson Bay. That venture failed because the HBC immediately went into its traditional defensive stance: it did nothing and waited for the impossible Hudson Bay climate to take care of its temporarily housed enemies. At the same time, the London-based Company's resident factors persuaded most of the Cree to stay away from the NWC posts, and after three years of lacklustre results the Nor'Westers razed their tiny forts and retreated from that unfriendly place. The NWC's agents had meanwhile been

---

* He even extended the scheme from furs to fish, planning to establish a new firm called the Fishery and Fur Company. Its whaling ships would trade items to the Northwest Coast from Nootka Sound, the harbour on the west coast of Vancouver Island that had sheltered Captain James Cook in 1778. He visualized posts being built at the mouth of the Columbia River and at Sea Otter Harbour, in the north. Mackenzie presented this plan to the Colonial Office in London twice in 1802, but no action ensued.

unsuccessfully tempting the HBC Governors to sue their firm for trespassing, hoping the resultant test case would reveal the royal charter's dubious legality. The Committeemen waited out their opponents and won the battle. The dynamics of delay had triumphed once again.

Mackenzie enjoyed a brief holiday in London before returning to Montreal, where he became a member of the Beaver Club and befriended the Duke of Kent, who had been sent to Quebec in command of the 7th Regiment of Foot (Royal Fusiliers). Although he was fully occupied as an agent in Simon McTavish's trading firm, Mackenzie became more and more interested in a Detroit-based interloper calling itself Forsyth, Richardson & Company. He was bound by agreement to remain a North West Company partner until 1799, yet he felt increasing irritation with McTavish's authoritarian style of management. The even more frustrated winterers began to regard him as their spokesman, although as the fifth of five co-partners in the McTavish trading company, he had no real power. Sensing his star partner's alienation and wanting to isolate him from the grumbling winterers, McTavish posted Mackenzie to New York as the NWC's resident agent. That transfer only served to whip up the explorer's anger because in his regular contacts with American fur traders he very quickly recognized they were about to outrun the Canadians to the Pacific.

The break came during the 1799 annual meeting of NWC partners at Grand Portage. At the very first session, Mackenzie rose in his place to declare that he would not be renewing his contract and had resolved to withdraw from the company. Agitated winterers immediately passed a resolution stating that Mackenzie alone enjoyed their confidence, asking him to reconsider. McTavish sat out the exchange in imperious, glacial silence, refusing to add his voice to those urging Mackenzie to stay. Mackenzie stalked out of the hall, later confessing that he had been so angry the gesture made him forget "that which we seldom lose sight of," his self-interest. Adding to the hurt, his place in the NWC partnership was taken by his beloved cousin Roderick. Describing the incident, Alexander Henry the Elder, who was there, noted: "The old North West Company is all in the hands of McTavish and Frobisher, and Mackenzie is out. The latter went off in a pet. The cause as far as I can learn was who should be the first—McTavish or Mackenzie, and as there could not be two Caesars in Rome, one must remove."

Mackenzie stormed back to Montreal and soon afterward embarked for England, where he sought solace among bluebloods who treated him as a colonial hero. He fitted perfectly into British society of the day, an exuberant, bearded fur trader fresh from his historic trek across an unknown continent— an ideal celebrity for the salons of aristocrats caught up in the patriotic fervour of that golden period in British history between Lord Nelson's victories at the Nile and at Trafalgar. He had his portrait painted by the King's Painter-in-Ordinary and with the aid of a ghostwriter named William Combe published a 550-page book about his exploits, bearing the imposing title *Voyages from Montreal, on the River St. Laurence, through the Continent of North America, to the Frozen and Pacific Oceans in the Years 1789 and 1793; With a Preliminary Account of the Rise, Progress, and Present State of the Fur Trade of That Country.*

The instant bestseller publicized Mackenzie's vision of a world-spanning trade organization, outlining details of his proposals for a grand coalition between the amalgamated Canadian fur organizations and the East India and South Sea companies. At another level, it was an exciting reprise of the explorer's discoveries, told without the exaggerated self-importance that characterized travel writing at the time.* "These voyages will not, I fear, afford the variety that may be expected of them," he wrote in his preface; "... I could not stop to dig into the earth, over whose surface I was compelled to pass with rapid steps; nor could I turn aside to collect the plants which nature might have scattered on the way, when my thoughts were anxiously employed in making provision for the day that was passing over me. I had to encounter perils by land and perils by water; to watch the savage who was our guide, or to guard against those of his tribe who might meditate our destruction.... Today I had to assuage the rising discontents, and on the morrow, to cheer the fainting spirits of the people who accompanied me. The toil of our navigation was incessant, and often-times extreme; and in our progress over land, we had no protection from the severity of the elements, and possessed no accommodations or conveniences but such as could be contained in the burden on our

---

* Among the volume's most interested readers was Napoleon Bonaparte. That French connection came to light years later in the correspondence of a Scandinavian monarch, Napoleon's former marshal Jean-Baptiste Bernadotte, who ruled as Charles XIV of Sweden. According to Bernadotte, Napoleon had intended to negotiate a treaty with the United States that would have permitted him to use New Orleans as a base of attack against British North America, with his troops sneaking up the Mississippi and taking Canada by surprise. The Mackenzie journals were purchased and translated into French, but the expedition was permanently delayed when Napoleon launched his disastrous Russian campaign instead. The special edition, stamped with Napoleon's personal eagle insignia, was found after his death among his possessions on St Helena.

shoulders, which aggravated the toils of our march, and added to the weari-someness of our way."

NWC spies sent back regular reports on Mackenzie's activities and remon-strations. "You know him to be vindictive," tattled John Fraser, the Marquis's cousin and London-based partner. "He has got an entire ascendant over your young Men, and if driven to desperation he may take steps ruinous to you. He has told myself Your Nt. West business will be completely ruin'd; to others he has thrown out most violent threats of revenge, and I have had some hints too extravagant to mention." But Mackenzie was reaping too much honour and glory to worry about such sniping. He attended a grand ball given in his honour by fellow Scots at Ayr, south of Glasgow, and early in 1802 was knighted by George III, in part thanks to the good offices of his friend the Duke of Kent. That knighthood, the first to be conferred by a British sover-eign on a Canadian fur trader, added a splendid patina of grandeur to all of Mackenzie's subsequent schemes.

He visited Montreal regularly, especially when he heard that plans had been hatched for a full-scale challenge to the North West Company's domi-nation, with Parker, Gerrard & Ogilvy, a large local concern, forming a combine to include the Forsyth, Richardson firm as well as Leith Jamieson, a Detroit partnership. By 1798 these disparate operations had been united into an organization officially known as the New North West Company but quickly dubbed the XY Company, a name derived from the "XY" insignia on its kegs and its bales of furs. (The initials were picked because they followed alphabetically the NW markings of its rival.) At first, the Nor'Westers dismissed the upstarts as "Potties"—a corruption of either *les petits* or *les potées*, a colloquialism meaning men made of putty. In other words, softies. The newcomers put together a small but highly efficient woods operation stretching all the way to the Athabasca that rocked the established trade of the Nor'Westers and cut further into the fur supplies reaching Hudson Bay.

The competition remained manageable until Mackenzie brought his pres-tige and active presence into the concern, which changed its name to Alexander Mackenzie & Company. The NWC was being hurt badly, and during the 1801 meeting at the head of Lake Superior, McTavish proposed a revamp-ing of the company, enlarging its scope of operations and raising its share capital as part of a new, twenty-year agreement. He was fifty years old now, tending to snap at lesser mortals, particularly when one winterer after another rose to complain that the Potties were moving in on their territories and gaining ever-larger portions of the trade. McTavish rewarded his most hardened and experienced traders with extra stock and sent them back into the critical fur regions with orders to drive the Potties out any damn way they chose. The battle had been joined.

By this time, the xy traders had built forts alongside many of the nwc establishments, including a miniature headquarters beside Grand Portage; prices were cut and wages inflated; all three companies were flooding the West with rum and brandy. The new partnership had only half the nwc force in the field, but its winterers were at least as tough and even more determined. Angry traders spied on one another, ambushed pemmican-laden canoes, bribed Indians with excessive trade goods and even more outrageous promises. The violence grew worse with each season, and because of the inaccessibility of the venue no legal action was taken. Crimes simply went unpunished. That changed, at least in theory, when an nwc clerk named James King was shot by the xy's Joseph Maurice Lamothe at Fort de l'Île on the North Saskatchewan in 1802. A band of nearby Indians had sent a message to the fort that they had valuable pelts to trade, and both men set off to claim them. They spent a night on the trail, sleeping together inside a leather tent, exchanging small talk, enjoying the camaraderie of the wilderness. They agreed that the best way to split the booty would be for each trader to deal with those Indians who had credit with his company. Next day, when King was loading his furs, several packs were missing, and his Indians told him they had already been bartered. Suspecting Lamothe, he walked over to his fellow trader, accused him of having broken their accord and asked for the furs back.

"Would you give them up if you were me?" an angry Lamothe demanded.

When King agreed that he would not, the enraged Lamothe yelled, "Then you will not have mine!"

As King reached for one of the packs, Lamothe drew his pistol and shot him dead, in full view of a dozen witnesses. The murderer was acquitted at a trial in Montreal because the presiding judge could not decide who had proper jurisdiction over the Indian Country where the crime had been committed. In direct response to this atrocity, the British Parliament passed the Canada Jurisdiction Act on August 11, 1803, ordering that offences committed in the Indian territories be tried in the courts of Lower or Upper Canada and that roaming magistrates (nearly all Nor'Westers, as it happened) be empowered to arrest anyone charged with a crime.

By 1802, the working capital of Mackenzie & Co. was nearly equal to that of the older NWC partnership. It had only 520 men in the field, compared with McTavish's 1,058 (assigned to 117 permanent trading posts), but was producing almost as much fur. Mackenzie had meanwhile been busy in England trying to buy control of the Hudson's Bay Company. The offer of £103,000 in Exchequer bills delivered through an intermediary was very nearly accepted. The deal was not consummated mainly because a majority of the HBC stock was held either by trustees or by minors who could not transfer their shares without a court action. This the Committeemen were determined to avoid, because they did not want news of the transaction made public.

THE ESCALATING VENDETTA came to an abrupt resolution when Simon McTavish, whose hatred of Mackenzie had fuelled so much of it, died unexpectedly on July 6, 1804, leaving a young wife, four children and his uncompleted dream mansion. They buried him in its garden, and the top-hatted mourners gathered for tea under the swaying pines.*

With the Marquis's autocratic presence removed, Mackenzie and William McGillivray, who succeeded McTavish, took only four months to negotiate a merger. The agreement provided for creation of a hundred shares in a revamped NWC, a quarter of the stock being allocated to the XY partners. But there was one codicil: because of his stormy temperament and because he had been so dominant in both companies, Mackenzie was precluded from actively participating in the new partnership. It was the supreme irony of Mackenzie's dashing career that his ambition nearly succeeded in wrecking the company he had sought to dominate; in the process, he lost his influence over the trade that might have allowed him to put into place some of his grander designs. Briefly elected to the Legislative Assembly of Lower Canada, he found political debate boring and except for one brief visit in 1810, he left North America for good in 1805.

---

* McTavish's vault, located just to the west of the half-finished building, was eventually covered with a mound of earth to keep out vandals, and today the founder of Montreal's commercial life lies in an unmarked and invisible grave. The mansion was demolished in 1821 and eventually made way for Ravenscrag, the estate built by Sir Hugh Allan, the shipping and railway magnate whose $356,500 contribution to the Tory party triggered the Pacific Scandal of 1873, causing the only post-Confederation defeat of Sir John A. Macdonald's government. Allan, who was a staunch Presbyterian, also managed to corrupt Montreal's Catholic clergy so thoroughly that he once had a priest demoted for not supporting a municipal subsidy for one of his railway projects.

Back in Britain, Mackenzie lived on his book profits and earnings, married a teenage member of his own clan in 1812 (Geddes Mackenzie of Avoch*) and retired to his father-in-law's Ross-shire on Moray Firth not far north of Inverness and Culloden. In his last preserved letter, written like so many others to his dear cousin Roderick, he complained about his health ("I have at last been overtaken with the consequences of my sufferings in the North West") but seemed more concerned about his distance from the scene of the action, lamenting: "Most of the prominent events I learn from the public prints." That final communication is muted, concluding on a domestic note: "... Lady Mackenzie is sitting by me, and the children are playing on the floor...."

A few months later, on his way by stagecoach from Edinburgh to Ross-shire, he was suddenly taken ill near Dunkeld and died at a roadside inn. Fifty-six years old, Mackenzie was probably the victim of Bright's disease, which had progressively destroyed his kidneys. Some years later, a fire swept through the estate at Avoch, burning most of his manuscripts and papers.

The Mackenzie legend has outgrown the man. "In a longer vista of time than we at present command," concluded Roy Daniells, his most thoughtful biographer, "Canadians will probably see the voyages to the Arctic and Pacific as the Greeks saw the fabulous voyage of the Argonauts to fetch the fleece."

There is implicit in the life of Sir Alexander Mackenzie, who came by land to taste the brine of the Pacific, an enduring sadness that this monument of a man who vowed to alter the world to his specifications could not have had his way.

---

* It certainly was a close-knit family. Not only Geddes herself but her great-grandfather, grandfather, father and twin sister all married within their own clan. Her great-grandfather George married twice, fathering thirty-three children.

Storming
of the West

"We had to pass where no human being should venture...."—Simon Fraser

FOR A FULL DECADE AFTER Mackenzie's magnificent forays, the distant territories west of the Rockies' height of land were left undisturbed. The rivers that slithered off the eastern shoulders of the mountains had become the turnpikes of the fur trade, coursing through the prairie lands and forests towards the great trading depots at Fort William and York Factory. But west of the unnamed peaks of the forbidding ranges there was nothing—no probe for an exit to Pacific tidewater when it was becoming desperately urgent to find one.

Short-term greed for pelts continued to drive the NWC winterers into untrapped districts, especially regions beyond the reach of the Hudson's Bay men, but in the longer term the company realized that American advances might soon close off overland access to the Pacific. The treaty that ended the American War of Independence and the Louisiana Purchase of 1803 had transformed the former Thirteen Colonies from a seaboard nation to half a continent. No longer were the Nor'Westers free to range down the bountiful valleys of the Mississippi and Missouri into what is now the American heartland. By 1805, Lewis and Clark had crossed the main ridge of the Rockies at Lemhi Pass (on the present-day Montana–Idaho border) and followed the Clearwater and Snake rivers to the estuary of the Columbia.

The struggle to discover an economic passage through the Canadian Rockies took more than ten years to resolve.

Simon McTavish's nephew William McGillivray, who had served his apprenticeship as the company's first non-French inland clerk and had taken over command of his uncle's company, knew his most pressing priority was to gain trading access to the Pacific. Because the Nor'Westers were cut off from Hudson Bay, only an accessible route across the Rockies (connected to England via Cape Horn) could ease the killing expense of maintaining his company's continental transportation network, and only a link into the lucrative fur trade with China could gain the profits necessary to keep the whole enterprise afloat.

Of the large rivers that fall west of the mountains, the Skeena, Nass and Stikine discharge too far north to have been useful to the fur trade, leaving only the Columbia and Fraser to be profitably explored. That last, then-unnamed, river, which had already been partly travelled by Mackenzie, was chosen for the initial assault on the misty province beyond the setting sun.

Picked to undertake this perilous enterprise was Simon Fraser, the most heroic and least attractive of the NWC explorers. Grumpy and forbidding, this brooding Vermont-born Scot demonstrated all the obstinacy but little of the charm of his heritage. His soft, pasty face, sloping forehead and trout-mouth gave him a permanently sour look. He was an awkward, uninspiring man. His mother, Isabella Grant (daughter of the Laird of Daldregan), had fled to Canada when her husband died in prison during the American War of Independence, and had settled in Cornwall Township on the St Lawrence River. After two years' schooling, Simon became a clerk in the North West Company and in 1801, at the age of twenty-five, had been promoted to full partnership. During the company's conclave at Fort William four years later, he was assigned twin tasks: to lead the expedition that would establish a new Western Department by planting a string of trading posts past the Great Divide, and to follow what the Nor'Westers believed to be the Columbia River to its mouth. Little was known about that rumoured waterway except that dependable captains of three countries—Bruno Heceta of Spain, W.R. Broughton of England and Robert Gray of the United States—had located its broad mouth at about latitude 46° north. Sir Alexander Mackenzie had correctly suggested that the river provided the most plausible access to the Northwest, but wrongly assumed he had travelled along its upper waters in 1793. If American competition on the Pacific was to be forestalled, Simon Fraser had to move fast.

That first winter Fraser and his small party followed Mackenzie's route along the Peace and Parsnip rivers, building several trading posts, among them Fort McLeod, the first permanent white establishment between Alaska and California. The following season he moved deeper into unknown territory and reached Stuart Lake, where his men erected a squat of huts known as Fort St James, which would evolve into a pivotal outstation of the fur trade. Fraser was so entranced by the majestic beauty of the landscape that he named the district New Caledonia, after the Scotland of his mother's fables.* He was determined to start down the mysterious "Great River" (which he confidently assumed to be the Columbia) in the summer of 1807, but supplies reached him too late in the season. He waited, fretting, until the spring of 1808.

According to Bruce Hutchison, who wrote its definitive portrait, Fraser's river (eventually named after him) "is one of the basic political and economic facts of America.... The life of Canada from the beginning has flowed mainly down two channels, the St. Lawrence in the east and the Fraser in the west.... Measured by size, by economic consequence, by political influence, the Fraser is a continental force." The river itself shoots 850 miles from its source near Yellowhead Pass on the western slopes of the Rockies north, west and south to the Pacific in a vaguely S-shaped descent between rugged mountainsides and through snarling cataracts.

At five o'clock on the morning of May 28, Fraser and his two lieutenants, John Stuart and Jules Quesnel, plus nineteen voyageurs and two Carrier Indians, set out in four canoes aptly christened with such brave names as *Perseverance* and *Determination*. Floating down the relatively calm waters between Fort George (now Prince George) and Soda Creek, they sighted a succession of Indian villages. The moccasin telegraph had been working over-time, passing along news of the intruders' progress and, curious to learn his intentions, the natives gathered in one of the larger settlements and invited Fraser ashore. The Nor'Wester made the most of the occasion, donning his topper and having himself grandly carried to land on the shoulders of two brawny voyageurs. Speaking through an accompanying interpreter, Fraser addressed an open-air rally, attempted some faith-healing by treating sick youngsters with tincture of opium and demonstrated the power of his "thunderstick." "These Indians," he noted in his journal, "had heard of fire arms but had never seen any, and they evinced a great desire of seeing ours and obtaining explanations as to their use. In compliance, we fired several shots whose reports astonished them so as to make them drop off their legs."

---

* The country was known to the Romans as Caledonia, and the term "Scotland" was first used in the eleventh century. Scots who emigrated kept establishing New Caledonias wherever they went.

The impressed natives donated a slave to the expedition. Although the man was touted to be useful as a guide, Fraser dismissed his warnings of impassable waters ahead that would swallow his canoes as the whimperings of a superstitious primitive. His attitude towards Indians, in this and other matters, was oafishly condescending. The diary he kept mentions that "their singing makes a terrible racket" and "their women's hair is dirty and smelly." He thought the several dyed dog-hair blankets given him attractive mainly because "they resembled, at a distance, Highland plaid." Although he was serenaded and feasted at one Interior Salish village, Fraser noted sarcastically that "however kind the savage may appear, I know that it is not in their nature to be sincere in their professions to strangers. The respect and attention, which we generally experience, proceed, perhaps, from an idea that we are superior human beings ... at any rate, it is certain the less familiar we are with one another the better for us."

After this interlude, the exploration party was swept once more into the canyons of the Fraser, a stretch of the roughest water ever traversed. "In a sense the Fraser does not flow at all," wrote Hugh MacLennan in his study of Canadian rivers. "It seethes along with whirlpools so fierce that a log going down it may circle the same spot for days as though caught in a liquid merry-go-round. It roars like an ocean in storm, but ocean storms blow themselves out while the Fraser's roar is forever." Spumes sluice down the narrowing riverbed, force-fed by the melting snow, moving with such speed and power that they hurl large fish bodily from the current.

Travelling through this maelstrom had less to do with boat handling than with acrobatics. The Nor'Westers had entered a world without choice: to attempt the only available portages—which meant hacking precarious footholds in the rock-faces overhanging the mad stream—made just as little sense as staying in their flimsy birchbark canoes and braving this hellish excuse for a river. Even Fraser's taciturn nature yielded to the terrors facing him. In the journal tallying each harrowing escape along the route, he uncharacteristically allowed himself the use of an exclamation mark in lamenting the nature of his mission: "... a desperate undertaking!"

Having decided to proceed, Fraser and his men inched along rock ledges so narrow it was often difficult "even for one person sideways" to make headway, and all but impossible to portage canoes: "We cut steps ... fastened a line to the front of the canoe ... some of the men ascended in order to haul it up, while the others supported the canoe upon their arms.... Our lives hung as it were upon a thread; for failure of the line or a false step of one of the men might have hurled the whole of us into eternity."

On June 9, at French Bar Canyon, about halfway between the mouth of the Chilcotin River and present-day Lillooet, the men faced a gorge with sheer walls and cliff edges almost meeting at the top, forming a roof over the cascades below. "Here," Fraser noted on what must have been water-soaked pages, "the channel contracts to about 40 yards, and is enclosed by two precipices of great height, which, bending towards each other, make it narrower above than below. The water, which rolls down this extraordinary passage in tumultuous waves and with great velocity, had a tremendous appearance. It being absolutely impossible to carry the canoes by land, all hands without hesitation embarked as it were *à corps perdu* upon the mercy of this Stygian tide. Once engaged the die was cast, and the great difficulty consisted in keeping the canoes within the medium, or *fil d'eau*, that is to say, clear of the precipice on one side, and of the gulfs formed by the waves on the other. However, thus skimming along like lightning, the crews, cool and determined, followed each other in awful silence, and when we arrived at the end, we stood gazing on our narrow escape from perdition."

Near Jackass Mountain, south of present-day Lytton, the going got even rougher. One of the voyageurs rode an overturned canoe three miles downstream, holding on for dear life with his legs and dancing with his spine as if he were on the back of a bucking bronco.

No relief. At Black Canyon, downstream from the present twin railway communities of North Bend and Boston Bar, expedition members were forced to claw over slimy outcrops, dangle from primitive rope ladders and balance on precariously hung log booms devised by local tribes. The men were by now exhausted beyond endurance and discouraged beyond caring. The conquest of each new trial-by-terror only meant encountering yet another, even worse, obstacle. Hell's Gate was next. The river narrowed into a giant crevice where torrents eighty-five feet deep had been heightened an extra hundred feet by the spring runoff. "I have been for a long period among the Rocky Mountains," Fraser confessed to his diary on this ultimate rainy day of his soul, "but have never seen anything like this country.... I cannot find words to describe our situation at times. We had to pass where no human being should venture...."

But even here there was a footpath indented into the precipice by Indians who had come this way for generations. Fraser described "steps ... formed like a ladder or the shrouds of a ship, by poles hanging to one another and crossed at certain distances with twigs, the whole suspended from the top to the foot of immense precipices and fastened at both extremities to stones and trees," and how he and his crew scrambled up these flimsy supports like grateful monkeys on a string.

That final hurdle behind them, the waterlogged Nor'Westers headed towards the ocean. Gulls were wheeling overhead. Just beyond the river's silty delta they could see a broad gulf set with jewelled islands. But true to the character of this expedition, Fraser's problems were far from over. On July 2, 1808, just before they broke through to tidewater, the boats were surrounded by hostile Musqueam Indians. Fraser noted that they were "singing a war song, beating time with their paddles upon the sides of the canoes, and making signs and gestures highly inimical." The following day, after more of the same, he wrote: "We, therefore, relinquished our design and directed our thoughts towards home." He did reach the ocean but had no time to look around and check his longitude, snatching only a fast latitude reading—just above 49° north. That was enough to confirm his worst fears: the muddy mouth of the river he had just run was clearly not that of the Columbia, which three master seamen had located near the 46th parallel.

The return voyage was worse than the original journey because the region's Indians, sure that the party of white men would perish in their attempt to ride the river, now did not want them to leave alive. Boulders were hurled down at the explorers' canoes; showers of arrows met some of their attempts to land for food. But thirty-three days after leaving the Pacific foreshore, Fraser and his men were back at Fort George, having accomplished little beyond proving decisively that what they had discovered was not the Columbia and that the Fraser was not a navigable fur-trade route.

AFTER BOTH MACKENZIE and Fraser had proved it was impossible to send freight canoes through the mountains, it became evident that the only effective way to move goods to the Pacific side was to go around them. That required a successful expedition down the serpentine Columbia to its saltwater mouth. The Nor'Wester who accomplished that difficult task as well as the mapping of one-third of the previously blank subcontinent was a remarkable geographer named David Thompson.

Thompson stood out among his colleagues. He was not Scottish but of Welsh descent, and was not only prodigiously literate but left behind thirty-nine volumes of journals that rank (or should) as major contributions to the early history of Canada. He cared little for the fur trade but walked and canoed fifty-five thousand miles, pacing off the country he was determined to chart. During his stewardship as chief topographer of the North West Company, Thompson not only mapped the Columbia River system to the Pacific but also pinpointed the sources of the Mississippi, explored the upper region of the Missouri and the southeastern interior of British Columbia. He also did the original surveys of the Muskoka country between the Ottawa River and Lake Huron and laid out Quebec's Eastern Townships. He later surveyed much of the border between Canada and the United States. "Elliott Coues's description of Thompson as the greatest geographer of his day in British America errs, if it errs, only in being an understatement," wrote Professor Richard Glover in his introduction to a modern edition of Thompson's journals.

Despite his sterling qualifications, Thompson seemed ill-fitted for the crude ethics of frontier life. His upright approach to the circumstances in which he found himself prompted the modern explorer Joseph Burr Tyrrell to exclaim that Thompson continually bore "the white flower of a blameless life." Such attempts at beatification were based less on Thompson's professional accomplishments than on his carefully groomed appearance and personal habits. He didn't smoke, swear or drink and not only had thirteen children by his country wife but stayed faithful to her for sixty years. His idea of relaxing after a strenuous paddle was to gather his voyageurs around him and read aloud in French from the New or Old Testament, explaining the Word of God to his uncomfortable charges.

According to his contemporaries, he was an immensely talented storyteller. Dr J.J. Bigsby, who helped him survey the boundary between Canada and the United States, described how Thompson could "create a wilderness and people it with warring savages, or climb the Rocky Mountains with you in a snow storm, so clearly and palpably, that you only shut your eyes and you hear the crack of the rifle, or feel the snow flakes melt on your face as he talks."

Thompson not only denied himself alcohol but also tried to deny it to others. No post under his jurisdiction was allowed to use liquor in the trade. On one trip into the Kootenays, he was ordered by his superiors to include two kegs of rum among his provisions. He fastidiously tied them onto the back of his most spirited packhorse; within hours the kicking, bucking animal had staved in both barrels, and Thompson wrote an accurate report in clear conscience to NWC headquarters about what he had done.

His view of Indians bordered on reverence. He blamed Europeans for every wrong committed in the New World, paying elaborate homage to the natives'

140°W.

The Voyages of
Simon Fraser
and
David Thompson

Great Bear
Lake

Mackenzie R.

Great
Slave
Lake

Liard R.

Slave R.

R O C K

Stikine R.

Lake
Athabasca

Nass R.

Finlay R.

NEW CALEDONIA

Peace R.

Clearwater R.

Skeena R.

Fort
McLeod

Parsnip R.

Athabasca R.

North Saskatchewan R.

Stuart Lake

Fort George

M

Fort
St James

Soda Creek

Bella Coola R.

Fraser

Boat
Encampment

Athabasca Pass

Howse Pass

O

Rocky Mountain House

50°N.

Chilcotin R.

Fraser R.

French Bar
Canyon

Thompson R.

U

Columbia R.

Thompson

N

South Saskatchewan R.

PACIFIC

Hell's Gate

T

Kootenay R.

Lillooet

Okanagan Lake

Okanagan R.

Pend d'Oreille R.

A

Lytton
(present-day)

I

Kettle Falls

Pend Oreille Lake

N

Astoria

Salish House

O C E A N

Columbia R.

Spokane House

S

120°W.

Snake R.

way of life, their ethics, religions and customs. He believed nature had been in perfect balance with the red man until the rum-besotted traders had dese-crated the natural paradise. "Writers on the Indians," he complained in his journal, "always compare them with themselves, who are all white men of education. This is not fair. Their noted stoic apathy is more assumed than real. In public, the Indian wishes it to appear that nothing affects him. But in private, he feels and expresses himself sensitive to everything that happens to him or his family. On becoming acquainted with the Indians I found almost every character in civilized society can be traced among them—from the gravity of a judge to a merry jester, from open-hearted generosity to the avari-cious miser."

There was a wide mystical streak in the man. He worshipped beavers as deities and claimed to have been challenged to a card game by the Devil. (Thompson reported that he beat Lucifer, but as a result of that match, he swore off cards forever.) The Indians called him *Koo-Koo-Sint* ("the man who looks at stars") and marvelled at his extraterrestrial obsessions. "Once after a weary day's march," he noted, "we sat by a log fire. The bright moon, with thousands of sparkling stars, passed before us. The Indians could not help enquiring who lived in those bright mansions and, as one of them said, he thought he could almost touch them with his hand. I explained to them the nature of these brilliant planets. But I am afraid it was to no purpose. The Indians concluded, 'The stars are the abodes of the spirits—of those who have led a good life.'"

As ardent a naturalist as he was a navigator and astronomer, Thompson described every species of moss he could find; while being bitten by mosqui-toes he studied the insects' devouring tactics under a magnifying glass, and he was the first to take the temperature of a reindeer's blood. As he led three suffering companions on a leash through a winter whiteout, he discovered that one factor governing the severity of snow blindness is eye colour; blue-eyed people suffer the most, dark-eyeds the least. He compiled Indian language dictionaries, could speak four Indian tongues (Chipewyan, Mandan, Peigan and Kootenay) and some of his bird observations have never been equalled for their evocative sensitivity: "No dove is more meek than the white prairie grouse, with its pleasing cheerful call of *Kabow-kabow-kow-a-e*.... I have often taken these birds, with their deep chocolate feathers against background of beautiful white brilliance, from the nest. I provoked all I could without injur-ing them. But all was submissive meekness. Rough humans as we were, sometimes of an evening we could not help enquiring, 'Why should such an angelic bird be doomed to be the prey of carnivorous animals and birds?' But the ways of Providence are unknown to us."

With these and other virtues being paraded at every available opportunity, it was little wonder that his contemporaries tended to dismiss him as being too good to be true. The modern fur-trade historian Richard Glover shrewdly rejected the geographer's goody-goody reputation by pointing out that the man "may perhaps be correctly diagnosed as suffering that common Puritan disease, a consciousness of his own virtue which was too strong and determined to enable him to recognize when he was doing wrong; and if he ever did realize that he made mistakes he was certainly not in the habit of admitting them."

In the end, what really mattered was his skill as a surveyor—and that was superlative. Thompson's map of the NWC empire, displayed at Fort William's Great Hall, became the matrix for every atlas of western Canada published in the next seventy-five years. His almost uncanny ability to delineate the contours of the wild land owed little to any privilege of his upbringing. Born of Welsh parents, he was fatherless when he was two, and his mother, unable to support her family, placed him in a charity institution called Grey Coat School, near Westminster Abbey. The young Thompson spent his free time reading adventure books such as *Robinson Crusoe* and touring the abbey memorizing the epitaphs of the great men and women buried there. He studied navigation in hopes of a career in the Royal Navy but joined the Hudson's Bay Company as an apprentice instead, leaving England in 1784 when he was fourteen. His first assignment was to Churchill, then under the distinguished governorship of Samuel Hearne. The youngster helped him copy some of his famous journal, though no real friendship developed between them.

After a brief stint at York Factory, Thompson was sent inland to serve at a post on the South Saskatchewan River. Two days before Christmas 1788, while hauling a sled of firewood, he fell and fractured his leg. That accident, which laid him up at Cumberland House for most of the next year, temporarily removed him from the daily pressures of the fur trade. It was Thompson's great good fortune that Philip Turnor, the HBC's resident surveyor, spent a winter with him explaining the rudiments of surveying. His mentor gave him an old Dollond sextant, and ever afterward Thompson took sightings wherever he went, gradually filling in the vast empty spaces on his map.

After several unsuccessful attempts to find a direct navigable route from Hudson Bay to the Fur Country of the Athabasca, Thompson decided to leave the HBC and defect to the service of its chief rival. Certainly, he must have been bored during his early service on Hudson Bay, feeling that his skills were severely underutilized and confiding to his journal, "... for all I had seen in their service neither writing nor reading was required. And my only business was to amuse myself, in winter growling at the cold and in the open season shooting Gulls, Ducks, Plover and Curlews, and quarrelling with Musketoes and Sand flies." Thompson's own rationale for his decision was that it was against his honest nature to pretend any longer he was interested in trading furs when what he most wanted to do was survey the country. When he received a letter from Joseph Colen, his supervisor at York Factory, forbidding him to spend Company time on any more surveys, he knew he had to resign. Just before he left, Thompson had been offered a promotion with the unusual title "Master to the Northward." If he had accepted that grand post, the fur trade would have had to become his full-time occupation. More to the point, he would have had to expend all his energies not only in commercial pursuits but also in the active leadership of his fellow traders. Despite his talents, Thompson did not feel qualified to manage the lives of others, preferring to commune silently with the sun and stars through his instruments. That obses-sion may have been the ultimate reason for his desertion. His actual defection took place in the spring of 1797, when Thompson walked the seventy-five miles from an HBC post on Reindeer Lake to Alexander Fraser's house on the Reindeer River, having made certain before his irrevocable act that the NWC would welcome him into its service.

AT THE NWC'S ANNUAL CONCLAVE the following summer Thompson was assigned to survey (at four times his HBC salary) the new boundary between the United States and the company's territories. He traced the Red and Assiniboine rivers, found the gurgling springs where the Mississippi originates (in what is now northern Minnesota) and at Lac la Biche met and fell in love with a gentle fourteen-year-old Mixed Blood named Charlotte Small, the daughter of a prominent NWC *bourgeois*, who proved to be an invaluable life-time helpmate. During the next half-decade he surveyed many of the lakes, rivers and trading posts of the Northwest, all of it the perfect preparation for his journey down the Columbia.

That confusing river had baffled the early geographers. Its tributaries, joining it from nearly every quadrant of the compass, are often substantial rivers in their own right—the Kootenay, which at one point runs parallel to the Columbia but in the opposite direction; the placid Okanagan; the Pend d'Oreille; and the magnificent Snake, whose drainage area would one day become the HBC's main trapping preserve. The source of the Columbia is a cool lake high in the Rocky Mountain Trench south of present-day Windermere, B.C. From there, the river wends deceptively for most of two hundred miles northwest before it doubles back on itself, then surges past the Selkirk Range and winds south and west towards the ocean. Its drop of 2,650 feet between source and sea makes it the most powerful of the West Coast rivers.

Thompson first sighted the upper reaches of the Columbia in 1807, after setting out with Charlotte and their three young children from Rocky Mountain House. The small party reached the azure glaciers of the high Rockies and, looking towards his river of destiny, Thompson prayed that God in his mercy would guide him to where its waters joined the ocean.

That quest would take another four years to satisfy. In contrast to the commando tactics of Mackenzie and Fraser, the sensitive Welshman chose to blend into the territory, spending the next three seasons on exploratory journeys to various sections and tributaries of the Columbia but never able to commit himself to its full exploration. Then, in 1810, as he was on his way back to Fort William, Thompson was ordered to the Pacific.

He set off immediately with a large, well-equipped party up the North Saskatchewan River, bound for Rocky Mountain House. In his conquest of the Columbia, Thompson had to overcome not only the river's geographical puzzles but the active resistance of the Peigan Indians who guarded the routes to its headwaters. The Peigans feared the white intruders would disrupt their trading patterns by supplying guns directly to their traditional enemies, the Kootenays. Thompson's most immediate problem was that one angry band of Peigans, who knew he had traded guns to the Kootenays, blocked Howse Pass (roughly halfway between the modern resort towns of Jasper and Banff), the entry point he had used for his previous treks into the mountains. Thompson divided his party into two groups. He left the main canoe flotilla behind and rode ahead on horseback with his own companions to scout and hunt for food. When he got back to the previously arranged rendezvous, the canoes had not yet arrived. He sent his Indians forward to reconnoitre, warning them not to fire their guns in case they tipped off their presence to the Peigans. The search party promptly came crashing back. They had run up against the Peigan blockade, fired a warning shot and fled. At this point, Thompson lost his nerve.

Instead of waiting for his main force to arrive, he ran for his life and spent the next three weeks cowering alone in a wooded gully in the nearby hills. There he nearly starved to death, being too paralysed with terror to sneak out and shoot game.

The main flotilla of canoes had meanwhile passed Thompson's hiding place and arrived uneventfully at Rocky Mountain House. Alexander Henry the Younger, an NWC partner on his way west to join Thompson, got to the post on October 5. Assuming that Thompson was upriver, having originally gone to scout *ahead* of his troops, Henry set himself the difficult assignment of sneaking the canoes upstream past the Peigan war party. Hostile Indian scouts were hanging around the post, looking intentionally ominous, and when Henry tried to send boats through on a dark night, they were stopped and ordered back to the fort. The problem was that the Peigans assigned to loiter near Rocky Mountain House sent word to their platoons on the river as soon as any canoe activity was sighted. To fool them, Henry dispatched empty canoes downstream, and invited the Peigans at the fort in to drink. He laced their rum with opium and, when they blissfully passed out, ordered the canoes back, loaded them and managed to slip past the river guards who had received no warning of their departure.

Henry was congratulating himself on his successful ruse when a voyageur who had been with the advance party arrived to report that Thompson was on the *other* side of Rocky Mountain House. An exasperated Henry marched back and finally located the trembling geographer on the north bank of the river at the top of a hill three hundred feet above the water, in a gully so thickly treed that he did not spot Thompson's tent until he was within ten yards of it. The grounded explorer had been living mainly on berries for twenty days and seemed beyond the point of being able to make rational choices.

Henry urged him to join the main party upriver, pointing out that even if the Peigans were on the warpath, they were dependent for their arms and ammunition (and rum) on the Nor'Westers and would hardly dare spark too decisive an incident. But Thompson, still wild-eyed, could not be persuaded. He insisted on abandoning the North Saskatchewan and Howse Pass route, deciding instead to break through the mountains at an unknown dip near the headwaters of the Athabasca River. The month-long delay, Thompson's refusal to take the easier route through the Rockies, and the three months he spent in a winter camp waiting for the weather to yield cost him valuable time. During the nightmarish trek through Athabasca Pass, all but three of his original thirteen companions deserted him, arriving back at Rocky Mountain House cursing the weather and Thompson's faltering leadership.

Thompson reached the Columbia at Boat Encampment, near the confluence of the Columbia, Canoe and Wood rivers, and here his men built a new boat. Only a quartet of survivors managed to get down the length of the Columbia, having made an unnecessary, six-hundred-mile detour when Thompson chose to avoid Howse Pass and seek a new route to the north. They finally built an awkward canoe out of split cedar held together by pine roots. But instead of floating down the river, they decided, in a search for added manpower, to *ascend* the Columbia and cross over to the Kootenay.

On July 12, 1811, they found seals playing around their boat, smelled salt in the air and broke out the company flag. Two days later, Thompson rounded Tongue Point. Four newly built log cabins were already holding that hallowed ground. The newcomers had arrived by sea on March 22, representing John Jacob Astor's Pacific Fur Company, an offshoot of the American Fur Company. They feasted the Nor'Westers with a magnificent duck dinner, urging Thompson to abandon his vow of abstinence and join in the Madeira toasts to his exploits. He refused. After canoeing to the open Pacific the next day, he set out on his return journey. That undertaking was just as complicated as his original trip, taking more than a year to complete.

After such hardship Thompson decided to leave the Northwest permanently. "Thus I have fully completed the survey of this part of North America from sea to sea," he summarized in his journal, "and by almost innumerable astronomical observations have determined the positions of the mountains, lakes and rivers, and other remarkable places on the northern part of this continent; the maps of all of which have been drawn, and they are laid down in geographical position. This work has occupied me for twenty-seven years."

David Thompson retired from the fur trade the following year to Terrebonne, Quebec, and spent the next twenty months completing his ten-foot-long map of the Northwest, delineating the 1.5 million square miles of the territories he had travelled and showing the precise location of the North West Company's trading posts.

JOHN JACOB ASTOR, who had beaten the Nor'Westers to the Pacific Coast, is best remembered as the man who made his fortune by being the first person to grasp the real-estate potential of New York, capturing ownership of more houses, commercial buildings and entire downtown blocks than any other individual has been known to own in one large city. He not only became the richest American of his generation but also founded one of the most enduring family dynasties, his descendants achieving dominant status within the United States and, later, British circles. The Astors could automatically count themselves as high society on both sides of the Atlantic at a time when the Vanderbilts were still struggling for social recognition and J.P. Morgan was dismissed as being *nouveau riche*.

He may have been a role-model for a fledgling society emulating anyone who had hacked a fortune from the new land, but John Jacob Astor was in fact a monumental boor—a vulgar barbarian in morning coat whose manners were damned in the diary of James Gallatin, a son of Thomas Jefferson's Secretary of the Treasury: "He dined here last night and ate his ice cream and peas with a knife." The less well-known coda to that famous gaffe was Gallatin's report of another meal at which Astor after the main course not only wiped his dirty fingers on the gown of the lady seated next to him but also shattered the cozy postprandial atmosphere by blowing his nose into his cupped hand.

A self-made man who worshipped his creator, Astor was born at Walldorf* on the fringes of Germany's Black Forest and left his father's butcher shop in 1779 at sixteen to follow his brother George to England, where he helped run a small musical instrument business. Three years later he had saved enough to buy a steerage ticket to America and left for the New World carrying his total wealth (£5) and seven flutes. On the way across the Atlantic he overheard some Hudson's Bay Company officials discussing how much money could be made in furs by traders operating independently of the large companies. His fellow passengers remembered Astor mainly because every time a storm came up, he would put on his best clothes, explaining that if the ship went down and he was rescued, at least he would have saved his one good suit.

The New York in which he landed was a swamp with a population of less than thirty thousand, no sanitary facilities and a future downtown that was still farmland. Astor's start as a pedlar of sweet cakes along the settlement's streets soon gave way to a better job (at two dollars a week) beating the dust

---

* The namesake of New York's Waldorf-Astoria Hotel, built by John Jacob's great-grandson, William Waldorf Astor, in 1897.

out of furs and packing them for shipment to the London auction markets. From that, it was a quick step to becoming an apprentice fur trader, venturing into the Iroquois territory north of Albany with a sixty-pound pack on his back, tramping through twenty miles of bush a day. The young Astor was inordinately successful because he managed to drive a hard bargain while ameliorating his technique by playing the flute and speaking to the Indians in their own languages—a skill first exhibited when he had to learn English virtually overnight after leaving Germany. Persuading the Indians to part with their pelts for a fraction of their worth was what had originally attracted him to the business. But when a New York fur merchant sent him to England and he realized that beaver skins traded for inferior trinkets could fetch 900 percent profit, Astor knew he had found his true *métier*.

In New York, he had married Sarah Todd, the daughter of his Scottish landlady, who not only brought him a sizeable dowry—and free room and board—but turned out to be a fine businesswoman. As their trade grew, she eventually charged him a usurious $500 an hour to grade the furs he collected on his treks through the Catskills, the thick forests of New Jersey and Long Island swamps—and he was glad to pay it.

By the turn of the century Astor, who was rumoured to be worth $250,000, decided to enter the China trade. That exotic commerce was centred at Canton, the busy port upstream from the Pearl River Delta that had become the trading capital of the South China Sea. The East India Company had operated there since 1685 and eventually thirteen "factories" had been opened to buy and sell most of China's imports and exports. The most unsavoury—and most profitable—aspect of that trade was the Turkish and Indian opium brought in by British merchantmen and sold to the Chinese. Profits from that degrading commerce were used to buy the tea and silks imported across the Pacific. Because one of the most desired western goods in China was luxury fur, a quarter of the pelts auctioned off in London found their way into the Chinese market.

With the French Revolution and other European discontinuities, that flow was disrupted, and Astor, seeing an opportunity to trade directly with Canton, dispatched his first chartered vessel there in 1800. It was loaded with 30,573 seal skins, fox, otter and beaver pelts and 132 barrels of ginseng, a root-plant then harvested in America that had become a popular Chinese aphrodisiac and cure-all. Vessels in the China trade, which had tea as the main return cargo, could take up to three years for the round trip. But the profits were so

phenomenal that soon Astor had built himself a fleet to exploit the trade.*
He envisaged a world-spanning business empire that would give him
supremacy over a triangular, highly lucrative commerce. It involved gathering furs from the untapped regions of the Pacific Coast (the Chinese were
willing to pay $100 for sea otter pelts, available mainly in Pacific waters);
transporting them to Canton; loading up the ships there with tea (plus
spices and silks) for the run to New York; reloading with trade goods (beads,
bells, blankets, rum) for the sail around Cape Horn and back to the
American West Coast—where the Indians supplied the furs. What this
grandiose but entirely feasible scheme required was a tidewater port on the
Pacific Coast—and the mouth of the Columbia River, so recently charted
by Lewis and Clark, was the ideal spot. That distant and as yet unoccupied
harbour was to become the capital of Astor's fur-trading empire, drawing its
pelt supplies from the trading posts he eventually established up the
Missouri and Columbia. This, roughly, was the Oregon Country, a vast,
temperate stretch of forests, mountains and valleys on the Pacific side of the
continent, still *terra incognita,* its only boundaries the northern margin of
California, occupied by Spain, and the even less clearly determined southern edge of Alaska.

Later, during the run-up to the War of 1812, a U.S. embargo suddenly
forced ships to stay in port. Astor already had the *Beaver* loaded and ready to
go. To lobby for an exemption, Astor sent a "Distinguished Mandarin" named
"Punqua Wing-chong" dressed in fine silks to Washington, claiming his father
had died and that he had to return home immediately—aboard the *Beaver,* of
course—for the state funeral. Permission was granted and the ship sailed off—
without its exalted passenger, who returned to his former incarnation as an
Oriental deckhand on another of Astor's vessels. Because the *Beaver* was the
only tea carrier to return with a cargo that season, Astor raised prices and
cleared a $200,000 profit.

---

* Its flagship was a 111-foot steam-powered sailing ship, the *Beaver,* which could cut the
passage time to Canton in half. When Astor launched a sister ship called the *Magdalen,* John
Cowman, its newly appointed captain, reported that the insurance company underwriting the
vessel insisted she be equipped with a chronometer. Astor refused to buy the instrument,
claiming the $500 cost was the captain's responsibility. Cowman quit his command and, six
weeks after *Magdalen's* departure under a new master, sailed for Canton in a rival vessel. His
navigation skills brought him back to New York well ahead of the *Magdalen,* in time to outdo
Astor at local tea auctions, causing his former employer a $70,000 loss.

Although Spain, Britain and Russia all laid claim to the Pacific Coast of North America, John Jacob Astor was determined to put forward Washington's rights by the authority of occupation. "Oregon was the specific prize at the centre of the conflict," wrote Kenneth Spaulding in his study of the Far West, "bounded by the Louisiana Purchase on the east, by Russian Alaska and the territory of the North West Company on the north, by the Pacific Ocean on the west, and by Spanish settlements on the south, it lay like a hollow center among contending interests and nations.... The beaver were there and the price was right; the risks were to be assumed with the rewards.... The country was open, beautiful, untrodden, and the hostile Indians would help keep it that way."

Astor chartered, as the instrument of the monopoly he hoped to establish, the Pacific Fur Company, and persuaded four fairly senior but disaffected Nor'Westers and a dozen experienced canoeists to join his new firm. In typically boisterous fashion, the boatmen arrived from Montreal for their New York posting in proper voyageur style. "They fitted up a large but light bark canoe," reported Washington Irving, "such as is used in the fur trade; transported it in a wagon from the banks of the St. Lawrence to the shores of Lake Champlain; traversed the lake in it, from end to end; hoisted it again in a wagon and wheeled it off to Lansingburg, and there launched it upon the waters of the Hudson. Down this river they plied their course merrily on a fine summer's day, making its banks resound for the first time with their old French boat songs; passing by the villages with whoop and halloo, so as to make the honest Dutch farmers mistake them for a crew of savages. In this way they swept in full song and with regular flourish of the paddle, round New York, in a still summer evening, to the wonder and admiration of its inhabitants, who had never before witnessed on their waters, a nautical apparition of the kind."

Staking claim to the trans-shipment port at the mouth of the Columbia River required a complicated exercise in logistics. Astor sent one group by land and another by sea. The foot party of sixty-four men and one woman was placed in the charge of a U.S. Cavalry captain named Wilson Price Hunt, who earned his reputation as a man who could be depended upon to bungle, so that whenever a decision had to be made about which way to go, he inevitably headed down the wrong trail. His party travelled most of two years, covering more than twice the actual distance involved because Hunt so often had to double back over his own path. By the time they staggered to their destination in the winter of 1812 they had eaten all their horses, including the nag whose hide they tried to make into a boat, which promptly upset, drowning its occupants. One of their party, John Day, had lost his mind; some of the others were on the point of insanity and all were well into the throes of starvation.

To command the *Tonquin*, the ship designated as the sea element of Astor's drive to the Pacific, he recruited a loony naval officer (on leave of absence) named Lieutenant Jonathan Thorn, who had taken part in the U.S. Navy's raid on Tripoli in 1804. His behaviour made the ill-starred Captain Hunt seem saintly. The kindest assessment of Thorn was that of the former Nor'Wester Alexander McKay, who whispered to one of the ship's mates: "I fear we are in the hands of a lunatic."

The captain of the *Tonquin* treated his ship's company of thirty-three sailors, clerks, partners and voyageurs with wanton cruelty, during an era when any sea voyage was hardly a benign occupation. Thorn's response to the mildest questioning of his most ludicrous orders was to draw his pistol and threaten to shoot anyone within range. He ordered all lights out by eight o'clock, promising to blow off the head of anyone caught not obeying his instructions. When the ship stopped off at the Falkland Islands to take on water, three of the most senior fur traders aboard and five other men went ashore, where they found two neglected graves whose headstones required repairs. They were completing this task when Thorn ordered the vessel under way. The shore party tumbled into their beached rowboat and desperately tried to catch up with the *Tonquin*. The distance between the two vessels widened and it was only when the cousin of one of the men in the small boat put a gun to Thorn's head that he hove-to and allowed the frantic rowers to catch up. When the ship reached the Sandwich Islands (Hawaii), some of the crew deserted, but one seaman named Aymes was so conscientious that when he missed the liberty boat, he hired a native canoe to take him out to the *Tonquin*. An entry in the journal of Gabriel Franchère, a clerk on the voyage, describes what happened: "On perceiving him, the captain ordered him to stay in the long-boat, then lashed to the side with its load of sugar-cane. The captain himself got into the boat, and, taking one of the canes, beat the poor fellow most unmercifully with it; after which, not satisfied with this brutality, he seized his victim and threw him overboard!"

By the time the ship arrived off the mouth of the Columbia on March 22, 1811, the crew was ready to mutiny—but the ordeal was not yet over. The estuary was obstructed by a dangerous sandbar. Thorn insisted on launching a boat to sound the channel even though a storm was brewing and the water was far too rough for safe navigation. The boat overturned, drowning five men, but instead of waiting out the high winds, Thorn ordered another boat into the channel and lost it too, with three more casualties. Two weeks later, the survivors had selected an appropriate site for Astor's western headquarters, christening it Astoria. On June 5, the *Tonquin*, with twenty-three of her original crew aboard, sailed north to barter for sea otter skins. When the ship put into Clayoquot Sound, one of the many inlets that scallop the west coast of Vancouver Island, Thorn lost his temper with the local chief, flung a pelt in his face and ordered him off the ship. His mates, sensing that the insult might have dire consequences, begged Thorn to hoist sail and leave, but that only persuaded the obstinate captain to stay. Next morning, large canoes arrived, their occupants waving otter skins above their heads—indicating willingness to trade. Thorn beckoned them aboard. Soon more canoes arrived, one after another, and the Indians crowded the decks. Two of the Nor'Westers warned Thorn that the situation was getting out of control, but that blinkered martinet kept exchanging furs for more and more knives, confident his guns could handle any trouble that came along. At a pre-arranged signal, the Indians drew their daggers. With a war whoop they attacked the crew, slashing throats and pushing the surviving wounded over the side, where the women in newly arrived canoes finished them off with their paddles. Thorn was quickly put out of his misery. One survivor was the Indian interpreter who eventually made his way back to Astoria with the gory details; the other was James Lewis, the ship's clerk, who though grievously wounded managed to pull himself near the *Tonquin*'s powder magazine. Next morning the Indians climbed back aboard to claim their booty and loot the ship. Lewis waited until he sensed that the full complement of boarders was preoccupied, then lit a fuse and blew them—and himself—skyhigh.

DESPITE THIS DISASTER, the morale of the traders at Astoria remained high. Not only had they reached their objective and erected John Jacob's new West Coast terminus, but the unexpected arrival of David Thompson had prompted them to expand their sphere of operations inland, certain they could meet the Nor'Westers on their own ground and triumph. Astor's agents built trading posts on the Okanagan and Kootenay rivers, at Spokane, and all the way up the Okanagan Valley and across to the Thompson River at what is now Kamloops, B.C. They inevitably became trade rivals of the NWC, but for the first while it was only token jousting, as this report of a duel between an Astorian and a Nor'Wester indicates: "Mr. Pillet fought a duel with Mr. Montour of the North-West, with pocket pistols, at six paces; both hits; one in the collar of the coat and the other in the leg of the trousers. Two of their men acted as seconds, and the tailor speedily healed their wounds."

In the summer of 1812, while Napoleon was preparing to invade Russia, the United States declared war on Great Britain and for the next two years invaded and harassed its territories in North America. Using that conflict as a pretext, in the autumn of 1813 the NWC decided to pursue its Oregon venture and dispatched a hundred men under the command of John George McTavish and John Stuart down the Columbia. They laid siege to Astoria, aided by rumours of war that threatened the continued safety of its occupants, specifically that the Royal Navy's twenty-six-gun sloop HMS *Racoon* was on her way around Cape Horn assigned to shell the embattled fort. The former Nor'Westers occupying the American outpost felt they had been abandoned by their own supply ships and began to talk surrender. (Astor had actually dispatched two ships to Astoria. The *Beaver*, then trading furs in Alaska, continued on to Canton where, hearing of the declaration of war, she stayed put. Another supply ship, the *Lark*, was wrecked off Hawaii.) It was hardly one of history's more savage sieges. The Astorians, most of whom were former Nor'Westers, were decidedly uncomfortable defending a fortress flying the Stars and Stripes when their home country was at war with the United States. They had not only friends but relatives among the besiegers, so whenever the attackers ran out of food, the defenders would quietly sneak out and offer them a snack. Finally, on October 16, 1813, Duncan McDougall, who was in charge of the fort, had the bright idea that instead of surrendering he would sell Astoria to the friendly invaders. The price was a bargain, with the inventory (worth about $100,000) of otter and beaver pelts going for less than half-price (about $40,000). Part of the deal was that McDougall and most of the senior Astorians would be admitted back into the NWC as partners.

HMS *Racoon*, her Royal Navy colours flying, appeared eight weeks later. William Black, her captain, could hardly believe his bad luck in having sailed eighteen thousand miles to this collection of shacks, which his four-pounders could have flattened before breakfast. Worse still, the purchase of Astoria by the Nor'Westers had deprived him of the right to claim the furs as prize money. He was so annoyed he decided to stage the takeover ceremony anyway. The voyageurs were rounded up, equipped with muskets and drilled to distraction by the ship's officers into a wobbly formation resembling a guard of honour.

Resplendent in his dress blues, Black ordered the Union Jack majestically hoisted. He broke out a bottle of Madeira, toasted His Majesty, renamed the post Fort George and ordered his quasi-militia to fire a proper salute. This they achieved in three rowdy rounds, one of the Nor'Westers very nearly shooting himself in the face.

Astor was beside himself when he was told of his fort's ignominious surrender, exclaiming: "While I breathe and so long as I have a dollar to spend, I shall pursue a course to have our injuries repaired!" He collected dividends of more than $1 million on his fur operations well into the 1830s, but Astor had by then become more intrigued by real estate development, riding nightly through the New York suburbs so he could foreclose on the properties of overextended farmers.

By 1844 Astor had acquired a fortune of $20 million in a country with private-sector capitalization of little more than $200 million. His last days were pitiful. He was North America's—and probably the world's—richest man, and yet he complained bitterly that one of his grandchildren had put more butter on his bread plate than he could possibly eat. Critically ill, Astor was kept alive to his eighty-fifth year by taking his daily nourishment from a wet nurse and being tossed about every morning in a blanket to get his circulation going. Only days before his death, he insisted that a destitute elderly woman pay the piffling rent for a flat in one of his houses. When his agent informed Astor that she was too sick and too poor to meet her obligations, he flew into a rage and demanded that the man go back and force her to pay up. The agent reported the conversation to Astor's son William, who gave him the equivalent of the unfortunate woman's rent so that the realtor could go back to Astor and claim the bill had been paid. The millionaire grumped with satisfaction: "There, I told you she would pay it, if you went the right way to work with her." John Jacob Astor died a few days later on March 29, 1848, presumably a satisfied man.

TO CONSOLIDATE THEIR HOLD on the strategically important mouth of the Columbia, the Nor'Westers had decided at the 1812 Fort William meeting to dispatch a sea party as a supplement to the overland expedition under John George McTavish. This contingent, commanded by Donald McTavish (Simon's first cousin) and John McDonald of Garth, boarded the 350-ton *Isaac Todd*, an armed merchantman built at Trois-Rivières, Quebec. They sailed to England with a load of pelts—and a crew of voyageurs to man the NWC's future trading canoes on the Columbia. The furs took many weeks to sell, and it wasn't until March 1813 that the *Isaac Todd* was ready to sail away in convoy with the Royal Navy's thirty-six-gun frigate *Phoebe*. McTavish and McDonald were dining at the main hotel in Portsmouth on the eve of departure, when word came that most of their voyageurs, who were celebrating their departure with a drinking spree, had been shanghaied by a Royal Navy press-gang and were already aboard a training ship. McTavish freed them by interceding with the port admiral, who happened to be a relative of the NWC agent's brother-in-law, Lord Grey, then leader of the Whigs.*

Armed with twenty guns, the *Isaac Todd* took an unprecedented thirteen months to reach Astoria. "It might have been better if she had only six guns well managed," McDonald of Garth noted in his journal. "We had on board cannon balls enough for a line-of-battle ship. She proved to be a miserable sailer, with a miserable commander, a rascally crew and three mates." The *Phoebe* was diverted to fight the American frigate *Essex*, which she captured off Valparaiso harbour, and the *Isaac Todd* finally slipped alone into Astoria on April 23, 1814.

That same season, the battered little ship took on a load of furs and sailed another eight thousand miles to Canton, as did the NWC's 185-ton *Columbia*, which arrived at Astoria three months after the *Isaac Todd*. Trade through Canton, operating under the East India Company's monopoly, was complicated by Byzantine customs regulations. A special edict allowed the Nor'Westers to sell their furs for cash instead of merely bartering them for Oriental products like most other importers, but it proved to be not a particularly profitable venture. "The expense attending the sending of our own vessels to China is too heavy," complained William McGillivray in April 1816. "The Partners of the North West Company do not understand

---

* One extra passenger did sneak aboard the *Isaac Todd* that night—a spunky Portsmouth barmaid named Jane Barnes, who signed on, according to her personal claim, to do whatever needlework might be required on the voyage. Described as being "coarse" and "illiterate," the first white woman on the Columbia did not have an easy time of it. McTavish himself took up with her, but then found an alternate entanglement with a Chinook woman. The other traders could only laugh at Barnes's social pretensions and resented her insulting attitude towards native women. On the way back to England via Canton she found a husband in the ship's commander and returned to Astoria briefly in 1819. According to Alexander McKenzie, a clerk serving there at the time, she had not improved with age. "I should offend your modesty," he wrote to a friend, "were I to mention specimens of what she intended as wit and humour during her stay with us."

the management of ships or captains. Collecting and trading skins is their real business."

That business was under intense pressure from the Hudson's Bay Company in the Northwest and from American freebooters in the Southwest. The American case rested mainly on that costly display of pretension by Captain Black of HMS *Racoon*. The protocol-encrusted naval officer's formal takeover of the tiny fort on behalf of his monarch lent authority to the case that Astoria had not been sold but captured as an act of war and, according to the terms of the Treaty of Ghent, all territories seized by force had to be returned. The British, who regarded the western coast of North America with an attitude that could not even be dignified as benign neglect, surrendered their claim. But the Nor'Westers dug in. Their take of furs from the district had doubled, they had financed the establishment of a chain of inland posts and felt very much at home in the lush Pacific land, free from the burden of having to struggle against the fierce climate of their northern territories.

Late in 1817, the *Ontario,* an American naval sloop, sailed into the mouth of the Columbia carrying a government commissioner named James B. Prevost to retake formal possession of the fort. When James Keith, then the NWC's resident chief, flatly rejected the appeal, Prevost tacked his proclamation on a board nailed to a tree and left. Shortly afterward, the *Blossom,* a British man-of-war, arrived with orders from the Colonial Office that the post should be handed over. That too carried little weight with Keith. The Stars and Stripes was hoisted over the post, but the American and British governments eventually signed a convention that allowed the Oregon Country to be used jointly by citizens of both jurisdictions, and this arrangement lasted until 1846.

But at headquarters these Pacific pursuits were relatively minor in the North West Company's lexicon of priorities. It was suddenly being threatened by a revived Hudson's Bay Company, whose factors were challenging the Montrealers at every river bend.

Howling with the Wolves

"When you are among wolves, howl."　　　　　　—Colin Robertson
NWC/HBC Trader

IN THE CHARGED ATMOSPHERE of multiplying confrontations, the two companies fought one another with hardening determination and, once the Bay men had moved fully inland, with the bravado reminiscent of a civil war. The chief victims of that wilderness imbroglio were not the men who traded the furs but the Indians who supplied them.

Canadians have traditionally prided themselves on the fact that after the turn of the nineteenth century there were relatively few armed confrontations between white and red men—certainly nothing on the scale of the Indian wars fought by the U.S. Cavalry. But this difference does not justify the smug assumption that white men north of the 49th parallel treated the native population with compassion and respect. On the contrary, the unrestrained use of liquor in the Canadian fur trade ranks as one of history's more malevolent crimes against humanity.

The Nor'Westers and the Bay men were equally guilty of encouraging and benefiting from that debauching commerce—though the London Company did not initiate the practice and gradually put an end to it once the two firms were amalgamated. In *The Owners of Eden*, Robert MacDonald, an Alberta historian highly sympathetic to the Indian cause, has noted that "'The Honourable Company' ... opposed the liquor trade, until the time when they felt the competition had made its sale a matter of economic survival." The late Frank B. Walker, former editor-in-chief of the *Montreal Star* and before that an executive with the HBC's head office in Winnipeg, once made the argument that it was impossible for isolated Company post managers to persuade Indians to bring in their furs except by treating them with justice. "That applied particularly to the liquor trade," he claimed. "It wasn't profitable to have drunken Indians. They weren't good trappers and they could be highly dangerous. Canada was not at all like the American experience, with a big fort and cavalry standing by. Usually, it was one Bay factor and his nineteen-year-old clerk, surrounded by four or five hundred Indians at trading time. There was no way the HBC wanted them drunk. You can't stare down four hundred drunken Indians."

Unfortunately, that kind of retrospective reasoning had little impact on what happened in the Canadian Northwest during the early 1800s.

Liquor became the currency of the fur trade. The initial utility of rum and brandy was based mainly on the fact that it was the most cost-effective item to carry inland, much less bulky in its concentrated form than such standard goods as blankets, axes, guns and bolts of cloth. Also, once addicted, the Indians could not get enough of the white man's deadly nectar and lost their ability or willingness to bargain patiently and shrewdly for their booty of furs. It was not long before the buyers of both companies realized that the way to manipulate their trading standards most profitably was by diluting the liquor rations with water. The Nor'Westers, who purchased their liquor supplies in Montreal from Caribbean exporters, would mix a nine-gallon keg of powerfully concentrated (132-proof) rum with anywhere from thirty to seventy gallons of water. This so-called High Wine was diluted according to whatever minimum the traffic would bear. In Cree or Assiniboine country, three to four parts water was the going formula; for the Blackfoot, the brew was reduced to seven or eight parts water, giving birth to a frontier cooler known as "Blackfoot Rum." The Indians, incidentally, quickly caught on to the white man's cheating ways. They would test the strength of any vintage by spitting a mouthful on a fire: good liquor would flame up dramatically, but if it were too weak, the potion would quench the flames. And that was how the term "firewater" originated.

As much as fifty thousand gallons of liquor was imported into the Fur Country each season. When mixed with water that probably amounted to at least a quarter of a million gallons—an appalling total, considering that the interior at the time had a native population of about one hundred and twenty thousand, including women and children. More than a third of the NWC freight stowed in the canoes heading west consisted of ninety-pound kegs of rum. As well as being a straight-out swap for pelts, alcohol served as an integral part of the gift-giving ceremony that preceded the actual trading process. While the possession of adequate stocks of rum and/or brandy (and tobacco) became essential, the traffic in such staples as guns, axes and blankets continued to predominate at most posts.

In 1786, the HBC's William Tomison had become so upset at the Montrealers' indiscriminate abuse of rum that he led a group of his colleagues in dispatching an official letter to the resident British Commander-in-Chief for Canada. "Good Sir," read the petition, "it grieves us to see a body of Indians destroyed by a set of Men, merely for self Interest, doing all in their Power to Destroy Posterity, so we hope that your Excellency will make such regulations as will preserve Posterity, and not be Destroyed by fiery double Distilled Rum from Canada." After a journey up the Saskatchewan the following year, Tomison complained to London that "the Canadians is [sic] going through the Barren Ground with Rum, like so many ravenous Wolves, seeking whom they may devour."

Yet less than half a decade later, the Bay men were openly trafficking in a potent concoction called English Brandy, trading booze for furs with as much aplomb as the Nor'Westers they had so recently condemned. The formula for making English Brandy was nothing if not simple: raw gin plus a few drops of iodine to simulate the ochre shade of the Nor'Westers rum.* Nor was any attempt made to hide the shameful commerce. When there was a ban in England on the domestic distillation of grain during the Napoleonic Wars, the London Committee dispatched stills to be erected at York Factory, Albany and Moose. By 1820 even a small HBC post like Fort Waterloo on Lesser Slave Lake was distributing its quota of 369 gallons per season; that meant dragging nearly two tons' worth of the concentrated grog across portages and rivers 1,350 miles from the nearest supply point. The HBC gained such a black reputation for its liquor trade that many years afterward, during a parliamentary debate, Lord Palmerston, the British Prime Minister, crudely interjected that "the Company's function should be to strip the local quadrupeds of their furs—and

---

* When iodine supplies ran low, a squirt or two of chewing tobacco provided the appropriate hue. A slightly more sophisticated blend was featured by the American Fur Company, which added to me base of water and raw alcohol doses of a medicinal painkiller (tincture of opium), overfermented wine, pepper and sulphuric acid. These and similar recipes raise the valid question whether the Indians who drank such rotgut got drunk or became sickened by the bizarre mixtures.

keep the local bipeds off their liquor." The most devastating summary of the HBC's attitude, which accurately reflected the prevailing frontier ethic of the time, was Douglas MacKay's comment in *The Honourable Company*, a lively Company history by an HBC official. "Drunken Indians," observed MacKay, "were among the casual inconveniences of fur trading."

Even if their field tactics varied little, the approaches of the two companies were subtly different. The Nor'Westers seemed convinced that drunken Indians were jolly hunters, as reflected in this typical entry from Duncan McGillivray's journal. "The love of Rum," he enthused, "is their first induce-ment to industry, they undergo every hardship and fatigue to procure a Skinfull of this delicious beverage, and when a Nation becomes addicted to drinking, it affords a strong presumption that they will soon become excellent hunters." The HBC factors believed the opposite: that the only good trapper was a sober trapper. But no matter what they thought or said, both concerns continued ladling out the booze. The daily tot was habit-forming, and once under the influence most Indians would trade only if firewater was included in the transaction.

The effect on their minds and bodies, on their families and culture, was ruinous. Firsthand reports from the Northwest described scenes so distressing that hardened fur traders could barely find words to express what they had seen. When he returned from the Blackfoot Country, Duncan McGillivray confided to his journal what he had witnessed: "Men, women, and children promiscuously mingle together and join in one diabolical clamour of singing, crying, fighting, &c and to such excess do they indulge their love of drinking that all regard for decency or decorum is forgotten:—they expose themselves in the most indecent positions, leaving uncovered those parts which nature requires to be concealed—a circumstance which they carefully avoid in their sober moments, and the intercourse between the sexes, at any time but little restrained, is now indulged with the greatest freedom, for as chastity is not deemed a virtue among most of the tribes, they take very little pains to conceal their amours, especially when heated with liquor." At about the same time, Daniel Harmon, the puritanical New England fur trader, recorded in his diary this sad scene from a trip into the northern reaches occupied by Chipewyans: "To see a house full of drunken Indians, consisting of men, women and chil-dren, is a most unpleasant sight; for, in that condition, they often wrangle, pull each other by the hair, and fight. At some times, ten or twelve, of both sexes, may be seen, fighting each other promiscuously, until at last, they all fall on the floor, one upon another, some spilling rum out of a small kettle or dish, which they hold in their hands, while others are throwing up what they have just drunk. To add to this uproar … a number of children, some on their mothers' shoulders, and others running about and taking hold of their clothes, are constantly bawling, the older ones, through fear that their parents may be stabbed, or that some other misfortune may befall them, in the fray. These shrieks of the children, form a very unpleasant chorus to the brutal noise kept up by their drunken parents, who are engaged in the squabble."

Another report described in explicit detail some of the worst abuses that resulted from too much drinking: "Every one knows the passion of the savages for this liquor, and the fatal effects that it produces on them.… The village or the cabin in which the savages drink brandy is an image of hell: fire [i.e., burning brands or coals flung by the drunkards] flies in all directions; blows with hatchets and knives make the blood flow on all sides; and all the place resounds with frightful yells and cries.… They commit a thousand abominations—the mother with her sons, the father with his daughters, and brothers with their sisters. They roll about on the cinders and coals, and in blood."

Diamond Jenness, the New Zealander who became recognized as Canada's most knowledgeable anthropologist through his studies of native cultures, flatly declared in his definitive work, *The Indians of Canada*, that "whisky and brandy destroyed the self-respect of the Indians, weakened every family and tribal tie, and made them, willing or unwilling, the slaves of the trading-posts where liquor was dispensed to them by the keg.… Disease and alcohol demoralized and destroyed the Indians just when they needed all their energy and courage to cope with the new conditions that suddenly came into existence around them. The old order changed completely with the coming of Europeans."

There were innumerable testimonies to the havoc caused by liquor, but one of the most brutal was reported by Alexander Henry the Younger. "We may truly say that liquor is the root of all evil in the North West," he wrote, and went on to detail a horrifying example of its effects: "The Indians continued drinking. About ten o'clock I was informed that old Crooked Legs had killed his young wife.… By sunrise every soul of them was raving drunk—even the children.… In the first drinking match a murder was committed. L'Hiver stabbed Mishenwashence to the heart three times … Grande Gueule stabbed Capot Rouge, Le Boeuf stabbed his young wife in the arm … Old Buffalo, still half drunk, brought me his eldest daughter, about nine years of age, in hopes I would give him a keg of liquor...." On another occasion Henry described what happened to an elderly Indian who, suspecting his young wife of infidelity, got blind drunk and stabbed her three times. When the woman had recovered, she plotted with her family to get even. After a drinking match, her relatives held her husband down while she "applied a fire brand to his privates, and rubbed it in. She left him in a shocking condition, with the parts nearly roasted."

How progressively hardened the frontiersmen became to the agony they had caused is dramatically revealed in this afterthought from Henry's journal: "Little Shell almost beat his old mother's brains out with a club. I sowed garden seeds."

Such inhumanity amounted to the anaesthetizing of the First Nations and helped promote the then-prevalent stereotype of Indian as "abject supplicant or outrageous maniac." Blair Stonechild, the head of the Department of Indian Studies at Saskatchewan Indian Federated College in Regina, has argued persuasively: "On the subject of alcohol abuse, Indians have not been dealt with fairly. Everyone is familiar with the stereotype of the 'drunken Indian,' and the Indian inability to deal with liquor. In Central America, where Indians had developed alcoholic beverages, a very firm approach was taken. Under the laws of Nezahualcoyotl, any official of high rank found intoxicated was immediately executed. Commoners were dealt with more leniently. The first time, the person's head was shaved in public and his house was knocked down. The second time, he was publicly executed. Surely these laws were more effective than today's approach of sending drunkards to halfway houses."

Historian Robert MacDonald made a telling point about why the natives took to liquor with so much abandon: "The Indian had never before tasted alcohol. He had no customs of social or convivial drinking. But he did have beliefs and rituals which required hallucinogenic experiences such as visions. Here, suddenly, was a surprising and powerful intoxicant. The trader encouraged him to use it to excess—the missionary exhorted him not to use it at all; *never* was it represented to him as something to be used *in moderation*." That was true, but most of the fur traders misinterpreted the Indian's reaction to the rum and brandy, concluding he was in some genetic or chemical way inferior. Typical of this view was the comment of historian Robert Pinkerton, who viewed Indians as childish savages devoid of morals. "It is commonly understood that liquor has an entirely different effect on an Indian than on a white man but few comprehend the degree of that difference," he pontificated. "The jovial exhilaration we know and enjoy is forbidden to the Red man. Mayhem becomes the mildest of his desires."

Some modern anthropologists have rejected the notion that alcoholism among Indians stems from their physical and nervous systems being somehow void of immunity to liquor. Bruce Cox, a Carleton University anthropologist who specializes in the field, concluded that "Indians develop alcoholism at about the same rate as the rest of us, and (on average) drink no more than the general population. Indians *may* metabolize alcohol a little differently to the general population, but differences are not large and in any case this is a trait they share with other groups who are not known as alcohol abusers." A more complicated explanation is the theory set out in *Drunken Comportment* by two California anthropologists, Craig MacAndrew and Robert Edgerton. "Across a continent, the Indian observed the dramatic transformation that alcohol seemed to produce in the white man," they noted, "… and, reaching into his repertoire of available explanations, concluded that 'Brandy was the embodiment, or was the medium through which an evil supernatural agent worked.' Thus it was that the Indian came to see that changes-for-the-worse were to be expected during drunkenness, for at such times the drinker was temporarily inhabited by an evil supernatural agent. And from this, the Indian reached the entirely reasonable conclusion that since he was thus possessed, his actions when drunk were not his own and he was not responsible for them. After all, the Indians' precontact cultures already contained an ample array of *time out* ceremonies and supernatural agents (such as witchcraft, dreams, spirit possession, and so forth) under whose influence a man became less than strictly responsible for his actions. The notion that the state of drunkenness was excusing of those transgressions committed while 'under the influence' was entirely consonant with the model the white man provided."

Not all social scientists agree. Writing in a recent issue of the University of Saskatchewan's *Native Studies Review*, Lillian E. Dyck has made a strong case that the pattern of alcohol-metabolizing enzymes differs in Orientals and Caucasians, making the Japanese much more susceptible to the unpleasant effects of alcohol. "If it does turn out that some Indian peoples have a genetic aversion to becoming alcoholic, as does a large percentage of the Japanese race," she concludes, "and if the rates of alcoholism are higher amongst such Indians than in the Caucasian population, then one could speculate that these Indians are over-exposed to other factors which lead to alcoholism. Though a particular group of Indians may be resistant to developing alcoholism, perhaps they can still become alcoholic because of the presence of unusually high levels of environmental stress." Dyck also added the important proviso that "in White urban areas, Indians look different, are a minority and, therefore, are noticed and remembered. A Caucasian drunk who behaves in the same way will not be noticed to the same extent because he is not expected to behave in this manner and because he is considered to be the exception rather than the rule. Consequently, we do not mentally tally up the number of Caucasian drunks we see, but we do note and remember the drunken Indians we encounter."

The problem with this sensible thesis is the difficulty of substantiating the white man's drinking behaviour from historical records. While there is no shortage of descriptions of drunken Indians, there are few memoirs about equally crazed whites. It was only the occasional visiting outsider who commented on drinking orgies such as those that regularly took place at the meetings of Montreal's Beaver Club, for example.

One exception is the description by Daniel Harmon of a New Year's Day drinking spree in New Caledonia: "Some of the principal Indians of the place desired us to allow them to remain at the fort to see our people drink, but as soon as they (our people) began to be intoxicated and quarrel among themselves, the Natives were apprehensive that something unpleasant might befall them also, therefore they hid themselves under beds and elsewhere and said they thought the white people had become mad. [Later] I invited several of the Sicaany and Carrier Chiefs and most respectable men among them, to come and partake of what we had remaining—and I must acknowledge that I was surprised to see them behave with so much decency and even propriety as they did in drinking off a flaggon or two of rum and after their repast was over they smoked their pipes and conversed rationally on the great difference there is between the manners and customs of civilized people and those of savages."

Nearly every departure or arrival of brigades of traders and voyageurs at any terminus was enough to set off a drinking spree. A typical scene, involving the white inhabitants of the Fur Country, was caught in the journals of Alexander Ross, who visited Michilimackinac, the staging depot at the juncture of Lakes Huron and Michigan, in the early 1800s: "To see drunkenness and debauchery with all their concomitant vices, carried on systematically, it is necessary to see Mackinac … for in the morning they were found drinking, at noon drunk, in the evening dead drunk, and in the night seldom sober. Hogarth's drunkards in Gin Lane and Beer Alley were nothing compared to the drunkards of Mackinac at this time. Every nook and corner in the whole island swarmed, at all hours of the day and night, with motley groups of uproarious tipplers and whiskey hunters. Mackinac at this time resembled a great bedlam, the frantic inmates running to and fro in wild forgetfulness...."

The alcohol problem on the frontier was bigger than either the NWC or the HBC—much more complicated and serious than its effect on the fur trade alone. The North West Mounted Police was established by the dominion government partly to counter the influence of American traders who came into southern Alberta to trade whisky with Blackfoot Indians for buffalo hides. Johnny Healy, the notorious Dubliner who went west with the U.S. Army and later founded the infamous Fort Whoop-up, the worst of the Canadian West's rotgut emporiums, once boasted to Isaac Gilbert Baker, a Montana liquor supplier, "I'll fix up 'coffin varnish' so strong, you'll be able to shoot an Injun through the heart, and he won't die till he's sobered up."

The Indian response to this decadence was not always passive. In the Athabasca Country, some Chipewyans quit the fur trade, retreating (as did many other bands across the Northwest) to their more tranquil, traditional tribal ways. But others, feeling they had been betrayed by the white man and his wicked brew, fought back.

In the summer of 1804, six Nor'Westers were killed during an Indian attack on Fond du Lac, a small fort near the eastern tip of Lake Athabasca, and four others were ambushed while hunting near Fort Chipewyan. Armed hostility on the prairies had begun as early as 1780 in the Eagle Hills of present-day Saskatchewan when an irresponsible Montrealer put an extra dose of opium into some trading rum. In the ensuing rumble there were serious casualties on both sides.

But the most vicious outbreak of violence was only partly due to liquor. As the fur trade moved west, guns became the decisive instruments for settling intertribal wars, and as a result, whichever fur company sold arms to any particular tribe's opponents would automatically be included among its enemies. During the 1790s the Gros Ventres, or Big Bellies (so named because of the sign language they used: the gesture for the tribe was a hand covering the solar plexus), had been defeated in several bloody encounters with the fur-rich—and therefore well-armed—Cree. The Gros Ventres had little to trade but wolf skins, which had tumbled in value on the London markets, prompting the companies to cut their standard price for the pelts in half. The Indians interpreted this as a hostile act and in 1793 raided the HBC's Manchester House on the North Saskatchewan, escaping with its store of rifles. The following summer, they rode out, a hundred strong, along the South Saskatchewan, eager for combat. While getting ready to attack an NWC installation on the river, they were spotted by a scout named Jacques Raphael, who, in the approved scenario of American Westerns, rode hell for leather to warn the post, was chased by menacing Indians and just made it inside the closing wooden gate. The ten-man garrison rushed to the barricades and maintained enough of a barrage to discourage a successful frontal attack. The Indians retreated when their war chief, L'Homme de Calumet, was killed. They then turned to a nearby HBC post. It was little more than a clutch of huts with no protection. Three of the resident traders were slaughtered where they stood. The fourth, John Cornelius Van Driel, hid under a rubbish heap and watched in horror as the tiny outpost's inhabitants were unceremoniously butchered. Having completed their carnage and appropriated what little booty there was, the Indians set the buildings ablaze. Forced from his hiding place, Van Driel waited until the conflagration was at its fiercest; then, using the smoke as a screen, he made a dash for the river, jumped into a canoe—and eventually reached safety with his grisly report.

THAT BLOODY ENCOUNTER was not typical of the fur trade, but during the decades straddling the turn of the century, the rivalry between the two main trading companies produced its own escalating violence. By 1806 the HBC's servants had opened five dozen inland stations, half of them within twenty miles of the already existing trading posts of their Montreal rivals.

During the early stages of the struggle between the two companies, both had a common motivating force: to ship the maximum number of pelts to the London fur auctions. Other than that, the two coalitions of traders were so different it was hard to believe they were in the same business. The Hudson's Bay Company continued to rely on functionaries hired more because of their ability to cope with subsistence wages than for any excesses of imagination or courage. Their every move was directed by an overseas court whose members were so indifferent towards the territories they were administering that no HBC Governor visited Hudson Bay for an unconscionable 264 years after the Company's original incorporation in 1670. (Sir Patrick Ashley Cooper, the twenty-ninth man to hold the office, finally managed a fast-paced ceremonial tour in 1934.) In contrast, the senior Nor'Westers were in business for themselves. They dealt with the monopoly proclaimed in the HBC's vaunted charter by the simple stratagem of ignoring it, taking the not unreasonable position that the forests they had explored should be a hunting ground for *all* British subjects, Canada having been formally ceded to England by France in 1763. Since legal sanctions within the Fur Country were uncertain, the Nor'Westers—and eventually the Bay men as well—increasingly resorted to physical intimidation to achieve their aims.

The geographical odds in that wilderness decathlon decidedly favoured the HBC. The location of its posts in the centre of the continent meant the Bay men could get their furs to England in six to eight weeks, compared to the four months it took the Nor'Westers to lug the pelts from Athabasca to Montreal, and then another four weeks to London. With the variables of climate taken into account, the HBC could gather its furs and sell them within the same annual cycle, while the Montrealers faced a minimum two-year turnaround. This was a crucial difference.

Apart from that admittedly overwhelming advantage of location, most of the other natural benefits accrued to the Montrealers. The valleys of the St Lawrence basin were covered with forests that contained plenty of the splendid birch trees whose bark was essential for canoe building, but birch grows only around the most southern reaches of Hudson Bay. The parishes of Quebec provided a surplus of voyageurs jostling to enlist their skill and muscle in the fur trade, but the only white labourers at the bay were the dour Orkneymen who worked as "servants" to the factors in charge of the HBC posts. At ease navigating in the tempests that buffeted their home islands, they could not or would not handle a canoe or shoot a rapid. This left the Company with two choices—either to employ local Indian crews or try training the recalcitrant Orkneymen as canoeists. Neither option worked. The Indians had little intention of voluntarily surrendering their profitable middleman function by paddling the traders inland—and for the same reason refused to help the whites build canoes, even when the HBC moved far enough west to claim its own birch trees. (At the same time, the Company was not particularly keen to tie up too many Indians as paddlers or boatbuilders because that kept them away from their pursuit of beaver pelts.) The Orkneymen, most of whom were in the Fur Country on three-year hitches, demonstrated little initial inclination to become voyageurs; some eventually did learn to handle canoes, mainly because after 1793 the Company agreed to an incentive pay scheme pegged to the number of miles logged on trips inland.

The problem by then was how to attract *enough* new manpower into the HBC's service. During the half-century after the NWC's formation, England was at war for half the time, and throughout those harsh days, press-gangs roamed Britain's streets and docks, draining the labour market of healthy young men, and forcing the Company to hire dotards, cripples, dwarfs and teenage boys as temporary help.

Apart from these difficulties, the HBC's stumbling progress inland had become seriously disrupted by internal dissension among various Chief Factors, overeager to curry favour with their employers by producing larger catches at their posts than those of their neighbours on the bay. The major initial organizational shift recognizing the growing importance of the hinterland commerce was the appointment in 1786 of William Tomison, an energetic if temperamental Orkneyman, as the Company's first Chief Inland. This made him senior to Joseph Colen, a sophisticated and articulate Englishman then in charge at York Factory. The two men clashed not only about the parochial concerns of the imposing depot on the bay, but about Tomison's obsession with organizing competition against the Montrealers along the Saskatchewan while ignoring the fur-rich ponds of the Athabasca. At the same time, the smaller brigades sent out by the HBC factories at Churchill, Moose and Albany were competing with one another for a thinning harvest of beaver. Overtrapping had dangerously depleted the animals, but when Colen suggested that the underpopulated areas be left temporarily idle to allow the rodents to propagate, he was roundly ridiculed.* The London Committee finally resolved the internecine warfare in 1799 by establishing clearly delineated routes inland and specific boundaries of jurisdiction for each of the bay forts. In the process, York Factory, once the Company's great tidewater trading centre, took on an important new role as an emporium, warehouse and distribution centre. By 1810, the post's business had become so routine that after the shipping season, its Chief Factor, William Hemmings Cook, could disappear into the bush to go hunting for three months, leaving his steward in charge.

The HBC as a whole was never that leisured; indeed, it was woefully undermanned and undersupplied. The Company's first hesitant probe westward, the

* Tim Ball, a professor of geography at the University of Winnipeg and a leading expert on northern Canadian climate, has argued that "Colen was right, but for the wrong reasons. A major cause of the lower beaver yields was the dramatic change in climate going on during these decades. The similar conditions that George Washington faced in his winter battles are described in his comments such as 'Indeed this winter has been so far the most remarkable for scarcity of provisions for neither Englishman or Indians can find anything to kill.'"

setting up of Cumberland House at Pine Island Lake in 1774, was typical of
the scale of its operations. The eight men assigned to the venture huddled in
a low log bunker, thirty-eight by twenty-six feet, with moss as caulking and a
leaky plank roof, while the nearby Montrealers, who had arrived half a decade
before, were solidly entrenched, more than a hundred strong, in a fort worthy
of the term. As late as 1811, when the Company became determined to move
inland with a vengeance, it had 320 men in the field facing 1,200
Nor'Westers. A considerable portion of the HBC's trade goods was inferior:
tobacco that wouldn't light despite attempts to improve it with small doses of
molasses, and guns that exploded in hunters' hands. William Auld, the
Edinburgh surgeon who was in charge of Churchill and spent the winter of
1808–9 at Reindeer Lake, complained that the HBC post there was "the most
miserable hovel that imagination can conceive. Surely such abominably
disgraceful styes must affect the Natives. Dirty as they are, they must make
shocking comparisons to our disadvantage. Such temporary shelter, infinitely
below what an Ourang-Outang would have contented himself with, can only
bespeak the glimmering dying lights of an expiring Commerce, not the residence of Britons, not the Settlements of the Adventurers of England."

At first, competition between the two camps was friendly enough that
traders would get together for joint celebrations of St Andrew's Day, Christmas
and Hogmanay, deliver each other's mail and, in some cases (as at Fort
Vermilion and later Terre Blanche on the Saskatchewan), build rival posts
within a common palisade. At Fort George on the Fraser, Angus Shaw invited
the HBC's William Tomison to a typical homecoming ball, which *must* have
been friendly, since seventy-two men, thirty-seven women and sixty-five children were entertained in his NWC trading hut that measured twenty-two by
twenty-three feet. On May 7, 1805, Daniel Harmon of the NWC described a
lively celebration he attended at Fort Alexandria: "When three-fourths of the
people had drunk so much as to be incapable of walking straight the other
fourth thought it was time to put an end to the ball, or rather brawl. This
morning we were invited to breakfast at the Hudson's Bay House … and in the
evening to a dance. This, however, ended more decently than the one of the
preceding evening."

Such camaraderie was due partly to the natural brotherhood generated by
the traders' being isolated together, but in their amicable overtures the Bay
men, at least, were also obeying orders. In its annual message issued to Bay
posts in 1806, the London Committee instructed its men "to avoid any discus-

sion or disagreement with those people" and to "maintain the utmost peace and harmony with your opponents." The Company's directives went even further, absolving employees from trying to outdo the rambunctious Nor'Westers. "The great and first objective of our concerns," the lords of the HBC decreed, "is an increasing trade to counterbalance the very enormous and increasing Expences of it. We do not expect returns equal to those of our more powerful Opponents but we ought to receive such returns as are adequate to the quantity of goods you are annually supplied with."

That sensible-shoes policy may have impressed them on Fenchurch Street, but out in the trenches it did little but grant the North West Company licence to plunder. The Montrealers organized blockades to keep the Indians away from the HBC posts and, having few fixed standards of trade, often won their business, even when (or sometimes *because*) they already had credit outstanding with the HBC. In 1800 at a post near Nipigon, an NWC clerk named Frederick Schultz murdered one of his assistants for defecting to the HBC. Imperceptibly, the mood was changing. In the autumn of 1806, John Haldane broke into the English company's warehouse at Bad Lake, overpowered its manager, William Corrigal, and stole 480 beaver skins.

Three years later, Corrigal was in charge of the HBC post at Eagle Lake, east of Lake of the Woods, when a party of rowdy Nor'Westers, led by Aeneas Macdonell, pitched camp only forty yards away. On the gloomy evening of September 15, an Indian arrived to trade and settle his debts. Not being able to pay in full, he offered to leave his canoe—provided that he could borrow it back long enough to paddle his trade goods home. Next morning, the Indian was packing up his clothing and ammunition when he was accosted by the NWC's Macdonell, armed with a cutlass and a brace of pistols, claiming that since the Indian was still indebted to the NWC, his canoe and merchandise were being impounded on the spot. The HBC commander, watching the shouting match, sent two of his assistants—James Tate and John Corrigal—to prevent the confiscation. They ran down the hill to the shore and tried to calm the situation. Macdonell let out a whoop, drew his sword and lunged at Tate, aiming to cut his head open. The unarmed Bay man shielded himself with his hands and had his left wrist deeply slashed and part of his throat cut. Macdonell then took off after John Corrigal, who dived into the river. The Nor'Wester waded in after him and, following a brief tussle, drove home a sword thrust that laid Corrigal's arm above the elbow open to the bone. Macdonell took another broadsword swipe at the Bay man's head, aiming with such ferocity that a heavy canoe paddle used to ward off the blow was cut in two. The fight then moved towards the post, where several Bay men, including a labourer named John Mowat, were just arriving from a round of fishing. They dispersed at the sight of the blood-mad Macdonell charging up the hill after them—all except Mowat, who was lame and couldn't move fast enough. The Nor'Wester's first sword lunge came close enough to slash Mowat's waistcoat at his chest. Macdonell was winding up for a final killing blow when Mowat fired a pistol into his heart. The Nor'Wester staggered backward, stumbled down the incline, stuck his sword defiantly into the ground, and died.

"Then all our people came into the house, and us that was wounded got our wounds examined and tied up," James Tate calmly noted in his journal. "My handkerchief and the pad that was in the inside of it and the collar of my shirt was all cut through by the stroke that I got on my neck. Our floor was all over of blood from John Corrigal and me in such a manner that two of our people was nigh fainting at the sight. When the bustle was all over and everything quiet the Indian made his escape through the wood and we saw no more of him."

Mowat gave himself up when the surviving Montrealers surrounded the HBC post, angrily threatening to incite local Indians to slaughter them, even if it cost them a keg of rum for each HBC scalp. He was taken in irons to Rainy Lake for the winter and later to Fort William, where he languished in a windowless six-foot-square cell. Then he was moved to Montreal for trial before some obliging judges, relations of local NWC partners, who found the protesting Mowat guilty of manslaughter. Sentenced to six months in prison (and branded on the hand with a hot iron as a felon), he was offered a pardon but refused on the sensible grounds that he should never have been condemned for a clear act of self-defence in the first place.*

AN IMPORTANT NEW ELEMENT in the changing scene was the arrival, in the spring of 1806, of the first white woman to settle permanently in the West—Marie-Anne Gaboury of Maskinongé near Trois-Rivières, Quebec, who had married a free-trader named Jean-Baptiste Lagemodière. She had her first baby, Reine, at the HBC post at Pembina on January 6, 1807, but the occasion

---

* The unfortunate Mowat served his sentence and, disillusioned, decided to return home. He was drowned while crossing a river during freeze-up on his way to board a New York packet bound for England.

of her second delivery nineteen months later was more dramatic. "She was riding her horse, a spirited buffalo runner," wrote Sylvia Van Kirk in *Many Tender Ties*, "with young Reine tucked snugly in one of the saddle bags when she suddenly came upon a herd of buffalo. The horse immediately gave chase and the young mother could only cling desperately to the horse's neck until she was finally rescued by her husband. Later that night, Marie-Anne gave birth to a son, nicknamed La Prairie; within three days she was on her horse again riding back to Fort Edmonton. Marie-Anne* and her children were objects of much interest to the Indians; in fact one Blackfoot woman so coveted her little son that she reputedly tried to kidnap him."

It was typical of the HBC's somnambulism that even though in 1754 Anthony Henday had been the Company's first white employee to view the western mountains, having marched from York Factory to within forty miles of what would later be Rocky Mountain House, nothing was done to consolidate that discovery for more than half a century. Even then it was a puny affair that drew no follow-up for another decade. The sensitive son of a brazier, Joseph Howse, who was educated in Latin, French and Italian before he left England for Hudson Bay in 1795, had made a brief journey into the mountains from Edmonton House in 1809. The following season he spent a full year in the Rockies, crossing the continental divide and wintering near present-day Flathead Lake, Montana. Although Howse carried no instruments to prove where he had been, William Hemmings Cook, the York Factory chief, reported that he had "explored a Country European feet had never trod" and his ledger showed that the expedition, mounted at a cost of £576, had produced thirty-six packs of fur with a profit margin of 75 percent. Howse had many other adventures but was never assigned to the Rockies again, and the HBC blithely left that highly lucrative sphere of operations to be harvested by the Nor'Westers.†

This policy of retreating in the face of competition also initially held true for the fur-rich Athabasca Country. The Nor'Westers had developed a gainful trade there well before 1800, establishing posts westward along the Peace and northward down the Mackenzie, cutting the flow of pelts that had previously sustained the HBC post at Churchill. The first Bay man into Athabasca was

---

* Through her daughter Julie, Marie-Anne became Louis Riel's grandmother.
† Howse himself retired from the Company in 1815 and devoted the next thirty years of his life to compiling the first published *Grammar of the Cree Language*, which became a standard text still cited by linguists.

Philip Turnor, the Company surveyor, who arrived in 1790 so ill-equipped he had to borrow a fishing net from the Nor'Westers, and so ill-provisioned that he survived mainly by shooting rabbits. But he did report back that the local Indians, remembering the fair way they had been treated on the bay, were friendly, while feeling "a settled dislike for the Canadians" who traded in the area, particularly because these Nor'Westers had the practice of seizing women as payment "for their Husbands or Fathers debts and then selling them to their [North West Company] men [for] from five hundred to two thousand Livres and if the Father or Husband or any of them resist the only satisfaction they get is a beating."

When Turnor arrived back at York Factory, he recommended that the Company adopt the aggressive trading methods of the Nor'Westers and volunteered to march back to establish a permanent Athabasca trading post. No one paid any attention.

Turnor mapped many of the waterways running inland from Hudson Bay, but his chief legacy to the HBC was his ability to spot and train promising newcomers. Besides teaching David Thompson the surveying skills that turned him into the NWC's greatest mapmaker, Turnor apprenticed Peter Fidler, a lesser known but also significant figure in the early probes of the western frontier. Fidler came to the western territory from Bolsover, Derby-shire, as a labourer in 1788, quickly rising to become a writer. He was stationed at Cumberland House just as Turnor was preparing to leave for Athabasca, and when Thompson broke his leg, the HBC surveyor took young Fidler with him instead. Turnor's main assignment was to prove that the Athabasca district could be reached by a river draining into Hudson Bay, which would have made it legally part of the original HBC grant. That proved impossible (because of a clearly defined watershed at Methy Portage), but this first incursion did provide the HBC with vital data and Fidler with valuable training. Not only did he become a qualified surveyor but he spent a full season living in a Chipewyan camp on the Slave River. There is a touching entry in his journal when, realizing how deeply assimilated into native life he has become, he marvels that for the first time he has dreamed in Chipewyan.

Finally, in 1802, Fidler was assigned to lead his own trading party into the Athabasca and establish a trading post near Fort Chipewyan known as Nottingham House. In its miniature "Big House," Fidler, his Swampy Cree wife, Mary, and sixteen Orcadian assistants spent the next four winters, living mainly on frozen fish, rarely daring to venture outside for fear of the wild, ravenous dogs roaming the snowdrifts. That first winter Fidler recorded, in his scientific way, the freezing temperatures of various substances: his English brandy froze at –26°F, rum at –23°, Holland gin at –17° and "blood out of the body" at 25°F. Fidler spent his time trading furs, studying French, operating a small hand-press and bindery—and jousting with Nor'Westers.

His first tormentor was a stout Highlander named Archibald Norman McLeod who flounced around Fort Chipewyan in a scarlet military uniform of his own design, complete with sword and cocked hat. McLeod warned Fidler that he had no right to be in Athabasca and that "the proprietors of the NWC were resolutely determined that the servants of the HBC should walk over their bodies rather than they would allow an Indian to go into the Hudson's Bay Company House." McLeod's most effective tactic was to command one of his clerks, Samuel Black, to harass the HBC employees. Unlike most of his fellow Nor'Westers, who treated the Bay men with either respect or contempt, Black was a terrorist who took pleasure in his violent activities. He led raiding parties that plundered the Chipewyan camps trading with the HBC, slashed Fidler's fishing nets, set ablaze his winter reserves of firewood, uprooted his garden and personally moved into a tent pitched right at the Nottingham House gates to prevent any Indians from entering. The best description of this frontier brigand was provided by George Simpson, when he was making notes on the personalities of the men (including such former NWCers as Black) under his command to see who might—and might not—be suitable for promotion. Of Samuel Black, he wrote: "The strangest man I ever knew. So wary & suspicious that it is scarcely possible to get a direct answer from him on any point, and when he does speak or write on any subject so prolix that it is quite fatiguing to attempt following him. A perfectly honest man and his generosity might be considered indicative of a warmth of heart if he was not known to be a cold blooded fellow who could be guilty of any Cruelty and would be a perfect Tyrant had he had power. Can never forget what he may consider a slight or insult, and fancies that every man has a design upon him. Very cool, resolute to desperation, and equal to the cutting of a throat with perfect deliberation: yet his word when he can be brought to the point may be depended on. A Don Quixote in appearance—ghastly, raw boned and lanthorn jawed, yet strong vigorous and active. Has not the talent of conciliating Indians by whom he is disliked, but who are ever in dread of him, and well they may be so, as he is ever on his guard against them and so suspicious that offensive and defensive preparation seem to be the study of his Life having Dirks, Knives and Loaded

Pistols concealed about his Person and in all directions about his Establishment even under his Table cloth at meals and in his Bed. He would be admirably adapted for the Service of the North West coast where the Natives are so treacherous were it not that he cannot agree with his colleagues which renders it necessary to give him a distinct charge. I should be sorry to see a man of such character at our Council board."*

Having to deal with Black's outrageous bullying tactics did nothing for Fidler's trading record, and he ended that first season with a disappointing total of only 253 skins. Ordered to stay where he was, he did even worse in the second season. Black had started trailing the Bay men's duck hunts; armed with a savage-looking cutlass, he would leap up to startle the birds at the crucial moment. He burned down the HBC watch-house near Fort Chipewyan and torched the lumber that had been collected to build another outstation. Still, enough Indians braved Black's blockade that Fidler grew determined to remain another season. That was a mistake.

Black declared psychological warfare at a more primitive level, denying the Bay men any sleep. Each night, he would pace outside their compound howling like a wolf and hurling rocks at their wooden walls. He once placed a heavy piece of bark atop the chimney, nearly asphyxiating the snoozing occupants, and even killed and ate their pet dog. He denied the Indians access to the English fort with the threat of shooting and so wore down Fidler and his crew that in June 1806 they decided to give up the venture and leave. But there was one more blow to come. Fidler had signed an agreement with an NWC winterer that in return for quitting the Athabasca district for two years, he would be given five hundred pelts and repaid the expenses incurred in establishing Nottingham House. Now that he was ready to depart, the Nor'Westers went back on their word and Fidler left empty-handed, lamenting in his journal: "We are so very few—they so numerous!"

Four years later, Fidler was posted back to the Athabasca gateway at Île-à-la-Crosse, only to be subjected once again to the guerrilla tactics of Black, aided this time by a young NWC recruit named Peter Skene Ogden, who swaggered about with two daggers in his belt. The Nor'Westers used the Company's flag and weather-vane for target practice, stole Fidler's fishnets,

---

* Despite this devastating analysis, Simpson promoted Black, who in 1823 joined the HBC he had so hated, to Chief Trader and eventually to Chief Factor and placed him in charge of the Kamloops district, where he was killed by an Indian on Feb. 8, 1841.

carried away his firewood, diverted Indians who arrived with furs and, finally, invaded his fort. "I told them both to return the same way they came and that they should not pass through our yard in the insulting manner they indicated," the Bay man dutifully noted in his journal. "I told one of our men to shut the west gates—which was at last done—they persevered in passing when I struck Mr. Black with a stick two or three times—Ogden immediately drew his dagger and cut two large holes in the side and back of my coat and pricked my body—but no further—Mr. Black then took up part of the stick I had broken over him and struck me on the thumb close at the upper end of the nail and smashed it to pieces—Ogden also struck me twice with a stick—all our men looking on the whole time without giving me any assistance—Mr. Black and Ogden yet followed me into my room with their guns and daggers and abused me very much while my thumb was dripping...."

After that, the Nor'Westers (outnumbering the Bay men twenty-six to eight) forbade any of Fidler's men to leave their posts and shot at his twelve-year-old son, Charlie. Faced with circumstances so stressful that he feared outsiders would not believe him, Fidler logged in his diary on January 21, 1811: "Some people in reading this journal might very naturally suppose, that many of the Ill actions that has been done was by people in a state of inebriety—but they are very sober people—it is a systematic plan that has been laid at the Grand Portage to harass and distress us and determine to expel us from these parts of the country where they get the greater part of their prime furs at very little expense...."

Before Fidler left that unhappy post the following summer, Black and Ogden had one more torment in store. Because the post depended for its food on fishing, they induced an Orkneyman named Andrew Kirkness, who was the Company's best angler, to defect to the NWC. As bait they used his Indian wife, who had defected to the Montrealers' camp a few months earlier. Fidler had tried to get her back, having heard that she was unhappy. The Nor'Westers not only refused but threatened to cut off her ears if she left. Shortly after his desertion, Andrew Kirkness changed his mind and decided he wanted back into the HBC post, but according to Fidler's journal, Black told him that "if he offered to go to us, they would make every Canadian in their house ravish his woman before his eyes." Three days later, Kirkness deserted anyway, departing without his wife. As Fidler was leaving the post for the last time, the Indian woman tried running after the departing Bay man, but was yanked back inside the NWC Post. "They have now given her to a Canadian," the hardened Fidler scribbled in his journal, adding, "Calm, hot weather."

When Fidler got back to Hudson Bay, William Auld, his superior, derided him for his "mean and spaniel-like behaviour." The surveyor remained with the Company until he died on December 17, 1822. During the last decade of his service, Fidler became the HBC's chief cartographer of the interior plains, drawing thirty-two invaluable maps of the area within the HBC's jurisdiction. After he retired at fifty-one, he was allowed to languish as a supernumerary clerk in the Swan River district of what is now western Manitoba. The last mention of this worthy geographer in HBC documents is a brief note describing him as "a faithful and interested old servant, now superannuated, [who] has had a recent paralitic affection [sic] and his resolution quite gone, is unfit for any charge." A typical Canadian hero.

THE HBC'S DISPIRITING ATTEMPTS to compete with the Nor'Westers in the Athabasca—and everywhere else for that matter—led its London-based proprietors to the verge of taking the Company out of the fur trade altogether. During these years, administration of the Company's affairs had fallen into the flabby hands of a closed clique of interrelated and interconnected fiscal aristocrats whose idea of a truly daring act was to be the first among their circle to try out the new French restaurants then dotting London. Samuel Wegg, whose family connections with the HBC went back a century, was succeeded in the governorship in 1799 by Sir James Winter Lake, the last of the Lake family that had dominated the Company's board for most of eight decades. The only fresh voice among the Committeemen was that of George Hyde Wollaston, son of a theologian and brother of a mathematician, who produced a dispassionate analysis of the Company's prospects and decided it had none—at least not in a fur trade by then overwhelmingly dominated by the Nor'Westers.

After studying the alternatives in April 1809, Wollaston presented his fellow directors with a bold initiative. Since the fur business had become prohibitively unprofitable and unsold pelts were piled high in the HBC's London warehouse while the supply of timber for Royal Navy masts, spars and decking was in dangerously short supply (because the Napoleonic Wars were cutting off England's traditional Baltic sources), he proposed transforming the HBC into a timber company. The London-based plutocrats, never having visited the place, had no firsthand idea of how little usable wood grew around Hudson Bay. (In fact, York Factory had just used up a six years' accumulation of its precious spare timber merely to erect two tiny outhouses.) There were small forests twenty miles inland from Moose Factory, at the southern end of the adjoining James Bay, and Wollaston eventually arranged to have a steam engine shipped so that a sawmill could be built. The engine, manufactured by Boulton & Watt, was reassembled by Alexander Christie, a Scotsman hired specifically by the Company to pursue timber sales. The trade never developed. Not only was the supply of raw materials inadequate but the Royal Navy was learning to evade Napoleon's blockades.

But something had to be done. By 1809, the Hudson's Bay Company's balance sheet was showing losses of £19,000. Dividends, which had declined to 4 percent, had to be eliminated, and the value of the Company's stock, which had sold for £250 a share, had declined to about £60. In 1808, the Committeemen had petitioned the British government for relief from custom duties. The Treasury granted a one-year reprieve, then looked the other way. Three Committee members had already lent the Company £25,000, and it was carrying a £50,000 overdraft with the Bank of England.

The quandary was resolved when Wollaston's negative influence on the HBC Committee was replaced by the drive of two remarkable men: Andrew Colvile and John Wedderburn Halkett. They both purchased substantial share positions in the Company during 1809, and while Halkett did not become a member of the governing Committee for another two years, Colvile, who had previously been a successful London sugar broker, assumed a position of power almost immediately. He was determined to move the HBC away from his predecessor's counsel of despair. Colvile had the intellect and lively sense of resolve, but it was a renegade Nor'Wester named Colin Robertson who provided the winning idea. The same day Colvile took up his seat on the Committee, Robertson had made a forceful presentation to the board arguing that instead of cowering before the Nor'Westers the HBC should attack them, mainly by mounting an expedition from Montreal to conquer the Athabasca fur lands. He also advocated that the Company revise its compensation arrangements so that its senior traders would, much like the Nor'Westers, be paid as incentive-inspired partners. He was particularly vehement in his arguments on behalf of the Athabasca venture. "Good God! See the Canadians come thousands of miles beyond us to monopolize the most valuable part of your Territories," he told the Committee. Robertson was adamant in his view that the HBC's incumbents in the field were "drones and drivellers" who "may as well attempt to take hold of the moon with their teeth" as beat the Nor'Westers at their own game. But it was by enlisting Colvile's support for the new pay arrangements that Robertson won the day. Known as the Retrenching System, the scheme provided for setting aside half the profits for the officers in the fur trade, granting men in the field more incentives and greater freedom of action. What made this prospect so significant was its ultimate aim of allowing the HBC, for the first time, to stand on its own feet as a commercial trading corporation instead of remaining as it had started—a royally chartered and protected monopoly.

Robertson, who had served the NWC as a clerk and been fired the previous year after a fistfight with John McDonald of Garth, was a new kind of man in the service of the Hudson's Bay Company. His personal motto, "When you are among wolves, howl," accurately summed up his operating philosophy. He was a proud and combative Highlander and made the most of each new situation in which he found himself. The Committee expeditiously adopted his recommendations that the Company seek its future traders in Scotland's Western Isles, in the Shetlands and among the heather of the Highlands.

But the most essential recruit in that unexpected surge of newly found energy was Andrew Colvile's brother-in-law: a Scottish nobleman known as Thomas Douglas, 5th Earl of Selkirk.

A Fearful Innocence

Unable to bridge the gap between noble aspirations and distasteful realities, Lord Selkirk tarnished his cause and eventually succeeded in destroying himself.

HE WAS THAT MOST DANGEROUS of combinations: a blend of moral fastidiousness and spiritual intransigence. A frail Scottish earl with his lungs and soul on fire, Lord Selkirk recruited himself as an agent of destiny, determined to alter the course of history.

That he achieved. His actions triggered the demise of the North West Company, and the Highland settlers he brought to the Red River established Western Canada's founding community.

Yet there is an incomplete quality about his remarkable saga—an enduring uncertainty as to whether he was fool or saint that still haunts the descendants of his people. Cursed as a blight on the landscape by his many enemies and chided for being a misguided visionary by his few friends, Selkirk followed his self-imposed mission, blissfully ignorant of Newton's Third Law of Motion—that for every action there is an equal and opposite reaction. Unable to bridge the gap between noble aspirations and distasteful realities, Lord Selkirk tarnished his cause and eventually succeeded in destroying himself.

Selkirk was driven by his personal sense of guilt over the Scottish crofters' sufferings and by frustration at his own illness, that most falsely energizing of conditions, incurable tuberculosis. The disease racked his every breath during the last dozen years of his life. While devoting his whole being to the Red River Colony, he was trying to muffle in lace handkerchiefs the blood-coughs from his chest—and fighting to keep down the bile he felt at the chicanery of his opponents.

Although he became known mainly for his bold experiments at colonization, Selkirk's more important contribution was geographical. His relentless determination to settle the western lands extended Britain's tenuous hold on the northern half of the North American continent during a critical decade, drawing the attention of London's colonial authorities to a region that might otherwise have gone by default to the United States. The very fact of the Red River Colony's existence proclaimed Britain's transcontinental intentions by planting a vested interest in the path of expansion-minded politicians to the south.

The ragtag diaspora of approximately 270 displaced Highland crofters who settled on the Red River was the Prairie equivalent of the Pilgrims who had emigrated to the Plymouth colony aboard the *Mayflower* nearly two centuries earlier. Few contemporary maps noted Red River's location; no gazetteer listed its existence. Yet the tiny agricultural enclave at the junction of the Assiniboine and Red rivers developed into a pivotal community, quickly evolving its own social structures and home-grown middle class, its own tensions and pretensions and, eventually, a full-scale rebellion.

Selkirk himself visited Red River only once—in 1817, five years after its founding—and stayed for one fleeting summer. This was his one brief season as benevolent king of his personal domain. He spent the long Prairie afternoons tramping the grasslands under the slanting sun, bestowing land on worthy recipients, planning roads and bridges, setting aside tracts for churches and schools, giving shape to his dream. Legend transmuted those thirteen weeks into a hallowed interlude, perpetuated in the community's still extant folklore as affirmation of its founder's compassion and his affinity for the land.

LAND HAD BEEN THE CHIEF PREOCCUPATION of the Douglases since the thirteenth century, and from 1300 to the Reformation no family had played a more conspicuous part in the affairs of Scotland. Its members, having intermarried eleven times with the Scots royal family (and once with that of England), had been involved in nearly every armed effort to guard and extend Scottish sovereignty.

Thomas Douglas was born on June 20, 1771, at St Mary's Isle, his family's ancient seat in southwestern Scotland. He was still a youngster when he suffered the traumatic experience of having his home invaded by a raiding party under the command of John Paul Jones, the Scottish-born naval hero of the American War of Independence. Jones was determined to impress his potential for greatness on the noble family he felt had spurned him during his youth. The son of a maid and a gardener at nearby Kirkbean, Jones harboured a deep resentment of the Douglases based on more than the great family's master-servant relationship to his parents. Unlike those of his sisters, John's own name did not appear in the register of births at the parish of Kirkbean, and he believed himself to be an illegitimate and unacknowledged offspring of the Selkirks.

Apprenticed as a cabin boy on a merchantman at twelve, John Paul had become chief mate on a Jamaican slaver and in 1772 killed the ringleader of a mutiny aboard his vessel. To escape charges, he added the anonymous-sounding surname "Jones." When the 1775 revolutionary war broke out in the Thirteen Colonies, he joined the new Continental Navy. In command of the *Providence*, he swept the North Atlantic, capturing or sinking a dozen British ships. Later, in charge of the newly commissioned *Ranger*, he sailed to France, where Benjamin Franklin, then the American envoy to Versailles, ordered him to harass shipping off the British Isles and, if possible, kidnap a well-known personage who could be exchanged for American prisoners held in England. These assignments found the *Ranger* on April 23, 1778, nosing into Solway Firth to anchor off the Douglas mansion. Her captain, in full dress uniform, was nervously pacing the quarterdeck, planning an early morning landing party to kidnap Dunbar Hamilton Douglas, 4th Earl of Selkirk. His motive may have been deeply personal, but Jones's bold foray in plucking one of Scotland's leading aristocrats out of his own hall would have been a great coup for the future Republic.

Despite his elaborate preparations, Jones decided at the last moment not to lead the raid in person, assigning that delicate duty to his two chief lieutenants, Simpson and Wallingford. As the longboat landed at the family dock, a governess snatched young Thomas from where he was playing in the garden and whisked him to safety. When the two naval officers, leading their armed troop of disreputable-looking matelots, knocked on the mansion's great door, something akin to drawing-room comedy ensued. The family butler, Daniel, his professional sang-froid hardly ruffled, acidly pointed out that if the visitors were a Royal Navy press-gang, there was no one home to "press." The Americans huffily identified themselves, just as Lady Selkirk came out of the breakfast room to see what all the fuss was about.

With that genteel mixture of total calm and utter contempt that takes generations to cultivate, Lady Selkirk motioned the two officers into her drawing-room and demanded to know what they wanted. The explanation that they intended to kidnap her husband to be bargained for American prisoners was waved away with the curt comment that the Earl was not home— clearly implying that even if he were, he would hardly stoop to entrust himself to such uncouth colonials. When Lieutenant Wallingford cheerfully replied that it didn't really matter, they would kidnap instead the youngster they had passed in the garden, Lady Selkirk drew herself up to her full height and matter-of-factly declared they would have to take her life first. She then offered any *objects* in the house that appealed to them.

The discomfited officers looked around, spotted the silver service from which breakfast had so recently been served, and allowed that perhaps the tea and coffee pots and silver salver might be appropriate. Lady Selkirk ordered Daniel to pack the silver in a stout sack, then offered her visitors a glass of wine, asking the butler to pass some whisky to the crewmen waiting outside. The ever-faithful Daniel had no intention of surrendering all of the family's Georgian treasures to the ragamuffins from across the sea, and while packing some of the silver into the sack, substituted lumps of coal wrapped in paper, temporarily secreting a valuable urn beneath a maid's ample apron. The raiding party and Lady Selkirk were meanwhile proposing increasingly spirited toasts to one another's health. The visit came to an end when the waving sailors rowed off in their little boat, clutching the bag of silver—and coal.

Back aboard the *Ranger,* Jones was furious with his two officers. Instead of impressing the Douglases with his greatness, his subordinates had made him out to be a common thief. He decided to buy back the booty from the Navy, pay his crewmen their prize money and return the goods to Lady Selkirk. The following month, he sent her a flowery letter apologizing for the raid. "MADAM," it began, "it cannot be too much lamented that in the profession of arms the Officer of fine feelings, and of real responsibility, should be under the necessity of winking at any action of persons under his command, which his heart cannot approve. But the reflection is doubly severe when he finds himself obliged in appearance to countenance such Action by his authority.... Knowing Lord Selkirk's interest with his King, and esteeming as I do his private Character, I wished to make him the happy instrument of alleviating the horrors of hopeless captivity when the brave are overpowered and made Prisoners of War. It was perhaps fortunate for you, Madam, that he was from home, for it was my intention to have taken him on board the *Ranger* and to have detained him till thro' this means, a general and fair exchange of

Prisoners as well in Europe as in America, had been effected … but some offi-cers who were with me could not forbear expressing their discontent, observ-ing that in America no delicacy was shown by the English, who took away all sorts of movable property…. I have gratified my men, and when the plate is sold, I shall become the purchaser, and I will gratify my own feelings by restor-ing it to you, in such conveyance as you shall be pleased to direct."

That bit of purple rationalizing should have been the end of the exchange, but Lord Selkirk haughtily sent word to Jones on the family's behalf that he could not possibly countenance return of his silver without consent of the Continental Congress. The objects, which had cost Jones £50, became the issue of protracted legal negotiations before they were returned seven years later, the silver pot still containing dried tea-leaves from the interrupted breakfast.*

The harmless incident did much to spread the reputation for courage of Lady Selkirk (who wrote to a friend, "… I frankly acknowledge my composure to be constitutional"), but it had a lasting impact on the future Lord Selkirk. "This was a momentous event in my life," Thomas later confessed. "I was terri-bly frightened…. I developed an antipathy for the United States due almost solely to the buccaneering of John Paul." *In his Red River Valley*, John Perry Pritchett claims that the raid in fact had profound consequences: "Perhaps this may help to explain why the Earl, when considering possible sites in America for colonization projects, was decidedly in favour of districts lying in British territory rather than in the more temperate regions of the United States."

The young Thomas was educated in liberal arts at the University of Edinburgh, where he came under the influence of Dugald Stewart, a brilliant exponent of the Scottish "common sense" school of philosophy, which held that thought should flow from scientific evidence unfettered by metaphysical speculation. Stewart impressed on his youthful charges the notion that univer-sal benevolence was the prime virtue, insisting that "only a man whose ruling or habitual principle of action is a sense of duty, or a regard for what is right, may be properly denominated virtuous." Counter to the prevailing tenet of the

---

* Jones went on to assume command of the *Bonhomme Richard*. He was on her quarterdeck when, in answer to a demand for surrender during an engagement with the Royal Navy's *Serapis* on September 23, 1779, he uttered his famous riposte: "I have not yet begun to fight!" He later became disillusioned with his adopted country and joined the Russian Navy (then fighting the Turks) as a rear-admiral but, plagued by discontented subordinates, returned to Paris. There he died a broken man in 1792.

time, this system of beliefs demanded from its followers the active social involvement and aggressive individual initiation of good works that would become the hallmarks of Selkirk's life.

At university, Thomas also befriended Walter Scott (he later met and admired Lord Byron),* but the most romantic influences on his youth were tales of his family's exploits, which stressed audacity above every other virtue. Sir James—the famous Black Douglas who had led Robert the Bruce's army into England—was an ancestor. A scarlet, crowned heart is still the centre-piece of the family's coat of arms, honouring James's vain attempt to carry out Bruce's dying wish to have his heart buried in the Holy Land. When he was outnumbered during an encounter in Spain with the Moors on his way to the Middle East, Douglas had thrown the silver chalice containing the organ into the advancing phalanx of his enemies, shouting, "Pass first in fight as thou wert wont to do and Douglas will follow thee or die!"—and fought his way towards his beloved friend's heart. He was slain just before he reached it.

Having seven centuries of fighting blood in his veins was not a heritage easy to live down, especially for young Thomas, who had no aggressive inten-tions for his own future. Unlike his elder brothers, he was not trained for the law or military service. But having been awakened to the new enlightenment sweeping continental Europe during his university years, he decided to visit France with his brother-in-law, Sir James Hall of Dunglass. That progressive baronet had many close links with some of the intellectuals behind the French Revolution, including the Marquis de Lafayette (a leader of the liberal aristo-crats demanding restrictions on the absolute power of the French monarchy), Pierre-Samuel du Pont de Nemours (a reform-minded economist who advo-cated free trade) and Jacques-Pierre Brissot de Warville (the moderate reformer who took delivery of the keys to the Bastille after it was stormed in 1789). It was here in the sensitized salons of revolutionary France that the young man's social conscience took root. His humanitarian sensibilities were awakened to a realization of how urgent political imperatives can turn patri-cian intellectuals into effective men of action. At the same time, he became

---

* The Douglases also knew Robert Burns. It was in the Selkirk house at St Mary's Isle that he wrote the celebrated Selkirk Grace:

> Some hae meat, and canna eat,
> And some wad eat that want it;
> But we hae meat and we can eat,
> And sae the Lord be thankit.

acutely aware that any society failing to alleviate the plight of the poor might suffer violent consequences *à la guillotine*. These two notions—that thoughtful aristocrats were not precluded from implementing social reform, and that *not* to initiate reform was by far the riskier course—became Thomas Douglas's motivating impulses.

After his return to Scotland, he astonished his father and brothers by choosing to work on the family farm, labouring from dawn to dusk as hard as any tenant, ploughing the black earth, scything the stalks of oats and barley. As part of his growing enthusiasm for improved land use, Selkirk began to take private journeys northward into the Highlands. There he came face to face with the notorious Clearances.

A DEAD HAND had lain on Scotland since the defeat of the clans at Culloden, that windswept moor of lost hope where the Jacobites under the Young Pretender were slaughtered by the English redcoats on April 16, 1746. Five thousand starving Highlanders equipped only with broadswords and stout hearts were confronted by a well-drilled cadre of professionals backed by cavalry and cannon. The odds were already uneven enough, but the Scots were also divided by internal jealousies. Many of the Macdonalds, for example, refused to fight because they had been placed on the left wing of the defending formation instead of on the right, which was considered the place of honour.

The battle lasted less than an hour, but 1,200 Scotsmen were killed (compared to 76 Englishmen) and once the fighting was done, the British decided not only to quell the Highland uprising but also to destroy the society that had given rise to it. The stragglers from Culloden were hunted down and killed, and the glens were invaded and occupied. The Highlanders' houses were burned, their herds appropriated, weapons banned, parish records destroyed; the powerful clan system was methodically dismantled. And then the British got serious: they outlawed wearing of the kilt and forbade playing of the bagpipes.

The traditional feudal bond between lords and followers broke under these measures, and Scottish society began to disintegrate. The clan chiefs, shorn of their authority, seemed to lose even the most basic concern for their own people. During the century after Culloden, the decision to disperse their crofters resulted in the glens and braes being turned into huge sheep farms. There was a ready market for mutton and wool—and sheep, unlike some of the poorer crofters, did not line up for a monthly dole. But clearing the land for pasturage meant driving out the men, women and children who had farmed it for generations. This was done with the help of police and soldiers or just by allowing flocks of Cheviot sheep to swarm over the Highlanders' crops.

The Clearances were a time out of joint. No one then (or now) could calculate exactly how many people were dispossessed in favour of sheep. According to one estimate, two-thirds of the Highlanders in the northern counties of Inverness, Caithness and Sutherland lost their homes. The forced evacuation was most vicious in Sutherlandshire. The Duke of Sutherland had landholdings of 1,332,000 acres, the largest in the realm. From 1811 to 1820, fifteen thousand people were evicted from Sutherland estates to make way for sheep. The valley of Strathnaver in northern Scotland, for example, was evacuated on one day's notice, leaving sixteen hundred people homeless. "The destruction was begun in the west at Grummore," reported British historian John Prebble. "Messengers were sent ahead to all the other townships warning the people that they had an hour in which to evacuate their homes and take away what furniture they could. 'I saw the townships set on fire,' recalled Roderick Macleod, who was a boy at the time. '… It was sad, the driving away of these people. The terrible remembrance of the burnings of Strathnaver will live as long as a root of the people remains in the country….' The timber of three hundred buildings burned in the thin May sunshine. The valley was filled again with terrible noise, the crying of women and children, the hysterical barking of the dogs the Northumbrian shepherds had brought with them. 'Nothing but the sword was wanting,' said Macleod, 'to make the scene one of as great barbarity as the earth ever witnessed.'"

The confiscated livestock of the evicted farmers was herded into large enclosures and left there to starve, with cows, goats and bulls goring and trampling one another. Some cattle were allowed to die by the roadsides, their eyes pecked out by ravens, still alive as they bellowed their final anguish.

Such were the scenes witnessed by the impressionable young Selkirk, and they created an obsession in him to find homes for the displaced crofters. His notion of sponsoring their exodus was hardly novel, since between 1760 and 1808 at least forty-two thousand people fled Scotland for sanctuaries overseas. Because he felt that too many Highlanders were being dispersed to lands where they were lost not only to their native country "but also to the British Empire," he decided to direct at least some of the migrants to British North America.

His prestige and ability to influence events were unexpectedly enhanced in

1799, when at his father's death, as the sole survivor among his brothers, he became the 5th Earl of Selkirk. The new lord used his inherited fortune and authority to purchase landholdings on Prince Edward Island, where in 1803 he successfully settled eight hundred Highlanders. The following year he shipped fifteen families to the twelve hundred acres he had bought at Baldoon in Upper Canada, but the experiment proved a failure; the land was poorly drained and during the War of 1812 the settlement was pillaged by the Americans.

THESE PRELIMINARY FORAYS brought Selkirk to Montreal, where he was treated to a lavish Beaver Club dinner by the nabobs of the North West Company and heard for the first time intriguing tales about North America's lucrative interior. He had read Alexander Mackenzie's recently published *Voyages* and was enthralled by its references to fertile lands owned by the HBC in the Red River Valley, with its 170-day growing season and plentiful buffalo herds to supply fresh meat. When Mackenzie approached Selkirk with the idea of trying to gain control of the Hudson's Bay Company, the Earl readily agreed— though their unspoken aims were diametrically opposed. Mackenzie was the stalking horse for the Nor'Westers, who had by now determined that the only way they could be certain of gaining access to furs using the shorter route via Hudson Bay was to buy out the Company. To Selkirk, the fur trade seemed to provide an ideal entry-point for his colonization scheme at Red River.

The Earl was already interested in the HBC. In 1807, the year before Mackenzie approached him, he had married Jean Wedderburn, the vivacious twenty-one-year-old beauty whose family was about to make large investments in the Company. Her brother Andrew was named to the HBC's governing committee in 1809, and Selkirk had not long before obtained written opinions from London's leading legal firms indicating that Prince Rupert's original charter was not only valid but that it clearly assigned the right to grant parts of the Company's huge domain for the establishment of permanent colonies. By May 24, 1809, Selkirk had invested £4,087 in HBC stock, Andrew Colvile had purchased a further £4,454 and their kinsman John Halkett, £3,717. The price per share, which only two years before had been quoted at £250, was down to £50. The HBC at this point had a capitalization of £103,950, but there were only seventy-seven shareholding accounts in existence and fifteen of those were held by estates in names of the dead. Historian K.G. Davies, who referred to the HBC as "this dollhouse company," noted that "many of the shares were being held in chancery pending settlement of claims. One share-holder in 1802 was a lunatic; another, King George III, was intermittently mad…. [Neither] took an active part in the company's affairs."

As soon as Mackenzie realized Selkirk's true aims, he threatened a lawsuit but dropped it in favour of urging NWC partners William and Simon McGillivray to start buying stock on their own to thwart the Scottish peer's plans. He correctly estimated that it would take an investment of only £20,000 to capture control of the Company. At their 1811 conclave at Fort William, the Nor'Westers voted enough funds to achieve that total—but they did not move fast enough. Selkirk eventually purchased stock worth a further £15,000, which with his own and his relatives' previous holdings allowed them to domi-nate the HBC's affairs. Trade in HBC shares had been so inactive that the stock was not regularly quoted on the London Stock Exchange until 1820. The average number of shareholders who attended the Company's annual courts between 1801 and 1813 was eleven, which included each year's retiring Committeemen and their successors—very often the same individuals, voting to reappoint themselves.

Selkirk's motives in using the HBC charter as a means of establishing the Red River Colony were not entirely altruistic. Because he felt the Family Compact's hold over Upper Canada was so powerful that no large tracts of public land would be available to him,* he saw the charter as an ideal vehicle to further his colonization scheme. In that decision he weighed the possibil-ity of ultimate profits, but wanted mainly to inaugurate a plan to benefit his countrymen. When he formally proposed to the HBC Committee that the Company establish an active colony at Red River, he was disappointed to find little support. Except for Colvile, the directors felt hesitant about investing funds of the cash-poor Company in such a risky venture. They were much more interested in restoring dividend payments, which had been halved in 1801 and done away with altogether in 1809. Most of the Committeemen were ready to dismiss Selkirk's idea as a nuisance proposition that would only add to the red ink already much too visible on the debit side of the Company's ledgers.

---

* The Family Compact consisted of the small group of self-appointed aristocrats who presided over Upper Canadian society until the 1830s. They were linked by Tory ideals, family connec-tions, hostility towards the United States and patronage. They provided a governing elite so rigid that it prompted the rebellion that led to a more moderate form of politics.

Instead of asking the Company to assume the operating risks of the venture, Selkirk decided to finance the new settlement himself, and on March 7, 1810, presented the HBC board with his revised proposal. Having been relieved of any obligation to back his colonization scheme with corporate funds, the Committeemen were quick to recognize the venture's advantages. It would affirm once and for all the validity of the HBC charter, at least in the sense that granting the land for colonization would clearly signify that the HBC had owned it in the first place. Existence of the colony would also neatly dovetail into Colvile's Retrenching System, which called for dramatically increased inland activity and the replacement of expensive imported food supplies with local provisions. Two other corporate reasons supported the colonial thrust: an indigenous settlement in the Fur Country would supply much-needed new recruits to the business and at the same time provide a welcome retirement community for the increasing number of HBC traders with Indian wives wishing to stay in the country at the end of their contracts.

After considering the details of Selkirk's request for nearly a year, the HBC Committee agreed to the terms of the land grant. The Scottish nobleman and his heirs would be responsible for settling a thousand families in the Red River district within ten years; the colony would supply at least two hundred men each year to the Company's fur-trade operations; and HBC officers in the field would each be allocated two hundred acres in the settlement when they retired. In return for these hardly onerous conditions (and a nominal payment of ten shillings), Selkirk was granted a land empire of stunning proportions. Stretching over 116,000 square miles (the equivalent of 74,240,000 acres), the area covered territory four times the size of Scotland, or only about 5,000 square miles less than the combined land surfaces of the British Isles, including all of Ireland. The grant's borders (see accompanying map) extended into the present states of Minnesota, North Dakota and the northeast corner of South Dakota. Its western margin was deep in what is now Saskatchewan, almost to the source of the Assiniboine River. That bountiful domain contained what would later prove to be some of the earth's most fertile agricultural land with its self-contained waterways system, reaches of grass (for buffalo grazing) and the lush prospect of an inland empire. It was as magnificent a gift as was ever bestowed on a would-be colonizer. However dominant Selkirk's altruistic impulses, he must have known a bargain when he saw one, having already spent £10,000 on the soggy 1,200-acre settlement at Baldoon. He was now buying more than 74 million acres for ten shillings.

The understanding was accepted by the HBC board on March 6, 1811, with only the approval of the Company's annual Court on May 22 required to make it valid. The transaction quickly became a public issue. Protesting Nor'Westers toured London's coffee houses, whipping up support for their opposition. Pamphleteers published stories describing the Red River territory as a primeval solitude not suitable for human habitation, fit only as a breeding ground for wild animals. While walking in Pall Mall one afternoon, Selkirk was approached by an acquaintance who asked: "By God, Sir, if you are bent on doing something futile … why do you not plough the deserts of Sahara, which is so much nearer?"

At the shareholders' meeting, Sir Alexander Mackenzie delivered such a passionate objection to the Selkirk proposal that he won adjournment of the proceedings to May 30 and the Committee's undertaking that a recorded vote would be taken at that time. The Nor'Westers lobbied the Company's major shareholders and drew up a lengthy document detailing the dangers of the scheme to the Company's fur trade. But the following week, of the shareholders who made an appearance, twelve voted with Selkirk, five abstained, while only six were opposed—and three of those ballots were declared invalid because the stock they represented had been held less than six months. Amid loud complaints from the Nor'Westers that the land should have been offered at public sale and that the settlers would inevitably be exposed to slaughter by Indians, the meeting was adjourned, and thirteen days later Lord Selkirk received his grant.

The exasperated Nor'Westers reacted with barely contained fury. This silly anachronism called the Hudson's Bay Company was supposed to be dying, or dormant at best; what right did it have, they demanded, to reincarnate itself in vigorous new directions, especially in the very heart of the Fur Country? Simon McGillivray, one of the senior partners then in London to direct the attack, wrote to his wintering confrères: "... The Committee of the Hudson's Bay Company is at present a mere machine in the hands of Lord Selkirk, who appears to be so much wedded to his schemes of colonization in the interior of North America, that it will require some time, and I fear cause much expense to us, as well as to himself, before he is driven to abandon the project, yet *he must be driven to abandon it,* for his success would strike at the very existence of the [fur] trade." Other Selkirk critics attacked this peer who, they sneered, was "governed by the moon," and portrayed his colonizing initiative as "a cloak thrown over [his] avaricious designs to become a monopolizer of the fur trade."

The Nor'Westers' objections were easy enough to understand. At the most rudimentary level, the HBC had just handed over to Selkirk the land on which half a dozen of the Montreal company's most important trading forts were located (Pembina, Bas-de-la-Rivière, Dauphin, Gibraltar, Espérance and La Souris) and across which lay its main supply routes from Fort William westward. More important, the valleys of the Red River basin were the main source of the buffalo-based pemmican the NWC needed to feed its canoe brigades, and any interference with that life-giving traffic would endanger the NWC's entire operation. Linked with these immediate concerns was the sinking feeling that nagged the more thoughtful Nor'Westers: that the long-term intention of the Bay men was to use Red River as a natural supply base to wedge themselves into the Athabasca Country, the NWC's most lucrative fur preserve.

Selkirk listened to the objections but was incapable of absorbing their content. To him, the Red River grant made eminent good sense, bringing together as it did his love of land, the crying need to relocate the Scottish crofters and timely reaffirmation of the HBC charter—thus furthering, in all its aspects, the imperialist ideal so popular among British aristocrats at the time. He shut his eyes and thought of England. "I really don't believe Selkirk realized what he was doing when he planted the Red River Colony right across the North West Company's main lines of communication," insists Dr W. Kaye Lamb, the internationally known fur-trade chronicler. "He just visualized a vast empty country and thought, 'Well, why can't they go five miles north or south of my colony?' never realizing he was cutting off the NWC's access to watercourses vital to their trade." Such naïveté was to haunt the Red River Colony's formative years. Selkirk could never bring himself to understand why his settlers could not simply be farmers without becoming pawns in the fur-trade wars. "It is a business," he wrote to Lady Selkirk about that commerce, "which I hate from the bottom of my heart."

Only four days after the HBC's dramatic shareholders' meeting, the Nor'Westers appeared at Hudson's Bay House with a new plan to prevent the bloodshed they could foresee if Selkirk received his grant. They suggested partitioning the Fur Country, permanently reserving Athabasca and the territory west of the Rocky Mountains for themselves, with the Red River Valley awarded to neither company. But having restored their self-confidence (by moving ahead with the Retrenching System) and their earnings (by 1811, profits were £57,860, compared with a loss of £19,000 for 1809), the HBC directors rejected the NWC offer without much thought or analysis. Accepting the NWC compromise might have prevented the tragic events that followed; turning it down meant moving beyond the possibility of averting the fatal consequences.

SELKIRK'S FIRST EXPEDITION should have been a logistical and emotional triumph; instead, it was a misadventure of such proportions that the suffering of its participants became its dominant legacy. The crofters, recruited throughout Scotland, were asked to pay £10 per person for transportation to Red River and a year's provisions. Each head of family would then be granted a hundred acres at five shillings an acre, with Selkirk (through the HBC) responsible for marketing excess produce. The settlement was to have its own school and church with a Gaelic-speaking minister of the Presbyterian faith. The plan was to dispatch an advance party from Stornoway (that rocky burgh in the Outer Hebrides where Harris tweed originated) under the command of Miles Macdonell. A Scottish-born former captain in the Loyalist Royal Canadian Volunteers, Macdonell was hired by Selkirk to prepare the colony for permanent settlement. A high-strung martinet who had been frustrated in his army command, Macdonell suffered from the worst aspect of the military mentality: the notion that giving orders persistently and loudly enough can alter any annoying reality. If he had been hired as a double agent by the Nor'Westers to sabotage the project (which he was not—his loyalty to Selkirk was one of his few redeeming qualities), Macdonell could not have behaved much differently than he did. It was as if he were determined to make true the anti-settlement propaganda being spread throughout the Highlands by Simon McGillivray, writing under the pseudonym "The Highlander": "Even if the emigrants escape the scalping knife, they will be subject to constant alarm and terror. Their habitations, their crops, their cattle will be destroyed, and they will find it impossible to exist in the country."

Most of the ships serving the emigrant traffic out of Scotland at the time were little better than slave traders; a little worse, really, because the death of a slave in transit meant lower profits, while the unfortunate settlers paid their steerage fares in advance, and so their health and well-being upon arrival were of little concern to the agents and captains in charge. There is documentation of a brig that sailed for the Carolinas with 450 passengers crammed for eleven weeks into a hold measuring sixty by eighteen feet. Dysentery, typhus and scurvy claimed all but a handful. No wonder the departure of the ships was such a wrenching experience for those leaving and those who remained, as both groups instinctively realized they were likely never to see one another again. "The Highlanders were like children, uninhibited in their feelings and wildly demonstrative in their grief," wrote John Prebble. "Men and women wept without restraint. They flung themselves on the earth they were leaving, clinging to it so fiercely that sailors had to pry them free and carry them bodily to the boats.... Hands were wrung and wrung again, bumpers of whisky tossed wildly off amidst cheers and shouts; the women were forced almost fainting into the boats; and the crowd upon the shore burst into a long, loud cheer. Again and again that cheer was raised and responded to from a boat, while bonnets were thrown into the air, handkerchiefs were waved, and last words of adieu shouted to the receding shore, while, high above all, the wild notes of the pipes were heard pouring forth that by far the finest of pibroch tunes, *Cha till mi tuille*, We Shall Return No More!"

The scene at Stornoway in the summer of 1811 was no exception. If, indeed, these Scottish crofters were the Western Canadian equivalent of the Plymouth Pilgrims, their ship, the *Edward and Ann*, was a poor excuse for the *Mayflower*. Undermanned, with a crew of only sixteen boys, and commanded by a temperamental wharf-rat named Hanwell, she had been a derelict recommissioned especially for this journey, and there had been no visible upgrading from her former state of unseaworthiness. The grey sails were mottled with age, the rigging was loose and torn; the hull leaked and some of the caulking was coming off in large, dried chunks. The hold below decks was not divided into cabins, even though the three dozen regular HBC clerks who were being transported on the same ship to York Factory had been promised separate accommodation, as befitted their relatively exalted station.

The disorderly circumstances of the delayed departure were due in part to the fact that the Collector of Customs at Stornoway was John Reid, whose wife was an aunt of Sir Alexander Mackenzie—who had so recently been frustrated in his attempt to abort the Red River land grant to Selkirk. Reid did his best to postpone the ship's departure. During the embarkation process, his son-in-law, a roustabout who called himself "Captain" John McKenzie, circled the *Edward and Ann* in a bumboat, trying to recruit emigrants into the King's army. With windy promises of good treatment in the military he mixed lurid descriptions of the hellish conditions on the other side of the Atlantic.

On July 25, 1811, James Robertson, Reid's chief assistant, took his customs pilot boat out to the *Edward and Ann* to check the final muster. "Captain" McKenzie was at his usual station, yelling at the passengers, urging them to sign up for the army while simultaneously accusing those who had already accepted the King's Shilling of being deserters from His Majesty's forces. The HBC clerks were loudly voicing their dissatisfaction with their quarters, indignant that they were being forced to share the crowded lower deck with the emigrants, with only a stretched sail fastened to the bulkheads dividing their quarters.

The emigrants themselves at first seemed subdued, miserable at having to say their family farewells and feeling more than a little overwhelmed by the havoc. Then Robertson, the customs officer, following the practice of the day, announced to the assembled ship's company that, according to British Admiralty law, no one was obliged to depart against his will. That did it. Pandemonium. Half a dozen passengers rushed the rails and jumped overboard. Others commandeered one of the *Edward and Ann*'s lifeboats and rowed ashore. Several more escaped by crowding aboard Robertson's pilot boat and refusing to budge. Some of the deserters were recaptured, but early next morning Captain Hanwell, fed up with all the delays, weighed anchor and put out to sea, leaving at least 20 of the original 125 emigrants behind. It was July 26, the latest departure date for Hudson Bay ever recorded.

William McGillivray and family

Voyageurs at Dawn, 1871

Sir Alexander Mackenzie

Thomas Douglas,
5th Earl of Selkirk
(1771–1820)

Simon Fraser

The Battle of Seven Oaks, June 19, 1816

William McGillivray

Simon McGillivray

Edward ("Bear") Ellice

Cumberland House

Dr. John McLoughlin, "Father of Oregon," at age 76

Sir George Simpson in his later years

The grand canoe reception on the St. Lawrence given by Simpson for the Prince of Wales

Prairie Camp—Sunset

Shoppers at Fort Edmonton, 1866

The nightmare voyage took sixty-one days, so that by the time the *Edward and Ann* dropped her rusty anchor at Five Fathom Hole off York Factory, it was far too late in the season to chance an overland journey to Red River. Because York Factory's food supplies were particularly strained that season and the incoming HBC employees were granted first call on the post's limited accommodation, the Selkirk party was left huddling in makeshift quarters at Nelson Encampment, twenty-three miles to the west. The diet of deer and ptarmigan, limited in any event, could not prevent a bad outbreak of scurvy, and by breakup the next spring, fewer than half the men were mobile. When Macdonell finally departed on July 6, leading four crude boats up the Hayes River, his followers numbered only twenty-two.

The move south, through wild unknown country along the boiling rivers and across moody Lake Winnipeg, took most of two months. Finally, on August 30, more than a year after leaving Scotland, the bewildered labourers arrived at the junction of the Assiniboine and Red rivers, traditionally a summer meeting place of local Indian bands and the very spot where, in 1738, Pierre Gaultier de Varennes, Sieur de La Vérendrye, had set up the advance depot he had named Fort Rouge. By 1810 there was a small HBC post in the district and the Nor'Westers had established Fort Gibraltar at the river junction under the command of Alexander Macdonell, Miles's cousin. The newly arrived Macdonell chose the west bank of the Red River, just below the Assiniboine and only a mile from the NWC post, as the site of Fort Douglas, which he hoped would soon be recognized as the new colony's headquarters. Guests from the establishments of both companies were invited to the formal ceremonies on September 4 at which Miles Macdonell officially took possession of the land on behalf of Lord Selkirk. A cannon was fired, flags were raised, and the usual "regale" of rum was offered to the Indians and Mixed Bloods watching the transfer of their lands with puzzled goodwill. After he was duly sworn in as governor, Macdonell acknowledged the seven-gun salute, then retired to his tent for snacks. Significantly, he spent his first evening celebrating the founding of the settlement at nearby Gibraltar, the NWC fort. The Nor'Westers not only tolerated but compassionately helped feed the newcomers during these early months, convinced that their venture was a foolish aberration that was bound to fail. A clerk named Willard Wentzel, the son of a Norwegian wool merchant, neatly summed up the Montreal company's attitude when he described the newcomers as "victims sacrificed to the sinister views of a noble imposter."

The ordeal endured by the Selkirk colonists during their first decade at Red River is usually tallied in terms of various armed confrontations with the Montrealers' local agents. But initially, the Nor'Westers did nothing to hamper the settlers. They didn't have to. Nature was a much more dependable enemy.

The newcomers may have been simple crofters from the Highlands, but they were men and women of inordinate fortitude and resourcefulness. They came not with ploughs but with hoes and spades to scratch the impervious surface of the great prairie; they boiled buffalo grease for soap and made starch from potatoes; they learned to pound pemmican, and flavoured it with sturgeon eggs. They survived, mainly because there was nowhere else for them to go.

When Sioux or Mixed Bloods attacked, the settlers hid their children under mats of sod or marsh grass; they knew that the nearest possible source for significant reinforcements was York Factory, more than seven hundred miles away. It might as well have been seven thousand. Wolves, wild dogs and blizzards killed their few precious cattle; for two successive summers clattering plagues of grasshoppers destroyed every edible thing, plugging even the wells and chimneys. The Red River washed away what fragile crops had been planted on its flood plains, and drought withered the remainder of the valiantly rooted vegetation. Rats, wild pigeons, blackbirds, mites—the Red River settlers fought one after the other. When they survived the growing seasons (harvesting only two good crops in the first ten years), they were left to face the winters. Flesh shrivelled in the howling wind, and even the Clearances must at times have seemed more benign than staying alive in this frozen blankness. It was so cold, went the local legend, that you could shout outside in winter without being heard, because the sound of voices froze in the thick, frigid air—but come spring, the woods would be filled with an eerie hubbub as the preserved shouts thawed in the warming sun.

About two hundred and seventy settlers arrived in the first five years—Sutherlands, McKays, Gillespies, McLeods, McPhersons, Mathesons, Polsons, McBeaths, Campbells, Harpers, Bethunes, Isbisters, Finlays, McLeans, Johnstons, McKinnons, Malones, McDonalds, Mathewsons, Murrays, McBeths and Bannermans, among others—beating upstream from York Factory, sometimes led by a piper, always propelled by hope.

THE COLONY'S RELATIONSHIP with the Indians (except for occasional raids by the Sioux) was amicable, the local Saulteaux helping the people at every turn. Not so the Métis. The original settlers of these river banks, they quickly became the most distinctive element in the battles for tenure and supremacy that followed the arrival of the Scottish (and a few Irish) crofters. Métis, a word probably based on the Spanish *mestizo* (mixture), is an elusive term applying to anyone whose culture and genealogy combine the customs, living styles and values of their roots, European and aboriginal. It is, quite simply, the French expression for 'Mixed Blood' peoples, Don McLean of Regina's Gabriel Dumont Institute, which attempts to preserve their records, has noted. "The Mixed Blood people—French and Indian, mainly Cree—who acted as the original work force for the North West Company during the fur trade epoch were known as Les Métis. On the other hand, those mixed blood people who became the major element of the work force for the HBC were mainly Scots or English and Indian. They were known as 'Halfbreeds.' ... Until recent times, the terms Métis and Halfbreed did denote the different European ethnicities of the Mixed Blood peoples, Métis indicating French, and Halfbreed English-Scots. Recently, however, Halfbreed has been seen as a pejorative term, and now all Mixed Blood people refer to themselves proudly as Métis."

A defiant people who prided themselves on being more than the sum of their bloodlines, the Métis enjoyed the natural grace of body proportion of their Indian ancestors, yet they rejected the traditional nomadic mode of life to become guardians of their own turf. Their land, as it became an essential element in their identity, was one of the primary flashpoints between them and the newcomers. This was true especially after 1813, when HBC surveyor Peter Fidler arrived and, using the river-lot system common to Lower Canada, carefully laid out long narrow strips fronting on the river, the aim being to allow the Scottish families to live closer together and relatively near the protection of Fort Douglas. With the Métis linked to the fur-trading interests of the Nor'Westers just as firmly as the Highlanders were to the Hudson's Bay Company, the land tenure issue escalated the potential for conflict between them. "Lord Selkirk, philanthropist and humanitarian," wrote McLean, "seems to have been used as a tool by his more 'hard-nosed' business companions within the Hudson's Bay Company's London Board of Directors. Selkirk, wishing only to find a place to locate the destitute survivors of the Highland clans, was duped into founding the 'Selkirk settlement,' consisting of potential farmers and settlers who were to provide supplies for the Hudson's Bay Company. But this settlement was placed directly under the guns of Fort Gibraltar, in the heart of North West territory, where a trained paramilitary force of Métis cavalry held sway."

What had honed the Métis into a "paramilitary force" was the great semi-annual buffalo hunts. The shaggy beasts were just as vital to the fur trade as the beaver because their meat, pounded into pemmican, provided essential food for the voyageurs and traders criss-crossing the country. The Red River district had become the chief source of pemmican for the Nor'Westers, and the livelihood of most Métis was based first on producing the edible tack, then taking it to the depot at Bas-de-la-Rivière on the Winnipeg River.*

Before the rise of the Métis, buffalo herds were the exclusive prey of the Plains Indians—the Assiniboine, Blackfoot, Cree, Gros Ventres, Peigan, Blood and Sarcee. By herding the animals over cliffs or funnelling them into pounds, the tribes increased the effectiveness of their hunts, but it was the introduction of horses in the first half of the eighteenth century that really multiplied the kill.

The buffalo was a walking emporium. Besides providing the meat that was its prime asset, it had a hide that could be used to make moccasins, leggings and tunics. When tanned, the hides became teepee covers; in the raw, they were cut into sleeping robes and winter coats. The inch-thick skin of a bull's neck could be toughened over a fire until it was strong enough to be a warrior's shield. The bladder made a fine waterproof carrying bag; the sinew was used for bowstrings; the long facial hairs were braided into rope. The animal's bones could be fashioned into cutting and scraping tools, the horns made perfect drinking cups and the tail, a handy flyswatter. The shorter body hairs could be stuffed into the saddle pads of warriors' horses. The buffalo's curved rib-cage yielded ideal sleigh runners; its incisor teeth could be strung into spectacular necklaces; and some of the spinal bones were polished and squared to make gambling dice. The greatest delicacies of all were buffalo tongues, which were salted and painted with molasses for shipment to the world's gourmet tables. Even the buffalo's dried dung was useful; it provided ideal fuel for fires. The hollows in the ground created by wallowing buffalos saved many lives by becoming small but essential reservoirs of water along the parched prairie. It was little wonder that with such a range of life-sustaining attributes these animals were thought to possess magical powers.

The Métis dominated the Red River hunts, which eventually spread south-westward into central Montana and later as far as the Cypress Hills in what are

---

* The boats used in this traffic were so roughly built that at the end of each voyage they were burned, with the handmade nails that had held them together carefully salvaged and carried back to the Red River to pin together the next fleet.

now Alberta and Saskatchewan. Hunting parties would rendezvous near present-day St Boniface, on the east bank of the Red River, and march sixty miles south to Pembina, where a tent city was erected. (The number of hunters swelled through the nineteenth century, reaching a peak of sixteen hundred, with four hundred horses and five hundred dogs, in 1840.) At Pembina, an overall chief and ten captains were elected to enforce the rules of the hunt. These regulations differed with each chase, but there were usually four points of conduct and the same number of precise punishments for disobeying them:

1. No buffalo to be run on the Sabbath.
2. No party to fork off, lag behind or go before without permission.
3. No person or party to run buffalo before the general order.
4. Every captain with his men, in turn, to patrol the camp and keep guard.
5. For a first offence against these laws, offender to have his saddle and bridle cut up.
6. For the second offence, the coat to be taken off the offender's back and be cut up.
7. For the third offence, the offender to be flogged.
8. Any person convicted of theft, even to the value of a sinew, to be brought to the middle of the camp and the crier to call out his or her name three times, adding the word "Thief!" each time.

Every morning the loaded carts fanned out from the encampment (during the 1840 hunt carrying 740 guns, 1,300 pounds of shot, 150 gallons of gunpowder and 6,240 spare flints) and followed the column of mounted riders until scouts had spotted a sizeable herd. The horsemen, four hundred abreast, would rein up in a long prancing line a mile or two from the peacefully grazing animals, waiting for the signal from the chief of the hunt. "*Commencez!*" came the command, and the horsemen approached the herd, slowly at first, then at a trot and finally at full gallop, thundering out of the sun. Too late, the bulls sensed danger, curving their tails and pawing the ground in gestures of magnificent if futile defiance. Flight was their only defence, and it usually came too late. The riders, their mouths filled with bullets, plunged into the mêlée of disoriented animals. Guiding their horses with their knees, the Métis kept their hands free to reach the loose gunpowder in the pockets of their buckskin jackets. After each shot, a palmful of powder was quickly poured down the barrel of the muzzle-loader and shaken home by hitting the gun butt against the saddle. Once he was riding alongside his chosen prey, the hunter would spit a bullet into the muzzle, the saliva making it adhere to the powder during the split second needed to depress the barrel, aim it just below and behind the buffalo's shaggy left shoulder, and puncture the animal's heart. Experienced hunters reloaded and fired fast enough to down three animals in the space of an acre's gallop. Each man threw a cap or scarf onto the body of his prey to identify specific animals for the women, who would later skin the carcasses. The kill seldom lasted more than an hour, with five hundred or so dying buffalo strewn over six square miles of trampled prairie. Some of the wounded animals stood stock-still in their tracks, with fountains of blood pumping through their mouths and nostrils, dying by ounces under the noonday sun. The hunters, their foam-flecked mounts snorting with excitement, rode triumphantly among the mounds of magnificent, expiring animals, boasting of their count.

Even the prolific buffalo could not long withstand massacre on this scale. They had once covered the prairie (in fact, the entire pasture region from Great Slave Lake down to Texas) like a sepia carpet. Naturalist Ernest Thompson Seton estimated that in 1600 there were sixty million in North America. Reports of herds fifty miles long and half as wide taking days to pass a given point were common. Paul Kane, the artist-explorer who toured the Canadian West in the 1840s, described the rich profusion of the animals. "During the whole of the three days it took us to reach Edmonton House," he wrote, "we saw nothing else but these animals covering the plains as far as the eye could reach, and so numerous were they, that at times they impeded our progress, filling the air with dust almost to suffocation. We killed one whenever we required a supply of food, selecting the fattest of the cows, taking only the tongue and boss, or hump, for our present meal, and not burdening ourselves unnecessarily with more."

As white men with their repeating rifles began to participate in the hunt, it degenerated into a blood sport; a million animals a year were killed, though often only their coats and many times only their tongues were utilized. (Buffalo Bill Cody, when he was employed to supply food to workers on the Kansas Pacific Railway, personally shot 4,280 of the animals in one seventeen-month period.) By 1889, only a meagre scattering of wild plains buffalo remained on the continent.* During the winter of 1886–87, starvation prevailed among Indian tribes who had only recently lived bountifully on the buffalo. "Owing to the destruction of game, the Indians, both last winter and last summer, have been in a state of starvation. They are now in a complete state of destitution, and are utterly unable to provide themselves with cloth-ing, shelter, ammunition, or food for the coming winter," a petition to the Canadian government signed by local missionaries reported in 1888, going on to detail "consequent cannibalism" and how a party of twenty-nine Cree Indians had been reduced to three during the winter. The proud Plains Indians were soon forced to eat their horses and dogs, then beg for sustenance wher-ever they could.

Buffalo herds in the United States blocked early train travel, and passen-gers often shot the beasts for fun. The animals loved rubbing themselves on telegraph poles, destroying links in the communications system faster than they could be repaired. To avert the damage, sharp spikes called bradawls were installed, but the effect was not anticipated. According to one report published in Kansas after the earliest installations, "From the first time they came to scratch, they seemed to have felt a sensation in their thick hides that thrilled them from horn to tail. They would go fifteen miles to find a bradawl. They fought huge battles around the poles containing them, and the victor would proudly climb the mountainous heap of rump and hump of the fallen, and scratch himself into bliss until the bradawl broke, or the pole came down."

If the buffalo was the Métis equivalent of the fur trade's beaver, the Red River cart was its canoe. These creaky wooden conveyances were so impor-tant to their early way of life that the Métis were sometimes called "wagon-men" and in the Indian sign language of the time were described as being "half cart and half human." An integral part of the buffalo culture (there were 1,210 Red River carts employed in the 1840 hunt), the two-wheeled carts,

---

* Paradoxically, the buffalo contributed to the welfare of their tormentors even after they vanished from the plains. Their bones (22,000 tons of them littering the Canadian West) were collected, processed into fertilizer and resold to nourish the soil of what had once been their dwelling place. When natural history museums learned how fast the buffalo were disappearing, there was a mad rush to collect specimens before they did become extinct. The descendants of the plains buffalo now number about 40,000; some are free-ranging, some are in parks and zoos. Some are raised commercially for their meat, and there are still places where they are hunted and shot as game. The largest concentration (5,000) is in Wood Buffalo National Park, strad-dling the border between Alberta and the Northwest Territories.

like the birchbark canoe, had the advantage of being manufactured entirely out of locally available materials. Their wooden frames were held together with wooden pegs instead of nails or screws, and even the tires were made from buffalo hide, which had been stretched on the wheels when wet and allowed to shrink as it dried. The high, concave wheels could be removed and placed inside the main box of the cart, which, when enclosed in a buffalo-hide tarpaulin, could be paddled across lakes and rivers. The single axle was never greased because that would have attracted dust and grit, and the result-ant noise was comparable to that of five thousand fingernails drawn across a thousand blackboards. Pulled by oxen or over-the-hill horses, the Red River carts travelled in long, undulating caravans down to St Paul, over to Portage la Prairie and across to Fort Qu'Appelle.

The Red River carts, buffalo hunts and, above all, the land on which they had settled gave the Métis a sense of belonging—and that, in turn, meant that unlike the other non-Indian inhabitants of the Fur Country, they had a specific place of their own to defend. They were not, at least not yet, a "New Nation," as some of their more radical adherents maintained, but they were already a political force—Western Canada's first nationalists, a populist move-ment in search of a cause.

That cause was provided by the arrival of the Selkirk settlers. Here was a group of cast-offs from another continent insisting *they* had been granted title to the very land the Métis claimed by right of occupation—not to mention descent from Cree and Saulteaux ancestors who had been its original inhabitants.

Given the rallying cry of driving out the unwelcome intruders and the fact that the discipline of the buffalo hunts and their brushes with the Sioux had toughened the Métis into effective warriors, all they needed to launch Canada's first war of liberation was someone to command them.

Showdown

"If we are to be poor for three generations, we must absolutely fight this out."
—Lady Selkirk

THE LEADER WHO EMERGED to fill this pivotal role at the crucial moment was Cuthbert Grant, embodying in his person (and later in his actions) the coming together of the two pressures building up against the Selkirk settlers: the Métis's growing sense of nationhood, and the avowed strategy of the Nor'Westers to stop the Hudson's Bay Company from interfering with their trade by driving out the land-squatters threatening their supply lines. Grant may have been manipulated by one side or the other in this unusual melding of commercialism and chauvinism. But he didn't have to be. At that point in his life, he really was *both*, a Métis patriot and a loyal Nor'Wester.

The son of a Cree mother and a distinguished NWC wintering partner, also called Cuthbert, who had led the way to Great Slave Lake and become a leading member of the Beaver Club, Grant was baptized a Presbyterian at the Scotch Church on St Gabriel Street in Montreal and sent to school in Scotland. Orphaned when he was six, young Cuthbert grew up as a ward of the man appointed executor in his father's will—William McGillivray, who later became effective head of the NWC. That exalted sponsorship won him admittance to the inner circles of the Montreal trading concern virtually from childhood, so that Cuthbert was marked as special from the beginning. In 1812, at nineteen, after having spent eleven years in the apprenticing pursuits of a well-tended Scottish schoolboy, he was sent out to the Qu'Appelle River as an NWC clerk, destined for rapid advancement. His sister had married the current master of Fort Gibraltar, the NWC's installation at Red River, and shortly after he went west, Cuthbert fell in love with and married Elizabeth McKay, whose brother was head of a nearby HBC trading post known as Brandon House.

These diverse kinship links and his demonstrated abilities as a hunter, horse-
man, organizer and warrior quickly moved him into a position of natural leadership. When the NWC decided to appoint him to the vague office of "Captain
of the Métis," it was only confirmation of his already existing status as the
recognized leader of his community. "He was able to identify himself with the
new Métis nation, and stands at the beginning of their history, as Louis Riel
stands at the end," concluded historians Margaret MacLeod and W.L. Morton.

It was the provocative tactics of Miles Macdonell, governor of the putative
Selkirk Settlement, that united the Métis as never before. A Roman Catholic
of Loyalist stock with the sublime faith that characterizes both, Macdonell had
with one stroke removed any vestiges of doubt as to whether the settlers would
interfere with the essential flow of pemmican from Red River to depots along
the NWC trading routes. Two more boatloads of newcomers had arrived, and
Macdonell didn't have enough horses to hunt his own buffalo. His puny farms
were years from being self-sustaining; his people were hungry; yet pemmican
by the ton was being shipped out of Red River to feed the NWC's distant
brigades. Arguing that the life-sustaining food was being produced on land
owned by Lord Selkirk, he issued the proclamations that would become
opening shots in the Pemmican War: an edict forbidding further exports of the
staple from Red River without his permission, and a prohibition against the
hunting of buffalo from horseback within the Selkirk territories. He followed
these foolhardy initiatives by confiscating four hundred bags of NWC pemmican and moving it under armed guard to Fort Douglas, boasting that he had
force enough "to crush all the Nor'Westers ... should they be so hardy as to
resist ... authority."

As if bent on self-destruction, Macdonell then escalated the antagonism.
He sent notices to the commanders of NWC forts on Selkirk lands ordering
them to evacuate their posts within six months. That was too much. At their
annual council meeting in the Great Hall at Fort William, the Nor'Westers
pledged to force the colony out of existence, first by weakening it with efforts
to persuade the settlers to desert, and later by inciting the Indians and Métis
against any who remained. As a third step, Miles Macdonell was to be arrested
on charges of illegal seizure of pemmican and sent to Montreal for trial,
leaving the survivors leaderless. The partner placed in charge of these tactics
was Duncan Cameron, a veteran harasser of the HBC, who arrived at Red River
resplendent in the scarlet uniform of a British army major, complete with
epaulettes and dangling sword. That bit of theatre, with hints that he held the

King's Commission, cowed the settlers whenever he arrived at their farms, accompanied by a restless retinue of Métis on wild-eyed horses, offering free transport and land in the balmy acreage of Lower and Upper Canada. (One of his aides-de-camp was Cuthbert Grant, wearing the uniform of an ensign in the Voyageurs Corps that had fought in the War of 1812.) Cameron's appeals, phrased in the Gaelic so dear to the settlers, often did the trick. His propaganda was aided by the nocturnal visits of hooting Métis firing shots in the air, riding over crops and occasionally burning a barn. Among the most active participants in these nightly missions was Grant, now clearly in charge of his people, convincing the Métis that they were the true lords of this rich soil and that their freedom depended on defying the settlers' legal pretence to ownership of the Red River Valley. From a camp at Frog Plain commanding a broad reach of the Red River, he participated in several shoot-outs, stealing the remaining settlers' implements and torching their houses. By summer's end of 1815, all but thirteen families had abandoned Red River, and their one cannon had been removed from Fort Douglas and mounted at Fort Gibraltar. Hoping to avert bloodshed, Macdonell surrendered to Cameron at the NWC fort and was promptly spirited away, first to Fort William and then to Montreal.

Disoriented and unprotected, the remaining straggle of settlers retreated by boat to temporary quarters near the north end of Lake Winnipeg. In the former colony, bands of Métis razed farms, burned buildings, attacked Fort Douglas and the small adjoining grist mill. The settlers' last sight of their utopia was smoke wafting in the soft summer breeze and the rampaging Métis spurring their buffalo-runners across the fields, trampling the precious wheat, barley and potatoes. For a while, the only sign of life left at the Selkirk Settlement was a salvage group of four Highlanders (John McLeod, Hugh McLean, Archibald Currie and James MacIntosh) who braved the taunts of the Métis to gather some of the abandoned tools and seed grains. Later, as if signalling some symbolic resurrection, the wheat, barley and potatoes did recover and ripen, unmatched, under the golden summer sun.

ON HIS WAY FROM MONTREAL to reopen the Athabasca Country trade, the HBC's Colin Robertson had by chance met the Red River refugees and persuaded them to return just in time to harvest the crops. That autumn another group of Scottish immigrants arrived, led by Robert Semple, the colony's new governor. Semple was a Boston-born Loyalist and popular travel writer whose innocence of cunning was matched by his overburden of self-importance. His commission provided dramatic proof of the Nor'Westers' and Métis's contention that the Selkirk Settlement was little more than an agency of the HBC, since he had been simultaneously appointed the colony's new governor and chief of the Company's Northern and Southern departments. That fall and winter, Colin Robertson took it upon himself to woo the Métis. A rogue with rusty sideburns and a long nose that swung around menacingly like a compass needle, Robertson was six feet tall and not afraid of any man's shadow. He had gained well-deserved notoriety as a scrapper but never uttered an oath stronger than "Oh for the love of beaver!" The Don Quixote of the Fur Country, he was one of the few traders who had read most of Shakespeare's works and could recite the main soliloquies. He had spent much of his energy—both in the Northwest and during his visits to England—trying to persuade the Bay men to drop their "slow, jog-trot manner" and adopt more of what he called "the glittering pomposity" of the Nor'Westers.

Robertson's entreaties to the Métis to remain neutral in the confrontation between the two fur companies worked mainly because Cuthbert Grant was not in residence at Red River, having moved to Qu'Appelle to be with the beloved Bethsy, as he called his wife, Elizabeth. Without him, there was no strong spokesman as a focus for their pride and heritage. On March 17, 1816, when Robertson attacked and temporarily captured Gibraltar, the NWC stronghold, and arrested Duncan Cameron, none of the Métis joined in the fort's defence. Inside Cameron's desk Robertson found documentary evidence that the Nor'Westers intended to engineer the final destruction of Selkirk's settlement that summer.

Robertson left the colony early in June, warning Semple to prepare for war. On the very day of his departure, the impulsive Semple ordered that the captured Fort Gibraltar be demolished. Some of the logs from its ramparts were rafted downstream to Fort Douglas, and whatever couldn't be moved was set ablaze. The Métis gathered in sullen clusters to watch the NWC stronghold burning. "The sight of the great fort in flames was too much," wrote Marjorie Wilkins Campbell, for "soon the fire which had been smouldering in every one of them also burst into flame. To each the destruction of the North West Company post was a warning of what might happen to his own small home. Like a prairie fire, news of the destruction of Fort Gibraltar raced from post to post, and from camp to camp wherever Métis and Indians gathered to hunt buffalo. The ancient war spirit of their Indian mothers, augmented by many a strain of fighting French and Highland Scots paternity, urged them to defend their existence; and the Nor'Westers were no longer in any mood to enforce restraint."

Here was the final, unforgivable act. Led by Cuthbert Grant, recently promoted by the NWC to be their "Captain-General," the Métis unfurled the New Nation's flag (blue with a horizontal figure 8 on its fly), cleaned their guns and waited.

Some friendly Saulteaux tried to warn Semple of the incipient dangers, but he would not listen. He did order one of his subordinates, the hard-drinking Lieutenant Ener Holte, late of the Swedish Navy,* to arm the cannon on the colony's schooner. The thirty-five-foot keelboat, brought in from Norway House, was anchored at the mouth of the Red River to intercept incoming NWC canoes. In the tradition of his service, Holte saluted and delivered himself of a Nelsonian pledge: "I will be in my proper glory and will give the N.W. scoundrels a drubbing if I can!"

The target of Cuthbert Grant's first attack was the HBC installation at Brandon House, then commanded by Peter Fidler. After plundering the fort, Grant gathered his troops and, taking his orders from a group of Nor'Westers recently arrived from Fort William, decided to run Semple's blockade at the Red River junction. He had with him sixty-two men, most of them done up in war paint. Thus began the assault on Red River. This was no longer an informal bunching of malcontents out to make trouble; this was an army on the march.

INSIDE FORT DOUGLAS, Governor Semple had just received word of danger. Moustouche Boutino, a Métis who was on friendly terms with the settlers because Dr James White, the colony's doctor, had treated his recent wound, had arrived to warn that Grant and his armed band were on their way to capture the fort. The governor ignored the warning even when, late in the afternoon of June 19, 1816, a lookout spotted the advancing troops.

Still convinced that diplomacy might win the day, Semple decided to meet these marauders and read them a proclamation forbidding Métis to commit acts of violence against the colony. He ordered Lieutenant Holte and Captain John Rogers of the Royal Engineers, who was serving as his second-in-command, to round up two dozen men to accompany him. Asked whether

---

* Exactly how an alcoholic Swedish naval officer came to be stationed in the middle of the Canadian prairies at this crucial juncture remains unclear.

they should take the fort's three-pound field-piece with them, Semple replied that it would not be necessary: his only intention was to discover what the intruders wanted.

Grant and his mounted men had reached a cluster of trees known locally as Seven Oaks. The two groups met there in the early twilight of the late spring day. The Métis halted in half-moon formation. Semple and his men advanced in single file. And then all grew quiet—a silence more intense than the absence of noise, with even the sweet sounds of nature temporarily stilled. A horse snorted. The Métis, reinforced by new arrivals at the edges of their formation, began to tighten their half-circle, pressing Semple's irregulars towards the river bank. Grant signalled one of his subalterns, a Métis named François Firmin Boucher, to order the governor and his men to lay down their arms or they would be shot. As Boucher urged his horse forward, Grant covered Semple with his gun. The stilted dialogue that followed caught the supercharged tensions of the moment:

"What do you want?" asked Boucher.

"What do *you* want?" demanded the affronted governor.

"We want our fort," was the spitting reply.

"Well, *go* to your fort!" Semple snapped back.

"Why have you destroyed our fort? You damned rascal!"

No Métis was going to call him, Governor of Rupert's Land, a rascal. Semple shouted something like "Scoundrel? Do *you* tell me so?" and made a grab for the stock of Boucher's gun while seizing the reins of his horse.

Cuthbert Grant pulled the trigger, wounding Semple in the thigh, and that shot set off the slaughter. Lieutenant Holte was the first to die. As if pulled by an invisible string, the Métis slid down behind their horses and levelled their guns across the animals' backs, while the Fort Douglas contingent milled in confusion around Semple to see if he was badly hurt. They were thus exposed to the full fury of the Métis cross-fire, and they began to die, returning random fire as best they could. When the Métis threw themselves on the ground to reload, the Semple survivors thought they had all been felled and with a cheer threw their hats in the air. Before those hats had landed, another multiple blast resounded. Rogers, the Royal Engineer, charged the Métis with his bayonet and was halted in his tracks, dying on his knees.

Within fifteen minutes, Semple had been killed by a Métis named François Deschamps, who placed his gun against the governor's chest and pulled the trigger. Twenty of his men lay dead at Seven Oaks. Only one of the Métis had been killed and only one prisoner taken—John Pritchard, an NWC deserter now in Selkirk's service, who feigned death, then begged for mercy, and was used by Grant to deliver a surrender demand to Fort Douglas. The settlement gave in without resistance, terminating the Selkirk Settlement for the second time in two years as its inhabitants departed once again to their temporary shelters at the north end of Lake Winnipeg.

But the day's horror was not yet done. At Seven Oaks, the bodies of the dead were stripped and dismembered in an orgy of mutilation. The best summing up of that chilling encounter is by Don McLean of the Gabriel Dumont Institute: "The nameless, faceless directors of the Hudson's Bay Company had placed the Highland Scots and Irish labourers into the mouth of a loaded gun; the Métis hunters, dupes of the North West Company, joyfully pulled the trigger."

THOSE FIFTEEN MINUTES at Seven Oaks changed everything. No longer a commercial contest with the occasional skirmish and post-burning, the struggle between the Nor'Westers and Bay men had turned into a guerrilla war, fought along a four-thousand-mile front with unreliable troops and scheming generals. The Northwest became a land to flee across, as leaders of both sides gradually realized victory was impossible. Success would be determined by survival.

What changed most was that for the first time in the long rivalry between the two companies, the fur trade itself had become subordinate to their struggle for supremacy. No restraint or discipline was applied to the trapping of the beaver (even their sucklings were being skinned), to the distribution of rum and brandy (any excess was permissible) or to the tactics used in pillaging competitors' forts (at one point forty-two murder charges had been sworn out against Nor'Westers). Because the social contract had been so blatantly flouted, Lord Bathurst, the British colonial secretary, moved to appoint a commission to investigate the mass murders, and the Governor-in-Chief of Canada issued a royal proclamation on May 1, 1817, in the name of the Prince Regent, against "open warfare in the Indian Territories."

Selkirk himself had meanwhile returned to Lower Canada during the autumn of 1815 to introduce Lady Selkirk to Montreal society. He hired a lawyer named Samuel Gale to protect his interests and had discussions about the fur trade with the NWC's William McGillivray. After preliminary negotiating postures, Selkirk was handed an astonishing proposal: the two companies should merge for a trial period of seven years, with the Montrealers supplying two-thirds of the goods and capital (and receiving two-thirds of the profits) while the Hudson's Bay Company retained the balance as a junior partner. The scheme was turned down because of the proportions being demanded and the NWC's reluctance to recognize the validity of the HBC charter, but the idea of amalgamation had been broached.

Having requested and been denied an official military escort for his intended inspection journey to Red River, Selkirk recruited instead four officers and a hundred members of the de Meuron and de Wattville regiments—Swiss, German and Middle European mercenaries who, after fighting in the Napoleonic battles, had been detoured to Malta and brought to Canada during the War of 1812. They accepted Selkirk's offer of free land at Red River in return for military service as it might be required, and the expedition moved west. Selkirk had himself sworn in as a justice of the peace, hired a hundred voyageurs, arranged for the canoes, and set off; he planned to bypass Fort William, hoping to reach his troubled settlement without provoking the Nor'Westers. He left Montreal in mid-June of 1816, and it was at Sault Ste Marie that news of the Seven Oaks killings reached his party. At this point Selkirk's tuberculosis was so far advanced that his accompanying physician, Dr John Allan, hesitated to pass on the gruesome details. But when Selkirk heard the facts, he vowed to lead his mercenary band against the very heart of the villainous Montrealers' enterprise by capturing their great depot at Fort William.

On August 12, 1816, after most of the winterers had departed westward, Selkirk's armed flotilla swept out of Lake Superior and set up camp on the bank opposite the fort's main gate. Selkirk soon learned that William McGillivray himself was among the fifteen senior Montreal partners in residence and charged him with treason, conspiracy, and being an accessory to murder.

Hardly able to credit the outrageous message from Selkirk's emissary, McGillivray, accompanied by two of his senior lieutenants, Dr John McLoughlin and Kenneth McKenzie, decided to humour his visitors and pay what he imagined would be a routine courtesy call on this crazed aristocrat who seemed unaware of who ruled these woods. Selkirk promptly had the trio arrested. McGillivray submitted to the indignities, whispering loudly enough to be heard that it really was a dishonour to be fooled by this "piddling lord." Selkirk then ordered one of his assistants, John McNab, late of the Glengarry Fencibles, to arrest the twelve other partners still known to be at Fort William.

McNab later remembered the ensuing events as follows: "We landed, and proceeded to the gate, as before, where several of the proprietors were standing and a number of men (their servants) and many Indians were assembled. The warrant was served on two of the gentlemen, but, on approaching the third, resistance was actually made, and a declaration uttered, that no further submission would be given to the execution of my duty, till Mister M'Gillivray was given up. In consequence I was nearly shut out of the fort by attempts to close one leaf of the gates.... At this moment I expressed the necessity of support to Captain D'Orsonnens [the de Meuron commander], who with much alacrity, aided by several of his men, instantly rushed in, and prevented the gate from being closed.... They ran forward, and, in a moment, took possession of two small cannons that were placed in the court within the gate."

The partners were herded into the Great Hall. They stood there beneath the bust of their patron saint, Simon McTavish, not quite sure whether to laugh or cry at the antics of this wearisome and apparently deranged Scottish earl. But Selkirk was in no mood to be gentle with anyone representing the North West Company. As far as he was concerned, these vicious woodsmen had murdered twenty-one of his people, and he was determined to "cut up by the roots one of the most abominable combinations that was ever suffered to exist in the British Dominions." He ordered the detainees to produce their papers, hoping to find evidence proving they had been responsible for ordering Cuthbert Grant's attack. But weakened by his illness and the day's excitement, Selkirk could not continue the interrogation. He impounded the documents and had seals placed on their containers, naively admonishing these "agents of infamy" not to touch the files until next morning.

Barely was he out the door on his way to rest at his camp across from the fort when the Nor'Westers began to scurry around frantically gathering up the documents by the armload, pitching them into the oversized stove of the Great Hall's kitchen. All night the papers burned, shooting sparks into the starlit sky. "The news of Seven Oaks," John Morgan Gray, the best of the Selkirk historians, has speculated, "meant much more guilt than most were prepared to shoulder. The group seems to have behaved as if morality were a matter of being found out; judged on this basis, they were guilty of a great wrong." That night, the Nor'Westers stealthily placed guns in hidden caches on the property for a possible attack on the Selkirk camp.

Alexander Fraser, the NWC blacksmith who had spent such a pungent eternity in the fort's privy-like prison, deserted the next morning, crossed over to the enemy camp, and told Selkirk about the bonfire of documents and the hidden arms. The guns were soon discovered and confiscated, and a careful search of the partners' premises turned up an overlooked fragment of incriminating evidence in the form of a list of the rewards presented by the NWC to the Métis who had participated at Seven Oaks. After a desultory attempt to interrogate the Nor'Westers, Selkirk sent them back to Montreal under guard, with only one partner, a weak-kneed boozer named Daniel McKenzie, staying behind. The departing partners suspected him of being a turncoat, and as they were being pushed into the canoes, Kenneth McKenzie (no relation) whispered to Daniel McKenzie: "If ever I am acquitted [of murder], I'll blow out your brains!" (The threat was never carried out because Kenneth McKenzie and eight others were drowned on Lake Superior during the return trip to Montreal.)

Realizing that his ravaged colony at Red River could not hope to feed his accompanying army, Selkirk decided to winter at Fort William. He moved into the partners' suites adjoining the Great Hall and, walking about that alien fort, felt a long way from the elegant mansion at St Mary's Isle. His only consolation during that dreary winter was the correspondence he received from his beloved wife, Jean, in Montreal. "Everything in your expedition turns out for the best," she reported, cheerfully putting the best face on the situation, "and last of all the great armada, with all the warrants and constables, partners, clerks, Iroquois and guns and Congreve rockets, melts away and disappears, and a little canoe comes dropping in now and then, and one after another of the partners return to Montreal looking very foolish, while all the world are laughing at them."

Using some fairly dubious tactics, Selkirk persuaded the faltering Daniel McKenzie to approve sale of the fort's food stores for £3,000, then dispatched his mercenaries westward to recapture Fort Douglas. This they accomplished in a surprise night attack without firing a shot, rushing the fort under the cloud-concealed moon and scaling its walls using pre-cut tree branches. The victorious troops captured several other NWC outposts, notifying the settlers who had scattered north towards Lake Winnipeg after the Seven Oaks débâcle that they could return to their land. By June they were joined by Lord Selkirk himself. Here at last, more than half a decade after he had first dreamed of providing a sanctuary for his beleaguered crofters, Selkirk was able to see for himself the hardship they had faced and the small promise their situation held out to them. Seized by the feverish exhilaration of disease and the infectious beauty of the prairie summer, he walked among his people like a kilted messiah, granting freedom from further land payments to some two dozen of his most deserving disciples.

By early autumn, knowing that he must deal with the barrage of charges and countercharges stemming from his illegal occupation of Fort William, Lord Selkirk returned eastward to face the uneven scales of Canadian justice.

THE TURMOIL AT RED RIVER had galvanized the Hudson's Bay Company into unaccustomed activity. Since the survival of the colony continued to menace the NWC's supply lines, this was the moment for the HBC to strike at Athabasca itself, the heart of the northwestern fur trade. Because that distant territory clearly lay beyond Prince Rupert's 1670 charter, the Nor'Westers had long regarded its fur-rich stretches as their own.

Selkirk's vivid exploits had demonstrated the vulnerability of the Montreal traders and instilled in the HBC officers and servants renewed vitality and pride of place. They felt ready at last to challenge their rivals in their home territory. Besides, a recent analysis of returns by individual posts had yielded the unexpected information that even those stations most fiercely competing with the NWC for a share of the catch were showing higher profits than the peaceful but fur-poor forts around Hudson Bay.

During the five years after Seven Oaks, the continent-wide rivalry between the NWC and HBC was nowhere contested more bitterly than within the Athabasca Country. Here the last violent clashes between the two companies determined the outcome of their protracted quarrel.

Athabasca became the Culloden of the fur-trade wars.

Infuriated by Selkirk's capture of Fort William, the Nor'Westers immediately seized the five tiny posts the Bay men had established in Athabasca during their tentative 1815 foray. That expedition, originally led by Colin Robertson, who broke away to help lead the settlers back to Red River, ended in disaster. Command was assumed by John Clarke, a thirty-four-year-old Montrealer with the nasty habit of flicking specks of gunpowder into his opponents' eyes. He had served a decade in Athabasca as a clerk with the NWC, leaving it to join Astor's Pacific Fur Company, and had come within a hair's breadth of being scalped after he hanged an Indian for stealing a silver goblet in the Spokane River country and was attacked by the victim's brothers seeking revenge. He returned to Montreal, where Robertson hired him, mainly for his fighting ways. Nicknamed "Bon Garçon," Clarke loved

swinging the diamond-studded cane given to him by John Jacob Astor—
especially in the thick of a fight.

Clarke had launched the Company's return to Athabasca by building Fort
Wedderburn on Potato Island, right across the channel from the Nor'Westers'
headquarters at Fort Chipewyan. It was moved when Samuel Black, the NWC
bully who had so thoroughly tormented Peter Fidler, drew a line in the sand
and dared any Bay man to cross it. Three did and were "fatally pricked in the
body." Clarke constructed several other small trading outlets on Great Slave
Lake and along the Athabasca River. Then he took fifty canoemen up the
Peace to establish the Company's presence there. He carried no supplies,
hoping to catch enough game along the way to keep them alive, but the
Nor'Westers chased the animals from his route and threatened any Indians
willing to help feed them. The embargo worked so well that sixteen Bay men
eventually starved to death, bringing the Company's seasonal death toll in
Athabasca to nineteen, close to the Seven Oaks total. By the time Clarke and
his desperate survivors stumbled back to Fort Wedderburn, all the HBC posts
had been captured and Black arrested the Bay men for theft. (Some
Nor'Westers had planted small quantities of pemmican in the path of the
starving men, and it was this food, which they had gobbled down, that
provided the excuse for the arrests.) They were allowed to depart only when
they took an oath to stay away from Athabasca for another two years. By the
summer of 1818, the Athabasca venture had cost the HBC three dozen lives
and £50,000. Yet the Company was barely able to retain one tiny fishing camp
in the area.

Realizing that only a massive assault could turn the tide, the HBC commissioned Colin Robertson to lead an attack brigade of nearly two hundred armed
men into the disputed territory. The flotilla was equipped to Robertson's
extravagant tastes, with plenty of buffalo tongues and kegs of Madeira. "The
lady with the ring in her nose is now holding a plum cake and with her delicate brown fingers is picking out the fruit," reads an enigmatic entry in the
journal of his voyage west.

His determination (and Madeira) quickly proved effective in attracting the
Indians; within weeks of his arrival, Robertson had restored Fort Wedderburn
and was trading with four dozen Indian chiefs who had previously been loyal
NWC customers. The Montrealers called in reinforcements, led by Simon
McGillivray, Jr., the Mixed Blood son of that company's reigning grandee. But
the day-to-day harassment was, as usual, left to the malevolent Samuel

Black—though sometimes with mixed results. "Black the Nor'Wester is now in his glory leading his bullies," Robertson noted. "Every evening they come over to our fort in a body, calling on our men to come out and fight pitched battles. One of their hair-pulling bullies got his challenge accepted and an unmerciful thrashing to boot from a little Frenchman of ours—Boucher.... Our men are in high spirits. The Indians have regained confidence in us and boldly leave the Nor'Westers every day for the Hudson's Bay."

Then, on October 11, 1818, while Robertson was outside the HBC fort reading the funeral service for one of his men who had been drowned in a fishing accident, Black, accompanied by the young McGillivray, seized him at gunpoint and bundled him off into Fort Chipewyan. Robertson's diary vividly described his arrival inside the enemy camp: "Landing, I dashed for their Indian Hall and at once ... called on the Indians, representing that the cowardly attack was an effort to reduce *them* to slavery; but Black rushed up to stop me. Seizing a fork on the hall table I kept the vagabond at bay. I loaded him with every abuse and evil name I could think of, then to the Indians: 'Do not abandon the Hudson's Bay on this account! There are brave men at our fort to protect you! That fellow was not brave enough to *seize* me; he *stole* me, and he would now rob you of your hunt if it were not for the young men I have left in my fort. Tell Clarke not to be discouraged. We will be revenged for this, but not like wolves prowling in the bushes. We will capture them as we captured them at Fort William, with the sun shining on our faces.' At this moment, the Indian chief came up and squeezing my hand, whispered, 'Never mind, white man, we are your friends.'"

Robertson was soon pinioned and confined inside a small shack next to the fort's privy. There he stayed for eight months. Apart from not having access to his Madeira (or ladies with rings in their noses), Robertson's main worry was that his troops had been left leaderless. Daily operational decisions had to be made to maintain and expand the HBC's beachhead. He persuaded his captors to allow him a keg of Madeira and devised a complex but literate code for sending out messages: "I began to arrange all our Posts, Gentlemen, Principal men with those of opponents in numbers, then all the monosyllables on which the meaning of a sentence rested, also sentences intimately connected with the affairs of this country ... untill my numerical figures amounted to 600. When the cypher was completed, the most difficult task remained, to convey the copy to my friends at Fort Wedderburn, which was effected by means of a small keg. First the cypher was written on long strips of paper having a pretty large margin on each side, then rolled up so tight as not to admit water beyond the first fold. Both ends were sealed; this finished, I perforated a small hole with a bent gun worm close by the bung, through which I passed a piece of holland twine, then hooked it up from the bunghole and attached to the end of the twine my Packet, repassed it through the bunghole, drew it up from the small aperture close to the stave of the keg. To fasten the letter I drove a small peg into the hole, over which I rubbed a little dust, that neither the hole nor the sound of paper could either be seen or heard."

That may have been ingenious, but there was no way for Robertson to inform his men how to locate the message—or to tell them there was a message there at all. The empty barrel was flushed out and put into storage without being examined for its hidden contents. Robertson next requested his personal volume of Shakespeare. He devised another code by annotating *King Henry IV,* and his men soon caught on. But he was eventually spotted scribbling out the coded instructions, and the Nor'Westers decided to pack him off to Montreal, still under arrest. On the way, the canoe in which he was travelling overturned in the rapids at Île-à-la-Crosse. No foul play was ever proved, but two of his NWC guards, both expert swimmers, mysteriously drowned, while a smiling Robertson bobbed out of the stream and waded to shore. He made his escape when they were passing Cumberland House by the simple stratagem of asking, on his word of honour, if he could step inside the HBC fort to say his farewells. Once inside, Robertson had the doors bolted and refused to come out. The angry Nor'Westers continued on without him.

In one of the messages he had managed to sneak past his guards during his imprisonment, Robertson had warned William Williams, the HBC's recently appointed Governor of Rupert's Land, that the Nor'West partners would probably be returning to Montreal loaded with furs and could be ambushed at Grand Rapids, the rendezvous near the juncture of the Saskatchewan River and Lake Winnipeg. This was a popular resting place for the NWC brigades heading east; while the voyageurs took the canoes through the rapids, the *bourgeois* could stroll down the portage trail swapping the tittle-tattle of the fur trade.

Williams, who had received the Robertson dispatch, was a new breed within the HBC's service. Because the Company was now engaged in war as much as in trade, it hired this truculent former East India Company sea captain to look after its affairs. As successor to the murdered Robert Semple, Williams required little motivation for the fight with the Nor'Westers. On the strength of Robertson's message, he left Red River aboard the colony's armed schooner with a detachment of twenty de Meuron soldiers, cannon loaded, and a sheaf of warrants. As the annual NWC brigades arrived at Grand Rapids, the accompanying *bourgeois* were apprehended by Williams's troopers. The trap netted five senior NWC partners, including Benjamin Frobisher, the son of an NWC founder. Each was spirited away to a temporary enclosure on a nearby mosquito-infested island. One of the partners, pleading a call of nature, disappeared in the bush. To thwart pursuit, he left a suicide note claiming he had drowned himself by jumping into the lake with a stone tied around his neck. That was not a brilliant improvisation because the lake at that point was only two feet deep, but no one went after him. The remaining prisoners were eventually taken to York Factory, but Frobisher, who escaped along the way, starved to death trying to get to the NWC post at Moose Lake.

The Grand Rapids affair (and the fact that along with the partners and the loads of fur, Williams captured documents incriminating the NWC in Seven Oaks and other incidents) seriously undermined the Montrealers' morale. "Our opponents," Robertson wrote to Williams, "have lowered their tone; they talk now of conducting their business on amicable principles…. The North West Company's servants have the old story of a junction in their heads … whatever their prospects may be, there is certainly a great change in their conduct; the affair of the Grand Rapids has not so much as produced a menace."

But the North West Company was not done yet. Outraged by Williams's behaviour, its partners promptly issued warrants for his arrest. During the following summer the Nor'Westers mounted their own ambush at Grand Rapids and were highly pleased when Colin Robertson, on his way east from a winter on the Peace River, fell into their hands. He was arrested and kept under close guard in preparation for shipment to Lower Canada.

Well aware that there were more warrants papering Montreal courtrooms calling for his arrest as soon as he stuck a foot into Lower Canada's jurisdiction, Robertson again mustered his natural talent for survival. He escaped by flinging a dish of biscuits in his captors' faces during a meal break and, after holding them off with a stolen gun, made a run for the U.S. border. Once in New York, he immediately sailed for London to participate in the negotiations rumoured to be leading towards amalgamation of the two fur-trading concerns. On his way across the Atlantic aboard the Western Ocean packet *Albion*, he found himself in the company of two arch-enemies, the NWC partners Dr John

McLoughlin and Angus Bethune. As the ship was about to land and the passengers were lining up to sign chits for gratuities to the dining-room stewards, Robertson and his friend, a Roman Catholic monsignor, happened to be standing between Bethune and McLoughlin.

"Come, [Abbé]," chided the irrepressible Robertson, "put down your name; I don't like to sign between two North Westers."

"Never mind, Mr R.," came the reply. "Remember our Saviour was crucified between two thieves."

AT THE END of his Red River visit, Lord Selkirk, Robertson's hero, was struggling to extricate himself from the final and most traumatic episode of his Canadian misadventures. He had spent most of the interval since returning from that brief happy summer at Red River in stultifying courtrooms, first in Montreal and later at York (Toronto), pursuing the 170 charges he had preferred against the NWC and its partners. Characteristically, he entertained no doubts about their total guilt and his utter innocence, yet he was being forced to justify his own actions.

Selkirk spent, besides his time and the last of his energies, £100,000 out of his own pocket (and another £40,000 out of the HBC's) defending himself against a bewildering array of mischievously worded charges, trying to extract justice from a variety of contemptuous witnesses, corrupt judges and a colonial administration barely able to suppress its fervent wish to be rid of him. "If we are to be poor for three generations," the faithful Lady Selkirk wrote to her husband, "we must absolutely fight this out." Although the grand juries returned eighteen true bills against various NWC partners and associates, only one man was found guilty, and his sentence was never carried out. Not a single marksman from Seven Oaks was convicted of anything. Cuthbert Grant jumped bail and escaped by canoe back to Red River. All charges against him were later quietly dropped.

The bewildered Selkirk at first blamed the fact that most of the magistrates sitting in judgment over him were either associates or relatives of the Nor'Westers he had brought to trial, but other weighty factors were in play. Selkirk's quixotic idealism threatened the sanctity of Lower Canada's social and economic establishment, dominated as it was by the partners and agents of the North West Company. When the trial's venue was moved to York, Selkirk encountered the equally vehement opposition of the Family Compact, that self-perpetuating oligarchy of reactionary judges, bureaucrats, politicians and theologians. These unyielding clusters of privilege were abetted in their anti-Selkirk efforts by the Colonial Office in London. Its secretary, Lord Bathurst, and more particularly his influential Under-Secretary, Henry Goulburn, openly favoured the NWC's claims, though both men tended to dismiss the feud as a routine commercial quarrel. One of Bathurst's dispatches, accidentally included in a sheaf of papers delivered to Selkirk, urged the attorney-general of Quebec to ensure the Scottish lord's prosecution and conviction.

Selkirk's London supporters took his case directly to the British prime minister, Lord Liverpool, hoping to bypass Bathurst and Goulburn, but the Family Compact's influence turned out to be too powerful. John Strachan, the rector of York's St James's Church, who also served on the colony's executive council and could claim the moral leadership of his circle, attacked Selkirk for being an irresponsible land speculator who had lured the poor Scottish settlers into a "polar region where even the minimal agriculture economy was impossible" since Red River was fit only as "a residence for uncivilized man." Strachan and his supporters saw in Selkirk's progressive views and colonial ambitions a threat to their own positions, believing that even if successful, the Red River Settlement "was so completely isolated from British civilization that, in the interests of mere survival, it would gravitate toward the southern republic." At the end of the lengthy litigation, Selkirk was assessed £2,000 for damages while not a single Nor'Wester was fined or imprisoned. Not waiting to hear this ludicrous verdict announced, Selkirk had returned to London, his health finally broken. "For pity's sake," Lady Selkirk begged her husband, "make up your mind to let the wicked flourish; they cannot take from us our own good conscience, and if we do not allow them to bereave us of health and tranquility, we can be happy without the right being proved."

But it was too late. His chronic consumption, seriously aggravated by the courtroom ordeal, had left her husband hardly able to breathe without retching blood. Following the practice of the day, doctors applied leeches to reduce his blood flow, but that only weakened him further. When his brother-in-law, James Wedderburn, objected that funds from his dangerously reduced estate were still flowing into Red River, Selkirk dictated a reply that might have been his valedictory: "... my honour is at stake in the contest with the North West Company and in the support of the settlement at Red River. Till that can be said to be fairly out of danger and till the infamous falsehoods of the North West Company are finally and fully exposed, expenses must be incurred which it is utterly impossible to avoid.... It is to be hoped that this state of things will soon be over, and when that is the case I will retire to St Mary's Isle and live on sixpence a day till I am out of debt."

His time was running out. Selkirk's illness was claiming so much of him that in September 1819 he was forced to leave England for the drier climate of Pau in the Pyrenees foothills of southwestern France, accompanied only by his doctor and the stalwart Jean. In the half-year remaining to him, Selkirk tried to reconstruct how the tumble of events had soured his generously motivated Red River venture.

He died on the morning of April 8, 1820, not yet forty-nine. Because Pau had no Protestant cemetery, he was buried in a plot at nearby Orthez, between two oak trees. Probates revealed that his once-magnificent estate consisted of £160,000 in debts plus the bankrupt kingdom on the Red River.*

It had been Lord Selkirk's fate to juggle desirable ends with destructive means, and he had not always made the right judgments. Perhaps his greatest sin was that he believed too fervently in his difficult cause, and thus lost the objectivity to create the ameliorating circumstances that might have allowed it to flourish. In the end, he lost everything except the self-esteem that mattered more to him than life itself.

---

* There was one more group expedition to Red River in this period organized by Captain Rudolf de May, one of Selkirk's former de Meuron subordinates. It numbered 165, mainly Swiss pastry cooks and clockmakers plus their families. Promised free land on which to grow bananas and other tropical fruits, they left Basle in 1821. After being barged down the Rhine to Rotterdam, they crossed the Atlantic and entered Hudson Strait, where they were trapped by ice. The young people danced on the icebergs by the light of the aurora borealis, but their parents may have begun to realize this was not citrus country.

VI EMPIRE TRIUMPHANT

A Marriage of Great Convenience

The moribund feudalism of the hbc took on the rampaging capitalism of the Nor'Westers and, in the process of winning, transformed itself into a mirror image of the enterprise it was trying to defeat.

THE DEATH OF LORD SELKIRK and, only twenty-seven days earlier, the passing of the bravest of his opponents, Sir Alexander Mackenzie, combined to exert a liberating influence on the battle-weary fur trade. Andrew Colvile, Selkirk's powerful brother-in-law, in his mourning expressed the family's true feeling about the late earl's obsession when he revealed to a friend how vehemently he wished the Red River Colony "had been in the Red Sea twenty years ago."

Colvile and his fellow Committeemen were confronting a profound problem in continuity of their operational management. William Williams, the overseas governor, was under threat of imminent arrest following his allegedly illegal detention of the Nor'West partners at Grand Rapids and, with no successor in place, the HBC's affairs in Rupert's Land were in danger of floundering. The vacuum developed at a particularly crucial moment. The tragedy at Seven Oaks had temporarily exhausted the furies at Red River, but a final duel between the two companies was in the wind, and, according to the prevailing consensus, whichever side won the Athabasca fur-trade war would dictate the terms of any amalgamation agreement. That required forceful leadership. To provide it, the HBC's governors made a startling decision.

Instead of entrusting the Company's overseas operations to yet another professional warrior like Williams, or to a fur-trade veteran such as Colin Robertson, they chose a youthful novice named George Simpson. The selection of a man still in his early thirties, with no claim to background in the complexities of the fur trade or any demonstrable qualifications to assume such burdensome responsibilities, was audacious—and probably the most important appointment ever made by the London board. Simpson was chosen because he had not been tainted by the internecine warfare of the previous decade, because he could bring to the Company the counting-house mentality it needed, and because he carried himself with that manner of self-confident authority the circumstances demanded. That he had been London-trained but Scottish-bred was also significant, for if the HBC were to emerge dominant, it would have to deal quickly and effectively with the proud Highlanders in charge of the North West operations.

Simpson's heritage definitely had deep Highland roots, but its exact path was less certain. Born out of wedlock to an unknown mother and George, the wastrel son of a Calvinist minister named Thomas Simpson, he was raised mainly by his aunt Mary at Dingwall, a small port town in the northern county of Ross-shire. Having shown some promise in mathematics at the local school, the young George was offered an apprenticeship by his uncle, Geddes Mackenzie Simpson, at his London sugar brokerage, Graham & Simpson, a partnership that expanded in 1812 to include Andrew Colvile. Not much is known about the dozen years he spent in the counting-house at 73 Tower Street, but Simpson impressed his seniors enough that his nomination by Colvile in 1820 as locum tenens Governor-in-Chief of Rupert's Land and possible replacement for the embattled Williams was unanimously accepted. Thus began a lifelong alliance between two men of different backgrounds and generations. "To you," Simpson later wrote to Colvile in a confidential communication from York Factory, "I feel that I am solely indebted for my advancement in Life, and it will ever be my study that your good offices have not been misapplied." In other letters, Simpson confided some of his inner-most and sometimes heretical thoughts to his mentor, such as his harsh dictum that "an enlightened Indian is good for nothing." Throughout his stewardship with the HBC, Simpson enjoyed the unparalleled benefit of having a man who felt (and acted) like a surrogate father dominating the Company's London head office. (Colvile served as the Hudson's Bay Company's Deputy Governor from 1839 to 1852 and Governor from 1852 to 1856.)

Ordered to leave for his new posting at only five days' notice, Simpson was entrusted by Colonial Secretary Lord Bathurst with two important messages. Identically worded, they required that both the NWC and the HBC strictly obey the 1817 proclamation that had been issued by Sir John Sherbrooke, Governor-in-Chief of Canada, requiring that all parties in the fur-trade war refrain from hostilities and restore captured goods and forts. Simpson was charged with passing on this official communiqué to his own troops and specifically instructed to deliver its duplicate to the Nor'Westers' stronghold at Fort William.

On the thirty-one-day passage from Liverpool to New York, Simpson observed with interest the women passengers ("precious nymphs [who] were confined to their cabins the greater part of the Voyage, and if the Steward's [word] be true, solaced themselves with copious brandy draughts to the downfall of the House of Bourbon") and became irritated with the arrogance of his American dining companions, haughtily assuring them that "John Bull merely wanted the opportunity to chastise them for their presumption and insolence."

His trek from New York to Montreal was a portent of many journeys to come. Spring thaw had turned the rutted trail between the two cities into a syrupy quagmire, slowing ordinary travellers to a careful crawl. Not Simpson. He rented an open horse-drawn cart and drove himself nineteen hours at a stretch, enduring with impatience at least fifty spills, to arrive at the southern shore of the St Lawrence in only seven days. Dodging floating ice and other debris of spring breakup, he was among the first across the river that season.

As an HBC executive obviously on the rise, Simpson was immediately accepted by Montreal society, and fêted by the resident mavens of Mount Royal as an important personage, and a vibrant bachelor to boot. The lightning transformation from counting-house clerk to courted celebrity at the nightly masquerade balls and theatre parties tilted his equilibrium. With unbridled bravado that sounded like a declamation more fit for Boy's Own Annual, Simpson wrote to friends in England vowing that once in the wilderness he was determined to "show my Governors that I am not wanting of courage if necessity puts it to the test. There is a possibility that I may be obstructed in my route as the N.W. Coy, a band of unprincipled Lawless Marauders, stick at nothing however desperate to gain their ends; I am however armed to the teeth, will sell my Life if in danger as dear as possible and never allow a North-Wester come within reach of my rifle, if flint steel and bullet can keep him off."

His introduction to the North American hinterland was the journey along the voyageur route from Lachine to Fort William. While delivering Lord Bathurst's admonition he was able to assess first hand the Nor'Westers' impressive physical facilities and size up their fragile morale. The fort was in a state of high excitement because just a few days before, a party of sixty armed men had been dispatched to harass the HBC at Grand Rapids. Camouflaging his intense curiosity and behaving as if he were little more than an interested traveller, Simpson left the fort and headed north. At Norway House, he met Governor Williams, and while delivering the HBC's copy of Lord Bathurst's message was apprised of the recent capture by the Nor'Westers of the elusive Colin Robertson. That left the Athabasca brigade, due to depart at any moment for that distant territory, without a leader. Having little choice, Williams accepted Simpson's offer to take charge himself.

The transformation in the tyro was instantaneous. Not only did Simpson assume the partisan abhorrence of the Nor'Westers that had become every local Bay man's second nature but he quickly entered into the spirit of the occasion by taking a country wife.* Placed in command of a grand brigade of sixty-eight, Simpson issued each man a musket, a bayonet and ten rounds, pledging to "maintain the rights and interests of the Honourable Company, and defend their property and our persons" by every means within his power. He set a gruelling pace, shaking his voyageurs awake long before sun-up and keeping them at their paddles well past sundown. By September 20, 1820, having passed several NWC canoe flotillas en route, he arrived at tiny Fort Wedderburn, a mile and a half from the imposing quarters of the Nor'Westers at Fort Chipewyan. His Athabasca adventure was about to begin.

SIMPSON PLUNGED INTO THE FRACAS of the Athabasca fur trade with boyish enthusiasm. Observing his rush to learn, some of the curious Nor'Westers mistook his eagerness as the mark of a naïve and ineffective novice. "Mr Simpson, a gentleman from England, last Spring ... being a stranger and reputed a gentlemanly man, will not create much alarm," was the initial assessment of the NWC clerk Willard Wentzel.

His assessment of Simpson could not have been more wrong. The "gentleman from England" quickly proved to be just as determined as the redoubtable Colin Robertson had been—but unlike that worthy renegade, he managed to

---

* On his way west, Simpson camped at Cedar Lake on the lower Saskatchewan close to the memorial erected for Benjamin Frobisher, the Nor'Wester who had starved to death attempting to escape HBC detainment at York Factory. The tablet bearing the inscription was missing after Simpson left the area, and the Nor'Westers never forgave him that act of desecration.

garner the respect of the Nor'Westers while beating them at their own game. His first task was to gain the respect of his own crew. This he achieved by absorbing their knowledge and experience, then assimilating it into his own very precise set of priorities. Instead of concentrating only on enlarging the post's fur catch (which he increased that first season by £726), he imposed severe cost-cutting measures (saving £1,054), which he labelled "Œconomy." Fish, not meat, became the daily ration, and every customary extravagance was curtailed or eliminated. Local Indians, for example, had kept the price of sled dogs high by eating them after every trapping season, forcing the HBC to purchase new teams each autumn. Simpson ordered that bitches be kept in Company kennels with an eye to producing his own cut-rate dog teams. (His experiment to domesticate the passing caribou as handy beasts of burden was a dismal failure.) He travelled eighteen hours a day, poking his Scottish nose into every aspect of his territory's commerce, busily imposing his version of proper discipline. Whenever flattery or reprimands failed, he had no hesitation about placing defiant underlings on short rations or handcuffing them until they came around to his way of doing things. When one of his post managers, Joseph Greill at Berens House, was found to be drinking too much, Simpson sent him a pointed rebuke: "It has been hinted that you are rather addicted to the Bottle; this report I cannot believe until it is substantiated on conclusive evidence, and I trust your conduct will be so perfectly correct as to challenge the strictest examination; a Drunkard you are aware is an object of contempt even in the eyes of the Savage race with whom we have to deal in this country."

Despite such advice, at this novice stage of his experience in the fur trade, Simpson's method of dealing with Indian traders was to ply them with liquor—and cajole them with words. He boasted in his journal about being in top form during one of his orations to a group of elders ("they look upon me as the greatest man who ever came into the Country"), cynically noting that "a little rum operates like a charm on the Indians. They cannot resist the temptation, and if the bait is properly managed, every skin may be had from them." With remarkable success he persuaded at least some local natives that he could cast magic spells and that he would *know* if they surreptitiously traded pelts with the Nor'Westers. He gained this reputation in part by casting a spell on the unfaithful wife of a Chipewyan who had eloped with a fellow tribesman. When she was recaptured, the husband demanded guarantees from Simpson that she would remain faithful during the forthcoming winter.

Simpson assured him that she would be—and she was. (He achieved this bit of magic by taking the lady aside and assuring her she would turn into a dog if she strayed.)

Samuel Black, the veteran nemesis of every HBC trader in the Athabasca since Peter Fidler, soon appeared on the scene, and when they met again on the Pacific Coast three years later, Simpson noted in his journal: "Black could at first scarcely look me in the face, he recollected my Athabasca Campaign, and never will forget the terrors in which he was kept that Winter ..." The rivalry between the two companies in that faraway outpost of empire centred on the line of demarcation between two particular forts. The Nor'Westers had built a small raised blockhouse on Potato Island only a dozen yards from Fort Wedderburn's main gate and had angled its back window so that they could observe the comings and goings at the rival post, taking careful note of which Indians were trading there in order to harass them later. Simpson decided to erect a palisade that would shield his post from the Nor'Westers' spies. When his men were set to the task, the younger Simon McGillivray, son of the NWC's chief executive officer and then in command at the company's Fort Chipewyan, decided to retaliate by moving the NWC blockhouse even closer to the HBC fort. As soon as Simpson noticed that McGillivray had trespassed twenty-four inches inside HBC property, he stormed out to protest.

His Scottish terrier, Boxer, waddled across the dividing line, and Simpson, pretending exasperation, ostentatiously ordered the animal to repent its sins: "Come here, Boxer, you do not seem to be aware that you are committing a trespass!"

"We have no intention to molest your dog, Sir," retorted the proud McGillivray.

"Nor shall you his Master with impunity," Simpson hissed over his shoulder, and walked away.

Shortly afterwards, Amable Grignon, an HBC clerk, arrived at Fort Wedderburn, bearing a Montreal warrant for McGillivray's arrest that he grandly intended to exercise. Simpson read it over, suspecting that it was really meant for the elder Simon McGillivray (his Athabasca opponent's uncle) but limited himself to an unctuous promise that he would, of course, never think of interfering with the law of the land. Promising Grignon armed support if McGillivray resisted arrest, Simpson pushed two loaded pistols under his belt and called out: "Mr. McGillivray, I should be glad to have some further explanation with you on the subject of this boundary line."

As soon as McGillivray was within grabbing distance, Grignon collared him, shouting: "I arrest you in the King's name!"

The Nor'Westers were furious, threatening reprisal, but the armed Bay men stared them down. McGillivray was beside himself, cursing in turn Grignon, Simpson, the HBC and his fate. He reluctantly settled into his imprisonment, made easier when Simpson allowed his country wife and children to join him. The Nor'Wester was permitted to dispatch letters back to his post, but they were censored by Simpson, who was not averse to enclosing his own version of the events being described before forwarding them. He often supped with McGillivray, hoping to learn more about the Nor'Westers' mentality, and the two men grew, if not friendly, at least mutually respectful. Then, early on the morning of December 4, 1820, while Simpson was falling asleep, congratulating himself on having "got to the blind side of these Argus-eyed Gentlemen," McGillivray made his escape.

Simpson had been abruptly alerted at one o'clock by a guard who reported a great commotion at Chipewyan and that Nor'Westers bearing torches were running back and forth from the NWC fort to their bastion outside Wedderburn. Expecting an attack, Simpson roused his men, armed them and fortified them against the bitter cold with a dram of rum. But no attack came. It seemed to be a false alarm. An HBC interpreter named Joseph Bouché was sent on a secret mission to reconnoitre the enemy bastion.

"The English are up," he heard one of the armed Nor'Westers whisper to his partner.

"Yes," was the reply, "and one of them is now listening close to the Port Hole of the Bastion."

Bouché tiptoed home. Fast.

Simpson served another dram of rum and ordered the post fiddler to lead the assembled troops in a reel to keep toes from frostbite. But nothing seemed to be happening. Next morning, when a tired duo of HBC servants went to the lake for a bucket of water, an NWC clerk inquired mischievously whether Mr McGillivray had danced to the music he had heard coming from the HBC fort. When he received a confused reply, the Nor'Wester exploded with the gleeful news that Simon McGillivray was back among his friends at Fort Chipewyan.

McGillivray's country wife at first insisted that he had vanished up the chimney, but it was too small for human passage. She then confessed that McGillivray had bribed his HBC guard, a former de Meuron soldier named Johann Knipe, and had escaped disguised in her nightgown. The recalcitrant guard was interrogated in English, French, Italian and Spanish—languages he had previously been heard speaking—but all he would say was that unfortunately he could answer questions only in German, which happened to be beyond the range of everyone else at the post.

That bloodless episode was more of an occasion for laughter than reprisal, and for the next seven months the traders of both companies concentrated on gathering pelts from the Indians. Simpson left Wedderburn on May 23, satisfied that his personal star was in the ascendancy. He had, in effect, won his field commission, having dealt effectively with Indians as well as Nor'Westers and, of more importance, having won the confidence of his own men. When he arrived at the foot of Grand Rapids a month after leaving Athabasca, rumours reached him that the London negotiations between the HBC and the North West Company had been completed. Instead of being elated that he was now heir apparent to their combined operations, he complained that the Nor'Westers could have been beaten in the field, presumably by himself, in a fight to the finish.

IN MOST WARS based on differing value systems, opposing armies tend to dissolve into composites of the causes driving the individuals who fight them. But if hostilities continue long enough, and if they are being waged in a region isolated from outside influences, the participants tend to become interchangeable, employing one another's strategies and ethics and gradually losing sight of the aggressive impulses that originally stirred them. The feud between the North West and Hudson's Bay companies was no exception. Professor K.G. Davies compared their struggle to the English Civil War that drove Charles I from the throne: "On one side were the North Westers, the Cavaliers of the fur trade, flamboyant, extravagant, preoccupied with the 'honor of the concern,' dashing but defeated. On the other side stood the Hudson's Bay Company, the Roundheads: sober, persistent, concerned above all with their own rightness and winning the charge at the end of the day." Davies made the telling observation that the Roundheads beat the Cavaliers "not by being right but with better cavalry; and as the competition for the fur trade proceeded to climax, the Hudson's Bay Company threw some of its traditions overboard and fought the Nor'Westers with their own weapons."

This was what decided the bitter contest's outcome: the moribund feudalism of the HBC took on the rampaging capitalism of the Nor'Westers and, in the process of winning, transformed itself into a mirror image of the enterprise it was trying to defeat. The HBC lost most of the battles but won the war, partly because it eventually recruited the quality Highlanders previously sought out only by the North West Company, and because it adopted the Montrealers' field tactics. With the escalation of hostilities, the London Governors expanded their inland facilities and incurred expenses with a momentum that had hitherto been the exclusive trait of their opponents. They also established an aggressive policy to drive their rivals out of competing fur areas by deliberately setting their barter exchange rates with the Indians at levels ruinous to the Nor'Westers. As the long fight wore on, the once-quiescent royally chartered company emerged in the guise of a band of merry adventurers determined to surpass the derring-do of the Montrealers. "By 1821," concluded Davies, "the Hudson's Bay Company had become an organization the North Westers could join."

Conversely, the Montrealers were ultimately defeated because the metamorphosis did not, indeed *could* not, work both ways. Their British rivals could adopt the Nor'Westers' methods and ethics simply by altering their strategy and personnel, never losing the sustaining advantages of access to long-term credit from the Bank of England, a supportive bulwark of highly placed politicians willing to respect the monopoly bestowed by an antique charter—and, above all, a management committee whose members, awash in alternative sources of income, could afford to skip dividends and, if necessary, help tide the Company over with personal loans. These were privileges more easily envied than copied. Even at the height of its power, when the North West Company's domain extended from Lachine to the Arctic, over to the Pacific and back again, it lacked secure long-term financing. When the grandiloquent Marquis, Simon McTavish, had been in charge, no British prime minister would lift a finger in response to his entreaties that the HBC's monopolistic privileges be abrogated. Neither McTavish nor his successors enjoyed any significant claims to British money at a time when most investment funds emanated from London.

To outsiders observing the pride and the arrogance, the fight and the flux of the Nor'Westers the impression was one of omnipotence; the reality was much closer to frailty. The same qualities that had made the North West Company great inexorably drove it to the wall.

The Montrealers could never overcome the handicap of their pathetically overextended transportation network—the interminable and prohibitively expensive hauls in and out of the heart of the continent in which the HBC was already entrenched. Here was ultimate proof of the animating notion propounded by those original caesars of the wilderness, Pierre-Esprit Radisson and Médard Chouart, Sieur Des Groseilliers. They had first ventured into this wild country in 1659 and then sped to England to persuade the British they should bypass the French fur buyers on the St Lawrence by trading directly into Hudson Bay. The commercial enterprise spawned by this daring idea had survived pitched battles and every kind of challenge—frost and starvation, parliamentary plots and coupon-clipping neglect—through the simple stratagem of keeping a keen and undistracted eye on profit margins and fiscal stability. Because the Governors and Committeemen were not owners, they could afford the tight-fisted policy of keeping dividends at a minimum—or not paying any at all (as between 1691 and 1717, or 1809 and 1815) even while maintaining reserves and credit facilities against the inevitable down cycles in fur sales.

The North West Company operated on the opposite principle. Because its managers were also its proprietors and their extravagant style of living depended on their dividend income, ever larger payouts *had* to be made, year after year, and that drained most of the NWC's working capital at the end of each season. Maintaining this quixotic situation required multiplying profits annually, which in turn demanded constant territorial expansion. But once the Nor'Westers' march westward was stopped short by the Pacific Ocean, and once the Bay men began to respond with their own brand of vigour and trading panache, the Montreal company faltered. And having faltered, it cracked.

By the autumn of 1820, the companies had reached an impasse that a merger alone could resolve. Beyond their commercial imperatives was the pressure being applied by the Colonial Office for an extension of British influence across the North American continent. Such an objective could be achieved only by a single, financially sound trading company. That was why, not long after Selkirk's death, Lord Bathurst assured representatives of both firms that if they could hammer out the financial details, he would sponsor an Act of Parliament approving their amalgamation. And there was a further inducement to the union promised by the Colonial Secretary: the new, amalgamated company would be granted exclusive trading privileges west of Rupert's Land all the way to the Pacific Coast. To promote such a merger, Bathurst enlisted one of Britain's most successful power brokers, the enigmatic Edward ("Bear") Ellice.

A PARAGON OF MERCANTILE PRAGMATISM, Ellice had earned his nickname, not out of any predisposition to ferocity, but because, like a bear, he was considered well greased in his dealings with friend and foe alike. He appeared playful—his cherry-cheerful face grooved by the laugh lines of inner self-confidence—but he could be deadly if crossed. Although he was a pivotal influence within the governing Whig party for half a century, Ellice's main function was to act as an honest or at least expedient broker between men, ideas and money on both sides of the Atlantic. Not much happened within Britain's governing circles without his unofficial blessing, which led an associate, the diarist Charles Greville, to label him as a "very serviceable man." Ellice had more wit than irony, acted as everybody's mercenary and nobody's intimate, and was grand master of that penchant peculiar to the British upper classes for looking down one's nose while talking through it. His capacity for moral suasion prompted more than occasional resentment, such as this complaint from the acid-tongued social observer Emily Eden to a member of the Clarendon set: "I never could see why the Bear was not only allowed to assume that he advised and managed and thwarted and assisted all the distinguished men of the age, but was also the authority by which every assertion was to be met and refuted. 'The Bear says the country does not like it'; 'the Bear thinks Lord Grey a fool'; 'the Bear says the Queen is unpopular,' etc., etc."

As well as depending on his innate sense of occasion, his solid background and family fortune, Ellice used his two marriages to advance his social standing—the first, to Lady Hannah Althea Bettesworth, the widow of a gallant sea captain and sister of Prime Minister Earl Grey; the second, to Anne Amelia, Dowager Countess of Leicester and daughter of the 4th Earl of Albemarle. Elected Whig member of Parliament for Coventry in 1818, Ellice served as an mp for all but four of the next forty-five years, rising to Secretary of the Treasury and, later, Secretary of War in the Earl Grey government.

Almost as if he led a double life, the Bear was at the same time deeply involved in the Canadian fur trade. His father owned the quarter-million-acre Beauharnois seigneury in the St Lawrence Valley, his two brothers had served in the Canadian Fencibles and he had himself spent much time in Montreal, becoming a senior NWC partner as well as the company's chief London agent. Five months before Selkirk's death, Ellice had approached the HBC's Andrew Colvile, offering to buy the consumptive earl's shares at his own valuation, while pledging to maintain all existing obligations to the Red River settlers. Selkirk dismissed this option as "all bunkum," but it wasn't. What was left unmentioned in this flash exchange—although Ellice and Colvile may or may not have been aware of it—was that the North West Company's bargaining status had been grievously undermined at its 1820 conclave in Fort William—and that it would soon either have to buy out the HBC or be bought out instead.

By this time, two generations of NWC winterers had expended their lives fighting the Hudson's Bay Company. Even though the Royal Adventurers seemed to stumble from one defeat to the next, they were often cowed but never vanquished. Although the Nor'Westers had endured all the hardships of the trade, they had not become its chief beneficiaries. Now they were being asked to renew for another decade the partnership agreements signed in 1802 and 1804 that were due to expire on November 30, 1822. Aware that their company was in perilous financial condition, worried about their own futures and those of their country families, weary of the violence and debauchery that had become such easy riders of the fur trade, they took out their resentment on the Montreal agents. William McGillivray tried to hold the mutineers in check, but for the first time in the NWC's reign, the country partners would not listen. Instead, eighteen of the most senior winterers voted their proxies to two of their own, Dr John McLoughlin and Angus Bethune, charging them with a momentous mission: to sign a peace treaty with the Hudson's Bay Company—in effect, replacing McGillivray and his London agent with the Royal Adventurers. It was this rebellion of the wintering partners more than any other catalyst that swung the ensuing negotiations in favour of the HBC.

Of the duo chosen for this delicate task, one lacked impressive credentials. Angus Bethune, who had been marginally involved in the NWC's takeover at Astoria and was briefly in the company's China trade, was later characterized by George Simpson as "a very poor creature, vain, self sufficient and trifling, who makes his own comfort his principal study; possessing little Nerve and no decision in anything: of a snarling vindictive disposition, and neither liked nor respected by his associates, Servants or Indians. His Services would be over-paid by the victuals himself and Family consume."

But McLoughlin was a man of very different composition. The son of an Irish subsistence farmer at Rivière-du-Loup in Lower Canada, he completed his Quebec City medical studies in 1803 and became a Nor'Wester under unusual circumstances. McLoughlin and his lady friend, the story goes, had been walking up a narrow Quebec street when they came to a plank lying across a puddle. Midway across, they met a drunken British officer in full regalia who was trying to balance himself as if he were walking a tightrope. He rudely ordered them off the narrow plank. When they refused to move, the officer shoved McLoughlin's companion into the mud. With a yelp of fury, the young doctor picked up the startled redcoat, lifted him over his head and threw him into the mud face down—epaulettes, sword, shiny boots and all. McLoughlin left town that evening to join the NWC. After a brief apprenticeship in the fur trade, he was appointed resident physician at Fort William during the summer rendezvous. Named a partner in 1814 and the next year placed in charge of the fort, McLoughlin quickly emerged as a natural leader.

Bent on their covert mission to London on behalf of the winterers, McLoughlin and Bethune first stopped in Montreal, where they contacted Samuel Gale, Selkirk's legal counsel, to inquire whether the HBC might enter into a new partnership with them. Gale expeditiously communicated the offer to London, so that Andrew Colvile was aware of the Nor'Westers' internal dissension before serious and more public negotiations on amalgamation got under way. The arrival in London of the two hot-eyed wintering partners accelerated everyone's timetable. Ellice and the McGillivrays knew this was the last available moment if they wanted the HBC to negotiate with them instead of with the envoys of the mutineers. Colvile, who had been charged with formulating the union on behalf of the HBC, also realized there would never be a better time to strike a deal.

As they moved among the classical Georgian façades of the City, London's financial district, the negotiators were determined to hammer out an agreement, figuratively looking over their shoulders at the looming shadows of Dr McLoughlin and his sidekick, who were prepared to throw the winterers' support to whichever side would give them most leverage. Ellice chaired the crucial discussions, but it was Simon McGillivray and Colvile who cut the final deal. "Simon Pure and I," exulted the triumphant Bay Committeeman, "settled it in a quarter of an hour.... We retain the power of management and get paid for our stolen goods, and they kiss the rod."

The twelve-thousand-word contract, signed March 26, 1821, was a complex and sophisticated document, but its effect was simple. When one of the NWC winterers finished reading it, he looked up from its convoluted clauses and exclaimed: "Amalgamation? This isn't amalgamation but submersion. We are drowned men!" Certainly, the HBC's seventy-seven shareholders had little to complain about—particularly since their stock moved up 100 percent on news of the merger.

The contract was to be effective for twenty-one years, commencing in 1821; its multiple provisions provided for amalgamation of the Hudson's Bay Company and North West Company assets, each valued at £200,000. The new business would clearly be operating under the HBC name and charter. A joint board established to advise on management of the fur trade included Ellice and Simon McGillivray, but it was dominated by Bay Committeemen, and the stock split guaranteed control by the HBC. Profits were to be divided into a hundred shares, with a block of twenty going to the HBC directors and the same size of holding going to the Montreal partners, five to the Selkirk estate and two and a half each to Ellice and McGillivray. Ten more were to be invested by the HBC as a floating reserve. The remaining forty shares were subdivided into eighty-five equal parts, two of which were dealt out to each Chief Factor in the reorganized Company, one to each Chief Trader and seven to eminent retirees. Because the new partners were chosen on the basis of ability rather than seniority, fifteen of the twenty-five Chief Factors selected were Nor'Westers, as were seventeen of the twenty-eight Chief Traders. "The union of the North West and Hudson's Bay companies created an enterprise of power unequalled in the history of the fur trade," concluded John S. Galbraith, the pre-eminent American scholar of British Empire history. "The resources, experience and business acumen of the Hudson's Bay Company blended with the energy of the Nor'Westers to give unusual vitality to the monopoly that came into being in 1821."

That monopoly was legally strengthened and geographically expanded by Lord Bathurst, as his promised reward for the merger, through an Act of Parliament passed on July 2, 1821. For an annual token payment of five shillings, the new organization was granted monopoly control, renewable in twenty-one years, over the whole of British North America except for the colonies already occupying the Atlantic shore and the St Lawrence–Lower Great Lakes area. The empire-sized grant extended the Company's territorial domain beyond Rupert's Land into Athabasca, across the Rocky and Coast mountains to the edge of the Pacific and well into the Oregon Country— although trading rights below the 49th parallel were held jointly with the Americans. Sir Alexander Mackenzie's twenty-year-old dream of a trans-continental trading empire had finally come true.

Because the parliamentary grant was made jointly to the McGillivrays and Edward Ellice, as well as to "the Company of Adventurers of England Tradeing into Hudsons Bay," it seemed at least theoretically possible that a rival coalition of frustrated interests might find an opening to enter the trade. Ellice, who immediately upon the amalgamation had characteristically transmogrified himself into a rabidly loyal Bay man, feared that those Nor'West winterers who had been excluded from the new concern might be tempted to fight the grand coalition. In the interests of a peaceful changeover, the new HBC Committee made an unprecedented decision: it would send one of its British members on tour of the most important posts of its overseas territories. The candidate, selected mainly because he was the only bachelor on the board and any journey into "Indian Territory" was taken at the individual's own risk, was Nicholas Garry. A former Baltic timber merchant fluent in German, French and Russian, Garry was a sensitive soul, perfectly attuned to the touchy nature of his mission. He left London, accompanied by the two McGillivrays, only three days after the coalition agreement had been signed, bound for the crucial 1821 gathering of wintering partners at Fort William. After being appropriately lionized in Montreal, he was paddled to the head of Lake Superior, and vividly recorded his impressions along the way. "At the [foot] of this magnificent fall," he wrote about one nocturnal stopover, "we dined and a power of imagination and description might picture it in the most enchanting colours. Indeed to my feelings there is something very animating and inspiring in the life of a voyageur. In Nature's wilds all is independence, all your luxuries and comforts are within yourself and all that is pleasurable within your own minds; and after all this is happiness, if there is such a thing in the world; which no mortal can say. Indeed there is no reasoning unhappiness. Our whole life is spent on wishing for something which, when we acquire it, often becomes insipid and new objects and new views crowd upon the mind, producing dissatisfaction with the present and a longing or desire for something in the future."

For both Garry and William McGillivray, this would be more of a pilgrimage than mere passage through the wilderness. For the HBC Committeeman, whose health had never been robust, it was to be his last great adventure. Declared to be of unsound mind in 1835, he would spend the last twenty-one years of his life confined to an asylum. For McGillivray, it meant the end of his dream of empire. He had been transported this way for most of two decades, to be feasted and hailed at Fort William as king of all he surveyed, haranguing his freebooting battalions against the British intruders. Now, he was making his final journey to the scene of his former triumphs—if not physically a prisoner certainly feeling like one. The express canoe in which they were travelling arrived at the dock of Fort William just eighteen days after leaving Lachine, and it was Nicholas Garry, not one of the McGillivrays, who was lodged in the senior partner's quarters.

There was no dancing or coquetry in the Great Hall now. On July 10, the grim-faced winterers filed in to be told their fate. The reading of the documents of amalgamation was met with shouts of protest. Why should they surrender the territory they had fought so hard to claim? How could the McGillivrays have agreed to the substitution of York Factory on bleak Hudson Bay for this magnificent fort as the centre of the continent's fur trade? What about the men not specifically named in the Deed Poll that listed those Nor'Westers being retained by the new organization? Many good questions; not many good answers.

As the McGillivrays and winterers glared at one another in that one-sided debate, each group was aware of what the other was thinking: we could have struck a better deal if only we had remained united. It had been the mutiny, staged in this very place only thirteen months before, that had triggered the NWC's collapse. Then another thought began to dominate the gathering. As the dour farewells were exchanged and claimants set out to fill their new postings, they were struck by the chilly realization that they would never meet here again. Fort William's glory days as the great entrepôt of the Canadian fur trade were done.*

Setting off for York Factory via the Red River Settlement, Garry noted that he had never in his life left a place with less regret. But William McGillivray, in one final gesture of defiance, made a presentation to the fiercest of the HBC's enemies, Samuel Black. It was a ring, bearing the telling inscription: "To the most worthy of the Northwesters." His point made, McGillivray decided he was too exhausted spiritually to journey any farther with the victorious Bay executive and asked his brother Simon to go in his stead. He then sat down and wrote a long letter to his friend the Reverend John Strachan of muddy York, who had fought so hard against Lord Selkirk in the Upper Canadian courts. That epistle, penned in the ghostly confines of the Great Hall after his once-loyal legions had dispersed for the last time, was a touching valedictory not only for a man but for his time:

---

* Relegated to the status of an ordinary supply depot within the new HBC's trading system, Fort William lingered in a state of accelerating decay until it was closed in 1878. Five years later, the derelict structures were flattened to make way for the Canadian Pacific Railway's lakehead freight yard. The reconstruction carried out under the sponsorship of Ontario Premier John Robarts in the early 1970s has produced a thoroughly authentic monument to the early Canadian fur trade, seven miles upriver from the original site.

"I avail myself of the opportunity of Mr. Alexr McDonell going down by York, to tender you my devoirs.—I have been at this place since the 1st inst: settling a most important Business—the carrying into effect the various Deeds and Covenants entered into on the part of the North West Company in London with the Hudson Bay Company;—these arrangements are happily completed, and I part with my old troops—to meet them no more in discussions on the Indian trade—this parting I confess does not cause me much regret—I have worked hard & honestly for them, and I am satisfied that I have at least done my duty. I have been an Agent or Director, since 1794—and Chief Superintendent since 1799, the management has not been easy, for we had too many storms to weather from without, and some derangement in the Household. But thank God! the whole is closed with honour—and the trade will be productive if well managed, after the Country shall have been restored to order, which it will require a couple of years to effect,—thus the Fur trade is forever lost to Canada! the Treaty of Ghent destroyed the Southern trade—still the Capital and exertions of a few individuals supported the Northern trade, under many disadvantages, against a Chartered Company, who brought their goods to the Indian Country at less than one half the Expense that ours cost us—but it would have been worse than folly, to have continued the contest further. We have made no submission—we met & negotiated on equal terms—and rating the N.W. Co. collectively—they hold now 55 out of 100 shares.... My own fortunes have been singular as connected with the N W Fur trade—I was the first English Clerk engaged in the Service of the N.W Co., on its first Establishment in 1784, and I have put my Hand and Seal to the Instrument which closes its career—and name in 1821...."

During a short stopover at Red River, Garry and Simon McGillivray noted that the colony was still clinging to existence, numbering 419 people, 221 of them the original Selkirk settlers. Along the way, at Slave Falls on the Winnipeg River, Garry had recorded another of his moody epiphanies. "Our dinner table," he scribbled in his journal about a particularly beautiful campsite, "was a hard rock, no table cloth could be cleaner, and the surrounding plants and beautiful flowers sweetening the board. Before us the waterfall, wild, romantic, bold. The River Winnipic here, impeded by mountainous rocks, appears to have found a passage through the rocks, and these, as if still disputing the power of water, show their heads, adding to the rude wildness of the scene, producing whirlpools, foam, loud noise, and crystal whiteness beautifully contrasted with the black pine. This again is softened by the freshness and rich foliage of the ash, maple, elm, red willow and occasionally the oak bringing to the mind England and all the delightful recollections this happy country produces, and showing in fact all the folly of my opening phantasy of a want of happiness in this life."

The meeting at Norway House near the foot of Lake Winnipeg was even more crucial than that at Fort William for the new coalition because in its customary diplomatic wisdom, the company had allocated the most coveted assignments to the best of the Nor'Westers, and Garry would now have to convince the gathered traders that such an arrangement was worthwhile. This he achieved, mainly by making it clear that executive direction would remain firmly in HBC hands. The trading system was divided into a Southern Department based at Moose Factory, under the continuing stewardship of William Williams, and the much more significant Northern Department placed under the command of the newly promoted George Simpson. His mission successfully completed, Garry sailed back to England from York Factory aboard the *Prince of Wales,* noting in the final entry of his diary: "I was not insensible to the kind, flattering manner in which the gentlemen of York Fort took leave of me.... Thus has terminated my mission to Rupert's Land, the last gun fired from the Fort.... All parties satisfied except those who have sinister & sordid views."

THE HARD-WON TERMS of amalgamation stayed in place for barely three years. In 1824 the original profit-sharing agreement was abrogated and under the new arrangement the former NWC agency partners were issued common stock instead.* They thus lost their votes and influence in the HBC's affairs

---

* The occasion of the 1824 agreement was also used to straighten out the Company's accounts with royalty. Stock had originally been granted to the Duke of York, the HBC's second governor, who had become King James II of England in 1685. Dividends were paid only until 1764; after an 1812 claim for back payments by financial advisers to the royal household was disallowed, no further action was taken. An 1824 resolution of the HBC Committee placed the King's stock permanently in an unclaimed account.

Rumour persists that the royal family retains holdings in the Hudson's Bay Company. In a 1980 interview Lord Adeane, then financial adviser to Queen Elizabeth II, confirmed this fact to the author but refused to divulge details. The HBC's own registry of stockholders shows no entry for the royal family, but many shares are held in "street names" or through surrogates such as British merchant banks. Possibly the best clue to the true status of the monarch's shareholders was a brief exchange between Prince Philip and HBC Governor Don McGiverin during the 1977 Canadian royal tour. At a noisy reception in Winnipeg, Philip sidled over to McGiverin and whispered in his ear: "How are we doing?"

and, worse, had to put up a bond of £50,000 to meet the many legal claims being made on their former partnership. Their financial affairs had reached crisis proportions. The McGillivrays' firm, which had been appointed the HBC's Montreal agency, was in such fiscal chaos that Thomas Thain, their accounting partner, who was also a vice-president of the Bank of Montreal, was spending all his time trying to balance the books. He finally gave up, locked the records in his private office, placed the key in his pocket and fled across the Atlantic to seek permanent and presumably more peaceful sanctuary at a Scottish insane asylum.

William McGillivray died suddenly on October 16, 1825, while on a visit to London, leaving instructions in his will that Simon satisfy the family's mounting debts. The surviving brother, who had been in England trying to raise money by selling his art collection, rushed back to Montreal, discovered the company's records in Thain's locked office and declared bankruptcy. The McGillivrays' creditors eventually received only ten shillings on the pound, and to make even that settlement possible, Ellice had to contribute £110,000. William McGillivray's daughters remained in London, living out their days in destitute circumstances, while the penniless Simon fled to Mexico, where he found employment as a "gold commissioner."

True to form, of all the Nor'West agents, only Edward Ellice prospered following the union. He gained a seat on the HBC's Committee after the 1824 reorganization and remained as one of its senior members until his death in 1863. The Bear became so influential within HBC affairs that in 1858, when Simpson suggested that trade goods be sent into Red River through St Paul, Minnesota, instead of via York Factory, approval of the current Governor and his Committee was contingent on consent of the seventy-five-year-old Ellice.

The so-called amalgamation, which had now been clearly revealed as the takeover it always was, launched the Hudson's Bay Company's golden age. By the summer of 1821, the HBC was chartering clipper ships to supply its newly won bases on the Columbia and farther up the Pacific Coast. "For another quarter of a century," noted the Canadian historian Chester Martin, "the commercial empire of Hudson Bay remained a marvel of lucrative fortune and efficiency."

Not so the empire on the St Lawrence. When McGillivray lamented that "the fur trade is forever lost to Canada," he had in mind the century-old route stretching from Montreal westward. Not only was Fort William downgraded and allowed to rot but the main artery of the fur trade—the voyageur trail to

Lake Superior—was left largely unused, not to be revived for another sixty years, when parts of it were traversed by the Canadian Pacific Railway.

The North West Company, that defiant alliance of voyageurs and Highlanders whose audacity had established Canada's first indigenous national enterprise, vanished almost overnight. Instead of spawning dynasties, the NWC partners left their few heirs deep in debt, and the capricious castles at the foot of Mount Royal turned out to be only monuments to their self-indulgence. They had set down the matrix of a country and had been its uncrowned rulers but were brought down by overextending their reach. "The feudal state of Fort William," eulogized Washington Irving, "is at an end; its council chamber is silent and desolate; its banquet-hall no longer echoes to the auld-world ditty; the lords of the lakes and the forests are all passed away."

The Birchbark Napoleon

A bastard by birth and by persuasion, George Simpson dominated the HBC during four crucial decades, the agent of a muscular corporate ethic that overwhelmed friend and foe alike.

THEY CAME FROM EVERY QUADRANT of the recently amalgamated Hudson's Bay empire. Deep in the summer of 1821, the triumphant traders of the Company of Adventurers and the vanquished wintering partners of the now-defunct North West Company, both freshly transformed into Chief Factors and Chief Traders of the newly created Northern Department of the HBC, converged on York Factory.

They were there to attend a banquet arranged by their untested governor, George Simpson. Most of the traders of the two recently warring concerns would be meeting face to face for the first time, although they might have seen each other previously while sighting down rifles and cannon.

As the brightly decorated express canoes rounded the final downstream curve of the Hayes River, the Nor'Westers caught first glimpse of the three dozen whitewashed structures that made up the HBC's tidewater headquarters on Hudson Bay. In the distance, beyond the hexagonal cupola of the great depot building, they could see the London supply ship riding impatiently on its anchor chain, apt symbol of the direct sea link so crucial to the Company's supremacy.

The paddlers and retinues of the various regional power barons gathered on York Factory's broad foreshore—Cree, Iroquois and Métis, serving different white masters but bound together by the brotherhood of the rivers. They were soon tending bonfires, singing, arm-wrestling, setting off the occasional fireworks, drinking and playing cards long into the starry night, gradually melding into an amicable unit.

Inside the walls, there was as yet no parallel sociability. The two groups eyed each other with suspicion, the gaunt cast of their weather-ravaged faces and their self-conscious gestures reflecting the tensions of the occasion. Even though many of the former Nor'West winterers had retained command of the richest and most extensive fur districts—New Caledonia, Columbia, Athabasca and the Mackenzie River basin—they stood about glaring defensively at the Bay men who were taking over most of the fiercely defended Saskatchewan River posts. However favourable the transitional arrangements might be, the HBC men were now in charge, and the fact that this victory celebration was taking place on Hudson Bay rather than at Fort William underlined that galling fact. Among the banquet guests was John Tod,* a young HBC clerk whose notes provide eyewitness evidence of what happened after the dinner bell rang and the two groups filed into the mess hall. Conspicuously silent and looking appropriately grave, the assembled dinner guests initially showed not the slightest inclination to mix with those who had once been their enemies.

"Evidently uncertain how they would seat themselves at the table," the observant clerk reported, "I eyed them with close attention from a remote corner of the room, and to my mind the scene formed no bad representation of that incongruous animal seen by the King of Babylon in one of his dreams, one part iron, another of clay; though joined together [they] would not amalgamate, for the Nor'Westers in one compact body kept together and evidently had no inclination at first to mix with their old rivals in trade." It was George Simpson, appearing "all bows and smiles," who acted as social director and great conciliator, getting them to shake hands and even eliciting the occasional ghost of a smile from the dour Highland countenances. There were some highly awkward moments. A volatile old Nor'Wester named Allan McDonell found himself seated directly opposite his mortal foe, Alexander Kennedy, the HBC Chief Factor with whom he had crossed swords in a bloody

---

* A native of Glasgow, Tod spent forty years with the HBC, in charge of several important northern and western outposts. When he left the service in 1849, he became the first person to choose Victoria as his retirement home and brought with him a teenage bride from Kamloops (his fourth wife) named Sophia Lolo, who gave birth to the last seven of his ten children. His one-time residence at Oak Bay is still reported to be haunted by the most assertive of his former spouses.

duel only months before over control of the Swan River fur catches. "One of them," noted Tod, "still bore the marks of a cut on his face, the other it was said on some less conspicuous part of the body. I shall never forget the look of scorn and utter defiance with which they regarded each other the moment their eyes met. The Highlander's nostrils actually seemed to expand, he snorted, squirted, spat, not on the table, but between his legs and was as restless as if he had been seated on a hillock of ants; the other looked equally defiant, but less uneasy and upon the whole, more cool. I thought it fortunate that they were without arms … it seemed not improbable they might yet renew the combat, which probably was only prevented in time by a side movement from the upper end of the table, where sat that plausible and most accomplished gentleman Simon McGillivray who used to talk of the 'glorious uncertainty of the law' and the 'nullity of the H.B.C. Charter.' He, seeing the state of affairs near my quarter, sent a request couched in the most gracious terms to [McDonell] to be allowed to take wine with him, which bye the bye had to be repeated more than once before the latter could be induced to remove the glare of his fierce eye from the person of his adversary.… Kennedy too, by similar means, put in operation by one of his friends at hand, was also induced to adopt the appearance of peace and tranquility."

The lavish courses of venison pie, roast partridge, basted wild duck and grilled Arctic char washed down with generous refills of sherry and old port soon had their mellowing effect. The feast, so carefully choreographed by the wily Simpson, developed into a garrulous mutual admiration society. They began to compare notes, laughing at how they might have bested each other in this or that confrontation. By dawn both groups were swearing allegiance to one another—and to George Simpson, now their acknowledged leader.

A BASTARD BY BIRTH and by persuasion, George Simpson dominated the HBC during four crucial decades, the agent of a muscular corporate ethic that overwhelmed friend and foe alike. "To dare and dare again" might have been his motto—though his family coat of arms bore the enigmatic inscription, *Avis nutrior* ("I am fed by birds"). He was one of the few men who lived up to his own Napoleonic pretensions.

The Bonaparte tag was no mere historical allusion. Simpson had triumphed over the Nor'Westers in Athabasca by employing a battlefield dictum followed by the Corsican: One must never interfere with the enemy while he is in the process of destroying himself. He went on to rule an empire larger than any in

Napoleon's most fanciful dreams. A painting of the French Emperor decorated the anteroom of Simpson's office. Like his idol, the wilderness autocrat laid claim to uncommon privilege that was nurtured by the obsequiousness of lieutenants in the field, deferring to his certitude. In height and bearing he even resembled the "Little Emperor."

Simpson's small, darting eyes betrayed the tensions of a setter constantly on point; his hair curled tightly against the back of his neck like fleece. John Henry Lefroy, who toured the Canadian Northwest in 1843–44 making magnetic observations for the British army, noted that Simpson was the toughest-looking man he had ever seen, "built upon the Egyptian model, height two diameters, or like one of those short, square massy pillars one sees in an old country church.... He is a fellow whom nothing will kill." His critics reviled George Simpson as a malevolent wraith—ruthless, chauvinistic and petty. Yet if the history of countries and great institutions flows from an interplay between character and circumstance, he was strictly the right man in exactly the right place at precisely the right time.

His style of buccaneering capitalism belonged less to an age than to a system. At a time when the Hudson's Bay Company's counterparts, the once-glorious East India Company, for example, were collapsing beneath administrative overloads, the HBC under Simpson's whip hand was transformed into an ornament of Empire. Its outriders carried the Union Jack (with its qualifying HB.C. initials in the fly) across the North American continent. While the early patriots of a nascent Canada in the old fiefdoms of the St Lawrence basin were struggling for responsible government, Simpson became an engine of manifest destiny, surging across the boundless reaches of his domain.

The most capable field marshal the HBC ever had, Simpson achieved the daunting task of re-establishing the Company's monopoly after four decades of fierce competition with the Nor'Westers. He did this by sending search-and-destroy teams of his most ruthless traders into the outer reaches of his empire with orders to eliminate putative rivals. The territories south and east of the Columbia River, which Simpson realized might one day be claimed by the United States, were trapped clean in a deliberate scorched-earth tactic meant to confound the American mountain men. Where encroachment by other activities, such as lumbering in the Ottawa Valley or fishing in the Great Lakes, already existed, the HBC launched itself into these enterprises, absorbing such sizeable deficits to capture the market that its opponents retreated in disarray. In the southern extremities of the HBC holdings, Simpson licensed independent trappers to carry their trade into the forests dominated by the American Fur Company, eventually forcing it to abandon the field. On the Pacific Coast, the Governor negotiated an agreement with the Russian-American Company for trapping and maritime rights, displacing the Yanks and then the Russians themselves. When nothing else worked, the HBC distributed liquor on the frontiers of its territories to attract the Indian trade, although alcohol was gradually proscribed elsewhere.

To diversify the Company's holdings to the full, Simpson traded lumber, cranberries and frozen salmon with Hawaii, started the first factory farms on North America's West Coast and even sold ice to Californians. In the 1850s, when San Francisco's population was swollen by the Gold Rush and ice had to be shipped around Cape Horn, the HBC leased some of its glaciers in the northern Pacific to American entrepreneurs, who cut and shipped the ice south. It proved such a success for meat preservation that at one time six large ships were participating in the trade.

By protecting the flanks of his empire, Simpson was able to regenerate the HBC's fur monopoly inside the Rupert's Land boundaries, jealously guarding it from intruders. Except for the traffic in and out of the Red River Settlement, during Simpson's long reign few outsiders were allowed to visit his magic kingdom. Those who did receive permission were mostly artists bent on glorifying the Governor's deeds, members of the British aristocracy engaging in a spot of buffalo hunting, botanists and other natural scientists sent out on behalf of the Royal Society, or land surveyors confirming the full extent of the HBC's impressive holdings.

During Simpson's stewardship, the Company's dividends reached unprecedented levels, rising from 4 percent in 1824 to 10 percent the following year, 20 percent by 1828 and 25 percent a decade later. In the process, the Company's capitalization was increased from £103,950 to £400,000, yielding inordinate capital gains to its stockholders. "Simpson represented in purest distillation the zeal for efficiency which dominated the managers of British industrial life in the early nineteenth century," concluded John S. Galbraith, the Little Emperor's biographer. "He became a nearly perfect instrument of Company policies ... preoccupied with the life of the Company with which he fully identified his own."

While it was certainly true that within the galaxy of his personal universe the Company meant everything, Simpson's psyche was more complicated than that. Like some red-headed magpie with quivering beak and glittery eye, he hoarded private grievances against anyone brave enough to question his iron will. He was a masterly politician, picking his surrogates and underlings with a view to advancing the Company's interests—and perpetuating the personality feuds that would leave him in place as the one indispensable presence. He played his associates off against one another and, like most charismatic leaders, maintained a luminous distance between himself and lesser men. He was so determined to retain this aura of mystery that even in 1841 when he was knighted and the editor of Dod's *Peerage, Baronetage and Knightage* requested the usual personal details required for publication, Sir George refused to supply anything beyond his name, position and address.*

The small arts of popularity found little place in Simpson's business make-up. He was in charge of a wilderness empire under siege by jealous competitors and would-be settlers; his officers were mostly Highland-bred Nor'Westers who regarded any form of corporate discipline as something good only for spayed weaklings. His servants—and few occupied territories have ever been held by such a thinly spread garrison—were mostly stolid Orkneymen, Métis on short-term contracts and ambitious but inexperienced apprentice clerks. To parlay such a corporal's guard into an effective work and occupation force was a magnificent achievement. Simpson drove himself and his men mercilessly, expecting flawless performance and hardly ever taking into account human fallibility. His audacity, his compulsive work habits and the brute force of his manner when he was riled left lesser men gasping for forgiveness, but it was seldom forthcoming. He had little patience with underlings brazen enough to suggest that considerations other than the maximization of profit (such as the welfare of the Indians) might govern the conduct of the fur trade. "It had occurred to me," he wrote to one would-be emancipator, his quill pen dripping with sarcasm, "that philanthropy is not the exclusive object of our visits to these Northern regions." On another occasion, justifying a harsh personnel

---

* The precise date of Simpson's birth remains a mystery, with estimates ranging between 1786 and 1796 and no parish records at Loch Broom in Ross-shire available to provide the correct data. In the Canadian census of 1851, his age was given as fifty-five (making 1796 the year of his birth), but since he was in England when it was taken, he was not the data's source; a register from the paddle steamer *Caledonia*, when she docked at Boston in 1841, listed him as a passenger and gave his age as fifty (which would mean he was born in 1791), but that information is believed to have come from his secretary, E.M. Hopkins. *The Times* of London, in its 1860 obituary, gave Simpson's age as sixty-nine, but his gravestone in Montreal's Mount Royal cemetery states that he was seventy-three when he died. Having studied the available evidence, Galbraith concluded that 1787 was most likely Simpson's birth date.

decision, he noted that "nine out of ten men are captivated with the phantom, Popularity"—and pointedly added that he was not one of them.

His own cousin Thomas Simpson, who left a brilliant academic career at King's College in Aberdeen to join the HBC and later became a noted Canadian explorer, recorded one of the harshest contemporary assessments of his senior kinsman: "His Excellency miscalculates when he expects to get more out of people by sheer driving. By assuming a harsh manner towards me, he should have known ... that the necessary effect on a young and generous mind would be a reciprocal repulsiveness, perhaps hatred; but I know his real sentiments and forgive his apparent, though unnecessary, unkindness.... On a nearer view of his character than I before had I lost much of that internal respect I entertained towards him. His firmness and decision of mind are much impaired: both in great and small matters he has become wavering, capricious and changeable.... He has grown painfully nervous and crabbed, and is guilty of many little meannesses at the table which are quite beneath a gentleman and, I might add, are indicative of his birth."

Even more telling—though the source was suspect because the Governor had refused its author a promotion—was John McLean's *Notes of a Twenty-Five Years' Service in the Hudson's Bay Territory.* "In no colony subject to the British Crown," complained the disappointed Chief Trader, "is there to be found an authority so despotic as is at this day exercised in the mercantile Colony of Rupert's Land; an authority combining the despotism of military rule with the strict surveillance and mean parsimony of the avaricious trader. From Labrador to Nootka Sound the unchecked, uncontrolled will of a single individual gives law to the land.... Clothed with a power so unlimited, it is not to be wondered at that a man who rose from a humble situation should in the end forget what he was and play the tyrant."

McLean also issued a more general warning to any future recruits contemplating service with the HBC: "They may learn that from the moment they embark in the Company's canoes at Lachine or in their ships at Gravesend, they bid adieu to all that civilized man most values on earth. They bid adieu to their families and friends, probably forever, for if they remain long enough to attain the promotion that allows them the privilege of revisiting their native land (twenty or twenty-five years), what changes does not this life exhibit in a much shorter time? They bid adieu to all the comforts and conveniences of civilization to vegetate at some solitary post, hundreds of miles perhaps from any other human habitation, save the wigwam of the savage, without any society other than that of their own thoughts or of the two or three humble persons who share their exile. They bid adieu to all refinement and cultivation, not infrequently becoming semi-barbarians, so altered in habits and sentiments that they not only become attached to savage life, but lose all relish for any other."

George Simpson's career and personality left few observers neutral—even in retrospect. Many historians have praised his accomplishments as the man who rescued the HBC from its fragile status following amalgamation and turned it into a profitable enterprise and an effective instrument of empire. But Alan Cooke, the head of Montreal's Hochelaga Research Institute, roundly condemns the Little Emperor for his money-grubbing single-mindedness: "Simpson must have been one of the best-hated men in North America.... He existed only as a man of business. More than any Indian, he was a slave—a willing slave—of the exploitive machinery of nineteenth-century mercantile capitalism. Although he achieved power, prestige and wealth, his only satisfaction came from work and his only pleasure was in incessant rapid travel.... He is an outstanding example of an immature ego possessed by personal complexes, which he projected onto his colleagues, and by an archetype he did not understand. He had unrivalled opportunities for personal growth but did not seize them."

THE MAIN REASON Simpson aroused so much loathing among some of his contemporaries was his obsession with "Œconomy"—his Draconian version of cost-cutting—which was precisely what was needed to get the business back on track and thus earned him such high esteem among the Company's London proprietors.

At the time of the 1821 merger, the HBC had seventy-six trading posts and the NWC ninety-seven. Within the next half-decade, the geography of the trade was completely reorganized. Norway House, not far from the foot of Lake Winnipeg, became the main distribution depot, its Chief Factor acting as continental dispatcher for the floating brigades that left in their various directions with the precision of express trains. Trading posts were strung at logical intervals along the North Saskatchewan River, with pemmican depots positioned at strategic crossings. Cumberland House was the transit point from the Saskatchewan north to the Churchill River. From Edmonton House, the Athabasca brigades swept on to the Mackenzie and the Peace, while packhorses carried furs and trade goods back and forth through the Okanagan

Valley to Fort Vancouver on the Columbia and, later, by other routes, to Fort Langley on the Fraser.

This proved to be such an efficient system that during the four years after amalgamation, the number of HBC employees was reduced from 1,983 to 827. Although the London Committee initiated the economy drive, Simpson stretched its directives to extremes, reducing wages one-quarter below the official requests and methodically eliminating most of the perquisites and European imports the Chief Factors and Traders had come to regard as their due. He fired many of the trade's veterans and instituted such meticulous cost accounting that he knew to the smallest item the contents of every fur-storage room and larder at each post. An example of the trivia that occupied Simpson was the following provision concerning protocol passed at one of his northern councils: "That all Chief Factors and Chief Traders for whom no special provision is made, accompany their loaded craft from the Depot inland, and all Chief Factors coming out to Depot, be allowed to precede their loaded Craft, thither for the purpose of attending Council, provided no loss of Freight is sustained thereby, and provided measures are concerted to enable two or more to embark in the same Craft." Willard Wentzel, the former NWC clerk who had once welcomed Simpson into the country as a gentleman who would not cause much alarm, now reversed his opinion. "The Northwest," he lamented, "is beginning to be ruled with an iron rod."

No detail seemed to escape Simpson's attention. Leaky boats, the proper manner of observing the Sabbath, declining buffalo tongue harvests, the going rate for Mexican silver dollars, how much mustard should (or should not) be used at each post, tea rations, even cutlery were dealt with in minutest fashion. In a typical missive, he ruled what must constitute a proper set of meal utensils: "The Table Appointments throughout the Country have hitherto been upon much too large a scale, far exceeding the consumption of most respectable families in the civilized world, and I think you may safely reduce the usual supplies by 50 p Cent—the descriptions to be of the cheapest, vizt. Tin plates: ... no table cloths, which with Towels are considered private property. No [earthenware] Dishes: a few Tumblers which answer for Wine glasses. Knives and Forks ought to last at least half a dozen years—in private families they sometimes last 20."

The most significant effect of Simpson's omnipresent Œconomy was felt by the Indians. They were essential to the fur trade, since they did nearly all the work, trapping and skinning the animals and bringing the pelts to the trading posts. But Simpson viewed them as immature creatures, fortunate beneficiaries of the Company's peculiar brand of paternalism.* In an 1822 letter to London explaining the effect on the Indians of the NWC/HBC merger, Simpson set down the tenets he would follow during his governorship: "The late arrangements [absorption of the North West Company] have given mortal offence to Indians.... Their immediate wants have been supplied, but of course the scenes of extravagance are at an end, and it will be a work of time to reconcile them to the new order of things. I have made it my study to examine the nature and character of the Indians and however repugnant it may be to our feelings, *I am convinced they must be ruled with a rod of iron, to bring and to keep them in a proper state of subordination, and the most certain way to effect this is by letting them feel their dependence upon us.* In the woods and Northern barren grounds this measure ought to be pursued rigidly next year if they do not improve, and no credit, not so much as a load of ammunition, given them until they exhibit an inclination to renew their habits of industry." At times, Simpson's condescension got the better of him. In 1825, during his first tour to the Pacific Coast, he noted in his journal: "Two Nez Percés Chiefs arrived to see me from a distance of between [200 and] 300 miles; my fame has spread far and Wide and my speeches are handed from Camp to Camp throughout the Country; some of them have it that I am one of the 'Master of Life's Sons' sent to see 'if their hearts are good' and others that I am his 'War Chief' with bad Medicine if their hearts are bad. On the whole I think my presence and lectures will [do] some good."

During the commercial war between the NWC and HBC, Indian trappers had become adept at playing off one company against the other, often arranging for credit at one post and later bartering their season's catch at another. They developed a sophisticated business network complete with well-connected middlemen, but once Simpson took over, that seesaw technique was diluted as more detailed accounts were kept, reducing the Indians' nomadic preferences. Simpson also did away with the granting of presents, which had become an accepted tradition during the annual trading ceremony. The Company reduced and eventually eliminated the use of rum and brandy for inland trading. While this was a long-term benefit, the changes tended to colonialize

* To impress the Indians, Simpson had a tiny music box attached to his dog's neck in such a way that when it was wound up, music seemed to come from the animal's throat. Generations later, the Carrier were still referring to George Simpson as "the great chief whose dog sings."

the relationship between trader and trapper—breaking down the sense of mutual exploitation that had once characterized their dealings.

The most contentious ruling by the HBC's Governing Council for the Northern Department was passed at its 1841 meeting: a strict limit was imposed on the beaver catch. This was meant as a sensible conservation measure aimed at allowing the doughty animal to rebuild its lodges and supply of offspring, but native trappers construed it as unwarranted interference with their way of life. Traders at individual posts enforced the regulations with a vengeance. George Gladman, then stationed at Norway House, proudly wrote to the Governor: "… an Indian brought me a Beaver skin the other day. The animal being recently killed, this being against the rule, I slapped his face with it!" To ensure obedience from some of the less enthusiastic subscribers to his creed, Simpson issued one of his typical no-nonsense edicts: "[If] it be found that gentlemen disregard this instruction, as they have done many others issued from time to time for the same object, it is [resolved] That the Governor and Committee be respectfully advised to give notice of retirement from the Service to such Gentlemen as may not give effect to the Spirit and the letter of the resolution now passed for the preservation of Beaver."

SIMPSON KNEW that the most effective operational economies must eventually mean replacing canoes because of their relatively puny payloads. He substituted the sturdy York boats on all possible routes, although primitive versions of the craft had been in use for many seasons. Based on an age-old Orkney design, which in turn was derived from the shape of Viking longships, the vessels had been built from time to time at Fort Albany since the 1740s. Called York boats because York Factory was initially their most frequent destination, the reliable craft were capable of carrying three times the payload of the *canot du nord*. They could run most rapids, were more stable in rough lake-crossings than canoes and were resistant to floating ice during spring breakup. Their raised bow and stern posts, mounted with a 45-degree rake, allowed them to be easily backwatered off sandbars. Along portages, the little ships had to be rolled on pre-cleared paths of logs, but this proved to be not an impossible task.

Crewing these larger craft, far less finicky than canoes, required more muscle than skill. Six or eight oarsmen would man the twenty-foot sweep-like oars, rising in their seats to get a purchase on the water, then, bracing themselves with one foot, falling back onto their thwarts—a series of movements that if elegantly executed was not dissimilar to the cadence of Venetian gondoliers. The bowsman would fend off rocks, the stern man steer. A large sail, used as a tent at night, could be hauled up a makeshift mast in following winds. The flat-bottomed vessels were strengthened by being clinker-built, with the overlaps of spruce planking dispersing the impact of steep waves and rocky outcrops.

A York boat, which took two skilled men only two weeks to build, would last three seasons with minimum maintenance. The trickiest part of the construction process was to find the proper piece of spruce or tamarack for a seaworthy keel. Samples were tested by being placed on stocks and a pocket watch held against the butt at one end. The builder listened for the tick at the other. Only if the ticking resonated loudly and clearly through the wood was it judged suitable to withstand the stresses of being carved into a keel. Little effort was expended on aesthetics; outside surfaces were tarred, interiors left unpainted.

As the West began to be settled, the York boats were used for general traffic as well as for the fur trade. The bells in the St Boniface cathedral at Red River arrived by York boat, for example, as did the settlement's first piano.*

These boats may have been fine for everyday traders, but they were not nearly fast enough for George Simpson himself. He did accompany a brigade of the pudgy craft to the Athabasca Country in 1822 to demonstrate their utility along northern routes, but most of his travel time was spent in his own express canoes manned by a praetorian guard of Iroquois boatmen from the Caughnawaga (Kahnawake) band across the St Lawrence from Lachine. A dozen men paddling at speeds up to sixty strokes a minute could propel the boat, measuring thirty-three feet with a five-foot-three beam, ninety to a hundred miles a day.†

The Governor's travels were legendary. During all but three of the thirty-nine years he spent in charge of the HBC's northern fur trade, Simpson ranged across the continent in furiously paced forays, inspecting his posts, hectoring

---

* The final York boat brigade arrived at York Factory in 1871, though York boats continued to be used at isolated posts for many years after that. The last commercial York boat was built at Norway House in 1924; several are still there for summer races on nearby Little Playgreen Lake.

† In 1889, the *Rob Roy* was discovered at Fort Timiskaming. Measuring a full seven fathoms (forty-two feet) long, it was authenticated as one of Simpson's personal craft and would have been one of the largest birchbark canoes ever built.

discouraged Factors, preaching the doctrine of cost efficiency and loving every minute of it. He was constantly in motion. He crossed the Rockies at three latitudes, completed twelve transatlantic round trips, eight visits to Boston and New York, and three great journeys to forts on the Columbia River in the Oregon Country. His most trying trek was by snowshoe during the winter of 1822–23, when he went from Lake Athabasca to Great Slave Lake and back, up the Peace River to Fort Dunvegan and across Lesser Slave Lake to Edmonton House. Simpson loved being on the move, wafting through the melodious forests of the great Northwest, dictating memoranda to his accompanying secretaries and being treated everywhere like a resplendent emperor on an imperial progress. "It is strange," Simpson once wrote to his friend John George McTavish, "that all my ailments vanish as soon as I seat myself in a canoe."

Simpson drove his crews sixteen hours or more a day, determined to demonstrate his own immunity to human weakness and demanding by example that they do the same. *"Levez! Levez! Levez nos gens!"* he would call out at two or three o'clock in the morning before plunging into some nearby lake or river to flaunt his own *joie de vivre*. After that morning dip and half a dozen hours of hard paddling, he would call a brief halt for breakfast and, three or four hours later, another for a quick lunch stop, his crewmen munching pemmican while he sat back and allowed his manservant to present him with tidbits and wine. The Governor had a habit of dozing off between meals but his crews were never allowed to relax. While he appeared to be asleep he would trail the fingers of one hand over the gunwale, testing the cruising speed by noting how high the water splashed up his wrist. The killing pace never let up. One steersman became so exasperated on one of the longer stretches that he picked the Governor up by the collar, lifted him over his head and pitched him into the river—then, with immediate remorse, dove in to help him out. Paradoxically, Simpson never had any trouble recruiting crews of men proud to test their endurance.

He set speed records that have never been beaten (or even attempted), and when he ran out of challenges in North America, he embarked on a voyage around the world. He was the first man to circle the earth by what was then called the "overland route"—and may have been a model for the hero of Jules Verne's *Around the World in Eighty Days*.

Simpson's travels were relieved by many diversions. He once took a sauna during a quick visit to Alaska, and his description of that "castigation" is a classic example of his humour and unexpected self-deprecation: "While at Sitka, I took a bath, which might be a very good thing for those that liked it. On entering the building, I was much oppressed with the steam and heat, while an ill-looking, long-legged, stark-naked fellow was waiting to officiate, as master of the ceremonies. Having undressed in an antechamber, so far as decency would permit, I made my way into the bathroom, which was heated almost to suffocation. Having thus got me into his power, the gaunt attendant threw some water on the iron furnace, while, to avoid, as far as possible, the clouds of steam that were thus raised, I squatted myself down on the floor, perspiring profusely at every pore. I next seated myself on a bench, while bucket after bucket of hot water was thrown on my head; and then, making me stretch myself out, my tormentor soaped me all over, from head to foot, rubbing and lathering me with a handful of pine-tops.... Once more taking his bucket, the horrid operator kept drenching me, the successive pailfuls descending gradually from nearly a boiling heat to the temperature of fifty degrees. The whole process occupied about an hour. I then returned to the antechamber, where, after being dried with hot towels, I was very glad to put on dry clothes. It was impossible, however, to make my escape immediately, for I was so relaxed as to be obliged to recline on a sofa for a quarter of an hour; and then I withdrew, inwardly resolved never again to undergo such another castigation."

One reason for his whirling-dervish approach was that Simpson wanted to catch his post managers off guard so he could check up on the efficacy of their daily rounds. He relocated posts, opened a few and closed many more. To heighten the patrician impact of his cavalcade on the woebegone little forts, Simpson arrived at each major stop with a sequence of punctilious flourishes worthy of a pope presuming worship. The pomp nearly always outdid the circumstance. Simpson's party, which usually included an escorting canoe or two, would put in to shore just before entering any settlement to give the Governor time to don his beaver topper and his paddlers a moment to spruce up in their best shirts. Ready and set, they would sweep towards the fort's tiny log dock at top speed. Once they were within sight and sound of the HBC fort, the performance would begin. A bugler, an occasional bagpiper and the voices of his chanting paddlers would meld into an impressive orchestration. This was how Chief Trader Archibald McDonald, who accompanied Simpson in his own canoe during the 1828 inspection tour to the Columbia, described the spectacle: "As we wafted along under easy sail, the men with a clean change and mounting new feathers, the Highland bagpipes in the Governor's canoe, was echoed by the bugle in mine; then these were laid aside on nearer approach to port, to give free scope to the vocal organs of about eighteen Canadians to chant one of those voyageur airs peculiar to them, and always so perfectly rendered.... On the signal hill of rock, from a tall Norway Pine shaft, floated the 'grand old Flag'. From the 'hollow rocks'—the world of rocks—all around us, awoke the wild echoes, by 'the bugle', 'set flying'. Then the grand thunder—skirrl of 'the bag pipes', with their 'Campbell's are coming, hourray! hourray!' or some such 'music of our mountain land', loud droned out to the very vault of heaven. And then—as a cadenza of soothing, gladdening, exqui- site charm—the deep and soft and so joyously toned voices of those full throated voyageurs, timed with a stroke—so quick—of glittering paddle blade, singing with such heart their 'La Claire Fontaine', or some such loved air of their native land—our own land, let us say ... when the Governor's canoe, with its grand high prow rounded, and brightly painted, flashed out of the dark rock 'at the point' into our full view, and gracefully turned into the little 'port' at our feet, the heart seemed to swell with admiration and delight at the sight. Never; never, had anything so grand and splendid, and delightful withal, been seen in those primitive wilds!"

Flags flying, cannon blasting, his piper leading the way, the Governor would step ashore in his theatrical Royal Stuart tartan cloak with collar of soft Genoa velvet. Simpson's insistence on being convoyed by a piper was only partly vanity. What better, what more emotional way to reach the hearts and souls of his men in these lonely huts than with the mantra of the glens? Those eerie wings must have been the equivalent of the trumpet flourishes that paced Giuseppe Garibaldi's march on Naples—their sound described by British historian G.M. Trevelyan as ringing "through the noonday stillness like a summons to the soul of Italy." Simpson's piper was Colin Fraser, who arrived in 1827 at York Factory from Kirkton, in Sutherlandshire. To win the £30-a- year job, he was asked to walk in front of a carriage the twenty miles to the point of embarkation, playing all the way; Fraser was the only one of three candidates who made it.

The bagpipes may have wowed the Highlanders, but Simpson's caravan left behind many puzzled Indians. According to one anonymous and quite possi- bly apocryphal story, a Cree who heard Colin Fraser play at Norway House reported to his chief. "One white man was dressed like a woman, in a skirt of funny color. He had whiskers growing from his belt and fancy leggings. He carried a black swan which had many legs with ribbons tied to them. The swan's body he put under his arm upside down, then he put its head in his mouth and bit it. At the same time he pinched its neck with his fingers and squeezed the body under his arm until it made a terrible noise."

BY 1824, Simpson's energy and single-minded dedication to reforming the fur trade within the confines of Rupert's Land was paying dividends, but on the other side of the Rockies and to the south along the West Coast, the so-called Columbia Department was still showing serious losses. It was in part a problem of sovereignty: Alaska was Russian, California remained Spanish, and the territories in between, jointly administered by the United States and Great Britain, were loosely occupied by the Hudson's Bay Company.

To reorganize and invigorate that Pacific operation, Simpson appointed as Chief Factor Dr John McLoughlin, the former Nor'Wester who had led the wintering partners' rebellion prior to amalgamation. McLoughlin left York Factory for his new assignment at Astoria on July 26, 1824, vowing that despite the Governor's reputation for speed, he would be first to reach the Columbia. Simpson had decided to await the arrival of the annual supply ship so that he could catch the season's incoming mail from the London Committee. He waited three full weeks, and when the vessel had still not arrived, he set off accompanied by a Chief Trader named James McMillan to teach the proud McLoughlin a lesson.

Instead of following the good doctor up the Hayes River, he chose the much more difficult but shorter route up the Nelson, setting daily speed records along the way. Less than five days out of York Factory, he exulted in his journal: "I believe there is nothing known in the annals of Rupert's Land travelling, equal to our journey so far." Six weeks later on the banks of a shallow river, at seven o'clock one dewy morning, McLoughlin and his party were still trying to stretch themselves awake when the Governor's canoes hove triumphantly into view. Despite his twenty-day head start, McLoughlin had been beaten, and he was anything but pleased by the speedy Governor. Simpson's description of the hulking wilderness doctor was appropriately unsentimental: "He was such a figure as I should not like to meet on a dark Night in one of the bye lanes in the neighbourhood of London dressed in Clothes that had once been fashionable, but now covered with a thousand patches of different Colors, his beard would do honor to the chin of a Grizzly Bear, his face and hands evidently Shewing that he had not lost much time at the Toilette, loaded with Arms and his own herculean dimensions forming a tout ensemble that would convey a good idea of the highwaymen of former days." The joint party reached the Pacific in eighty-four days' travel time, cutting three weeks off previous records, though Simpson complained all the way that he had been forced to slow down "to give the Dr. an opportunity of keeping up with us."

Simpson's return journey was even more dramatic. Although he realized that he was due to preside at a Northern Council meeting in Norway House during early June, he did not leave the Columbia until late April 1825—and that meant fighting his way against spring flood waters. Because some prearranged horses did not show up, he and his party had to walk through the tortuous Athabasca Pass in the Rocky Mountains, crossing the rushing Wood River seventeen times. "Some of the people were so numbed with the cold," he dispassionately observed, "that on getting out of the water, they actually could not stand." After a second such nightmare tumble down the range's eastern slope (crossing the icy Whirlpool River twenty-seven times), he finally clambered into a waiting canoe and sped down the North Saskatchewan to Fort Carlton, an old HBC post on the boundary of the Plains Indians' hunting grounds. The Indians were on the warpath, and his retinue was too frightened and physically spent to continue. Not Simpson. He commandeered some horses and, with half a dozen volunteers, rode off over the hostile prairie. They eventually reached the juncture of the Qu'Appelle and Assiniboine rivers. Both were in full flood and there seemed no way across. "The water was too wide; there was no wood of any kind to make a Raft; several of our people could not swim.... I however being more at home in the Water than any of my fellow travellers and anxious to save the lives of the poor animals [horses], stripped and Swam across with a few things; three others followed my example and by making several crossings in this way we got the whole of our little Baggage over; the Horses were driven across, those people who could not Swim holding on by their Tails.... In like manner we got across the Assiniboine River."

His personal servant, Thomas Taylor, and a trader named George Bird got lost while hunting for food. Simpson coolly noted that if they were to meet any hostile Indians along the way, "they will lose their scalps as a matter of course." (Taylor and Bird did eventually stumble into an HBC Post.) By the time the Simpson party reached White Horse Plain, sixteen miles from Fort Garry at the Red River Settlement, none of the Governor's companions could continue. His melodramatic final dash is best described in his own journal entry: "I got on my old charger 'Jonathan,' gave him the Rein with a smart cut across the haunches and commenced a furious attack on the Gates of Fort Garry at 12 midnight, was immediately answered by a most hearty welcome from Mr. McKenzie and every person at the Garrison and here I purpose taking a rest for Eight Days after having performed one of the most dangerous and harassing journeys ever undertaken in the Country through which, thank God, I have got with no injury or inconvenience worthy of Notice."

At the Norway House meeting that followed this exploit, Simpson was rewarded by tangible evidence of the London board's esteem—a raise in pay of £200 to £1,200 a year, plus a £500 bonus. At the same time, he received a resounding vote of confidence from the assembled Chief Factors, who praised his "unremitting exertion … masterly arrangements and decisive measures." Significantly, the testimonial was signed by such hard cases as the former Nor'Wester Samuel Black.

Simpson's next venture to the Pacific three years later was even more rushed, covering the 3,261 miles from York Factory to Fort Langley near the mouth of the Fraser in a breathtaking sixty-five days. Accompanied by Chief Trader Archibald McDonald and Dr Richard Hamlyn, Simpson embarked to the (compulsory) three cheers of York Factory's permanent staff and a seven-gun salute at one o'clock in the morning of July 12. The two passengers were assigned the duty of waking up the crews at precisely two each morning, and since there were no alarm clocks, that meant each could sleep only on alternate nights. For the first time, Simpson was also accompanied by his country wife, Margaret, the Mixed Blood sister of his servant, Thomas Taylor. "The commodity has been a great consolation to me," was the chauvinistic tribute to his female companion in a letter he sent from Stuart Lake, along the way, to his friend McTavish.

Except for its furious pace, the journey was uneventful until they crossed the Rocky Mountains. Because Simpson realized that the Company could not hold on forever to its trading rights in the Oregon Country and would therefore lose the access to the Pacific afforded by the Columbia River, he was set on discovering an alternative route. He thus decided to explore the Fraser River and its great tributary, the Thompson, both of which their discoverer, Simon Fraser, had so eloquently declared to be unnavigable only twenty years previously. Simpson had also been warned by local traders that he would never descend those rocky torrents alive. That, of course, ensured he would make the attempt. After facing the terrors of the Thompson, which he admitted "made whitened countenances of the boldest among us," he tackled the relentless Fraser with its perpendicular canyons and deadly whitewater shoots. Though Simpson praised his Iroquois bowman for being "nearly amphibious," even he was forced to concede that passage down that river of hell was certain death and disappointedly ruled it out as a trade route. That also eliminated Fort Langley as the HBC's future Pacific terminus, though it remained an important regional trading post well into the 1880s.

DURING THESE AND OTHER EXCURSIONS, Simpson devoted most of his time to assessing the strengths and weaknesses of his men in the field. He could be occasionally compassionate and frequently cruel. As in James Thurber's cele-brated metaphor, Simpson knew how to cut off a man's head so that he didn't realize it was severed until he tried to sneeze. He displayed little sympathy for the Company's veterans. In a confidential letter he wrote to the London Committee's Andrew Colvile in 1826, he explained: "Many of our principal Clerks are nearly worn out and I should not consider it good policy to allow them to have commissions as the step from a Chief Tradership to a Chief Factorship I think ought to be gained by important active services which none except such as are in the prime and vigour of Life should be qualified or required to perform. I consider it highly injurious to the general interests to have old worn out men in our councils, they are timid, indolent and helpless and would be of no manner of use in cases of difficulty danger or emergency. Worn out Indian Traders are the most useless helpless class of men I ever knew and the sooner the Company can get rid of them after their days of activity and labor are over the better; but that will always be a difficult matter as they become attached to the Country to the half savage Life they have been accustomed to lead and to their women and Families and will not move unless actually forced away."

Still, Company morale during most of the Little Emperor's reign was high, partly because service with the HBC had become something of a family affair. Youngsters had been following fathers and uncles into the Company for five or more generations. Out of touch with their extended families in Scotland, many of the more isolated traders nurtured a filial relationship with Simpson, seeking him out for advice about their lives, personal as well as corporate. They asked for his help in finding wives, lost children or new postings; they turned their savings over to him for investment and often named him executor of their wills. Loved or hated, he was the great patriarch of the clan.

Among his closest associates were John George McTavish, the former Nor'Wester in charge of Fort William at amalgamation, who was transferred to similar responsibilities at York Factory; Alexander Christie, who lasted forty-two years in the HBC; Duncan Finlayson, a talented veteran who spent his last three years with the HBC as a member of its London Committee; James Hargrave, a crusty fur trader also remembered because of his hospitable and literary wife, Letitia; and Angus Cameron, the Fort Timiskaming Chief Factor, who received what was probably the Governor's highest compliment: "From what I have seen of you, I consider you worthy of whatever can be done for you, command me therefore when you may think I can be useful."

But Simpson's favourite fur trader was John Rowand, son of a Montreal doctor, who had joined the North West Company as a fourteen-year-old apprentice and for thirty years ruled the HBC's key Saskatchewan district with something close to inspired tyranny. Simpson promoted him to Chief Factor at Edmonton House in 1823, took him along for part of his round-the-world tour and treated him as a confidant rather than an employee.

Edmonton House and its NWC counterpart were relocated on several occasions, sometimes as much as 125 miles at a time, from the original 1794 site. It became a key post because the old canoe route to the Athabasca and Pacific via the Churchill River and Methy Portage was abandoned after 1824 in favour of the North Saskatchewan water route and later along the Carlton Trail. Pioneered by Simpson on his dramatic return journey from the Columbia in 1825, this land route became a major artery, eventually worn clear by more than three hundred Red River carts making round trips at eighty-day intervals.

Aside from being a key conduit, Edmonton under Rowand's direction quickly became the most productive fort in the territories, in terms both of its impressive fur catch and as a production centre for York boats and bags of pemmican. Rowand developed the West's first horse-breeding spread, complete with a two-mile racetrack, and his sixteen-hand chestnut hunter was the object of much envy. A vital trading centre for tribes in the Plains group (the Assiniboine, Cree, Blackfoot, Sarcee, Gros Ventre, Peigan and Blood), the hexagon-shaped enclosure at Edmonton soon sprouted a dozen warehouses, residences and workshops. All were smeared with the red earth found in the neighbourhood, which, when mixed with oil, produced a shade called "durable brown."

The most imposing structure of all was Rowand's own "Big House," his residence and office, which boasted the Northwest's first glass windows. (They had been shipped from England in barrels of molasses to minimize breakage.) Known to the locals as Rowand's Folly, the three-storey extravaganza had an outside gallery running the length of the building where the resident piper could tread his measured path, wheezing the call of the Highlands to the fort's population of 130. Off the second-storey gallery was a gentlemen's mess on one side and the Northwest's only ballroom on the other. Under the high-pitched roof were the bedrooms and on the ground floor the armoury, kitchen and stewards' quarters. Rowand used the ballroom mainly to hold court and impress visiting Indian chiefs, but at Christmas he could entertain 150 at a single sitting for dinner and dancing. Itinerant artist Paul Kane, who was there to enjoy the 1847 repast, wrote glowingly of a meal that included boiled premature buffalo calves, dried moose noses, wild goose, and whitefish delicately browned in buffalo marrow. "The walls and ceiling," he reported, "are painted in a style of the most startling, barbaric gaudiness, and the ceiling filled with centre pieces of fantastic gilt scrolls, making altogether a saloon which no white man would enter without a start and which the Indians always looked upon with awe and wonder." Although Rowand forbade most Indian and Mixed Blood women from dining with "the gentlemen," they were welcomed in for the dances that followed, enjoying mightily the famous Red River jig and toe-tapping theatrics of the local fiddler. *Harper's Magazine* described a typical Métis dance of the period in its October 1860 issue: "Jigs, reels, and quadrilles were danced in rapid succession … fresh dancers taking the place of those on the floor every two or three moments. The men were stripped to shirt, trousers, belt and moccasins; and the women wore gowns which had no hoops … a black-eyed beauty in blue calico, and a strapping Bois Brûlé, would jump up from the floor and outdo their predecessors in vigor and velocity—the lights and shadows chasing each other faster and faster over the rafters; the flame, too, swaying wildly hither and thither; and above the thumps of the dancers' heels, and the frequent 'Ho! Ho!' and the laughter … rose the monomaniac fiddle-shrieks, forced out of the trembling strings, as if a devil was at the bow."

The fountainhead for all this merriment, John Rowand, stood even shorter than Simpson but was known as the Big Mountain for good reason, his ample girth* being supported by equally outrageous quantities of bombast and bluster. His temper made even Simpson seem a bit of a milquetoast. When several of his servants came down with a serious malady, Rowand accused them of shirking their duty and decreed that "… any man who is not dead within three days' illness is not sick at all." His operating philosophy was summed up in the terse credo: "We know only two powers—God and the Company!" On one occasion, when he and the well-known Catholic missionary Albert Lacombe were out riding across the plains, they were resting at a campfire when they suddenly found themselves surrounded by two hundred Blackfoot, clearly on the warpath. Rowand marched up to the chief and roared, *"Stop, you villains!"*—then turned his back and resumed his meal. Recognizing his opponent, the chief not only called off the raiding party but was so abject in his apologies that according to the piper Colin Fraser, who reported the incident, many of the Indians "actually cried with vexation."

That was an obvious exaggeration, but Rowand's influence did help keep the Prairies free of antagonistic incidents at a time when the American Plains ran with the blood of Indian wars. Rowand's affinity for his regions' inhabitants was no doubt influenced by his romantic first encounter with Louise Umphreville, his Mixed Blood country wife. As a young man he had gone buffalo hunting one morning, riding out alone through the gates of Fort des Prairies, where he was then stationed. She had noticed his departure, and when his horse returned riderless, she became alarmed and jumped on a pony and followed the horse to where Rowand, who had been thrown by his mount, was lying immobilized with a broken leg. She set his limb, binding the splints with strips from her leather garments. They fell in love while she was nursing him back to health, and although their marriage was never officially consecrated, they stayed together for thirty-nine years, and Louise became the proud chatelaine of their wilderness chateau.

In the spring of 1854, Rowand was leading the Edmonton brigade down the Saskatchewan, planning to take a year's furlough prior to retirement. While at Fort Pitt, where his son was Chief Trader, he noticed two Métis crewmen

---

* It was a family affair. His wife weighed in at only 322 pounds, but Rowand's daughter Margaret reached 336 pounds, while his son John, Jr., was an even 350. When Margaret married an HBC trader named James McKay (364 pounds), an observant guest at the wedding noted that the moment the four of them got up to jig, 1,372 pounds hit the dance floor. McKay, later a Manitoba minister of agriculture, was so huge that when he and his bride went for rides in their hackney carriage, they had to sit one behind the other.

having a fight. He stepped between them, his face flushed, temper rising. Without warning, he clutched his chest and dropped dead of a heart attack. His bereaved son and members of the little outpost's garrison buried the staunch trader with full honours.

Then the fun began. Rowand had stipulated in his will that his bones should rest in Montreal, his birthplace, and George Simpson was not about to ignore his friend's final request. In the spring of 1855, Rowand's body was disinterred and an elderly Indian was instructed to boil the flesh off the bones, which were then stored inside a keg that was carefully filled with rum as a preservative. (The women at Fort Pitt utilized the considerable amount of residual fat to make soap.) Simpson sent his own canoe to bring the remains to Red River, but the superstitious crew threw the keg over the side of the express canoe during a storm on Lake Winnipeg, believing that the dead man's unrequited rage had caused a tempest to swamp them. The barrel was eventually recovered and trundled onward to York Factory.

Since there was no direct link between Hudson Bay and Montreal, the makeshift coffin was loaded on a supply ship heading for London. There, the HBC Committeemen tendered the battered barrel a magnificent funeral service, complete with muffled drums and standardbearers. The keg was then taken to Liverpool, where it was for a time lost in a storage shed but ultimately loaded on a Montreal-bound steamer.

Nearly four years to the day after his death, John Rowand's remains were ready to be buried at Mount Royal cemetery. When the peripatetic barrel was finally pried open, it was full not of rum but of water.

The Viceroy

*Under George Simpson, the hbc tacitly agreed to serve as an informal
territorial agency of the British Empire, ensuring that there existed a modicum
of law and order in this far corner of Queen Victoria's globe.*

MASTERMINDING THE THIN VANGUARD of Bay functionaries holding
together a territory ten times the size of the Holy Roman Empire, George
Simpson acted with the lordly hauteur of a man in charge of his private
universe. But he was in fact a viceroy—one who ruled his province as the
representative of an external sovereign power and exercised his authority in
its name.

Every summer while the trade was slack and the rivers were flowing
wide, the Council of the Northern Department of Rupert's Land met either
at York Factory or, more often, at Norway House. Unlike the bonny
reunions of the Nor'Westers at Fort William, which were as much excuses
for great parties as discussions of policy, these HBC conclaves were sonorous
business sessions, with the gathered Chief Factors and Traders exchanging
views and auguries, but being very much guided by the Governor's every
word and gesture.

The most practical advice on how to deal with Simpson was tendered by a
veteran Chief Factor named John Stuart, who told Donald Smith, his newly
arrived Scottish nephew (who would one day hold Simpson's office), that
there was only one way to cultivate the Governor's sponsorship: "No man is
more appreciative of downright hard work coupled with intelligence.... It is
his foible to exact not only strict obedience, but deference to the point of
humility. As long as you pay him in that coin you will quickly get on his sunny
side and find yourself in a few years a trader at a congenial post, with promotion in sight."

Even though many of the Chief Factors who sat pondering around the conference tables at the Northern Department Council meetings were formerly high-spirited Nor'Westers who had come within a breath of beating the HBC at its own game, they realized only too well they were no longer "lords of the lakes and forests"; they had become integral cogs in an efficient transcontinental fur-gathering machine. Members of the Council had the right to nominate their own successors, but it was Simpson and the London Committee who made the final selections. "They could outvote me, but it has never been so," Simpson wrote, referring to the Council as "my own government." He presided at these gatherings flanked by his recording clerks and listened to the debates with ill-concealed, foot-tapping boredom. Although it was not true, as alleged by his critic John McLean, that he wrote the minutes of the meetings *before* they took place, the renegade trader's verdict on how much power the Council actually had was chillingly accurate: "The few individuals who compose it know better than to offer advice where none would be accepted; they know full well that the Governor has already determined on his own measures before one of them appears in his presence. Their assent is all that is expected of them, and that they never hesitate to give."

Simpson was much too wise to make it appear that he was not heeding the advice of his pastoral parliament. When he asked John George McTavish to substitute for him at one of the meetings, the Governor explained the secret of his approach. "Keep your temper," he advised, "and do not allow yourself [to] be drawn into altercation with any of those who may be there; you can gain neither honour nor glory by quarrelling with them, but can twist them around your finger by setting about it properly." Despite his deftness in dealing with his troops and scattered lieutenants, Simpson came under heavy criticism for playing favourites and bypassing established procedures. (Chief Traders were supposed to be appointed only after nine years as clerks, while to become a Chief Factor required at least sixteen years in the service.) But he had many more claimants for preference than he could possibly satisfy, and even at their worst, Simpson's personal likes and dislikes did little to prejudice the profitable conduct of the trade.

Like everything else he did, Simpson judged the character of the Highlanders under his command in a methodical manner that revealed as much about himself as it did about them. In a secret Character Book, he analysed with absolute candour the personalities and motivations of his senior people. The pocket notebook's entries, which delved into his subalterns' lives both private and professional, was strictly for his own use. It was not listed as being in the HBC's Archives until 1923, and its code (he numbered each entry instead of using names) was found separately on a piece of scrap paper by an archivist named K.E. Pincock. Professor Glyndwr Williams of Queen Mary College, London, who edited the document for publication, noted that "as a feat of memory and sustained reportage the Character Book is a *tour de force*.... The men who helped the Hudson's Bay Company to its period of greatest dominance in the North American fur trade ... emerge not as names in an official letter or signatures at the end of a formal report, but as human beings, usually fallible, sometimes frail and inconsequent. Many are shown in a harsh, ungenerous light which magnifies the imperfections and deepens the shadows."

Even Simpson's friends received objective reviews. John George McTavish was one of the Governor's closest companions, sharing personal as well as professional concerns. Yet in his Character Book, the Governor pointed out that McTavish was "generous to extravagance ... unnecessarily dignified and high minded which leads to frequent difficulties with his associates by whom he is considered a 'Shylock' and upon many of whom he looks down ... has of late Years become very heavy unwieldy and inactive; over fond of good living and I much fear is getting into habits of conviviality and intemperance." Not even John Rowand escaped criticism. Simpson extolled his boldness and added that he "will not tell a lie (which is very uncommon in this Country) but has sufficient address to evade the truth when it suits his purpose...."

A sampling of Simpson's little red book leaves open the question of how he managed to run an empire with such an emotionally crippled crew. These are a few typical examples of his more negative assessments:

Antoine Hamel: ... A stout strong illiterate common kind of fellow who was employed during the opposition in River St Maurice because he could walk well on Snow Shoes and had the name of being a tolerable bruiser. Can drink, tell lies and Swear.

Charles Ross: ... A good classical scholar and a man of very correct conduct but so nervous at times that it is quite painful to see him. Very Slovenly both in business and in his appearance.... I have often thought that he was not quite of Sound Mind and am much mistaken if he has not shown decided symptoms of Madness although it has been carefully concealed by those about him.

Thomas Dears: ... A flippant, superficial, trifling creature—who lies more frequently than he speaks the truth, can take a Glass of Grog and I strongly suspect is given to pilfering: altogether a low scampish fellow, but active, can make himself useful either at a Trading Post or Depot and has a facility in acquiring a smattering of the Indian Languages. Was picked up in Canada during the opposition when character was not much enquired into and I suspect him a Gentleman's Servant "out of place."

Leslie Bryson: An Irishman.... Was attached to the Commissariat in the Peninsular War, but I should think in one of the lowest capacities ... is evidently a fellow who has been accustomed to live from hand to mouth by his Wits. Deals in the Marvellous but his fiction is harmless.

Francis Ermatinger: ... A stout active boisterous fellow who is a tolerable clerk and trader and qualified to be useful where bustle and activity without any great exercise of judgment are necessary. Talks a little at random but will not descend to a deliberate falsehood. Got into disgrace lately in conse-quence of having employed one of the Company's Servants in cutting off the Ears of an Indian who had had an intrigue with his Woman, but which would not have been thought so much of, had it been done by himself in the heat of passion or as a punishment for Horse Stealing.

It was when he harboured a personal dislike for one of his officers that Simpson's sarcasm really struck home. Characteristic entries dealt with two of the most distinguished pre-amalgamation Bay men, John Clarke and Colin Robertson.

John Clarke: A boasting, ignorant low fellow who rarely speaks the truth and is strongly suspected of dishonesty; his commanding appearance and pompous manner, however, give him a good deal of influence over Indians and Servants; and his total want of every principle or feeling, allied to fair dealing, honour and integrity, together with his cruel and Tyrannical disposition render him eminently qualified for playing the lawless, cold blooded Bravo in opposition. He is in short a disgrace to the "Fur Trade."

Colin Robertson: A frothy trifling conceited man, who would starve in any other Country and is perfectly useless here: fancies, or rather attempts to pass himself off as a clever fellow, a man of taste, of talents and of refinement; to none of which I need scarcely say he has the smallest pretension. He was bred to his Father's Trade an operative Weaver in the Town of Perth, but was too lazy to live by his Loom, read Novels, became Sentimental and fancied himself the hero of every tale of Romance that passed through his hands. Ran away from his master, found employment for a few months as a Grocer's Shopman at New York, but had not sufficient steadiness to retain his Situation. Pushed his way into Canada and was at the Age of 25 engaged as *Apprentice* Clerk by the N W Co for whom he came to the interior, but found so useless that he was dismissed from the Service. His age about 55 and his person of which he is exceedingly vain, large, soft, loosely thrown together inactive and helpless to infirmity. He is full of silly boasting and Egotism, rarely deals in plain matter of fact and his integrity is very questionable. To the Fur trade he is quite a Burden, and a heavy burden too, being a compound of folly and extravagance, and disarranging and throwing into confusion whatsoever he puts his hand to in the shape of business. The concern would gain materially by allowing him to enjoy his situation a thousand Miles distant from the scene of operations instead of being taxed with his nominal Services in the Country.

This last was the most ill-considered of Simpson's entries, jumping as it does from Robertson's early NWC days to his later, somewhat tarnished years without taking into account his magnificent contributions to the HBC's survival in between. Simpson shunted Robertson aside by giving him insignificant assignments such as the Chief Factorship of New Brunswick. He was retired in 1840 after thirty-seven years' service and a year later was elected member for the Lake of Two Mountains riding in the Legislative Assembly of Canada.

The Character Book was an important if covert guide to Simpson's decisions because once an entry had been made, the Governor seldom altered his view of officers and clerks, no matter how their performance might improve or deteriorate. The real source of his authority flowed from the fact that he was the London Committee's man in North America. He held a tight grip over the HBC's Northern Department from 1821 onwards, but it was another five years before he supplanted Governor Williams of the Southern Department to head both districts, and he was officially accorded the grand title of Governor-in-Chief of Rupert's Land only in 1839. By then he was running the company's everyday affairs, although as late as 1846 the London board vetoed his request that he be allowed to appoint clerks in the Montreal Department without their approval.

The overseas Governor's most important leverage in his struggle for expanded authority was the slowness of the communications system with London—the days of transatlantic cable transmissions still being well in the future, conveniently after his time. As it was, a letter forwarded aboard the Company's spring supply ship to Hudson Bay was delivered in late summer, duly answered, and the reply received in England only by late autumn—to be acted upon the following spring in time for the vessel's return to York Factory, a full year after the original inquiry. By the time this annual cycle had run its course, most operational decisions had already been taken. At that, Simpson had few substantive arguments with his corporate parent, except that he wanted to exercise greater daring than the London Committee could stomach. He was also a more enthusiastic British Imperialist (and devout anti-revolutionary), urging London in 1824, for example, on no account to give up any Oregon territory north of the Columbia River.

In his dealings with London, Simpson enjoyed the incalculable advantage of having in his corner his original mentor, Andrew Colvile, that most influential of the HBC's Committeemen. For the first thirty years of Simpson's term, the London Governor in charge was Sir John Henry Pelly, who had already spent more than a decade on the HBC's board. He served simultaneously as a director and ultimately Governor of the Bank of England. Cultivated, clever and cordial, Pelly viewed the making of money as something of an intellectual tumbling exercise. His father, grandfather and great-grandfather had all been skippers in the service of the East India Company, and he himself enjoyed four years in command of his own ship. He insisted on being called Captain Pelly ever afterwards, and his official portrait shows him wearing the gold-braided Royal Navy jacket of Nelson's vintage, posing beside the model of a light-house. The beacon's presence was more authentic than his assumed RN captaincy, since Pelly was Deputy Master of Trinity House, Britain's pilotage and principal lighthouse authority.*

---

* Master of Trinity House at this time was the Duke of Wellington, a close friend and associate of Sir John's. During Pelly's term at the Bank of England, the nation's credit position grew so precarious that £2,000,000 had to be borrowed from the Bank of France. In the ensuing riots, Pelly (as the bank's former governor) invited Wellington to inspect the building's paramilitary defences, including the gun positions on its roof, in case there was a run on the bank. They knew how to deal with creditors in those days.

Pelly's lengthy tenure conveniently consolidated the Hudson's Bay Company's status within the British financial establishment. The reticent and largely self-perpetuating oligarchy that controlled most of its stock operated out of the Company's headquarters at Numbers 3 and 4 Fenchurch Street, near the corner of Gracechurch. Corinthian columns flanked the red brick building's arched front gate; inside, the height of the hall's white ceilings was set off by tall mahogany doors, brass lamps and velvet swags up the staircases. Each Wednesday at high noon the Governor, Deputy Governor and half a dozen Committeemen would gather to consider the Company's affairs, exchange City gossip and speculate on the government's evolving policies towards North America.

Herman Merivale, the Colonial Office's permanent undersecretary, voiced no objection to the HBC's occupation of the Prairie region on condition that the Company improve the social and economic situation of the native peoples within its purview. Under George Simpson, the HBC tacitly agreed to serve as an informal territorial agency of the British Empire, ensuring that there existed a modicum of law and order in this far corner of Queen Victoria's globe. In return, it was understood that the British government would help keep out settlers and prevent free trade in furs. Either incursion would have weakened or destroyed the HBC's monopoly, which the London bureaucrats recognized as being an essential deterrent if the territory in question was not to degenerate into a killing ground similar to the American West. "The reason for this situation was clear," commented historian David McNab. "If the Company did not treat its skilled native labour humanely, then there was always a distinct possibility that the Company's supply of furs would be either disrupted or curtailed altogether in any particular region. Using this reasoning, Merivale marshalled his arguments and concluded that, for the circumstances existing in Rupert's Land in the mid-nineteenth century, the best ruler was the Hudson's Bay Company." This practical attitude was of necessity based on third-hand information, with the Colonial Office dependent on reports from the HBC's London headquarters about what was really happening west of Lake Ontario.

One plaintive countervailing voice of protest was that of Alexander Kennedy Isbister. The articulate son of an HBC clerk and a Cree mother, he had joined the Company and served with distinction at Fort McPherson, then its northernmost outpost, which he had helped establish. Angered by what he considered Simpson's reluctance to promote Mixed Bloods, he resigned. After spending some years at Red River, he enrolled in the University of Aberdeen, was admitted to the bar, and eventually became dean of an important British teachers' college. He used his prestigious position to lobby Westminster and the Colonial Office on granting free trade to the Red River Métis, but his speeches, articles and books went unnoticed. His petition remains one of the most eloquent and unanswerable indictments of the Hudson's Bay Company's treatment of the Indian peoples: "When we assert that they are steeped in ignorance, debased in mind, and crushed in spirit, that by the exercise of an illegal claim over the country of their forefathers, they are deprived of the natural rights and privileges of free born men, that they are virtually slaves, as absolutely as the unredeemed negro population of the slave states of America—that by a barbarous and selfish policy, founded on a love of lucre, their affections are alienated from the British name and government, and they themselves shut out from civilisation, and debarred from every incentive thereto—that the same heinous system is gradually effacing whole tribes from the soil on which they were born and nurtured, so that a few years hence not one man among them will be left to point out where the bones of his ancestors repose—when we assert all this in honest, simple truth, does it not behoove every Christian man to demand that the British legislature should not continue to incur the fearful responsibility of permitting the extinction of these helpless, forlorn thousands of their fellow creatures, by lending its countenance to a monopoly engendering so huge a mountain of human misery? For the honour of this great country, we pray it will not be; and, sincerely trust we, some few voices will respond earnestly, Amen."

The native peoples had succumbed in dramatic numbers to the 1837 smallpox epidemic. That summer, the dreaded infection spread up the Missouri from St Louis, carried by crewmen of an American Fur Company supply ship who spread the virus at every stop. The Indians who went south to trade brought the disease back into Rupert's Land, and the virulent plague wiped out about three-quarters of the Plains people in one wave. A frightened traveller noticed there was no smoke rising from the Indian lodges. "Not a sound can be heard to break the awful stillness, save the ominous croak of the ravens, and mournful howl of wolves fattening on the human carcasses that lie strewed around. It seems as if the very genius of desolation had stalked through the prairies, and wreaked his vengeance on everything bearing the shape of humanity."

IN 1838, the British government had renewed the Company's licensed monopoly for a further twenty-one years, and during the next three years Queen Victoria had rewarded John Pelly with a baronetcy and George Simpson with a knighthood—ostensibly for their support of Arctic exploration.

It was an auspicious moment. The young Queen was restoring the popular splendour of the monarchy, and although there is no firsthand record of Simpson's visit to Buckingham Palace, it would have been a grand occasion. The past triumphs of Lord Nelson and the Duke of Wellington, followed by its magnanimous treatment of France, had made England the pre-eminent leader among nations; the Royal Navy patrolled three oceans, ready to sink unbelievers at a moment's notice. The Empire was already being touted as an instrument of Christian destiny, and burgeoning London was the arbiter of world commerce and culture. It was a splendid time to be a member of the British gentry, and Simpson had just been initiated into its golden circle. He might be only the viceroy of an empty land, but he was still a worthy field marshal in the imperial obsession of Anglicizing the outer reaches of what was condescendingly defined as "the civilized world."

The Hudson's Bay Company was in a similar state of euphoria. Its Rupert's Land monopoly had been successfully extended in every direction; no significant rivals had replaced the Nor'Westers; American settlers had not yet captured the Oregon Country; the monetary returns of the Company's operations had never been higher; its Governor and his Committeemen had Britain's leading politicians in their pockets; and even if changing fashions were depressing the price of beaver hats, the Company's commercial prospects were sound. Sir George was being accorded most of the credit for this halcyon state of affairs. The Northern Department Council's forty-three Chief Factors and Traders presented Simpson with an ornate sterling silver trophy weighed down with scampering beavers and naked dancers. That spontaneous vote of confidence, and his freshly minted knighthood, permanently altered Simpson's outlook. Gone was the wilderness administrator; the Governor now ranked himself a diplomat and international financier.

His first venture into diplomacy had occurred three years before, when, along with Pelly, Simpson had visited St Petersburg to negotiate a new Alaskan fur-trade treaty with the Russian fur company. The dispute had lengthy historical roots. The commerce had its start in 1742 when the handful of starving survivors of Vitus Jonassen Bering's doomed expedition reached Petropavlovsk with valuable sea-otter pelts. After three decades of private trading, the largest operators in the region, the Shelikhov-Golikov Company and the Mylnikov Company, united in 1797 to form the Russian-American Company, which was granted a twenty-year monopoly of the North Pacific fur trade. Under its energetic resident governor, Alexander Baranov, an abundance of seal skins was harvested and the company's operations were extended north and south along the Alaskan coastline. Its headquarters was built on the west coast of the Alexander Archipelago at Novo Arkhangelsk, now Sitka. So far from home base and operating in an agriculturally inhospitable climate, Baranov was forced to purchase food and trade goods from visiting Boston skippers. As an imaginative alternative, he sent an expedition southward to establish a factory farm near Bodega Bay, California. Some of the field crops did well and the company herds numbered fifteen hundred sheep and three thousand head of cattle. But the farm was not productive enough and too far away to be a dependable field kitchen.

By 1821, the combination of American privateers and Russian trappers had so depleted the quality and quantity of the Alaskan maritime fur catch that Tsar Alexander I issued his famous ukase unilaterally decreeing the North Pacific Coast, down to 51° north (just north of the tip of Vancouver Island), Russian territory. No foreign ships were to be allowed shore access within that boundary. Few paid much attention to this grand proclamation, least of all the Russians on the spot, who still needed what food they could get from the holds of visiting Yankee trading ships. It was at this point that the HBC entered the negotiations, boldly demanding that the Russians retreat northward beyond the 60th parallel of latitude. Eventually the border was set at 54°40´N, and the HBC gained the right to navigate international rivers across the Alaska Panhandle to its inland posts in what is now British Columbia. The uneasy peace was broken by the appointment of a charismatic naval officer, Baron Ferdinand Petrovich von Wrangell, to the post of Russian-American Company governor,* where he reigned with his nineteen-year-old bride, the Baroness Elizabeth Rossillon. Wrangell expanded the California farms, encouraged the detailed exploration of his territory, sponsored the first significant ethnological studies of Alaskan natives—and forced a confrontation with the HBC.

---

* The Baron's best-known modern kinsman was George Wrangell, the debonair fellow with the patch over one eye who posed as the Man in the Hathaway Shirt for advertising campaigns during the 1950s.

In 1834, Simpson dispatched one of his toughest traders, Peter Skene Ogden, to establish a Company post up the Stikine River. Aware that the attempt would be made, Wrangell hastily set up a blockade at the river mouth, fortifying a nearby Indian village (which he grandly renamed the Redoubt of St Dionysius) and anchoring the fourteen-gun *Chichagoff* under the command of a ferocious captain named Zarembo at a strategic turn in the channel. When Ogden appeared aboard his little brig, the *Dryad*, Zarembo fired a shot across her bow and ordered the HBC ship back into the Pacific. Ogden and the Russian captain argued their respective positions ever more loudly for eleven days. Characteristically, the HBC beat a strategic retreat, only to win by diplomacy what it dared not take in open combat.

The ambassadors chosen for this touchy assignment were Simpson and the HBC's British Governor, John Pelly. They left London in the summer of 1838, bound for St Petersburg, but detoured briefly to Copenhagen where Simpson challenged a local swimming champion to a race in the harbour, and won. "Few," he boasted, "can overmatch me in the water." They toured Pelly's Scandinavian timber estate, which Simpson was surprised to learn provided most of the wooden blocks used to pave London streets at the time. During a state dinner at Christiania (Oslo), Simpson purred when he heard himself described as "head of the most extended Dominions in the known world, the Emperor of Russia, the Queen of England and the President of the United States excepted." But his vanity was a bit deflated later that evening when he had to spend an hour in his hotel room mending his clothes: "… retired at 11, occupied till 12 Sewing Buttons on my Shirts and mending my breeches and Waistcoat. Damned bad Needles, worse thread and Villainous Sewing!"

During his journey Simpson complained about the homeliness of European women. "Indeed," he noted, "I have not observed what I should call a pretty looking woman in the course of my travels through these northern Regions: our Canadian and half breed women of North America are angels compared with them." At St Petersburg, Simpson and Wrangell met for the first time, and they immediately recognized each other as kindred spirits. "An extraordinary looking, ferret-eyed, red-whiskered little creature in full regimentals," was Simpson's comment on his negotiating opponent, adding, "Wrangell and I are very thick … a nice, intelligent clever little man." The arrangement they signed allowed the HBC trading rights across the Alaska Panhandle in return for supplying fresh produce from its farms in Oregon and paying an annual rental of two thousand prime sea-otter skins. The pact, which endured until Alaska was sold to the United States in 1867, was so mutually beneficial it survived hostilities between the two companies' parent governments that broke out as the vicious Crimean War in 1854.

The impressive results of that initial foray into statesmanship fed Simpson's already substantial sense of self-importance. Feeling that his bush empire was no longer a stage significant enough for his airs and graces, he set his mind on becoming the first man to circle the world via British North America, Hawaii, Alaska and Siberia, through Europe and back to Canada. He even hired a ghost writer to record his progress across the continents. Only two months after he had been knighted and appropriately fêted in London, Simpson was ready to begin the first lap. Accompanied by two young British aristocrats (Lords Caledon and Mulgrave) who were headed west on a buffalo hunt, he intended to leave dockside at Lachine in grand style. The two dozen Iroquois paddling his two canoes were each supplied with specially dyed red feathers for their caps and the Company boat flags were to have been unfurled simultaneously. But a spring snowstorm came up, and they barely managed to get across Lake St Louis without being swamped.

Up the Ottawa–Mattawa route the canoes rushed, across the upper reaches of Georgian Bay and along the northern shore of Superior—the old voyageur journey—reaching Fort Garry in record time. There his two companions disembarked and Simpson set off on a breakneck ride across the Prairies. He covered at least fifty miles a day, using relays of horses to save time. The description of his caravan's departure from Fort Garry, at five in the morning on July 3, 1841, is typical of the overblown sense of drama attached to Simpson's journey by Adam Thom, his ghost writer: "While we defiled through the gates into the open plain with an horizon before us as well defined as that of the blue ocean, the scene resembling the moving of an eastern caravan in the boundless sands of Arabia—a medley of pots and pans and kettles, in our single vehicle, the unruly pack horses prancing under their loads, and every cavalier armed to the teeth, assisting his steed to neigh and caper with bit and spur. The effect was not a little heightened by a brilliant sunrise, the firing of cannon, the streaming of flags and the shouts of spectators."

Getting across the western mountains and down to the Columbia River had taken six weeks and five days of hard riding. Although Simpson was well into his fifties by then, he was never in the saddle less than eleven hours a day. He inspected all the posts en route, reorganized his Company's Pacific fur trade, and took an unexpected detour to the Company's southernmost station. Yerba Buena, named for the Spanish mint plants that covered the area, had a population of fewer than fifty, and the area (renamed San Francisco in 1847) did not really flourish until after the mid-century gold rush. But there were furs to be traded, so the HBC had opened a small outpost and put William Glen Rae in charge of it.

Brigades of Bay men had actually been venturing into the area for most of a decade but had been run out of the country for buying mustangs from Indian horse thieves. Rae, who was the son-in-law of Dr John McLoughlin, Chief Factor at Fort Vancouver on the Columbia, arrived at the post six months earlier than his wife, Eloisa, and almost immediately got into personal and political trouble. The local government at the time was in debt to London financiers for the equivalent of about $50 million, and the sudden appearance of the HBC on what was still Mexican territory alarmed local citizens, who feared it might be a plot to turn California over to the British bondholders instead of repaying the loan. These rumours were fanned by Rae's support of the revolutionary leaders, Juan Bautista Alvarado and José Castro. When they were defeated in 1842 by General Manuel Micheltorena, who remained in California as governor for three years until driven out by the rebels, they were carrying arms and ammunition worth the equivalent of $15,000, advanced for future considerations by Rae's HBC outlet. At the same time, Rae was known to be drinking too much and indulging in a torrid affair with a Spanish woman; he had also been overheard in boasting that while it had cost £75,000 to drive Yankee traders from the Columbia, the Hudson's Bay Company would drive them out of California if it cost a million. Worst of all, the rebels did not honour their debts, and his little post began to show serious financial losses.

When Simpson arrived at Yerba Buena in December 1841, he accused Rae of departing from Company policies by granting credit too easily and was so unhappy about the manager's various misadventures that he ordered the outpost closed. Wishing to give his son-in-law another chance, McLoughlin delayed implementing the order for a few seasons, but on January 19, 1845, Rae short-circuited the dilemma by blowing his brains out. When his servant, William Sinclair, rushed in at the sound of the shot, he found a swooning Eloisa, an empty pistol, a bottle of opium potion and a note explaining that the victim had fallen into difficulties through the malice and intrigue of others.*

Simpson did not tarry long in California but sailed off aboard the HBC brig *Cowlitz* to Hawaii, then still known as the Sandwich Islands. France had already colonized Tahiti; New Zealand had come under British control; and Hawaii was attracting the ambitious attention of the United States, France and Britain because of its relatively prosperous economy. Once merely a provisioning way station for whalers and a fur-trade trans-shipment point between London and the Columbia River, Hawaii had begun to export sugar, molasses, salt and arrowroot in return for imports of flour, lumber and machinery. As the island's economy became more sophisticated, the once semi-clad women were evangelized by New England missionaries, and their muumuus became the voluminous badge of their conversion.

The HBC had maintained an agency on the islands since the early 1830s, manned by George Pelly, the British Governor's cousin, mainly as an outlet for the sale of salted salmon and timber from the Pacific Northwest. Located at the corner of Honolulu's Fort and Queen streets, the Hudson's Bay post was yielding a significant profit. Simpson's arrival coincided with an alteration in status of the Hawaiian king, Kamehameha III, who had recently surrendered some of his personal power by voluntarily signing the islands' first constitution. After looking over the situation, the HBC Governor emerged as a militant champion of Hawaiian independence, mainly because he recognized that the most likely alternatives—French or American occupation—would be bad for business. Although he became an energetic spokesman on behalf of Hawaiian freedom, in his private correspondence with London, Simpson speculated about buying the island nation's territory and reselling it (at enormous profit) to the Russians, who were intently seeking a warm-water port in the Pacific. In his consultations with Hawaii's royal circles, Simpson made a particularly strong impression on the Reverend William Richards, a Congregational missionary who had wormed himself into the islands' prime ministership. He arranged for Richards to meet him back in London, where he promised to help argue the case for Hawaiian independence and even negotiated an HBC loan of £10,000

* The HBC post, which was on the west side of what is now Montgomery Street, between Sacramento and Clay, was permanently closed in 1849. Nine years later, when workmen were excavating for sewers on nearby Commercial Street, they found a glass-covered coffin containing Rae's headless remains.

to back the cause of liberty—at 12 percent interest, of course. Once back in England, Simpson did in fact prove genuinely helpful to the Hawaiian cause, accompanying the islanders' delegation to Paris and Brussels. Britain, France and Belgium committed themselves to recognizing Hawaii's independence, but the islands were eventually annexed by the Americans.

After his Sandwich sojourn, Simpson sailed back to Alaska. Then he crossed over to Siberia and, accompanied by an escort of Cossacks, rode by horse and carriage across seven thousand miles of inhospitable terrain, the momentum broken only by sumptuous banquets along the way tendered by local governors. When they fed him pyramids of caviar he reciprocated with a delicacy of his own: hors-d'oeuvre of travel-weary pemmican. Simpson arrived in St Petersburg too exhausted to participate in the Tsarist court's piquant social scene and was back in London nineteen months and nineteen days after leaving on his round-the-world adventure. The final page of his diary records no more substantial conclusion about his momentous voyage than the fact that the prettiest girl he had seen along the way was in Gotland, a Swedish island in the Baltic.

GEORGE SIMPSON'S RELATIONS with women were legendary. When he was referred to as "the father of the fur trade" it was sometimes with a nudge and a knowing wink. Grant MacEwan, a former lieutenant-governor of Alberta and a popular Western Canadian historian, claimed the Governor had "fathered seventy sons between the Red River and the Rocky Mountains." That is an unlikely if mathematically possible proposition, but he did spend ten years in the Fur Country and certainly made the most of his bachelorhood. After he had married his eighteen-year-old cousin Frances in 1830, there was no indication that Simpson was anything but a faithful husband. But before he joined the HBC, Simpson had already acknowledged two children born out of wedlock in Britain, and during the decade between his arrival in Canada and his marriage, he had at least five other children by four women.

His derisive references to Indian Country women as "bits of brown" are only the best known of what are now considered sexist comments. In a letter to his friend McTavish from Île-à-la-Crosse, where three babies were born during his brief visit, he remarked that "the White Fish diet of the district seems to be favourable to procreation, and had I a good pimp in my suite I might have been inclined to deposit a little of my Spawn...." His lechery, not uncommon for the times, was unabashedly rampant.

In the same letter to McTavish at York Factory, in which he asked him to arrange a "private or separate entrance to my apartments" to make it easier for his nocturnal female companions to come and go, he instructed his friend to "turn off" Betsey Sinclair, the first of his wilderness loves. The daughter of Chief Factor William Sinclair and his native wife, Margaret Nahoway, she had borne him a child. "Simpson continually violated the custom of the country, creating confusion and anguish. Fur-trade society thought it appropriate, for example, to consider Betsey Sinclair as 'Mrs. Simpson', but to Simpson she was just a mistress of whom he soon tired," Sylvia Van Kirk, the University of Toronto historian who is a specialist in social aspects of the fur trade, has noted. "… He never really served an apprenticeship in the country which might have conditioned him to the 'custom of the country' and his attitude coincided with the first missionaries' attacks on country marriages." Once he wanted to be rid of her, his instructions to McTavish were crude and precise: "My Family concerns I leave entirely to your kind management, if you can dispose of the Lady it will be satisfactory as she is an unnecessary and expensive appendage. I see no fun in keeping a Woman, without enjoying her charms which my present rambling life does not enable me to do; but if she is unmarketable I have no wish that she should be a general accommodation shop to all the young bucks at the Factory and in addition to her own chastity a padlock may be useful; Andrew is a neat handed Fellow and having been in China may perhaps know the pattern of those used in that part of the World."

Simpson's longest-lasting country relationship was with Margaret, the daughter of George Taylor, York Factory's sloop master. She accompanied him on his 1828 Pacific adventures. When he left her pregnant on Hudson Bay during another journey, he gave these curt instructions to McTavish: "Pray keep an Eye on the commodity and if she bring forth anything in proper time and of the right color let them be taken care of but if any thing be amiss let the whole be bundled about their business.…" Simpson had two sons by Margaret, referred to her brother Tom as his brother-in-law and treated her family with special consideration. He also had at least two other simultaneous affairs (and a child each), one with Mary Keith, the daughter of Chief Factor James Keith, the other with a Montreal mistress named Ann Foster. "He was utterly ruthless, and introduced the regency-buck approach to women into Western Canada," the fur-trade historian Irene Spry has concluded. "His sex-object attitude to women was largely responsible for the breakdown of marriage à la façon du pays, which was a humanly decent type of relationship. He created a total dislocation in what had been a perfectly valid type of society."

Unlike the American West, where the so-called squaw men living with Indian women were regarded as inferior, in the Canadian Northwest, country marriages were respectable liaisons, many lasting their partners' lifetimes. Even the courts occasionally recognized the special status of such unions. William Connolly had married a native woman called Suzanne Pas-de-Nom in a country ceremony; they were together thirty years and had six children. But when Connolly retired to Montreal, he officially married a white woman, his cousin Julia Woolrich. On his death his eldest Mixed Blood son sued for a share of his father's estate. The courts ruled that the marriage was valid and declared the son a legal heir. John Macdonell, who retired in 1814, took his country wife, Magdeleine Poitras, out of the Fur Country and married her in a church ceremony forty-six years after she had joined him at the age of twelve on the Qu'Appelle River. When the wife of Chief Trader Nicol Finlayson died of dropsy, he penned this moving obituary: "I have not got over the shock of my severe bereavement. My hearth is desolate. I have not even a domestic animal to caress me when I enter my house from a journey.... I feel greatly the loss of her prattle, as it beguiled me for many a solitary hour."

In the absence of officiating clergy, these country weddings were an accepted and lasting phenomenon that had evolved within fur-trade society. In effect, they were a form of civil marriage. Besides being the Bay men's sexual partners, the women, proficient in comfort and survival skills, gave meaning to life in the raw land.

As with most other aspects of daily existence in the bush, the Nor'Westers had been more progressive about recognizing the benefits of these domestic arrangements in terms of furthering trade, particularly if a local chief's daughter were involved and kinship connections came into play. After initially attempting to outlaw such relationships, the HBC Governors relented, heeding the advice Simpson sent to London in a report dated May 18, 1821, from Fort Wedderburn in Athabasca. "Connubial alliances are the best security we can have of the goodwill of the Natives," he wrote. "I have therefore commended the Gentlemen to form connections with the principal Families immediately on their arrival, which is no difficult matter as the offer of their Wives and Daughters is the first token of their Friendship and hospitality."

To discourage transferred or retired traders from leaving families across the Northwest to be nourished at Company expense, the HBC at its 1821 council meeting adopted a tough (if unenforceable) resolution stating that "all officers or servants of the company having women or children and wishing to leave the same in the Country on their retirement therefore be required to make such provision for their future maintenance, more particularly for that of the Children as circumstances may reasonably warrant and the means of the individual permit ... all those desirous of withdrawing the same from the country be allowed every facility for that purpose and none be allowed hereafter to take a woman without binding himself down to leave 1/10 of his annual wages in the hands of the Company as a provision for his family in event of Death or retirement from the country...."

One of Simpson's peeves was those country wives who insisted on advising his resident officers on how to deal with the Company. He lamented the influence of "petty coat politicians" and was particularly incensed with Mrs McDonald, wife of the Chief Trader at Fort Qu'Appelle, whom he described as "a stout good looking Dame" but condemned for trying to run the post with her backstage "persuasion and cunning."

Most of the country marriages worked well, even if the women had fewer rights than church-wedded wives of the time. After 1823, their HBC husbands had to sign marriage contracts and whenever a Bay man left his country wife, besides supporting their children, he had to find her another suitable provider.

It was Simpson himself who disrupted this cozy arrangement by marrying a white woman and importing her into the Fur Country as his consort. "[He] led the stampede among the active and retired officers for a European marriage with a British-born white wife," noted John E. Foster, the University of Alberta historian. "It was no longer acceptable to have a grandmother, let alone a mother or wife, who smoked a pipe as she strung snowshoes." The fact that it was the Governor—their role model—who had irrevocably altered the pattern of what had become an accepted practice had cataclysmic consequences. Once the Bay men began to marry in Scotland and England, Indian women, on whose kindness and energy the vast fortunes of the fur trade had largely been built, were relegated to inferior status as either workhorses or mistresses. "The coming of white women to the Indian Country," argues Sylvia Van Kirk, "brought into disrepute indigenous social customs of the fur trade. Marriage à la façon du pays was no longer acceptable, especially with the presence of missionaries intolerant of any deviation. The presence of white women underlined the cultural shortcomings of mixed-blood wives, particularly in more settled areas where their native skills were no longer required. Unfortunately, European ladies themselves, by zealously guarding what they considered to be their intrinsically superior status, actively fostered an increasing stratification of fur-trade society."

When Simpson decided to visit England in hopes of finding a suitable bride, he sent his country wife, Margaret Taylor (then with child), to Bas-de-la-Rivière at the mouth of the Winnipeg River, presided over by Chief Factor John Stuart, whose own country wife was Margaret's sister. Simpson told them nothing of his plans, and by the time he received a letter from Stuart telling him the news of his newly born, bonny wee son, the Governor was within two weeks of marrying his beautiful cousin Frances, twenty-six years his junior.

THE WOOING OF FRANCES by the middle-aged Governor had to be sandwiched between business meetings with his London principals. At one point he asked his faithful sidekick McTavish, who was in Britain at the same time and bent upon a similar mission, "Let me know if you have any fair cousin likely to suit an invalid like me," noting, "I see you are something like myself, shy with the fair, we should not be so much so with the Browns...." Within weeks of the writing of this missive, both men had chosen their loves and married—McTavish in Edinburgh to Catherine Turner, the Governor in a suburban London church (Bromley St Leonard's) to Frances, the daughter of Geddes Mackenzie Simpson, who two decades earlier had given the young George a first job with his London sugar company. The two happy couples decided to sail across the Atlantic and spend their honeymoons together, proceeding inland by canoe.

Their lighthearted mood was shattered in a dramatic domestic confrontation when they reached Montreal. McTavish had also abruptly abandoned a country wife, but his relationship had been much longer and seemed more solid than Simpson's. He had lived with Nancy McKenzie, the Mixed Blood daughter of a distinguished Nor'Wester, for seventeen years, and they were the parents of six living children. When he sailed away from York Factory on his British courting venture, he took one of his daughters with him and left all his personal effects behind, which must have reassured Nancy that he intended to return. McTavish allowed others to break the news of his overseas marriage and had his personal possessions shipped to Moose Factory, where the sympathetic Governor had found a good posting for him. "I owe it all to Geordy," he breezily confided to a friend.

McTavish finally did pay a lump-sum dowry of £200 to an HBC veteran named Pierre Leblanc willing to marry his Nancy. The prospective bridegroom was even granted a week's leave of absence by the Company for courtship duty. Margaret Taylor, the Governor's last country wife, was similarly "placed" with an HBC employee, Amable Hogue by name. Simpson took great trouble to hide his previous brood from his new wife—although Frances later confessed she "was always terrified to look about her, in case of seeing something disagreeable." Most Chief Factors, themselves devoted to their country wives, felt bitter about what had happened and, afraid of criticizing the Governor, turned their scorn on McTavish. "What could be your aim in discarding her whom you clasped to your bosom in virgin purity and had for seventeen years with you?" demanded John Stuart, who had known Nancy McKenzie from childhood. "She was the wife of your choice and has borne you seven children, now stigmatized with ignominy ... if with a view of domestic happiness you have thus acted, I fear the aim has been missed and that remorse will be your portion for life ... I think it is well our correspondence may cease."

When the newlyweds arrived in Montreal, McTavish's thirteen-year-old daughter, Mary, who was attending school nearby, surprised them one evening by being ushered unexpectedly into their private dining quarters. According to the only report of the scene that followed, McTavish introduced her to his new wife, "who got stupid, but shook hands with the Miss who was very pretty and mighty impudent.... [Mrs McTavish] got white and red and at last rose and left the room, all the party looking very uncomfortable except [her husband] and the girl. [Mrs Simpson] followed and found her in a violent fit of crying, she said she knew the child was to have been home that night, but thought she would have been spared such a public introduction."

These awkward unpleasantnesses behind them, the quartet set out from Lachine on May 2, 1830, for their wilderness honeymoon. Only George Simpson would have chosen a departure time of 4 A.M., but he did allow a brief breakfast pause five hours later, the gentlemen being carried ashore on the backs of the Iroquois paddlers and the ladies being cradled carefully in their brawny arms. At Lake of Two Mountains a deputation of Algonquin chiefs gathered to pay the Governor homage, and an eight-year-old girl presented Frances with a bouquet of cherry blossoms.

They were later entertained at Bytown by the wife of Lieutenant-Colonel John By, who was busy building the Rideau Canal between the Ottawa and

St Lawrence rivers. After leaving the Ottawa, the two canoes turned west along the Mattawa, and Frances recorded her impressions of the passing panorama: "On either side are stupendous rocks of the most fantastic forms. Some bear the appearance of Gothic castles, others exhibit rows of the most regular and beautifully carved corinthian pillars; deep caverns are formed in some, while others present a smooth level surface, crowned with tufts of pines and cedars. From the upper end of the portage is seen a beautiful waterfall, which dashes over immense masses of rocks thro' which it had worn itself many a channel foaming and roaring to a considerable distance, the spray glittering in the sun with all the varied hues of the rainbow."

Through Georgian Bay, across the North Channel of Huron and along Superior they went, and after a brief stopover at Fort William (where they changed to smaller canoes), they reached what Frances described as "the Savage World." Three of the paddlers had deserted by then, worn out by Simpson's relentlessness. The portages were getting tougher. At one half-mile crossing rendered all but impassable by fallen trees and slippery rocks, the water was waist-deep in places. "To cross this," noted the exasperated Frances, "baffled the skill both of Mrs. McTavish and Myself (good walkers as we flattered ourselves to be) and accordingly after mature deliberation, it was agreed that each should be carried by a man chosen for the purpose. Tomma Felix took me up in his arms, and Nicholas Monique, an old Indian, volunteered his services in transporting my companion across the miry portion of road which lay before us. Tomma pushed on, despite of every difficulty making however many stumbles and false steps—but Nicholas' load being rather heavier, he absolutely came to a stand still, in the midst of a bog, and declared he could not take the Lady a step farther in his arms, but if she would get on his back, he thought he might accomplish the journey. Mr. Simpson who was coming on after us, persuaded Mrs. McTavish (with some difficulty) as a last resource to do as Nicholas recommended, which she at length agreed to, and on the back of Nicholas accordingly mounted: the scene however was so ludicrous that the by-standers could not resist a laugh, in which Mrs. McTavish joined so heartily, that poor Nicholas was thrown off his equilibrium, stumbled forwards, fell on his face, and gave his unfortunate rider a summerset over his head, into the mud: throwing her into a situation the most awkward, and ridiculous that ever a poor Lady was placed in."

At one encampment, having slogged the entire day through a succession of rain squalls, members of the bedraggled little expedition were awake until eleven at night drying their clothes—only to be rudely roused by the hated shout *"Levez! Levez!"* a few minutes after midnight. Honeymoon or not, Sir George was determined to break yet another speed record.

Along the way, Frances Simpson was paid a personal honour. At the far end of the aptly named Rainy Lake at a trading post then known as Fort Lac la Pluie, she made such a luminous impression on its drenched inhabitants that they decided to rename their community Fort Frances. The Governor's lady later recalled her guided tour of the lilliputian settlement by Chief Trader Thomas McMurray: "... old and weather beaten as he was, he surpassed all the Gentlemen I had met with in these Wilds, as a Lady's Man but altho' our walk did not occupy an hour, it quite exhausted all his fine speeches, and the poor man seemed as much relieved when we returned to the house ... as if he had just been freed from an attack of the Night-Mare."

On the final lap into Fort Garry, they travelled the clock round and arrived at midnight. Riders had spotted the Governor's party and had warned the settlers of his coming, so there was a lively torchlight parade mustered to meet them. "The reception I here met with," Frances recalled, "convinced me that if the inhabitants of this remote region were plain and homely in their manners, they did not want for kindness of heart, and the desire of making every thing appear favorable, and pleasing, to the eye and mind of a stranger."

When the Simpsons eventually settled there, it turned out to be a far from happy experience. Instead of trying to repair the existing Fort Garry at the juncture of the Red and Assiniboine rivers, which had been devastated by the flood of 1826,* the Governor built himself a new official residence above the flood plain, nineteen miles to the north. Known as Lower Fort Garry, it covered thirteen choice acres and took eight years to complete. Its limestone bastions were erected by the best masons in the territory. No expense was spared during construction, and the Governor uncharacteristically tried to hide the expenditures from London, not reporting any

---

* The last of several forts built at or near this location, it remained the HBC's inland adminis-trative headquarters for thirty-five years, becoming the seat of the Métis Provisional Government during the Red River Rebellion. Everything but its north gate was demolished in 1882 to permit the straightening of Winnipeg's Main Street.

disbursements for a whole year and then claiming the cost had really amounted to little more than the provisions consumed by the workmen. The grandeur of the imposing buildings was enhanced by the installation of an elegant pianoforte, provision of sets of monogrammed cutlery, and all the most fashionable furnishings worthy of turning the new fort into the community's social as well as economic centre. The Simpsons moved into the Stone Fort (as it quickly became known) in 1832, but it was soon clear that the *beau monde* pretensions of the Governor and his lady would never be realized.

Their first child, George Geddes, was so frail at birth that he survived only seven months, and both parents suffered serious depression and subsequent maladies. Simpson talked vaguely about quitting the fur trade but could not afford to retire because he had lost £4,000 in a bad investment. His over-supply of energy found so few outlets that he expended most of it picking quarrels with the fort's cook. He spent his time at Red River brooding about why a Governor of his repute and accomplishments should have to count his days in such godforsaken outskirts of empire. He refused to accept the Mixed Bloods of the settlement as appropriate company for himself or Frances, and was particularly insulting to HBC officers for living with and loving country wives—even though he had himself been an ardent champion of the practice for most of the preceding decade. When Colin Robertson tried to visit the Stone Fort with his Mixed Blood wife, Theresa Chalifoux, Simpson was enraged at such impropriety. "Robertson brought his bit of Brown with him to the Settlement this Spring in hopes she would pick up a few English manners before visiting the civilized world," he noted with disdain, "but it would not do—I told him distinctly the thing was impossible, which mortified him exceedingly." Only two country-born women, both maids, were allowed into Mrs Simpson's sanctified presence. (Ironically, one of these servants was Nancy Leblanc, McTavish's former country wife.)

Having rebuffed the idea of social intercourse with most of the colony's population, the Simpsons were thrown upon the company of the few white settlers, mainly the missionaries' wives, who suited the Governor's temperament even less. "I am most heartily tired of Red River," he wrote to McTavish, complaining that his bride had made no friendships there and recounting peevishly the social shortcomings of the local clerics' wives. "Mrs. Jones is a good unmeaning Woman whom we merely see for half an hour occasionally," he wrote, "and Mrs. Cockrane [Cockran] whose assumed puritanism but ill conceals the vixen, shines only when talking of elbow Grease and the scouring of pots and pans."*

By 1833, it had become obvious that the Simpsons would have to move away from their wilderness fort.† The Governor transferred his management operations permanently to Lachine and took Frances back to England where she remained for the next dozen years, seeing her husband only occasionally while raising their four children, Frances Webster (Fanny), Augusta D'Este (Gussy), Margaret Mackenzie (Maggie) and John Henry Pelly (Moses). Within the limitations of Simpson's expedient boorishness towards women, theirs was a workable and occasionally loving relationship.

Simpson treated Frances as a prized but almost inanimate possession, seldom allowing her to express any will or view of her own. After she returned to live with him at Lachine in 1845, she continued to be heartsick for London, enduring her chatelaineship of the Canadian fur trade with well-trained grace but no enthusiasm. Her husband was impatient with the formalities of the times, even with such simple rituals as reciting grace before meals, and at one formal dinner, when Frances insisted he do so, Simpson embarrassed her by abruptly blurting, "Lord have mercy on what is now before us," then immediately digging into the first course.

Their mansion on the north flank of the old Lachine Canal (large enough that it had once been an inn) became the Company's overseas headquarters, although most commerce still flowed in and out of York Factory. By moving to Lachine, Simpson for the first time tied the Hudson's Bay Company into Montreal's commercial mainstream. Here at last he found an outlet for his social aspirations, quickly earning his place as a key member of the fledgling metropolis's Establishment. To exploit that function to the full, he converted his house into a showplace, permanently exhibiting paintings and objects from the continent's hinterland. Besides the portrait of Napoleon in his antechamber, the house was filled with a dozen oil portraits from the Indian

---

* Simpson was especially miffed when the Reverend William Cockran arrived late at a formal dinner riding a cow, with the lame explanation that his horse was snowbound.
† Lower Fort Garry served as a barracks for British soldiers stationed at Red River in the mid-1840s and later became the residence of Eden Colvile when he was associate governor of Rupert's Land. The fort languished as a minor trading centre, a North West Mounted Police training depot, a prison and an asylum until 1911. Two years later it was leased to the Manitoba Motor League and became known as the Manitoba Motor Country Club. Lower Fort Garry was later transferred to the government as a National Historic Park; its restored quarters are open to the public.

Country by Paul Kane and other artists, Indian bark boxes with porcupine quill embroidery, ornamental canoe paddles, a model Indian bark tent, buffalo robes and glass cases brimming with stuffed birds.

From a large office overlooking Lake St Louis on the main floor of the magnificent residence, the aging Sir George ruled his empire. He entertained visiting dignitaries, dispensed rough justice and, in calm possession of authority, comforted himself with the certainty that his tenure was fulfilling heaven's command.

Galahads
of the Pacific

"Necessity has no laws."

—Peter Skene Ogden

THE WILDEST SHORES of George Simpson's trading estate were the HBC's Columbia and New Caledonia departments, stretching from the Gulf of California to the southern edge of Alaska. Separated from the U.S. eastern seaboard and the Company's main sphere of influence across British North America, the people of these mountain valleys and jagged coasts obeyed their own laws.

Within a few decades the two satrapies were transformed from Indian hunting grounds into HBC fur-trapping preserves. The Americans, driven by the gravitational pull of their manifest destiny, were bent on extending their Union westward to encompass the continent; the British stepped in to claim Vancouver Island and mainland British Columbia. "An imperial tide lapped the shores of the Northwest Coast," wrote historian Barry M. Gough, "and in doing so changed the character of human occupation, and it brought with it at the flood new political, legal and social institutions whose legacies are still apparent." For the two countries destined to share the upper part of the North American continent, the takeover of these westernmost lands meant having to confront the Hudson's Bay Company. For Great Britain, which initially claimed both regions, the process strengthened the conviction of its wiser statesmen that trade, not dominion, constituted the wealth of nations.

The Company's Pacific affairs, while ultimately governed by the whims and dictates of George Simpson acting on behalf of the HBC's London Committee, were in the hands of a defiant triumvirate of Galahads: Dr John McLoughlin, Peter Skene Ogden and Sir James Douglas, former Nor'Westers all, who ruled their distant provinces with unorthodox methods and astounding results.

ONE OF SEVERAL ELEMENTS making the Pacific fur trade different from that of the rest of the continent was its use of horses instead of canoes, because of the difficult topography and formidable river systems. The animals became essential to the trapping outfits, lugging in trade goods and provisions, carrying out the pelts, finding their own forage along the way—and, in the last resort, being themselves a handy food supply for starving trappers. Burdened with wood-frame packs, the horses had a tough time of it. To thwart nocturnal thieves, the animals were tethered so close to their sleeping owners that they could rarely reach enough grazing ground to regain their strength from the day's exertions. The steep, rocky trails and absence of inland smithies to provide new shoes meant that their battered hooves were soon worn away, curtailing their usefulness as beasts of burden. Because every trapper required three or four animals each season, the Indians realized that the horse trade could be at least as profitable as the bartering of fur, and made the most of the situation by selling the white man their culls—wild-tempered mustangs or nags more suitable for the boneyard.

Nor were Indian–HBC relations nearly as peaceful as in other Company territories. The Oregon Country's American mountain men had introduced the violent tradition of their breed, competing directly with the Indians for furs and treating them as a species less worthy than beaver. Violence and murder were so common that Senator Thomas Hart Benton, who championed westward expansion during his three decades in Congress, estimated that by the end of the 1820s at least five hundred of the American trappers had been killed in skirmishes with Rocky Mountain tribes.

The Northwest Coast Indians were ruled by an elite of slave-owning chiefs with a highly developed culture and powerful brigades of war canoes. Relieved of having to expend most of their energies in the daily hunt for food that hampered the evolution of inland Indian societies, the Haida, Nootka, Bella Coola, Tsimshian, Kwakiutl and Coast Salish geared their year to the rush of salmon swarming up Pacific inlets. One early explorer claimed the fish filled the rivers, so that "you could walk across on their backs."

At first, the coastal and inland peoples viewed the white invaders as very strange indeed: they were all males and carried "magic sticks," as muskets were first described. But once the newcomers and their demands became known, they were treated as envoys from distant tribes—in other words, as potential enemies, especially when they began interfering with the traditional slave trade. Many of the Northwest Coast Indian tribes kept slaves, valued at from eight to fifteen blankets for a healthy male and more for an agreeable female. Regular slave auctions were held not only in Oregon but in what is now Canadian territory near Fort Simpson on the Nass River of British Columbia. Yankee skippers regularly bought slaves at Cape Classet, the present-day Cape Flattery, at the northwest tip of Washington State, and at Nahwitti, near the northern end of Vancouver Island, trading them to the Haida of the Queen Charlotte Islands for sea otter skins. Driven by their Company's paternalistic impulses, HBC traders did their best to eradicate such practices, granting protection to runaway slaves and treating all Indians as British subjects. But George Simpson was not above manipulating personal lives in an effort to develop trade. In April 1825 he instructed John Work, one of his Columbia Department officers, to marry the daughter of a chief of the Cayuse, uncharacteristically promising that the ceremony would be at Company expense, because its traders would be travelling through Cayuse territory and the lady (whom Simpson ordered taken along on every journey) might afford protection to the Company's brigades.

Unlike the Cree, who provided most of the pelts at the posts around Hudson Bay, Pacific Coast Indians were rarely lured into the fur trade. In the Oregon Country, their places were taken by so-called Freemen, usually discharged or retired HBC servants who wanted to remain in the wilds. Most of them had Mixed Blood backgrounds, but they missed the permanent home base of the Red River Colony that provided the Métis with personal stability and communal support. Simpson described them as "the very scum of the country and generally outcasts from the Service for misconduct ... the most unruly and troublesome gang to deal with in this or perhaps any other part of the World." He was not far wrong. They were impossible to control, fought constantly among themselves, abandoned their trapping parties on impulse to go hunting on their own and accumulated debts at Company stores they had no intention of paying—simply trading their next catch to the competition.

That competition was American, based in St Louis on the Mississippi River; the Missouri route to the west coast tracked by Lewis and Clark was too circuitous and dangerous for easy trade. Originally held back by sheer distance, the disruptions of the War of 1812 and the fury of the rampaging Blackfoot, the Americans by the mid-1820s began moving into the HBC's domain, seriously undermining the Company's commerce. Simpson regarded this intrusion as highly dangerous, not only in terms of daily trade but because he saw the mountain men as the inevitable precursors of colonization. As it turned out, the more significant forerunners of the U.S. claim on Oregon were the missionaries who started arriving in the mid-1830s and immediately recognized the country's economic potential; they soon became effective evangelists for its emancipation into the waiting arms of the American Union.

The vast expanse of the Oregon Country had been officially declared open to joint occupation by the 1818 Convention between Britain and the United States, a policy that was expediently renewed in 1827. Because these accords provided only for equal freedom to occupy, both the American and British governments were anxious to strengthen their claims to more enduring possession. Washington felt its case was particularly strong because the Columbia River had been discovered by the Boston trader Captain Robert Gray in 1792 and first explored by Lewis and Clark a dozen years later. The first permanent settlement in the region had been the trading post established by John Jacob Astor's Pacific Fur Company at Astoria. In its counter-claim, London pointed out that while Gray might have discovered the mouth of the Columbia, Captain George Vancouver's men had ascended the river and mapped it and that even if Astoria had been there first, the North West Company had captured it. Besides, the territory was currently occupied by the Hudson's Bay Company with its growing chain of trading posts—and possession was nine points of the law. Ironically the Americans were determined to seize British Columbia's coast, while most British jingoists felt more strongly about claiming and holding Oregon. Although ambassadors on both sides lacked any realistic idea about the character of the land in dispute, their multiplying claims made diplomatic compromise difficult to negotiate.

The stage was set for an escalating conflict not only between the Company and the American free traders but also between two irreconcilable views of the world. The American frontier ethic was highly individualistic, disinclined to collective, corporate or governmental solutions—stressing instead the virtue of challenging authority at every turn. The Yanks felt they were entitled to all the pelts they could nab on any given day, especially on what they considered to be their home turf, and dared anyone to show them otherwise. The Hudson's Bay Company represented a very different set of values, being a bureaucratic monopoly run by absentee landlords employing mostly wage-earning functionaries. Its traders were all too aware that they were stewards in a foreign land. Discouraged from being too blatantly aggressive, they were seeking comfortable survival rather than self-motivated adventure.

AT THE 1821 amalgamation, the Hudson's Bay Company was not entirely certain it wanted to keep the half-dozen posts south of the 49th parallel it had inherited from the North West Company. They were known to be difficult and expensive to maintain and had been producing little if any profit. But the Company's London Committeemen, well aware of the American craving for the desirable New Caledonia Department north of the disputed territory, decided that the Oregon Country—stretching north from California to include the present-day states of Oregon, Washington and Idaho, southeast into Nevada and across Utah all the way to Wyoming and north to Montana—was potentially too lucrative to surrender without a fight. At worst, its tenure would act as a buffer against Washington's ambitions to extend the United States' territorial reach northward. Simpson was ordered to survey the district, cut its expenses and reorganize its trade, keeping in mind that the international boundary would most likely be eventually fixed at the 46th parallel—which happened to coincide with the line of the Columbia River's westward flow.

When the HBC Governor arrived at Astoria on November 8, 1824, accompanied by Dr John McLoughlin, his designated commander of the Columbia Department, he found that the peculiar stories he had been hearing about the self-indulgent habits of its occupants were all too true. The warehouses held not only the standard fur-trade items but such luxuries as silk stockings, umbrellas, ostrich plumes and jewellery. Seating at dinner was strictly by rank, and the hierarchical protocol was carried to such ridiculous extremes that three grades of tea were poured, sweetened with three grades of sugar—refined loaf, common crushed and inferior brown. At Spokane House, the traders had built themselves a ballroom that fit well into the decadence of their daily— and nocturnal—pursuits.

Noting that "everything appears to me on the Columbia on too extended a scale *except the Trade*," Simpson not only jolted the local fur society into an abrupt appreciation of his Œconomy but cut the staff by half and ordered the Company's headquarters moved about a hundred miles inland to a pastoral plateau on the Columbia River's north shore, six miles past the mouth of the Willamette. The site, more easily defensible, offered opportunity for growing local food crops, thus saving the funds that had been spent supplying Astoria with European delicacies. At sunrise on March 19, 1825, Simpson broke a bottle of rum on the fledgling post's flagstaff and portentously declared: "In behalf of the Honourable Hudson's Bay Company I hereby name this establishment Fort Vancouver. God Save King George the Fourth!" That evening he noted in his journal that the object of naming the post after the distinguished British navigator was "to identify our claim to the soil and trade with his discovery of the river and coast on behalf of Great Britain." During his visit Simpson also devised a daring plan to keep the mountain men at bay south of the Columbia. He left instructions that the area was to be trapped bare of every last beaver kit, so that there would be little incentive for the Americans to occupy it. This scorched-earth policy would produce short-term profit and neatly fit the Company's strategic master plan. The area in question consisted mainly of the Snake River's immense drainage basin, a convoluted pattern of unclimbed mountains and torrential streams stretching from Wyoming (its source) into the northwest corner of Utah, northeastern Nevada, much of Idaho and slices of what are now the states of Oregon and Washington.

One of the Company's first traders assigned to the Snake was Finan McDonald, a six-foot-four Highlander with a bushy red beard whose first (and, some swore, only) language was Gaelic. At the end of his 1823 venture, which had included running battles with Blackfoot war parties (McDonald's men killed sixty-eight Indians, while sustaining half a dozen casualties), the weary Bay man wrote to a friend: "I got home safe from the Snake Cuntre, thank God, and when that Cuntre will see me agane, the beaver will have gould skin." To head up the methodical destruction of animal life that would create the fur desert he had in mind, Simpson appointed Peter Skene Ogden as Chief Trader in charge of the Snake River campaign.

An odd character to find in the fur trade, Ogden was the son of a prominent Montreal jurist who had joined the North West Company out of a sense of adventure.* In 1810, while stationed at Île-à-la-Crosse with Samuel Black, he had tormented the HBC trader Peter Fidler and was later involved in the murder of an Indian suspected of trading with the HBC. To place him beyond reach of the criminal indictment that followed the

---

* Ogden's voice never changed from its pre-puberty soprano, so that even though he completed some legal training before leaving Montreal, he accepted the fact that he could never be a convincing court advocate.

incident, he was transferred to the Pacific and spent the last three years before the NWC's absorption as one of its Oregon agents. Left off the original list of transfer appointments because of his violent anti-Bay activities, Ogden was eventually rehired as a Chief Clerk and soon promoted to Chief Trader. The reason for plucking this relatively obscure daredevil for the key assignment on the Snake was revealed in the secret assessment of Ogden in Simpson's Character Book: "A keen, sharp, off hand fellow of superior abilities to most of his colleagues, very handy and active and not sparing of his personal labour.... Has been very Wild & thoughtless and is still fond of coarse practical jokes, but with all this appearance of thoughtlessness he is a very cool calculating fellow who is capable of doing anything to gain his own ends. His ambition knows no bounds and his conduct and actions are not influenced or governed by any good or honorable principle. In fact, I consider him one of the most unprincipled men in the Indian Country, who would soon get into habits of dissipation if he were not restrained by the fear of their operating against his interests, and if he does indulge in that way madness to which he has a predisposition will follow as a matter of course. A man likely to be exceedingly troublesome if advanced to the 1st Class as the Trade is now constituted, but his Services have been so conspicuous for several years past, that I think he has strong claims to advancement."

During the course of his six forays into the Snake River basin between 1824 and 1830, Ogden had plenty of opportunity to put into practice his personal credo: "Necessity has no laws." Bolstered by his combative nature, he faced brutal challenges and survived them all. Besides trapping beaver,* he became the first white man to explore parts of Idaho, California, Nevada, Utah and Wyoming, outwitting the rampaging mountain men and hostile Indians along the way. He judged each tribe on its merits, forming attachments with the Nez Percés and Cayuse but having nothing but contempt for the Blackfoot and especially the Snakes of Oregon. In the

---

* Ogden was one of the few HBC traders who demonstrated even momentary consternation at the indiscriminate slaughter of the animals, noting in his journal on April 28, 1829, while camped on Bull Run Creek in southeastern Oregon: "It is scarcely credible what a destruction of beaver by trapping there has been at this season; within the last few days upwards of fifty females have been taken and on an average each with four young ready to litter. Did not we hold this country by so slight a tenure it would be most to our interest to trap only in the fall, and by this mode it would take many years to ruin it."

winter of 1828, when the Americans offered to join the British in a punitive war against the troublesome Snakes, he confessed to his journal: "I
would most willingly sacrifice a year and even two to exterminate the whole
Snake tribe, and in so doing I am of opinion could justify myself before God
and man."

In his personal life, Ogden married, country-style, first a Cree woman
and later the legendary "Nymph of Spokane," Julia Mary Rivet, the step-
daughter of a French-Canadian trapper. Ogden nicknamed her his Princess
Julia (she called him M'sieu Pete) and they became inseparable for the rest
of their lives. Julia's exploits, such as the time she dove into a turbulent
river to retrieve a runaway raft loaded with furs, were the talk of the
Oregon Country. When the Ogden expedition's horses were stampeded by
marauding American mountain men led by Joe Meek, she was horrified to
discover that one of the vanishing mounts was carrying her first-born son
in a moss satchel dangling from its saddle straps. She jumped on another
horse, rode straight into the enemy camp, found the missing horse with
baby attached, leaped from one saddle into the other and galloped off to
her home base—leading a stolen Company nag loaded with furs behind her
for good measure.

Peter Skene Ogden commanded his Snake River platoons, which
numbered as many as 75 men and 372 horses, as if they were military units,
with rotating rosters of night watches, advance and retreat strategies worked
out beforehand and Spartan discipline. When one of his men got lost in the
wintery bush, Ogden went up a hillside to fire rifle shots and built a large fire
to guide the missing trapper home. But when the stray finally showed up the
following morning without his outfit, suffering from exhaustion and frostbite,
Ogden fed him a cup of hot broth and sent him right back out again to recover
his missing horse, blanket and furs.

Ogden's most humiliating brush with his American competitors
occurred at Deserter Point on the Weber River in Utah on May 25, 1825,
when a group of mountain men, led by Johnson Gardner, a member of
William Ashley's Rocky Mountain Fur Company, persuaded a dozen of
Ogden's Freemen to desert (along with their horseloads of furs) by telling
them they were in U.S. territory and would be freed of their debts to the
Hudson's Bay Company. Gardner and Ogden got into a heated argument,
with the American claiming that the expedition was violating U.S. territorial sovereignty and the Bay man insisting that the fate of the Oregon

Country had yet to be determined, and at present was mutually occupied by Great Britain.*

Apart from being constantly harassed by the Americans and hostile Indians, Ogden and his men suffered from a strange malady peculiar to the area. Like all trappers they ate beaver meat after the animals had been skinned but now they found themselves afflicted with racking pain that immobilized their limbs. The beaver, it turned out, had been feeding on poison parsnip (water hemlock) and even though they grew fat on the plants, humans consuming their meat became violently ill.†

Ogden's final Snake River expedition in 1829–30 was marred by tragedy, when nine men drowned and five hundred beaver skins were lost in the turbulent cascades of The Dalles on the Columbia River. "This life makes a young man sixty in a few years," he complained in the privacy of his Journal. "A convict at Botany Bay is a gentleman at ease compared to my trappers. Still they are happy. A roving life suits them. They would regard it as a punishment to be sent to Canada." The toll on his followers was appalling. When Joseph Paul, a youthful companion from his earliest forays, died at twenty-nine of the beaver disease, Ogden lamented, "There remains now only one man living of all the Snake men of 1819 and rather extraordinarily all have been killed, with the exception of two who died a natural death." He summed up his feelings for the country whose exploration became his monument, while suffering from heat prostration, camped near Goose Lake (California) where the only available drink was liquid mud: "This is certainly a most horrid life … without exaggeration Man in this country is deprived of every comfort that can tend to make existence desirable."

THE TRADER IN CHARGE of the troublesome Columbia Department for twenty-two years was John McLoughlin, the former North West Company doctor who had impressed Simpson as a man of integrity able to get things

---

* They were both wrong. Being south of the 42nd parallel, they were in Mexican territory. Under a treaty concluded between the United States and Spain on February 22, 1819, and proclaimed two years later, that parallel of latitude (the present northern boundary of California, Nevada and the western part of Utah) from midway across what is now southern Wyoming to the Pacific Ocean was declared to be the dividing line between the two countries in North America.

† The remedy was equally violent. Ogden discovered that he could obtain relief only by drinking liberal doses of a cocktail with the ultimate kick: pepper and gunpowder mixed in creek water.

done. Although he had privately criticized McLoughlin for being far too conscious of social rank and for believing too firmly in his own incorruptibility, the Governor realized that to run the Company's outposts in the potentially explosive Oregon Country he would have to hire no ordinary fur trader. What he needed was a Chief Factor capable of attracting other men to his own and the Company's cause. McLoughlin, who had by this time spent more than two decades in the fur trade, not only fit the part but looked it. A six-foot-four mountain of a man with a mane of loose-flowing, prematurely white hair, he resembled a born-again Elijah. His stern jaw, the disciplined set of his face and eyes, his grace of movement and careful speech—all lent his presence natural authority.

Fort Vancouver, where McLoughlin ruled with such benevolent effectiveness that he was posthumously accorded the title "Father of Oregon," was a community of forty wooden houses inside a twenty-foot-high stockade, including a two-storey lodging for the Chief Factor's family. Because he recognized that fur was a finite resource, McLoughlin also set up sawmills and flour mills and established large farming and fishing operations manned by servants who lived in a sizeable village outside the fort's gates. The day's work was run with shipboard exactness, the clanging of bells marking changes of shift and activities. Workmen were issued weekly rations of eight gallons of potatoes and eight salted salmon plus bread, and occasionally meat. The lives of the officers were considerably more gracious. Nightly, the Company's traders and visiting dignitaries of varying ranks and purposes gathered at the Fort Vancouver officers' mess to trade tall tales in the warm light of candelabra, lolling at tables laden with crested cutlery, crystal glasses and blue earthenware dishes. Roast beef and pork, boiled mutton, baked salmon, beets, carrots and turnips were the fare, plentifully and elegantly served, with McLoughlin leading spirited exchanges of ideas that spun on long into the convivial nights.

What impressed the Indian chiefs who came to call was McLoughlin's sense of justice. Anyone—white or Indian—caught breaking the Chief Factor's concept of permissible behaviour was sentenced to be lashed while tied to the fort's cannon. Flogging was common in those days, but few Chief Factors were even-handed enough to mete out the same punishment regardless of the culprit's skin colour. That did not mean McLoughlin was soft on Indians. On the contrary: when provoked, he could be brutal. In 1828, after the Clallam Indians on Puget Sound had murdered HBC clerk Alexander MacKenzie, McLoughlin dispatched his men on a series of punitive expeditions.

Twenty-three Indians were killed and their camps at Port Townsend and New Dungeness burned before the assassins were executed by their own families to placate the Company's death squads. A year later, the HBC's supply ship *William and Ann* was wrecked on the Columbia River bar, and Clatsop Indians appropriated the salvageable trade goods. When McLoughlin demanded restoration of the stolen property, the local chief insolently sent back a used ship's broom and an old scoop. An armed schooner was sent to teach him a lesson, and three Indians died in the mêlée that followed. Throughout these and other incidents, McLoughlin managed to retain the Indians' respect, becoming known far and wide as The White-Headed Eagle.

His relationship with the Americans arriving in growing numbers was more ambivalent. The HBC's presence acted as a deterrent to their territorial aspirations while at the same time providing the only available support system for lost or hungry mountain men and would-be settlers. McLoughlin was too good a Christian to turn anyone away from his fort, even those who had come specifically intending to drive the British intruders into the sea. Acting against orders from his own principals in London and Lachine, who saw no good reason to extend succour to enemies, McLoughlin not only welcomed all comers but granted them supplies on extended credit terms, thus encouraging the very settlements that inevitably strengthened the American hand in the Oregon Country's eventual disposition.

One of McLoughlin's favourite visitors was Jedediah Smith, a bible-quoting mountain man of extraordinary endurance and sagacity who confessed to having "a bump of curiosity the size of a goose head" for exploring the outer reaches of the Oregon Country. Only thirty-two when he died at the point of a Comanche lance near the Cimarron River, during his eight years in the fur trade Smith became the first white man to reach California by land from the east and the first to cross the Sierra Nevada and Siskiyou Mountains. Although a Methodist teetotaller, he was one of the founding organizers of the annual Rocky Mountain Rendezvous, the combination trade fair and debauchathon where mountain men met to trade gossip, merchandise and women. When Smith was attacked by Umpqua Indians, who killed all but two of his companions, McLoughlin not only gave Smith and the other survivors shelter but sent out an HBC party to recapture their purloined furs. They were purchased by the Company at a fair price and Smith spent the winter of 1828–29 enjoying McLoughlin's hospitality. Ironically, Smith's reports home about McLoughlin's ability to handle Indians and successful agricultural ventures were so glowing they prompted a succession of independent backers to mount expeditions to share Oregon's bounty.

One of Fort Vancouver's more eccentric visitors was a near-sighted Boston schoolteacher named Hall Jackson Kelley, who arrived via Mexico, dressed in a white slouch hat, blanket capote and leather pants with a red stripe down the seam—"rather *outré*, even for Vancouver," McLoughlin noted in his journal, with raised eyebrows, no doubt. Kelley (who boasted of having ruined his eyesight as a young man reading all of Virgil by moonlight) claimed to have experienced a heavenly vision that had assigned him the task of colonizing the Oregon shore. For reasons that were then (and remain) obscure, McLoughlin viewed Kelley as a common horse thief and treated him shabbily during his four-month sojourn at Fort Vancouver, ostracizing him to a hut used to gut fish. Ever afterwards, Kelley blamed the HBC for most of the many mishaps in his misspent life, claiming at one point that he had been thrown into debtors' prison at the instigation of "an unscrupulous hireling of the Hudson's Bay Company in the shape of a lawyer, living in a dark alley in the City of Boston." When his wife left him, Kelley plaintively observed that she "probably felt sad, though her affectionate regards had been somewhat alienated by deceiving monsters."

One of the few Kelley disciples who eventually reached Oregon was Nathaniel Wyeth, a handsome Boston merchant who had made a small fortune ferrying ice around Cape Horn to tropical ports. McLoughlin was delighted with his company but when Wyeth built his own trading posts on Sauvie Island, west of Fort Vancouver, and at Fort Hall on the Upper Snake, the HBC Chief Factor organized a boycott among the Indians and paid them extra until the intruder gave up and sold out to the Company in 1837. There followed troops of missionaries. The best known of them was the remarkable Marcus Whitman, a scholarly and courageous medical cleric who arrived with seven companions, including his bride, the beautiful Narcissa, aboard the first wagon to cross the ranges from Wyoming. McLoughlin was enchanted by the pair, giving them extended credit at the Company store, and free horses and cattle to start a settlement in the Willamette Valley. The Whitmans ignored McLoughlin's advice and decided to move deeper inland, into the domain of the volatile Nez Percés.

The preachers sent messages back East, and their description of the idyllic life in Oregon aroused so much attention that President Andrew Jackson decided to send a secret agent disguised as "a private gentleman" to gather

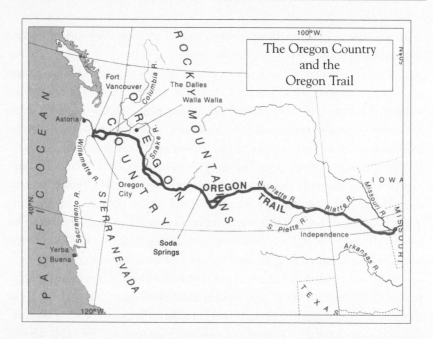

The Oregon Country
and the
Oregon Trail

firsthand observations of the area. Captain William Slacum arrived at Fort Vancouver aboard the U.S. brig *Loriot* in late December 1836. It didn't take McLoughlin long to detect Slacum's real motives, but he entertained the visitor anyway and lent the American a canoe to make a brief tour of the surrounding territory. Slacum's subsequent report described Oregon as the world's finest grazing country and accused the HBC of having established an immense foreign monopoly that supplied arms to the Indians to perpetuate the institution of slavery. Slacum recommended that Washington take firm and immediate action to possess the territory once and for all.

THESE INCURSIONS were only the most visible manifestations of John McLoughlin's increasingly difficult tenure at Fort Vancouver. His real battle was within his own ranks. The combination of his generous treatment of potential American settlers, his diversification into non-fur enterprises and several other simmering issues had roused George Simpson's ire. The main problems were based on personality, distance and the peculiar circumstances of the Oregon trade.

Unlike Simpson, who regarded himself primarily as a colonial administrator, tough and efficient but only marginally concerned with the welfare of the people and land where the HBC operated, McLoughlin felt he was in the process of founding a new society. Given the choice between fattening the Company's balance sheets and acting according to the dictates of his conscience, he opted for the latter. Not that he was disloyal to the HBC's interests, but he viewed them as part of a much more extended horizon, certain that the Company's future would be best served by his sometimes costly efforts to treat the growing influx of settlers as potential customers rather than unwanted pests. He was constantly expanding his influence—building a new sawmill on the Willamette River and setting up trading posts inland, as well as establishing a major farming community on Puget Sound and a string of coastal depots north towards Alaska. These actions suggest McLoughlin had in mind the possibility that the tentative British claim to the territory would lapse and that only a reservoir of goodwill would permit continuation of the Company's impressive revenue flow. Instead of measuring these efforts within the context of the Company's eventual benefits, Simpson regarded McLoughlin as a self-centred and vainglorious rival busy erecting foundations for an American republic on the Pacific—a Chief Factor bent on creating his own constituency so that he might slip beyond the Governor's authority.

Both men's assessments were awry, and the lack of rapid communication over the immense distances involved meant that their differences grew ever deeper. Simpson was certainly correct in maintaining the position that none of his Chief Factors would act on his own in what appeared to be a deliberate flouting of corporate edicts. But he was uncharacteristically myopic in refusing to recognize that no matter how unorthodox McLoughlin's methods appeared, they worked. Within a decade of Fort Vancouver's founding, both the Missouri Fur Company and the Rocky Mountain Fur Company, which had been the HBC's main American rivals, were bankrupt, and the Snake River basin had been swept clean not only of beaver but of mountain men.

One reason there was so little understanding between the two men was that they hardly ever saw each other. McLoughlin so closely identified his physical presence with Oregon's welfare that he could not bear to leave even on a brief furlough, and interrupted his twenty-two-year stewardship with only one journey to England. Similarly, during his nearly forty years in charge of the HBC's North American operations, Simpson visited Fort Vancouver only three times, and his initial foray hardly counted, because the post was barely established and none of the subsequently divisive issues were yet in train. His longest stay was during 1828, when he lingered at Fort Vancouver for five months and thoroughly inspected every aspect of McLoughlin's operations. He lavishly praised the good doctor's efforts, noting with satisfaction that "eatables and drinkables no longer fill the precious space in the holds of the supply ships arriving from England," concluding that "never did a change of system and a change of management, produce such obvious advantages in any part of the Indian country, as those which the present state of this Establishment in particular, and of the Columbia Department as a whole, at this moment exhibits."

But there were already signs of strain. The main burr of irritation was whether emphasis was to be placed on ships or trading posts in developing the Company's business along the Pacific Coast. During the early 1820s, that area had been dominated by intrepid skippers sailing out of New England in late summer, their holds crammed with trade goods and casks of rum. Rounding the Horn in December (the Antarctic's summer), they would touch at Hawaii to replenish their food supplies before setting sail for the Alaskan coast in spring. There they would spend the summer bartering with the Indians for pelts, then set off for Canton, stopping once again at Hawaii to load up with sandalwood. In China, their precious fur and lumber cargo would be exchanged for tea, silk and nankeen (a buff-coloured cloth used in making work clothes) bound for markets in Boston or New York.

At its zenith, more than a dozen ships were engaged in this risky transoceanic commerce and McLoughlin was determined to compete—or, better yet, to drive them out of the trade—by establishing permanent posts that would monopolize pelt supplies the year round. Langley was well placed near the mouth of the Fraser; other forts were added: Nisqually, Simpson, McLoughlin, Rupert, Taku and Stikine. Governor Simpson, on the other hand, insisted that an expanded fleet of Company trading ships would be more effective, even when McLoughlin produced figures showing he could maintain four small land forts for the cost of one vessel. His pleading could not dint Simpson's determination to build up the Company's Pacific flotilla. The Governor appointed his kinsman Aemilius Simpson head of a new marine department and this fur-trade "Admiral" had under his command a formidable armada, consisting at various times of the *Vancouver* (324 tons, 6 guns, 24 men), the *Cadboro* (71 tons, 4 guns, 12 men), the *Dryad, Eagle, Isabella* and *Broughton*.

McLoughlin was disillusioned not only with having to account for this disproportionately powerful fleet but with having to mollycoddle the restive crews and drunken captains. In that regard, at least, George Simpson agreed with him. "Captain Davidson's talent as a Navigator I know nothing about," he noted, "but his talent as a Grog drinker I understand is without parallel and I shall be agreeably surprised if he and his ship ever reach the Port of Destination."

The nautical squabble between the two men reached its crescendo over the acquisition in 1835 of the *Beaver*, the first steamship to be commissioned under HBC colours. Launched at a Thames shipyard in the presence of a crowd of cheering onlookers, the 101-foot paddle-wheeler had gone by sail around the Horn (her Boulton & Watt engines safely stored in the hold) to arrive 227 days later at Fort Vancouver. Simpson recognized two advantages in adding the steamer to the HBC's fleet: unlike other Company sailing vessels, the *Beaver* could move into tiny coves even when there was no favouring wind, thus stealing a march on American skippers bidding for the same cache of furs, and its novelty would, as he put it, have the effect of "overawing the natives."* McLoughlin saw the whole enterprise as a waste of money and suggested that if the main purpose was to impress Indians, the *Beaver* ought to be treated as a travelling circus, steaming from post to post to hoot its whistle and belch smoke—that she was far too ungainly and expensive to be involved in the serious business of the fur trade. The crusty Chief Factor certainly had a point in terms of the little ship's wood consumption: it took about ten cords of wood a day to keep the *Beaver* under way, and she had to carry thirteen woodcutters and four stokers to chop and haul the fuel for her insatiable boilers. Despite these and other quirks (or perhaps because of them) the *Beaver* became a symbol of the Hudson's Bay Company's early dominance on the Pacific Coast. After thirty-one years in its service, and twenty-one as a survey vessel, *ad hoc* tug and log-boom towboat, she went aground in 1888 at Prospect Point near the entrance to Vancouver Harbour.†

McLoughlin could never see the *Beaver*'s brave prow without being reminded that the presence of the belching little paddle-wheeler represented

---

* At least one group of Indians, the Bella Bella, was so taken by the ship that they told John Dunn, an HBC clerk, they intended to build their own version of the *Beaver*. A few days after this boast, a thirty-foot contraption, black with painted white portholes, hove into the Bay man's view, apparently propelled by red wooden paddles at each side. The copy had been built atop a hollow log, inside which crouched panting Indians frantically turning a crank that moved the paddles, producing a respectable cruising speed of three knots.

† After half a century's service, she was still sturdy enough to survive four years of battering by the sea on her involuntary rocky perch. The *Beaver* was finally sunk in 1892 by the wash of a passing HBC freighter; her remains have recently been discovered near the Lions Gate Bridge by divers from Vancouver's Underwater Archeological Society.

Simpson's repudiation of the authority originally delegated to him. These feelings came to a head during the Governor's next (and final) visit to the Oregon Country in 1841, as part of his whirlwind world tour. Only a week after arriving at Fort Vancouver in late August, he went north to satisfy himself that the Americans had been driven out of the Alaska fur trade. Scrutinizing the southern tip of Vancouver Island along the way, Simpson appraised its excellent harbours, abundance of timber and moderate climate, carefully noting that it would be worth colonizing.

When he returned from his coastal sidetrip, Simpson had devastating news for McLoughlin. The Chief Factor was peremptorily ordered to dismantle most of the northern forts. The trade was to be conducted from the decks of the *Beaver* instead. The doctor was beside himself. The successful trading system he had created was to be wiped out on the strength of an apparently wilful gesture based on one superficial tour. Not only had Simpson made his momentous policy decision without consulting McLoughlin but he had already announced it to the various subordinates stationed in the posts he had visited along the way. "I am not aware that these subjects have been discussed," McLoughlin complained to the Governor, "as it is perfectly out of the question, to talk of discussion, when there are only two persons at the discussion, and one has the power to decide as he pleases and does."

Having delivered himself of his kangaroo verdict and dismissed McLoughlin's objections as based on nothing more substantial than the Chief Factor's regret that he had not originated these "reforms," Simpson set out for Alaska once again, this time on his way to Siberia for the longest leg of his round-the-world odyssey. When he arrived at Fort Stikine, Simpson found the Company flag at half-mast and was told that four nights earlier its commanding officer, John McLoughlin, Jr., the Chief Factor's son, had been killed by one of his men during a drunken orgy. Instead of investigating the tragedy properly, the Governor dismissed the affair as "justifiable homicide" and turned the actual murderer, a tripman named Urbain Heroux, over to the Russian authorities at Sitka. Because he felt that any further inquiries would only embarrass the Hudson's Bay Company, he wrote a heartless letter to the dead man's father condemning the son's behaviour and strongly advising the elder McLoughlin not to press charges.

The distraught father, already shell-shocked by Simpson's destruction of his trading system, vowed to clear his son's name. "Instead of conducting the examination so as to endeavour to find out what had led to the murder," he wrote to Simpson in one of his milder missives, "you conducted it as if it had been an investigation into the moral conduct of the Deceased, and as if you were desirous to justify the conduct of the murderers." Evidence that young McLoughlin had in fact not been drunk on the night of his death began to mount, with several visitors to Fort Stikine swearing affidavits that he had hardly touched a glass in their presence. His personal liquor ration was found to be untouched. Pierre Kanaquassé, an HBC servant who shortly afterwards visited Fort Vancouver, matter-of-factly explained that the youthful McLoughlin had been murdered because he would not allow his traders to have Indian women in their rooms overnight and because he punished those of his men who stole Company goods to give their mistresses. The assassination had been no spur-of-the-moment crime but a long-standing plot by frustrated employees to rid themselves of their commanding officer, who seems to have been guilty of nothing more than defending the Company's interests. Kanaquassé coolly outlined how he himself had made three attempts on McLoughlin's life and produced a written pact, signed by all but one of Fort Stikine's staff members, swearing to murder McLoughlin and cover up the crime.

When an independent investigation confirmed that the murder was premeditated, the elder McLoughlin expected some form of vindication or apology. What he got was further abuse. Simpson ignored the incontrovertible evidence that his snap verdict had been wrong and instead berated McLoughlin for allowing his judgment to be sacrificed to his feelings. When the aggrieved father finally managed to have the real murderers extradited to York Factory, he was censured for sending them so far without permission, then told they could be tried only in England at a cost of at least £10,000, which he personally would have to pay.

The resulting impasse forced McLoughlin to drop the case, but it solidified his bitterness. He was by then facing trouble from another quarter. On May 2, 1843, during a meeting at Champoeg, the Oregon missionaries and settlers decided to organize a provisional government, an idea secretly planned at so-called "wolf meetings"—informal get-togethers, ostensibly convened to discuss the threat of predators to their flocks of sheep and herds of cattle. The following season fourteen hundred new settlers arrived, and by 1845 the Willamette Valley boasted a permanent population of more than six thousand. The tentative rivulet of immigrants into the Oregon Country from the eastern United States had become a torrent. Trains of covered wagons, after gathering at Independence on the Missouri, lurched two thousand miles across the arid midlands towards the mountain ranges, along the Oregon Trail, carrying bright-eyed pioneers anxious to share the bounty of the new land.

The election of James K. Polk (the original "dark horse" candidate) who came out of the backwoods of Tennessee politics to win the U.S. presidency in 1844 on the slogan "Fifty-four forty or fight!" served to hurry the process. By thus setting the southern tip of Alaska as their territorial target, the Americans forced Westminster to reach a workable compromise on Oregon. Britain was by this time much more interested in maintaining good trading relations with Washington than in arguing about rights to a faraway colony on behalf of an already prosperous trading monopoly. The issue came up for decision at a time when the British government was facing many more significant questions, including strained relations with France and a threat that repeal of the Corn Laws would destroy its political base. These and other internal strains prompted the London politicians to negotiate a relatively quick agreement. The Oregon Treaty, signed on June 15, 1846, salvaged for the HBC the mainland territory north of the 49th parallel plus Vancouver Island, but the Company lost its rights in Oregon.*

For John McLoughlin, these political manoeuvres had become academic. By the spring of 1844, the London Committee had decided to be rid of the old-timer by terminating his superintendency of the Columbia Department, demoting him to temporary membership in a trio of HBC officers who would take over management of Fort Vancouver and Oregon's fur trade. The Committeemen had anticipated the effect on the Chief Factor's pride correctly. Deeply offended by their treatment of him, McLoughlin resigned. "Gentlemen," he wrote, with laudable understatement, "I will serve you no longer."

He retired to Oregon City at the falls of the Willamette River and applied for U.S. citizenship, but the Americans didn't treat him any better than his former employers. Suspicious because he was British, a Catholic and a former Bay man, the settlers whom he had helped now turned on him and arranged to have his property confiscated. At the same time, Simpson insisted that

---

* Despite the treaty, the Company did not immediately abandon its Oregon-based operations. The last of its American trading posts was closed in 1871. Legal proceedings to compensate the HBC for its original rights of possession dragged on for most of another decade after that, but the U.S. Government eventually paid the Company $650,000 (including $200,000 for the agricultural lands on Puget Sound) in gold bullion.

McLoughlin pay back out of his own pocket the balances outstanding for the goods he had sold on credit to help the incoming settlers. They refused to honour their debts, dismissing their former benefactor as a traitor. "By British demagogues," McLoughlin lamented in one of the justifiably bitter epistles of his last dozen years in exile, "I have been represented as a traitor. What for? Because I acted as a Christian, saved American citizens, men, women and children, from the Indian tomahawk.... American demagogues have been base enough to assert that I had caused American citizens to be massacred by hundreds of savages—I who saved all I could.... I founded this settlement and prevented a war."

The unheralded "Father of Oregon" died on September 3, 1857, bitterly indignant to the end. "I might better have been shot forty years ago," he wrote to a friend shortly before his death, "than to have lived here and tried to build up a family and an estate."

BEFORE THE HBC FADED from Oregon's history, a dramatic event shook the new settlement's tranquility. The Reverend Dr Marcus Whitman and his wife, Narcissa, had been living at Waiilatpu, in the dangerous Walla Walla country, for eleven years, trying to minister to their charges' spiritual lives but finding themselves dealing more and more with their physical ailments. According to Indian belief of the day, medicine men were only as good as their latest cures; occasionally their own shamans were put to death if a chief died following unsuccessful treatment. The Whitmans had lost several native patients of high station, and the young men from a nearby Indian village were angry with the missionaries for larding the melons in their garden with laxative to discourage theft. Years before, Indian–white relations in Oregon had been poisoned by the stupid boast of former Nor'Wester Duncan McDougall, who had tried to disarm an unruly mob of Indians by playing on their understandable fear of smallpox. He had shown their leaders a small black bottle, claiming that it contained the dreaded smallpox virus, and threatened to pull the stopper. After a family of newcomers arrived in the Whitmans' precinct afflicted with measles and several Indians caught the disease, their chiefs planned a war party against the mission.

Early in the morning of November 29, 1847, as the doctor and Narcissa were starting on their rounds, an unusually large number of Indians gathered on the premises, hiding weapons under their blankets. As one of the chiefs engaged Whitman in animated conversation, another tomahawked him from behind, and the massacre was on. In the next hour, Narcissa and twelve other white people were killed and forty-seven women and children taken prisoner.

A week later, a Métis reported the massacre to Fort Vancouver, then co-commanded by Peter Skene Ogden, late of the Snake River expeditions. Ogden had spent most of the intervening years on HBC duty in Alaska as well as New Caledonia, and was now in the process of settling the Company's affairs before its forced move out of Oregon. Although the territory's provisional government was already in place and the HBC had no authority or responsibility in the situation, Ogden set off at dawn the next morning, determined to free the hostages. He went unarmed with sixteen paddlers up the Columbia, travelling light to gain time. When he reached Walla Walla, he realized that a full Indian uprising was brewing. The white captives had been dispersed to several Indian camps, so he sent a message to the chiefs of the Nez Percés and Cayuses that he wished to meet them for a parley. When they were assembled, he entered their longhouse alone and spoke in their own tongues. "The Hudson's Bay Company has been with you more than thirty years without bloodshed," he began, in what was to unroll as an all-day oration. "We are traders, and of a different nation than the Americans. But we are of the same colour, speak the same language, and worship the same God. Their cruel fate causes our hearts to bleed. Besides this massacre, you have robbed the Americans passing through your country, and you have insulted their women. We have made you chiefs, but you say that you cannot control your young men. They are cowards, and you are responsible for their deeds. If the Americans begin war, you will have cause to regret, for you will be exterminated. I know that many Indians have died; so have white people. Dr Whitman did not poison those Indians who died. You now have the opportunity to make some reparation. I advise you, but I promise you nothing should war be declared against you. The Hudson's Bay Company has nothing to do with your actions in this trouble. Deliver to me these captives and I will give you a ransom. That is all."

The Cayuse chief Tiloukaikt gave a long and dignified reply, concluding with this promise: "Your words are Weighty. Your hairs are grey. We have known you a long time. You have had an unpleasant journey to this place. I cannot therefore keep the captives back. I make them over to you, which I would not do to another younger than yourself." The prisoners were delivered unharmed six days later, and Ogden paid the ransom of sixty-two blankets, sixty-three cotton shirts, twelve muskets, six hundred loads of ammunition, thirty-seven pounds of tobacco and twelve flints.

The suspected murderers of the Whitmans were eventually captured by a posse and taken to Fort Vancouver, which had become a U.S. Army camp. Five of the Cayuse tribesmen who were thought to have killed the missionaries were lined up on makeshift gallows, and Joe Meek, the former mountain man since promoted to U.S. marshal, released each drop with a tomahawk blow. Thus Oregon's time as a "Company town" came to a bloody and abrupt end.

British Columbia's Mulatto King

James Douglas turned parsimony into an art form.

THE COMPANY'S WEST COAST pursuits now passed into the hands of James Douglas, a mulatto of elegant mien whose character was a perplexing combination of endearing romanticism and glacial tenacity. In his actions and person, he guided British Columbia's metamorphosis from savage fur farm to British colony to Canadian province—and played a dominant role in all three incarnations.

He was imperious, penny-pinching, obsessed by detail and ritual; his swarthy complexion would cloud over dangerously if subordinates failed to jump at his many commands. Described by one contemporary as "a cold brave man ... with a wooden hard face, which said very plainly, I am not afraid," Douglas had been in the fur trade since before his seventeenth birthday and knew all its tricks and subtleties.

Paternal despotism was his operational code, though his devotion to duty (as he defined it) made him seem more pompous than he really was. He could (and did) make a terrible fuss to ensure that his family's croquet lawn was laid out precisely thus and so, yet in 1853 at Cowichan he sat stock-still on a camp-stool for most of a day, staring down two hundred armed and angry Indians. On that occasion, he smoked his pipe, a pile of gifts ready at one hand, his cutlass firmly grasped in the other, impassively waiting for the band to surrender one of their kin who had murdered an HBC shepherd. When they gave in, he walked away with his prisoner, making a mental note to order a more serviceable sword for future confrontations. He was so stiff and formal that his men referred to him behind his back as "Old Square-Toes," yet he was sentimental enough to retain in his watchcase a shilling given him by a grandchild as a birthday gift to "spend as he liked," and at the age of sixty-nine could still be seen nearly every morning skipping rope on his veranda.

Self-possessed and self-serving, he moved so carefully within the reefy confines of the HBC's internal politics that *both* sides on any given issue usually praised his behaviour and his decisions. Perhaps because he was so far removed from any countervailing authority and thought himself to be the personification of almost kingly powers, he practised a policy of social superiority that suited neither his background nor his circumstances. Joseph Watt, an Oregon immigrant who had met him, noted: "Douglas ... would step around in a way as much as to say: 'you are not as good as I am, I don't belong to your class.'" He was so taken with postures and titles that at one point he was signing official documents over the self-composed description: "His Excellency, James Douglas, Governor of Vancouver Island and its Dependencies, Commander-in-Chief and Vice-Admiral of the same."

James Douglas turned parsimony into an art form. He was so obsessed with money that when he was receiving handsome salaries while serving as both the local head of the Hudson's Bay Company and Governor of Vancouver Island, he requested additional payment for acting as Lieutenant-Governor of the Queen Charlotte Islands though that function involved no duties. A few years later, when he was far and away the richest man in British Columbia, he wrote a long letter to his London outfitters instructing them to ship his clothes in as small a package as possible because local customs officers judged parcels by size rather than by weight. In the same letter, he asked the British company to subtract his 5 percent rebate for prompt cash payment from the total cost in advance because that way he could save a fraction on the 20 percent *ad valorem* duty.

Despite such microscopic attention to mundane matters, Douglas could also be a visionary. He was the first man to urge the building of a trans-Canada highway, for example, advocating as early as 1862 a cross-country route that would have "the peculiar advantage of being ... remote from the U.S. frontier and traversing a country exclusively British, which from its position, and general resources can hardly fail ... to become the seat of a large population." Douglas was literate, seldom spending a night without dipping into his prized leather-bound forty-five-volume set of English classics, and could be poetic in his insights. Reminiscing about the departure of the annual express from Fort Vancouver to York Factory, he wrote in his journal: "A day highly suggestive of the past, of fresh scenes, of perilous travel, of fatigues, excitement and of adventures by mountain and flood; the retrospect is full of charms; images of the morning breezes, the bright sky, the glowing sunrise, the rushing waters, the roaring cataract—the dark forest, the flowery plains, the impressive mountains in their pure white covering of snow, rise before me, at this moment, as vividly as ever and old as I am, my heart bounds at the bare recollection of scenes I loved so well … I can recall nothing more delightful than our bivouac on a clear moonlit May night, near the Punch Bowls—the highest point of the Jasper Pass. The atmosphere was bright, sharp and bracing, the sun set in gorgeous splendour, bringing out the towering peaks and fantastic pinnacles dressed in purest white, into bold relief. Our camp was laid and our fire built, on the firm hard snow which was about 20 feet deep. As the daylight faded away, and the shades of night gathered over the Pass, a milder light shot up from behind the nearest Peak, with gradually encreasing brilliancy until at last the full orbed moon rose in silent majesty from the mass of mountains shedding a mild radiance over the whole valley beneath."

Born out of wedlock to John Douglas, a Glasgow merchant who owned sugar estates in Demerara, British Guiana, and Martha Ritchie, the daughter of a black freewoman from Barbados, the young James was taken to Scotland, where he passed his preparatory grades at Lanark and was later sent to a boarding school at Chester in England. He joined the North West Company in 1819 as an apprentice and two years later went over to the HBC, eventually being assigned to Fort St James in the New Caledonia Department. There he served as a clerk under William Connolly, whose fifteen-year-old Mixed Blood daughter Amelia he married in 1824. The posting was almost his last. A pair of Carrier Indians had killed two HBC employees at nearby Fort George some time before, and the employees' bodies had been eaten by dogs. When one of the murderers arrived back at a camp near Fort St James, Douglas and a group of Bay men set out to apprehend him. He was discovered hiding in a sick woman's tent under a pile of pelts and, while attempting to escape, stabbed Douglas with an arrow. In the fracas that followed, the Indian was hanged on the spot and his body fed to wolves.

When Kwah, the local Carrier chief, returned from a hunt and discovered what had happened, he marched into Fort St James at the head of a war party. Connolly was away, and Douglas was quickly overpowered and pinned down on a table. Tloeng, the Indian chief's assistant, held a knife to the HBC clerk's throat, ready to pierce the jugular. At this precise moment, Douglas's wife,

Amelia, who had been hiding in an upstairs storeroom, began to throw tobacco, blankets and other goods at the Indians' feet, the customary compensation for an Indian death, begging for her husband's life. Chief Kwah accepted the offer, waved the dagger away from Douglas's neck and, suitably placated, retreated from the fort. Later in his HBC career, Douglas enjoyed fairly good relations with local tribes, so much so that some Vancouver Islanders resented it. "Though the Governor is a wonderfully clever man among the Indians, he does not seem to be governing a white population at all," complained Lieutenant Charles William Wilson, a visiting Royal Navy officer.

Transferred to Fort Vancouver in 1830 as an accountant, Douglas was promoted to Chief Trader in 1834 and Chief Factor in 1839. If McLoughlin was the Oregon Country's king, Douglas was its prime minister, having served the Company's interests in the Columbia Department faithfully for nearly twenty years before being placed in charge of its relocated headquarters on Vancouver Island. "The place itself appears to be a perfect 'Eden,' in the midst of the dreary wilderness of the North west coast," he wrote to a friend when he first reconnoitred the new territory in 1842, "and so different is its general aspect, from the wooded, rugged regions around, that one might be pardoned for supposing it had dropped from the clouds into its present position."

The new HBC installation was first named Fort Camosun, then very briefly Fort Albert, but after December 12, 1843, it was known as Fort Victoria in honour of the young queen of England. With its tiara of mountains reflected in a jade sea, the island's unspoiled beauty astonished most newcomers, especially those who ventured along its west coast, where rugged slashes of rock elbowing into the Pacific surf etch some of the earth's most spectacular landforms. But not everyone was impressed. When the Honourable John Gordon, brother of the Earl of Aberdeen, the British Foreign Secretary, arrived as captain of the fifty-gun HMS *America,* he took a look around and concluded that he would "not give one of the bleakest knolls of all the bleak hills of Scotland for twenty islands like this arrayed in barbaric splendor."

Fort Victoria was planned with its future significance in mind. Its quadrangle, more than three hundred feet on a side and surrounded by a stockade of pointed eighteen-foot pickets, enclosed a dozen buildings including an octagonal bastion three storeys high mounting nine-pound guns. To forestall the possibility of invasion by American settlers from the Oregon Country, Vancouver Island was granted to the HBC by the British government in 1849—

the Company thus being utilized as a colonizing agent by the Crown. The Mormons of Utah had already been in touch with London seeking to claim the island and James Edward Fitzgerald, a private British entrepreneur, had submitted a detailed proposal to Westminster for exploiting the colony at its southernmost tip. The HBC did not particularly wish to take on the responsibilities of colonization, but it certainly had no intention of allowing anyone else to grab its advantageous new Pacific site. The Royal Adventurers were charged by the government with establishing "settlements of resident colonists, emigrants from Our United Kingdom of Great Britain and Ireland, or from other Our Dominions …" and disposing of "the land there as may be necessary for the purposes of colonization." Although the Company agreed it would sell land to settlers at a fair price, they had to purchase at least twenty acres at a time, and anyone buying larger spreads had to bring out five single men or three married couples at his own expense, for each hundred acres under cultivation. Land costs were set at £1 an acre. These stringent regulations, ostensibly meant to discourage squatters and land speculators, were in truth designed to perpetuate Britain's agricultural class system, so that the new colony would attract gentleman farmers and not fall prey to the populist agitations that had shaken the established orders of Lower and Upper Canada during the 1830s.

Although its grant specifically stated that the HBC would lose jurisdiction over Vancouver Island at the end of five years if it had not fostered a successful colony, the Company showed little enthusiasm for its assigned task, treating the outpost as little more than an ideally located bulwark for its mainland fur preserves. At the end of that period, only seventy men, women and children had arrived and no more than five hundred acres had been settled. Typical of those early pioneers was Captain Walter Colquhoun Grant, son of Wellington's chief intelligence officer at Waterloo and late of the Scots Greys, who arrived aboard the *Harpooner* in the summer of 1849, preceded by eight workmen. Bankrupted by a bank failure, he secured his passage from the Company by claiming to be a competent land surveyor. He brought few instruments with him but managed to supply himself with the necessities of a gentleman travelling to the colonies: a fancy carriage harness, a large library, two small brass cannon and a plentiful supply of cricket wickets. He chose to settle at Sooke, twenty-five miles west of Fort Victoria, and on his thirty-five-acre estate erected a log manor house complete with circular driveway. His duties as the Company's land surveyor were considerably hampered by the fact that he lacked all sense of direction, and once got lost for five days trying to make it from Sooke to Fort Victoria. Although he was the life of many a party at the officers' mess (on one notable occasion he challenged anyone to a duel after demonstrating his skill by snuffing out a candle with one swipe of his cutlass and splitting it in half with another), he soon grew peevish and by the winter of 1851 was contemplating suicide. To cheer himself up (and to escape James Douglas's well-founded suspicion that he was a hopelessly incompetent surveyor), Captain Grant hopped on a Company ship and spent two winter months in Hawaii. It was there that he made his most lasting contribution to Vancouver Island. He brought back with him seeds of the broom plant (given to him by the local British consul) and broadcast them around his estate, thus introducing the yellow-flowered shrub that now blooms profusely throughout the island's southern parts.

To govern its new island colony, the British Cabinet appointed Richard Blanshard, an ambitious thirty-two-year-old barrister who had already seen service in the West Indies and was eager for further experience that might lead to higher government appointments. He left England under the impression that he would receive a grant of a thousand acres of free land, occupy a suitable governor's mansion and generally be able to exercise the considerable power then vested in colonial officials. When he arrived aboard HMS *Driver*, Blanshard discovered that he was slated for no land and no residence and that James Douglas had no intention of sharing his authority with the newcomer. The only recognition of his exalted station Blanshard ever received was a seventeen-gun salute from Fort Victoria on his arrival. After that there was silence. He submitted regular dispatches about his increasingly futile daily rounds, twitched his walrus moustache in frustration, diverting himself with lonely horseback rides and cursing his solitary fate. Douglas made certain that he had no advisers, no budget, no proper accommodation and no prospects. When Blanshard finally unearthed from the regulations something that he felt even a governor with his restricted mandate could do—clear ships officially in and out of Victoria Harbour—he was flattened when Douglas himself pointedly gave clearance to the HBC trading vessel *Cadboro*. Blanshard promptly took Douglas to court and tried to jail him inside Fort Victoria. This proved awkward because Blanshard commanded no law enforcement facilities and Douglas was the fort's commanding officer. In weary desperation, Blanshard bound Douglas over to appear for sentencing at some indeterminate future date and sent in his resignation. The poor fellow even had to pay his own passage home.

Blanshard's tenure had the makings of a minor Gilbert and Sullivan operetta, but he did leave behind one important legacy. When a group of settlers headed by Captain James Cooper, a retired HBC skipper and cranberry broker who had been put out of business by the Company, petitioned him to set up an executive council, he agreed. Blanshard appointed Cooper, the retired HBC trader John Tod, plus Douglas, to the newly instituted council in what was the first, however feeble, step in the colony's evolution to representative government. That trend seemed to reverse itself a few weeks after Blanshard's departure, when Douglas became Vancouver Island's Governor—without being asked to give up his HBC appointment. The potential for conflict of interest was so obvious that the British government insisted he establish a functioning elected assembly. Douglas went through the motions, but by allowing absentee landlords to vote through their locally appointed agents, he made certain that loyal HBC men held the balance of power. The Speaker of the new House was John Sebastian Helmcken, the Company doctor, and, not incidentally, Douglas's son-in-law; the colony's collector of customs was a retired HBC Chief Trader; the colony's chief justice was Douglas's brother-in-law, David Cameron; and so forth. All revenues from the sale of lands, timber and minerals went straight into Company coffers, with only the fees from licensed taverns being directed towards general expenditures. That was a source of revenues hardly liable to dry up, but it was not enough to provide a counterweight to the HBC's continued dominance of the island's affairs.

A more profitable venture proved to be mining. Coal had been discovered at Beaver Harbour (later renamed Fort Rupert) on the northeast coast, but when Scottish miners were brought in, they dug seventy feet down and found the seam no more than eight inches wide. Then an elderly chief from a Nanaimo Indian band arrived at Fort Victoria one winter day to have his gun repaired. While watching the blacksmith at his forge, he noticed the coal and mentioned that there was plenty of such black rock up his way. Offered a bottle of rum and no charge for the gun repairs, he arrived back a few months later, his canoe filled with coal—and the rush was on. A major coal deposit was soon outlined at Nanaimo, and the miners, Robert Dunsmuir among them, were ferried back from Fort Rupert. Coal was mined at Nanaimo for most of the next century, first by the HBC and later by the Dunsmuir family. (The pits employed three thousand miners at the height of their productivity.)

The colonists' attention was soon diverted northward to the ethereal Queen Charlotte Islands, a scimitar-shaped archipelago visited by James Cook in 1778. An Indian woman had found a gold nugget on a local beach in 1850 and when it was traded at Fort Victoria, Douglas dispatched an HBC ship to Mitchell Harbour on Moresby Island to investigate. A quartz vein, said to be a quarter pure gold, was pinpointed, and thirty miners were sent to work the lode, but the Haida strenuously protested the removal of their heritage. "They arrived in large numbers, say thirty canoes," reported Chief Trader W.H. McNeill, a former captain of the *Beaver* in charge of the expedition. "When they saw us blasting and turning out the gold in such large quantities, they became excited and commenced depredations on us, stealing the tools, and taking at least one-half of the gold that was thrown out by the blast. They would lie concealed until the report was heard, and then make a rush for the gold; a regular scramble between them and our men would then take place; they would take our men by the legs, and hold them away from the gold. Some blows were struck on these occasions. The Indians drew their knives on our men often. The men who were at work on the vein became completely tired and disgusted at these proceedings, and came to me on three different occasions and told me that they would not remain any longer to work the gold; that their time was lost to them, as the natives took one-half of the gold thrown out by the blast, and blood would be shed if they continued to work at the digging; that our force was not strong or large enough to work and fight also. They were aware they could not work on shore after hostility had commenced, therefore I made up my mind to leave the place."

Not enough gold was found on the Queen Charlottes to make mining ventures worthwhile, but the fever was in the air. More nuggets were spotted along the Thompson River near its junction with the Fraser and by 1858 a full-scale rush had started, with California's Forty-Niners leaving behind their worked-out claims and scurrying north. Because Victoria was the only supply depot in the region, the California miners headed for Vancouver Island. On Sunday, April 25, 1858, the fort's citizens emerged from church to find an American paddle-wheeler disgorging half a hundred red-shirted men lugging pickaxes, panning equipment and tent poles. The little settlement's population doubled in one afternoon, and the ensuing building boom irremediably altered its character. That year thirty thousand impatient miners passed through the streets of Victoria. On one July morning two San Francisco steamers landed twenty-eight hundred men. Land values rose a hundredfold almost overnight; gambling saloons, opium dens and brothels promptly opened for business. All was set for one of history's most frenetic gold rushes. "The entire population of San Francisco—merchants, capitalists, businessmen of all descriptions, as well as the ever-present gamblers—were alike seized by the insane desire to sell out their businesses, their homes and any other property they were possessed of, for any sum that would bring them and their outfit to the golden banks of the Fraser," American journalist H.B. Hobson reported in his description of these hectic times. "Pieces of valuable real estate on Kearney and Montgomery streets, and in other desirable locations in San Francisco, were sold for less than the cost of the improvements by the excited people in their haste to get to the new gold fields. It is needless to dwell upon the many trials and hardships of these pioneers of British Columbia. A comparatively small number reached their goal and succeeded beyond their most sanguine expectations; many fell by the wayside, and many more returned to their deserted homes in California—sadder, poorer, but wiser men."

For those who got as far as Victoria, the most daunting problem was to find transportation across the Strait of Georgia's tide rips to the Fraser River delta and beyond. Since few sailing vessels were available, the crossing was attempted in commandeered skiffs and even canoes, often with fatal results. The miners' knowledge of local geography was so sketchy that some of them navigated strictly by tasting the water to see how salty it was—the theory being that it would get sweeter as they approached the mouth of the Fraser River.

By the end of 1859, the sandbars of the Fraser had been panned clean for two hundred miles and the rush subsided as suddenly as it had started—until the late autumn of 1860 when word came from the high interior that even richer deposits had been found in the Cariboo Country, far to the north. There, as it turned out, the yellow metal had been deposited in highly concentrated form. One miner named J.C. Bryant retrieved an incredible ninety-six ounces out of one pan.* The miners worked their way up the Fraser, eventually taking out gold then worth $50 million, using the more complicated sluice boxes and rockers instead of the rudimentary pans. The instant city of Barkerville (named after a Cornish sailor who struck it rich there) soon boasted every civilized facility, including thirteen saloons—and the largest population north of San Francisco and west of Chicago.

---

* An 83.2-ounce nugget was later found on Spruce Creek, east of Atlin near the Yukon.

Because Simon Fraser's river was as impassable as ever, alternative transportation arteries had to be created, the most sophisticated of them being the Cariboo Road built under James Douglas's sponsorship from Yale to Barkerville by Royal Engineers imported from Britain. Mule teams were the customary beasts of burden, but a group of imaginative trail-blazers imported two dozen camels from Manchuria via San Francisco, probably because they thought the animals were sure-footed and would not require much food. The odd thing was that the theory proved true, and several camel trains eventually swayed their way into Barkerville. The problem was smell. The spoor of the animals spooked every horse and mule in the district, setting off many a stampede. The camels also had unforeseen feeding habits. Contemptuously refusing the hay and other forage offered by their keepers, they seemed to hunger only for miners' shirts and socks, preferably unwashed. The animals were eventually set free and vanished into the wilds, with only the occasional sighting (one as late as 1905) to indicate any had survived.

Throughout the gold-rush period, the Hudson's Bay Company represented the only form of law enforcement on or near the Fraser, and even though Douglas had no authority on the mainland, he decreed that miners would require licences to be allowed into the diggings—and that he was the only source of such permits, obtainable at twenty-one shillings a month, payable in advance. This was partly a revenue-raising device, but it also served as a practical way to exert British sovereignty over the suddenly valuable territory. It was Douglas's further insistence that all supplies had to be purchased at Fort Victoria, Fort Langley or from HBC ships anchored off the Fraser River that prompted the British government to intervene. (The last straw was when Douglas ordered the seizure of any ships selling non-HBC goods.) On August 2, 1858, British Columbia was declared a Crown colony and the Company's exclusive trading licence in New Caledonia was permanently revoked. The boundaries of the new colony stretched from over the summits of the Rocky Mountains to the Pacific and from the Finlay branch of the Peace River in the north to the 49th parallel in the south, with the Queen Charlottes but not Vancouver Island included for the moment.

The administration of the new colony was to be headed by a governor with wide powers—and no one seemed better qualified to wield them than James Douglas. "I trust and think he is a safe and sensible man, barring his too close connection with the Company," wrote Herman Merivale, the British

Undersecretary of State for the Colonies, in an internal memorandum. "If he is, detailed instructions will only hamper him. If he is not, they will do him no good." Douglas was appointed for a six-year term (at £1,000 per annum) but was ordered to sever his ties with the Hudson's Bay Company and required to organize a Council and eventually to hold elections for an Assembly.

But first the new Crown colony had to be officially proclaimed. On one of those rainy days when the sky appears painted permanently gunmetal-grey, Douglas and his retinue (Rear-Admiral R.L. Baynes, Commander of Her Majesty's naval forces, Pacific Station; David Cameron, the Chief Justice of Vancouver Island; Matthew Baillie Begbie, judge designate of British Columbia; plus a naval guard of honour) boarded HMS *Satellite* for the trip across the Strait of Georgia to Point Roberts, where they transferred to the HBC ship *Otter* and later set course for Fort Langley aboard the *Beaver*. The next day (November 19, 1858) Douglas disembarked at the post's muddy shore to the tune of an eighteen-gun salute, and before an audience of a hundred cheering, if drenched, spectators administered the oath of office to Begbie, who in turn read aloud Queen Victoria's commission appointing him British Columbia's first Governor.

Begbie, who became known for his fairness on the bench and never really earned his sobriquet, "The Hanging Judge," helped Douglas administer the fledgling colony, as did a detachment of 150 Royal Engineers under the command of Colonel Richard Moody, sent out by the British Government to survey the land and pick a new capital. Moody promptly chose New Westminster, a freshwater port on the north bank of the Fraser; that site found little favour with Douglas, who much preferred Victoria and seldom visited the mainland. By 1860, settlement had spread to Cowichan and Chemainus and to Saltspring, the most luxuriant of the Gulf Islands. Douglas's administration erected lighthouses and built bridges and roads, providing the new colony with everything except democracy. The Governor insisted on legislating by proclamation, so that he could keep control of the government firmly in his grasp. That rigid attitude fed ammunition to his critics, chief among them being Amor de Cosmos, publisher first of the *British Colonist* and later of the Victoria *Daily Standard*.

Born William Smith, at Windsor, Nova Scotia, the crusading journalist had changed his name by California edict to "Lover of the Universe" as being a more appropriate reflection of his aspirations. After arriving in Victoria from California, he established the *British Colonist* to promulgate his emphatic views.* In the newspaper's first issue, dated December 11, 1858, he attacked the Governor's record: "He wanted to serve his country with honor and at the same time preserve the grasping interests of the Hudson's Bay Company inviolate. In trying to serve two masters he was unsuccessful as a statesman. His administration was never marked by those broad and comprehensive views of government, which were necessary to the times and to the foundation of a great colony. It appeared sordid; as exclusive and anti-British and belonged to a past age. A wily diplomacy shrouded all.... The great mistake of the administration occurred early. Instead of taking the responsibility to throw the country open to free trade and colonization; instead of sinking all sordid considerations for the public good, we fear our Executive gave honeyed words to those whom he would partially prohibit; made his policy approximate to 'masterly inactivity', published obstructive proclamations for acts; and excused all by a doubtful claim to exclusive trade and navigation."

By late 1863, the pressures from England for Douglas to summon a legislative assembly had grown irresistible and the Governor was ordered to organize an election. The opening session of British Columbia's first Legislative Council sat at New Westminster on January 22, 1864, but Douglas felt allergic to all that populism. He resigned a few weeks later and huffily retired from public life. He had been knighted by Queen Victoria the previous year and now decided to indulge himself with the fortune he had built up during his half-century in the fur trade. He led his family on the grand tour of Europe and, on his return, settled down at James Bay as Vancouver Island's wealthiest citizen. Formal to the end, he decreed that only male guests could attend his retirement dinner; the ladies were allowed merely to "look on."

His HBC associate John Tod, who came to call on the former Governor during that final period (Douglas died on August 2, 1877), reported in a letter to his friend Edward Ermatinger: "You probably think me unjustly severe on our old friend, but it is with sorrow I say it, that to all those who have known him for years, he has even appeared cold, crafty and selfish; and justly merits the reward he now reaps of isolation and desertion of all who have known him from early times."

---

* He was premier of British Columbia for fourteen months in 1872–74 while holding down an MP's seat in Ottawa, where he sat as a Liberal from 1871 to 1882. A firebrand for responsible government and later a pro-Confederationist, he was described by George Walkem, his successor as premier, as having "all the eccentricities of a comet without any of its brilliance."

By 1862, the Crown had taken back all rights over Vancouver Island, so that the Hudson's Bay Company was reduced to the status of any other enterprise, its only enduring advantage being long tenure and physical presence. The Pacific empire forged by Peter Skene Ogden, John McLoughlin and James Douglas had come to a peaceful end, which is more than can be said of most empires. Their legacy was to maintain the British presence on North America's western shore just long enough to ensure that Canada would one day stretch eastward and westward from coast to coast.

VII END OF EMPIRE

Unravelling the Fur Monopoly

George Simpson's opinion of missionaries verged on the benign, but he could never concede that there might exist a presence within his empire claiming allegiance to any authority higher than himself.

BY THE MIDDLE OF THE nineteenth century, precise knowledge of Canada's hinterland had scarcely moved beyond the "HERE BE DRAGONS" inscriptions on early exploration charts. The navigable lakes and rivers were familiar, but much of the rolling prairie and most of the tundra to the north had been viewed only in passing.

Fort Edmonton was the largest settlement west of Red River; the postage-stamp farms comprising Fort Langley, near the mouth of the Fraser River, and Fort Victoria on Vancouver Island were the only communities of any conse-quence on the Pacific. Known as the "Great Lone Land," the fertile prairie was cut off from Upper Canada (renamed Canada West in 1841) by eight hundred miles of wilderness. The famed voyageur route from Lachine to Lake Superior had been abandoned, its portages overgrown with weeds, being used mainly by George Simpson's express canoes on his annual dashes to inspect the inland posts. The grandiosely named North West Transportation, Navigation and Railway Company obtained a government contract to deliver mail to Red River at $1,000 a trip, but on its first run between Collingwood on Georgian Bay and Fort William, the company's steamer carried only fourteen letters. Red River residents were so unimpressed they consigned only two letters to the vessel's return journey, and the service folded soon afterwards.*

---

* To test the reliability of the service's claimed rapid delivery, Simpson mailed two letters from Lachine on October 12, 1858—one by way of the U.S. railway route, the other via

The most dangerous threat to the HBC's monopoly should in theory have been the agitation for annexation of its lands by leaders of public opinion in the Canadian provinces. There was no shortage of windy political rhetoric on the issue, and George Brown, the founding editor of the Toronto *Globe*, wrote thunderous editorials claiming that only the extension of Canada's borders westward to the Pacific would revive the colony's stagnant economy. But there was little initial response. The politicians were all too aware of the inadequacy of their treasuries; taking on the administrative cost of the huge HBC territories seemed neither desirable nor realistic.

Then, with the suddenness of a summer storm, this standoffish attitude changed. The realization struck home that if nothing was done, Red River and what would someday become the Canadian heartland might be annexed by the United States. American expansionists had been mobilized by their discovery that steam was about to redraw the map of the continent. Although a few short "portage" rail lines were built in the Canadian provinces during the 1830s and 1840s, the first really major rail project was the Grand Trunk, completed between Lévis and Sarnia in 1859. In contrast, American entrepreneurs had been pushing steel across their country at a much faster pace; by 1860, thirty thousand route-miles of track had been laid. Whatever territory was not made accessible by snorting locomotives had been or was being exploited by steamboats, the belching paddle-wheelers that were turning the Missouri and Mississippi into riverine freeways. By 1858, Minnesota, just south of the original Selkirk grant, had attained statehood and was a nest of 150,000 expansion-minded citizens.*

These and other stirrings prompted the nationalists of Canada West to rally against the possibility of Red River annexation and eventually against the monopoly of the Hudson's Bay Company itself. The early Canadian capitalists, especially the competition-conscious owners of the lumber and grist mills, began to express their revulsion at this foreign, feudal and forbidding enterprise, which, as a petition from the Toronto Board of Trade complained,

---

the North West Transportation, Navigation and Railway Company. The former arrived on November 10, 1858; the latter on March 2, 1859—141 days after it was mailed.

* There is a documented instance of an ingenious American, during the 1862 Sioux uprising at Mankato, Minnesota, hoisting a British flag. He was the sole white man to escape the massacre alive—and the only possible explanation was that the Indians, having become familiar with the Red Ensign through their connections with the HBC, considered him to have kindlier designs and spared his life.

"assumed the power to enact tariffs, collect custom dues, and levy taxes against British subjects, and has enforced unjust and arbitrary laws in defiance of every principle of right and justice."

After nearly two centuries of having taken its mandate for granted, the HBC was facing a fierce and widespread challenge to its hegemony: a wave of populist sentiment that viewed its monopoly as the chief obstacle to dreams of free trade, settlement and transcontinental nationhood.

AT RED RIVER ITSELF, a much more subtle undercurrent touching racial, social and religious confrontation was changing the character of the settlement and its people. The most jarring disruption to the Colony's stability had been the arrival of Frances, Simpson's British bride. Distinctions of class and parentage that had largely been ignored over a generation of HBC and NWC occupancy suddenly surfaced to upend family and community equilibrium. "There is a strange revolution in the manners of the country," James Douglas noted later. "Indian wives were at one time the vogue, the half breed supplanted these, and now we have the lovely tender exotic torn from its parent bed...."

This shift in the pattern of sexual liaisons and marital unions was fundamental. It did much more than alter the lives of the specific men and women involved. It meant that the status of the country marriage, which had proved to be such an integral and essential element of the fur trade, was permanently downgraded, disrupting what had been considered the natural order of things.

Worse still, the arrival of well-meaning but narrow-minded missionaries in Rupert's Land led to imposition of a moral code on fur-trade society that branded most of its traditions, including the honourable custom of country marriage, as not only wrong but sinful. According to the earnest tenets of these righteous ranters, native women had to be indoctrinated with what they considered to be the proper wifely attitudes. "A good wife must be clean and industrious in her habits and docile and obedient to her husband," wrote Sylvia Van Kirk, outlining the rigid value system missionary wives tried to inculcate in the schools they established at Red River. "Above all she must be sexually pure. Every vestige of the sexual freedom to which Indian women had been accustomed was to be stamped out; chastity, it was impressed upon young mixed-blood women, was their greatest virtue and responsibility. According to contemporary British sentiment: 'A woman who has once lost chastity has lost every good quality. She has from that moment all the vices.'"

Although such a state of vestal purity was presumably difficult to attain retroactively, the missionaries insisted on sanctifying by formal church service the informal unions of HBC traders and their country wives. In some instances this proved a happy arrangement, but some Chief Factors and Traders seized the moment as an excuse to "turn off" their native partners and marry younger overseas brides instead.

To compound the complexities, the missionaries also insisted on identifying Christian conduct with their own vision of civilized behaviour. While agricultural pursuits fell within their reckoning of acceptable conduct, hunting did not. They equated the Indians' nomadic life with barbarism. Their culture and struggle for survival were disparaged as distractions from opportunities to contemplate the nature of existence and the eternal mysteries of Christianity's God. Proud hunters who had survived unimaginable hardships by following their own ancient codes were told that worshipping the white man's God, handling a fork correctly and using handkerchiefs would save their souls. What these opinionated parsons really meant when they railed about converting "the heathen savages" was that they were determined to make Indians not quite so outrageously un-British. "They struggled to recreate the English rural parish," wrote the historian Frits Pannekoek, describing the itinerant clerics' aspirations, "a little Britain in the wilderness, with the parson as a major landowner, teacher, custodian of charities, and law giver. They saw themselves as sharing these tasks with the other members of the elite: the squirearchy, the Company's officers and the settlement's Governor. The Anglican clergy's plans for this society placed them at the helm and made outcasts of all who did not comply. Firm in their conviction that 'civilization must go hand in hand with Christianity,' they preached what they assumed were the virtues of nineteenth-century England as fervently as the Gospel."

Except for an occasional visit, such as the solitary season spent at York Factory by the Reverend Thomas Anderson in 1693, the HBC had historically welcomed few evangelical diversions within its territories. As late as 1815 there was not a single church in Rupert's Land, but Lord Selkirk invited Father (later Bishop) Joseph Norbert Provencher to establish a Catholic mission in 1818 and had arranged for the dispatch to Red River of a Church of England chaplain named John West two years later. Since nearly all the colony's Protestant settlers were staunch Presbyterians, West's brief stay was not a happy one. He felt overwhelmed by the size and nature of his mandate and established little empathy with his parishioners. But he did build a small school and a chapel, performed a grand total of sixty-five marriages and inaugurated an auxiliary of the British and Foreign Bible Society for Rupert's Land at York Factory. There he welcomed his successor, the Reverend David Jones. That worthy was an even harder-shell divine who would not baptize country wives before their church weddings and refused to marry them if they were not baptized, insisting that it would be sacrilege to pronounce "our excellent Liturgy" over such "heathens." Officially, Jones worked under the auspices of Britain's Church Missionary Society, but his real sponsor was Benjamin Harrison, brother-in-law of the HBC's long-time Governor John Pelly. Harrison himself served as an HBC Committeeman from 1807 to 1854, including a four-year stint as Deputy Governor. A member of the Clapham Sect, a group of Evangelicals within the Church of England, Harrison sent more than three dozen missionaries to Rupert's Land. By the mid-1850s, Red River alone boasted eight churches, and there were forty-two missionary stations within the HBC lands, a dozen of them Catholic, five Wesleyan, one Presbyterian and the rest Church of England.

George Simpson's opinion of missionaries verged on the benign, but he could never concede that there might exist a presence within his empire claiming allegiance to any authority higher than himself. Besides, the nosy parkers favoured free trade in furs and diverted the Indians from trapping. In his mind, that categorized the lot of them as necessary evils at best. In a letter to London, he complained that the diffusion of Christian doctrine within Rupert's Land really did little good other "than filling the pockets and bellies of some hungry missionaries and rearing the Indians in habits of indolence."

The most troublesome man of the cloth called to the Fur Country was the appropriately named Herbert Beaver, who arrived with his wife, Jane, at Fort Vancouver in 1836. He was a creature of fathomless rectitude whose idea of imposing his rigid ethics on the wilderness fort was not helped by an awkward personality, a squeaky voice and pretensions of grandeur that exceeded spiritual boundaries. The clash between Beaver and Dr John McLoughlin, the post's Chief Factor, was not long in coming. At first it concerned trivialities: Jane Beaver wanted boiled salmon, though the resident cook usually baked it, and the room assigned to the parson and his wife was enclosed only by a thin partition. Beaver complained that he had not been assigned proper servants (having rejected the Sandwich Islander and his wife who had been offered by the HBC) and snivelled about the liquor rations he had been allocated—yet fort records showed that from August to October 1838 alone he had been issued 143 3/4 gallons of brandy, port, sherry and porter. What drove Beaver to self-righteous frenzy was the idea that men and women could live together without benefit of a church ceremony. His sermons, delivered in a high-pitched whine, disparaged women partners in country marriages as little better than concubines and condemned their men as fornicators. This doctrine was inappropriate enough while he was apportioning damnation indiscriminately among the fort's residents, but when Beaver deliberately homed in on McLoughlin and Marguerite McKay, his country wife of twenty-six years, that was a fighting matter. In a report to the HBC Committee in London that fell into McLoughlin's hands, Beaver referred to the respected chatelaine of Fort Vancouver as "a female of notoriously loose character" and the "kept Mistress of the highest personage at this station"—charging that the fort's officers were practising concubinage. That was too much for the good doctor. When the two men met in the yard, McLoughlin demanded an explanation.

"Sire," replied Beaver, "if you wish to know why a cow's tail grows downward I cannot tell you; I can only cite the fact."

The enraged Chief Factor delivered a hard right to the reverend gentleman's jaw, then grabbed his walking stick and thrashed him with it, roaring: "You scoundrel! I'll have your life!"

Only the hysterical intercession of Mrs Beaver prevented her husband from being seriously injured. McLoughlin later apologized for his outburst, but the parson would not be quieted. He threatened to sue the Company and wrote the draft of a book exposing the iniquities of its employees. Beaver's crusade ended when he was fired and paid £110 in compensation for his claims of mistreatment.

The incident was not important in itself—particularly because, unbeknownst to the eager Beaver, McLoughlin and Marguerite had actually been formally married at that time. (Because McLoughlin was a Catholic and wanted no part of the clergyman's militant brand of Protestantism, the ceremony was performed by Fort Vancouver's second-in-command, James Douglas, in his capacity of Justice of the Peace.) A later episode at Red River, which also involved the conflict between Victorian morality and indigenous culture, had deeper and more enduring consequences. The old familiarity of the Fur Country, the sense of belonging, of sharing a prevailing sense of values, was threatened by the Foss–Pelly sex scandal of 1850. It threw into doubt the position of Mixed Bloods among the Red River elite of the mid-nineteenth century. The cast of this wilderness soap opera was almost too stereotyped to be real, and its denouement seems less appropriate to the historical record than to the purple-plot purveyors of supermarket romance novels. Yet it served to underline the racial prejudices tethered within the respectable society of Red River.

John Ballenden, the Chief Factor at Fort Garry, had married Sarah, the exquisitely beautiful Mixed Blood daughter of Chief Trader Alexander McLeod. Her striking appearance and natural vivacity were so compelling that her social achievements easily eclipsed those of the local white women. As the Chief Factor's wife, Sarah gave dinner parties and organized masked balls; she presided over the Upper Fort Garry officers' mess, and quickly became the object of intense male attention and even more intense female buzz. When Mrs Robert Logan, a school teacher, remarked that Mrs Ballenden was the type who "must always have a sweetheart as well as a husband," everybody at Red River knew which lover she had in mind. According to the settlement's gossips, Sarah had repelled the ardent advances of A.E. Pelly, the fort's accountant, but was rumoured to have found more pleasant accommodation with Captain Christopher Vaughan Foss, a rambunctious Irishman who had arrived in Red River two years earlier as part of the British garrison. Local tattlers were maliciously pleased to whisper that Foss was parking his boots under Sarah's bed.

The breezes of innuendo turned into a gale when Anne Clouston, daughter of the HBC agent in the Orkneys, arrived at Red River as the wife of Mr. Pelly, Sarah's rejected admirer. Since Pelly was a member of one of the HBC's most distinguished families, the bride assumed that her mere presence would catapult her to the top of the colony's social register. She dressed the part, bringing with her from Scotland five new bonnets and other finery. But her aristocratic pretensions and tendency to protest each imagined slight by carefully choreographed fainting spells soon made her a figure of fun at the Red River officers' mess. In retaliation, the Pellys withdrew from that circle and Anne began to interrogate Sarah Ballenden's German maid, Catherine Winegart, about her mistress's rumoured adventures. Convinced that she had valid evidence of Sarah's dalliances, Mrs Pelly petitioned Major William Caldwell, governor of the colony, to take action. Caldwell, who had been Foss's commanding officer, was stymied. He had a high regard for John Ballenden, was fond of Foss, yet feared the Pellys' powerful London connections and hoped that the whole tempest would be forgotten. But Sarah and Captain Foss were determined to strike back. Mrs Ballenden obtained a sworn affidavit from her maid confirming that she, Catherine Winegart, had in fact no evidence of her mistress's immorality. Foss for his part posted a public notice on the door of the fort's general store denouncing Anne Pelly and proclaiming his intention of suing her for defamation of character.

John Ballenden himself, who never doubted his wife's public denials of unfaithfulness but spent a lot of time away on company business, was forced to resign as Chief Factor after Anne Pelly obtained a sworn deposition from the Fort Garry mess cooks, John Davidson and his wife, implicating Sarah and Foss. The issue became a *cause célèbre* when the persistent Pellys repeated the charges in front of George Simpson during one of the Governor's visits, and Captain Foss promptly launched his threatened lawsuit.

The three-day trial, which started on July 16, 1850, became the sensation of the territories. According to Alexander Ross, the best of the contemporary fur-trade historians: "Writs were carried to every hole and corner of the colony, in high and low life: Knights, Squires, Judges, Sheriffs, Counsellors, Medical men, all the Nabobs of the Co., the Clergy, Ladies and Gentlemen, down to the humblest pauper were summoned, a glorious turn out. I happened to meet one of the officials, and he alone had no less than 52 summonses! ... A special court was summoned and 50 jurors were in attendance. A jury was impanelled, and The Court, and same jury sat ... three solemn days. The bible in the hands of the Clerk of the court might well be hot!"

The trial itself was more farce than formality. The resident clerics' wives pursed their lips in well-practised disgust as they testified against the aggrieved couple, presenting billows of rumour but little hard evidence. At one point, Adam Thom, the presiding judge (who was godfather to one of Sarah's children), stepped down from the bench, walked over to the witness box and spoke glowingly about her honesty and strength of character. The twelve Anglophone Métis who made up the jury found the defendants guilty of defamation of character, and Judge Thom awarded Foss damages from the Pellys of £300. That should have ended the drama, but instead it only helped fan the embers of racial prejudice. Sarah Ballenden continued to be ostracized by the white women. Most of the settlement polarized into opposing factions. "All the inhabitants," Simpson noted with considerable dismay, "thought it proper to espouse one side or the other and to regard the verdict as a personal triumph or a personal injury."

When Eden Colvile arrived to take Red River Governor Caldwell's place, he found himself trapped into playing straight man in the ongoing skit. "Today," he wrote to Simpson about a visit from the Right Reverend David

Anderson, "the Bishop and his sister were calling on us, & in the middle of the visit I heard a knock at the door and suspecting who it was rushed out & found Mr. and Mrs. Ballenden. I had to cram them into another room till the Bishop's visit was over, but as he was then going to see the Pellys he had to pass through this room, so that I had to bolt out and put them into a third room. It was altogether like a scene in a farce."

Colvile reinstated the Ballendens in Red River's good graces, and when John Ballenden had to visit Scotland for medical treatment, Colvile allowed Sarah to move in with his family at Upper Fort Garry. Shortly afterwards, an unsigned letter believed to be in Sarah's handwriting inviting "darling Christopher" to visit her turned up anonymously. She later went alone to his lodgings for an afternoon's visit. At this point, Thom and some of her other supporters deserted Sarah, but her husband did not, later writing to Simpson: "I entreat you, for my sake, if not for hers, to cease and let her rest in peace— if that is now possible."

It wasn't. When Ballenden was posted to Fort Vancouver, Sarah's deteriorating mental and physical health kept her from following him. Alexander Ross lamented that "if there is such a thing as dying of a broken heart, she cannot live long." Sarah died of consumption at thirty-five, only three years after the trial, but not before she and her John (who had been invalided home) met in a tearful, final reunion at Edinburgh. Sarah Ballenden's gothic tale exposed the tensions and pretensions of the pioneer community. The affair had pitted white against Mixed Blood, clergy against laity and placed the HBC—as the defender of established authority—uncomfortably in the middle.

THE ROOTS OF THESE CONFLICTS had been planted long before. After the death of Lord Selkirk, the colony had languished. Its presence provided living proof of the HBC's charter rights, yet nearly every active Bay man resented Red River's intrusive influence on the fur trade. In 1836, the Selkirk family had moved to rid itself of the unhappy land asset by selling it back to the HBC for stock worth £84,000, which eventually brought returns many times the late Earl's losses. Despite the severe flood of 1826, the settlement had grown, with imported livestock, new grist mills and the continued buffalo hunt providing the chief economic mainstays. Its population had mushroomed from less than 300 in 1818 to 4,369 by 1840, but by mid-century less than 12,000 acres had been settled, although land was priced at only five shillings an acre.

Red River continued to expand not only geographically but socially, sprouting five distinct communities. There were the Scots of Kildonan, the brave remnants of the original Selkirk immigrants, who eschewed the buffalo hunt and the fur trade. They concentrated on farming, conversed in the Gaelic and whispered to their own God under Presbyterian auspices. They had become isolated, like the stranded inhabitants of an island within an island, feeling morally superior but too proud to acknowledge their declining influence and numbers. Nearby lived the retired Hudson's Bay factors and their families, who treated Red River as a fur-trading post over which they claimed natural managerial rights, living out old glories and supporting the influx of Anglican missionaries. They quickly became the settlement's self-appointed leaders, sharing, in W.L. Morton's wonderful phrase, "neither the Ishmaelite wildness of the Métis nor the careful poverty of the Kildonan Scots." To the south and west of the river junction lived the Métis of the Upper Settlement and White Horse Plain, the most dynamic element in the region; their way of life focused on the seasonal buffalo hunts and fostered increasingly militant aspirations to control their own destinies. Finally, there were the villages of Swampy Cree in St Peter's, above the Red River Delta, and the band of Saulteaux at Baie St Paul up the Assiniboine. The census of 1849 also listed one Pole, one Dane, one Norwegian and a Dutchman.

Nearly all the would-be Swiss settlers who had come to the Selkirk Settlement in 1821 had left Red River soon after arriving and taking a good look around. They moved to Fort Snelling, near modern-day St Paul, Minnesota, as did most of the De Meurons. The mercenaries' departure was hastened by the fact that immediately after the 1826 floods had scattered local dairy herds, the De Meurons suddenly had quantities of beef and hides for sale, while the Scottish settlers never did locate their lost animals. Thirteen families came out from Lincolnshire in 1836 to work the HBC's experimental farm, but the colonization of Red River did not become a mass movement. This minimal inflow meant that it was the indigenous population of Mixed Bloods who assumed natural dominance within the settlement.

The problem with Red River as a farming community seemed at times extra-terrestrial, as if a committee of vengeful archangels had decided to twist the indifferent forces of nature into a malignant conspiracy to prevent agriculture from flourishing there. Thirty crop failures, resulting from early frosts, locusts and alternations of drought and flood, blighted the land between 1813 and 1870.

The Selkirk colony shared with many other Canadian communities the problem that at least one of the rivers on which it was located flows north, from a harsh climate into one even more severe. This means that spring breakup occurs on the upper parts of the stream first, with the thawing waters, impounded behind the ice of still-frozen river mouths, flooding the lower banks. The 1811 spring flood on the Red, just above its junction with the Assiniboine, for example, raised water levels by fifty feet. (One of the few men known to have taken advantage of this phenomenon was Alexander Griggs, captain of the river steamer *International*, en route to Fort Garry from the United States with a load of liquor destined for the Hudson's Bay Company. On May 10, 1873, a new tariff that would have cost the Company extra duty was due to come into effect. The skipper was having trouble manoeuvring his vessel along the flooded river because he couldn't see the usual shorelines. According to a report in the *Manitoban*, he turned the ship "out of the bed of the river and made a short cut over the prairie ... thereby reducing the distance materially and gaining the Customs House" before the midnight tax deadline.

Apart from natural hazards, the Red River economy was difficult to sustain because nearly everything had to be imported. Most goods and provisions brought from England were subject to mark-ups of 110 percent—33 percent for ocean freight, 20 percent for land transport from York Factory and 57 percent for HBC profit. Yet the Company could purchase locally produced grain at almost any price (usually as low as two shillings sixpence a bushel) because there were no other buyers. The farmers could not engage in the fur trade, which was an HBC monopoly, and were excluded from the settlement's main cash crop—production of pemmican for export into the Fur Country—since that was the preserve of the Métis.

Simpson launched a series of experiments, hoping to diversify Red River's revenue base, but none worked. The Buffalo Wool Company of 1822 was supposed to process the animal hair for export to British textile mills, but the harvesting expenditures and transportation charges raised the manufacturing cost to $12.50 a yard for cloth that sold at only $1.10. The HBC then tried to start an export business in tallow—the hard fat rendered from butchered cattle, widely used in making candles and soap. Two particularly tough winters and an invasion of predator wolves reinforced by the colony's wild dogs killed the hundred cows allocated to that enterprise, and Simpson turned his attention back to the wool industry. This time he planned to raise sheep, dispatching two HBC traders to purchase 1,471 of the animals at St Louis or in Kentucky. The duo was more familiar with the habits of beaver, and so many of their charges died along the fifteen-hundred-mile journey that by the time the two unlucky shepherds returned to Red River, only 241 sheep were trotting after them.

These and other equally disastrous ventures proved to the settlers that their only economic salvation lay in precisely the option the Hudson's Bay Company was bound to resist most fiercely: free trade in furs with the United States.

THE HBC HAD NEVER generated much loyalty from its employees at Red River. Because Simpson preferred to recruit his new officers in Scotland, he promoted few if any Métis. The York boat crews were hired locally on a per-trip basis to take the pemmican from Red River to Norway House. The trade goods (brought in from York Factory) were then shipped to Athabasca, where pelts were loaded for the return journey. The four-month round trips were joyless excursions, and the tripmen developed little affinity for the Company.

Simpson had no mixed emotions about Red River. He hated it. Dealing with the settlers, he complained, was like training what he called a "Libyan tiger"—the more you try to tame it, the more savage it becomes. "[They] are a distinct sort of beings," he groused, "somewhere between the half Indians and overgrown children. At times they need caressing and not unfrequently the discipline of the birch, in other words the iron rod of retribution. But in the present instance the latter not being within our reach, it behooves us to attempt by stratagem what we cannot compass by force."

Paradoxically, his choice of agent to defend the Company's interests was none other than Cuthbert Grant, leader of the death squad that had savaged the HBC's settlers at Seven Oaks a decade earlier. After that bloody episode, Grant had been part of the NWC contingent dispatched to guard Grand Rapids and at a nearby rendezvous had become involved in the killing of the HBC's Owen Keveny, leader of the second group of Selkirk settlers. Following amalgamation of the two companies, Grant spent eleven months in disgrace before Simpson invited him back into the fur trade as a constable-clerk at Fort Garry.

With a group of followers Grant founded the village of Grantown (now Saint-François-Xavier, Manitoba) at White Horse Plain on the Assiniboine. Promoted by Simpson in 1828 to Warden of the Plains, Grant was eventually sworn in as a justice of the peace and was later also named a magistrate and sheriff. He became an influential voice on Company matters within the Council of Assiniboia, the HBC's puppet colonial administration. Grant's official assignment was to police the border with his volunteer cavalry units against free traders, but his real function was to co-opt the rebellious spirit of the Métis. This he achieved, at least temporarily, but neither Simpson nor Grant could long hold back the forces gathering to engulf the settlement.

The edgy situation at Red River attracted its share of freebooters and soldiers of misfortune, none more bizarre than "General" James Dickson (who also called himself Montezuma II), whose self-imposed mission was to recruit a Métis army for a march on Santa Fé, where he intended to free the Indians and establish his own kingdom. He first materialized in Montreal during the spring of 1836, equipped with the gold-inlaid sword of a British general and exquisitely tailored uniform to match. He wore a fierce-looking false beard (which he frequently switched from a suitcase filled with spare vandykes and moustaches) and carried with him a coat of mail in which he presumably intended to mount his Santa Fé throne. Dickson had enough money to recruit a sixty-man advance guard and promptly set off for Red River to sign up his invasion force. By the time the General and his party arrived at Red River, Simpson had formulated a strategy to prevent the exodus of Métis who might be tempted to follow him. The HBC store refused to honour the General's drafts, thus depriving him of funds, and the Company hired away most of his saner lieutenants.

The frustrated Dickson stomped around Red River during the winter of 1836–37, changing beards and uniforms to suit his darkening mood. He made friends with Cuthbert Grant, and that spring the Métis leader arranged for a guide to start Dickson on his way to Santa Fé. The General had the last word. "You are the great soldier and leader," Dickson told Grant. "I am a failure. These belong to you...." With that, he took off his epaulettes, fastened them to Grant's shoulders, handed over his sword and rode away into the sunset, never to be heard from again.

On a more serious level, Simpson decided to meet the mounting challenge of competition by realigning the Assiniboia trading system, allowing settlers to barter furs with the Indians under Company licence. His hope was that he could defuse some of the resentment of the HBC's monopoly and thus gather pelts that might otherwise be smuggled across the border. The theory was valid, but in practice, giving outsiders a taste of the mark-ups to be gained only drove them to the conclusion that they would benefit most by going into the fur business for themselves. Donald MacKenzie, the HBC's Chief Factor at Upper Fort Garry, tried his best to halt the fur pirates, arresting the worst offenders, searching the Red River carts heading south and, in summer, poking sticks up the chimneys of settlers' cabins in search of secret pelt caches.

The free traders soon began to move both ways across the international boundary. A Mixed Blood named Alexis Bailly, employed by the American Fur Company, had driven a herd of cattle to Red River as early as 1821 and sold the animals at great profit. Even the HBC's general store at Fort Garry had competition—Andrew McDermot, an ambitious former HBC clerk, claimed his newly opened shop could supply anything except second-hand coffins. The most articulate leader of Red River's free-trade movement was James Sinclair, the British-educated son of an HBC Chief Factor, whose sister Betsey had been abandoned by George Simpson.

The fragile equilibrium of the situation changed dramatically in 1843 when Norman Wolfred Kittson, an emigrant Lower Canadian serving with the American Fur Company, opened a trading post at Pembina in North Dakota, about seventy miles south of Fort Garry. His instructions were to capture the Red River fur trade, and he set about it with energy and cunning. He drew Sinclair, McDermot and many other independent traders, including an outspoken Mixed Blood named Pierre-Guillaume Sayer (son of a former NWC winterer), into his orbit. By the late 1840s, free traders had infiltrated so much of the commerce that Simpson realized the continued existence of the Red River Colony was at stake. Using the threat of American incursion as their fulcrum and lever, the London Committee persuaded the British government to dispatch three companies (340 men) of the 6th Regiment of Foot (the Royal Warwickshires) to maintain the peace. They arrived by way of York Factory and hacked their way to Red River, dragging a nine-pound cannon and three six-pounders behind them.

The presence of the soldiers provided a deterrent to free trade, but there was little in the colony to allay their own sense of ennui. The 6th had been at Fort Garry only three months when Wemyss Simpson, the Governor's brother-in-law, reported: "They are not too fond of the country, as they have so very little amusement and so little occupation. They tried to get up races, but did not succeed. Mr. Mosse, one of the ensigns, walked from the Upper to the Lower Fort in three hours, 39 minutes, for £5 sterling. The men are very orderly, and there have only been a few rows. One man was stabbed by a half-breed, who was jealous of him. Two others were tried and flogged, one 100 lashes, the other 50. They did not say a word during the whole time of the punishment, and therefore saved themselves from being laughed at. The people in the settlement were never so well off, as the Government spends about £30 per day, and the Company also spends a great deal, buying all the cattle, pigs, sheep and grain. McDermot and the Scotch settlers are making fortunes. The soldiers buy great quantities of beer, and give any price for it, and there are few houses in the settlement where they cannot get it."

After two years, their place was taken by a dubious rabble of fifty-six British Army pensioners under the command of Major William Caldwell, who was also appointed Governor of Assiniboia. Each man was promised twenty free acres if he made the journey, and though they were not so much an occupying army as policemen, the Red River resident who condemned them as worse than useless was overly generous in his assessment. The only distinction any contemporary observer could attach to Major Caldwell was the fact that he was unusually tall. The agitation for free trade, which had languished during the pacifying interlude of the Warwickshires, now came alive with a vengeance. Kittson's take of furs, greater than ever, was threatening to dominate the trade. Using the flimsy excuse that Caldwell's appointment had separated local governing authority from the Company's orbit of influence, HBC Chief Factor John Ballenden arrested Pierre-Guillaume Sayer and three other Métis on charges of illegal trafficking in pelts. Ballenden never questioned that a proper verdict would be returned, reinstating the Company's monopoly.

The Métis harboured no such illusions. The trial was set for May 17, 1849 (the Feast of the Ascension, their priests carefully noted), and neither the hunters nor the tripmen went out that day. Their protests were organized by a Committee of the New Nation. One leader of that militant confederacy was Jean-Louis Riel, known as "the miller of the Seine" because he had dug a nine-mile channel from the Red River to increase the flow over his mill wheel on a little river named for the local custom of seining fish. An ardent Métis nationalist (whose first-born and namesake would become the patron saint of French Canadian rebels), Riel père had dreamed of establishing a wool factory in the region, but his efforts had been frustrated by the HBC's monopoly. The Sunday before the trial, the Métis leader had read a public letter urging every man in the church to attend the proceedings armed and prepared to assert his rights.

On the day of the trial, Riel addressed the three hundred Métis gathered near the steps of St Boniface Cathedral, exhorting them to liberate Sayer and assert freedom of trade for the New Nation. Riel then led the armed buffalo hunters across the river to the courthouse presided over by Adam Thom, the recorder of Assiniboia, who had a well-earned reputation for being both anti-French and anti-Catholic. Some of Riel's more militant sharpshooters threatened to pick off the judge on his bench. Inside the courtroom, James Sinclair, acting as Sayer's counsel, was following a carefully plotted legal course. Members of the empanelled jury—seven English and five French—settled into their seats with powder horns and shot pouches at their belts and guns on their knees.

The testimony droned on into the long afternoon, with various witnesses contradicting one another on the extent of Sayer's free trading habits. When Donald Gunn, the jury foreman, finally delivered the verdict, it was divided into two parts. Sayer was found guilty of trading furs, but the jurors also recommended mercy "as it appeared that he thought he had a right to trade as he and others were under the impression that there was a free trade." Ballenden committed the strategic error of unthinkingly accepting this mixed verdict and compounded his mistake by setting Sayer and his co-defendants free on the spot.

As the doors of the courtroom opened and Sayer stepped into the sunshine, Riel and his troops came to the instant (and as it turned out, irrevocable) conclusion that their fellow Métis had been acquitted—and that the fur trade had officially been set free. "*Vive la Liberté! Le commerce est libre!*" went the victory shouts. Musket-fire exploded skyward as the exhilarated Métis rode out to spread the news—the HBC's monopoly had been broken at last.

Maybe. In line with its usual strategy, the Hudson's Bay Company simply switched horses. Instead of trying to defend its trading rights, which had been ended by popular reaction if not yet by invalidation of its legal position, the Company immediately started undercutting the free traders by offering higher prices for furs (eventually putting Kittson out of business) and by agreeing to most of the Métis' political demands. Simpson removed Adam Thom from his post as recorder even though the controversial Scottish-born lawyer had acted as a good HBC man, merely following orders. Use of the French language in the settlement's courtrooms was allowed, and the first independent Métis representatives were appointed to the Council of Assiniboia.

One inadvertent victim of the Sayer trial was Cuthbert Grant. He no longer commanded the loyalty of the Métis, who had pointedly ignored his presence on the Council when demanding representation. They noted with dismay that he had been on the bench during the Sayer trial as one of the associate magistrates. With Grant's usefulness to the Company exhausted, Simpson fired him as Warden of the Plains after twenty-one years of faithful HBC service. Grant spent the half-decade before his death (from injuries sustained falling off a horse) as a token totem, entertaining gentleman buffalo hunters.

Although the Company maintained a dominant share of the business, free traders were now swarming across its territories and had defiantly built a storehouse on the banks of the Red within sight of Fort Garry. By 1858, six hundred Red River carts were running a commuter line between Red River and St Paul, Minnesota. That ambitious city's newly formed Chamber of Commerce offered a $1,000 prize to anyone daring enough to run a steamboat into Fort Garry.

A nautical daredevil named Anson Northup first persuaded the Chamber to double the reward, then bought a derelict stern-wheeler that had been beached at St Anthony Falls on the Mississippi River and floated her up to Crow Wing just before freeze-up. To drag the hull and 11,000-pound boiler the 160 miles to the Red River, Northup put together a land caravan consisting of thirty teamsters to drive the seventeen span of horses and thirteen yoke of oxen through snowdrifts and over makeshift bridges. The vessel, reassembled in six spring weeks, was christened after her owner, and the little thumper set off merrily down the Red River, past Grand Forks and Pembina and across the border towards Assiniboia. Ninety feet long, twenty-two feet wide, with a draft of only fourteen inches, the ungainly contraption could carry fifty tons of cargo; passengers slept in open berths that extended along the main saloon. The ship's silhouette resembled nothing so much as a log cabin mounted on a washbasin, with a smokestack sticking up its middle. One of the vessel's later captains, C.P.V. Lull, described her as "a lumbering old pine-basket, which you have to handle as gingerly as a hamper of eggs."

Without advance warning, the *Anson Northup* pulled into Fort Garry on June 10, 1859. "Within moments there was pandemonium," reported Theodore Barris in *Fire Canoe*, his wonderful book on prairie steamboats. "Panic-stricken Indians fleeing to the river forks cried out that a fiery monster was pounding down the river towards them. Then the 'monster' appeared, as suddenly as an apparition … the *Anson Northup*, shrouded by swirling steam and woodsmoke, rounded the final bend and bore down on the Red River Settlement. The Red River was in its annual flood, but even the tumult of the rushing water was drowned by the violent thrashing of the Northup's stern paddlewheel. The Hudson's Bay Company colours rose above the fort walls to greet the Stars and Stripes flying from the prow of the ungainly vessel.... Horses with buckskin riders, oxdrawn two-wheeled carts from the fields, and cautious Indians clad in feathers, leggings, and moccasins streamed to the fort landing. Children thronged at the riverside to see 'an enormous barge, with a watermill on its stern' emerging from the wilderness like a demon churning up water and spitting sparks."

The HBC's response to this daring incursion threatening its transportation system was once more in character: the Company bought out the *Anson Northup* to assert its monopoly over the water route, then raised the freight rates to prohibitive levels on any goods carried for its competitors. But there was a hurdle: American law at that time did not allow foreigners to own U.S.-based properties. No problem. Simpson recruited the best man to head the secret partnership that controlled the small but vital one-boat line: Kittson, the displaced free trader from Pembina, who was now mayor of St Paul. To sweeten the deal, Simpson promoted Kittson to "Commodore"—a rare rank in those parts.

The most important piece of cargo ever carried by the little stern-wheeler was a printing-press that would give the community its first newspaper, the *Nor'Wester*. Edited by two young Englishmen, William Coldwell and William Buckingham, who had been reporters for Toronto newspapers, the weekly took up the cause of Red River's annexation by Canada. It was becoming increasingly clear that either the Canadian or the British government would soon have to take decisive action against the HBC's charter. Red River historian Alexander Ross must have sensed the impending power-shift when he astutely remarked that instead of fighting to preserve Red River, the Hudson's Bay Company was treating its once-treasured colony with "the cool and languid care of a stepmother."

Death of
a Titan

*Like a latter-day King Lear raging against his own mortality, Simpson was
now dragging himself painfully across the land he had once ruled.*

BY THE 1850S, SIR GEORGE SIMPSON must have been aware, however reluctant
he may have been to admit it, that his brand of absolute power could no longer
hold men or causes. Now that he was in his mid-sixties, the coils of wrath having
retreated deep inside him, he assumed the mantle of the fur trade's elder statesman and turned his attention to profitable investments on his own account.

With free trade a reality not only at Red River but spreading like a flash
fire through the Company's once insulated territories, the HBC's days of
dominance were clearly numbered. Yet its daily operations ticked on as
methodically as before.

As in the past, the Company treated a shift in its commercial environment
as a circumstance to be carefully co-opted, not as a reason for any sudden
switch in strategies.

The Hudson's Bay Company's 152 posts, manned by 45 Chief Factors and
Traders, 5 surgeons, 154 clerks and postmasters, and 1,200 servants, plus the
crews of the inland canoes, York boats and seagoing supply ships, were
conducting business as usual. Dividends of the British shareholders (in 1850
only 4 of the 232 proprietors had Canadian addresses) were still rolling in at
such a profitable rate that the stock was listed in London at premiums of 220
to 240 percent. When Sir John Pelly, who had been the Company's British
Governor for thirty years, died in 1852,* he was replaced by Andrew Colvile,

---

* Pelly had been so influential that Company wags suggested the HBC's Latin motto, PRO
PELLE CUTEM (roughly translated as "A skin for a skin"), should really have been changed

which reduced Simpson's influence not one whit.

The overseas Governor's burden had been reduced somewhat by the appointment in January 1849 of Andrew's son Eden Colvile as Associate Governor of Rupert's Land, to be resident at Red River. Although the younger Colvile's remuneration (£1,000 annually) was deducted from Simpson's salary, his presence at least relieved the senior Governor of having to handle the daily goings-on at the settlement that had always worn his patience to a nub. Only eight years out of Eton and Cambridge, the young Colvile proved equal to his assignment and became such an enthusiastic Bay man that he was later appointed to the Company's London Committee, and from 1872 to 1889 was its Deputy Governor and then its Governor. (The Colviles, father and son, spent no fewer than seventy-nine years directing the HBC's affairs.)

Simpson still sallied forth on his annual inspection tours, but they had evolved into royal processions, staged more for show than specific purpose. His declining energies were concentrated on building up his private portfolio in Montreal's expanding banks, railway companies, canal construction firms, shipping lines and other enterprises. A shrewd assessor of each business proposition's risk–reward ratio, Simpson purchased (from the estate of Sir Alexander Mackenzie) some of the most desirable land in the centre of Montreal (between what are now Dorchester and Sherbrooke streets) and subdivided it into small building lots; he was first a director of the Bank of British North America and was later associated with the Bank of Montreal. He became part of the syndicate that built the original Beauharnois Canal, invested heavily in the commercial boat operations that dominated the Ottawa River, was one of the founders of the Montreal Mining Company set up to explore Lake Superior's north shore, and was a co-sponsor of the railway line between Montreal and Lachine that was expanded to the U.S. border and eventually bought out by the Grand Trunk. He also purchased a partnership in the enterprises of Hugh Allan, the shipping magnate who was Montreal's wealthiest businessman at the time. When the Allan Line bid against the Canadian Steam Navigation Company for a valuable mail contract, Simpson

---

to PRO PELLY CUTEM. Certainly, no other HBC Governor is so amply commemorated on the Canadian landscape. Wherever northern explorers went they affixed his name to the geography as a mark of gratitude for the Company's co-operation: the Pelly River in the Yukon; Pelly Bay on the Arctic Coast in the Keewatin District; Pelly Island on the Arctic Coast in the Mackenzie District; Pelly Lake on the Back River in Keewatin; Pelly Mountain on Victoria Island in the Franklin District; and Pelly Point on Victoria Island, in the eastern Arctic.

was assigned the task of lobbying the two Canadian politicians responsible for awarding the tender: Premier Francis Hincks and John Ross, Solicitor-General for Canada West. As in most of his political pressure plays, Simpson used the services of his trusted go-between, Stewart Derbishire, then the provincial government's Queen's Printer. Simpson loved handing out buffalo tongues to his favourite legislators, and when one politician jokingly complained that acceptance of such wilderness delicacies might undermine his credibility, Derbishire assured him, with a twinkle in his eye, that "Sir George ... pleaded his cause with many tongues." Simpson gave away birchbark canoes, boxes of cheroots, Indian tents and, more than once, large sums of money. Hincks and Ross collected "10,000 golden reasons" between them when Simpson was trying to get a tugboat contract for the Allan Line, a bribe that helped make Ross a staunch supporter of the HBC and all its works.

Although Simpson's name appeared on the prospectus of nearly every important new Montreal business venture, his major concern remained conduct of the HBC's overseas operations. That no longer meant dashing from one wilderness outpost to the next trying to catch some hapless Chief Trader with an incomplete inventory tally. Instead, it required intense lobbying in both London and Montreal to keep the politicians on both sides of the Atlantic aware of why the Company and its royal charter still ought to be accorded such extraordinary privileges.

One of his problems was that the fur trade itself, at least in beaver hats, had declined precipitately almost from the instant Prince Albert, Queen Victoria's consort, had appeared at a public function in 1854 wearing a topper not of beaver felt but of silk. A trend towards the much less expensive substitute swept European society, forcing the HBC to trade for secondary animals such as marten, lynx, fox, wolf, otter and even swans for what were called "fancy" furs.

That switch was disruptive enough, but what was really at stake was the continued existence of the Hudson's Bay Company as a continent-spanning monopoly. As usual, the most intense campaign against the Company originated at Red River. The local activist Donald Gunn officially complained to Philip Vankoughnet, president of Canada West's Executive Council, that the HBC was charging up to 400 percent mark-up on goods sold in its stores. The Red River colonists also sent petitions to Westminster claiming that "Hudson's Bay Company's clerks, with an armed police, have entered into settlers' houses in quest of furs, and confiscated all they found. One poor settler, after having his goods seized, had his house burnt to the ground, and afterwards was conveyed prisoner to York Factory.... On our annual commercial journeys into Minnesota we have been pursued like felons by armed constables, who searched our property, even by breaking open our trunks; all furs found were confiscated."

This was followed up with a formal request that Red River be either incorporated into Canada or allowed to establish its own independent government. Even George Moffatt, who had been one of the useful intermediaries in the 1821 amalgamation negotiations, quietly informed Simpson that he intended to move a motion in the Canadian Legislative Council calling for abolition of the HBC's monopoly. A British Army major named Robert Carmichael-Smyth, who visited the Prairies, came back with the recommendation that a railway be built across the empty territory as the "great link required to unite in one powerful chain the whole English race." He added that all this could be achieved with the utmost economy by using convict labour. Just such a scheme (minus the convicts) was proposed by a Toronto group of promoters led by Allan Macdonell, who had pioneered mining developments north of Lake Superior. He based his approach on the advantages of building "a highway across the Continent, westward, thereby establishing a short route to the possessions in India, as well as other Asiatic Marts." Macdonell's idea was to purchase from the HBC (at a quantity discount, of course) a sixty-mile-wide strip of land across its territory to build the railway and grow food for its construction crews. He was denied his wish because the government of the day judged his scheme to be visionary but premature; in the longer run, its effect was to draw attention to the potential uses of the vacant hinterland.

The main problem Canada's politicians had in dealing with the HBC was that they were not daring enough to confiscate its land and did not have the necessary funds to buy it. Their solution was to fight the Company on the legally slippery ground that its charter was no longer valid and that as heirs of the French who had originally claimed most of its real estate, they had full rights to all the territory west of Lake of the Woods. George Brown, editor of the reformist Toronto *Globe*, was still championing his version of manifest destiny, which meant acquiring Rupert's Land from the HBC. Brown was now able to rally not only his own Clear Grit supporters but some of the most articulate Quebec politicians in his crusade. Simpson's spy Derbishire reported that he had overheard the *Globe* editor complaining to a Toronto bookstore proprietor that the HBC had debauched the Indians by importing, in one year alone, a million hogsheads of liquor into the fur trade. That kind of propaganda was reinforced by the continuing agitation at Red River and formal resolutions of the Canada West Executive Council calling ever more urgently for the country to reach out to the Pacific.

Free traders had meanwhile infiltrated all the Company's territories except two of its northernmost districts, and nearly as many goods were flowing in and out of Red River through St Paul as via York Factory. In October 1846, Chief Factor John Swanton, then in charge of Fort Garry, informed Simpson that Lieutenant Colonel C.F. Smith, commanding officer of an American cavalry unit stationed in the Dakota plains, had notified him that the Métis would no longer be allowed to run buffalo south of the border and that he intended to build a military post in the Red River Valley. These belligerent gestures were enough for Simpson and his London principals to persuade the Colonial Secretary to dispatch a detachment of 120 officers and men of the Royal Canadian Rifles to defend the Company's interests. The presence of the troops strengthened the Company's hand, though they actually did nothing except escort a band of twenty visiting Sioux away from the settlement in case of attack by local Métis. This irrelevant show of force only angered the settlers, who set up the Assiniboia Committee to monitor the Company's actions and safeguard their own interests.

It was not a powerful or even representative group, but the Committee organized the settlers' anti-HBC campaign, which was rapidly accelerating where it really mattered—in London, among the British politicians and bureaucrats who would soon be responsible for dealing with the Company's request that its licence be renewed before it expired, in May 1859. Late in the summer of 1856, Simpson had warned the London Committee that the Company was "… in a very critical position, the authorities being overawed by the numerical strength of the Halfbreed race; so that, at any moment an unpopular measure or accidental collision might lead to a general rising against the Company and the destruction of their establishments. In the meantime, by tact and forebearance, we contrive to maintain the peace and are making large returns—a state of things which may continue one, two or more years, although at all times liable to be interrupted suddenly."

But the London Committee could be of only limited assistance in helping to avert this portent. British public opinion was swinging against the Company, not so much for any specific Canadian reasons but because it had so clearly become an anachronism. The East India Company was in the process of being wound up, the Royal African Company was long gone, and

the originating justification for these and other royally chartered enterprises—
to encourage exploration of unknown continents by rewarding groups of
investors in such ventures with trading monopolies—had become irrelevant.
The HBC was under attack in the British House of Commons by the influential social reformer (and future prime minister) William Ewart Gladstone, who
despised monopolies in any form. "In England," wrote James Morris in his
monumental history of the period, "the trend of empire was against the
Company. The radical imperialists wanted all of Canada open to settlement.
The evangelists wanted every valley exalted, the financial community
resented the tight-lipped and privileged manner of the Company.... Even Lord
Palmerston thought commerce was not enough in itself as justification of
empire."

THE ISSUE CAME TO A HEAD when Henry Labouchere (afterwards Lord
Taunton), Secretary of State for the Colonies in Lord Palmerston's first administration, called for a Select Committee of the House of Commons to investigate the case for renewing the HBC's trading monopoly—and appointed
himself its chairman. Among that august body's nineteen members were some
of the great notables of British politics at the time: Sir John Pakington, a
former Secretary of State for War and for the Colonies; Lord John Russell, the
great Whig leader who had been prime minister from 1846 to 1852; Lord
Stanley, later the Earl of Derby; Gladstone, who had already been Colonial
Secretary under Peel; Robert Lowe, later Viscount Sherbrooke, one of the
leading classicists of his time and subsequently Chancellor of the Exchequer;
John Arthur Roebuck, the radical free trader and disciple of John Stuart Mill;
and Edward Ellice, son of the veteran parliamentarian and former Nor'Wester
who had become one of the HBC's staunchest advocates. It was the senior
Ellice who would act throughout the hearings as the Company's counsel for
the defence.

And so the Hudson's Bay Company and its charter were put on trial at last.
The committee sat eighteen times and cross-examined twenty-five witnesses,
asking 6,098 questions. The transcript of its hearings covered 450 pages. First
to be heard was John Ross, the former Solicitor-General for Canada West, who
had already been bribed at least once by Simpson and was president of the
Grand Trunk Railway. His testimony was so favourable that the Governor
later congratulated him on his "able handling" of the parliamentarians' questions. Even though he wanted the Grand Trunk to cross the West, Ross was

quite definite in advocating that the HBC remain the continent's landlord. "I think it would be a very great calamity if their control and power in that part of America were entirely to cease," he told the committee. "My reason for forming that opinion is this: during all the time that I have been able to observe their proceedings there, there has been peace within the whole territory. The operations of the Company seem to have been carried on, at all events, in such a way as to prevent the Indian tribes within their borders from molesting the Canadian frontier; while, on the other hand, those who have turned their attention to that quarter of the world must have seen that, from Oregon to Florida, for these last thirty years or more, there has been a constant Indian war going on between the natives of the American territory, on the one side, and the Indian tribes on the other. Now, I fear very much that if the occupation of the Hudson's Bay Company, in what is called the Hudson's Bay territory, were to cease, our fate in Canada might be just as it is with Americans in the border settlements of their territory."

Next on the witness stand was William Henry Draper, later Chief Justice of Ontario, representing the Macdonald-Cartier government's claims to the great lone land. Associated with the Family Compact so influential in governing the colony, Draper was also a friend of Simpson's; in fact, the Governor had just recently arranged a job for his son. After lauding the HBC, Draper went on to advocate a tougher line on colonization: "I do not think that the interests of a trading company can ever be considered as compatible with the settlement of the province … I hope you will not laugh at me as very visionary, but I hope to see the time, or my children may live to see the time, when there is a railway going all across that country and ending at the Pacific."

There followed bishops, explorers, army officers, admirals and retired employees, all testifying to the essential decency of the Company's stewardship, emphasizing how HBC Factors had often saved Indian bands from starvation, and repeatedly stressing the differences between the relatively benign occupation of the Canadian Prairie and the savage Indian wars of the American West. But two bits of evidence damaging to the HBC did emerge from the preliminary testimony. Dr John Rae, the Orkney surgeon who had spent most of his life in the Company's service as a doctor, trader and explorer, testified that its servants were forced to pay a 50-percent mark-up for goods they bought on their own accounts, while Indians were charged the equivalent of 300 percent over British costs. Other testimony confirmed that the HBC was still using large quantities of rum in its Indian trade. Ellice admitted that liquor was employed, but blamed its necessity on American competition.

One of the most telling attacks was the brief from the Aborigines' Protection Society, which claimed that the HBC charter had "given unlimited scope to the cupidity of a Company of traders, placing no stint upon their profits, or limits to their power ... [with the result that] the unhappy race we have consigned to their keeping, and from whose toil their profits are wrung, are perishing miserably by famine, while not a vestige of an attempt has been made on the part of their rulers to imbue them with the commonest arts of civilized life, or to induce them to change the precarious livelihood obtained by the chase for a certain subsistence derived from cultivation of the soil."

Several hostile witnesses, including A.K. Isbister, the chief British advocate for the people of Red River, and Richard Blanshard, the first governor of Vancouver Island, condemned the Company as a barrier to enlightenment and civilization, stressing its obnoxious monopoly and tyrannical ways. Unlike the previous witnesses who had praised the HBC as a universally benevolent force, these critics were specific, showing with actual examples why the lack of competition meant the loss of freedom for the 158,000 inhabitants (11,000 of them whites and Mixed Bloods) of the HBC's licensed territories.

The main issue before the Parliamentary Committee was not so much the Company's past reputation as its future credibility, especially in terms of its own insistence that there could never be any economically viable settlements in its territories beyond its trading posts and the already established enclaves at Red River, Fort Langley and Victoria.

On February 26 and again on March 2, 1857, the politicians appeared in full regalia, puffed up with self-importance as they welcomed to the stand the witness whose testimony they believed would decisively sway their verdict. As he stepped tentatively into that Westminster committee room, Sir George Simpson looked all of his biblical span of threescore and ten years. He felt uncomfortable in his surroundings. His rectitude had always been taken for granted, but here were these politicians in their dandy vestments, none of whom would last an hour hiking up a stiff portage, asking *him* to account for his actions—to justify what he considered to be the Company's natural position. He had never felt himself accountable to anyone except the HBC's proprietors, and he was not about to indulge these popinjays with his confidence. Yet there was nothing for it but to keep his temper as he resigned himself to answering what he expected would be silly little questions.

As it turned out, the questions were chillingly sensible, and, for the first time, Simpson must have felt publicly humiliated by his performance.

When Labouchere, the committee chairman, asked the Governor to describe how suitable the Company's territories might be for cultivation and colonization, Simpson replied: "I do not think that any part of the Hudson's Bay territories is well adapted for settlement; the crops are very uncertain."

"Would you apply that observation to the district of Red River?"

"Yes."

"Why so?"

"On account of the poverty of the soil, except on the banks of the river. The banks of the river are alluvial, and produce very fair crops of wheat; but these crops are frequently destroyed by early frosts; there is no certainty of the crops. We have been under the necessity of importing grain within these last 10 years from the United States and from Canada, for the support of the establishment."

A little later, when asked whether he was familiar with the characteristics of the Pacific Coast, Simpson answered confidently: "Yes. I have gone along the coast from Puget's Sound to the Russian principal establishment at Sitka."

"Do you believe that coast to be altogether unfit for colonization?"

"I believe it to be quite unfit for colonization."

This was a careless assertion for Simpson to make since previous testimony had already confirmed that the HBC's Fort Langley, near the mouth of the Fraser—which Simpson had just described as worthless—was enjoying great success as a Company farm. More damaging still to his credibility had been his cursory dismissal of the agricultural future of Red River and his later direct reference to the uselessness of the land around Fort Frances.

"If I understand you rightly," interjected one of the committee members, reaching into his briefcase for a book, "you think that no portion of Rupert's Land is favourable for settlement, but that some portions might be settled?"

"Yes."

"In your very interesting work of a *Journey Round the World*, I find at page 45 of the first volume this description of the country between the Lake of the Woods and the Rainy Lake: 'From Fort Frances downwards, a stretch of nearly 100 miles, it is not interrupted by a single impediment, while yet the current is not strong enough materially to retard an ascending traveller. Nor are the banks less favourable to agriculture than the waters themselves to navigation, resembling, in some measure, those of the Thames near Richmond. From the very brink of the river there rises a gentle slope of green-sward, crowned in many places with a plentiful growth of birch, poplar, beech, elm, and oak. Is it too much for the eye of philanthropy to discern through the vista of futurity this noble stream, connecting, as it does, the fertile shores of two spacious lakes, with crowded steamboats on its bosom and populous towns on its borders?' I suppose you consider that district favourable for population?"

"The right bank of the river is favourable, with good cultivation; that is to say, the soil is favourable; the climate is not; the back country is a deep morass, and never can be drained, in my opinion."

"Do you see any reason to alter the opinion which you have there expressed?"

"I do see that I have overrated the importance of the country as a country for settlement."

"It is too glowing a description, you think?"

"Exactly so; it is exceedingly beautiful; the bank is beautifully wooded, and the stream is very beautiful...."

"Will you allow me to remind you of one other sentence in your interesting work. It is at page 55 of volume 1: 'The soil of Red River Settlement is a black mould of considerable depth, which, when first tilled, produced extraordinary crops ... even after 20 successive years of cultivation, without the relief of manure or of fallow, or of green crop it still yields from 15 to 25 bushels an acre! The wheat produced is plump and heavy; there are also large quantities of grain of all kinds, besides beef, mutton, pork, butter, cheese, and wool in abundance.'"

Not an exchange to make the earth move, but enough to plant a seed of doubt in the minds of the parliamentarians about Simpson's—and the Hudson's Bay Company's—believability. Gladstone later noted in his auto-biography that the HBC Governor "in answering our questions had to call in the aid of incessant coughing."

In other testimony the hearings revealed that the Company's shareholders had been enriched by dividends totalling £20 million. Even though the HBC had been praised for many of its practices, the most generous-minded among its proponents based their defence mainly on the notion that whatever its corporate sins, the Company had at least prevented the slaughter typical of the American frontier. This was a valid if slightly simplistic point of view, but hardly a rallying cry stirring enough to justify prolonging the HBC's despotic powers over such a large and potentially lucrative chunk of geography. "The disclosures laid bare by this accumulation of testimony, letters, petitions, memorials and other evidence produced before the Parliamentary Select Committee, made the deepest kind of a public sensation," wrote Gustavus Myers in his *History of Canadian Wealth*. "For nearly two centuries the Hudson's Bay Company had represented itself in England as the grand evangel of religion, colonization, and civilization among the Indians; for nearly two centuries it had assiduously spread abroad its pretended reputation; and by insisting long enough upon its assumed virtues had been credited with them by the large mass of the unknowing. Now the truth was revealed, and bad as it was, yet it was regarded as undoubtedly only part of the whole. Imminently threatened, as the Hudson's Bay Company now was, with judicial and legislative extinction, it had to adopt some hurried expedient to save itself."

That expedient proved to be the production of one last witness before the committee adjourned to write its report. He was Edward ("Bear") Ellice, now in his mid-seventies, still respected by the parliamentarians and very much a force within the HBC's governing councils. He had been associated with the Canadian fur trade for half a century and, after a rambling lecture on its historical importance, electrified the committee with his reply to the chairman's question: Would it be difficult to make an arrangement between the Canadian Government and the Company for the extension of settlement into Hudson's Bay territory?

"Not only would there be no difficulty in it," replied the Bear, as if on cue, "but the Hudson's Bay Company would be [only] too glad to make a cession of any part of that territory for the purposes of settlement, upon one condition, that Canada shall be at the expense of governing it and maintaining a good police and preventing the introduction, so far as they can, of competition within the fur trade."

"You think it would be advantageous to the Company to withdraw, as it were, to the more Northern part of their territory, and leave for gradual settlement the Southern portion of their country?"

"I am of [the] opinion that the existence and maintenance of the Hudson's Bay Company for the purpose of temporarily governing this country, until you can form settlements in it, is much more essential to Canada and to England than it is to the Company of Adventurers trading into Hudson's Bay."

After that exchange, the committee's report was a foregone conclusion. As if by magic, the future of the Canadian West had suddenly become negotiable. The committee's majority recommendations, though mildly phrased, were hard-boiled in their intent: the Company must surrender its claims to Vancouver Island immediately and to the adjacent mainland (where a colony was to be created) soon afterwards; the Red River and Saskatchewan districts were to be annexed eventually to Canada; only those portions of the Indian territory considered unsuitable for settlement were to remain under the HBC's monopoly control for another twenty-one years. The Company of Adventurers could no longer claim, as it had in the original charter, to be "true and absolute Lords and proprietors" of the land beyond the westering sea. In the hush of that wood-panelled committee room, it seemed as if the epitaph of the sprawling enterprise had been written.

But such a pessimistic interpretation was based on an underestimation of the HBC's boundless pragmatism. If the impatient realm of Canada had transcontinental pretensions, that was fine: the Company would sell its land at the highest bid. No corporate officer adopted this unexpected detour with greater enthusiasm than Simpson himself, calculating that the Company's assets should fetch about £1 million cash, including £408,000 for its posts. His prescription for survival was simplicity itself—the HBC would pocket the money and continue to maintain its trading dominance within its territories, but as a private enterprise rather than an odious and "privileged" monopoly. The only problem was that this happy formula required a purchaser with ready funds—and there was none available. While the Macdonald-Cartier government was issuing brave declarations on the issue (mainly to disarm George Brown's more militant supporters), its treasury was bare, and London was not about to make the purchase of HBC lands a burden on the British taxpayer.

That, roughly, was the situation in 1859, when the Company's position was renewed on sufferance. Since neither Canada nor Britain would vote the funds required to govern the Indian territory, the Hudson's Bay Company continued to operate much as before. Its ever-staunch defence of the status quo had triumphed, one more time.

SIR GEORGE SIMPSON RECOVERED quickly from his parliamentary ordeal, but the illnesses that had periodically plagued him now came on more frequently and with debilitating consequences. Waves of fatigue left him so weak he could hardly dress without help. Doctors kept leeching him, but his pulse remained abnormally slow. He was liable to bouts of fainting and occasional seizures. He had suffered two mild apoplectic strokes in 1851 and two years later was devastated by the terminal illness of his beloved

Frances; her delicate health had broken after the birth of their second son in 1850.

The Governor could still work up the energy for his annual visits inland, but as one of his former comrades-in-arms, Edward Ermatinger, remarked: "Our old Chief, Sir George, ... tottering under the infirmities of age, has seen his best days. His light canoe, with choice of men, and of women too! can no longer administer to his gratification."

In the early summer of 1858, feeling a bit more chipper, Simpson travelled west for the first time by train, from New York through Chicago and Milwaukee to St Paul. His companion was none other than the Bear, come from England to spend time with his favourite compatriot. A few years Simpson's senior, Ellice had heard about the wonders of the American rail-roads, and the two old men sat nodding at one another, assuring themselves that they had come by rail to investigate the possibility of using this southern supply route as a replacement for York Factory on Hudson Bay. Simpson did briefly visit the Council meeting at Norway House and, after some ill-tempered remarks, retreated the way he had come.

Before the following season's inland journey, he penned a confidential letter to the London Committee. Suffering from periods of near-total blind-ness, he had somehow shrunk into himself, and his clothes hung loosely on his once-imposing frame. "In February next, I shall have completed forty years Service with the Hudson's Bay Company," he wrote. "During that very long period I have never been off duty for a week at a time, nor have I ever allowed Family ties and personal convenience to come in competition with the claims I considered the Company to have on me.... It is high time, however, I rested from incessant labour. Moreover, I am unwilling to hold an appointment, when I cannot discharge its duties to my own satisfaction. I shall therefore make way for some younger man, who I trust may serve the Compy. as zeal-ously and conscientiously as I have done." Before receiving a reply he set off westward on his annual inspection tour, but when he reached St Paul he was too ill and too exhausted to continue. After a few days' rest he returned to Lachine.

NOT FAR FROM LACHINE on August 1 of that summer, two other old men met for their final reunion. Eighty-three-year-old Simon Fraser, who had explored the restless river named after him, visited the house of his old friend John McDonald of Garth, who had fought every battle in the

Northwest worth fighting. There the two Nor'Westers composed a memorandum. "We are the last of the North West partners," it began, "we have known one another for many years—which of the two survives the other we know not—we are both aged—we have lived in mutual esteem and fellowship—we have done our duty in the stations allotted to us without fear, or reproach—we have survived many dangers—we have run many risks—we can not accuse one another of anything mean or dirty through life—nor done any disgraceful actions—nor wrong to others—we have been feared, loved and respected by natives—we have kept our men under subordination—we have thus lived long lives—and as this is probably the last time we meet on earth—we part as we have lived in sincere friendship and mutual good will."

McDonald of Garth lived another seven years; Fraser died destitute three years later. The most worthy of the Nor'Westers, David Thompson, had passed away two years earlier. After completing his service in the Fur Country and for another decade mapping the Canadian-American border, he had spent most of thirty years trying to eke out a living as a freelance surveyor. He mapped the Eastern Townships for the British American Land Company and most of the Muskoka Lakes country and, as he became poorer, various street and lot locations in Montreal for anyone who would pay him enough for a meal.

Carrying his surveying tripod on his back, trying to find sustenance for himself and his thirteen children, Thompson eventually had to sell his precious instruments and even pawned his winter coat. "Offered Lake Superior chart to a friend for five dollars," he scribbled in one of the final pages of his journal. "He would not take the chart but gave me the five dollars. A good relief, for I have been a week without a penny."

Despite his failing eyesight, Thompson started to edit his journals for publication and devised an elaborate scheme for financing his writings. He decided to try recruiting a group of patrons who would pay him a dollar a day for the maintenance of his family during his literary endeavours—in return for half the profits from the book. There were no takers. So at seventy-four, half blind and without sponsors, he started to write the memoir of his adventurous life.

Before the work was completed Thompson died on February 16, 1857, in privation at Longueuil, Quebec. The thirty-nine parts of his personal journals were not published until 1916 and then only because of the inspired sponsorship of Dr Joseph Burr Tyrrell, the Canadian mining engineer and explorer who had retraced Thompson's journeys and found his astronomical observations faultless.

WALKING IN THE SIBILANT RAIN falling hard on the granite blocks of the Lachine Canal, Sir George Simpson was most likely unaware of these and many similarly plaintive episodes. Reflecting on how alone he really was, he realized that Frances, John George McTavish, McLoughlin, Ogden, Rowand, Pelly and many others who had shared his life were dead. Ellice would live another four years, but the two men would never meet again. Somehow it didn't seem fair that they had all abandoned him. Like a latter-day King Lear, raging against his own mortality, Simpson was now dragging himself painfully across the land he had once ruled.

Rather than at Lachine, he spent much of his time on nearby Dorval Island, where he had purchased a large summer home four years earlier. One of his few remaining pleasures was to attend Sunday services at St Stephen's Anglican Church, so that he could stamp out as noisily as possible whenever he disagreed with the sermon.

At this point, his ordered life was enlivened by a distinguished visitor. The Prince of Wales, the future Edward VII but then an awkward eighteen-year-old, was on his way to be the officiating dignitary at the opening of the Victoria Bridge spanning the St Lawrence. Simpson decided to give him a treat and called out his Iroquois paddlers from Caughnawaga one last time. Having put in a lifetime's apprenticeship at playing the *grand seigneur*, Simpson scurried around for weeks beforehand, making certain that details of the magnificent tableau he intended for the travelling prince would be exactly right.

On August 29, 1860, His Royal Highness inspected a military parade on the Champ de Mars in a thunderstorm, then at noon was driven to Hudson's Bay House at Lachine and welcomed under eight triumphal arches made of pine boughs. As the sun burst from behind the clouds, the royal entourage left their carriages and set out in two barges belonging to the frigate HMS *Valorous* (anchored downstream from the rapids in Montreal Harbour) towards the wharf at Dorval Island, a quarter of a mile away. Near the foot of the island Simpson had assembled a flotilla of ten birchbark voyageur canoes, their HBC flags flapping in the summer wind. Each was manned by twelve Iroquois in full regalia of red flannel shirts, blue trousers and round caps decorated with dyed feathers pretending to be ostrich plumes.

As soon as the Prince's barge pushed off, the canoes darted out to meet him. Chanting voyageur songs, the paddlers allowed the royal party to pass among them. Then, suddenly wheeling around in perfect formation, the colourful convoy escorted the Prince to his landing place, where Sir George was waiting.

Simpson's island home had been temporarily rented out to Lieutenant-General Sir Fenwick Williams, commander-in-chief of the British forces in Canada, and it was he who acted as host for the ensuing luncheon. Simpson had devised a guest list of forty, inviting only those he considered socially worthy of meeting His Royal Highness. That meant mostly visiting celebrities, such as the Colonial Secretary, the Duke of Newcastle; the British Minister to Washington, Lord Lyons; the Marquess of Chandos; the Earl of Mulgrave, Lieutenant-Governor of Nova Scotia; Admiral Sir Alexander Milne, Commander-in-Chief of the North American and West Indies station; Lord Hinchingbrooke, heir to the Earl of Sandwich; Major-General Robert Bruce of the Prince's staff; and only three women—his niece, his private secretary's wife (the artist Frances Ann Hopkins) and her sister, one of the four other daughters of the Arctic explorer E.W. Beechey.

At four-thirty, the party embarked in the Indians' canoes, the Prince in one and Newcastle and Simpson in another. They wheeled about perfectly in line and crossed to Caughnawaga, where the Iroquois paddlers showed off their passengers to the people of the village, more than two thousand of them watching along the St Lawrence shore. With twilight painting the scene a golden amber, Simpson and his Prince were paddled back to Lachine, where they parted.

That day in the sun with the future king had been Sir George Simpson's formal farewell. Only two days later, still flushed with the exhilaration of the royal occasion, the Governor was stricken with apoplexy. On the morning of September 6, his attending physician, Dr William Sutherland from Montreal, came into his sick room to hear Simpson say: "Well, doctor, this is the last scene of all …"

"Yes, Sir George. Where would you wish to be buried?"

"In the Montreal Cemetery, of course."

"Would you wish to have a monument erected over your grave?"

"There is a monument there already."

"Would you wish any particular inscription to be put on it?"

"That," said the dying Sir George, in his last words and final show of temper, "is the business of my executor, not yours …"

By morning he was dead.*

The Caughnawaga canoemen, chanting a wild but doleful dirge, crossed the
river to escort the cortège from his house to the landing, where a special train
was waiting, and Simpson's body was borne by railway car to Montreal. He was
buried beside Frances under a simple headstone. The surest sign of his greatness was that those who felt most diminished by his passing were his enemies.

---

* The official cause of Simpson's death was stated to have been "haemorrhagic apoplexy,
attended with epileptiform convulsions" but historian Frits Pannekoek maintains he died
from tertiary syphilis. Simpson's estate was worth more than £100,000; his residence was
sold to the Sisters of St Ann, who demolished it in 1888 to make room for a convent. It
was at what is now 1300 St Joseph Boulevard in Lachine, where the only reminder of the
fur trade is a small warehouse on the other side of the canal, now a lively fur-trade
museum run by Parks Canada. Simpson's summer house on Dorval Island stood for
another eighty years. When it was finally torn down in 1939 as a safety hazard, its rubble
was carted away in thirty-one scow loads, at two dollars each.

Surrender

"What? Sequester our very tap-root? Take away the fertile lands where our buffaloes feed? Let in all kinds of people to squat and settle and frighten away the fur-bearing animals they don't kill and hunt? Impossible!"
—HBC Governor H.H. Berens to the Colonial Secretary, 1863

THE LITTLE EMPEROR WAS dead, but his Company still ruled the West. Although the HBC's monopoly was not renewed in 1859, its charter remained the object of universal envy and its commerce continued much as before.

Sir George Simpson's successor as Governor of Rupert's Land was Alexander Grant Dallas, a capable if colourless businessman who had started his career in China with the powerful trading house Jardine, Matheson & Company. He had spent most of the five years before his appointment as the Company's main representative on Vancouver Island as President of the Council. During James Douglas's term as Governor of British Columbia, the two men quarrelled but made up long enough for Dallas to marry Douglas's second daughter, Jane.

Dallas moved the centre of operations to Red River from Lachine, sensing that the influx of land-hungry migrants into the once-isolated Selkirk Settlement would become the HBC's most sensitive dilemma. "As the country comes to be occupied without our leave," he grouched, "they will bye and bye not even give us thanks."

For the moment, fur sales continued to bring in 10- and 15-percent annual dividends, despite the best efforts of the free traders who had invaded the Company's territory. But the Bay men themselves, deprived of Simpson's disciplinarian leadership, had gone soft. Many of them insisted that salutes be fired whenever they left or arrived at a fort and that Company servants doff their caps to them. Some dined on white linen, wielded monogrammed silverware, sent their sons to English or Scottish schools and their daughters to Toronto or Montreal to be tutored in singing and the piano.

The HBC's Governors realized only too well that they could not maintain their feudal proprietorship much longer. No private corporation could hope to possess the moral authority or spend the funds necessary to govern a region the size of Rupert's Land, once it had been settled. As they scrutinized their long-term prospects, the London-based Committeemen were not at all dismayed. The change in circumstances would gain them a potentially hefty profit on their land—an asset they had not previously considered valuable except as free range for fur-bearing animals. The trick was to win the highest price possible, even though the new Canadian nation lacked the necessary money and the mother country didn't want to spend it. The negotiations that ensued were long and convoluted because the Canadians thought that Rupert's Land should be surrendered without payment, and yet there was really no faction prepared to tackle the Company head on.

The issue tightened into a more serious matter than satisfying the already well-heeled HBC shareholders with the emergence of not very subtle aspirations by American annexationists to grab the virgin territory—that, and the increasingly loud urgings of ambitious railway promoters to use a Canadian land route to connect Europe with the Orient. The mainland of British Columbia had achieved colonial status in 1858, and that provided an incentive for the provinces favourably disposed towards Confederation to pump for the inclusion of the vast empty lands between Canada West and the Pacific Coast. "There can be no question," thundered George Brown's *Globe*, "that the injurious and demoralizing sway of that Company over a region of four millions of square miles, will, ere long, be brought to an end, and that the destinies of this immense country will be united with our own. It is unpardonable that civilization should be excluded from half a continent, on at best but a doubtful right of ownership, for the benefit of two hundred and thirty-two shareholders."

Until the 1864 meetings at Charlottetown and Quebec City's St Louis Hotel, Canadian politics was deadlocked between Brown's Clear Grits and John A. Macdonald's oddly named Liberal-Conservatives, because the two leaders had almost nothing in common except their mutual dislike. The largely agricultural and French-Catholic Canada East and the commercially enterprising Protestant Canada West shared equal representation in the Legislative Assembly. Decisions required a double majority (of the two provincial caucuses) as well as overall approval, and that system stifled new initiatives. British free-trade policies had ended the preferential treatment of Canada's exports. Then on March 17, 1866, Washington permitted the lapse of the Reciprocity Treaty of 1854 (which had allowed free U.S.–Canada trade in most commodities), causing the Canadian economy to suffer a severe recession.

The American Civil War had just ended, and the U.S. government was intent on using British North America as the "Achilles heel of the Empire" to exert pressure on London. The Irish vote was too essential to American politicians for them to prevent the unruly Fenians from carrying out raids across the Canadian borders. These forays were based on the Fenians' erroneous conviction that harassing Canadians would prompt the English to "free" Ireland. While most Americans viewed Canada "with an indifference at times amounting to benevolence," many U.S. politicians genuinely believed that citizens of the nascent Canadian state required help to escape the yoke of British imperialism—and recognized no contradiction in the fact that they were attempting to substitute their own. Washington had even dispatched agents northward to measure the strength of the annexation mood. Israel Andrews, who had been sent to Montreal, enigmatically reported that "if people had more brains and officials weren't corrupt, the future would be clearer."

Others had no such doubts. The *New York Herald* was calling for annexation, "peaceably if possible, forcibly if necessary." Most Americans saw the largely unoccupied plains of the Canadian Midwest as a happy hunting ground for their frontier desperadoes, who could shoot buffalo, Indians and each other just as well north as south of the 49th parallel. Because no one else was actively claiming the land and the Hudson's Bay Company just hunkered there assiduously gathering furs, "the British prairies had now become part of the American horizon." During his 1865 tour, a Boston journalist named Charles Carleton Coffin extolled the region's fertile belt as "boundless savannas fragrant with flowers in spring time, and warming with verdure in summer"—with no visible limit to its agricultural and mineral potential.

One of the main agitators for the American takeover of the HBC's real estate was James Wickes Taylor. A special agent of the U.S. Treasury Department, Taylor was stationed in the Midwest for most of the 1860s, part of the time at Red River (where he was later accredited as U.S. Consul between 1870 and 1893), with orders to promote the progress of American interests. His annexationist views never wavered as he reported that here "was an area large enough to make five states equal in every way to Minnesota." When Taylor was asked by the House of Representatives to analyse commercial relations between the two countries, he overstepped his mandate and drafted an act for the admission to the Union of Nova Scotia, New Brunswick, Canada East, Canada West and "the territories of Selkirk, Saskatchewan and Columbia," proposing to pay the HBC $10 million for the surrender of its claims. The measure was formally introduced in Congress by Nathaniel Prentiss Banks of Massachusetts in July 1866, given two readings, then relegated to the Committee on Foreign Affairs for what turned out to be permanent study. Two years later, the U.S. Senate passed a resolution offering $6 million for the HBC's territorial rights, but it too was shelved.

At Red River itself, which by the late 1860s had a population of more than ten thousand (only sixteen hundred of them whites), the mood was more difficult to read. Because absorption by either the U.S. or Canada was bound to inundate the settlement with newcomers who would eventually outnumber the Mixed Bloods and relegate them to a minority position, annexation by any outside agency had limited appeal. The Canadian lobby was led by a blond giant named Dr (later Sir) John Christian Schultz, who had arrived at Red River in 1861, bought into the weekly Nor'Wester and founded the small but noisy Canadian Party. An acquaintance once remarked that in Schultz, "fate had manufactured a scoundrel out of material meant by nature for a gentleman," but he was an effective propagandist, uniting the pan-Canadian sentiments of Toronto Orangemen with local anti-HBC agitation, portraying the Company as a relic of empire obstructing Canada's inland aspirations.

It was less as a response to such trouble-making than as a defensive measure against the threat of American manifest destiny veering northward that John A. Macdonald finally acted. "I would be quite willing, personally," he wrote as late as March 1865, "to leave that whole [HBC] country a wilderness for the next half century, but I fear if Englishmen do not go there, Yankees will." He accused the Hudson's Bay Company of "spoliation and outrage" but was well aware, as his biographer Donald Creighton has pointed out, "that the only way in which British North America could ensure its survival as a separate autonomous power in North America was through the union of all its territories in a single transcontinental state."

Any proposed step by the Canadian government to absorb Rupert's Land was, at least initially, regarded by most Montreal politicians as part of a plot by Brown and his followers to disrupt the delicate political balance between Canada East and Canada West. After the Charlottetown and Quebec conferences of 1864 had dispelled much of this suspicion, and as the act of Confederation moved closer, French Canada's politicians, particularly George-Etienne Cartier, came around to accepting the notion that compensation would have to be paid to the HBC for its unexpired rights. "Canada," wrote an eloquent Macdonald in an official note to the British government, "looks forward with interest to the day when the valley of the Saskatchewan will become the back country of Canada, the land of hope for the hardy youth of the provinces when they seek new homes in the forest ... when Canada will become the highway of immigration from Europe to those fertile valleys."

The British North America Act, the statute enacted by Westminster on March 29, 1867, providing for Canadian independence, contained a clause to allow Rupert's Land into the forthcoming Confederation. Later that year, during the first sitting of the country's new parliament, Public Works Minister William McDougall, who had been an active Clear Grit under Brown and had changed party affiliations so often he was nicknamed "Wandering Willie," moved a seven-part resolution calling for action on the Rupert's Land issue. British Columbia made building a railway the condition of entering Confederation, and international financiers were pressuring Ottawa to push the rails westward. The time had come to settle the issue of the Hudson's Bay Company's lands once and for all.

SUCCESSIVE BRITISH COLONIAL SECRETARIES, governed by their own pressing priorities, had spent inordinate time and energy on the issue of nationalizing the HBC, but the burdensome corporate dinosaur never seemed long off their agendas. Immediately after the 1857 parliamentary hearings, the British government decided to dispatch an independent expert to Rupert's Land to help sort out some of the contradictory testimony by investigating at first hand what was really there. Chosen for the assignment (co-sponsored by the Royal Geographical Society) was Captain John Palliser of the Waterford Militia, who had written a book on a similar mission to the western plains of the United States, where he had wrestled a bear, shot a prize panther and been tossed on the horns of an enraged bull buffalo. Accompanied by a botanist, a doctor, an astronomer and an artillery officer turned naturalist, the Palliser expedition surveyed the land-mass between Lake Superior and the Pacific, reporting back on the location of fertile valleys, coal deposits, valuable forests and a possible railway route.*

---

* One memorable entry in Palliser's diary concerns his meeting with an Indian chief at Fort Frances on Rainy Lake. As translated by a local free trader, the chief's message was sadly prescient: "I know that you have come straight from the Great Country, and we know that no men from that country ever came to us and lied. I want you to declare to

At the end of his three-year study, Palliser drew up a comprehensive plan for a new Crown colony bounded by the 49th and 54th parallels, strongly recommending that it be created promptly to prevent its loss as a British possession. When the government of the day approached the HBC with the Palliser plan, the Company's response was handled by Edward ("Bear") Ellice, who replied matter-of-factly: "The Hudson's Bay Company are quite willing to dispose of their territory and their establishments. It is a question of a million of money. If either this Government or the Government of Canada wish to take the affair into their own hands I can tell them the cost of the undertaking. But in my mind, as far as the maintenance of order and peace throughout that vast territory is concerned, that is the smallest part of the question." The "million of money" quoted by the Bear was precisely that: £1,000,000 cash.

The Colonial Secretary who first tested the HBC's mettle by issuing an ultimatum to its governor was Sir Edward George Earle Lytton Bulwer-Lytton, who came into office with the Derby-Disraeli government of 1858. A popular novelist (now mainly remembered as author of The Last Days of Pompeii), he was nearly stone deaf and suffered from a severe speech defect—political handicaps he overcame by minutely rehearsing every speech and lip-reading his opponents' replies. Determined to create the colony sketched out by Palliser, he threatened to remove the HBC's trading rights unless the Company agreed to test the validity of its charter before the Privy Council, hinting that the verdict was almost certain to be negative. That danger was removed when Lord Palmerston returned to power, and the Duke of Newcastle moved into the Colonial Office.

Unlike his predecessors, Newcastle had at least been to Canada, as one of Sir George Simpson's guests during the Prince of Wales's Montreal visit in 1860. He was an informed and intelligent advocate of colonizing Rupert's Land. Realizing that neither Canada nor England would invest the required capital, he turned to the private sector, particularly to the British financiers anxious to build a railway and telegraph system across the upper part of North America.

Enter Edward Watkin. A former manager of the Manchester, Sheffield, and Lincolnshire Railway, Watkin had been hired by two of London's most reputable merchant bankers, Glyn, Mills & Company and Baring Brothers, to

---

us truthfully what the Great Queen of your country intends to do to us when she will take the country from the Fur Company's people. All around me I see the smoke of the white men to rise. The Long Knives [the Americans] are trading with our neighbours for their lands and they are cheating them and deceiving them. Now, we will not sell nor part with our lands."

help resolve the problems of Canada's troubled Grand Trunk Railway, which they had financed. He studied the situation and quickly decided that the best prescription for the Grand Trunk's salvation was to build a railway from the Atlantic to the Pacific. As a first step, he organized the Atlantic and Pacific Postal and Telegraph Company, requesting a ten-mile-wide right-of-way across Rupert's Land for telegraph poles and a wagon road, presumably a precursor of the railway line. On November 17, 1862, the Duke of Newcastle, who heartily endorsed the idea, visited Henry Hulse Berens, then Governor of the HBC, to sound him out on the Watkin proposal.

The twentieth man to hold the office since Prince Rupert of the Rhine, Berens, who was also a director of the Bank of England, had spent thirty years gracing the HBC Committee, upholding a staunch family tradition. His great-grandfather Herman Berens had been a member of the Committee from 1765 to 1794; his grandfather Joseph Berens, Sr., from 1776 to 1795; and his father, Joseph Berens, Jr., from 1801 to 1822. The Colonial Secretary approached the touchy issue at hand as moderately and gently as he could. He presented the promoter's idea of slashing a strip across the heart of the HBC territory as a patriotic gesture to tie the Empire together. Berens's reply was as indignant as it was emotional. "What?" he blustered. "Sequester our very tap-root? Take away the fertile lands where our buffaloes feed? Let in all kinds of people to squat and settle and frighten away the fur-bearing animals they don't kill and hunt? Impossible! Destruction—extinction—of our time-honoured industry...."

That emphatic defence of his turf having been delivered, the Governor reverted to type and, shrewdly squinting at the Duke, queried: "If these gentlemen are so patriotic, why don't they buy us out?"

"What is your price?" calmly inquired the Colonial Secretary.

"Well, about a million and a half."

The price had gone up because Berens could sense that Newcastle's determination to tame Canada's West would attract the necessary funds. He was right. Less than a month later, Watkin and his banking principals appeared in Berens's office (which the promoter derisively described as being dingy, the old wooden chairs black with age and the table covered with a faded green cloth), and the deal was cut. The purchasers set only one, highly reasonable, condition: before spending £1,500,000, they wished to examine the Company's books.

In response, Berens produced an eighty-five-year-old accountant named Mr Roberts, who insisted that the ledgers not be removed from Hudson's Bay House. One item Watkin gleaned from his brief inspection of the balance sheets was that the Company had disposed of one thousand acres of prime land in the heart of San Francisco just before the 1849 gold rush for only £1,000 because two Factors had quarrelled over its disposition.

The sales agreement was concluded on June 15, 1863. To raise the large amount of cash demanded by the Governor required greater assets and more risk than were represented by the two bankers backing Watkin. The financial conglomerate that came up with the £1,500,000 called itself the International Financial Society. Incorporated only a month earlier by a consortium of City bankers, the IFS would eventually float debentures that financed a land company in Mauritius and the building of railways in Eastern Europe, but its HBC investment was handled as a share flip. The IFS paid the purring HBC proprietors £300 for each share of £100 par value, up to the £1.5 million total. The Company was then immediately recapitalized (an elegant term for having its stock watered) at £2 million, and the shares were sold to the public in £20 units. Thus the HBC's stock, which had been purchased for three times its nominal value, had quadrupled in price with no real change in revenue prospects having taken place. The transactions left the International Financial Society's owners with a net gain of £300,000; then, having disposed of its shares, the IFS faded from the scene. For the first time since the Company's founding in 1670, HBC stock was now widely distributed among seventeen hundred shareholders, each one of whom expected a hefty return. The *Times* of July 3, 1863, called the plan "one of the most important proposals, both in a financial and national sense, ever introduced on the London money market."

Perhaps the only man in London who despaired of the Company's sale to a group of promoters was Edward Ellice. When one of the IFS negotiators met the Bear, then bent with age and only months away from death, in a London arcade, he reported that the old man had confronted him for some moments without speaking, in a state of confused abstraction. "Then he passed on, like a man endeavouring to recollect a long history of difficulty, and to realize how strangely it had all ended."

The prospectus that had attracted so many eager shareholders listed the Company's assets at £370,000 in cash; £1,023,500 in physical plant such as trading posts, ships and offices; and 1.4 million square miles, or 896 million acres of land. "The Southern District will be opened to European Colonization under a liberal and systematic scheme of land settlement," spouted the offering circular. "The Company can, without creating any new and costly establishments, inaugurate a new policy of colonization and at the same time dispose of mining grants."

That pledge meant very little, but shareholders were reassured by the quality of the new Committeemen who took over the Company's direction. (The only important holdover from the former board was Eden Colvile, whose lengthy tenure and experience at Red River provided essential continuity.) In addition to three of the City's best-known merchant bankers—James Hodgson, John Henry Schröder and Daniel Meinertzhagen—the Company's new Deputy Chairman, Curtis Miranda Lampson, a former American fur trader who had moved to London in 1830, was one of the City's most able financiers. On the Duke of Newcastle's suggestion, Sir Edmund Walker Head was installed as Governor of the reconstituted HBC. He had served as Lieutenant-Governor of New Brunswick and later as Governor-in-Chief of British North America (1854–61). An Oxford honours graduate in classics, an author, poet and philologist, Head was a thoughtful statesman, genuinely concerned with developing Rupert's Land in an orderly fashion. But he soon found himself overwhelmed by Edward Watkin's impatience. The promoter had hurried to Canada as an agent of the new Company and on his own authority had dispatched surveyors into the field, ordered two hundred tons of copper wire and let a contract (with Hugh Allan's Montreal Telegraph Company) for construction of the line from Fort Garry to Jasper House.

Head could not condone such outrageous flouting of his authority, particularly since Watkin's own reports made it clear that the Canadian government had expressed no intention of helping finance construction of the telegraph line. The Company did send Dr John Rae, the retired HBC Chief Factor and Arctic explorer, to survey the route, but absence of government support had already killed the project. What the minor crisis did accomplish was to reactivate Canada's official pressure on the British Colonial Office to resolve the Hudson's Bay territorial dispute. "What a glorious program it would be," Macdonald later wrote to Charles Tupper, his chief Nova Scotia lieutenant, "to go down to Parliament next session with Nova Scotia pacified, Newfoundland voluntarily joining and the acquisition of Hudson's Bay."

A powerful Canadian delegation, headed by Cartier and McDougall, arrived at London's Westminster Palace Hotel during October 1868 in a mood for serious bargaining about expropriating the new HBC. Earl Granville, the Colonial Secretary in the Gladstone government, had thoroughly absorbed the department's files on the issue and had decided to act much more quickly and decisively than any of his predecessors. Correctly estimating that the Company and the Canadian delegates would reach their usual impasse, he presented both parties with a twelve-paragraph ultimatum on March 9, 1869, noting with a touch of deliberate sarcasm that his conditions would no doubt be found unacceptable to both sides, but that on further consideration they might realize that breaking the deadlock would benefit each of their joint and separate interests. The Canadians were the first to capitulate, and after that the Company had no choice; Granville had made it crystal clear that no other alternative was or would be available. Despite loud protests from HBC shareholders, who regarded the Colonial Secretary's terms as a betrayal of their trust, the deal was approved. On November 19, 1869, the Hudson's Bay Company signed the Deed of Surrender (which became valid on July 15, 1870) that extinguished its much-coveted monopoly rights.

While there was no direct charge to the Treasury of the United Kingdom, it did agree to guarantee a loan to the Canadian government of £300,000 (then the equivalent of $1,460,000) that was to be the HBC's cash compensation. Among the other conditions of the transfer (apart from such trivialities as paying for the aging telegraph wire stored at York Factory) the HBC was allowed to retain:

1. A grant of more than forty-five thousand acres around its 120 existing trading posts. Only four of these forts were in what was then considered to be the fertile belt, but the acreage around Fort Garry alone had immediate cash value.
2. A right to claim, during the ensuing fifty years, blocks of land set out for settlement within its former territory, not to exceed one-twentieth of the fertile area. (This was defined as the region bounded on the south by the American border, on the west by the Rocky Mountains, on the north by the North Saskatchewan River, and on the east by Lake Winnipeg, Lake of the Woods and the waters connecting them.) This grant amounted to seven million acres of some of the best agricultural land in Western Canada.
3. A guarantee of the continuance of its trade without hindrance and with no special taxes or tariffs.

Enemies of the Company interpreted the surrender as the HBC's death blow. "The old lion has been shorn of its mane," one of them gloated, "his roar is no longer heard in the great North-West." The Company's original charter may have been reduced to a decorative parchment, but the HBC was still the largest private landholder in Western Canada—and had been handed a rich ransom for relinquishing holdings that, from the Canadian point of view, it ought never to have been allowed to possess. Most significantly, the Company had been relieved of the responsibility of administering those lands just when settlement was promising to make that function dangerous and expensive.

The terms of sale were routinely ratified by Canada's Parliament, and the physical takeover was slated for December 1, 1869, with William McDougall being named Lieutenant-Governor of Rupert's Land. When he arrived at the frontier village of Pembina, instead of being greeted by a delegation of delighted former colonials, he was handed a proclamation signed by Louis Riel forbidding him to enter Red River. The brief and bitter rebellion that followed has been thoroughly documented and is well beyond the scope of this volume, but the uprising was a perfectly appropriate response to the Company's treatment of what should have been its most valued constituency—the field hands holding down the ground its London proprietors had sold to satisfy their shareholders.

In 1863, when the International Financial Society purchased the HBC, the Company's servants in North America were notified so tardily they felt, as one of them remarked, as if they had been "sold like dumb driven cattle." It was only when they threatened to resign in a body that their plight finally caught London's attention. The Committeemen realized how effectively their own fur traders could compete if they should choose to organize themselves as independents. Governor Head intended to discontinue the winterers' 1821 Deed Poll (which guaranteed them 40 percent of profits), placing all employees on straight salaries. But faced with mounting opposition from across the Atlantic, he agreed to pay a lump-sum settlement of £157,055 to terminate the practice of shared ownership—and specifically excluded the Canadian-based personnel from future land sale profits.

Six years later, when the Company gave up its territory to Canada, neither the citizens of Red River nor the HBC traders scattered across Rupert's Land were officially notified of the proceedings leading to the sale. William Mactavish, the last Governor of Rupert's Land, complained to a Métis acquaintance during the final phase of the negotiations: "I can guarantee nothing. Times are changing. I myself know nothing. Am I still the governor? It seems that everything gets settled in London, but they don't tell me anything."

Least consulted and most directly affected of all were the Indian peoples. As land sales rather than fur barters became the HBC's prime concern, their traditional way of life lost its *raison d'être*, and hunger was the result. Indians begging for food at white settlements became a common sight, as did the sad spectacle of natives having to subsist on a meagre diet of gophers caught by pouring water down their holes and snaring the tough little animals as they emerged. On April 13, 1871, Chief Sweet Grass and a delegation of Plains Cree from the Edmonton and Carlton House districts came in stately procession to address W.J. Christie, the Chief Factor at Edmonton, asking him to transcribe and submit a petition to the Governor at Fort Garry. "We heard our lands were sold and we did not like it," went the proclamation. "We do not want to sell our lands; it is our property, and no one has a right to sell them. Our country is getting ruined of fur bearing animals, hitherto our sole support, and now we are poor and want help—we want you to pity us. We want cattle, tools, agricultural implements, and assistance in everything when we come to settle—our country is no longer able to support us."

Indian claims to the grasslands were gradually muffled, and the interracial fur-trade partnership that had shaped day-to-day contact over most of a continent for much of two centuries was irrevocably severed. A native heritage was regarded as a liability, not an asset, as tent towns grew into villages and villages expanded into towns and cities. The buffalo herds were gone, their mournful bellowing replaced by the echoing hoots first of steamboats and then of locomotives. York boats rotted on the riverbanks, and Sir John A. Macdonald boasted to his friend Sir Hastings Doyle, Lieutenant-Governor of Nova Scotia: "We have quietly and almost without observation annexed all the country between here and the Rocky Mountains."

The last meeting of the Northern Department of Rupert's Land was held at Norway House in July 1870. Only seventeen years later, no further commissioned officers were appointed by the HBC and, four years after that, all of the time-honoured titles of the fur trade were withdrawn. But for this one final occasion, the Chief Factors and Chief Traders sat around the great oak table where Sir George Simpson had once ruled, and where generations of their predecessors had traded quips and empires.

They must have felt as if they were living out the final act in some much-told tale, these ordinary men caught in extraordinary circumstances. Later in life, nodding by a fireside back in the Highlands, England or Montreal, they must have had trouble remembering the details of all those glory days and earthy nights. Like some greybeard who runs his forefinger along his duelling scar as he recalls the bravado of his youth, each of them must have given thanks to his deity for having survived—and yet not on any account would he have forgone the experience.

VIII LABRADOR SMITH

The Man Who Became a Country

"Who is Smith? What is Smith? … Why, Smith is not a name, but an occupation!"
— Thomas Wilson

IF THEY REMEMBER HIM AT ALL, most Canadians retain only a vague folk memory of Donald Alexander Smith as the centrepiece of their country's most famous historical photograph. He is that bearded gentleman in the stovepipe hat awkwardly hammering home the last spike of the Canadian Pacific Railway at Craigellachie, a hastily erected caboose-town in Eagle Pass of the Monashee Mountains on November 7, 1885.

But from there the fuzzy public memory ends.

He had, after all, been neither head of the CPR (that was George Stephen) nor the railway's builder (William Van Home), and the reason for his prominence during that improvised ceremony was as mysterious at the time as it appears in retrospect. Typically, he said not a word at this most memorable of his life's occasions; he just bashed in that big nail.

Although he spent considerable energy cultivating the myth of being an enigmatic presence in crowded landscapes of his own choosing (or even making), in retrospect, there was nothing very profound or mystical about Smith—or the faith he worshipped: his own pocketbook. The institution he served during an astounding seventy-five-year association was the Hudson's Bay Company, which he transformed from a haphazardly linked collection of wilderness outposts into a profitable commercial enterprise.

In terms of modern Canadian history, Smith was there at the creation. His roster of accomplishments, self-serving as they may have been, distinguishes him as a giant among the decision-makers who transformed Canada from colony to nation. Preferring to dominate events from behind the scenes rather than directly confront rivals, Smith staged a dazzling sequence of commercial and political *coups d'etat* that made him the richest and most powerful Canadian of his day. He became the role model for his peers. Smith won every available public honour, including two university chancellorships, the close confidence of four Canadian prime ministers (each of whom he betrayed), the friendship of two British monarchs, a knighthood and a barony for which he chose the tongue-paralyzing title: "Baron Strathcona and Mount Royal, of Glencoe, co. Argyll, and of Mount Royal, Quebec, Canada."

No one felt neutral about Smith. "As a Canadian," proclaimed the Very Reverend Daniel M. Gordon, vice-Chancellor of Queen's University, "I am grateful to God for the large service He has enabled Lord Strathcona to render for Canada." In contrast W.T.R. Preston, then chief Liberal organizer for Ontario and a close observer of his methods, wrote: "The Smith syndicate was entirely responsible for using [the] Canadian Parliament for the most improper purposes that ever became operative among a free people."

Smith's catlike career enjoyed endless reincarnations. Each move irrevocably led to another opening, with Smith propelling himself from one opportunity to the next without a touch of diffidence or backward glance:

The last of the great historical figures associated with governance of the HBC, Smith spent most of three mind-numbing decades as one of the Company's Labrador fur traders before being anointed last Chief Commissioner, first Land Commissioner, and, for a tense quarter of a century, London-based Governor. The first apprentice-clerk to attain such exalted rank, Smith turned out to be an indifferent administrator, but he did move the Company away from its genesis in bartering animal pelts to real estate, transportation and the beginnings of retailing. He thus ensured the HBC's survival after the Company lost its trading monopoly when the Dominion of Canada purchased the original land grants in 1870. Smith was fully as significant a figure in the HBC's history as that great Caesar of the Wilderness, Sir George Simpson, who had governed the operating arm of the Company during four adventurous decades from, his express birchbark canoe.

For forty-two years a director of the Bank of Montreal, as well as its second-largest shareholder, and for seventeen years its president, Smith turned the Bank into Canada's most profitable and North America's safest financial institution. At the same time, he treated the Montreal as a private financing instrument for his various ventures—Canadian history's fattest piggy bank.

A director of the CPR and member of its executive committee for thirty-two years, Smith took little interest in its building or operation. But as anchorman of the road's private- and public-sector financing, Smith had the fiscal perseverance that allowed completion of the Confederadon-fulfilling project. Patriotic as it may have appeared, this effort did not force Smith to stray too far out of character. As one of the railway's main shareholders, he benefited mightily from the stock's extravagant long-term rise. Members of his syndicate purchased CPR treasury stock for their own accounts at twenty-five cents on the dollar and grabbed control of the Canada North-West Land Company, which sold 2,200,000 acres of the Crown land granted the CPR as a construction incentive.

Smith's most successful railroading venture had nothing to do with the grandeur of the CPR. Along with three partners, he invested a borrowed $250,000 in the bankrupt St Paul, Minneapolis and Manitoba Railway, which, following a decade of stock manipulation and minimum construction, increased in value to a cool $60 million. Even considering the gutter ethics of late nineteenth-century railway promotion, acquisition of the St Paul earned pride of place as the most shameless of swindles.

Along the way, Smith became founding president of the Royal Trust Company, now one of Canada's largest trusts. He co-owned a textile mill at Cornwall, Ontario, and a rolling-stock manufacturing plant in Montreal; his will documented many other discreet but significant holdings.

Smith's political influence equalled the impressive impact of his commercial activities. His crucially timed intervention settled Louis Riel's Red River Rebellion; his personal vote defeated Sir John A. Macdonald's second Canadian administration; he served eighteen years in the House of Commons, much of that time as the powerful pro-consul for western Canada—known in Parliament as Minister for the Hudson's Bay Company.

Some of Smith's more positive legacies included recommendations that led to formation in 1873 of the North West Mounted Police, predecessor of the Royal Canadian Mounted Police, and to the founding of Canada's reserve army. Convinced that it was a sin for a Scot to die rich, he became one of the most generous and creative philanthropists of his age, helping establish Montreal's Royal Victoria Hospital and significantly expanding McGill University. He won the admiration of a grateful British Empire by personally donating a regiment of Canada's best horsemen to help fight the Boer War and by funding the start of Lord Baden-Powell's Boy Scout movement. He gave away more than $20 million and left many benevolent Canadian and imperial legacies, including funds for a leper colony and plans for the so-called All-Red Transportation and Telegraph route that was supposed to circle the globe.

The first HBC executive to evaluate correctly the agricultural potential of the fur country, Smith foresaw that much of the Prairies would become fertile farmland. To position the HBC (and himself) as recipients of the revenues from sale of those acres, Smith became one of the principal promoters of immigration responsible for settling the West.

Smith spent eighteen years as Canada's High Commissioner to the United Kingdom, quickly becoming as influential in Britain as he had been in Canada. He bankrolled and became chairman of Burmah Oil and the Anglo-Persian Oil Company, the innovative energy firms that later spawned the giant British Petroleum. At the personal behest of Winston Churchill, then first Lord of the Admiralty, Smith's companies guaranteed security of oil supply for the Royal Navy as it prepared for the First World War.

It hardly seems possible that any man could have engaged in so much activity in a single lifetime, since until the relatively advanced age of forty-nine Smith was fully occupied by the mundane business of trading furs with Indians in a remote corner of Labrador, then justifiably known as "the world's jumping-off place." Part of the explanation for Smith's long roster of achievements was the extraordinary stretch of his life. Donald Smith was born in 1820, the year of George III's death, and arrived in Canada within months of Queen Victoria's accession, while the odd soldier who had fought under Wolfe or Montcalm on the Plains of Abraham still tottered along the streets of Quebec. He died in his ninety-fourth year on the eve of the First World War. His crowded lifetime spanned Canada's evolution from wilderness to urbanization. He headed west when the buffalo still roamed the plains, and died just before tanks rolled into the fields of France.

It was an astonishing life of significant tenures:

75 years with the HBC
42 years with the Bank of Montreal
32 years with the CPR
23 years with the St Paul Railway
18 years as Canada's High Commissioner in London
18 years in the Parliament of Canada
15 years as president of Royal Trust
6 years as chairman of Burmah Oil and Anglo-Persian Oil
4 years in the Manitoba Legislature.

Smith of course held most of these positions simultaneously. He had the knack of switching from one business to another, from yet another enterprise to politics and back again, without any derailment of consecutive thought or action. In 1905, for example, he was at one and the same time Governor of the Hudson's Bay Company, president of the Bank of Montreal, director and executive committee member of the Canadian Pacific Railway, president of Royal Trust, Canada's High Commissioner to Britain, chairman of Burmah Oil and the Anglo-Persian Oil Company, all the while remaining a major influence in Canadian and British public affairs and masterminding recruiting efforts in Europe to populate the Prairies. Not that 1905 was a particularly busy year—and he was eighty-five at the time.

Smith's compulsion to increase his wealth and expand his power when he already possessed a surfeit of both baffled and disturbed his supporters and critics alike. His contemporaries shared a sense of disquieting inevitability about Smith's amazing career. Considerable as they were, his accomplishments seemed less man-made than imposed by a force of nature. He was like the first rain of a monsoon season: nothing much could stop or pacify him.

Thomas Wilson, one of his many political opponents, best summed up the puzzle of Smith's obsession when he demanded, during a Manitoba by-election campaign: "Who is Smith? What is Smith? Is the palladium of our destinies to be entrusted to a Smith? What has a Smith done that he should seek to grasp the Ark of the Covenant with the one hand and with the other wrestle for the sceptre of the Almighty? Smith! Why, Smith is not a name, but an occupation!"

UNLIKE THE CHRONICLES of most public individuals, Donald Alexander Smith's life and times were impossible to separate. He so frequently advanced his career along with whatever historical forces he happened to be commanding or diverting at the time that he eventually stopped differentiating between his personal ambitions and the national interest. In his mental calculations these diverse objectives could be joined in a singular path: his own.

That intuitive leap had curious consequences. It meant that while at the beginning of his career Smith was driven by the same devils that push any self-respecting swashbuckler, he eventually came to see himself as an instrument of the national will, convinced that his personal success and the nation's destiny were inextricably linked. He failed to recognize any conflict of interest between the public good and his private benefit. According to this self-imposed credo, the consequences of his decisions could flow either way, there seldom being any difference in the spelling of the name of their ultimate beneficiary.

At first glance, this monumentally self-centred view of the world appears to collide with the fact that during most of his life Smith sought to advance the estate and well-being of the Hudson's Bay Company. Not necessarily. For many years Smith was the largest individual shareholder of the Company, so there was in this, as in his other endeavours, little absence of common cause.

Not only did Smith hypnotize himself into following such dubious logic but others began to believe it too. McGill historian John Macnaughton wrote of Smith in his later years: "That old man was Canada. In him, the whole history of our country, from the mink-trap and birch-bark canoe, down to the grain-elevator and ocean-liner, lived and breathed and moved and walked about ..."

Smith's egotistical approach was not unusual for his day. "God helps those who help themselves" was less an anachronistic cliché than an eleventh commandment. The myth, perpetuated in the simple-minded Horatio Alger books of the late nineteenth century (really one book rewritten a hundred times over), that thrift and hard work secured wealth, which in turn guaranteed virtue and godliness, had ignited the ambitions of a generation. Since it was clearly God's design that the virtuous become wealthy, to gain riches meant gaining Divine Sanction. Anything to be nearer, my God, to Thee.

Having thus created his own fiscal universe and a self-sustaining ethic to go with it, Smith seemed genuinely puzzled when he was accused of bribery and corruption. He wished to be remembered as a man who had never sinned and indeed had been intrinsically incapable of sinning. Yet he virtually invented insider trading, and double-crossed both his political allies and one-time HBC comrades in the field. He regarded his House of Commons seat as a patriotic trust and refused to accept his Member's salary. But he was tossed out of Parliament for bribing voters, and the success of his syndicates depended directly on bribing politicians. As the British social historian Jan Morris noted, "All his life Smith was attended by a detectable aura of double-dealing ... he was ... without many principles but admirably resourceful."

Even in an age when the slightest evidence of business ethics was considered a sign of dotage, Smith's juggling of loyalties was breathtaking in its scope and audacity, outrageous in its absence of accountability or sound auditing practices. "Apart from their illegibility, Smith's letters reveal a man preoccupied with politics, railways, steamboats, furs, and lands—in that order," concluded Alan Wilson, who studied Smith's surviving correspondence. "Many of his reports would appall a modern business practitioner by their lack of sufficient data, of attention to detail and sufficiently regular review.... For one who had close relations with some of Canada's leading bankers, he had a curious distaste for accountancy in his own administration."

That careless approach to detail was hardly startling. When the burden of a nation's future rests upon one's shoulders, who has time for balance-sheet trifles? The notion of an individual personifying a civilization now seems bizarre in any context outside an insane asylum. Yet in Victorian times the idea was not that preposterous. Those who, like Smith, subscribed to the efficacy of the British Empire—and it then ruled a quarter of the world—saw the expanding arc of their authority as a means of elevating mankind. Smith believed that immigrants hailing from anywhere in the British Isles were endowed with a very special mission. It was perhaps best described by the Earl of Carnarvon, a Secretary of State for the Colonies, who mused that in the far reaches of the Empire there were "races struggling to emerge into civilization.... To them it is our part to give wise laws, good government, and a well-ordered finance.... This is ... the true strength and meaning of imperialism."

The concepts of parliamentary government, the value of gentlemen's clubs, fiscal stability, free trade, chivalry, Rudyard Kipling and the supremacy of the Royal Navy were all part of Smith's gospel. Canadian reaction to his imperialistic sermons was divided into predictably opposing viewpoints. Canadian nationalists of the time—a minority, then as now—believed this message was nonsense, that their burgeoning new country could find strength and identity only by cutting its cross-Atlantic apron-strings. The young nation's business and political Establishments preached just as fiercely that the only way for Canada to attain international stature was to expand the British link by gaining influence within the empire's highest councils. Despite his Scottish origins and Presbyterian roots, Smith was an acknowledged leader of the second faction, behaving like a born-again Anglophile yet being fiercely (if somewhat patronizingly) proud of his rarefied brand of Canadianism.

Constantly cultivating the reclusion of a great man in the service of an all-consuming mission, Smith was stubbornly uncommunicative in an age when business tycoons pranced across front pages, dispensing avuncular advice and dropping marginally relevant comments. Smith stayed mum. He knew how to wait and he had a nose for power. Whatever nefarious fiction (or truth) might be written or repeated about him, he realized how valuable it was to allow legends to marinate undisturbed—that however useful a reply might be, silence was even better. He destroyed nearly all his early papers and was seldom interviewed. He managed almost always to take the credit for his achievements without bearing the burden of his failures. "There were always others willing to accept the responsibility," noted W.T.R. Preston. "He developed his power in this direction into a science. He never allowed himself to show resentment. So far as possible he avoided arousing thoughts of reprisals in the hearts of his opponents. However the end might justify the means, the reason for the means was not in evidence—his hand was never visible."

Portentous and solemn, terminally obscurantist in his manner of speech, Smith, as one contemporary observer put it, kept "his own counsel, his sixpences, the Sabbath, and everything else he could lay his hands on." George Stephen, first president of the CPR and his closest business associate for forty-eight years, once confided to a friend about Smith: "What a strange creature he is, so Indian-like in his love of mystery and secretiveness." Smith was obsessive about not committing incriminating facts to paper. Even though he and Stephen spent most of a half-century cutting the youthful Dominion's important business deals, nearly went bankrupt together, and ultimately fathered Montreal's essential philanthropies, Smith wrote Stephen few letters, preferring to discuss important issues personally, even if it meant crossing the Atlantic to do so.

Because the first three decades of his career were spent in the Labrador wilderness, cut off from the events in which he longed to play a part, Smith developed a need for self-assertion that never left him. But instead of signalling what he was doing through public displays or pronouncements, he simply acted and allowed others to catch up with him if they could. His formative years, insulated from the kind of lively discourse that prepared men for the anterooms of power, led Smith to distrust words, written or spoken. He developed a sense of boldness that required no validation from others. If there was one quality that characterized everything he said and did, it was aversion to revealing his innermost feelings. "He loved the solitude of a crowd, a privacy of mild light, from which he shone benevolently on all alike and upon no one in particular," wrote Professor Macnaughton, who also noted that "his really fine manners" were "more impenetrable and isolating in their lubricant defensiveness than crocodile's scales."

Smith's appearance helped create the air of some enigmatic Old Testament prophet who spoke in public so seldom that his occasional pronouncements were given more weight than they deserved. His imperturbable composure served him well during financial negotiations. Because Smith was photographed only after he left Labrador, the record of his physical aspect is almost entirely that of his later years—grey-bearded, tall and slight, elegant yet wiry, all bone and gristle at a time when distended bellies were regarded as a sign of affluence. His body language was a lexicon of military precision, but his most marked physical features were those bristling eyebrows, hiding eyes of feral flint. His sight had been injured early by snow blindness and the intensity of his gaze lent his glance a telescopic effect. One of his characteristic gestures was to turn his hands outward, showing the insides of his wrists, then to lean forward in a semi-bow that granted others in the room permission to speak—without having uttered a word himself. Whenever he did condescend to say something, there was little head-nodding for emphasis and nary a quiver in his meticulously trimmed beard. He lacked any flash of wit or mischief and left the task of abusing his enemies to underlings.

His solemn manner and demand for unquestioning obedience had their roots in instincts Smith acquired during his sojourn in Labrador. It was there that he learned to husband his energies and ration his emotions; survival often required both. Compliance with orders was equally important because dereliction of duty, however minor, could place human life at risk. The stern code of behaviour implanted during those formative years never left him. Work, to Smith, was less an occupation than a compulsion; his operational code was the maxim: "To rest is to rust."

THE KEY TO UNDERSTANDING Donald Alexander Smith is the Scottishness of the man—Scottish to the marrow of his soul, despite his English airs and Canadian domicile. Like all good Scots, he knew how to maximize the authority of pursed lips and disapproving glances, how to parlay endurance into salvation, and, above all, how to fight.

The Scottish clans had always been fighters—against the Romans, the Anglo-Saxons, the Danes, the Anglo-Normans, the English—and, when there was no one else to fight, one another.* Scottish soldiers served as mercenaries

---

* Of the Scottish clan wars, Andrew Strome Carmichael-Galloway, Bannerman to the 30th Chief of the name, has noted that there were MacDonalds and Campbells who hated one another in the west; Armstrongs and Carmichaels who hated one another in the south; Mackays and Gunns who hated one another in the north; Lindsays and Ogilvies who hated one another in the east; MacGregors in the centre whom everybody hated, and Douglases who hated everybody everywhere.

of French kings, German princes and Scandinavian knights, and provided the human cannon fodder used in the defence of the wilder margins of the British Empire. "Scotland's history," the noted military writer John Keegan has observed, "is bloody with battles ... and her national heroes ... are men of the sword. The military ingredient of Scottish life goes deeper than that. For to the Scots ... war has been something of a national industry."

That bellicose nature was a useful trait Smith and his fellow Highlanders enlisted in the service of the Hudson's Bay Company. Sparse of speech but swift in action, they had temperaments perfectly suited to the fur trade—the meld of perseverance and self-sufficiency, of endurance and courage that Donald Smith epitomized so perfectly. It was their gravity of demeanour and curiously rolling gait, their gloomy cast of countenance and habit of being close with money and emotions—their determination that even moments of pleasure or splendour must appear accidental—that was the Scottish way.* Scotsmen like Smith embraced the burden of hard work as Calvinism's earthly path to salvation. They were theological hybrids—Presbyterian Jesuits who believed that a fixed dose of piety could be exchanged for a prescribed sprinkling of grace.†

With all that self-righteousness burning inside him, Smith could never forgive himself for having taken up with Isabella Hardisty, then another man's wife. It had happened in Labrador under perfectly understandable circumstances, and his own marriage to Isabella lasted sixty-one years, but the whispers never let up. As late as 1888, two decades after Smith had left the North, Sir Henry Tyler, president of the Grand Trunk Railway, confided to Lady Tyler that Smith's "wife is said to have another husband." Smith grew so desperate to quell such rumours that at nearly every important juncture of his career, he remarried Isabella—no fewer than four times.

An equally serious source of guilt was Smith's sly betrayal of his fellow fur traders. Although he had been one of their number for most of three decades

* "The Scots," observed R.B. Cunninghame Graham, one of their wittier essayists, "fornicate gravely but without conviction."
† Scottish puritanism knew few limits. Canadian novelist Hugh MacLennan recalled that Sir William Dawson, the renowned Scottish-educated geologist who became principal of McGill University in 1855, once led fifty-seven other members of the congregation out of the Presbyterian church on Montreal's Stanley Street when the minister dared install an organ. The choir had previously used only a tuning-fork to pitch their hymns, and Dawson was convinced that the new musical instrument would sully the austere purity of the service.

and they had entrusted him with their savings and with representing their case for better working conditions to the London board, Smith instead struck a deal that allowed the Company to acquire for next to nothing the traders' legitimate 40-percent share of profits. The once proud partners were reduced to ill-paid employees, shut out from revenues generated by sale of the land they and their predecessors had claimed and protected for two centuries.

All in all, Donald Alexander Smith may have been the most intriguing rogue in Canadian commercial history—a distinction that covers a lot of territory. Certainly, he was the most successful.

Growing Up Cold

"A man who has been frozen and roasted by turns every year must be the tougher for it, if he survive it at all." —Donald A. Smith

DONALD SMITH'S PEREMPTORY ARROGANCE was particularly galling to those aware of his inconspicuous beginnings. He was born on August 6, 1820, at Forres, a storied Scottish trading town in that brooding countryside where Shakespeare's Macbeth and Banquo encountered the prophetic trio of witches. One of three sons and three daughters, he was much less influenced by his father, a shopkeeper clinging to solvency with alcoholic indecision, than by his mother, Barbara Stuart, the feisty and admirable Highland dame who brought up the family.* "Her voice was low, and she disliked loud noises," her son remembered. "She set great store by courtesy and good manners, and our bonnets were always off in her presence. She insisted on scrupulous cleanliness in house, person, and apparel, and herself set an example of perfect neatness in dress." Among other things, she taught young Donald to recite metrical versions of the Psalms then popular in Scotland, one of which he repeated "without error, pause or confusion" on his deathbed.

While his elder brother attended the University of Aberdeen and studied medicine at Edinburgh (he became a doctor on the northwest frontier with the East India Company and a major in the Army Medical Corps), young Donald was articled to Robert Watson, Town Clerk of Forres. He spent most

---

*Alexander Smith, the father, was a brother of George Stephen's mother; Barbara Smart was a Grant on her mother's side, distantly related to Cuthbert Grant, the Métis leader who staged the massacre at Seven Oaks. (See Chapter 22.)

of his time hand-copying documents, but apprenticing to succeed Watson was far too humdrum a prospect to enlist his energies or talents. He was much more excited by the arrival on retirement leave of his mother's brother John Stuart, a doughty former Nor'Wester who had been second-in-command during Simon Fraser's daring exploration of the Fraser River in 1808 and later served as a Chief Factor with the HBC. Stuart promised to recommend the youngster to George Simpson, the HBC's all-powerful overseas Governor, and Donald set out on foot from Forres to Aberdeen, where he caught a London-bound schooner. Armed with his uncle's letters of introduction to Simpson and other influential Montrealers, Smith sailed for North America on May 16, 1838, aboard the *Royal William*, a 500-ton timber-trade windjammer. Just before leaving, Smith wrote to his mother, breathlessly enumerating the wonders of the British capital: "I have already visited the West End of town, walking all the way from the Mansion House, where the Lord Mayor resides, to Hyde Park, where the aristocracy are to be seen riding and driving…. Here the trees and flowers are a good month in advance of ours in Scotland, or at least in Forres. Had I been in the Park an hour later or earlier, I should have been rewarded by the spectacle of Her Majesty. The Queen and the Duchess of Kent, her mother, drive every day, I am told; so I shall hope to enjoy the privilege."

Much of Smith's fifty-day voyage was spent studying the only reference book aboard, Francis Evans's *The Emigrant's Directory and Guide*, which stuffily advised: "Canada is a country where immigrants should not expect to eat the bread of idleness, but where they may expect what is more worthy to be demonstrated as happiness—the comfortable fruits of industry." Smith landed in Montreal at a time when nationalist stirrings had reached their culmination in the Papineau rebellion, and his vessel passed the steamer *Canada*, carrying the last of the Patriotes of the 1837 uprising to Bermudan exile. British North America then had a population of 1.2 million, with most of the lands north and west of what is now Ontario belonging to "The Governor and Company of Adventurers of England Tradeing into Hudsons Bay." Montreal was a crude bush settlement numbering scarcely 30,000 inhabitants, its only patch of sidewalk being in front of the Cathedral of Notre Dame. On dry days, blinding limestone-powdered wind eddies made walking difficult, while rain turned the streets of the hilly town into mudslides that made getting about all but impossible. McGill College consisted of a medical faculty staffed by only two part-time professors.

Smith walked upriver to Lachine, where Simpson administered the Hudson's Bay Company's 170 trading posts, scattered not only across the Prairies to the Pacific but also down to the Oregon Country, through half a dozen future American states, south to San Francisco, and as far west as Hawaii. The young Scot was hired at "£20 and found" a year and assigned to counting muskrat skins in the Company warehouse.*

The initial drudgery in the Lachine warehouse was a useful lesson for Smith in learning how to differentiate the various qualities of pelts, and he soon graduated from muskrat to grading beaver, marten, mink and otter, learning to judge the value of a silver fox by the number of white hairs in its glossy patina. Buoyed by his uncle's introductions, he spent a memorable evening mingling with some of Montreal's leading citizens, including his host, the international financier Edward Ellice, HBC Arctic explorer Peter Warren Dease, Duncan Finlayson, then about to leave for his new assignment as Governor of Assiniboia at Fort Garry, and Peter McGill, chairman of the Champlain and St Lawrence Railroad and president of the Bank of Montreal. The Forres apprentice would leave Lachine soon afterwards and not return to Montreal permanently for another thirty years, but the memory of the sweet adrenalin of social acceptance he had experienced that brief magic evening never left him.

The circumstances of Smith's departure remain mysterious. One version involves Frances Simpson, the Governor's vivacious wife, twenty-six years younger than a husband who spent most of his time away on inspection tours. According to a fellow apprentice, the lonely Mrs. Simpson, who "took a friendly interest in the 'indentured young gentlemen'… was attracted by the simplicity and gentle address of the new-comer's manners."

---

* At the time, apprentice-clerks worked five-year terms at a gradually increasing salary that culminated at £50 in the final twelve months. If their records were acceptable, they could then sign up for another five years at £75. A third contract with a £100 maximum was offered to the best of them, followed, after a total of at least fifteen years of loyal and efficient service, by a chance to be promoted to a Chief Trader's and, eventually, Chief Factor's commission. These two ranks were eligible for shares in the Company's annual profits that ranged as high as £2,000. Retired commissioned officers received half-pay for seven years. All HBC personnel were granted free board but had to buy such basic goods as soap and boots from Company stores, at a one-third discount. They were responsible for providing their own bedding and room furniture. Typical yearly food rations consisted of 240 pounds of flour, 20 pounds of tea, 120 pounds of sugar, 10 pounds of raisins, and 5 pounds of coffee or cocoa per person. Their annual liquor allowance was two gallons each of sherry, port, brandy, rum, Scotch whisky, and all the lime juice they could drink.

They seem to have enjoyed an innocent flirtation, the odd boating excursion on Lake St Louis and several cups of tea. Harmless it may have been, but the Governor was not amused. He called Smith into his office soon after his return and was heard shouting that he was not about to endure "any upstart, quill-driving apprentices dangling about a parlour reserved to the nobility and gentry." Smith was abruptly banished to the Company's career purgatory, the King's Posts district at Tadoussac.

Owned by the French Crown before 1760 and mainly by British monarchs thereafter, the seven tiny trading locations had been leased in 1830 by the HBC, which also rented the more easterly Seigniory of Mingan. Trade was slow because most of the territory had been beavered out and the Company did not enjoy the monopoly there it had elsewhere. Assignment to the region was regarded as an unwelcome alternative to being fired.

Tadoussac itself was one of the oldest trading points in North America; this was where Jacques Cartier had obtained his furs in 1535. Summers were cool and damp, the winters bitterly windy; nothing disturbed the rugged, sterile geography—certainly not the huddle of huts in the hollow of a mountain without even the presumption of a stockade, near the confluence of the broad St Lawrence and the deep Saguenay. That was the Tadoussac of Smith's initial assignment. He spent seven of his most unhappy and unproductive years in the area, trading principally for fox, marten and sable pelts with the Montagnais Indians, who paddled down annually from the Quebec-Labrador plateau. "You would have to travel the whole world over to find a greater contrast to the Scotch than these same Indians," the young trader wrote home. "If civilisation consists in frugality and foresight, then the Montagnais are far worse than dogs, who at least have sense enough to bury a bone against an evil day. In some of their lodges even before winter has properly begun their rations have come to an end. Everything about the place has been swallowed that can be swallowed, and starvation stares them in the face. They stalk in the tracks of a solitary caribou, and in their excitement forget their own hunger, but this does not make their families forget theirs. The caribou eludes them. They wander farther afield and at length bring down a bear. They cut him up and return to find their families dying or dead, which is what happened last month near Manwan Lake."

Smith tried to keep his spirits up by reading such classics as Plutarch's *Lives* and Benjamin Franklin's *Correspondence*, but often he found himself scanning every line of outdated copies of the Montreal *Gazette* and Quebec

Mercury left behind by travellers. At this point he also suffered a strange "second sight" experience, dreaming that Margaret, his favourite sister, on a sickbed in Forres, was muttering "Donald! Oh, Donald" with her dying breath. Letters that reached him later revealed she had indeed died, of smallpox, on January 12, 1841, at the very hour, allowing for difference in longitude, of Smith's nightmare.

Eventually placed in charge of Mingan, the most remote of the King's Posts (opposite North Point on Anticosti Island) and an even more dreary locale than Tadoussac, Smith incurred the wrath of Simpson, who arrived for a surprise inspection in the summer of 1845. The post's account books, which to Simpson were the Company's secular bibles, were far from satisfactory. Following his visit, the Governor sent the young clerk this devastating assessment: "Your counting house department appeared to me, in a very slovenly condition, so much so that I could make very little of any document that came under my notice. Your schemes of outfits were really curiously perplexing, and such as I trust I may never see again, while letters, invoices and accounts were to be found tossing about as wastepaper in almost every room in the house ... if you were but to give a few hours a week to the arrangement of your papers your business would be in a very different state to that in which I found it."*

Smith hoped to redeem himself by submitting a neater set of accounts the following season, but on September 29, 1846, his house burned down. He had been briefly away on an errand, and one of his assistants had salvaged most of his belongings. With the Company records destroyed, Smith turned so despondent that he descended into a highly uncharacteristic public display of anger and frustration. According to eyewitnesses, he danced around the still-burning pyre of the tiny post, feeding the flames with his clothes and private papers, cackling incoherently: "Let them go, too, if the Company's goods have gone!"

The following winter he suffered from snow blindness and feared he might become permanently sightless without medical attention. Not bothering to wait for official permission, he boarded the HBC's Montreal-bound supply ship *Marten* and reported his condition to Simpson. The Governor immediately

---

* Smith's successors at the various King's Posts where he had kept the books had similar complaints, and the originals in the HBC Archives are scrawled with frustrated notations such as "Hang Donald S.!" or "Damn Donald Smith, I cannot make head or tail of this!" But there is evidence that Smith, rather than being careless, was beginning to exercise his penchant for secrecy and that the accounts were kept in a code to which he alone had the key.

ordered an eye examination. When the attending physician found no clinical problem, Simpson accused his clerk of malingering, then interrupted his catalogue of Smith's perfidies in mid-flight to offer him another chance.

It was not a typical Simpson gambit. Smith had now been with the Company most of a decade. He was twenty-eight and had done little to distinguish himself. Yet Simpson must have sensed a potential in the intense but sensitive young Scot that Smith himself probably didn't recognize. At the time, the HBC was busy trying to revive its Labrador district, partly to counter competing freebooters moving in from Newfoundland and also to prevent nomadic Indians from evading their Company debts as they migrated from one post to the next.

Simpson's business acumen was attracted by that mammoth, frigid Labrador peninsula for precisely the reason no sane man wanted to go there. For its latitude, it was the coldest place on earth. Mercury froze in thermometers. Snow fell early and deep; it stayed so long that winter stretched over nine months. To survive in that harsh climate, animals had to grow extra thick, tight pelts that fetched premium prices at the HBC's London auction house. As early as 1828, a Company trader named William Hendry had sailed up the Ungava coast from Moose Factory in James Bay as far as Richmond Gulf and explored an overland route into Ungava Bay. Two years later, Nicol Finlayson established Fort Chimo about thirty miles above where the Koksoak River flows into Ungava Bay. There he waited twenty months for the local Naskapi to appear. When they finally did, Finlayson described them as "the most suspicious and faithless set of Indians I ever had to deal with ... they must be sharply dealt with before they are properly domesticated." The primitive tribe, then numbering less than three hundred, suffered from having no internal political structure—no chiefs, no social organization larger than the family, no ritual ceremonies to facilitate trade, no formal alliances with any other groups. They were subsistence hunters, living off migrating caribou, and it was mainly their addiction to the HBC's rum and tobacco that prompted them to become trappers. As trade expanded, Simpson opened Fort Nascopie on the northwest arm of Lake Petitsikapau (near present-day Schefferville) and purchased from some Quebec merchants their post at North West River on Esquimaux Bay (now known as Lake Melville) about halfway up the eastern Labrador coast.

Just before Smith came to Lachine with his eye problem, word had reached Simpson that Chief Trader William Nourse, then in charge of that faraway region, had been incapacitated and badly needed medical attention. The

Governor directed the "malingering" Smith to leave immediately at the head of an emergency winter relief party to North West River. Although he had come out of the bush seeking solace for bruised eyes and for an even more seriously damaged ego, Smith now found himself with a challenging option. The bristle of his Scottish nature had been touched: if Simpson was mean enough to issue such an order, Donald Smith was too proud not to obey it. Accompanied by a young HBC clerk named James Grant and three Iroquois boatmen, Smith accomplished the thousand-mile journey in record time, almost starving to death along the way and being lost for extended periods in snowstorms. It was the toughest physical ordeal of his life. Years later he refused to dwell on the details, though it is known that two additional Indian guides hired along the way starved to death.

Once in Labrador, Smith found Nourse paralysed, the victim of a serious stroke. While Grant stationed himself at North West River, Smith took temporary charge of the smaller but more strategically located post at nearby Rigolet. The North West River station (near modern-day Goose Bay airport) was tucked into a clearing on the shore of a 110-mile-deep salt-water gash in the frowning eminence of the unexplored Labrador coast, with mountain ranges rolling out of both horizons. Rigolet sat nearer the Atlantic, at the mouth of the rocky gorge that joined Hamilton Inlet to Esquimaux Bay. The unpredictable riptides of those treacherous narrows had already claimed many an over-confident vessel, including the British man-of-war *Cleopatra*. Smith placed the gravely ill Nourse aboard the annual supply ship, and by September his successor, Chief Trader Richard Hardisty, had arrived from Montreal. Smith was promptly relegated to his earlier rank of clerk, though he was delighted to welcome his new superior and especially his accompanying family. Hardisty, who had served in Wellington's army as an ordnance officer in the Peninsular campaign and the Battle of Waterloo, came to Labrador accompanied by his Mixed Blood wife (Margaret Sutherland) and their lively daughters, Isabella, Mary and Charlotte.*

---

* Each of Richard Hardisty's six sons joined the HBC, with varying degrees of career success. The best known of the sextet was his namesake Richard, who rose to the rank of Inspecting Chief Factor and in 1888 was appointed the first senator for the old Northwest Territories, representing the district of Alberta. Richard's granddaughter Isabella, known as Belle, married James Lougheed, himself named to the Senate for the Northwest Territories in 1889 and knighted in 1916. One of Senator Lougheed's grandsons, Peter Lougheed, was the longtime premier of Alberta.

While the Hardisty family moved inland to live at North West River, Smith remained at Rigolet. Under his direction, the little station became more than the mother post's maritime outlet. He met head-on the marauding free traders who were attempting to lure the Naskapi to their shore trading posts, ranging far back into the fur country to finalize his trades and claim *de facto* exclusivity over a territory outside the HBC's Charter.

Though he could move fast on snowshoes, Smith acquired few of the proficiencies of frontier life. He was a terrible shot, attempting to down birds by firing without first taking the trouble to aim, and there is a record of his bagging a lone wolf which he noted proudly in a letter to his mother. He never learned to ride, though he introduced the first horses to Labrador, and could not properly handle a canoe. He very nearly drowned when a kayak he was attempting to paddle overturned after only a few yards. "I went straight home and took a glass of wine," he later recalled, confessing, "the only time, by the way, I ever tasted liquor by myself." Yet he could be brave, too, and when the *Marten*, sailing out of Rigolet, ran aground, he personally commanded the rescue boats that saved cargo and passengers—though not the captain, who committed suicide rather than face the wrath of the HBC Governor.

By the autumn of 1850, Smith was writing letters directly to Simpson, not exactly disparaging Hardisty's efforts but clearly implying that the Company might expect better returns from the district if a younger Chief Trader from, say, Forres, were in charge. For his part, Hardisty seemed genuinely impressed with Smith, recommending him to Simpson at every turn. These exchanges produced results in 1851, when Hardisty requested permission to leave Labrador on furlough the following year. As soon as it was agreed that Smith would temporarily replace the older man (though still in his rank of clerk), he grew bolder in his criticisms. He wrote to Simpson that Hardisty was much more suited to a great inland post than to the actively competitive Labrador situation and criticized the Chief Trader for not seizing the local commerce more energetically. He openly attacked Hardisty's slackness in the face of increasingly vicious competition and criticized his plans for diverting staff and funds to improve some of the local Company posts. None of this backbiting seemed to disturb Hardisty. "He is all fire, and indefatigable in his endeavours to promote the interests of the Company," he wrote to Simpson about Smith, "and having a thorough knowledge of the business carried on in this district, I consider him in every respect competent to succeed me...."

On July 8, 1852, only four years after arriving in Labrador, Smith was formally promoted to commissioned rank and placed in charge of the Esquimaux Bay District. "I have much confidence in your energy and desire to turn the business to good account," Simpson wrote, adding an important codicil, "but trust you will adopt a greater degree of regularity and system than characterized your management at Mingan. You no doubt remember that on my visit to that place while you were in charge, I had occasion to note what appeared to me a want of method and punctuality in your household arrangements, as well as in the shipping office business. I now revert to this matter in the most friendly spirit with a view to putting you on your guard against a repetition of such a ground of complaint which in your present more important charge might be productive of greater injury...." Smith took the admonition under advisement and moved out of the barren clapboard hut at Rigolet to the much grander Chief Trader's residence at North West River, which boasted a winter fireplace and a summer veranda.

The senior Hardistys departed alone. Their youngest daughter, Charlotte, had recently died, while Mary had wed an HBC clerk named Joseph McPherson and moved away to Kibokok, a small post northwest of Rigolet. Isabella, who was twenty-three when she first arrived in Labrador, had shortly afterwards married James Grant, Smith's companion on the long overland trek from Montreal. Because there were no clergy in that empty place, the ceremony was performed by the bride's father. He had no official authority to do so since he was neither a clergyman nor sanctioned to perform marriages by his HBC commission because Labrador lay outside the Company's Charter territory. Such country marriages were routinely performed by anyone or no one, requiring only the consent of the couple involved. James and Isabella had a son named James Hardisty Grant in 1850 but shortly afterwards separated when, as Donald Smith explained, Isabella's husband exercised "no command of his passions." Just before Richard Hardisty left Labrador, Isabella and Smith decided to marry and went through an informal ceremony on March 9, 1853. The presiding official at that wedding was none other than the groom himself. Smith later claimed that he had been appointed a lay preacher by the Governor of Newfoundland and thereby had properly sanctioned Isabella's first real wedding (to himself), making an ostentatious fuss about the illegitimacy of her previous match.

The following year saw the arrival of Margaret Charlotte, Isabella and Donald's only child. To everyone's embarrassment, including his own, James

Grant remained at the post another two years. Smith did his best to undermine his rival's career, complaining to Simpson that young Grant "has [very] much to learn before becoming an experienced trader, his long residence at North West River having been anything but advantageous to him, as while there he had little or nothing to do with the trade, and literally got no insight into the manner of keeping accounts which beyond a blotter or an invoice, he was rarely, if ever, permitted to see." In the same letter he lied to the Governor about his own romantic involvement: "It is just possible these remarks might lead to the supposition that I myself have been an unsuccessful suitor, but the case is so far otherwise that up to the present time I have not been so presumptious [sic] as to aspire to the hand of any fair lady."*

It took Smith seven years to acknowledge his marriage in correspondence with Simpson. Even then he referred to having wed a "Miss Hardisty" rather than any "Mrs. Grant." Although it was a routine event in the bush ethic of the time, the episode was magnified and made infinitely more wicked by the rub of Donald Smith's Presbyterian conscience—a flexible instrument that failed to censor some of his far more questionable pecuniary ploys.

DURING HIS TWENTY YEARS in Labrador, Smith developed the cold insensibility that allowed him to betray political and business associates at will. The pressures that made him one of the most frigid, class-conscious aristocrats of his era had their origins here in Smith's lonely treks through the boreal wilds of Labrador, apparently forgotten by the glittering world he had barely glimpsed before his exile. He never admitted that there might have been a dramatic event to blame for his bitter turn of spirit. All he would say was that Labrador had toughened him. ("A man who has been frozen and roasted by turns every year must be the tougher for it, if he survive it at all.")

The Naskapi who traded in Smith's territory experienced grave difficulty adapting their lives and seasonal cycles to the white man's requirements. Their main source of food was the enormous herds of caribou migrating semi-annually across their turf. The Naskapi had to stalk the animals through deep snow, which required infinite patience and great skill—until, of course, the

---

* James Grant left Labrador and the HBC in 1855, moved to New York, remarried, and became a successful stockbroker. His son with Isabella used Smith's name and was mentioned in Smith's will, but when the family left Labrador, he lived apart from their household.

local HBC posts supplied them with guns and powder. These made the hunt relatively simple: so simple, in fact, that the old skills were quickly lost, and the hunters soon could not survive without weapons. Their independence had been broken. "Because the HBC controlled the supply of ammunition," the late Dr Alan Cooke of the Hochelaga Institute pointed out, "the Naskapis were obliged to spend part of their time trapping furs, mainly marten, whether or not they preferred to hunt caribou. When they abandoned their traditional techniques of hunting caribou for the new technology of guns and ammunition, they gave themselves into the traders' hands. There was no return."

The Naskapi were further endangered because the marten-trapping and caribou-hunting seasons coincided. The marten is one of the few woods animals that carries almost no edible meat, so the Indians were caught in a vicious circle: they could hunt caribou—their sustaining food supply—with guns and ammunition that the traders would provide only if they turned in good marten skins. But they couldn't keep themselves alive long enough to trap the pelts because that diverted them from pursuing the caribou. This dilemma could be avoided if the local HBC trader was understanding and advanced them the necessary ammunition, assuming that over several seasons he would come out ahead. (One such Company clerk, Henry Connolly, himself part Indian, did just that and found himself reprimanded for having been too generous in his allotments.)

During the winter of 1843, three families of Naskapi numbering twenty souls starved to death within sight of the HBC's Fort Nascopie, then managed by Donald Henderson. Three winters later, three dozen more Naskapi died, and in the winter of 1848 there was mass starvation in the area. Most of this was caused by Henderson's denial of enough ammunition to the local hunters. Henderson eventually left the service; but word of the disaster had spread, and Simpson demanded an explanation. As Alan Cooke observed: "Indians starving to death was, of course, regrettable, but the loss of hunters in a sparsely populated region that produced valuable furs was a serious matter.... During the space of six years, a 'proud' and 'independent' population of 276 persons had been reduced to about 166, with what hardship, misery and sorrow, and with what effects on family and social life no one today can imagine or understand."

These tragic events at Fort Nascopie had taken place before Smith's arrival, but there is evidence that he was directly involved in the subsequent famines of the mid-1850s, the worst of them all. For one thing, it was well-documented knowledge within the service that "no matter how poor the post might be, Donald Smith always showed a balance on the right side of the ledger." At this time he was trying to make the best possible impression on Sir George Simpson and his principals in London by maximizing fur returns at any cost. During the 1857 deliberations of a British Parliamentary Select Committee studying the HBC, a letter was tabled that former Chief Trader William Kennedy had received from a Company clerk at Mingan. "Starvation has, I learn, committed great havoc among your old friends, the Nascopies, numbers of whom met their death from want last winter; whole camps of them were found dead, without one survivor to tell the tale of their sufferings; others sustained life in a way most revolting, as [sic] using as food the dead bodies of their companions; some even bled their children to death, and sustained life with their bodies!" In another undated note, Kennedy's correspondent stated that "a great number of Indians starved to death last winter, and _____ says it was _____'s fault in not giving them enough ammunition." Since these blanks appeared in the Committee's final report, Smith's name was not officially linked with this harrowing episode, but he was in charge of the region at the time, and because of the very tight control he maintained over trade expenditures, it is not unreasonable to assume that the famine, which wiped out so many lives, was his direct responsibility.

Smith's own reminiscences of Labrador mention few specific Indians; the natives were simply there, like trees or the wind. As the HBC's Chief Trader, he was North West River's community leader and that often meant medical duties as well. He achieved modest success treating wounds with a pulp made from the boiled inner bark of juniper trees, a method authenticated by Lord Lister, who introduced the principles of antiseptics to surgery in 1865.*

At night, the vast Labrador stillness was interrupted only by the hoot of a hungry owl, the subdued yelp of a dreaming dog or, during spring breakup, the thud and groan of heaving ice. Smith stayed up late, writing to his mother, reporting on each day's events even though his letters could be sent out only once a year via the HBC's supply ship. That vessel also brought Smith annually from London issues of *The Times*, which he carefully perused over breakfast— each newspaper exactly one year after publication. On Sundays he held religious services with his household, HBC staff, and a dozen or two Indians as the

---

* Fifty years later, Smith, now Lord Strathcona, delivered a lecture on his primitive but effective techniques to medical students at Middlesex Hospital in London.

congregation. "To-day we all assembled for prayers in Mrs. Smith's parlour—every mother's son scrubbed and brushed up to the nth—even old Sam, who looked positively saint-like with a far-away expression, although he was probably only counting the flies which were buzzing on the windowpane," one of Smith's clerks later recalled. "We sang three hymns, I coming out particularly strong in the Doxology."

To provide his family with a proper diet, Smith sent to the Orkney Islands for hardy seed grains, poultry, and cattle and to Quebec for horses, sheep, goats, and an ox. On seven painstakingly cleared acres, fertilized by fish offal, he grew cucumbers, pumpkins, potatoes, and peas, ripening more fragile fruits and vegetables in a large greenhouse. Charles Hallock, afterwards head of the Smithsonian Institution in Washington, was exploring "bleak and barren Labrador" when he happened on Smith's farm. "Then the astonished ear is greeted with the lowing of cattle and the bleating of sheep ...," he wrote of his visit in *Harper's New Monthly Magazine*. "In the rear of the agent's house are veritable barns, from whose open windows hangs fragrant new-mown hay; and a noisy cackle within is ominous of fresh-laid eggs.... Donald Alexander Smith, the intelligent agent of the post, is a practical farmer, and, by continued care and the employment of proper fertilizing agents, succeeds in forcing to maturity, within the short summer season, most of the vegetables and grains produced in warmer latitudes." To complete the tableau, Smith built a two-mile track from his house to the farm—Labrador's first road. In summer he would take Isabella for sundown outings aboard his ox-drawn carriage.

North West River hosted another distinguished visitor in 1860, Captain (later Admiral) Sir Leopold McClintock, then in command of HMS *Bulldog*, a Royal Navy survey ship, who had gained prominence during the search for the Franklin Expedition. His log provides one of the few physical descriptions of the Labrador Chief Trader at this point in his life: "Smith ... was about forty years old, some five feet ten inches high, with long sandy hair, a bushy red beard, and very thick, red eyebrows. He was dressed in a black, swallow-tail coat, not at all according to the fashion of the country, and wore a white linen shirt.... His talk showed him to be a man of superior intelligence." McClintock in later years told Smith that he had foreseen at the time of the visit "Labrador won't hold this man...."

To prove his worth to Simpson, Smith not only reported unprecedented fur-trade returns but began diversifying the district's sources of revenue, expanding into a salmon fishery (and eventually cannery), exporting barrels of seal oil, and even sending out rock samples for geological tests. "I believe," he predicted, "that there are minerals here which will one day astonish the world."* The most beneficial consequence to Smith of these activities was that the fishery, which involved shipping the iced or canned salmon to England, gave him an excuse for corresponding directly with HBC headquarters in London, bypassing his aging benefactor, Sir George Simpson. The Company eventually formalized this arrangement by separating Labrador from its Lachine administration, so that Smith now reported to London on all his activities. In one of his last letters, Simpson warned his ambitious protégé against being heavy-handed trying to impress his British superiors: "When you want to bring any point strongly under notice, it will have a better chance by putting it in a few clear and appropriate words than by spinning out the theme so as to make it look important by the space it occupies on paper."

Smith ignored that advice and his letters grew embarrassingly verbose. As soon as he felt a promotion might be in the works, Smith did what he would always do in later life: he remarried Isabella. This particular wedding, performed either by an itinerant missionary or a visiting sea captain, must have been staged so that Smith could not only salve his conscience but also specifically refer to the sanctioned ceremony in his London correspondence.

He was appointed Chief Factor shortly afterwards at the age of forty-four, and in 1864 decided to take his first home furlough in twenty-six years. After visiting his mother, who was now almost blind, he hurried to London and spent the balance of his leave trying to ingratiate himself with the bigwigs at the HBC's Fenchurch Street head office. He met the Governor, Sir Edmund Walker Head, his deputy, Curtis Miranda Lampson, Eden Colvile, a future Governor, and most of the other important Committeemen. "Smith, the officer in charge of our Esquimaux Bay District," Colvile reported to Lampson, "... gives a good account of our affairs in that region, where he has been stationed for many years. As he is just the sort of man you would like to meet, shrewd and well-informed upon every topic relating to that *terra incognita* of the British Empire, I have asked him to dine with us on the 14th." Lampson, in turn, had been predictably charmed by the visitor who from now on was a marked man in the Company's future planning. There was one small hitch. As

---

* Simpson ignored the rocks, but Smith proved to be correct. The area he pinpointed as having valuable mineralization later proved to contain a huge iron-ore body, as well as lesser quantities of titanium, lead, zinc, nickel, asbestos, columbium and uranium.

was their custom, on the eve of the departure of the supply ship (which would carry Smith home), the Company directors proposed hearty toasts to the well-being of its Commissioned Officers. But when he was called on to reply, Smith had vanished. Overcome by a fit of shyness, the Labrador trader (who had known he would be requested to speak and had prepared his notes) could not face the distinguished gathering, afraid that he might somehow blot his copybook. It was the first public evidence of Smith's well-deserved reputation as a clamshell.

Smith was back in North West River by August 1865, but the visit had transformed him. He now knew there was still a chance for him to participate in the great events of his time. Despite his geographical isolation, Smith's reading of the Company's prospects was amazingly accurate. Perhaps because he had never been there and had no vested interest in the HBC's main fields of operation in the West, he could clearly see that the future would not run with the buffalo hunters or fur-trade canoes but with the oxcarts and ploughs of settlers come to claim new lives in the new land. "I myself am becoming convinced that before many decades are past," he wrote to a friend at the time, "the world will see a great change in the country north of Lake Superior and in the Red River country when the Company's licence expires or its Charter is modified.... You will understand that I, as a Labrador man, cannot be expected to sympathize altogether with the prejudice against settlers and railways entertained by many of the western commissioned officers. At all events, it is probable that settlement of the country from Fort William Westward to the Red River, and even a considerable distance beyond, will eventually take place and with damaging effect to the fur trade generally."

Within a year, the newly self-confident Smith had decided to visit Boston, New York and Montreal. Ostensibly, his trip was to view the sights of the city he had left twenty-seven years earlier. "The object I most wanted to see ...," he explained, "was the Victoria Bridge, which is truly one of the wonders of the world, and gives Montreal an unbroken railway communication of 1100 miles...." In reality, he was seeking belated acceptance in the milieu he felt had suddenly become accessible to him.

The most important part of his trip, at least in retrospect, was a call on his cousin George Stephen. The son of a Banffshire carpenter, Stephen had emigrated from Scotland at twenty-one to become a clerk in his cousin's Montreal drapery business, in which he eventually purchased a controlling interest. He studied banking and had become associated with some of

Montreal's leading entrepreneurs. The cousins' initial meeting was hardly propitious. The Smith family had gone shopping, and Donald had purchased a gaudy crimson carpet-bag for his Labrador journeys. Later, he wouldn't discuss his encounter with Stephen, but when Isabella was asked whether his cousin had been happy to see Smith, she burst out: "Really, why should Mr. Stephen be glad to see country cousins like us—all the way from Labrador? I wish ... [my husband] had waited until he had met Mr. Stephen before buying that red carpet-bag. But he wouldn't let me carry it and the rest of us waited outside." Still, Stephen did condescend to introduce his country cousin to friends at the Bank of Montreal and leading members of the city's shipping circles. All the talk was about domestic electricity, still considered a risky innovation, William Gladstone's surprising eloquence in the British House of Commons, Alfred Tennyson's latest verses and the prospects for Canada under Confederation, then only a year away.

Smith reluctantly returned to North West River, but mentally he had already left Labrador behind. Simpson had died in 1860, and his successor, Alexander Grant Dallas, had transferred the Company's North American headquarters to Red River, closer to its main field operations. Since Smith was already in charge of the Labrador District, all that remained in Lachine was direction of the relatively minor Montreal District, which included the King's Posts along the St Lawrence as well as trading forts up the Ottawa and Mattawa rivers. After the retirement on June 1, 1869, of the Montreal District's Chief Factor, E.M. Hopkins, "Labrador Smith," as he had become known in the Company's service, was appointed to the job.

And so Donald Alexander Smith came out of the wilderness at last. He was forty-nine years old, his skin permanently blackened by two decades of snow tans, his nerves as taut as those of a sprinter about to start his championship turn.

Montreal by then had a population of about 100,000, its streets had been paved and its harbour dredged, and the city (North America's tenth largest) was becoming an important rail and steamship terminus. Smith fitted in as if he had never left. "I called today to pay my respects ...," reported a startled HBC Factor shortly after Smith's arrival, "and was surprised to find him so affable and assuming, with no trace of the ruggedness you would associate with the wilderness. You'd think he had spent all his life at the Court of St James instead of Labrador...." One reason Smith was treated as an equal by members of the city's financial élite was that in a modest way he was already one of them. During most of his time in Labrador he had put away virtually his entire HBC earnings (arriving in Montreal with a grub-stake of $50,000), but starting in 1853 with the purchase of two shares, he had also quietly been accumulating stock in the Bank of Montreal. Coincidentally, George Stephen had been doing the same thing, and within the next four years the two cousins would become the Bank of Montreal's second-largest shareholders.

Overnight, Smith seemed to be launched on the urban business career that had been his long-postponed dream. Then a confluence of circumstances intervened and hurled him into the vortex of a strange rebellion gathering momentum halfway across the continent.

Bringing Louis Riel to Heel

Louis Riel remains the perfect martyr of the prototypical Canadian tragedy: a well-meaning yet deluded mystic who died prematurely by pretending to be sane.

THE COUNTRY WHOSE HISTORY Smith was about to affect still seemed more an idea than a reality. Canada in 1869 consisted of Nova Scotia, New Brunswick, Quebec and Ontario (the latter two minus their present northern areas), plus the huge but nearly empty western territories then in the process of being acquired from the Hudson's Bay Company.* After protracted negotiations, the Canadian government had agreed to purchase Prince Rupert's original land grant for £300,000 ($1,460,000) through a loan guaranteed by the Treasury of the United Kingdom. In addition to receiving cash, the HBC was granted unhindered trading privileges and 45,000 acres around its 120 trading posts as well as the right to claim, during the ensuing fifty years, one-twentieth of the fertile land (about seven million acres) between Lake Winnipeg and the Rocky Mountains. The transfer that would extinguish the HBC's long-coveted monopoly rights was to take effect on December 1, 1869.

In the decade after Confederation, most of the 3.6 million citizens of the new Dominion scratched for a living in rural isolation; only 390 square miles were occupied by two dozen embryonic towns and cities. Montreal was the largest at 100,000 people, with Quebec and Toronto competing for second place at about 60,000 each. Across the broad continent west of the Lakehead, there was almost nothing. "The plains were as thousands of years

---

* For details, see pages 550–61.

of geological and climatic change had made them," wrote W.L. Morton, the bard of western Canadian historians. "The grasses flowed, the prairie fires ran in the wind; the buffalo grazed like cloud shadows in the plain; the buffalo hunt raised a flurry of dust in the diamond summer light; the rivers sought the distant sea unchecked; summer made green, autumn bronze, winter white, spring gray.... What had been wrought lay unchanged until it became the setting for the last frontier."

Because the HBC had for two centuries kept nearly everyone who was not a Company employee out of its domain, the new Canadian West remained in the public mind a territory not far removed from those mysterious hunks of geography labelled on ancient charts "Here Be Dragons." Returning missionaries and the odd free spirit had brought out fragmentary reports of the land's contours and habitability, but it was the American, not the Canadian, West that attracted most settlers. The larger population base of the United States, its better climate and the mood of egalitarianism that characterized the self-confident republic made it a good place to start new lives. The notion of upward mobility still seemed foreign in Canada, which remained trapped in perpetuating vestiges of the British class system.

Canada's West was isolated more because of the absence of transportation facilities than as the result of geography. There were only three means of entry: by ship to York Factory through Hudson Bay; by Red River cart northward from the headwaters of the Mississippi River in Minnesota; or by canoe along the historic fur-trade routes from the upper end of the Great Lakes. Local HBC post managers had from the beginning been encouraged to live off the land, but except for the tracts of cultivation at Red River and a tiny spread at Cumberland House, the pioneer trading post opened by Samuel Hearne in 1774, only a few kitchen gardens had taken root. That began to change with the report by John Palliser, a Dublin-born explorer and buffalo hunter who was commissioned by the Royal Geographical Society to report on the region's potential. He not only defined a fertile land crescent across the prairie and noted deposits of coal and other minerals but also explored six passes through the Rockies for possible future railway construction. His optimism was somewhat tempered by the conclusion that no railway could be built across the treacherous bogs north of Lake Superior; the Red River settlement would have to be provisioned from the United States, via Chicago and St Paul.*

---

* For the founding of Lord Selkirk's colony, see pages 369–410.

By the late 1860s, Red River's inhabitants, including the offspring of the dispossessed crofters from the Scottish clearances, had turned the fifty-mile area around the HBC post at Fort Garry, near the junction of the Red and Assiniboine rivers, into a relatively prosperous, if insular, community of about ten thousand souls. Half were proud buffalo hunters descended from the mixed marriages of voyageurs and HBC clerks with Cree, Saulteaux, Blackfoot, Chipewyan, Dogrib and Slavey women. Their spiritual centre was the grey stone cathedral in the parish of St Boniface, presided over by the shrewd Roman Catholic bishop, Alexandre-Antonin Taché. The tiny village of Winnipeg at the edge of the HBC fort had grown into a miniature business centre, with half a dozen saloons, hotels and stores, supplied by the Red River cart brigades that maintained the link between Fort Garry and St Paul.*

Red River's hermetically sealed world revolved around the Hudson's Bay Company's Canadian headquarters at Fort Garry, its busy compound enclosing the Governor's residence, storehouses, clerks' and officers' quarters, sales and trading shops, the powder house and a scatter of outbuildings. Here in summer came the Indian canoe flotillas, loaded to the gunwales with pelts. The trading chiefs—big men with deliberate limb movements and the rhythmic lope of hunters—would hump the fur packs through the fort gates, eager to acquire guns, blankets, copper kettles, and the increasing range of household goods brought over by the HBC from England. Most summer days, Red River carts would he pulling in from St Paul or pulling out, their ungreased wooden wheels screeching in the sunlight, to supply the HBC's outposts along the North Saskatchewan River all the way to Fort Edmonton. They would return three months later bulging with the inland fur harvest.

Inside the fort, where each arrival and departure was accompanied by the yelps of a swirling chorus of mongrels, the walls had been painted scarlet, yellow and orange to offset the monotony of nature's blues and greens. Local courts sat here, as did the district's administrators, ruling for half a century through an insipid body known as the Council of Assiniboia, headed by the resident HBC Governor, its roster padded by tame Company appointees. James Ross, an English Mixed Blood who had gone east and graduated from the

---

*The first saloon was opened in 1859 by "Dutch George" Emmerling, who arrived with a barrel of whisky and sold the diluted rotgut at sixpence a shot. The sleazy emporium was eventually purchased by Robert Atkinson Davis who promoted it as "a haven of warmth, rest and billiards." Davis reluctantly quit the saloon business in 1874 to become Manitoba's fifth premier.

University of Toronto before returning to Red River, complained sourly about "the incubus of the Company's monopoly—the peculiar government under which we *vegetate*—it cools our ardour—destroys our energies—annihilates our very *desires* for improvement."

Even William Mactavish, the HBC's incumbent Governor, declared himself disgusted with "the greedy London directory" and the "arrogant Dominion Government," since neither had exercised the courtesy of informing him directly about the impending changes of circumstance. Although negotiations agreeing to terms that would surrender the HBC lands and monopoly had been concluded in London on April 9, 1869, by November of that year Mactavish had still not received notification of the transfer. In the absence of reliable information, rumours swept the HBC compound, so that Mactavish's already difficult position became untenable.*

The Edinburgh-born Mactavish had joined the Company as an apprentice in 1833. He was trained mainly at York Factory and worked his way up through the accounting department with few operational commands until he was promoted to the HBC's highest overseas office. A dreamy yet disenchanted Highlander, Mactavish was an amateur phrenologist who believed that a person's character could be read by the shape of his or her skull. He had accepted the governorship of Assiniboia under protest and later lamented he would rather have served as "a stoker in hell." His unhappy tenure was made all the more agonizing by the fact that he was suffering from advanced tuberculosis and had to expend most of his waning vitality fighting the awful lassitude inflicted by the disease. As a result, no matter what the provocation, no matter how seriously the Company's authority was challenged, Mactavish retreated into a stupor of inactivity and apparent indifference. Yet had Mactavish been the most enlightened and energetic of men, neither he nor any other Bay official could have turned back the gathering storm at Red River.

The tiny settlement, with little of the required infrastructure to provide channels for common cause, housed almost as many factions as families. A

---

* He said little publicly about the impending transfer, which would terminate his authority, and his official journal is equally reticent on the subject. Mactavish expressed his real feelings in a letter to his brother, Chief Factor Dugald Mactavish, in Montreal. "I will not speak of our dignity," he wrote, "but it is more than flesh and blood can bear that we who have conducted the government of this country for years, with a view to the welfare and best interests of all classes of the inhabitants, should be summarily ejected from office, as if we were the commonest usurping scoundrels."

small but vocal Canadian Party led by Dr John Christian Schultz, a militant Protestant and publisher of the local paper, the *Nor'Wester*, demanded union with the Dominion; equally loud were the proponents of immediate annexation to the United States. There were Irishmen fulminating against everything British, Highlanders trying to replicate their ancient clannish ways, even importing nightingales to make themselves feel at home, and agents of Napoleon III* vainly resurrecting wispy dreams of French empire along the vanished trails of the *coureurs de bois*. The best-organized Red River grouping was that of the Métis. They were united by concern for the buffalo herds, their main source of income and pride, which had been relentlessly gunned down and dangerously thinned out. The magnificent beasts were often shot solely for their tongues, that commodity when pickled having become a delicacy in fashionable European restaurants. The advance of agriculture and decline of the fur trade—the main market for buffalo meat in the form of pemmican— threatened their livelihood. They were restless and they were angry. They had opened up this country and now saw little future on their home turf. Their temperament was much too volatile to turn in their guns for the restraints of urban domesticity. Since they recognized that evolving circumstances would neither restore their past nor validate their future, the Métis decided to draw on their French and Indian roots to fashion a peculiar world of their own—a new nation, *their* nation, on the edge of civilization.

TROUBLE CAME FIRST in the form of Colonel John Stoughton Dennis, a United Empire Loyalist and cavalry veteran commissioned by William McDougall, Minister of Public Works in Sir John A. Macdonald's first administration, to chart the new territory. He arrived at Red River unannounced in August of 1869, four months before the transfer was due to take place, charged with making a survey so that the unoccupied Red River lands could be subdivided in a radically new pattern. The land had traditionally been laid out according to the Quebec seigneury style, with long, narrow rectangular lots fronting on the Red and the Assiniboine. Most of the farms occupied about four hundred feet of riverbank, then arched two miles or so through

---

*The French Emperor had dispatched Norbert Gay, an army captain, to Red River to "report on the situation," because a majority of its population was French-speaking and its political future seemed uncertain. Although Gay did little spying, he helped train the Métis buffalo hunters into a formidable fighting force.

fields and woodlands to the drier prairie soil, where "hay privileges" were shared with neighbours. Ownership was based on original HBC and Selkirk grants or, more often, squatters' rights.

Following instructions from McDougall, Colonel Dennis and his military surveyors began to lay out square townships designed for large-scale grain production from ploughed land. As practical as that may have sounded to Ottawa bureaucrats busy preparing the way for occupancy by ambitious newcomers from Ontario, the system ran directly counter to the Métis way of life and farming requirements. On October 11, a survey party led by Captain Adam Clark Webb unexpectedly arrived at the hay privilege of André Nault. The distraught Métis sent a messenger to fetch his cousin, Louis Riel, who came at the gallop with fifteen unarmed but defiant companions. An elegant and remarkably self-possessed gent with a high forehead overhung by clusters of black curly hair, Riel theatrically placed his foot on Captain Webb's measuring chain and solemnly declared: "You go no farther." The surveyors eventually went away and nine days later the Métis formed a committee, based on the old buffalo-hunt governments, with the twenty-five-year-old Riel as secretary. He quickly emerged as the group's real leader.

At this point, onto the stage of western Canadian history stumbled William McDougall, former minister of public works, now designated first lieutenant-governor of the Northwest Territories. Picked for the Red River assignment mainly because Macdonald considered him pompous and inflexible enough "to keep those wild people quiet," McDougall was one of the Prime Minister's more serious miscalculations. Known as Wandering Willie because he had served so many political faiths, McDougall turned out to be as stupid as he was pompous—not an easy accomplishment.

When McDougall's caravan, consisting of sixty carts loaded with his official entourage, relatives, fox-hunting dogs and an ornate viceregal throne of state, arrived at the customs house in Dakota Territory on October 30, McDougall was handed a note from Le Comité National des Métis de la Rivière Rouge, refusing them entry into Rupert's Land. Three days later, an unarmed Riel, riding at the head of more than 120 armed followers, seized Fort Garry, explaining to a compliant Mactavish that his purpose was to prevent bloodshed and guard the fort against unspecified dangers. Although the HBC Governor was confined to quarters, there seemed to be remarkably little hostility between him and the rebel leader. McDougall later accused the Company of opening the fort gates to the Métis and welcoming the invaders.

Viewing the escalating pace of events with increasing alarm from Ottawa, Sir John A. Macdonald hastily dispatched two messages. The first went through the correct political channels to the HBC in London, pointing out that since McDougall was being denied entry to Red River, the land purchase would have to be postponed until peaceful possession could be assured and advising the Company not to expect its £300,000 payment until the official transfer could take place. His second letter was to McDougall, telling him to stay put. "I hope," cautioned the Prime Minister, "no consideration will induce you to leave your post—that is, to return to Canada just now. Such a course would cover yourself and your party with ridicule, which would extend to the whole Dominion."

Encamped on the American side of the border and unaware of the postponement, McDougall was determined that the transfer date as he knew it would not go unnoticed. On the afternoon of December 1, he drew up a bogus royal proclamation. "Victoria, by the grace of God, of the United Kingdom of Great Britain and Ireland, Queen," it began, then appointed, of all people, "our trusty and well-beloved William McDougall" to hold supreme governmental authority over the disputed territories. That night, in one of the great comic turns of Canadian history, McDougall had his carriage driven through a twenty-below blizzard into Canada. He was accompanied by seven puzzled functionaries and two pointer dogs casting curious glances to left and right as they approached the ceremonial moment. Then, having reached the courtyard of an abandoned HBC post, McDougall ostentatiously positioned himself in a proper Nelsonian stance and, while one of his minions unfurled a Union Jack and another held a guttering lantern, sonorously read his proclamation to the empty prairie sky. He stood there, the parchment in his mittened hands, baying at the polar moon. The winds blew, the dogs howled, the functionaries snickered into their beards—and McDougall basked in the glow of his self-anointed glory.

The absurd deed done, the nocturnal caravan, led by the pair of bounding pointers, quickly headed back to the warmth and safety of its temporary American quarters, satisfied with a long night's work well done. It had indeed been an occasion to remember: the night the Honourable William McDougall finally stepped over the slippery line between pomposity and idiocy. McDougall's document carried the weight of no authority. He had none of his own and had counterfeited the Queen's imprimatur. His impetuous act turned the federal government into the object of frontier hilarity.

None of this bothered the Ottawa emissary (thereafter known as "*Silly Wandering Willie*"), who actually expected Macdonald to reward him for his "prompt display of vigour [that] will inspire all inhabitants of the Territory with respect for your Representative, and compel the traitors to cry, 'God Save the Queen.'" The Prime Minister ignored McDougall's bluster, angrily denounced him for having "done his utmost to destroy our chance of an amicable settlement with these wild people," and recalled him to Ottawa. Before leaving, McDougall appointed the surveyor, Colonel Dennis, as his "Lieutenant and Conservator of the Peace" and ordered him to clear the rebels out of Fort Garry—in effect inviting Dennis to launch a civil war. McDougall also dispatched copies of his worthless proclamation to Fort Garry, so that Mactavish and the Hudson's Bay Company would be officially aware they had just been deposed. The HBC Governor, his chest on fire with advanced tuberculosis, was beyond caring. He spent most days sitting alone at his deserted council table, coughing and staring into space.

Red River did have an effective government, and Louis Riel was at its head. When the Métis leader called a community meeting to establish the terms of his provisional administration, English-speaking delegates asked Mactavish whether he still considered the HBC to be Red River's prevailing authority. The gravely ill Governor advised them that McDougall's mission, however foolishly conceived, would soon terminate his powers, and that since he was "a dead man," they had better construct a government to maintain peace.* Riel named himself President of the Provisional Government of Rupert's Land and the North-West (then the world's second-largest republic) and raised over Fort Garry the new Métis flag (a golden fleur-de-lis and a green shamrock on a white ground).† To emphasize his authority, Riel transferred the new Government House furniture that had been prepared for McDougall's arrival to another part of the fort, which became his office as chief of state.

---

* John Bruce, a local magistrate and president of the National Committee, later testified that Mactavish had told him McDougall and his successors should be resisted because Canada's taking possession of the territory was "an injustice to the people and to the officers of the Hudson's Bay Company, since the Government had given them no part of the £300,000 paid for their country."

† The fleur-de-lis was the proud standard of Samuel de Champlain, the Father of New France. The shamrock was added to recognize the treasurer of the Métis Governing Council, a professional Irishman named W.B. O'Donoghue, who taught mathematics at St Boniface College.

The rebellion, if that's what it was, had been achieved with force but no bloodshed. With the subtlety of a seasoned politician, Riel had drawn enough consensus from the diverse elements of the colony to govern Red River. While the Canadian government dithered, American annexationists were quick to realize the potential of the situation, offering Riel flattering entreaties and generous cash donations if he would throw in his republic's lot with the Stars and Stripes. Insignificant as Red River was, Washington politicians recognized it as the ideal entry point for a takeover of Canada's West—and eventually the entire continent. "The tendency of North American events is plainly towards the consolidation into one great nation," chirped the New York *Sun*. "From the Polar Sea to the Isthmus of Darien, there will in time be only one national government—that of the United States. Who among us can say that ours is not a glorious destiny or reflect without exultation that he is an American citizen?" Macdonald understood these sentiments all too well, lamenting that while he would gladly neglect the West for the next half-century, if Englishmen didn't go there, Yankees would. Something had to be done fast to bring Riel's upstart republic to heel.

SUCCESS BY INADVERTENCE did not figure prominently in Labrador Smith's cunningly conceived career path, but at this pivotal moment in Canadian history Sir John A. Macdonald's ignorance intervened to place the still-obscure fur trader at centre stage. Sir George Simpson, who for most of forty years had operated the Hudson's Bay Company as a private preserve out of his headquarters of Lachine, just west of Montreal, had such an enormous personal impact on Canadian public life that Macdonald quite naturally assumed the secretive Company was still run out of Montreal, even if he no longer knew who was in charge. That had not been true since Alexander Grant Dallas, Simpson's successor, had moved the headquarters to Red River in 1860 and had himself been succeeded by William Mactavish four years later. Ensconced in Montreal for less than a year, Smith had Company rank only of district manager, and his department was the HBC's smallest and least typical, taking in eastern Canada and Labrador. The Prime Minister had never met or heard of Smith, but it was a normal reflex for him to call on the highest accessible HBC official to help settle troubles on the western front in what was, after all, still Company territory—particularly since he had been recommended by George Stephen. Smith, who had never even visited a Company post west of Lachine, was the last man on earth to try to set Macdonald straight. As he later explained, it was no part of his duty "to volunteer to correct any man's opinion or delusion unless it were in the general interest."

Summoned to Ottawa on November 29, 1869, Smith was closely questioned by Macdonald on the difference in attitudes between the HBC's London head office, anxious to complete the transfer and get its money, and local Company officers reported to be encouraging the insurrection. Not averse to involving himself in a situation he knew nothing about, Smith laid much of the blame on the government for not securing Governor Mactavish's co-operation before dispatching McDougall to the territory. To counter claims that the HBC was helping the rebels, he insisted that adjustment of the present difficulty would be of great advantage to both the Company and its field officers, then delivered a patriotic sally he must have known would please the Prime Minister. "If no settlement occurs," said he, "there will be no transfer, and if there is no transfer of the territory law and order and property will be at the mercy of the most lawless members of the community until the Americans step in and annex it."

Macdonald interrupted to ask Smith whether he would go to Fort Garry and help settle the dispute, and later the same day sent a memorandum to Joseph Howe, the cabinet minister in charge of the Red River negotiations, praising Smith: "I am now strongly of opinion that we should make instant use of D.A. Smith. In the chat I had with him to-day he took high ground, declared himself a staunch *Canadian* and lost no opportunity of emphasizing his own complete impartiality as well as the desire of the Company to effect a speedy settlement of this unhappy business. If the Hudson's Bay officers are implicated in fomenting the disturbance, Smith can, from his position, discourage them...."

Smith was shortly afterwards appointed Dominion Commissioner to Inquire into the North West Rebellion and charged with endeavouring to arrange some system of concerted action in the pacification of the country. The term "pacification" correctly identified his real mission. He was to use the moral suasion of the royal proclamations he carried with him plus whatever bribes might be necessary to create a political movement that would oppose and, if possible, overthrow Riel, laying the groundwork for future negotiations, not with any puppet administration but directly between the citizens of Red River and the Canadian government. Smith left Ottawa on December 13, accompanied by a brother-in-law, Richard Hardisty, and Dr Charles Tupper, one of the Fathers of Confederation and former premier of Nova Scotia, now a prominent Tory Member of Parliament. Tupper (after 1879 Sir Charles) came along ostensibly to inquire into the whereabouts of his son-in-law, Captain D.R. Cameron, who was serving on McDougall's staff, but was probably included by Macdonald as his personal spy. The party took the fastest route available—by train to Toronto, Chicago, St Paul, and the end of steel at Breckenridge, Minnesota (the last miles aboard the St Paul and Pacific Railway), then by stage and canvas-covered sleigh to the Canadian border.

They met McDougall on his way back to Ottawa and were briefed on the horrors of Red River. But what Smith recalled most vividly about that trip was the fertile land along the tracks of the St Paul and Pacific, the bankrupt railroad originally chartered to reach Oregon on the Pacific Coast. For Tupper, one of the more curious moments of the journey was Smith's unexpected attack of megalomania. The fur trader, less than a week after taking on his government assignment (and less than two weeks after anybody in Ottawa even knew his name), demanded to be named a member of the august Privy Council, then Canada's highest civilian honour. When Tupper pointed out that, if sanctioned, this should have been done before they had left Ottawa, Smith stopped at the next telegraph post and wired the suggestion to Sir John A. Macdonald, who just as quickly turned him down. The trio fought their way across the frigid plain towards Red River, stopping to rest and warm up at Fort Abercrombie, where the landlord took them to his shed. Six woodland caribou were standing there, like horses in stalls, frozen stiff, and the Abercrombie cook hacked off a hindquarter for the travellers. After leaving his royal proclamations at an HBC trading post along the way, Smith arrived at Red River on December 27.

He was received civilly enough by Riel, but when asked to promise he would not try to upset the provisional government's legality Smith declined and was detained for most of the next two months in a cramped room at Fort Garry. Allowed an unlimited flow of visitors and using his well-connected brother-in-law to recruit the right people, he persuaded several of the settlement's moderates to support Ottawa's intentions of integrating Red River with the growing Dominion. When persuasion failed, Smith had at his disposal several thousand dollars to bribe wavering Métis, credits to hand out at HBC stores for winter supplies, and jobs as tripmen for next summer's canoe and cart brigades. Realizing that his support was beginning to drain away, Riel demanded that Smith demonstrate the legitimacy of his mission by showing him the royal proclamations. Smith dispatched Hardisty to fetch the documents. Métis raiders tried to stop him, but some of the Smith converts escorted Hardisty to the fort, spreading the word that there was among them a fully accredited representative of the Canadian government and Queen Victoria with important news for Red River citizens. Riel could not refuse Smith's demand that everyone be brought together the next morning to hear his message.

JANUARY 19, 1870, DAWNED SULLEN AND COLD, the sun hugging the horizon as if hesitant to venture into such frigid surroundings. It was twenty below zero Fahrenheit, and the wind snarled across the flat landscape, obliterating most points of reference with snow. The good burghers of Red River came, more than a thousand strong, to hear the Ottawa emissary. They arrived aboard horse-drawn sleds swathed in buffalo robes, on snowshoes or by puffing dog trains from the outer settlements and gathered in a field inside the fort. They lit small fires, stamping circles in the snow to keep the blood flowing, and, as the temperature dropped, tucked mittened hands inside their HBC blanket capotes for extra body-warmth—or indulged in some liquid glow. The steam of their breathing had almost obscured the enclosure by the time Riel and Smith climbed onto a hastily erected platform to begin the historic proceedings.

For five hours Smith read aloud from various documents, his words faithfully translated by Riel, including the text of the original commission to the misguided McDougall, proving that the Prime Minister's original emissary had acted entirely on his own. Smith read the lengthy proclamation from Sir John Young, reiterating the Governor General's wordy pledge that the "Imperial Government has no intention of acting otherwise, or permitting others to act otherwise than in perfect good faith towards the inhabitants of the Red River district of the North-West.... The people may rely upon it that respect and protection will be extended towards the different religious persuasions; that titles of every description of property will be carefully guarded; and that all the franchises which have existed, and which the people may prove themselves qualified to exercise, shall be duly continued or liberally conferred." Except for the occasional mild tiff between Smith and Riel about which papers should be promulgated, the mutual respect that seemed to flow between the two men impressed members of the audience. By mid-afternoon, the sun was settling into the southwest, and the cold had become intolerable; the small boys who had been collecting wood to keep the fires aglow were too chilled to continue.

The meeting was adjourned to ten o'clock the next morning.

On the following day, lectured at for another five hours, the crowd—except for the Métis riflemen patrolling its edges—started to swing towards Smith. It wasn't so much anything specific he said or promised as the cumulative effect of his documents, their carefully drafted and often stilted phrases demonstrating the fact that central Canadian politicians really did care about Red River's welfare. And it was Smith himself, looking fully his fifty years, the leathered skin reflecting his two decades in Labrador's primitive fur trade, who made his arguments persuasive. He told them, as if it were a hard-wrung confession, that he was married to a Hardisty whose mother had been a Red River Sutherland, and that his own mother was a Grant, related to the great Métis leader, Cuthbert Grant. He seemed somehow incorruptible in his dour Scottishness, the tiny beard-icicles bobbing to the rhythm of his earnest pledges. He kept reading all those long documents, with their high-sounding cadences, transmitting the subliminal message that anyone taking this much trouble to sound *officious* had to mean it. He read a personal greeting from Queen Victoria (delivered through Lord Granville, the Colonial Secretary) assuring his listeners they would enjoy the same status as British subjects in any other part of Canada. At the end of that interminable second day, Smith set aside the dreary documents and spoke from the heart. "I am here to-day in the interests of Canada," he intoned, "but only in so far as they are in accordance with the interests of this country.... As to the Hudson's Bay Company, my connection with that body is, I suppose, generally known; but I will say that if it could do any possible good to this country I would, at this moment, resign my position in that Company. I sincerely hope that my humble efforts may, in some measure, contribute to bring about, peaceably, union and entire accord among all classes of the people of this country."

Not eloquent, exactly, but after ten hours of mind-numbing proclamations, at least genuine, and Smith was cheered for his effort. A chastened Riel now took the stage and moved that a convention of twenty Métis and the same number of English-speaking representatives meet to consider Smith's commission and draw up a list of rights for submission to Ottawa. When a listener objected that his statement cast doubt on the legality of Smith's documents, Riel replied matter-of-factly that the Bay man's commission was valid and that it should be implemented. Riel's agreement to set up a constituent assembly outside the sponsorship of his own purview meant that Smith had achieved precisely the breakthrough Sir John A. Macdonald had recognized as the crucial element in any solution: that Canada be able to negotiate directly with representatives of Red River instead of Riel's unelected and radical provisional government. Three delegates to the Ottawa talks were eventually elected and a Bill of Rights framed under which the people of Red River were willing to become part of Canada. Riel was chosen—by representatives of the entire community this time—to continue as head of the provisional government. As a sign of good faith, he later released most of the Fort Garry prisoners, including HBC Governor William Mactavish, who left for his ancestral hearth in Scotland.*

A few days before Smith was due to leave for Ottawa to report on his mission, Red River's fragile tranquillity was shattered by a series of bizarre blunders. A hundred English-speaking malcontents from Portage la Prairie, west of Red River, marched towards Fort Garry determined to hang Riel. Norbert Parisien, a young Métis they had taken prisoner, escaped, snatching a double-barrelled shotgun, and started running across the frozen Red River. When Parisien encountered a popular young settler named Hugh John Sutherland, who happened to be passing by, he shot him in the chest. His pursuers, seeing the mortally wounded Sutherland, recaptured Parisien and kicked him to death. Members of the rowdy, now bloodied gang, including a boisterous Irish Protestant drifter named Thomas Scott, were arrested by Riel's riflemen. Not much was known about the twenty-eight-year-old Scott because there wasn't that much to know. He was one of those marginal frontier characters who substituted racial and religious prejudice for personal motivation and had spent the past year cursing and harassing the Métis. Once in the Fort Garry jail, Scott jeered at the guards, insulted their religion, called them cowards, and at one point physically attacked Riel. The situation deteriorated to the point where Scott's guards could no longer maintain discipline and bluntly told Riel they would shoot *him* if he didn't execute Scott. The Métis leader's more militant followers were already angry that he had ordered the release of so many other prisoners, and Riel had to find a way of quickly reasserting his authority. Scott was brought before a court martial, found guilty of insubordination and sentenced to death. When Smith pleaded with Riel not to spoil his bloodless record with a senseless execution, the Métis leader shrugged and replied, "We must make Canada respect us."

---

*Mactavish reached Liverpool on July 21, 1870, and died two days later.

At noon on March 4, 1870, the Reverend George Young, a local Methodist pastor, led the terrified Scott to a ditch outside the fort. His hands were bound, he was blindfolded, and a firing squad of six Métis shot the trembling Irishman in the chest. When Scott was heard moaning, François Guillemette, one of the executioners, pulled out a revolver and at close range put a bullet through his left ear; it came blasting out through his mouth. Refused burial at Red River's Presbyterian cemetery, Scott's body was placed in a rough coffin and taken to a shed, where, according to George Young, five hours after the execution he was heard still pitifully moaning, "Oh, let me out of this. My God, how I suffer!" Riel dispatched two guards to deliver a *coup de grâce*. Scott was buried inside a deep hole in Fort Garry's stone battlements, but a year later when his remains were being disinterred for transfer to a proper graveyard, diggers found his coffin empty—except for the rope that had been used to tie his hands at the execution. According to one report, just before the original burial, Scott's body was removed from the coffin by a Métis guard named Elzear Goulet, weighted down with chains, and dropped through a fishing-hole in the Red River ice. "The secret of Thomas Scott's burial will likely never come out ...," Alexandre Nault, whose father was one of Scott's executioners, told the Winnipeg *Tribune* in 1961 on his eighty-seventh birthday. "An oath was taken never to tell."

Scott's lively ghost harmed no one more grievously than Louis Riel.* The many shots that killed the Irish renegade destroyed any chance of peaceful transfer of the HBC lands. Dr Schultz, leader of Red River's rabid pro-Canadian party, toured Orange Ontario brandishing a rope that he claimed had bound Scott's hands during the execution and a vial of the martyr's blood.† Schultz and others whipped up public outrage, demanding revenge on those the *Globe* in Toronto labelled as desperate, depraved, devilish Papists. In Quebec, Riel and his praetorian guard of Métis were raised to the status of folk heroes— champions and victims—of French Canada's crusade against Anglo-Saxon bigotry. It was one of the many ironies of the situation that only five days after Scott's execution, Bishop Taché arrived in Red River bearing word from Sir John A. Macdonald of a general amnesty and the promise of welcoming Red

* After Louis Riel was hanged for treason in Regina on November 16, 1885, one of the jurors at his trial admitted, "We tried Riel for treason, and he was hanged for the murder of Thomas Scott."
† Volunteers must have provided refills, since Schultz freely sprinkled blood on the handkerchiefs of tearful women at the climax of his melodramatic lectures.

River into Confederation as a province, to be called Manitoba. Riel immediately released all remaining prisoners and prepared to join Confederation. The trio of Red River delegates—a priest, a magistrate and a store clerk—left for Ottawa to negotiate the terms of what became the Manitoba Act, passed into law on May 12, 1870. It included nearly all of Riel's demands, such as guarantees for the French language and Catholic religion, and set aside 1.4 million acres for the Métis, preserving their precious river lots.

DONALD SMITH DEPARTED RED RIVER a changed man. No longer the obscure fur trader, he was hailed as the heroic peacemaker of the North-West. His report on the events of the past three months recommended, among other reforms, recruitment of a permanent paramilitary force to maintain law and order in the North-West. Smith's future was assured. It was whispered that even Benjamin Disraeli, the British Prime Minister, kept a copy of Smith's submission on his desk to show visitors how such documents should be drafted.

On his way back to Montreal, Smith had a memorable encounter with James Jerome Hill, a one-eyed St Paul entrepreneur (born at Rockwood, Ontario), who was on his way to assess Red River as a location for future business opportunities. Hill had arrived in the Minnesota capital as a teenager and immediately became part of the steamboat scene, at first providing fuel, then becoming a partner in some of the operations. An aggressive and unpleasant deal-maker, he tended to intimidate people with the stern look of his one good eye, the other having been lost in a youthful archery accident. Hill and Smith had heard of one another by reputation and it didn't take them long to find a common interest. The two men shared a wilderness meal and spent the night in a tent, trading dreams, discussing the need for a railway to link Red River with the civilized world.

Back in his HBC office, Smith was besieged by cablegrams from London soliciting his counsel on the Company's future affairs. Treated as the HBC's overseas chief operating officer, he was shortly afterwards promoted to President of the Northern Department (a new title for William Mactavish's former position) and transferred to Fort Garry. Smith's most urgent priority was to meet with his northwestern Chief Factors and Chief Traders, gathering in late July at Norway House near the upper end of Lake Winnipeg. This was to be the last of the great Northern Council meetings to be held at Norway House, initiated by George Simpson half a century earlier. It was here, seated around the great oak table where they had traded so many quips and empires, that the Hudson's Bay Company's seasoned veterans first met their new viceroy. The understandable hesitation of pledging loyalty to this awkward stranger who had mysteriously been promoted over their heads gave way to respect as Smith conducted the meeting with the same resolute dignity that had marked his debut as an orator at Red River. In the end, the HBC field hands empowered him to represent them in negotiations with London for their rightful share of the £300,000 transfer fee. After the meeting, Smith went by canoe to Fort Alexander, a post on the southeast side of Lake Winnipeg ninety miles from Fort Garry, originally built in 1792. There he impatiently awaited arrival of the troops Sir John A. Macdonald had dispatched to claim the North-West.

To appease the anti-Riel backlash and assert Canada's authority, the Prime Minister sent an army detachment to Red River under the command of Colonel Garnet Wolseley, a prematurely stuffy Anglo-Irish officer then serving as Deputy Quartermaster-General in British North America. The contingent, numbering 2,213 officers and men (a quarter of them British regulars) and 700 voyageurs, was officially described as a "benevolent constabulary," but its prevailing mood was that of a punitive military expedition. The sentiment was appropriately caught in Wolseley's private journal. "Hope Riel will have bolted," he confided to its pages, "for although I should like to hang him from the highest tree in the place, I have such a horror of rebels and vermin of his kidney that my treatment of him might not be approved by the civil powers." A vintage hawk who, as a viscount and field marshal, would later command the British Army, Wolseley loaded the soldiers and their equipment aboard 140 boats and heaved them across the mudpie labyrinths West of the Lakehead. The Manitoba historian Reverend R.G. MacBeth was being restrained when he described the task as "more suitable for aquatic animals than for human beings." The agony of strong-arming the heavy equipment across forty-seven punishing portages lasted ninety-six days, and at times the lead and last boats were as much as 150 miles apart. After Smith joined the Wolseley troops on their way through Fort Alexander, they marched in battle formation towards Fort Garry.

Pleased with the passage of the Manitoba Act and still brimming with Victorian ardour, Riel had planned to welcome the British troops in elegant fashion. Elaborate arrangements were made for bonfires and salutes on the south bank of the Assiniboine, with Riel himself presiding at the turnover ceremony at the head of a hundred crack Métis cavalrymen. Expecting to benefit from the general amnesty granted by Ottawa, the Métis leader had even drilled a guard of honour for Wolseley's inspection when the British colonel reached Fort Garry. For once, he seemed alone in his faith. Reports began to arrive that many of the Canadian volunteers were Ontario Orangemen boasting they would avenge Thomas Scott's execution by lynching the papists and watching them squirm. That was enough for most of Riel's lieutenants, who began drifting away, mumbling excuses about going home to check on relatives.

By sunrise, only Riel and O'Donoghue were left in the fort, pacing its echoing battlements, peering through the rain, trying to decide which way to turn. They lowered the brave Métis flag, suspecting it would never fly again. Wolseley's 60th Royal Rifles could easily be spotted stumbling unprotected through the mud, and Riel must have glanced at Fort Garry's thirteen silent cannon with something close to regret. The two men escaped through the fort's front gate barely ahead of the troops, scurried to the river, which they crossed on a raft hastily fashioned out of fence posts tied with their sashes. Riel cut the cable of a nearby ferry to prevent pursuit, but he needn't have bothered. Colonel Wolseley was too busy strutting around the fort, firing royal salutes, raising the Union Jack, boasting how he had routed the "banditti." Deprived of their quarry after the hardship of their long march, the troops took out their frustrations on the local Métis, looting their homes, raping their daughters (including seventeen-year-old Laurette Goulet, the child of a Riel supporter, who died after being assaulted by four drunken soldiers), and murdering most of the provisional government's ministers. Elzéar Goulet, a member of Scott's court martial, was chased into the Assiniboine and stoned until he sank and drowned. Another of the men who determined Scott's fate was left for dead on the American side of the border, while a third, François Guillemette, was shot.*

Riel himself had initially escaped to the United States but soon returned, still anxious to assist in Manitoba's transfer to Canada, and even helped organize the Métis to counter an abortive invasion by a band of Fenians from the States. Macdonald didn't want Riel arrested because that would have played badly in Quebec. But he didn't want him casually strolling around Red River,

---

* Ambrose Lépine, who presided at both the trial and the execution, was convicted of murder in 1875 and sentenced to be hanged. The Governor General, the Earl of Dufferin, commuted his sentence, and Lépine died in 1923 at the age of eighty-three in rural Saskatchewan.

either, because Ontario's Orangemen still had a price of $5,000 on his head. Resorting to the political ethic of his day, the Prime Minister eventually sent a bribe of $1,000 (supplemented by £600 from Smith) through Archbishop Taché to get Riel out of the country. On February 23, 1872, he was unceremoniously escorted outside his "country" under police protection.

And so the Red River Rebellion ended in both victory and defeat, its objectives achieved, its founding spirits shot or disowned. Ironically, Red River's ostensible liberators had inflicted far more moral and physical damage than the rebels themselves. Most of the regular troops departed five days after they arrived; it was the last British military operation in North America.

As the HBC's presiding officer, Smith stayed on to head a reconstituted Company government that ruled Red River until McDougall's permanent successor arrived. The new lieutenant-governor of Manitoba and the Northwest Territories was a sensible Maritime lawyer-politician named Adams G. Archibald, who had been Macdonald's first Secretary of State and now would negotiate the first two treaties with the Indians of the North-West.

"I yield up to you my responsibilities with pleasure," said Smith.

"I really do not anticipate much pleasure on my own account," said Archibald.

With that insipid exchange the Hudson's Bay Company finally surrendered its bountiful monopoly over the largest empire ever ruled by a commercial enterprise.

A DETAILED ANATOMY of the Red River Rebellion and the North-West uprising that followed in 1885 is beyond the scope of this book—except as Louis Riel was manipulated by and influenced the Hudson's Bay Company. His tragic saga, particularly the 1885 trial for treason, when he refused to hide behind a justified plea of insanity that might have saved his life, is Canada's most enduring myth. A compelling rebel in a nation of cloying conformists, Louis Riel remains the perfect martyr of the prototypical Canadian tragedy: a well-meaning yet deluded mystic who died prematurely by pretending to be sane.

Riel's dominant characteristic was his sense of ambiguity. Caught between Métis nationalism and Victorian loyalty, he could never let go of either emotion, trapped in a polarization of his own making. He was constantly trying to overthrow an entrenched Anglo-Saxon hegemony in order, as he paradoxically kept insisting, to gain "our just rights as British subjects." In one moving address after passage of the Manitoba Act, the Métis leader was glowing with *bonhomie* as he praised his followers for bowing to the Queen— the same Queen whose forces were at that very moment marching west to destroy him. "I congratulate the people of the NorthWest," he said, "... on having trust enough in the Crown of England to believe that ultimately they would obtain their rights." The man's fundamental dichotomy was symbolized even by his dress: during eight months as President of the North-West Republic, Riel received visitors wearing hand-sewn buffalo-hunt moccasins— and a formal Victorian frock coat.

Had it not been for Scott's execution, Riel would have been elected the province's first legal premier and could justifiably have claimed to be the Father of Manitoba. But in Canada, civic monuments are erected to functionaries, not rebels. Riel's resistance had salvaged the French element in Canada's North-West and in the process bestowed on the Métis a degree of self-confidence and self-assertion they had never before possessed.

Riel has inspired idolatry and contempt in equal measure, being condemned by English Canadians as a traitor who deserved to be hanged, while Quebeckers still worship him as a victim of Anglo-Saxon racial and religious prejudice.* Hartwell Bowsfield, a York University historian, best summed up the heroic revolutionary's contradictions: "He was a man of intelligence and authority who was mentally unstable; a reasonable protester against legitimate grievances who turned fanatic and dictatorial; a gentle man whose name became associated with violence even though he himself never took up arms; a simple man of great personal appeal who developed grandiose pretensions as a spiritual and political leader; a visionary and an erratic religious mystic who inspired unquestioning faith in the Métis people."

That faith was unrequited because Louis Riel's conflict was as ancient—and as contemporary—as Canada itself: a clash between the semi-articulated *collective* demands of the Métis and the stubbornly held *individual* rights of English Canadians.

---

* Honoré Mercier climbed to power in Quebec on Riel's execution. Ironically, in 1990 the bridge named after Mercier became the focal point in Indian-French disputes. Mercier used Riel to get at the Conservatives in Quebec and at the Tories in Ottawa. Where did it get his descendants?

The Great
Fire Canoes

The Northcote may or may not have been the first warship to fight an engagement in waters thirty-six inches deep—twice the depth of a children's wading pool. But she was the only man-of-war ever to proceed into combat with a billiard table as armour.

DONALD SMITH RULED THE NORTH-WEST for only eight days—and his main public edict was to close the saloons at night—but he was the perfect transitional figure between the Hudson's Bay Company's two centuries of sullen monopoly and its transformation into a dominant but vulnerable commercial enterprise. He differed from every other senior Bay man in the territory because his heart was not in the West; his Labrador background made it easy for him to deal unemotionally with the new circumstances. He came to the job with enhanced credibility through his diplomatic triumph at Red River, moved by restless aspirations for his own and the Company's advancement that had not been in evidence among the HBC's overseas managers since Sir George Simpson's day.

The first sign of the Company's reduced status appeared when Colonel Wolseley called for tenders to supply stove-pipes for the barracks of the remaining army volunteers. The HBC submitted a high bid, assuming it would get the business automatically. A local merchant named James H. Ashdown sent in a much lower quote but lost the contract when Smith convinced army officers the newcomer wasn't equipped to do the job. Once the HBC got the contract, Smith discovered there were no tinsmiths on his staff and ordered Ashdown to do the work under HBC auspices. When Ashdown refused, Smith asked the colonel to force the fellow into line. Wolseley cancelled the HBC's contract instead and asked Ashdown (who went on to found western Canada's largest wholesale hardware house) to produce the stove-pipes at his original bid. The minor incident reflected the competitive new world in which the ancient fur-trading company would have to operate.

Smith's initial order of business was to settle accounts outstanding from the Red River Rebellion. It was typical of their corporate ethic that the HBC's London Pooh-Bahs viewed Louis Riel's agonizing struggle on behalf of his people strictly as a bookkeeping entry. The uprising had disturbed the business of the Company, and now it was claiming refunds from the Canadian government for missing fur stocks, lost trading opportunities and six months' interest, at 5 percent, on the delayed transfer payment of £300,000—a total of £32,508, not counting the amounts Smith had paid out in bribes. It took a dozen years to settle the dispute, and the Company received very little cash because Ottawa subtracted the costs of surveying its territory, but the claim hurt the HBC's already poor reputation. "A corporation has no conscience," observed Captain W.F. Butler, Wolseley's intelligence officer, whose familiarity with the West produced its most evocative early literary portrait, *The Great Lone Land*. "From a tyrant or a despot you may hope to win justice; from a robber you may perhaps receive kindness; but a corporation of London merchants represents to my mind more mercenary mendacity, and more cowardly contempt of truth and fair play, than can be found in the human race."

Despite such condemnation, there were some genuine worries about the HBC's loss of stature. The Company had become vital in the daily lives of the North-West's Indians. Natural gathering places, its trading posts were the natives' only source of the barter goods that made wilderness life more bearable—the guns, blankets, axes and other items they had grown to depend on. "The sudden withdrawal of the Company's operation from any part of the Indian country will cause widely spread misery and starvation and the consequent disorders and embarrassment to the Government which spring from such scenes," William Mactavish, Smith's predecessor, had warned, "nor can any other company ... be in a position ... to supply the Indian tribes with the requisite regularity with those necessaries of life at present provided them. This is the secret of the Company domination—its existence is a necessity to the Indian." That was true enough, but the fur trade itself was in a highly volatile state. Felt hats made from Canadian beaver had enjoyed a momentary fashion revival in the 1860s. The headgear took the shape of wide-brimmed adaptations of the "wideawake," a name invented by the humour magazine *Punch* for a hat that had no nap. But now the new seamless silk toppers were much more in vogue, having been worn by the Prince Consort, the Prince of Wales and President Abraham Lincoln. Although there was continued strong demand for specialty pelts from North America, London's fur industry was turning towards other, less expensive sources, and to nutria, the skin of coypu rats, being harvested in Brazil and Argentina by the million. The most immediate impact on the North-West was the final downgrading of York Factory, which for two centuries had been the flourishing centre of the North American fur trade. By 1875, the headquarters of the HBC's Northern Department had been moved to Fort Garry and the magnificent tidewater depot was reduced to a regional trading post.

That shift drew attention to the staggering realization that a full century after James Watt had perfected his steam engine, the Hudson's Bay Company was still depending on a primitive transportation system of horse- or ox-drawn carts, birchbark canoes and York boats. Apart from the immense manpower expenses, which were mounting now that the Métis no longer thought of themselves as slaves, use of such primitive technology meant that it took the Company four years to realize returns on invested capital. As one frustrated shareholder exclaimed at the Company's 1871 annual meeting, "Gentlemen, this Company has not been very celebrated for doing things in a hurry. It is really very much like Rip Van Winkle waking up in the year 1871 and finding out that steam engines and steam boats will be of advantage to the trade."

Right on cue, Donald Smith wrote to William Armit, the HBC's secretary, on November 6, 1871, recommending that the fur trade's cost structure be streamlined by the use of steamboats along the North Saskatchewan River, its main traffic artery. That would radically reduce costs and, ideally, bring the furs out in a season or two instead of four seasons. On top of these benefits, Smith recognized the possibility of perpetuating the Company's monopoly over western Canada, this time by controlling its commercial traffic flows.

The Hudson's Bay Company decided to relaunch itself as a prairie shipping line, using a brand-new fleet of what the Indians quickly dubbed Fire Canoes.

INCREDIBLE AS IT NOW SEEMS, an awkward but sporadically effective flotilla of sternwheel steamboats for a time supplied the Canadian West. These ships, chugging along at a respectable five knots, became a common sight in what everyone then—and now—assumed to be a landlocked prairie. They not only carried the materials of the fur trade (two or three trips in the high-water season easily handled the cargoes previously consigned to the large and expensive brigades of carts and fleets of York boats) but quickly branched out into ferrying the necessities of the new civilization being born on the Prairies. Ploughs and scythes, tea and bacon, threshing machines, and their accompanying pioneers crowded the decks and cabins.*

The perky vessels' steam whistles could be heard up to Edmonton on the 1,200-mile flow of the North Saskatchewan River; along the South Saskatchewan past Saskatoon to Medicine Hat and beyond; on the Assiniboine, from Fort Pelly and Fort Ellice to Lake Winnipeg; and up the Red to Fargo in Dakota Territory which had connections to the railway networks of the northern United States.

By 1879, seventeen ships, not all owned by the HBC, were regularly employed on prairie rivers. Getting there was all the fun. Constant stops had to be made for cordwood to fire the boilers.† The flat-bottomed sternwheelers, difficult to control under the best of conditions, didn't so much travel the river routes as bounce their way through them. New obstructions were always being encountered, or a bumping acquaintance with old ones was being renewed. Flood times were the worst because the surging waters hid dangerous rocks and made the keelless vessels impossible to steer. Occasionally a bold skipper would take advantage of the high water to invent a shortcut. On May 10, 1873, Captain Alexander Griggs was en route to Fort Garry aboard the *International*, carrying a large liquor consignment for the Hudson's Bay Company. He had to reach the border by midnight or his cargo would be liable for a new tariff. Cursing the day's delays and gazing at the waters spilling over the banks of the Red and flooding the plain, Griggs "coolly turned the boat out of the bed of the river," as reported later in the *Manitoban*, "and made a short cut over the prairie ... thereby reducing the distance very materially and gaining the Customs House" in time.‡

---

* Passenger fares aboard the HBC boats from Fort Garry (Winnipeg) to Edmonton were forty dollars one way for cabin space, twenty dollars for a perch on the open promenade deck. Freight was carried at four dollars a hundredweight.

† Finding it could get tricky. The HBC's *Lily*, desperate for firewood, pulled into the tiny enclave of Red Deer Forks when her crew noticed two Métis log cabins whose owners were out hunting. In minutes the buildings had been dismantled, their timbers loaded, and the ship was hastily puffing her way along the Saskatchewan.

‡ Another example of overland navigation was the *Assiniboine*'s astonishing sweep down the main street of Emerson, Manitoba, to rescue and bring relief supplies to Red River flood victims in 1897.

Summer low water was a much more common problem. Ships' captains, mostly recycled wharf rats from the Mississippi River trade, often ordered crew and passengers overboard to help push or warp the vessels through shallow sections. Warping meant literally walking the ship over an obstacle. This was achieved by using four strong spars hinged to double derricks on either side of the bow. When aground, the vessel could lift itself over the obstruction by the manipulation of ropes running through these derricks to turn the poles into stilts. One skipper was exaggerating the shallowness of the river only slightly when he yelled at a settler who was dipping his pail into the Assiniboine, "Hey! You put that water back!" Stuck in the ankle-deep backwaters of the North Saskatchewan above Cumberland Lake, Captain Aaron Raymond Russell of the *Marquis* ordered his crew members overboard with picks and shovels to dam every creek flowing out of the main channel. The extra inches obtained this way made it possible for him to tiptoe his way downstream to deep water.

"We go from one bank to the other," complained Lady Dufferin in August 1877 when she and her husband, the first Governor General of Canada to tour the West, were aboard the *Minnesota* on their way to inspect the Red River settlement, "crushing and crashing against the trees, which grow down to the waterside; I had just written this when I gave a shriek as I saw my ink-bottle on the point of being swept overboard by an intrusive tree.... The consequence of this curious navigation is that we never really go on for more than three minutes at a time.... Our stern wheel is often ashore, and our captain and pilot must require the patience of saints." Later that day Lady Dufferin saw another ship, the *Manitoba*, approaching in the dark. "It looked beautiful," she reported, "with two great bull's-eyes, green and red lamps and other lights on deck, creeping towards us; we stopped and backed into the shore, that it might pass us. It came close and fired off a cannon and we saw on the deck a large transparency with 'Welcome Lord Dufferin' on it, and two girls dressed in white with flags in their hands; then a voice sang 'Canada, Sweet Canada,' and many more voices joined the chorus, and they sang 'God Save the Queen' and 'Rule, Britannia', and cheered for the Governor General as they began to move slowly away disappearing into the darkness."*

---

* "O Canada," with music by Calixa Lavallée and words by Adolphe-Basile Routhier, was not written until 1880, and not widely sung outside Quebec until the early years of the twentieth century. Its use as the national anthem was approved by Parliament in 1967, and it was officially adopted in 1980 under the National Anthem Act. Lavallée, who had

During the viceregal visit, Lady Dufferin hammered in the last spike of western Canada's first railway, a primitive four-mile-long, narrow-gauge tramway built by the Hudson's Bay Company where the waters of the Saskatchewan roared down the Grand Rapids to Lake Winnipeg. The wilderness link provided horse-drawn wagons to handle goods en route between Edmonton and Fort Garry, bypassing the steep limestone canyon where the river dropped almost a hundred feet in three miles, causing painfully long portages. For a time, using a specially trained white horse, the little railway actually ran itself. Trains consisted of a car laden with the merchandise being trans-shipped, followed by an empty carriage. At the height of land, a platform was built the same height as the cars. Having been taught the drill, the animal would pull the two carriages up from one or the other terminus, slip out of its own harness, walk onto the platform and into the empty car, which would then glide down behind the load to the end of steel, banked to provide an automatic brake.

Once this barrier was conquered, the prairie ships grew in size and appointments. Captain Peter McArthur's *North West* boasted a five-thousand-dollar grand piano and two bridal chambers. First-class passengers aboard the *City of Winnipeg* dined in soft leather chairs in a carpeted and chandeliered Grand Saloon. According to the *Manitoba Free Press*, one of their number was so overcome by the ambience—and presumably the booze—that he "was trying to waltz across the deck with an umbrella … for a partner." Inevitably, the intoxicated passenger made one uncalculated twirl and "without trying, waltzed off most beautifully into the river."

THE FIRST STEAMSHIP on the Canadian Prairies was a prototype of the bizarre fleet that was to follow. The *Anson Northup,* which arrived at Red River from Georgetown, Minnesota, on June 10, 1859, was ninety feet long and twenty-two feet wide, though she had a draft of only fourteen inches. She looked like

---

served as a bandsman with the Union forces in the U.S. Civil War and favoured U.S. annexation of Canada, spent much of his adult life in the United States and died in Boston in 1891. Routhier was a judge of the Superior Court of Quebec from 1873 who later became chief justice of that court and was knighted. In English-speaking Canada, a popular national song for many years was "The Maple Leaf Forever," written in 1867 by Alexander Muir, a Toronto teacher. Its emphasis on the Britishness of Canada tended to rule out its use in French Canada. The English translation of "O Canada" now in use is a modified form of the words written in 1908 by R. Stanley Weir, an author of legal texts and later judge of the Exchequer Court of Canada.

a log cabin mounted on a washbasin with a toy smokestack stuck in the middle, but she could carry fifty tons of cargo as well as passengers, and her arrival caused great excitement. "Horses with buckskin riders, oxdrawn two-wheeled carts from the fields, and cautious Indians clad in feathers, leggings, and moccasins streamed to the fort landing," wrote Ted Barris in *Fire Canoe*, the definitive study of prairie steamboats. "Children thronged at the riverside to see 'an enormous barge, with a watermill on its stern' emerging from the wilderness like a demon churning up water and spitting sparks. The few carriages available rushed to the scene with flounced and furbelowed ladies attended by bearded gentlemen in tall hats—the [HBC] Governor's entourage."

The Hudson's Bay Company reacted by purchasing the *Anson Northup* through a dummy U.S. company and later bought a slightly larger sister ship, the *International*, reasserting its transportation monopoly by raising rates to prohibitive levels on goods carried for its competitors. The monopoly was broken in the spring of 1871 by the sudden appearance on the river of the much larger *Selkirk*, which could carry 125 passengers and 115 tons of freight. Owned by J.J. Hill, the St Paul entrepreneur Donald Smith had met on his way back from settling the Red River Rebellion, the new venture represented enough of a challenge that Smith negotiated a partnership deal that gave the two men control over a new entity called the Red River Transportation Company, which secretly granted the HBC a one-third preferential freight rate. It became so profitable that 80-percent dividends were not uncommon. Within four years, grain was being exported by Manitoba farmers, adding further impetus to improve a transportation system that was already handling more river traffic than moved along the Mississippi between St Paul and St Louis. When the competing Merchants International Steamboat Line launched the *Manitoba*, Red River Transportation Company captains proved that subtlety was not their long suit. Acting on orders from Smith, on June 4, 1875, the skipper of the *International* rammed the *Manitoba* abreast of her stacks and sank her.*

The HBC's own shipbuilding adventures verged on slapstick. First to be completed was the *Chief Commissioner* (named for Smith), launched on May 7, 1872. Her draft turned out to be too great to navigate her intended route along the Saskatchewan, so the ship was reassigned to Lake Winnipeg,

---

* Jerry Webber, the captain of the *Manitoba* and other sternwheelers, was known mainly for the fact that he kept a tame raven with red ribbon tied around its wings on his bridge.

where the absence of a keel made her wallow too violently to be of much use. Another HBC ship sank the following summer near Grand Rapids, a day into her maiden voyage. The next project was an expensive (£4,000) steel-hulled vessel built at the Clyde shipyards of Alfred Yarrow & Company for reassembly in North America. The *Lily* was fast and she was beautiful; but an anonymous marine architect had designed her draft four inches too deep, and the North Saskatchewan's margins for error were so narrow that this was enough to keep her out of practical service. After many modifications the *Lily* finally fought her way up the South Saskatchewan nearly as far as Medicine Hat, hit a submerged rock, and sank.*

The Company's most durable vessel was the *Northcote*. Launched in 1874, she was 150 feet long, had a 30-foot beam, and drew only twenty-two inches— about the same as a loaded York boat. Her boilers and high-pressure engines had been brought all the way from Cincinnati and could produce 39.72 horsepower. On her maiden voyage, the *Northcote* made it to Carlton House after only ten days' steaming, recouping her cost in one trip. On July 22, 1875, she reached Fort Edmonton with a cargo that had left Fort Garry only thirty-three days earlier, turned around after three days in port, and was back at Grand Rapids on August 5. Later seasons were less successful because of low water levels and trans-shipment delays from Fort Garry.

This lack of reliability plus steep insurance premiums and the unwillingness of the Canadian government to help remove some of the more obvious hazards to navigation gradually cooled the Company's shipping ardour.† The fleet was

---

* The best-known skipper on the South Saskatchewan was the appropriately named Horatio Hamilton Ross. He built eight ships (including the *O'Hell*) and sank them all. His most famous encounter was with a bridge in Saskatoon, which the local paper correctly described as "the greatest marine disaster in the history of Saskatoon." At the wheel of the 130-foot SS *City of Medicine Hat* and aware that spring flooding had raised river levels, Ross was navigating carefully under the city's bridges, even removing part of the smokestack to lower the height of his ship's superstructure. But the *Medicine Hat's* rudder snagged in some telegraph wires, and the ship was impaled on the 19th Street pedestrian bridge just as a few head of cattle were being herded across. The cattle stampeded, as did their keepers, and, according to an onlooker, everybody aboard the ship "scrambled up onto the bridge to safety, except the engineer. He popped out of the engine room and jumped into the water. By the time he reached the river bank, he had drifted a mile downriver, the current was so strong...."

† The premiums were high both because river beds were strewn with rocks that seemed drawn to the flat-bottomed hulls and because the ships' stacks emitted live sparks. Every riverbank farmer knew that if his barn or haystack caught fire, it was far more profitable to let it burn and claim the insurance than attempt to fight the blaze.

eventually folded into two independent transportation companies that allowed the HBC preferential freight rates with no need for further capital expenditures. The arrival in Winnipeg on October 8, 1877, of the *Selkirk* pushing a barge that carried the West's first locomotive signalled the terminal phase of the Prairies' brave steamships.*

But the HBC's sternwheeler *Northcote* had one more great adventure in store. She went to war.

When Louis Riel returned to Canada from his dispiriting American exile in the summer of 1884, the Métis of northern Saskatchewan enlisted his fervour in what was to be the bloodiest expression of agrarian protest in Canadian history: the North West Rebellion of 1885. Apart from acting as principal provisioning agent for the troops dispatched by the Canadian government to quell the uprising, the Hudson's Bay Company's main contribution was to charter the *Northcote*, at $250 a day, to Major-General Frederick Dobson Middleton, the blimpish, walrus-moustached former commandant of the British military college at Sandhurst, who had been placed in charge of the Canadian militia. Riel and his shrewd field marshal, Gabriel Dumont, were massing Métis warriors and their Indian allies at Batoche, a small farming community on the South Saskatchewan River southwest of Prince Albert, while the *Northcote* was being used by Middleton's staff to ferry troops across the river at Saskatchewan Landing to help relieve the siege at Battleford.

On April 23, 1885, the ship was assigned the dangerous task of carrying ammunition into the war zone, towing two barges loaded with ordnance supplies behind her. Middleton's plan to oust the Métis, snugly dug into their rifle pits at Batoche, called for the *Northcote* to provide an amphibious second front for his land attack. Aboard the saucepan-bottomed wooden tub was one of North America's ace Indian fighters, Arthur "Gat" Howard, late of the

---

* The engine was the *Countess of Dufferin*, named after the wife of the Governor General who visited Manitoba that year. Five years old when Joseph Whitehead, a pioneer railway construction man, bought her, the locomotive was built at the Baldwin yards in Philadelphia and had been in the service of the Northern Pacific. After arriving in St Boniface, the *Countess* was put to work by Whitehead building a southbound line along the east side of the Red River to Pembina, where a connection would be made with the U.S. railroad to St Paul. The little locomotive ended up on the scrapheap at Golden, B.C., after working for the Columbia River Lumber Company. In 1908 R.D. Waugh, later mayor of Winnipeg, found her there and persuaded the lumber company to donate her to the Manitoba city. The CPR hauled her back to Winnipeg and restored her to become a municipal historic artifact.

Connecticut National Guard, who had been seconded to the militia contingent because of his marksmanship with the hand-cranked, multi-barrel Gatling gun. In addition to this rapid-fire weapon, which had never been used in Canada before, the *Northcote* carried a nine-pound cannon mounted on her weather deck, and thirty-five sharpshooters lined her railings. That arsenal was formidable enough, but it required armour for protection, not an easy commodity to come by in these parts. The *Northcote* may or may not have been the first warship to fight an engagement in waters thirty-six inches deep—twice the depth of a children's wading pool. But she was the only man-of-war ever to proceed into combat with a billiard table as armour. On her way downriver, the HBC vessel had passed the plundered homestead of Gabriel Dumont, and the *Northcote's* crew protected her gun emplacements with his billiard table and two-inch-thick planks torn from his barn door. The table was reinforced with Dumont's mattress and bags of oats, not to mention his washing machine and his wife's sewing machine.

And so the *Northcote* steamed to war, a floating apparition sure to dismay her friends and comfort her enemies.

Middleton had arranged to rendezvous with the ship at a loop in the river just above Batoche, near Gabriel Dumont's ferry crossing. The plan was to launch a co-ordinated assault, his land forces marching to the fanfare of their bugle boys, while the *Northcote* would provide a diversion by sailing towards the centre of the Métis position to the hoot of its three-note steam whistle.

The *Northcote* had firepower of a kind and armour of a lesser sort, but she had no camouflage. It is not simple to hide a 150-foot ship, chugging through a 3-foot-deep river on the plains of Saskatchewan. Métis scouts reported on her every lurch downstream, and on the morning of May 9, when she rounded the final bend of the river, her crew was greeted with concentrated fire from Métis troops lining the banks. Her captain promptly assumed his battle station by lying prone on the wheelhouse floor, doing his best to guide the ship's wheel—with several of its spokes shot off—by peeping through a rifle hole. As the *Northcote* reached the ferry terminal at Gabriel's Crossing an hour early, Dumont ordered the ferry cables, normally slung high above the river, lowered astern and ahead of the ship, crippling her manoeuvrability. The forward motion of the vessel when she hit the taut wire sheared off the smokestack and most of the pilot-house, loading spars and steam whistle, disabling the prairie warship but allowing her to drift onto a sandbank below Batoche.

Thus ended the HBC vessel's Gilbert-and-Sullivan naval engagement, but the doughty and awkward steamboat, having successfully run a five-mile gauntlet of murderous rifle fire, was still more or less afloat. Certainly her presence had been intimidating enough for Louis Riel to pray, "O my God, I pray you, in the name of Jesus, Mary, Joseph and St. John the Baptist, grant that you use the cable of our ferry to upset the steamboat; that we may have the provisions, the useful things the boat contains, the arms and the ammunitions."

After the Battle of Batoche, the *Northcote* was beached at Cumberland Lake in a meadow opposite the Pas River, a bullet-scarred hull the only evidence of her brief moment of glory. She died nineteen years later, the victim of evangelical zeal. A Catholic priest who discovered that local teenagers were using the *Northcote's* cabins to flirt away long summer evenings persuaded the HBC's Cumberland House manager to give an Indian named Jimmy Greenleaf enough coal oil to torch the proud ship's remains.*

Completion of a railway link between Winnipeg and St Paul in 1878 brought Red River's commercial water traffic to an effective halt, though one ship, the *Grand Forks*, didn't make her final run until 1909. There were still three vessels operating on the North Saskatchewan as late as 1887, and the *North West* ran a tramp service along the river for another dozen years.†

One by one the ships disappeared. Their final resting place was seldom at dockside. They died where they had lived, at river bends or at the edge of rapids. They were left to sink where they had rammed their final rock or crunched into their last riverbank. Eventually, their superstructures disintegrated into driftwood, and their rusting remains were blanketed by the shifting sands and weeping willows.

---

* According to Ted Bards, the *Northcote's* bell "now beckons a congregation to the Duck Lake Anglican Church each Sunday; while a hundred miles away the Gardiner Presbyterian Church—now Fred Light's tiny museum in the old town of Battleford—houses the *Northcote's* three-tone steam whistle. And three feet of *Northcote* deck plank functions as a ... cribbage board in one Prince Albert living room."

† Only the *Keenora*, converted from steam to diesel during her career and restored by the Marine Museum of Manitoba, now survives. Of the scores of passenger steamers of the inland waterways of the West, only four sternwheelers—the *Klondike* and *Keno* in Yukon and the *Moyie* and *Sicamous* in British Columbia—remain.

Progression and Betrayal

"Fine promises butter no parsnips."   —HBC trader James Lockhart

TRAVERSING THE STILL UNOCCUPIED WEST by steamboat and canoe, on foot and snowshoe, aboard sleighs and buckboards, Donald Smith spent most of a decade after the Red River Rebellion and the subsequent surrender of the HBC's monopoly holding the Company together long enough to transform its core business from fur trading to real estate. Apart from laying down a drastically altered operational code in line with the HBC's new competitive environment, Smith's main concern was to deal with the increasingly strident demands of the Company's wintering partners for their share of the Canadian government's £300,000 cash down payment on Rupert's Land.

According to the 1821 and 1834 Deed Polls, which set down the rules of their engagement, Chief Factors and Chief Traders were not employees but partners. To them belonged 40 percent of the Company's equity divided on a share basis according to rank, and they were thus entitled to the same proportion of its net profit. This was not some form of earnings incentive; the dividends plus a modest subsistence allowance represented their sole income. Having suffered through many downturns in fur prices, they seemed entitled to participate in the Company's cash windfalls. They argued convincingly that Rupert's Land was available for sale mainly because they and their predecessors had legitimized and expanded Charles II's original land grant through right of occupation. They felt particularly deserving because the transfer to Canada, which had destroyed the monopoly that made the fur trade so profitable, was bound to endanger their livelihood. At least one favourable court judgment had upheld the basis of their claim. When the

Company's headquarters building on Fenchurch Street was sold at a profit five years earlier, London's Chancery Court had ruled the wintering partners were entitled to two-fifths of the proceeds, since the original purchase price had been paid out of the fur trade's gross income. Using that precedent, the overseas officers also claimed two-fifths of the $450,000 the Company had recently been awarded for giving up its Oregon territories to the United States.

When these points were raised by his Chief Factors and Chief Traders at the Northern Council meeting held at Norway House in the summer of 1870, Smith promised to make their case in London. Even if he was a stranger, the field men thought they recognized in the man they appropriately nicknamed "Labrador Smith" a colleague who had connections with the powerful and who could salvage their estates. "Our immediate destiny is in your hands," one of the Chief Factors pleaded with him. "You know our life—you know how arduous our labours are. In nearly every instance they involved long servitude, separation from friends and relations, many hardships which we feel more sensitively as time wears away…. These might be, as they often are, borne cheerfully even for a long period, were the prospects of retirement on an adequate competency in sight; but failing this hope, they are almost insupportable."

Sir Stafford Northcote, who was named HBC Governor when the Earl of Kimberley resigned to become Lord Privy Seal in the Gladstone government, balked at sharing the £300,000 award, insisting that the value of the wild land had not been improved by the fur traders' activities. In fact, Northcote enjoyed little manoeuvring room. For the first time in its long history, the Hudson's Bay Company was no longer controlled by the London Committee. Since the sale to the International Financial Society in 1863 there were no more "sleeping partners" who could be counted on to vote automatically with the directors on the conduct of the fur trade.* Instead, the stock was actively traded on the London Exchange, and annual meetings were swayed by whatever coalition of shareholders emerged on any particular issue. These new-style investors, hard City men with long pedigrees but little sense of history, felt no allegiance to the traditions of the Company; their only concern was to increase stock yields. During some of the early years after the end of the Company's monopoly, net revenues had been so paltry that winding up the HBC and splitting up its assets seemed entirely

* For details of this transaction, see pages 557–60.

appropriate—but no one was quite certain how such an ancient royally chartered enterprise could be extinguished.

Smith spent the summer of 1871 in London advancing his officers' claims. Even as he was arguing their case, he was haunted by that train ride he had taken eighteen months earlier on his way to Red River, through the fertile farmlands lining the railway tracks north and west of St Paul. With the HBC about to receive title from Canada to seven million acres of what was the northward extension of that rich soil, he was convinced of something most of his Chief Factors only vaguely suspected: that furry animals would not be the main source of the Company's profits much longer. He realized that where buffalo roamed, cattle would one day graze, and had ascertained that much of the land about to come into the Company's possession was favoured with two more hours of sunshine a day during the wheat-maturing season than other farming areas. But that was only the beginning of Smith's vision. He knew that to switch the prairie economy from fur to grain would require large-capacity transportation—a railway network, initially down to St Paul, Minnesota, and eventually right to the Pacific. Reverting to character, Smith merged his own aspirations with the country's future and turned the combination into a personal mission. He became determined that in some as yet unpredictable way he would participate in construction of a railway across the Canadian West.

Although he was only two years out of Labrador, circumstances had conspired to place Smith at the vortex of a historic transformation. Despite his very recent promotion, he suddenly commanded enormous leverage within the councils of the HBC. The Red River incident had made him all but indispensable in rearranging the Company's overseas affairs. He had proved during his long Labrador stewardship to be a capable fur trader, worthy of the Company's confidence. In his dealings with Riel he had gained the respect of Canada's Prime Minister, the confidence of the North-West's settlers, and the trust of the HBC's officers. Having accomplished all this so quickly, Smith began to sense that his destiny was not on the gumbo streets of Fort Garry or even in the relatively sophisticated offices and curtained salons of Montreal. It was in London, among the patricians of Empire transacting the world's important commerce, that he wanted eventually to claim his roost.

As a first step, Smith set out to ingratiate himself with the Hudson's Bay Company's directors, especially Governor Northcote, a seasoned political juggler who had honed his skills as secretary to Prime Minister William Ewart Gladstone, President of the Board of Trade and Secretary of State for India. He intended to show Northcote and the HBC Committeemen that he was really one of *them*, that he had the Company's best long-term interests at heart rather than the dispensable concerns of the wintering partners. He did this by suggesting a workable compromise to resolve the fur traders' demands that they share in the government's £300,000 payout. Northcote later won shareholder approval for the scheme, which provided the winterers with a one-time payment *of* £107,055. It also guaranteed continuation of their 40-percent equity position and perpetuated their 40-percent share of trading profits. In return, they had to sign a new Deed Poll that specifically exempted them from proceeds of future HBC land sales.

Having expected little, most of the fur traders were pleased with the suggestion, particularly the cash, since the service then had virtually no pension provisions. When he returned to Montreal, Smith was feasted by the outback veterans, who presented him with a silver serving set worth £500. Only a few of the more astute characters realized that Smith had signed their professional death warrants. By giving up future land profits, the one-time lords of the forests had been rendered powerless and poor. The appropriately grateful London board showed its appreciation by immediately promoting Smith to Commissioner at a generous annual £2,000, and a year later to Chief Commissioner, with a healthy salary increase.

The Factors held desultory discussions about resigning to establish a new independent fur-trading company and several retired on the spot. Among those who quit in disgust was Chief Trader Roderick McKenzie. "If we had insisted in participating in the sale of lands there might be some hopes of a certain remuneration for our services, which under the present régime with all the expense is very doubtful," he wrote to a colleague in the Peace River country. Another senior trader, James Lockhart, noted: "It is all very well for Donald A. Smith, with his £2,000 secure annually, to puff the new arrangements. But 'fine promises butter no parsnips,' and you will all find yourselves fooled.... For your sake and the sakes of a few other true friends of mine still in the service, I hope things may turn out all right, but I do not expect it, and would advise you to do as others have done, i.e. send back their commissions with the note, 'Declined with thanks.'" Still, under pressure from Smith, most of the traders signed the fateful Deed Poll.

Northcote, by then Lord Iddesleigh, returned to British politics in 1874, becoming Chancellor of the Exchequer and later Foreign Secretary in Lord Salisbury's second ministry. He was succeeded in the HBC Governor's office by

George Joachim Goschen, later first Viscount Goschen, who had attained a Bank of England directorship at the age of twenty-seven and had more recently served as first Lord of the Admiralty in the Gladstone government. Instead of trying to offset bad times by branching out into retail stores or aggressively pursuing government contracts, the HBC under Goschen withdrew into a form of suspended animation. He tried sporadically to revitalize the fur trade; but initial progress in land sales was slow, and revenues dipped so steeply that HBC stock prices in London slipped from £38 to £12. One of his few positive contributions was to strengthen the HBC board by recruiting Sir John Rose, partner in the London merchant banking house of Morton, Rose & Company, who had served as finance minister in Macdonald's first Canadian government and had since become the country's unofficial ambassador to London's financial district.

The trio of patrician governors—Kimberley, Northcote and Goschen—who ran the Hudson's Bay Company between 1868 and 1880 raised its social profile but accomplished little else. The Company's unostentatious headquarters in a former silk warehouse of the East India Company on Lime Street had only a tiny permanent staff that was made up of the corporate secretary, an accountant, a warehouse keeper, a few shipping clerks and some fur graders. Governors presided over fur auctions two or three times a year but measured annual time spent on HBC affairs in hours rather than days. The head office's budget, which in 1870 barely exceeded £13,000, had *dropped* by £2,000 thirty years later. Once a month or so the Committeemen would meet in the Governor's office to debate policies and prepare for the semi-annual gathering of shareholders (still quaintly referred to as General Courts of Proprietors), held at the London Tavern or the City Terminus Hotel. Even when these assemblies were stormy, the election of directors was customarily confined to approving candidates from the Governor's house list, and most Committeemen contributed little beyond their physical presence.

INTO THIS VOID STEPPED Donald Smith, the freshly minted head of the HBC's North American operations. The fur department, which had been without strong leadership since the death of Sir George Simpson in 1860, had suffered during the decade of neglect, and badly needed Smith's brand of energy and dedication. Curiously, it didn't get it. Smith's heart was no longer in the fur trade. Since leaving Labrador he had participated in grander events and had expanded his personal agenda in too many new directions to be drawn back into daily concern with the messy business of buying pungent pelts and selling them on a reluctant market. He did manage to keep the fur trade going, but he continued having trouble with its mundane bookkeeping details (as he had had while a youthful clerk), failed to maintain his inspection timetable to outlying districts, and allowed the HBC infrastructure to slide into dilapidation. "The Chief Commissioner cares nothing and hopes nothing from the fur trade," complained Chief Trader Lockhart.

Despite his preoccupation with more weighty issues of state—politics and railways—Smith's position at the head of the HBC's Canadian operations required him to live and work at Red River, which had been incorporated as Winnipeg in 1873. In the spring of that year Smith purchased Silver Heights, a comfortable mansion in the St James district, where he could spend time with his wife, Isabella, between trips to Montreal, Ottawa, London and St Paul.

Captivated by the potential of real-estate speculation, Smith resigned his fur-trade posting in the spring of 1874 to become the Company's first Land Commissioner and moved his main office to Montreal. He was succeeded as head of the fur trade by a cheerful nonentity named James A. Grahame, a Chief Factor then in charge of Victoria and the Western Department's sub-commissioner. His main historical legacy seems to be that his beard was even longer than Smith's. When he switched responsibilities to what was then the more junior posting, Smith made certain he preserved his valuable privilege of reporting directly to London. In a circular letter to Chief Factors and Traders announcing his decision, Smith added a telling postscript: "It may not be out of place for me here to add that I shall informally give my attention to the personal interests of my friends connected with the service who have investments with 'private cash' in my hands. This latter, as you are aware, having throughout been entirely inde-pendent of my relations to the Company as their Conunissioner...."

Here was the first hint of Donald Smith's most daring gamble—and the source of his betrayal of his one-time fur-trade colleagues. He had not only deluded them into giving up their share of the HBC's land sales profits but he also intended to buy control of the Company right out from under them—using their money to do it.

The scheme that made this possible had originated with Sir George Simpson. As overseas Governor, he had helped the Company's thrifty back-woods Factors invest their earnings. He eventually controlled a large block of funds, adding to his clientele such churchmen as Alexandre-Antonin Taché and Henry Budd, and the famous plainsman James McKay. As early as 1848, when Smith was still in Labrador, he had started buying shares in the Bank of Montreal and later in the Hudson's Bay Company. His reputation for shrewd money decisions attracted fellow Factors, who turned to him for investment management after Simpson's death. By the early 1870s, Smith was running thirty-seven trusts with considerable financial leverage—a fact the Bank of Montreal recognized in naming him a director. Whenever one of his investors retired or wanted to withdraw from the money pool, Smith would pay out the capital and agreed-upon 3-percent annual return, but purchase the shares for his own account. He eventually became first president and chief shareholder of the Royal Trust Company, specifically established to handle these transactions, which were quickly making him very rich. Smith used these funds—plus his generous credit lines at the Montreal—to purchase large blocks of HBC stock at depressed prices when termination of the Company's monopoly triggered a market panic. Smith, who was all too aware of the HBC's underlying land values, could thus pick up stock at £9. (Within his lifetime those shares would become worth more than £130 each—an increase of 1,300 percent.*) These strategically timed purchases and his subsequent dealings in HBC stock confirmed Smith as Canada's father of insider trading. Granted, there were no laws against using privileged information to play the stock market in those days, but Smith abused the system mercilessly—and deliberately didn't share his knowledge with the fur traders whose financial destinies had been entrusted to him.[†]

"WHERE EVERY MAN'S A LIAR—that's where the West begins!" That anonymous boast, quoted by Prairies historian Grant MacEwan, caught the exuberant spirit and somewhat less glorious reality of history's greatest voluntary migration. The movement of new settlers into the West didn't really begin on a mass basis until the last half-decade of the nineteenth and the first decade of the twentieth centuries, but the people who eventually occupied

---

* That capital gain does not take into account the Company's generous dividend payouts. Between 1872 and 1911 the HBC's entire capital stock was repaid to shareholders six times over in special bonuses. To maximize returns on the profits generated once the real estate started to move, the nominal par value of shares was reduced and the difference paid out in cash directly to shareholders. In the fifteen years after surrender of the HBC's monopoly, for example, HBC shares were written down from £20 to £13, with £700,000 distributed to stockholders.

† At about this time Smith also purchased major equity interests in the Paton Manufacturing Company of Sherbrooke, Quebec, a spinning and weaving mill, and the Cold Brook Rolling Mills Company of Saint John, New Brunswick.

fifty-eight million acres of the Canadian plains were driven by a common motive. What lured them was less rumours of fortune than the personal freedom they might gain. Here, as ploughs creased the startled land, came the supreme blessing of a new start. Men and women could till the good earth and make fresh lives without having to face an entrenched aristocracy, established church or preordained political order.

All they had to pledge was their youth, strength and endurance—and it certainly wasn't easy, freedom or no. Settlement of the land was painfully slow. It was delayed by absence of railway transportation, an economic depression triggered by the collapse of American financier Jay Cooke's debt-burdened Northern Pacific Railway, the casual gait of government surveyors and the HBC's determination to get a better deal. Under the original Deed of Surrender, the Company could retain about 45,000 acres around its major posts and had the right to claim, over fifty years, one-twentieth of any township within the Prairies' "Fertile Belt"—the desirable agricultural tracts enclosed by the American border, the Rockies, the North Saskatchewan River, and (on the east) Lake Winnipeg and Lake of the Woods. That amounted to a valuable seven million acres, but no one seemed certain how the HBC's actual acreage within each township should be chosen.

The Dominion Land Act had established a survey system based on the American model, with each township divided into thirty-six square sections of 640 acres each (plus road allowance) to ensure that farms would be large enough for commercial wheat production. Originally the HBC lands were to be chosen by lot or chance, but Smith prevailed on the government to allocate the same pattern of sections in each township. Purchasers of HBC land were allowed fairly generous terms: a down payment of one-eighth the market price, with the balance payable in seven annual instalments at 7-percent interest. (A similar arrangement spread over five years applied to town lots.) In a typical ten-year period (1879–89), the HBC sold 514,009 acres and had to repossess all but 195,150 acres when breaking the land broke the farmers instead.*

* To the HBC went Sections 8 and 26 in every fifth township, and in all other townships all of Section 8 plus the southern half and northwest quarter of Section 26. Of the remaining sections, two (29 and 11) were set aside as educational endowments, and all even-numbered sections were reserved for homesteads, available to heads of families for a nominal ten dollars plus the requirement of carrying out specific improvements. The odd-numbered sections were reserved for later sale at one dollar an acre, with a limit of one to a customer, When the CPR claimed its land grants, the odd-numbered sections four deep on either side of the tracks became railway property.

Although Smith had lobbied for the job as HBC Land Commissioner, his record in that office was no more impressive than his time as head of the fur trade—and for the same reason. His interests had grown too diverse. He was too deeply immersed in railway manipulation and politics to devote his prime energies to being the Company's chief real-estate agent. Typically, the Hudson's Bay Company sat on its land, allowing prospective buyers to make bids but doing very little to promote sales. No effort was made to lure railway builders towards its territory, and London even turned down the opportunity of acting as paymaster, on Ottawa's behalf, for the newly created North West Mounted Police. During Smith's tenure, little farmland was sold. He did open a land office in Winnipeg, though he himself stayed mostly in Montreal, and successfully auctioned off town lots in Winnipeg and Portage la Prairie. The urban plots, measuring fifty feet by a hundred, were sold at the equivalent rate of $7,000 an acre.*

An enduring mystery of this interregnum in his career is why, as the HBC's senior representative in North America, Smith didn't even attempt to convince his British principals that they should take advantage of the HBC's primacy in the North-West. Although he was right at the centre of the action, in charge of the HBC's most future-oriented department, he did little to expand the Company's revenue base and nothing to involve the HBC in railway construction. Smith put up a small hotel at Portage la Prairie, built a few grist mills, and began operating a ferry service across the Assiniboine at Fort Ellice—and that was the full extent of the HBC's diversification during his stewardship. Asleep at the edge of the rapidly awakening new territories, the HBC land department under Smith's direction gave up its head start by default and lapsed into a period of ill-tempered hibernation. It was typical of the HBC's mentality that while great opportunities were being lost, the Company was concerning itself mainly with such fusty detail as setting rates on the Fort Ellice ferry. Crossing tariffs were minutely differentiated at twenty cents for a cart with one horse or ox and thirty cents for the same vehicle drawn by two animals. Foot passengers were charged a straight eight cents.

As the Canadian historian Michael Bliss astutely noted in his epic history of Canadian business, *Northern Enterprise*, "If ever an organization had a head

---

* The HBC presented fifty acres to the new Government of Manitoba as sites for office buildings. The first sale from the HBC's 500-acre Fort Garry Reserve was to the Canadian Pacific Hotel Company for $838 per lot; the first land sale, 640 acres near Emerson, Manitoba, was to William McKechnie for six dollars an acre, or $3,840.

start on the commerce of an area it was surely the Hudson's Bay Company in the lands that became western Canada. If the Company of Adventurers of the 1860s and 1870s had been as shrewd and supple as its founders had been two centuries earlier, it would have diversified and adjusted its organization to exploit the new order being brought about by Canadian expansion. It would have dominated, if not monopolized, trade and development in the new West. It would have been a leader in transportation—one of the Company's historic strengths." Bliss is right. Although the CPR was built by a syndicate in which Smith was a dominant influence, there is no record in the HBC archives of any suggestion by him that the Company become involved in railways.

The inevitable and hardly surprising conclusion is that, once again, Smith applied his self-serving code to the situation and chose the CPR instead of the HBC as his favoured instrument. The railway, at least in those years, must have seemed to him an attractive personal investment with the possibility of unlimited perks for early shareholders; the HBC, on the other hand, was only his employer, and it would be another decade before Smith would hold enough stock to control its policies. For more than forty years he lived with a deepening conflict of interest between the two organizations—at first in terms of which group would build the railway and later in terms of whose land he would try harder to sell. This meant appraising the conflicting geographies of the two companies: the HBC's infrastructure glued to the rivers that had once been highways for the fur trade while the new population centres followed the ribbons of steel. When he eventually became the dominant shareholder of both, Smith was free to balance the land-sales policies of the CPR and HBC, which at least in their time frames were complementary rather than competitive. Interested in building up traffic along its new tracks, the Canadian Pacific was anxious to sell its land sooner than the Hudson's Bay Company, which regarded real estate as part of the price for surrendering its monopoly and was determined to obtain top dollar, no matter how long it had to wait. Certainly it was no accident that by 1914, the year of Smith's death, only one of the fifteen prairie towns with HBC department stores (Fort Qu'Appelle) was not served by CPR trains.

It took five years for Smith to lose his patience with the land business. When he finally decided to resign in 1879, his departure was applauded by the London board, fed up with his inability to keep the books straight. "Looking to the small amount of work connected with the accounts of the Land Department it was hoped that the details would have been promptly and regularly rendered," HBC Secretary William Armit had scolded, "but as the Committee are again disappointed in this respect, they direct me to state that a minute was passed directing your special attention to the matter and calling upon you to render the accounts in question regularly." Smith had grown exasperated by the slow pace and bureaucratic nature of the Land Department. Real-estate sales seemed to be in remission until the advent of the railroads, and title transfers of the few acres that were sold could be handled by clerks. Smith was by now more of a railroader than a Bay man and for the next four years occupied no official post with the Company.

It was a sign of the times that he was succeeded as Land Commissioner by a railwayman, Charles John Brydges, who had been general manager of the Grand Trunk and general superintendent of government railways under Alexander Mackenzie's administration. A confidant of leading Canadian politicians, a good friend of Sir John Rose, who was about to be appointed the HBC's Deputy Governor, Brydges carried himself with an air of righteous enthusiasm. "His arrival in Winnipeg," observed historians Alan Wilson and R.A. Hotchkiss, "... was like that of a great administrative juggernaut. Extensive surveys began in prospect of a 'Manitoba Fever'; new administrative, legal, accounting, and advertising machinery emerged; contracts for supplies to Indians and the North West Mounted Police became competitive; new hotel and milling facilities enhanced the value of HBC lands; a subsidiary bridge company for the Red and Assiniboine rivers at Winnipeg was formed; the retail stores were reorganized under new men, not those only 'accustomed to the barter system with the Indians'; supervision of barge and steam transport of goods and passengers was wrenched from the hands of 'incompetents'; and, finally, executive operations were permanently moved from Montreal to Winnipeg in November 1880. Within a year the HBC was recognized as the most reliable source for information on settlement and commerce in Manitoba and the North-West Territories." This was good news to everyone but Smith, who didn't want any successor showing him up. He had refused Brydges the courtesy of a briefing and didn't even pass on his correspondence files, though the new Commissioner discovered unpaid seven-year-old HBC tax bills in Smith's desk.

At the same time as the business tempo in Canada was picking up under Brydges, a similar transformation was taking place at the Company's head office. With Goschen's return to politics in 1880, the energetic Eden Colvile was appointed Governor. He stood out from his twenty-four predecessors in two important respects: he understood something about the fur trade and he had actually visited Canada's North-West.

The son of Andrew Colvile, who had served the HBC for most of three decades as Deputy Governor and Governor in the mid-1800s, the younger Colvile had been sent to Rupert's Land as Associate Governor in 1849. Only eight years out of Eton and Cambridge, he had apprenticed brilliantly under Sir George Simpson's direction and became a lifelong HBC enthusiast. He turned head office into a far more interventionist agency and was determined to rid the Company of Donald Smith's corrosive influence. Colvile's love of the Company made him distrust Smith, who had so cavalierly mishandled his last two appointments, and the British Governor specifically instructed Brydges to displace the vestiges of Smith's authority and to downgrade the Fur Commissioner, James Grahame, so that he could be responsible for the entire North American operation.*

Unlike Smith, who regarded life in Winnipeg as a necessary but melancholy inconvenience, Brydges threw himself into community activities, becoming head of the Manitoba Board of Trade, chairman of the Winnipeg General Hospital, head of the local Anglican church's building committee, and president of the Manitoba Club, the exclusive gentlemen's watering-hole incorporated only eight months after the city itself.† Brydges succeeded in

---

* For his part Colvile returned some of the lost grandeur to the Company by acquiring a flotilla of impressive ships to serve its West Coast operations directly from England. Pride of the fleet was the graceful tea clipper *Titania*, then the world's second-fastest vessel—next only to the *Arid* and faster than the *Cutty Sark* or the *Thermopylae*. Two hundred feet long, she made the 14,000-mile journey from Victoria to London in a record-breaking 104 days. Built in 1866 by Robert Steele at the Steele yard on the Clyde, she was designed by his brother, William Steele. Basil Lubbock, the authority on clipper ships, said of *Arid* and *Titania*: "[They] carried all before them in the tea races, besides being the most beautiful and yacht-like merchantmen that ever sailed the seas." Flying the Company's pennant for six years, the *Titania* was luckier than most of the HBC's Pacific squadron—the *Labouchere*, *Lady Lampson* and *Pacific*, which all foundered on the intertidal rocks of the West Coast.

† No other Canadian private club has symbolized so directly the concentration of economic authority in any province, institutionalizing its decision-making process from the beginning. Membership in the Manitoba Club, according to W.L. Morton, remained "the symbol of success and the Club itself the centre of the informal exchange of opinion and information—access which marks the 'insider.'" If you were male, that is. F.M. Macklin, an early member who served for many years as general manager of the *Winnipeg Free Press*, explained during a Club debate on whether or not to admit women that he gloried "in the progress women have made. I rejoice in the liberty they enjoy. I would

altering the local image of the HBC as a distantly run, shadowy presence. His spans across the rivers (inevitably known as "Brydges' bridges") drew people from east and south of the city to the Company store, and he even persuaded municipal politicians to site the terminus of the city's first streetcar line on HBC property.

Between the summers of 1880 and 1883, Winnipeg, by then known as the Bull's Eye of the Dominion or the Chicago of the North, exploded into a land boom. Some 1,300 lots were sold in Winnipeg alone, with other town-sites at Portage la Prairie, West Lynne (adjoining and later absorbed by Emerson) and Rat Portage (Kenora) filling up equally fast, while in a single year (1882) some 341,588 acres of farmland worth $2,235,308 were sold—sixteen times the previous annual total. "The office now is like a fair," Brydges happily reported to London, "and the people stand in a row waiting their turn to reach the counter. It is like the crowd at the entrance to the pit of a London theatre...." and two months later, "Bedlam let loose was a mere incident to the scene in our office.... I never saw Winnipeg in such a state of frantic excitement."

The boom quickly degenerated into a speculative frenzy; Winnipeg's streets "were more crowded than Broadway." The initial lake shipment of Manitoba grain was delivered by James Richardson & Sons in 1883. The Harris Company of Brantford, Ontario, established its first Winnipeg agricultural implement dealership in 1878 and signed up seventeen agencies across the West. One of the main real-estate investors was Donald Smith. He used the knowledge he had gained as the HBC's Land Commissioner to purchase properties on his own account, even utilizing Bain & Blanchard, the HBC's Winnipeg legal firm, to negotiate the contracts. Not surprisingly, he chose the lots within the four-mile belt along the Assiniboine, then thought to be the most probable route of the CPR being built by a syndicate to which he belonged. He also invested in the new CPR hotel. He not only obtained a $15,000 loan from the Company to purchase the hotel property but also demanded that Brydges turn over to him gratis two of the HBC's most desirable

---

extend that freedom to embrace the granting of every privilege they might ask, every wish they might express, save one, the privilege of admission to the Manitoba Club. I appeal to you, preserve one little spot on this planet where the swish of women's skirts and the music of their voices are not heard.... It would prove a great boon to many of us who for an hour or two every now and then want to live the simple life." Women members (and Jews) were finally admitted in 1974, though neither group has since taken much advantage of the privilege it took only a hundred years to achieve.

town lots. Brydges refused, and, fearing an end run, wrote to London recommending against the grant.

Preoccupied as he may have been with his railroading schemes, Smith had no intention of losing touch with the Hudson's Bay Company's intimate corporate affairs and never ceased expanding his stockholdings. He hired spies inside Brydges's office to keep him informed of the Land Commissioner's correspondence with London and even rented space in the new Winnipeg real-estate building to keep a personal eye on who came to call on Brydges and for how long. "I am satisfied that there has been a long pending scheme to wreck the H.B. Co. and buy it up as a wreck," Brydges complained to London about Smith, "and there is much chagrin & disgust that the scheme did not succeed. Mr. Smith has been very outspoken in denouncing the trade operations of the Co as at present conducted, and his friends talk very openly & very publicly in the same way. He has talked in that sense to me several times but I have simply listened. His course is altogether too sinuous."

Smith resented the confidence Governor Colvile had placed in Brydges, even though he had done little to deserve it himself. An honest man enthralled by his mission to breathe new life into the Company while helping to nurture the new West he had come to love, Brydges recognized early how essential it was for the Company to assume community leadership.* "Armed with ... [a] sense of the Board's confidence, he seldom hesitated to set his mark upon every aspect of the Company's operation ...," concluded historian Alan Wilson. "He operated from instinct and mandate as if he were Chief Commissioner, not Land Commissioner—and as if it were *his* task to create a new image of the Hudson's Bay Company as a citizen of the Canadian North West." Even when the Manitoba land boom fizzled and the HBC had to repossess property worth $900,000, Brydges managed the negotiations without harming the Company's reputation.

The clash between Smith and Brydges finally came into the open over the railways clawing their way towards Winnipeg. The Grand Trunk, Brydges's former employer, had been trying hard to discredit the CPR on world money markets, and, despite his vigorous denials, the Land Commissioner got some of the blame. More seriously, Brydges became involved in the controversy

---

* Brydges had a romanticism of his own. He claimed a link to the old barony of Chandos, whose holders owned Sudeley Castle, since the Civil War of the 1640s one of the great ruins of the English countryside.

over location of the CPR, whose engineers favoured crossing the Red River at Selkirk instead of Winnipeg because of spring flooding dangers. Brydges offered the railway twenty acres of prime land for a station and lobbied so strenuously and so successfully on behalf of the Winnipeg route that he permanently alienated not only Smith but also Charles Tupper, then federal Minister of Railways and Canals, and Sandford Fleming, the railway's chief engineer, who was also a director of the HBC.* Brydges supported the strong representations of Winnipeg business leaders against the CPR's branch-line monopoly and recommended the HBC grant city land to the Northern Pacific, an American railroad, to offset Canadian Pacific's influence. He gradually found himself with many local friends but just as many—and much more powerful—distant enemies.

The first hint of Smith's counter-attack was in a private letter Brydges received from Governor Colvile alleging irregularities in some of the Winnipeg land sales. The issue was brought up by Smith at the Company's 1882 shareholders' meeting, and a committee was struck to investigate the charges—specifically, that Company officials, including Brydges, had person-ally profited from buying fifty-six Winnipeg lots, eleven of which were later resold for almost the total purchase price. Except for HBC Deputy Governor Sir John Rose, the committee members—including Sandford Fleming and HBC Secretary William Armit—were solid Smith partisans, but even they found nothing to condemn Brydges for except the vague charge of having "erred on the side of prodigality." They recommended that HBC land auctions should be held only once a month with firm upset prices, and that no Company land be sold within five miles of the railway right-of-way. Like Smith, Fleming had a double loyalty to the HBC and CPR, and, like Smith, he usually came down on the side of the railway. "I do not believe in mixing up our land sales with anyone else," Brydges objected. "The proposal puts the

---

* A Scottish immigrant, Fleming surveyed routes for four pioneer railways, lithographed the country's first large-scale surveyor's maps, designed Canada's first postage stamp (the three-penny brown, featuring his drawing of a beaver, which turned the animal into a national emblem), wrote an interdenominational prayer book, founded the Royal Canadian Institute, laid the Pacific cable between Vancouver Island and Australia, was chancellor of Queen's University for thirty-five years, and served as an influential HBC director for more than a quarter of a century. Frustrated by trying to run trains across a country where every town set its own clocks, he invented standard time, which divided the earth into twenty-four fixed zones of fifteen longitudinal degrees each. Canadian territory, spanning a quarter of the earth's day, was divided into five time zones.

whole matter in the hands of the CPR." Sir John Rose's report totally vindicated Brydges. The Deputy Governor had even gone to the trouble of
personally examining the cancelled cheques for all the transactions
involved. As he wrote to Sir John A. Macdonald, "We ... trace all these
reports & complaints ... to Donald Smith. He has evidently a great enmity
towards [Brydges]...." None of the specific accusations against Brydges were
ever substantiated, and he was even awarded a cash bonus of £1,500 to
compensate for the mental stress he had suffered.

Smith wouldn't let up. At the 1883 General Court he revived the accusations as if no investigation had been made, and despite Rose's defence of
Brydges (which filled thirty pages of transcription) the Land Commissioner
remained under a cloud. After verbally approving the Company's annual
report, most of the shareholders departed the meeting. These included some of
the Committeemen, who assumed that, as was the custom, their re-election
would be routinely based on the "Governor's list." Instead, Smith got up and
proposed his own Committee slate, which included himself and one of his
financial allies, the noted barrister Charles Russell, later Lord Russell of
Killowen and Lord Chief Justice of England. A surprised Colvile called for a
secret ballot, and when the votes had been counted, thirteen of the fourteen
shareholders still present—everyone but Smith—supported the Governor's
list. But if Smith didn't have the numbers, he had the weight. His ballot represented 4,000 shares, far outnumbering the other votes. Smith took his seat on
the board, and when questioned by *The Times* about his successful *coup d'état*,
he piously declared, "My long connection of 40 years with the Hudson's Bay
Company and being, perhaps, the largest registered holder of the shares on the
books of the Company, should offer to my fellow proprietors some guarantees
that I am unlikely to take any course prejudicial to their interests."

A more incisive summary of the dubious manoeuvre was the verdict of
Shirlee Smith, a close student of the Company's history and until the autumn
of 1990 Keeper of the HBC Archives in Winnipeg. "Smith's actions were
certainly unethical and probably illegal," she wrote, "... but two of his great
strengths were strategy and timing. He now had a seat on the London
Committee and was thus in a position to have an even greater say in the Land
Department." And he did. At the following shareholders' meeting he championed a resolution appointing two directors (himself and Fleming) to form a
subcommittee in charge of supervising Canadian affairs. Smith insisted that
Brydges would have to report directly to the new subcommittee as well as to

the London board. Poor Brydges must have known the trap was closing on him, but he agreed to go along with the scheme, only to find that Smith never would see him, even when they were both in Winnipeg at the same time—and would then complain that Brydges wasn't accountable enough.

When Sir John Rose died suddenly in the summer of 1888 while stalking deer on the Scottish estate of the Duke of Portland, Smith's last critic on the HBC board disappeared, and he moved immediately to have himself named Deputy Governor. Within a week of his appointment, Smith returned to his campaign of harassment, forcing Brydges on the defensive by repeatedly asking him to justify his work and his salary. Sensing disaster, Brydges wrote to his friend Sir John A. Macdonald to complain that Smith's behaviour had "every appearance of a desire to worry me out." But it was too late. On January 17, 1889, a tired and exasperated Eden Colvile retired as HBC Governor, and Donald Smith was "elected" in his place. With the retirement of Colvile most management traditions were cast aside. Never again would an HBC Governor "take charge of the hammer" at the Company's fur auctions. The very day of the takeover, Brydges was sent a letter dispensing with his services.

Thus ended the feud between the conscientious Charles John Brydges and the fur trader turned autocrat who, during fifty-one years in the service, had advanced from muskrat grader at Lachine to Governor of the Company of Adventurers. Brydges didn't live long enough to receive his termination notice. On February 16, 1889, while inspecting the Winnipeg General Hospital, one of his favourite philanthropies, he died of a heart attack. The correspondence between the two men provides a telling example of Donald Smith's pettiness. He was indeed, as the *Dictionary of National Biography* noted in his entry, "A good hater ... resenting the success of other men's ideas."

WITHIN THREE YEARS OF ASSUMING the Governorship, which he was to hold for the next quarter-century, Smith had packed the board with money men who would do his bidding. Because he was both Governor and the Company's largest shareholder, the semi-annual meetings became more subdued affairs, particularly since he treated net land revenues as profit, which he distributed annually as dividends. Now that he was in charge, he could apply his thrifty policies freely on the expense side of the ledger, cutting the budget of the Land Department in half, for example.

Smith dismissed the fur trade as a doomed enterprise run by ill-starred eccentrics too stubborn or too ignorant to accommodate themselves to their fates. Although the proceeds of the fur trade kept the Company alive until the western land boom, that once buoyant commerce had deteriorated drastically since its heyday. Fur prices hit a twenty-year low in 1876, but trade was bolstered by diversification into new varieties. Instead of concentrating on beaver, the Company shipped out twenty-four categories of pelts, including muskrat, marten (Canadian sable), lynx, mink, otter, skunk, ermine, wolverine and seal, and muskox and buffalo robes.

Between 1876 and 1878, fur prices at London auctions declined by half, and wheat surpassed fur as Manitoba's leading export. Because the Company suffered continuing losses in the mid- and late 1870s, the Chief Factors and Traders who depended on dividends for their livelihoods were threatened with having to serve at their own expense. They retaliated by organizing themselves into a quasi-union called the Fur Trade Party to demand an annual guaranteed minimum dividend of £200 a share—but quickly grew quiescent when London offered £150. The oldtimers' feeling of abandonment was best expressed by Chief Factor James L. Cotter, descendant of an Irish baronet, who had been a Bay man for thirty years, mostly at Moose Factory.* "I ... see no prospect of ever being able to retire on anything beyond a mere pittance," he wrote to a fellow Factor. "My health is delicate, and I could not now go at anything else in the way of business; so I am beset with difficulties and anxieties on all hands.... We work as if at the pumps of a sinking ship. It is a strained and unhealthy state of mind."

Money was not the only problem. Although the fur trade enjoyed another fifty years of impressive activity, these hardy traders who had so diligently manned and maintained the HBC's land preserve felt dispossessed. The comforts, sophistications and relatives they had left behind in Scotland, England or the populated parts of Canada had become as disconnected from them as the rapidly changing contours of the once-immutable landscape of Rupert's Land. They had nowhere to turn. "While competent in the woods, I was inferior to John, the H.B. Co.'s messenger boy, in city life," complained George McTavish, a York Factory Chief Trader on a visit to Victoria. "My greatest fear was that I should display my ignorance, be laughed at and taken advantage of if I asked the price of everyday necessities, say a box of matches.

---

* Cotter also took the first pictures of the Hudson Bay area with a homemade camera, a tradition carried on by his grandson, George Cotter, who is the HBC's best contemporary documentary film-maker.

When my old schoolmate, Arthur Robertson, secured a place for me at the festive board of Miss Coates on Fort Street ... I was as a fish out of water. The table talk was unintelligible to me."

Chief Commissioner James Grahame, who had succeeded Smith in charge of the fur department, was replaced in 1884 by Joseph Wrigley, a vaguely connected Yorkshire businessman who proved so ineffective that he managed to give banality a bad name. The first Commissioner with no background in the fur business, he was hired strictly as an overseas agent to enforce London's will. And London's will under Smith's direction dictated that the fur traders be deprived of their 40 percent of the Company's profit. Wrigley promptly called a meeting of all the Chief Factors and Chief Traders—the Northern Council—for August 30, 1887, at the Queen's Hotel in Winnipeg.

They came from as far away as the Arctic Circle and the verdant forests of the Pacific slopes, the historic hovels around Hudson Bay and the modern if still primitive shops of the southern Prairies. There was great excitement as they journeyed to the Company's Canadian headquarters because there were rumours this would be the very last time the Northern Council, which had traditionally ruled their professional lives, was to meet.

The Winnipeg that greeted them was less a frontier settlement grown large than a commercial entrepôt, the hustling metropolis of the West, close to the height of its importance. The Grain Exchange was being organized—later to include the Bawlfs, Bells, Roblins, McMillans, Gaits, Mitchells, Atkinsons, Spinks, McBeans, Hastingses, Maulsons, Richardsons, Parrishes—and the new grain families were busy spawning their fortunes. The thriving community had not only its own private banks (Alloway & Champion was the biggest) and the West's best bordellos (on Annabella Street) but also a theatre and opera house (at the corner of Notre Dame and Adelaide) and even a telephone exchange (560 subscribers, with a special long-distance hookup to Selkirk, twenty-two miles away).

As they gathered for that final time, an anonymous photographer snapped a group portrait, revealing the fur traders as large but not fat. They have few double chins, no flabby, swollen bellies—just rib-cages as solid as if held together by barrel hoops. They boast trim beards and wise country eyes. The British poet Stephen Spender once remarked that for him the division between the past and the present was the French Revolution because he always imagined that before it, everyone wore fancy dress. The photograph catches that *fin de siècle* quality—the quandary of being out of one's place and time, knowing the world is wrong but being unable to change it. At one level, the picture evokes the sombre mood of men attending their own funerals, awkward in their Sunday suits, trying to position their age-dappled hands as if to show how very hard they had toiled. But a second look reveals these hard-etched faces glowing with a touch of swagger, the pride of having practised the continent's ancient commerce and survived.*

The meeting dealt with such mundane problems as the Northern Department's scale of allowances, which carefully equated rations to rank, so that, for instance, an Ordinary Interpreter would receive three pounds of tea a year, a Mechanic five pounds, an Apprentice Postmaster eight, a Postmaster ten, an Apprentice Clerk fifteen, a Clerk twenty and a Commissioned Officer thirty. Wrigley confirmed the traders' worst expectations that not only would this be the last Northern Council meeting but that no new commissions would be issued to those who had entered the service after the 1870 land transfer. That meant it was only a matter of time before their partnership with the Company would be dissolved. They would have to give up their 40-percent ownership and become bureaucrats instead of proprietors. "This very startling information threw a wet blanket over the entire Service and produced in many cases very unfavourable results in the Company's interest," reported N.M.W.J. McKenzie, a junior trader at the time. "The only interest the majority of their servants have had since then was their weekly, monthly or annual salary."

Wrigley was replaced within two years of the Winnipeg meeting by a Smith servitor named Clarence Campbell Chipman, a former secretary to Sir Charles Tupper. He closed down posts, hounded veteran traders out of the service, and dropped the apprentice plan that had kept the fur trade fuelled with new energies. "Here was a great scatteration, a breaking up of family ties so to speak," lamented N.M.W.J. McKenzie.

In 1893, Smith—speaking through Chipman—abruptly terminated the vestiges of the Deed Poll and extinguished the former wintering partners' equity positions. Some of the Chief Factors bewailed their fate ("I have

---

* Among those in attendance was Canada's least-heralded explorer, Robert Campbell, who had explored most of Yukon and once had snowshoed 3,000 miles from Fort Simpson on the Mackenzie River to Crow Wing, Minnesota, on the Mississippi. He was extraordinarily robust and seems never to have been ill. The day before Campbell died in 1894, at the age of eighty-six, he placed his hand on his forehead and declared in a puzzled tone, "I have a pain here. I suppose that is what people call a headache." It was his first and his last.

waited so long for promotion, and have worked so hard to make and keep affairs prosperous, that I have lost heart and do not care what is done," wrote J. Ogden Grahame); others became angry ("The *fiat* has gone forth and Attila is to ravage and destroy the handiwork of the 'Company of Adventurers,'" fumed Roderick Ross). But they all knew who was to blame.

Reduced from patriarchs of the forests to supervised employees, the winterers at last realized how the colleague they had so fervently hoped would champion their cause had betrayed them. A Factor named Duncan MacArthur summed up their rage when he termed Donald Smith "the prince of humbugs and probably the worst enemy the Company ever had."

Steal of Empire

Smith vacillated in his support between the Conservative and Liberal parties, equally disloyal to both and trusted by neither.

THE PUZZLE OF DONALD SMITH's straining for most of three decades to promote himself within the Hudson's Bay Company's hierarchy, rising to head its fur and, later, land operations, then treating these highly coveted positions as minor annoyances was explained by his obsession with having control of the Company instead of trying to run its functional parts. More to the point, at this midstage in his career Smith was preoccupied with politics and railways, faster and financially much more rewarding paths to power.

In contrast to most of his contemporaries, who sought wealth as an avenue to political influence, Smith recognized that in the primitive environment of his time it was infinitely easier to parlay political connections into lucrative private ventures, often supported by the public purse. "For forty years his personality stands out in every political crisis in the Dominion," noted W.T.R. Preston, one of Smith's many political foes. "He has had far more to do with the defeat and victory of political parties since Confederation than all other influences combined.... On many important occasions Parliament, without being aware of the fact, simply registered his decrees."

Smith's view of public life paralleled his approach to business. He believed political parties were no different from commercial corporations—handy conveyances to be boarded and abandoned at will, according to which one best served his personal purposes at any given moment. Smith was aware of no conflicts of interest in his adroit manoeuvrings between the private and public sectors because *his* interests never conflicted; they were, one and all, designed to advance his fame and his fortune. "His philosophical disposition to accept the inevitable never deserted him," noted Preston. "His standard of political honour was not high, but it served."

Smith vacillated in his support between the Conservative and Liberal parties, equally disloyal to both and trusted by neither. He once complained that he would not consign ownership of his grandmother's toothbrush to the ordinary politician—even if his own record proved the understatement of that taunt.

The buccaneering that characterizes developing economies found its most virulent expression in Canadian railway promotion. By 1915, when major construction ran out of steam, Canada had 40,000 miles of rails, built with government cash, subventions or bond guarantees worth more than $1.3 billion—plus the giveaway of 65,000 square miles including some of the finest wheat-growing land on earth. Yet despite these extravagant provisions, nearly every mile of every track was privately owned. Financing a new railway usually meant its promoters would set up secretly controlled construction companies, then negotiate inflated contracts with themselves, collecting hefty profits at both ends of each deal. At the same time, they would award themselves bloated debenture offerings in return for artificial corporate services, reducing their balance sheets to rivers of red ink. They would then turn to Ottawa and demand subsidies to cover fiscal overruns, either bribing ministers to ensure bailouts or threatening to embarrass the government by halting construction—or both.

And yet the railways did get built, and they provided the essential infrastructure for the transcontinental economy, yanking an embryonic Dominion into the new century. The railways' promoters and operators became folk heroes, Canada's version of the great American robber barons— reviled and envied, riding about in their ornate private cars, gesturing with fat cigars, collecting old masters and young mistresses. Apart from the obvious chicanery in the link between politicians in power and these railway manipulators, the industry corrupted the electoral process itself. Railways and politics in nineteenth-century Canada became interchangeable black arts, only marginally more ethical than piracy on the high seas.

DONALD SMITH'S DEBUT in Canadian politics followed his successful arbitration of the Red River Rebellion in 1870. He contested and won the Winnipeg and St John seat in Manitoba's first provincial election and was simultaneously appointed to the executive council of the Northwest Territories. Unhappy with its municipal status as a "police village," Winnipeg in 1872 requested the right to incorporate itself as a city, but the new provincial legislature adjourned without dealing with the issue. Feelings ran so high that when enactment of the measure was delayed by Dr. Curtis James Bird, a local physician who had been elected the legislature's Speaker, he was lured out of his home on a phony nocturnal house call and waylaid by constituents who dragged him from his sleigh and poured a bucket of tar over him. Popular outrage had been roused by a belief that Bird was helping Smith oppose incorporation so that the HBC could avoid paying city taxes. Insinuations of corporate favouritism were fanned by the fact that the province's first lieutenant-governor, A.G. Archibald, lived on Company property and his successor, Alexander Morris, toured his domain aboard HBC steamers. Before Manitoba's first bank was incorporated in 1873, the Company acted as the provincial treasury and repository for funds collected by customs officers. This official status, added to the retroactive bitterness over the HBC's long monopoly, had jelled into an enduring resentment of the Company and all its works. Dr John Christian Schultz, the charismatic leader of Manitoba's pro-Canadian movement, summed up popular sentiment when he labelled the Hudson's Bay Company "a curse to the country."

The act of incorporation was finally passed in the closing days of 1873. Winnipeg's original street surveys followed the Métis river lots and boundaries of the HBC's Land Reserve, its five-hundred-acre holding around Fort Garry.* The settlement's muddy alleys ("a mixture of putty and bird-lime") had been graded and planked, but there was nothing tame about Winnipeg's roughneck inhabitants, who turned the settlement into Canada's closest approximation to the American Wild West. The gin mills and mug-houses were there, as were the prostitutes brazenly auctioning off their sexual wares. "Winnipeg and Barrie are the two most evil places in Canada," went a typical report of the time.

Smith sponsored few initiatives in the Manitoba Legislature mainly because he was hardly ever there. Quickly growing dissatisfied with the constraints of provincial and municipal venues, he won the Selkirk federal

---

* Winnipeg's original coat of arms featured a buffalo, a steam locomotive and three sheaves of wheat. This was slightly fanciful, since the buffalo had long vanished from the city's environs, the first train would not arrive until 1878, and there would be no substantial grain exports for another five years.

seat in 1871 and held it in the next three campaigns.* He showed no favouritism, being elected twice as a Conservative and twice as a Liberal. The contests were hard fought, with boozing and brawling part of each run-up to election day and axe handles across the head frequently used to persuade dithering voters. Smith's margins of victory, ranging from a high of 196 ballots in 1872 to only 9 in 1878, reflected the bitterness of these contests.

The first Manitoba representative to arrive in Ottawa, Smith didn't take his parliamentary career too seriously and spent little time in legislative pursuits; debating the fine points of new laws was not a profit-producing enterprise. But from the moment he walked into the House of Commons, Smith knew that within the shifting alliances of that resplendent chamber there was significant personal authority to be gained, and he intended to grab it. The great issue of 1871 was British Columbia's entry into Confederation. The twelve thousand white residents of the former HBC territory and British colony had decided to enter Confederation as Canada's sixth province on condition they be linked to the rest of the country by a railway within ten years. The only regular passage across the Rockies north of the forty-ninth parallel was by HBC-owned pack mules. The animals, fitted with *aphareos* (Mexican-style pack saddles), gathered at the Punch Bowl, near what is now Jasper, to transfer loads and passengers.†

The entrepreneur who first undertook to build a railway across the Canadian West was Sir Hugh Allan, yet another Scottish immigrant, who had expanded his Montreal shipping line into the North Atlantic's largest merchant and passenger fleet. Allan had most leading Conservative politicians, including Sir John A. Macdonald, Sir John Rose and Sir George-Étienne Cartier, in his pocket and regularly obtained lucrative subsidies and mail contracts for his maritime operations. Named to the Bank of Montreal board, Allan also expanded his coal and steel interests, and built himself Ravenscrag, a magnificent house on a fourteen-acre estate on Mount Royal that had originally been owned by the greatest of the Nor'Westers, Simon McTavish. Modelled on a fifteenth-century Tuscan villa, the house had thirty-four rooms including

---

* The constituency Donald A. Smith represented was known as Lisgar in his time. In 1891 the name was changed to Selkirk. Some sources list Smith as Member for Lisgar, others for Selkirk.
† HBC packtrains, numbering three hundred or more animals, were led by a guide followed by a bagpiper and an HBC Chief Factor, who usually carried a Bible and a bottle of gin in his saddlebags, consulting both along the way.

an imposing ballroom complete with a minstrels' gallery to accommodate a large orchestra. From the estate's seventy-five-foot tower Allan could scan the horizon for glimpses of his steamers returning from their weekly run to Glasgow or setting off to supply the sloping riverbank settlements along the St Lawrence. (These luxurious surroundings contrasted harshly with conditions at Allan's east-end Montreal cotton mill, which employed ten-year-old street waifs who didn't earn enough to buy shoes in winter.)

When the Macdonald government decided to honour its railway commitment to British Columbia, Sir Hugh Allan was the logical choice to head the construction syndicate. His lawyer, John J.C. Abbott (later Canada's fourth prime minister), incorporated the Canada Pacific Railway Company to take advantage of Ottawa's offer to grant the builder $30 million in cash and fifty million acres of land, plus an undertaking to extinguish Indian title along the way. Donald Smith was originally recruited as a member of Allan's syndicate to ensure the Hudson's Bay Company's cooperation in gaining use of its existing infrastructure through western Canada, but his name was not included in the final offering memorandum. To guarantee that he would be granted the Pacific railway charter under Ottawa's generous terms, Allan pledged secret subscriptions of $100,000 to Macdonald's 1872 campaign fund and even arranged for his Merchants' Bank to cancel $80,000 of Macdonald's personal debts.

The great Pacific Scandal that followed, one of the most thoroughly documented instances of bribery in the country's political history, involved more than $500,000. Its least subtle manifestation was the telegram Macdonald sent to John Abbott, the Allan lawyer, at the climax of the 1872 campaign: "I MUST HAVE ANOTHER TEN THOUSAND. WILL BE THE LAST TIME OF CALLING. DO NOT FAIL ME. ANSWER TODAY—J.A. MACDONALD." Abbott consulted with Allan and hastily replied: "DRAW ON ME FOR TEN THOUSAND DOLLARS." When the Montreal *Herald* published these and other incriminating documents, a royal commission was established to investigate the bribery allegations. It found the Tories guilty as charged. Macdonald had won the 1872 election with a dismal margin of only two seats, and his government seemed doomed—unless he could somehow retain Parliament's confidence. Macdonald quickly realized the fate of his administration hung on one vote, that of Donald Smith. "Upon you and the influence you can bring to bear," he wrote to the HBC executive, "may depend the fate of this administration."

Smith was in Fort Carlton, halfway from Fort Garry to Edmonton, on an inspection trip at the time, but immediately rushed back to Ottawa. He set a record of only five days returning to Fort Garry, six hundred miles to the east. Angus McKay, then a fifteen-year-old HBC apprentice, witnessed that mad dash across the Prairies. "We first noticed a cloud of dust on the big salt plain near Humbolt [sic]," he wrote in his journal. "Then we saw a buckboard, a Red River cart and a bunch of loose horses, driven by two men on horseback. When they met our freight train [of Red River carts], they stopped for a few minutes to ask questions while the men changed a tired horse for a fresh one, driving on again and leaving the tired one on the prairie. [Smith] was strapped crossways on his breast with wide strappings and onto the seat of the buckboard to prevent his falling out when asleep. It was the fastest journey ever made between Carlton and Winnipeg with horses."

Smith was in his seat when the Commons met on October 23, 1873. He hoped that Macdonald might take this occasion to grant Louis Riel the amnesty that had originally been promised and to pay back the $3,000 Smith had spent bribing the Métis leader and his followers during the 1870 Rebellion. The debt was long overdue, and Smith rightly maintained that he had been carrying out Ottawa's instructions, but had to pay the money out of his own pocket because there were no banking facilities in Red River at the time. The Prime Minister never disowned the debt, but he didn't honour it either. He was all too aware of how precarious the Conservatives' political situation was and that if word of any amnesty or payments to Riel leaked out, he would lose his remaining support in Orange Ontario.

The Prime Minister's cronies buzzed around Smith, trying to ensure his support, and eventually arranged a private meeting between the two men. Macdonald had been drinking for most of three days and took exaggerated offence when Smith calmly requested repayment of his loan and then advised the Prime Minister to confess his political sins and ask the country for forgiveness. Instead of trying to appease his western MP, Macdonald dared him to make the Riel bribe public, boasting with the false courage of the bottle that he could win Ontario in another election, no matter what Smith said about him. That barely coherent bombast was followed by a stream of woozy obscenities, as the Prime Minister worked himself up into red-faced ferment and finally passed out.

The performance didn't impress the puritanical Smith. He let it be known he would probably go against the administration but agreed to postpone his final decision until the night of the vote. Smith met with a sobered-up Prime Minister two days later, on November 4, and yet again asked for his Riel money back. Macdonald wearily agreed, had Smith write out an invoice, and promised he would he paid $3,367.50 the following morning. (Smith had characteristically added an interest charge.) The two men parted warily, as if they had not yet taken the full measure of one another.

The Commons session that evening was jammed with so many political ward heelers and lobbyists that they were crowded into the space on either side of the Speaker's dais. The busiest spot on Parliament Hill was the bar in the Commons basement, as MPs used any excuse to sneak away and toast their fortunes or drown their sorrows.*

At five minutes after one on that moon-washed autumn night, when the question on the government's amendment to the non-confidence motion was put, Smith finally rose to speak. The House of Commons hushed as its members tried to size up the enigmatic "member for the Hudson's Bay Company," the penthouse of his eyebrows masking any signal of his intentions. Barely four years removed from the Labrador wilderness, Smith was about to determine whether Canada's founding ministry would survive. He began hesitantly, as if suddenly aware of how far he had come and how much depended on his decision. He condemned the Liberal Opposition for establishing a case against the government on the basis of purloined letters and telegrams, defending the sanctity of private correspondence. He meandered on about Manitoba's need to have its own railway, then seemed to harden in his discourse by declaring that the. Prime Minister had certainly not taken Sir Hugh Allan's money with any corrupt motive. That satisfied the Tory Whip, who led a troop of relieved Government benchers to the bar, where they lifted tumblers charged with champagne "To the health of Donald A." It wasn't long before they were chanting "Rule, Britannia!" and

---

* There has never been anything unusual (then or now) in having drunken MPs on the floor of the Commons, but tactics in those days were slightly more crude. Whenever the sozzled members got excited, they would throw parliamentary papers (or, on one occasion, firecrackers) into the air, mimic roosters, dogs or bagpipes, perform jigs up and down the aisles—or just go to sleep. An inebriated James Domville, president of the Maritime Bank and MP for King's, New Brunswick, is on record in Hansard as having addressed the Commons with the fly of his pants open, and Colonel C.J. Campbell, the MP for Victoria County, Cape Breton, once prostrated himself at the feet of the Speaker, bellowing a drunken challenge for anyone in government, on Parliament Hill or from the whole universe to come and fight him.

"God Save the Queen"—the echoes of their ribaldry drifting up to the Commons floor.

There the mood had changed. Donald Smith had turned sour. "I would be most willing to vote confidence in the Government," he said, baiting the trap, "if I could do so conscientiously." Then, with that special brand of righteousness reserved for middle-aged Scots with long beards, he pronounced his verdict: "For the honour of the country, no government should exist that has a shadow of suspicion resting upon it; and for that reason, I cannot give it my support." A page hastily whipped down to the bar to inform the revellers: "Donald A. has gone over to the Grits." Members rushed back to vent their fury at the treachery of their colleague from Red River.

The Commons was adjourned without a recorded vote, but the government knew it was beaten and resigned the following afternoon. As Sir John A. Macdonald walked out of the chamber that momentous night, he turned to one of his cronies and remarked with bitter bite: "I could lick that man Smith quicker than hell could frizzle a feather." In the parliamentary basement, the Liberals now had their own bellies to the bar, singing "Sir John is dead and gone forever," to the tune of "My Darling Clementine."*

Behind Smith's switch in allegiances was a web of motives that became clear only in retrospect. Charles Tupper, in an 1877 speech at Orangeville, Ontario, described the HBC executive's 1873 tactics: "Mr. Smith was a representative of the Hudson's Bay Company and he had been pressing a claim on his Right Hon. friend [Macdonald] for public money; Sir John had been holding back, and Mr. Smith came to the conclusion that it would be just as well to jump the fence if there was to be a change of Government. But Mr. Smith was a canny man; he held back and sat on the fence and watched the course,

---

*Ironically, Macdonald's last act before leaving office was to implement one of Smith's recommendations in his report on the Red River Rebellion: creation of a North West Mounted Police to rid the plains of American whisky pedlars and proclaim Canadian sovereignty. (In the summer of 1873, twenty-two Assiniboines were massacred by the rotgut traders in the Cypress Hills of what is now southeastern Alberta.) Their first commanding officer, Lieutenant-Colonel George French, head of the Canadian Militia Gunnery School at Kingston, treated his troops more as a cavalry regiment than a police force. That impression was heightened by their first uniforms: red jackets modelled on the British Army's red coats, cut to resemble those of Hussars, black breeches with red stripes as worn by the British cavalry, lances like those carried into battle by the doomed Light Brigade in the Crimean War, and pillbox hats held on with chinstraps—later replaced by Texas Ranger stetsons.

certainly not in the interests of his country, because he did not want to jump too soon and find that he had jumped into a ditch. But, when he came to the conclusion that the Government was going out, he made the bolt, and he (Dr. Tupper) had no doubt but that he had had a great deal of reason since for congratulating himself on having jumped as he did." But beyond such strategic considerations was Smith's ambition to build the Pacific railway himself. In their wonderful *Lords of the Line,* popular historians David Cruise and Alison Griffiths unlock the mystery. "The key to Smith's actions most likely lay in the awarding of the Pacific railway contract, in which he had a clear personal interest. Certainly no one knew better than he the potential wealth of the northwest, and he wasn't anxious that the lush Red River territory be entrusted to the whims and self-interest of Hugh Allan...." That imputing of motives rings true, but it doesn't do full justice to Smith's baser side. There was yet another reason for his betrayal of Macdonald.

By aligning his syndicate with Jay Cooke's Northern Pacific, Allan had virtually guaranteed that his Canada Pacific Railway Company would have to utilize an extension of the American promoter's railway from the international boundary to Winnipeg. Cooke had for years wanted to expand the Northern Pacific into Canada, and this would have been his ideal opportunity. But a competing syndicate, led by Smith and including his cousin George Stephen, had already applied for a railway charter to serve the link between the border town of Pembina and Winnipeg—just sixty miles away. Smith was also protecting his private investment in the Pembina venture.

In the 1874 election that followed, Smith ran as a Liberal supporting Alexander Mackenzie, the Sarnia stonemason who became Canada's second Prime Minister.* Smith's political antics had begun to concern London. The HBC Governor pointedly wrote to James Grahame, the Company's Canadian Chief Commissioner: "We are now simply a trading corporation and wish to confine ourselves to our own business, cultivating the most friendly relations with those in authority, but taking no side with one party or another...." Smith paid no attention to such admonitions and won his seat with a 102-vote margin. At one meeting, local Tories, furious at his defection, pelted him with raw eggs until he was unrecognizable. "Few figures in political history apart

---

* Mackenzie's background contributed to his reputation as Canada's most close-mouthed Prime Minister. While he was working as a stonemason, a hunk of cut stone weighing more than a ton dropped on his toes. He uttered not a sound—and during his five years in office said very little about anything important.

from Benedict Arnold ... have incurred the opprobrium directed at the member from Selkirk," noted the business historian Gustavus Myers.

Back in Ottawa as one of Mackenzie's most influential advisers, Smith began to lobby for his Pembina charter. The Liberal Prime Minister had assumed the Public Works portfolio himself, determined to build the transcontinental railway as a government enterprise without increasing taxes or pledging incentives to greedy promoters.

At about this time, Smith's interest quickened in an awkwardly named relic of American railway speculation called the First Division of the St Paul and Pacific line. That preoccupation dated from his first meeting with James J. Hill, the Canadian-born entrepreneur from St Paul, Minnesota. The two men had tented together in 1870 when Smith was returning to Ottawa from settling the Red River Rebellion. They had jointly acquired the Red River Transportation Company—possibly the most profitable steamship line in North America.* Now that their shipping monopoly was threatened by the advent of railways, Hill came to Ottawa early in 1876 and stayed with Smith at the Bank of Montreal's residential "Cottage" on O'Connor Street. He had arrived late in the afternoon of St Patrick's Day in the vanguard of a fierce blizzard, and the two men talked for most of two days about what could be done. Their thoughts quickly turned to the First Division of the St Paul and Pacific, which had gone bankrupt and was being reorganized by a trustee, John S. Kennedy, and the line's receiver, Jesse P. Farley. The main bondholders were six hundred Dutch investors, headed by Johan Carp, who were owed $28 million. Hill knew they had become disillusioned by long-overdue payments and were open to offers. The two promoters agreed that Hill would obtain more details about the insolvent property, reach a realistic estimate of what salvage price the Dutch might accept, and put feelers out to the railway's receiver.

Smith had frequently travelled aboard the unfinished St Paul and Pacific on his way to and from Red River. Seldom out of bankruptcy, the ravaged

* With their partners Norman Kittson and Captain Alexander Griggs, Hill and Smith had turned the Red River Transportation Company's monopoly into a formidable cash cow. Although it discounted HBC transportation invoices by one-third, helping to maintain the London firm's oligopoly in the area, the transportation company still turned such a huge profit that annual dividends of 80 percent were not unusual. One of Smith's critics calculated that regular freight charges along the Red River Transportation Company's three hundred miles of slack navigation cost customers double the rates paid for taking grain across the Atlantic and that freight could be sent the length of the Mississippi for half as much.

company maintained the link between St Paul and Breckenridge with an increasingly decrepit railbed. By 1873, the right of way was littered with rotting ties and twisted remains of collapsed bridges. The tracks were a crazy-quilt of fifteen different types of rail, all made of iron instead of steel so that passage of a train made the whole rusty works tremble. Several stretches could be crossed only by handcar. James J. Hill's investigation revealed that despite its grotesque physical plant, the road was still an immensely valuable property. He discovered that an investment of only $5.8 million (most of which could be borrowed from the Bank of Montreal) would be enough not only to buy out the Dutch bondholders but also to complete the tracks to St Vincent, a town on the international boundary, which was the cut-in point for the 2.6-million-acre state grant that the woefully underfinanced railway had never been able to trigger. The road also had an exclusive charter to build up to the Canadian border. Because most of the land in the grants was in counties that were now well settled, Hill estimated that the bankrupt railway's real-estate assets alone were worth at least $20 million.

To complete the deal, Smith enlisted the cousin, George Stephen, he had first met while still a Factor in Labrador. Stephen had meanwhile become president of the Bank of Montreal and a dominant figure in Canadian finance. He was sufficiently interested to visit Amsterdam, where he obtained an option to buy the Dutch bonds at a third of their nominal value. He then arranged to have the Bank of Montreal underwrite a loan to take out both the railway's mortgage holders and the Netherlands group, while Smith, Hill and their partner Norman Kittson rolled their Red River Transportation Company shares over into railway stock. In 1878, the Smith-Hill-Stephen-Kittson partnership won clear title to the line and renamed it the St Paul, Minneapolis and Manitoba Railway. They put up only $283,000 in cash for what turned out to be a bonanza. Within a decade the railway would be worth $60 million and over the next thirty years Smith and his partners received an estimated $500 million in interest-bearing securities, not including dividends, from the once-defunct property.

The full potential of the renamed St Paul line could only be realized with completion of the Canadian link to Winnipeg. Prime Minister Mackenzie had promised to build that branch line to provide citizens of the newly incorporated province of Manitoba with outside access. Construction was painfully slow, but by the spring of 1878 the Pembina Branch was snaking the sixty miles to the American border. The first spike had been driven on

September 29, 1877, in St Boniface when the Governor General, Lord Dufferin, and his wife had each driven a silver spike into the first tie. The viceregal couple had been entertained by Smith at Silver Heights, his estate outside Winnipeg. "It is impossible to describe to you," Dufferin wrote to Mackenzie about that visit, "all that Donald Smith has done for our comfort. Had he been a great Duke in the old country receiving the Queen, he could not have made greater assertions,—in fact, I am quite vexed about it as the expense of his preparations must have been very considerable, and they quite exceed what we needed, for instance, he has built a large Reception Room, and two offices for the Colonel and myself, which are quite equal to those at Rideau, and in the minutest details has forgotten nothing...."

Stephen had lobbied the Prime Minister hard to allow his St Paul syndicate to lease the new line, but Smith's participation in the project was a complicating factor. The Liberal leader knew that no undertaking with the Smith name attached to it would be approved by Sir John A. Macdonald and his Tories, who remained so angry with Smith that they left the House of Commons *en masse* whenever he rose to speak. When Mackenzie introduced the bill to lease the line on March 18, 1878, he not only left out Smith's name but also pointedly denied that Smith had any connection with the project. The Opposition Tories quickly turned the routine bill into a major issue, with Macdonald insisting that the legislation was a fraudulent measure because it would only "put money in [Smith's] own pocket." Mackenzie used his Commons majority to ram the lease through, but it was vetoed by the Tory-dominated Senate. Smith informed the Prime Minister that if the roadbed could not be legally leased, his syndicate would be happy merely to rent running rights. When Mackenzie approved that compromise, Macdonald could no longer hold himself back. In a stunning attack on Smith, the Tory leader commended the Senate's action, "which would put a stop to their [the government's] bargain with the honorable member for Selkirk to make him a rich man and to pay him for his servile support."

Smith rose in the Commons the following afternoon (the last day of the session) to defend his honour. The House was all set to prorogue for a general election, but the Selkirk member's question of privilege halted the proceedings and turned Parliament into a rowdy day-care centre. When George Brown, founding editor of the Toronto *Globe* and at the time a Liberal senator, described the scene that followed as "the most disgraceful in the annals of the Canadian House of Commons," he was indulging in understatement. Members' shouts escalated from "liars" to "treacherous liars" and many cruder epithets that Hansard reporters chose to ignore. Just as the Commons was on the verge of bedlam, the sonorous knock of Black Rod, the parliamentary official whose entry signals termination of sessions, could be heard. The Speaker, trying to invite him in, as protocol demanded, could not make himself heard, so the poor man kept on knocking. "Finally ... Black Rod entered," reported W.T.R. Preston, then a parliamentary page. "He bowed, as usual. His lips moved, but no sound reached the frantic House. The Speaker stood up and evidently made an announcement. He was not heard—the 'Faithful Commons' continued to shout at one another with unabated fury! Finally, with what dignity he could muster, the Speaker stepped down from the dais, the Sergeant-at-Arms shouldered the mace, and preceded by Black Rod, they slowly made their way to the lobby leading to the Senate. The Cabinet followed, and then as excited a mob as ever disgraced the House of Commons...." Preston himself was caught up in the swaying, belligerent crowd and at one point found himself pushed against Smith, just as "Tory members reached out to strike his grey top hat."

As usual, Sir John A. Macdonald had the last word. The final insult recorded in Hansard during that stormy parliamentary sitting was attributed to Macdonald. "That fellow Smith," he declared, "is the biggest liar I ever met!"

The Liberal government's final official act was to grant Smith, Stephen and their partners the ten-year running rights on the Pembina Branch line they had requested. It was soon connected with their St Paul, Minneapolis and Manitoba tracks, giving them a monopoly on western Canadian freight. In the election that followed, which easily returned Macdonald to power, the Tories singled out Smith as a special target. "Now, Sir John, if you want that prince of old scoundrels 'Smith' beaten, use your influence to get William Ogilvie to consent to run ...," advised John C. Schultz. "Donald Smith has I think lost just about the last vestige of character he ever possessed here, since the accounts of the closing scene of the House have come to hand. Smith's challenger turned out to be an even more formidable choice, Alexander Morris, who had been a minister in Macdonald's first administration and served as Manitoba's first chief justice. When Morris pointed out his opponent's obvious conflict of interest between what was best for land sales in Manitoba and best for him as one of the proprietors of the St Paul, Smith reacted with a dose of righteousness improbable even for him. With a straight face he explained that "the primary object of the railway was for the benefit of Manitoba and not for the purpose of making money."

Realizing that his re-election bid was in serious trouble, Smith tried to enlist the organizational assistance of J.H. McTavish, a popular HBC Factor, but London head office firmly directed Winnipeg to "keep the Company neutral ... the Fur Trade officers must take no part in the election as such." Smith attempted to protect himself by pretending he was politically inde-pendent,* pledging that he had "no favour to ask and nothing personal to desire from any Government" and would "support only such measures as are conducive to the advancement of Manitoba...." Just in case this high moral ground might prove too slippery, Smith transferred several gangs of Métis who were on the Company's payroll to his riding and ordered twenty-six HBC families to be temporarily moved into his jurisdiction, then bribed them to vote for him. Even these outrageous manoeuvres barely turned the trick. He won the election by a hair's-breadth margin of nine votes. On the night of his modest victory, as his cheering supporters led him through Winnipeg's main streets, the salute guns of Fort Garry boomed happily in the background. Smith was magnanimous in his triumph: he donated $750 to the Knox Church Building Fund.

A petition charging Smith with bribery and corruption was immediately filed, but when it was heard before Mr. Justice Louis Bétournay in the Manitoba Court of Queen's Bench, Smith was confirmed in his seat. That verdict was tarnished by the fact that Smith held a four-thousand-dollar mort-gage on Bétournay's house, granted at highly favourable terms. When the deci-sion was overturned, a by-election was called for September 10, 1880. Smith ran as an independent, bolstering his political stance with bribes that totalled more than $30,000. But the voters refused to be bought. Smith was decisively beaten. His subsequent comment to James Cole, an HBC Factor who had acted as his campaign manager, easily ranks as Canadian history's longest snort. "I am sorry to say," Smith complained, "that a majority of the intelligent elec-torate of my late Selkirk constituency have, in the exercise of their undoubted privilege and the right to choose the most fit and proper person available for the purpose of representing them in the Dominion Parliament, seen fit to reject my own humble, not hitherto unacceptable person."

"The damn voters," shot back the more succinct Cole, "took your money and voted against you!"

"You," intoned Smith, "have properly expressed the situation."

---

*Which, in a way, he was—his sole allegiance was to himself.

HIS POLITICAL CAREER temporarily abandoned, Smith could concentrate on his long-standing ambition to be a fiscal animator—and personal benefici-ary—of building a railway across Canada. His involvement with that project was to be the central public accomplishment of his life, forever perpetuated in the history books by the photograph of his driving in the last spike. Because it was the CPR that finally destroyed the HBC's dominance in western Canada, its construction, at least as briefly summarized in the pages that follow, is part of the Company's history. Smith had resigned his post as the HBC's Land Commissioner in 1879, but he continued buying up stock. By 1883 he had become the HBC's dominant shareholder and a year later was appointed, along with Sandford Fleming, to head a Canadian subcommittee that controlled the Company's overseas operation—all this before the CPR had been completed.

The building of that railway probably ranks as Canada's greatest achieve-ment, "A new current was in motion within the mainstream of human history," wrote Ralph Allen in his evocative *Ordeal by Fire*. "The railways opened up a new caravan trail for the restless, the driven, and the questing and led them to the heartland of Canada."

By 1880, all the elements of Smith's career seemed to combine in pushing him to join his cousin George Stephen in becoming a decisive figure in the railway's realization, A fringe benefit of the Minnesota railway venture had been to provide Stephen with an opportunity to view the West at first hand. He had travelled over the St Paul's rickety tracks in the autumn of 1877 and was then driven north to Silver Heights, where Smith and Stephen discussed the railway project's future. "The immensity of the treeless Prairie landscape affected him deeply, indeed disoriented him, as it does most people when they see it for the first time," W.L. Morton wrote of Stephen's reaction. "He could at last imagine what Smith had all along been telling him—that people would come to this emptiness, that they would survive and prosper, and that the railway would be the instrument of this population—that it would bring the population to its lands, and those people would provide it with its future earnings."

Because the revelation of his association with the project would have killed its chances, Smith was deliberately kept in the background, but it was his determination that proved essential in financing the epic venture. He had roused Stephen's interest in both railroading and the great North-West, and though the cousins both tended to hoard their emotions too much to develop an easy friendship, theirs was an enduring partnership.

Stephen was unassuming in private and invisible in public. He loathed the circuitous mouthings of politicians but knew how to rent them—and occasionally buy them. He believed devoutly that man's salvation lay in hard work and besting one's enemies. His only recreation was fishing, and he owned the rights on two rivers to prove it, the Matapédia (later sold to the Ristigouche Club in New Brunswick) and the Mitis, where he regularly cast a most beautiful fly. He was a tall man, thin, with a hangdog look and brooding eyes that, complemented by his droopy moustache, endowed his face with a cast of melancholy wisdom. His position as the Bank of Montreal's president together with his experience in reviving the St Paul line made him a natural choice when the newly re-elected Sir John A. Macdonald began his search for a syndicate to build the long-delayed transcontinental railway. "This was the climate in which the CPR Syndicate was eventually formed," noted Pierre Berton in his lively history. "For all the controversy served to illuminate one fact: there was now available a remarkable group of successful men who had experience in both railway building and high finance. In the summer of 1880, the Macdonald government was looking for just such a group. It was John Henry Pope, the homely and straightforward minister of agriculture, who had first drawn his Prime Minister's attention to the St Paul associates.

"'Catch them,' he said, 'before they invest their profits.'"

And "catch them" Macdonald did, with as generous a mark-up as was ever offered any businessman not selling snake-oil. According to W.T.R. Preston, it was "the most stupendous contract ever made under responsible government in the history of the world." To complete the transcontinental tracks from North Bay, Ontario, to Port Moody, at the head of Burrard Inlet in British Columbia, within ten years, the syndicate was granted an eventual $206 million in cash, subsidies and stock guarantees in addition to 25 million acres in land grants, with the shortfall in fertile acreage made up in other regions.* According to John Gallagher, a historical researcher, when all the tax benefits and value of the land exchanges are taken into account, the CPR received gifts from the country worth $106,300,000. The CPR's authorized history, written by its publicity manager, John Murray Gibbon, was called *Steal of Empire;* a more appropriate title might have been *Steal of Empire*.

The new Canadian Pacific Railway syndicate, granted its charter on October 21, 1880, included George Stephen, James J. Hill, J.S. Kennedy (the

---

* Between 1893 and 1930, the CPR sold 23 million acres worth $178 million.

New York banker who had acted as trustee of the St Paul), Duncan McIntyre, who controlled the Canada Central Railway running between Ottawa and North Bay, Sir Stafford Northcote, twenty-second Governor of the Hudson's Bay Company, and Richard Bladworth Angus, yet another Scot with a nose for money, who had been named the Bank of Montreal's general manager when he was only thirty-eight.*

Building a Pacific railway was the dominant issue in Canada's fledgling Parliament for thirty years. One CPR lobbyist boasted that whenever the Speaker's bell rang for a division, there were almost always more MPs in his apartment, swilling free liquor and puffing complimentary cigars, than anywhere else in Ottawa. The CPR directors dispensed bountiful "bonifications," as they preferred to call them, to smooth parliamentary obstacles. Most of these bribes were in the form of CPR share options deposited in secret bank accounts.†

From the beginning the railway was difficult to finance. Most of the government's largess was scheduled to kick in only after completion targets had been met, and most sophisticated international investors had been disillusioned too often to gamble again on North American railway bonds. Stephen at first could not get any stock exchange to list the CPR shares, and by December of 1881, Stephen and Smith were already forced to borrow on their own signatures $300,000 in working capital from the Bank of Montreal.

That same month, the railway's prospects brightened considerably with the recruitment of William Cornelius Van Horne as the CPR's general manager in charge of constructing the rail line. His assignment was to complete twenty-nine hundred miles of track through a sparsely explored land mass, across the

---

* Unlike most of his confrères, Angus rejected the offer of a knighthood—twice—though he was a founder of the prestigious Mount Royal Club and his neo-Romanesque home was ample enough to eventually house McGill University's Conservatory of Music. His great hobby was cultivating orchids. One of his daughters married B.T. Rogers, founder of British Columbia Sugar, amalgamating what became two great Canadian fortunes. Angus, along with Stephen and Smith, dominated the Bank of Montreal for most of four decades, raising its asset base from $38 million to $350 million. Angus was its general manager from 1869 to 1879 and president from 1910 to 1913; Stephen served as vice-president and president between 1873 and 1881; Smith occupied the same positions from 1882 to 1905.
† At the CPR's incorporation, the company directors sold to themselves at least 200,000 common shares at twenty-five cents each. Stephen's holding of 31,000 shares later produced a net dividend income (in equivalent 1990 dollars) of $3.9 million a year, and Smith's was at least as large.

Rocky Mountains and around Lake Superior, stretches that even daring rail-roaders considered impassable. During the 1881 construction season, only 161 miles of road across the flat prairie had been completed, and the entrenched staff of British engineers resented the intrusion of the fat Yankee with the big cigars who cursed like a spike driver and seemed immune to sensible objections to his outrageous demands. "We did not like him when he first came to Winnipeg as general boss of everything and everybody," J.H.E. Secretan, a CPR surveyor, complained to his diary. "His ways were not our ways ... he told me that if he could only teach the section men to run a transit, he wouldn't have a single damn engineer about the place."

Van Horne boasted that he would lay five hundred miles of track in 1882. By train and steamer or on horseback he ranged the Prairies—firing, hiring, ordering people and obstructions about. The snow had not left the ground when ten thousand men and seventeen hundred teams of horses began to push the rails westward, advancing two, three, and even four miles a day—once as much as twenty miles in three days. By the end of the 1882 season, 417 miles of track had been completed. When construction was held up by an engineer's refusal to drive his locomotive over a swaying trestle, Van Horne climbed into the cab himself.

"Well, if you ain't afraid of getting killed, with all your money, I ain't afraid either," reasoned the reassured driver.

"We'll have a double funeral—at my expense, of course!" Van Horne shouted back across the lurching engine as it successfully pirouetted across the deep divide.

Even tougher to cross were the two hundred miles along the north shore of Lake Superior. It is a land drowning in its own juices, with muskeg, quicksand and matted spruce forests making any kind of orderly traverse impossible. One particularly bitter stretch of muskeg cost $750,000 to cross, swallowing the tracks seven times along with three locomotives. To the east, between Sudbury and Cartier, a lake had to be lowered ten feet to secure a foundation for tracks, and three miles of curve were needed to go around Jackfish Bay, although the straight jump across the water was less than half a mile.

The unexpected ruggedness of the terrain rapidly drained the company's treasury. The normally placid Stephen was beside himself with worry and at one meeting with Smith despondently predicted the railway would go bust. "It may be that we must *succumb*," Smith calmly replied, "but that must not be as long as we individually have a dollar." The Macdonald government grudgingly advanced another loan of $30 million, but within six months Van Horne sent Smith a coded cable with the blunt message: "HAVE NO MEANS PAYING WAGES, PAY CAR CAN'T BE SENT OUT UNLESS YOU SEND IMMEDIATE RELIEF, WE MUST STOP." Stephen begged Macdonald for an additional $22.5 million, and even though the Prime Minister at first told the CPR president he might as well ask "for the planet Jupiter as for more money," a bill for the further extension of funds was hastily presented to the Commons. The Liberal benches exploded with outrage, their critic charging that for six months a year the new railway would become "an idle, ice-bound snow-covered route," while party leader Edward Blake predicted its mountain section "would not pay for the grease on the axles."

The Tories finally rammed the extra loan through, but caucus demanded a dividend for their support. It took the form of humiliating Donald Smith by forcing him to agree, the story went, that he would run for Parliament in a future election not merely for the Conservatives, the party he had betrayed in 1873, but as a personal admirer of Sir John. As the CPR's troubles became more serious, Smith had emerged more and more into public view. "He was the great controlling spirit in all the principal business of the syndicate," Preston wrote of Smith, who officially became a CPR director in 1883 and remained the most influential member of the board's executive committee for the next thirty years. He was more or less reconciled with Macdonald over a bottle of Scotch at a 1883 meeting arranged by Stephen. In his typical self-centred way, Smith reported that the Prime Minister felt better for it: "I know—without his saying it—that he is today a much happier man."

Stephen hurried off to London and by pledging Smith's and his own personal credit was able to negotiate a £77,000 loan, which would tide them over until the government's guarantees were formally approved. "Once again the partnership of company and government, the partnership of Donald Smith, John A. Macdonald, and himself, had triumphed," Donald Creighton wrote of this moment in The Old Chieftain, the second volume of his magnificent Macdonald biography. "They were all Scotsmen, all Highlanders, all, ultimately, sons of the same river valley.... He remembered the river itself, winding onward, peat-black between the high banks, and brown, like old ale, over the shallows. He remembered the great rock, which had given the Clan Grant its rallying-place and its battle slogan. The rock of defiance. Craigellachie.... He took a telegraph form, addressed it to Donald Smith in Montreal, and wrote a message of three words only: 'Stand fast, Craigellachie!'"

Less than a year after the $22.5-million bailout, the CPR was on the verge of bankruptcy again. Stephen and Smith borrowed yet another $650,000 from the Bank of Montreal. By March 1885, they were pleading for another one million dollars to provide Van Horne with construction funds for one more month, but even their Bank of Montreal credit facilities had been exhausted, and to try tapping another bank would have triggered panic. The desperate situation prompted from Smith a totally unexpected retort: a short, declaratory sentence. "It's to the government, or to the penitentiary," he told Stephen, who had lapsed into his customary silence.

It was, of course, to the government that the CPR turned because, as one of the railway directors correctly pointed out, "The day the CPR busts, the Conservative Party busts the day after." Whatever his personal feelings, Macdonald didn't dare ask his followers to approve yet another loan. He was on notice that at least three cabinet ministers would resign if he allowed the insatiable railway to feed at the public trough one more time. At a dispirited directors' meeting, Smith and Stephen agreed to see what credit they might raise from their personal possessions. Stephen stood quietly by in the study of his $3-million house as evaluators assessed his paintings, statuary, cutlery, furniture, linen and imported piano. But the CPR president didn't have to surrender these luxuries. His railway was saved by Louis Riel.

WILLIAM VAN HORNE later claimed the CPR should erect a monument to the Métis leader, and he was right. Since fleeing Canada, he had spent time in a Montreal lunatic asylum, become a naturalized American citizen, and taught in a Montana mission school. When settlers along the South Saskatchewan River became radicalized by Ottawa's insensitivity to their demands, they joined forces with local Indians and Métis who invited Riel to champion their cause. Once back on Canadian soil, he declared, "The time has now come to rule this country or perish in the attempt." Riel's exile had transformed him from the dreamy statesman of Red River into a hectoring, hard-edged prophet, preoccupied with theological theories. Riel spent little time on political or military strategy, formulating instead new catechisms and decreeing such oddities as new names not derived from pagan gods for the days of the week. He declared Bishop Ignace Bourget of Montreal his new Pope and himself a Messiah.

The rebellion, which was backed by Big Bear's and Poundmaker's Cree warriors, grown aggressive with the frustrations of lost land and impending starvation, as well as the Métis demanding aboriginal title similar to that granted their Manitoba cousins in 1870, was masterminded by Gabriel Dumont. Grandson of a voyageur, illiterate yet fluent in six languages, a crack shot, permanent chief of the buffalo hunt and head of the first local government between Manitoba and British Columbia, Dumont was a worthy predecessor of Ernesto (Che) Guevara, the Argentine revolutionary who perfected modern guerrilla tactics as Fidel Castro's lieutenant. Appeals to Ottawa having been either ignored or rejected, Riel set up a provisional government at Batoche, a fording place on the South Saskatchewan River thirty-seven miles southwest of Prince Albert, and appointed Dumont his adjutant-general. In a preliminary skirmish at nearby Duck Lake, Dumont's Métis easily routed a North West Mounted Police detachment from Fort Carlton, killing twelve constables and several volunteers. A dozen whites were massacred at Frog Lake; Battleford was ransacked by Chief Poundmaker; local HBC posts were looted and burned; lodges of Assiniboines were already marching east; and the powerful Blackfoot nation was threatening to join in.

In Ottawa, Stephen and Smith were back in their customary pose, palms outstretched for yet another government handout. The CPR had run out of payroll money and notes worth $7 million would be maturing by June 1885. Failure to redeem them would push the company into the bankruptcy courts. In British Columbia, a band of three hundred strikers demanding back wages was being held at bay by the NWMP, and the company's stock was in a free-fall on the New York and London exchanges. On March 26, Macdonald gave Stephen the hard news that the federal treasury was shut tight to any further CPR grants or guarantees.

That also happened to be the date of the battle at Duck Lake, and as word of the massacre was flashed to the Dominion's capital, everything changed. Having barely prevented the Métis takeover of Manitoba in 1870, Macdonald knew he had to move fast or the Métis leader might have the entire North-West up in arms. Yet there seemed to be no practical way of enforcing the federal power; Riel might as well have been on Mars.

William Van Horne, who was in Ottawa to backstop Smith and Stephen, announced that if the government put two batteries of men in his care, he would guarantee to have them on the Qu'Appelle River, next to Riel's encampments, in twelve days. Forty-eight hours after the Prime Minister agreed to the daring scheme, CPR trains were pulling into Ottawa to load the soldiers. Singing "The Girl I Left Behind Me," the men marched to the station for one of the most remarkable train rides in Canadian history. Macdonald had been right. There was no practical way to move the militia west; the railway's Superior link was incomplete, with four gaps totalling eighty-six miles yet to be filled in. Much of that country was nearly impassable for lone hunters; to move more than three thousand men with supplies, ammunition and heavy artillery pieces across these quagmires seemed impossible.

Van Horne routed trains across temporary rails laid only hours earlier and at each end of steel loaded the troops into hastily fashioned freight sleds, feeding the soldiers steak and roast turkey to keep up their spirits. Fifteen years earlier it had taken Colonel Wolseley ninety-six days to move his volunteer army from Toronto to Red River. Van Horne's army made it in seven, and two days after that they were safely on the banks of the Qu'Appelle. By mid-April, the entire force was in place except for one Halifax battalion, and the troops moved into battle. Dumont's brilliant hit-and-run tactics at Fish Creek had won the initial encounters, but only two hundred Métis sharpshooters remained to face the full onslaught of more than eight hundred soldiers at Batoche. Riel had refused to heed Dumont, who had advised continued guerrilla warfare. Instead, the Métis were placed in siege formation; without any artillery, they had no chance. The four-day battle ended with Dumont fleeing to Montana while Riel surrendered to three Mounted Police scouts.*

True to form, the Hudson's Bay Company reacted to the battle by trying to exploit its profit potential. Immediately after the Duck Lake massacre, the Company ostentatiously placed itself at the disposal of the Dominion authorities and assured Minister of Militia and Defence Adolphe Carron that it would provision his forces in the battle area. Trade Commissioner Joseph Wrigley set the tone of the HBC's patriotic contribution when he sent an urgent letter to Chief Factor Archibald McDonald at Fort Qu'Appelle, the field force's main jumping-off point. "All supplies furnished by you to the Military Expedition," he ordered, "must be charged at wholesale prices ... get receipts!" By the end of hostilities, the Company submitted bills for $2 million, which included a $96,000 profit. The HBC then claimed a further $207,115.84 for damaged buildings and stolen furs but collected only $163,768.54.

---

* The Métis leader was at first to be taken to Winnipeg for trial, but when he reached the CPR main line at Moose Jaw his party was rerouted to Regina for what, it was explained, were judicial reasons. The real reason was that under Manitoba law, prisoners had the right to demand half the jury be French-speaking. The Northwest Territories, where Regina was located, had no such provision.

In gratitude to the nascent railway for transporting the troops west, Parliament voted to authorize the guarantee of a temporary $500,000 loan. It wasn't much, but it was enough to save the line. An impatient creditor was about to push the company into receivership. When Van Horne and a group of CPR executives got the news, they went wild. "We tossed up chairs to the ceiling; we tramped on desks; I believe we danced on tables. I do not fancy that any of us knows what occurred, and no one who was there can ever remember anything except loud yells of joy and the sound of things breaking." Soon afterwards Parliament guaranteed most of a final $35-million issue of mortgage bonds,* and Stephen hurried over to London where Lord Revelstoke, head of Barings, the famous merchant banking firm, purchased the balance.

Because Smith was forced by political circumstances to stay under cover during much of the CPR's construction, it was Stephen and Van Horne who got most of the public credit for the project's completion. But a few years later before a London audience, Sir Charles Tupper, who as Macdonald's minister of finance had been in the centre of the bargaining, declared that "the Canadian Pacific Railway would have no existence to-day, notwithstanding all that the Government did to support that undertaking, had it not been for the indomitable pluck and energy and determination, both financially and in every other respect, of Sir Donald Smith."

CHOSEN TO HAMMER IN THE CPR'S LAST SPIKE, Smith had travelled west aboard his private railway car, *Matapedia*, as part of a small train that included Van Horne's *Saskatchewan*, a baggage car and the engine. As they puffed across the country, crews were racing to lay the final links through Kicking Horse Pass. The rails from east and west were due to abut at Eagle Pass, a forlorn spot in the Monashee Mountains that Van Horne had named Craigellachie, after the clan stronghold of Smith's and Stephen's ancestors in Moray.

In the United States, comparable last-spike ceremonies had inevitably included fireworks, marching bands, extravagant speechifying, free liquor for construction crews and gold-plated spikes. At the last-spike ceremony of the first transcontinental U.S. railway at Promontory, Utah, two gold and two silver spikes had been driven into polished laurel cross-ties. Telegraph offices along the line were manned, their specially wired keys left open so that an

---

* At this crucial moment, Smith reportedly presented Lady Macdonald with a necklace worth $200,000 to influence her husband to grant the new loan. Stephen later confirmed the "bonification" but stoutly maintained it was "a personal gift."

account of the hammer blows could be heard across the country. In contrast, the Craigellachie celebration was to be a very Canadian occasion with no pomp and little ceremony. A discarded boxcar had been set aside to serve as a temporary railway station. From the Pacific side arrived a mixed work train, and a small party of labourers gathered to watch the final spike being driven home. Lord Lansdowne, then Governor General, had commissioned a silver spike for the occasion, but Van Home was his usual practical self. "The last spike," he decreed, "will be just as good an iron one as there is between Montreal and Vancouver, and anyone who wants to see it driven will have to pay full fare."

On the misty morning of November 7, 1885, Major A.B. Rogers, who had found the pass for the railway through the Selkirk Mountains, held the tie bar under the final rail in place for the ceremonial finish. Smith's first feeble blow merely turned the designated spike's head, bending it. Roadmaster Frank Brothers yanked it out, replaced it with a new one, and Smith carefully tapped it home. Alexander Ross, the hunchback photographer from Winnipeg, took his famous shots, but except for a thin cheer there was little rejoicing. The only sound that reverberated in that historic canyon was the thump of Smith's maul. For a long moment there was silence, as if those present were remembering all the anguish that had led to this moment. "It seemed," recalled Sir Sandford Fleming, the CPR director who had first suggested the practicability of a transcontinental railway twenty-five years earlier, "as if the act now performed had worked a spell on all present. Each one appeared absorbed in his own reflections."

Smith said nothing. Van Horne gruffly allowed that "the work has been done well in every way." But it was the conductor of the little train, now cleared to head due west, who pronounced the ceremony's most dramatic line when he shouted: "All aboard for the Pacific!"*

It was a moment that changed Canadian history. Louis Riel, whose two

---

* The engine that pulled the train west was scrapped and the *Matapedia* burned on her trucks at Princeton, B.C., in 1925, but Van Horne's private car has been preserved by the Canadian Railroad Historical Association. The maul used by Smith to pound in the last spike was last seen in the basement of his Montreal house being used to break up coal lumps for the furnace. There is considerable controversy about the fate of the last spike, but in a letter to the author dated March 10, 1989, the present Lord Strathcona explained what happened: "The last spike was an ordinary nail and is still in place. The 'one-from-last' spike was bent and pulled out. Small pieces were cut out and incorporated into spike-shaped diamond brooches for Lady Strathcona, Lady Shaughnessy, and the wife of the Governor-General. In the Shaughnessy one, an emerald has been put in place of iron. We still have a slightly larger brooch with iron disc. The 'one-from-last' spike, with pieces cut out, was presented by me to the CPR at a centenary ceremony on rebellions had unintentionally opened up the West, was hanged for high treason in Regina nine days later, clearing the way for prairie settlement. The closed world so jealously guarded by the Hudson's Bay Company for two centuries was now irrevocably breached. The spider's web of waterways and prairie trails, worn out of the wilderness by decades of Red River carts hauling goods from Fort Garry to Edmonton, from Qu'Appelle to Battleford, and on westward to Red Deer Forks and all the way to Peace River Junction, had been rendered obsolete in a day. The great HBC installations at Fort Canton and Fort Pitt shrank to inconsequence.

By throwing most of his energies into financing the CPR instead of enlisting the HBC's London board to sponsor or at least propose a joint venture for the railway through its former territory, Smith threw away the Company's future as a major player in the evolution of Canada's modern economy. "The Canadian Pacific Railway," Michael Bliss pointed out in his *Northern Enterprise*, "was created by westerners and fur traders. But not by the Hudson's Bay Company. The fur-trading concern was not able to maintain the monopoly it gained in 1821 or use its advantages to diversify into new lines.... New men, some of whom began as pipsqueak fur traders challenging the mighty Company, became the key to the Canadian Pacific—in alliance with one of the HBC's own former Factors. The former fur traders organized the CPR syndicate and built the road after central Canadian capitalists had bungled the job and given up. They succeeded without the help of the Hudson's Bay Company, and by their success they put it permanently in the CPR's shadow."

The first scheduled transcontinental left Montreal for Port Moody on June 28, 1886. Its engine was draped with flowing silk ribbons as the Pacific Express pulled out of Dalhousie Square Station to cheers and a fifteen-gun salute. It completed the 2,907-mile journey in 139 hours, just over five and a

---

condition it was put on display. It is on permanent loan to the Transport Museum in Ottawa, probably still sitting on a teak block made by me." Craigellachie itself never prospered and was all but abandoned after the Second World War. Its tiny train station was closed, though location of the last-spike ceremony was landscaped for a 1985 centennial re-enactment. The CPR did not bother to maintain the site, and in January of 1990, the railway company withheld permission for the final run of its last transcontinental passenger train to pull in at Craigellachie. Told they couldn't stop, the crew decided to throw a wreath off the train at the appropriate spot. But when the engineer slowed down, he forgot to notify the rest of the crew, and nothing happened. "They didn't tell us they were going to let us throw it off," explained a befuddled employee. If Paris was worth a mass, Craigellachie was worth a stop—but no one at the CPR cared.

half days. Once it became fully operational, the CPR plugged Canada into world trade. The Silks—non-stop express trains hurtling eastward from Vancouver—provided a link for consignments of Oriental textiles dispatched from Hong Kong and Siam to Montreal and on to London. The dream of a North West Passage had been achieved at last—even if it was a century late and over land instead of water.

AN EXHAUSTED GEORGE STEPHEN retired to England and turned the CPR over to Van Horne, who transformed it into an integrated transportation system, building grain elevators, hotels and steamships, as well as infusing the railway with the same gusto that had allowed him to build it in the first place. He later threw railways across Cuba and Guatemala but his first loyalty was to the CPR. "Building that railroad," he said on the day he renounced his American citizenship, "would have made a Canadian out of the German Emperor."*

On the way back from the last-spike ceremony, Van Horne had sprung a surprise on Smith. Without the elder man's knowledge, a spur line had been built from Winnipeg to his country house at Silver Heights. Smith and his party of railway executives were so busy talking no one paid any attention when the engine was being driven in reverse until they were almost pulling up to his house. "Now, there's a very neat place," Smith remarked, looking increasingly puzzled. "... who is it that has Aberdeen cattle like that? I thought I was the only one. This is really very strange ... I must be going crazy; I've lived here many years and I've never noticed another place so exactly like Silver Heights." The mystery was explained when the conductor called the stop: "Silver Heights!" For once, Smith was overwhelmed. Proud of his

---

* One of Van Horne's favourite ploys was to test future employees with his cigar trick. When a firm of cut-rate tobacconists had capitalized on his fame by calling a five-cent brand the "Van Horne," he ordered several boxes of the leafy horrors, removed their bands, and mixed them with expensive perfectos in his humidor. Prospective employees, wishing to acknowledge his reputation as a connoisseur, would inhale the tarry mixture, then ecstatically compliment him on the "delightful aroma." They could only smile icily at Van Horne's crude guffaw that followed his explanation. He once hired a man mainly because he had butted one of the dud cigars after his first whiff and demanded: "How much does the stable boy charge you for these things?" During Van Horne's final illness, his doctors limited him to three cigars a day. He meekly agreed. But by next morning he had a box of specially rolled two-foot-long perfectos brought to his bedside, and so puffed contentedly the prescribed three a day, four hours each, until he died on September 11, 1915.

homestead, he had raised a small herd of buffalo there and entertained four governors general. Smith could never do enough for his visitors. When the Marquess of Lorne, the Queen's son-in-law then Canada's Governor General, came to visit, the façades of Silver Heights' main buildings were transformed into a copy of Inveraray Castle, the viceroy's ancestral home.

Success of the railway had converted the trio of capitalist desperados who had built and financed it into high-Establishment figures. Queen Victoria honoured Stephen with a baronetcy while Smith and Van Home were dubbed Knight Commanders of the Order of St Michael and St George. By 1887, Smith was named the Bank of Montreal's president, having become one of its dominant shareholders, second only to Sir William C. Macdonald.* Smith ran for Parliament as a Sir John A. Macdonald supporter in the 1887 election and sat as a largely quiescent MP for the next nine years. During that period, he took some time out to savour his accomplishments and become a significant philanthropist. He donated at least $2.5 million to McGill University, of which he became the chancellor, directing that some of the funds be used to provide for the admission of women.† Together with Stephen, he financed the building of the Royal Victoria Hospital in Montreal and donated two ships to Dr Wilfred Grenfell's mission in Labrador.

To display his wealth and influence properly, Smith built a mansion on two properties at the corner of Fort and Dorchester streets. The exterior was brownstone, brought from the Ontario Credit Valley, and the front door opened onto a magnificent three-storey, $50,000 mahogany staircase, carved by artisans who dovetailed all the parts so that not a single nail was used in its construction. The second-floor ballroom was overlooked by a marble balcony to accommodate the musicians. Smith understood little about painting, but his private collection included works by Raphael, Titian, Gainsborough, Reynolds, Romney, Constable and Millais. The dining-room opened into a garden for summer receptions attended by more than two thousand neck-craners.

Below stairs and out of hearing was a row of eight rooms for more than a dozen maids and flunkeys, including an English butler, inevitably named James. Fitted more by temperament than by birth for the aristocratic life,

---

* Macdonald was a Prince Edward Islander who had amassed a fortune selling tobacco during the American Civil War.

† In his honour, McGill's first eight female graduates, who received their Bachelor of Arts degrees in 1888, called themselves the "Donaldas."

Smith ruled his household with humourless mastery. Once, while he was eating breakfast with Dr Grenfell, he watched the lamp under the hot-water kettle falter and die. When the missionary wanted to relight it, Smith stopped him and angrily summoned the butler.

"Remember, James," he said, "you have only certain duties to perform. This is one. Never, under any circumstances, let such an omission occur again."

Smith was a snob to the point of keeping a private guest tally categorizing his visitors according to their social rank. The impressive roll call included a future king and queen of England, a prince and princess, eight dukes, seven marquises, twenty-one earls, six viscounts, six governors general, seven prime ministers, twenty-seven provincial premiers, four archbishops, seventeen bishops, fourteen chief justices, twenty-nine supreme court judges, thirty-one mayors and fifty-eight generals. The tally even separated this last group into forty-seven generals of the Imperial Army and eleven commanders of colonial troops. The future king and queen were George V and Queen Mary, who came to Montreal as the Duke and Duchess of Cornwall and York. On that occasion, Smith not only refurnished their rooms but had a special balcony built off the second floor so that the royal couple might have a better view of the fireworks display lighting up the top of Mount Royal in their honour.*

Through Smith's involvement with the building of the CPR he had become a significant figure on the world's financial stage, and in his corporate dealings he now reverted to concentrating his wiles and energies on the Hudson's Bay Company. Within three years of the last-spike ceremony he would become the Company's Deputy Governor and, less than twelve months later, its Governor.

---

* According to Freeman Clowery, the former archivist at the Bank of Montreal, Lady Strathcona presented the Duchess with a spray of maple leaves fashioned of gold, diamonds and pearls that had been made by Henry Birks & Sons for $1,600.

Canada in a Swallow-Tail Coat

Becoming a peer of the realm was no trifling matter. So Smith did what he always did on such watershed occasions. He remarried Isabella. The secret ceremony ... reunited the bride and groom (then seventy-seven) for the fourth and final time.

DURING THE TROUBLED WINTER of 1895–96, there were whispers that Donald Smith would become Canada's sixth Prime Minister. Mackenzie Bowell, the fusty Ontario Orangeman who occupied the nation's top political office at the time, governed with a degree of incompetence that decisively distinguished him among the uneven quartet who succeeded Sir John A. Macdonald. In his bumbling way of dealing with nearly every issue threatening the still fragile Dominion, Bowell demonstrated an unerring instinct for his own jugular. His inability to manage the ordinary business of government, much less such politically charged issues as the Manitoba Schools Question, prompted seven ministers, half his cabinet, to walk out and demand a new leader.

Smith, who had by then been the loyal Tory member for Montreal West for most of a decade, was immediately nominated for the job. "There is one man, and one man alone," declared Sam Hughes, MP for the Ontario riding of Victoria North, "who can save the Liberal-Conservative Party from falling to pieces, and also who can command the respect and confidence of the whole country, and that is Sir Donald A. Smith." The cry was taken up by others, but the Hudson's Bay Company Governor, ever faithful to his creed of self-advancement, saw no point in tying his future to the leadership of a party that had the smell of a dying political movement. Still, he used the occasion to help manoeuvre circumstances that would help him realize what was, to his way of imperialistic thinking, a more attractive alternative: appointment as Canada's High Commissioner to the Court of St James's.

Since that office was held by Macdonald's veteran lieutenant, Sir Charles Tupper, Smith made a great show of eschewing personal ambition and with mock modesty helped lever the holder out of the post he wanted to occupy. "I have no claim [to the prime ministership]," he humbly insisted, "while such a statesman as Sir Charles Tupper is alive and active, and prepared to assume the burden should the latter prove too great for Sir Mackenzie Bowell." Tupper rushed back to face the thankless task of leading his party into its disastrous electoral confrontation with Wilfrid Laurier. When Smith began to lobby him hard for the London job, the new Prime Minister, delighted at the prospect of having an ocean between himself and his one-time nemesis, undertook to appoint the HBC Governor High Commissioner, though the neophyte diplomat was seventy-six years old.

True to form, Smith followed his standard procedure whenever faced by an important career move: he remarried Isabella. Using the excuse that he had mislaid his marriage certificate, on March 9, 1896, he and his wife went through their third wedding ceremony in the Wall Street office of John Stirling, Smith's New York lawyer. Staged to put an end to whispers about the couple's murky marital past, this masquerade only drew attention to Smith's relentless sense of Presbyterian guilt. Tupper served only ten weeks in office before being beaten by Laurier, but on April 24, 1896, he appointed Smith to London and in a touching move also named him a Privy Councillor, the title Smith had coveted when the two men had ridden together to Red River twenty-six years earlier.

The British posting was Canada's most important (indeed, only) diplomatic appointment, but its occupant was under few legal, partisan or economic constraints. Sir Alexander Tilloch Galt, the railway promoter who became Macdonald's finance minister and later served as Canada's first High Commissioner, used the prestige of the office to help finance exploitation of the coalfields his son had discovered on the Belly and Little Bow rivers near Lethbridge in southern Alberta. Tupper himself held the posting while still a member of Macdonald's cabinet and regularly returned home to fight election campaigns.*

---

* The post has gone ever since mainly to superannuated politicians. During the Second World War it was occupied by former Liberal organizer Vincent Massey, who later became

Although he served as his country's ranking representative *in* the glittering capital of history's greatest Empire, the High Commissioner devoted most of his time and energy to more mundane pursuits, acting as Canada's main immigration recruiter, chief financial facilitator and manager of the national debt. London was the centre of world trade and finance, while Canada's money markets were still too primitive and much too modest to capitalize the new Dominion's rapid expansion.

The 1896 election spawned a new age in Canada. The once vital era of Macdonald, which had sputtered to a dreary conclusion after the death of its guiding spirit, was replaced by the tantalizingly optimistic "ministry of all the talents" headed by Wilfrid Laurier, the forceful yet pragmatic nationalist who was to govern Canada for the next fifteen years. Suddenly, everything seemed possible. The new Prime Minister personified the young nation's hopes with his assertion that the twentieth century belonged to Canada.* Laurier didn't agree with Tupper on very much, but it didn't take the Liberal Prime Minister long to decide that Smith, who had spent most of two decades subverting the Liberal cause, was far less dangerous in London than back in Canada. The Hudson's Bay Governor, who also retained his presidencies of the Bank of Montreal and Royal Trust and his seat on the executive committee of the CPR, was quickly reappointed by the new government.

Smith, who as a youth sixty years before had worshipped British royalty from afar, could now participate in history's grandest festival of Empire, Queen Victoria's Diamond Jubilee, celebrated in the shimmering summer of 1897. The Empire on which the sun dared not set then encompassed more than a quarter of the earth's land surface occupied by 372 million people, whose representatives came to parade for their Queen. "There were Rajput princes and Dyak headhunters," rhapsodized Jan Morris in her epic *Farewell the*

Canada's first native-born Governor General. While in London Massey vividly recalled receiving a letter from a worried British housewife with a unique complaint. "A Canadian soldier on leave has visited my house," she wrote. "As a result both my daughter and I are pregnant. Not that we hold that against your soldier, but the last time he was here he took my daughter's bicycle which she needs to go to work."

* Even if he didn't really say it. The closest Laurier came to coining that aphorism was during his Canadian Club speech in Ottawa on January 18, 1904. "Canada has been modest in its history, although its history is heroic in many ways," he declared. "But its history, in my estimation, is only commencing. It is commencing in this century. The nineteenth century was the century of the United States. I think we can claim that it is Canada that shall fill the twentieth century."

Trumpets, "there were strapping troopers from Australia. Cypriots wore fezzes, Chinese wore conical straw hats. English gentlemen rode by, with virile moustaches and steel-blue eyes, and Indian lancers jangled past in resplendent crimson jerkins. Here was Lord Roberts of Kandahar.... Here was ... Wolseley, hero of Red River, Ashanti and Tel-el-Kebir.... That morning the Queen had telegraphed a Jubilee message to all her subjects.... The occasion was grand. The audience was colossal. The symbolism was deliberate. The Queen's message, however, was simple. 'From my heart I thank my beloved people', she said. 'May God bless them.'"

And He did. The forces that held the British Empire together seemed at times to be more theological than political. True adherents felt little confusion about what to believe or how to behave: God, Queen, Union Jack and family were the icons that mattered; being patriotic, disciplined, uncomplaining, frugal, chivalrous, stiff-upper-lipped and not too expert in any one thing (the cult of the all-rounder reigned supreme)—these were the coveted virtues. "The British as a whole," Jan Morris astutely observed, "would have been shocked at any notion of wickedness to their imperialism, for theirs was a truly innocent bravado. They really thought their Empire was good ... they meant no harm, except to evil enemies, and in principle they wished the poor benighted natives nothing but well." The passion in which the Empire was held is difficult to exaggerate. Typical was the story of Warburton Pike, an Englishman who had graduated from Rugby and Oxford but spent most of his adult life trapping, hunting and hiking in the Canadian wilderness. An archetypal imperial adventurer who took many risks exploring the outer edges of the northern tundra, he never forgot his British roots. Fifty-four when he reached home to enlist shortly after the outbreak of the First World War, he was rejected as too old. Pike was so upset he hiked to Bournemouth, walked into the sea, and plunged a knife into his heart.

At this high noon of Empire, the pervasive influences of what O.D. Skelton, the great Canadian public servant, called "the dervishes of Anglo-Saxondom" were in full and glorious flight. The Jubilee was pure light opera, with Edward Elgar writing the score and Rudyard Kipling the libretto. British society had little conception of how to treat the slightly awkward representatives of their newest "self-governing colony." One London matron who had condescended to include colonials at her garden reception addressed a special request to the Canadians suggesting that Wilfrid Laurier and his party kindly appear in their "native costumes." Canadians at home found themselves caught up in the fever of the occasion, with local parades, fireworks, floral arches across main streets and patriotic speeches. "As a warm darkness fell on the exhausted town that evening," June Callwood wrote of the elaborate Jubilee celebrations held in London, Ontario, "fireworks spelling VICTORIA hung for a long, poignant moment in the black sky. People watched it sputter out and were transfixed. It seemed something important had happened to them, to the whole country It felt like a flowering, a future greatness just opening to enfold them all."

The Jubilee rewarded Smith with a royal accolade. Summoned to Windsor Castle, he received a barony from Queen Victoria. Becoming a peer of the realm was no trifling matter. So Smith did what he always did on such water-shed occasions. He remarried Isabella. The secret ceremony, held according to Anglican rites at the British Embassy in Paris, reunited the bride and groom (then seventy-seven) for the fourth and final time. That requisite guilt-pacifier out of the way, Smith set about finding a title, crest, motto and coat of arms appropriate to his elevated rank. The crest was easy: a beaver gnawing at a maple tree. The motto was one exquisitely apt word: "PERSEVERANCE," the coat of arms a canoe paddled by four HBC traders, and a hammer with nail to symbolize the last spike. But the title proved more difficult. Queen Victoria usually referred to him as "Your Labrador Lordship," but Smith finally settled on a characteristically convoluted moniker—in the words of Burke's *Peerage*, "Baron Strathcona and Mount Royal, of Glencoe, co. Argyll, and of Mount Royal, Quebec, Canada"—in tribute to both his Canadian domicile and the large estate he had recently purchased in western Scotland.*

The freshly minted peer's love of Empire knew no bounds. In a speech during the launching ceremony of the steamer *Mount Royal* at Wallsend in the summer of 1898, Strathcona laid down some new definitions. "I do not," he trumpeted, "care to speak any longer of Canada and the other countries constituting the Empire, as Colonies. They are constituents of an Empire, one and indivisible. They are English quite as much as is Great

---

* The *Strath* in Strathcona is the Gaelic equivalent for *glen* or *valley*. The difference between being just plain Donald Smith and becoming Lord Strathcona was most visible in the new peer's signature. The Bank of Montreal at that time issued its own currency bearing the printed autograph of its president. As Donald A. Smith he had signed his name unobtrusively, the neat, tiny letters taking up only thirty-nine millimetres on the bank-note; the bold new scrawl, *Strathcona*, could not be contained in its alloted space, spreading over ninety-five millimetres and jutting into the bill's margin.

Britain, and to remain so to all time is the desire of Canada and all other possessions of the Empire."

Strathcona and some of his more imperialist-minded friends conceived the idea of girdling the globe with telegraph wires and a transportation service, to be known as the All-Red Route, that would link railway lines with accelerated British steamship schedules. Telegrams, mail, people and merchandise could then move aboard conveyances inviolably British. Express timetables called for a twenty-knot service across the Atlantic, with sailings from Liverpool to Halifax taking only four days. "The All-Red Line," declared Sir Sandford Fleming, one of the project's enthusiasts, "would, in some respects, resemble the spinal cord in the human body; it would prove to be the cerebro-spinal axis of our political system, and give origin throughout its length to many lateral groups of nerves ... through which would freely pass the sensory impressions and the motor impulses of the British people in every longitude." Using a slightly more comprehensible metaphor, Strathcona's doctor once remarked to his patient just before a heart examination, "Now we must attend to the All-Red Route, my Lord." Strathcona tried hard to promote the project, but the fact that it would have required government subsidies of more than $100 million considerably cooled the ardour of its supporters. The Hudson's Bay Company Governor turned his attention to more practical pursuits.

THE SECOND-STOREY WINDOW of the Canadian High Commission on Victoria Street glowed through London's nocturnal smog into so many long evenings that passersby nicknamed it "the Lighthouse." Here Strathcona spent eighteen years, occupied with the business of his life. While he placed the HBC's affairs at the top of his agenda, actively participating in the Company's daily management and ongoing policy formation, his energies were dispersed in many directions.

He sat in his office, signing cheques, justifying accounts, writing letters (always by hand, because he considered typewritten correspondence a breach of courtesy): to the Queen's Chamberlain, asking for special seats at a royal ceremony for a visiting politician; to an old fur trader at Temiskaming, thanking him for a box of lightly salted deer tongues; to another former HBC Chief Factor, forty-three years in the service, bitter about having to live out his days with no Company pension; to his cronies at the Bank of Montreal, requesting them to approve a loan to help James J. Hill "fight off the Harriman forces."* His cable messages flew around the world. He bargained for tea and silk shipments from Yokohama and sent timber to the Orient; he settled Lewis crofters in northern Saskatchewan and sold Labrador sable to Chinese aristocrats; he tied down a Canadian company that would give him a monopoly on salt production; he shipped flour from Vancouver to Fiji; he arranged for the Bank of Montreal to underwrite the bonds for construction of the New York "El"; and he approved plans to expand the HBC's department store in Vernon, B.C. The work never stopped, and even if being Governor of the HBC was his dominant concern, he seemed frantic to keep expanding his reach, as if he could never have enough money, power or prestige.

Calculation of an individual's private wealth was not a suitable topic for public discussion in Victorian England, but Strathcona arguably ranked as one of the Empire's richest men. His vast holdings of HBC stock returned record dividends; the Bank of Montreal, with himself as its second-largest shareholder, was Canada's most profitable bank; and the CPR shares that he had purchased for $25 or less appreciated to $280 in his lifetime. Besides holding these highly visible directorships and major stock positions in these companies, he enjoyed similar arrangements with Royal Trust, the Canada North-West Land Company, the Canadian Salt Company, the Commercial Cable Company, the Great Northern Railway, the Minnesota Imperial and Colonial Finance and Agency Corporation, the London & Lancashire Fire Assurance Company, the Manitoba South Western Colonization Railway, the New Brunswick Railway Company and the St Paul, Minneapolis and Manitoba Railway. He was also an important shareholder of Barings, the London merchant bank he helped rescue after the 1890 crash. Strathcona continued to use the Bank of Montreal (which during his term as High Commissioner was hired as Canada's chief fiscal agent abroad) as his private cash dispenser and in his first nine years in London did not surrender the bank's presidency. In 1905, on his eighty-fifth birthday, Strathcona decided it might be time to give the young bucks a chance. He allowed himself to be named honorary president and was succeeded by Sir George Drummond, who was only seventy-six. Drummond in turn was followed five years later by Richard Angus, then a spry seventy-nine.

The High Commissioner still returned regularly to Montreal (once estimating he had crossed the Atlantic at least a hundred times), but his heart

---

* Although he was offered a thousand dollars a share by E.H. Harriman for his Northern Pacific Railway stock, Strathcona stuck with his old friend Hill, rescuing him from bankruptcy—and he didn't even send Hill a bill for use of his proxy.

belonged to London. Although he had long ago achieved life's highest social and economic peaks, Strathcona continued to labour like a man possessed, with no detail small enough to escape his fussy attention. More pathetic than admirable, his devotion to duty finally affected his health—though he always remembered the warning of a leading London physician, Sir Andrew Clark, that for him to stop work would be fatal. After one of Strathcona's bouts of illness, Sir Thomas Shaughnessy, then president of the CPR, reported in mock serious tones to an Anglo-Canadian gathering in London that "yielding to the earnest entreaties of his physician ... [Lord Strathcona] has decided to relax his energies. He has succumbed to the united pressure of his medical man, his family, and his friends, and has been induced to promise to leave his office at 7.30 each evening instead of 7.45." During a holiday in rural England, Strathcona began dictating letters to his newly hired secretary early Sunday morning. The assistant politely but firmly declared he could not work on the Sabbath. The High Commissioner courteously agreed to indulge the young man, then spent most of the day impatiently pacing his room. Promptly at midnight he woke the startled clerk with the command: "The Sabbath is over. We must make haste with those letters!"*

His daily office labours done, Strathcona spent most evenings hosting or attending dinners and receptions at the Athenaeum Club, the Imperial Institute, and the Savoy or Westminster Palace hotels. As these and other venues proved insufficiently exclusive for the grand scale of the High Commissioner's hobnobbing, he eventually acquired seven houses and did most of his own entertaining. In Canada he had, retained his magnificent dwelling on Dorchester Street in Montreal,† Silver Heights near Winnipeg, with its buffalo pound, and Norway House, his stone mansion at Pictou, Nova Scotia. In London his first town residence (at No. 53 Cadogan Square) was

---

*Such work habits were not new. Dr Wilfred Grenfell, the Labrador medical missionary, noted how he had been granted an appointment to see Smith at Hudson's Bay House, on Montreal's St Peter Street, one Christmas Day. "I still remember vividly the deserted streets ... the silence and entire absence ... of any living thing," he later told a friend, "and at last the great, towering portals of the world-famous Company's offices. I climbed the steps with no little trepidation, and the bell startled me, when its echoes rang out, as if in some long-deserted haunt of men. Finally, the great door swung, open, and there stood, quite alone, the smiling old gentleman, apologizing for keeping me waiting."

† The Smith mansion was sold in 1927 to Lord Atholstan, publisher of the *Montreal Star*, who converted it into a home for elderly Presbyterian ladies from good but bankrupt Montreal families. In 1941, the contents were auctioned off and the following year the mansion was demolished to make way for an office building.

replaced by the much larger five-storey Grosvenor Square house (No. 28). As his country residence, he at first leased Knebworth in Hertfordshire, the ancestral home of the Lyttons (of *Last Days of Pompeii* fame) where Oliver Cromwell had met in solemn conclave with his followers to consider how England could rid itself of a tyrant king and a corrupt parliament. He later purchased Debden Hall in Essex and the Inner Hebrides islands of Oronsay and Colonsay, which included a beautifully sheltered manor house built from the ruins of a priory. But his most impressive property was the magnificent mansion he built in Black Corries of Glencoe, the rugged 64,000-acre estate he purchased in the west Highlands of Scotland, near Ballachulish. The place had an ominous background, and Dickens said that part of Argyllshire was "perfectly terrible."

Strathcona loved taking friends on grouse shoots in the Highland wilds, but his more serious entertaining was focused on pet causes. "Lord Strathcona presides most afternoons and every evening at some meeting or another," noted Gaspard Farrer, a young London merchant banker who moved in his circle, "and speechifies with great aplomb on art, music, medicine, science, university extension, French Employment, and every other interest that is glad to enlist the dear old gentleman's presence—and purse." Strathcona's most elaborate social function was the reception he threw for the four-hundredth anniversary of Aberdeen University. Named Lord Rector of the university in 1899 and later Chancellor, he realized there was not a hall on campus large enough to seat the 4,500 graduates and dignitaries invited to attend. He had a temporary building erected at his own expense on a three-acre site that could accommodate 2,500 at dinner and 4,740 in rows of chairs for the official ceremonies. Since no Scottish caterer was equipped to handle such a mob, he imported 650 waiters and their equipment (including 25,000 plates and 12,000 glasses) from London by special train. The actual graduation ceremonies and handing out of honorary degrees proved an anticlimax because by the end of the day the badly ventilated building was so fogged with cigar smoke no one could see which of the platform notables was speaking. When Andrew Carnegie, the American robber baron, couldn't make out the notes for his convocation address, he stopped in mid-sentence and explained, "I have given the eloquent speech which I had prepared, and from which I had hoped to elicit your cheers, to the myriad-mouthed press, and you will read it there in full tomorrow morning." Carnegie never did officially get his doctorate because when he walked up to Chancellor Strathcona, who was presiding, for his "capping," the two elderly men, who had started from nothing to reach this pinnacle, looked into one another's eyes and, moved by the emotions of the moment, shyly hugged one another instead of going through the degree ritual.

As he became ever richer, Strathcona turned himself into one of the Empire's more imaginative philanthropists. On top of the usual donations to hospitals and various funds for the unemployed (it then being cheaper to do good works than pay good wages), he also provided seed money for the establishment of Major-General Sir Robert Baden-Powell's Boy Scout movement and helped finance Captain Joseph Bernier's explorations of Canada's Arctic coast in the steamer *Arctic*. He purchased the auxiliary barquentine *Discovery* used by Captain Robert Falcon Scott in his Antarctic exploration of 1901–4, assigned the vessel to the HBC's northern trade for five years, then donated her to the Boy Scouts.* All requests for funds were placed on a silver tray, and every Sunday Strathcona would fish out a dozen or so. Those that satisfied his strict tenets of being "properly deserving" received a donation. One exception to this ritual occurred when an arrogant tramp appeared at his office and ordered the secretary to inform the High Commissioner that he was the son of the man who had driven young Donald to Aberdeen when he had left home to sail for Canada. Given a £5 note, the tramp was back the next day. When he was announced, Strathcona quietly told his secretary, "Give the gentleman another five pounds and tell him he need not return. You may add that his father did not drive me to Aberdeen. I walked."

Besides granting him automatic access to the Empire's most distinguished soldiers and statesmen, Strathcona's peerage made him a member of the Imperial Parliament. Until 1910 the Lords and Commons exercised equal constitutional powers, and the upper chamber contributed Prime Ministers of the realm into the twentieth century. It was two years before Strathcona made his first speech in these august surroundings, and when he did, it was on a curious subject. On June 28, 1898, he introduced a bill to legalize in the United Kingdom colonial marriages with sisters of deceased wives. It was a quirky, rather risky topic for him to champion, and Queen Victoria, who resented such excursions into ecclesiastical law, was quick to take offence. "His Labrador Lordship," she pointedly remarked, "should be the last to meddle in these matters." Strathcona was careful to point out that his proposal would

---

* She was later docked at the Thames Embankment in London as a memorial to Scott and moved to Dundee in 1986.

leave untouched marriages to brothers' widows and wives' nieces, but even though the Lords passed the bill, the government refused to take it up in the Commons.

His slightly strained relations with the royal household improved on Queen Victoria's death in 1901 and the succession of her eldest son, Bertie, the fifty-nine-year-old Edward VII.* The two men struck up a friendship so close that Edward treated the HBC Governor almost as a member of the royal household, referring to Strathcona as "Uncle Donald" and consulting him on matters of state as well as personal finance. Edward fondly remembered his 1860 tour of the Canadian provinces as Prince of Wales, particularly the great canoe pageant staged for him by the HBC's overseas Governor, Sir George Simpson, at Lachine.† But what had really won the heart of the British Monarch and most of his subjects was Strathcona's magnificent gift of Empire, the regiment of rough-riders he personally donated to help the British fight the Boer War.

THE APPOINTMENT OF JOSEPH CHAMBERLAIN, an impatient Birmingham screw manufacturer, to the Colonial Office in 1895 had hardened the face of British imperialism. A dandy who sported a monocle, Chamberlain didn't just preach white supremacy—he actually believed in it. The main flashpoint for the inevitable counter-thrusts that followed his sabre-rattling was South Africa, a pivotal outpost along the Empire's eastern trade routes. It was occupied by "black pagans" and, among others, intractable Huguenots from Holland, Germany and Belgium known as Boers (and later as Afrikaners) who had gradually withdrawn inland to the Transvaal and Orange Free State, while in the nineteenth century the British settled in the Cape Colony, Natal and Rhodesia. A major gold strike in the highlands near Johannesburg disturbed the uneasy equilibrium, and a pre-emptive strike by the Boers into British territory on October 11, 1899, served as a declaration of war. British troop commanders, most of whom had not evolved their tactics much beyond the stolid battlesquares of Waterloo, were easily outmatched by South Africa's territory-wise opponents, who did battle in everyday clothing, elected their

---

*Victoria, who died in the arms of the Kaiser at eighty-one at Osborne House, her beloved country seat on the Isle of Wight, had become a powerful force for perpetuating the status quo in her country's life and exemplified it in her own, having her husband's shaving water taken to his room every day for four decades after his death.
† For a description of this unique ceremony, see pages 548–49.

officers, and knew the contours of every gully in the veld. By winter, the proud British battalions, still rigidly close-advancing into battle to the wail of bagpipes, were in disarray.

Canada's defence force at the time consisted of a weak militia commanded by British generals, with eight steel-clad Royal Navy cruisers patrolling the coasts. Although Laurier had responded to Chamberlain's 1897 plea that the colonies come to the aid of Mother Britain in times of need by declaring "Let the watch fires be lit on the hills and Canada will be the first to respond!" the Canadian Prime Minister now felt much more ambivalent. Henri Bourassa, the Quebec activist who later founded *Le Devoir*, resigned from the Liberal party to protest Laurier's intention of dispatching Canadian troops to the African killing-ground. Watching his adopted country dither, Strathcona decided to act. On the last day of 1899 he offered the British War Office a mounted Canadian regiment, recruited, armed and payrolled at his own expense. This grand one-million-dollar gift, Strathcona's most deliberately spectacular gesture, taught the public imagination on both sides of the Atlantic.

The patriotic troop of 540 mobile scouts was placed under the command of Colonel Sam Steele, the most impressive of the young North West Mounted Police officers who had helped establish law and order during construction of the CPR and the Klondike Gold Rush. Recruiting quotas for Strathcona's Horse were oversubscribed several times in five days, some 600-odd Arizona cowboys willing to supply their own guns and horses having been turned down. The final roster included many a renegade British aristocrat along with former army officers glad to serve as privates (known as "gentleman-rankers"), at least one fugitive from the law of the United States, as well as cowpunchers, bushwhackers, whisky-priests and the toughest frontiersmen Steele could find. When this motley assembly was inspected at an Ottawa march-past by Governor General Lord Minto, he complained to his diary of "the useless ruffians, the halt, the lame and the blind." The regiment may not have pleased Minto's fastidious Sandhurst standards, but other Ottawans, especially the young girls, loved these wild-eyed soldiers of fortune, colourfully clad in stetsons, high yellow boots, and charcoal-hued greatcoats. As the troops journeyed by train to Halifax they were cheered at every stop before embarking for the long journey to the front.

Never at a loss to capitalize even on his patriotism, on the very day his soldiers sailed for Cape Town, Strathcona began to apply pressure on

Chamberlain to make an important change in his barony, which, according to accepted custom, would have descended to his eldest son. Since he and Isabella had only a daughter (Margaret Charlotte, who had married Dr. Robert Howard of McGill), he wanted to have a change made so the title would remain perpetually in the family. The adjustment required proclamation of a royal decree, and Chamberlain replied, through a letter to Sir Charles Tupper, that "there were great difficulties in the way of such an unusual grant." These problems were magically resolved by the intervention of Sir John McNeill, a Victoria Cross winner in the Maori War of 1864 and a friend of Strathcona's (they first met when the Scots officer was on Wolseley's staff at Red River), who now served as an equerry to the royal household and arranged for the required patent to be issued in the summer of 1900. It must have been a happy coincidence that shortly afterwards Strathcona purchased his Hebridean islands (Colonsay and Oronsay) from Sir John for £30,000.

In South Africa, the Canadian irregulars quickly gained a well-deserved reputation for matching the Boers' own guerrilla tactics with commando raiding parties and daring thrusts to sever the enemy's supply routes. Steele's contingent looked hopeless on the parade square, but in the field, where mobility, courage and innovation counted, no one could match the Canadians. Originally hardened by their ability to survive on their home turf, they had been toughened by their commanding officer's brutal approach to discipline. When half a dozen of his soldiers complained they were suffering from piles, for example, Steele ordered them to gallop bareback for five miles to burst the source of their complaints. "Of all the regiments, British or Colonial," reported London's *Daily Express*, "... Strathcona's Horse among the Boers were the most dreaded, and, strange to say, the most respected." Strange indeed, because Steele's men were reported to have lynched some Boer prisoners, and when a British officer remonstrated, they threatened to lynch him, too.

On the way back to Canada, Strathcona invited his regiment to London, where King Edward presented its battle colours, pinned each man with a medal, and rewarded Steele with the Victorian Order. Strathcona later dined the entire unit at an elaborate banquet. "The occasion of his own toast being drunk," trumpeted *The Times*, "produced the wildest enthusiasm, the officers and men springing to their feet, making the roof echo with their ardent cheering." At a special reception for officers in the great drawing room of the Savoy Hotel, attended by the Empire's leading dignitaries, Strathcona launched into yet another laudatory address, but Steele would have none of it. "He arrived a bit tight and grew tighter," recalled Agar Adamson, one of Steele's subalterns, "insisting on making a speech in the middle of which Lord S. pulled him up and said that they would have speeches on other occasions. He insisted upon continuing, in the middle of which [Steele] wanted to pump ship. He left the table ... lost his way, and found himself in a kitchen, on the stove of which he relaxed nature. He then returned, and wound up being sick on the carpet." Despite such lapses, Steele was given important Canadian army commands and Lord Strathcona's Horse fought with distinction in both world wars and Korea.*

Revered as the Empire's pre-eminent visionary, Strathcona became London's favourite colonial character. Ever courteous, more British than the British, painfully anxious to please, Strathcona as he grew older caused minor protocol problems for his London hostesses. He could never quite remember the proper precedence. One regal maven complained that "it was very difficult indeed to persuade him to 'stand in the order of his going.'" But the highly publicized generosity of his South African contribution had earned Strathcona wide repute and rescued the Hudson's Bay Company from social oblivion. "He is Canada in a swallow-tail coat," marvelled A.G. Gardiner, editor of the London *Daily News*. "You talk with him, and it is as if Canada stands before you, telling her astonishing story."

---

*During the 1980s, the regiment, now armoured and 500 strong, fielded Canada's last ceremonial cavalry troop consisting of a configuration of fourteen horses and eighteen men as riders and equipment personnel. It was saved from extinction by another Scottish-born philanthropist, Alan Graham, head of Calgary's Cascade Group.

The Reckoning

Too weak to stand or even to read his own remarks, he sat before a representative gathering of the Company's shareholders like a stuffed effigy of himself—mute, barely emitting any vital signs, yet still there, the Governor and a Bay man to the end.

THE BOER WAR HAD CRACKED THE MIRROR of imperial glamour. While the British could claim a military victory, it had been achieved in a sequence of senseless slaughters. The Empire finally had to mass 450,000 troops to crush 35,000 elusive Boer warriors. In the process, the invaders ravaged the countryside, burned the Boers' farms, and imprisoned their families in detention camps. There, 20,000 women and children died, some of the youngest casualties being victims of ground glass mixed into their morning porridge. The conflict put an end to the naïve Victorian notion of "gentlemen's wars," and Britain's "splendid" isolation now became real. At the same time, technological change was making the grip of Empire less tight. Electricity began to take over from steam, and Marconi's transatlantic wireless transmissions shattered dreams of cable and telegraph monopolies.

Few of these momentous changes disturbed Lord Strathcona's personal world. His already spectacular financial prospects changed only for the better. The CPR was finally realizing its traffic potential, the Bank of Montreal was setting new profit levels, and the somnambulant Hudson's Bay Company became one of the London Stock Exchange's most fashionable investments. While trade in furs faced an uneven future, the Company's landholdings took on new significance. Since 1898, settlers had been funnelling into the Canadian West in ever-increasing numbers, and as they became successful farmers, even more were attracted. The influx triggered a land rush. Three million immigrants settled the barely inhabited Prairies before the outbreak of the Great War. Land values doubled, then doubled again. By 1903, the HBC was able to sell nearly 400,000 acres to willing homesteaders at five dollars an acre, though Strathcona would live to see the price quadruple to more than twenty dollars.

As land values soared, stock quotations shot up. The *Economist*, which hadn't thought about the HBC for thirty years, noted that the Company was showing "remarkable vitality in its old age." Share prices moved from £20 in December 1889 to £129.5 in November 1906, while dividends reached 24 percent and rocketed up to 50 percent—their highest level since 1688— though even at 50 percent this worked out to only 3.1 percent on the par value of the stock.*

Instead of sharing some of this new-won affluence with the field hands whose efforts had created and maintained the HBC's land empire, at the Company's 1904 annual meeting Strathcona delivered these worthy veterans the *coup de grâce*. He proposed that a pension plan be established (paying a top annual rate of $1,500 to Chief Factors with thirty years' continuous service) but specifically excluded aiding those who were already retired. Not only were the former traders to be deprived of any sustaining income but the £50,000 left in the Servants' Pension Fund after abrogation of the fur partnerships by surrender of the Deed Poll in 1893 was absorbed into general corporate revenues. When retired Chief Factor Roderick MacFarlane complained, urging Strathcona "to aid in doing the right thing by those [who] have suffered many hardships, and endured many privations in the performance of their onerous duties in the interior," his pathetic appeal was dismissed with a curt note pointing out that it was really quite useless to trouble the board with correspondence relating to a period with which the existing Hudson's Bay Company had only "an historical concern."

That brutally dismissive phrase relegating more than two centuries of stead- fast dedication by generations of loyal employees to the oblivion of "historical concern" served as the corporate epitaph to the HBC's fur traders, if not the fur trade.

---

*A fringe benefit of the fortunes made from the rise in value of HBC stock was the found- ing of Dublin's renowned Abbey Theatre. Forerunner of the Little Theatre movement and the first state-subsidized stage in any English-speaking country, the Abbey was able to open in its own building in 1904 thanks to £1,300 in HBC stock profits donated by Annie Horniman, a London theatre manager.

It seemed an easy, if heartless, decision because the land boom kept accelerating. When Rudyard Kipling came back from a trip to Medicine Hat (where he had seen flares of natural gas blazing like torches) and reported the town had "all Hell for a basement," Strathcona quickly realized the underground potential of mineral rights and ruled that the HBC would henceforth retain them on all the lands it sold. The High Commissioner's interest in speeding up the already hectic pace of land sales was not limited to his mandate as Governor of the Hudson's Bay Company. He was also a controlling investor of the Canada North-West Land Company, formed in 1882 to acquire five million acres of the original CPR land grant. In case emigrants to Canada failed to enrich his purse through purchase of a homestead, there was always the shipping line. During Strathcona's London tenure the CPR, in which he remained a dominant shareholder, established steamship connections between Liverpool and Montreal. The new fleet immediately became part of J.P. Morgan's North Atlantic maritime cartel, which was estimated to have extracted from newcomers to North America a surcharge of $44 million until U.S. courts broke the back of the trust in 1911. Canadian Pacific vessels used in the service were already subsidized by the Canadian government. Yet both, Sir Richard Cartwright, the Liberal Minister of Finance (and later of Trade and Commerce), and his Tory successor, Sir George Foster, substantially increased these subventions, then enacted regulations that only goods travelling to Canada on steamships sailing directly to Canadian ports would be eligible for preferential British tariffs.

The rush to Canada was partly the result of the propaganda flooding Great Britain. The new Dominion was variously described as "the dutiful daughter of Empire," "a hunter's paradise," "the wild and woolly west" and "the land of golden opportunity." "It little mattered ... if the Rocky Mountains sometimes penetrated into Saskatchewan or that no foothills ever dotted the fictional landscape," noted R.G. Moyles and Doug Owram, who have studied the promotional literature, "or whether the intrepid hero really could, simply by 'turning to the right-hand seek the rugged haunts of the grizzly bear ... or, by turning to the left, ride after the buffalo on his own undulating plain.' ... It was best that nothing be too specific or accurate; that setting be an *impression* only, an impression of a 'great wilderness' where ... 'the red man and the buffalo roamed at will, and the conventionalities of civilised life troubled them not.'" Settlers' guides were distributed on British street corners; every railway station featured a poster glorifying some aspect of

Canadian agriculture. Adventure novels of the period even hinted at erotic murmurs in the grain fields. ("Caleb would stand for long moments outside the fence beside the flax. Then he would turn quickly to see that no one was looking. He would creep between the wires and run his hand across the flowering, gentle tops of the growth. A stealthy caress—more intimate than any he had ever given to woman.")

The reality faced by immigrants was very different, of course: after the Atlantic crossing, cramped into steerage bunks, to be unloaded, cattle-like, in Halifax or Quebec; then the climb aboard wooden railway cars equipped with cookstoves but no mattresses for the long journey west. There the newcomers were dumped onto the flat, slough-pitted prairie to scrub for a hidebound life. But at least their fate was their own, and within the cycle of the seasons they cultivated the virgin soil, bought an ox, then a horse, built a house, made a life. Out of their labours emerged not only a new land but a new nationality.

Much to the surprise of almost every official involved (except Strathcona, who had been on the ground and appreciated the area's rich potential), the Prairies turned out to be almost as good as advertised. Even better, when Charles Saunders, an inspired cerealist working at a federal experimental farm, perfected a strain of wheat that required two weeks less to ripen than the standard Red Fife and produced top-quality flour. Even earlier, the prairie had been producing more than 100 million bushels of wheat, and as farmers consolidated their holdings, villages, towns and eventually cities simmered up. The local HBC trading posts were quickly overshadowed by general stores, train stations, grain elevators and bank branches—opened by young clerks sent west from head offices in Montreal and Toronto with a thousand-dollar bill pinned inside their coats to provide the initial capital. "There isn't a tinhorn gambler left in Nevada," exclaimed an American journalist after touring the West. "They're all selling town lots in Canada!"

Winnipeg came fully into its own. By 1911, it was Canada's third-largest city, and, at the height of the land boom, Winnipeg's hotel accommodations were so hard to come by that proprietors charged travellers willing to sleep on stairways a dollar a night. By 1904, Winnipeg's railway yards had grown into the world's largest—and busiest—with as many as 1,800 cars shunted through per day. While the city's North End became the centre of immigrant cultures, mansions of Winnipeg's rapidly expanding merchant class were thrown up on the south bank of the Assiniboine, forming Wellington Crescent and its environs, where many of the leading figures in Winnipeg gathered. They included, over the years, the Aikins family, the Allans, Alloways, Ashdowns, Bawlfs, Drewrys, Eatons, Galts, Heimbeckers, Heubachs, McMillans, Nantons, Oslers, Pitblados, Richardsons, Rileys, Searles and Sellerses.

In the summer of 1909, when Lord Strathcona paid his first visit to Winnipeg in two decades, the local business establishment turned out in force. They organized a two-mile triumphal parade from the Canadian Pacific railway station to Government House, under arches and banners glorifying (and exaggerating) his connections with the city. Giggles of maidens dressed in white spread flowers before his carriage, and the crowds cheered at the very mention of his name. It was a marked contrast to his first furtive visit forty years earlier, when as Donald Smith he had slipped into town and was promptly placed under house arrest by Louis Riel. Strathcona enjoyed the celebration but could not find it in himself to forgive Winnipeggers for having voted against him in the 1880 federal election. When a local deputation asked him for a million dollars to help establish the Selkirk Exhibition, he politely heard them out and said he would give his decision on his return through Winnipeg from a journey to the Rockies. On his instructions, the CPR scheduled that arrival to bring his private coach into the Winnipeg station at midnight. The organizers were on the platform, but no one was invited to enter his darkened and shuttered railway car.

Such incidents aside, Strathcona, assisted by W.T.R. Preston, who had been appointed Commissioner of Immigration for Europe by Laurier, threw himself into the recruitment drive for new Canadians with typical enthusiasm—and was almost arrested for his trouble. Not satisfied with trying to boost emigration from Britain, he visited Hamburg to preach the gospel to German booking agents. They seemed impressed that a British lord had taken the trouble to address them, but the German authorities, particularly anxious not to lose any farmers, had a different reaction. The Minister of the Interior, Count von Posadowsky-Wehner, officially complained about the visit to the British government, threatening to arrest the High Commissioner if he ever returned. "The arrogance of the Canadian, Lord Strathcona, and the utter disrespect shown by him for the laws of the Empire in publicly conducting his emigration propaganda on German soil in the very teeth of the authorities, demand that vigorous representations should be made at once to the British Government …," editorially thundered the *Hamburger Nachrichten*. "Apart from the weakening of the Fatherland which the success of such propaganda entails, the attempt to lure our fellow countrymen to this desolate, sub-arctic region is, upon humane grounds alone, to be denounced as criminal."

SHORTLY AFTER THE TURN OF THE CENTURY—only a few decades too late—the Hudson's Bay Company nervously began to develop retail stores. Although there had been a tiny tuck shop for local customers in a corner of the compound at Fort Garry since 1830, it was not until twenty-eight years later, during the Fraser Gold Rush, that the Company opened, in Victoria, its first real store.* In 1881, a modest drygoods, hardware and grocery emporium was built at the intersection of Winnipeg's Main and York streets, and there the Company stubbornly remained for forty-five years while most of the city's commercial development took place several crucial blocks away at Portage and Main, later Canada's best-known intersection. Sensing that the HBC was not intending to capitalize on Winnipeg's remarkable growth, in 1905 the Toronto-based T. Eaton Company opened a magnificent five-storey department store at Portage Avenue and Donald Street—the latter, ironically, named after Smith. Spread over 6.5 acres and using all the latest merchandising techniques, it employed beautifully groomed high-stepping delivery horses that were soon the talk of the town.

Eaton's had revolutionized the Canadian retail trade by selling merchandise strictly for cash with a satisfaction-or-money-back guarantee. A militantly Methodist abstainer who drank buttermilk instead of water because he didn't believe merchants should patronize anything that was free, the chain's founder, Timothy Eaton, had established a reputation for scrupulously honest dealings. Among other things, he had eliminated the so-called wet sales. This was a shabby trick used by merchants of the day to market fabrics by pretending they had been slightly water-damaged on their way across the Atlantic and could therefore be purchased at unbelievable savings. The merchandise was actually old stock nobody wanted to buy that had been carefully sprinkled with salt water from barrels kept specifically for that purpose in the storekeepers' basements.

In contrast to Eaton's innovations, the HBC persisted in its parsimonious and conservative ways, losing trade to rambunctious new competitors throughout the West. That lassitude was best expressed by Strathcona at the Company's 1908 annual meeting. When shareholders objected that little effort was being

---

* Other small outlets, mostly glorified versions of the original trading posts, eventually appeared in Vancouver, Kamloops, Vernon and Nelson in British Columbia; at Pincher Creek, Edmonton, Calgary, Lethbridge and Fort Macleod in Alberta; at Prince Albert, Battleford, Yorkton, Fort Qu'Appelle and Whitewood in Saskatchewan; at Shoal Lake, Portage la Prairie, Deloraine and Lower Fort Garry in Manitoba; and at Kenora, Fort Frances, Fort William and Mattawa in Ontario.

expended to turn existing trading posts into attractive sales centres, the Governor haughtily replied that this was unnecessary because "the Hudson's Bay Company by their dealings, their administration, and their management in the past ... acquired a prestige, which is not possessed by others in the West.... The name of the Hudson's Bay Company is an advertisement of itself, and our stores do not require so many embellishments." If this had ever been a fact, it certainly wasn't true now. New immigrants, who constituted the overwhelming majority of prairie customers, had never heard of the HBC; many of the oldtimers, who knew it only too well, had unsettled scores with the Company and would gladly have walked or ridden miles to shop elsewhere.

THE FIRST SIGN OF CHANGE, though it seemed a natural and not particularly important appointment at the time, was the election in 1907 to the HBC board of Leonard Cunliffe to replace the retiring Sir Sandford Fleming. An important City animator involved with the financing of Harrods department store, Cunliffe did what few other British HBC directors of the day had ever done: he went on a Canadian inspection tour, accompanied by Harrods' resident impresario and managing director, Richard Burbidge. It was Burbidge who had converted a modest groceria into the world's largest department store, with, eventually, 220 departments and 20 acres of selling space. Under his influence, Harrods became recognized as a social rendezvous, with bevies of elegant dogs chained outside its entrances, waiting for their owners who were shopping or relaxing at one of three watering holes: a Georgian-style Gentlemen's Club done up in rich mahogany, a Ladies' Club in the Adam style, with figured satinwood and windows of stained glass, or the palm court tearoom, which featured its own orchestra. Burbidge was also known for engaging daughters of the nobility to model fancy underclothes. Paid £20 a week, debutantes considered the assignment quite a thrill.*

Cunliffe and Burbidge returned from Canada shocked by the inadequacy not only of the HBC's pitiful retail outlets but also by the absence of any admin-

---

* Among other innovations, Harrods pioneered the use of department-store escalators, with attendants stationed at the top of the first flight to serve jiggers of cognac to anyone flustered by the ride. Harrods' cable address was, and remains, EVERYTHING— LONDON. The store much later became part of the business empire of the mysterious Egyptian billionaire Mohamed al-Fayed, who grew so enraptured with his possession that he vowed it would remain in his family for a thousand years. He announced that when he died he would be mummified and laid to rest in a tomb atop Harrods.

istrative structure capable of capitalizing on the prairie boom. There was nothing particularly outrageous in their carefully worded report except its unmistakable subliminal message that Lord Strathcona was running the Hudson's Bay Company into the ground. The few stores that had been opened were so badly stocked and so poorly operated that they were turning over their merchandise only once every twelve to forty-eight months, and their accounting techniques were a century out of date. Strathcona's determination to govern the firm through a centralized London bureaucracy only vaguely in touch with Canada's startling new realities and, above all, his unwillingness to mobilize the HBC's financial resources to modernize its operations made it crystal clear that only the Governor's removal from effective authority could revitalize the Company.

Strathcona was yet again trapped in his own myth. He genuinely believed—as he always had—that what was beneficial for him personally would naturally benefit the Company. That may briefly have been true when both the man and the HBC were on their earlier growth curves, but the ever-increasing land-sale revenues and his own fattening purse had lulled the Governor into a false sense of corporate security. From his own narrow vision, it may have made sense to minimize expenditures on stores and to concentrate on marketing land. But such a shortsighted approach also meant that the Company was forfeiting its future. If current trends and management continued, the Hudson's Bay Company would have been virtually out of business the day it sold its last acre.

The most devastating condemnation of Strathcona and his methods was contained in an unpublished history of the HBC, written by Philip Chester, who was named the HBC's first General Manager for Canada in 1930 and had access to all the records. "Company policies were not changed by [Strathcona]," Chester alleged; "in fact he accentuated that [policy] of taking every possible dollar out of Canada, as he apparently believed the Deed of Surrender committed the Company to a slow, lingering death, which would come about when the acreage it had received as part of the purchase price of its monopoly had been sold. He established for himself a network of spies among employees in Canada, which contributed to denuding the organization ... of good administrators and managers. The vital qualities of restless energy and expansion of the Simpson era were crushed by apathetic policies, and as civilization gradually pushed the Fur Trade into the North, the Company left the rich opportunities of a growing Canada to its young and aggressive competitors. In those years Canada became a nation and enjoyed great economic and social expansion, but the Company failed to meet these favourable circumstances, and the natural opportunity to become a great mercantile Company in Canada was lost."

While Strathcona was ensconced in the Governor's chair and still the Company's largest single shareholder, not much could be done to dislodge him. But in 1910 a powerful stockholders' alliance was formed to combat his regressive policies by challenging his sway over the HBC's board of directors. After a London court of appeal had ruled that receipts from the sale of HBC land were a return on capital and therefore not liable to income tax, a group of City financiers associated with the American interests of J.P. Morgan started to put pressure on Strathcona to increase the number of outstanding HBC shares so that they could participate in the potential growth of the company. At the 1910 annual meeting the Morgan interests won four out of the nine directors' seats, gaining significant influence. Thomas Skinner, a financial adviser to the Canadian government, a director of the CPR and the Bank of Montreal, and chairman of the Canada North-West Land Company, was promoted to Deputy Governor, along with the four Morgan representatives:

Robert Molesworth Kindersley, chairman of the merchant bankers Lazard Brothers & Company and Whitehall Trust; he was also a director of the Bank of England, and managed large private shipping interests. Within five years he would be elevated to Governor of the Hudson's Bay Company.

Vivian Hugh Smith, a partner of Morgan, Grenfell & Company, later Lord Bicester, who served as Governor of the Royal Exchange Assurance for forty-two years and was one of the City's most distinguished financiers.

Richard Burbidge, the managing director of Harrods, who immediately obtained the HBC's British goods purchasing account (at 2.5 percent commission) and had his second son, Herbert, appointed Commissioner of the Company's stores. Harrods was also granted exclusive rights to merchandise HBC furs, the first time the pelts had been offered publicly in London since the Company's founding in 1670. The only other display of the Company's products had been at the Colonial Exhibition of 1886.

William Mackenzie, the Ontario-born teacher-turned-entrepreneur who was founding chairman of Brazilian Traction and president of the Canadian Northern Railway, completed from Halifax to Victoria in 1915. He was the first Canadian-born director and revelled in the honour.

This powerful quartet's first decision was to divide the HBC's operations into three separate departments, each with a new commissioner, in charge of the fur trade, land sales and retailing. The Company's stock was split on a ten-for-one basis and its capitalization doubled through issuance of 200,000 cumulative £5 preferred shares, which raised £1 million for store expansion. To advise on overseas growth, a fledgling Canadian Committee was appointed consisting of three eminent Winnipeg businessmen, Sir Augustus Nanton, George Gait and Sir William Whyte, a retired CPR vice-president. Almost at once they got down to the business of transforming the Hudson's Bay Company into a modern corporation. Construction of a major chain of department stores was commissioned, starting with Calgary and Vancouver in 1913. By the end of that year, the HBC had fifteen sales shops in operation, with $5 million invested in expanding the facilities.

Strathcona continued to occupy the Governor's majestic office, but the Company was beginning to slip away from under him.

AS TOUGH AS OLD PEMMICAN, Strathcona had finally begun to betray signs of his advanced age. During his 1909 Canadian visit when he had been on a buggy tour of the Okanagan Valley, the horses stumbled while going downhill and his carriage overturned. Both of the driver's legs were broken, but the eighty-nine-year-old High Commissioner survived intact except for a slightly strained arm. The same summer when he was back in England, a Royal Navy flotilla sailing up the Thames fired a salute salvo that exploded too close to Strathcona's eardrums. He was temporarily deafened and grew cranky and even more fusty than was his habit. When he heard that W.H. Duff-Millar, Agent-General for New Brunswick, had ordered a ceremonial uniform for a royal reception, he personally tracked down the tailor, walked into his shop and, waving his cane for emphasis, insisted that work on the garment be stopped immediately because provincial agents-general had no official standing and were not entitled to special dress.

In the spring of 1910, feeling poorly and having reached the great age of ninety, Strathcona reluctantly offered Laurier his resignation. The Prime Minister just as reluctantly accepted it and officially announced the High Commissioner's retirement at the Dominion Day banquet in London the following summer. The resignation having been offered and accepted, nothing more happened. There was an election in the air, and neither of Canada's political parties wanted to press for the old man's departure. Any partisan demand for the High Commissioner's scalp would have left the offending politician open to Strathcona's wrath and the possibility of financial aid to his opponents. And so Strathcona was able to stay on through a simple stratagem: neither of Canada's political parties wanted him back because each was fearful of his possible support of the other.

Laurier had earnestly tried to accommodate Strathcona's every whim during the fifteen years of their political partnership. But in 1911, as the Liberal Prime Minister faced his toughest election campaign, advocating support for a reciprocity agreement with the United States, Strathcona remembered the one disagreement of their relationship and publicly came out against Laurier's trade scheme.*

Laurier's subsequent electoral defeat brought the Conservatives back into office under Robert Laird Borden. That pleased Strathcona because one of the new Prime Minister's first decisions was to order construction of three dreadnoughts as Canada's contribution to the Royal Navy. Borden and Strathcona had first met during a London visit by the then Opposition Leader two years earlier. "(Lord Strathcona) was most kind and attentive in every way," Borden later recalled. "I was struck at that time with an almost pathetic earnestness in the discharge of even the minor duties of his office.... He was in evidence on every occasion. He met us at the station upon our arrival in London; he regularly called upon us at our hotel; when I left to visit Paris, I found him (to my great astonishment) waiting for me at the hotel door early in the morning in order to accompany me to the train. On that occasion he reproached me for not having given him formal notice of my departure; and he seemed to feel that his failure to attend would have been almost a disgrace." Once in office, Borden reappointed Strathcona—now in his ninety-second year—unaware that the old man had turned his mind to one final project.

STRATHCONA'S LAST ADVENTURE, historically his most significant, ensured that in the decisive run-up to the First World War the Royal Navy would have adequate fuel reserves to take on the Kaiser's fleet.

---

* Strathcona was still nursing his recollection of the time the heir to the throne had visited Canada and stayed at his Montreal residence. When the royal party left for the West, Laurier would not allow the High Commissioner to attach his private car to the royal train—even though Strathcona promised to ride along only as far as Calgary. Another, more weighty reason for umbrage involved Laurier's enthusiastic support for construction of two transcontinental railways, the Grand Trunk Pacific and the Canadian Northern, that cut into the CPR's earnings.

Strathcona had been interested in petroleum exploration since it was reported to him that a CPR construction crew drilling for water in southern Alberta had struck gas. Besides retaining the Company's rights to minerals found on the lands it sold, he also instructed the new Canadian Committee to search for oil. Not much happened at first, but Strathcona was rewarded with a rich geological sample of oil seepage formations found near what is now Norman Wells in the Northwest Territories.* Through his Scottish connections, the High Commissioner had meanwhile obtained control of Burmah Oil, a firm founded in 1886 by Glasgow engineers who pioneered the extraction of oil from shale. The company's deposits up the Irrawaddy River in central Burma were not particularly extensive, but at least they were under British control.

That suddenly became important as development of marine engines fired by oil instead of coal began to revolutionize the world's navies. The Royal Navy had continued to act as the guardian of the Empire, protecting garrisons "on every rock in the ocean where a cormorant could perch," as the parliamentary reformer Sydney Smith had caustically observed. The silent service's self-esteem remained unaffected by the Boer interlude. Admiral Algernon Charles Heneage habitually removed his jacket while reciting his morning prayers because he considered it unthinkable for a uniformed British officer to fall on his knees. Another salty character, Admiral Sir Robert Arbuthnot, was such a martinet that when, shortly after he passed command of his ship to his successor, a seagull defecated on the foredeck, a chief bosun's mate deadpanned: "That would never have happened in Sir Robert's day." The navy's progressive element, led by the First Sea Lord, Sir John Fisher, was more concerned with transforming its obsolete coal-fired vessels to oil. Coal engines took eight hours to flash up and some ships took days to coal; oil propulsion was faster, more efficient, produced less telltale smoke and nearly doubled the effective action radius of warships.

The Royal Navy's predicament was that 94 percent of the world's oil supplies were under Russian or American control, with Royal Dutch/Shell and the Rockefeller-dominated Standard Oil interests uneasily sharing the western oligopoly. Apart from the tiny Burmah Oil operation, Britain's only potential petroleum source was Persia (modern Iran), where William Knox D'Arcy, the wealthy developer of the Mount Morgan goldfield in Australia, had obtained

---

* Located on the Mackenzie River, the little settlement did eventually strike an economic oilfield and still produces a million barrels of crude a year.

a sixty-year oil exploration concession for only £20,000 and 10 percent (later 16 percent) of net profit. He risked most of his fortune drilling the concessions, but his Polish and Canadian field crews reported only dry holes. Afraid that D'Arcy would be tempted to join the Shell or Rockefeller cartels, a delegation headed by Fisher secretly called on Strathcona and asked him to become chairman of a reconstructed and refinanced major oil consortium that would combine the Burmese and Persian properties.* Briefed on the strategic significance of the Royal Navy's maintaining defensible oil supplies, Strathcona immediately agreed to help finance the new oil firm and become its chairman.

A new Anglo-Persian syndicate was hurriedly incorporated, D'Arcy was pushed aside, and at least £1.5 million was personally contributed to the oil hunt by the HBC Governor. He received 75,000 shares for his trouble, and by the very act of agreeing to become chairman of the highly risky enterprise provided the credibility required to raise more exploration funds. The joint venture struck oil at Maidan-i-Naftun soon afterwards and quickly outlined a major oilfield. At the personal urging of Winston Churchill, then First Lord of the Admiralty, Strathcona signed over the Persian concessions to the British Crown for £2.2 million, guaranteeing the Royal Navy twenty years of oil at a price that Churchill estimated saved British taxpayers enough money to have paid for construction of all its pre-war dreadnoughts. The Anglo-Persian reserves fuelled the fleet that gave Britain the edge at sea over Germany in the First World War. "It was not as a mercantile company that I looked upon it," Strathcona explained, "but really from an Imperial point of view."†

BY THE SUMMER OF 1913, Strathcona looked and acted his ninety-three years. The old man's proud chin no longer jutted out before him but looked more like a manmade jaw in which the paraffin was melting. Ethel Hurlbatt,

---

*D'Arcy had in fact been negotiating with both rival concerns. At one point Shell had hired a freelance master-spy identified by British Intelligence as Sidney George Reilly to intercept D'Arcy during talks he was holding with the Rockefellers aboard a Rothschild yacht anchored off the French Riviera. Reilly dressed up as a priest and, inveigling his way aboard the vessel on the pretext he was collecting money for a nearby orphanage, took D'Arcy aside and on behalf of Shell offered to improve any Rockefeller offer.

† The Anglo-Persian Oil Company eventually grew into British Petroleum, the $50-billion London-based petroleum giant that now ranks as the world's third-largest oil multinational. In January 1975, Burmah Oil sold its 21.5-percent interest in British Petroleum to the Bank of England for $426 million.

the Warden of McGill's Royal Victoria College, who met him at the time, poignantly recalled his "detachment of manner, as if he had already passed some boundaries of time and space beyond his fellows, and while occupied and keenly interested and ceaselessly concerned with work and duty and service, [he was] really alone with himself."

On June 13, 1913, Labrador Smith presided for the last time over the Hudson's Bay Company's annual Court. Too weak to stand or even to read his own remarks, he sat before a representative gathering of the Company's shareholders like a stuffed effigy of himself—mute, barely emitting any vital signs, yet still there, the Governor and a Bay man to the end. The news was all good: £300,000 had been invested in the building of larger stores in Calgary, Vancouver and Victoria; the year's dividend declaration of £5 on each share of £10 value set a modern record; land was being disposed of at an unprecedented $20.06 an acre, and 4,032,860 acres were still to be sold.*

The High Commissioner's final public function was the giant Dominion Day reception he had given every July 1 at Queen's Hall. He tirelessly shook 2,300 hands, but his voice, never very strong, had given out. "The whole scene was exceedingly beautiful," noted the Reverend J.W Pedley, a visitor from Canada. "The great hall with its brilliant illumination, its fine decorations ... its orchestra discoursing the sweetest music, and crowded with the elite of London's social life ... all arrayed in their best, flashing with jewels and adorned with knightly orders, presented a spectacle of light and color and animation, which was not only charming but wonderfully impressive." A month later, Strathcona decided on a lightning visit to Canada to inspect his latest investment, the Ritz-Carlton Hotel in Montreal. His wife, Isabella, herself a frail eighty-nine, had always accompanied him everywhere, but, having suffered several mild strokes, was not feeling healthy enough to go along. When Strathcona gently reminded her that he might not be well enough to return, she insisted on going to Euston Station so she could see him off. He last saw her there on the platform, lifted by four young men, gazing directly into the window of his private carriage, waving her fond farewell.

On the morning of November 7, after walking her Yorkshire terrier in Grosvenor Square, Lady Strathcona collapsed. Her cold developed into

---

* A further million acres had been sold by 1923, with most of the balance of the land-bank moved in the following two decades. By 1954, the HBC had only 18,250 acres in its inventory; the last major parcel of fifty acres was donated to the University of Victoria by the Company in 1961 when Richard Murray was Managing Director.

pneumonia, and she died five days later. Her husband of sixty years—and four weddings—was devastated. His grief caused him to make a fatal mistake: he stopped working.

Ten weeks later, on January 21, 1914, in his ninety-fourth year, Lord Strathcona died of "great prostration and heart failure." Incredibly, on his deathbed he was still worrying about the legitimacy of his marriage to Isabella, as if unwilling to carry the burden of that imagined sin to his grave. His two physicians, Sir Thomas Barlow and William Pasteur, signed a legal declaration with a firm of London solicitors testifying to his last words.*

In their tributes, Strathcona's contemporaries attempted to outdo each other with purple praise. "We need not fear exaggeration in speaking of Lord Strathcona," declared Sir Charles Davidson, Chief Justice of the Quebec Superior Court. "In especial degree has he enriched and uplifted Canadian life. May we emulate even if we cannot in the mean while at least reach to the lofty standards of his public and private careers." Sir William Peterson, the principal of McGill University, had little trouble topping that "Duty was his guiding star," he said of Strathcona, "duty and conscience. We ought to be glad, too— ought we not?—in our day and generation, that Canada can boast of him as a man of unspotted integrity." Even Sir Wilfrid Laurier seemed overcome by grief. "Since Sir John Macdonald's time I do not know that there has been any Canadian who, on departing this life, has left behind him such a trail of sorrow as Lord Strathcona.... He came as a simple clerk to the Hudson's Bay Company, and from that station he rose step by step until he became ... at first in fact, and afterwards both in fact and name, the governor of that historic company, a position which he held to the last day of his life." *The Times* summed up his amazing career most succinctly: "With no advantages of birth or fortune, he made himself one of the great outstanding figures of the Empire."

---

* "Lord Strathcona," the affidavit stated, "said he knew he was dying and asked us to come close to the bed and listen to what he was going to say.... He said his wife's first marriage was performed by a man who had not the legal power to do it in that district. The man to whom his wife was first married was called Grant. Grant treated her so badly that life with him became impossible. They separated. Before Lord Strathcona married his wife he consulted several persons including Sir George Simpson ... and they all advised that [he] would be justified in marrying her. The domicile of Lord Strathcona being Scotland and he being a Scotchman he had no doubt about the validity of the marriage. The marriage was subsequently repeated in New York...." Oddly, his last Paris marriage, the only one accompanied by full religious rites, was not mentioned by the expiring peer.

The Dean of Westminster had suggested the High Commissioner's remains be preserved in a sepulchre in the Abbey among Britain's most distinguished sons, but Strathcona had stipulated that he wished to rest beside his beloved Isabella at Highgate Cemetery in North London.* Still, the Abbey was the scene of his funeral, a state occasion of grand proportions attended by the Empire's noblest citizens. His coffin, carried in to the sombre cadence of Chopin's funeral march, was followed by a single wreath of lilies and heliotrope orchids. Attached to it was a card from the Dowager Queen Alexandra: "In sorrowful memory of one of the Empire's kindest of men and the greatest of benefactors."

By the time he died, Lord Strathcona had outlived most of the violent animosities he had created as Donald Smith. Yet his carefully drafted will perpetuated many of his earthly quarrels. Although the document was a model of philanthropic generosity, spreading funds across three continents, it never once mentioned Winnipeg. The former fur trader's snobbery also extended beyond the grave. His legacy establishing a leper colony was conditional on a strict entrance test: only leprous English gentlemen of good standing might apply. More than $25 million—the bulk of his estate having been distributed to family members before his death—was dispersed to McGill, Queen's, Yale, Cambridge, and Aberdeen universities, as well as a dozen poor divinity schools and underfunded hospitals. He left small inheritances (£50) to a number of HBC traders and set up the Strathcona Trust for Physical and Patriotic Education in the Schools, which still operates from Ottawa.

The will's strangest revelation was an obscure paragraph that stated: "I remit and cancel the debts owing to me by (1) the estate of the late *Right Hon. Richard Cartwright*, (2) the estate of the late *Lieut.-Colonel William White*, one time Deputy Postmaster-General of Canada, (3) the *Hon. George E. Foster*." Cartwright had been the Liberal finance minister who made his reputation denouncing politicians who had sold their souls to the CPR syndicate, yet shortly after formation of the Laurier government he became highly sympathetic to the railway and later authorized huge handouts to Canadian Pacific steamship lines. Foster, a former professor of Classics at the University of New Brunswick, who had risen to be minister of finance in five Tory administrations, had similarly helped out the CPR while in office; the favours procured from William White were never revealed, though the CPR received

---

* Thus sharing the graveyard with Karl Marx (1818–83).

many valuable mail contracts during his tenure. The heirs of the three men could now officially keep Strathcona's bribes—but only at the cost of sullied family reputations.

IT HAD BEEN A HELL OF A RUN. The minor HBC clerk who began his career for "£20 and found" had during his seven and a half decades with the Company not only preserved it and drastically altered its character but, unlike most of its modern Governors, had also become a pivotal figure in Canadian history. Here was a man of little privilege, unbridled ambition, and the mindset of a conquistador. For a time, he personified his country.

IX | QUEST FOR A NEW EMPIRE

On the Trail
of the Arctic Fox

*"Most masters of the Company's posts is lak kings.... Yo kin be birthed and
died without [their] consent but dat's 'bout all."* —Annie Redsky

HAVING LOST ITS EMPIRE in the western Canadian plains, where the influx
of railways and settlers had reduced its influence to the kind of commercial
competition for which the HBC had little skill and less stomach, the Company
set out to establish a new kingdom on Canada's northern frontier. Many things
about this frigid realm were radically different: the climate and terrain; the
pelts the Company traded (Arctic fox, not beaver); the aboriginal people who
did the work—Inuit instead of Indians; and the animals that fed and supplied
the hunters—seal and northern caribou rather than deer and buffalo. But
nearly every other aspect of the Hudson's Bay Company's shift north had an
equivalent in its earlier sweep west.

The move into the Arctic took place mostly in the twentieth century, but,
as in the plains, the Company had been operating successfully on the fringes
of its new spread for most of two hundred years. While the pace of its expansion was at the speed of a funeral slow march, the HBC eventually prospered in
the harsh new environment—as it had in the Prairies—but only as long as it
could maintain a monopoly. Eventually, the HBC became the dominant retailer
in each region, its initial customers being mainly the aboriginals whose way of
life its presence had robbed of self-sufficiency.

In both places, the Company's expansion was essential to its own—and
Canada's—future. During its western and northern hegemonies the HBC exploited
a territory that was commercially untouched. Just as its slow but persistent move
across the continent laid down the matrix of subsequent prairie settlement, its
invasion of the land mass North of Sixty carved into that bleak landscape the lines

of human traffic that would become its permanent pattern of habitation. Of the fifty main population centres in the modern Northwest Territories, three-quarters had been former fur-trading stations. As in the West, the Company served to protect Canada's sovereignty from outside, mainly American, pressures, not by heroic gestures or patriotic deeds, but simply by being there.*

"For at least 150 years," William Watson, a professor of economics at McGill University, noted, "the Hudson's Bay Company dominated the northern economy, both as a monopsonist [the only buyer] in the market for furs and a monopolist [the only seller] in the market for finished goods. There can be little doubt that it was The Bay—and not northerners, whether white or non-white—that was best served by this system." A simpler rationale for the Company's domination of the North was offered by Bob Chesshire, a veteran Bay man in charge of its fur-trade department in the 1940s. "At one time," he said, "we dispensed all the welfare in the Arctic, and the Government took the position that since we had a monopoly, we could bloody well provide the relief. I told them that was all right but that we only had a monopoly because no one else could operate in the damn country."

Except for explorers trying to find the North West Passage, or each other, Canada's far northern reaches had remained almost entirely outside the white man's purview until the nineteenth century, with only the whalers or the occasional missionary, looking for new positions, daring to break its silence. First to appear were the Moravians, who in 1771 established a mission at Nain, on the Labrador coast. Members of the world's oldest Protestant church, founded on the teachings of Jan Hus, the Bohemian martyr burned at the stake by Catholic persecutors in 1415, these dedicated men of God provided solace and support where little was available.†

---

* Canada's claim to ownership of the mainland portion of the Northwest Territories was based on its inclusion in the 1870 transfer of the HBC's charter lands to the recently formed Dominion. The islands of the Arctic archipelago were ceded to Canada through the British Colonial Office in 1880 "to prevent the United States from claiming them, and not from the likelihood of their proving of any value to Canada."

† Early missionaries had some unexpected problems with their gospel, which claimed that those who obeyed the Ten Commandments would go to heaven, where it was very beautiful, while those who sinned would go to hell, where it was very hot. To the preachers' shivering listeners, hell didn't sound so bad. When Father Pierre Henri, the Catholic missionary at Pelly Bay in 1935, told his flock about how Jesus Christ had once walked on water, he was surprised to find they were singularly unimpressed. When the good Father asked why, a member of his congregation replied, "What's so difficult about that? We walk on water all winter."

By the 1890s, Canada's North had become an area of intense theological competition, with various denominations attempting to carve out spiritual monopolies. There is a documented story of Father Henri Grollier, OMI, racing Archdeacon James Hunter down the Mackenzie River in the winter of 1858–59 to evangelize new districts around Aklavik. (The Catholic beat the Anglican.)

With Roald Amundsen's epic 1903–6 east-to-west journey across the roof of North America, the 400-year quest for the fabled Passage came to an end. The Arctic became, if not more accessible, at least less mysterious and more frequently visited. As more southerners ventured beyond the tree-line, they encountered the Inuit.* Because the white man entered a climate that defied his own survival, he had to manufacture a set of myths to account for the ability—and willingness—of the Inuit to endure. Such mythologies were expressed in many dubious ways, but the underlying message from those early contacts was that the people of the North were happy campers, frolicking in the snow—"Nanooks of the North" done up in polar-bear pants, their children playing with litters of photogenic puppies in cute igloos. "The Eskimo makes his or her appearance with a smile," wrote the northern expert Hugh Brody in a devastating parody of this silly stereotype. "[He] is an eternally happy, optimistic little figure; a round, furry and cuddly human with a pet name; a man or woman who amazes and delights our European representatives with innocent simplicity. Gorge themselves as they might on raw meat and blubber, a stereotypical Eskimo of the impossible north wages his battle against environment in astonishing good humour." Brody also pointed out the difference between Inuit and Indians: "The 'Eskimo' smiles from the sidelines; the Indian is cunning, warlike and stands in our way. This distinction between the two peoples is a geographical and anthropological myth, but the double stereotype has nonetheless persisted.... The one at war with nature, the other with settlers."

---

* "Eskimo" is the Indian (most likely Montagnais or Naskapi) name for the northern aboriginals. It was the designation originally used by whites because a Jesuit in 1611 had heard Indians refer to the northerners as *Eskimantsiks*, a derogatory term meaning "eaters of raw flesh," It is used in this chapter only when authors or resident HBC Factors refer to the aboriginal population by that word. Inuit, the more contemporary term, simply means "people." (Inuk is the singular of Inuit.) Canada's 25,000 Inuit are divided into eight tribal groups: Labrador, Ungava, Baffin, Iglulik, Caribou, Netsilik, Copper and Western Arctic. They speak a common language, Inuktitut, which has six dialects. Dwellers in the Western Arctic have in recent years coined a new word, "Inuvialuit," to distinguish themselves from other Inuit. Those who live in Northern Quebec (Ungava) are "Taqramiut" (people of the shadow); they call the aboriginal citizens of Labrador "Siqinimiut," people of the sun, which rises in their land first.

Other observers have noted differences in their philosophical approaches to life, with the Indians tending to be more introverted and generally less mischievous. One example: for a time during the 1950s many Indians and Inuit suffering from tuberculosis were lodged at a hospital near Moose Factory in northern Ontario. "The Eskimos were very smart," recalled J.J. "Woody" Wood, a local HBC Factor. "They never complained but could get their point of view across. When there was an economy drive, the cook kept serving spaghetti. Nobody said anything, but I remember one supper hour when the hospital was unusually quiet. As the nurses started making their rounds again, they found everything—the light fixtures, toilet bowls, door knobs—decorated with spaghetti. That was a creative protest and very unlike anything the Indians might have done." Stuart Hodgson, the first resident Commissioner of the Northwest Territories,* notes that one of the main differences between the Indians (Dene) and the Inuit is that Dene settlements or camps are usually along a lake or river, whereas the Inuit are seldom far from salt water.

Inuit survival had a lot less to do with mischief or good humour than with an environment that daily stretched the limits of human endurance. Generations of men and women grappled with the exigencies of a frozen world that held out no advantage, except that it was home. The many historical instances of starvation, cannibalism and infanticide were eloquent evidence of how agonizing it all had been—the numbing cold, the constant quest for sustenance, and the unremitting search for shelter and for driftwood for cooking fires.

To cheat nature they had to be tough. E.J. "Scotty" Gall, a veteran HBC Arctic trader, recalled that while building a boat at Tuktoyaktuk, he once saw his Inuk assistant pull nails out of the hardwood planking with his teeth. That story may or may not be true, but Father Frans Van der Velde, the veteran Arctic missionary, reported that an Inuk used his teeth like a third hand. The Inuit developed quite extraordinary ways to deal with their surroundings.

---

* A Grade 8 dropout and successful union organizer, Hodgson was an improbable appointee to head what was, before his arrival, a colonial old boys' club, the Northwest Territories Council. (During his union days he headed an organizing drive for the International Woodworkers of America in Newfoundland, where union-busting goons nearly killed him. He was terrified by his narrow escape. The next morning, when he looked into a mirror, he found his hair had turned white. Only later did he realize that in his nervousness he had put toothpaste instead of Brylcreem on his head.) During his dozen years as Commissioner (1967–79), when he actually lived in the NWT, Hodgson shook up the council and left a permanent and enlightened imprint on the North. "The Arctic does funny things to you," he once observed. "It's a jealous lover and it *doesn't* forgive."

While the wind that howls across the flat tundra prevented them from using such primitive communication methods as yodelling or Tibetan "far-away singing," they learned to *feel* movement a horizon away, so that they could communicate with arm-signals at great distances.

Until a version of Cree syllabics was introduced by the Reverend E.J. Peck in 1894, the Inuit had no written language, transmitting their myths and history through songs, stone carving and elders' recited memories. The half-dozen dialects of their spoken language catch the underlying sophistication of their culture. They use different words when addressing dogs or people, and some verbs possess a dozen tenses, so that instead of merely a past, present and future there are a near and a distant future, an imperative, a negative past and present, an interrogative, a subjunctive and so on. Many words describe snow because its exact condition is so important for hunting or trekking.*

In the early days, Inuit lived entirely off the land and sea, lighting fires by rubbing driftwood or striking bits of pyrite together, fashioning cooking pots out of soapstone, and making garments from sealskin with needles of goose or gull wing bones. Driftwood and whalebone were carved into harpoons; fish strips were frozen into thick, smooth packets to build sled-runners—providing basic rations in emergencies. No part of an animal was wasted. Seal windpipes were used as snow-house windows, ptarmigan bladders made children's balloons, fish eyes were snacks—a munchy Arctic version of Smarties. Inuit in the Western Arctic lined the hoods of their seal jackets with wolverine fur because frost won't stick to it. But the main source of nourishment, clothing and equipment was the caribou. Like the buffalo of the plains and the deer of the forests, the animal was a walking emporium, its skin used for tents, cloth-ing, sleeping bags, ceremonial drums, hunting bags, gloves and buckets; its antlers turned into bows and arrows, thimbles, sled handles and anchors. Its migration cycles fitted in with native life (or vice versa). Herds of caribou moved like great quadruped tides from the margin of the boreal forest to the edge of the Arctic Ocean, migrating between their rutting and calving grounds, involuntarily feeding man and wolf along the way. While he was stationed at Baker Lake in the 1920s, Archie Hunter, who spent thirty-five

---

* Some of the more common are *igluksaq*, which is snow suitable for shelter-building on long journeys; *pukak*, a powder snow; *ganik*, falling snow; *piqtuq*, snow being blown about by a bliz-zard; *mauya*, soft, deep snow.

years with the HBC, watched the caribou go by: "One could look across Baker Lake by telescope to the rolling land around the mouth of the Kazan River and, at first, see nothing," he recalled. "Then, as the glass was focussed, what appeared to be a sea of antlers came into view and then the caribou themselves. The hillsides seemed to be moving. In whichever arc the glass was turned there were the animals, thousands upon thousands of them. One old native told me of watching a caribou herd during the fall migration which took three days to pass where he was camped."

The herds are supposed to have originally numbered a hundred million, and as late as 1907, the naturalist Ernest Thompson Seton estimated Canada's caribou population at thirty million, though both figures were probably exaggerations. According to calculations compiled for the Fourth International Reindeer/Caribou Symposium, held at Whitehorse, Yukon, in 1985, the North American caribou count had by then declined to between 2.3 million and 2.8 million animals, of which only half the herds were increasing in number. The gradual decimation of the life-sustaining critters was bad news for all but the Company. "The sooner the caribou are gone the better ... for then more food-stuffs can be imported and the natives will be forced to trap and become fur producers or starve," a trader told Philip Godsell in 1934. Godsell, who himself spent two decades in the Company's northern service, abhorred that attitude, commenting in his memoir, *Arctic Trader*, that it was "a case of the Indian and buffalo over again. As long as the caribou are plentiful the Eskimo is independent of the white man but once the caribou are gone he becomes nothing but the white man's slave."

The Company attitude of encouraging the Inuit to become dependent on its goods was reminiscent of Sir George Simpson's edict, outlined in an 1822 letter to the HBC's London Committee: "I have made it my study to examine the nature and character of Indians and however repugnant it may be to our feelings, *I am convinced they must be ruled with a rod of iron to bring and keep them in a proper state of subordination, and the most certain way to effect this is by letting them feel their dependence upon us.*" J.W. Anderson, who spent his life with the HBC in the Canadian North, had a more thoughtful approach. "There is an optimum period in the dealings of any primitive people with the white man," he concluded. "This might be described as the period of time when the aborigines have sufficient of the white man's material civilization to ease the *burden* of life, but yet not enough to disrupt their *way* of life—muzzleloading guns instead of bows and arrows; twines and lines for fish nets and snares, instead of tree and willow roots ... steel traps instead of deadfalls. And one must not overlook those undoubted and perhaps harmless comforts, tea and tobacco, two of the greatest amenities we have given to the original inhabitants of Canada." The Inuit reached that turning point in the middle of the twentieth century; their treatment ever since has been a patronizing mixture of neglect and manipulation. But in the lexicon of villains that most Inuit feel have threatened their way of life, government ranks first, the missionaries second—and the Hudson's Bay Company a distant third. This is not because the HBC was particularly benign but because it was interested in selling them goods, not—as was the case with Ottawa and the churches—in converting them to new ideologies or ways of living.

THE HUDSON'S BAY COMPANY moved into the Far North with the founding of Fort Churchill south of the Arctic Circle early in the eighteenth century, but its commerce was with the Cree arriving from woodlands to the south. The only trade with the Inuit was from Company sloops irregularly dispatched into the upper reaches of Hudson Bay to barter harpoons, knives and lances for sealskins and whalebone. "So fond are these poor people of ironwork, that they lick it with their tongues before they put it by; indeed, I have seen them so transported with pleasure as to fall into dreadful convulsions," reported Andrew Graham, with his usual style of operatic exaggeration, after leading one of the earliest expeditions out of York Factory. The first regular trading station set up specifically to deal with the Inuit was Fort Chimo (Kuujjuak), at the south end of Ungava Bay, established by Nicol Finlayson in 1830. Not much business developed because the aboriginals had few items worth trading, but the Bay men hunted beluga whales and set up other whaling stations along Hudson Bay's east shore. In 1860 alone, twenty-three hundred white whales were harpooned off the Little Whale and Great Whale river posts, but within a decade overkill had ruined the hunt.

European whalers had been active in Davis Strait since the early eighteenth century. In pre-petroleum days the bowheads' blubber was valuable as a lighting oil and lubricant, while their baleen (horny tissue in the mouth with the consistency of human fingernails that allows whales to filter food from the sea) was used instead of spring steel or celluloid in many applications, including buggy whips, umbrella ribs and stays for women's corsets. Whale tongues were an exotic delicacy, and whale oil was so valuable that the profit from a pair of harpooned animals was enough to pay for a new ship. At the peak of the east-coast hunt, in the decade after 1820, some 750 vessels took part, landing more than eight thousand whales. The commerce was so lucrative that men spent their lives in pursuit of the huge mammals; one Scottish harpooner named Peter Ramsay died of old age aboard the *Erik* while on his fifty-sixth annual whaling expedition into Baffin Bay. It was a rough trade. Interminable tedium alternated with moments of mortal danger as crews scrambled to answer the cry, *"Thar she blows!"*

"It was not some primitive blood lust which prompted these sailors to endure the intense danger and prolonged monotony of a whale hunt," Daniel Francis wrote in his *Arctic Chase*. "The whalers probably served the most commonplace of masters, the need for a living wage. Today whaling is widely regarded as a slaughter of the innocents, but the men who engaged in it believed themselves simply to be doing a job—more perilous than most, less lucrative than many. Like those who engage in any task demanding skill, physical endurance, and bravery, the men had a fierce pride in their work, and popular writers found it easy to transform them into folk heroes." Only very occasionally did a whaler mildly lament the nature of his calling, such as this entry in the log of Captain William Scoresby, one of the most successful hunters: "There is something extremely painful in the destruction of a whale ... yet the object of the adventure, the value of the prize, the joy of the capture, cannot be sacrificed to feelings of compassion."

As the business grew more competitive, the whalers began to set up shore stations to process the oil and to afford themselves the chance of profiting from a second summer in the whaling grounds. Tiny communities sprang up at Cape Fullerton in Hudson Bay and in sheltered coves such as the eventual sites of Pond Inlet and Pangnirtung on Baffin Island. It was at these makeshift camps that the first prolonged contacts between whites and Inuit took place. The Inuit found most ships' captains happy to barter almost any item aboard their vessels for polar bear and fox skins. The whalers hired the aboriginals to help man the harpoon boats and to trap for furs that could be taken back and sold at highly profitable rates, while the Inuit were, for the first time, exposed to the iron-and-steam-age goods of their employers. Eager to acquire axes, pots, copper kettles, blankets, knives, needles and guns as well as the steel traps that allowed them to catch the animals whose pelts boosted their "gifts" from the white men, the Inuit came to treasure the imported wares. Having acquired rifles and inherited the clinker-built harpoon boats left behind by the whale hunters, the relatively small number of Inuit involved with the hunt gradually moved away from their traditional emphasis on the seal hunts to seek fur-bearing land animals, impatiently waiting for more white men to appear with more goods.

The trade grew even faster on the continent's west coast. The first whaling ships into the Beaufort Sea were a fleet out of San Francisco, and when one vessel—the *Grampus*—came back with twenty-two bowheads worth $250,000, even more whalers followed. A wintering station was set up at Pauline Cove on Herschel Island, a rocky outcrop northwest of the Mackenzie Delta, and soon as many as six hundred whalers were living there, trading with the Inuit. Unfortunately, that exchange, which went on for two decades, was not limited to food and fur. From late September to early July the ships were frozen in, with most of their crews gradually dispersing to aboriginal settlements that had sprung up nearby. Unlike their east-coast counterparts, the western whalers distributed large quantities of liquor to the local population and participated in such uninhibited sexual orgies that a disgusted witness described Herschel as "a paradise of those who reject all restraint upon appetite and all responsibility for conduct; when a dozen ships and five or six hundred men of their crews wintered here, and scoured the coasts for Eskimo women. I do not think it extravagant to say that the scenes of riotous drunkenness and lust which this island has witnessed have probably rarely been surpassed." Another observer noted that "when girls were not obtainable, wives were enticed away from their husbands, or men induced to rent out their wives." On August 7, 1903, two North West Mounted Police constables were finally posted to Herschel to enforce order, but they mainly collected customs duties in response to the HBC's complaints that the whalers were introducing cheap goods into the region.

By 1910, kerosene had taken the place of whale oil and the whalebone-structured corset had gone out of style, driving the price of baleen from a high of fifty dollars a pound to forty cents.* After trying to survive by slaughtering fleets of walrus and sea otters, the whaling crews departed the North, leaving behind an Eskimo population with a taste for European goods that the Hudson's Bay Company was only too happy to satisfy. Because the Company

---

* Whaling, on a reduced scale, has continued to the present day, with the magnificent animals' various body parts providing a fatty base used in the manufacture of margarine, fertilizer, food to fatten ranch-bred mink, and a special grade of oil used to lubricate the guidance systems of intercontinental ballistic missiles.

proceeded at its usual snail's speed, accomplishing in a decade what should have taken a season, former whaling skippers quickly established themselves as private traders. The most notorious of them was Captain Christian "Charlie" Klengenberg, who in his autobiography boasted about one of his typical commercial encounters with the Copper Eskimos: "They were so innocent a people of so long ago that I had not the heart to take advantage of them in trade, so all I took was most of their clothes and stone cooking pots and copper snow-knives and ice picks for steel knives and frying pans and a supply of matches. They had no raw furs with them, but their garments would be useful for my family and some of my rascally crew." Klengenberg, who had arrived in the territory from Denmark as the cabin boy on an American whaler, turned his ship, the *Maid of Orleans,* into a floating department store, serving, among others, the many Mixed Blood sons and daughters he had sired along the Arctic coast. One of his most popular items was trading rifles for furs, but the weapons lasted a long time. When the resourceful captain found there were few repeat customers, he rose to the occasion by handing out steel rods which, he explained, should be used to clean out the gun barrels. After a few applications, the rifles wouldn't shoot straight. Not unexpectedly Klengenberg was standing by, ready to sell replacements. When the Company persuaded the police at Herschel Island to ban the Danish swindler from the country, he begged to be allowed to take his ship on one more round, so he could supply his extended family. The local police inspector placed Constable Slim Macdonald aboard the *Maid* to make sure the trade was limited to the captain's relatives. When the ship returned to Herschel in the autumn without the constable, Klengenberg lamely explained that the policeman had unfortunately fallen overboard off Rymer Point on Victoria Island. There were no witnesses and the Dane was never charged, but his northern exploits—and Herschel's evil legacy—had come to an end.

The mainland sector of the Western Arctic, which lay to the south and east of Herschel Island, was far more accessible than the sub-Arctic regions on Canada's east coast because it had the Mackenzie River for a spine. With the connecting Liard, Peace, Athabasca and Slave river systems, the Mackenzie's drainage basin covers an area the size of Western Europe, most of it within relatively easy access—especially during the four precious months when the rivers aren't frozen. Though North of Sixty, this was mostly Indian, not Inuit, country and had been a highly profitable fur-trading preserve ever since Alexander Mackenzie's downstream dash to tidewater in 1789, because the frosty climate prompted its woodsy creatures to grow thick fur.* By the 1880s, the HBC had put steamboats on the Mackenzie and the Athabasca, with the *Grahame* running from Fort Chipewyan to Fort McMurray, where the Clearwater and Athabasca rivers meet, while the *Wrigley* served the lower Mackenzie. By then the HBC was maintaining eleven trading posts in the area, with Fort McPherson, less than 150 miles south of the Beaufort Sea, its northernmost installation.† The area's commercial potential received a big boost when a CPR branch line linked Edmonton to Calgary, and Waterways (part of the present location of Fort McMurray) became the Company's regional transportation terminus. The HBC ships looked like awkward floating verandas, with picket-fence rails around their decks, but they fundamentally altered the area's human geography. To push the trade northward, roads were built bridging the Mackenzie's only navigation hazard—the sixteen miles of rapids south of Fort Smith.

Accommodation aboard these early northern "fire canoes" was even more primitive than on their prairie counterparts, as attested to in this diary entry of Elizabeth Taylor, an early traveller down the Mackenzie. She had originally been assigned the *Athabasca River*'s best stateroom but was bumped to an ordinary cabin by an HBC Factor. "Mine, a single, had a hay tick only as furniture, no toilet articles whatever, and no bedding," she noted with mounting dismay. "I unpacked my blankets and went to bed. Had just settled for the night when a big drop fell on my nose and then another. I got up, spread the mackintosh over the slats above, and lay down again. But from the pattering above me, I saw that I should soon be deluged, so I rose, balanced myself uncertainly on the edge of the berth, and untied my bag of camping things, placed a frying pan under the leak, and tried to sleep again. But the leaks came faster and faster, and in fact I spent the entire night in warfare with the waters."‡

A later passenger, on the sternwheeler *Fort McMurray*, was Jean Godsell, who went down the Mackenzie on her honeymoon in the 1920s. The ship was loaded with Mounted Police inspectors, priests, trappers, traders, cardsharps, Indians and "Improved Scotsmen," as she facetiously called the Mixed Bloods. The captain, decked out in gold braid and brass buttons, was

---

* For a detailed description of Mackenzie's magnificent journey, see pages 306–8.
† Founded in 1840 by an HBC explorer named John Bell, the first white man up the Peel River, Fort McPherson became known for the longevity of one resident Factor, John Firth, who was in charge from 1893 to 1920 and died there in harness in 1939.
‡ The Company stopped carrying passengers on the Mackenzie in 1948.

constantly on the bridge, bellowing orders to crew members who paid absolutely no attention, except occasionally to bellow back some appropriate obscenity. The newly married Godsell spent most of her time with husband Philip in the *Fort McMurray's* "Bridal Suite," which consisted of "a number of sacks of flour upon which we spread our bedroll; a dirty tarpaulin, stretched on hoops of willow, being our only protection from the snow flurries and fall rains which frequently beat down upon the heavily laden craft." The ten-day journey to Fort Smith allowed Mrs. Godsell time to ruminate on the HBC outports she passed along the riverbank. "The unutterable loneliness of these little outposts of civilization—clinging like birds' nests to the riverbank, a hundred and fifty to two hundred miles apart—strikes one forcibly. Cut off for nine months of the year the life is one of extreme solitude yet, at boat time, they manage to surround themselves with somewhat of a gala spirit."*

Despite the relative ease of entry afforded by the Mackenzie and the predisposition of local Inuvialuit towards European trade goods, the HBC delayed its move into the far reaches of the Western Arctic until the second decade of the twentieth century, when it opened posts at Herschel Island, Baillie Island, Bernard Harbour on Banks Island, and Aldavik in the Mackenzie Delta. Even then, trade at these outstations grew slowly, easily surpassed by the busy commerce developing along the Mackenzie. In the Central and Eastern Arctic, whaling had also vanished, with the *A.T. Gifford* making her last voyage into Hudson Bay in 1915. As if masterminded by some benevolent deity, the decline of whaling coincided almost exactly with a dramatic rise in demand and price for Arctic fox. It was a time when furs ceased being strictly an extravagance, becoming much more popular and affordable. The fox pelts were fashionable not so much as garments but as trimmings—collars, muffs, neckpieces, and floor-length stoles that dripped with heads, tails and paws. White fox was ideal for the purpose because, unlike beaver or muskrat, it had a luxurious appearance without being unduly expensive and could be dyed almost any colour, with light grey, beige and black most in demand.

---

* A few years later, while stationed with her husband at Fort Fitzgerald, Jean Godsell created a scandal when she publicly beat up the wife of an RCMP corporal who had been spreading gossip about her. "Blinded by a curtain of flaming red, I reached out, caught her by the coat-collar and smashed my fist in her face," she recalled with obvious relish. "For the next few minutes, I thrashed the snivelling creature within an inch of her life, and sent her crawling and moaning back to the barracks with the warning that if, on any future occasion, she as much as dared mention my name this would be but an infinitesimal sample of what she would get the next time."

Although the market for Arctic fox was firmly established by the turn of the century, it took the Hudson's Bay Company the usual decade to react. Finally, in 1909, at Erik Cove on the south shore of Hudson Strait, which its vessels had been traversing for 240 years, the Company established its first Eastern Arctic post dedicated to trade with the Inuit. A treeless notch at the top of the Ungava Peninsula, the tiny harbour had been visited three centuries earlier by Henry Hudson and named Wolstenholme, after one of his financial backers. The HBC Factor placed in charge of the new venture was Ralph Parsons, who would quickly become a dominant force in the Company's northward expansion. Born at Bay Roberts on the west shore of Newfoundland's Conception Bay, Parsons was schooled at the local Church of England academy, then went to Labrador as tutor to an HBC Factor's children. He joined the Company himself as an apprentice at Cartwright in 1898 and spent six years commuting between Rigolet and North West River, the wilderness posts once managed by Donald Smith. Given only a week's notice to get the expedition to Wolstenholme organized, Parsons arrived at the desolate spot aboard the Company's supply ship *Pelican,* and after instructing his accompanying carpenter to start building the post, set off in a dinghy with two Inuit boys to seek customers. Finding none, they put in for the night sixty miles along Hudson Bay's east coast, and while they were asleep their boat and provisions were washed away by the tide. They had no choice but to walk back across hilly terrain, circumventing the fords that serrate the coast. The rocky ground cut to shreds first their boots and then their feet. Staggering along the tundra for four days, exhausted and starving, the two boys gave up (but were rescued later) while Parsons was reduced to crawling on all fours as he approached Wolstenholme. He waited at the new post a full two years before the first customers showed up. "Snowing fast, very tough wind," he noted in his journal on April 20, 1909. "This place should have been called 'Windhome' or something worse. Great place for a lunatic asylum, that sort of thing would *pay*." Once the Inuit found Parsons, the trade grew briskly, and by the summer of 1911 he felt confident enough to establish the Company's first Baffin Island post at Lake Harbour on the opposite side of Hudson Strait. Within the next eighteen years, Parsons inaugurated a dozen more posts (including Cape Dorset, Pangnirtung, Pond Inlet and Port Harrison), and a further twenty HBC stores were opened while he was in charge of the Eastern Arctic.

Parsons ruled over an immense empire with the righteousness of a latter-day Cromwell. The Company was everything to him, not just his job but his religion. He even made sure that the licence plates on his Newfoundland-based automobile always bore the numbers 1670, commemorating the year of the HBC's founding. He married Flora May House in 1918, and they had a son born the following year. After his wife died in childbirth the year after that, Parsons never remarried and wore a black tie for the rest of his life. "He was naturally reserved, independent, self-controlled," recalled Archibald Lang Fleming, first Anglican bishop of the Arctic, who knew Parsons intimately. "He also had amazing powers of detachment and never appeared to be surprised no matter how unexpected or absurd a report or incident might be. These qualities enabled him to rise step by step in the company's service until he became Fur Trade Commissioner in charge of the whole extensive and complicated transportation system.... He raised the whole tone of the fur trade. He was ruthless in his determination to stop drunkenness and immorality, not perhaps because of any deep religious conviction, but because he knew that these spelled ruin to both trapper and trader." Reflecting on that same single-track mentality in less kindly fashion, Captain Henry Toke Munn, who had run a trading post at Pond Inlet before being bought out by the HBC, commented in his memoirs: "The Company is a hard taskmaster and Parsons serves it with cold-blooded efficiency. He had been a Company trader at Lake Harbour, on Baffin's Island, for some years, and knows the Eskimos well, but I do not think he has ever understood them. He neither likes nor dislikes them, but regards them merely as instruments to serve the great Company."

THE HBC'S NORTHERN COMMERCE expanded gradually, with the Inuit trading in polar bear pelts, Arctic wolf and weasel skins, white whale hides (processed into shoe laces), the occasional find of mica (used for electrical insulators) or garnet crystals from Lake Harbour, eiderdown from Cape Dorset, and sealskins, used to make school satchels, boots and windbreakers. But such items were all incidental to the fox. The sharp-eared, fluffy animal that fed mainly on the remains of caribou brought down by wolves or the leavings of seal caught by polar bears lived everywhere north of the tree-line, often wintering on floes. Unlike its more wary red or silver cousins foraging in the forested south, the Arctic fox is less clever than it looks. The animal's most noticeable feature is its tail, a portable Linus blanket that can be used in close encounters to blind attacking predators but more commonly serves as a heating pad when the fox is curled up against the cold, guarding its exposed nose and footpads from the frost, acting as both a wrap and a respirator. Before the white man's arrival, the Inuit had little use for fox pelts because they are too flimsy for clothing. Their only application was as a hand or face wipe—a kind of furry Kleenex—or for trimmings on children's clothes. The foxes' meagre back legs, their meatiest part, provided little nourishment.

Too curious for its own good, the Arctic fox has an unerring instinct to investigate any physical change within its field of vision. Trappers tell of foxes watching from a distance while they are setting a trap; the moment they're out of sight, the animal is already poking at it, often the victim of its iron jaws. If the fox doesn't freeze to death in the trap's deadly embrace, trappers kill it by diverting the animal's attention with an outstretched hand and when it lunges, hitting it across the snout with a snow knife, so that the stunned animal can then be removed from its leg-hold.*

Valuable and relatively simple to catch though the white fox was, it had one drawback as a staple for the Inuit trade: its appearance in the North was subject to irregular birth rates, peaking quadrennially according to the life cycle of the lemming, the fox's main diet. HBC posts would collect five thousand pelts in a good year and a hundred in a down-cycle season.† Since the Inuit had become dependent on the white man's goods, the fox trade became essential. But few realized how fundamentally the switch from hunting to trapping would disrupt their traditional society.

BEFORE THE HUDSON'S BAY COMPANY moved into the North, Inuit life had followed specific seasonal patterns based largely around sea animals. Frozen water was a form of liberation because dog teams could whiz sleds along its smooth surface at much faster and safer speeds than over the fissured terrain of the tundra, allowing families to visit one another and to hunt together. Summers were spent at temporary fishing camps established at river mouths where the Arctic char wiggled towards their spawning grounds. The catch was stored for dog food; then, within a month, the hunters were out in their kayaks, after seal. In October there was fishing from stone weirs at river mouths and seal hunting through breathing-holes in the ice. Much of this

---

* An alternative trapping method was used in capturing wolves and even polar bears. Small seal bones were filed to sharp points, then bent into a U shape, the ends loosely tied together with sinew, and the whole thing wrapped in a piece of meat, which was allowed to freeze. A wolf would gulp down the package; once inside its stomach, the meat would thaw and the bone would spring out, piercing the animal's stomach, causing a speedy death.

† A record 30,000 white fox pelts were exported from the Canadian North by the hbc in 1943.

catch was used to fuel dog teams during the inland hunt for migrating caribou. Since the average Inuit family and its dogs consumed forty pounds of meat a day, this often caused a serious logistical problem. An inland Inuk had to kill at least two hundred caribou annually to keep his family and dogs alive. The constant search for food in a land with severely limited resources meant that each family had to hunt over a large area. Except for the temporary shelters thrown up to hold the traditional family reunions early each autumn, there were few real settlements or communities. The Inuit lived on the hunting trails or in temporary, widely dispersed fishing and seal-hunting camps. Inuit life was nomadic, coastal (except for the caribou forays), proud and independent.

In those early days, the Inuit lived in small, related family groups sprinkled along the coastline, and their visits to HBC posts were usually limited to two a year. In the dead of winter, the head of each family would arrive alone by dog team to trade and renew his essential supplies; in summer, whole families would come to greet the annual HBC supply vessel and mingle with kinfolk. Like the whaling ships, the Company's posts were there providing goods, but their presence was incidental to the seasonal rhythm of Inuit existence. As the fur trade accelerated, such HBC supplies as rifles, hatchets, needles, matches, tea and tobacco became necessities instead of supplements, and everything changed. To satisfy these essentials, the Inuit had to abandon their subsistence mode of life and concentrate on the only "cash crop" there was: fox pelts.

This shift from the primary role of hunter to trapper involved a radical switch in the aboriginals' sense of self-worth. Unlike trapping, hunting—especially of seal and polar bear—was a test of manhood, a dignified and courageous occupation in which each family celebrated the day's bounty. To be a hunter was to be an *Angut*—"a Man, preeminently." The fox had to be trapped in winter when fur was at its prime, which meant abandoning most of the seal and caribou hunts. That in turn meant not only having to change social customs but also having to buy from the HBC the clothing and tools previously obtained as byproducts of seal and caribou kills. To maximize their trade and retail selling opportunities, the HBC encouraged the concentration of the Inuit into villages or settlements. The location of few HBC posts was chosen by aboriginals; sites were picked for their proximity to safe supply-ship anchorages and their nearness to areas where the abundance of Arctic fox promised profitable commerce. At least once, the HBC moved whole Inuit communities to their trading posts; in 1934, fifty-three Inuit volunteered to be transferred (with their 109 dogs) from Cape Dorset, Pangnirtung and Pond Inlet to Dundas Harbour on Devon Island in the High Arctic, where the Company had set up a new store.*

THE FIRST PRIMITIVE POSTS RALPH PARSONS planted in the Eastern Arctic—consisting of a trading store, twin warehouses and a staff house (which was the only heated structure)—set the physical pattern for the HBC's northern presence over the next four decades. The buildings were makeshift, slapped together and not insulated. Painted or limed white on the outside, with green trim and black roofing (changed to red in the 1930s), the compounds stood out from those of such later arrivals as the Royal Canadian Mounted Police, who customarily occupied quarters in two tones of grey, and most missionaries, who chose brown. The inside walls of the HBC stores were unpainted and there was no attempt at decoration except for the Coleman lamps and dog chains suspended from the ceiling. Merchandise was divided into three categories: provisions (flour, cornmeal, jam, baking powder, sugar, tobacco, tea, candles and matches); dry goods (canvas and duffel, tartan shawls, mirrors, toys, yard goods and the utilitarian panties known as "joy-killer bloomers"); and hardware (rifles, ammunition, files, traps, knives, pots, pans, hand-powered sewing machines, and coal oil or kerosene). Since few customers could read, colours were important in arranging the displays: five-pound tins of HBC tobacco were bright red, while the cheaper Ogden's brand came in light green; red-label tea was stronger than the green-label tea; red boxes held 12-gauge Imperial shotgun shells while blue boxes were used for Dominion shells, yellow boxes for rifle cartridges, and so on.†

Because stores were unheated and even on warm winter days indoor temperatures hovered at a chilly –20°F, the Bay men attended them only at trading time and seldom removed their outdoor clothing. They learned to sign counter-slips while wearing hairy caribou-skin mittens and standing in their

---

* Later mass transfers, based on Ottawa's absurd excuse of using the Inuit presence as a symbol of Canadian sovereignty occurred between Port Burwell and Coral Harbour on Southampton Island and from Port Harrison to Resolute on Cornwallis Island and Grise Fiord on Ellesmere Island, well north of any other habitation.
† These basic stock lists were gradually expanded to include accordions, axes, blankets, ostrich-feather boas, beads, boots, buttons, belts, tailor-made cigarettes, dresses, gingham, harmonicas, hats, mitts, needles, fish and mosquito netting, paints, perfumes, prepared and canned foods, snowshoes, soap, spectacles, sweaters, tents, toboggan boards, towels, tools, twine and waders.

deerskin boots on dogskin mats. "I'd go in there and stay as long as my feet didn't freeze," recalled Scotty Gall. "It was so cold that nail heads on the inside walls were coated thick with frost and if there were too many people in the store, you couldn't see anything because of their condensed breath. In those days we seldom dealt with fine articles, mostly trading in bulk items. Because it was too cold to use scissors, we'd premeasure and cut the calico into six-yard lengths." No glass goods were safe in the frosty environment, and one trader recalled that the approach of winter was heralded by the popping of ketchup bottles. The only vaguely fresh vegetables offered were potatoes, brought in aboard the annual supply ships by the barrelful.

The official reason stores weren't heated was that coal (at a hundred dollars a ton) was too expensive; the real reason was that the Company wanted the Inuit out trapping foxes instead of relaxing around a welcoming warm stove.

Much like the Indians' stories of dealings with the HBC, too often the folk memory of the Inuit recalls the trading relationship with the Company as a simple exchange: fox pelts for goods. It was in fact a more complicated transaction, with each side slyly certain it was exploiting the other. The Inuit wondered why the white men wanted the perfectly useless fox and polar bear pelts, since neither could be made into warm or comfortable coats. The Bay men, on the other hand, knew only too well what these "worthless" furs were fetching on the London auction market. In 1923, for example, a .30/30 Winchester rifle sold for twelve skins, even though "the market value of a rifle was not much more than a single white fox pelt."

The actual swap was relatively uncomplicated.* When an Inuit family arrived to trade, they were lodged in what the HBC managers called their "Eskimo Kitchen," a small room adjoining the staff house where the visitors warmed themselves, and enjoyed a "mug-up" of tea and hardtack. When the trader felt the family might be ready to go into the store, he would casually inquire whether they had trapped lots of foxes. "The man would answer, in the old Eskimo manner," recalled Duncan Pryde, who served eleven years with the HBC before being elected a member of the NWT Council, "always belittling himself and his own efforts. 'Well, I've only got a few skins—really poor—hardly worth bothering to show the trader,' and then as likely as not he would bring out some of the loveliest hides you could ever wish to see. The Eskimos

---

* This was in sharp contrast to the complicated ritual of Indian HBC trading, as described on pages 165–71.

really enjoyed the trading. A man and his wife might come in with ten white foxes worth $200 ... and we would know we were in for a long session in that frigid room. They would look all around the store as if they had never seen it before, and they would wander around—not that we minded, but all the time we would be getting colder and colder even though we were dressed like the Eskimos, in a full set of skins."

The Bay men had been schooled in how to detect faults in pelts such as rubbed shoulders in an animal that had suffered from fleas and had scratched itself too vigorously. Fur that was too flat indicated the fox had spent part of the winter in a burrow, instead of running about improving his coat's condition. "These fellows in the early stores worked under very poor conditions, often at night holding a coal-oil lantern in one hand, the pelt in the other," according to J.J. "Woody" Wood. "The customer might owe you a thousand dollars and be your best trapper, so you had to be psychologically very careful about what you said and what credit you gave. But whenever we overpaid for furs, we'd get a hot letter from Winnipeg." After the price was agreed to, trading tokens were placed on the counter and, as goods were chosen, they were withdrawn to make customers aware of how much each purchase was worth and how much they had left to spend.*

The quality of the HBC's early trade goods reflected the Company's monopolistic priorities. "It sold good rifles and traps, the best flour, tea and ammunition—all the items needed for a successful trapping expedition," noted Al Hochbaum, the Manitoba artist-naturalist who became one of the HBC's liveliest critics. "But otherwise there was much junk on the HBC's store shelves—bargain-basement stuff that wouldn't sell in Toronto or Montreal. Why, over the long trek, did they bring in frying pans so thin that food burned, or canvas tents so fragile that the wind whistled through and the insides became wet after only a light rain? Peter Arvelek once told me at Rankin Inlet that the frypans were thinner than the beer can he was holding." It was one of the very few retailing relationships anywhere in which the merchant decided what goods his customers needed and how much they should be charged. The hunters who had been turned into trap-

---

* These tokens, matches or wooden sticks and brass, copper or later aluminum coins, had no monetary value outside the stores. (In 1926, the HBC's London Governor ruled that cash should be substituted for tokens at all HBC posts, but the order was ignored in remote areas and tokens were still being used in Ungava, for example, until the 1960s.)

pers were gradually becoming consumers in a market economy that allowed them little freedom of choice.

Apart from having to trap for a living, the very idea of bartering for the goods they wanted was a new discipline for the Inuit. Their tradition allowed everyone to take whatever the reluctant land would yield; the notion of private property, money or material possession lay outside normal thought or discourse. In the pre-HBC period, Inuit society followed a pure form of communism (in the sense of a social order in which property is held in common), with protection and survival of the group (which usually meant family) being far more important than any one man's or woman's wishes. The Inuit were so determined to play down any sense of individualism that they would periodically exchange dwellings. Such a communal approach was essential on the tundra or when aboard some errant floe where all the available food had to be shared or someone could starve. But once the Company moved in and established its stores, individual possessions became a status symbol, and the basis of Inuit society was compromised. "The new barter economy—furs in exchange for the goods of civilization—made life harder instead of easier, more complicated instead of more simple," wrote Diamond Jenness, an early student of native cultures. "The commercial world of the white man had caught the Eskimo in its mesh, destroyed their self-sufficiency and independence, and made them economically its slaves."

THE RELATIONSHIP OF HBC TRADERS with the Inuit had its furtive aspects, too, and no part of that interchange was more carefully hidden from view—or more open to misinterpretation—than the sexual liaisons between them. The Bay men's perceptions of these sensual assignations varied according to their own experiences. "It was the accepted thing to do when I was up there as a kid," recalled Scotty Gall. "You went to the husband and asked for the wife, and you paid him in goods or ammunition and her in so many yards of calico or whatever she wanted." Chesley Russell, on the other hand, who spent from 1921 to 1960 in the HBC's northern service, claims none of it ever happened. "The Eskimos were just as jealous of their women as we are, and never traded off their wives to anybody," he insisted. Certainly, there was much gossip among the Inuit about the Bay men's sexual appetites. "They are not only in the North to make money but they're in it for a fast buck and a good piece of action, but they always forget they're dealing with human beings."

Cecil "Husky" Harris, the HBC Factor at Poorfish Lake on the edge of the tundra, had three Inuit wives at the same time and even visited Winnipeg with them all in tow, staying at the Empire, then known as the Hudson's Bay Hotel. "Harris' wives were quite a mixed lot," reported his colleague Sydney A. Keighley. "One was old and ugly, one was young and pretty, and one was very short and very homely. Eventually he decided to limit himself to one wife and he chose to keep the old, ugly one, who was the mother of his three children. Alfred Peterson bought the young, pretty one, and George Yandle bought the short, homely one. I never managed to find out what sort of price he got for them." Gontran de Poncins, the French adventurer who spent the winter of 1938 at the HBC's King William Island post, remembered asking Paddy Gibson, the local manager: "What would happen if I asked one of these Eskimos for his wife?"

"Very likely he'd let you have her."

"Without a word? Without any—er—bargaining about it?"

"Oh, quite! In the first place, it's done. And then, you see, it's something of an honor. The fact that out of them all you, a white man, picked her, would make the rest think more highly of her. And so far as the husband goes, of course he'd expect something in exchange…."

"And suppose I asked for her several days running?"

"That wouldn't upset him. He might say to you, 'Tomorrow: I want her myself tonight.' But chances are that you could have her. And her husband and the rest would sit round in the igloo, laughing and chatting about you. The husband would be congratulated upon having made a rich friend. Probably he would let the others talk on while he dreamt of the things he'd get out of you."

No Bay man was more explicit in his sexual confessions than Duncan Pryde, whose exploits once prompted him to boast that "every community should have a little Pryde." Stu Hodgson could vouch for that reputation. "Duncan took on all comers," Hodgson recalled. "One time, I had a party travelling with me and I arranged to pick him up at one of the far northern settlements. I couldn't find him. There were thirteen houses near the beach. Suddenly Duncan came running out of the twelfth and said, 'Wait a minute—I have only one more to go,' and he dashed into the thirteenth. The local missionary came along, wringing his hands, saying, 'Please take him with you.' When we left, I am sure it was the first peaceful night he'd had in three weeks."

"Of all the Bay men who came north in the last sixty years, Duncan Pryde was probably the best linguist and he gained an immense amount of respect among Inuit people," recalled Gordon Wray, an HBC veteran from Baker Lake who later became the Territories' minister of tourism and economic development. "But he destroyed himself because he did something that I don't believe he should have done. He wrote a book about his sexual dalliances, and mentioned names. He was forced out of the North, and people said they would kill him if he ever went back to the Central Arctic. He broke the rules. He was taken into Inuit life in ways that very few white men ever are, and he used it for his own personal gain; he broke the code of silence, and by using people's real names embarrassed a lot of people. Last I heard he was in London. He had lost an eye in a bar fight and was driving taxi."

Each tale of sexual liaisons under the polar moon may have tallied with specific moments and local circumstances, but the notion that Inuit women could, be bought and that they couldn't wait to climb into the white men's beds distorts the rigid Inuit code of sexual ethics. Marriage was—and is—at the core of Inuit society. Men and women depended on one another not only for love and moral support but to carry out the division of labour so essential to the functioning of the Arctic family unit. Spouse-sharing did take place in the hunting days as a way of formalizing the sustaining alliances required for survival—less an expression of sexual licence than an essential social mechanism. "Far from being the casual and promiscuous affair that it is generally pictured to have been, 'wife-trading' was a very serious matter to the Eskimos," observed the American sociologist Ernest S. Burch Jr. "We now know that it was an integral part of their system of marriage, which also included polygamous as well as monogamous forms of union. Both 'wife-trading' and polygamy, once thought to be manifestations of 'anarchy,' turn out to have been components of a complex but well-ordered system." An exception was "putting out the lamp"—a game played to relieve the tension of long winter nights. Nude couples shuffled about in their host's *iglu* until, at a given signal, they embraced the nearest person of the opposite sex.*

"My experience with Inuit on the land suggests that it is difficult for one man to exist without a woman," reminisced Commissioner Hodgson. "The man builds the snow house, looks after the dogs, hunts, traps, looks after the

*And yes, in the early days Inuit did rub noses because kissing was considered unsanitary. The smaller and flatter a girl's nose, the more desirable she was deemed to be.

equipment and handles all of the chores outside the home. As the hunter goes, so goes the family. The woman does everything else: prepares the food, raises the family, makes the clothes, keeps the home, skins the animals, prepares the skins and so on. One can't make it out on the land without the other."

"There are those that will tell you that the Hudson's Bay men were rapers and pillagers and there are those who will deny it ever happened. The real truth lies somewhere in between," Wray has pointed out. "Baker Lake is my home, and there are young and middle-aged Inuit whose features and mannerisms relate them to well-known HBC men. As a Bay clerk in a northern post—and I was one—you were, to a certain extent, the lowest caste or the lowest member of a caste system among the white community. There were two reasons for this: almost all of us were very young, seventeen, eighteen, nineteen, while most of the other white people were professionals in their thirties and forties—missionaries, government administrators, managers, Mounties and so on. We had nothing in common with the other white people in the community. So the HBC clerks would gravitate to Inuit their own age. Most of us were Scots, and we very easily assimilated into Inuit society; it wasn't the other way around. All our friends were young Inuit men and young Inuit women, and naturally a lot of us had girlfriends. I mean, there was nothing else to do.

"As a result, we became much more in tune with the goings-on within the Inuit community and because we were, that caused even more resentment among the older whites. There was this unwritten rule that the whites would stay together and have their own little parties and mix with the Inuit only when business dictated it. And so that put us down even more at the bottom of the totem pole to the point where we wouldn't be invited to their get-togethers, whatever. Almost always the relationships we developed were with people our own age who were Inuit. I'm now forty years old and I came north when I was eighteen. This talk about people swapping wives and limit giving you wives, I never saw that. Inuit men were very jealous of their wives, and in fact a lot of the murders in the old days that went unreported were caused by jealousies. I'm not saying that it didn't happen, but it was rare. Even then, it was often done with sets of pre-conditions, and I don't think it was as loose as everybody made it out to be. But the Bay boys clearly had a bad reputation, no question about that. In fact, most self-respecting Inuit girls wouldn't go to the Bay staff house until it was dark."

The Company had many informal rules against its employees marrying Inuit women and on May 8, 1940, issued a policy directive to that effect that included a remarkably muddle-headed paragraph on the subject: "The Board also discussed the question of the line of demarcation to be drawn as between 'native' and other women, Fullbred Indian and Eskimo women would obviously be classed as 'natives', but the distinction to be applied as between these and half-breeds and other women whose blood-relationship to 'natives' is more remote still, would appear to be a problem."

The young clerks served a five-year apprenticeship and learned to speak Inuktitut before being promoted to junior traders; if found incompatible with their surroundings, they were quietly dismissed. What they achieved upon promotion was a combination of freedom and responsibility. "So here we were," wrote J.W. Anderson about his first posting, which received mail twice a year, "on our own in the far interior, with no doctor and no means of communication with the outside world. We had to be prepared for all the hazards of life—fire, flood, famine, sickness and sudden death. This dependence on our own resources, and particularly inner resources, comes as quite a shock to the fur trade novice, though for my part I had made my peace with the country and its hazards during my first winter at Moose Factory." Anderson was fortunate compared to a trader named Charles Duncan, stationed at Payne Bay, where ice conditions were so bad it took two years to deliver a telegram notifying him of his father's death in a car accident.

WHETHER OR NOT IT HAD ANY CONNECTION with stories of nocturnal goings-on, the northern service was the HBC's most coveted posting. For an employee of an enterprise steeped in history, being an Arctic hand revived memories of the HBC's glorious genesis on Hudson Bay, and even though they were strictly a twentieth-century addition, the northern stores were often referred to as the Company's "founding department." Running an Arctic post was curiously similar to being captain of a Royal Navy ship-of-the-line, constantly at sea. The Company's headquarters in London and Winnipeg were belittled as "home ports" where uncomprehending desk-bound "admirals" schemed to produce irrelevant, bureaucratic red tape. The naval analogy was heightened by the HBC's insistence on dressing up its Factors in blue blazers with Company crests stitched on left breast pockets and special caps to exhibit the wearer's rank. An interpreter's or junior clerk's headgear had only a red enamel HBC flag on it; the flag on senior clerks' hats was surrounded by a cluster of gold leaves; post Factors or managers (as they were called after 1930) sported the flag and the cluster plus another spread of gold leaves (known as scrambled eggs) on their caps' peaks. "It was really the comradeship that bound us together," recalled Scotty Gall. "You felt you belonged."

Resident Factors derisively referred to anyone living South of Sixty as "on the Outside" and it was part of their rigid belief system that while they themselves spent most of their waking hours cursing the Company, any outsider who dared to agree with them did so at his own—often physical—peril. "The northern traders' loyalty had to be seen to be believed," noted Bob Chesshire, who was in charge of the northern posts during much of the transitional period to modern stores. "In some ways, it was a dangerous type of loyalty, because the Company could do no wrong, according to these oldtime Bay men." Bill Cobb, a Newfoundlander who joined the HBC as an apprentice clerk and retired thirty-seven years later as Deputy General Manager of Northern Stores, agreed: "God was the Company—and the Company was God. Let some outsider criticize the HBC and their life was in jeopardy." The Bay men knew no other life. When Cobb was at Rigolet in Labrador, the HBC employed a local cooper named Jim Deckers. He had spent his entire career making barrels at the post without ever bothering to collect his salary, though he had repeatedly been told there was a large savings-account balance available to him. "When the time came for Jimmy to retire," Cobb remembered, "he got quite upset and asked Ralph Parsons, 'Is that money you told me about still there?'" When he was assured that it was, Deckers offered to buy the cooperage, just so he could keep working there. The Company allowed him to stay on the job till he died, and he never did collect his accumulated pay.

An HBC Factor named Jimmy Bell was known as a character, even among the oddballs who populated this frozen outback. He served much of his time at Arctic Bay near the top of the Borden Peninsula on Baffin Island, where he devoted himself mainly to eating. He could gulp down ten pounds of seal meat at one sitting with no effort at all, and as one observer described the process, "it disappeared into him just as if he were a polar bear." Bell soon began to *look* like a polar bear, so that his 350-pound frame had to be lowered into his peter-head boat by block and tackle. Eventually transferred to Cape Dorset, Bell started to lose weight and vomit blood. He was diagnosed as having stomach cancer, but before leaving Dorset he told a companion that he wanted to be buried in the North. "When I die," he vowed, "my spirit is going back to Arctic Bay. That's the place I really love most...." And that was exactly what happened. Although Bell was eventually treated at a Winnipeg hospital, where he died after six weeks, and was buried in a nearby urban cemetery, from the moment of his death, Bell's ghost began to appear in the Arctic Bay staff house. Doors opened mysteriously, footsteps were heard in empty rooms, shadows moved along the walls, noises and moans sounded for no explicable reason. One night, the HBC trader who had taken Bell's place heard his kitchen dishes rattling, and, finally fed up, he yelled out, "Leave the goddamned dishes alone, Bell, and get the hell out of here!" That made Jimmy so mad he bounced the dishes right out of their cupboards. The phenomenon was eventually reported to the RCMP, which carried out a formal investigation, but they couldn't get their ghost. Bell's old shack had to be abandoned in favour of a new post building.

The hardy stock that produced such dedicated eccentrics had previously generated the HBC's advance across the Prairies. They were hard-bitten Scots whose loyalty was beyond question even if their Company-supplied equipment was often beyond salvage—wilderness men who had more muscle than imagination and less introspection than courage. "They called us North Sea Chinamen," recalled Scotty Gall, proud to be one of them, "because we took the work cheaper than anybody else and we stayed with it. We were tough little guys; they could beat us into the ground with a hammer, and we'd spring up again." Recruited as youngsters in the Orkneys, Hebrides and Highlands, they signed on for twenty dollars a month to serve the HBC by day or night, pledging to protect with courage and fidelity the property of the Company with their lives if necessary. The youngsters could be sent anywhere within the HBC's domain, but North was where they all wanted to go. Apart from the adventurous aspect of these postings, advancement was faster and the Arctic posts were far more informally run than the western or even sub-Arctic stations. Philip Godsell, who left an entertaining account of his twenty-year HBC service, was posted to Norway House not long after arriving in Canada. Although it was located three hundred miles north of Winnipeg, Norway House was not considered a northern post and was run in the old-fashioned way. "We lived in a sort of semi-feudal state," Godsell later reminisced. "At regular hours the bell rang and we paraded to the messroom. Here, with much pomp and ceremony, presided the bewhiskered Donald McTavish, and although we were literally in the back of beyond, woe betide the person who appeared at table unshaven or without a white collar on. Once only I appeared with a spotted scarf knotted around my neck. Hardly was I seated ere I found myself transfixed by old Donald's astonishing and disapproving gaze. A string of expletives crackled off the old man's tongue as he demanded to know whether I considered they were all barbarians in this country.... I was forth-with ordered to proceed to my room and put a collar on." As late as 1912 at York Factory, HBC employees had to swear oaths of allegiance that obliged them "never to purchase any fur excepting for [their] personal use, and never to betray any business information that might come into [their] possession." The local cook, a marvellous, earthy Mixed Blood named "Lame Annie" Redsky best summed up the HBC's operational code: "Most masters of the Company's posts is lak kings.... Yo kin be birthed and died without [their] consent but dat's 'bout all."

THEIR DOMAINS WERE VAST IF NEARLY EMPTY, but within these icy realms the HBC traders were kings. They acted as their subjects' shopkeepers, meteorologists, bankers, dentists, doctors and welfare officers as well as father confessors and, until the RCMP arrived, administrators of justice. "When I was in charge of a post," declared Cornwallis King, who spent forty-one years with the HBC in the Northwest Territories, "if orders were good, I carried them out. If not, I handled them in my own way. I was willing to be judged by results. Sometimes the orders from England were absolutely idiotic.* All right for London, perhaps, but no good in the Mackenzie River District fur trade. I did not look for credit for myself. If my own decisions brought the desired results, I let the honour go to the district manager. We were above money considerations. *We were the Company* [emphasis added]."

The Company kept a fairly tight rein on its employees, with regular visits by district managers and inspectors, but the most potent self-regulator was the journal in which every Factor was obliged to document his daily rounds and business transactions. Until the advent of radio and air travel, these diaries, kept in duplicate and forwarded annually to Winnipeg and London, were treated extremely seriously, so much so that on the inside cover of each journal there was pasted this admonition: "Your ability to keep this book in a neat and intelligent manner will be an indication of your character and ability as Post

---

* London's suggestions included turning seal meat into dog food, processing Chesterfield Inlet mud into cement and building their famous hoot-chewing machine. The traditional way to soften sealskin for boot-making was for Inuit women to chew the pelts until they were flexible enough to be sewn. This eventually wore their teeth down to the gums, which caused them great difficulty in eating. The HBC's Development Department built a device to soften the hides. It was based on the principle of an old-fashioned clothes wringer and had brass teeth mounted in it. One of the contraptions was actually installed at Port Burwell, but it didn't work.

Manager." Some Factors grew bored and exasperated with trying to describe each day's largely repetitive activities. When Pierre Mercredi ran Fort Resolution on Great Slave Lake, one of his jobs was to haul firewood with a team of oxen named Bill and Tom. For twenty-one days his journal carefully noted the weather, how much wood was moved and so on. Each entry was virtually identical, and finally he could take it no longer. On the twenty-second day, his journal notation was reduced to two words: "Tom Balked."

The Company handled its staff with hard-fisted parsimony. "It was a pretty primitive existence," recalled Bill Cobb. "The furniture in staff houses was mostly home made, and some of the post manager's houses were real shacks." Architecturally, the worst example was the post manager's house at Repulse Bay on the Melville Peninsula. For reasons known only to himself, George Cleveland, who built the structure, reversed its windows so that they opened *into* the house and the windowsills sloped inward. That meant winter storm-windows had to be uselessly attached on the inside, allowing condensation to run into the rooms, where it froze. Local Factors vainly complained for decades that every winter at Repulse Bay was a nightmare, but the faulty building remained in place.

To cheer up post managers' wives, who began to move north in the 1930s, the HBC allowed them to pick their own staff-house colour scheme. One stir-crazy lady painted the ceiling of her living-room black, a foot-wide border at the top of the walls white and the rest of the surfaces a shocking pink; another applied various combinations of mauve and yellow. These early Company installations had no indoor plumbing, and there were serious logistical problems with outhouses. Any hole dug into the frozen ground caused the permafrost to thaw and the opening to widen, so that eventually the whole flimsy structure would sink into its own cesspool. When William Duval, a Cumberland Sound free-trader who had become a hermit, died, the Inuit, who had liked the strange white man, thought he deserved a proper Christian burial. There being no wood in the area to build a coffin, they interred him in the only wooden structure available: his own outhouse.

One area of significant discretion granted the Factors was the amount of credit they could allow various customers when Arctic fox prices were low and times turned bad. The problem was that no one could explain the basic laws of supply and demand to Inuit whose lives had come to depend largely on their ability to harvest furs. When fox prices at international auctions were at their lowest, the trappers worked extra hard because it took more pelts to obtain the supplies they wanted. That, of course, turned the classical supply/demand equation upside down, since conventional wisdom would have required the trappers to hold their goods back until the market turned up again. Understandably, they had little idea of what governed the price of a fur that seemed worthless to them—but that the white men wanted without being able to decide exactly what it was worth. Stuart Hodgson recalled how he once tried to explain the fluctuation in muskrat prices to an Indian on the Mackenzie.

"One day this fellow came up to me and said, 'Commissioner, how come I only get twenty-five cents for my rats?'

"'Well, I'll tell you, it's like this. There's a guy in Paris by the name of Christian Dior, and one day he decided women would wear H-form dresses, which meant using short-hair furs for trim. So orders went out to the London fur auction houses to buy seal, and the Bay told its post managers to set a lower price for longhair muskrat.'

"The Indian listened to the long-winded explanation with a stony expression, and shot back: 'Yeah, I know all about that. But how come I only get twenty-five cents for my rats?'

"'Because that's all they're worth.'

"'Well, why didn't you say so in the first place?'"

Because market prices and fox populations were both cyclical, on many occasions Inuit came into the HBC posts with no furs to trade or not enough pelts to obtain significant store credits. Some, if not most, of the HBC Factors responded with compassion, or at least as much compassion as was allowed within the limits of their headquarters-imposed credit lines and quantities of available supplies. But the extent of the HBC's generosity in those hard days before there was a federally sponsored welfare system remains an issue of active controversy. Charlie Watt, the Inuk who became a Canadian senator in 1983, has defended the Company. "When things were not going well, as they often did in those days ... the Hudson's Bay Company dispensed assistance to widows and people in need. Inuit were given per family per week: eight pounds of flour, half a pound of tea, half a pound of lard, half a pound of baking powder, two pounds of molasses or two pounds of sugar."

Others disagree. When he was Grand Chief of the Grand Council of the Cree of Quebec, Billy Diamond charged there was a graveyard ninety-five miles south of Rupert House on James Bay where twenty families had starved to death because the local HBC store would not give them credit. "The Bay *would* grubstake people," Stuart Hodgson maintained, "but they also kept good records and never lost a dime." Bernie Weston, a private fur trader wise in the ways of the North, argued that the HBC did carry starving people in off-season fur droughts, but that those who were helped later had to sell their pelts at whatever prices the Company set, even if it was less than they could get from competing traders.

Peter Ernerk, a former president of the Keewatin Inuit Association at Rankin Inlet and one of his people's more youthful spokesmen, put it this way: "The Hudson's Bay Company was necessary in our time as a trader of furs. It got rich from the native people in the North as well as throughout Canada and took advantage of the native people, especially in the area of furs, handicrafts and carvings. Inuit got very little return for their goods. It also lacked hiring native people, although this situation has improved in recent years. When I was growing up in Repulse Bay, which is my home town, I felt that. On the other hand, the Company provided a service which no one else was able to provide. So, from that point of view, it was positive. The Company's staff also acted as jack-of-all-trades besides being traders. They provided medical supplies and also acted as paramedical doctors. This was good."

Gordon Wray, the former Bay man who married an Inuk, is not as harsh in his assessment. "The missionaries were the ones who really changed people's ways and thinking," he claims. "When we joined the HBC, they said: 'The only way you can serve your customers is to understand that customer.' That's why they forced us into learning to speak local dialects and how to run a trapline. They made our lives hard because they wanted us to understand the people we were serving. But they never tried to change the Inuit in terms of how they did things or how they thought or to stop the drum dances or any of that stuff.

"The old people still have a lot of respect for the Bay. Some of it was out of fear, there's no question, but also some of it was genuine respect because the Bay appeared at a time when the Inuit were in trouble; there was a lot of star-vation. The Bay was seen to a certain extent as having saved a lot of Inuit people because the Company appeared on the scene with better hunting equipment that allowed them to get more food and they did a lot of early medical stuff. But there was a sort of a safety net around that didn't exist before. So among the old people, you'll never hear a bad word said about the Hudson's Bay Company. The younger people are a different story. To them it was just another store. But not among the older people. The Bay is much more than just a store, it's part of their life, part of their culture almost."

Within two decades of its decision to seek a new empire in Canada's Arctic, most of the Company's infrastructure was in place and its business was reaching new levels of prosperity. Unaware that they were destroying aboriginal traditions in the process, the Factors who pioneered the HBC's northern service pointed with pride to the Inuit they had rescued from starvation. Closer examination revealed it was mainly the families of reliable trappers who were granted most of the store credit—and that the real reason for subsidizing them was that dead customers paid off no debts.

Killing the Competition

"To open up a store against the Bay, that was heresy. Why, you were committing an act against God. It was God who gave the Hudson's Bay that land!"
                                        —HBC Trader Bill Cobb

THE WORLD OF THE TWENTIETH CENTURY was not smaller, but it was faster. When Guglielmo Marconi tapped his first wireless telegraphy signals across the Atlantic in 1901, it was only a matter of time before prices at London auctions were instantly being flashed to posts in Canada's beaver swamps. Ever dependent on fickle fashion, the HBC faced the most serious threat yet to its long-established trading system, with independent operators able to move in and out of fur categories and, by taking advantage of the new advances in communication, turn over their capital several times a season. Installation of regular telegraph services shattered *what* was left of the Company's monopoly because it demystified the fur trade by allowing everyone access to the latest market information.

At the same time, economic prosperity had returned to North America and stocks of luxury furs diminished as not only elegant women wished to buy the glamorous garments but also men, driving the new open motor cars, wrapped themselves in enormous coats that made them look like pregnant mountain goats. "Growing numbers of fur buyers and traders, many of whom were Americans, were drawn into the Canadian north seeking new sources of supply," noted Arthur Ray, a University of British Columbia historian who specializes in the fur trade. Canada's northern edges—though not yet the Arctic—were being opened up through the Klondike gold rush and construction of railways towards Port Nelson on Hudson Bay and into the Peace River country. Traders and merchants poured into the Mackenzie River Valley and Great Slave Lake territory so fast that the hamlet of Fort Resolution eventually boasted six retail stores, and Fort Chipewyan on Lake Athabasca counted more than a dozen fur-trading posts clustered around the HBC's historic fort. Because these newcomers enjoyed much lower overheads and were not subject to decisions made by boards of directors on the other side of the world, they cut deeply into the HBC's established business. At the same time, consignment and mail-order houses appeared in Canada for the first time, buying and selling furs on commission, allowing competitors quick and simple entry into the trade.*

Occasionally, the HBC deliberately—and deviously—competed with itself. John Montague of North West River in Labrador recalled, with a touch of humour and an exaggerated accent, how he had once been fooled into selling to an "independent," with unexpected results: "I remember one time for sure when I had quite a little bit of fur and there was this feller come from Cartwright. Martin he was, Jim or Frank, I fergits now. I thought this feller was a fur buyer, not from HBC at all. I took my fur to HBC and they priced it. I took my fur to Martin and he didn't offer me quite as much, but I sold it to 'em anyway because I wanted to encourage him to come back. After he was gone I found out he was buyin' fer HBC. That was wonderful funny." But more often, the competition was real, and it nearly drove the Company's fur business to the wall.

First to follow the HBC into the Mackenzie district was Hislop and Nagle, which eventually opened twenty-four posts between Athabasca Landing and Arctic Red River, built three steamships, and even had its own sawmill and engineering shop. James Hislop, a mathematician and civil engineer from Pictou, Nova Scotia, had gone West as a surveyor on the Pembina Branch of the CPR and later moved to Edmonton. His partner, Edmund Barry Nagle, was a millwright who had served with the St Hyacinthe Infantry Company during the Fenian raids and had taken part in Métis buffalo hunts out of Fort Garry before joining Hislop in Edmonton. "They were considered outlaws at the time, because the Hudson's Bay Company behaved as if it still had a monopoly," noted Jordan Zinovich, who studied the history of the enterprise. "When Mrs. Nagle arrived at Fort Resolution, the HBC Factors and their

---

* The impact of these innovations forced the HBC in 1920 to abandon its 250-year-old policy of auctioning only its own furs and to begin moving consignment pelts as well. Competitors opened alternative auction houses in London (C.M. Lampson & Company and A.W. Nesbitt), New York (New York Fur Auction Sales Company), St Louis (International Fur Exchange), Winnipeg (Fur Auction Sales Company), Vancouver (Little Brothers), Montreal (Canadian Fur Auction Sales Company) and Leipzig (G. Gaudig & Blum).

wives would not talk to her. She was so socially ostracized that she had to bring in a 'professional friend' from the Outside." After harvesting fur worth $200,000, Hislop and Nagle in 1913 sold out to the Northern Trading Company of Edmonton, which eventually manned thirty-two small posts, obtaining financial sponsorship from London's A.W. Nesbitt and temporarily diminishing the HBC trade. When Nesbitt went bankrupt in 1919, Northern was pushed into receivership. A group of Winnipeg auctioneers led by Max Finkelstein and fronted by Colonel J.K. Cornwall (the celebrated Alberta entrepreneur known as Peace River Jim) obtained control and moved its headquarters to Fort Smith, but it never fully recovered and went bankrupt in 1931; the HBC picked up its remaining assets.

Lamson and Hubbard Corporation, Boston's leading fur dealers, arrived in Canada right after the First World War, erecting a dozen outlets on the Mackenzie and two short-lived Arctic posts at Chesterfield Inlet and Baker Lake. The firm moved in like an invading army, or rather navy, launching an impressive sternwheeler (the SS *Distributor*) that shuttled between Fort Smith and Fort McPherson, two other steamers, a pair of large gas boats, several gas-powered tugs and a fleet of fifty twenty-ton scows. Within six years its heavy overhead sank the firm, with the HBC yet again absorbing the pieces. Several smaller trading outfits tried to buck the Company, but none succeeded. The most tragic attempt was that of a group of retired British naval officers who incorporated the Sabellum Trading Company in 1911 and for the next dozen years dispatched trading vessels to Baffin Island. One of their ships, the *Enne*, was blown up by a German submarine; another, the *Vera*, a forty-four-year-old wooden Cowes-built racing yacht, proved comically unsuitable for Arctic voyages. Sabellum managed to land only one representative on Baffin, an elderly stone-deaf gunnery officer named Hector Pitchforth, who starved to death in his ten-by-fifteen-foot shack at Cape Kater on the isolated Brodeur Peninsula during the cruel winter of 1927. The following year Sabellum sold its few belongings to the HBC.*

THE ONLY SERIOUS LONGTERM RIVAL faced by the HBC in the North was Revillon Frères of Paris. Like that of the Nor'Westers who had challenged the

---

* Another inglorious venture backed by British interests was the Arctic Gold Exploration Syndicate, inaugurated by Captain Henry Toke Munn, formerly of Pond Inlet. Munn persuaded Lord Lascelles and others to back him in seeking gold on Baffin Island, mainly by showing them art photographs he had taken of some "naked Inuit girls reflected in pools."

Company's hegemony a century earlier, Revillon's assault lasted for most of four decades and was led by far more enterprising spirits than the bureaucratic duffers who inhabited the HBC's middle management. Exactly like the Nor'Westers, Revillon ultimately failed because it expanded too fast, and its backers—unlike the Hudson's Bay Company, which had put aside adequate financial reserves and enjoyed access to guarantees from the Bank of England—were unable to withstand long periods of financial drought. A successor firm to the veteran (1723) French furrier François Givelet, Louis Victor Revillon's company had revolutionized the industry. It broadened the market by selling fur coats through drygoods shops. Instead of purchasing all its pelts from wholesalers, it established its own trading outlets to obtain the raw product from Russian and Canadian trappers. At the turn of the century, Revillon purchased a string of Mackenzie River posts from Colonel Cornwall, and also established half a dozen stores on the north shore of the St Lawrence and up the Labrador coast.

Revillon's assault on Hudson Bay, planned for the summer of 1903, was predicated on impressing local trappers by installing one of its prefabricated stores beside nearly every HBC outlet. The necessary staff and material were gathered in Montreal and loaded on the *Stord*, a Norwegian-built merchant ship, which promptly ran aground at Pointe des Monts in the Gulf of St Lawrence. To get into the Bay before freeze-up, Revillon chartered the 820-ton *Eldorado*, then employed on the London-Liverpool run, whose skipper, Captain William Berry, had never ventured beyond England's coastal waters. He successfully crossed the Atlantic, picked up the *Stord's* crew and cargo, then somehow muddled his way through Hudson Strait. The crew and passengers, numbering forty-seven, included Revillon's Montreal representative, a Monsieur d'Aigneaux, who was travelling with his wife, daughter and a governess, a doctor, four clerks and fourteen Quebec carpenters hired to erect the stores. Drawing a deep sixteen feet and carrying 1,450 tons of cargo, the *Eldorado*, her decks crowded with sections for the prefabricated buildings, lumbered into Hudson Bay bound for Fort George on the eastern shore of James Bay. After several close calls, the ship rammed a reef nine miles out of the settlement. "When the tide fell, she listed so badly that her decks became almost vertical," Third Engineer George Venables wrote in his journal. "… So serious were matters now that the captain insisted that the ladies, child, and other passengers should go in boats to Fort George, so as to be safe. It was well this was done, for on the Wednesday [September 2, 1903] a terrible storm came on, the ship bumped up and down on the cruel rocks, and finally tore a great hole in her bottom, through which the water rushed in volumes. We saved what food we could, and, with some clothes, got away to an island ere the doomed vessel was lost."

Donald Gillies, the HBC Factor resident at Fort George, counted the four dozen survivors and quickly realized his spare supplies would feed them for only two days. He lent them boats and advised them to hurry south to Charlton Island, where an HBC steamer, the *Lady Head*, was due to leave for London. After a hazardous passage the *Eldorado's* crew reached Charlton the day after the steamer's departure—which was lucky, because the *Lady Head* was shortly afterwards wrecked on Gasket Shoals. The unhappy travellers made their way down to Moose Factory in borrowed HBC lighters, then had to travel five hundred miles up the Moose and Abitibi rivers before they reached civilization. It was a harrowing journey. "When we got up each morning," wrote Venables, "it was invariably to find that the blanket with which each person was provided was a solid piece of ice, as hard as iron, and we had to get it thawed and free as best we could.... We endeavoured to bake some of the flour into cakes each night; but as we had no baking powder you can imagine what the result was like. Our rations at best did not run to more than half a cake each per night, and we began to feel very weak and ill from being so underfed and so much exposed." When they came out of the bush at New Liskeard, without having lost a soul along the way, a correspondent for the Toronto *Globe* who interviewed the survivors wrote that they had portaged their "lifeboats" around the rapids through a terrain "as unknown to the party as if it had been in the heart of Africa."

The mishap set back Revillon's Hudson Bay venture, but by 1908, with supplies brought in on the 2,500-ton icebreaker *Adventurer*, Revillon had seven posts on line, including a dock and warehouse at Strutton Island in the lower bay. The *Adventurer* was eventually wrecked in Hudson Strait, but not before she helped erect other Revillon posts at Baker Lake, Repulse Bay and the Belcher Islands.*

---

* Revillon commissioned the explorer/film-maker Robert Flaherty to shoot *Nanook of the North* on the Belchers and at Port Harrison during the winter of 1920–21. The first documentary of its kind to achieve world-wide distribution, the movie was an instant hit, so much so that Americans marketed a new brand of ice-cream called Nanook, while Germans sold Nanook ashtrays. Brilliantly shot and edited, the film helped perpetuate the stereotype of Inuit as happy victims of their environment.

The French concern eventually operated forty-seven Canadian trading posts, mostly concentrated in the northwest. The firm's huge warehouse in Edmonton, its stock supplied from Montreal aboard a special twenty-six-car freight train, became the West's largest department store, offering everything from food products, china, fabrics and farm equipment to bronze bells and missionaries' chasubles. Revillon was soon doing annual business in excess of $5 million, including supply contracts for the Indian treaties and Mounted Police on the Peace and Yukon rivers, but like the HBC it had great difficulty supplying some of its western land posts. To move goods from Edmonton to Hudson's Hope on the Peace River, for example, required taking them by sleigh in January as far as Athabasca, where they were stored for the rest of the winter. In spring they were poled over by scow to Lesser Slave Lake, where they were stored again until the primitive road to the Peace River became passable. That oxcart passage was followed by another scow expedition to Hudson's Hope—the entire one-way journey having taken eight months.

It was typical of the Bay men that, although they had lost their official monopoly in 1870, they still behaved more than a generation later as if they owned the country. "Only those who have worked for the Company," explained Philip Godsell, "can understand the feeling that existed against the average opposition trader, and the perhaps misguided sense of loyalty which would, literally, cause a Hudson's Bay man to push even his own brother to the wall if he happened to be trading in opposition to the 'Gentlemen Adventurers.'" Bill Cobb, who traded against Revillon, echoed the thought. "To open up a store against the Bay, that was heresy. Why, you were committing an act against God. It was God who gave the Hudson's Bay that land!" he recalled in mock anger forty-eight years later, adding, "I laugh about it now, but that's the way I felt—and still do, to some degree."

In the field, competition between the two firms quickly turned vicious. Startled Inuit and Indians were treated to the sight of the only two white men in their settlements childishly squabbling over each pelt, spying on one another, outbidding each other's prices. It became standard practice for HBC Factors to decree that any trapper caught trading with Revillon could no longer sell to the Company. The Cree sensed this was a potent threat; their name for Revillon was *Tustowichuk*—the "people between them and the Company." The French firm's post managers complained that their customers refused to trade in the daytime lest they be spotted by the HBC traders, who had ostentatiously trained telescopes on their competitors' front doors. Even at night, exchanges at the Revillon posts had to be carried out behind drawn blinds.

Revillon's first managers were mostly retired French army and navy officers and superannuated bureaucrats, more familiar with wine vintages than the crude ways of the Canadian frontier. They underestimated their opponents and patronized their customers. The Bay traders derisively referred to Revillon as "the Frenchmen" and were not above delivering some low slurs. One Christmas at Moose Factory, a Revillon trader was celebrating alone while there was a big party at the Bay post. The Anglican missionary R.J. Renison, later an archbishop, who was visiting Moose Factory, urged the Bay man to go over and invite his rival. After grumbling about the idea for most of a morning, the Factor, a humourless Scotsman, agreed. But the Revillon man didn't show up. When Renison demanded to know how the invitation had been issued, the burred reply was: "I just asked him who won the Battle of Waterloo—any goddamned Frenchman should know that." Revillon eventually switched to recruiting in Dundee, Scotland. It signed on good men—at forty dollars a month, all found, twice the wage offered by the HBC—but its traders could not compete in the down cycles of the fur trade. Wallace Laird, who was one of them, claimed that he had never been at a Revillon post "that showed a profit. The cost of goods was so high ... that a generous mark-up was still not sufficient to keep the posts out of the red."

By the spring of 1925, Revillon's owners initiated discussions with the HBC on a cooperative agreement that would reduce expenditures of both concerns. The contract, signed on July 17, 1926, was in fact a takeover, with the HBC agreeing to acquire 51 percent of Revillon Canada for up to $918,000 during the next eight years. Ralph Parsons was named the HBC's representative director on the Revillon board; the French firm had Canadian assets of $2,981,214 and current liabilities of $879,642 at the time. There was no doubt about the HBC's motives for the takeover. "Arrangements should be definitely made, for the fixing of the prices of Furs and Merchandise at all Posts affected directly, or indirectly, by the competition of Revillon Frères," stated an internal memo prepared for the HBC management. "These prices can be fixed periodically by the District Managers concerned, with Revillon managers. Competition between the companies for employees will be eliminated; thus eliminating salary increases unwarranted for any reason, other than the possibility of injury being done to our trade by a transfer of an employee."

Revillon continued to operate into the 1930s as a quasi-independent entity. By then an exasperated Jean Revillon was writing to the HBC Governor: "After more and more consideration on the subject, we came to the final conclusion that the active management of the Hudson's Bay Company's Trading Posts: i.e. Mr. Parsons and his subordinates, were so deadly opposed to any competition held out against the Hudson's Bay Co., even though this competition be afforded by the Revillon Frères Trading Co. in which the Hudson's Bay Company holds the majority of shares, that they did everything in order to crush Revillon Frères Trading Company and the conclusion reached was that it was preferable for this Company to have a single owner."

When the Bay argued about the price it would pay for his firm's remaining assets, Jean Revilion didn't hide his anger: "We have good grounds to claim that the present state of Revillon Frères Trading Company is due to misman-agement on the part of your Winnipeg office," he wrote to the HBC Governor. "The co-operation in the North, which was an important factor of our 1926 Agreement, and carried most weight towards our acceptance of it as far as our interests were concerned, was not lived up to by your managers. The results have proved disastrous.... The assets of the Revillon Frères Trading Company have been stripped and laid bare to the bone, which has been a wise policy on your part, as it certainly favours your claim when establishing the price of shares." By this time, net assets had been reduced to $1,158,000, and the HBC purchased all of Revillon's outstanding shares for $380,000. Liquidation of the French firm's Canadian holdings was completed during 1937, with twenty-two of its seventy-three employees joining the Bay.

There then followed a bizarre mop-up operation. The HBC didn't intend to stop at having beaten its rival; the Company wanted to obliterate Revillon's every trace, so that no other freebooter would again be presumptuous enough to assume the North belonged to anyone but the Company of Adventurers. When Revillon decamped, one of its district inspectors, a former French naval captain named Jean Berthe, decided to remain in the Arctic as an indepen-dent trader. A highly civilized Parisian with a wry sense of life's absurdities, he found pleasure in the eternal solitude of the Ungava Peninsula and, gathering a few trading supplies, settled near Burgoyne Bay, on the south shore of Hudson Strait. The Hudson's Bay Company panicked. Determined to hound the Frenchman out of the North, Fur Trade Commissioner Ralph Parsons placed three of his toughest subordinates—Alex Stevenson, John Stanners and Bruce Campbell—in charge of mobile trading posts code-named U-X,

U-Y and U-Z. The outfits were dropped at locations near Berthe's camp and loaded into peterhead boats, so that as soon as the French trader made a move in any direction an HBC post could immediately be set up near him to undercut his trades.

They chased him for three months and finally cornered Berthe at Payne Bay, where the Bay men erected their instant shop to head off the Inuit trappers. After two seasons of mounting losses, the French naval captain departed, his purse empty but his dignity intact.*

The Revillon episode was a turning point. The Company won, but the cost had been high. The North, like the West, could not much longer remain the private preserve of any commercial enterprise.

---

* A happier tale was the adventure of the American biologist Clarence Birdseye, who purchased Revillon's abandoned post on Sandwich Bay, near Cartwright in Labrador, for a fur-farming venture. He watched the catch of native fishermen freeze in -50°F weather, the moment the fish were taken out of the water. "Months later, when they were thawed out," he noted, "some of those fish were so fresh that they were still alive!" Applying similar techniques to meats and vegetables, he gradually perfected the famous frozen food products that bear his name.

The *Nascopie* Chronicles

"Signifying many things to many people and, on occasion, everything to a very few, Nascopie *acquired a unique personality endowed with almost human characteristics."*
—Henny Nixon

CHIEF AGENT OF CHANGE in the Canadian North was not a man ot a company, but a ship. On July 10, 1911, Lord Strathcona had commissioned construction of a 2,500-ton supply vessel from Swan Hunter of Newcastle-on-Tyne. The coal-burning *Nascopie's* unique design—her stern cut away like a yacht from above the waterline, a semicircular hull and undercut bow, every steel plate reinforced and slightly curved to deflect the ice—fitted the vessel ideally for the treacherous journeys that would earn her pride of place among the ships that altered the perception of Canada's northern geography.*

Not precisely an icebreaker—though often used as one—the *Nascopie* was designed to open a seapath by sliding over the ice, then shattering it under her own weight. She had a bottom as smooth and rounded as that of a racing shell and no bilge keel, so that ice pressure around the sides would lift rather than crush her. Her bow was fitted with a "shoe"—a sturdy casing riveted to the keel plate that occasionally allowed her to batter ice formations until a crack appeared wide enough to sail through. "Signifying many things to many people and, on occasion, everything to a very few, *Nascopie* acquired a unique personality endowed with almost human characteristics," wrote Henny Nixon, an Ottawa maritime historian.

---

* The *Nascopie* took her name from the Montagnais designation for the local tribe of Ungava and Labrador Indians, whose own name for themselves was Nenenot—"true men."

After her maiden voyage across the Atlantic, the *Nascopie* was employed in the Newfoundland seal hunt before setting off on her first voyage into Hudson Bay and the Eastern Arctic. When she arrived at the Charlton Island supply depot near the bottom of the Bay, local natives, astounded at *Nascopie's* size, got balls of string to measure her 285-foot hull, and later they would stretch out the twine and explain to friends up the coast that the great new ship was "as long as that!" At the end of her 1915 voyage, with the Great War presenting new problems, the *Nascopie* was assigned to the Brest-Murmansk-Archangel supply run and armed with a three-pounder Hotchkiss, a gun built in 1857 to help quell the Indian Mutiny. The ancient weapon's range was uncertain, but it made as much noise as a six-incher. On June 14, 1917, when the *Nascopie* was attacked by the German submarine U-28 off Archangel, she drove off the boat with four well-placed shots. Later that year, command of the *Nascopie* was assumed by Captain Thomas Farrar Smellie, one of the few mariners who had master's papers for both sail and steam. For most of the next thirty years he sailed the largely uncharted waters of the Canadian North, turning his ship and himself into a legend. "There may have been some 'luck' about it," wrote Roland Wild, the *Nascopie's* lively biographer, "but the happy partnership of Captain and ship was based on a much surer foundation. These partners knew one another, they each had sturdy beginnings; you could say they had each been built by craftsmen, each knew the qualities and endurance of the other—they were as one, not Captain and ship, but a unit."

The *Nascopie* made thirty-four trips to resupply the HBC's Eastern Arctic and Hudson Bay posts, bringing back furs, mail and rotating personnel, serving an area then not otherwise accessible. She went about her risky business in waters virtually unmarked by navigational aids, sailing through latitudes where compasses were useless because of underwater iron ore deposits and proximity to the north magnetic pole. In parts of Hudson Bay, the earth's magnetism is so powerful that compass needles point nowhere, except down; at the entrance to Pond Inlet, the earth's variation is more than 100 degrees, so that ships have to be steered 10 degrees east of north to be heading west. Available maps were so amateurish Captain Smellie once complained that if he followed the Admiralty charts at his disposal, his ship's position would be 150 miles inland. The distances the *Nascopie* had to cover in the brief season of open water between the widely dispersed HBC posts were immense; each trip averaged 10,500 miles—Arctic Bay, then the northernmost of the HBC outposts, was 2,800 miles by sea from Montreal.

Each voyage was an adventure. Smellie was tough; he had to be. A steward who served under him recalled a hazardous climb to the bridge as the ship, battered by blizzards and waves higher than her funnel, seemed ready to pitchpole. The steward managed to reach the captain and shouted in his ear: "Would you like anything to eat?"

"Bowl of soup!" Smellie yelled back.

The steward laboriously climbed down to the galley, was instructed to carry the bowl not on a tray but in the hollow of a napkin held by its four corners, and climbed back up to the bridge, almost losing the soup and his life in the process. Feeling that he had been miraculously spared from the elements to fulfil his mission, he proudly presented the still-steaming brew to his captain. Smellie took one look at the soup bowl and bellowed: *"Where's the spoon?"*

THE *NASCOPIE*'S JOURNEY NORTH from her berth in Montreal quickly became a ritual. Her decks, noisy with penned sheep, chickens and pigs bound for traders' skillets, also carried an occasional milk cow. Her holds bursting with supplies, the vessel was so overloaded that shipping officials and Smellie had to play an unusual game. "When the Port inspectors made their routine check before departure," Roland Wild observed, "the Captain would show them the port side first, and give a vague kind of opinion that the ship must be listing to port, since the Plimsoll Line was invisible. When the inspectors repaired to the starboard side, the ship must have suddenly listed to starboard, for there was little sign of it there either.... Rather than order the ship to be unloaded of a hundred tons or so of vital cargo, they [the inspectors] seemed to have arrived at a remarkable conclusion: the *Nascopie* was a ship that listed on both sides at the same time." Fully loaded, the ship would sound her siren and, her pennants flying, cast off lines and steam half-astern to midstream. With all the ships in harbour blowing their salute whistles, the *Nascopie* would puff proudly out to the St Lawrence and set course for Labrador. Aboard would be not only HBC executives and post replacements but also red-coated Mounties, explorers, geologists, missionaries, doctors, nurses, postmasters and government administrators of every description.

The ninety-day voyage was a race against tides and weather. None of the three dozen or so ports of call had a dock, so the ship anchored off each post while goods were loaded and unloaded from wooden scows. This could be tricky. The HBC's Archie Hunter recalled putting into Chesterfield Inlet on a rough day: "When we arrived no one from shore dared venture out to meet us, with the exception of one hardy soul. Out he came battling the white-capped waves in a Lac Seul canoe until he finally made it to the ship. I still remember his introduction of himself, 'They call me Crazy Mac but you ought to see the rest of them ashore.'"*

The fox pelts were brought aboard in bales of one hundred, stamped with each trading post's name and a silk-cloth destination label that read: "Beaver House, Great Trinity Lane, London, England." The day of arrival was very special as the residents of each settlement read their annual ration of mail. Then the stevedoring started. "At every port where we stopped," complained Ernie Lyall, an old Arctic hand, "we had to work with the crew and hump cargo all the time. I think that's about the time that 'Heavy Bloody Cargo' got tacked on to the HBC initials." Local Inuit would help out, and some remembered the magic of those occasions. "The sight of these great vessels entering the world where we lived made thrills go through our hearts," recalled Alootook Ipellie, a Frobisher Bay artist and carver. "This was during high tide and everyone worked as a unit, just like a circus setting up the big tents and other things to get ready for the opening night. There was laughter among the people, a sign of happiness which never seemed to stop as long as the ship stayed." The traders themselves held a less romantic view. The second-best day of the year was when the Nascopie arrived, they said. The best was when she left.

By early September, winter would begin to set in and the stops became shorter, the unloading even more frenzied. Smellie once steamed for an hour past the largest iceberg on record: an ice island a hundred feet high and ten miles long. In those pre-radar days he had to "smell" the presence of ice in fog or in the dark, and his ship didn't always stay out of harm's way. Smellie had three spare propellers on board, and whenever one was damaged, he would back his ship onto some deserted northern beach at high tide, wait for a tide shift, then change props. Heading north through Baffin Bay or into the rip-tides of Hudson Strait, ships had no protection from the grey swells, mountains of water thirty feet high, claiming the ocean for themselves.

THE NASCOPIE'S IMMEDIATE PREDECESSOR was the Pelican, a former British man-of-war and slave-chaser, purchased by the HBC in 1901. The 290-ton

* Crazy Mac had by this time been north with the HBC for fifteen years without a furlough. He left that season aboard the Nascopie, got off at Halifax, and promptly married a bishop's daughter.

auxiliary sloop also beat off a German submarine (on August 26, 1918, off Cardiff) and continued in the Company's service until 1920. She was joined in 1905 by the *Discovery*, the heavily reinforced exploration barquentine that carried Captain Robert Falcon Scott's 1901–4 expedition to the Antarctic, which made the last annual supply voyage to York Factory in 1914.

Many a brave Company crew undertook the annual supply voyage, and the HBC even fought a major naval battle to protect its sea lanes, but many more vessels departed than returned.* The last HBC sailing ship to ply the Bay, the three-masted barque *Stork*, went down in a storm off Rupert House in 1908. Ice crushed the *Bayeskimo*, while the *Bayrupert* piled up on Hen and Chickens Reef, on the Labrador coast.† The fifty-six-ton *Fort Churchill*, a ketch that arrived at York Factory in the late autumn of 1913 with a load of coal from Falmouth, England, was left unattended at anchor some distance up the Nelson River. She vanished during a three-day easterly gale, only to be found two years later washed up on one of the Belcher Islands.

The potential for east-west trade across the top of North America was first demonstrated in 1930. The HBC's schooner *Fort James* (built in Shelburne, Nova Scotia, as the *Jean Revillon*) had sailed out of St John's to spend two winters frozen in at Gjoa Haven on King William Island. When the HBC's western-based supply ship *Fort McPherson* pulled in and anchored near her, it was the first time the North West Passage had been bridged— even if by two ships—since Amundsen's history-making crossing of 1903–6. In 1934, when the *Fort James* was transferred to the Company's western division, she went through the Panama Canal and eventually back into the North; she got as far east as Cambridge Bay—only two hundred miles west of her 1928–30 wintering place. Had she closed that short gap, the *Fort James* would have been the first vessel in history to circumnavigate North America. Both the *Fort James* and the *Fort McPherson* as well as the *Fort Hearne* were later wrecked in Arctic gales.

The Company's maritime experience in the Western Arctic wasn't much luckier. After several sinkings of chartered and purchased vessels, the HBC decided in 1920 to build a ship specially designed for the job, the auxiliary

* For details of this epic sea engagement, see pages 104–7.
† The HBC manager at Wolstenholme had put away his salary for years to purchase a piano, which went down with the *Bayeskimo* in 1925. Two years later he had saved enough to order a replacement, only to have it sink aboard the *Bayrupert*. He found a new hobby.

wooden schooner *Lady Kindersley*. Her ribs were mounted so close together that with planking and sheathing the hull had an overall thickness of nearly twenty-two inches, while her bow was reinforced with thick metal sheets. She sailed out of Vancouver on June 27, 1924, carrying not only a year's worth of HBC re-supplies but also a powerful government radio transmitter, due to be installed at Herschel Island. Imprisoned by the floes and hummocks off Point Barrow, *Lady Kindersley* had to be abandoned after a month of attempting to free herself.

Other ships were assigned to the west-coast run, but few hulls could withstand the battering of the ice around Alaska's northern coast. Originally built as a Baltic coaster and taken by the British as part of German postwar reparations, the HBC's supply ship *Baychimo* was the largest vessel to trade in the North West Passage. The 1,500-tonner successfully completed nine expeditions to the Company's eight Western Arctic posts, but on her return journey in 1931 she got stuck in ice off Point Franklin, near Point Barrow. Since she was carrying a million dollars' worth of fur there was no question of abandoning her, but when the vessel seemed in danger of being crushed, Captain S.A. Cornwall ordered the crew to set up a temporary shelter on shore, two miles away. Although some passengers and HBC officials were flown out by rescue planes, the captain and sixteen of his crew retreated to their makeshift dwelling to await a change in the weather, so that they might free their ship. On November 24, a blizzard howled in. It turned so ferocious the sailors had to close off their little dwelling, huddling together for warmth and comfort, taking turns sitting next to the gasoline drum that had been converted into a stove. When they dug themselves out three days later, the *Baychimo* had disappeared. She was seen a few months after that drifting alone through pack ice by an Inuk travelling from Herschel to Nome.

Two years later, the *Baychimo* was boarded by Isobel Wylie Hutchinson, a Scottish botanist bound for Herschel aboard the schooner *Trader*. The ghostly *Baychimo* had been sighted twelve miles off Wainwright, and the *Trader's* captain had brought his little vessel alongside. "A strange spectacle the decks presented," Hutchinson later noted in her journal. "The main hold was open to the winds, but its half-rifted depths still contained sacks of mineral ore, caribou skins, and a cargo of various descriptions.... Writing paper, photographic films, ledgers of the Hudson's Bay Company, typewriter ribbons—all were here for the taking! In a wooden crate was an unsullied edition of *The Times History of the Great War* in many tomes. Charts of all seas of the world lay scattered upon the decks of the pilot-house.... A breakfast menu tossed in the doorway indicated that the crew of the unlucky ship were at least in no danger of starvation, for there was a choice of some six courses."

The *Trader's* first mate determined that the *Baychimo's* engines were in perfect condition and that all she needed was to have her spare propeller mounted before she could sail away under her own steam, but the weather closed in and the visitors scrambled off the doomed vessel as fast as they could. The sightings continued. In 1936 Captain Parker of the cutter *Northland* pulled alongside, and in 1961 she was spotted by a party of Inuit between Icy Cape and Point Barrow. A DEW Line supply superintendent from Vancouver named Don Roderick reported seeing her off Cambridge Bay in 1965. That any ship—manned by ghosts or men—could survive the awesome force of the polar ice pack for three decades seems beyond reason, but the HBC's *Baychimo* did just that, and since no one actually saw her sink, she may be out there still ...

SCOTTY GALL, THE HBC TRADER who had been one of the last crew members to get off the *Baychimo*, reacted to his ship's fate with the typical aplomb of a good Company man. "Pity," he said. "She still had twenty bales of fur on her." Gall was back north six years after the *Baychimo* disappearance on what would turn out to be the greatest sea adventure of his career. In the spring of 1937, the Hudson's Bay Company decided to establish a connecting link between its western and eastern operations by building a trading facility in the Central Arctic at the bottom of Somerset Island on Bellot Strait. The new outpost was to be named Fort Ross, after the two British naval officers, uncle and nephew, who had first explored the area in the 1820s and 1830s. The *Nascopie's* itinerary called for her to pick up some Inuit families at Arctic Bay for resettlement at Fort Ross, then rendezvous with the small (thirty-ton) schooner *Aklavik* at the eastern entrance of Bellot Strait.*

No steel-hulled vessel had ever entered these waters, and no ship of any kind had been here since the visit of Leopold McClintock, the Irish-born Royal Navy captain who found documents and relics indicating the fate of the Franklin expedition while on an 1859 sledge journey from his ship, frozen in

---

* These were the same Inuit who had been uprooted from their homes at Cape Dorset, Pangnirtung and Pond Inlet by the HBC in 1934 and taken to Dundas Harbour, where the ice turned out to be too rough and thick for either sled or boat travel. In 1936, Dundas Harbour was closed and the Inuit were transferred to Arctic Bay. Now they were being displaced again.

near the entrance to the strait. Bellot Strait, where Fort Ross was to stand, had been discovered by Joseph-René Bellot, a French naval sub-lieutenant, poking around the North mainly because he was in love with Sir John Franklin's widow, Jane, and hoped to gain heroic status by finding her husband's remains. Barely navigable, the strait was an important link in the North West Passage, dividing the Arctic archipelago from the North American continent. Scotty Gall, who spent forty-three years in the Company's northern service, had learned his navigation in the Mackenzie Delta. "I knew where all the reefs were; I'd hit every one," he remembered. "Some of the Scotsmen who came north were linguists, others studied the Inuit. I was much more interested in finding out how the aboriginals can travel without any navigation aids. I came to believe they have an inherent sense of direction, reading the sun, wind, snowdrifts or the lichen on rocks." It took Gall twenty years to hone his own instincts and crossing Bellot Strait was his greatest test.

The passage is twenty miles long and often less than a mile wide. Eleven-foot tides flood in from its western end, causing an eight-knot current. Just as he was steering the *Aklavik* into the strait, his engine (a 35-h.p. Fairbanks-Morse) failed; he replaced a faulty fuel strainer just as the little ship was about to run aground. The motor sputtered to life, but it would operate only at half speed. "The current was running pretty fast," Gall recalled, "and I couldn't get much way-on, so I turned the boat around, pointed my nose into the current, which gave me more control against side-slips, and we went through the Bellot backwards!"*

At noon on September 2, 1937, Gall traded his cargo of furs for supplies aboard the *Nascopie*, then anchored at Depot Bay, just off the Fort Ross site. The transaction made Gall the first man in history to have turned the North West Passage into a commercial reality. He was not impressed. "It's all bunk about the North West Passage, it gives me a pain," said he. "We could have done it any time, and gone higher north. But that was no advantage to us. We were traders, and we went where the fur was. There was nobody to the north

---

* Known as a crack navigator, Gall also had the reputation of being the worst cook among the HBC's northern hands. "He couldn't even make a pot of tea," recalled Woody Wood, one of his colleagues. "He'd eat all his meat raw because he was always hungry and couldn't be bothered cooking it—though he usually killed the animals first. I remember one time, Scotty shot an owl, and his wife cooked it because it was Christmas, and once served on a platter it looked a bit like turkey. When it was put in front of him, Scotty took one bite, and smacking his lips with pleasure said, 'Oy, it tastes like premasticated mouse meat to me.' I never had roast owl again."

of us. What the hell good would it have done to run right through the Passage, when there were no Eskimos, and we didn't have any trade there?"

The *Nascopie* had not found easy passage because Prince Regent Inlet, which leads to the strait, was choked with blue ice that year. She had a tight margin of only seven days in which to reach Fort Ross, establish the post, and steam out again to free water. J.W. Anderson and Paddy Gibson, a chief Trader normally in the Western Arctic, went ashore to select the site, having first paid silent tribute at the cairn left behind by McClintock, the Admiralty sailor who had made five futile attempts to sail through Bellot Strait nearly a century before. HBC carpenter Clem James, aided by two Company traders, Lorenz Learmonth and D.G. Sturrock (who had arrived the same day after a harrowing journey from Gjoa Haven, mainly on foot, carrying a sixteen-foot canoe), erected a store, staff building and warehouse. By the evening of September 7, the work had been nearly completed and the HBC flag was raised over the Company's last new post devoted to the fox trade. Learmonth stayed behind (with interpreter-trader Ernie Lyall) as Fort Ross's first manager. The *Nascopie* landed her Inuit passengers, and just before she was due to sail away an HBC hand named Donald Goodyear, incongruously dressed in a three-piece suit, topped off with a fedora (because he was on his way out on furlough), rowed himself ashore, determined to help Learmonth finish building the post. The *Aklavik* tooted her whistle and the *Nascopie* blew her horn as the ships parted, headed back to their separate oceans, knowing their meeting had made a four-hundred-year dream come true. On shore, Goodyear was waving his silly fedora and Lyall a dishcloth; Learmonth gave a salute. Fort Ross was in business.

But not for long. In 1942 and 1943 unusually thick pack ice prevented the *Nascopie* from resupplying Fort Ross, then manned by W.A. Heslop, his wife, Barbara, and a clerk named Darcy Munro, who also operated the post's new short-wave radio. "One evening in September [1943], we sighted the *Nascopie* about fifteen miles off shore," recalled Mrs Heslop. "We thought our worries were over; but it was not until later that we were to realize they were just beginning. For three days we saw her, or her smoke, on the horizon and it was evident she was having difficulty in the ice-pack. That was an anxious three days, but we didn't give up until we finally saw her heading north with black smoke belching from her funnel."* Food was so short that both HBC men spent

---

* Captain Smellie had intended to stay longer, but on the afternoon of the third day, a group of crewmen led by two Newfoundland lightermen confronted him on the bridge. They issued

most of their time hunting. By November, a U.S. Army Air Forces plane was sent in to rescue the staff and leave food for the Inuit.

The post was reactivated the following summer, but by 1947 it was clear that Fort Ross was too remote, too expensive and too risky to keep open. It was closed and its Inuit families were moved yet again, this time to Spence Bay, 180 miles to the south. Fort Ross vanished from the Hudson's Bay Company's rosters, but its memory survived. All those involved knew that they had for a brief time been part of a brave experiment on the very edge of the world. Lorenz Learmonth, long after he had retired from the HBC, managed to find commercial passage to Bellot Strait. For a week he rummaged around the ruins of that lonely little outpost, pining for the forgotten dreams of a land that seemed to exist north of hope.

CAPTAIN SMELLIE RETIRED IN 1945 and was succeeded by James Waters, who had served as the *Nascopie's* first officer since 1941. On his second run, during the early afternoon of July 21, 1947, Waters was nosing the *Nascopie* into Cape Dorset when the ship struck an uncharted reef off Beacon Island. J.W. Anderson, then in charge of the fur trade's Eastern Arctic Division, was aboard and vividly remembered the grounding: "Dashing out on deck, I could see what had happened, but the tide was falling and notwithstanding the reversing of the engines she stuck fast in a perfectly upright position. Well, I thought, if this is going to be a shipwreck, it is quite a civilized one...." Another witness was Peter Pitseolak, a local artist who had customarily piloted HBC ships into Dorset but on this, of all occasions, had been rebuffed by Waters, who thought he could outdo Smellie by bringing the ship in himself. A few hours after the vessel went aground, the captain ordered everyone ashore in lifeboats, but the mood was still buoyant because it was a beautiful windless day and except for her ten-degree list to stern, the ship seemed unharmed. Anderson and the other HBC managers expected the lightened vessel could be refloated at high tide. Helped by kedged anchors, that was exactly what happened—the ship worked her way off the reef. But in so doing, she grievously holed her hull. The Arctic waters rushed in, flooding her engine room. At 3 A.M. a gale came up, smashing the vessel into another rock. She

---

an ultimatum: if he didn't turn the ship around by dusk, they would refuse to work it because they feared being frozen in for the winter. Smellie recognized the truth, if not the manner, of that advice, headed his ship back to sea, and did not lay any mutiny charges.

was now down by her bow, her decks at a thirty-degree angle, her screw high out of the water, her bilge pumps useless. At 5 A.M. the order was given to abandon ship.

Captain Waters, standing on shore watching his doomed vessel, asked one of his mates, a colourful Newfoundlander named Willis Warren, to go back aboard and rescue some warm clothes for his wife, who had been travelling with him. "Willis got into a dory and rowed back to the ship, climbing up her stern on a jacob's ladder that had been left hanging there," the HBC's George Whitman said later. "This was all done to a gallery of smirking Inuit who had been watching the white men make fools of themselves, running their ship into a rock. Warren went below into the captain's cabin, vanished for a while, then stuck his head out a porthole and waving a pair of Mrs Waters's pink bloomers, yelled: 'Would these be what ye wants, Captain?' The assembly burst into laughter, with the Inuit dancing out their joy, jumping up and down, wildly clapping their hands. Then the ship lurched a little and Warren got out of there fast."

The *Nascopie* remained poised on the reef for an incredible three months. Battered by gales and ice, she showed off her seaworthiness one last time, finally slipping under at midnight on October 15, 1947. Peter Pitseolak, Cape Dorset's Inuit pilot, quoted her fitting epitaph, voiced by his friend Kululak: "Our big helper has hit the bottom."

Northern Gridlock

"There was a big war. It was between the Bay and the Germans. The Bay won."
—Octave Sivanertok

A PAINTING OF THE NATIVITY that hung in the Anglican Cathedral in Aklavik until it burned down in 1975 depicted a crowd of Inuit celebrating the blessed event. Clearly identifiable among them were a missionary, a Mountie and an HBC Factor.

The theme and juxtaposition were entirely appropriate to the birth of the modern North except that in many of the really isolated Arctic posts, Bay managers frequently handled both spiritual and legal functions on top of their commercial mandates. "The real boss of each settlement was the local Bay man," recalled Ed Spracklin, who served in half a dozen posts. "Everybody came to you for advice, even on family and medical matters. I was also acting as commissioner of oaths and registrar for family allowances." Bay men were not medically trained and their stores carried only such nostrums as Minard's Liniment, Dodd's Kidney Pills, Perry Davis's Pain Killer (30 percent alcohol), Carter's Little Liver Pills and Gin Pills (which achieved little except to turn the urine green), but the Factors were often faced with medical emergencies. "One time, this Eskimo interpreter of ours at Cape Dorset got a nick in his left elbow, and it turned septic," recalled Chesley Russell, a veteran of the service. "There was a young fellow from Scotland with me as clerk, and we decided we'd take his arm off above the elbow. We put him on the kitchen table, and I found some morphine in the first-aid kit. It was outdated by a couple of years, so I figured we'd give him a double dose. We overdosed the poor son of a gun and every hour or so we'd have a look to find out how bad it was. One of the symptoms was to watch his eyes and see how much they had contracted. His pupils got as small as pinpoints. He was really overdosed. The first-aid book said the remedy was to keep him moving. But he was out for the count. He couldn't move. So we got him off the table, and my clerk would roll the poor bugger across the kitchen floor one way, and I'd roll him back. Every once in a while we'd skin back the eyes to see if they were dilating, and we were just about exhausted when he began coming around. To hell with cutting his arm off after that. We forgot about it. In a day or two he started to get better. It was the exercise that had started up his circulation again. He came around. Otherwise, we'd have taken his arm off—we had the saws and everything ready...."*

The best of the Bay men in the Arctic—characters like Ches Russell, Lorenz Learmonth, Scotty Gall, Sandy Lunan, Bert Swaffield, Jimmy Ford, John Stanners, Bob Cruickshank and J.W. Nichols—became true northerners, growing grey in the service, and as Leonard Budgell, who was one of them, remarked: "[We] accepted a more intimate responsibility for [our] customers. It was a good way to live, no matter what today's experts will tell you ... we could not have existed without that paternal feeling ... no one will ever convince me that it was not right in its time and place." Certainly that streak of paternalism characterized the HBC's dealings. P.A.C. Nichols, who for a time was in charge of the Arctic stores, referred to the Inuit as "these simple, primitive folk of the Arctic" who had remained "unspoiled" but some of whom could now "see no reason to struggle for survival if the wherewithal to live can be acquired with little effort" so that "the temptation to relax and be looked after often becomes too strong to conquer." That attitude was institutionalized in *The Eskimo Book of Knowledge,* published and distributed by the Company in 1931. Its author, an HBC Factor and Oxford graduate named George Binney, utilized biblical cadence to praise the Company not only as an agent of the British King but as a Divine presence. "Take heed," ran a typical passage aimed at the Inuit, warning them against doing business with independent fur traders that threatened the HBC's monopoly, "strange traders will come among you seeking only your furs ... these wanderers are like the

---

* Apart from their rough but ready medical skill, some of the post managers were unusually ingenious, even inventing a better mousetrap. "Using a large ten-gallon pail, half filled with water, I laid narrow pieces of board against it," recalled Hugh Mackay Ross. "Then I dangled a juicy piece of salt pork from a nail directly over the pail. When the mice smelled the pork, they ran up the boards to get at it, and overbalancing, fell into the water and drowned."

drift-ice; today they come with the wind, tomorrow they are gone with the wind. Of these strangers some will be fairer than others, as is the nature of men; but whosoever they be, they cannot at heart possess that deep under-standing of your lives through which our traders have learned to bestow the care of a father upon you and upon your children."

The northern field men may have been patronizing in their outlook and dictatorial in their methods, but they certainly weren't in the HBC's service for the money. "Sometimes we could be trading in the store for over twenty-four hours at a stretch without stopping," Ernie Lyall remembered. "We never got any overtime for this sort of thing, of course, or for any of the extra work we did evenings or weekends.... I was getting $120 a month when I started in Spence Bay in 1949, and $185 when I left the HBC in 1962."

The Company's influence grew in the first half of the second decade of the twentieth century, as the HBC became determined to take advantage of its monopoly by significantly expanding its northern presence. The move prompted Winnipeg's *Free Press* to comment approvingly: "The Company will make a last stand against civilization at the Arctic Ocean." But when the First World War disrupted European trade, the British government suspended London fur auctions, forcing pelt prices into dramatic, if temporary, decline. In the 1914–15 season, for the first time in its long history the Company halted its North American fur purchases, forbidding its traders to grant the natives new credit. Some of the HBC veterans ignored the sour directive and continued to distribute limited quantities of food and essential supplies to the Inuit and Indians, entering these shadowy transactions in "purgatory ledgers" that didn't show up in their posts' regular accounts. But enough aboriginals were deprived of rations for one deadly season that, as the HBC's Philip Godsell later observed, "I think any experienced trader will agree that the Hudson's Bay Company never fully regained their old-time prestige." In 1916, as the American fur market expanded, prices surged upward, more than doubling to $38 per white fox skin within the next four years, then nearly doubling again to $70 in 1928. The trade became so lucrative that in some posts along the Mackenzie, the HBC owed considerable amounts in trade goods to its customers. By 1924 the Inuit of Aklavik had purchased a private fleet of thirty-nine auxiliary-powered schooners and twenty-eight whaleboats, valued at $128,000.

The HBC was operating more than two hundred northern posts, opening new stores as high in the Arctic as Gjoa Haven, where Amundsen had wintered during his traverse of the North West Passage, and for a time even maintaining a string of trading outlets in eastern Siberia. Despite this rapid expansion, or perhaps because of it, the HBC began behaving like a bloated dinosaur—big, awkward and almost totally disconnected from its shifting environment. Writing of the trade along the Mackenzie, Heather Robertson noted in her evocative memoir of the HBC's Richard Bonnycastle that "the Company had lost control in the north. The economy was changing: Imperial Oil was developing the oil field at Norman Wells; prospectors were searching for gold and silver; fly-by-night free traders had introduced a cash economy among the natives. The Company's political base, the Indians—once the proud wives and children of famous post factors, the loyal 'family' of a mighty patron—had been reduced to patients and pupils, cooks and chore boys; and the great factors themselves ... once feared as demi-gods, were more often than not the objects of laughter and ridicule for their pompous manners and foolish brass hats. The unthinkable was happening—the Hudson's Bay Company was losing money."

It was a measure of the Company's fiscal desperation that its directors took seriously the suggestion of an old Arctic hand to turn a fortune in breeding reindeer as a cheap substitute for beef. Vilhjalmur Stefansson, the Icelandic-Canadian who became the Arctic's most accomplished non-Inuit sledge driver, won fame leading three daring expeditions that added one hundred thousand square miles to the maps of Canada's Far North, charting its last size-able unknown islands. Like Samuel Hearne and John Rae before him, Stefansson was able to dash across the Arctic by adopting Inuit survival techniques instead of being burdened by what he derisively described as "the portable-boarding-house school" methods of British adventurers. Stefansson genuinely believed that exploration required less courage than driving a New York taxicab, with preparation and adaptability taking the place of mock heroics. "I know nothing whatever about courage," he was fond of pointing out. "Everything you add to an explorer's heroism you have to subtract from his intelligence." He predicted Canada's North could support thirty-five million reindeer because its grazing territory was superior to most semi-arid sheep lands—but nobody took him seriously except the HBC. In 1920, the Company approved his scheme to establish a subsidiary to breed the ungainly beasts on Baffin Island, purchased 14,000 Lapland reindeer in northern Norway, hired a dozen herders, and shipped the first contingent of 689 animals (plus 3,000 sacks of moss) across the Atlantic aboard the *Nascopie*. Only 550 reindeer were still alive by the time the ship anchored off Amadjuak on the south coast of Baffin Island, the spot chosen by one of Stefansson's associates as having the best moss. A storm immediately dispersed the seasick reindeer, and though there was indeed plenty of moss, it turned out to be the wrong variety. (The reindeer wanted to munch on *Cladonia rangeferina*, which grew out of the soil in Lapland and thus contained delicious nutrients; the Baffin moss, which sprouted out of bare rock, contained no nutritional equivalent.) "We soon found," reported Captain John Mikkelborg, the HBC official charged with the loony venture, "that the pastures would not permit us to keep a large herd under restraint; if we did, they would starve to death. Consequently, we had to divide them into flocks and let them spread over a wide area, after the style of the caribou.... Sometimes the caribou would come and mix with our reindeer—more often the reverse—and that was the last we would see of them." Only 210 animals survived the winter, and with expenses still mounting, HBC accountants calculated by the end of 1922 that each beast was now worth $80.22. The $200,000 venture was eventually written off, though the Hudson's Bay Reindeer Company was still on the HBC's books as late as 1956.

Because the HBC operated in an area virtually inaccessible to visitors, its spreading northern presence was immune to criticism; any outsider wanting to live in the Arctic depended on its supplies. That protection from censure was challenged in 1927 when Dr Frederick Banting, the co-discoverer of insulin, went on an Arctic expedition with his sketching companion, A.Y. Jackson, a founding member of the Group of Seven, whose work caught the enduring beauty of the Arctic's desolation. The two men went along as guests aboard the Department of the Interior's supply ship *Beothic* and visited most of the HBC's stations in the Eastern Arctic. Banting had embarked on the journey as an amateur painter badly in need of a vacation, but his medical training and essential humanity could not long be denied. His journal contained many astute observations, such as that "a native cannot live on white man's food or in white men's dress," a correct diagnosis of the unsuitability of woollen and cotton goods for Arctic wear and of salted and canned provisions for Arctic food. But he was harshest in his assessments of the HBC. "The company have systematically possessed themselves of this country," he noted. "They have at each post an interpreter who puts before the native the company's view & teaches them that the great company will look after them & is their savior. While at the same time they hire them at ten dollars per year to 'retain' them as their men. They buy their furs very cheap—in trade—tea—tobacco—woollens etc.—which are by no means as good for the native as his former life without these things. At this port [Arctic Bay] we took on 23 bales of fox furs & there are said to be one hundred skins per bale—They sell at $50 to $60 per skin. 2300 x 50 = $115,000. Now where does the native come in? He hunts $100,000 worth of furs & the Company takes the profits."

In a *Toronto Star* interview after his return (given to a reporter while he thought he was speaking off the record), Banting expanded on his criticism, charging that the Inuit were getting goods worth only $5,000 in exchange for fox skins marketed at $100,000 and that the natives' resistance to disease was being lowered by the diet the Company encouraged its northern customers to eat. In a subsequent letter to an official at the Department of the Interior, he recommended that the Canadian government "take over full control of the fur trade throughout Eskimo territory. From the profits of the trade, proper administration could be carried out and steps be taken to improve rather than destroy the chances of the Eskimo race." The doctor, who because of his Nobel Prize was one of the best-known and most trusted Canadians of his day, went on to comment that "the native should be encouraged to lay up a reserve of money or credit in time of plenty to take care of the inevitable lean years ... generally speaking, the policy of the trader has been to keep the Eskimo in his debt."

In the face of this and Banting's many other criticisms, Governor Charles Vincent Sale wrote a twenty-seven-page letter to Deputy Minister W.W. Cory in which he denied the charges, claiming that "it is obvious that we must be interested in their [the Inuit] welfare since they are the people who, given reasonable opportunities, can best occupy and make use of the snow covered regions in which we operate, and where we have embarked so much of our capital." Banting's attack was a timely indication that the HBC could no longer insulate itself against outsiders questioning its divine right to rule. The North, especially the Arctic's western sector, was exploding with activity that would change the fur trade forever.

THE MACKENZIE RIVER HAD BECOME a comfortable superhighway through the Western Arctic, with the HBC's impressive fleet of thirteen ships leading the way. By 1927, the Company was offering tourists thirty-five-day round-trip cruises on the Mackenzie as far north as Aklavik for $325, including meals, and was unable to accommodate all the passengers who swarmed in every summer to take advantage of the journey, advertised as being "2000 MILES

OFF THE BEATEN TRACK."* Ships such as the *Athabasca River* boasted a cruising speed of thirteen knots, electric lights, and luxury salon accommodation for fifty-eight passengers. Those were great days on the river. "You had time, for there was no schedule but the riverboat's own," recalled Laco Hunt, a former HBC Factor who took the journey many times. "You had time to muse on the legends you'd heard about the great Northern lakes whose names echoed with history; about the fur-trading forts and the men who'd fought to put them in the wilderness.... The long procession of days brought a new rhythm to your life; it seemed to fall in with the pattern made by the mornings and afternoons filled with the sounds of birds, and the swift undercurrents of water, dark blue with reflected sky."

That romantic vision was disrupted by construction of the Alberta and Great Waterways Railway, known to every northern hand as the Muskeg Limited, which tapped the Mackenzie Basin into the country's main transportation network. The most disturbing influence was the dramatic mineral strike in the region by a Toronto prospector named Gilbert LaBine. On the unseasonably cold morning of May 16, 1930, at a forlorn inlet on the eastern shore of Great Bear Lake, a day's walk from the Arctic Circle, he found a plum-sized glob of rock that turned out to be pure pitchblende. This would become the great Eldorado Mine, the source first of radium and later of the uranium that was used in the atomic bomb dropped on Hiroshima. The find, which trebled the world stock of radium (before LaBine's discovery, supplies of the precious metal amounted to only half a pound, worth $22 million), set off a mining rush. Would-be prospectors included a Russian prince who arrived with his princess, accompanied by a bearded valet, and an Arab sheikh who wandered aimlessly along the shores of Great Bear, his robes catching in the stunted conifers. The most ingenious method of discovering surface traces of the radioactive ore was that used by Tom Creighton, a veteran sourdough who had earlier helped stake the Flin Flon mine in northern Manitoba. He dropped undeveloped film on likely-looking rocky outcrops; the presence of pitchblende would show up as streaks of light.

*The meals the Company advertised received mixed reviews. When one of the steamer captains asked a passenger, the Reverend Gerald Card, to say grace, the Anglican minister refused. "Indeed, I won't," he thundered. "After paying the Hudson's Bay Company fifty cents for a meal, against which even my stomach registers the most vigorous and continual protests, I fail to see any reason why I should lift my voice in thanks to God!"

At about the same time, major gold deposits were discovered at Beaverlodge, on the north shore of Lake Athabasca, while a Cominco prospector named Spud Arsenault struck gold at Yellowknife. Most of the bushwhackers and goldseekers who poured into every part of the North arrived by airplane. LaBine himself had first spotted the pitchblende deposit from the back seat of C.H. "Punch" Dickins's primitive biplane. Peering through the aircraft's humming shrouds, he noticed rocks smudged with the peach-red hues that indicated cobalt bloom, one of the clues associated with radium deposits—a mineral strike that would eventually create a world-scale mine. "I suddenly realized," he later recalled, "that I was in elephant country."

The first prospecting flight into the North had actually taken place a decade earlier, when Imperial Oil purchased two German-built 175-h.p. Junkers monoplanes to supply drilling crews during the oil rush at Norman Wells. The monoplanes got only as far as Fort Simpson, where one of them crash-landed, breaking its propeller. The aircraft was able to take off again after an HBC carpenter named Walter Johnson fashioned a substitute out of toboggan boards held together with babiche—glue distilled from moose hoofs. Those early bush pilots became reluctant heroes as they peered over the sides of their open cockpits to verify their bearings, nervously checking their watches against fuel gauges, adjusting their goggles, praying that the far distant dot on the tundra for which they were heading was actually there. The Inuit, who had never seen a streetcar or automobile, could easily distinguish a Junkers from a Fokker, Norseman, Beechcraft, Gypsy Moth or Beaver, but as one of their elders at Chesterfield Inlet remarked when gazing for the first time at a flying machine, "That is a bad thing to know just a little about." In the tradition of the voyageurs who dared to tread where others only dreamed of going, the fliers, most of them beached veterans of Great War dogfights, transformed the North. Probably the most enterprising pilot on those early runs was Leigh Brintnell, whose tiny Mackenzie Air Service won the government mail contract for most of the Western Arctic. His arrangement with Ottawa called for him to be paid according to how many pounds of mail he delivered to each settlement. He had been granted the contract by drastically underbidding his rivals, who were certain he couldn't make a profit on existing traffic. They were right. But that didn't stop Brinmell. He purchased airmail subscriptions to the Edmonton *Journal* for nearly every log shack along the Mackenzie, automatically increasing his payload and trebling his income. W.R. "Wop" May, who had duelled with Germany's Red Baron and flown under the High Level Bridge at Edmonton on a bet, became the first idol of Canada's air age, closely followed by Punch Dickins.

With its customary foresight, the HBC refused to participate in a new scheduled air service between Edmonton and the Mackenzie Valley. But it did employ Dickins on contract to fly bales of fur out of Fort Good Hope and in the winter of 1930 financed him on a medical mercy mission into Coppermine. The Company purchased its first plane—a twin-engined Beechcraft equipped with wheels, skis and floats—in 1939, only eleven years after nearly everyone else in its territories had taken to doing business by air. Paul Davoud, the HBC's first pilot, calculated that George Simpson's eighty-four-day dash by canoe in 1824 on his famous inspection tour from Lachine to the Pacific would now take only ten hours. Davoud flew HBC executives on their first aerial inspection tour in the summer of 1940, much to the unwelcome surprise of local store managers, used to getting warnings of visits by Company brass via the staff moccasin telegraph. "We landed at Fort Resolution at five in the morning," Davoud recalled. "The post manager, with about a five days' beard on him, was down on the dock, scratching his belly, wanting to know who I had aboard. When I told him I had 'the works'—the chief of the fur trade, head of Canadian operations, and the Governor, over from London—he groaned and was sure he'd be fired. He wasn't, but I don't think he was the same man after that." When the Beechcraft set down at Fort Rae, one of the local aboriginals was shown through it. Pointing at the plane's luxurious fittings, an HBC executive asked the visitor whether he admired the white man's marvel. "Sure," was the laconic reply. "We paid for it."

An incursion into the North of a very different sort was the railway built to Churchill, on Hudson Bay. Proponents of the railroad claimed that exporting grain through the Bay would force the CPR to reduce freight rates and cut the cost of trans-shipping Liverpool-bound goods at Montreal. The project had been kicking around Parliament since 1884, awaiting funds and legislative sanction. Nine charters were approved, but actual construction didn't start until 1910. The line was originally planned to terminate at Port Nelson, near York Factory, and a $6-million, seventeen-span steel bridge was erected to a man-made island, where the new harbour was to be built. The First World War intervened, and when the railway was finally completed in 1929, Churchill was its terminus, leaving Port Nelson abandoned, the sub-Arctic's most expensive white elephant. Two years later, the *Farnworth*, a tramp steamer out of Newcastle-on-Tyne, loaded Churchill's first commercial wheat shipment. For a time the harbour handled general goods, but soon its only customer was a reluctant Canadian Wheat Board, and the dream of building an alternative grain-export route faded.*

The failure of Churchill was partly due to its inauguration on the eve of the Depression, which also cut deeply into HBC profit and the fur trade in general. Arctic fox prices declined as much as 800 percent, and silver fox pelts plummeted in value from $450 in 1920 to only $9 by 1939. The problem with that luxurious variety was not only the Depression but the new customers it attracted. Nearly every prostitute in London and Paris suddenly decided she couldn't successfully walk the streets unless she was decked out in a silver fox stole—and with more and more tarts adopting the fur as a badge of office, the bottom fell out of the market. The Depression cut severely into Company budgets. Operational costs were dramatically reduced by the closing of a hundred stores. At one Arctic settlement, coal rations grew so short that the HBC manager had to dismantle and burn his warehouse to keep warm. The HBC's presence in the Western Arctic was reduced to only three posts: Coppermine, Cambridge Bay and Tuktoyaktuk.

The Depression only aggravated the Company's less than generous staff policies. Post managers were usually moved to lower-paying positions for the last few years of their tenures, so that the pensions due them, calculated as a percentage of their final years' pay, could be reduced. But the HBC's manage-ment did come up with the occasional generous and humane decision. When Hugh Mackay Ross was appointed manager of the Saskatchewan district, he wanted to pension off Jock Mathieson, the veteran post manager at Beauval, who hadn't many years to go in the service and was the main stumbling block to Ross's reorganization plans. Ross sent his recommenda-tion to the Company's Canadian headquarters, where his request for remov-ing the old trader was denied. "They had carefully studied Mr. Mathieson's dossier," he later recalled, "and had concluded that because his son was attending the local school, it would be a hardship for the family to be sent

---

* The train from Winnipeg to Churchill was still operating in the 1990s, but in a typical year it attracted only 5,616 passengers, so that a $11.5-million annual federal subsidy—or $2,047 a passenger for its thirty-four-hour run—was required. Adam Corelli of the *Financial Times of Canada* calculated that the same trip in a rented Mercedes limousine would cost only $1,566— if only there were a road.

where no school was available. They further concluded that Mr. Mathieson's abilities as a competent post manager had always been in doubt, but no action had been taken by the Company. The fault, therefore, was the Company's, and not Mr. Mathieson's, and he should remain at Beauval until he reached full retirement." Ross pondered the ruling and after his initial disappointment had to admit that it was a wise decision, one that made him feel proud to be a "Bay man."

About the only improvement the Company made to its northern facilities during the 1930s was installation of short-wave transmitters that for the first time connected the isolated outposts with each other and the outside world. Except for the annual supply-ship visit and the occasional winter dog team, the Company's servants received no personal or corporate news until these radios were installed, starting with Arctic Bay, Leaf River, Cape Dorset and Cape Smith in 1937. The twelve-watt Morse code sets were powered by windmill-operated generators and twelve-volt storage batteries that were nursed like colicky babies, kept warm by claiming the place of honour behind each staff house stove. The network grew to fifty-four stations—the country's largest—and was eventually converted to single sideband, and later to voice and radio telephones.

A more daring departure was the first modern Canadian beaver preserve, established near Rupert House on James Bay. The area's beaver ponds had been almost totally trapped out, leaving the Cree with nothing to trade, when the local HBC manager, James Watt, and his wife, Maud, persuaded Company authorities to leave the few remaining beaver houses alone, so that the animals would have a chance to multiply. Quebec designated a 7,200-square-mile beaver sanctuary, which was so successful that by 1940 trapping could begin again.

During the Second World War several northern locations were used for temporary airfields, as staging areas for military manoeuvres and for Ferry Command operations. The largest undertaking was the great Canol project, which piped oil from Norman Wells on the Mackenzie River six hundred miles to a refinery built at Whitehorse for use in the North Pacific theatre of war. As the Arctic expert Graham Rowley noted, "In a country where old lard pails had been treasured, 45-gallon drums, not always empty, were discarded." One measure of the HBC's dominant influence among the Inuit at that time was this description of the Second World War, given by Octave Sivanertok of Repulse Bay in a 1979 interview with the CBC's Lorna Kusugak: "There was a big war. It was between the Bay and the Germans. The Bay won." Yet in at least one way, the war years were merely an extension of the Depression. The Canadian government, pressured by more urgent priorities, perpetuated its benign neglect of the North.

What changed all that was the precipitous dive of white fox prices from thirty-five dollars to three dollars between 1946 and 1948. With their only cash crop all but wiped out, the Inuit found their social and economic framework altered. They had abandoned their hunting ethic to become trappers, and now, cut off for at least a generation from living off the land, they could not subsist on the low fur prices. Epidemics of such white men's illnesses as measles, influenza, tuberculosis, diphtheria and venereal diseases were spreading across the North. Families were starving and sled dogs dying, further reducing the ability of the Inuit to hunt. There were some work opportunities, such as the opening of a nickel mine at Rankin Inlet, which operated between 1957 and 1962, employing up to eighty Inuit, and construction of the ninety-eight Distant Early Warning stations across the North in the mid-1950s. But they were too limited to have much impact. According to a 1960 survey, only 307 Inuit (out of a total population of about 12,000) had jobs that year, and only 63 of them worked for non-government agencies: 58 for North Rankin Nickel Mines Limited, 2 for missionaries and 3 for the Hudson's Bay Company. With such narrow employment opportunities, the Northerners grew increasingly dependent on government welfare. As Ottawa became more concerned about their ability to survive, the Inuit themselves were being urbanized, a process that significantly raised their individual and collective aspirations. Paradoxically, the most significant of these urbanizing influences was tuberculosis, which at one time afflicted a third of the Inuit population. "Endemic upper respiratory diseases like tuberculosis, emphysema, and bronchitis motivated movement of the people into white men's settlements, mainly to hospitals in the South," recalled R.G. Williamson, an anthropologist at the University of Saskatchewan. "New lifestyle expectations were created during their time at the treatment centres, as they watched television and visited white people's homes in Winnipeg, Brandon, Hamilton, Toronto, and Montreal. As material expectations were raised, the Hudson's Bay Company had to modernize its merchandising methods and expand its lines. It began to stock tailor-made cigarettes and moved from selling mainly high-protein foods to such high-carbohydrate (and high mark-up) items as sweet biscuits, soft drinks, candy, and other junk foods.

That was a big change to the old fur trade posts, where keeping 2 ½-inch nails in stock was thought to be a bit of a luxury."

As the economic plight of the Inuit developed into a political issue and it became evident that the fur trade could no longer sustain them, Ottawa moved north with a vengeance, formally accepting the fact that education and welfare were its responsibilities. Well-intentioned teachers, nurses, doctors, welfare officers and administrators galore arrived in the Arctic. To monitor the behaviour of the new arrivals, the Royal Canadian Mounted Police increased its northern presence, being charged, among other duties, with distributing family allowances and old-age pensions.* Government handouts were issued not as cash, which was still not a generally accepted means of doing business in the North, but as entries in RCMP ledgers. The police would itemize precisely what goods the people could receive and send the tally over to the HBC store, which then handed out the merchandise. A typical 1945 monthly family ration consisted of fourteen pounds of flour, a pound of tea, three pounds of sugar, three pounds of rolled oats, two pounds of rice, six packages of Pablum and a gallon of coal oil. Not much to build a dream on, but better than starving. The notion of receiving goods free from HBC stores that had previously traded them for furs was disturbing and not always understood. "The Mountie told me I could go into the trading post and buy anything I needed because I had family allowance," recalled Matthew Innakatsik of Baker

---

* Some of their patrols were amazingly infrequent. When an RCMP constable arrived in the Belcher Islands on April 11, 1940, it was the first police visit since 1919. Official calls too were rare. "When I went to the Belchers in 1969," said former Commissioner Smart Hodgson, "it was the first public meeting that had ever been held there. As I recall, it was in a little one-room schoolhouse that had been dumped off in the southern end of the Belchers rather than the north. As a consequence, a few houses were built for the local people, as their children were going to school. Essentially, the main settlement was in the north end of the island. In any event, the meeting started about six o'clock and by midnight there were only myself and the interpreter left. The rest of our party had retired. At 2.00 A.M. as the meeting developed into a sort of lull, I asked the people (all the locals were there—grandparents, parents, children and babies—the entire settlement) if perhaps they would like to adjourn the meeting and they said, 'Oh, no.' At 2.30 I again put the question to them, 'Have you anything more to talk about?' and they said no. I said, 'Well, perhaps we should adjourn the meeting,' and they again replied no, to which I said, 'Why not?' The reply was both astounding and humorous. They simply said that they had never had a meeting before and they thought it was a lot of fun. I was up the next morning at six o'clock. We had breakfast and left at seven to see the people at the north end of the island. When the plane landed and I opened the door, I was astonished to see the same people. They asked, 'Are we going to have another meeting?' They had travelled fifty miles overland that night in order to be there for another meeting."

Lake. "It didn't make any sense because I had never received anything for free before and I was afraid to do it."*

The combination of nervousness about Canadian sovereignty, the paranoid influences of the Cold War, which gave the Arctic unexpected strategic significance, and the growing awareness in southern Canada that the Inuit were severely deprived lent impetus to the government's involvement. Free match-box houses were provided for Inuit families in the main settlements, with electricity and water at nominal cost. The North became fashionable. Experts arrived by the hour, it seemed—scientists and human manipulators, all eager to carry the white man's burden. Minnie Aodla Freeman, a wonderfully wise Inuit from Cape Hope Island, summed up the effect of the influx most succinctly when she commented that the ideal Arctic family now consisted of a husband and wife, four children and an anthropologist.†

After 1960, family allowances and old-age pensions were sent directly to the intended recipients. Not only did some managers insist that old debts be paid before they extended any credit to their customers (a policy the Company claimed was not contained in their directives), but natives who dared send order forms to Eaton's catalogue department or any other competitor claimed their letters were occasionally mislaid. Even when orders did get through, usually on a cash-on-delivery basis, they could not always be claimed. Jean Godsell, whose husband was stationed with the HBC in Fort Smith, recalled a typical scene when the long-expected mail-order goods finally arrived and the customers came to collect them: "One by one, they appeared at the wicket, their dusky faces wreathed in smiles which soon turned to black anger when they found they could not take the parcels off in debt, as was the case with the trading stores. Naturally, most of the parcels went back, but others came in on

---

* Relations between the Mounties and Inuit were not limited to welfare. "Almost all the single RCM Policemen had native girlfriends," observed E.G. Cooch, a Canadian government ornithologist who specialized in on-site Arctic studies. "It was no big deal. But I remember being told about a young constable posted to Pond Inlet who was a very fastidious individual and apparently afraid of women, behaving like a bashful monk. One time, when his senior colleague had to go on patrol to Arctic Bay, he was out about five hours when he remembered something and went back. He could hear noises from the ground-floor bathroom, so he looked in and there was the monk in the bathtub with one of the local girls, scrubbing her back. There was a candle and a bottle of wine beside them and my friend, Cliff, said he didn't have the heart to walk in and disturb them."

† She married one—Milton Freeman, a professor of anthropology at the University of Alberta—and went on to write some of the best of the northern books, including *Survival in the South* and *Life Among the Qallunaat*.

the next plane; still more came in on the steamer, and it was quite some time ere the mail-order houses realized that Marie Chandelle, Rosalie Squirrel, Elsie Lame-Duck et al. were not, despite their substantial orders, the type of customers they desired."*

Best of the newcomers to the North was James Houston, a Toronto artist who spent fourteen years on Baffin Island under contract to the Department of Northern Affairs, teaching the Inuit how best to market their soapstone creations. Carving, an intrinsic skill of the Inuit, had been used to fashion out of bone, stone and ivory the snow goggles, parka toggles, harpoons, arrowheads, ice-chisels, spoons, fish spears, talismans and toys that were part of their everyday existence. In 1949, Houston, assisted by Norman Ross, the HBC store manager at Port Harrison, collected a test group of Inuit carvings for the Canadian Handicrafts Guild in Montreal, which successfully sold the items. Gradually a market was built up for the best of the pieces. After a false start trying to produce bookends, ash trays and such, the carvers, under Houston's guidance, let their imaginations soar. By the late 1950s, the carvings had achieved international stature. The work was so successful partly because the carvers' own longing for a return to their ancestors' hunting days, expressed in their art, coincided with the southern buyers' romantic notions of what "Eskimos" were all about. The native artists responded to the material they were working. Their sculptures were not as much artistic as ritualistic, the crystallization of moments in time. "These are not cold sculptures of a frozen world," Houston noted. "They reveal to us the passionate feelings of a people aware of all the joys and terrors of life. They also reveal an enormous freshness and ingenuity, a hunter's sense of observation." Once the soapstone trade was established, Houston and his then wife, Alma, moved to Cape Dorset. "Oshaweetok, a famous Eskimo carver ... sat near me one evening casually studying the sailor head trademarks on two identical packages of cigarettes," Houston later recalled. "He noted carefully every subtle detail of color and form, and he suggested to me that it must be tiresome for some person to sit and paint every one of the little heads with exact sameness on an endless number of packages.... Looking around to find some way to demonstrate printing, I saw an ivory walrus tusk that Oshaweetok had recently carved.... Taking an old tin of writing ink that had frozen and thawed many times ... I dipped

---

* The men had their own problems with mail-order catalogues, especially those pages featuring women's underwear. One trapper, gazing with fascination at the suggestive layouts, wrote away for "the lady on the far right of page 59."

up the heavy black residue and smoothed it over the tusk. Taking a thin piece of toilet tissue, I laid it carefully on the inked surface and rubbed it lightly and quickly. Stripping the paper from the tusk, I saw that by good fortune we had a clear negative image of Oshaweetok's incised design.... 'We could do that,' he said. And so we did." That was how Cape Dorset's block printing and sealskin stencil printing industry was born, its evocative images later gracing museums and private collections the world over. By 1960, the HBC was buying forty tons of "Eskimo" carvings a year for resale in southern Canada.*

The prints and carvings grew so profitable that the following year a native-run West Baffin Eskimo Cooperative was opened at Cape Dorset to market the art. Nineteen similar outlets were soon opened in other communities, over stern protests from the HBC. "They were strongly against the move," recalled Ben Sivertz, then Commissioner of the Northwest Territories and a co-op advocate. "But the Eskimos took to it like ducks to water. We didn't have to tell them what to do. They took over from the Hudson's Bay post manager the business of setting carving prices. Jim Houston told me he was away when it happened, but when he got back to Cape Dorset he was invited to a meeting where everybody brought in their carvings. Each one was put on a table and all the carvers wrote down what they thought it should sell for; they then averaged that out, and that was the set price. They did that on their own in place after place. The pieces were sent to Ottawa, where we distributed them to the Handicrafts Guild and other merchandisers—in San Francisco, Paris, London and anywhere. The money was then sent back to the carvers, and that in fact was how cash on a large scale first came to the North—though it still had to be spent in Hudson's Bay Company stores."

As retailing competition grew more intense, so did the scrutiny of the HBC's methods and mark-ups. The Company maintained that its objective for mature northern stores (those established five years or more) was a 23-percent return on net assets (before interest and taxes). Some outlets exceeded that average and many others, particularly in the more remote areas, fell below it

---

* A less serious Company sideline was the U-Paddle Canoe rental service for adventurous holi-dayers who wanted to spend part of their summers following the trade routes of the voyageurs or exploring the wilder shores of the continent's sub-Arctic rivers. The Company purchased twenty-eight seventeen-foot aluminum canoes in 1964 and distributed them to posts at likely locations. There were enough rentals (at twenty-five dollars a week) to allow the HBC to break even, and by the time the U-Paddle service was abandoned twenty years later, the Company had a fleet of eighty canoes, renting for a weekly $125.

because of higher transportation costs. Testifying before the Northwest Territories Council on May 27, 1981, Marvin Tiller, then head of the HBC's northern operation, gave a rare insight into corporate pricing policies. The retail price of non-perishable goods, he stated, included a mark-up of up to 25 percent on top of landed costs, with the margin rising to one-third on most perishable items. He pointed out that stock in the North turned over only one and a half times a year, compared with eleven or twelve times in the South. Instead of trying to refute the accusation that perishables at the HBC's Frobisher Bay store were selling at 70 percent more than comparable items in Montreal, Tiller boasted that "to lay down fresh produce in Frobisher at only 70 percent more than Montreal prices is, in our view, a remarkable achievement of planning and organization." Goods at the HBC stores were—and are— expensive, but most of the added margin is accounted for by transportation costs. In 1981, a five-pound bag of potatoes at Pond Inlet, for example, sold for a ridiculous $7.10. But its actual freight cost was $5.15. "We are probably regarded as large and prosperous from money made out of the natives," Dick Murray, the HBC's managing director, complained in 1966. "The fact that in ninety-eight cases out of one hundred our men are able and dedicated, and work under conditions that most Canadians would refuse to work under for any length of time, is simply not taken into consideration."

Perception of the HBC was changing. Clearest summary of that evolution was the observation of Adrian Tanner of Memorial University, writing in *Queen's Quarterly*. "When I lived in an Arctic trading post community in the late 1950s, where trade with the Inuit was still conducted using Hudson's Bay Company tokens rather than cash, the two subjects which we learned to avoid at the segregated social gatherings of the white inhabitants were religion and impact of the Hudson's Bay Company on the native people. We who did not work for the Company found it remarkable that all Hudson's Bay employees, from the old-time traders to newest clerks who had just arrived from across the Atlantic, had a staunch and unquestioning loyalty to their employer and its past actions, and that when a subject like this was raised they seemed to quickly be reduced to irrational argument and wounded feelings.... By the time I went north again in the mid-1960s the Hudson's Bay Company fur trade and its effects on the native people had become something of a dead horse which the Canadian public was only too willing to flog, thanks to authors like Farley Mowat, and to some of the native political leaders. However, my own attitude to the recent situation, if not to the past history, had by then become less harsh. The Hudson's Bay Company's operation of its contemporary monopoly in the north seemed to be a model of benign responsibility, in comparison both to the European exploiters in other parts of the colonial world, and to the other 'marginal men' who were by then taking over power in the communities—government administrators, policemen, missionaries and teachers."*

"THE IMAGE OF THE CLASSIC ESKIMO is still that of Nanook of the North, the indomitable hunter clad in a sealskin anorak and polar-bear pants, his harpoon poised for the kill," concluded Sam Hall, an Arctic documentary film-maker, in a 1987 study. "In the Arctic today, this vision is as ludicrous as that of Caesar, his toga flowing behind him, a bunch of grapes in one hand and a silver chalice in the other, striding through a traffic jam in Rome." That's true enough, but the Inuit still live in both worlds. They left behind the last vestiges of the Stone Age only four decades ago; most were born in sealskin tents by the light of whale-oil lamps. The Inuit, caught between past and present, must find their refrigerators, VHS recorders and Yamaha trail buggies just as unreal as their fathers' and grandfathers' walrus-meat sledge runners, whalebone eye goggles and *iglus*. All those stately *kayaks*, *umiaks*, York boats and peterheads were displaced by functional 14- or 24-foot square-stern aluminum canoes, weighted down with 25- or 45-h.p. Evinrudes. For long journeys, there were the de Havilland Twin Otters operated by the many airlines criss-crossing the North; for short trips, snowmobiles.

That switch—from dogs to snowmobiles—was the final farewell to tradition. The few dog teams that remained were seldom used, except as rentals to film-makers or white tourists pretending they were Scott of the Antarctic. It was the whine of the snowmobiles' supercharged 250-cc motors that shattered the Arctic dream. Soon there were more skeletons of dead SkiDoos than caribou carcasses around the community dumps. Local teenagers spent endless

---

* One of the major changes in the Arctic was the introduction in 1960 of legally sold liquor. Previously, with no legal booze available, some of the more desperate Arctic hands, both aboriginal and white, had been swilling Aqua Velva after-shave lotion, Lysol or anti-freeze. HBC employees for a while enjoyed a tastier and more literary potion. Because the ink used by store managers to mark ledger entries kept freezing in their unheated stores, an enterprising Boston manufacturer introduced a new variety of red ink that contained so much alcohol it didn't turn solid. Once the HBC field hands discovered they could drink the stuff as well as write with it, orders for the scarlet concoction multiplied rapidly. But the Company caught on and went back to filling inkwells with less delectable thirst-quenchers.

hours aimlessly racing the machines in and out of settlements, the unmuffled roar of their engines giving voice to their desperation and their anger.

In this troublesome context the HBC became a natural target for discontent. Despite the natives' steady incomes, from government handouts, it was a strict Company rule never to grant an Inuk a Bay credit card. At the same time, the Company came to be perceived as an agent of destruction of the old values. "The Hudson's Bay Company ... helped the government practice genocide of Eskimo dogs, by providing the necessary hardware in which Inuit were to become assimilated into Canadian society," charged Josh Teemotee of Frobisher Bay. "This would also place the Inuit into a credit situation. Whether it was a commercial plot to assimilate Inuit is not known, but it seems coincidental that civil service posts would open up where Hudson's Bay stores located." Billy Diamond, Grand Chief of the Grand Council of the Cree of Quebec, complained that as late as 1970 the HBC store at Rupert House was not paying interest on funds it was holding for its customers—yet charging interest on credit overdrafts. "I was just starting out as Chief at Rupert," he recalled, "and you had to buy everything at the Bay store. After your furs had been auctioned off by the Company, the money went directly to the store and they told you how much your furs had been worth, though there was no way of verifying it. Then you dealt for goods, but the store kept the balance and paid no interest. Even if you deposited money for safekeeping with the Bay— and I heard of people who had $25,000 with the Company—you got no interest.... It was only my generation that said, 'Listen, there's much more to life than the Hudson's Bay Company. There's a world out there!'"

Reduced in their function to local supermarkets, the stores began to expand their merchandise racks, featuring such southern specialties as soft-porn magazines, canned lobster, Poly-fil parkas with Velcro pocket fasteners and every possible variety of junk food. The surfeit of Kool-Aid, Coca-Cola, chocolate, bubble gum and potato chips from the HBC store meant that most young Inuit lost their teeth by the time they were teenagers.*

The HBC's presence had radically altered the Inuit way of life, and while it was easy enough to be critical of the Company's impact, there was no permanent escape from the malignant forces of the white man's civilization. Within that context the Bay demonstrated remarkable restraint, and many of its local

---

* The 500-year-old remains of an Inuit woman found in 1978 in a Greenland cave had a near-perfect set of teeth.

managers earned their reputations for fair treatment of their customers. "I got
to know probably twenty or thirty of the Bay managers and I never knew one
who was a rascal," recalled Ben Sivertz. "It was life of a specialized kind and I
think that the rectitude and decency of the Bay men was remarkable, though
I'm not talking now about sexual relations with Eskimo women. That's one
aspect that needs special interpretation. But all that stuff about how mean
they were about the prices they paid for fur, that was Company policy. I am not
sure there was any other way to do it." Even Billy Diamond relented in his
criticism of the modern HBC. "The Company took a look at our needs and has
tried to adapt to what we're doing up there and at the same time they're trying
to give us a chance to take control of a lot of things," he admitted. "They used
to be the only guys selling gas, outboards and Ski-Doos. We've taken over all
that and the local trappers' association is ordering its own canoes and supplies.
The Hudson's Bay Company really streamlined its operations to bringing in
the groceries, appliances and clothing. It's no longer a credit outlet." Nellie
Cournoyea, an Inuk born in Aklavik and currently Minister of Health,
Minister of Energy, Mines and Petroleum Resources and Minister of Public
Works in the Northwest Territories, agrees: "I'm indifferent to the Bay. To us
it is just another store with no particular significance."

Under the HBC's—and later the government's—sponsorship, life was
certainly better for the old and the sick, and having a box of matches was an
improvement on rubbing sticks together to light a fire. But the argument about
whether the Inuit were happier then or now can never be resolved. "I know
people were happier in the old days," said William Kuptana, an elder at Sachs
Harbour. "But I know for sure they were not happy every day." Former
Commissioner Stuart Hodgson recalled asking Jimmy Kilabuk at Pangnirtung
the same question. "I don't know," was the reply. "But I'll tell you this: when I
was a young man, I can never, ever remember being warm."

Minnie Aodla Freeman, the Inuit author, placed the Company in its proper
perspective when she told a 1980 conference that it had "made easier lives for
Inuit since 1670. They were in my home area of James Bay long before I was
born, fur trading with my ancestors.... I think one of the reasons why Inuit
welcomed the Hudson's Bay Company was the fact that the Company never
tried to change Inuit ways of behaving or thinking. Yes, they changed our
equipment, to better steel knives, steel saws, steel nails, steel axes and manufactured cloth. Inuit understood it was the furs that the Hudson's Bay
Company were after. Inuit hunters had employment through the Hudson's Bay

Company. It was the familiar job Inuit enjoyed. We still hear older Inuit today saying that the Hudson's Bay Company is most useful in Inuit lands.... Hudson's Bay Company sold Fort Garry tea to Inuit first, before it was sold in Bytown ... pity!"

X MERCHANT PRINCES

The Lords and the Good Old Boys

"In England we gave them knighthoods; in Winnipeg they became directors of the Hudson's Bay Company." —Joe Links, HBC Director

THE TRANSITION OF THE BAY MEN from merchant adventurers to merchant princes was slow, painful and absolute. By the end of that long cycle, the Hudson's Bay Company had become a major retailing empire with no sense of privilege or feeling for history. But in the half-century leading up to that lapsed state of grace, the Company's top management went through a series of stops and starts, serious internal wrangling and several boardroom convulsions.

The protagonists in this jousting for control were the governors, deputy governors and their ennobled retinues trying to *rule* the Company from London pitted against a group of fiercely proud, down-home Good Old Boys trying to run the Company from Winnipeg. The two groups did battle with the obdurate conviction of crusaders, each side serving the righteousness of its cause.

On the surface, it seemed an uneven contest. The British lords and knights were exquisitely aware of the subtleties of their clout and class. Their authority was so persuasive because it flowed not from any divine right or self-proclaimed sense of superiority. They really *were* the best and the brightest in the upper crust of a society that took breeding and intelligence for granted, and they genuinely represented the interests of the HBC's shareholders, 97 percent of whom were domiciled within the United Kingdom.

Arrayed against these British proprietors and their distinguished proconsuls was a tightly knit posse of Winnipeg's finest. Midwestern squires, they were good if limited men, frontier-tough and damned if they were going to kowtow to these haughty strangers wearing spats and with handkerchiefs up their sleeves. Yet they loved being involved with the Company that had once ruled the West and eventually viewed themselves as a kind of apostolic succession, smoothly following one another as members of the HBC's Canadian Committee. That tenure became such a desirable badge of office among the local business élite that Joe Links, the British board's wittiest member, once quipped: "In England we gave them knighthoods; in Winnipeg they became directors of the Hudson's Bay Company."

In a very real way, Canadianization of the Hudson's Bay Company was part of the decolonization of the British Empire. Victory through gradualism. In the fifty-eight years between formation of the first Canadian Advisory Committee in 1912 and permanent transfer of the Company's charter across the Atlantic in 1970—between the governorships of Lord Strathcona and Lord Amory—a sequence of tippytoe measures was reluctantly taken to shift authority from London to Winnipeg. Although provision of a domestic registry for Canadian shareholders had been suggested as early as 1908, it wasn't until forty-five years later, in 1953, that it was actually put into effect. On October 16, 1958, the Hudson's Bay Company board convened in Winnipeg, the first time its directors had met outside London in 288 years. It took another half-decade before the British shares were listed on the Toronto Stock Exchange. A year later, for the first time the Company's dividend cheques were paid to Canadian shareholders in Canadian dollars instead of British pounds, and it was 1970 before the annual report was printed in Canada.

The transfer of substantive decision-making authority didn't really begin until 1930, when Winnipeg was granted power of attorney to deal with the Company's day-to-day operations. In 1957, the Canadian Committee's members became directors of the mother firm, though it took a further six years before they were allowed to outnumber their British colleagues. "The Canadians were always trying to grab more authority," remembered Peter Wood, for thirty-eight years the Company's senior financial officer, "but the Brits kept hanging on, putting little roadblocks in the way, standing about with long faces, stressing the risks and disadvantages, so that it was difficult to be enthusiastic. They were such a distinguished and respected group that it was hard to ignore them. Besides, they held the power."

The nature of that power was limited at best, authority and responsibility being divided between two continents, with London possessing the former but unable to impose the latter. It was one thing to draft policies in the hush of

the HBC's City boardroom but quite another to police how—or whether—
those directives had been followed in the field. Accountability was always the
pivotal issue, yet making orders stick was never satisfactorily resolved. The
mesmerizing effect of the HBC's unique history made everyone cautious about
allowing authority to be dispersed too quickly or too widely. The Canadian
Committeemen had the local knowledge but not the breadth of experience to
run a major trading company; the London directors possessed the necessary
expertise but were too far removed from the trenches to have much practical
input.

The operating heads of the Company in Canada quickly realized that
their main leverage lay in how much or how little data they transmitted
across the Atlantic, and being astute about it—knowing full well that
rationing performance statistics would only make London suspicious—they
tried to overwhelm the HBC's British headquarters with tidal waves of facts.
Sheaves of weekly returns enumerated each post's fur intake and each
department store's inventory of socks; every transaction was meticulously
documented and transmitted overseas. What went missing was any feeling
about the exciting new economy sprouting up north of the 49th parallel.

That omission was less by design than by the character of the Canadian
operation. The Committee, in fact, knew very little about the new Canada
evolving outside Winnipeg's municipal boundaries. Its members stubbornly
resisted lifting their sights beyond regional concerns, leaving others, as they
haughtily declared, "to go whoring in the East." The dynamics of delay ruled
the Company's affairs.

THE TENSION THAT PERMEATED RELATIONS between the British directors
and Canadian Committeemen even touched their social lives. Sir Eric
Faulkner recalled his first visit to Winnipeg in the mid-1950s when he was the
HBC's Deputy Governor: "I was viewed with enormous suspicion by the
Canadians and subsequently learned they were told to invite me to their
houses for a drink, but under no circumstances to serve me a meal until they'd
taken my measure. I went to have a drink with Stu Searle, who turned out to
be a delightful man. After a whisky, he suddenly exclaimed, 'Do you realize
I'm not allowed to ask you to dinner? This is bloody nonsense, but since
there's no food in the house, let's go out and eat.' We finally changed our
minds and had scrambled eggs while sitting on his living-room floor, and that
was the beginning of a friendship that lasted all our lives."

In a letter to the last British Governor, Lord Amory, the last Chairman of the Winnipeg Committee, David Kilgour, betrayed the Canadians' real feeling about the visitations of London dignitaries. "I confess," he wrote, "we are probably unduly annoyed by individuals who have that austere superiority which we Western Canadians ascribe to some Englishmen...." Joe Harris, one of the Canadian Committeemen, was more blunt. "When a North American wants to insult you," he explained to Amory, "he calls you a son of a bitch, laughs with you about it over a drink at lunch, and forgets it by evening. A Britisher, on the other hand, does it in the most thoughtful courteous language that can be devised—and writes it into the Minutes."

The Canadians' standoffish attitude was demonstrated in the smallest gestures. Most of the Winnipeggers owned lodges in the duck-hunting marshes northwest of Winnipeg, and even though the aristocratic visitors loved shooting, invitations were seldom forthcoming. "It was soon clear that ... the Winnipeg Establishment didn't want them at their lodges and sent them out to Delta for me to take care of," wrote Al Hochbaum, then in charge of the local waterfowl research station. "I remember especially what fine specimens of the human race were Tony Keswick [the HBC's Governor] and Sir Henry Benson [then Deputy Governor]. I kept wondering why Winnipeg society didn't wish to have them for a weekend. They shot like gentlemen, drank like gentlemen, swore like gentlemen—and didn't mind the outdoor toilets." The British visitors tended to be overpolite, slightly patronizing and more than a little puzzled by the Winnipeggers' provincialism. "I once asked Con Riley, the first time I met him after he was appointed to head the Canadian Committee," Keswick recalled, "exactly what Winnipeg was famous for. I've never forgotten his answer. He said very quietly, without looking left or right, 'Nice people,' and left it at that."

Both groups were so internally cohesive it was difficult for either side to comprehend the other. Except for one attempted *coup d'état* in 1963, the British directors were so compatible they didn't bother taking votes on any significant issue. "I was going to say we never voted on anything," recalled Joe Links, a twenty-eight-year board member, "but we actually did hold one vote when we were getting some new china for serving tea in the boardroom. Some of us wanted green, some wanted yellow. I think the yellows had it."

The British directors received virtually no perks, and none of them needed either the prestige or the token stipend (£500 annually). Yet there never seemed to be a shortage of top-drawer candidates. "We frankly had the pick of the best men in the City," boasted Lord Amory. "I don't remember any directors whom we thought of turning us down, no matter how high their calibre. Whereas the Canadian Committee people were big men only in Manitoba, but had little contact with the rest of Canada."

The executive committee of the British board met at noon every Tuesday (with the entire directorate attending once a month); sherry was served at quarter to one, though several of the more robust members would have preferred gin and tonic. Seated under the portraits of past Governors and surrounded by silver objects, some dating back to 1670, they discussed Company business, mainly reports of the Canadian Committee, which met each previous Thursday. Over lunch they would lapse into a wider discussion of public affairs, occasionally touching some such tangent as dismissing the latest biography of Lord Keynes for being the work of an Oxford man struggling to understand a Cambridge mind. The east wall of the walnut-panelled boardroom was covered with a map showing the Company's posts and operations, visited yearly by the Governor or his deputy. Most shareholders' annual meetings (still called "Courts") were quick and tame affairs; an elapsed time of seventeen minutes in 1957 was the record for speed. "One frail old proprietor," recalled Links, "used to refer at the annual Court to the previous speaker, equally frail, as 'the adventurer who has just sat down,' probably correctly, since we were 'the Governor and Company of Adventurers of England, trading into Hudson's Bay.'"

Immediately after the Second World War, bankers became significant on the HBC board, mainly in the person of Sir Eric Faulkner (later chairman of both Lloyds Bank and Glyn, Mills). He had won a football Blue at Cambridge, participated in the retreat at Dunkirk, fought against Rommel, done all the important things expected of an all-round English gentleman of his generation, yet he regarded his dozen years with the HBC as very special. "During the 1930s when I first went to Glyn's," he recalled, "I thought that if I ever did succeed in getting up the ladder and was allowed to take outside directorships I would love to be invited one day to join the board of the Hudson's Bay Company. By chance fate dealt the cards that way. I well remember saying laughingly at one of our board meetings, 'God, what a Company this is, never a moment of peace. There is always turbulence somewhere.'" Sir Martin Jacomb, another distinguished banker who also served on the HBC board, reached a similar conclusion. "Some institutions," he said, "although they are only legal entities, do have real organic personalities. The Bay transmits that feeling to anyone who comes in contact with it."

One of the HBC's great strengths was the active interest in its financial welfare displayed by the Bank of England. The Old Lady of Threadneedle Street had actually been founded twenty-four years *after* the Hudson's Bay Company—a fact successive central bank governors were never allowed to forget—but the two institutions remained very close. Half a dozen Bank of England governors and directors had been either governors or directors of the HBC, including Sir John Henry Pelly, Henry Hulse Berens, George Joachim Goschen, Sir Robert Molesworth Kindersley, Sir Patrick Ashley Cooper, Lord Cobbold and, above all, Sir Edward Peacock. The Canadian-born financier had for two decades been a dominant figure in the Bank of England and later became senior partner of Barings, the London money house the Due de Richelieu, premier of France, had in 1818 dubbed Europe's "Sixth Great Power," alluding to the continent's economic order being ruled by England, France, Prussia, Austria, Russia and Baring Brothers. Peacock, who became an HBC director in 1931 and stayed on the board for the next nineteen years, was also an adviser to the Royal Family and had been intimately involved in matters financial and otherwise concerning Edward VIII's abdication. His influence on the HBC's economic deliberations over two crucial decades was considerable, and it was highly conservative.

Because of existing tax laws, the English shareholders much preferred capital gains to income, so that stock splits were more desirable than dividends. The Company's capital funds were grossly inadequate to keep it expanding along with the Canadian economy because until 1960 the HBC refused to borrow. "We all hated borrowing and considered any loan a blister on the balance sheet," Keswick confirmed. "Mum told us you mustn't overspend your allowance, and that was the British discipline. We were against borrowing because we saw all around us people borrowing tremendously and getting into difficulties, and we didn't want our beloved Hudson's Bay Company to get into trouble. We may have missed some tricks, but we were old-timers and had seen accidents happen before."

The real paradox was that despite their "blister on the balance sheet" attitude and the rigid corporate directives that flowed from that bias, the London directors were often less averse to risk than the Winnipeggers. "It always seemed to me that we were more anxious than the Canadians to modernize and keep up with the times," Faulkner recalled. "Few of the Winnipeg directors got around the country or the Company, and so were inclined to miss opportunities. We could never persuade them to travel much outside Winnipeg. They might have a look-in at the Vancouver store if they happened to be there, but we'd often add a week or two to our tours and go to the really remote places, into the Saguenay country or way up into the Arctic, where we were welcomed by the staff who were delighted to see a director, even an English one."

THE DICHOTOMY OF THE MENTALITIES at work in Winnipeg and London reached far deeper than that. The Canadian West is a land of long memories. At the turn of the century, Winnipeggers had felt at the very forefront of Canadian civilization. The *Winnipeg Telegram* proudly reported in its January 29, 1910, edition that the city had nineteen millionaires, pointedly adding that Toronto, many times its size, had only twenty-one. An American journalist who arrived the following year waxed enthusiastic about the Manitoba capital as the Chicago of the North, "a gateway through which all the commerce of the east and the west, and the north and the south, must flow. No city, in America at least, has such absolute and complete command over the wholesale trade of so vast an area. It is destined to become one of the greatest distributing commercial centres of the continent as well as a manufacturing community of great importance."

Instead, completion of the Panama Canal gradually eliminated Winnipeg as the transportation and distribution linchpin of the Canadian economy's spread to the Pacific coast, although the population of Vancouver surpassed that of Winnipeg only in 1931.* No longer a potential Chicago, Winnipeg became Canada's Vienna—a city-state without an empire. Geared to supply a hinterland half a continent wide, it became an economic backwater, its geographical significance drastically reduced by history's tides. Most Winnipeggers responded to the change by leaving or sending their children to carve out lives and careers elsewhere; certainly the city's most valuable export

---

* The Panama Canal was only one factor in Winnipeg's decline, though a major one. Also at fault was the post-war collapse of the local wholesale business, when prosperity allowed carload lots to be shipped across the West instead of being broken up by wholesalers in Winnipeg, which meant that the three provinces west of Manitoba began to deal directly with the large eastern companies and institutions. As that trend intensified, Winnipeg tapered off to being a provincial capital, even though more cultured than most. At the same time, the financial functions of Winnipeg changed. First, British Columbia banking executives were allowed to report directly to head office in Montreal or Toronto. Later, because of the 1947 oil boom, the same became true of Alberta. The service industries, especially insurance, followed the pattern of the banks. Until the late 1940s Winnipeg was the regional centre of the entire West for these industries, but it declined rapidly after that.

was its people. Those who stayed either accustomed themselves to living in a pleasant, unspectacular place or—like the Hudson's Bay Committeemen—scarcely acknowledged Winnipeg's demise. Bound together by fear of their own irrelevance, the Bay men dug in. W.L. Morton, the Manitoba historian who understood his province better than anyone else, concluded that the local business community—from which the Hudson's Bay Company's Committeemen had been drawn—was "cautious, canny, reactionary, untravelled, fearful of ideas and of imagination."

The most unyielding point of dispute between London and Winnipeg directors was location of the Canadian headquarters. In the mid-1930s the British Governor hinted that a move to Toronto might be desirable, to take better advantage of the country's future opportunities. The Winnipeg Committee immediately threatened to resign *en masse,* and a lame compromise of naming a few token non-Manitoba directors was finally accepted. Still, the Winnipeggers howled in anger and frustration—even though the appointees ranked among Canada's best-connected businessmen. J.W. McConnell, for example, was a dominant figure in St Lawrence Sugar, Ogilvie Flour Mills, the Bank of Montreal, CPR, Canada Steamship Lines, Brazilian Traction, Dominion Bridge, Sun Life, Inco, Royal Trust and later the *Montreal Star,* while another, D.C. Coleman, was senior vice-president of the CPR (as well as a director of Metropolitan Life and Canadian Marconi) and had only recently moved away from Winnipeg. The then resident HBC managing director assured London that these two Eastern members were "of no practical value to the Company" and that "in any case, it was impossible to justify paying them the same fees as the Winnipeg members who did all the work" so that "if the Board wished to keep them, their fees should be reduced to $50 a meeting." As late as 1966, the Canadian managing director, Richard Murray, wrote a four-page, closely spaced memorandum to the then Governor, Lord Amory, explaining that the HBC's headquarters had to stay in Winnipeg "both now and in the future" because it was Canada's geographical centre, had adequate Telex and air services, and that even if executives had to be paid a premium for being willing to relocate there, it meant lower turnover because there would be less "job hopping." What Murray failed to mention was that this was true mainly because there was nowhere to hop to—and that maintaining headquarters in Winnipeg almost guaranteed being out of touch with the mainstream of Canada's business community. "The actual benefits from such contacts," he huffed, "are intangible, vary with individuals, and are impossible to calculate ... [but] this affects a very small portion of the total number of executives and thus cannot be given too much weight."

Not only did the HBC's Canadian pastorate limit itself to a Winnipeg parish but its membership was circumscribed by directorships in a handful of local companies. A dozen HBC Committeemen who held office between 1913 and 1970 were also directors of Great-West Life Assurance, for example, and David Kilgour, who was the head of both concerns, once assured the British Governor that "the Canadian Committee of the Hudson's Bay has perhaps very parallel objectives so that it is wholly natural that there should be some duplication between the two Companies." The other Winnipeg-based firms that spawned succeeding generations of HBC Committeemen included Monarch Life, Beaver Lumber, Northern Trusts, Canadian Indemnity, Manitoba Bridge & Iron Works, Osler, Hammond & Nanton and, most important of all, the Richardson group. The successive generations of Winnipeg Establishment men who ran these commercial concerns were entwined corporately, socially and even genetically. The Hudson's Bay Company in Canada was run by a clique of buddies with limited horizons and a common mentality. Part of that mindset was their determination to break the hold on the West of St James Street in Montreal and Bay Street in Toronto by establishing strong corporate principalities in Winnipeg. Local control of the HBC was an essential element in that strategy.

BETWEEN 1911 AND 1926, the Hudson's Bay Company built or purchased its fleet of flagship downtown department stores in Victoria, Vancouver, Edmonton, Calgary, Saskatoon and Winnipeg, opening smaller versions in Kamloops, Vernon, Nelson, Macleod, Lethbridge, Yorkton and Kenora, all of them initially successful as the transcontinental railways deposited tens of thousands of new customers on their doorsteps.* Despite the proliferation of department stores across the country, their share of the retail dollar remained constant—at 10.23 percent in 1923 and exactly the same percentage three decades later, which meant fierce competition among the

---

* The HBC was actually a latecomer among Canadian department stores. As well as the major Eaton's and Simpsons chains originating in Toronto, there were Jas. A. Ogilvy's, Morgan's and Dupuis Frères in Montreal; Bowring's in St John's; Wood Brothers in Halifax; Manchester, Robertson, Allison in Saint John; Paquet's and Pollack's in Quebec City; Charles Ogilvy's in Ottawa; Robinson's in Hamilton; Smith's in Windsor; Goudie's in Kitchener; Smallman and Ingram's in London; Williams's in Regina; Spencer's in Victoria; and Woodward's in Vancouver.

existing players and minimal profit margins. Figures released by Harry Stevens's 1934 Royal Commission on Price Spreads showed that only the HBC's coal sales were keeping the retail operation in the black, and Peter Wood estimated that the stores had actually never made a profit.*

By the time Lord Strathcona had completed his interminable governorship in 1914, the HBC was accurately described as being "more of an historical curiosity than a vital enterprise, because it had failed dismally to keep pace with the Dominion." Although London retained its power under Strathcona's immediate successors (Sir Thomas Skinner and Sir Robert Kindersley), the Canadian Advisory Committee named in 1912 had no authority beyond helping London keep in touch with local conditions. It included Sir William Whyte, the Winnipeg-based retired vice-president of the CPR's western division, and George Galt (a nephew of Sir Alexander Tilloch Galt, one of the Fathers of Confederation), who had established Blue Ribbon Limited, a Winnipeg wholesale grocery house, and become a director of three of the city's touchstone companies: Great-West Life, Northern Trusts and Manitoba Bridge & Iron Works. The Galt family lived at 460 Wellington Crescent, described as "the finest house from Fort William to the coast," and George Gait remained on the Canadian Committee until 1928. Augustus Nanton, the third of the original Committee members, was a central figure in Winnipeg financial circles who served on the boards of Great-West Life and Manitoba Bridge & Iron Works and turned the investment firm of Osier, Hammond & Nanton into a major player in prairie land and resource ventures.†

Nanton could not exercise much Canadian influence on the HBC because the land and fur-trade commissioners reported directly to London. Even worse, the key department-store operation was run by Herbert E. Burbidge, whose

---

* HBC earnings between 1947 and 1983, for example, totalled $897.5 million, while income from all non-merchandise sources (including land sales, fur auctions and oil royalties) amounted to $954.2 million. That meant a *loss* of $56.7 million attributable to the department stores in thirty-seven years. (The calculation assumed the stores had to finance their own debt loads and did not take into account the fact that operating the outlets increased their real-estate values.)

† The extent of Nanton's participation showed up in the fact that twelve western towns and cities have streets named after him, and there is still a Nanton, Alberta, between Calgary and Fort Macleod. An early nationalist, Nanton protested when an American firm was hired to make a film commemorating the HBC's 250th anniversary in 1920 and prohibited the abbreviation U.S.A. from appearing anywhere in the presentation. When Nanton became a key animator in the citizens' committee organized in 1919 to quash the General Strike, his farm was a target for demonstrators, who burned down the stable.

father headed Harrods and was a London-based director of the Bay. Only thirty years old when he was handed responsibility for the Canadian retail outlets, clearly modelled on the Harrods Brompton Road department store, the young Burbidge moved the headquarters of the retailing division to Vancouver, where he was comfortably settled, and allowed the individual units to fend for themselves. This meant giving up the advantage of mass buying, with the manager of every department in each store free to set his own mark-ups and credit policies. The chain soon became unmanageable—even if in 1914 its profit (£63,757) for the first time surpassed that of the fur department (£55,008). By 1919, Burbidge, who turned out to be allergic to hard work, was fired and later supplanted by Edward Fitzgerald, a former CPR assistant purchasing agent, who was appointed the Canadian Committee's full-time Deputy Chairman. He had little merchandising experience, found himself the pawn of games played between Winnipeg and London, and within six years returned to the relative calm of railroading. His main legacy was that during his stewardship the Canadian Advisory Committee (from now on simply called the Canadian Committee) was granted slightly more authority, including the naming of some senior appointees, but the Company had meanwhile acquired a much more profitable sideline.

SIR ROBERT MOLESWORTH KINDERSLEY, who served as Governor from 1915 to 1925, was also chairman of the London affiliate of Lazard Frères, the Anglo-French merchant bank, and it was through his Paris connections that the HBC gained a unique opportunity. Using Jean Monnet, wartime organizer of the French government's emergency International Supply Committee (and later father of the Treaty of Rome that spawned Europe's Common Market), as a go-between, he negotiated appointment of the Hudson's Bay Company as the French government's transportation agency for the duration of the First World War.* The contract would eventually net the Company £1,265,000 for five years' involvement, the most profitable single transaction in its long history, but it took a lot of doing. Thrown into disarray by the initial German advances, the French government had moved to Bordeaux and was desperately seeking a way of supplying its population with foodstuffs and its troops with ammunition. There being no effective

* As a reward, Monnet later was granted a £40,000 "loan," most of which was written off. Its existence was not mentioned in Monnet's memoirs or in the hbc's annual reports.

French merchant marine available, Alexandre Millerand, France's war minister, named the HBC the country's chief purchasing agent to arrange international credits and charter the ships required to deliver the goods.

The Company's 1-percent commission on these transactions was well earned. The Bay Steamship Company, a hastily set-up subsidiary, chartered 286 merchant ships totalling 1.58 million tons deadweight, which carried 13 million tons of supplies to French ports. In addition to grains from Canada, Argentina, Algeria and Australia and sugar from Cuba, Java and Martinique, their cargoes included coal from England and the United States, groundnuts and palm-kernels from Morocco, and airplane parts from Casablanca.

By war's end, the Company was operating the world's third-largest merchant fleet, loading 11,000 tons of goods daily—the equivalent of the *Nonsuch's* cargo every seven minutes.* It had been contracted to carry out similar supply missions for Romania and the White Russian Army (following the Bolshevik Revolution), through an agency at Archangel. The Company's house flag—the Red Ensign with the letters HBC on the fly—became a recognized and proud symbol in ports the world over, the more so since German submarines, storms, icebergs and fires at sea sank 110 of the Bay ships. The maritime commerce was highly profitable but horrendously complicated. Towards the end of 1917, for example, the HBC undertook management of four large Russian liners capable of carrying 13,000 passengers that became international ferries, taking Central Europeans, Belgians, Romanians and Argentines out of Russia before collapse of the Tsarist regime. The German steamer *Prinz Heinrich*, interned in Portugal where she had been requisitioned by the government, was chattered by the British government, then sublet to the French government, which turned her over to be operated by the HBC. The Company used her to repatriate Russian Jews who preferred returning home to service in the British Army. (Each passenger had to be provided with kosher rations for the long railway trip from Murmansk to Petrograd.)

Co-ordinating such complex arrangements and handling assignments for the Company's 145 purchasing agents went far beyond the HBC's existing

---

* One problem was that the Company soon ran out of titles for its expanded fleet and began using such forms as *Bayford, Bayleerran, Bayfield, Baynwunt, Baysoto, Baychattan* and so on. The names, one of the HBC's senior officials explained to Jean Monnet, should be limited to "10 letters, that is including the first three [Bay], the reason being that they can then be telegraphed as one word, and this, over the course of a year, makes quite a little economy compared with the names which cost two or three words."

knowledge or established facilities. The London staff was expanded from 10 to 120, and to head the operation Kindersley hired, as the HBC's full-time Deputy Governor, Charles Vincent Sale, president of his family's firm of coal shippers, F.G. Sale & Sons, whose unoriginal motto was "Coals to Newcastle." Sale and Kindersley had swung many deals together, providing rails to the Japanese for construction of the Manchurian Railway as well as trading arms, cotton, coal and metals between the United States, Belgium and the Orient. Both men were close to Lord Cowdray, Minister for Air in Lloyd George's wartime cabinet, and had made friends with Sir John Anderson, who as Lord Waverley would subsequently become an HBC director. A tall, pink-faced workaholic, complete with white military moustache, bowler hat and wing collar, Sale was pompous and could be fussy. Dora Darby, who was his secretary, recalled that he sometimes came into the HBC offices on Saturdays and "checked the girls' work stations searching for cosmetics. He put any he found on their desks to indicate they did not belong in an office. He was very strait-laced, and when he was in charge, every stenographer knew not to cross her legs in front of a man while taking dictation." Bob Chesshire, who worked for the Company at the time, remarked, "He was a peculiar sort of chap who suffered from a tropical liver and was quite likely to pick up a dictionary and heave it at someone he didn't like."

THE SHARPEST BREAK IN THE CONTINUITY of the old executive system in the Company was caused by the war. The immense profits from the French engagement perpetuated the illusion of management by the London Governor and directorate while the end of the temporary profits eventually made all too plain the dilapidation of its Canadian affairs.*

Ignoring this underlying weakness, the Company chose this very moment to stage the most elaborate and most expensive pageant in its history. The Hudson's Bay Company celebrated its 250th birthday on May 2, 1920, and Sir Robert Kindersley decided to visit Canada—only the third reigning Governor

---

* One business that briefly flourished around that time was bootlegging. Canadian provinces had passed laws prohibiting the sale though not the manufacture of alcoholic beverages, but since each province could enforce laws only within its own borders, booze could easily be transported for sale in other jurisdictions. The HBC immediately established a dozen mail-order houses from Kenora to Revelstoke and installed a Winnipeg bottling plant, capable of turning out four hundred cases daily, to supply its own brands to these outlets. Income peaked in 1917 at $2,260,627.

ever to do so.* Each Company unit, including every northern post, was given a grant to join in the festivities and every employee received a month's extra wages.† Philip Godsell, an imaginative veteran who after joining the Company in 1906 had travelled more than 100,000 miles by dog team, snowshoe and canoe, was placed in charge of planning the celebration. It was to be the last great Company occasion, and Godsell made the most of it.

On May 1, 1920, Kindersley addressed the Winnipeg staff at a gala dinner in the Hotel Fort Garry. He quickly got the guests on side by announcing a relatively generous non-contributory pension plan and pledged $1,225,000 to its trust fund. "I look to the future of the fur trade with a feeling of utmost confidence," he declared. "The last three years have shown the best results of any years in the history of the Company." The speech prompted loud cheers, several choruses of "For He's a Jolly Good Fellow," and a new Company song to the tune of "There's a Long, Long Trail A-Winding." The fur traders, ships' captains, department store managers, clerks and servants formed a happy, chanting line, marching around the dining-room enmeshed in nets of paper streamers.‡

Climax of the Canadian celebrations was the great spectacle Godsell staged at Lower Fort Garry, once the proud domicile of Sir George Simpson. Indian chiefs and their retinues came from every corner of the HBC's former empire— Swampy Cree from Hudson and James bays, Saulteaux from Lake Winnipeg, Ojibwas from the Nipigon country, Sioux from the Portage Plains, and mighty warriors from the Peace and Athabasca valleys. "For a while," Godsell noted, "the atmosphere of earlier and more picturesque days hovered about the Old Stone Fort. Silhouetted against the painted tepee covers at night the shadowy figures carried the mind back to days of long ago.... Within the walls all was quiet and silent though the tent occupied by the two Mounted Policemen who kept watch was dimly lighted with a coal-oil lantern. An occasional light flickered from the Governor's residence and there was a peculiar tranquillity

---

* The others had been Sir Stafford Northcote, who had briefly visited Montreal and Ottawa in 1870, and Lord Strathcona, though that was a special case because he had been the only Governor in the Company's history to work his way up through the HBC's Canadian service.
† The Company's assets at the time consisted of eleven major department stores, six wholesale houses, three hundred fur-trading posts, eighty-six steam and motor vessels, twelve hundred canoes, six hundred sledge dogs and 2.5 million acres of desirable prairie agricultural land.
‡ At a dinner for the London staff, Deputy Governor Sale gave a similar oration, handing out 134 long-service medals. One warehouse worker topped the list with sixty years of servitude. In Winnipeg, John George McTavish Christie was presented with a special medal; his family had served a combined 238 years with the Company.

permeating the old fort and its surroundings, so different from the bustle of the city but a few short miles away." The following morning the Governor took the salute as birchbark canoes, York boats and dugouts sailed by the great stone fort, and cheering Winnipeggers lined the riverbanks. Salute guns boomed, the Governor's flag snapped in the wind, and Godsell introduced each tribal chief to the six-foot-six Governor, who looked exactly the way a benign despot should look. Godsell had arranged for the Company interpreter to censor the Indians' comments, so that when the Chief of the York Factory Cree, for instance, complained because the Company was not feeding his dogs, the comment was translated into a flowery tribute to "the Great Master of the Company." Long into the night could be heard the screech of fiddles and the tattoo of moccasined feet stamping out the Red River Jig and Eightsome Reel. "As I gazed at the flickering lights of the tepees and watched the shadowy forms of the old Indians passing the pipe once more from hand to hand," Godsell lamented, "I realized with a keen pang that history had been made that day, and that, with its passing, the old fort and the traditions which surrounded it had taken another long step towards antiquity."

The most important legacy of the celebrations was Kindersley's decision to establish *The Beaver,* a magazine "Devoted to the Interests of Those Who Serve the Hudson's Bay Company." It eventually became a superb journal of record chronicling the history of the Northwest. But under its first editor, a Chicago advertising man named Clifton Moore Thomas, *The Beaver* limited itself mainly to a hodgepodge of curling scores from the Saskatoon store, news of an engagement in Kamloops, photos of an office picnic in Victoria, the results of a pie-eating competition at Fort à la Corne, word of new tennis and quoits courts for the Winnipeg staff—all interwoven with hair-raising fur-trade accounts and glued together with bad Irish jokes and harmless homilies on how to increase sales.*

Kindersley also signed a contract with Bruno Weyers, a New York business agent who'd had previous dealings with the Company, to produce films. The subsidiary eventually purchased two Hollywood studios and during the next decade produced thirty-seven two-reel films featuring such stars as Buster Keaton, Helen Morgan, James Melton, the Easy Aces and the Pickens Sisters. Some of the films premiered in Broadway's best first-run houses, but the

---

* *The Beaver*'s scope and quality improved dramatically under its subsequent editors, Robert Watson, Douglas MacKay, Clifford Wilson, Malvina Bolus, Helen Burgess and Christopher Dafoe.

advent of the big Hollywood productions killed the business, and the HBC wrote off its investment.*

THE PROFIT WINDFALL from its shipping operations had camouflaged its financial instability, but the Company could not compete in the volatile post-war market because its traditional methods emphasized conservative mark-up policies instead of customer-enticing price cuts and quality of service ahead of high volume. Charles Vincent Sale took over as Governor from Kindersley in 1925 and a year later the new Winnipeg super-store was opened. It covered an entire city block and had all the latest equipment. Its two massive banks of six elevators each faced one another on the street floor in a concave configuration. "The consequence of this layout," noted James Bryant, who worked there at the time, "was that every customer wishing to visit any floor other than the main one, congregated in the elevator lobby. It was so restricted in size and shape that even small crowds caused utter confusion.... Customers ran back and forth to catch elevators, only to have doors close as they reached them. Many became convinced that all the elevators on one side only went up and those on the other side only went down, an idea encouraged by some management trainees who, despite the scarcity of jobs, were not above having a little joke at the customers' expense."

Sale, who enjoyed risk and knew the Company desperately needed to diversify, had entertained an unusual visitor in his London offices before coming to Canada for his annual inspection tour in 1926. He was Ernest Whitworth Marland, born at Pittsburgh in 1874 when oil was $2.70 a barrel, who had struck his first gusher in West Virginia and soon founded his own Marland Oil company with headquarters in Ponca City, Oklahoma.

Applying his practical grasp of petroleum geology and his natural instinct for the hunt, he hit it big in 1911 with the ninth well drilled on land owned by Willie Cries-for-War near the Osage Indian Reservation. He went on to develop Marland Oil into a major company but spent his money even faster than he made it.

---

* The Company commissioned a forgettable eight-reeler about itself called *The Romance of the Fur Country,* and jealously guarded its reputation. When another film-maker produced a shoddy thriller entitled *The Lure of the North,* the HBC's lawyers got changes made in the print depicting a heroic-looking free trader being crushed by a brutal (unnamed, but British) fur monopoly whose agents burned his shack, stole his provisions, then dispatched him across something ominously called The Long Traverse.

Marland fenced in a tract of four hundred acres near Ponca and turned it into a pseudo-upper-class British estate, complete with polo fields, peacocks, ponies and hounds. Across the savage prairie of Oklahoma Marland and his pals would spend long afternoons, mounted on British hunters, following British hounds on the scent of British foxes. The son of a Scottish mother and an English father, Marland was so infatuated with Anglophile values that he went to grade school dressed in a kilt, and arrived in the wild Indian country during his oil-hunting days wearing a belted tweed jacket, knickerbockers and spats. He often visited London to recharge these pretensions and on one such trip made a deal with the Hudson's Bay Company to exploit the mineral rights it had retained (from 1910 onwards) on 4.5 million acres of the Canadian West, checkerboarded across Manitoba, Saskatchewan and Alberta.

Sale and Marland worked out a simple arrangement: in return for providing the technical knowledge and paying all exploration expenses, Marland was granted a twenty-five-year option to lease any parcel of land for drilling purposes, with the HBC receiving a royalty on any oil or gas produced.* Three years later, when Marland's personal spending habits caught up with him and he had to amalgamate his company with Continental Oil, the two concerns formed Hudson's Bay Oil & Gas (HBOG), with the HBC owning 25 percent (later reduced to 21.9 percent) of the stock.

By the mid-1920s, when the shift from Kindersley to Sale took place, chairmanship of the Canadian Committee passed from Nanton to George Allan, who was soon joined by such Winnipeg worthies as James Armstrong Richardson, Robert Gourley, Conrad Riley and Hugh Lyall. They had all the required credentials: Richardson was president of his family's firm, head of the Winnipeg Grain Exchange, a director of the CPR and the Canadian Bank of Commerce, and in the decade that ended in 1929 accumulated one of Canada's great fortunes. Richardson's horizons, unlike those of most other HBC Committeemen, reached far beyond Winnipeg. The Richardsons have always had all of Canada for a playground.† Gourley was the animating force in Beaver Lumber and a director of such other Winnipeg touchstone compa-

---

* Significantly, the partnership missed leasing the Athabasca tar sands, said to hold the world's largest oil reserves, because it viewed them only as a substitute for asphalt in road building. The two companies opened only one filling station, near the HBC's Winnipeg store, which sold Marland lubricating products but gasoline supplied by Imperial Oil.
† When Richardson died of a heart attack at sixty-four in 1939, the *Winnipeg Free Press* lowered the flags on its building to half-mast.

nies as Monarch Life and Manitoba Bridge & Iron Works, and had been Canadian curling champion. Riley had worked for seven years on the Northern Pacific Railway before moving to Winnipeg to take a job in his father's Canadian Fire Insurance Company. He was, of course, also a director of Beaver Lumber and Great-West Life. Lyall had slightly different connections, being one of the rare HBC Committeemen who was not a director of either Monarch or Great-West, but he did establish Manitoba Bridge & Iron Works, was on the board of Northern Trusts, and president of Dominion Tanners, both companies controlled by the Rileys. George Allan, who had been a Committee member since 1914, remained Chairman until 1940. True to form, he was a director of Great-West Life and Northern Trusts, but, unlike his predecessors and successors, he devoted most of his time to the Company's affairs. A graduate of Upper Canada College and Trinity University in Toronto, he had co-founded one of Winnipeg's largest law firms (Munson & Allan) and had been responsible for channelling millions of dollars' worth of British investment into the Canadian West. A Conservative MP from 1917 to 1921, he was a political traditionalist, once complaining in a letter to London that "democracy has its valuable and strong features, but it certainly has its weak ones. I suppose it is natural that during a long drawn out period, activities of crooks, cranks, university professors, school masters and a clergyman with extreme socialistic views [J.S. Woodsworth], miracle workers and pedlars of paradise, should have their innings and their place under the sun, and that the product of their combined efforts should be a Social Credit Party, a CCF Party, a Communist Party and a Labour Party."

London, too, had been undergoing important physical and personnel changes. Governor Sale was coming under increasingly virulent attack for the Company's inability to turn adequate earnings on its huge department stores. Despite these uncertainties, the Company invested the bulk of its wartime profits in a new head office building on Great Trinity Lane, opposite the famed Church of St Ethelburga the Virgin in Bishopsgate.* Designed by Oscar Faber, Hudson's Bay House was a curious, turreted edifice that needed a large formal garden around it to bring out its lines. The Company also built Beaver House on Garlick Hill in the 1920s, and for the first time in two centuries, the HBC's

---

*To prevent any variation in light quality, the walls and floors of these grading chambers were glazed with sand-blasted non-reflecting battleship-grey tiles.

fur auction could once again be held at its own premises. Inside, there was refrigerated storage space for two million pelts and large fur-grading rooms under double windows with a northern exposure.* The halls and boardroom were decorated with paintings of former governors, narwhal tusks and ship models in cases. After the Hudson's Bay House building was sold, this structure also accommodated the Company offices.

In Canada, the Company's stores were being transformed. Through the direct intervention of Deputy Governor Sir Frederick Henry Richmond, managing director of Debenhams, a large London department store, the HBC's retailing outlets were placed in the charge of P.J. Parker, a former Boston merchandiser who had set up his own store across the road from the HBC's Calgary outlet and had been bought out to obtain his services. A tiny creature who appeared to have walked straight out of the pages of *Pickwick Papers*, he had rosy cheeks and always wore gloves and matching spats. But Parker was a misanthropic presence who angered his fellow employees with his lusty ways, and he lasted for less than a year. In his place was appointed an obscure British accountant named Philip Chester, who would exercise almost as significant an impact on the Hudson's Bay Company as had Sir George Simpson a century earlier.

---

* It was at this stone sanctuary, dating back at least to 1430, that Henry Hudson received communion on April 19, 1607, before setting off on the voyage of exploration that would eventually provide the Company with its initial base of operations.

Trans-Atlantic Blood Feud

*The Governor and the hbc's Canadian General Manager understood that,
like two scorpions in a bottle, only one would emerge the victor.*

WHILE PHILIP CHESTER WOULD TURN OUT to be the dominant force in
creating the modern Hudson's Bay Company, neither his tenure nor its success
would have been possible without the operational matrix set down by Charles
Vincent Sale. Eventually deposed as the HBC's Governor in a shareholder
revolt triggered by charges of self-dealing, during his sixteen years in the
Company's two top jobs Sale turned its operations upside down. Not only was
he largely responsible for generating the wartime profit that financed its
growth through the uncertain 1920s but he also transformed the HBC from
mainly a fur-trading house and general-store business into a mass retailer.
Unlike most of his predecessors, he took more than a passing interest in
Canada, spending three months of every year touring the Company's stores,
and, as a parting gesture, granted the Canadian Committee most of the
authority it had always wanted. At the same time, he widened the Company's
horizons by throwing its archives open to historians and hiring a young Oxford
zoologist (Charles Elton) as a consultant to study fluctuations in Arctic animal
populations.

What really brought Sale down was the Depression. The great department
stores he had built across the West were transformed almost overnight from
luxurious merchandising palaces into drafty nightmares with huge overheads.
The new Winnipeg store alone had an annual carrying charge of $3.3 million,
while Vancouver, at $2.6 million, was nearly as expensive. Gross margins had
to be increased to 38.5 percent of selling price just to meet overhead costs,

making it difficult to turn any profit. Between 1929 and 1931, operating losses in the retail division jumped from $182,000 to more than $2 million. Sale's plight was aggravated by shareholder expectations. "Many of them had acquired their shares in the same confidence of steady returns with which they would have opened a savings account," wrote HBC archivist Anne Morton, and, "bitterly disappointed, were now out for blood. Sale was the obvious scapegoat."

London's initial response to the Depression's onset was to dispatch Lord Ebury, one of its senior directors, to Canada for a first-hand report.* He was appalled at the laxness of some of the staff, condemning P.J. Parker, then in charge of stores, as being unfit for the job. "Amongst his chief weaknesses— apart from Drink—are a tendency to jump into action without proper fore- thought," Ebury reported. "He fails to appreciate the supreme importance of ... living up to agreements and promises, and he is inclined to be a bit of a 'slick.'"

In contrast, Ebury had nothing but praise for Philip Alfred Chester, who had been assigned to Canada by Sale as Chief Accountant in 1925 after having joined the London staff as a junior two years previously. "Mr. Chester," wrote Ebury, "is, in my opinion, brilliantly clever and certainly one of the quickest thinking men I have come across in a long time." The visiting peer added a prophetic footnote: "He suffers from high blood pressure and needs careful nursing; one of the drawbacks of Winnipeg is that this man is never free of his work, or thinking or talking shop." Ebury strongly recommended that the Canadian Committee, then headed by George Allan, be given power to deal with the Company's staff appointments and daily operations. His suggestion was confirmed at the Court of proprietors on June 27, 1930, and put into effect by Sale himself during a Winnipeg visit shortly afterwards.

The essential element in the reorganization that followed was the appoint- ment of Chester as General Manager for Canada, at an annual salary of $20,000. Although the London board's resolution had conferred on the

---

* Francis Egerton Grosvenor, 4th Lord Ebury was one of the most-decorated officers of the Canadian Expeditionary Force in the First World War. He came out from England and spent the early years of the century in the Kootenays as an assayer for smelters at Trail and Nelson, and after 1910 worked on the Duke of Sutherland's land-settlement plan in Alberta. He joined the 29th Battalion CEF (Tobin's Tigers) in Vancouver in 1914, and won the DSO and bar, the MC and bar, and the Croix de Guerre with palm. He was mentioned in dispatches five times, was wounded, and ended the war staff officer with the 4th Canadian Division. He served on the board of the HBC and another City institution, the Royal Exchange Assurance.

Canadian Committee "full powers of attorney" and all necessary arrangements "for the due exercise thereof," the true meaning of these phrases would be argued over for the next forty years. "There seemed afterwards to be some misconception of what was really arranged with the then Governor on this side of the water and what apparently was the conception at head office," admitted Allan in a speech to his Calgary staff, "but that was very soon washed away.... As I put it, if they desired us to relieve them and take over the management, administration and control, that it might as well be one hundred percent, and that the horns had better go with the hide."

The HBC's affairs were clearly in crisis, and its proprietors began demanding a drastic shakeup. In London, the fight to unseat Sale and his board was led by a solicitor named Charles Louis Nordon. A highly effective campaigner on behalf of minority shareholders' rights and dividend incomes, he was incensed with the Hudson's Bay Company's dismal earnings record and eventually fought the Company of Adventurers to a standstill. "My father considered it to be one of his greatest legal triumphs," recalled Keith Nordon of his father's clash with the HBC, "in that he was well and truly up against not only an enormous Company but also against almost the whole of the City of London in that, in the big dispute, the City naturally sided with the powerful Hudson's Bay." At one point, things got so nasty that Nordon (who held 740 shares in 1927 and whose family had been investing in HBC stock since 1873) was physically barred from one of the HBC's annual Courts and had to sneak in through a fire escape.

Nordon had first challenged Sale on the fact that between 1920 and 1925, the Company had sold land worth £1,987,738 while paying out £1,750,922 in taxes—a levy which, when added to administrative expenses, meant the land sales had been a futile waste of potential future assets. It was a perfectly reasonable criticism, but Sale chose to ignore it because Nordon was too insignificant a shareholder. Nordon continued to bombard the directors with meticulously researched queries in the later 1920s so that even proprietors who had at first considered him a noisy nuisance began to pay attention. He was particularly incensed by the revelation that in 1927, which was not an especially bad year, the Company had been able to earn only £151,909 on its £6,779,656 investment in the fur trade and sales shops.

Having been barred from corresponding with the Company, Nordon began issuing a series of circulars condemning its fiscal performance and the integrity of its directors. He organized a shareholders' vigilante group that included several major investors including Captain Victor Alexander Cazalet (the HBC's largest stockholder with 40,500 shares), who demanded action.* The shareholders were particularly frustrated by the Company's practice of diverting profits to something called a "dividend equalization fund," which was really a reserve account, preventing more generous dividend distribution.

But it was Nordon's pointed attacks on the Governor's integrity that finally broke Sale's hold and reputation. Nordon had accused Sale of self-dealing in the 1920 purchase by the HBC, for £60,000, of a 15-percent interest in the Merchant Trading Company, owned mostly by the Sale family. Used during the Great War as a purchasing agency for the shipping operation, the firm had continued in business but returned the HBC almost no dividends. Although it was never identified as such, the HBC acquisition of Sale's shares had been more in the nature of an interest-free loan to reward the then Deputy Governor for his wartime services. Sale's great mistake was to pretend that it had been a legitimate business transaction, thus trapping himself into defending the indefensible.

At the 1930 annual Court, Nordon asked that an internal committee be set up to investigate the Company's affairs. Its report, tabled five months later, vindicated Sale but suggested the HBC's stores be run by a newly established, Canadian-domiciled HBC subsidiary. Since Sale had just approved a similar arrangement, or at least granted the Canadian Committee all the authority it could handle, there seemed to be no reason for him to resign. Yet he left the governorship just before publication of the report, leading contemporary observers to believe there had been a secret deal: that Sale would be officially exonerated from the accusations of self-dealing by his peers in return for clearing up all the suspicion surrounding the Company by agreeing to abandon his post.

The resignation took place during an extraordinary Court, held at the City Terminus Hotel on Cannon Street on January 16, 1931. Company records pointed to a loss of £746,334 for the fiscal year, which meant there would be no cash for dividends. With the worth of its assets reduced by an astonishing £2 million in the previous twelve months—and facing the prospect of an

* Four times the British (and once the Canadian) squash champion, Cazalet had attended Eton and Oxford (where he earned four Blues), fought with distinction in the trenches during the Great War, and was later elected a Member of Parliament. He inherited the HBC stake from his father. He was killed with General Wladyslaw Sikorski, the Polish premier in exile, in the crash of a Liberator bomber off Gibraltar in 1943.

extended economic downturn—the Company seemed well on its way to technical bankruptcy. Shareholders nearly went berserk, calling for the resignation of the entire board and nominating members of the Nordon committee to take their place. Chaired by Deputy Governor Sir Frederick Richmond, the noisy meeting would not allow Sale to speak. When he rose briefly to reassert his innocence in the Merchant Trading affair, he was shouted down and could barely be heard, lamenting: "For my shortcomings I ask your forgiveness." Five other directors eventually stepped down, and were replaced by three Nordon nominees, including Cazalet. A new board was elected, led by the redoubtable Edward Peacock, but the most important item on the agenda was the appointment of a new governor.

THE MAN PICKED TO RESCUE THE COMPANY at this difficult moment was Patrick Ashley Cooper, and his selection was no accident. In an act of direct, almost brutal intervention unprecedented in the HBC's long history, Montagu Norman, Governor of the Bank of England, personally assigned Cooper to the job, then went on to choose Sir Alexander Murray, one of the City's ablest financiers, to be Cooper's Deputy.* In case there might be any doubt about the weight of authority behind his nominations, Norman sent a letter to C.L. Nordon not only affirming his personal regard for Cooper but placing the Company of Adventurers in its appropriate context. "I alone selected Mr. Patrick Ashley Cooper and recommended him as suitable for the Governorship of the Hudson's Bay Company," he wrote. "I am not concerned with the affairs of the Hudson's Bay Company except as regards the Governorship and that owing to the prestige and imperial importance of the Company." Norman stressed the same historical link during a private briefing with Cooper. "Your task," said the Governor of the Bank of England to the Governor of the Hudson's Bay Company, "is to rebuild a bridge of Empire."

A tall, awkward Scot with round tortoise-shell glasses and a crisp military moustache, Cooper could be kind and approachable, though he never softened his attitude of trying to run the firm like the headmaster of a rowdy boys' school. With the sombre suits he favoured draped over his six-foot-four frame,

---

* Yet another of those peripatetic Scottish financiers who held the Empire together, Murray had spent three decades in India, occupying most of its important administrative positions, including a five-year stint as Governor of the Imperial Bank of India. He later became a director of Lloyds Bank and the Bank of London and South America, remaining a solid influence on the Hudson's Bay board until 1946.

he commanded instant attention—and got it. Born in middle circumstances at Aberdeen, Cooper attended Fettes College in Edinburgh (Scotland's Eton), then read law at Aberdeen and went on to Trinity Hall, Cambridge, where his long arms helped him win an oar. Badly wounded in the back while serving as an infantry major during the Great War, he became a City accountant and did so well that the Bank of England began asking him to act on its behalf in helping salvage near-defunct British companies around the globe. At forty-three and married to the beautiful Welsh heiress Kathleen Spickett, he became an important figure in London society, having won kudos for success-fully liquidating the Banco Italo-Britannica in Milan and rescuing the Primitiva Gas Company of Buenos Aires. He had accepted the difficult job of turning the Hudson's Bay Company around in the bearpit of the Depression on condition that his initial salary of £5,000 be raised when the economy improved. Despite his relatively meagre stipend, Cooper brought the July 1931 proprietors' Court to its feet with the offer to reduce his pay by 10 percent. "Are we to devote ourselves," he demanded, "to searching in the past or build-ing for the future?"

"Both!" cried out an Adventurer.

"No. It cannot be both. You must make up your minds whether you are going to ask us to dig into the past, or go forward into the future, and *that* is the decision I shall ask you to make." It was a clever ploy because the Company's proprietors had become so mesmerized by recent troubles they had lost sight of the future. For the next three years that future was grim indeed, with losses totalling £3.6 million. Cooper threw himself into his new job, leaving almost immediately for Canada, eager to meet Philip Chester, the new General Manager.

The omens were not good. Just before he left England, Cooper was informed by the Canadian Committee that henceforth communications to London would be dispatched monthly instead of weekly and that, oh yes, P.J. Parker, the Canadian operation's highest-ranking executive in charge of stores, had just been fired. In reporting these changes to the Governor, Chester—speaking through Canadian Committee Chairman George Allan—lamely apologized for not having first consulted or even notified the London board. "It was purely an oversight," Allan explained, "… caused by very great stress of work at the time."

Cooper arrived in Montreal on September 3, 1931, and the first entry in his private diary reflected his sour mood: "Went to Ritz-Carlton. General

Manager of the HBC in the Hotel and still in bed." His outlook didn't improve at the breakfast he had next morning in the Windsor Hotel. He ordered "a pot of tea. Dry toast, butter on the side. *English* marmalade and two eggs boiled three minutes ... three minutes precisely." When the waiter arrived, all was as requested, but there was only one eggcup with *one* egg perched on it. Cooper, according to his breakfast companion, berated the hotel employee mercilessly, calling him a "stupid colonial" and similar epithets. He stopped only when the waiter, with white-gloved hand and beatific smile, lifted the eggcup to reveal the missing egg, boiled three minutes precisely.

The Governor's mood brightened considerably when he was summoned to Ottawa for a private meeting with the Prime Minister, only to find that the Right Honourable R.B. Bennett was, as Cooper confided to his journal, "cordial and helpful, but most critical of the Company, its higher personnel and policy." Still, he stayed at Rideau Hall, the Governor General's official residence, with the Earl of Bessborough and went swimming in the Chateau Laurier pool wearing a bathing suit borrowed from CNR Chairman Sir Henry Thornton that had "room for myself and two others." In Toronto he met most of the men who mattered—Sir Joseph Flavelle, Sir John Aird, E.R. Wood, W.E. Rundle—and was shown around Eaton's (by R.Y. Eaton) and Simpsons (by C.L. Burton). He then went off to Winnipeg and a tour of the Company's retail operation, at one point "driving down the main street of Kamloops to examine our competitors' windows." By the time he left, two months later, Cooper was not at all pleased with what he had seen. "I was dismayed at what I found," he noted. "As soon as I arrived in Winnipeg, it was perfectly obvious to me that the state of misunderstanding and tension between London and Winnipeg had almost reached an open breach...." Later, Cooper summarized the areas of serious concern he had uncovered. He had found not one department or subsidiary operation that wasn't losing money; "great and thoughtless extravagance in all directions," he noted in his diary, "a sense of unthinking security throughout the whole staff," and "no general comprehension that the Company was nearing complete collapse...." As if that diagnosis wasn't gloomy enough, Cooper wisely concluded that his main problem would be learning to live with Chester, the thirty-five-year-old General Manager installed under Sale. Chester, the Governor felt, should have a different attitude towards London, one that would show loyalty to the British board and shareholders.

Fat chance.

MOST FACES BETRAY THE CHARACTER of their owners, reflecting the balance between their generous natures and niggardly emotions. But Chester's facial features were smooth and uncommunicative, like those of the masked man in *The Phantom of the Opera*—not ugly, but expressionless, designed to evoke in others emotions complementary to his own. His eyes were as blank as gun barrels, tinted pewter-grey, revealing nothing. His three-piece suits were all the same: immaculately tailored (by Lloyd Brothers in Toronto or one of the bespoke shops in Savile Row), but interchangeable; no one ever remembered anything he wore. Even his handshake was bereft of feeling. "Like taking hold of a piece of cold fish," one Bay employee recalled. "There was no squeeze. You let go quickly, because you got no response."

He grew up in a harsh and sterile place—Long Eaton, an industrial town in the working-class region of Derbyshire, where his mother (a Rhinelander) worked as a governess and his father as an intermittently employed millhand. In 1914, Philip, who was then barely eighteen, volunteered for the King's Royal Rifle Corps. The day he was set to leave for the Front—already dressed in his uniform and ready to board the troop train—his mother wanted to snap a picture of him with her Brownie. She aimed the camera, but young Philip's grandmother smashed it out of her hands with the admonition: "Not on the Sabbath!"

Chester won a field commission (to Staff Captain) and was severely wounded, both times on January 10, first in France and later on the Isonzo Front in northern Italy. He saved his gratuities and had just enough money to put himself through accounting school, then joined the Hudson's Bay Company's London office. He grew to love the Company, but his feelings were poisoned by his intense awareness that no matter what he did, no matter how successful within the HBC's hierarchy he might become, its upper-class directors would make him feel he didn't quite measure up, that he was of lowly birth, a man who had emigrated to make his way in a former colony. "However nice they are to you, they'll never accept you, because they know where you came from by the sound of your voice," Frank Walker, his executive assistant and later editor of the *Montreal Star*, had warned Chester after he had been feted at a social function by members of the London board. Years later, Lady Cooper, Sir Patrick's widow, confirmed that diagnosis. "Socially," she recalled, "Chester wasn't in the same group as the other people he worked with. They were all on a higher plane in London. He thought they were always looking down on him, which made him feel mad. He was absolutely off his head. My husband was being invited to stay at Sandringham ... the King would invite him to go down. Then he was made a director of the Bank of England, and Chester hated him more than ever. He'd never even *met* the Governor of the Bank of England. My husband was moving in those circles—miles above Philip."

But Chester knew the rules of the game and how it was played. Confronted by the icy nuances of the British class system, he decided to find a suitable exit. He couldn't change his birthplace, but he could fix his speech, and eventually he did. He invented a new persona for himself to bypass the upper-class English habit of accepting or dismissing individuals on the basis of their accents. His voice, melodious, incongruously rich coming through those pursed lips, marked him as a certified gentleman. "He never achieved the 'oink' of an old Etonian," remembered Charles Loewen, the Bay Street broker who married Chester's daughter, Susanne. "His became an unidentifiable English accent, a sort of Alistair Cooke inflection."

That transformation, as significant as it may have been to his future, had to be put on hold until Chester could deal with the crisis of confidence at the Company's Canadian headquarters and impose discipline on an organization that had spun out of control. Chester began a major reorganization of the fur department under the direction of Ralph Parsons and later Bob Chesshire, while Western Arctic Manager Dudley Copland winnowed the number of posts from nineteen to fourteen. He had Company engineers experiment with and use insulation materials for the northern posts, masterminded development of a radio medical network and initiated research into permafrost. In charge of retail operations he placed a Massachusetts-born merchandising specialist named Francis F. Martin. It was not a popular choice. "He was a rude, ruthless, egoistical despot," recalled John Enright, then in charge of the sewing machine department. "Even dress regulations were laid down, with salesladies expected to wear conservative black or navy and short sleeves permitted only if they were at least four inches below the armpit." Chester and Martin would reassign the coal-department manager from one store to run the corset department of another.

Even if his methods were crude, Chester shook up the stores' bureaucratic lethargy and moved them into the twentieth century. He insisted that the Company be a leader in personnel and wage administration policies; the HBC was one of the first national companies to name a woman (Joan Whiting) to an executive post. Chester was responsible for starting a preparatory course in merchandising in the Company. Advertising was increased; selection and variety became as important as mark-ups; self-service food floors were introduced; executive salaries were raised; training and profit-sharing became part of senior employees' fringe benefits. The unprofitable Lethbridge store was sold, and the cost-benefit ratio of each outlet was examined and re-examined. A strict rule against hiring relatives of existing employees was put into effect. Decentralized purchasing and consolidated management techniques allowed individual store managers freedom to match their merchandise selection more closely with their own communities' needs, while the central buying office in Winnipeg handled such staples as HBC blankets, sheets, towels, dried fruit and so on. To collect its bills from hard-pressed customers, the HBC employed its own bailiffs. Fred Herbert, who occupied that office in Vancouver, boasted that he was kindness personified while repossessing unpaid-for articles: "If there's kids in the house, I'll never take a stove, but I'll take a radio or gramophone goddamn quick."

Within a year of Chester's appointment, store profits were up 60 percent, and by 1937, though the Depression had hardly abated, most divisions had begun to prosper again.* What Chester achieved was to break the psychology, widespread among Company executives when he arrived, that it was their right to demand the trade of the public. The HBC's monopoly had been dead for more than half a century, but they had yet to react to the news.

Chester's store inspections were legendary. "He was positively vicious," recalled Bob Chesshire. "He would raise so much hell, you wouldn't know whether you were standing on your head or your feet. He wouldn't miss a thing, find ten things wrong on every floor, had everybody scared out of their wits, because we were all hanging on to our jobs by our eyebrows at the time. He used to place a lot of emphasis on cleanliness of toilets, and one poor store manager got into deep trouble because he hadn't finished having the washrooms painted, so Chester couldn't get in to see if they passed muster." Another time, in the Calgary store, Chester happened to pass a suggestion box. He asked how often it was cleared, and when he was assured it was at least

---

* Not so lucky was the HBC's oil investment. Chester had tried unsuccessfully to sell the Company's share in Hudson's Bay Oil & Gas to the Anglo-Ecuadorian Oilfields Company, and further investment funds in oil and gas exploration were cut off after September 1931. Three years later, HBOG signed a deal with the Northwest Company, a subsidiary of Imperial Oil, and eventually renewed it to June 1951, to allow the Esso subsidiary to explore the Company's holdings in return for a 50-percent share in the findings.

once a day, demanded it be opened. He read every suggestion, found one two weeks old, and sacked the store supervisor on the spot.

"Why must I be surrounded by bloody fools?" he often complained to anyone in range of his wrath. One senior executive who had momentarily displeased Chester was astounded to find the General Manager staring at him for a long moment, then pronouncing his verdict: "You know, whenever I look at you, I think we're a man short." George Weightman, who worked at head office at the time, had been assigned to produce an inventory of HBC blankets. He had trouble collecting the necessary documentation and one afternoon found that Chester had quietly stolen up behind him. "He stood looking silently on for a few minutes and then said: 'You know what's the matter with you, Weightman? You've got more records than we have blankets.'" Chesshire remembered being summoned into Chester's office (known as the holy of holies) only to find his temper in full flight. *"You!"* Chester began, an accusing finger pointed at Chesshire. *"You!* I *told* you what to do and they've buggered up the whole thing! Now you're just sitting there, with nothing to say!" Chesshire, one of the few head-office functionaries not actively terrified of Chester, calmed him down by investigating the situation and reporting back. "Chester made a lot of preposterous statements to deliberately get under your hide," he observed, "because he felt that it was sometimes the only way to get all the facts."

Chester was always testing people. Almost every conversation became an interrogation. But anyone brave enough to face him down usually won. "He was sitting in my office when I accused him of not having told me the truth about something," recalled Frank Walker. "'Are you calling me a liar?' he demanded. I calmly replied that to be a liar, he would have had to make a habit of not telling me the truth. Well, he marched out of there, and I didn't see him again until next morning, when he came in to apologize. I said there was no need to apologize; all he had to say was that he hadn't told me the truth. That got him fired up all over again, and he stormed out. He had been willing to be decent, but I was being a son of a bitch and had brought the issue up again. Finally, he came in just before lunch and mumbled, 'That's all you want me to say, that I didn't tell you the truth?' I told him that he didn't really have to say anything, so he shot back: 'All right, I didn't tell the truth'—and marched out of my office in high dudgeon, for the *third* time."

"There's no question that Chester used his outbursts to get precisely what he wanted, especially from the British board," mused John de B. Payne, the

HBC official who had hired Walker as one of Chester's executive assistants. "His temper was never vindictive, never personal, just temper really, as in, 'I've got an idea and this is the way I'm going to fight for it.' He was driven by an obsession for excellence and in seeking it was as harsh on himself as with others." Chester himself, looking back on his stewardship, wrote to E.F. Newlands, secretary of the Canadian Committee: "While I was a tough bird—perhaps too tough on many occasions—it was because of my constant urge to keep a first-class office and to be an example for the rest of the old Company. I had seen and lived in the sad Winnipeg H[ead] O[ffice] of the late twenties, which was a disgrace and a big contributor to the mess in which the Company found itself in those years."

While most HBC employees (who made up a new translation for the Company's initials as "Here Before Chester") viewed him as "living on Mount Olympus, occasionally hurling a thunderbolt," they were fairly often exposed to his exquisite political tactics. "He used to brief a group of us before each Canadian Committee meeting," recalled Pete Buckley, who worked with Chester at the time, "and we'd have to rehearse everything he wanted us to say, so that by the time we presented our case the Committee members could only agree. It kind of shocked me."

THE MAIN VICTIM of Chester's temper tantrums was Patrick Ashley Cooper, a target so perfect that if he hadn't existed he would have to have been made up. The Governor and the HBC's Canadian General Manager understood that, like two scorpions in a bottle, only one would emerge the victor. Once the Company had been turned around, the blood feud between Chester and Cooper over corporate territoriality took on the extra dimension of competing to get the credit for its hard-won return to profitability. For Chester, the great advantage of having Cooper to shoot at was that the British Governor had little sense of humour and never really understood his opponent. He genuinely believed that Chester's mood swings were physiological rather than tactical and could never figure out any way of controlling or silencing his Canadian colleague—apart, perhaps, from somehow court-martialling him or challenging him to a duel. The British Governor and the Canadian Manager both became obsessed with keeping one another at bay, studying every nuance of every letter they exchanged—the slant of the signature, the way the paper was folded—as though it were written in hieroglyphics signalling a wealth of hidden motives and meanings. Each was convinced that only his way of doing things was correct and that anyone who strayed one inch from his particular path to righteousness was a write-off. "They just didn't get along," recalled Cooper's widow. "They disagreed about everything, and each prickled when the other was near. Chester set out to run the Company from Canada, and my husband, from the moment he heard that, put his foot down, saying, 'Never. Over my dead body. It was founded by Prince Rupert. It has always been in London and will always be in London!' They were poles apart."

"Chester is so changeable," Cooper bitterly complained to his diary (August 2, 1934). "When he is in control of himself, a pleasure and anxious to do what he can for us ... but then again, swept by brain storms, he takes a ridiculous attitude almost amounting to open opposition to London, fighting over every detail." The diary bristles with complaints about Chester's behaviour. *November 27, 1936:* "Long talk with Chester. If the English language means anything, he was entirely reasonable and satisfactory. I fancy it was all eyewash." *January 7, 1943:* "Chester's behaviour abominable. He sat with a face black as thunder and contributed nothing except one or two outbursts ... he was very narrow minded and difficult. I was glad however that his ill temper and bad manners were exposed to the board." On his first trip to London as General Manager for Canada, Chester expressed his contempt for the annual Court proceedings. "I was given a seat on the rostrum so that I could look over a selection of our proprietors," he wrote to Allan, "and to me, the gathering resembled that of the representatives of a Diocese assembled together for the induction of a new Archbishop, rather than a bunch of intelligent and disturbed shareholders."

The two men had little in common except that they happened to have been born on the same island. Winnipeg was such a long way from London in those days, and the Governor seemed untouchable. He led a charmed life. Hexton Manor, his country seat, near Hitchin, in Hertfordshire, dates back to 1030, is mentioned in the Domesday Book and has been occupied by only sixteen different families since. If, as Noel Coward once pointed out, the stately homes of England existed to prove that the upper classes still had the upper hand, Cooper's home was a grand example of the genre. Set on a private lake in a 4,000-acre estate, it had twenty-eight rooms and that feeling of elegance-as-a-throwaway-gesture that marks the British gentry. The Coopers were invited to dine with the Prince of Wales at St James's Palace ("Another milestone!" he triumphantly noted in his diary on

February 21, 1934); he was named a director of the Bank of England ("From now onwards I enter the Bank as of right, and have a peg on which to hang my hat with my name over it!"—April 6, 1932); and on January 16, 1935, he and Kathleen went to Sandringham—the first HBC Governor to be invited to a royal residence since Sir Bibye Lake in 1713. ("Down to dinner where I met … Sir Herbert and Lady Fetherstonhaugh. Lady Meade-Fetherstonhaugh's first husband was Hesketh Pritchard who was at Fettes 7 years before me. I sat on the Queen's left.… When the ladies left the room the King called me around to sit by him and was full of questions about the Eskimos.")

Into the early 1950s, the HBC was still reckoned as something of a viceregal presence among Canadian companies, and the Governor's tours resembled a royal procession, with the Coopers treated like visiting heads of state, accompanied by flag-bearers and trailed by a retinue of flustered flunkies.* They would cross the Atlantic aboard one of the great liners, occupying a suite of two bedrooms, sitting room and bathroom on A deck, being seated nightly at the Captain's table. In Montreal, Cooper called on the greatest capitalists of the day, including Sir Herbert Holt, Sir Charles Gordon, Sir Edward Beatty and Arthur Purvis, the head of Canadian Industries Limited, the first Canadian executive to have a private airplane, who won the admiration of his peers for having chaired meetings in Montreal, Ottawa and Toronto on the same day.† Then on to Ottawa. "We were received by the Prime Minister, provincial premiers, and, of course, stayed at Government House—with the Bessboroughs, Tweedsmuirs, Athlones and Alexanders," recalled Lady Cooper. "They would lend us their private railway cars to travel in, and my husband

---

* One of the stranger legacies of Cooper's stewardship was his insistence that *The Beaver* publish photographs of him on safari. The magazine regularly featured candid shots of the Governor "shooting crocodile from the roof of a launch on the Kafue River in Northern Rhodesia" or the Governor "setting out on a duck expedition in the swamps of the Zambesi at Lealui village, ruled by King Yeta III." Exactly how this was supposed to raise the morale of the fur traders freezing their butts off at Baker Lake wasn't clear.

† On his 1939 visit, Cooper took a detour to meet Maurice Duplessis, the Union Nationale premier, in Quebec City. "The whole performance and atmosphere of his office was very like a provincial government office in the Argentine," he disdainfully noted in his diary [July 18, 1939]. "Unshaven secretaries sitting about and smoking innumerable cigarettes.… I went in and found the typical young Latin politician. He made it evident that he had no time to waste on me, for he kept one of the members of parliament with him.… During our short talk he made a few of his facetious remarks accompanied by winks, for which he is so famous."

had nicknames for all the young aides who worked at Rideau Hall. It was charming."*

After a triumphal stopover in Toronto (lunch at the Toronto Club with Principal W.L. Grant of Upper Canada College and calls, as always, on the heads of Simpsons and Eaton's), the caravan would roll into Winnipeg. The usual sparring with Chester and the Canadian Committee was followed by a visit to the Manitoba Club, where he gave a yearly address. "There were 63 present including the lieutenant governor, the premier, and almost everyone in Winnipeg of any importance," he noted of his visit on October 7, 1932. "George Allan introduced me with a speech of 35 minutes which was of unnecessary length, the first 25 minutes being taken up with sheer irrelevancies and before the end of his speech people were getting fairly restive. I rose in this atmosphere but was fortunate to find that I was able instantly to claim their attention and I thought that I held it without a break to the end." While in Canada, Cooper believed that he had the right to communicate directly with any Company official, which often caused annoyance, confusion and misunderstanding. "One thing that particularly riled Mr. Chester," remembered Winifred Archer, his loyal secretary, "was that when Governor Cooper visited Canada and was with, say, the manager of a large store, he would question the Canadian executive on matters not under the control of London. Mr. Chester felt this was not only unfair to himself, but also unfair to the manager." That didn't stop Cooper, and he always made a special point of inspecting the Winnipeg store. On one such occasion, his wife expressed a desire to view the competing Eaton's store, then managed by Bill Palk. "How do you like it?" Palk politely inquired, after she and Mrs Conrad Riley had spent some time touring several departments.

"Well," Kathleen Cooper replied, equally politely, "actually, I don't like it at all. 'We've just been all through the Hudson's Bay Company store and it's nice and quiet. You can do your shopping in peace. But here, the aisles are crowded and everyone is pushing you around all the time." Palk, who read the

---

* Cooper was happy to borrow His Ex's rail car but would far rather have had his own. Repeated entreaties to have the Canadian Committee purchase or lease one for him were manfully rebuffed by George Allan, who patiently explained that "we are, of necessity, driving our rank and file pretty hard these days of reduced salaries and wages ... and my own hunch is [that you should avoid] a breath of criticism by any member of the staff, no matter how Bolshevistic he might be.... Democracy in Canada has made great advances and Canadians ... are critical of people of importance from Great Britain and other countries visiting Canada...."

riot act to any department manager whose aisles weren't crowded enough to force him and his assistant to walk through in single file, knew at that moment why Eaton's was outselling the Bay.

The first Governor to undertake northern inspection tours by air, Cooper posed a special problem for his keepers. The Governor insisted that his official flag be fluttering *before* he arrived at any Company post.* Many stores, especially in the North, didn't have one, or it had been eaten by rats, and often the HBC Beechcraft kept circling for some time. Chesshire recalled being stuck in just such a situation, trying to land the HBC plane against an incoming low-pressure front, when Cooper exclaimed: "I can't see the Governor's flag flying!"

"But Sir," Chesshire replied, "they don't have a flag."

"Well, they should have."

"What good would it do?"

"The Indians would know the Governor's in town," explained Cooper. Chesshire had no answer for that except to shrug and turn his eyes heavenward.

Cooper inspected not just every store but every warehouse. While at Fort Chipewyan, he once found "numbers of horse collars, horse shoes although I ascertained that there were only two horses in the whole district. These have been written off the books but it is an obvious weakness that they are not moved somewhere where they can be sold" [September 16, 1932]. One problem with Cooper's northern sojourns was that he demanded a full press corps reception when he returned to Winnipeg. Local journalists obliged the first time but soon found more interesting copy. Murray Turner, then in charge of public relations, solved the problem by recruiting eight tea and coffee salesmen from the wholesale department, handing them cameras—but not film—from the retail store, and telling them to pretend they were photographing the Governor's every limb movement as he descended from the aircraft. That made Cooper very happy, but every year when he returned to London, he would puzzle about it. "Extraordinary," he would say. "I have lots of photographs taken when I'm in Canada—and they never let me see them …"

COOPER'S MOST NOTABLE—and most bizarre—adventure was his 1934 journey into Hudson Bay. "1933 was a year of depression and losses," Chester noted when the Governor's decision to go North the following summer was

---

* This was the Company's coat of arms on a white field, which today flies from all HBC stores.

being debated. "Within the Company the prospect of an Arctic pageant was received with misgivings and hopes that nothing would come of it. But as events quickly proved, such hopes were reducing the man and his plan to too simple a simplicity, as in no time at all London and Canada were organizing a voyage that would be the talk of Arctic circles for years to come." The *Nascopie* was turned over to a shipyard for reconfiguration of her passenger space to accommodate the Governor and his retinue. Bronze commemorative medals were struck featuring the profile of Cooper; hundreds of hunting knives were inscribed "From P. Ashley Cooper, Governor of the Hudson's Bay Company, 1934" on one side and "Be happy while you hunt" on the other; and an extra stock of Governor's flags was ordered.

On July 7, 1934, Cooper boarded the ship at her home berth in Montreal. With him were his wife, her maid, his secretary (G.R. Macdonald), a piper from the Black Watch of Canada (Pipe Sergeant Hannah) and Michael Lubbock, who was to act as Cooper's executive assistant and speech writer.* Aboard also were Ralph Parsons, the Company's Fur Trade Commissioner, a King's Scout (one a year was awarded the trip by the HBC), eight Mounties and several new HBC clerks, an archaeologist, an astronomer, an ornithologist and a newsreel production team. A thousand spectators lined the dock as the thirtieth Governor of the Hudson's Bay Company was piped aboard his ship for a six-week voyage into the Company's original territory that none of his predecessors had ever bothered to make.

The *Nascopie*, her pennants flying, steamed along the north shore of the St Lawrence, through the Strait of Belle Isle, then up the rocky coast of Labrador to Cartwright and later Port Burwell. The piper first did a round of the decks, frightening the caged chickens and sheep, then climbed into the bow of the ship's cutter and began playing "Oh where, tell me where, is my Highland laddie gone?" He was followed down the ladder by the Governor and his wife, Captain Smellie of the *Nascopie* and Parsons. "Sir George Simpson in his 30-foot canoe, with his beaver hat, piper and singing voyageurs, made no braver picture than this," rhapsodized R.H.H. Macaulay, a Company scribe. "A white motor boat of trim line—amidships, on a high-backed seat, the

---

* The highly educated son of a director of the Bank of England and a former director of the HBC, Lubbock was not unduly fond of Cooper. "He was almost illiterate," Lubbock claimed, "so that whenever I wanted him to express rather loftier sentiments, I would insert, 'as the seventeenth-century writer said'—and then put in my own words. I even got quoted in a number of papers, and I knew he'd never dare ask me who the writer was."

Governor and Mrs. Cooper, by the Governor's side the Commissioner. At the small wheel immediately behind the seat stood the 3rd mate in uniform, and by his side a uniformed seaman to tend the motor. Behind them, standing with arms folded, was the Captain, with his gold ribbon and oak leaves, and aft the Governor's flag. In the bow … the piper keeping time to his 'Highland Laddie' with one brogued and buckled foot, the ribbons decorating his pipes flying in the breeze." The Coopers inspected the tiny settlement, handed out the inscribed knives to the hunters, and mouth organs, toques, beads and rattles to the children, then officiated at the laying of a cornerstone for a new Bay store.* "It is no exaggeration to say," Macaulay reported with all the paternalism he could muster, "that those Eskimos were overcome by this unprecedented shower of gifts; never before in their lives had such a thing happened, and, in consequence, they could only sit and look at their presents, touching them gently every now and then to see that they were real, and, finding that they were, giving delighted little laughs."

As he would at all his stops, Cooper then showed his Inuit audience a film of King George reviewing the trooping of the colour, explaining through an interpreter that this was *their* King too. There is no record of local reactions to the movie—the first they had ever seen—or to the notion that somebody who usually went around on a horse was their King, but everybody's attention was soon distracted by a kayak race, a square dance and fireworks.† Next morning, as the *Nascopie* struck her anchor and pulled out of Cartwright on the way to Port Burwell, Cooper got ready for the broadcasts he intended to give just before his arrival or just after his departure at each stop. He would rush to the radio room and, sitting in front of a large microphone, drone on about how glad he was to be here, how the Eskimos should be more diligent in trapping foxes, how it had taken "many moons travelling" to reach them, and how they must always be loyal subjects of the King who was sponsoring this message.

---

* "Possibly arranged," as Chester later noted, "by the Post manager to express hopes for a new building; but after the *Nascopie* left, the ceremonial platform and inscribed cornerstone (a wooden crate filled with rocks and covered with concrete) were sadly dismantled."
† At Stupart Bay, the Governor gamely climbed into a kayak, got his balance, and paddled around the cove until his legs got cold. One highlight of the journey, recalled by Michael Lubbock, was stopping off at Lake Harbour, where the piper started to wail for a group of elderly Inuit. "I noticed they were in a sort of ring, shuffling around, and it suddenly struck me that they were going through the rudiments of a Scottish reel. It was a most curious spectacle, but of course the Dundee whalers used to come here regularly, and they were doing what they had been taught so many, many years ago."

Then, straining even his own considerable limits of condescension, the Governor would conclude with the admonition: "We ... leave you with confidence that you will work with our post manager as one large happy family, you following his advice as if he were your father, for he does the things which I tell him and I want you to do the things which he tells you."

There were three problems with the Governor's broadcasts:

1. Each settlement had only one radio receiver, usually in the store manager's staff house, so that the chances of an Inuk's actually hearing Cooper were remote.
2. He spoke in English, so that any Inuit who did listen would not understand a word Cooper was saying.
3. When Ottawa objected to an HBC official's speaking to Canadian subjects on behalf of the King, the plug was pulled on Cooper's microphone amplifier. As a result, his carefully rehearsed speeches were never heard outside the little shipboard studio. "They kind of went up in the air and never came down," Captain Smellie later confessed with a mischievous twinkle in his eye.

Cooper was not aware of any of this—then or later—and earnestly continued to perform his daily stint. The post managers had meanwhile been carefully briefed to praise him for his non-existent broadcasts wherever he appeared.

The voyage's most historic event was commemoration of Henry Hudson's voyage of discovery into the Bay, 324 years earlier. Cooper had been charged by Lord Jellicoe of the Royal Empire Society in London to cast a specially prepared wreath (which had been preserved in a huge block of ice) upon the waters near the spot where Hudson was thought to have been abandoned in a lifeboat by his mutinous crew. The previous evening the Captain had asked Arthur Reed, his Chief Steward, to prepare the wreath for launching. It could not be found, and Reed finally concluded it had mistakenly been left behind. "Make a wreath," ordered the skipper, adding, "by tomorrow morning." To create a circle of flowers held together by red ribbon on a supply ship in the middle of Hudson Bay might have daunted a lesser man, but Reed produced a realistic facsimile within twelve hours. It had been fashioned out of artificial blooms painted on and cut out of toilet paper by one of the passengers, mounted in moss that had been brought aboard by one of the scientists.

Cooper delivered one of his windier speeches, then solemnly heaved the contraption into the sea, while his piper appropriately played "Flowers of the Forest."

"On his triumphant return to Winnipeg the Governor gave a dinner for the Canadian Committee," Chester noted, barely able to rein in his sarcasm. "And after speaking about the great value which the Company, the C.C., and the Fur Trade Department would reap from his efforts, he called up each member to be pinned with one of his medals. To climax the subsequent silence.... G.W. Allan remarked: 'Governor, by God, never before in my long life have I received a medal and I shall always treasure this memorable occasion.'"

IN DRAMATIC CONTRAST to Cooper's chivalrous if extravagant approach, Chester's life in Winnipeg was remarkably routine. He lived on River Avenue, had an account with Bradley's Taxi, but usually walked to work and taxied home. He spent most of his limited spare time at the Manitoba Club, either playing bridge or trading gossip with members of the Sanhedrin. They were an informal group of thoughtful Winnipeggers led by John W. Dafoe, the great editor of the *Free Press* who customarily huddled in a corner of the club lounge (which always seemed redolent of ox blood), to dissect world events, talk up free trade, and spread the gospel of Manchester Liberalism. They resented the restraints placed on western development by the Montreal-Ottawa-Toronto axis and fervently believed that a prosperous West, exercising its financial independence, would strengthen Confederation. They were also an insular and extremely conservative bunch; having weathered the Depression, they vowed not to owe anybody anything ever again, encouraging Chester in his determination that the HBC should not borrow money to finance a move into Eastern Canada. When Owen Funnell, the ambitious and capable manager of the Calgary store, formulated plans for the Company to open a branch at the head of the Great Lakes in the grain-export town of Port Arthur, Chester cut off the discussion by proclaiming the community would not grow because the St Lawrence Seaway would never be built.

Chester's wife, Isabel, was an Ivey, the youngest child of a wealthy family from London, Ontario, who had made their fortune in Empire Brass and later branched out into life insurance and packaging. She had been planning to spend a season in Paris when she met Chester during a Great Lakes steamboat excursion, and they decided to marry. Their honeymoon at Beaver Point, the Ivey family summer compound on Ahmic Lake, near Burk's Falls, northwest of

Huntsville, was an appropriate portent of things to come. The happy couple arrived in style and were met by the bride's two maids, but within two days Chester had decided they were not good enough and fired them both. Chester eventually bought the place and spent six weeks every summer there. "Beaver Point had a magnificent main house with six bedrooms, an enormous stone fireplace, and its own electricity generating plant," recalled son-in-law Charles Loewen. "Chester kept pretending it was just a little country cottage and got very cross when some Boy Scouts, who had paddled the lake in a canoe, came to borrow a can opener and asked: 'Sir, what's the name of this hotel?' He did things with reasonable style, so that at breakfast, for example, there were always ten pots of different jams and you had to go through the ceremony of choosing one. I remember particularly one day having lunch with him on the dock. He was sipping champagne and offered me some. When I told him I'd rather have beer, he looked at me and exclaimed, 'Helot!' Now, that was interesting, because he was calling me a peasant but granting me the recognition that I was an educated one, and would know the Helots had been Spartan serfs. He had a fairly sophisticated sense of humour."

Life at the Chesters' was not always that placid. They had adopted a son in England named David Andrew, a sensitive, artistic child. He was sent to Trinity College School at Port Hope, was a good student in art, literature and jazz piano, but worked only intermittently as a journalist. So displeased was the father with his intellectual son that Chester kept him at an emotional distance. David's attractive wife, from whom he would later become estranged, was a trained speech therapist but had to take jobs as a cleaning lady to pay the grocery bills. Young David's recurring nightmare was his memory of the time his father forced him to eat some jelly dessert that he was allergic to. When he got so upset he threw up, Chester insisted he eat everything on his plate, including the vomit—but his mother intervened.

Despite his frustrations with the British overlords, Chester loved his visits to London. He would arrive on the *Queen Mary*, stay in a suite at the Dorchester, lunch at the Savoy Grill, and be the dinner guest at various functions hosted by resident directors. The trips tapered off during the Second World War, as nearly everyone was pressed into service. Chester himself served briefly as Acting Master General of Ordnance in Canada's suddenly mobilized defence department but left Ottawa two months later, frustrated by the impenetrable maze of regulations. When he returned to Winnipeg, his wife gave a celebratory dinner party for their friends. As the guests sat down to eat, they found each serving tied up in red tape, and they had to fill out forms in triplicate before they could begin the meal.

Cooper also served his country, as Director-General of Finance in the Ministry of Supply, and in 1944 was knighted for his efforts. The Company's London office was never hit by German bombs, but they came close. More than one directors' meeting was concluded with the directors crouching under the boardroom table, and the annual Court in 1944 was disrupted three times by buzz-bombs landing nearby. A spice warehouse just behind. Beaver House was hit and burned for a week, giving off a terrible smell. Several fire bombs landed on the front steps and roof of the Company building, but they didn't go off.*

The staff spent most nights huddled in the building's underground fur-storage vaults, occasionally relieving the tension by chuckling through one of the least authentic Hollywood films ever made.[†] Although there was a wartime embargo on importing fur, the HBC maintained the continuity of its operations by auctioning the pelts of British wild rabbits, used in the hat trade. On February 25, 1946, regular sales resumed, with £200,000 in turnover the first day alone. The HBC was back in business.

Cooper celebrated the end of hostilities by revamping his board. Much to everyone's surprise, but prompted by his directors, he named Chester a British director (replacing Victor Cazalet) and upgraded his title from General Manager to Managing Director for Canada. The Governor also recruited as new board members some of the war's most distinguished graduates. They included Field Marshal the Right Honourable the Viscount Alanbrooke, who had served as Chief of the Imperial General Staff and, according to the

---

*A typical wartime incident was the near escape of a Company employee named A.J. Pullen, who woke up in his southeast London house one Saturday evening just as a hundred-pound bomb penetrated his roof and buried itself in an upstairs floor. He borrowed a saw, removed enough floor boards to free it, attached it to a wire cable, and dragged it over his garden rail-ings into the street. He then hoisted the bomb—still ticking loudly in his ear—on his shoul-der and carried it towards a bomb disposal dump. He was accompanied in this perilous journey by his seventeen-year-old son, Harry, who explained to neighbours that he was along in case his father dropped it. When Pullen finally reached the dump, he was arrested and fined three pounds (which the Company paid) for "removing and tampering with a bomb dropped from enemy aircraft."

† *Hudson's Bay*, a clinker produced in 1940 by Twentieth Century Fox, starred Gene Tierney (as a beautiful Indian princess), Vincent Price (as Charles II), Virginia Field (as Nell Gwyn), Paul Muni (as Pierre Radisson) and a 309-pound Laird Cregar (as Médard Chouart, Sieur Des Groseilliers). The movie's grasp of Canadian geography was as real as the canvas canoes, painted to resemble birchbark, in which most of the action took place.

American general Douglas MacArthur, was "the greatest soldier that England has produced since Wellington"; Sir John Anderson, later Lord Waverley, one of Britain's most distinguished public servants, who had served as Governor of Bengal (where he earned the reputation of being the most shot-at man in the world) and wartime Chancellor of the Exchequer;* and William "Tony" Keswick, a brigadier on the staff of General Montgomery's planning group for the Normandy invasion, whose family controlled Jardine, Matheson & Company, a Far Eastern trading company.

The most interesting new post-war recruit was Joe Links, the head of his own firm of furriers that had been chosen by Royal Appointment Furrier to the Royal Household. A spritely and cultured gentleman with all the social graces and a novelist's eye for detail, he had written authoritative studies of Venice, Canaletto and the fur trade. Links made light of the fact that he was the first Jew to be invited on the board, and when asked whether he had encountered any prejudice, replied, "Of course not, neither then nor at any other time in my life. It's not so much that I was the only Jewish director, I was the *English* one—the only Englishman among six Scots or sons of Scots. So, perhaps I cannot acquit my colleagues altogether of prejudice." Described by a later Governor as "the most useful board member, his mind worked like lightning and he would always ask the kind of awkward questions that made us wonder why we had never thought of what he had just brought up," Links served on the board for twenty-eight years, an invaluable source of wisdom, humour and plain good sense.

The Canadian Committee also underwent drastic changes. In 1940, Charles Dunning, who had become Premier of Saskatchewan at thirty-six and

---

* Alanbrooke's honours and decorations: Knight of the Garter, Knight Grand Cross of the Bath, Order of Merit, Knight Grand Cross of the Royal Victorian Order, Distinguished Service Order (he was twice a DSO—in 1917 and 1918). He also held the French, Belgian and Czechoslovak Croix de Guerre and the Distinguished Service Medal from the United States, and his wife was from an old HBC family: a great-granddaughter of Sir John Henry Pelly, Deputy Governor 1812–22 and Governor 1822–52. Waverley's honours: Privy Councillor, Knight Grand Cross of the Bath, Order of Merit, Knight Grand Commander of the Star of India, Knight Grand Commander of the Indian Empire, Fellow of the Royal Society. He attended the universities of Edinburgh and Leipzig, and held an MA and a BSc. He was Home Secretary in the early years of the 1939–45 war, and the little air-raid shelters that dotted British gardens were known as Andersons after him. After the war he became chairman of the Port of London Authority and a director of the CPR. The Order of Merit is limited in number to twenty-four members, with provision for honorary foreign members. General Dwight Eisenhower was made an honorary OM in 1945. The Bath is a much larger order, with many degrees, including several of knighthood.

later served as federal minister of finance, was invited to join. Chancellor of Queen's University, chairman of Ogilvie Flour Mills and a director of eleven other major companies, he was one of the few distinguished non-Winnipeggers to join the HBC Committee. In Winnipeg itself, the Company's corporate traditions carried on through the appointment of Perley Banbury (Beaver Lumber), Stewart Augustus Searle (Searle Grain, and a director of Monarch Life), Colonel Hugh F. Osler (head of Osler, Hammond & Nanton and a director of Great-West Life) and Joe Harris (Canada Packers, Great-West Life and a director of Beaver Lumber).* Originally an executive in his father's meat packing-house (later merged into Canada Packers), Harris was a candid character who had the disconcerting habit of ending most lunches by pushing back his chair and, as he was turning to leave, informing his fellow diners: "Got to get back to the abattoir and stick a piggy."

After George Allan's death in 1940, the Canadian Committee chairmanship went to Conrad Stephenson Riley, an unassuming but effective financier who could divert most of Cooper's aggressive ploys with the simple: "Yes, Patrick, I'm sure that would be very nice. But no." A noted oarsman who became a member of Canada's Sports Hall of Fame, he succeeded his father as president of Northern Trusts and was a director of such Winnipeg touchstone companies as Great-West Life and Beaver Lumber. Under Riley, the Cooper-Chester feud quieted down a bit, with the Winnipeg Managing Director temporarily becalmed because of his new title and London appointment, while the British Governor, savouring his new knighthood, felt vindicated and slightly more immune to the Canadian's little plots.†

Within a decade, Riley was succeeded by J. Elmer Woods, who would run the Canadian Committee from 1950 to 1964. While he was cut from the same pattern as every other Winnipeg Committeeman (he was president of Monarch Life and a director of Beaver Lumber), Woods was an original. He was the ultimate insider, so trusted by Manitoba's political and economic élite that for a brief time he was chief bagman for both the provincial Liberal and Conservative parties at one and the same time. He took on the HBC

---

* A prominent member of a well-established Winnipeg grain family, Searle stayed on the Committee for fifteen years, but when he developed the habit of spending every winter in Florida, and thus missing an increasing number of meetings, he was not invited to stand for re-election.

† Chester was so relaxed that he even took on an outside directorship (his only one), naturally choosing the Great-West Life Assurance Company.

Chairmanship determined to move the Company's head office to its proper address, on Winnipeg's Main Street, and though he didn't succeed, he put in place most of the necessary groundwork. Prompted by Chester, he also reactivated the Hudson's Bay Oil & Gas operation. By the spring of 1943, the firm owned a dozen wells in Turner Valley, representing 10 percent of the field's production. Within the decade, the HBC had invested $8 million in exploration and HBOG had become the second-largest holder of known gas reserves (4.3 million acres) in Alberta, with eighty producing wells. A major exploration agreement was signed with Continental Oil, to expire June 30, 1951. That proved to be a bonanza because Continental at about this time named as its president L.F. McCollum, one of the great Texas oilmen, who invested $300 million in land acquisition and oil exploration in the next two decades.

A continuing controversy of the 1950s concerned the desirability of moving retail operations into Ontario and Quebec and whether or not the HBC should join other department stores in establishing satellite branches in suburban shopping centres. Chester's position, strongly supported by Elmer Woods, was nothing if not clear: he would never "go whoring in the East," and there was no point going into shopping centres because sales in such urban fringes would only reduce the core business of the Bay's magnificent downtown department stores. "if there were fuddy-duddies in the Company, they were to be found in Canada rather than London," claimed Joe Links. "Chester was instinctively opposed to buying other companies, believing the HBC could perfectly well build up any business it wanted and 'crucify' its competitors. Above all, Chester wanted the HBC to stay in the West—certainly to make itself competitive, to enlarge its big downtown stores, to build parkades, and open up new stores in unexploited areas, but not to challenge 'those whores in the East,' where an honest trader with Western Canadian principles would only get his fingers burnt. We in London felt the shopping centre movement gave HBC opportunities with its expertise in operating retail stores of widely differing sizes. Chester's argument that anything that might weaken our downtown stores must weaken the Company was an interesting reversal of a situation that arose in the HBC's pioneering days. When the French took to opening trading posts upriver in order to catch the Indians before they reached the HBC posts with their furs, the Bay men on the spot sought authority from London to go still farther upriver. But London foresaw a limitless leap-frogging and decided instead that better prices for furs and better trade goods would do more for the Company's reputation. I once reminded Chester of this story and saw him momentarily waver. If what he was saying had been said by those London bastards of the eighteenth century, then perhaps he might be wrong after all. But he was comforted by the thought that twentieth-century London didn't agree with him: this confirmed that he *must* be right." Peter Wood, the HBC's Treasurer, verified this: "If the London people had been overtly against the suburban stores, Chester would have been vehemently for them."

It was a costly dispute. Sears in the United States had opened its first suburban store at Aurora, a Chicago suburb, in 1928, and by the early 1950s shopping centres with department stores at each end were sprouting up all over America. Woodward's opened Canada's first shopping-centre store at West Vancouver's Park Royal in 1950 after the HBC had turned down an offer from the Guinness family, the centre's developers, to be the anchor store. Four years later Canada's initial double department store plaza was launched in a suburb of Hamilton, with Morgan's and Simpsons-Sears as anchor tenants. Eaton's put its first branch into Oshawa in 1956. George Weightman, a thirty-year Bay man who eventually became manager of market research, still laments the lost opportunities. "I wrote a long précis summing up the prospects for the Company and made a convincing argument, but when I finished my presentation, Chester just said, 'Young man, you can't see the woods for the trees,' and I thought to myself, 'Well, there you are.'" Part of the problem was that Chester was an atrocious driver, seldom drove his car and was not aware of the effect of people's new mobility on North American cities.

BY THE EARLY 1950S, Sir Patrick Ashley Cooper, now nearing his sixty-fifth birthday, began to send out feelers about having his term as Governor extended beyond normal retirement. He had a good case and made certain that it was promulgated in the Company's 1951 report. Share values, he reminded the proprietors, had fallen from 131s 3d in 1928 to 22s 6d in 1930, but since 1932 the Company had distributed £3 million in dividends and ploughed £8.5 million back into its treasury, raising assets from £10.7 million to £66.8 million. Cooper had introduced many enlightened policies, such as stressing promotion from within. He established the Hudson's Bay Record Society to take over publication of the Company's historic documents. He was the first Governor to hold summer picnics for the London staff at his home, and even demonstrated a sense of humour when he read out to an annual Court a letter he had received. "I got your letter about what I owe," wrote the troubled HBC customer. "Now be pachant. I ain't forgot you. Please wait. When I have the money I will pay you. If this was the Judgement Day and you was no more prepared to meet your maker than I am to meet your account you sure would go to hell. Trusting you will do this."

"I kind of liked Sir Patrick," remarked Scotty Gall, the old Arctic hand, who met the Governor several times. "He loved the feudal system, behaved like a baron coming around to inspect his serfs. But he was a keen business-man, too. He knew the right side of the dollar and gave nothing away." That was true enough, and there was no doubt that Cooper had rescued the Company from the Depression. But the post-war era demanded other qualities, and even if it was mostly Chester's fault, relations between Winnipeg and London had deteriorated beyond repair, so that no concerted expansion plan could be put into effect. Cooper's exaggerated sense of personal vanity had become even less endearing to Canadians than it was to the Londoners, and his Churchillian refrain, that he had not become Governor of the HBC in order to preside over its dissolution, was a brave stance but hardly a policy.

During his tenure at Beaver House, Cooper had acquired a collection of silver pieces made in 1670, the year of the Company's founding, and had special carpets woven in Kidderminster by four artisans especially chosen for the job. He also had his portrait painted, and as was then the custom, an extra copy was done for a record of the original. Cooper borrowed the copy to hang in his country house and one summer weekend in 1952 told R.A. Reynolds, the Company secretary, he was taking the original home to compare the two canvases. Reynolds had placed a secret mark on the primary painting and was not too surprised when Cooper returned on Monday morning, passing off the copy as the real thing.

It was a tiny incident, but it raised questions about Cooper's approach. There had been rumours that he was charging his London flat to the Company and that he accepted generous expense-account advances but seldom reported on them. Whether or not this amounted to any serious abuse of his fiscal responsibilities, it certainly was true that after more than two decades in the Governor's chair Cooper had lost the ability to differentiate between his personal considerations and those of the Company. There were, in those days, very tight foreign exchange controls in Britain, to the extent that executives travelling abroad were allocated ridiculously small spending allowances. The Bank of England agreed to grant Cooper, as HBC Governor, a special exemption to finance his journeys and required entertainments, yet

Company auditors discovered that he was withdrawing a similar amount from the Winnipeg office but sending his bills through to be paid in London. Cooper made his own rules and at one time even imported a tractor for his farm with the allowance granted him by the British central bank. The London board members deputized Lord Waverley to persuade Cooper that he should resign. The final confrontation, attended by Tony Keswick (by then promoted to Deputy Governor) and Waverley, left Cooper no escape.

Keswick recalled later, "We just said: 'The staff have lost confidence; it's no use trying to build it up. It must come to an end. There must be a change.'"

"Do I understand what that means?" asked a distraught Cooper.

"You understand what it means."

"Yes, I understand what it means. We won't discuss it any more."

And so, on November 19, 1952, Sir Patrick Ashley Cooper resigned as thirtieth Governor of the Hudson's Bay Company.

Chester had won.

Canadian at Last

"The British have the rigidity of red hot pokers without their warmth."
—Lord Amory

TONY KESWICK, WHO HAD BEEN BROUGHT on the board by Cooper in the mid-1940s, now took over as Governor, and his presence introduced a whiff of China Seas buccaneering to the HBC's deliberations. "He was a big man in every sense, a sharp trader, and I thoroughly enjoyed working with him," reminisced Eric Faulkner, who was for a time his Deputy, "although there were moments when one had to slightly pull on the reins and say, 'Tony, you're going a bit too far. There's too much bullshit in that, you must be more careful.'"

To such admonitions, mild as they were, Keswick preferred to reply with a parable and a fact. The fact was that during his stewardship, HBC profits climbed 320 percent; the parable had something to do with a mythical creature known as the Arctic Robin. "It had been snowing for a long, long time," went his oft-told tale, "and the poor bird, having had nothing to eat, said to himself, 'I think I'll turn up my toes and pack it in.' Just then, a farmer let his bull out of its pen near where the Arctic Robin was sitting. The bull had been overfed and after a while deposited an enormous pile, which allowed the Robin to have a delicious hot breakfast. The bird, feeling perky again, flew up a tree and started singing so loudly that it attracted the attention of the farmer's son, who fetched a catapult, took aim, and killed the Arctic Robin stone dead." The point of the story, as Keswick loved to explain through snorts of belly-pumping laughter, was that "if you get to the top with the aid of bullshit, you shouldn't sing about it."

Keswick came by his merchant adventurer's calling honestly, having been associated for most of his business life with Jardine, Matheson, the Hong Kong trading house. "Both companies, at different times and different places, lived dangerously and had to struggle against larger forces," he pointed out. "Whatever else, the life of a merchant adventurer is full of incidents." One such incident that illustrated Keswick's approach to life and adventure made good his claim that he may have been the only politician ever shot for making a budget speech. In the winter of 1940–41, when he was working for Jardine's along the South China coast, the invading Japanese had hived most of the surviving foreign community into the International Settlement, the European quarter of Shanghai. Elected head of the municipal council, Keswick was presenting his annual budget at an outdoor arena in Shanghai filled with five thousand ratepayers when Yukichi Hayashi, a Japanese radical opposed to the foreign presence, rushed on stage, took out a revolver and began firing at him. The first bullet went through his rib cage, causing Keswick to feel genuinely annoyed. "I told the Japanese fellow, 'For God's sake, stop that.' Then I fell on top of the little chap. Nearly killed him. He tried to send another bullet up my nose and took three fingers off the interpreter's left hand with his last shot. Seemed *very* upset."

His would-be assassin was hailed as a hero in Tokyo while Keswick escaped with only superficial wounds and eventually boarded the last plane to leave Singapore before the Japanese invasion. He had a good war, and later spent most of two decades as a director of the Bank of England. His many honours included membership in the Royal Company of Archers. "We're the Queen's bodyguard whenever she's in Scotland," he explained. "We have bows, arrows and little swords and stomp about protecting her." Scotland was also the site of his grouse moor, on a 6,000-acre estate in Dumfriesshire, sixty miles south of Glasgow. It was stocked not only with game birds, sheep and cattle but also with statues. Haunted by memories of Buddhas spotted in the Far Eastern landscape, Keswick planted, at strategic viewpoints throughout his estate, works of some of the twentieth century's most famous sculptors: two Rodins, Epstein's famous *Madonna* and half a dozen Henry Moores, including his resplendent *King and Queen*. "I have all the big boys," he allowed, "and they look very well in their natural surroundings against the sky—better than seeing them in some damn museum."

Perhaps because Keswick had such a powerful sense of self-worth and came to the HBC without having to prove anything, his thirteen years as Governor were very different from the stewardships of his predecessors. Unlike Cooper, Keswick placed the greatest emphasis on cultivating the staff, trying to raise morale by reigniting their pride in the Company. "He used to come around and sit in my office," recalled Arthur Frayling, who was in charge of London fur sales, "and say, 'Arthur, we're having a bad year, can you do anything for us?' I'd tell him that we would make a decent kick, and he'd put his hand on my shoulder and reply, 'We're counting on you.' That pompous old bugger Cooper would never have done that. He would have sent out four memorandums on how to reorganize the fur division." After his annual trips to Canada, Keswick would write a hundred or more personal letters to the Bay employees he'd met, and eventually knew nearly all of them by their first names.

Keswick's most serious assignment was to protect the Company against an attempted takeover by Max Bell of Calgary and H.R. Milner of Edmonton. The episode was referred to in the HBC's secret internal files as "The Bullfight" because the tactics employed by the Alberta investors were similar to those used in the takeover of the Matador Land & Cattle Company, a venerable Texas land outfit that had struck oil. The idea, novel at the time, was to seek representation on the board of the desired company and, with the information obtained, promote an offer to shareholders for control. Once their goal was achieved, the new owners would then sell off parts of the company to pay for their acquisition expenses. Had Bell succeeded, he would have spun off the HBC's retail stores to Simpsons or Eaton's and, in effect, obtained the HBC's petroleum reserves for nothing. An athletic-looking gent with a sporty brush-cut, Bell had made an early fortune in the Alberta Oil Patch, purchased half a dozen daily newspapers, and become a well-known horse breeder and racer. A fitness devotee, he would disconcert employees who had come to see him for a pay increase by walking across the office floor on his hands, urging them to state their case as money poured out of his upside-down trouser pockets. He owned the luxury yacht *Campana*, a pair of islands up the B.C. coast and several vacation palaces but had Spartan eating habits. "Max's idea of real debauchery," claimed his friend the sportswriter Jim Coleman, "is to have three flavours of ice-cream in the same dish."

There had been heavy buying of HBC stock on American stock exchanges in early 1952 and rumours began to grow that a New York syndicate, organized and headed by S.G. Warburg & Company, the British merchant bankers, would attend that year's annual Court to grab control of the Company. Because both the Canadian and the U.S. groups were attracted by the HBC's oil leases, Company management immediately began to negotiate a new long-term agreement with its exploration partner, Continental Oil, locking the two companies into joint ventures until 1999. Within a year of its original push, the Warburg group decided to unite with Max Bell. That gave the combined group sway over more than 200,000 shares (out of 2.5 million shares outstanding), nowhere near a control position but enough to worry management. Keswick decided to deal first with Siegmund Warburg. "I put on a clean white shirt and went to have tea with Mr. Warburg in the interest of 'shareholder relations,'" he wrote to Canadian Committee Chairman Elmer Woods. "After a sip of very indifferently made tea I took the opportunity of expressing my own views on the breaking up of the companies or selling off limbs, especially those with long histories and established success. I left him with no doubt that in principle I would find it very difficult to agree to any such policy and that I personally believed ardently in maintaining the united strength of our grand old Company."

After prolonged discussion and some bickering, Warburg agreed to vote his proxies with the board, but Bell held out. He had drawn up a forty-four-page report suggesting how the HBC could improve its profit potential, particularly in oil operations, and on March 17, 1953, Bell and Keswick met face to face. "At times he shouted like an undisciplined or spoilt boy unable to get his way too easily," Keswick recalled. "Curiously enough, the question of taxation never arose as a major criticism, nor did transfer, other than his recommendation that I should transfer myself over and settle down like a broody hen on top of the Canadian Committee. It could all be summed up in one generalization: that Mr. Bell feels that we lack drive and progressive management; we do not make the most of our assets; and that if we did we could treble and quadruple our profits.... It is good that we have shareholders as keen as this but I am glad there are not too many of them." Bell quite rightly concluded he was not being taken seriously and soon afterwards sold his HBC stock—at a $500,000 profit. The main impact of his raid was to bring a substantial block of stock across the Atlantic.

PERHAPS IT HAD SOMETHING TO DO with celebrating his victory over Bell, the first colonial to challenge London's vested authority, but more likely it was Keswick's intuition that his beloved Company could not much longer resist the pull westward and would soon be domiciled in Canada, that prompted him to stage one final, glorious pageant. Who better as the centrepiece of such a grand occasion than the most eminent Englishman of the century, Sir Winston Churchill? The wartime Prime Minister's ancestor John Churchill (later first Duke of Marlborough) had during his seven-year reign as the HBC's third Governor restored the Company to glory. Nine generations later, the eighty-one-year-old Sir Winston had reluctantly retired from active politics in 1955, and allowed Anthony Eden to succeed him with the immortal comment: "I must retire soon. Anthony won't live forever." He was working on his masterpiece *The Second World War,* and while his intellect seemed undiminished his health was poor and he was feeling left out of things. Word had come from Chartwell, his country house, that he might be open to an invitation to join the HBC in some manner because he felt there was no other commercial enterprise with which he could align himself without drawing criticism for favouritism. Lord Waverley had suggested the entirely honorific but appropriately historic title "Grand Seigneur of the Company of Adventurers of England Trading into Hudson's Bay," which had the advantage of playing up to Churchill's approach to the British Empire: its details had always bored him, but he was much attached to its ideal—"the spectacle of that immense estate enhancing the grandeur of England," as Jan Morris described it.

Churchill accepted Keswick's invitation but Winnipeg did not. When the Governor mentioned the idea to the Canadian Committee, Elmer Woods replied that he thought "any such position would be incompatible with the stature of Sir Winston. By the unthinking public it would be construed as a form of publicity, with unfavourable reactions...." Keswick forwarded copies of the Woods letter to his fellow British directors with the notation: "I have received the attached somewhat typical and ungracious unanimous disapproval," and paid scant attention to the Canadians. He decided the title would be conferred at a ceremony in Beaver Hall, followed by luncheon at Skinners' Hall on April 27, 1956, with the top layer of Britain's social, economic and political establishments invited to attend.*

"We had a hell of a job getting him up the Skinners' Hall steps," Faulkner recalled. "He appeared deathly pale and we had seats with little tables every fifty yards or so, equipped with helpings of Hudson's Bay fifty-year-old cognac.

---

* The banquet was catered by Ring & Brymer at forty-two shillings a head, with the menu consisting of Scotch salmon with hollandaise sauce; long fillet of beef with new potatoes and French beans; lemon posset and Savoy fingers—and two wine varieties to wash it down: Forster Fleckinger Riesling Auslese, 1953, and Château Léoville Poyferré, 1934. Warre's Port, 1927, accompanied dessert, and Fine Old Cognac was served with the coffee.

He would take a little slug of it and go on, so that by the time he got into the hall there was colour in his cheeks and he was happily coherent." Another HBC director, Lord Alanbrooke, who had been Churchill's senior military commander, was astonished at the transformation. "He is a marvel," the former Chief of the Imperial General Staff told Lord Moran, Churchill's physician, who was at the luncheon. "Before the Election in 1945 I said to myself: He is finished. I could not get him to decide anything.... He was burnt out.... That was eleven years ago, and look at him now."

Keswick and Sir Edward Peacock proposed glowing toasts to the old man, praising his magnificent accomplishments, pretending the office of Grand Seigneur was more than just a grandiose title. The former Prime Minister went along with the game. He rose to his feet, looking a trifle strange in what he must have imagined was a Grand Seigneur's uniform—a smoking jacket over a dress shirt decorated by a bright green bow-tie with large white polka dots—and mischievously told his delighted audience: "I must be very careful how I use the great power that has been placed at my disposal at this very agreeable and memorable function: If I were perhaps to interpret it too literally, it might need a lengthy explanation and I might not receive the full accord which it is in all cases desirable should be given to it and also given to the Grand Seigneur. I will not, therefore, attempt any strong action as a result of the post to which you have called me until and unless I have had further experience...."

Churchill concluded his remarks with a touching benediction. "This honour will be appreciated all my—," there was a long pause and his voice tightened, "—all my remaining life." Sensing they might not see him again, members of the audience grew still. The Grand Seigneur turned to leave. He stepped gingerly from the speaker's dais and, when he reached the bottom stair, faced the hall and gave everyone present a long, searching look; then his features broke into a cherubic smile. The ovation was deafening, lasting the long moments it took for the head table party to escort Sir Winston down to his car.*

---

* After the ceremony, Churchill wanted to know if he could do anything for the Company. Asked whether he might donate one of his paintings, the former Prime Minister replied that this would be difficult since he'd given them all to his wife. When Joe Links went to see Lady Churchill, she explained that while Sir Winston had painted about six hundred canvases, only twenty-five of them were any good, and she didn't want to give the Company either one of his bad ones or a very good one. They finally settled on "the twenty-sixth or twenty-seventh," a Marrakesh street scene that still hangs in the HBC Governor's office, now in the Simpson Tower at the corner of Bay and Queen streets in downtown Toronto.

HAVING VANQUISHED BELL and toasted Churchill, Keswick's main preoccupation became getting along with Chester. His style was certainly more accommodating than Cooper's. After visiting London late in 1952, the Winnipeg-based executive sent the Governor a comforting note. "I cannot attempt to describe the wonderful contrast of my first visit under your reign," he wrote; "it was so happy and enjoyable that I'll hop over any time, even for forty-eight hours." But Chester had by then been battling London for nearly a quarter-century, and his suspicion of British motives had marinated his brain, so that despite his early good intentions he could not stop fighting. "It was easy to follow Cooper," Keswick recalled, "because he was a puffed-up hot-air merchant. But my main task was handling Chester, who was very able, a piledriver intolerant of people not willing to work twenty-four hours a day, but he had a great capacity for sulking. At some of our board meetings, I could see him starting to lose his temper, and I'd say, 'Phil, you're turning black.' It was enormous fun." On one occasion while en route from Toronto to Vancouver, the plane in which the Governor was travelling experienced extreme turbulence in an air pocket over Winnipeg. "We all had to fasten our lap straps," Keswick recalled, "and the passenger next to me, who must have known who I was but hadn't uttered a word during the flight, said out of the side of his mouth: 'Phil Chester must be down below.'"

Even the London board members who admired Chester found him difficult. Deputy Governor Faulkner complained that "on his black-face-days, he was almost impossible to deal with." Yet Faulkner also believed that "Chester had saved the Company. He was a difficult man to like but easy to respect." That was a generous verdict because Faulkner's introduction to Chester had not been promising. "When I first went on the board, I arrived in Montreal and had breakfast with Chester at the Ritz-Carlton," he remembered—only too well. "I needed to blow my nose, so I drew a handkerchief from my left sleeve, where I always carried it. Chester saw me and said: 'It may offend you deeply, but for Christ's sake, don't wear those suede shoes in Canada, because the only people who wear suede shoes here are not the sort of people we would have as directors of the Hudson's Bay Company. Secondly, last week four Royal Canadian Navy captains returned from a course in the United Kingdom. They went on television, and when one of them blew his nose into a handkerchief he'd taken out of his sleeve, Canada went up in smoke, thinking this man's been corrupted. So, don't keep your handkerchief there and take off those shoes.' I remember thinking to myself, 'My God, what have I walked into?'"

Still, the Company under Chester's regime prospered. On August 29, 1946, he had been promoted to Managing Director and granted a $15,000 bonus, but not even that show of confidence satisfied him. "He would chip away at London's authority, chip away at it the whole time," HBC financial officer Peter Wood remembered. "They always said, 'We'll give in on the little things, but we're not going to give in on the main points.' By the time Chester had chipped away a hundred times, he had grabbed a fair amount of authority."

Records of the time reveal that despite Chester's constant complaining, he made not a single policy proposal that wasn't eventually approved by London, while the British directors seldom pressed him to do anything against his will. Yet the feud continued unabated. The enlarged Canadian membership on the London board—in 1957 and 1960—required new appointments that dramatically improved the calibre of the Canadian Committee. C. Gordon Smith, the scion of a well-known grain family with the appropriate Winnipeg credentials (directorships in Beaver Lumber and Monarch Life) joined the board, as did James Richardson, who became chairman and the fourth-generation member to head the family grain firm. (This particular Richardson later became minister of national defence in the Trudeau cabinet.) Two other previously named Committeemen, Stewart Searle and Joe Harris, joined the parent board.

But the most significant catch was Graham Towers, the former (and first) governor of the Bank of Canada, who during his twenty-year reign at the central bank had become universally recognized as the country's most respected economic thinker. In his time, Towers had preserved an unsullied reputation for business prescience, but he never lost his shy and self-depreciating presence. At one time he found himself at a Maritimes hotel without enough cash to settle his account. When a suspicious cashier demanded identification before he would cash a cheque, the Bank of Canada Governor tried with considerable embarrassment to avoid revealing who he was, but finally pulled out a dollar bill and reluctantly showed the startled hotel employee his signature, then decorating Canada's paper currency.

As the Canadian Committee grew in stature, the British board was under-going a similar metamorphosis. The distinguished but largely decorative Lords Waverley and Alanbrooke departed, while J.E.H. Collins, a thirty-six-year-old financier who later headed Morgan, Grenfell, the London banking firm, moved in, as did Henry (later Lord) Benson and Lord Heyworth. Collins put in a useful decade and a half on the board, questioning policies with youthful vigour, but it was Benson and Heyworth who caused the most trouble—and, in retrospect, the most regret. A distinguished Coopers & Lybrand accountant who had served as a colonel in the Grenadier Guards, Benson was a born troubleshooter, having chaired three dozen commissions and inquiries. Tough and unsentimental, he took a good look at the HBC and decided the make-up of its non-executive board of directors was all wrong. To help him with what he felt were the required reforms, he recruited to the board Lord Heyworth, the recently retired head of Unilever, one of the world's great trading companies. Heyworth had worked for the Anglo-Dutch soap and food multinational in Canada, had married a Canadian and was vitally interested in improving the HBC's administration.

The pair set down the necessary steps to reorient a firm whose earnings and performance record they felt had been deplorable. They recommended that the Company's most able operating executives be appointed to a revamped board that would include half a dozen Canadians of Graham Towers's stature; that the Company be immediately Canadianized by transfer of its charter across the Atlantic; and that the HBC's Canadian headquarters be moved from Winnipeg to Montreal or Toronto. The hidden item on their agenda was that Keswick, whom they considered too old-fashioned and too compassionate to wield a broad enough axe, be shoved aside and replaced by Heyworth as a full-time Governor with clear executive powers to modernize the Company and turn it Canadian. The rest of the board demurred, and even if nearly all of the directors would later admit that Benson and Heyworth had been right, not much happened.

What brought the impasse to a head was the move by Keswick to fill a British board vacancy with Lord Cobbold, the retiring governor (1949–61) of the Bank of England. A subsequent Lord Chamberlain of the Royal Household and later a permanent Lord in Waiting to the Queen, Cameron Fromanteel Cobbold was the perfect personification of the trend Benson and Heyworth had been protesting against: perpetuation of the Company's creaky command structure by the naming of yet another distinguished non-executive director with little knowledge of Canada and less of retailing to a board already top-heavy with such creatures. "Benson and Heyworth," Links later recalled, "argued that far from adapting ourselves to change, we were determined to perpetuate the traditional, decorative, and entirely ineffective board of the past. All of us agreed there was much to be said about the approach of appointing executive directors, but little to be done about it until the right people could be found. Interestingly, the Canadian members were aghast at the prospect and demanded that Benson and Heyworth resign immediately. There was no difficulty about this—neither of them wanted to stay under existing conditions. Heyworth just walked out of the board meeting but Benson, cerebrally superior to any of us, stayed behind to tell us not what he thought of the Canadians but what the Canadians thought of us, one by one. There was no malice in this, nothing more than a sense of duty to ensure that we did not continue under any delusions."

Keswick won that round ("They had no notion of the strength of the man they were up against," his wife later declared). It was a remarkable reflection on both men that after it was all over, Benson remained Keswick's personal accountant. Yet it was a hollow victory. Looking back on Benson's thwarted *coup d'état*, Peter Wood enthusiastically sided with the departed renegades. "They were absolutely right," Wood maintained. "If their advice had been followed, the Company would have moved to Canada ten years earlier and it would have been very different. For one thing, we could have got into the first instead of third generation of shopping centres, which would have meant grabbing a lot of the most desirable locations. We could never do that as long as Chester was around."

HAVING CONSOLIDATED HIS POWER and position, by the late 1950s Chester had changed. The provocative complainer of the Cooper period had been replaced by a far more equable and cultured presence who had become a fervent Canadian nationalist. He regarded his past battles with London as having been a microcosm of Canada's struggle to free itself from foreign domination, and in Winnipeg's case to become less dependent on the overwhelming influence of central Canadian bankers. He was part of the small but powerful circle of Manitoba capitalists—the Richardsons, the Rileys, the Gourleys and others—dedicated to halting at Winnipeg the flow of money eastward from British Columbia and the Prairies, which was why they launched financial service institutions and insurance companies.

Within that context Chester grew frustrated by his confinement to his Winnipeg circle and, incongruous as it seemed, enjoyed nothing so much as his semi-annual visits to London. Corporately, he desperately wanted to be the architect of the Company's patriation to Canada, realizing that it had become silly to have the HBC run from London. But personally, he loved the stays in his suite at the Dorchester Hotel, his dinners with the cultured members of the

HBC board at Claridge's and the St James's Street clubs, or at Greenwich. He enjoyed especially spending weekends at the country home of Joe Links, playing poker and discussing modern art. "He was totally dedicated to the HBC and everybody, both in London and Canada, knew it and respected him for it," Links reminisced. "We all liked his company, and above all, trusted him."

Chester did not plan to attend the Company's May 1959 Court because most of the board was due to be in Winnipeg during July in connection with the Queen's visit for the Rent Paying Ceremony. He did, however, go to London in February and either caught pneumonia or suffered a mild stroke. On his way home, he convalesced at Toronto's Park Plaza Hotel for a week. On July 23 at a Canadian Committee meeting in Winnipeg, one of the subjects discussed was enlargement of the Company board that would have made more room for Canadians while retaining the requirement that eight directors—including the Governor and Deputy Governor—should be U.K. residents. Chester stood alone in opposing the restriction, and when he recognized there would be no movement on the issue, orally submitted his resignation.

He was on the platform at the Rent Paying Ceremony at Assiniboine Park the next day and even gave a large garden party at his home immediately afterwards. Although his resignation did not officially take effect until September 30, he never again set foot in Hudson's Bay House.*

RICHARD MURRAY, WHO NOW BECAME the HBC's Managing Director, possessed the one quality that could never have been ascribed to Chester: he was a diplomat. High-strung, romantic and compassionate, with a wide-ranging mind and a set of beliefs stronger than the discipline required to contain them, he tended to be indecisive and dithering. Yet Murray was, in a way, the perfect trans-Atlantic gentleman—in awe of the Establishments on both sides of the ocean, yet their willing and capable instrument. He got along with the Canadians who mattered as well as with Keswick, and after one of the Governor's Canadian visits wrote him a typically effusive letter: "The atmosphere was indeed extraordinary when you arrived; in fact, it defied description

---

* Chester's final bonus and pension payment amounted to $505,000. The pressures of work removed, Chester lived another seventeen years. Although he resolutely stayed away from the HBC and didn't even shop at its Winnipeg store, in 1976, when he knew he was dying, Chester returned to the Company fold. He requested that his burial service be celebrated by Jack Dangerfield and Joan Whiting, HBC executives who had become Anglican priests. And so it was.

or analysis. Your direct, constructive and friendly approach to all issues and personalities in the short time you were with us did a tremendous amount of good." Murray was a true Bay man, outrageously proud of working for what he described as "the most hellishly modern old-fashioned company in the world," and boasted that the Winnipeg headquarters staff often came to work at 7:45 in the morning, although the office didn't officially open until 8:30, just to get an early start.* He wasn't a retailer, and swore he never would be, but loved what he called "the trading part" of the Company and was known to comfort employees complaining about their jobs with the slightly incongruous sally: "How would you like instead to be a vice-president of General Motors in charge of designing tail lights?"

A graduate in liberal arts and law from McGill University, Murray volunteered for the Royal Canadian Navy and served as a corvette signals officer, then joined External Affairs and was almost immediately posted to the Canadian Embassy in Washington. He worked under Lester Pearson, Hume Wrong, Clifford Clark, Norman Robertson, Wynne Plumptre and John Deutsch, the intellectual giants who dominated Canada's post-war recovery, and emerged from that magic apprenticeship as both a patriot and a Liberal.†

Unable to meet the expenses of his growing family on an External salary, Murray joined the HBC's fur department in Montreal and within two years was named head of the New York fur-sales operation. Thrust among the street-wise Jewish traders of Seventh Avenue, he surprised everyone, including himself, by successfully turning the HBC's auction house into a major profit centre that set the trade's pace and prices. By 1955, he had been transferred to Winnipeg as Chester's chief of staff and heir apparent.

Murray's first major move as Managing Director was his 1960 decision to purchase Henry Morgan & Company, a Montreal-based, family-owned department store with ten outlets and annual sales of $48 million. The move, financed with a rights issue and an increase in equity share capital, broke

---

*Murray fitted right in with the Company's Scottish traditions, although he had been born in Winnipeg. When he was out driving, he not only tried hard to make sure that the money he put into parking meters covered only his required time, but if he miscalculated and returned before the meter had expired, he'd sit in his car until it did.

† During the 1962 general election, when the upstart Quebec wing of the Social Credit party threatened the Liberal party's bastion, Murray was watching the outcome on television in the viceregal suite of the Royal York Hotel in Toronto with a group of HBC executives. As a news flash appeared on the screen that a Créditiste had captured the traditionally *Rouge* seat of Quebec East, Murray jumped to his feet and shouted, "It's a national disgrace!"

Chester's most sacred commandment that the Company not go "whoring in the East." Since Morgan's owned five shopping-centre branches, the purchase signalled the Bay's first venture into the suburbs, a move that Chester had also vehemently opposed. Morgan's staff organization and downtown store turned out to be riddled with problems and neglect, while Montreal's carriage trade, which had sustained the main store, promptly switched to shopping at Ogilvy's. "Those wheat farmers from Winnipeg moved in and catered to a wider market," Aird Nesbitt, who then owned Ogilvy's, disdainfully declared. "Now the Morgan family buys in *our* store."*

Despite its bold steps eastward, the Hudson's Bay Company retained its reputation as "the sick man of the Canadian retail business," its image tarnished by age and conservatism. There was growing evidence that the acquisition had been a desperately costly way to break into the East; $12 million had been spent to modernize its stores, and the chain had still to produce any profit. "A stroll through any Bay [department store unit] in the 1950s and 1960s indicated that the ingrained and rigid policies of the 1930s were not about to be abandoned overnight," reported James Bryant, a department store chronicler. "In a Bay store in the Boulevard Shopping Centre in the east end of Montreal, six years after the Bay had taken it over from Morgan's, the luggage department consisted of one camper's trunk and one suitcase. On them leaned a lonesome bicycle, the total stock in that category." Murray hired a top U.S. retailing consultant, Alfred H. Daniels, a former head of Federated Department Stores, to survey the scene. He found deep variances between both stores and departments. "There were no common denominators," Daniels reported. "You could have a fairly good shoe department in Vancouver, and the world's worst in Winnipeg. The Victoria store should have been sunk; it was a disgrace. None of the tricks of merchandising that had been developed in the previous decade were being used, or even heard of in many instances. They didn't know how to make a profit—the whole emphasis was on cost control. Don't spend a cent. They didn't even have records on profitability, so that prominent space in a store might be given to toothpaste and shaving cream, on which you hardly made a dime, while cosmetics, on

* A condition of the purchase was that Bart Morgan, the chain's chairman, be allowed to join the HBC board. He was welcomed, but Morgan seldom showed up, attending only 13 out of 147 HBC board meetings between April 13, 1961, and November 1, 1968, mainly the annual all-expenses-paid trips to the London annual Court. He almost never went to Winnipeg and was eventually dropped.

which you can make billions, were in the rear corner or some goddamn place.
The Bay had no understanding of the fashion business. They had a lot of klutzy
guys who could have been there or at Rupert's Landing, and had almost no
important women or Jews in the Company. Yet they had the best name in the
business, and problems that were both definable and rectifiable."

One of the rectifiable factors was finally moving the Bay into the shopping
centres sprouting outside Canada's main cities. The rush to the suburbs had
dramatically reversed the long-term dip in department stores' sales, so that by
1967, more than a third of their increased turnover was coming out of the
suburbs. Apart from the Morgan's acquisitions, the Hudson's Bay Company's
first shopping-centre branch—a Morgan's—was opened at Eglinton Square in
Metro Toronto in 1963, but it was a further six years before the first western
suburban store went on stream, in Richmond, outside Vancouver. That store
turned a profit in its first year, but it almost wasn't built. George Weightman,
a Company marketing executive, had taken Murray on a tour of Richmond,
parts of which lie very close to sea level and in those days had ditch drainage.
"There were these wide canals along the sides of each road, perpetually filled
with water, and every house had a footbridge for access," Weightman recalled.
"After I had been driving Dick Murray around for a few hours through the rain
between these canals, he drew himself up to his full height, gazed at the watery
view, and declared, 'As long as I'm Managing Director of this Company, we'll
never build a store in this swamp!'"*

At about this time, Murray presided over a sad historical event. York
Factory, the great tidewater headquarters on Hudson Bay where the HBC had
perfected the fur trade as a world-scale enterprise and the base from which the
first trader-explorers had set out to probe the Company's inland empire, was

---

* The Company followed up its free-standing suburban store in Richmond by opening later the
same year its first western shopping-centre outlet at Lougheed Mall in Burnaby, also adjoining
Vancouver, and in 1973 it built a shopping mall around its Richmond store. The failure to turn
a profit at Morgan's made Murray gun-shy of any further expansion and inhibited any move to
the suburbs. The Eglinton Square store was an exception—complete with a "parkade," which
now sits useless and dilapidated. Murray was finally persuaded to add another Montreal suburban store in Châteauguay. It was approved by the Canadian Committee, and Murray, who was
going to the United Kingdom for the annual Court, decided to stop off in Montreal on the way
and look at the site. He was appalled by what he saw—a sparse collection of blue-collar housing
developments bordering the Mohawk reserve—and he pulled the item off the agenda for the
Board meeting in London. Châteauguay ruined his appetite for further suburban expansion and
lowered his confidence in the judgment of Bay retail management.

turned over to the federal government as a national historic site. The object of a major naval engagement, invasions and bloody battles, York Factory had changed hands between the French and English ten times, eventually becoming not only the centre of the fur trade but also the venue for the annual meeting of the Council of the Northern Department of Rupert's Land, the body charged with governing the greater part of what would later become Canada. At one time, the depot had consisted of more than thirty buildings that included a haberdashery, ironmongery and even a perfumery; but in the 1930s all the structures but one were torn down for firewood. All that remained was the three-storey depot building, the "Big House" on the shore of the Hayes River, its hundred vacant windows yawning in the early sunsets. After 275 years of trading, the Company had abandoned the post in 1957, and now it was cutting the final ties. Even the handing-over ceremony didn't disturb York Factory's hibernation: it was conducted at Lower Fort Garry, more than five hundred miles to the southwest.

But York Factory couldn't entirely shed its heritage. The government did next to nothing with it, and the Big House started to be overrun with looters and loiterers, duck hunters who would come in off the Bay and set up bowling alleys on its main floor, using leftover cannon balls and empty beer bottles as pins. There was always the danger of fire; above all, it didn't seem right that this ghost of a wilderness metropolis should be given up to neglect and the ravages of nature. At least that was the feeling of Doug MacLachlan, a Winnipegger who had served briefly as an HBC apprentice clerk at York Factory in the late 1930s. A tight-end on the Blue Bomber championship football team of 1947, MacLachlan later ran his own fur-trading post at St Theresa Point on Island Lake in northern Manitoba, but his heart belonged to York Factory. After Ottawa took over, he became the desolate post's only permanent resident, tending the place, collecting relics (more than five thousand of them—candlesticks, strap-on skates, scissors and guns), guiding visitors, trapping to keep alive and setting up a chapel on the depot's second floor. "Sometimes you arrive at a place, and you feel as if you'd been there before," MacLachlan reminisced. "When I first got to York Factory, I knew where everything was, even the location of buildings no longer standing. It was kind of peculiar, but I felt that it should be properly protected, that there was something valuable here for the whole country." When the Canadian fur-trade historian Arthur J. Ray visited York Factory in the summer of 1982, he was discouraged by what he saw: "This summer marked the 300th anniversary of the founding of the first York Factory. At the end of each century the post has faced crises. In 1782 it was sacked and burned by the Comte de La Pérouse. In 1882 it was experiencing the trauma of readjusting to new economic and environmental circumstances.... In 1982 it is the heritage of the post that is threatened. Unless an aroused (and interested) public makes a concerted effort to make sure that appropriate actions are taken to save the architectural and archaeological heritage, too little will be done too late. I am not optimistic. I have a sinking feeling that the post is in its twilight years."

At the government turnover ceremony, Murray had joked about the absence of either adventure or profit in the exchange, but another decision caused a lot more harm to the Company's historical reputation. His management committee, concerned about lack of a national identity—Morgan's in the East, the Bay in the West—and a reputation for high prices and unfriendly service, persuaded Murray to hire a team of New York image-makers to come up with a solution. The result was the replacement of an inconsistent collection of mainly green signs and grey bags proclaiming in Old English script "Hudson's Bay Company" with a bright yellowish ochre designation in modern typeface that flatly stated "The Bay." An executive recalls that Murray had to be dragged along, protesting about tradition, and he personally vetoed a scheme for Beatle-influenced psychedelically coloured trucks.

By the mid-1960s, Murray had a more serious worry. His friend and mentor, Tony Keswick, decided to retire from the Governorship (though not yet the board) because, as he told friends, he would not personally preside over the Company's departure from Britain. Such a transfer had become an urgent necessity. Canadians on the British board had been officially notified on October 26, 1961, that none of the London members opposed the transfer except Keswick, who wished to go as soon as the time seemed propitious. Apart from the obvious efficiencies in having the Company run from the country where it transacted 90 percent of its business, tax considerations required the shift. At the 1965 annual Court, his last, Keswick bewailed the fact that under new British regulations on overseas trading companies, taxes on dividends would increase by about £800,000 a year, affecting shareholders' pockets in both the United Kingdom and Canada.* Having given his farewell address to

---

* Company documents revealed that in the preceding twenty years the HBC had suffered a tax disadvantage of approximately £2,500,000 by retaining its United Kingdom tax residence. If those taxes had been reinvested in the Company at 6 percent, its earnings would have been £3,750,000 higher.

the shareholders, Keswick would not allow anyone to tender him a retirement dinner as was the custom with departing Governors. He wrote to Murray that he was remaining on the board, but wanted to leave the Governorship "as quietly and as innocently as possible without any fuss whatsoever."

In Keswick's place arrived Lord Amory, destined to be the Hudson's Bay Company's last British Governor. Recently retired as British High Commissioner in Canada, Derick Heathcoat Amory had spent most of three lively decades in Conservative politics, having been minister of pensions in the post-war Churchill government and chancellor of the exchequer under Harold Macmillan. He had a distinguished military record that included twenty years in the Devon Yeomanry, where he trained as an expert in airborne warfare and during the dark days of the Second World War broke his leg in a parachute jump at the siege of Arnhem in the Netherlands. Taken prisoner, Arnory was about to have his left leg amputated when the Nazi doctor noted a pin identifying the Englishman as a master of the hunt. The two men swapped foxhunting stories as the German worked to save the limb.*

Amory lived modestly in a drab sixteen-guinea-a-week bachelor flat at Marsham Court, where he ironed his own shirts and made his own breakfast, although he could have afforded much more as chairman and part-owner of a large textile firm, John Heathcoat & Company. Shy and naturally secretive, he delivered a stern lecture to Roy Hodson of the *Financial Times* for "sensationalizing" news of his appointment to the HBC Governorship because the story had run under a two column headline.

He loved limericks and could deliver amusing speeches.† Eric Faulkner remembered the first time Amory was asked to speak at a Canadian HBC function: "We'd had about ten speeches already and everyone was absolutely speech-drunk when somebody called on Lord Amory, and to my horror he got to his feet. He had a habit of nibbling at the corner of his handkerchief and he started in his owlish way to talk about visiting our Montreal store and

---

* The wound never completely healed, and in November 1967 Amory had an emergency hip replacement. While still in hospital, he wrote to Murray: "I am now coming to life again with a new hip designed on most modern lines—stainless steel with plastic embellishments. I shall no doubt leave a trail of sparks behind me as I stride along unless I carry a grease gun for lubrication."
† His favourite was one of his own:
    There was a young lady of Kent,
    Who knew very well what it meant,
    When asked out to dine,
    Given cocktails and wine.
    She knew what it meant, but she went.

having had some difficulty disengaging himself from the chap who sold socks. Nobody knew how to react; there was a deathly hush, and I thought, 'Oh God, it's the first time the Canadians are seeing him. What are they going to make of him?' But he went on and on, talking about the sock salesman until some chaps began to realize he was pulling their legs, and there were a few titters. Soon the whole place was rocking with laughter. They made him go on for twenty minutes and after that, he had the whole top Bay executive in the palm of his hand. It was an extraordinary performance by a cunning old man."

Amory had been put in place because his influence with British politicians would grease the ways for the HBC's transfer. In that transaction, Dick Murray turned out to be an essential partner. The Canadian Managing Director had first demonstrated his political clout in 1960 when the Diefenbaker government introduced a 15-percent tax on dividends paid by branches of foreign companies operating in Canada. By quietly nurturing his contacts, Murray got the bill altered to exclude companies carrying on trade in Canada before July 1, 1867—an amendment that applied only to the HBC.

Circumstances were conspiring to accelerate the Company's trans-Atlantic shift: a 14-percent devaluation of the British pound to $2.40 made the investment in HBC shares more attractive to Canadian shareholders, and the prospect of British membership in the European Economic Community, now that the Germans supported Britain against the continuing French veto, had loosened Westminster's iron grip on the status quo. The Company's three hundredth anniversary, May 2, 1970, was chosen as the ideal symbolic date for patriation. Peter Wood moved temporarily to London and soon had all of the Company's accounting ledgers and systems transferred to Winnipeg.

At Amory's request, Joe Links did much of the preliminary negotiating with the Privy Council Office, conferring with lawyers and stock-exchange officials concerning the 92.6 percent of HBC shares then held in the United Kingdom. He recalled stalking the corridors of the Treasury—not his first visit, "but first as emissary of a former Chancellor of the Exchequer; it made a difference. The question we always asked ourselves was to whom control should be transferred, once permission was granted. To have transferred to a weak board and management would inevitably have resulted in a takeover followed by a breakup of the Company's assets, so that it would have ceased to exist. Could the Company have continued and prospered without a takeover bid, or fended one off, under the management available before 1970? We shall never know, but it did not seem likely to us. Why, then, did we not find the management we could hand over to, or go to Canada and run the Company ourselves? On this, perhaps, we shall be judged, as well as the wisdom of vesting control in a board of non-executive, part-time directors. As is so often the case with anomalous, unplanned developments, success or failure must be judged by whether they work. The HBC was certainly not a failure. For most of the twenty-five post-war years it was a success. Had we taken a different course it might have been more successful still. But the risk of failure was too daunting to contemplate."

When Lord Amory was taking the final poll on whether or not to go for transfer, he asked each board member for his views, and they agreed—but as Amory went around the table, all eyes were on Keswick, still a director and known for his antipathy to allowing the Company to leave England. The former Governor sat up a little straighter in his seat, tugged at the handkerchief in his sleeve, and in a clear, strong voice gave the verdict: "Mr. Governor, I would go. I would *go now*."*

Although double taxation was held out publicly as the main reason for the transfer, several other factors contributed to the move. Despite the British board's reservations about the quality of Canadian management, it was increasingly ludicrous to believe that an absentee board of part-timers could direct a modern retailing operation an ocean and half a continent away. It had become obvious that to stay in the race, the HBC would have to expand its retail operations significantly, which meant undertaking some serious public financing. In such transactions, the Company's dual citizenship was sure to depress credit ratings. Since no British trading company with a royal charter had ever moved abroad—and since the Canadian directors didn't really wish to lose that privileged status—some new corporate formula had to be discovered.

The man who found it was David Guest, a senior partner at Blake, Cassels & Graydon, the Toronto legal factory, who drew up a new Canadian Charter (to be granted by Elizabeth II in her capacity as Head of State of the United

---

* Keswick, who was knighted in 1972, later reminisced about that momentous day. "I had very mixed feelings. It was a bit like your child departing, you feel sad, but only momentarily because you know it's the right thing to do. I recognized that it should be done but didn't feel politically competent to handle the transfer to Canada. Politics is not my game. I'm just a dirty little merchant adventurer, with an eye on the main chance." In fact, Tony Keswick would probably not have voluntarily sanctioned the departure of his beloved Company for foreign parts in a thousand years. He retired from the board not long after the fatal vote and sold all his stock but never left the Company in spirit. Of all the modern HBC Governors, he alone magnified the grandeur of the HBC's past without using it to reflect glory on himself.

Kingdom and Canada) that would simultaneously keep the Company incorporated under the Royal Charter of 1670 and turn it into a Canadian corporation, subject to nearly all the standard provisions of the Canada Corporations Act.* Outlining the effect of Guest's approach, Murray wrote to Amory that it meant the "transfer is a historical move with certain economic consequences, rather than an economic move with historical consequences." That wonderfully meaningless phrase appealed to the Governor's sense of irony; he immediately wanted it translated into Latin and used on the crest of the new Canadian incorporation.

Before Guest had thought through his formula, both Michael Pitfield, the Clerk of the Privy Council in Ottawa, and Britain's Solicitor-General, the Right Honourable Sir Dingle Foot (eldest brother of Michael Foot, later leader of the Labour Party), had considered transfer impossible without winding up the Company in England first, which would have disrupted its continuity, cost much in new incorporation expenses and had dire tax consequences. When initially confronted by HBC officials advocating the transfer, the two men, who up to that time had not spoken, used the same metaphor to describe why they thought it could never be done. As if on cue, they said it was not technically feasible because it would be "like trying to reverse the immaculate conception." Following that rebuff, Murray recalled going to see Pitfield with the Guest opinion. "I had never met him before, and I stumbled into his office, as I often do, without having organized my sentences, but when I showed him Guest's letter, he read it, and like Rex Harrison in My Fair Lady telling Eliza Doolittle that she's got it, he said, 'My God, he's right. It can be done.'"

Prime Minister Lester Pearson had written a personal letter (drafted by Murray) to Prime Minister Harold Wilson advocating the HBC's transfer, and most of the outstanding questions seemed to be resolved when a new issue came up. Sam Bronfman, acting through Harris & Partners, a Toronto investment dealer, launched a takeover attempt to acquire 100 percent of the HBC's stock. Murray met the Bronfmans' intermediary, Noah Torno, who had become a minor partner in the Seagram business when his Danforth Wines

---

* The Queen granted a new Charter, the old one remaining but with a supplementary charter attached. The crucial work was done by the Clerk of the Privy Council in London. The Company's main exemption from the Canada Corporations Act was that the HBC would never have to use the word "Limited" in its name, because it is not and never was just another incorporated enterprise with limited liability. In his search for precedents, Guest found that the Victorian Order of Nurses and the Dominion Drama Festival had been granted similar privileged status.

was bought out in 1948, and told him that on no account would the Canadian government countenance a takeover of the HBC. Torno backed off, but the incident triggered a series of unexpected events.*

To prevent other takeover attempts, Murray started to lobby Ottawa for a special amendment that would not allow any investor to hold more than 10 percent of the Company's stock for a five-year period. A comparable ownership rule already existed for Canadian banks, but no other private-sector company enjoyed a similar privilege. The board had reluctantly accepted the notion, but there was one holdout: David Kilgour, who had succeeded Elmer Woods as head of the Canadian Committee in 1964. President of Great-West Life, son of a judge, father-in-law of a future prime minister and a pillar of the Winnipeg Establishment, Kilgour was debonair and worldly yet obstinately ambitious. During his three decades at Great-West, he had become used to behaving like a Chief Executive Officer and saw no reason to change his ways when he took on the HBC's Canadian Committee chairmanship. That quickly brought him into conflict with Dick Murray, who as Managing Director was charged with running the Canadian operation. The rift between the two men soon widened beyond repair.† Operational difficulties aside, their positions had hardened on the 10-percent ownership rule. Murray was now dedicated to achieving the five-year limit, while Kilgour had dug in at a full ten years and was personally lobbying John Turner, then the federal minister of justice, who had married his daughter Geills.

That not only subverted Murray's efforts at working through the proper Ottawa channels but also roused the ire of Amory because he and other board members were convinced Kilgour's real motive for backing the longer term was to guarantee himself a quiet decade as the HBC's first Canadian Governor. Amory had already indicated that a Canadian would be named to head the Company immediately after patriation, but no one had yet been picked.

---

* It was not the first time the Bronfmans had taken a run at the HBC. In 1952, Allan Bronfman, Sam's younger brother, approached Governor Cooper to buy Hudson's Bay Oil & Gas for Royalite Oil, which then managed most of the family's energy investments. Cooper turned him down but described the encounter in his diary: "The Bronfmans, who began as bartenders and bootleggers, have made a fantastic fortune and they seem to buy new companies almost every day.... I liked him and would have asked him to lunch, but Elmer Woods has advised me that Phil Chester hated him so much, he would have been most unhappy" [May 30, 1952].
† Their relationship turned so nasty that Amory called a special board meeting in the viceregal suite of the Windsor Hotel in the autumn of 1969 to discuss the impasse. Most of the directors backed Murray. The two men reluctantly shook hands; but nothing was really resolved.

Kilgour considered himself the ideal candidate, being familiar with the HBC's Canadian workings—and being dangerously close to the end of his steward-ship at Great-West Life. (Control of the Company had been purchased by Power Corporation in 1969, and Paul Desmarais, the Montreal conglomerate's chairman, was known to be unhappy with Kilgour's style of management.)

After Kilgour had been involved in several minor attempts at trying to usurp the authority of both the Canadian Managing Director and the British board, Murray's patience broke, and on February 14, 1970, he wrote to Amory requesting that Kilgour be immediately dismissed because he "had not only failed in his responsibilities as a director and as Chairman of the Canadian Committee, but had indeed violated the trust placed in him as the premier of the Canadian directors charged with special responsibilities for loyalty and cooperation with the Governor of this Company." Two weeks later Amory wrote to the Canadian Committee Chairman, demanding that he submit his resignation at a forthcoming Montreal board meeting because, as he put it, "not only is there a lack of mutual confidence between you and the Managing Director but increasingly between you and me." Kilgour refused to quit. Amory got tough. He sent a cable informing the recalcitrant Chairman that if he didn't offer his resignation he would be retired involuntarily. Kilgour kept his peers on edge until the last minute. They had misjudged their man. He may have overreached himself, but he was too proud to be humiliated by the swarm of former colleagues now baying for his blood. So as the first order of business at the March 6, 1970, directors' meeting he resigned with a flourish, wishing the Company a long, happy future, and walked out.

Not quite. A week later he wrote a stinging rebuke to Amory, denying all of Murray's accusations. "We reached exactly the right conclusion," he wrote, "but I was unhappy with the 'saturation bombing' you felt was required in getting there.... There was an amusing cartoon in the *New Yorker* a few years ago of a mild little man sitting at a Board room table with about a dozen big, red-faced, blustery Directors. He was shown breaking into their debate with the remark, 'Haven't you forgotten that I own 51 percent of the stock?' Some of us at times forget that in the Hudson's Bay Company Britishers own over 90 percent." Amory, ever the gentleman, replied: "During the unheroic years in which I served in the Army, I was taught that when in doubt deploy maximum fire power! However, I hated doing it and if I did overestimate, I can only ask you to forgive me.... It was, I think, one of your fellow countrymen who said that 'the British have the rigidity of red hot pokers without their warmth.'" Both men agreed to consign their vitriolic exchange "to the flames" so that it would not, someday, turn up in the Company Archives. When Amory made that request of Murray, who had been sent copies of the correspondence, the Managing Director enthusiastically agreed. "Your 'for the fire and ashes' exchange of letters with David Kilgour was waiting for me when I got home. They are returned for shredding in Mrs. Harron's hungry little machine," he wrote to the Governor.

There remained only the matter of choosing an appropriate farewell gift to the departing Canadian Chairman. Having been asked what he would prefer, Kilgour suggested a Canadian painting and a trip to the Arctic with his wife, Mary. In response, Murray immediately set a $2,000 limit on any canvas that might be purchased and had cost accountants do runs on what kind of expense would be involved in the northern expedition. "I am not too happy to have Mr. and Mrs. Kilgour go on a working trip," he wrote to Amory, "since [his] views on the English directors are so embittered.... I would prefer to see him go on a goose hunt in our Grumman Goose."

Kilgour was not thrilled about the wild-goose chase because he was told he couldn't take Mary along, and suggested that the two of them accompany a regular northern inspection trip. That idea threw Murray into a total panic. "It is incredible," he wrote to Amory, "but he can be as difficult (almost) in retirement as he was before. He has written to request a trip to the North with his wife—we thought we had gone rather far with the Goose Hunt offer."

Murray eventually got an auditor's opinion that any northern journey by the retiring chairman would be a taxable benefit, and in a curt letter on July 8 he withdrew the offer. Kilgour replied in kind: "God forbid that I should be involved in over-generosity by the HBC. I am going north, but completely happily on my own, and a painting from HBC would, on reflection, not be something I would welcome—so please forget it."

Kilgour's stormy departure left open the issue of who would succeed Amory and become the Company's first Canadian Governor. The clear choice of board members had been Donald Gordon, the dynamic former Bank of Canada deputy governor and chairman of Canadian National Railways, who had joined the HBC board in 1967. But he died within two years of his arrival, and the Bay insiders had to look elsewhere. In 1970, after only three hundred years, the Hudson's Bay Company recognized the existence of Toronto and appointed its first director from that trading post, A.J. MacIntosh, a senior partner in Blake, Cassels & Graydon. And it was from Toronto that the majority of the British directors wanted to recruit their first Canadian Governor. He was Allen Thomas Lambert, the high-school drop-out who had joined a Victoria branch of the Bank of Toronto at sixteen and was now chairman of the Toronto-Dominion Bank. "Lord Amory approached me and it was not something you would turn aside lightly," Lambert recalled. "I would have had to give the Company at least 40 percent of my time and I wasn't able to resolve in my own mind how I could do that and still be fair to the bank." Other suggested candidates included Senator Hartland de Montarville Molson, the former chairman of his family's brewing company, and Major-General A. Bruce Matthews, chairman of Excelsior Life Insurance, but in the end the job went to yet another Winnipegger: George Taylor Richardson.

The sixth Richardson to head the family business, he was a tall, imperial man who exuded a kind of easy institutional grace. Although he seemed on the surface to be the ultimate corporate bureaucrat, whose proudest boast was how many members of his company's twenty-five-year club were third-generation Richardson employees, there was an adventurous side to him as well, known only to his closest associates. An experienced helicopter pilot, Richardson would guide his Bell Jet Ranger across the Canadian landscape, swooping down on some lonely HBC post, skimming over the nocturnal terrain of the endless prairie, following the moving lights on highways and train tracks, hopping across the Rockies, and finally, like some giant mechanical hummingbird, dip his skids in the Pacific. A Bay man even as a youngster, Richardson ran a trapline near his old family home on St Mary's Road at St Germain, near Winnipeg, catching and skinning ermine, mink and the odd coyote, which he sold to the HBC. He lived there with his elegant wife, Tannis, hunting, riding his horses and puffing his Rea Belvedere cigars—guarded all the while by a rainbow of peacocks, gugalating trumpeter swans and a domesticated flight of ptarmigan.

The governance issue having been settled (though Richardson was not sworn into office until November 26, 1970), the Canadianization of the Company moved into its final phase. The cabinet in Ottawa had stamped the terms of the transfer (including a five-year, 10-percent ownership clause) on February 26, 1970, and two months later Lord Amory had received notification from the U.K. Treasury approving the move. On May 28, the British proprietors convened at Beaver House for the last time. The HBC had been founded on May 2, 1670, in Whitehall Palace, when Charles II handed Prince Rupert the Charter, naming him and his fellow Adventurers "true lords and proprietors" of all the sea and lands of Hudson Bay and its drainage system—

a grant that turned out to enclose a land empire of 1.5 million square miles, 40 percent of modern Canada plus several states of the northern United States. Now, three centuries later, the Company still mattered (it ranked fifty-sixth among U.K. firms in 1970) and, more than that, its uninterrupted existence was a reminder of the days when Britain had been great—just as its departure served notice that Britain was not quite so great any more.

"The die is cast, we're on our way to Canada!" exclaimed one of the elderly Adventurers after Amory proclaimed the transfer to Winnipeg; only four hands had been raised in protest when the Governor called for a vote. That evening, the directors adjourned to Nelson's Tavern at Greenwich, where the supply ships that ventured to York Factory had once been waved farewell. Joe Links had devised a menu replicating those early feasts; many toasts were proposed and many more were drunk, and while there may have been personal regrets, the mood was one of exhilaration. They had kept the faith, these quirky Scotsmen and their English cousins who privately respected history while publicly appearing to exist only for profit, kept the faith and dispatched the Company to its modern domicile, intact, ready to benefit from the breath of fresh life in a new world.

THAT SAME DAY IN OTTAWA, Governor General Roland Michener had been host to a small ceremony at Government House at which the HBC's new Canadian Charter was signed into law. Because the move required simultaneous proclamation on both sides of the Atlantic, there was some concern about delays. Ron Basford (born in Winnipeg, of course), who was Registrar-General of Canada at the time, asked his executive assistant, Tex Enemark, to handle the details, including the business of affixing the Great Seal of Canada on the new Charter. Enemark telephoned Louis McCann, the Deputy Registrar-General, who explained that he could get the charter from Government House, once it had been signed by Michener, and bring it back to his office to imprint the Seal, then return it for Basford's signature. "I asked McCann how long it would take," Enemark recalled, "and he said perhaps forty-five minutes at the outside, but that would have meant that the Hudson's Bay Company would have been homeless for most of an hour, so I said, 'Well, why don't you take the Great Seal up to Government House and make the impression there?'"

"Because it's bolted down," McCann replied, never having been confronted with such an order before.

"Why not unbolt it?"

"It weighs 350 pounds!"

"So, get a truck."

Although McCann firmly believed that the security of Canada depended squarely on the Great Seal's remaining bolted in place on the twelfth floor of the Canadian Building in downtown Ottawa, he did recognize that this was a special occasion and agreed—though he insisted the entire operation be classified as top secret and an armoured vehicle be rented from Brink's for the transfer. The HBC was represented at the brief ceremony by Graham Towers, the former Bank of Canada Governor who had served on the board; David Guest, the lawyer who had thought up the patriation formula, was also present. There, too, was the Great Seal of Canada, resting on top of the Governor General's writing desk, which was almost collapsing under its weight. "At this point, a noticeable change overtook McCann," Enemark remembered. "Here was a middle-level civil servant who had spent his whole life immersed in the monotony of the shuffling of the paperwork of officialdom.... Now, suddenly, there was this great national event wherein the oldest incorporated company in the world was going through the metamorphosis from being British to being Canadian, and there was Karsh's brother, Malak, taking pictures, while Louis was telling the Governor General, the Registrar-General and the former Bank of Canada Governor about where to sign. McCann became quite animated, showing His Excellency how to turn the screw on the Great Seal with such zest that I thought the desk would collapse for sure. After several attempts, the impression of the Seal was placed on the document, and the job was done."*

And that was how the Hudson's Bay Company came to Canada at last.

---

* At the date of its Canadian incorporation, the HBC's assets consisted of nine ships, three airplanes, 585 trucks, 33 large and medium-sized department stores, 218 northern stores, three of the world's largest fur-auction houses, merchandise worth $65 million, a payroll of 15,000, plus a 21.9-percent interest in 41 million acres of oil and gas rights across the Prairies. That was a considerable increase from its original stake in the country, three hundred years earlier, when the Company's total assets consisted of a leaky ketch, one abandoned canoe, three pairs of used snowshoes and fourteen employees. But then it also owned 38.8 percent of Canada— compared with only .0017 percent by 1970. It took a further four years for the Hudson's Bay Company Archives to be transferred from London. Shirlee Smith, the Keeper of the Archives, was posted to London in October 1973 and supervised the transfer of 4,200 linear feet of records, which were shipped in six twenty-ton containers, divided among different ships for safety across the Atlantic. In the fall of 1974 the documents were deposited in the Provincial Archives of Manitoba, where they are housed in an environmentally controlled vault on the second floor of the Manitoba Archives Building. This significant archive is consulted by national and international scholars and the odd journalist.

McGiverin's Run

He altered the HBC's corporate culture forever.

ONE OF THOSE UNWRITTEN CONDITIONS set by London before agreeing to the HBC's transfer was that a top retailer be hired to run what had become the Company's core business. No one was more anxious to recruit the right person than Dick Murray. The managing director was a great Bay man but a lousy merchandiser. Murray's restless energy and infectious enthusiasm had guided the smooth Canadianization of the Company, but it had also burned him out. (Suffering from nervous exhaustion, he signed himself into the Mayo Clinic but soon recovered.) More dedicated to the glorious *idea* of the Company than its often grubby daily realities, he began to have trouble making decisions. He would get his staff to work up proposals for construction of a shopping centre branch, approve their submission, then take it to the board and vote against the project. At the same time, he was facing an internal dilemma about the leveraging staff accountants were injecting into the Company's balance sheets. (Borrowing charges, instead of being shown under merchandising costs, were attributed to the overall operation, which made the retailing results look far better than they actually were.)

Murray's choice to head the department stores—though he must have known he was also picking his own successor—was Donald Scott McGiverin, then a Winnipeg-based group vice-president with Eaton's, who joined the Bay as Managing Director, Retail Stores, in September 1969. Born in Calgary (where his father spent the best part of his fifty-three years with Dominion Rubber, which later became Uniroyal) and educated in Winnipeg, McGiverin began working at Eaton's (selling men's shoes at $1.85 a day) on weekends and holidays, leaving only to earn an MBA at Ohio State. He was never good at sports. Referring to his lack of co-ordination, his father once remarked that his son "ran like a crowd." In Toronto, Donald quickly worked his way up the Eaton's corporate ladder, becoming a protégé of Chairman John David Eaton, and in 1961, at only thirty-seven, was appointed to the company's board, the youngest non-Eaton ever to be so favoured. Five years later he was transferred to Winnipeg and placed in charge of western operations.

One reason McGiverin worked so hard was his tragic home life. He married Margaret Ann Weld in 1950, and they had a son (Richard) and a daughter (Mary). In 1957, they were living just north of Toronto in Thornhill, which at that time had run-off ditches paralleling the streets. Richard, who was then four, had dressed up to celebrate his grandfather's birthday and went out to watch the water flow by. He lost his footing and drowned while his mother watched helplessly from a kitchen window. She never got over it and died eleven years later. Mary suffered from a rare disease of the spine called scoliosis that required special care including years in a body cast. Though she later fully recovered, her condition took its toll on McGiverin's spirit.

In Winnipeg, McGiverin at first had little intention of taking the Bay offer because he assumed he would have a shot at the top slot in Eaton's. But in the spring of 1969, when John David Eaton retired, his sons instead picked R.J. Butler, who was far less experienced. McGiverin took his daughter on a long European cruise aboard the *Michelangelo,* and somewhere under the Mediterranean moon decided that the Hudson's Bay Company was his destiny. That option was made considerably easier by an offer from Eaton's to work for Butler in a newly created but ill-defined post as vice-president, corporate development. "These guys were sending me east to do something I wasn't interested in," he told a friend. "I'm a sock salesman, after all. Corporate development, what's that? It probably meant dealing in property, but I did only two real-estate deals in my life—when I sold my houses in Thornhill and Winnipeg, and lost money on both—so I didn't feel qualified."

McGiverin and Murray worked well together, each glad he wasn't doing the other's job. During the next three years the Company purchased the A.J. Freiman department-store operation in Ottawa as well as 49.9 percent of the G.W. Robinson firm in Hamilton, and eight suburban stores were opened.

In the fall of 1972, after an Edmonton board meeting of Hudson's Bay Oil & Gas, Murray was called into the hotel suite of HBC Governor George Richardson and his Deputy, Alex MacIntosh, a tough Toronto lawyer named to the board in 1969.* They unceremoniously presented Murray with a memorandum that not only listed in precise, almost hourly detail the newly outlined duties of the job he had held for thirteen years but also spelled out in humiliating terms that he was henceforth not allowed to discuss any aspect of retailing with anyone except McGiverin, and that, effective immediately, he couldn't even enter an HBC department store without McGiverin's permission. On a recent visit to Montreal, Murray had entertained at lunch a French-Canadian executive who had just been hired by the Morgan's subsidiary. It had been a friendly, welcoming gesture, especially so since Murray was the only HBC executive who could speak French, and he wanted the newcomer to feel at home. But Richardson and MacIntosh used that incident as proof of his interference in the retail department. "It was grubby, grubby," Murray recalled. "So I just said, 'Oh, for God's sake, I quit.'"†

On November 17, 1972, McGiverin was appointed president of the Hudson's Bay Company. He hit the ground running. "At our first management meeting," he recalled, "we committed ourselves to becoming the preeminent department store in Canada." The Company had a long way to go. The year McGiverin took over, retail sales generated per square foot of store space were a dismal $57, compared with $88 for Woodward's and $100 for Simpsons. The stores were run according to a pathetically outmoded decentralized buying and distribution system, with each major unit having its own warehouse and purchasing agents. The HBC was very much the weak sister of Canadian retailing.

A born-again pragmatist with little concern for the Company's traditional survival syndrome, McGiverin set out on a massive acquisition spree to establish The Bay as *the* leading national retailer. Trying to catch up on two decades of hesitation, he projected the HBC's presence into suburban malls by accepting nearly every developer's proposal that came along. At the same time, he took over a major real-estate company (despite his self-confessed ignorance of the subject) and began to assemble and build his own shopping centres and shake up the HBC's oil investments in a huge gamble that almost paid off. In

---

* MacIntosh's family motto is "Touch not the cat without a glove."
† Murray later became head of the government's Foreign Investment Review Agency and, later still, president of the Federal Business Development Bank. He then retired as a gentleman adventurer, dividing his year between seaside dwellings in Maine and British Columbia. But the Company is not forgotten; above the bathtub in each of his houses hangs a full-colour painting of the *Nonsuch*, the ship that started it all.

the decade and a half of his dominance he expanded Company sales tenfold from $502 million to $4,829 million, and even if the impact of his stewardship was muffled by the recession of the 1980s, he altered the HBC's corporate culture forever.

But the bill was staggering. McGiverin, fully supported by the board, which was loaded with financial experts, leveraged the Company to the hilt so that its once modest "blister on the balance sheet" became a festering boil. Under McGiverin, the HBC's debt grew exponentially from $70 million to $2.5 billion while the number of issued shares nearly doubled. The pain resulting from the huge debt became intense when prime interest rates peaked at 22 ¾ percent in September 1981.*

McGiverin's priority assignment was to create a major retailing presence in Toronto, the country's largest marketplace. One problem was that he alone among his planning staff had ever lived there, and everyone except for his comptroller (Donald Wood, who was from Montreal), was a Winnipegger, totally unaware of the Ontario city's retailing geography. "We wanted to be at Yonge and Bloor because we would then be sitting on the crossroads of the subway system," Wood recalled, "but market research was of little help because they gave us a potential sales range of $15 million to $30 million. We opted for a $60-million, 260,000-square-foot flagship department store and made the final decision in the recreation room of Don McGiverin's house on a Sunday morning in the fall of 1971, with most of us not quite sure where Bloor and Yonge actually was."† That dramatic choice meant that McGiverin himself had to move to be near his massive investment, and that in turn meant the end of Winnipeg as the Company's operational head office.

Completion of the giant Toronto unit was celebrated to the rocking cadence of the Grease Ball Boogie Band on August 1, 1974. At the official opening a week later, so many customers jammed in to inspect the first downtown department store opened in the Ontario capital in forty-four years

---

*In early 1973, three Canadian brokerage houses, Richardson Securities, Harris & Partners and Wood Gundy Limited managed a syndicate that floated $100 million in convertible HBC debentures. The proceeds were delivered to McGiverin in the form of a huge cheque embossed on the back of a stretched beaver pelt, certified by the Canadian Imperial Bank of Commerce.
† The final decision on Bloor and Yonge made by the HBC board on November 19, 1971, was not unanimous. Rolph Huband, Company Secretary, recalls that "in my thirty years of attending Board and Canadian Committee meetings, almost all decisions have been by consensus with no opposition, but a vote was taken on both Bloor and Yonge and on the Freiman purchase, with three directors voting against in each case."

that after two hours the doors had to be shut and escalators closed down.*
McGiverin subsequently expanded the Company's national activities by
purchasing the 30,000 credit-card accounts of Montreal's bankrupt department store Dupuis Frères, creating an HBC travel agency, establishing a sixty-
three-outlet catalogue-store operation under the Shop-Rite banner, and
acquiring 35 percent of Eaton's life insurance and mutual fund marketing
agency, renamed Eaton Bay Financial Services Limited. But the most interesting non-retail diversification was the deal in 1973 with Siebens Oil & Gas.

Through a subsidiary, the Company still held mineral rights on 4.5 million
prairie acres; but depletion allowances had run out, and McGiverin decided
on a potentially more profitable—though much more risky—investment. It
involved turning the HBC's rights income over to Siebens, a company then
active in North Sea exploration, in return for 3.2 million Siebens shares
(35 percent of the total), mainly to come from its treasury. A brainchild of
Don Mackenzie, a savvy Calgary oil consultant who had joined the HBC
board a year earlier, the deal caught investors' imaginations because it gave
The Bay, which had money but few proven oil reserves, the chance to share
in a big potential strike, and it gave Siebens, which had potential oilfields
but little money, more cash for exploration.

Not long afterwards, McGiverin purchased control of Markborough
Properties, which owned a real-estate portfolio worth at least $100 million. In
a dramatic last-minute struggle with Robert Campeau, McGiverin outbid the
developer from Sudbury mainly because hysterical Markborough shareholders
wanted anybody but Campeau to buy their company. They kept The Bay in
the bidding and stormed Royal Trust offices five minutes before closing to get
back the stock they had already pledged to the swashbuckling financier.

Ironically, McGiverin, whose hiring as a first-rate retailer had been a condition of the U.K. directors for transferring the Company to Canada, was soon
spending most of his time on corporate affairs, acquisitions and strategy, while
Ronald Sheen, an uninspired executive who had been bypassed for McGiverin
in 1969, ran The Bay department stores through most of the 1970s. By the
spring of 1978, McGiverin had gathered around him a top-flight takeover

* The HBC honoured the launch by promising to donate three black beavers to the
Metropolitan Toronto Zoo. But the Company's trappers had done such a thorough job that
none of the subspecies could be found in Canada's backwoods. Three animals were finally
located at a breeding ranch near Salt Lake City, Utah. They were purchased for $200 and
shipped north.

team of financial experts including Peter Wood, John McIntyre, Iain Ronald, Donald Wood, Rolph Huband, Peter Nobbs and Douglas Mahaffy, while Marvin Tiller, aided by George Whitman, provided locomotion for the Northern Stores Division. McGiverin himself, usually jacketless, feet up on his desk and incessantly puffing on Camel cigarettes, had grown into the job, running the Company with good humour but little charisma. Dependent more on logic than emotion, he conducted the business not so much by issuing orders as by making suggestions—and repeating them if they weren't followed up. Irish in manner rather than Scottish—outgoing and breezy, not introspective and gloomy—he liked to pretend that he was really a small-town boy, hitching his pants up towards his armpits, telling stories with a grin on his lived-in face and rhapsodizing about the weekends he spent "getting a little plastered" at his "hut in a swamp" at Palgrave, Ontario. (He actually lived in a luxury apartment in the Manulife Centre in Toronto's upscale Bloor and Bay retailing district, and much preferred spending weekends at the Lyford Cay resort in Nassau, where he had a house.) One of his few eccentricities was that he never sold any of his cars, which he considered old friends. He still had his first purchase, a 1930 Ford coupe, but mostly drove his 1963 Falcon, his 1962 Cadillac convertible or the 1972 Lincoln—bought to celebrate his appointment as the HBC's president. He never got caught up in the Company's history except as a source for after-dinner anecdotes, and stoutly maintained that "you don't make money by reflecting on a glorious past…. There are no muskrat traps hanging from the rafters any more."

THE YEAR OF THE BIG CHANGE WAS 1978. McGiverin's acquisitive impulses reached their crescendo as, in a series of stunning corporate coups, he more than doubled the Company's revenues—as well as its longterm debt.

There were a few disposals: the sale of a minority interest in Glenlivet Distillers of Scotland to Seagrams for $6 million, realizing $4.4 million in profit; sale of the HBC's 35-percent interest in Siebens Oil & Gas to Dome Petroleum at $38.50 a share, generating a $94-million gain for a five-year hold, though the dream of striking it rich in the North Sea never materialized.

In early June, word came through from George Richardson's Vancouver office that Joe Segal, chairman of Zellers Limited, which operated cut-rate department stores, wanted to discuss some new merchandising concepts with McGiverin. When the two men met, Segal came right to the point: his great merchandising idea was to buy the Hudson's Bay Company. He proposed purchasing 51 percent of the issued shares at $28, about $7 over current market, though part of the value would be in Zellers shares. An astonished McGiverin replied that any offer would have to be for 100 percent, and all cash. Shortly afterwards, Jim Pitbiado, chairman of Dominion Securities, the country's largest brokerage house, phoned McGiverin to inform him that Dominion Securities would be acting for Segal, but only if it was a friendly takeover. Then came the kicker: Segal informed McGiverin that he had consulted his associates and that a 100-percent, all-cash offer was on its way. Segal matter-of-factly confirmed that he had the necessary funds ($450 million), and agreed to meet McGiverin in Winnipeg on July 7 to complete the takeover.

The Company of Adventurers went ape. Flying to that meeting (aboard the Company's new HS-125-400 $2-million jet), McGiverin and his advisers hurriedly pored over intelligence reports they had gathered about Segal. Born in Vegreville, Alberta, he had dropped out of school at fifteen to work in the Credit Arcade clothing store in Edmonton ("a quarter down and a quarter a week"), was a labourer during construction of the Alaska Highway, then lost his entire savings in an all-night poker game. After two years in the army, he was demobbed in Vancouver and launched a small army and navy surplus outlet, starting with some naval exhaust fans built to operate through portholes. He sold them off to tailor shops willing to have round exhaust holes cut in their store fronts. Subsequently he opened a clothing outlet called Fields near Woodward's main store. That was the beginning of a highly successful western chain that later included a hardware operation (Marshall Wells). He eventually used his Fields holdings for a reverse takeover of Zellers, a Canadian variety chain that had been sold in the 1950s to W.T. Grant, a U.S. marketing giant. At the time, Canada's business Establishment thought so little of Segal that the news of his takeover pushed down Zellers' already depressed stock $2.00 to a new low of $2.50. But within two years, Zellers was in fine shape and Segal was wealthy enough to purchase Vancouver's most beautiful house.*

Before he left Toronto for the Winnipeg meeting, McGiverin had tried to find out who was backing Segal and soon traced the Bank of Montreal as the

---

* Rio Vista, his palace at 2170 Southwest Marine Drive (sold to a Singapore billionaire in 1990), had its own terraced Italian garden, waterfall, tranquillity ponds and galleried conservatory where he grew grapefruit-sized lemons and melon-sized grapefruit. The mansion itself had ten fireplaces, eleven bathrooms, a sunken ballroom, a full-sized tavern with suede walls, not to mention a banquet-sized dining chamber, a billiards room decorated in tartan, a full-scale spa and so on—all done up in a mongrel mixture of elegance and Disneyland.

most likely suspect. When he got Fred McNeil, the Montreal's chairman, on the telephone, nearly everything McGiverin asked was met with stone-cold silence.

Finally the HBC president demanded, "May I assume that your bank is behind this takeover bid?"

"If I were in your position," McNeil replied, "that is the assumption I would make. But I didn't say it."

The Winnipeg meeting began warily. McGiverin and his advisers had concluded that only one move would defuse Segal's takeover strategy: a pre-emptive bid for Zellers.

"I recognized the Hudson's Bay Company as a sleeping giant with a tremendous, understated balance sheet," Segal later recalled. "The Company would have been the greatest leveraged buyout in history. Its breakup value was huge, except that I wouldn't have broken it up but would have maximized the value of its assets—and that meant merging it with Zellers to create the largest retailing entity in Canada. I didn't particularly care which of the two companies emerged on top, as long as it was done."

About halfway through Segal's presentation, his financial man, John Levy, mused—as if he'd just then thought of it—"Of course the real way to do it is for The Bay to take over Zellers."

McGiverin was delighted the suggestion—which was to have been his trump card—had been made. Three months later, on October 3, 1978, The Bay bought 57.1 percent of Zellers for the equivalent of $10 a share, with Segal receiving 452,177 HBC shares and a lump of cash for his 13-percent holding in the chain. For his $76-million purchase price, McGiverin obtained control of the 155-store Zellers and the 61-unit Fields chain. The transaction temporarily made the Vegreville entrepreneur the HBC's largest shareholder; becoming the first Jewish Governor of the Hudson's Bay Company was within his grasp.

But in two months, Zellers and Segal were overshadowed by the largest deal in the HBC's history.

SIMPSONS AND THE HBC had always been one another's favourite buyout targets. They each specialized in quality merchandise, considered themselves the country's best department stores, but unlike Eaton's had no national customer constituencies. To combine the western dominance of The Bay with the eastern presence of Simpsons seemed a perfect match. Back in the 1920s, Sir Augustus Nanton of the HBC's Canadian Committee had approached Sir

Joseph Flavelle on the possibility of a merger, but the Simpsons chairman declined on the grounds that he was reluctant at his age to launch new ventures. In October 1936, Philip Chester and George Allan, then running the Canadian operation, were hastily summoned to London by Governor Patrick Ashley Cooper. When they arrived, Cooper informed them he was about to complete negotiations for a merger with Simpsons and that the Toronto department store's chairman, Charles Burton, and its investment adviser (also a major shareholder), Harry Gundy, were on the way to London with the documents, ready to be signed. At a meeting the following morning, also attended by HBC director Sir Edward Peacock, Chester made a fervent plea against any such move. "I talked for about forty minutes," he recalled, "about Simpsons, the HBC Stores, the ruinous effect of the deal upon the future of HBC in Canada, and so forth.... As we filed out, Peacock called me aside and, putting his arm around my shoulder, said 'Don't you worry,' and left. A few days later Burton and Gundy arrived and proceeded to Hudson's Bay House to see Cooper. By accident or design, they were left in a small anteroom cooling their heels for well over an hour, saw Cooper for a few minutes, and left in a state of fury and consternation."*

The next attempt, in 1968, was much more sophisticated, involving G. Allan Burton, who had that year succeeded his brother Edgar as chairman of Simpsons, and Lord Amory, the HBC's last British Governor. Dick Murray had brought the two men together, and Amory felt quite excited by the prospect, since the combined chains would account for 22 percent of Canadian department-store sales. "There might be something really big for our old Company here," he wrote to Murray. "Anyway, if we do not like it, we can sing in Elizabethan style, 'With a hey nay ninny nonny-no!'"

Simpsons then had a market value of $280 million compared to The Bay's $320 million. In the minds of the HBC executives, there was no question whether this should be a merger; it was to be a takeover, pure and simple. Two main problems had to be overcome. The first was corporate. In 1953, Simpsons had signed an agreement with Sears, Roebuck & Company of Chicago to form a new enterprise, Simpsons-Sears Limited, which took over

* The following notation appears in Chester's unpublished history of the Company: "Some years later Charlie Burton wrote the story of his business life [A *Sense of Urgency*, published by Clarke, Irwin in 1952]. He told me it contained a chapter on these events with HBC and I urged him with all the power at my command to cut this out.... When the book was published I was thankful to see he had done so."

Simpsons' mail-order operation and launched an intensive drive to open branches in suburban malls. Among the many conditions of the partnership (which included a provision that Simpsons-Sears could not operate stores within twenty-five miles of a Simpsons outlet) was a firm undertaking that no Simpsons shares could be transferred without Sears' permission. When Burton visited Chicago, Sears executives granted him a hunting licence to follow up the possibilities but also made it clear they would retain veto power over the results.

The other problem was personal. Allan Burton, DSO, CM, ED, LLD, OSJ, KCLJ, had a proud pedigree, overdeveloped social graces and a keen sense of his own importance. His love of horses (he was Joint Master of the Eglinton Hunt for twenty-three years) led him to a commission with the Governor General's Horse Guards.* He fought with the regiment in the Second World War (winning a Distinguished Service Order on the Italian front) and later took over command.† Burton transferred his sense of military precision to Simpsons, trying, not always successfully, to operate his main store like divisional headquarters and its branches like outlying regiments—and he was not about to give up command easily. He ran Simpsons as a family concern, even though the Burtons and all the directors and senior officers together owned a mere 1.8 percent of the shares.

Burton saw The Bay offer as a way of both increasing his company's retail reach and making the combination so powerful it could never be overshadowed by Sears. The two sides decided to meet in secret on neutral ground at the Waldorf-Astoria Hotel in New York on January 15, 1969. Their venue was a large dining-room decorated like the Hall of Mirrors at Versailles, with a long green baize table down the middle and delegations seated on either side, as if they were negotiating a peace treaty. Burton had written out several "military appreciations" of the situation, and concluded that the new retailing giant emerging out of the deal should include all of the HBC's operations and be owned 40 percent each by Simpsons and the HBC, with Sears tacked on for the remaining 20 percent. The Bay executives wanted to include only their stores,

---

*The Burtons were pivotal members of the Canadian Establishment. Their youngsters played department store together with the Eaton boys in their Forest Hill recreation rooms, running a pretend shop named the Seaton Company.

† "The war toughened me up a great deal," he maintained. "For one thing, I overcame my quite noticeable stutter. That was from talking on a field wireless sixteen, seventeen hours a day. When I first started in action, I used to have to write out every single message before I tried to transmit it."

combining them with those of Simpsons and Simpsons-Sears into a package—owned 40 percent by The Bay, 40 percent by Simpsons-Sears and 20 percent by the Canadian public—all operating under the Hudson's Bay Company banner. Those deep differences guaranteed failure, and when it came, Burton blamed the impasse on the HBC's unwillingness to include its oil and gas holdings in the deal. In fact, the idea had been killed by Sears executives in Chicago who insisted they would not go along with any arrangement that didn't guarantee them 50 percent of voting shares.

A decade later, in 1978, coming off his successful takeover of Zellers, McGiverin examined Simpsons afresh. That had been a banner year for Burton. Simpsons-Sears was celebrating its silver anniversary, and in June he had entertained his twenty-five-year employees with a Sunday picnic at his country home. A month later he was host to an anniversary dinner for Edward Telling, chairman of Sears, Roebuck, the world's largest retailer with annual sales of $18 billion. During dessert, Burton brought up the fact that he felt his company was vulnerable to takeovers and that it might be best to move towards an outright amalgamation of Simpsons with Simpsons-Sears. Six weeks later Telling agreed, and on August 16 the merger was announced. The new company, with assets of $3.2 billion, would be Canada's seventh largest, and although Sears, Roebuck would retain a controlling interest, Burton would remain Chairman and Chief Executive Officer well past retirement age. The scheme required only the approval of the Foreign Investment Review Agency, which then had to confirm all major takeovers, before being implemented.

"There was really no alternative for The Bay but to try and buy Simpsons because had that merger been completed, Canada's retail trade would forever have been dominated by Sears," recalled HBC Governor George Richardson. "The timing was not our own, but it was now or irrevocably never, even if it extended The Bay more than we would prudently have done had the circumstances not been forced on us." McGiverin and Peter Wood were enthusiastic, but some of the acquisition team, notably Iain Ronald and Doug Mahaffy, as well as his top merchant, Evan Church, were opposed, pointing out that most of the earnings increases of Simpsons were attributable to Simpsons-Sears, while Simpsons itself had grown weary, top-heavy and unprofitable.* Martin Jacomb, a British director, strongly opposed the idea of further borrowing and

* Joe Segal, who was opposed to the acquisition of Simpsons and whose position in the HBC would be diluted by the shares issued under the takeover, resigned from the HBC board shortly after the deal's completion.

the overheated expansion, although he supported the proposed takeover. Richardson phoned Russ Harrison, chairman of the Canadian Imperial Bank of Commerce, and instantly secured a standby credit line of $70 million.*

Burton had initiated the merger talks with Sears to protect himself and his family against a takeover. Watching the HBC's rampaging growth, he realized that his store might be the next target. It was. At eight o'clock on the cloudy morning of November 17, the telephone rang at Limestone Hall, the four-hundred-acre farm that was the Burtons' main residence, near Milton, Ontario. The Simpsons chairman and his wife, the broadcaster Betty Kennedy, were about to leave for Florida. "Allan," said McGiverin, "this is Don. We're going to be making an announcement this morning, and I wanted to speak to you first. Our board has authorized The Bay to make an offer for your company. The specific terms will be made available on Monday." Good soldier that he was, Burton pressed his clipped white moustache into the mouthpiece, and calmly replied, "Thanks for letting me know."

McGiverin had actually been trying to get through to Burton for the past ten hours. He couldn't trust anyone else to place the call and seemed unable to find the number or to dial the right combination of digits when he finally got it. "What do you do?" Burton later complained to a friend. "A guy calls you up at eight in the morning and says he's going to take you over.... It screwed up the whole day."

Thoughts of Florida forgotten, Burton rushed downtown to confer with what he had already named his "war cabinet," which included lawyer Jim Tory, and Ian Sinclair, Tom Bell and several other top company directors. He reached Earle McLaughlin just as the Royal Bank chairman was boarding his jet for Bermuda and asked him for a $500-million credit line. McLaughlin's reply was brisk and to the point: "Canadian or American?"

Coming from the Company that had said nothing public for most of three hundred years, McGiverin's tactics were refreshing. He announced the details of The Bay's $310-million offer for Simpsons (at $8.27 a share, 27 percent over market price) on CTV's *Canada AM* and made himself constantly available to the media, which quickly became caught up in the "Store Wars" battle for

---

* An influential factor was a McLeod Young Weir report by Ray Beetridge claiming that Simpsons shares were severely undervalued, with the stock market assessing the firm as being worth $241 million ($5.13 a share) while the real value of the Simpsons-Sears stock alone held by Simpsons was $248 million—and that took no account of the department store's impressive facilities and valuable real estate.

control.* Each side issued earnings figures, equity and growth potentials, and lobbied hard in Ottawa to influence the Foreign Investment Review Agency.

In an imaginative defensive move, on December 11 Simpsons declared a dividend payable December 14 consisting of its entire holdings of Simpsons-Sears. This was supposed to blow the HBC bid out of the water as it reduced the value of the Simpsons shares to less than one-third of the hbc bid of $8.27 (Simpsons shares hit a low of $2.35 in December 1978). But in their haste to pay out the dividend, the Simpsons group had violated stock-exchange rules on notice of dividends and got themselves in trouble with the regulators. The Toronto Stock Exchange normally sets an ex-dividend date five days before payment, but Simpsons paid the dividend only three days after its declaration, which was clearly against the rules. Trading in Simpsons shares was suspended on December 14.†

On the same day, Trade and Commerce Minister Jack Homer announced the FIRA approval of the merger. McGiverin didn't miss a step, sweetening his offer (to $388 million by including the dividend as well as the Simpsons shares) and declaring he was still going after Simpsons and to hell with Ottawa.

Then, in the final hours of Sunday night, December 17, just before the hearings into the Simpsons irregularities by the Montreal and Toronto stock exchanges, Chicago torpedoed Colonel Burton. "In terms of an alternate merger proposal," Simpsons lawyer Jim Tory told a surprised group of reporters before the hearings started, "a disagreement with our American partners could not be resolved. It's a sad day for us." Burton, for once abandoning his code that the worse things are the more cheerful the commanding officer must look, could only gasp: "The toughest blow ... a partnership of twenty-five years, out the window...." He went home to Limestone Hall that night, walked among the pawing horses in his stables, watched the Canada geese bed down between

---

* Three of Toronto's most prestigious law firms were engaged in the Store Wars battle, but with a twist. When Don McGiverin phoned Alex MacIntosh to line up Blake, Cassels for The Bay, he was sheepishly told that not expecting a Bay move, they had some months earlier agreed to represent Sears in its merger negotiations. So McGiverin recruited McCarthy & McCarthy— Peter Beanie for the corporate work and Donald Macdonald, a former Liberal cabinet minister and later High Commissioner to the United Kingdom, for government relations. Tory, Tory acted for Simpsons.

† Burton wrote in his private diary that evening: "I no longer feel in charge because there are just too many legal manoeuvres going on from several directions at the same time. We must put our faith in Jim Tory and God...."

the big stone house and the pond, and saw the moonlight glistening cold and blue on the icy fields. Then he went to bed but just lay there, wondering what had happened to the world of loyalty and civilized behaviour that had sustained him until now.

What had happened was not simple to explain or understand. Certain conditions had been attached to the original deal, allowing Sears, Roebuck to back out. The main escape clause stated that if any third party accumulated more than 10 percent of the merged company's stock, Sears could withdraw its approval for the merger. Burton and his family had started out owning less than 2 percent of Simpsons, and he had diluted his position by the dividend so it was entirely likely that a financial institution such as Royal Trust could—even inadvertently—accumulate 10 percent and activate the escape clause. Without Sears reversing its conditions, the deal was not feasible, and Burton lacked the clout—or shares—to persuade Chicago.

Burton and Tory did their best. The Simpsons chairman was on the phone almost constantly with Sears chairman Ed Telling, all but begging him to lift the 10-percent restriction or at least give the issue a breather until after Christmas, when the Simpsons chairman could formulate fresh defence strategies. Tory meanwhile had been calling Jack Kincannon, known in the company as "a professional son of a bitch," then Sears' chief financial officer. By early Monday morning, Tory was tracking Kincannon and several other Chicago executives on their car phones as they were driving to work, making desperate appeals to have "that damn provision" waived. "We couldn't get them to move," he recalled. "We kept postponing the hearing to ten and then eleven o'clock, but at the end I told them, 'Okay, look, if you're not going to support us, we're walking away from the hearing, and we'll take what we get.'"

What Simpsons got was the dubious privilege of running up the white flag and surrendering to Don McGiverin.

Sears insiders gave a slightly different version of this dramatic exchange, pointing out that they had used the 10-percent provision as a handy escape clause because they lacked confidence in Burton, in Canada and in the idea of trying to run downtown department stores. They were angry that under the agreement Simpsons reached with the FIRA, their voice in Canadian retailing would have been considerably diminished. Just as in 1968, they were happy to have Simpsons' management do anything it wanted—providing Chicago had the final veto power. They had used The Bay's raid as an excuse to cut their links with Simpsons, convinced that a freestanding Sears operation in Canada meant less trouble and more profit.

Allan Burton's life was never the same after that. "It's different," he wrote in his diary. "I've been my own boss for thirty years, roughly, and I think that once you're not in the public eye and not in a top position, there is a very subtle erosion of power that you didn't even dream you had.... I don't think wealth can buy happiness or peace of mind, or anything else. But having the means to produce situations of happiness for yourself and other people is a very satisfying thing. I can conceive being happy within a cabin. I don't need all this. I'd like to have a nice wife like Betty; and I'd like to have a good horse, and a few things ..."

Just before Christmas, 1978, the final handover was completed. By the end of that year, Donald McGiverin had achieved his goal. The Hudson's Bay Company had become Canada's pre-eminent retailer. Now he could enjoy his new corporate stature, consolidate things, get back to walking around the floors of his stores chatting up the staff, have some fun. Little did he suspect that the Company he had built into the country's retailing giant was about to fall under the tight-fisted control of a most unexpected outsider—Lord Thomson of Fleet.

XI | FAREWELL TO GLORY

Young
Ken

The world's eighth-richest individual ... Thomson acts and looks as if he were a small-town bank-teller living near the poverty line.

HE SHAMBLES THROUGH LIFE, his limb movements a study in awkwardness, doing none of the things one would expect a man of his means and opportunities to venture and enjoy. Deferential to the point of absurdity—and stingy to a point far beyond that—Ken Thomson has turned self-effacement into an art form.

His astonishing communications empire swirls about him, throwing off $4.4 million a week into his personal dividend account, employing 105,000 on four continents, and threatening to become the world's largest media company. It already ranks fourth—after Germany's Bertelsmann, Capital Cities/ABC and Time Warner. Thomson publishes 175 newspapers (with a daily circulation of 4.5 million)—more than any other firm—and sells an incredible 40,000 other editorial products, including 145 magazines, 188 weeklies, and assorted books, directories, newsletters and softwear packages.

There's no corporate kingdom quite like it anywhere. Besides the Hudson's Bay Company and his publishing holdings, Thomson owns a real-estate arm (Markborough, with assets of $2.3 billion) and an overseas travel subsidiary that accounts for 40 percent of England's package tour business and owns five hundred Lunn Poly "holiday shops." He also is sole proprietor of Britannia Airways, the United Kingdom's second-largest airline, which in 1990 carried six million passengers aboard forty jets. (Sixteen more are on order.) Because the Thomson companies' debt ratios are unusually low and their credit lines are virtually unlimited, Ken is in the enviable position of being able to buy any $5-billion competitor. That would overnight make him the world's media king.

By mid-1991, Thomson's personal equity holdings were worth $7.7 billion. The July 22, 1991, issue of *Forbes,* which annually tallies the wealthy, ranked him as the world's eighth-richest individual. The listing placed Thomson well ahead of Gerald Grosvenor, sixth Duke of Westminster, who is England's richest man, and such celebrated moneybags as Italy's Giovanni Agnelli, Hong Kong's Li Ka-shing, the Gettys, the Rothschilds and the Bronfmans. He is also the richest Canadian.

Unlike these and other worldly figures who qualify as rich and famous—and behave as if they were—Thomson acts and looks as if he were a small-town bank-teller living near the poverty line. He spends virtually no money on himself and divulges no public clues to his private thoughts or personal motivations. Compulsively shy of personal publicity and seldom interviewed except about his art (and for this book), he would much prefer to be invisible, and he in fact almost is. "The lowest profile," he contends, "is the very best to have."

Although he seems scarcely aware of it, Thomson is caught in a time warp between the high-tech world of his communications conglomerate and the unbending Baptist ethic of rural Ontario where he simmered up. "We were raised on the principle that you kept yourself to yourself and that only the members of your close family were your true friends," recalls his niece Sherry Brydson, who grew up with Ken. "You played it close to your chest and believed that only with family could you let your hair down. Ken has taken it a step further. He's got to the point where he doesn't let his hair down with anybody."

Thomson, even in his dealings with longtime business colleagues, demonstrates that air of impenetrable reserve. It is entirely in character that his office, on the top floor of the Thomson Building at the corner of Queen and Bay streets in downtown Toronto, has a vertical moat. Public elevators run to the twenty-fourth floor, but only pre-screened and thoroughly vouched-for visitors are allowed into the private elevator that ascends to the twenty-fifth level, shared by Ken Thomson and John Tory, his chief corporate strategist. Thomson's office houses part of his art collection, including most of the 204 canvases by the Dutch-Canadian artist Cornelius Krieghoff that he owns— hanging there, looking about as comfortable as nuns in a discotheque.

Gathering Krieghoffs is Ken Thomson's most visible dedication, but his real cultural hero is a somewhat less exalted artist in a very different discipline: Clarence Eugene "Hank" Snow, the Nova Scotia-born country singer.

Thomson regularly visits Hank at the Grand Ole Opry in Nashville, owns all his records, has been to Snow's house in Tennessee, and once presented him with a gold Hamilton pocket-watch that had been a family heirloom.

Ken Thomson's psyche is so difficult to penetrate because he behaves like an accomplished actor, able to detach himself from whatever, crisis might be occupying his mind. Occasionally, very occasionally, a show of passion will flicker across his shuttered face, only to be withdrawn quickly, like a turtle's head back into its protective shell. Exceptions to his customary reticence come unexpectedly.

A FEW SEASONS AGO, Posy Chisholm, a sophisticated and vivacious Toronto socialite who looks smashing in hats, has a profoundly developed sense of the absurd and possesses a remarkable memory, found herself at Heathrow, about to board British Airways Flight 93 to Toronto. When she spotted Ken, the two acquaintances decided to travel together, though Chisholm had to trade down a class, wondering why Thomson was too cheap to travel in style and comfort.

"You know why I'm flying home?" Thomson asked, when they were settled in their narrow seats.

"No, I don't, not really," Posy replied.

"To give Gonzo his evening meal," the press lord matter-of-factly explained. "I've been away from my dog for five days now, and I miss him so terribly. We were half an hour late leaving London, and I'm really nervous they might give him dinner without me."

"Oh, Ken," Chisholm tried to reassure her agitated companion, "they'll make up time across the ocean."

"Gonzo is crazy in many ways, but very, very lovable," Thomson went on as Posy, crammed into steerage beside the fretting billionaire, began looking longingly down at the heaving Atlantic. "Gonzo is the sweetest dog. He's everybody's pal, especially mine. He's a Wheaton terrier, the colour of wheat, off-white. Actually, he's got a little apricot."

"How about some champagne, Ken? No? Oh well...."

"Gonzo leads a good life. I plan my trips abroad around him. I never go to annual meetings unless I've got him covered. I couldn't put him in a kennel; he's a member of the family. He seems to have an understanding of what's happening all the time. We communicate. We know what the other is thinking. We love each other."

"I suppose you take him walking ..."

"Oh, I take him out all the time. Early in the morning, late at night, and every time I can in between. If I can't get home for lunch, my man goes up and walks him. He might be there right this minute. Gonzo's got to have his exercise."

"Doesn't he have a garden?" asked Posy, grasping for relevance.

"He doesn't want to stay out all day. Gonzo's a people dog. He likes walking in the park and then he wants to come back inside."

It was going to be a long flight.

Chisholm remembered a friend's joking that if she was ever reincarnated, she wanted to come back as Ken Thomson's dog. So Posy told him, hoping the idea might amuse the single-minded tycoon.

"Well, she'd be well looked after," was the serious reply. "I tell you, Gonzo's a big part of my life. I know that sounds awfully funny. But it's a fact. I think of him all the time. I look after him like a baby."

"What about your wife—does Marilyn love Gonzo too?"

"One time, I was looking at Gonzo, and I said to Marilyn, 'Geez, he wants something.'

"She said, 'We all want something.'

"'Yes, but he can't go to the refrigerator and open the door. Gonzo can't tell you he's got a pain in his tummy. We've got to look after him, anticipate everything he wants. It might be a bit of food he needs, maybe to go out or just a show of affection.'"

At this point Thomson leaned forward to emphasize the significance of what he was about to reveal. "I tried to figure what Gonzo was really after," he confided. "It's a game we play."

"So, what did Gonzo end up wanting?" Posy Chisholm half-heartedly inquired—purposefully fumbling under her seat, hoping that was where they kept the parachutes.

"A bikkie!" exclaimed the world's eighth-richest man. "That's what Gonzo wanted—a bikkie!"

There followed a lengthy silence. Thomson seemed satisfied there was little point trying to top that remarkable bit of canine mind-reading.

About half an hour out of Toronto, he started to get restless because the 747 had been unable to make up the original delay and was not going to arrive at 1735, as scheduled. He put on his coat and complained so bitterly he might miss getting home in time for his dog's feeding that Chisholm suggested she take his luggage through customs and drop it off at his house— while he dashed through the terminal, bound for Gonzo.

KEN THOMSON SIGHTINGS ARE LIKE THAT. If he knows and trusts the person he's with, he will talk about his dog or his art collection, but that's it. He leaves few contrails. "The smartest thing those who have more than anybody else can do is not to flaunt it," he says. "It's resented and it's in terribly bad taste. It shows a poor sense of priority.

"Everybody has their own ways of doing things," he allows. "It's all a matter of temperament. A lot of people who make money fast spend it fast. It's very difficult to live a simple life and love your dog as much as I do. I spend as much time as I can with my family, walking Gonzo, watching a fair bit of television. I like to get in my car and fill it up with gas. So if you add up running the business with all the personal things I do, there's not an awful lot of time and energy left after that. I am as happy as can be."

Walking your dog and filling your car with gas may well be the path to eternal happiness, but those who know Thomson best insist that he is not as content as he claims. "He's not a man doing his choice of things," insists his niece. "If he had two or three brothers, he would never have chosen—or been chosen—to run the family empire. I get the impression of someone doing his duty. He is intensely loyal and was very attached to his father, so when my grandfather said, 'I'm going to start a dynasty and you're going to carry it on,' Ken said, 'Right.' It didn't really matter that he might have preferred to be the curator of an art museum—and now he's training his son David to take over, just as his father wished. He's doing it with good will but not much joy. Every morning when he wakes up he must say to himself, 'I'm unhappy being a businessman, but wait a minute, it's bringing me all this other stuff like my art collection that I couldn't otherwise have—so it's a trade-off.'"

Everything Ken Thomson says and does is to underline that he's fundamentally decent, that he would be quite happy to have his epitaph read: "What a Nice Guy." He *is* a nice guy, but he is much more than that—and despite his pose as the ultimate *innocente*, his self-assurance can be devastating. For instance, he readily conceded in early 1980 that "there is a limit to how many papers one man, or company, should own," insisting that his own firm had yet to grow to such "ludicrous" extremes. "We will know ourselves if and when we do," he reassured the dubious commissioners on the 1980 Royal Commission on Newspapers. Thomson then controlled one of the largest concentrations of press ownership in any democratic country.

The best evidence of Ken Thomson's success in perpetuating his anonymity is that most Canadians, even fairly sophisticated businessmen, still regard him as the youthful and untried inheritor of the publishing empire built up by his father, Roy Thomson. They dismiss the current press lord as "Young Ken," an immature figurehead whose main accomplishment was to be his father's only son.

"Young Ken" is in fact sixty-nine years old. "I'm not young any more, but I don't really mind being called 'Young Ken,'" says he. "My dad was such an unusual individual that nobody can expect to be anywhere near a carbon copy of him. He was one of a kind. He channelled his ambition in a single direction and everything emanated from that. Now it's a different world we live in."

Ken has force-fed his father's business empire from annual revenues of $725 million in 1976, when he took over, to $11.5 billion a decade and a half later. The total equity value of the companies he controls has sky-rocketed from less than $1 billion to more than $11 billion, exponentially surpassing Roy Thomson's impressive rate of annual growth.

In 1989, following sale of the Thomson Group's North Sea oil holdings for $670 million, its publishing and travel assets were combined into an umbrella organization (the Thomson Corporation). Ken uncharacteristically boasted that it would allow him to set his sights on any target. "I can't imagine any publishing company anywhere in the world that would be beyond our ability to acquire," he gloated.

KEN THOMSON LEADS A DOUBLE LIFE, and enjoys neither. In England—and most of non-North America where titles still mean something—he is Baron Thomson of Fleet of Northbridge in the City of Edinburgh, the peerage bestowed on his father on January 1, 1964, two days before he lost his Canadian citizenship for accepting a British title. "I regret giving up Canadian citizenship," Roy Thomson said at the time, "but I had no choice. I didn't give it up. They took it away from me. They gave me the same reward you give a traitor. If I had betrayed my country, that's the reward I would get—taking away my citizenship. Canada should allow titles. If you get a title from the Pope, there's no trouble accepting that."*

---

* Roy Thomson turned down Prime Minister John Diefenbaker's 1959 offer to appoint him Governor General of Canada. "It wouldn't have suited me very well because I'm too much of an extrovert for that," Roy declared at the time. "I can't conceal my feelings very easily. I talk too much, everybody says, but I talked myself into more deals than I ever talked myself out of, so I'm still ahead of the game. At any rate, it worked out for the best. Since then, I've got a hereditary peerage. And I'm a Knight Grand Cross of the Order of the British Empire, that's a GBE, which is the highest degree of the Order of the British Empire. That entitles you to be 'Sir.' If I hadn't got a peerage I'd be Sir Roy, so I'm right at the top of the heap."

During their visits to England, Lord and Lady Thomson live in a four-bedroom flat (purchased for £90,000 in 1967) in Kensington Palace Gardens, off Bayswater Road.* A secluded street with extra police protection, this is where many of the ambassadors to the Court of St. James's have their residences: 'While abroad, the introverted Ken and Marilyn Thomson of Toronto are transformed into the introverted Lord and Lady Thomson of Fleet, using their titles, with two sets of clothing and accessories as well as stationery and visiting cards. "I lead a dual life and I'm getting away with it," Thomson declares. "It actually works."

One place it doesn't work is in the House of Lords. Ken has never taken up his father's seat in Westminster's august Upper Chamber, nor does he intend to. The older Thomson glowed with pride the day he received his title. After celebrating by queuing up at Burberrys for a cashmere coat reduced from £75 to £40, he had his official coat of arms† carved on his office door, and when one elderly London dowager persisted in calling him "Mr Thomson," he barked, "Madam, I've paid enough for this goddamn title, you might have the good grace to use it."‡

Having been elevated to the House of Lords, Thomson seldom attended its sessions and didn't particularly enjoy it when he did. "I've made a lot of money, but I'm not the brightest guy in the world, by a hell of a long ways," he once commented. "I've found that out since I've been in the House of Lords. About 90% of the things they discuss there, I'm a complete ignoramus about. I've got a one-track mind, but I bloody well know my own business."

"For Dad, the title symbolized what he had achieved from nothing, and he made me promise I wouldn't give it up," Ken recalls. "He told me he'd like to see me carry it on because he rightly suspected I was the type of person who might not want to. I remember telling him, 'Well, Dad, I think you're a little naughty to ask me to do that. Because everybody should have the right to make his own decisions in this world. But after what you've done for me, if you really want me to, I'll make you that promise.' Now, I didn't promise him I'd

---

* During the Second World War the flat was used for interrogating high-ranking Nazi officers.
† It features the bizarre image of a beaver blowing an Alpine horn under the motto, "Never a Backward Step."
‡ The reason for the granting of a title is never promulgated, but in Thomson's case it was thought to have been mainly for his initiative in donating £5 million to establish a foundation to train Third World journalists. It is still active and recently helped revive the *New China Daily*.

use the title in Canada or that I'd take up my seat in the House of Lords. So now I'm happy to have it both ways."

Another of the inheritances from his father was the attitude that while making money was holy, spending it was evil. The Thomson style of penny-pinching—father and son—goes well beyond sensible parsimony. "Nobody has any sympathy for a rich man except somebody that's richer again," Roy once ruminated. "I mean, hell, I eat three meals a day and I shouldn't, I should probably eat two. And I only have so many suits of clothes, and I'm not very particular about my dress anyway, and I can't spend, oh, not a small fraction of what I make, so what the hell am I doing? I'm not doing it for money. It's a game. But I enjoy myself. I love work. I like to be successful. I like to look at another paper and think, Jesus, if only that was mine. Let's have a look at the balance sheet."

Roy Thomson's approach to spending was best summed up in the marathon bargaining sessions he staged when he was renting space for his Canadian head office at 425 University Avenue in downtown Toronto. The landlord, a promoter who had a Scrooge-like reputation of his own to uphold, despaired of reaching any reasonable rental agreement because Thomson's offer was so far below rates charged for comparable space else-where. When the press lord finally wore him down, the building's owner gasped in reluctant admiration, "Mr Thomson, you really are cheap!" To which an indignant Roy Thomson responded, "I'm not cheap! You're cheap! I'm cheap cheap!"

The photographs of the original Lord Thomson weighing his baggage so he wouldn't have to pay extra on his economy flights across the Atlantic, going to work on London's underground, or lining up for cafeteria lunches created a comic mask that somehow took the hard edge off his business deals. His outrigger spectacles, with lenses as thick as Coke-bottle bottoms, magnified his glinting blue eyes as he peered at the world with Mister Magoo–like good humour, hiding his touch of icy cunning. Thomson carefully cultivated the image of himself as the living embodiment of the profit motive on the hoof. Seated next to Princess Margaret at a fashion show, he spotted a lamé gown on one of the models. "My favorite color," he told the Princess. "Gold!" During Thomson's much-publicized 1963 encounter with Nikita Khrushchev the Russian dictator teasingly asked what use his money was to him. "You can't take it with you," said Khrushchev. "Then I'm not going," shot back a determined Thomson.

Ken Thomson's scrimping habits are equally mingy if less well known. Although he is a member of six of Toronto's most exclusive clubs—the York, Toronto, National, York Downs, Granite and Toronto Hunt—he prefers to have lunch by himself at a downtown yogurt bar, if he's not home walking Gonzo, that is.* He does most of his shopping on department-store bargain days. Murray Turner, a former HBC executive who knows Thomson slightly, was shopping in the Loblaws store at Moore and Bayview when he heard a shout, "Murray! Murray!" and saw Thomson beckoning to him. As he reached the side of the world's eighth-richest man, it was obvious that Thomson could hardly contain himself. "Lookit," he exclaimed, "lookit this. They have hamburger buns on special today. Only $1.89! You must get some." Turner looked in disbelief at Thomson's shopping cart, and sure enough, there were six packages of buns, presumably for freezing against a rainy day. "I'd walk a block to save a dime at a discount store," Thomson readily admits. On the same day he spent $641 million on a corporate takeover, Thomson met George Cohon, the Canadian head of McDonald's, and asked him for a toy Ronald McDonald wristwatch. Cohon sent him one of the free timepieces (used mainly for internal promotions), but the very next day Thomson's secretary was on the phone claiming the watch had gained four minutes over the past twenty-four hours and asking where His Lordship could get it fixed. Cohon ordered another watch sent to him, but the messenger had strict orders to bring back the original gift.

The press lord appears to dress well (his shoes are from Wildsmith's on London's swank Duke Street), but his suits are made for him by a cut-rate tailor in Toronto's Chinatown at $200 apiece from the discounted ends of bolts he picks up during his journeys to Britain. He lives in a twenty-three-room mansion behind a set of handsome gates at the top of Rosedale's Castle Frank Road, built in 1926 by Salada Tea Company president Gerald Larkin. A prime example of Ontario Georgian-style architecture, the dwelling is run down, its curtains left over from its first owner. The Thomsons (Marilyn's parents live with them in a coach-house) usually eat in the kitchen to save electricity, and the family is unable to retain housekeepers because of the low pay. Even the help's food is rationed. Most cookies are kept in a box with the Thomson name lettered on it. A strict allocation of two of Mr. Christie's best

---

* He occasionally frequents fancier restaurants but takes the uneaten portions home in a Gonzo-bag.

is placed on a separate plate to feed the rotating parade of disillusioned cleaning women.*

Thomson owns a Mercedes 300-E but usually drives his ancient Oldsmobile ("it clunks around but it's the car that Gonzo prefers") and once purchased a red Porsche turbo. ("Honestly, not one of my more practical expenditures. I was thrilled at first but I hardly use it—I've probably driven not more than twenty-five miles in it this summer." The car is for sale.) The Thomsons never entertain and seldom go out. When they do, preparations include discreet calls to find out precisely what other guests have been invited, whether anyone will be smoking or drinking, how soon they might comfortably leave, and so on.

The world's eighth-richest man is one of the country's most reluctant philanthropists. When Toronto-Dominion Bank chairman Dick Thomson (no relation) and Fred Eaton, head of his family's department store chain, called on Thomson to solicit funds for the Toronto General Hospital, a favourite Establishment charity, they were warned by a mutual friend that the only way they would get any money was to pledge construction of a veterinary wing to treat Gonzo. They thought it was a joke, and came back almost empty-handed.

There has been much argument among his headquarters staff over how much cash Ken Thomson actually spends per week. Some insiders claim it's twenty dollars; others insist it's at least forty. No one bids any higher. He has credit cards but seldom if ever uses them. "It's an idiosyncrasy," says John Tory, his chief confidant. "It's just very difficult for Ken to put his hand in his pocket and spend money. Yet he's extremely kind and generous. When we're rushing to a meeting and we're late, if he sees a blind man, he'll stop, miss a couple of lights, and help him cross the street." Tory didn't need to add that the blind man gets no money. Thomson himself won't discuss his spending habits. "I agree with my father that you should use only a small portion of your money on yourself and that you have some kind of obligation to do something useful with the balance. He thought the most beneficial thing you could do with money was to invest and reinvest it, to keep it growing—and so do I."

Ken's only excursion into philanthropy was his successful 1982 effort to have Toronto's premier concert hall, the magnificent structure designed by

---

*Besides the London flat, the only other Thomson residence is in Barbados, where he owns the Southern Palms Hotel. To maximize profits, Ken and Marilyn stay in a third-floor walk-up apartment whenever they visit instead of occupying one of the more luxurious main-floor suites. Toronto travel impresario Sam Blyth has occasionally booked them aboard West Indies cruises on a travel agent's discount.

Arthur Erickson, named after his father. He gave $4.5 million to the project, the largest donation ever granted the performing arts in Canadian history. "Dad would have been thrilled," he says. "I'm so proud to hear it on the radio sometimes—Roy Thomson Hall, my dad's name being mentioned—or see it in the *Globe* and *Star*. He was born on Monteith Street and loved Toronto. He even tried to use Lord Thomson of Toronto as his title, but the government wouldn't let him." Still, a cultural—especially musical—edifice hardly seemed an appropriate monument. "I could do without culture," Roy Thomson once confided. "I haven't got any, particularly. And I could do without art. I can do without the theatre. I can do without all these things.... Some people love culture. They live on it. They appreciate it and I rather envy them in a way. But, not for me. My favorite music is about the level of *Gigi*. I like tunes like the 'Blue Danube' waltz, 'Sailing Down the River,' and *South Pacific*."

The naming of Roy Thomson Hall caused a furore. Of the $39 million required to finance the building's construction, $26.5 million had been allocated by the federal, provincial and municipal governments; a further $12.5 million had been raised from corporate donors and individuals. The Thomson contribution was a welcome but hardly essential windfall to be used for future improvements, which to many minds did not warrant naming of the hall after Roy. Accountants quickly calculated that the magnificent gift would not cost Ken very much. The $4.5-million donation was divided into five annual instalments of $900,000, paid through a Thomson subsidiary. As well as saving Thomson $450,000 a year in deductible taxes, the delayed instalments earned annual interest of more than half a million dollars at the high rates prevailing at that time, leaving the benefactor to scrape up only $2 million.*

THE SAGA OF ROY HERBERT THOMSON, the Toronto barber's son who quit school at fourteen to become a five-dollar-a-week clerk and in 1931 leased a fifty-watt radio station in North Bay, Ontario, and another later at Timmins—so he could sell the radios he was lugging along country roads—is one of the sustaining legends of Canadian capitalism. Less well known is the way the hardships of the Great Depression permanently imprinted themselves on generations of the Thomson clan. "I'm still horrified by people who don't

---

* That's not all. When they attend Roy Thomson Hall concerts, Ken and Marilyn regularly phone down for free house seats—and get them.

make soup stock out of meat scraps," says Ken's niece Sherry, who spent her youth in the communal Thomson home at Port Credit, just west of Toronto. "And if you were making a custard with three egg yolks, you could have knocked me over with a feather the first time I saw a woman throw the egg whites down the drain. That just wouldn't occur to me; the whites are tomorrow's dessert. You used everything and got into the rhythm of making your own jam and freezing your vegetables."

The Port Credit household, which for a time included not only Ken but also his sisters, Irma (Sherry's mother) and Phyllis Audrey, and most of their children, was run according to stern, puritanical precepts. "Granddad loved us very much," Sherry recalls, "but the affection was always very gruff. It was a staunch, didn't-come-from-much kind of family, so that signs of affection came out almost by accident, as asides." It was a stern upbringing. She remembers her mother being locked out by Roy, the family patriarch, if she ventured home after midnight. This was not when Irma was a teenager but well into her thirties, divorced, with a nine-year-old daughter, and dating again. Luckily the family had German shepherds and a dog porthole had been cut into the sunroom door. Irma's dating partners still recall having to push her, 1940s dirndl and all, through the dog door after their goodnights. "They could only do that in the summer," according to Sherry, "because in other seasons, the ground got too wet. When I became a teenager I was locked out by my mother in turn, and had to climb up the trellis."

Young Ken had attended elementary school in North Bay, where he worked summers as a disc jockey in his father's radio station, CFCH. His main job was to play background noises meant to evoke the crowd sounds and clinking glasses of a ballroom, while big-band dance numbers were on the air, but he also fell in love with the music of Hank Snow and dreamed someday of actually meeting him. When the family moved to Toronto, young Ken was enrolled in Upper Canada College. After an unsuccessful year at the University of Toronto, he joined the Royal Canadian Air Force but was never promoted beyond Leading Aircraftman, the equivalent of an army lance-corporal, spending most of his time as an editorial assistant on *Wings Abroad*, a propaganda weekly. He took his discharge in London and spent two years at Cambridge, though the university had no discernible effect on him. After spending a year on the editorial staff of his father's Timmins *Daily Press*, he moved back to Southern Ontario where Roy Thomson had acquired the Galt *Evening Reporter* as one of four dailies he picked up in 1944. His five-year apprenticeship there was an important formative influence, as were the weekends he spent at the Port Credit house.

Roy Thomson had moved to Scotland in 1954 but returned to the family homestead in summer and at Christmas. The elder Thomson held court while watching the TV set in front of him, listening to the radio beside him, petting the Scottie dog at his feet, eating fruit with a little paring knife, all the while reading a murder mystery. Ken loved frightening his nieces and nephews, especially when they slept in garden tents during the summer. "He'd put a sheet over his head and ghost us," Sherry recalled. "Or he'd hide behind a bush and make fake owl noises. But we always knew it was him and we'd yell, 'Oh Kenny, stop it!' He was very much the tease."

By the late 1950s, Roy Thomson had not only acquired the prestigious *Scotsman* but had also won control, in what was the world's first reverse takeover bid, of the huge Kemsley chain that included London's influential *Sunday Times*.* Roy's lucky streak broke in 1967, when he acquired *The Times*, Britain's great journal of record.† *The Times* may not have lost its lustre under Thomson, but it lost him bags of money.

Thomson had by this time become a fixture among British press lords. He could always be depended upon to say something mildly outrageous and to pose for yet one more photograph showing off his skinflint habits. "They say business is the law of the jungle," was a typical sally. "I think it's the law of life.... If you want to prosper, you've got to be ambitious.... You've got to be ready to sacrifice leisure and pleasure, and you've got to plan ahead. I was forty years old before I had any money at all. But these things don't happen overnight. Now how many people are there that will wait that long to be successful, and work all the time? Not very many. Maybe they're right. Maybe I'm a bloody fool. But I don't think I am."

American tycoons J. Paul Getty and Armand Hammer approached Thomson in 1973, offering a 20-percent share in their Occidental consortium preparing to drill in the North Sea where Phillips Petroleum had already found valuable indications. Roy bet his family's (as opposed to his company's) fortune on the play, though oil was then worth only $3.60 a barrel. When

---

* At about that time his daughter Irma had to canvass funds from neighbours to get the roof of the Thomson house fixed because Roy refused to spend the money.

† The extent of *The Times'* authority was best summed up in a *Punch* cartoon, depicting a secretary walking into a British company president's office to announce: "Sir, the gentleman from *The Times* and the press are here."

Occidental struck the giant Piper field and later the Claymore—and prices climbed to $14 a barrel—Thomson almost overnight earned $500 million.

By 1976, Roy Thomson was in his eighty-second year and not at all well. Ken, who by then had married a graceful model named Nora Marilyn Lavis, had been brought across the Atlantic to assist the old man.* "Most people would say, 'I wouldn't want to do what you've done, even for your success," Roy reminisced in one of his last interviews. "They'd say, 'You've missed a lot out of life and success hasn't made it all worthwhile.' But it has to me. It's just a matter of ambition and determination, you keep plugging away. I learn more from my failures than I learn from my successes, because I learn bloody well not to do them again. Nothing has ever happened to me in my life that hasn't been for the best, now I accept death. I lost my wife. I lost a daughter, but those things, I mean, you can't measure them in terms of happiness or success or failure. I'm a very imperfect individual, and I've done a lot of things I shouldn't have done, but I honestly am not a person who caused anybody any suffering if I could help it."

Henry Grunfeld, former chairman of S.G. Warburg, the London merchant bankers who had helped finance Thomson, remembered his last conversation with Roy in the bank's Terrace Room at its Gresham Street headquarters. "It was about three weeks before his death and we both knew it was the last time we would meet. He told me he was worth about $750 million, or whatever it was, and complained bitterly how much he wished he could have made a billion. 'Why, haven't you got enough, Roy?' I remember asking, especially since he was so obviously very ill. He looked surprised, as if he had never considered the question, and shrugged, 'Henry, it's just for the fun of it …' It was pathetic."

Thomson died on August 7, 1976, and Ken was suddenly in charge. His father had passed away both too soon, because the younger Thomson was not ready to take over, and too late—because Ken was by this time fifty-three years old and had spent most of his adult life following his father, a tactful step behind like a commercial version of Prince Philip. Inheriting a father's

---

* Theirs is a wonderful marriage. But Ken seems to be deferential at home as well as the office. In an impromptu 1988 telephone exchange with a reporter from the *Financial Post*, Thomson admitted that he saved barbers' bills by having his wife cut his hair, but made the transaction sound curiously self-demeaning. "My wife made me have it cut commercially lately," he admitted, "but if I behave myself, she'll do it for me. I'd just as soon have her cut my hair. Nobody does it as nicely as Marilyn. The cost is for me to be nice to her for a few days."

business is difficult; succeeding an individual as powerful and articulate as Roy Thomson—recognized as a folk hero of capitalism—was impossible. Ken tried valiantly to turn himself into an extrovert but soon conceded that it was a mission impossible. "The nice thing about my dad was that he was so unusual. No one in his right mind could expect me to be the same. I'd be happy to go unnoticed. I've tried to be a good, sound businessman in my quiet way, but I can't say I've been a slave to business. I've tried to strike more of a balance between my personal and business lives." His father's friend and adviser, Sidney F. Chapman, summed up the situation more succinctly: "When you live in the shadow of a legend, you don't go flashing mirrors."

Ken's first major decision was to cut family ties with *The Sunday Times* and *The Times*, where union problems had forced suspension of publication for eleven months. During their stewardship the Thomsons, father and son, had poured £100 million into the properties without any significant return. Their loyalty to those great institutions without any apparent fiscal controls was totally out of character. Thomson sold the two papers for the value of the land and buildings to Rupert Murdoch, and gradually moved his businesses back to Canada.

The company owned forty-three daily and eleven weekly Canadian newspapers at the time. They ranged geographically from the Nanaimo *Daily Free Press* on Vancouver Island to the *Evening Telegram* in St John's, Newfoundland. What they had in common, apart from ownership, was a blandness so pervasive that no self-respecting fish could bear being wrapped in one of their pages. "Disliking Ken Thomson, let alone detesting him, is wholly impossible," confessed Richard Gwyn, a leading Canadian commentator who once worked for him. "He radiates niceness from every pore, down to the holes in the soles of his shoes. He's self-effacing, shy, unpretentious, soft-spoken. He peppers his conversations with engaging archaisms, like 'golly' and 'gee whiz.' But then you stop feeling sympathetic, because you realize that his innocence is just a synonym for timidity. And you realize at the same instant that the reason Thomson newspapers are bland is that they are led by the bland."

The Thomson operational code had been set down by Roy but it didn't initially change much under Ken. Both Thomsons regarded editors as expendable eccentrics, and Clifford Pilkey, then president of the Ontario Federation of Labour, once called their company "a vicious organization, certainly not compatible with what I describe as decent, honourable labour relations."

Reporters did not receive free copies of their own newspapers, and earnest bargaining went on to deprive delivery kids of half a cent in their meagre take-home pay. Most positions had fixed salary limits, so that anyone performing really well would inevitably work himself or herself out of a job. In pre-computer days, Thomson papers sold their used page mats to farmers as chicken-coop insulation and Canadian Press printers were adjusted from triple to double spacing to save paper. Each newsroom telephone had a pencil tied to it, so there would be no wasteful stubs floating around. "God help us if they ever realize there are two sides to a piece of toilet paper," one publisher was heard to whisper at a management cost-cutting meeting. In a thesis he wrote for the Carleton School of Journalism, Klaus Pohie, the former managing editor of the Lethbridge *Herald,* documented the Thomsonization of his former paper and coined the name for a sadly relevant and increasingly frequent process.

In January 1980, Thomson had used some of his North Sea oil proceeds to purchase, for $130 million, a major Canadian newspaper chain, FP Publications Limited, but that projected him into new and unfamiliar territory. FP had fielded an impressive Ottawa news bureau under the inspired direction of Kevin Doyle (later the editor of *Maclean's)* that included such stars of Canadian journalism as Allan Fotheringham, Walter Stewart and Doug Small. The bureau regularly beat the Parliamentary Press Gallery to the news, but it didn't fit in with Thomson's usual barebones operation. When FP's Edmonton bureau chief, Keith Woolhouse, who was working out of his one-bedroom apartment, asked for a wastebasket, that was enough to trigger the cost-efficiency instincts of Thomson's executive vice-president, Brian Slaight. Doyle tried to defuse the situation by offering to send out an extra wastebasket from the Ottawa office.

"Is it excess to the Ottawa bureau?" Slaight, ever the champion of independent editorial control, sternly demanded.

Doyle, about to break the news of Prime Minister Pierre Trudeau's resignation, calmly replied, "Well, if you mean, do we need it, no, we don't."

At last, a triumph for head office. Slaight could barely contain himself. "We have a truck that goes from Ottawa to Toronto to Winnipeg, then on to Edmonton. If we put the wastebasket on the truck, it will hardly take up any room, and won't cost us a cent!"

So the wastebasket journeyed jauntily across the country, and it took only a week and a half to reach its destination. But the Edmonton Bureau's troubles were far from over. Woolhouse wanted to rent an office and needed furniture. Slaight vetoed the initial $1,600 estimate but later approved a bid of $1,100 from a local repossession centre. That didn't save Woolhouse. He permanently blotted his copy book by purchasing his pens and paper clips on the open market instead of from the repossession house. The Edmonton bureau was soon closed, as was the entire FP news operation.

The FP purchase had also thrown the Thomson organization into the unusual position of having to operate newspapers against local competition, especially in Ottawa, where its *Journal* was up against the Southam-owned *Citizen*; in Winnipeg, where its *Free Press* was head to head with Southam's *Tribune*; and in Vancouver, where its *Sun* had to compete with Southam's *Province*. That ran strictly against Thomson's publishing philosophy, which perpetuated his father's dictum that what's important "isn't the circulation of one's own newspaper, it's the circulation of the opposition's. Even second-largest is no good. Only the largest is worth buying." The dilemma was neatly resolved on August 27, 1980, when Southam's closed the Winnipeg *Tribune* while Thomson shut the Ottawa *Journal*—throwing eight hundred employees on the street—and Southam's bought out Thomson's interest in the *Vancouver Sun*. The Ottawa move was particularly puzzling because the *Journal's* circulation had climbed 25 percent in the previous six months and its advertising image was the highest in eight years. But looking back on that Black Wednesday, Thomson wouldn't change a thing. "Nobody likes to see people lose their jobs," he says. "We didn't take any satisfaction in that. But the situation at the *Journal* was hopeless and it was never going to get any better. We couldn't give the paper away for a dollar. We tried nine different buyers. Nobody else wanted it. Somebody had to draw the curtain. So when Gordon Fisher of Southam's told us he was going to close his paper in Winnipeg, he suggested we close them both on the same day. I thought it was a good idea because I knew if he closed his paper first, people would come to me and ask, are you going to close yours, and I didn't want to lie to them. So when he said, 'Why don't we do it the same day?' I said, 'Oh boy, we'll be in real trouble—but let's do it.'"

Trouble came in the form of a Royal Commission, headed by Tom Kent, a former *Economist* and *Winnipeg Free Press* editor, who labelled the Thomson publications as "small-town monopoly papers [that] are almost without exception, a lacklustre aggregation of cash-boxes" and suggested the organization be forced to sell its flagship publication in Toronto, the *Globe and Mail*, purchased in 1980. The recommendation was not followed up, but the hearings brought into the public consciousness Thomson's utilitarian code of editorial independence. "We run our newspapers in a highly decentralized manner, delegating operating authority to publishers," Ken Thomson told the Commission's opening session. "We have vested in our publishers the responsibility and the autonomy to decide what news, information and comment should be published daily in their newspapers." That was true enough, and there was no more eloquent witness to that philosophy than Harold Evans, the former editor of both *The Times* and *The Sunday Times*, who wrote in his memoirs that the difference in ownership between the Thomsons and Rupert Murdoch was "a transition from light to dark." Neither of the Thomsons have, in fact, cast much of an editorial shadow over their publications. The problem is that editorial budgets ultimately decide any publication's content, and that was—and is—how the Thomsons exercise control. Since the Kent hearings, John Tory has impressively improved both the quality of Thomson papers and the working conditions under which they're produced.

The severest test of Thomson's hands-off attitude was the *Globe* story about the newspaper closings written by Arthur Johnson, quoting the press lord's heartless comment on the plight of those who had lost their jobs: "Each one has to find his own way in this world." Johnson firmly stuck to his version, but Thomson categorically denies having made the comment. "I explained for twenty minutes how we had gone way beyond our statutory obligations in severance arrangements, but that we were not prepared to see the company's assets dissipated because we didn't have the guts to face up to the flak. I never said anything about everyone having to make his own way in the world, even though that quote will go down in history with me. I would never say that. I know I'm not brilliant, but even I can figure that one out." He didn't phone the *Globe* to complain, but six weeks later he met publisher Roy Megarry at a Royal York Hotel reception and let him have it. "Jesus, Roy, the *Globe* misquoted me terribly," he complained. "They put the worst words in my mouth. I never phoned you about it, but I wish I had."

"Geez, Ken," Megarry replied, "I wondered at the time why you'd make such a statement and I talked it over with the editor involved, but he insisted that you had said it."

"You'll have to take my word for it. I didn't. I'm not that stupid."

Megarry, who persuaded Thomson to invest $65 million in turning the *Globe* into a national newspaper, insists there has been no editorial interference from the Thomson head office, a few blocks away. "It's one thing to own the Barrie *Examiner* and not interfere editorially," he says. "It's another to own the *Globe* in the city where you reside and resist the temptation to put on pressure. But they haven't." On Thomson's sixtieth birthday, Megarry edited a special one-copy issue of the *Globe*, substituted on his doorstep for the real thing, that had a front page with Ken's picture on it and several feature stories about Gonzo. "That morning, Ken did phone me," Megarry recalls, and said, "'What are you doing, you rascal?'—he frequently refers to me as a rascal—and admitted he had been stunned, because for a split second he thought it really was that day's *Globe*. 'It was a cute thing to do,' he told me, 'but I hope it didn't cost the company too much money.'"

DURING THE LATE 1970s, Ken Thomson enjoyed a unique problem. With oil prices up to as much as $34 a barrel, his share in the North Sea fields purchased by his father was throwing off annual revenues of $200 million. That's not the kind of sum you keep in a savings account. Tax reasons plus the wish to get into hard assets dictated new acquisitions, but the chain had run out of cities, towns and even villages where they could maintain monopolies. Thomson went shopping for a safe, timeless investment for his family.

While on a flight to London, John Tory passed over to Ken an annual report of the Hudson's Bay Company, with the comment, "This is one you should think about." That struck Thomson as a weird coincidence because he *had* been thinking about The Bay, ever since Fred Eaton at a party had mentioned that the HBC was lucky because so much of its profit flowed from non-merchandising sources. "It was like mental telepathy," Thomson recalled of the airplane conversation.* At first glance, the Hudson's Bay Company seemed a perfect takeover target. It certainly carried the kind of historic pedigree that would please a British-Canadian lord, it was widely held with no control blocks that would have demanded premium prices, and it was a well and conservatively managed enterprise, ideal for the Thomson habit of acquiring companies that turned decent profits without requiring day-to-day involvement. "It looked to me like a business that in the inflationary environment of that time would do quite well, because the top line was pushed up by price increases while many of the costs, including store leases, were fixed,"

---

* There is another theory why Thomson settled on The Bay. He walked Gonzo most often through Craigleigh Gardens, near his Rosedale home, and at night the most visible object from the shrubbery is the ochre neon sign at Bloor and Yonge, announcing "The Bay! The Bay!"

John Tory recalled. "Also I knew that Simpsons, which they had just taken over, was not well managed, so that a turnaround would have impressive bottom-line results."

On March 1, 1979, Ken Thomson and John Tory called on Don McGiverin to announce they were bidding $31 a share—36 percent over market value—for 51 percent of the Hudson's Bay Company. At The Bay's board meeting two weeks later, Governor George Richardson reported that in a meeting with Thomson the previous Sunday evening he had failed to persuade him to buy less than 51 percent. The board decided that the premium offered for control was not high enough and that $37 to $40 would have been a more appropriate amount. That consideration was aborted by the sudden entry into the bidding of grocery magnate Galen Weston, offering $40, for the same percentage, though part of it would have been payable in stock. Unlike Thomson, Weston hinted that he intended to fire most of the HBC executives, replacing them with his own.

In typical Establishment fashion, the first telephone call Thomson received after word of his intended takeover leaked out was from Fred Eaton. "I wish you luck. Welcome to the world of merchandising." The second was from Galen Weston, advising him of the competing bid.* By April 2, Thomson and Tory had raised their bid to $35 for 60 percent of the HBC stock. Weston countered with an improved offer ($40 for 60 percent), but once Thomson came in with an unconditional cash offer of $37 for 75 percent of the shares—$276 million more than he had originally been willing to pay (although for 75 percent of the shares rather than the original 51 percent)—the bidding was over. The Bay board met on April 4 to approve the takeover formally. The Thomson group made only three demands: a pledge that its equity position wouldn't be diluted by the issue of extra treasury shares; two seats on The Bay board for Thomson and Tory; and alteration of the Company's banking arrangements so that the two banks on which they sat as directors—the Toronto-Dominion and the Royal, which had financed the deal—could get some of the business. There was so little board discussion on these issues that when Richardson pointed out it was Don McGiverin's fifty-fifth, the directors burst into "Happy Birthday."

---

* It was a project the fathers of both men had desired. Galen's father, Garfield, had purchased 200,000 HBC shares in preparation for making his own bid, just before he died; Roy Thomson had told his sidekick Sid Chapman and his granddaughter Sherry that he someday wanted to own the Hudson's Bay Company.

Ironically, this all happened just five weeks short of the ten-year limit that Canadian Committee Chairman David Kilgour had wanted to include in the Company's patriation arrangements. "I don't like all this bloody publicity," was Ken Thomson's only public comment.*

KEN THOMSON DID LITTLE TO ENJOY his position as the HBC's proprietor, neither becoming its Governor nor taking part in any of its rituals. One exception was a summer journey he took to Baffin Island and Hudson Bay with his wife, Marilyn, two of their children, Lynne and Peter, and George Whitman, the Company's Vice-President of Public Affairs, a Second World War pilot who had fought in the Battle of Britain and had since earned a cross-Canada reputation as a social animator. They had just finished lunch at Ross Peyton's tiny hotel at Pangnirtung, on Baffin Island, and Whitman was relaxing on a small rise overlooking the town when up puffed Marilyn and said, "George, I want to do some shopping at that co-op you told me about. You got any money? Here I am, married to the richest man in the country, and he won't allow me to have any credit cards or anything like that. Can I borrow a hundred dollars? But don't tell Ken about it."

Whitman peeled off the bills and she skipped off down to the co-op. Just as she disappeared from view, as if on cue, the world's eighth-richest man came up the hill with the same request. "George, I want to go up to the Bay store and buy some fishing tackle. Can you lend me a hundred dollars?" Later that day, as they were fishing, Ken began to eye Whitman's down-filled vest so wistfully that the Bay man finally told him to take off his Eddie Bauer finery and slip it on. "If you like it, it's yours," Whitman offered, happily expecting to agree with Thomson's refusal. Instead, the press lord held out his hand and said: "Let's shake on it." And that was the last Whitman ever saw of the vest that had been his Linus blanket on many a northern expedition.

Later that day something significant happened, best recorded in Whitman's diary: "We were fishing on the Kulik River and I had gone back to the boat

---

* There was one strange incident in the takeover. George Richardson made a personal profit of more than $15 million by buying—through his own firm, Richardson Securities—1,059,800 shares of HBC stock in twenty-one separate deals between February 6 and 23, 1979, at an average price of $22.50, nearly $15 below the amount for which he traded them in six weeks later to Thomson. "Lucky George," as he quickly became known, defended his amazing good for me and the Ontario Securities Commission cleared him of any wrongdoing. But he was worried enough about accusations of insider trading that he devoted half his speech as Governor before the 1979 annual meeting to defending his actions.

with a double handful of char, when I heard Paul McIlwain, one of our pilots, shouting: 'George! George! Marilyn's hurt bad!' She was down between two river rocks and had a deep cut between her eyes and down her nose. I pulled my shirt and T-shirt off and bound up her head in them. I carried her to the boat where we met Ken and our Inuit guide. We started across the mile and three-quarters of iceberg-studded water to the first-aid station at Pang, Marilyn in the bow, weeping and still in a state of shock. Me on the motor, Ken amidships and the old Inuk, in front with Marilyn, telling her a story.

"'In the Kulik River, there's a big mother fish,' he was saying, 'but this year the fish was going to die and there would be no more char in the Kulik. But today you put some of your blood in that river and the mother fish is going to live and we'll always have char.' Having used a little applied psychology, the Inuk moved back and stood between Ken and me. He gave me a nudge with his elbow and, pointing at Ken, asked: 'He good man?'

"I didn't reply for about fifteen seconds because to have given a token response to a deeply personal question like that would have been perceived as flippant. So I waited, and then said, 'Yes, he's a very good man.'

"The Inuk, who was one of Pang's elders, turned to Ken, and carefully crafting his thoughts, said: 'You don't go home. You stay. We take boat, we go down Kingnait Fiord. You come. You catch big char, see polar bear, caribou. We live on the land. You stay with us, my wife, my family, George too.'

"Ken was absolutely mesmerized. He tried to mumble something, but nothing came out. He leaned over and whispered to me, 'Does he really mean it?'

"'Of course he means it.'

"'Well, I can go anywhere. I can go anywhere in the world for a holiday.'

"'Yes, but Ken, there are things that money can't buy. You've just been paid the most tremendous compliment that one man can give another. He's offering to share his life with you.'

"Poor Ken," Whitman noted in his journal, "that kind of generous gesture was completely outside his conceptual frame of reference—that some person from another culture would comfort his wife with a beautiful little made-up fairy tale and pay him the highest tribute that a person in a tribal society can extend to someone who comes from away...."

IF THERE IS ONE SANCTUARY where Ken Thomson can find peace it's in the private world of his art objects. Within these hushed precincts he can build his own aesthetic universe, indulging his whims without the budgetary problems that inhibit most collectors. He richly deserves his reputation as the premier collector of *habitant* scenes by Krieghoff (some selling for as high as $275,000), all of them magically revivified by one of England's best restorers. "He knows every picture the artist painted or attempted to paint and is constantly improving his collection," according to the Earl of Westmorland, a director of Sotheby's in London. "He's got a great eye and a passionate love of art," echoes Christina Orobetz, the president of Sotheby's Canadian company.

The best of his Canadiana collection (conservatively estimated as worth $20 million) is now displayed in a 5,000-square-foot gallery on the top floor of Toronto's main Bay store. "I've reached a plateau," he says. "I've got my collection basically together and have reached the point where I can be very selective with gathering my *objets d'art*." They include the only wood carving Michelangelo ever did, stunning boxwood and ivory carvings and some incredible miniatures by Octavio Jenilla. Death is a recurring theme of his collection, which includes any number of realistically rendered skulls—the carving of a sleeping child using a skull as a pillow, the tableau of a starving wolf being strangled by a skeleton, and a pearwood skull hinged to reveal a miniature Adam and Eve on one side and the Crucifixion on the other. The most unusual—and most treasured—objects in his collection are the ship models carved by French prisoners in British jails during the Napoleonic era. They carved to keep from going insane in their dungeons but had few tools or materials, so most of the hulls are fashioned out of the bones of their dead, the rigging braided out of their hair.

As with most enterprises, Ken Thomson's art collection is not exactly what it seems. It's controlled by Thomson Works of Art Limited, a company owned by his three children so the increase in value of the collection will be exempted from taxes on his death. The Krieghoff paintings offer their owner an extra incentive: every Christmas, Ken lends one or two canvases to Hallmark, which sends him free Christmas cards bearing the imprint of his painting in return. "They give me a thousand cards free and another four hundred wholesale," he admits.*

---

* The Thomson Christmas card list has carefully noted beside each name the year when it will be removed from his mailings.

IN RUNNING HIS COMPLEX OPERATION, Thomson of course enjoys the advantages of proprietorship, so that he can be wrong without triggering any adverse consequences. He also has the supreme luxury of belonging to a dynasty, so that financial results—good and bad—can be spread over generations instead of having to meet quarterly projections. The HBC's stock values didn't climb back to their original purchase price for more than a decade, but there was never a thought of liquidating or seeking other drastic remedies. "We never have to keep looking over our shoulders at people taking over any of our companies," John Tory points out. "Even when we make major acquisitions that have an initially negative impact on our profitability, in the longer term we'll have a broader base on which we're able to grow. It's really that simple."

Not quite. Tory's real function in the Thomson hierarchy is a source of constant conjecture within and without the organization. "I'm a professional and I never worry about my image," Tory says. "As a business person you can have too high a profile and there's no upside to that whatsoever. When we bought the Hudson's Bay Company there was a big fuss, but we didn't say much; when it was down for the count we said even less; and when it recovered we said nothing." Tory refuses to play the Bay Street game. "I don't need the kind of glory others seek," he says.

It's too easy to speculate that John Tory is the brains behind Ken Thomson, because that wouldn't be fair to either of them. Thomson is smarter than that and Tory is not that self-effacing. As president of most of the family holding companies, Tory exercises enormous influence. He acts as a kind of secretary-general of the $11-billion corporate confederacy, prodding, solving, appointing, acquiring, investing, trouble-shooting—running the damn thing—but never quite making the ultimate decision by himself. He is not exactly a surrogate because when he speaks no one knows whether it's really with his voice or Ken's. Veterans of the Thomson organization know that it's usually both, and leave it at that.

Tory reads at least two books a year that have nothing to do with business, loves to parse balance sheets, is happy to work sixteen-hour days, plays some golf and tennis, and skis, but when a friend asked him to go sailing discovered he didn't own a suitable short-sleeved shirt. The centre of his life is his family—four super-bright children (John, Jennifer, Jeffrey, Michael) and ten grandchildren. He plays a mean "After You've Gone" on a barrel-house piano and dabbles in bridge, but his most serious hobby is keeping up with his wife,

Liz, Toronto's shrewdest and busiest social animator. As well as his Thomson responsibilities he is a director of Sun Life, Rogers Communications, Abitibi-Price and, for the past twenty years, the Royal Bank of Canada. "If you asked almost anyone on the Royal board who was the most brilliant guy there," says former deputy chairman John Coleman, "they'd say John Tory. He asks the most pertinent questions and can see through a deal most quickly."

Thomson himself doesn't just admire Tory; he worships the man. "If you take the best qualities of the best people in all the different fields of business and roll them into one—that's John Tory," he says. "It's the same pleasure for him to work, the way I collect paintings and walk my dog. Above all, he's got a great wife, family and good friends. They have fun together."

That emphasis on family governs Thomson's own life. "He has so much love and affection with the family and Gonzo," says his son David, "we get so much pleasure just seeing him and trying to make him happier." David likes to quote the maxim of Meyer Guggenheim, the Swiss-born American industrialist who maintained a family dynasty by handing each of his sons a stick and asking him to break it. Each did. He then gave each a bundle of sticks, which none of them could break. "Stand alone, and you will be broken," he told them. "Stand together and no one will break you." The Thomson family very much sticks together; they are proud and protective of one another, especially in tragic circumstances.

Just two weeks before Christmas 1990, Gonzo died.

"I've had the loss of dear ones, human beings," Ken lamented, "but I've never experienced anything that shook me more than his death. Gonzo slept with me the last night. I held the little guy in my arms and I thought, I can't really stand this. I left the room and then I thought, no, he really needs me. I've got to be there. I felt him expire. I don't want ever, ever to go through such a thing again ..."

Disaster and Deliverance

"There are no merchants here. You're all a lot of bookkeepers."
—Harvard Professor Walter Salmon,
speaking to an HBC executive think-tank

FOR MOST OF THE FIRST TWO YEARS after they had attained control of the Hudson's Bay Company, Ken Thomson and John Tory were ecstatic about their new purchase. Contrary to everyone's expectations, they seldom intervened in board decisions, and Thomson evidenced no desire to become the Company's Governor. "I'm not on any ego trip," he said after George Richardson left the post and was succeeded by Don McGiverin. "I've got so much in my life that I'm grateful for and so much to be occupied with, that I don't need or want to be Governor. The future of the Company is largely in Don McGiverin's hands. He's an awfully nice guy. Nobody could represent the Company better. I'm much happier to have him do it than myself."

Thomson and Tory joined the board but, with one exception, seemed happy merely to be consulted, their input limited mainly to deciding the extent of dividend payouts and monitoring major capital expenditures. The exception was Tory's concern about Simpsons. The first item on his agenda was to advise McGiverin to merge the twenty-three-unit department-store chain with The Bay.* "We're absolutely delighted with our long-term investment ... happy with management and very hopeful the year's results will be quite satisfactory," Tory told the *Financial Post* in 1979, when the Company's operations showed a net of $104 million on sales of $3.4 billion.

---

* Had Tory's advice been followed, $500 million in operating losses and $600 million in interest carrying costs over the next decade might have been avoided.

By the early 1980s, inventory was turning over more slowly and interest rates had started to climb. That was a serious matter. The interest payments necessary to cover the $2.3-billion debt McGiverin and his board had incurred expanding the retailing empire quickly overwhelmed every other balance-sheet item. By 1982, The Bay had moved into a serious negative earnings position (a net loss of $128 million), and at a directors' meeting on June 22, Tory finally stepped in. "We can't keep growing by incurring more and more debt," he warned the board, threatening drastic measures if there was no bottom-line improvement by the end of the year.

What Tory came to realize was that the Company's management had become obsessed with expanding its share of market at the expense of profit. The quest for greater sales became a *jihad*. The Company, which had once confined its special pricing to semi-annual Bay Days, launched Super Dollar Days, In-Store Warehouse Sales, Big Deals, Scratch and Save Days, Price Blow-Outs and quarterly Bay Days each of which lasted two weeks. Customers reacted by cherry-picking the merchandise that was deeply discounted (up to 50 percent) and passing over the items with big mark-ups. To heighten the impression of a stock of bargain goods that had to be moved quickly, stores were over-inventoried; the typical sales floor looked like an untidy warehouse, with merchandise left in cartons to block the aisles. As they were picked over, the items usually spilled onto the floor, where they were trampled on—or stolen.* The pressure to produce advertising flyers promoting the many sales grew so intense that their pages were crammed with mistakes. A four-page HBC flyer published on August 20, 1989, for example, contained thirty-seven errors that had to be corrected in subsequent newspaper ads.

Such tactics proved costly in terms of both immediate profit and the HBC's long-term reputation. Richard Sharpe, who then ran the competing Simpsons-Sears (later Sears Canada) chain, reacted by issuing orders that his company would not even try to match the HBC price cuts. "We ignored them," he says. "They were giving the goods away and losing pailfuls of money. We lost some market share, but we were *making* money." Still, no expense was spared in trying to pump up the HBC's sales totals, which in 1984 had climbed by $1.4 million since the Thomson purchase—while earnings of $104 million for 1979

---

* There was a story going the rounds of Toronto's fashion district about the sales manager of a dress supply house, who told his staff, "There's a Bay buyer coming in this afternoon to see our line; lay it out on the floor, so she'll know what it will look like when it gets into the store."

had turned into a loss of $107 million in 1984. When one high-ranking Company executive defended that strategy of continual growth and praised the merits of spreading overhead costs through continual expansion, Tory shot back, "You can't eat market share—and you can't eat overhead, either." Not being a retail merchant, Tory didn't really know what was possible in the department-store trade, but he did know that as desirable as a growing market share might be, profit was much better—particularly since current cash flows were not enough to service existing debts.

FOR A TIME, THE COMPANY was barely under control, lacking direction or sensible forward momentum. Its executives had been taught how to expand the business, not how to change it. The Company's troubles were so serious that everyone was looking inward to prevent collapse, instead of outward to trigger resurrection. Most of the organization men who were moved in to run various departments had the necessary know-how, but they lacked soul. Walter Salmon, who taught retailing at the Harvard Business School, said as much, addressing the HBC's executives at a 1982 think-tank. "The problem with this company," he declared, gazing at the gathered suits, "is that there are no merchants here. You're all a lot of bookkeepers."

Sir William Keswick, the retired British Governor, observing the tribulations of his beloved Hudson's Bay Company from his retirement at Theydon Bois, shook his head in disbelief: "We handed over the Company in apple-pie order, and they went wild with it. If you borrow money at a certain percentage and invest at half that percentage, sooner or later it doesn't work. That's sort of elementary. But that was what they did."

"They imbued the staff with the notion that fiscal accountability was the highest virtue, and forgot that retailing is really showbiz," complained Shirley Dawe, a brilliant marketer who had joined the HBC as a trainee and rose to be a vice-president. "Don McGiverin had a wonderful rapport with everybody," she fondly remembered, "but he kept getting further and further away from the action."

One problem was The Bay's inability to keep up with the changing tastes of Canadian consumers. The Company still behaved as if its main competitors were other department stores when retailing was being fragmented in new directions, with specialty marketers such as Dylex, the Grafton Group, Leon's, The Brick and thousands of imaginative independents winning sales. Despite the Herculean efforts to raise it, between 1978 and 1984 The Bay's market share of Canadian retail sales actually declined to 5.3 percent from 5.7 percent—while profits plummeted at the same time. The Company did a lot of silly things, such as abandoning its pharmacy counters, which may not have produced an especially high gross (9 percent) but had been great traffic builders. Some areas—like the cosmetics department at the Winnipeg store with its $12-million face-lift—were overbuilt; others, such as the untidy, often filthy main floor in the Victoria store, were ignored. "If there is an example of abrogated opportunity in the history of corporate Canada," concluded a 1983 study of the HBC by Toronto's Yorkton Securities, "surely it is the Hudson's Bay Company."

The HBC became so obsessed with cutting costs that the basic rationale for its department stores—friendly service and a wide selection of merchandise— was lost. The Bay stores switched almost entirely into soft goods, emphasizing fashion at a time when more and more families were nesting in their homes, stocking many of the hard goods the HBC was abandoning. Even the fashion-driven clothing business faced an uncertain future. "Nobody knows what women want to wear any more," commented Marilyn Brooks, a leading Toronto fashion designer. Service at most Bay stores became virtually non-existent as thousands of knowledgeable and loyal employees were laid off and part-timers took their places. The temporary substitutes may have been untrained and disinterested, but unlike permanent employees they cost the company no pensions, paid statutory holidays, vacation times or other fringe benefits. Barry Wilson, manager of The Bay at Bloor and Yonge in Toronto, reported a 43-percent staff turnover at his store in 1987.

It was not always easy for Bay management to dismiss longtime employees. One of the mainstays of the downtown Vancouver store, for instance, was Helen Carson, who had managed the wool department for twenty-eight years and had a large following of local knitters. The Bay wanted to fire her because her salary had reached the maximum, but that would have cost a considerable severance allowance. Since she refused to quit, she was transferred to the children's wear department, where she had to move heavy boxes. Carson eventually injured her lower back and had to resign for medical reasons, leaving behind an untended—and unfrequented—wool department. Lynn Scully, who successfully built up the same store's book department, had taken great pride in her work. "My grandfather was a fur trapper and the whole family was excited when I got the job. We loved The Bay and I remember when it was a prestige store and people would actually come in just to buy our shopping bags." But

Scully left, as so many other department managers did, because not only had unrelenting cost-cutting made effective merchandising impossible but the Company had also turned into an impassive and uncaring bureaucracy. In her last year at The Bay, Scully was reporting to *nineteen* different managers.*

All through this time, the head-office bureaucracy continued to balloon. D.G. (Pete) Buckley, a Bay vice-president, once burst into McGiverin's office to dramatize the point. "Look, Don," he told the Governor, "when I first arrived at your head office, we had an internal phone directory five pages long. This one, published today, has two hundred pages and that doesn't include the whole data-processing group. We've got a problem."

"I was absolutely appalled by many of the attitudes and directions within the HBC," recalls David Thomson, Ken's elder son, who was training on the job in the HBC organization at the time. "There seemed to be a distinct separation between the people who felt themselves visionaries and the line operators facing the customer. The latter were less involved in the decision-making process, which in fact they were funding. The world was turned on its head. The system had come to a great human impasse."

Pierre Mignault, a brilliant merchandiser and later president of the Price Club of Canada but then head of the HBC's Quebec region, felt a similar frustration with "the grids of people coming at me from all angles out of that humongous Toronto head office. It was unreal. You didn't even know who to call about anything important. The Company became too big and too fat and didn't have the human-resource structure to handle its rapid expansion." Mignault experienced a good example of Bay bureaucracy in 1983 when the roof of the Place Vertu store started leaking. He had to put twenty buckets on the shop floor to catch the water whenever it rained, but couldn't find the appropriate vice-president in charge of fixing leaky roofs. Even though the local fire department temporarily

---

* Many people left the Company with understandable bitterness, none more so than Mark Blumes, who later started the successful Mark's Work Wearhouse chain. Blumes had been forced out of his job as a junior manager at the Calgary store because his many ideas and ambitions didn't fit the HBC mould. This diverted him from his objective of becoming the youngest—and only Jewish—senior executive of The Bay. He was not pleased. "For many years afterwards," he recalls, "if I felt a little lazy, and was thinking, 'Geez, I'm not going to bother opening up in Quebec,' or something like that, I'd drive down to the Bay store and just ride the escalators. The hate would wash over me and would fuel up my emotions, remembering all the times I had answered the page 'Blumes, call 555,' only to have my nose rubbed in it. So I'd come back and tell my staff, 'Let's go for it!'"

closed the store because of the danger of the ceiling's collapsing, Mignault never did get head office to sanction repairs to the building. He gave up the attempt after a year and ordered it done on his own. "Of course it cost much more than it would have originally," he recalls, "because after a year of dripping water, the carpets had to be replaced and I had to buy huge fans to get rid of the musty smell. It was awful. It was embarrassing."

To offset the neglect and losses, the Company launched an internal money-raising program that took the form of disposing of the balance of its Simpsons-Sears stock for $211 million to Sears, Roebuck, realizing a $48-million profit, and cashing in—for $455 million—the 7.7 million preferred shares in Dome Resources it had received in 1981 on the sale to the Calgary company's parent of its remaining interest in Hudson's Bay Oil & Gas.

That Dome transaction was a milestone in Canadian business history, because it was ultimately responsible for the toppling of the high-flying Calgary energy company and its even higher-flying chairman, Jack Gallagher. Dome had grown from a one-man operation in the early 1950s to a major energy player, but its corporate behaviour remained dominated by that same man, Jack Gallagher, whose dreams of grandeur knew no limits. At the heart of his fantasies was the desire to make Dome larger in Canada than Imperial Oil. To achieve that goal, in 1981 Gallagher went after Hudson's Bay Oil & Gas, a subsidiary of Conoco, the former Continental Oil, based in Stamford, Connecticut. He easily won control (53 percent) of HBOG but only by doubling Dome's debt load to $5.3 billion, a level that required interest payments of an agonizing $3 million a day. To lighten that load he desperately needed access to HBOG's $300-million annual cash flow, and that meant buying out all the minority shareholders, including the largest single block—the 10.1 percent still owned by the HBC.

Just before Gallagher had made his move on Conoco, he had offered Tory, through a Bay Street intermediary, $27 a share for the Company's HBOG stock. Tory, who had done his own calculations, considered it to be worth at least $50, though he had at one time been willing to sell HBC's position at $40 to $45. Now he dug in. Tory seldom loses his temper, but he still turns red thinking about that $27 bid, particularly since it was made just three days before Gallagher offered Conoco the equivalent of $52 for its HBOG stock. "That really stiffened our backbone," he recalls, "and when I met Gallagher I told him in no uncertain terms that I thought this was not the way ethical businessmen operated." He refused a trade of Dome shares for HBC's stake and would accept only a complicated retractable preferred-stock formula that made the HBC's 7.7 million Dome shares worth $57.50 each on or before December 31, 1984, with the money paid out of an escrow account that Dome management couldn't touch in the interval. Gallagher later claimed the deal was largely responsible for Dome's downfall, but for HBC the 1983 Dome redemption provided a badly needed infusion of $455 million in cash.*

By 1984, the HBC's pre-tax losses over the preceding four years amounted to more than $320 million. Thomson and Tory had grown exasperated with management's intransigence. One of the big problems was that the cost of the money involved in the HBC's expansions was never included in profit projections. Regional and departmental managers would make presentations to the board forecasting glowing revenues and operating profits for new store expansions without even mentioning returns on capital invested, interest costs, cash flows or tax considerations. At 5 P.M. on November 29, 1984, Tory, who had brought up the issue so many times he was fed up with bleating about it, arrived late at a Bay committee meeting attended by Governor Don McGiverin and HBC vice-presidents Wally Evans, Rolph Huband, Marvin Tiller, Don Wood, Al Guglielmin and Lorne Klapp. The outside directors present included Ian Barclay of Vancouver, Marcel Bélanger of Montreal and Dawn McKeag of Winnipeg. They had met to hear the presentation of C.W. "Chuck" Gerhart, then general manager of the Ottawa region, who reviewed his area's retail growth, projected sales and operating profits five years into the future, cheerfully predicting a net increase from $3.5 million to $12.1 million by 1989—this for a district that had a profit peak of $5 million in the past and had not recently been reaching its own sales targets.

For Tory, that was it. Keeping himself under tight control, he politely inquired whether Gerhart cared to acknowledge the fact that current profits had been realized only after investment of about $30 million to improve the main Ottawa store, linking it to the Rideau Centre, and pointed out that this expenditure had involved considerable financing costs. When the Ottawa manager replied with the equivalent of a shrug, Tory gave him a stern lecture about the impact of financing charges on cash flows and bottom-line profits.

---

* The HBC's only remaining oil investment was the small Calgary-based Canadian Roxy Petroleum (named after the Roxy Arcade, a New York roller-skating rink where its promoter, Robert Peters, had spent an enjoyable evening), bought in 1980 and sold seven years later to Westcoast Transmission for $82 million at a small profit.

"It really wasn't Gerhart's fault," he later admitted. "He was just part of the HBC's corporate culture. They were living in a dream world—only looking at operating profits and pretending everything else would take care of itself."

The next day, just after a revised quarterly profit outlook was tabled showing a further $50-million dip in a rapidly accelerating financial slide (the loss for the nine months ended October 31, 1984, was $7.67 a share, compared with $4.20 the year before), Tory addressed the Company's full board. It was the toughest speech he'd ever given, and would in retrospect become recognized as a watershed in the Hudson's Bay Company's long history. "When we acquired HBC," one of the directors recalls his saying, "it had just taken over Simpsons. I thought HBC was well managed and could help Simpsons, which had inferior management. Instead, the Bay's management screwed up Simpsons, and I've lost confidence in the HBC management. The major shareholder would not consider investing another cent in HBC at this time. I will review the situation with Ken and our people and will have recommendations for the Board at our next meeting in January." He stressed that the continued existence of the HBC was at risk because nobody seemed to be focusing on the real problem—that the Company simply wasn't generating enough cash to cover its daily requirements. An immediate freeze was placed on capital spending; drastic cuts in corporate overhead were ordered; new guidelines were established to focus objectives on cash flows and net earnings rather than sales totals and operating profits.

"When you look back," Thomson later ruminated, "it's a legitimate question to ask why we let it go so long. When we made the investment, we believed the HBC was a well-managed company, and there was very little reason for us to think otherwise, as profits grew in the first few years. Then, all of a sudden, with the downturn in business and upturn in interest rates, the sins of the past came home to roost. Now *that* doesn't make for a passive investment. Professional management was failing to meet budget objectives by increasingly wide margins. When I said the management of the HBC is great, I was right—I just got the tense wrong. Don McGiverin and his people had done a superb job, but the Company had turned into a sort of ivory-tower bureaucracy. We could have tried to get a hot-shot retailer from the States to take his place, but that wouldn't have been right. We could have sold off The Bay's real estate and broken up the Company, but I didn't want to do that. We could have merged the HBC with Thomson Newspapers, but that wouldn't have been fair to the shareholders who had invested in our publishing abilities. No, the best thing was to stick with it, and build it up again."

Right after that November 30 meeting, Tory had an encounter with McGiverin over costs of the Company's computer operation, which were climbing at an alarming 20 percent annually. Tory wanted independent cost-control experts to review the computer systems, but McGiverin refused to allow them access. Tory and Thomson quickly realized that the Governor's head would have to be included in any effective reform package. "I don't really think management realized how desperate the financial situation had become," Ken Thomson recalls. "They thought, 'Here's a 300-year-old company, and nothing will happen'—so they just kept doing things as before. We had waited and waited and waited, but finally we had to take action. Lookit, out of respect for the kind of person he is and what he had done in the past, we didn't want to hurt Don McGiverin. But he had to go, and he was gentlemanly enough, big enough to realize changes had to be made. We were able to maintain our mutual respect and friendship."

And so the merchant prince was stripped of his crown, if not his title. Feeling prouder of his run than bloodied because of the way it had ended, McGiverin lost not an ounce of dignity in the process of giving up his authority. "I hung in too long, I really did," he told a friend on the morning after his demotion. "But then, not every person's built for all seasons. If I had thought there was a better way of doing things, I'd have done it. God, I've been forty-five years in this thing, and I've been at it twenty hours a day. Still, the Chief Executive Officer can never have a bullet-proof vest. I've had a good run, and when they asked me to stay on as Governor, I told them I'd be delighted."

At a crucial board meeting on January 25, 1985, Tory, speaking on Thomson's behalf, announced that McGiverin had relinquished his post as Chief Executive Officer but would continue as Governor in a non-executive capacity. In his place, two executive vice-presidents—Iain Ronald and George Kosich—were being appointed to run the Company, with the former to be in charge of Zellers, wholesale, furs, real estate, the northern stores and the disposal of non-strategic assets, while the latter would take over control of the HBC's department stores including Simpsons as well as credit and information services. The directors (except Ronald and Kosich) thought this was a silly idea because the Company would not have a single responsible executive. They only approved the new structure subject to Tory's taking on the chairmanship of the management committee of the board, thus effectively turning himself into the Company's CEO, since neither Ronald nor Kosich could implement major policy shifts without first checking with him. For the next half-decade, John Tory, in effect, ran the HBC. It was a stormy five years, but in the end he saved the Company.

THE TORY-DOMINATED RONALD-KOSICH partnership represented a dramatic shift in direction, since Don McGiverin had by then been running the Company for fifteen years. While few had ever questioned his skills as a retailer, McGiverin had, since 1978, opted out of his chosen profession, spending nearly all his time and energy on takeovers. As a result of that neglect— plus the effects of the recession and the Company's astronomical debt load—the HBC's credit ratings were downgraded from AAA to a humiliating B. Between 1980 and 1982, operating profits declined 97 percent.*

Apart from cutting costs of its existing retail operations, The Bay under both McGiverin and Tory had also drastically trimmed the number of its operations. The Shop-Rite catalogue stores were closed in 1982 and its Marshall Wells hardware subsidiary was sold in 1985. Its travel business and its share of Eaton Bay Financial Services, Computer Innovations, Hudson's Bay Distillers and Toronto Credits were disposed of the same year.† In the summer of 1987, The Bay sold off its wholesale division, established in 1907 to handle liquor as well as grocery distribution, later adding candies and tobacco. With annual sales of $800 million, it was a big operation, but it never made much profit. After a partnership between Norman Paul, brother of a former president of Zellers, and Jimmy Kay (then chairman of Dylex) bought it for $133 million (about half of it down), the pair took not quite a year to run it into the ground, forcing its 1,200 employees on to the street and causing a $45-million write-down on the HBC's books, though much of it was later recovered.

Late on a Friday evening in January 1987, Marvin Tiller, head of the Northern Stores Division in Winnipeg, got a call from Iain Ronald, the HBC's executive vice-president, advising him to be in his office at 8:30 A.M. the following Monday. "When I got there, Ronald abruptly advised me that the

---

* At one point in 1986, things got so tight that the Company applied to take a $35-million surplus out of its employee pension fund. The application was withdrawn only when the Pension Commission of Ontario warned that it would be refused.

† The Bay's real-estate holdings, except those buildings occupied by its stores, were folded into its subsidiary Markborough Properties in 1984 and six years later Markborough was turned into a separate public company through the spinning off of its shares to the HBC's stockholders. With 78.4 percent of the parent company's stock, Ken Thomson could claim the same percentage of Markborough, which allowed him to realize a tax-free $315-million capital gain.

Northern Stores Division had been sold and that the new owners would be arriving in half an hour," Tiller recalls. "I told him that we'd like to have done an employee buyout, but sure enough, thirty minutes later Ian Sutherland and Raymond Doré, representing Mutual Trust of Waterloo, Ontario, rolled in, ready to take over."

Sale of the Company's historic Northern Stores Division had first been discussed at a management committee meeting on September 12, 1986. Ronald reported that he had been approached by a group of investors organized by Mutual Trust and that while profits for the operation might reach $35 million, it didn't have much opportunity for expansion. The item came up again at a January 23 meeting, where the selling price was set at $8 million over book value, with an 80-percent cash advance. Approval to jettison this most historic of the HBC's departments—the territory for which it had received its Charter 317 years earlier—was granted at the directors' meeting on January 28, 1987. The official minute hardly does that momentous decision justice: "The Board discussed the pros and cons of such a sale. On the one hand N.S.D. is profitable and represents to Canadians the heritage and pioneering spirit of the company. On the other hand, it operates in a total welfare environment with considerable risks of government intervention, it requires capital for modernization and has little growth potential. On balance, given the overriding need to substantially reduce debt, the Board decided to approve the sale."

Strangely, no outside directors attended that meeting, though they were polled by telephone. Only four executives, who also served on the board, were there to vote on the fateful motion to cut the ties with the HBC's own history.* "My recollection," recalled J.W. "Bud" Bird, one of the directors who was telephoned on the issue, "was of feeling a sense of loss, that we were really changing the character of the Company, but that it was sort of a side-battle in the mission to establish three main retailing giants and to concentrate where the volumes were and the super-store kinds of activity. The preservation of the origins of the Company was no longer commercially attractive to the main mission of the Company."

That seemed more of a retroactive rationalization than a reason. Northern Stores had been a dependable money-maker, clearing $28 million in operating profit on a $400-million sales volume the year the division was sold.

---

*They were: Don McGiverin, George Kosich, Iain Ronald, and Gary Lukassen. All the directors polled by telephone agreed to the sale.

Spinning the 178 stores off for $189 million reduced the parent company's debt by a net $150 million, about 6 percent of the total it then owed, which didn't make any material difference. Tiller was as puzzled by the decision as anyone. "I couldn't fathom how they could possibly come to that decision," he said, "particularly since we had a five-year profit trend that was right on target and was marching on and on. The most difficult experience for me was having to face my people, who all have an HBC stamped on their backsides, and tell them about it."

Rolph Huband, the HBC's vice-president and secretary, was the only Company executive who took note of the sale's historic dimensions. "The heritage and adventuring spirit of the Company is gone," he lamented. Dick Murray, the former managing director, came out of retirement to thunder: "Only unpardonable cowardice and incompetence could lead the Canadian owners of this great historic company to throw away these jewels in their crown. The Company now abandons the Canadian North; it severs generations of a trusting and respectful relationship between native peoples and traders—it deletes the words and discards the heart of its historic name: Company of Adventurers. One might just as well take the RCMP and sell it to Pinkertons." These sentiments were shared by former Deputy Governor Sir Eric Faulkner, who mourned: "If the HBC is alive three hundred years from now, it will be neither the fault of the Thomsons or of the Bay directors from 1970 on. If we had foreseen what would follow ... would we all have been persuaded to transfer to Canada?"*

On May 2, 1987, precisely 317 years after the Company of Adventurers had taken up Charles II's Charter to exploit the upper half of the North American continent, Derek Riley, the Winnipeg businessman who had been elected chairman of the offshoot company, folded the Governor's flag that had flown over the posts of the HBC's northern division and handed it back to Don McGiverin. Suddenly it was over—317 years of history cut adrift as if they had never happened. Ken Thomson's main interest in the transfer was to claim for the HBC the art works collected by the northern division, taking three-quarters of the Inuit sculptures, prints and historical paintings.

---

* The last of the great British directors, Sir Martin Jacomb, expressed his views of the sale by quietly investing in the successor company to the Northern Stores Division, which at George Whitman's suggestion became known as the North West Company.

He felt very much more strongly about getting rid of the Company's fur business. "I was just praying the Company would sell it," he confided after the decision had been made. "I think it's an anachronism. We don't need to kill animals to feed our vanity. They may not be a high order of life, but animals have the same right to live as we have. They can say what they like about animals being humanely trapped—it's not true. You can't kill an animal without making it suffer. So why should we kill creatures who are out there trying to survive? That's all they're doing, trying to survive. Over the coming years, people are just not going to be wearing fur coats. It's a dying business. I know that somebody else is still doing it, but it has nothing to do with my family." That was a revealing statement, because it was the one aspect of current HBC operations that Thomson really felt passionately about (except, of course, for losing all that money), yet he himself did nothing about it, allowing the Company's executives to work their way towards his conclusion on the issue—but only eight years after he became the Company's principal proprietor.

His son David confirms his father's reluctance to apply the force of his authority even in a cause he feels passionately about. "My father has never wished to dictate his will to the business operators," says he. "Power is always perceived; when it is used, it ceases to be. He had believed that the people within HBC supported the business and that it was beneficial to the Company. Although he made his personal feelings very clear on numerous occasions, he would never unilaterally end the fur business within the HBC."

The Canadian fur-sale operations near the Toronto airport were sold for $45 million to Len Werner, the previous manager. Disposing of the British facilities at London's Beaver House was a much more complicated affair. Hugh Dwan, the president of the HBC's British fur unit, received a phone call from Iain Ronald ordering him to be at the London offices of Morgan Stanley a day or two later to hear the details pertaining to the sale of his company. Dwan, who had up to then received no notice of the move, was just as puzzled as Marvin Tiller had been about jettisoning the northern stores, particularly since the auction house had been turning good profits and he had just recently submitted (and had approved) his optimistic budgets. The sale—to the Finnish Fur Sales Company, for $37.5 million—had been negotiated without his knowledge or consent. "They told me that selling the auction house would enable the Company to concentrate on their core business," he recalls. "In fact, the fur business in England was no drain at all on Canadian management because we didn't need them. The debt reduction benefits were a drop in the bucket. To me, their decision seemed like chopping up the kitchen furniture to feed the fire, and then finding out you have no place to sit.... They sold the company in the face of fast-rising fur prices, so if they had waited one more year, they could have got several million dollars more. It was an undignified scramble to get out."

Dwan had a devil of a time persuading London's fur traders that the HBC move was serious. Three centuries is a long time. "They thought it was some kind of reverse takeover for tax reasons and that the HBC would end up owning the Finnish co-operative," Dwan remembers. "There was strong feeling that the Company had let them down. In furs, the HBC was a mark of confidence all over the world." After his day at Morgan Stanley, going over the dreary details of the sale, Dwan walked to Earls Court, then took a taxi home. "I turned on the TV news," he recalls, "and there was young David Thomson, who had just purchased a Constable for £2 million, saying that as its new owner he was anxious the United Kingdom not lose its heritage, and that he therefore might not take it out of the country. I thought to myself 'They've just sold out the best trading name in the world,' and I cried."

On January 31, 1988, the fur men held a wake on the auction floor at Beaver House. It had been on January 24, 1672, that the first London HBC fur auction was held at Garraway's coffee house, near the Royal Exchange, where tea from dried leaves imported by the East India Company had originally been brewed. That first sale was a very special event attended by the Company's founder, Prince Rupert, his cousin, the Lord High Admiral, the Duke of York (who would become the HBC's second Governor and, as James II, King of England) and the poet John Dryden. Now it was all over, and from seven in the evening to midnight, a lot of rum was tasted, songs were sung, and stories told. Special arrangements had been made to transmit the Company's farewell telegrams and telephone calls that day, presuming there would be some form of official farewell wishes sent to mark the end of the Company's founding department. Incredibly, no message ever came. "They didn't even know we still existed," said a bitter Arthur Frayling, Dwan's predecessor and a sixty-eight-year veteran of the fur trade. "The greetings from head office in Canada were as they had been for some years previous— zero. They had actually established in their minds that the Company's great background and tradition was, in fact, a drawback. Now that I can't take. I'm sorry, I can't bloody well take it."*

The British fur trade ended with Frayling, well over six feet tall and with the bearing of the infantry colonel he once was, standing on the bidding stage at Beaver House and leading the mourners in song:

> *Dear old pals,*
> *jolly old pals*
> *all in together*
> *in all sorts of weather.*
> *Dear old pals,*
> *jolly old pals,*
> *Give me the solace*
> *of dear old pals ...*

THE RULE OF THE TORY-KOSICH-RONALD triumvirate ended on July 1, 1987, with the appointment of George Kosich as the HBC's president and chief operating officer. A University of British Columbia Commerce grad, he had spent twenty-seven years with The Bay, and even though his cutbacks had earned him the nickname George Carnage, he was a capable retailer with energy to burn, and brought to his position an optimistic outlook and determination to dismantle the deadening sanctions of head office.† Kosich's— and the HBC's—good fortune was to have at his side Gary Lukassen, the Company's chief financial officer, who became a key man in its resurrection.

Kosich was tough and as single-minded as a mountain mule, which didn't enhance his popularity. On October 24, 1988, an anonymous petition was

---

* Having divested itself of its northern stores and fur trade, the Company went on a kind of scorched-earth rampage, getting rid of the very last historic symbol it possessed. This was the collection of silver objects minted in 1670, the year of its incorporation, that had been gathered by various Governors and kept at Beaver House. The thirty hallmarked pieces were shipped without notice to New York for sale by Christie's, so that some of the former British HBC directors had less chance to buy them, or, as one former Governor intended, to donate them to the city of London.

† Iain Ronald resigned the same day Kosich was appointed, later becoming president of administration for the Canadian Imperial Bank of Commerce. "I just couldn't stay at The Bay a moment longer, because I have to look at myself in the mirror every day and can't shave with my eyes shut," he told a friend just after he quit. Doug Mahaffy, the HBC's senior vice-president, finance, also resigned within a few weeks of the Kosich appointment.

circulated at the HBC's head office, asking executives whether they respected Kosich's style of management. "Do you believe that the removal of George Kosich [as chief operating officer and president] would return the Company to a more stable and productive environment?" the questionnaire demanded. At the first management committee meeting after its distribution, John Tory began the proceedings by turning to Kosich and, with mock seriousness, explaining, "Before we start the business of the meeting, there is an announcement I have to make. It concerns the questionnaire that was circulated to the executive staff. We've tabulated the results. There were 175 replies that came in. Six percent voted for Ed Broadbent [then NDP leader], about 15 percent were undecided, and the others said they didn't know who George Kosich was." One of Kosich's problems in dealing with staff morale was his vocabulary. He was always talking about M.B.W.A. (which meant Management By Walking About—a reference to mingling with customers), eliminating T.N.M.J. (the That's Not My Job syndrome, when it came to helping close sales by using a little extra effort) and in a gush of participles, defined his formula for success as "downsizing, rationalizing, fine-tuning and refocusing."

With Ken Thomson's and John Tory's active backing, Kosich turned the Company inside out, closing unprofitable units but supporting success with ambitious retailing plans. The deliverance of the HBC was not nearly as dramatic as its near disintegration. It was largely a matter of rationalization and reorganization—the gradual reintroduction of the Company to its natural retailing audience.

Kosich eliminated layers of middle management and centralized buying and sales promotion to cut expenses. He used computer technology to provide better data for buying decisions and his merchandising flair to pick commodity winners, then spent money backing those premium items with more inventory and upgraded locations in the stores. At the same time he restored flagship downtown units to some semblance of their former glory by installing colourful, contemporary environments for housewares and women's and men's fashions.

It was at Zellers, the discount store that Joe Segal saved from bankruptcy and Don McGiverin bought at gunpoint, that Kosich and the HBC enjoyed their most spectacular success. When he and David Thomson took over Zellers in 1987, it was experimenting with an upscale format to distinguish itself from its discount competitors. Kosich declared that a discount store must look like a discount store and ordered the newly installed partitions and carpeting removed. He also insisted that in discounting, expenses are everything and put into effect the lowest operating costs in the industry. This allowed Zellers to reduce its prices and trumpet that at its stores "the lowest price is the law." Customers responded, driving sales up, expense rates down, and prices still lower. As a result, Zellers' operating profits tripled in the four years of the Kosich presidency and for the first time since the Thomson takeover, the owners opened the pursestrings in November 1990 to purchase the fifty-store Towers chain. By mid-April 1991, Kosich had their carpets removed, their expense rates reduced, and new Zellers signs installed.

In the meantime the Company had completed its transformation from a conglomerate to a retailer. "Disposal of the fur and northern departments was required to correct the daring excesses of the 1970s," maintains Rolph Huband, the Company's vice-president and corporate secretary. "The necessary corrections having been made, the HBC reset the course originally plotted in 1970—to become the most successful of Canadian business enterprises." With the distribution in August 1990 of Markborough Properties shares to its own stockholders, the HBC was for the first time since 1870 mainly in one line of business—retailing.

The only unit that never stopped bleeding was Simpsons. That upscale, Toronto-centred department store had proved a disaster since Don McGiverin had taken it over in the late 1970s. Simpsons had suffered through the tenures of eight presidents in a decade: Ted Burton, Charles MacRea, George Kosich, Al Brent, Bob Peter, David Thomson, Paul Walters and Bob Peter again. None of them could resurrect the sleeping elephant. The store had lost its audience. HBC management tried going first upscale and then downscale, firing sales personnel over thirty-five years of age, publishing yuppie ads, shutting down the Montreal and Regina units, combining purchasing offices, amalgamating advertising departments, putting in the country's—probably the continent's—most expensive food hall (in the basement), but nothing worked. The upscale shoppers didn't get upscale service— and so they stayed away. At any rate, there weren't enough of them to turn Simpsons into a northern Bloomingdale's. Even internally, Simpsons was treated as a joke, with Bay executives referring to its main Toronto store as "the Panty Palace." The Company became fed up with throwing people and money at the troublesome Simpsons division and finally in the summer of 1991 closed it down.

But that was all anti-climax. By the spring of 1989, the HBC's balance sheets reflected the dramatic turnaround that Tory had masterminded and Kosich had engineered: profits at $144 million were up 389 percent from the previous year's. The Company's salvation had been slow and painful but, against all odds, it had been achieved and its credit ratings had been restored. The Hudson's Bay Company was once more safely in the black.

Last Lord of the Bay

"I become excited at the thought of measuring myself in varied situations, alongside Wellington in India or being in a fighter, attacking a formation of bombers and being vastly outnumbered. It's an interesting way to test yourself because you set your own limits." —David Thomson

THE RICH DON'T HAVE CHILDREN; they have heirs. For the first-born male, growing up is a brief interval during which he matures into becoming his father's Son, with all the baggage of continuity and shedding of spontaneity that such a rite of passage implies. Youth involves being wafted through Father's private school and enrolled in his clubs at birth, experiencing all the right things (doing drugs means two Aspirins at bedtime), earning a Harvard MBA, and spending languid vacations at large summer homes on the manicured shores of cool green lakes.

These precocious progeny learn at their daddies' knees how to exude that air of besieged innocence that marks the Canadian Establishment's young— a mixture of being well bred and mentally inert. As a group, they seldom have an original idea, think it's daring to use an adverb and believe that culture means attending a Pavarotti gala in a tux. They are dull to the point of banality.

And then there is David Kenneth Roy Thomson.

His very name evokes the three-generation dynasty he represents, and he is, by quite a wide margin, the most fascinating of Canada's inheritors, being his own kind of pensive rebel and a recognized art connoisseur to boot. At thirty-five, David Thomson is Deputy Chairman of Woodbridge, the holding company that controls the family assets. The trust set up by Roy Thomson, who died in 1976 at eighty-two, having amassed a corporate flush then worth at least $750 million, appointed David, Ken's elder son, to be the next head of the Thomson Organization. He will also assume his grandfather's title, which will give him a seat in the House of Lords, never claimed by Ken. "David, my grandson, will have to take his part in the running of the Organization, and David's son, too," the dying Thomson wrote, spelling out the rules. "For the business is now all tied up in trusts for those future Thomsons, so that death duties will not tear it apart.... These Thomson boys that come after Ken are not going to be able, even if they want to, to shrug off these responsibilities. The conditions of the trust ensure that control of the business will remain in Thomson hands for eighty years."*

The scenario is predictable; its leading man is not. The young Thomson marches to his own drum corps. He is as private as Conrad Black—his only intellectual rival among Canada's young rich—is public. He has climbed to the second-highest position within the Thomson Organization with no profile, has yet to grant his first newspaper, television or any other interview (except for this book), and is so circumspect that his 1988 marriage to a fashion buyer for Simpsons was missed by Toronto's social columnists and not detected even by the nosy Rosedale mavens who surround his home. His conversation, which is what he must mainly be judged by, since he has yet to exercise much visible power, is an improbable mixture of introspective genius and post-industrial babble. Tall and wispy, with curly sandy hair and frigid blue eyes, he is light on both feet, betraying the easy grace born of his training in the martial arts. Intensity characterizes all his thoughts and actions. Ask him the meaning of life or the time of day and the brows furrow into deep scars (the forehead is too youthful to show supporting wrinkles), the eyes grow reflective, and the brain cells almost audibly start churning; there is never any small talk.

---

* Ken Thomson has two other children: Lynne, eighteen months younger than David, a stunning brunette who graduated from the acting faculty at Harvard and who was in Hollywood in 1991, working with a producer, and Peter, eight years David's junior, who participates in Southern Ontario racing circuits and dirt-rally events, practising his driving four or five hours a day. A graduate of the University of Western Ontario, he owns a substantial interest in a Toronto cable-TV company and has begun his career inside the Thomson Organization. To avoid succession duties, Roy Thomson's will stipulated that his personal fortune would be divided among his seven grandchildren. Roy Thomson's trust is administered by his son, Ken, his surviving daughter, Phyllis Audrey Campbell (the other daughter, Irma, died in 1966), his former chief of staff, Sidney Chapman, and John Tory.

DAVID THOMSON WAS EDUCATED at The Hall School in England and Toronto's Upper Canada College. He was (and is) painfully shy, staying away from the sports and military training in which both schools specialize. "I never understood the emphasis on playing games as the only forum for exhibiting manliness," he recalls. "The Upper Canada College Battalion was an unnecessary and wasteful commitment, illustrating the shallow nature of so many contemporaries in early life. As a chore, it was counter to the deep emotional issues which I sought to begin my journey." Not your average prom-date jock.

He read history at Cambridge, specializing in studies of the civil service in India from the late eighteenth to the mid-nineteenth centuries, particularly under Mountstuart Elphinstone, who rose from aide-de-camp to Colonel Arthur Wellesley (later the Duke of Wellington) to governor of Bombay and was one of the chief founders of state education in India. "My classmates were more interested in military battles," he remembers, "and I must say Wellington fought tactically superb engagements, greater by far than any of his European campaigns, including Waterloo. His tactics were similar to Hannibal's against the Romans after his crossing of the Alps, when he gained the higher ground at the battle of Lake Trasimene. But I was much more fascinated with the mundane aspects of how the British were able to educate and develop an infrastructure of modern government in that huge land mass. Legalities are very important and represent absolute regulation, constrictive and formal. I prefer frameworks to guidelines, because you're able to be creative within them. My mind works with associations and ideas. History taught me this above all else. At an early age, I realized that to not understand these life experiences would lessen my ultimate success and enjoyment in life." To lighten the academic load, Thomson played left wing on the 1976 Cambridge hockey team that beat Oxford for only the fourth time since 1930. "I like to think I was on the team because of my abilities," he laughs, "but I owned a Volvo, which afforded me a constant place."

David believes his most significant formative influence was the weekends he spent with his grandfather at Alderbourne Arches in Buckinghamshire. "He was very lonely and we conversed for hours about business and people," the young Thomson reminisces. "His curious mind was always questioning why things were done in a particular way, seeking to understand the forces that affect people's judgments. Granddad would relate his experiences with various personalities: Chou En-lai, Mao, Khrushchev, Beaverbrook, competitors, social companions, family. He always admired those people who could laugh at themselves amidst the negative circumstances that surrounded their lives. He was an optimist with an uncanny ability to seize opportunities that others could not see. This approach was in complete parallel to my own nature." There was another parallel: Roy Thomson unleashed the random thoughts that he credited with helping him resolve the most complex corporate problems by guessing the murderer in the dozen Agatha Christie and other whodunits he devoured every week. Those mystery stories were for him what art would become to his grandson, less an escape than a way to sharpen and exercise the mind for managing the exponential growth of the family fortune. (Every morning of every day David still puts on the copper bracelet Roy Thomson wore to ward off arthritis, as a reminder of the old man's spirit.)

It was at this time that his serious interest in painting took root. "Art came to mean more and more as I became involved with the lives of the artists and came to better understand the context in which they lived. For me, art has never been a financial or social game." Aware that any cultural hobby pursued by a rich kid was bound to be dismissed as dilettantish, David put in a long and arduous apprenticeship under Hermann Baer, who ran a small shop on London's Davies Street that rented antique props to the film industry and was also an articulate expert in medieval art. The other mentor in art has been his father, whose collection, David claims, "should be celebrated in its completeness; even the frame mouldings are harmonious. He has distilled his vision of a few artists into a handful of works by each. The result is sincere and compelling."

"David gets feelings that I never get from pictures," admits his father, Ken. "He never misses the technical aspect of art. He sees when something is well executed and when it's not so well executed. He talks about the soul, the true message of a painting and can sort of read what the artist had in his mind when he did it. I'm not that good. I can't figure those things out. He gets signals that I don't even understand. I just get an instant message that's probably much more shallow than David's." The relationship between the two men is close but not cloying, with the senior Thomson occasionally wondering if his son is tuned in to worldly business realities.

"Our private discussions evoke mixed emotions, but once agreed, we tackle issues with a single-minded tenacity," David insists. "I love him deeply, would do anything for him, and I am not alone. Many of my cohorts would defend him to the death." Of his son, Ken Thomson says, "He's a fine young man. The same sensitivity that he relates to his paintings, he relates to people and busi-

ness. It worries him if somebody isn't being treated right and all that sort of
stuff. He relates to quality. When he's involved in something he wants it to be
the best, but of course we can't always have the very best. In his position, he
could have just taken what's coming and enjoyed it, but that would have been
more shallow than his thinking. It wouldn't have been as satisfying."

DAVID THOMSON WORKS on the eighteenth floor of the Thomson Building
across the street from Toronto City Hall. A visitor entering the private headquarters of his personal holding company, Lavis Incorporated (after his
mother's maiden name), is struck by the sight of three incongruous objects: the
large-scale model of a 1920s U.S. Post Office monoplane, painted every colour
of the rainbow, that looks as if it had just landed out of a *Peanuts* cartoon; an
exquisite, life-sized thirteenth-century French limestone figure that appears to
be bending towards its owner in an attitude of gentle benediction; and the
dark green seat from a Second World War Nazi Luftwaffe fighter. The office
walls are covered with the striking canvases of Patrick Heron, a controversial
contemporary British artist who specializes in jarring colour patterns.

David usually works gazing out the window opposite his desk on which are
mounted several transparencies. "That one," he explains, "is a Constable, an
oil sketch he painted on his honeymoon in November 1816 of Weymouth in
Dorset, along England's south coast. These two are by Cy Twombly, the most
compelling of modern artists, who left the States in the 1950s and now lives
in Rome. That small transparency is a marvellous limestone figure from about
1260 and represents the beginning of sculpture in the full round. One must
travel backwards to pagan times before one encounters full relief sculpture."

In the same mood he produces out of his desk a coin from the Dark Ages,
a Merovingian gold Tremissis struck in Lyons about 675 A.D., modelled after
the Roman currency of the Emperor Justinian: "Hundreds of moneyers minted
crude coinage in the manner of Imperial Rome, inscribing their names and
cities on the reverse legend. The effigies are extraordinary in their vivid line
and spontaneous gesture; they evoke a most wonderful sense of expression and
power. For me, they are the beginnings of the small entrepreneur in the history
of coinage—they were created amidst the most barbaric circumstances by a
people in constant motion and are amongst the few objects that remain from
those distant days."

Thomson's most valuable acquisition was J.M.W. Turner's magnificent
Seascape, Folkestone, which Lord Clark, the former director of the National

Gallery (who once owned the painting), described as "the best picture in the world." David bought it at auction in 1984 for $14.6 million, outbidding the National Gallery of Scotland; five years later it was officially valued at $50 million. But his real obsession is with John Constable, the miller's son who with Turner dominated English landscape painting in the nineteenth century. Thomson's first purchase, at nineteen, was a page out of the artist's 1835 Arundel sketchbook, and his current collection of twenty major works and eighty-six of his drawings, as well as oil sketches, watercolours and letters, ranks as the world's finest private representation of Constable's art.

In 1991 Thomson published a lavishly printed and illustrated 328-page study, *Constable and his Drawings* (with text by Ian Fleming-Williams, Britain's leading Constable expert), which has been highly praised by English art critics. "In sharp contrast to formal art history monographs," he notes, "one can read this book without having studied fifteen previous works. This is about pure observation, not terribly different to the art itself. Constable's sensibility has had a strong influence on my personal philosophy, which I carry forward in all walks of life, including the business. So few people allow themselves to openly see and question scenes and events as he did. All too often subjects are viewed from a narrow perspective, with strong conclusions drawn in advance. Being possessed by imagination, curiosity and such dreamlike qualities doesn't mean one is incapable of pragmatism and tough decision-making. Whenever you lose that sense of idealism, you lose your reason for being. Constable for me has always represented the search for truth."

THAT SEARCH HAS TAKEN THOMSON into the soggy pastures of existentialism, at least in the sense that he believes men and women are diminished by not meeting the challenges they set for themselves. Intensely attracted by war and danger, because those circumstances force people to harness the peak of their physical and emotional energies, he owns a large library documenting first-hand experiences of aerial combat and the uses of camouflage ("creating patterns and colour combinations that transformed each aircraft into a work of art"). He often imagines himself in battle. ("I become excited at the thought of measuring myself in varied situations, alongside Wellington in India or being in a fighter, attacking a formation of bombers and being vastly outnumbered. It's an interesting way to test yourself because you set your own limits.")

Among his favourite documents is one of the last letters written by Antarctic explorer Robert Falcon Scott, found beside his frozen body in 1912, that Thomson regularly rereads as an example of an undaunted spirit facing death. "The existential idea of life's journey is very important," he contends. "It's all too easy to become cynical and to forget that we are all children at heart, that when you leave those youthful dreams behind you leave a great part of your being forever, you abandon your sense of wonder and astonishment, the idea that you can be spiritually moved by something or someone."

That sense of wonder is best caught in his house, an architect's jewel on a dead-end street in Rosedale where he finds sanctuary. He lives there with his wife, a pre-Raphaelite beauty named Mary Lou La Prairie, and their daughter, Thyra Nicole. He met Mary Lou in 1988 at Simpsons where she worked as a fashion buyer for young contemporary women's wear. ("Our love for one another was instantaneous. It was a fairy-tale romance. It has changed my life.")

David drives a 1984 Audi and owns a *pied-à-terre* in New York and a house in the Highbury district of London. His main interest is the collection at his Toronto house, which is less a home than an art gallery with a kitchen and some bedrooms attached. Every wall is crammed with paintings. The total effect is less than the sum of its parts because individual pictures have so little room to breathe; the eye cannot feast on any one canvas without being distracted by those on either side of it. Edvard Munch, Sir Stanley Spencer, Ilya Chasnik, Piet Mondrian, Eugene Jansson, Picasso, Ivan Kluin, Roger Hilton, Cy Twombly, Joseph Beuys, Ferdinand Hodler, Ernst Ludwig Kirchner, Mark Rothko, Paul Klee and a dozen other artists of equal international renown are represented. Strangely, except for a small drybrush by David Milne, there are no Canadian paintings. (Not a Krieghoff in sight.)

"I look forward to the day," he says, "when I can hang a room of empty frames. What an extraordinary experience that would be. Nothing can be more perfect than a frame and one's perception of balance and space, within and without its running pattern. This is sculpture. Immediately one thinks of the classic argument about what one chooses to leave out as opposed to what one puts back in. As with business, it is what we end up not expending that returns far more in the long run, well beyond any immediate cost savings or profits."

And then there are his art objects: a rare book on coloured fifteenth-century woodcuts, among the earliest printed and hand-coloured images in the history of art; facsimiles of the original texts of T.S. Eliot's *The Waste Land* and George Orwell's *1984*, showing the authors' corrections in ink; a study of fences from the Middle Ages ("one of the finest ways of dating objects and understanding the social order of those times"); an animation cell from Dr Seuss's *The Grinch Who Stole Christmas*; an Ethiopian book of holy scriptures in hippopotamus-hide binding from the year 1500; an original Schulz cartoon of Charlie Brown; a small woodcut from Lower Swabia, dated 1420; an eighteenth-century African bronze from Benin; and a magnificent depiction in wood of the Crucifixion, mounted on its original cross, which was the focal point of an unidentified church in South Germany during the last quarter of the twelfth century.

David and a visitor gaze at this icon. "The agony of Christ is pronounced with the hips slightly tilted," he explains. "The profile of Jesus' head is quite spectacular. In this piece, one confronts the beginnings of Gothic carving and the tremendous expressionism of the northern world ..."

"Look at those nails," the overwhelmed visitor offers helpfully, "how honest and raw they are ..."

"Well, no, actually I put them there myself; they're what the cross is hanging on."

The gallery is constantly being expanded but its paintings will probably never be exhibited. "One does not form an art collection to then have a representative of *Architectural Digest* come by and write an article that invades one's privacy," Thomson insists. He maintains an intelligence network in New York and London to hunt down the works he seeks. "The art world has taught me harsh lessons on human nature," he confesses. "Money does not open every door. A real collector will rarely sell a work unless he can replace it with something even greater that has more personal meaning. Sometimes the issue can only be resolved by a trade or an exchange. I rely on a few people to update me and avidly peruse books and catalogues. I'll take three or four volumes with me to bed every night. It's no different from my grandfather reading all those spy and detective novels."

Almost hidden from view in the basement of the Rosedale house are a few exquisitely fine lead-pencil drawings—of a fish pond, an oak tree, water lilies, wrecked cars. These are some of David Thomson's own. He has been drawing to express his innermost thoughts since childhood. One British critic who saw them while on a visit noted they were "very good indeed, highly detailed, well observed," but they will never be shown. "I sometimes say to Mary Lou, 'I must draw a tree now,' and go away into my world for several hours. I have to. I am absolutely compelled to follow my feelings, or I forfeit the right to live."

Thomson makes little effort to separate his passion for art from his devotion to business. In his mind, these twin strands are forever intertwined: "I take art so seriously because it's one of the few pursuits in which I can totally unravel my soul. For me, the act of creation comes through in a better appreciation of business…. I measure great achievements in information publishing [the Thomson newspapers] in the same way as I view a compelling work of art." He dismisses the criticism that Thomson newspapers fill the spaces between their ads with the cheapest boiler-plate copy available as being out of date. Instead, he praises employees such as Peter Kapyrka, publisher of the Barrie *Examiner*, for furthering his company's organic growth by adding a weekly real-estate supplement.

There is, according to the youthful inheritor, almost no aspect of art that can't be related to some section of the Thomson Organization's operational code. "If you look at Limoges and Mosan, two of the great French workshops producing art in the twelfth century, you might think, 'What the hell does that have to do with business?'" he says. "Limoges in central France made fantastic reliquaries and chalices for churches and cathedrals with very few variables. But the Mosan craftsmen were different. They worked the market between Liège and Cologne. Their representatives sat down directly with the local bishop and asked what he wanted to see in the holy shrine. They were, in effect, forming the first customer focus groups and producing castings that were far superior to the Limoges enamels. You can't do anything well in publishing without a highly developed sense of audience."

David's spiritual bible is a remarkable book-length essay entitled *Happiness: An Exploration of the Art of Sleeping, Eating, Complaining, Postponing, Sympathising, and, Above All, Being Free,* by Theodore Zeldin, an Oxford don who portrays Everyman's journey into paradise, comparing what he encounters with what he expected to find. "The book," Thomson summarizes, "is about having the courage to dream in a highly structured society and the corporate world. It's about having faith in one's intuition, about preserving one's childhood vision and curiosity, about the fact that dissent requires great moral courage, and that failure is as important as success." He is mesmerized by the fact that in his position and state of development he is free to make mistakes and believes that this may be the greatest privilege bestowed on him by wealth. It's the errors in judgment that really accelerate his learning curve; he takes the correct decisions for granted.

That learning curve received its most valuable spurt during the decade he spent with the Hudson's Bay Company.

DAVID THOMSON'S DEDICATION to the HBC seems incompatible with his artistic temperament and search for mental stimuli. Yet he spent ten years in the service of the Company—between the ages of twenty-four and thirty-four, his most productive business apprenticeship—as a hill-time retailer, right down to a term of selling socks at The Bay's downtown Toronto department store.

In the summer of 1982, when Ken Thomson took his family on a second northern journey to view the HBC's Arctic kingdom, their guide was once again the Company's George Whitman. The party was encamped on the Belcher Islands in the middle of Hudson Bay when Whitman bluntly asked the elder Thomson why he had bought the Hudson's Bay Company. When Ken explained that he had a sense of Canadian history and he did not want to see the Company swapped around, sold off, or allowed to disappear, Whitman turned to David and said, "It would really be nice to hope that someday you might become the Governor. How do you feel about that?" David, who was then looking for a place to light, allowed that he would indeed be interested but that he knew nothing about retailing. Sensing the young man's excitement, Whitman talked for hours about the Company's glorious history and its magical presence in the Canadian wilderness. He suggested to Ken that David not be parachuted into some senior position where he would be usurping the succession of staff climbing through the system but that a comprehensive training program be put together that would expose the young Thomson to the Company's inner workings, and vice versa.

"People were very careful about what they'd say to me and were told to be so, anticipating that I would not stay long," David recalls. "But this didn't happen because I became enthralled with many areas of the Company's then disjointed business potential. I have always been fascinated by how one motivates people in a negative situation. My business focus was entirely retail, and to learn it well I allowed myself no distractions or meanderings. I committed myself to the cause of making the HBC a great Company again." He began in the main Toronto retail store, then spent a year commuting to Quebec, Saskatchewan, Alberta (where he once forgot his pyjamas in a motel at Medicine Hat) and British Columbia in addition to the fur divisions in New York and Montreal.

Probably his most moving experience was the time he spent at a fur-trading post in Prince Albert. "The juxtaposition was dramatic," he recalls. "On July 4, 1980, I bid successfully for a Munch woodblock; the following week I was in Prince Albert, and I remember being taken to the post's back-yard where ten bear claws were positioned on the cement floor, with fresh bloodstains and tissue intact. One fellow proceeded to demonstrate the various new traps and took me through the back room, where numerous shiny models were hanging. He hinged several in open positions and tossed a branch into the claw. I shall never forget the powerful crescendo of the folding pincers. For one of the first times I enjoyed a completely unfettered response to life, isolated from big cities and the diversions of money. We drove along dirt roads, watched sunsets, merchandised the store, went fishing and talked of our childhoods. The experience was unforgettable and I developed a deep respect and empathy towards those real people."

That warm feeling described his reaction to the Company as a whole. During his travels, he kept a private journal, recording his thoughts—among them:

> *On store fixtures:* Chrome is poor choice. For specialty men's store in Toronto, would buy old barns which farmers glad to get rid of and refurbish our departments completely in cedar.
>
> *On display:* Spotlight the ring on a model's finger in a downtown window … use all senses, including the aroma of good cooking.
>
> *On old stock:* Things never die. One item from an unsuccessful line will become so popular, it becomes one itself.
>
> *On expansion:* To build a new shopping centre or store is an analytical decision with no feelings. Yet selling decisions are all feelings.
>
> *On selling:* Merchandising is the last frontier of the untrained intelligence.
>
> *On Zellers:* Slop it up. Far too clean.
>
> *On Fred Eaton:* Talk to any time. Get in touch. Ball is in my court.

In the course of his training, he spent twelve months with one of the HBC's most troubled units, Shop-Rite, which ran five dozen discount catalogue outlets, mostly in Southern Ontario, and was losing about $2 million a year. Pete Buckley, who then ran the division, recalls that David was an effective junior manager, particularly as a member of Shop-Rite's ball-hockey team, which challenged the company's warehousemen to a match. "I was the referee and it got pretty rowdy," he recalls. "As soon as the warehousemen saw David, I could hear them muttering, 'Get that sucker.' But he was the most competitive guy in there and just beat the hell out of some of them." The admiration was mutual. "I have a lot of respect for Buckley," Thomson says. "He told me on one occasion, 'David, do you know how to better understand your consumer? I'll tell you. At one time I lived in an apartment building and at night, using binoculars, I would scan people's apartments, to see what goods they were using.' I said, 'You're a bloody genius! That's so simple!'"

David's next and most important step, in July 1983, was his appointment as manager of the HBC's suburban Toronto Cloverdale store, which he ran for a year, raising its operating profit to 8.9 percent, among the chain's highest. He established a Grandmother's Boutique ("a fine opportunity to cater to all the empty-nesters in Cloverdale's trading area"), reduced inefficiencies and soon found other managers copying his methods. "For many, it made no sense that David Thomson would need to work, and I think it was a surprise because no one had ever seen me perform alone," he recalls. "That year's journey made me acutely aware of the pressures and discomforts some people felt from the mere thought of my presence." But he persisted, and the time at Cloverdale established his independent reputation among Bay executives. There followed a stint with Simpsons, where he became assistant to George Kosich, who, a year later, would be promoted to run both Simpsons and The Bay. They quickly formed a duo, cruising the HBC retailing empire's inner and outer limits, cutting costs, closing stores, laying off employees, recasting its merchandising philosophy. (What annoyed staffers most was that when Thomson and Kosich would arrive at a store, obviously preparing to wield the axe, they first spent a day walking around each department handing out jujubes.) "The system was at an impasse," David remembers, "and its dismal financial results mirrored my feelings, as did many conversations and pieces of information that came my way. I had clandestine meetings under stairwells in shopping malls and other places, as employees, torn between what they knew in their hearts was right and the security of their employment, confided to me about basic merchandising issues that were not being addressed. I felt the ground swell beneath me as I realized how passionately these people cared about the Company."

Others were critical of his methods, accusing him of grilling underlings about their superiors' performance, then attacking those in charge on the basis of what he'd heard. They claimed that he could operate at only *two* speeds, full throttle or total indifference, and recalled an HBC management meeting where he grew bored, slumped at his desk, and finally started reading a book. "David used to phone from Liechtenstein on a Sunday night and say, 'Hey boss, can I get Monday off?'" complained Marvin Tiller, then in charge of the HBC's Northern Stores, where the young Thomson put in some time.

Early in 1987, he had to decide whether to continue with retailing or switch to publishing. He flew to London, took a long walk on Hampstead Heath, and opted for the presidency of Zellers. That meant moving to Montreal and taking on his first major executive assignment. "David was only twenty-nine years old, an unknown quantity, his apparent qualifications confined to his shareholdings," recalls J.W. "Bud" Bird, an HBC director at the time. "We made the appointment, knowing it was an innovative move that could have a lot of precarious circumstances." With one exception, the investment community was not impressed. "I don't think it's appropriate," an investment analyst charged anonymously in the *Financial Times of Canada*. "He should not be allowed such a position just because of his father's influence, to take over such a large chain without working his way to the top." The exception was Don Tigert, an analyst with Burns, Fry, who commented, "I was very impressed with the guy. He said he was going to whack $80 million out of Zellers' expense structure and in just six months he did precisely that."

According to David, the franchise had to be brought back down to its pedestrian fundamentals, which had governed its earlier success, because its stores and merchandise were becoming too expensive and head office, in particular, needed some brutal trimming. "In the initial week," he recalls, "I summoned the head-office staff and announced my decision to lay off 250 employees who, in fact, were standing in that room. I remember someone questioning me about having butchered the Simpson organization a couple of years earlier. I always appreciated blunt opinions, and this was no exception."

He had a brief but spectacular success at Zellers (he raised operating profit by 45 percent), although some attribute a good deal of the credit to the influence of his mentor, George Kosich, who was now president of the HBC. It was followed by a frustrating term as president of Simpsons which, unlike Zellers, was no easy turnaround, and after a year he was discreetly promoted to part-time chairman and sixteen months later resigned to pursue his other business interests. Although his relations with Kosich have cooled noticeably and some question his continuing interest in retailing, he remains a director of the HBC and attends its Executive Committee meetings. "I have asked my father on many occasions," says he, "where the family might find a great franchise equal to the Hudson's Bay Company."

Most if not all Thomson employees who have come into contact with David respect him but eventually become overdosed on his intensity and his lingo. He told one dissatisfied British staff member that perhaps he should consider leaving the firm, that there were certain disadvantages and anxieties involved in working for someone like him. "But at the end of the day," he added, "you may say: 'You know, it's interesting working for David. Even if he's mad.' If that means I'm not normal, I'm perfectly happy with that. That's the type of dialogue I really enjoy because it not only gives me strength but allows so many wonderful initiatives to occur in the business."

DAVID THOMSON IS VOLATILE, as unpredictable as a hailstorm. He could become the leader of the new generation of Canada's Establishment, or he might seek permanent refuge in his art. He is just beginning his run, with each new experience providing the bounce that will determine his ultimate direction.

Not at all like the father he loves but very close to the grandfather he respects, he faces a future limited only by his ability to survive his own intensity. Perhaps he had an inkling of the fact that nothing could stop him except himself when he chose the quote to accompany his picture in the Upper Canada College 1975 graduation yearbook: "We are never so much the victims of another as we are the victims of ourselves."

Meanwhile, he goes on pontificating, turning dollars and flexing his expanding authority. "I wish," he says, "to prolong those inspired moments in life and see them continually manifested in all areas of endeavour.... My search is always to create new wealth."

Once a Thomson, always a Thomson.

"THE WORKING OF GREAT INSTITUTIONS is mainly the result of a vast mass of routine, petty malice, self-interest, carelessness and sheer mistake. Only a residual fraction is thought." So wrote George Santayana, the Hispanic-American philosopher, who might have been describing the history of the Hudson's Bay Company. Yet, as this book amply documents, it had its moments of glory, endowing the territory it occupied with a legacy of rough justice and Scottish stoicism that characterize Canadians still.

As well as the miracle of its commercial survival, the Company became one of the pivotal influences in the founding of Canada as the transcontinental state that allowed a brave huddle of like-minded survivors to prosper in North America's attic. It truly was a company that became a nation. Its traders were castaways in a tight-fisted land, yet they achieved something uniquely magnificent: they endured. And out of their endurance was born the matrix for modern Canada.

Despite its grandiloquent past, the HBC's fiscal heyday was late coming. Its sales didn't exceed $1 billion until 1977, and the Company's highest net profit ($80 million) was earned two years later. That was when Ken Thomson purchased control of the Company for $640 million (cash), a larger stake (76 percent) than any individual had ever before held. It then employed 70,000 people and enjoyed annual revenues of more than $7 billion. It remained the world's largest fur auctioneer; operated nearly five hundred retail outlets; owned Markborough, one of the world's poster real estate operations; and ran the giant downtown department stores it had built across the Canadian West between 1913 and 1968. In its retailing expansion mode, the HBC also took over Morgans in Montreal, Freimans in Ottawa and the Zellers discount chain.

Within a decade of Thomson's purchase, the Company voluntarily abandoned its historical roots, selling its remunerative northern store divisions (in May 1987) and profitable fur division (in January 1991), as well as spinning off the real estate arm. That left it exposed to a single revenue stream: the ultra-competitive retail business. It was thus reduced to a chain of middle-class department stores with a fancy crest in a market increasingly dominated by world-class retailers from south of the border.

The HBC's decline was a long descent from dominating a continent to becoming the troubled orphan of Canada's decreasing department store trade. While most of the one-time giants—Eaton's, Simpsons, Woodwards, Spencers, Robinsons and others—were forced to close shop, only the Bay among the indigenous commercial enterprises survived. Barely. It lost $76 million in the 1980s. Waves of modernizations, the heralded arrivals and abrupt departures of marketing geniuses, and any number of desperate measures to attract shoppers produced no permanent benefits but only served to underline its decline. (At one point it even hired professional shoppers to tag along and help customers choose merchandise and carry their bags.) "When one thinks of bland, uninspired retail space," wrote Richard Talbot, a Canadian retail consultant, "it's hard not to think of the Bay."

The root of the problem was the HBC's precipitous decline in market share triggered by the arrival in Canada of big box American operators such as Home Depot, Toys "R" Us, Costco and particularly that awesome eight-hundred-pound gorilla of world retailing, Wal-Mart Inc., whose Canadian sales catapulted 245 percent between 1994 and 2000.

To meet the killing competition of the Wal-Mart entry, the Company played its most desperate card in 1997 and hired away one of the American retailer's street-smart twenty-five-year veterans, William Fields. He expanded the Zellers chain by purchasing K-mart's Canadian operation and tried to subdivide the Bay's anchor units into separate specialty stores, but within twenty-two months he was pushed out—dangling at the end of an $6-million golden parachute.

By the end of 2002, the financial ratings services had reduced HBC's debt to "junk" status, citing "increased competition and the irreversible trend away from department store shopping." During 2003, the HBC's profits fell another 24 percent with a record thirteen consecutive quarters showing lower margins. The real situation was even worse because nearly all of the HBC's profit was derived not from the sale of merchandise but from providing credit facilities to customers. An even more telling calculation emphasized the problem: The Bay turned an annual profit of $169 per square foot of sales space compared to $284 at Sears Canada and $425 at the Canadian arm of Wal-Mart.

By mid-2004, Jerry Zucker, who ran a highly successful American vulture fund that took over undervalued companies and turned them around or sold off their assets, had acquired nearly 20 percent of HBC's stock. Since Lord Thomson's departure, the Company had been operating without a controlling shareholder, making it a natural takeover target, but Bay Street wondered out loud why any investor would be interested in the pitiful remains of the once magnificent Company of Adventurers. HBC CEO George Heller, who started his career as a fur trader at Fort Severn on Hudson Bay (and still knows how to skin a beaver), stuck to his prediction that the Company would boost its revenues to $9 billion and triple its profits by 2008, but few subscribed to his rosy forecast.

As this book goes to press, the future of the Hudson's Bay Company remains uncertain. It is tempting to speculate that since the Company has weathered so many crises during its stormy 334-year history, it will survive this one. Should it fail or emerge in different form, its achievements against impossible odds in a barely accessible part of the New World—its deeds and misdeeds, as chronicled in the preceding pages—will serve as its epitaph.

ACKNOWLEDGEMENTS

HAVING COME TO THE END of the nearly ten years that I devoted to this study of the Hudson's Bay Company, I find myself surrounded by a heavy load of literary debts.

The books that make up this volume could never have been written without the inspired determination of Shirlee Smith, then head of the HBC Archives in Winnipeg. She not only encouraged the idea of a popular history of the Company, but her reading of my chapters proved invaluable. John de B. Payne, a former HBC executive and political alchemist, was of immense assistance.

I greatly benefitted from generous professional advice and the personal support of such distinguished scholars as Tim Ball, Abe Rotstein, Blair Stonechild, Alan Wilson, Hartwell Bowsfield, W. Kaye Lamb, John S. Galbraith and the late Richard Glover. They and others encouraged this project because they understood what I was trying to accomplish. They subscribed to my notion that truth is not necessarily the sum of all the ascertainable facts but an interplay of character and circumstance.

The preparation of the sections of this book dealing with the North was greatly assisted by the wisdom of Stu Hodgson, the former commissioner of the Northwest Territories; NWT cabinet ministers Nellie Cournoyea and Gordon Wray; Senator Willie Adams; and Peter Ernerk. Janet Craig and Martin Lynch, who edited all my books, performed their usual magic, bravely attempting to make my overheated prose more comprehensible.

I was also privileged to meet the British governors and directors who nurtured the HBC's fortunes during and after the Second World War. I interviewed most of them and came to understand at last how the Company's huge domain could be run with such brave results for three hundred years. I must pay special tribute to Lord Adeane, Lord Amory, Lord Cobbold, J.E.H. Collins, Lady Patrick Ashley Cooper, James and Anne Cooper, Sir Eric Faulkner, Arthur Frayling, Sir William Keswick, Lord Tweedsmuir and, most of all, J.G. Links, by royal appointment furrier to the Queen and an HBC director from 1947 to 1975, whose sprightly and graceful observations made the Company's ethos come alive.

A special salute to George Whitman, the HBC's director of public relations, who took his job seriously, mainly in making sure that I was presented with facts instead of myths, authenticity instead of bafflegab. Al Hochbaum, a free spirit, artist and professional zoologist who made a fetish of being beholden to no one, gave me the invaluable benefit of his honest critiques. He taught me more than all the professional historians combined.

I gratefully acknowledge the invaluable contribution of Camilla Turner, then my wife, who was chief editor for the series; Cynthia Good, former publisher at Penguin Canada, whose dedication and enthusiasm made it possible; Mary Adachi for her copy editing; and Pat Harding, my indefatigable assistant, for coordinating my untidy life as well as my hectic work schedule. As always, a salute to the bravura *Artistry in Rhythm* of Stan Kenton, which kept me alive and kicking.

When I started work on my chronicles of the HBC, it seemed like an uncomplicated excursion into Canadian history. So many words and years later, I left the project, happy to have resurrected, however briefly, the many heroes and villains whose existence had too long been ignored by Canadians, convinced their country's history was dull.

It isn't, and never was. Trying to recreate 320 years of history was a tough assignment; attempting, as I have, to write it in the manner of an itinerant storyteller was harder still. This book owes its existence to many people, only the responsibility for its imperfections remains fully my own.

P.C.N.
August 1, 1987–September 24, 2004

ILLUSTRATION CREDITS

Radisson (standing) and Groseilliers
By Frederic Remington Photo courtesy of the Remington Art Museum, Ogdensburg, New York

Trading Ceremony at York Factory, 1780s
By Adam Sherrif Scott, R.C.A. Courtesy Hudson's Bay Company

Brigade of Boats
Painting by Paul Kane, 1848. Courtesy Royal Ontario Museum, Toronto. Neg. no. 63AA400; cat. no. 912.1.31

Governor George Simpson on a Tour of Inspection
Painting by Cyrus Cuneo for CPR. Copied by L.L. Fitzgerald for HBC calendar, 1926. Original by Cuneo stolen. Courtesy Hudson's Bay Company

Nineteenth-century portrayal of Henry Hudson
Painting by the Honourable John Collier. First exhibited 1881. Courtesy the Tate Gallery, London

Prince Rupert (1619–1682)
Portrait by Sir Peter Lely. Courtesy Hudson's Bay Company

The signing of the Hudson's Bay Company Charter
By unknown artist. Courtesy Hudson's Bay Company

The battle between the Hampshire *and the* Pélican, *1697*
Courtesy Norman Wilkinson for Hudson's Bay Company

D'Iberville's bombardment of York Factory in 1697 after the sinking of the Hampshire
From Bacqueville de la Potherie, Histoire de l'Amérique Septentrionale, vol. I (Paris, 1753)

Plans of York and Prince of Wales's Forts
Plate iii in James Robson, Voyage to Hudson's Bay, 1747. Courtesy Hudson's Bay Company

A southwest view of Prince of Wales's Fort
After a drawing by Samuel Hearne, 1769. Courtesy Provincial Archives of Manitoba

Mr. Samuel Hearne, late Chief at Prince of Wales's Fort, Hudson's Bay, 1796
Coloured engraving by unknown artist. Courtesy Hudson's Bay Company Archives

Portaging trade goods on the way to the fur country
National Archives of Canada c-82974

Coat of arms of the North West Company
Watercolour. National Archives of Canada c-8711

Shooting the Rapids, ca. 1879
Oil painting by Frances Ann Hopkins, wife of the Secretary to HBC Governor George Simpson. National Archives of Canada c-2774

Simon McTavish
Oil painting by unknown artist. National Archives of Canada c-164

One of four remaining Beaver Club medals. This one was presented to Saskatchewan fur trader Nicholas Montour, who purchased the seigneury of La-Pointe-du-Lac. McCord Museum of Canadian History, McGill University, Montreal

William McGillivray and family
Oil painting, 1806, by William Berczy. McCord Museum of Canadian History, McGill University, Montreal

Voyageurs at Dawn, 1871
Oil painting by Frances Ann Hopkins. National Archives of Canada c-2773

Sir Alexander Mackenzie
Oil on canvas by Sir Thomas Lawrence. The National Gallery of Canada, Ottawa

Thomas Douglas, 5th Earl of Selkirk (1771–1820)
Photogravure; from a painting ascribed to Raeburn. National Archives of Canada c-1346

Simon Fraser
Provincial Archives of British Columbia. Cat. no. pdp 2258

The Battle of Seven Oaks, June 19, 1816
Pen and ink drawing by C.W. Jefferys. National Archives of Canada c-73663

William McGillivray
Oil painting, 1820, attributed to Sir Martin Shee; National Archives of Canada c-167

Simon McGillivray
SM Oil painting attributed to R.R. Reinagle; National Archives of Canada c-176

Edward ("Bear") Ellice
National Archives of Canada c-2835.

Cumberland House
From a sketch taken by the Henry Youle Hind expedition of 1858. Hudson's Bay Company Archives, Provincial Archives of Manitoba

Dr. John McLoughlin, "Father of Oregon," at age 76
The Oregon Historical Society. Neg. no. ORHI 248

Sir George Simpson in his later years
Copy of a daguerrotype by Notman. Notman Photographic Archives

The grand canoe reception on the St. Lawrence given by Simpson for the Prince of Wales
Illustrated London News, 13 October 1860; print provided by the Metropolitan Toronto Library

Indian Camp—Sunset
Oil painting by Frederick Arthur Verner. Winnipeg Art Gallery.

Shoppers at Fort Edmonton, 1866
Photo coutesy Frederic Remington Art Museum, Ogdensburg, New York

INDEX

A *La Claire Fontaine* (voyageur anthem), 288–89

A.T. Gifford (ship), 715

Abbott, J.C., 648

Aberdeen, Earl of, 505

Aberdeen University, 680–81

Aborigines' Protection Society, 541

Abraham, John, 181, 181n

Adamson, Agar, 685

Adventurer (icebreaker), 739

Adventurers. *See* Company of Adventurers

Africa, 42, 59, 66 (*See also* South Africa; West Africa)

Agnelli, Giovanni, 869

Agnello, John Baptiste, 28

Aird, Sir John, 803

Aklavik (Mackenzie River), 706, 755, 757, 760

Aklavik (ship), 750, 751, 752

Alanbrooke, Viscount, 818–19, 819n, 830, 832

"Alarm Bird," 226–27, 226n

Alaska, 194, 212, 254, 342, 444, 447, 463, 464, 466, 469, 480, 494, 494, 496, 498, 500

Albanel, Charles, 83

Albany (modern), 30, 55

Albany (ship), 189, 190, 192

Albany Fort, vi, 94, 95, 102, 103, 107n, 109, 114, 120, 121, 123n, 129, 139, 153, 154, 173, 184, 196, 197, 198, 206, 245, 337, 348, 442

Albany Home Guard Indians, 198

Albany River, 83, 101, 186, 197

Alberta and Great Waterways Railway, 761

Albion (ship), 407

Alcohol, 138–41, 169, 171, 173, 198, 203, 233n, 240, 250, 260, 270–271, 286, 346–54, 348n, 399, 416, 436, 441–42, 540–541, 650, 650n, 712, 772n; bootlegging, 790n ; brewing operations, 140

Aldavik (Mackenzie Delta), 715

Alexander I (Russia), 464

Alexander Mackenzie & Company, 318, 320

Alfred Yarrow & Company, 619

Algonkian language, 163

Algonquin Indians, 45, 55, 186, 283

Allan, George, 794, 795, 802, 811, 811n, 798, 820, 859

Allan, Sir Hugh, 320n, 535, 559, 647–48, 650, 652

Allan, John, 400

Allan Line, 535–36

Allants et venants, 280

Allen, Ralph, 658

Allen, William, 104

All-Red route, 566, 677

Alvarado, Juan Bautista, 467

America (ship), 505

American Civil War, 553, 617n, 670n

American frontier ethic, 18, 19, 252, 483, 593

American Fur Company, 278, 335, 348n, 462, 529

American Revolution, vix, 237, 243, 322, 323, 370

American War of Independance (1861–65), 237, 322, 323, 370

Amory, Derick Heathcote, Lord Amory, 779, 781, 782, 785, 841–43, 841n, 845n, 846–47, 848, 849, 859

Amsterdam Exchange, 78, 78n

Amundsen, Raold, 706, 748, 757–58

Anderson, David, 523–24

Anderson, J.W., 709–10, 727, 752, 753

Anderson, Sir John. *See* Waverley, Lord

Silk hats, 44n, 536, 614
Silver fox, 764
Silver Heights (Smith homestead), 669–70, 679
Simba, Henry, 172n
Simcoe, Sir John Graves, 315
Simpson, Aemilius, 494
Simpson, Augustus D'Este, 478
Simpson, Lady Frances, 469, 473, 474–77, 478, 518, 546, 548, 550
Simpson, Frances Webster (Fanny), 478
Simpson, Geddes Mackenzie, 413, 473
Simpson, Sir George, 3, 7, 9–10, 13–14, 146, 150, 156, 175, 254, 257, 353–64, 412–19, 423, 428–29, 434, 435, 437n, 449, 454, 459, 463, 468–79, 536, 628–29: attitude to Indians, 440–41, 450, 469, 527, 709; attitude to missionaries, 520; business ventures, 535–36; champions Hawaiian independence, 468–69; Character Book, 456–59; children of, 469, 470, 477, 478; closest associates, 451, 540; conflicts with McLoughlin, 492, 493–97; cost-cutting measures, 439–42; credo of, 434–35; criticism of, 456; death of, 548–50, 550n; dealings with London, 460, 461; diversification efforts, Red River economy, 526–27; gov.-in-chief, Rupert's Land, 459; health of, 545–46, 549; knighted, 463; Napoleonic pretensions, 434–35; Northern Dept. meetings, 455, 456; official residence, 476–77; personality of, 482; and post-amalgamation celebration, 423, 433, 434; realigns trading system, 528–29; relationship with Donald Smith, 578, 579–81, 582–83; relationships with women, 469–73, 477–78; retires, 546; royal visit, 548–59; testimony before parliamentary committee, 541–43; and trade in Oregon Country, 482–83, 484–85, 496; travels of, 443–50, 466–69, 474–76, 496, 546; ventures into diplomacy, 463–69
Simpson, George Geddes, 477
Simpson, John Henry Pelly, 478
Simpson, Margaret Mackenzie, 478
Simpson, Thomas, 7, 413, 438

Simpson, Wemyss, 529
Simpsons (dept. store), 803, 811, 827, 900, 901, 909, 923, 926; merges with The Bay, 893; takeover, 858–65
Simpson-Sears Limited, 859–62, 862n, 894, 898
Sinclair, Betsey, 470
Sinclair, James, 529, 531
Sinclair, William, 470
Sioux, 56, 275, 392, 386, 517, 538, 792
Siqinirmiut (Inuit), 706n
Sivanertok, Octave, 765
Sivertz, Ben, 770, 774
Skelton, O.D., 675
Skinner, Sir Thomas, 694, 787
Skinners Company, 91
Slacum, William, 492
Slaight, Brian, 883–84
Slave Indians, 186, 186n, 225
Slave River, 306, 362, 713
Slave trade: Africans, 207; Indians, 177–78, 190, 274–75
Slavey Indians, 172, 177, 594
Small, Charlotte, 332, 333
Small, Doug, 883
Small, Patrick, 266
Smallpox, 163n, 241, 242, 274, 462, 499
Smellie, Thomas Farrar, 745–46, 747, 753, 753n, 813, 815
Smiles, Samuel, 41
Smith, Adam, 10, 111
Smith, Alexander, 575n
Smith, C. Gordon, 832
Smith, C.F., 538
Smith, Donald Alexander, 1st Baron Strathcona and Mount Royal: appearance of, 571–72; art collection of, 670; and betrayals/corruption, 566, 569, 573–74; and Boer War, 683–85; business ventures, 565–66, 567, 628–29; credo of, 568–71, 572; clash with Brydges, 636–39; critics of, 643, 644, 645, 653n, 655, 656, 657, 693–94; death/funeral of, 700–1, 700n; deputy gov., HBC, 671; directorships, 678; efforts to populate Prairies, 567, 568; friendships, 682; gift-giving of, 666n, 683; gov., HBC, 639, 671; and HBC land